D1087426

5

August 16–December 31, 1776

Paul H. Smith, Editor

Gerard W. Gawalt, Rosemary Fry Plakas, Eugene R. Sheridan
Assistant Editors

LIBRARY OF CONGRESS   WASHINGTON   1979

This volume is printed on permanent/durable paper.

Library of Congress Cataloging in Publication Data (Revised)

Main entry under title:

Letters of delegates to Congress, 1774–1789.

Includes bibliographical references and indexes.
Supt. of Docs: LC 1.34:5
CONTENTS: v.1. August 1774–August 1775.—v.2.
September–December 1775.—[etc.]—
—v. 5. August 16–December 31, 1776.

1. United States. Continental Congress—History—
Sources—Collected works. I. Smith, Paul Hubert, 1931–
JK1033.L47   328.73'09'033   76–2592
ISBN 0–8444–0177–3 (set)

ISBN for this volume: 08444–0276–1

For sale by the Superintendent of Documents, U.S. Government Printing Office
Washington, D.C. 20402
Stock No. 030–000–00111–7

Foreword

Well before the signing on July 4, 1966, of Public Law 89–491, establishing a national American Revolution Bicentennial Commission, the Library of Congress began considering how it could contribute to the Bicentennial celebration. With approval from Congress in 1968, the Library took as the theme for its program "Liberty and Learning" from James Madison, who asked: "What spectacle can be more edifying or more seasonable, than that of Liberty & Learning, each leaning on the other for their mutual and surest support." Reflecting the Library's rich resources for the study of the revolutionary era, its Bicentennial program ranges from compiling bibliographies and guides to recording folk music and presenting symposia.

In preparing the guide *Manuscript Sources in the Library of Congress for Research on the American Revolution,* the Bicentennial Office staff discovered large numbers of letters written by members of the Continental Congresses not published in Edmund C. Burnett's magisterial 8-volume edition of *Letters of Members of the Continental Congress.* As additional unpublished delegate letters turned up and as a cursory survey of other repositories suggested that even more existed, the Library decided that an expanded edition of letters would be a valuable Bicentennial project.

This edition has benefitted immensely from Burnett's path-finding work and from the generous cooperation of the editors of several other documentary publications with a common focus on the revolutionary era. From them the Library has borrowed heavily and to them it owes a debt it can never adequately acknowledge. It is a pleasure to give special thanks to the editors of the papers of John Adams, Benjamin Franklin, Thomas Jefferson, Henry Laurens, James Madison, and George Washington.

Thanks are also due the Advisory Committee on the Library's Bicentennial Program for support and encouragement. To the Ford Foundation, which supplied a generous grant to help underwrite the project, we are grateful. And, finally, we are beholden to the Congress of the United States for appropriations of funds for the publication of these volumes and understanding support of the Library's Bicentennial program.

Elizabeth Hamer Kegan
Assistant Librarian of Congress
for American and Library Studies

Editorial Method and Apparatus

In its treatment of documents this edition of delegate letters strives to achieve a middle ground between facsimile reproduction and thorough modernization. The original spelling and grammar are allowed to stand except in cases where editorial changes or insertions are required to make the text intelligible. For example, when a badly misspelled word is misleading, the correct spelling is inserted in roman type in brackets after the word. Moreover, words omitted through oversight have been supplied at appropriate places in italic type in brackets. Obvious slips of the pen and inadvertent repetitions are usually silently corrected. Capitalization and punctuation have been standardized according to certain conventions. Each sentence begins with a capital letter, as do all proper and geographic names as well as days of the week and months of the year. Doubtful cases have been resolved in favor of modern usage; otherwise the usage of the original texts has been followed. Generally, abbreviations, contractions, and monetary signs are preserved as they appear in manuscript except when they are ambiguous or misleading. On the other hand, the thorn and the tilde are consistently expanded. "Ye" always appears as "The," for instance, and "recvd" as "received." Likewise, "pr." and "p" are always expanded to "per," "pre," or "pro," as the case demands. Finally, superscript letters are always lowered to the line.

Gaps in the text are indicated by ellipses in brackets for missing words and by blank spaces in brackets for missing numbers. Conjectural readings are supplied in roman type in brackets, and editorial insertions in italic type in brackets. Material canceled in manuscript but restored to the printed text is included in italic type in angle brackets ("square parentheses"). Marginalia in letters are treated as postscripts, and postscripts which appear without explicit designation are supplied with a *P.S.* in brackets. Documents are arranged chronologically, with more than one document of the same date being arranged alphabetically according to writer. Documents dated only by the month or by the year are placed at the end of the respective month or year. Place-and-date lines always appear on the same line with the salutation regardless of their position in the manuscript.

A descriptive note at the foot of each entry provides abbreviations indicating the nature and location of the document when it was copied for this project, except for privately owned manuscripts whose ownership is fully explained. The descriptive note also contains

iv

information on the document's authorship if explanation is necessary, and endorsements or addresses are quoted when they contain more than routine information. Other editorial practices employed in this work are explained in the sections on editorial apparatus which follow.

TEXTUAL DEVICES

The following devices will be used in this work to clarify the text.

[. . .], [. . . .]	One or two words missing and not conjecturable.
[. . .]¹, [. . . .]¹	More than two words missing; subjoined footnote estimates amount of material missing.
[ ]	Number or part of a number missing or illegible.
[ ]¹	Blank space in manuscript; explanation in subjoined footnote.
[roman]	Conjectural reading for missing or illegible matter; question mark inserted if reading is doubtful.
[*italic*]	Editorial insertion in the text.
⟨*italic*⟩	Matter crossed out in manuscript but restored.

DESCRIPTIVE SYMBOLS

The following symbols are used in this work to describe the kinds of documents drawn upon. When more than one symbol is used in the descriptive note, the first to appear is that from which the main text is taken.

RC	recipient's copy
FC	file copy
LB	letterbook copy
MS	manuscript
Tr	transcript (used to designate not only contemporary and later handwritten copies of manuscripts, but also printed documents)

LOCATION SYMBOLS

The following symbols, denoting institutions holding the manuscripts printed in the present volume, are taken from *Symbols of American Libraries*, 11th ed. (Washington: Library of Congress, 1976).

CSmH	Henry E. Huntington Library, San Marino, Calif.
Ct	Connecticut State Library, Hartford
CtHi	Connecticut Historical Society, Hartford
CtY	Yale University, New Haven, Conn.

DLC	Library of Congress
DLC(ESR)	Library of Congress, Early State Records Collection
DNA	National Archives and Records Service
DNDAR	Daughters of the American Revolution, Washington, D.C.
DeHi	Historical Society of Delaware, Wilmington
ICHi	Chicago Historical Society
InU	Indiana University, Bloomington
M–Ar	Massachusetts Archives, Boston
MB	Boston Public Library
MH–H	Harvard University, Houghton Library
MHi	Massachusetts Historical Society, Boston
MWA	American Antiquarian Society, Worcester, Mass.
MdAA	Maryland Hall of Records, Annapolis
MdAN	United States Naval Academy, Annapolis, Md.
MdBJ–G	John Work Garrett Library, Johns Hopkins University, Baltimore, Md.
MdHi	Maryland Historical Society, Baltimore
MeHi	Maine Historical Society, Portland
N	New York State Library, Albany
NHi	New–York Historical Society, New York
NHpR	Franklin D. Roosevelt Library, Hyde Park, N.Y.
NN	New York Public Library, New York
NNC	Columbia University, New York
NNPM	Pierpont Morgan Library, New York
NRCR	Colgate-Rochester Divinity School, Rochester, N.Y.
Nc–Ar	North Carolina State Department of Archives and History, Raleigh
NcU	University of North Carolina, Chapel Hill
Nh–Ar	New Hampshire Division of Archives and Records Management, Concord
NhD	Dartmouth College, Hanover, N.H.
NhHi	New Hampshire Historical Society, Concord
Nj	New Jersey State Library, Trenton
NjFrHi	Monmouth County Historical Association, Freehold, N.J.
NjHi	New Jersey Historical Society, Newark
NjP	Princeton University, Princeton, N.J.
NjR	Rutgers University, New Brunswick, N.J.
OClWHi	Western Reserve Historical Society, Cleveland, Ohio
PHC	Haverford College, Haverford, Pa.
PHarH	Pennsylvania Historical and Museum Commission, Harrisburg
PHi	Historical Society of Pennsylvania, Philadelphia
PPAmP	American Philosophical Society, Philadelphia
PPL	Library Company of Philadelphia

PPRF   Rosenbach Foundation, Philadelphia
PU   University of Pennsylvania, Philadelphia
R–Ar   Rhode Island State Archives, Providence
RHi   Rhode Island Historical Society, Providence
TxU   University of Texas, Austin
Vi   Virginia State Library, Richmond
ViHi   Virginia Historical Society, Richmond
ViStrR   Robert E. Lee Memorial Association, Stratford, Va.
ViU   University of Virginia, Charlottesville

ABBREVIATIONS AND SHORT TITLFS

Abbreviations and short titles for works frequently cited in the present volume are identified below.

Adams, *Diary* (Butterfield)
   Adams, John. *Diary and Autobiography of John Adams.* Edited by Lyman H. Butterfield et al. 4 vols. Cambridge: Harvard University Press, Belknap Press, 1961.
Adams, *Family Correspondence* (Butterfield)
   Butterfield, Lyman H., et al., eds. *Adams Family Correspondence.* Cambridge: Harvard University Press, Belknap Press, 1963–.
Adams, *Writings* (Cushing)
   Adams, Samuel. *The Writings of Samuel Adams.* Edited by Harry A. Cushing. 4 vols. Boston: G.P. Putnam's Sons, 1904–8.
Am. Archives
   Force, Peter, ed. *American Archives: Consisting of a Collection of Authentick Records, State Papers, Debates, and Letters and Other Notices of Publick Affairs.* 4th series, 6 vols. 5th series, 3 vols. Washington: U.S. Government Printing Office, 1837–53.
Austin, *Life of Gerry*
   Austin, James T. *The Life of Elbridge Gerry, with Contemporary Letters to the Close of the American Revolution.* 2 vols. Boston: Wells and Lilly, 1828–29.
Burnett, *Letters*
   Burnett, Edmund C., ed. *Letters of Members of the Continental Congress.* 8 vols. Washington: Carnegie Institution of Washington, 1921–36.
DAB
   Dictionary of American Biography. Edited by Allen Johnson and Dumas Malone.
Evans, *Am. Bibliography*
   Charles Evans. *American Bibliography.* 12 vols. Chicago: Privately printed, 1903–34.

Franklin, *Writings* (Smyth)
    Franklin, Benjamin. *The Writings of Benjamin Franklin.* Edited
    by Albert Smyth. 10 vols. New York: Macmillan Co., 1905–7.
Greene, *Papers* (Showman)
    Greene, Nathanael. *The Papers of General Nathanael Greene.*
    Edited by Richard K. Showman et al. Chapel Hill: Published for
    the Rhode Island Historical Society by the University of North
    Carolina Press, 1976–.
Jay, *Papers* (Morris)
    Jay, John. *John Jay; the Making of a Revolutionary: Unpublished
    Papers, 1745–1789.* Edited by Richard B. Morris et al. New York:
    Harper & Row, 1975.
JCC
    U.S. Continental Congress. *Journals of the Continental Congress,
    1774–1789.* 34 vols. Edited by Worthington C. Ford et al. Washing-
    ton: Library of Congress, 1904–37.
Jefferson, *Papers* (Boyd)
    Jefferson, Thomas. *The Papers of Thomas Jefferson.* Edited by
    Julian P. Boyd et al. Princeton: Princeton University Press, 1950–.
Journals of N.Y. Prov. Cong.
    New York. *Journals of the Provincial Congress, Provincial Conven-
    tion, Committee of Safety and Council of Safety of the State of
    New York, 1775–1777.* 2 vols. Albany: T. Weed, 1842.
Md. Archives
    Archives of Maryland. Edited by William H. Browne et al. Balti-
    more: Maryland Historical Society, 1883–.
Md. Hist. Magazine
    Maryland Historical Magazine.
Morgan, *Naval Documents*
    Morgan, William James, et al., eds. *Naval Documents of the Ameri-
    can Revolution.* Washington: Department of the Navy, 1964–.
N.C. Colonial Records
    North Carolina. *The Colonial Records of North Carolina.* Edited
    by William L. Saunders. 10 vols. Raleigh and Goldsboro, N.C.:
    P.M. Hale et al., 1886–90.
N.C. State Records
    North Carolina. *The State Records of North Carolina.* Edited by
    Walter Clark. Vols. 11–26. Winston and Goldsboro, N.C.: M.I. and
    J.C. Stewart et al., 1895–1914.
N.H. State Papers
    New Hampshire. *Provincial and State Papers.* 40 vols. Concord,
    1867–1943.
NYHS Collections
    Collections of the New-York Historical Society.
OED
    Oxford English Dictionary.

Pa. Archives
Pennsylvania Archives. 9 series, 119 vols. in 120. Philadelphia: J. Severns & Co., 1852–56; Harrisburg: State printer, 1874–1935.

Pa. Council Minutes
Pennsylvania. *Minutes of the Supreme Executive Council of Pennsylvania, from its Organization to the Termination of the Revolution.* 6 vols. Colonial Records of Pennsylvania, vols. 11–16. Harrisburg: Theo. Fenn & Co., 1852–53.

Paullin, *Marine Committee Letters*
Paullin, Charles O., ed. *Out-Letters of Continental Marine Committee and Board of Admiralty, August, 1776–September, 1780.* 2 vols. New York: Printed for the Naval History Society by the De Vinne Press, 1914.

PCC
Papers of the Continental Congress. National Archives and Records Service. Washington, D.C.

PMHB
Pennsylvania Magazine of History and Biography.

PRO
Public Record Office. London.

Rodney, *Letters* (Ryden)
Rodney, Caesar. *Letters to and from Caesar Rodney, 1756–1784.* Edited by George H. Ryden. Philadelphia: University of Pennsylvania Press, 1933.

Rush, *Letters* (Butterfield)
Rush, Benjamin. *Letters of Benjamin Rush.* Edited by Lyman H. Butterfield. 2 vols. Princeton: Published for the American Philosophical Society by Princeton University Press, 1951.

Shipton, *Harvard Graduates*
Shipton, Clifford K. *Biographical Sketches of Those Who Attended Harvard College.* Sibley's Harvard Graduates. Boston: Massachusetts Historical Society, 1873–.

Susquehannah Co. Papers
Boyd, Julian P., and Taylor, Robert J., eds. *The Susquehannah Company Papers.* 11 vols. Ithaca, N.Y.: Cornell University Press, 1962–71.

Warren-Adams Letters
Warren-Adams Letters, Being Chiefly a Correspondence among John Adams, Samuel Adams and James Warren. 2 vols. Massachusetts Historical Society Collections, vols. 72–73. Boston: Massachusetts Historical Society, 1917–25.

Washington, *Writings* (Fitzpatrick)
Washington, George. *The Writings of George Washington.* Edited by John C. Fitzpatrick. 39 vols. Washington: U.S. Government Printing Office, 1931–44.

Wharton, *Diplomatic Correspondence*
Wharton, Francis, ed. *The Revolutionary Diplomatic Correspondence of the United States.* 6 vols. Washington: U.S. Government Printing Office, 1889.

Acknowledgments

To the Library of Congress, the Congress of the United States, and the Ford Foundation this edition owes its existence. It is fitting, therefore, that we take this opportunity to acknowledge the foresight of the Library's administration in planning a timely and comprehensive observation of the American Revolution Bicentennial, of the Congress in funding a Bicentennial Office in the Library, and of the Ford Foundation in making a generous grant in support of this project as a scholarly contribution to the celebration of the Bicentennial era. It is with the most profound gratitude that the editors acknowledge their appreciation to all those who bore responsibility for the decisions that made possible these contributions. Our appreciation is also extended to the innumerable persons who have contributed to enriching the holdings of the Library of Congress to make it the premier institution for conducting research on the American Revolution.

The photocopies of the more than 20,000 documents that have been collected for this project have been assembled through the cooperation of several hundred institutions and private persons devoted to preserving the documentary record upon which the history and traditions of the American people rest, and it is to their work that a documentary publication of this nature should ultimately be dedicated. Unfortunately, the many individual contributors to this collecting effort cannot be adequately recognized, but for permission to print documents appearing in the present volume, we are especially grateful to the following institutions: the American Antiquarian Society, American Philosophical Society, Universiteitsbibliotheek van Amsterdam, Archives du ministère des affaires étrangères (Paris), Archives nationales (Paris), Boston Public Library, Chicago Historical Society, Colgate-Rochester Divinity School, Columbia University, Connecticut Historical Society, Connecticut State Library, James S. Copley Library, Dartmouth College, Daughters of the American Revolution, Historical Society of Delaware, Donaldson, Lufkin & Jenrette, John Work Garrett Library, Harvard University, Haverford College, Henry E. Huntington Library, Indiana University, Robert E. Lee Memorial Association, Maine Historical Society, Maryland Hall of Records, Maryland Historical Society, Massachusetts Archives, Massachusetts Historical Society, Monmouth County Historical Association, Pierpont Morgan Library, National Archives and Records Service, New Hampshire Division of Archives and Records Management, New Hampshire Historical Society, New

Jersey Historical Society, New Jersey State Library, New-York Historical Society, New York Public Library, New York State Library, North Carolina State Department of Archives and History, University of North Carolina, Pennsylvania Historical and Museum Commission, Historical Society of Pennsylvania, University of Pennsylvania, Library Company of Philadelphia, Princeton University, Public Record Office (London), Franklin D. Roosevelt Library, Rutgers University, Rhode Island Historical Society, Rhode Island State Archives, Rosenbach Foundation, University of Texas, United States Naval Academy, Virginia Historical Society, Virginia State Library, University of Virginia, Western Reserve Historical Society, and Yale University. And in addition we express our thanks and appreciation to the following persons: Mr. Ronald von Klaussen, Mr. J. Woodward Redmond, Mrs. Elsie O. Sang and Mr. Philip D. Sang, Mr. C. Stribling Snodgrass, Capt. J. G. M. Stone, Mr. Robert J. Sudderth, Jr., Mr. Justin Turner, Mr. Paul Francis Webster, and Mrs. John G. Wood. Finally we owe thanks to the historians who have served on the Advisory Committee on the Library's American Revolution Bicentennial Program, and especially to Mr. Julian P. Boyd, Mr. Lyman H. Butterfield, and Mr. Merrill Jensen, who generously act as an advisory committee for the *Letters* project.

Chronology of Congress

August 16   Censures Commodore Esek Hopkins.

August 19   Orders Commodore Hopkins to resume command of Continental fleet; adopts extensive new instructions for Indian commissioners in middle department.

August 20   Reads draft Articles of Confederation and orders them printed in preparation for debate in committee of the whole.

August 23   Authorizes additional troops on Continental establishment for frontier defense.

August 26   Adopts measures for relief of disabled soldiers and seamen.

August 27   Resolves to encourage foreign mercenaries to desert from British army.

August 30   Adopts plan to improve postal system.

September 3   Receives Gen. John Sullivan's written report on Lord Howe's proposal for peace conference.

September 6   Designates Benjamin Franklin, John Adams, and Edward Rutledge to meet with Lord Howe.

September 9   Revises style of Continental commissions, replacing "United Colonies" with "United States."

September 11   Committee meets with Lord Howe on Staten Island.

September 16   Adopts new plan for a Continental Army of 88 battalions and system of bounties for recruitment of officers and soldiers.

September 17   Adopts Plan of Treaties; receives report of the committee appointed to confer with Lord Howe and orders it published.

September 20   Adopts Articles of War.

September 22   Sends committee to New York "to enquire into the state of the army."

September 25   Resolves to send committee to Ticonderoga to improve administration of northern army.

September 26   Appoints Silas Deane, Benjamin Franklin, and Thomas Jefferson as commissioners at Paris.

September 28   Adopts "letters of credence" for commissioners at Paris and plan for their maintenance.

October 1   Appoints Thomas Mifflin as quartermaster general to replace Stephen Moylan; appoints committee to bring in plan for military academy.

October 2   Refuses to accept Gen. Philip Schuyler's resignation as commander of northern department.

October 3   Resolves to borrow $5 million and establishes system of loan offices to transact the business.

October 7   Receives Gen. Charles Lee's personal report on southern department and advances $30,000 indemnity to him for loss of property in England.

October 9   Appoints John Morgan and William Shippen, Jr., director of military hospitals "on the east side of Hudson's river" and in New Jersey, respectively.

October 14   Accepts the report of the committee on the appeal of the libel case *Joshua Wentworth* v. *the Elizabeth* from the maritime court of New Hampshire.

October 18   Appoints Thaddeus Kosciuszko colonel of engineers in Continental Army.

October 22   Appoints Arthur Lee to replace Jefferson as commissioner at Paris; instructs commissioners to procure eight line-of-battle ships in France.

October 28   Appoints committee to conduct inquiry into monopolizing and engrossing of military supplies.

October 30   Rejects Maryland proposal to substitute money for land as an additional bounty; adopts new formula for division of prize money in Continental Navy.

November 2   Resolves to emit additional $5 million.

November 6   Resolves to appoint naval board in Philadelphia "to execute the business of the navy, under the direction of the Marine Committee."

November 11   Directs Board of War to confer with Pennsylvania Council of Safety on defense of Philadelphia.

November 15   Adopts new pay plan for Continental Navy.

November 18   Adopts lottery scheme to raise Continental funds.

November 20   Resolves to enlarge navy by eight additional ships.

MARYLAND

Robert Alexander
   Elected: July 4, 1776
   Did not attend under this election
Charles Carroll, Barrister
   Elected: November 10, 1776
   Attended: December 7–31, 1776
Charles Carroll of Carrollton
   Elected: July 4, 1776
   Did not attend under this election after August 16, 1776
Samuel Chase
   Elected: July 4, 1776; November 10, 1776
   Attended: September 16–28; November 19 to December 12, 1776
Thomas Johnson
   Elected: July 4, 1776; November 10, 1776
   Attended: September 16 to October 4? 1776
William Paca
   Elected: July 4, 1776; November 10, 1776
   Attended: September 16?–28; November 21 to December 12? 1776
   (traveled on a mission to the army in New Jersey, ca. November 25 to December 5)
Benjamin Rumsey
   Elected: November 10, 1776
   Attended: November 19?; December 12, 1776
Thomas Stone
   Elected: July 4, 1776; November 10, 1776
   Attended: August 16 to October 22? 1776
Matthew Tilghman
   Elected: July 4, 1776; November 10, 1776
   Attended: December 2–11? 1776

MASSACHUSETTS

John Adams
   Elected: January 18, 1776
   Attended: August 16 to October 12, 1776
Samuel Adams
   Elected: January 18, 1776
   Attended: October 25 to December 31, 1776
Elbridge Gerry
   Elected: January 18, 1776
   Attended: September 2 to December 31, 1776 (traveled on a mission to headquarters at New York, September 21–30)

November 23	Receives news of evacuation of Fort Lee and British crossing of Hudson River.
November 25	Urges Pennsylvania to mobilize militia for six-week emergency.
December 1	Holds emergency Sunday session; authorizes General Washington to order troops from east of Hudson River to west side.
December 5	Hears address of Indian delegation.
December 8	Holds emergency Sunday session.
December 11	Proclaims day of fasting and humiliation; instructs General Washington to contradict report that Congress was preparing to adjourn from Philadelphia.
December 12	Adjourns to Baltimore; leaves Gen. Israel Putnam to direct defense of Philadelphia.
December 20	Reconvenes in Baltimore; inquires into treatment of Gen. Charles Lee since his recent capture by the British.
December 21	Appoints George Clymer, Robert Morris, and George Walton an executive committee of Congress at Philadelphia.
December 23	Authorizes commissioners at Paris to borrow "two millions sterling," arm six vessels of war, and seek information on Portugal's hostile actions toward American ships.
December 26	Appoints committee to prepare plan "for the better conducting the executive business of Congress, by boards composed of persons, not members of Congress."
December 27	Confers extraordinary powers on General Washington for six months.
December 30	Approves new instructions for American commissioners abroad and votes to send commissioners to "courts of Vienna, Spain, Prussia and the Grand Duke of Tuscany."
December 31	Receives General Washington's announcement of his victory over Hessian garrison at Trenton.

List of Delegates to Congress

This section lists both the dates on which delegates were elected to terms falling within the period covered by this volume and the inclusive dates of their attendance. The former are generally ascertainable from contemporary state records, but the latter are often elusive bits of information derived from the journals of Congress or extrapolated from references contained in the delegates' correspondence, and in such cases the "facts" are inevitably conjectural. It is not possible to determine interruptions in the attendance of many delegates, and no attempt has been made to record interruptions in service caused by illness or brief trips home, especially of delegates from New Jersey, Delaware, Maryland, and Pennsylvania living within easy access of Philadelphia. For occasional references to such periods of intermittent service as survive in the correspondence and notes of various delegates, see the index under individual delegates. Until fuller information is provided in a consolidated summary of delegate attendance in the final volume of this series, the reader is advised to consult Burnett, *Letters*, 2:xxxix-lxxiii, for additional information on conjectural dates of attendance. Brief biographical sketches of all the delegates are available in the *Biographical Directory of the American Congress, 1774–1971,* and fuller sketches of more than half of the delegates can be found in the *Dictionary of American Biography.*

CONNECTICUT

Eliphalet Dyer
  Elected: October 10, 1776
  Did not attend August–December 1776
Titus Hosmer
  Elected: October 12, 1775
  Did not attend in 1776
Samuel Huntington
  Elected: October 12, 1775; October 10, 1776
  Attended: August 16 to October ? 1776
Richard Law
  Elected: October 10, 1776
  Did not attend in 1776
Roger Sherman
  Elected: October 12, 1775; October 10, 1776
  Attended: August 16 to October 8, 1776 (traveled on mission to headquarters at New York, September 21–30)

William Williams
  Elected: October 12, 1775; October 10, 1776
  Attended: August 16 to November 12, 1776
Oliver Wolcott
  Elected: October 12, 1775; October 10, 1776
  Attended: October 1 to December 31, 1776

DELAWARE

John Dickinson
  Elected: November 8, 1776
  Did not attend as a delegate from Delaware in 1776
John Evans
  Elected: November 8, 1776
  Did not attend Congress
Thomas McKean
  Elected: October 21, 1775
  Attended: September 24 to October 18? 1776
George Read
  Elected: October 21, 1775; November 8, 1776
  Attended: August 16–24?; December 2–12? 1776
Caesar Rodney
  Elected: October 21, 1775
  Attended: August 16 to October 5, 1776

GEORGIA

Nathan Brownson
  Elected: October 9, 1776
  Attended: December 20?–31, 1776
Archibald Bulloch
  Elected: February 2, 1776
  Did not attend in 1776
Button Gwinnett
  Elected: February 2, 1776
  Did not attend after August 16, 1776
Lyman Hall
  Elected: February 2, 1776; October 9, 1776
  Attended: August 16 to November 2; December 20–31, 1776
John Houstoun
  Elected: February 2, 1776; October 9, 1776
  Did not attend in 1776
George Walton
  Elected: February 2, 1776; October 9, 1776
  Attended: August 16 to November 2; December 12–31, 1776 (appointed to Executive Committee at Philadelphia on December 21)

John Hancock
  Elected: January 18, 1776
  Attended: August 16 to December 31, 1776
Robert Treat Paine
  Elected: January 18, 1776
  Attended: August 16 to December 10, 1776

NEW HAMPSHIRE

Josiah Bartlett
  Elected: January 23, 1776
  Attended: August 16 to October 26, 1776
John Langdon
  Elected: January 23, 1776
  Did not attend under this election
Matthew Thornton
  Elected: September 12, 1776
  Attended: November 4 to December 31, 1776
William Whipple
  Elected: January 23, 1776
  Attended: October 24 to December 31, 1776

NEW JERSEY

Abraham Clark
  Elected: June 22, 1776; November 30, 1776
  Attended: August 16–17?; October 28? to November 9?; December 3–31, 1776
Jonathan Elmer
  Elected: November 30, 1776
  Did not attend in 1776
John Hart
  Elected: June 22, 1776
  Attended: October 25? to November 5? 1776
Francis Hopkinson
  Elected: June 22, 1776
  Attended: August 16 to November 18? 1776
Jonathan Dickinson Sergeant
  Elected: November 30, 1776
  Attended: December 20?–31, 1776
Richard Stockton
  Elected: June 22, 1776; November 30, 1776
  Attended: August 16 to November 23? 1776 (traveled on a mission to Ticonderoga, September 26 to November 22?)

John Witherspoon
  Elected: June 22, 1776; November 30 1776
  Attended: August 16 to December 31 (traveled on a mission to the
  army in New Jersey, ca. November 25 to December 5)

NEW YORK

George Clinton
  Elected: April 21, 1775
  Did not attend after August 16, 1776
James Duane
  Elected: April 21, 1775
  Did not attend August–December, 1776
William Floyd
  Elected: April 21, 1775
  Attended: August 16 to October 8; November 14 to December 12,
  1776
John Jay
  Elected: April 21, 1775
  Did not attend August–December, 1776
Francis Lewis
  Elected: April 21, 1775
  Attended: August 16 to September 2?; September 20? to December
  31, 1776
Philip Livingston
  Elected: April 21, 1775
  Attended: August 16 to December 12, 1776
Robert R. Livingston
  Elected: April 21, 1775
  Did not attend after August 16, 1776
Lewis Morris
  Elected: April 21, 1775
  Attended: September 9 to 24? 1776
Philip Schuyler
  Elected: April 21, 1775
  Did not attend in 1776
Henry Wisner
  Elected: April 21, 1775
  Did not attend after August 16, 1776

NORTH CAROLINA

Thomas Burke
  Elected: December 20, 1776
  Did not attend in 1776

Joseph Hewes
  Elected: September 2, 1775; December 20, 1776
  Attended: August 16 to September 26? 1776
William Hooper
  Elected: September 2, 1775; December 20, 1776
  Attended: August 16 to December 31, 1776
John Penn
  Elected: September 8, 1775
  Attended: August 16 to October 26, 1776

PENNSYLVANIA

George Clymer
  Elected: July 20, 1776
  Attended: September 26? to December 31, 1776 (traveled on a mission to Ticonderoga, ca. September 28 to November 22?; appointed to Executive Committee at Philadelphia on December 21)
Benjamin Franklin
  Elected: July 20, 1776
  Attended: August 16 to October 25, 1776
Robert Morris
  Elected: July 20, 1776
  Attended: August 16 to December 31, 1776 (appointed to Executive Committee at Philadelphia on December 21)
John Morton
  Elected: July 20, 1776
  Attended: August 16 to August ? 1776
George Ross
  Elected: July 20, 1776
  Attended: September 6? to December 12? (traveled on a mission to the army in New Jersey, ca. November 25 to December 5)
Benjamin Rush
  Elected: July 20, 1776
  Attended: August 16 to December 12, 1776
James Smith
  Elected: July 20, 1776
  Attended: August 16 to November 24? 1776
George Taylor
  Elected: July 20, 1776
  Attendance after August 16, 1776, not known
James Wilson
  Elected: July 20, 1776
  Attended: August 16 to September 13?; October 14? to December 31, 1776

RHODE ISLAND

William Bradford
  Elected: October 28, 1776
  Did not attend Congress
William Ellery
  Elected: May 4, 1776
  Attended: August 16 to December 31, 1776
Stephen Hopkins
  Elected: May 3, 1776
  Attended: August 16 to September 7, 1776

SOUTH CAROLINA

Thomas Heyward
  Elected: February 16, 1776
  Attended: August 16 to September 4; December 24?–31, 1776
Thomas Lynch, Jr.
  Elected: March 23, 1776
  Attended: August 16 to November 2? 1776
Arthur Middleton
  Elected: February 16, 1776
  Attended: August 16 to November 29? 1776
Edward Rutledge
  Elected: February 16, 1776
  Attended: August 16 to November 24, 1776
John Rutledge
  Elected: February 16, 1776
  Did not attend in 1776

VIRGINIA

Benjamin Harrison
  Elected: October 10, 1776
  Attended: November 5 to December 31, 1776
Thomas Jefferson
  Elected: June 20, 1776
  Attended: August 16 to September 2, 1776
Francis Lightfoot Lee
  Elected: June 20, 1776
  Attended: August 16 to December 31, 1776
Richard Henry Lee
  Elected: June 20, 1776
  Attended: August 27 to December 31, 1776

Thomas Nelson
Elected: June 20, 1776
Attended: August 16 to September 21; November 10 to December 31, 1776
Mann Page
Elected: December 4, 1776
Did not attend in 1776
George Wythe
Elected: June 20, 1776
Attended: September 14? to December 12? 1776

Illustrations

"An East Prospect of the City of Philadelphia; taken by George Heap from the Jersey Shore, under the Direction of Nicholas Scull Surveyor General of the Province of Pennsylvania." This detail is from an engraving by Thomas Jefferys based on an etching of the city published in Thomas Jefferys, *A General Topography of North America and the West Indies. Being a Collection of All the Maps, Charts, Plans, and Particular Surveys, That Have Been Published of That Part of the World, Either in Europe or America* (London: R. Sayer, 1768).

Edward Rutledge, a conservative South Carolina planter and lawyer who attended Congress almost continuously during the first two years of the Revolution, made a vivid impression on several of his fellow delegates. Silas Deane thought him "young, and zealous—a little unsteady, and injudicious, but very unnatural and affected as a Speaker," and John Adams confided to his diary that "Young Ned Rutledge is a perfect Bob o' Lincoln—a Swallow—a Peacock—excessively vain, excessively weak, and excessively variable and unsteady—jejune, inane, and puerile." On the other hand, his moderate political views commended him to a number of like-minded New Yorkers and led to the development of personal and political friendships with John Jay, Robert R. Livingston, and Philip Schuyler.

Rutledge was a reluctant supporter of American independence in Congress. Although convinced that British actions and policies—especially Lord Dunmore's offer of freedom to Virginia slaves—made separation between the colonies and mother country inevitable, he maintained that independence should be preceded by the formation of a confederation among the states. At the same time he opposed the draft Articles of Confederation prepared by John Dickinson in June 1776 because of his belief that they would subordinate the states to the central government. His ambivalence about the timing of the Declaration of Independence is also suggested in his behavior during the conference with Lord Howe that he attended with John Adams and Benjamin Franklin on September 11, 1776, when he repeatedly expressed a wish for cordial relations between Great Britain and an independent United States. In later years Rutledge

November 23	Receives news of evacuation of Fort Lee and British crossing of Hudson River.
November 25	Urges Pennsylvania to mobilize militia for six-week emergency.
December 1	Holds emergency Sunday session; authorizes General Washington to order troops from east of Hudson River to west side.
December 5	Hears address of Indian delegation.
December 8	Holds emergency Sunday session.
December 11	Proclaims day of fasting and humiliation; instructs General Washington to contradict report that Congress was preparing to adjourn from Philadelphia.
December 12	Adjourns to Baltimore; leaves Gen. Israel Putnam to direct defense of Philadelphia.
December 20	Reconvenes in Baltimore; inquires into treatment of Gen. Charles Lee since his recent capture by the British.
December 21	Appoints George Clymer, Robert Morris, and George Walton an executive committee of Congress at Philadelphia.
December 23	Authorizes commissioners at Paris to borrow "two millions sterling," arm six vessels of war, and seek information on Portugal's hostile actions toward American ships.
December 26	Appoints committee to prepare plan "for the better conducting the executive business of Congress, by boards composed of persons, not members of Congress."
December 27	Confers extraordinary powers on General Washington for six months.
December 30	Approves new instructions for American commissioners abroad and votes to send commissioners to "courts of Vienna, Spain, Prussia and the Grand Duke of Tuscany."
December 31	Receives General Washington's announcement of his victory over Hessian garrison at Trenton.

List of Delegates to Congress

This section lists both the dates on which delegates were elected to terms falling within the period covered by this volume and the inclusive dates of their attendance. The former are generally ascertainable from contemporary state records, but the latter are often elusive bits of information derived from the journals of Congress or extrapolated from references contained in the delegates' correspondence, and in such cases the "facts" are inevitably conjectural. It is not possible to determine interruptions in the attendance of many delegates, and no attempt has been made to record interruptions in service caused by illness or brief trips home, especially of delegates from New Jersey, Delaware, Maryland, and Pennsylvania living within easy access of Philadelphia. For occasional references to such periods of intermittent service as survive in the correspondence and notes of various delegates, see the index under individual delegates. Until fuller information is provided in a consolidated summary of delegate attendance in the final volume of this series, the reader is advised to consult Burnett, *Letters*, 2:xxxix-lxxiii, for additional information on conjectural dates of attendance. Brief biographical sketches of all the delegates are available in the *Biographical Directory of the American Congress, 1774–1971*, and fuller sketches of more than half of the delegates can be found in the *Dictionary of American Biography*.

CONNECTICUT

Eliphalet Dyer
 Elected: October 10, 1776
 Did not attend August–December 1776
Titus Hosmer
 Elected: October 12, 1775
 Did not attend in 1776
Samuel Huntington
 Elected: October 12, 1775; October 10, 1776
 Attended: August 16 to October ? 1776
Richard Law
 Elected: October 10, 1776
 Did not attend in 1776
Roger Sherman
 Elected: October 12, 1775; October 10, 1776
 Attended: August 16 to October 8, 1776 (traveled on mission to headquarters at New York, September 21–30)

William Williams
Elected: October 12, 1775; October 10, 1776
Attended: August 16 to November 12, 1776
Oliver Wolcott
Elected: October 12, 1775; October 10, 1776
Attended: October 1 to December 31, 1776

DELAWARE

John Dickinson
Elected: November 8, 1776
Did not attend as a delegate from Delaware in 1776
John Evans
Elected: November 8, 1776
Did not attend Congress
Thomas McKean
Elected: October 21, 1775
Attended: September 24 to October 18? 1776
George Read
Elected: October 21, 1775; November 8, 1776
Attended: August 16–24?; December 2–12? 1776
Caesar Rodney
Elected: October 21, 1775
Attended: August 16 to October 5, 1776

GEORGIA

Nathan Brownson
Elected: October 9, 1776
Attended: December 20?–31, 1776
Archibald Bulloch
Elected: February 2, 1776
Did not attend in 1776
Button Gwinnett
Elected: February 2, 1776
Did not attend after August 16, 1776
Lyman Hall
Elected: February 2, 1776; October 9, 1776
Attended: August 16 to November 2; December 20–31, 1776
John Houstoun
Elected: February 2, 1776; October 9, 1776
Did not attend in 1776
George Walton
Elected: February 2, 1776; October 9, 1776
Attended: August 16 to November 2; December 12–31, 1776 (appointed to Executive Committee at Philadelphia on December 21)

MARYLAND

Robert Alexander
Elected: July 4, 1776
Did not attend under this election
Charles Carroll, Barrister
Elected: November 10, 1776
Attended: December 7–31, 1776
Charles Carroll of Carrollton
Elected: July 4, 1776
Did not attend under this election after August 16, 1776
Samuel Chase
Elected: July 4, 1776; November 10, 1776
Attended: September 16–28; November 19 to December 12, 1776
Thomas Johnson
Elected: July 4, 1776; November 10, 1776
Attended: September 16 to October 4? 1776
William Paca
Elected: July 4, 1776; November 10, 1776
Attended: September 16?–28; November 21 to December 12? 1776
(traveled on a mission to the army in New Jersey, ca. November
25 to December 5)
Benjamin Rumsey
Elected: November 10, 1776
Attended: November 19?; December 12, 1776
Thomas Stone
Elected: July 4, 1776; November 10, 1776
Attended: August 16 to October 22? 1776
Matthew Tilghman
Elected: July 4, 1776; November 10, 1776
Attended: December 2–11? 1776

MASSACHUSETTS

John Adams
Elected: January 18, 1776
Attended: August 16 to October 12, 1776
Samuel Adams
Elected: January 18, 1776
Attended: October 25 to December 31, 1776
Elbridge Gerry
Elected: January 18, 1776
Attended: September 2 to December 31, 1776 (traveled on a mis-
sion to headquarters at New York, September 21–30)

John Witherspoon
    Elected: June 22, 1776; November 30 1776
    Attended: August 16 to December 31 (traveled on a mission to the
    army in New Jersey, ca. November 25 to December 5)

NEW YORK

George Clinton
    Elected: April 21, 1775
    Did not attend after August 16, 1776
James Duane
    Elected: April 21, 1775
    Did not attend August–December, 1776
William Floyd
    Elected: April 21, 1775
    Attended: August 16 to October 8; November 14 to December 12,
    1776
John Jay
    Elected: April 21, 1775
    Did not attend August–December, 1776
Francis Lewis
    Elected: April 21, 1775
    Attended: August 16 to September 2?; September 20? to December
    31, 1776
Philip Livingston
    Elected: April 21, 1775
    Attended: August 16 to December 12, 1776
Robert R. Livingston
    Elected: April 21, 1775
    Did not attend after August 16, 1776
Lewis Morris
    Elected: April 21, 1775
    Attended: September 9 to 24? 1776
Philip Schuyler
    Elected: April 21, 1775
    Did not attend in 1776
Henry Wisner
    Elected: April 21, 1775
    Did not attend after August 16, 1776

NORTH CAROLINA

Thomas Burke
    Elected: December 20, 1776
    Did not attend in 1776

John Hancock
  Elected: January 18, 1776
  Attended: August 16 to December 31, 1776
Robert Treat Paine
  Elected: January 18, 1776
  Attended: August 16 to December 10, 1776

NEW HAMPSHIRE

Josiah Bartlett
  Elected: January 23, 1776
  Attended: August 16 to October 26, 1776
John Langdon
  Elected: January 23, 1776
  Did not attend under this election
Matthew Thornton
  Elected: September 12, 1776
  Attended: November 4 to December 31, 1776
William Whipple
  Elected: January 23, 1776
  Attended: October 24 to December 31, 1776

NEW JERSEY

Abraham Clark
  Elected: June 22, 1776; November 30, 1776
  Attended: August 16–17?; October 28? to November 9?; December 3–31, 1776
Jonathan Elmer
  Elected: November 30, 1776
  Did not attend in 1776
John Hart
  Elected: June 22, 1776
  Attended: October 25? to November 5? 1776
Francis Hopkinson
  Elected: June 22, 1776
  Attended: August 16 to November 18? 1776
Jonathan Dickinson Sergeant
  Elected: November 30, 1776
  Attended: December 20?–31, 1776
Richard Stockton
  Elected: June 22, 1776; November 30, 1776
  Attended: August 16 to November 23? 1776 (traveled on a mission to Ticonderoga, September 26 to November 22?)

served as a South Carolina legislator, associate justice of the United States Supreme Court, and governor of South Carolina, the office he held at the time of his death in 1800.

Engraving by J. B. Longacre from a painting by Ralph Earl. LC–USZ62–40478

Drafted by John Adams, amended by Congress, and adopted on September 17, 1776, the "Plan of Treaties" was intended to guide the American commissioners sent to deal with France and other European countries. By its offer of commercial reciprocity, the plan sought to win European support for American independence by holding out to continental countries the prospect of a share of American commerce, which before 1776 had been monopolized by Great Britain. In this sense it was a superb example of the willingness of the members of Congress to manipulate the European balance of power in the interests of the revolutionary cause.

From the Papers of the Continental Congress, National Archives and Records Service.

Lewis Morris, a landed aristocrat from New York, was the third and last lord of the manor of Morrisania. In Congress Morris spoke little, devoting himself instead primarily to routine administrative work and to Indian affairs. After his appointment as a brigadier general of New York militia during the summer of 1776, he left Philadelphia in September of that year to assume his command, boldly declaring that "he would never return until he has conquer'd." But military glory proved to be elusive and, despite his brave words, Morris returned to Congress for a brief term of service in the spring of 1777. Thereafter he stayed in New York for the remainder of the Revolution and attended to his duties as a country judge, militia officer, and state senator.

Painting by Charles Flagg. Independence National Historical Park Collection.

The man who once seemed content to be known as B. Franklin, printer, but became known instead as the most versatile and famous American of his generation opened a new chapter in his public career when on May 10, 1775, at the age of 69, he took a seat in the Second Continental Congress. Although initially distrusted by many persons as too sympathetic to the mother country because of his long residence in England and his campaign to substitute royal for proprietary authority in Pennsylvania, Franklin gradually allayed such suspicions by remaining somewhat in the background during most of his months in Congress and carrying a heavy load of committee responsibilities. Franklin not only influenced the creation of a Continental postal system and foreign service but he also undertook demanding missions to New England and to Canada in 1775 and 1776 and served on such key committees as those entrusted with drafting the Olive Branch Petition and the Declaration of Independence. Despite his advanced years and the arduous nature of the demands that would be placed upon him, he accepted appointment as a commissioner to the court of France in September 1776 and embarked upon still another career the following month, one that brought him fame as America's premier diplomat but kept him from his native land until 1785.

Pastel drawn from life in 1777 by Jean Baptiste Greuze. Photograph courtesy of the Diplomatic Reception Rooms, Department of State, Washington, D.C.

George Wythe   516

A Virginia jurist and statesman, George Wythe had served in Congress for more than a year before returning to Virginia in December 1776 to work with Thomas Jefferson and Edmund Pendleton on the monumental task of revising the commonwealth's laws according to republican principles. While in Congress Wythe was a member of the "committee on hostilities" in October 1775 and served on the committee for Indian affairs in 1776. A staunch republican, Wythe supported the resolution on independence, and although he was attending the Virginia Convention during July and August 1776, he signed the Declaration upon his return to Philadelphia in September. However, Wythe's major long-range contributions were in the field of American jurisprudence, where his most distinguished leadership occurred during his tenure as professor of law at the College of William and Mary, 1779–90, and as judge of the Virginia high court of chancery from 1778 until his death in 1806.

Engraving by J. B. Longacre. LC–USZ62–33513

Committee of Congress Resolves, November 24, 1776   541

On November 23, 1776, Congress appointed a committee "to devise and execute measures for effectually reinforcing General Washington, and obstructing the progress of General Howe's army." After meeting the following day, the committee issued a series of resolutions for mobilizing the militia, which were distributed as a broadside to the commanding officers of the various battalions of Pennsylvania associators. Although the resolutions were never entered on the journals of Congress, they contained a Continental fiscal commitment and carried the force of official congressional resolves.

For additional information on this unusual episode and a sample of the committee's correspondence, see its letter to Gov. William Livingston of November 25, 1776, printed below.

From the Papers of the Continental Congress, National Archives and Records Service.

John Morgan   560

John Morgan, a noted Philadelphia medical practitioner and theorist who was appointed director general and physician in chief of the Continental Army in October 1775, had an unhappy term in office. His efforts to provide medical service for Continental soldiers were plagued by numerous problems—including restricted authority, untrained staff, inadequate supplies, the jealousy of regimental surgeons, and ineffective congressional support—that were never wholly solved. Morgan's difficulties worsened during the long period of American reverses that began with the battle of Long Island, when complaints about the adequacy of the medical care he offered mounted. Simultaneously Dr. William Shippen, Jr. (an old rival— and the brother-in-law of Francis Lightfoot and Richard Henry Lee, who coveted Morgan's position) circulated charges that Morgan was guilty of corrupt practices. As a result, Congress dismissed Morgan from office on January 9, 1777, and subsequently replaced him with Shippen. Vigorously protesting his ouster, Morgan eventually obtained as a partial concession from Congress the explanation "that the general complaints of persons of all ranks in the army, and not any particular charges against him, together with the critical state of affairs at that time, rendered it necessary for the public good and the safety of the United States, that he should be replaced."

Painting by Angelica Kauffman, 1764. Washington County Historical Society, Washington, Pa.

Lottery Tickets   569

Lottery tickets were issued as a result of the adoption of a national lottery by Congress on November 18, 1776. Congress resorted to this expedient in order to raise money for the campaign of 1777 and to avoid the need for another emission of paper money, which, it was widely feared, would accelerate the depreciation of Continental currency. Unfortunately for its sponsors, the lottery failed to accomplish either of these goals. Owing to a number of delays, the drawings for the first class of tickets were not held until May 1778, and the final drawings were not completed until four years later. For additional information on this intriguing episode in congressional fiscal management and a perceptive comment by a Virginia delegate on the lottery's future, see the letters of William Ellery to Nicholas Cooke, December 4, 1776, and Thomas Nelson to Robert Morris, January 25, 1777.

Continental Congress Broadside, no. 16, Rare Book and Special Collections Division, Library of Congress.

William Paca   587

Paca, a well-to-do planter and lawyer trained in the law at the Inner Temple in London, was one of Maryland's four signers of the Declaration of Independence. A member of the Maryland legislature at the beginning of the Revolution, he was elected to the First and Second Continental Congresses as well as to the Maryland Council of Safety and the state's constitutional convention in 1776. Following his tenure in Congress, which spanned the years 1774–78, Paca accepted a judicial appointment in Maryland, and he served three terms as the state's governor, 1782–85. He was a member of the Maryland convention that adopted the federal constitution in 1788, and the following year he was appointed a federal district judge by Washington, holding the post until his death in 1799. As a member of Congress he was approvingly labeled a "deliberator" by John Adams, who also noted that despite Maryland's lukewarm support for independence Paca had behaved "generously and nobly" on the issue.

Painting in oil on mattress ticking by Charles Willson Peale, ca. 1772. The Maryland Historical Society, Baltimore.

Address to the People of America   593

Drawn up by a committee consisting of Samuel Adams, Richard Henry Lee, and John Witherspoon, approved by Congress on December 10, and printed in both English and German editions, this address was a ringing call for American resistance to the British advance on Philadelphia. The moral force of this call was undoubtedly weakened by Congress' decision on December 12 to adjourn from Philadelphia to Baltimore, however, and it was Washington's action at Trenton rather than Congress' exhortations that brought about a reversal of American fortunes. In any case the address is deeply revealing of Congress' anxiety about the seemingly irresistible march of General Howe's veteran army through New Jersey, and not even the timely American victories at Trenton and Princeton sufficed to remove all apprehensions among the delegates.

Continental Congress Broadside, no. 18, Rare Book and Special Collections Division, Library of Congress.

Oliver Wolcott   668

Oliver Wolcott, a Litchfield, Conn., judge and delegate to Congress, 1776–78 and 1780–83, was Connecticut's sole representative in Congress during the last seven weeks of 1776—weeks in which increased military demands, the departure of many delegates, and the flight to Baltimore threatened to halt Congress' operations entirely. Wolcott's letters to Connecticut during this troubled time particularly stressed his anxiety about the slow progress of Continental enlistments. His active duty during the summers of 1776 and 1777 as a general of Connecticut militia undoubtedly increased his sensitivity to General Washington's plight and he accordingly served on several ad hoc committees concerned with supplying and improving the condition of the army. Having served as an Indian commissioner for the northern department since July 1775, Wolcott was appointed to the standing committee for Indian affairs in April 1776. He was also Connecticut's representative on the committee of claims and the committee on qualifications. Retiring from the national scene in 1783, except for brief service as a commissioner at the Treaty of Fort Stanwix in 1784, Wolcott remained active in Connecticut politics. He was elected lieutenant governor in 1786, a delegate to the Connecticut ratifying convention in 1788, and governor in 1796, in which post he remained until his death the following year.

Painting by Ralph Earl. Museum of Connecticut History, Connecticut State Library, Hartford.

Robert Morris   699

Robert Morris, who was called "the virtual prime minister of the Continental Congress" when he served as superintendent of finance from 1781 to 1784, played a key role in the development of Congress' commercial and foreign policies during the early years of the Revolution. A partner in the prestigious Philadelphia firm Willing, Morris & Co., Morris took a seat in Congress in the autumn of 1775 and for the next three years remained near the center of Continental power as a member of the Marine Committee, Secret Committee, and Committee of Secret Correspondence. Determined to remain in Philadelphia until the last possible moment when the British threatened the city in December 1776, he was strategically placed to supervise Congress' affairs there when the delegates fled to Baltimore, and he was consequently appointed to the "executive committee," along with George Clymer and George Walton, which Congress appointed for that supervisory purpose on December 21. A vigorous nationalist, who often aroused suspicions because of his pursuit of private profit and readiness to subordinate local to Continental concerns, Morris retired from Congress in 1778, already having become a symbol of the commercial and financial influence that many Americans feared threatened the virtue of the republic.

Nevertheless he accepted Congress' call to take over its financial affairs during the crisis of 1781 as superintendent of finance and served largely under terms of his own making. Although equal to the challenge confronting the country, he remained under fire from his enemies, and as nationalist influence waned after the cessation of hostilities he returned to private life. The following decade several of his financial ventures failed, and he eventually spent over three years in debtors prison, the victim of western land speculation.

Painting by Charles Willson Peale, ca. 1782. Independence National Historical Park Collection.

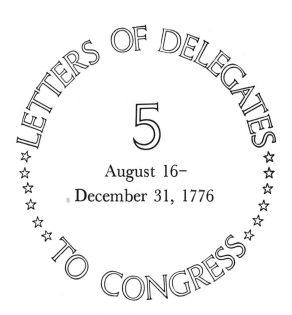

LETTERS OF DELEGATES

5

August 16–
December 31, 1776

TO CONGRESS

John Adams to Francis Dana

My dear Sir.   Philadelphia August 16. 1776

Your obliging Favour of July 28 I duely received.[1] Am glad to hear that your third Freshmanship is a busy one. I think you commence a fourth at Philadelphia very soon. I have presumed to lay before the Gen. Court a Proposal to choose Nine Delegates.[2] That their Duty may be discharged here in Rotation. The service here is too hard, for any one to be continued so long: at least for me. Who will be thought of, I know not. I wish they may be Characters respectable in every Point of View. Mr Bowdoin, Dr Winthrop, Major Hawley, Gen. Warren, Dana, Lowell, Sewall, Sullivan, Serjeant, present themselves with many others and cannot leave the Court at a Loss.

You inform me, that the House have taken up the subject of Government, and appointed a Committee to prepare a Form—and altho they have not joined the Board, in this important Business, yet I hope they will prepare a Plan which the Board will approve. I fear I was mistaken, when in my last to you, I foretold that every Colony would have more than one Branch to its Legislature. The Convention of Pensilvania has voted for a single assembly, such is the Force of Habit, and what surprizes me not a little is, that the American Philosopher should have so far accommodated himself to the Customs of his Countrymen as to be a zealous Advocate for it. No Country ever will be long happy, or ever entirely safe and free, which is thus governed. The Curse of a Jus vagum will be their Portion.

I wish with you that the Genius of this Country may expand itself, now the shackles are knocked off, which have heretofore confined it. But there is not a little danger of its becoming still more contracted. If a sufficient scope is not allowed for the human Mind to exert itself, if Genius and Learning are not sufficiently encouraged, instead of improving by this Revolution, We shall become more despicably narrow, timid, selfish, base and barbarous.

The little Pamphlet you mention was printed by Coll Lee, who insisted upon it so much that it could not be decently refused.[3] Instead of wondering that it was not enlarged, the Wonder ought to be that it was ever written. It is a poor Scrap. The Negative given in it to the first Magistrate will be adopted nowhere but in S. Carolina. Virginia has done very well. I hope the next sister will do equally. I hope the Massachusetts will call their Government a Commonwealth. Let Us take the Name, manfully, and Let the first Executive Magistrate be the Head of the Council board, and no more. Our People will never submit to more and I am not clear that it is best they should. The Thoughts on Government were callculated for Southern Latitudes, not northern. But if the House

3

should establish a single Assembly as a Legislature, I confess it would grieve me to the very soul, and however others may be, I shall certainly never be happy under such a Government. However, the Right of the People to establish such a Government, as they please, will ever be defended by me, whether they choose wisely or foolishly.

Mr. Wrixon has found hard Luck in America as well as in Europe. I have never seen nor heard of any Reason to doubt the Sincerity of his Professions of regard to our Country. But he is about returning. I am sorry that he has just Cause to return. The Baron is dead —has not left a very good Character.[4]

There is one Particular, my Friend, in which our Province uses her Delegates here very unkindly, and by the same Means injures herself, and all the united States. I mean in not sending Us your Journals. To this Moment I dont know one step that has been taken to raise the Troops for N. York and Ticonderoga, nor the Name of one officer, nor when they marched. The Interest and Reputation of our Province suffers beyond Measure by such a confused way of doing Business. We ought to be minutely informed to the Characters and Connections of all the officers you send into the service as well as of their Names. You ought to Rank and Number the Mass. Regiments and publish a List of all the officers Names.

Mr Ellery is very well. He says he dont intend to write you again till you answer his Letter.[5] I made him very happy, by letting him know that Mrs Dana and her little son were in a good way.

LB (MHi).
[1] Dana's July 28 letter is in the Adams Papers, MHi.
[2] See John Adams to John Avery, July 25, 1776.
[3] See John Adams to John Penn, March 19–27, 1776, note 1.
[4] Baron de Woedtke. See John Hancock to Baron de Woedtke, March 19, 1776.
[5] Not found. Dana was married to Ellery's daughter Elizabeth.

John Hancock to George Washington

Sir   In Congress Philada 16 Augst. 1776

I have only time to acknowlege the Rec[eip]t of your Letter of 15th, and to Transmitt the Resolves pass'd since my last, which you will find Inclos'd.[1]

That the allwise Disposer of Events may Crown your Arms with Success is the hearty wish of, Sir, Your very hum sert,

                                                    John Hancock Prest.

RC (DLC).
[1] Washington's letter is in PCC, item 152, 2:413, and Washington, *Writings* (Fitzpatrick), 5:438. The enclosed resolves, which were passed by Congress on

August 13, 14, and 15, dealt with a treaty between Massachusetts and certain Indian tribes, a plan for encouraging Hessian deserters, the appointment of Antoine Felix Weibert, and the raising of Canadian volunteers by James Livingston. *JCC*, 5:651, 653–57. On August 13 Hancock had written the following note to Washington: "I have nothing in charge from Congress to communicate to you. Had not the honour of a letter by the post. I judge the return of the express is on the road, by whom wish to have an agreeable account of the state of the Army." Washington Papers, DLC; and *Am. Archives*, 5th ser. 1:930.

Philip Livingston to the New York Convention

Gentlemen   Phila. 16 Augt. 1776.
Your favours dated the 22d July Inclosing Copy of Mr. Alsops lettr. to the Convention & a Resolve of your body acceptg his resignation of his Seat in Congress we recd & Agreable to your directions Communicated the Same to the Congress & delivd. a Copy to Mr. Alsop, who had not Attended for Some Days before, tho' we did not then know the reason of his Absentg himself.[1]

Your favours of the 7th Instant with Inclosures we recd. & Communicated to Congress.[2] The Spirited behaviour of your body so Very Conspicuous in your Resolves was very pleasing indeed. We Cannot conceive the reason that the Connecticut Militia does not Come forward at this Alarming Crisis. Those from the Massachusets are we Suppose now with you. They passed thro' Providence Last Monday. Their Number we are not Informed of. There is not the Least Doubt but your Rangers will be taken into Continental pay. The Southern Colonies are raising Troops for the like purpose & we intend in Conjunction with them to Apply to Congress on that head. The Gentn. representg these Colonies wish to have the Application defered for some time, but We are of opinion you ought Not to defer raising the men. The People on the frontiers Most Certainly Will not be Easy nor, we fear, Safe, Without such Security. We are Confident Congress means to be At the Expence Incurred & to be Incurred in Obstructg. the Navigation of Hudson's River & Will in Our Next Acq[uain]t you with their Explicit Ansr. on that head.

Collo. James Livingston has orders to raise a Regt. out of the People who were friendly to the United States in Canada.[3] Will it not be best that Capt. Jas. Stewarts Company Shd. make part of that regiment? We have requestd. Collo. Livingston to Confer with you on that Subject under the Greatest Anxiety for what is Speedily to happen at N. York. We remain, Gentlemen, Your Most Obedt servts.   Phil Livingston

RC (NHi).
[1] See John Alsop to the New York Convention, July 16, 1776, note.

² The convention's August 7 letter to the New York delegates, which was apparently presented to Congress on August 12, is in *Am. Archives*, 5th ser. 1:1482–83.

³ See *JCC*, 5:657.

Marine Committee to
William Hallock and John Paul Jones

Sir   Philada. Augt. 16th. 1776
    You will find inclosed herein a paper sent us by the Captn. of a French Sloop that is now daily expected from Martinico with Arms and Ammunition Which we are very Anxious should be got safe in.¹ Therefore we desire you to keep a good look out for her and if you fall in with her, make such Signals as will make you known for a Friend. She mounts twelve Guns with Sixty Men. You'l please to deliver this letter and it's inclosure to Capt. Hallock who must hire a pilot Boat and man her with an officer & four or five men to Cruize about the Capes for this sloop Observing to make the Signal desired and give them the needful information to get safe in here.
    When the Wasp goes down she will Convey further Orders respecting this matter Unless the sloop arrives safe in the meantime. We are Sir, Your Obedt Servants,   John Hancock

                          Robt Morris   Frs. Lewis

                          Frans. Hopkinson   Joseph Hewes

Tr (DNA: PCC, item 58). Addressed: "To Jno Paul Jones Esqr. of sloop Providence. Wm Hallock Esqr. of sloop Hornet."

¹ This "paper" consisted of a drawing of a flag accompanied by these notes:
    "Flagg of the Queen of Hungary. Six Black Carrs [bars] & Six Yellow Carrs [bars].
    "The Capt of the Pilot Boat will put his Flagg in the Foremost head of a Pilot Boat.
    "Carefully Recommended to the Care of Mr. Paul Siemen." See PCC, item 58, fol. 169. Force misleadingly printed this enclosure as a postscript to the present letter. *Am Archives*, 5th ser. 1:977–78.

Robert Morris to John Bradford

Sir,   Philada. August 16th 1776
    I have recd your favour of the 8th Inst.¹ and still find you will be disapointed about Money, therefore to prevent all further delay I will Cause ten thousand Dollars to be put up & sent with a Sum of money now going from the Treasury to Mr. Ebenezer Hancock

paymaster of the Troops at Boston. This money will be directed to you & Mr Hancock will deliver it. The remainder whatever it may be, you may either draw for or I will send it by some future Conveyance. I hope Mr. Merkle will arrive safe & sail immediately in the Dispatch, Capt Cleveland. I beg the favour of you to deliver the enclosed letter to Capt Cleveland; it is of some Consequence to me & Contains a few bills of Exchange. Give the Captain a Memorandum with the letter desiring him to put it in the Post office at the first Port he arrives at in France or if he goes to Havre to deliver it himself, but shoud he be taken desire him to break it open, take out the bills & destroy the letter, and then to Convey the bills to Mr. Andw Limozin, Mercht at Havre de Grace, the first opportunity he has. Pray excuse me for giving you this trouble & command freely on all occasions.

Sir, Your Obed hble servt,   Robt Morris

P.S. I beg my Compts & best Wishes to Mr Merkle.[2]

RC (Donaldson, Lufkin & Jenrette, New York, New York, 1975).
[1] Bradford's August 8 letter to Morris is in Morgan, *Naval Documents*, 6:114–15.
[2] For the continuation of this letter, see the first letter of Morris to Bradford, August 27, 1776.

John Morton to Anthony Wayne

Dear Sir,[1]   Philada. Aug 16th 1776
I reced your favor of third of July but Want of Opportunity to write and my Engagements to make out the Commissions for our Militia who are all on their march to New Jersey to Oppose Lord How, who is Encampt on Staten Island with About 27000 men Including devil Dunmore, Clinton and the Hessians, and my attendance in congress has taken almost all my time. I hope I Shall stand Excused. Our Politicks here have taken a Turn that I have Expected some time. The people whom you know have all along held back, joyned to some Others who were the Proprieatary friends Chosen by Virtue of A late Law for Enlarging the representation in the City of Philadelphia and the back Counties, became at last too heavy to drag along and A Convention have taken place Consisting of 8 members out of each County and 8 in the City who are to form A New government. They have made but little progress yet having only formed a Bill of rights and tis said they are to have but one branch to Ligislate, to wit an Assembly only, which I am afraid will not do if the Assembly went too slow as I Beleive they did. These Gentlemen will I doubt not make up the Leeway as they make ordinances and do Some things which people did not Expect

as it was give out at the time of Choice they were only to form a new Government. Our army of Militia in New Jersey is now Aforming under the Command of Generals Mercer, Roberdeau & Ewing to face the Enemy on the Jersey side. Our army at New York are rather Weak but Increasing and are very well provided to receive the Enemy. May god grant them the Success to End this Cruel & Unatural war by Totally defeating our Enemies. Your Family and friends were well A few days ago. I Saw Captain Vanlear on his march to Jersey. Our Privateers take many Prizes chiefly sugar ships. Some French Merchant Ships arrive to trade with us; two are here now. We look on this time as the most Critical perhaps that may happen during this war. If we defeat them I think the rest of our work will be Easie; if the advantage should be on their side god only Knows the Effect that it may have on our affairs. I Conclude my self sir and beleive me to be, Yr most Obedt humble Servant,   John Morton

RC (PHi).
    [1] Anthony Wayne (1745–96), colonel of the Fourth Pennsylvania Battalion since January 1776 and commander of the garrison at Ticonderoga during much of 1776. He was appointed to the rank of brigadier general in February 1777. *JCC*, 4:24, 7:141; and *DAB*.

Roger Sherman to Jonathan Trumbull, Jr.

Dear Sir   Philadelphia August 16th 1776
    I have not been favoured with a letter from You Since You was appointed to the office You now Sustain. I now take the liberty to begin a correspondence with You, which I wish may be continued for the future. There have been great complaints for want of money in the Northern department. That want has been partly owing to a neglect of making application to Congress for it, as Paper currency might have been Sent at any time, but a Sufficient Supply of Specie could not be obtained to Support the Army in Canada, therefore Supplies of provisions &c ought to have been Sent from the Colonies. Who is most blameworthy for the neglect I shall not undertake to Say.
    500,000 Dollars were Sent forward to You about a fortnight ago which I hope are Safe arrived. As Many more were ordered yesterday, to be forwarded immediately, So that I hope You will in future have Sufficient Supplies of that article, especially as Congress has directed the Paymasters to make returns weekly of the State of their Military Chests, which returns 'tis expected will be Sent by the Post.[1]
    I should take it as a favour if You would as often as may be

conveniente, write to me the State of Affairs in that department & the remarkable occurrences. The Enemy have now a very formidable force at Staten Island, and a Battle may soon be expected at New York which will probably be attended with very important consequences to the United States. Hitherto the Lord hath helped Us, On him may we Still depend, and find Him a present help in every time of trouble & danger. The enemy have now collected their whole force at New York & Canada, with intention, no doubt to open a communication between their two Armies by the way of Hudson's River. A vessel Arrived here this week with 100 Barrels of Powder & 50 Tons of Lead and a large quantity of Duck for the Use of the United States. Ammunition hath also been lately brought in at Several other Ports so that we have a good Supply at present.

My Son William, to whom the enclosed letter is directed, is appointed Paymaster to Colo. Warner's Regiment.[2] I dont know where he resides, but request You to forward the Letter to him as soon as may be. I wish to know what progress Colo. Warner has made in raising a Regiment. I am Sir, with due regards, Your humble Servant,   Roger Sherman

RC (CtHi).
   [1] On August 2 Congress ordered $200,000 to be sent to Paymaster Trumbull, and on the 15th authorized an additional $500,000 for the northern department. See JCC, 5:627, 659.
   [2] William Sherman had been appointed paymaster to Col. Seth Warner's regiment on July 6. JCC, 5:523. Sherman's letter to his son has not been found.

Charles Thomson to John Dickinson

Dear Sir.   Summerville Aug 16. 1776.
   I did not receive your letter of the 10th till yesterday,[1] at which time by the advices received and the movements made I apprehend the difficulties you mention are in a great measure removed. Besides the very same cause that occasioned those difficulties operates so strong in the Army, as to prevent their being removed at this time by the measure proposed. Had Mr. M[ercer] when he moved for rank, moved for the appointment, there would have been no obstacle; or had Mr. W[ilson] on receipt of your former letter, which I communicated to him, agreed to support it; or if he had not resolved to oppose it, I am of opinion there would then have been no opposition.[2] There is a tide in human affairs, which if improved, things go on smoothly, but if neglected, tis in vain to lose from the wharf.
   You and I have differed in sentiment with regard to the propriety

of certain public measures. Not so much about the measures themselves, as the time, which you thought was not yet come. But from
the prejudices, that I find prevail, & the notions of honour, rank &
other courtly Ideas so eagerly embraced, I am fully persuaded had
time been given for them to strike deeper root, it would have been
extremely difficult to have prepared men's minds for the good seed
of liberty.

I know the rectitude of your heart & the honesty & uprightness
of your intentions; but still I cannot help regretting that by a
perseverance which you were fully convinced was fruitless, you have
thrown the affairs of this state into the hands of men totally unequal
to them. I fondly hope & trust however that divine providence,
which has hitherto so signally appeared in favour of our cause, will
preserve you from danger and restore you not to "your books
& fields" but to your country, to correct the errors, which I fear
those "now bearing rule" will through ignorance—not intention—
commit, in settling the form of government.

There are some expressions in your letter, which I am sorry for;
because they seem to flow from a wounded spirit. Consider, I beseech you and do justice to your "unkind countrymen." They did
not desert you. You left them. Possibly they were wrong, in quicken-
ing their march and advancing to the goal with such rapid speed.
They thought they were right, and the only "fury" they showd
against you was to chuse other leaders to conduct them. I wish they
had chosen better; & that you could have headed them, or they
waited a little for you. But sure I am when their fervour is abated
they will do justice to your merit, And I hope soon to see you restored to the confidence & honours of your country.

I am glad to hear you continue hearty. We have flattering accounts from Canada by some Canadian officers who have joined our
Army. I hope they will prove true.

Order and harmony are returning to our northern Army, and if
it please providence to dispel the dark cloud, that hovers over New
York, I fondly hope the sun of peace will quickly shine upon us.
May that gracious providence in which I know you place your confidence, protect & preserve you.

I called yesterday to see cousin Polly & Sally. They are both well.

Your cousin Hannah remembers you with great affection, & so
do the rest of your cousins at Summerville.

Adieu, I am your sincere & affectionate friend,

Chas. Thomson

RC (PHi).

[1] Dickinson's letter to Thomson of August 10 is in the Charles Thomson Papers,
DLC.

[2] Dickinson had explained to Thomson that Gen. Hugh Mercer had recently
spoken to him of "the appointment of the person I mentioned to You in a

former Letter," by which he undoubtedly meant that Mercer also supported the promotion of Col. Samuel Miles, a move that James Wilson apparently opposed. See ibid.; and Charles Thomson to John Dickinson, July 29, 1776.

John Adams to Jonathan Dickinson Sergeant

Dear sir   Philadelphia August 17. 1776

Yours of the 13 came by yesterdays Post.[1] You have not acknowledged in it, the Receipt of a Letter I wrote you, 21 of July.

I dont like your Elections at all. County Elections are never worth much. Divide your Counties into Towns and give a Representative to every Town. The Ballot is of great Importance, and ought not to be given up; if you have lost it for once, you was in the Right, not to let up. It is so ridiculous a Farce, that it brings Elections themselves into Contempt, and it is a never failing Source of Corruption. I hope nevertheless, that your County will have the Wisdom, the Cunning and the Selfishness to choose you.

Your Convention have done worthily in ordering out so many of the Militia.

You ask the Reason of the New Englandmens Backwardness, this Campaign. If there was a Backwardness it might easily be accounted for Several Ways. The Small Pox is more terrible to them than any other Enemy. There has been another severe Drought this year, which obliges them to double their dilligence to get Bread. Besides there has been enough of successfull Pains taken to disgust them, particularly in the affair of officers. But notwithstanding all this, I deny the Fact. The Massachusetts has more than Ten Thousand private Men at N. Y. and Ticonderoga, besides all that are employed in defending their extensive Sea Coast, and in garrisoning the Fortifications in Boston Harbour, or on Board the armed Vessells. N. Hampshire and Connecticutt have Numbers in Proportion. R. Island has not been called upon. The Brigade of Militia ordered from the Massachusetts, has arrived at N. York under General Fellows. It is composed of Holmans, Smiths, and Carys Regiments. Your Negro Battallion will never do.[2] S. Carolina would run out of their Wits at the least Hint of such a Measure. I am

LB (MHi).

[1] Sergeant's August 13 letter to Adams is in the Adams Papers, MHi.

[2] Sergeant had enclosed a plan for a battalion of blacks to be raised in New Jersey as a home guard to replace the militia then being called up for service at New York. Anticipating a hostile reaction to the proposal, which he had prepared for publication, Sergeant remarked: "However, I rather apprehend it to be heretical: if so commit it to the Flames, or deal with it in what other Manner You think best." After considering Sergeant's recommendation, Adams apparently decided simply to file the plan in his papers with Sergeant's letter, where it still remains.

The heart of Sergeant's proposition reads: "Suppose the Congress to enlist under proper Officers a Number of Slaves within a certain Age sufficient to form a Battalion, paying their Masters according to a certain Rate (say fifty pounds apiece) & as a farther Compensation for their additional Value let the Master be exempted from bearing Arms. Many Slaves would willingly enlist & I Suppose a great many Masters would be glad to purchase an Exemption from bearing Arms upon these Terms.

"Let every one of these Slaves become free as soon as by Stoppages from his pay or otherwise he can reimburse the Money advanced for his purchase."

John Adams to James Warren

Dear Sir   Philadelphia August 17. 1776

I had a Letter from you, by the Post yesterday.[1] Congratulate you, and your other Self, on your happy Passage, through the Small Pox.

I must intreat you to embrace the earliest opportunity, after the General Court shall assemble, to elect some new Members to attend here, at least one, instead of me.[2] As to others they will follow their own Inclinations. If it had not been for the critical State of Things, I Should have been at Boston, e'er now. But a Battle being expected at New York, as it is every day, and has been for Some Time, I thought it would not be well to leave my Station here. Indeed if the Decision Should be unfortunate, it will be absolutely necessary, for a Congress to be Sitting and perhaps I may be as well calculated to Sustain Such a Shock, as Some others. It will be necessary to have Some Persons here, who will not be Seized with an Ague fit, upon the occasion. So much for froth: now for Something of Importance. Our Province has neglected some particular Measures, apparently of Small Moment, which are really important. One in particular let me mention at present. You Should have numbered your Regiments, and arranged all your officers, according to their Rank, and transmitted them to congress, at least to your Delegates here. I assure you, I have suffered much for Want of this Information. Besides this has a great Effect upon the Public. The five and Twentyeth Regiment from the Republic of Massachusetts Bay, would make a Sound. New York, New Jersey, Pensilvania, Virginia, &c are very Sensible of this. They have taken this political Precaution, and have found its Advantage. It has a good Effect too upon officers. It makes them think themselves Men of Consequence, it excites their Ambition, and makes them Stand upon their Honour.

Another Subject of great Importance, We ought to have been informed of, I mean your Navy. We ought to have known the Number of your armed Vessells, their Tonnage, Number of Guns, Weight of Metal, Number of Men, officers Names, Ranks, Characters—in Short you should have given Us your compleat Army and Navy List. Besides this, one would have thought We Should have been informed,

by Some Means or other, of the Privateers fitted out in your State—
their Size, Tonnage, Guns, Men, officers, Names and Characters.
But in all these Respects I declare myself as ignorant, as the Duke
de Choiseul, and I Suspect much more so.

Our People have a curious Way of telling a Story. "The Continental Cruizers Hancock and Franklin, took a noble Prize." Ay!
but who knows any Thing, about the Said Cruisers. How large are
they? How many Guns? 6, 9, 12, 18 or 24 Pounders? How many
Men? Who was the Commander! These Questions are asked me
so often, that I am ashamed to repeat my Answer. I dont know.
I cant tell. I have not heard. Our Province have never informed me.
The Reputation of the Province, the Character of your officers, and
the real Interests of both, Suffer inexpressibly, by this Inaccuracy
and Negligence. Look into Coll Campbells Letter. With what Precision he States every particular of his own Force, of the Force of
his Adversary and how exact is his Narration of Facts and Circumstances, Step by Step? When shall We acquire equal Wisdom. We
must take more Pains to get Men of thorough Education, and Accomplishments into every Department, civil, military and naval.
I am as usual.

[*P.S.*] My Horse, upon which I depended is ruined. How and where
to get another to carry me home I know not. I wrote to my Partner
to Speak to some Members of the G. Court, to see if they could
furnish me with a Couple of good Saddle Horses. If not She will be
put to some Trouble I fear.

RC (MHi). In Adams' hand, though not signed.
  [1] Warren's August 11 letter is in *Warren-Adams Letters*, 1:267–68.
  [2] For Warren's response on the indifferent reaction in the Massachusetts General Court to Adams' proposal for additional delegates to Congress, see Warren
to Adams, September 19, 1776, ibid., p. 273.

John Hancock to George Washington

Sir,   Philadelphia August 17th. 1776. 5 O'Clock P.M.
Your Favour of the 16th Inst. per Post this Minute came to Hand,
& shall be laid before Congress on Monday.

I do myself the Pleasure to enclose sundry Resolves for your Information, and likewise to forward the Commissions ordered by a
Resolve of Congress of the 10th Inst., a Copy of which I transmitted
in my Letter of that Date.[1]

With the most ardent and sincere Wishes for your Health & Prosperity, I have the Honour to be, with perfect Esteem, Sir, your most
hble Sert.   John Hancock Prest.

[*P.S.*] This morng. I Rec'd the Box by Coll Reed, & am Directed by Congress to Take care of it, which is done.[2]

RC (DLC). In the hand of Jacob Rush, with signature and postscript by Hancock.

[1] Washington's letter to Hancock of August 16 is in PCC, item 152, 2:417, and Washington, *Writings* (Fitzpatrick), 5:439–40. The "sundry Resolves" Hancock sent to Washington were passed by Congress this day and dealt with the conduct of Gen. David Wooster, the appointment of an assistant quartermaster general to reside in Philadelphia, prisoner exchanges, the raising of two more Maryland battalions, and supplies for the flying camp in New Jersey. *JCC*, 5:664–66. Hancock also wrote the following note to Commissary General Joseph Trumbull this date: "I have this Minute received your Favour by Post, and can just acquaint you, that the Bills you have Drawn shall be paid. No more Time. God Bless you." Joseph Trumbull Papers, Ct. For Trumbull's "Favour," see Trumbull to Hancock, August 15, 1776, in PCC, item 78, 22:105, and *Am. Archives*, 5th ser. 1:966–67.

[2] In anticipation of an attack by Howe, Washington had taken "all the papers in my hands respecting the Affairs of the States," put them "in a large Box nailed up," and sent the box to Congress in care of "Lieutenant Colonel Reed, Brother of the Adjutant General." Washington, *Writings* (Fitzpatrick), 5:426–27.

William Hooper to Robert R. Livingston

Philadelphia August 17. 1776.

Will you excuse me, Dear Sir, if I trespass so far upon your time, at present devoted to the important purpose of struggling yourself and inducing others to struggle for the dearest rights & privileges of mankind, as to awaken your remembrance of an old friend. I know I am in your debt; circumstances which I could not avoid have contributed to make it of long continuance. I am now in your Neighbourhood; Opportunities frequently offer & I intend to repay you with ample interest.

Since I had the pleasure of seeing you I have experienced all the vicissitudes which change of Climate could afford & been in as perilous situations as ever St Paul was and am thank God safe and sound without the aid of a Miracle. That hopeful youth Governour Martin made a Bonfire of a countryhouse of mine, fortunately my family were absent from it, and as the buildings were not compleated I suffered little more than the mortification of having given Martin an opportunity to triumph at my expense. The accidental Circumstance of my being upon a party from home with my family for a day, prevented my being kidnapped by a Boat from the Cruizer Man of War which was sent within 100 yards of a house I have on the sea side; for that pious purpose. But why do I teize you with what can be of no consequence to any one but myself. In truth I hear so much of the figure in Rhetorick called the *Egomet* that I have taken the infection; and you'll easily conjecture the respectable source from which I derive it, & forgive it if it was ten times more criminal when you consider the dignity of the examples I adopt for imitation. When I see you I'll give you a glossary. Times are critical.

We wait with anxiety the day which may bring Generals Howe and Washington in contact. Two the most formidable Armies that ever were in America under two such able Generals, with the aid of a most formidable Navy, to contest not the fate of a province, but in the result, perhaps the fate of this western world, is an object almost too enlarged for human Contemplation. May heaven crown our cause with the Success which its justice entitles it to and prosper your well meant endeavours to promote the happiness of your fellow beings.

Where is Duane? I wish to hear that he is busied in calling forth the strength of his Neighbourhood to oppose the Miscreants of Britain. Upon no other terms can I excuse his absence. I miss his nocturnal Whiff, I am sick of regularity, in bed before ten o Clock, judge what Company I keep. Pray return to us, and urge him to his duty here as soon as you can be spared from your present employment. Adieu. Health & happiness be your portion is the sincere Wish of, Dear Sir, your Obed Sert,   **Will Hooper**

RC (NjP).

Rhode Island Delegates to Nicholas Cooke

Sir   Philadelphia Augt. 17th. 1776.
We have the Pleasure to inform you that by late Advices from the Northern Army great Harmony prevails among the Officers there, and that the Jealousies and Suspicions which had distracted the Troops had almost subsided,[1] that our Fleet had increased to a very respectable Number and was still increasing,[2] that the Treaty with the Six Nations had closed and that they had solemnly agreed not to take up Arms against Us. They requested our Officers to join with them in deploring the Death of One of their Sachems, who was killed by the Party under the Command of Major Sherburn at the Cedars, which was refused because he fell fighting against Us.[3] General Schuyler had been informed that a Company of Hessians had deserted from Carlton; but they had not reached Ticonderoga when the Express came off. We wish it may prove to be true. We have the Pleasure also to acquaint you that a Continental Trading Ship arrived here a few Days ago with a large Quantity of Duck, Upwards of fifty Tons of Lead, and between 7 and 8 Tons of Powder.

We have now sufficient Lead and Powder. We wish We may have a sufficient Number of Troops at New York to use those Articles, when

Howe shall make an Attack on New York, which is daily expected. Much depends upon the Event of the Battle which will soon be fought. God grant Success to our Arms. Commodore Hopkins, who was charged with Disobedience of Orders, hath been heard in his Defence. Congress Resolved that his Answers were by no means satisfactory, and thereupon further Resolved "that he should be censured and he is censured accordingly." [4] Judge Greene arrived here yesterday. We shall move Congress for the Payment of the Money requested by the General Assembly.[5]

We have not urged an Appointment of a Brigadier General to the Command of the Troops in our State; because We think it would be imprudent to bring them in View at this Time least they should be ordered to New York and our State be left defenceless.

We should be very glad to receive a Letter now and then from the Assembly [and] you. However We shall continue [to] pursue the Rule We have prescribed to Ourselves, [and are] with great Respect, your Honor's most obedient, humble Servants,   Step Hopkins

William Ellery

RC (NN). Written by Ellery and signed by Ellery and Hopkins.

[1] On August 8 Congress had read letters from Generals Gates and Schuyler expressing satisfaction with Congress' resolution of the recent dispute between them about command of the northern army. See Gates to Hancock, July 29, and Schuyler to Hancock, August 1, 1776. *Am. Archives*, 5th ser. 1:649, 714–15. See also *JCC*, 5:526, 638; and Hancock's letters to Gates and to Schuyler, July 8, 1776.

[2] The state of the American fleet on Lake Champlain was one of the subjects discussed in Gates' August 5 letter to Hancock, which was read in Congress on August 15. See *Am. Archives*, 5th ser. 1:795–97 (where Gates' letter is misdated August 6); and *JCC*, 5:659.

[3] For the proceedings of Schuyler's conference with representatives of the Six Nations at German Flats from August 6 to 13, which were transmitted to Congress by Washington in his August 23 letter to Hancock, see *Am. Archives*, 5th ser. 1:1030–49; and Washington, *Writings* (Fitzpatrick), 5:477. Although the Iroquois did reaffirm their neutrality at the end of this conference, Schuyler's August 7 letter to Hancock—the latest account of the conference available to the Rhode Island delegates on August 17—clearly stated that he still could not predict whether the Iroquois would "engage to take an active part with us, . . . promise to remain neuter, or give evident marks of an unfriendly disposition." PCC, item 153, 2:248–52; *Am. Archives*, 5th ser. 1:856–57 (where Schuyler's letter is misdated August 8); and *JCC*, 5:659.

[4] See Thomas Jefferson's Notes on the Inquiry into Esek Hopkins' Conduct, August 12, 1776.

[5] On July 13 the Rhode Island Assembly had appointed John Collins and William Greene to go to Philadelphia and ask Congress for $120,000 "on account of the moneys due to this state, for the expense of the brigade, taken into Continental pay;" and on August 31 Congress approved the payment of this sum "in favour of the delegates of Rhode Island, for the use of that state, which is to be charged with the same." *JCC*, 5:728; and John R. Bartlett, ed., *Records of the Colony of Rhode Island and Providence Plantations in New England*, 10 vols. (Providence: A. Crawford Greene, 1856–65), 7:594.

John Adams to Abigail Adams

Philadelphia August 18. 1776

My Letters to you are an odd Mixture. They would appear to a Stranger, like the Dish which is sometimes called Omnium Gatherum. This is the first Time, I believe that these two Words were ever put together in Writing. The litteral Interpretation of them, I take to be "A Collection of all Things." But as I said before, the Words having never before been written, it is not possible to be very learned in telling you what the Arabic, Syriac, Chaldaic, Greek and Roman Commentators say upon the Subject.

Amidst all the Rubbish that constitutes the Heap, you will see a Proportion of Affection, for my Friends, my Family and Country, that gives a Complexion to the whole. I have a very tender feeling Heart. This Country knows not, and never can know the Torments, I have endured for its sake. I am glad they never can know, for it would give more Pain to the benevolent and humane, than I could wish, even the wicked and malicious to feel.

I have seen in this World, but a little of that pure flame of Patriotism, which certainly burns in some Breasts. There is much of the Ostentation and Affectation of it.[1] I have known a few who could not bear to entertain a selfish design, nor to be suspected by others of such a Meanness. But these are not the most respected by the World. A Man must be selfish, even to acquire great Popularity. He must grasp for himself, under specious Pretences, for the public Good, and he must attach himself to his Relations, Connections and Friends, by becoming a Champion for their Interests, in order to form a Phalanx, about him for his own defence; to make them Trumpeters of his Praise, and sticklers for his Fame, Fortune, and Honour.

My Friend Warren, the late Governor Ward, and Mr. Gadsden, are three Characters in which I have seen the most generous disdain of every Spice and Species of such Meanness. The two last had not great abilities, but they had pure Hearts. Yet they had less Influence, than many others who had neither so considerable Parts, nor any share at all of their Purity of Intention. Warren has both Talents and Virtues beyond most Men in this World, yet his Character has never been in Proportion. Thus it always is, has been, and will be.

Nothing has ever given me, more Mortification, than a suspicion, that has been propagated of me, that I was actuated by private Views, and have been aiming at high Places. The Office of C[hief] J[ustice] has occasioned this Jealousy, and it never will be allayed, untill I resign it. Let me have my Farm, Family and Goose Quil, and all the Honours and Offices this World has to bestow, may go to those who deserve them better, and desire them more. I covet them not.[2]

There are very few People in this World, with whom I can bear to converse. I can treat all with Decency and Civility, and converse with them, when it is necessary, on Points of Business. But I am never happy in their Company. This has made me a Recluse, and will one day, make me an Hermit.

I had rather build stone Wall upon Penns Hill, than be the first Prince in Europe, the first General, or first senator in America.

Our Expectations are very high of some great Affair at N. York.

RC (MHi). LB (MHi). Adams, *Family Correspondence* (Butterfield), 2:99–100.

[1] In the LB Adams had included this sentence. "There is a great Deal of Selfishness under the Masque and Disguise of it."

[2] In the LB Adams lined out the following passage, which he had undoubtedly penned with his fellow delegates John Hancock and Robert Treat Paine in mind.

"I have been wounded, more deeply than I have been willing to acknowledge, more deeply than the World suspects, by the Conduct of those Persons, who have been joined with me, here. The sordid Meanness of their Souls, is beneath my Contempt. One of them covers as much of it, as ever disgraced a mortal, under the most splendid Affectation of Generosity, Liberality, and Patriotism. I have acted in Conjunction with such Characters, while it was necessary to do so, but when that Necessity ceases, I will renounce them forever. I had rather shut myself up in the Cell of an Hermit, and bid adieu to the human Face, than to live in Society, with such People."

For additional information on Adams' conflict with Paine and Hancock, see Robert Treat Paine to Joseph Hawley, January 1; John Hancock to Thomas Cushing, January 17; John Adams to James Warren, February 11, 1776; and John Adams to Samuel Adams, this date.

John Adams to Samuel Adams

Dear Sir   Philadelphia August 18 1776

I had the Pleasure of a line from you, at Princetown, and yesterdays Post brought me another from New York.[1] I thank you for this Attention, and for the encouraging Account you give of the State of our Affairs at New York and Ti. The last is agreable to the Official Letters We have from G. Gates who has at last Sent Us a general Return of the Army and Navy upon a more distinct, accurate and intelligible Plan, than any which I have seen before. Among other Particulars which are new, is a Return of the State of the Hospital— in one Column the Number admitted in July, in another the Number discharged, the Ballance remains by which it appears that between 4 and 500 got well in that Month, and he has distinguished the Regiments to which they belong, by which it appears that the Pensilvania, N. Jersey and N. York Battallions are as sickly in Proportion to their Numbers, as the N. England ones.

Confederation has not been mentioned Since you left Us. We have spent the Time upon the two old Bones of Contention, the old Gen. and the Commodore.[2] The first We voted blameless. The last We voted censurable, because the Reasons given for not complying litterally with his Instructions, were by no Means satisfactory. My two Colleagues [3] differed in opinion from me, upon those Questions concerning the Ad[miral]. 6 Colonies ay, 3 No, 3 divided. I am afraid this will hurt the Fleet, but Time must determine. We have ordered the old Hero to his Command.[4]

Before the Receipt of your Letter, what you advise concerning Meigs and Dearborne was done.[5] The Board of War recommended it and it was done, but not without opposition from 5 or 6 Colonies, who thought that there ought to be no Distinctions made, but a general Exchange of the Prisoners of Arnolds Party, or none.

Let me intreat you, Sir upon your Return to Watertown, to promote an Inquiry concerning the Massachusetts Forces. Let a List be collected and published of all the Regiments raised in that State. The Names of all the officers. Let the Regiments be numbered and the officers ranked. Let us know for what Periods they were inlisted.

Let me suggest one Thing more. I am in doubt, whether our Province have had returned to them all the Powder, they furnished the Continent from the Town Stocks, as well as the Provincial Magazines. Pray inquire and if they have not, let it be demanded. There is by a Return from G. Ward 3 or 400 Barrells of Powder there belonging to the Continent, and if this opportunity is not embraced, another so fair may not present itself.

I wish to know the armed Vessells in the Service of the Province, their Number, Size, Guns, Weight of Metal, Number of Men &c.

As soon as the G. Court shall assemble I hope you will promote an Election of Some fresh Delegates, at least of one, to take my Place. Mr Hawley, I hope will be perswaded to come. It will be a fine season to have the Small Pox here, and Rush will insure him through, almost without a sigh or Groan. Warren is the next, Dana the third and Lowell the fourth. If the Province should approve the Plan of choosing Nine, these four will make up the Number. But if there are objections to these there are enough others.

Some of us here, are tremblingly alive, at the Prospect of a Battle, but whether it will be fought this year, or not, I cant Say. The two gratefull Brothers may loose Reputation with their fellow Tyrants, if they dont attack but I hope they will loose more, if they do. My most respectfull Compliments to your good Lady. I am, your Friend and servant, John Adams

RC (NN). LB (MHi).

[1] Samuel Adams' August 13 and 16 letters are in Adams, *Writings* (Cushing), 3:309–11.

[2] David Wooster and Esek Hopkins. *JCC*, 661–62, 664–65. For Adams' autobiographical account of the struggle in Congress over the behavior of these men, see Adams, *Diary* (Butterfield), 3:405–9.

[3] John Hancock and Robert Treat Paine. See Adams to Abigail Adams, this date, note 2.

[4] As this action concerning Hopkins was officially taken on August 19, Adams

apparently added this sentence after he had completed writing the letter. *JCC*, 5:667.

⁶ On August 17 Congress had ordered a special prisoner exchange for Return Jonathan Meigs and Henry Dearborn. *JCC*, 5:665.

Josiah Bartlett to William Whipple

Sir   Philadelphia August 18th 1776
   Since you left this City the Ship Morris is arrived from France. She has Brou't for the Congress above 100 Bolts of Sail Cloth which Cost above 3,000 pound Stirling. She has also Brou't for this Colony 53 Tons of Lead & 15,000 lb of Powder &c. A ship has also arrived from Lisbon which place she left the latter end of June. She has Brou't some necessaries for the Congress. The master Contradicts the report of the Portuguese Seizing American vessels and informs us of several of our vessels being at Lisbon when he left it and had free Liberty of trading. A French vessel from the West Indies & a Dutch vessel from St Eustatia have arrived & have Brou't about 10,000 lb of powder.
   I fear the confederation will not be finished in time to be laid before our Assembly at their next setting.[1] Last week passed without Looking at it, other affairs have taken up the whole time. Near two days were taken up about Comodore Hopkins, and we had the pleasure to be, for the greatest part of that time, Entertained by the Eloquence of some of our southern Brethren, particularly that polite Speaker, Middleton.
   The Congress at last found Hopkins Guilty of not paying proper attention to his orders and have ordered him to be censured; thus stands that affair at present. The Report concerning General Wooster is at length agreed to.[2]
   By Gen. Gates letters of the 7th inst.[3] it appears that our affairs in that Department wear a much more favorable aspect than for some time past. 6 or 700 of our Militia had arrived. Col Bedel was Cashiered, Butterfield Cashiered & rendered incapable to hold a Commission under the Congress.
   I am sir your friend and humble servant,

                                                    Josiah Bartlett

P.S. August 20th. Comodore Hopkins is ordered to his Command.[4] Yesterday York's Brig arrived at Egg Harbor from the West Indies. 'Tis said she has Brou't 600 Stand of arms & ten tons of powder. This is the third voyage she has made since last winter for the continent. A vessel has just arrived from Statia. Dont hear what she has Brou't.[5]   J. B.

RC (Ronald von Klaussen, state of Florida, 1976).

¹ Congress had last considered the articles of confederation on August 8 and took them up again on August 20. *JCC*, 5:639–40, 674.

² See *JCC*, 5:661–62, 664–65.

³ Undoubtedly Gates' August 5 letter to Hancock, which is printed under the date August 6 in *Am. Archives*, 5th ser. 1:795–97. See also John Adams to Horatio Gates, August 13, 1776, note 4.

⁴ *JCC*, 5:667.

⁵ In his September 2 response to this letter, Whipple made the following report on his activities during his recent journey home. "I called on Govr Trumble, on my way thro' Connecticut, who informed me of the state of affairs at the Lakes, which as you observe have a much better appearance then they had some time ago. At Providence I endeavored to get Guns for the Frigate but found that the owners of the Furniss were determined to take every advantage of the times. They talked of £90 Lawful Money per Ton but would not contract at that unless half the Money was paid at the Signing of the Contract. I think it better to comply with their extravegant Terms then to let the ship lay here, while one of the Enemys ships (the Milford) is taking everything on our coast. I therefore have advised Mr. Langdon to get the guns on the best terms he can, he talks of seting off for Providence to morrow. If he gets the guns the ship will soon be ready for sea. I have sometimes laugh'd at Mr. Langdons Panegyric on this Ship, but I am now convinced he has said no more in her praise then she deserves. She is really the Best ship by far, of the Nine which I have seen, & is as well Officer'd as any ship in the Service. I hope justice will be done these Gentlen in Ranking them, they really deserve to be high on the list. Were they known to the Committee I am sure they would be. I found on my arrival that our assembly had Emitted £23,000, in addition to the 60,000 Emitted before I went to Philadelphia. I could not help Expressing my surprise to the Committee at their taking this step without asking a supply from the Continental Treasury. I think it very wrong to issue such Quantities of paper Money." Fogg Collection, MeHi.

John Morton to Persifor Frazer

Dear Sir   Philada. the 18th Augt. 1776

Your favor of the 31th Ultimo is received.¹ I thank you for your Inteligence, it may be useful to me and in some way so to the publick but am sorry to hear of the Extream distress of my dear Countrymen. There is nobody Abhors Peculation more than I do, how can people attend to such things in this time of distress, surely good cannot Come of such doings. Pennsylvania Never see such days as now on Account of Arrival of so large an Armament at N York. The Enemy now Consisting of 27000 or as some Accounts say 30,000 men all Encampt on Staten Island. Our Militia are march'd to A man Out of Chester County (Except some few that ran of[f] and hid Themselves) and so they have from all the Counties to the Amount in the whole of Upwards of 15000. The Spirit of the Association on this as well as on Other Occasions does them much honor and I have good reason to hope at this time they will be the salvation of North America. 4000 more will soon arrive from Maryland and the Delaware Counties and two Battalions of Regulars also on their march from Virginia for New York and General Lee is also on his way there by order of Congress. I hope If we can stand it this Campain the spirit of our Enemies will be broke and our Business will then be Easie. We have Arrivals of Powder, and Military stores frequently make a great deal and are in no want of that Article nor of Lead. Our Malitia are Stationed at Amboy, Woodbridge and Elizabeth Town point, are in health though Some of them that went from this City about A Month Ago are I am told somewhat uneasie to return. Our army at New York at present Not so Numerous as I Could wish but Increases every day. General Washington Expects an Attack every hour, is well provided with every thing, and I am sure our Troops will sell their lives dear or Conquer. They have my prayers and yours I am sure for their success. Your friends and Relations I have reason to beleive are well. It is a Very healthy time here as I have known or Else there is no body to be sick the strep being mostly gone. I had almost forgot to mention the Arrival of Devil Dunmore and Clinton who are both at N York and all their troops. With my best Respects to you and prayers for your health I am sir with real Esteem your most Obedt, humble sevt,   John Morton

P.S. write freely to me—no fear of Injury to you. Subscribe P.F. Sketchleys Compliment to you, he marches this day to Jersey from this place.

Augt 21th. News has just now arrived from Martinique that the Governor will receive our Vessels to trade freely, Protect that trade and receive and Suffur us to sell our Prizes there; that the French are preparing for war, which will soon take place agt the English; this may be depended on.

RC (MH–H).
    [1] Frazer's letter is filed with Morton's at MH–H. Frazer, a captain in Col. Anthony Wayne's Fourth Pennsylvania Battalion, was at Ticonderoga.

John Adams to Samuel H. Parsons

Dear Sir.   Philadelphia August 19. 1776
    Your Favours of the 13th and 15th are before me.[1] The Gentlemen you recommend for Majors, Chapman and Dier, will be recommended by the Board of War, and I hope agreed to in Congress.[2]
    I thank you for your observations upon certain Field officers. Patterson, Shepherd and Brooks make the best Figure, I think upon Paper. It is my Misfortune that I have not the least Acquaintance with any of those Gentlemen having never seen any one of them,

or heard his Name till lately. This is a little remarkable. Few Persons in the Province ever travelled over the whole of it, more than I have, or had better oppertunities to know every conspicuous Character. But I dont so much as know from what Parts of the Province Shepherd and Brooks come, of what Families they are, their Educations, or Employments. Should be very glad to be informed.

Lt Coll Henshaw has been recommended to me by Coll Reed for Promotion as a usefull officer. But upon the whole, I think the List you have given me dont shine. I am very much ashamed of it. I am so vexed sometimes as almost to resolve to make Interest to be a Coll myself. I have almost Vanity enough to think that I could make a Figure in such a Group. But a treacherous, shattered Constitution is an eternal objection against my aspiring at military Command. If it was not for this insupperable Difficulty I should certainly imitate old Nol Cromwell in one Particular, that is in launching into military Life after forty, as much as I dislike his Character and Example in others. But enough of this.

I wish I could find Materials any where in sufficient Quantities to make good officers. A brave and able Man, wherever he is, shall never want my Vote, for his advancement: nor shall an ignorant, awkward Dastard, ever want it for his Dismission. Congress must assume an higher Tone of Discipline over officers, as well as those over the Men.

With Regard to Encouragement in Money and in Land, for Soldiers to inlist during the War, I have ever been in favour of it, as the best œconomy and the best Policy and I have no doubt that Rewards in Land will be given, after the War is over. But the Majority are not of my Mind for promising of it now. I am the less anxious about it, for a Reason which does not seem to have much Weight however with the Majority. Altho it may cost us more, and we may put now and then a Battle to a Hazard, by the Method we are in, yet We shall be less in danger of Corruption and Violence from a standing Army, and our Militia will acquire Courage, Experience, Discipline and Hardiness in actual service.

I wish every Man upon the Continent was a Soldier, and obliged upon occasion to fight, and determined to conquer or to die.

Flight was unknown to the Romans. I wish it was to Americans. There was a Flight from Quebec, and worse than a Flight at the Cedars. If We dont attone for these disgraces We are undone.

A more exalted Love of their Country, a more enthusiastic arder for military Glory, and deeper Detestation, Disdain and Horror of martial Disgrace must be excited among our People, or We shall perish in Infancy. I will certainly give my Voice for devoting to the Infernal Gods, every Man high or low, who shall be convicted of Bashfullness in the day of Battle.

P.S. Since the above was written Congress has accepted the Report of the Board of War, and appointed Dier and Chapman, Majors. I had much Pleasure in promoting Dier, not only from his own excellent Character, but from Respect to my good Friend his Father.

LB (MHi).
    [1] Parsons' letters of August 13 and 15 are in the Adams Papers, MHi.
    [2] For the appointments of James Chapman and Thomas Dyer by Congress this day, see Adams' postscript to this letter; *JCC*, 5:667–68; and William Williams to Joseph Trumbull, August 20, 1776.

Josiah Bartlett to John Langdon

Dear Sir: Philadelphia, August 19, 1776.
    Your favour of the 5th instant has come to hand, and am much pleased to hear of the success of the *New-England* privateers in capturing *British* ships.[1] May they go on to distress the *British* trade, till they are taught wisdom by misfortune, since nothing else will effect it. I opened your letter to Colonel *Whipple,* agreeable to your order, in which I find you want information about the agency and marine affairs; but as Colonel *Whipple* will be able to satisfy you as to those matters, (who will be with you before this,) I shall say nothing about them.
    Since Colonel *Whipple* left us the ship *Morris* arrived here from *Havre-de-Grace,* in *France.* She has brought on Continental account above one hundred bolts of sail cloth, amounting to between fifty and sixty thousand yards. She has also brought for this Colony fifty-three tons of lead, and seven and a half tons of powder, &c., &c.
    A ship has likewise arrived from *Lisbon,* with necessaries for the Continent, but cannot give the particulars. She left *Lisbon* the latter end of *June,* and left several other of our vessels there, who were permitted to trade freely, notwithstanding the report which lately prevailed, that the *Portuguese* had seized all *American* ships in their harbours.
    One vessel from *'Statia,* and one vessel from the *French West-Indies,* have also arrived, and have brought in about five tons of powder, &c. By a letter from *'Statia,* dated 28th *July,* we are told that the *Dutch* have refused to renew the prohibition for sending out arms and ammunition; that the *English* have seized two of their ships, and sent them into *England,* under pretence of their supplying us with arms, &c.; that in consequence, the *Dutch* had ordered sixty ships of war to be fitted out, and to raise twenty thousand additional land forces, and had refused to lend *England* the *Scotch* regiments, as they had before agreed to. What dependence is to be placed in this intelligence, I can't certainly say, but believe some

part of it, at least, is true, I hope all. By sundry letters, it appears that both the *French* and *Dutch* are very fond of our trade, and have sent and are sending to the *West-Indies* large quantities of arms, and every other article that we are like to want.

The insolence of the commanders of the *British* men-of-war in the *West-Indies,* is become intolerable. It seems that one of them some time since went into the harbour at *'Statia,* and after waiting some days, attempted to take possession of some *American* vessels there, but was prevented by the *Dutch.* She then left the harbour, and the next day seized a ship bound from *'Statia* to *Amsterdam,* and carried her into one of the *English* Islands, and there he detains her. This has so exasperated the *Dutch,* that the Governour of *'Statia* has (it is said) ordered the Captains of the ports to fire on any *English* man-of-war that comes within reach of their guns. This looks like kicking up a dust.

I am, your most obedient, humble servant,

Josiah Bartlett

P.S. *August* 20th. Yesterday a vessel arrived at *Egg-Harbour,* that was sent to the *West-Indies* on the account of the Congress. It is said she has brought six hundred stand of arms and ten tons of powder. The particulars of the fire-ships attempting the men-of-war, and burning a tender, and of the men-of-war getting down by *New-York,* you will hear before this reaches you. *Ut sup.*   J. B.

MS not found; reprinted from *Am. Archives,* 5th ser. 1:1060.

[1] An extract of Langdon's August 5 letter to Bartlett is in Morgan, *Naval Documents,* 6:56.

Edward Rutledge to Robert R. Livingston

My dear Robert   [August 19? 1776] [1]

Your Favour of the 6th Instant came to Hand on Thursday; your last I received Yesterday after the Post had left Town. It will give me real Pleasure I assure you to do Justice to Mr. Cortland & promote your Brother to the Rank which his Services and Situation in my opinion demand. But as we must pursue opposite Rules in advancing those Gentlemen, the one rising according to Seniority, the other Regimentally, and as the Congress will I believe act with great Caution in their *next* Arrangement of your Forces I submit to you whether it would not be best to get a Recommendation from your Convention on this Subject. I think there should be no difficulty in giving Lt. Colo. Cortland, McDougall's Regiment, & your Brother, Clynton's, because I know it is the Opinion of Genl. Washington & the Board of War to whom that Opinion was given, that

Promotions should in common be Regimentally, but that that Rule
should give way in extraordinary Cases. This Principle will then
exactly apply supposing that your Brother had no peculiar Merits,
but with Me he has, and if the House shall think as I would wish
them, he will have Merit with them likewise. But as I have already
mentioned, lest they should run retrograde, a little Jog from your
Convention would not be amiss. The Promotion of General officers
gave us a good deal of trouble. Woorster had more Advocates for
his Advancement than his Abilities entitled him to. His Friends
threaten'd us with his Resignation if he was passed by. This was
conclusive with some of us, but he has not as yet justified our Expectations, and we begin to fear that his Attachment to 120 Dollars
a Month will prevent the good work. We found some difficulty in
getting Clynton made a General. Phil. Livingston proposed him &
I advocated his Promotion. It was confessed on all Hands that he
had done more & suffered more than McDougal, but a Mr. Varnum
of Rhode Island & Maxwell of Jersey were opposed to him. Our
Exertions however prevailed.[2] I shall be doubly fortunate if by my
Endeavours two valuable officers can be rewarded. You who have
served so long in Congress will confess it is not often that we do
much good in one day. Most of the last Week was taken up in
trying old Hopkins, for a Breach of Orders. The Fact was clearly
proved, his Excuses were trifling to the Last Degree, to say the least
of them, the Congress in opposition to the Eastern Colonies found
him guilty, and have censured him for his Conduct. Some of us
pressed his Removal, from the Command, but a tenderness or
rather weakness for his Brother,[3] and an opinion that he would
resign in Consequence of the Thunder of the House, obstructed the
passing of the Motion. I wish he would resign, for I am satisfied
that he is totally unfit for the Department, & that we shall be disgraced so long as he shall continue at the Head of our naval Affairs.
We are doing every thing in our Power to reform the Pay of the
Army & put the Forces under better Regulations than they have yet
been. The Committee of Spies (of which you, Jefferson, Adams & I
were Members) who were desired to revise the Articles of War &
bring in such Amendments as they thought proper, have reported to
the House the British Articles as far as local Circumstances will
admit, and the Congress is in a fair way of adopting them. If we
can carry them thro' compleatly it will have a most happy Effect.[4]
I know not how we shall so soon purge the Army of the Men you
mention, as by prevailing upon them to resent their own Quarrels.
To shew you how exactly we concurr'd in Sentiment upon this
Subject, I must tell you that when the Congress were employing a
little Leisure Time some days ago in considering the new Articles,
& before I received your Letter, I proposed to strike out that Article
which prevents the sending of Challenges, and pressed it as a

Measure that would tend to make their officers Gentlemen, or at least induce them to act as such, whilst in Company with Gentlemen. Stone seconded & supported the Motion, but we could not carry the Point. I believe we must leave it to time. We have done nothing with the Confederation for some Days, and it is of little Consequence if we never see it again, for we have made such a devil of it already that the Colonies can never agree to it. If my opinion was likely to be taken I would propose that the States should appoint a special Congress to be composed of new Members for this purpose—and that no Person should disclose any part of the present plan. If that was done we might then stand some Chance of a Confederation, at present we stand none at all. We have not as yet touched the Treaty—and Independence has been declared upwards of Six Weeks! We have heard of Deane's arrival in France but no Letters from him. I am much pleased with the Spirit of your Convention. God grant they may receive the Blessings of Liberty, & by a wise Government fix those Blessings upon a strong and lasting Foundation. Exert my good Friend all your Abilities in the accomplishing of this delicate Business, so that you will be beloved by Posterity as truly as you are by your most affectionate,

Edward Rutledge

P.S. Remember me affectionately to Jay. We have sent to the Southward for General Lee, lest any Accident should befall Washington (which God prevent) & our Army be without a proper Head. You did not inclose me Mr Cortland's Letter as you thought.

RC (PPRF). Endorsed by Livingston: "Edward Rutledge Esqr. Recd. Augt 1776."
   [1] This letter was written after Congress censured Esek Hopkins on August 16 but before debate on the Articles of Confederation was resumed on August 20. It has been assigned the date August 19 because of Rutledge's references to impending action on the revised articles of war, which were debated for a time this day.
   [2] For Congress' recent action in regard to the appointment of general officers, see JCC, 5:641.
   [3] Stephen Hopkins of Rhode Island.
   [4] On June 14 Congress had directed the committee on spies "to revise the rules and articles of war." This committee brought in a revised set of articles on August 7, which was considered by Congress on August 13 and 19 and September 19 and finally approved on September 20. JCC, 5:442, 636, 652, 787-807, 6:1125-26. For John Adams' autobiographical account of the revision of the articles, explaining why they were essentially "the British Articles of War, totidem Verbis," see Adams, *Diary* (Butterfield), 3:409-10.

John Adams to Joseph Ward

Sir   Philadelphia August 20. 1776
   Your Favours of 28th July and 8 August are before me.[1] I have a Favour to ask of you, that is to Send me an exact Account of the

Number of Continental Cruisers fitted out in the Massachusetts, the Tonnage of the Vessells, the Number of Guns belonging to each, the Weight of Metal, the Number of Men, the Names of the Vessells and the Names of All the officers, that is to say, the Captains and Lieutenants, the Sailing Masters and Mates, and the officers of Marines.

You complain that there has not been a sufficient Number of Promotions among the Massachusetts officers—perhaps with Justice. But what is the Cause of the Disinclination in Massachusetts Gentlemen, to the service. Ward, Fry, and Whitcomb have resigned. If We go out of the Line of succession among the Collonells, to make a Brigadier General, We give Discontent. And can you lay your Hand upon your Heart and recommend the oldest Collonells for Generals as they stand upon the Line. We have now made Nixon a General. I know neither him nor his Qualifications. Prescott would have been a General long ago. Nay there is no Advancement to which he would not have been pushed for his Conduct and Intrepidity on Charlestown Heights. But you know there is a fatal objection.

You ask if it was not in Contemplation to send two Southern Generals to command you, in Defence of yourselves? I answer it was, and that at the earnest Solicitation of the principal Gentlemen in the Province who in their Letters pressed for it. They had two Reasons for this. One was that a Stranger would be likely to have more Authority among the People there than a Native. Another was that a Southern Gentleman would be likely to give more Satisfaction to the middle and Southern Colonies. I will tell you a plain, frank Truth, Mr Ward, the People of our own Province have not much Confidence in their own Generals. I am extremely sorry for it—nothing has made me more unhappy, but so the fact is, and I cannot alter it.

You Speak of a General Mifflin who was young in Experience, and in the service. I wish our Massachusetts Collonels, old as they are, had as much Activity and as extensive Capacities and accomplishments as that young General. However he is not so very young. He is old in Merit in the American Cause. He has the utmost Spirit and Activity, and the best Education and Abilities. He is of one of the best Families and has an handsome Fortune in his Country. He has been long a Member of the Legislature here, and of Congress. He was long the most indefatigable and successfull Supporter of the American Cause in this Province, where it has laboured more than any where else. He was the prime Conductor and the Creator of Motion to that association, which has compleated the Restoration of this Province to the American Union, and has infused a martial Spirit into a People who never felt any Thing like it before. You can Scarcely name a Man any where who has more Signal Merit.

There is a Number of young Gentlemen, of our Province, whom I wish promoted. But to advance them over the Heads of a long Line of Colonells, would ruin the service—and I wish you would tell me, which of our Collonells you think most fit for Generals. I wish you Promotion with all my Heart, because I think your military and literary Qualifications would do Honour to your Country. But you know that to shoot you up into high Command, over the Heads of a hundred officers, would destroy the Army.[2]

[*P.S.*] Since the foregoing was written Congress has requested General Ward to continue in Command.[3] I hope he will. The Fortifications in Boston Harbour must be compleated, otherwise the two gratefull Brothers may seek Winter Quarters there.

LB (MHi).
[1] Ward's July 28 and August 8 letters are in the Adams Papers, MHi.
[2] This day Adams also wrote a letter to his wife, which although concerned primarily with personal affairs contained a brief reference to Admiral Howe's peacemaking efforts. "Lord Howe seems afraid to attack and has got to the old Work of Amusement and Chicanery. But he cannot catch old Birds. They are aware of the snare." Adams, *Family Correspondence* (Butterfield), 2:102–3.
[3] On August 21, Congress resolved that Gen. Artemas Ward "be authorized and requested, if his health permit, to continue in the command of the forces in the service of the United States, in the eastern department, until farther orders." *JCC*, 5:694. On August 8 the Massachusetts Council had written to President Hancock requesting the early replacement of General Ward if he retired. Richard Derby, Jr., to John Hancock, August 8, 1776, PCC, item 65, 1:105; and *Am. Archives*, 5th ser. 1:859–60.

Benjamin Franklin to Lord Howe

My Lord   Philada Aug 20. 76 [1]

The Temper ⟨*& Disposition*⟩ of the Colonies as professed in their several Petitions to the Crown was sincere. The Terms they proposed should then have been closed with, and all might have been Peace. I dare say your L[ordshi]p as well as myself, laments they were not accepted. I remember I told you that better wd never be offered, & I have not forgotten your just Comparison of the Sybyl's Leaves. But the Contempt with which those Petitions were treated, none of them being vouchsaf'd an Answer, and the cruel Measures since taken, have chang'd that Temper. It could not be otherwise. To propose now to the Colonies ⟨*a Return to the State of Subjection they were formerly in to the*⟩ a Submission to the Crown of Great Britain; would be ⟨*useless*⟩ fruitless. The Time is past. One might as well propose it to France, on the Footing of a former title.

FC (PPAmP).

[1] Perhaps drafted in response to Howe's letter of August 16—which is available in Franklin, *Writings* (Smyth), 6:462—but undoubtedly not sent. In a subsequent letter, Franklin explained that he had received Howe's letter of August 16 but "did not immediately answer it, because I found that my corresponding with your Lordship was disliked by some members of Congress." See Franklin to Lord Howe, September 8, 1776.

John Hancock to George Washington

Sir   3 oClock P M, Congress Chamber 20 Augst 1776
Your Letter by Express with its several Inclosures I yesterday Rec'd, & yours by Post this moment came to hand. I have laid the whole before Congress, & am directed to keep the Express.[1] I shall therefore only by the Return of the Post Inclose you Two Commissions which please to order to be Deliver'd, Referring all other matters to be Sent by the Express.[2]
I have the honor to be, Your most Obedt sert,
                                             John Hancock Prest.

RC (MdHi: Middendorf deposit, 1972).

[1] Washington's second letter to Hancock of August 12, which was read in Congress on August 19, is in PCC, item 152, 2:385, and Washington, *Writings* (Fitzpatrick), 5:419. Enclosed in it were "the proceedings and judgment of a court martial against Colonel Donald Campbell." *JCC*, 5:667. See also Hancock to Washington, August 22, 1776, note 1. Washington's letters to Hancock of August 18 and 19, which were read in Congress on August 20, are in PCC, item 152, 2:433–34, 443–46, and Washington, *Writings* (Fitzpatrick), 5:450–52, 463–64.

[2] Hancock probably sent Washington commissions for James Chapman and Thomas Dyer. *JCC*, 5:667–68.

Samuel Huntington to Jabez Huntington

Sir   Philadelphia 20th August 1776
I am this day favoured with yours of the 15th Instt. The affairs of the nothern department have lain heavy on my mind for a long time, & much hath been said here on that Subject by Some of the member[s]. At present things have a better prospect in that department, hope it may continue. Am glad to hear Troops are coming from Connecticut at this Critical Season, alltho that State hath gone so far beyond their proportion. The American Cruisers have in many parts been Successfull, hope we shall have a good account of Captains Niles and Hardin in due time.[1]
By deserters lately from Staten Island we are told Ld Dunmore with his fleet are arrivd there, that he had divided his troops into three departments, the sick were sent to Hallifax, the well which

were few were landed at Staten Island, & his Black Regiment were Sent to the West Indies for Sale. The Indians have Committed Some depradations at the southward on the backs of the Carolinas, & Troops are Sent against them which I hope will bring them to good terms, but in the middle & northern department the latest advices are more favourable. The Indians Seem disposd to observe a neutrality which I cannot but hope will take place among them if our unnatural Brethren Should not get any advantage against us which God prevent.[2]

We have Just recivd advice that the Ships which went up the north river returnd last Sunday with the advantage of the wind & tide & run by the batteries. Believe they were weary of their Situation.

Am Sir with Esteem your Humble Servant,

Samll Huntington

RC (CtHi).

[1] Jabez drafted his August 15 letter to Samuel on the verso of Samuel's July 31 letter to him. He reported that 14 regiments of Connecticut militia had been ordered to New York, "many of which are on their March & the others Like to Come on Soon," that Robert Niles, captain of the Connecticut schooner *Spy*, "is Lately Sailed on a Cruse," and that Capt. Seth Harding "in a verry fine Bermuda Brig Late Purchased by Govt. will Sail in a few days." Samuel Huntington Papers, CtHi. For additional information on Harding's orders, see Morgan, *Naval Documents*, 6:16–17, 154–55.

[2] For the August 19 report of the committee on Indian affairs, see *JCC*, 5:668–70.

Thomas Jefferson to John Page

Dear Page   Philadelphia Aug. 20. 1776.

We have been in hourly expectation of the great decision at New York but it has not yet happened. About three nights ago an attempt was made to burn the two ships which had gone up the river. One of the two fire-rafts prepared for that purpose grappled the Phenix ten minutes but was cleared away at last. A tender however was burnt.[1] The two ships came down on Sunday evening and passed all our batteries again with impunity. Ld. Dunmore is at Staten Isld. His sick he sent to Halifax, his effective men he carried to Staten Isld. and the blacks he shipped off to the West Indies. Two gentlemen who had been taken prisoners by the enemy have made their escape.[2] They say they are now 20,000 and that another division of 5000 foreigners is still expected. They think Ld. Howe will not attack these 10 days, but that he does not wait for his last division, being confident of victory without. One of these informants was captain of a continental vessel going for ammunition. The mate and crew rose and took the vessel. They fell in with the division of the Hessians which came with the Hessian general and were brought to. The general learning from the dethroned captain what had happened, immediately threw the piratical mate into irons and had the captain to dine with him every day till they got to Halifax where he delivered him, vessel &c. over to the English. A gentleman who lived some time in this city, but since last winter has become a resident of St. Eustatia writes that by a Dutch ship from Amsterdam they have advice that the states of Holland had refused to renew the prohibition on the exportation of powder to the colonies, or to cede to the English the Scotch brigade in their service, or to furnish them with some men of war asked of them by the British court. This refusal so piqued the ministry that they had been induced to take several Dutch ships, amongst which he sais were two which sailed from that island and were carried to London, another to St. Kitt's. In consequence of this the Dutch have armed 40 ships of war and ordered 60 more to be built and are raising 20,000 land forces. The French governor in chief of their W. Indies has not only refused to permit a captain of a man of war to make prize of our vessels in their ports but forbidden them to come within gun shot of the ports. The enemy's men of war being withdrawn from our whole coast to N. York gives us now fine opportunities of getting in powder. We see the effect here already.

Two Canadians who had been captains in our Canadian regiment and who General Gates writes us are known in the army to be worthy of good credit made their escape from St. John's, and came over to our army from Tyonderoga; and give the following intelligence.[3] The enemy did not fortify any place we abandoned. They had 2000 men at Isle aux noix under Genl. Fraser, 2000 at St. John's under Carleton and some at Montreal. 250 only had been left at Quebec. It was reported that 4000 English troops which were to have been a part of that army had perished at sea which gave great uneasiness. The fleet brot over timber &c. for 50 boats which they attempted to transport by land from the mouth of Sorel to St. John's, but could not for want of carriages which had been destroyed. Carleton therefore employed Canadians to build batteaux at St. John's. He has rendered himself very odious to the Canadians by leving contributions on them in general and confiscating the estates of all those who followed our army or who abscond. Great numbers of the Germans desert daily and are anxiously concealed by the inhabitants. 70 Brunswickers disappeared in one day. Their officers are so much afraid of bush-fighting and ambushes that they will not head any parties to pursue the runaways. The men have the same fears, which prevents them from deserting in so great numbers as is supposed they will when once our fleet shall appear cruising on the lake to receive and protect them. Between the 22d and 24th July Carleton and the other generals abandoned all their posts on this side Sorel except St. John's with as great precipitation as our poor sick army had done, carrying with them their artillery and provisions. This was occasioned by the arrival and mysterious manoeuvres of a fleet at Quebec supposed French, hoisting different colours and firing at Tenders sent from the town to enquire who they were. 200 men were left at Isle aux noix to send them intelligence of our operations, who they say will go down the river if we return into Canada. For this event the Canadians are offering up prayers at the shrines of all their saints. Carleton sometime ago hearing that we were returning with a considerable reinforcement was so terrified that he would have retired immediately had not some of his spies come in and informed him of the deplorable situation to which the small pox had reduced our army. They are recovering health and spirits. Genl. Gates writes that he had accounts of the roads being crowded with militia coming to his assistance. 600 from New Hampshire came in while he was writing his letter, being the first. His fleet had sailed from Tyonderoga to Crown point. Their number and force as in the margin.

	Guns				Swivels	Men
1 Schooner	12,	4 lbrs.			10	50
1 Sloop	12,	4s			10	50
1 schooner	4,	4s	4,	2s	10	35
1 do.	2,	4s	6,	2s	8	35
2 Gallies, each	1,	12	2,	9s	8	45
2 do. each	3,	9s			8	45
2 do. not quite rigged						

8 more gallies would be ready to join them in a fortnight when they would proceed down the lake. General Arnold (who is said to be a good sailor) had undertaken the command. We have 200 fine ship carpenters (mostly sent from here) at work. I hope a fleet will soon be exhibited on that lake such as it never bore. The Indians have absolutely refused Carleton in Canada and Butler at Niagara to have any thing to do in this quarrel, and applaud in the highest terms our wisdom and candour for not requiring them to meddle. Some of the most sensible speeches I ever saw of theirs are on this head, not spoken to us, but behind our backs in the councils of our enemies. From very good intelligence the Indians of the middle department will be quiet. That treaty is put off till October. Were it not that it interferes with our Assembly I would go to it, as I think something important might be done there, which could not be so well planned as by going to the spot and seeing it's geography. We have great fear that the sending an agent from Virginia to enlist

Indians will have ill consequences. It breaks in upon the plan pursued here, and destroys that uniformity and consistency of counsels which the Indians have noticed and approved in their speeches. Besides they are a useless, expensive, ungovernable ally. I forgot to observe that a captain Mesnard of Canada had come to Genl. Gates after the two abovementioned and confirmed their account in almost every article. One of the German deserters travelled with him to within 20 miles of our camp, when he was obliged to halt through fatigue. He passed 3 others of them. Baron Woedlke is dead. No great loss from his habit of drinking. The infamous Bedel and Butterfeild were ordered by Congress to be tried for their conduct. They have been tried by a Court martial, condemned and broke with infamy. We inclose to you all the Commissions mentioned in the last letter of the delegates,[4] except Innis's to be forwarded to the Eastern shore immediately, and Weedon's and Marshall's who we are informed are on the road hither. Would to god they were in N. York. We wait your recommendations for the 2 vacant majorities. Pray regard military merit alone. The commissions now sent do not fix the officers to any particular battalion so that the commanding officer will dispose of them. Cannot you make use of any interest with Lee or Lewis to call Innis over to the Western shore. He pants for it, and in my opinion has a right to ask it. Adieu, Adieu.

[*P.S.*] Davis with the 4000 lb. of gun powder and 90 stand of arms for Virga. got into Eggharbour. We have sent waggons for the powder to bring it here, and shall wait your further order. We were obliged to open Van Bibber & Harrison's letter to the Council of safety of Virga. in order to take out the bill of lading without which it would not be delivered.[5]

RC (MWA). Jefferson, *Papers* (Boyd), 1:497–501.

[1] For Gen. William Heath's eyewitness account of the August 16 engagement between Washington's galleys and H.M.S. *Phoenix* and *Rose*, see Morgan, *Naval Documents*, 6:217–19.

[2] Washington's August 17 letter to Congress and the enclosed intelligence obtained from Isaac Favier and Capt. Alexander Hunter are in *Am. Archives*, 5th ser. 1:995–96.

[3] For the accounts of Captains L'Oiseau and Allain and other military intelligence regarding Canada and northern New York transmitted in Gen. Gates' August 5 letter and read in Congress on August 15, see ibid., 1:795–800.

[4] This Virginia delegate letter has not been found. These Virginia officers had been promoted on August 13. See *JCC*, 5:649.

[5] Van Bibber & Harrison's July 25 letter to the Virginia Council of Safety is in Morgan, *Naval Documents*, 5:1224–25.

North Carolina Delegates to the
North Carolina Council of Safety

Gentlemen   Philadelphia August 20 1776.

You will receive by the five Waggons which accompany this 4 tons of Gunpowder and several other articles which in obedience to your orders we have procured for the use of the State of North Carolina. The inclosed will shew the particulars with which the Waggons go charged, & what remains still to perfect what by your last letters you gave in command to your delegates.[1] The Cartridge paper, the pamphlets upon the making of Salt are ready & will be sent off by Waggons which will follow these in a few days.

We find great difficulty in procuring Salt pans. We flatter ourselves however that we shall be able to effect that important purpose tho not so speedily as we could wish and the circumstances of our state seem to require. We have applied for directions as to the size, shape and quality of those made use of in Shrewsbury and have obtained such information as will put it in the power of the Blacksmiths here to make agreeable to the specimen, as soon as rolled plates can be procured for them to work upon. As the Mechanicks belonging to this City are chiefly in the Jersies at present, a delay will be unavoidable, tho the Council may be assured that their delegates will use their utmost endeavours to expedite this measure and answer the Wishes of the Council of Safety.

We anxiously expect to hear from you & to receive any other Command, which you may have for Gentlemen, Your obed Humble Serts,   **Will Hooper**

Joseph Hewes

John Penn

P.S. The five Waggons & Horses are purchased on the account of the Province and are put under the direction of Henry Hinckle Waggon Master who is to receive wages at the rate of Five pounds Ten Shillings per Month 'till he returns, allowing one day for every Twenty five Miles after he is discharged in Carolina to return home. The other Waggoners are to have four pounds per month in like manner, all of them are paid up to this day. They have agreed to take the Waggons to any part of the Province that you may direct and deliver them to such persons as you may Order to receive them, a guard by order of Congress accompanies the Waggons.[2]

RC (Nc–Ar). Written by Hooper and signed by Hooper, Hewes, and Penn. Postscript added by Hewes.

[1] According to "An Account of the Packages sent in the Five Waggons to North Carolina," the delegates sent the council of safety 8001 lbs. of gunpowder of various sorts as well as these books and pamphlets: "144 Setts of Sime's

Military guide, 2 Vol. each. 24 New System of Military Discipline. 24 Wither-spoon's Sermons. 32 Van Sweeten's & Jones's Cures for Armies. 48 Principles of the English Constitution (Pamphlet)." *N.C. Colonial Records,* 10:755–56.

² For an agreement between Hinkle and the North Carolina delegates, dated August 21, and two receipts from Hinkle to the delegates, dated August 20, see ibid., pp. 756–57.

Secret Committee to Comte d'Ennery

Sir,¹   Philadelphia August 20th 1776
It is impossible that at this date you can be a stranger to the im-portant contest subsisting Between Great Britain and her (late) colonies, Neither can it be necessary for us to enter into any detail of the Origin, or history of the progress of the dispute, sufficient it is for our present purpose to inform your Excellency, that the good people of America grown quite impatient under the yoke of tyranny, and sore with the crueltys' Daily practised against them, have at length determined to shake of[f] the yoke and oppose at the revoque of every thing that is sacred and dear to mankind the future oppera-tions of that government w[h]ich had determined to seize with a strong hand their property, and in violation of all natural, moral & Civil obligations to annihilate their liberty.²

These being the avowed purposes of the court of Great Britain, pursued with the utmost violence, notwithstanding the many and frequent representations, and supplications of this people, their dele-gates in General Congress did resolve in July last to shake of[f] their dependence on such oppressors and to set up for free and inde-pendant States, as you will see by the printed declaration wich we have the honor to inclose.

We depend principaly on the Virtue and Strength of our people to support this state of independancy, wich was loudly called for by them and received with universal marks of joy and approbation, but that we might not be wanting in any part of that duty we owe to ourselves, and posterity, we have sent a person ³ to the Court of France to represent our present situation, and to sollicit a favour-able disposition toward [us] as we are well assure[d] of the mutual and important advantages that will arise to both Country's from an alliance founded on just principles and supported by commercial intercourse.

The Court of France Cannot be insensible to her Own interest, and we have (uncertain) information that our resident is arrived and has meet a most favourable reception, but from himself we have not yet received any advice.

We have also sent a young Gentleman ⁴ to reside for some time at Martinico for commercial purposes. He has been favourably received, and informs us by authority of the general, that our Commerce will meet with Encouragement and protection in that island.

As we Know well that the island of Hispagnolia has Constant occasion for the produce of these states, and Vice Versa, these states will require large supplies of the produce of that island, we have been led by the consideration of mutual benefits to intrude upon your Excellency['s] time and to solicit your protection, and Encouragement of the Commerce Carried on between our inhabitants and yours. We do not Mean by this to Express a Wish that your Excellency should depart from the line of your duty, or that our people should interfere with the municipal laws and regulations of your Country: but we are well assured that the favorable Countenance of a Governor will greatly Encourage an infant commerce, and will paliate and Excuse such errors, neglects or crimes against the rules or laws as arise from ignorance of them.

The great painstaking and the vigilance used by our Enemies to deprive us of the necessary supplies of arms and ammunition, has made it necessary for the Congress to institute a trading Committee, stiled the Secret Committee with full powers to pursue such commerce as may be most likely to procure the articles wanted for the public Service. We the undersigned are members of that committee and members of the general Congress as will appear by the Certificate from our president & Secretary. In consequence of the power we are Vested With, and of advice we have lately received of arms and ammunitions being now very plenty in your island, we have sent a young Italian Gentleman that had resided here a Considerable time and is warmly attached to our Cause, to Cape Francois, where We propose he s[h]ould remain for the purpose of receiving the Cargoes we send him, and shipping in return the articles we may order. His name is Mr Stephen Ceronio a Gent'n of good family at Genoa, and of exceeding good character and we beg to recommend him to your Excellency['s] Patronage, and protection during his Stay on the island, not doubting but his Own Merit will recommend himself to your friendship and Civilities, Should he at any time have opportunitys of purchassing Such goods as we Want, and not have sufficient effects in hand we beg your Excellency would in such Cases assure the Owners of them, that we shall Constantly remit him sufficient to discharge all Contracts he makes for our Account.

We hope a Favourable acceptance of this application and have the honor to be, your Excellency, your obedient and Very humble Servts.

Robt Morris	Fras Lewis
Joseph Hews	Josiah Bartlett
	Phil Livinstong [Livingston]

Tr (Archives nationales. Marine B⁷, 458). Endorsed: "Pour copie conforme a l'original, Thiery."

[1] Victor Thérèse Charpentier, comte d'Ennery, was governor of the French colony St. Domingue.

[2] Archibald Bulloch, governor of Georgia, wrote a similar letter to d'Ennery on August 28, 1776, asking his support for trade with merchants from Georgia. Archives nationales, Marine B⁷, 458, no. 17.

[3] Silas Deane.

[4] William Bingham.

Roger Sherman to Zebulon Butler

Sir   Philadelphia August 20th. 1776

I received by Mr Swift Your Letter of the 6th Instant with the representation made by the Authority, Selectmen & Committee of Inspection concerning their apprehentions of trouble from the Indians, upon which we applied to Congress to raise Some Companies upon the Continental Establishment.[1] The application was referred to the Delegates of Connecticut and Pennsylvania who reported for raising three Companies in the Town of Westmoland to be under the Command of a Major, which now lies before Congress not acted upon, as also a report for raising a Battallion in Pennsylvania for Defence of the Frontiers of that State. Since these applications were made we have had favourable accounts from the Indians that they refused to comply with the Solicitations of Butler & others to take up arms against the colonies and are determined to remain Neuter. I dont know what will be finally done about raising Troops to defend the Frontiers, but if any are raised in Pennsylvania 'tis probable You will be allowed to raise three Companies. We shall pay proper attention to the affair and if anything is done about it Shall give You the earliest Notice.[2] I hope your people will have restitution of their effects taken at the Warriours run, after the State of Pennsylvania hath Settled a regular Government.

I remain Your humble Servant,   Roger

RC (CtY).

[1] The August 6 letter of Westmoreland officials to the Connecticut delegates is in *Susquehannah Co. Papers*, 7:18–20.

[2] On August 23 Congress authorized Westmoreland to raise two companies at Continental expense and ordered six companies to be raised in Pennsylvania to protect the frontiers in Northampton and Northumberland counties. *JCC*, 5:698–99.

William Williams to Joseph Trumbull

Dear Sir   Philadel. Augt 20 1776

I recd your favr of the 17 yesterday informg of the Attack by the Fire Ships. They have done something worth atchieving, if they have not paid too dear. Happy, if they had succeeded with the Phenix. We are just informd that they dont incline to sustain any more such encounters, & are pushd back by your Batteries & joind the fleet, have not the certainty of it yet.

Convinced that it was the surest way I had sundry times pressed sev[era]l of the board of War, to recommend Cap Dyer for a Majr. They promised to consider it &c & yesterday brot in a report reccomending him & Cap Chapman of Tylers, & after some Consideration, the votes were calld for & they are both appointd.[1] Conclude the Pres[iden]t has or will send their Comissions. Your Letter came just Time enough for me to strengthen the Recomenda[tion] by informing the House that the objection of Rank was removed. I just knew of the Conveyance by Mr Colt, & had but a minutes Time. Pray let me know every thing material passing among you. I am your affect. Friend & Bror.   W Williams

RC (Ct).
[1] See *JCC,* 5:667–68.

John Adams to Abigail Adams

Philadelphia August 21. 1776

Yesterday Morning I took a Walk, into Arch Street, to see Mr. Peele's Painters Room. Peele is from Maryland, a tender, soft, affectionate Creature.[1] He shewed me a large Picture containing a Group of Figures, which upon Inquiry I found were his Family. His Mother, and his Wifes Mother, himself and his Wife, his Brothers and sisters, and his Children, Sons and Daughters all young. There was a pleasant, a happy Chearfulness in their Countenances, and a Familiarity in their Airs towards each other.

He shewed me one moving Picture. His Wife, all bathed in Tears, with a Child about six months old, laid out, upon her Lap. This Picture struck me prodigiously.

He has a Variety of Portraits—very well done. But not so well as Copeleys Portraits. Copeley is the greatest Master, that ever was in America. His Portraits far exceed Wests.

Peele has taken General Washington, Dr. Franklin, Mrs. Washington, Mrs. Rush, Mrs. Hopkinson. Mr. Blair McClenachan and his little Daughter in one Picture. His Lady and her little son, in another.

Peele shewed me some Books upon the Art of Painting, among the rest one by Sir Joshua Reynolds, the President of the English Accademy of Painters, by whom the Pictures of General Conway and Coll. Barry [Barré] in Fanuil Hall were taken.

He shewed me too a great Number of Miniature Pictures, among the rest Mr. Hancock and his Lady—Mr. Smith, of S.C. whom you saw the other day in Boston—Mr. Custis, and many others.

He shewed me, likewise, Draughts, or rather Sketches of Gentlemen's Seats in Virginia, where he had been—Mr. Corbins, Mr. Pages, General Washingtons &c.

Also a Variety of rough Drawings, made by great Masters in Italy, which he keeps as Modells.

He shewed me, several Imitations of Heads, which he had made in Clay, as large as the Life, with his Hands only. Among the Rest one of his own Head and Face, which was a great Likeness.

He is ingenious. He has Vanity—loves Finery—Wears a sword—gold Lace—speaks French—is capable of Friendship, and strong Family Attachments and natural Affections.

At this shop I met Mr. Francis Hopkinson, late a Mandamus Councillor of New Jersey, now a Member of the Continental Congress, who it seems is a Native of Philadelphia, a son of a Prothonotary of this County who was a Person much respected. The son was liberally educated, and is a Painter and a Poet.

I have a Curiosity to penetrate a little deeper into the Bosom of this curious Gentleman, and may possibly give you some more particulars concerning him. He is one of your pretty little, curious, ingenious Men. His Head is not bigger, than a large Apple—less than our Friend Pemberton or Dr. Simon Tufts. I have not met with any Thing in natural History much more amusing and entertaining, than his personal Appearance. Yet he is genteel and well bred, and is very social.

I wish I had Leisure, and Tranquility of Mind to amuse myself with these Elegant, and ingenious Arts of Painting, Sculpture, Statuary, Architecture, and Musick. But I have not. A Taste in all of them is an agreable Accomplishment.

Mr. Hopkinson has taken in Crayons, with his own Hand, a Picture of Miss Keys, a famous New Jersey Beauty. He talks of bringing it to Town, and in that Case I shall see it, I hope.

RC (MHi). Adams, *Family Correspondence* (Butterfield), 2:103–4.

[1] Charles Willson Peale (1741–1827), Maryland born artist, whose works are described in Charles C. Sellers, *Portraits and Miniatures by Charles Willson Peale, Transactions of the American Philosophical Society*, n.s., vol. 42 (Philadelphia, 1952).

John Adams to Harriet Temple

Madam
Philadelphia August 21. 1776

I had the Honour of receiving your very polite Letter of the Tenth instant by yesterdays Post. I sympathise with you, most sincerely, in your peculiar situation, and nothing would give me greater Pleasure than to be able to contribute any Thing, towards procuring you Relief and Redress. I have the Pleasure to congratulate you on Mr Temples arrival in the Fleet. General Washington has given Leave for him to come to New York and return to New England, which the Congress have approved, so that I hope he is now on his Way home, and that you will have the Happiness to see him before you receive this Letter.[1]

Upon the Receipt of your Favour, I went immediately to Mr Hancock and inquired of him concerning your former application to him. He says he received your Letter in May, at a Time when the General was here to whom he shewed your Letter. The General expressed the utmost Concern for Mrs Temple and her Family, and wished her Relief, but there were so many other Persons in the same unhappy Predicament, that he did not see how one could be relieved without establishing a Precedent for all. The Multiplicity of avocations which constantly engage Mr Hancock, have no doubt been the Cause that he has not answered your Letter.

I have shewn your Letter to me, Madam, and the Copy of that to Mr Hancock, to Mr Hooper of N. Carolina, and several other Gentlemen and intend to shew it to more, and to move that it may be considered in Congress. But whether any Relief will be granted you, I cannot say. I wish it may with all my Heart, and it shall not be my fault if it is not.

I thank you, Madam, for your kind Visit to my dear Mrs Adams in her Distress, and for the agreable Account you give me of her Recovery. Be pleased to make my most respectfull Compliments to Mr Temple, and believe me to be, with great Respect, Madam, his and your most obedient, humble Servant.

LB (MHi). Endorsed: "Sent by Post Aug. 23d."

[1] Harriet Temple, daughter of the late Massachusetts governor William Shirley and wife of Robert Temple of Charlestown, Mass. Robert had gone to England in 1775 and had obtained permission from Generals Howe and Washington to return to Boston. Following the receipt of her August 10 letter (Adams Papers, MHi), Adams presented her request—for permission for her husband to return to Boston—to Congress on August 23. Congress granted its approval on August 28 and also authorized the payment of damages for the cutting of trees on Temple's property by the Continental Army. After numerous delays Congress, on March 6, 1779, granted Temple £6702, less the £2500 already paid him by the Massachusetts government for the damage done to his farm. Temple finally left Massachusetts in 1780 for Ireland. See W. H. Whitmore, "An Account of the Temple Family," *New England Historic and Genealogical Register* 10 (January 1856): 75–76; *JCC,* 5:699, 713, 13:260, 288–89; Adams, *Family Correspondence* (Butterfield), 2:87n.2; *Warren-Adams Letters,* 1:21n.1; and William Howe to George Washington, August 13, and Washington to Howe, August 17, 1776, in *Am. Archives,* 5th ser. 1:932, 1026.

John Adams to James Warren

Dear Sir   Philadelphia August 21 1776

Yours of August 11 reached me yesterday.[1] Mrs Temple shall have all the assistance which I can give her, but I fear it will be without success. It will be a Precedent for so many others, that there is no seeing the End of it. I shall answer her Letter by the next Post,[2] and if I cannot promise her any Relief, I can assure her of Mr Temple's Arrival, and of his having Leave to go home, which I presume will be more welcome News.

The success of your Privateers is incouraging. I lament with you the Langour and Inattention to the Fleet. I wish I could explain to you my Sentiments upon this Subject, but I will not. I am determined you shall come here and see and hear, and feel for yourself, and that Major Hawley and some others shall do the same. I must not write Strictures upon Characters. I set all Mankind a Swearing, if I do. I must not point out to you, not even to you, the Causes of the Losses, Disgraces and Misfortunes that befall you. I make the Faces of my best Friends a mile long, if I do. What then shall I do? Just what I have long Since determined; go home, and let two or three of you come here and fret yourselves, as long as I have done, untill you shall acknowledge that I had Reason.

There is a Marine Committee, who have the Care of every Thing relating to the Navy. Hopkins and his Captains, Saltonstall and Whipple, have been Summoned here, and here they have lingered, and their Ships laid idle. I cannot, I will not explain this Business to you, because if I should, it would get into a News Paper, I suppose. You must come and see.

We suffer inexpressibly for Want of Men of Business. Men acquainted with War by sea and Land. Men who have no Pleasure but in Business. You have them, send them along.

Have you got Boston Harbour sufficiently fortified? If not take no Rest untill it is done. Howe must have Winter Quarters, somewhere. If he cant obtain them at New York, he must attempt them at the Southward or Northward. It will be your Fault, if you are not prepared for him, in the North. I took a Hint from your Letter, and this day obtained a Resolution, authorizing and desiring General Ward to continue in the Command in the Eastern Department, untill further orders. I hope he will comply.[3] He has some good officers about him, and he does very well. We give him the Credit in the War office of making the best Returns, that we receive from any Department. The Scene brightens at Ticonderoga—and We have a very numerous Army at N. York. By the last Return We have more than Eight and twenty thousand Men including officers, at New York, exclusive of all in the Jerseys. Since which Men have been pouring in from Connecticut. Massachusetts I think is rather lazy this Campaign. Remember me with all possible Respect to your good Lady and believe me to be, as usual

[*P.S.*] Since the foregoing was written I have procured Mrs Temples Letter to be committed. I must depend upon the Gen. Court to send me a couple of good Saddle Horses.

RC (MHi). In Adams' hand, though not signed.

[1] Warren's August 11 letter is in *Warren-Adams Letters*, 1:267–69.

[2] See Adams to Harriet Temple, this date.

[3] See John Adams to Joseph Ward, August 20, note 3; and John Hancock to Artemas Ward, August 26, 1776.

Caesar Rodney to Thomas Rodney

Philada. Augst 21st 1776

Last night by the Post I received an account of your defeat in the Election and in Which I was not disappointed being Convinced You Continued to be Sanguine in your Expectations without taking the necessary steps to Carry a point of that Sort. Added to all the rest of your bad policy you Suffered Caldwell's Company to March away just before the Election When there was no necessaty for it, as the other Companies were not half full in any of the Counties.[1] Parke tells me the Conduct of yr Light Infantry heretofore, had Drawn down the resentment of the people Which put it in the power of that party who were opposed to you, to make this use of it. As to the order Which Hodgson has on me, He Cannot Stand in need of the Money for knowing that I Could not be down, and that Mr. McWilliam had not Wherewithall to Satisfie his order. The Delegates procured of Congress three thousand Dollars for the purpose of advancing a Months pay to the Soldiers and Contingent Expences, fifteen hundred of Which have been sent down to Coll. Patterson.[2] However as you have paid him forty odd pounds in part, it is so far well. I hope you have taken his Rect—but Cannot tell how you ascertained Hunn's Debt, as you had not the Bond. As Mr. Read will go the Convention and our Colony Requires two delegates to make a Representation, I shall come home next week if Possible, but if I should not be down in time enough, pray attend to the orphans Court.

The present Convention is solely for the purpose of frameing Government,[3] and will not be allowed to go out of that line unless it be so far as may be necessary for Supplying the flying Camp with such things as may be heretofore omitted. The people may therefore perhaps think better of this matter next time they Choose.

I am yrs.   Caesar Rodney

[*P.S.*] Orne Woodcock at Willmington has been speaking to me about a privateer he was applied to, to build, by Captn. Pope. He says he has a parcel of Carpenters sent to him and Cannot go on for want of the Iron Work, Rum &c. Some persons among you ought to go Imediately and Enter into the Contract with him, and fix the means of Supplying him.

RC (Paul Francis Webster, Beverly Hills, Calif., 1975).
¹ See Thomas Rodney to Caesar Rodney, August 19, 1776, in Rodney, *Letters* (Ryden), pp. 103–4.
² *JCC*, 5:644.
³ Rodney is referring to the Delaware Constitutional Convention, which began its session on August 27 in New Castle. The Delaware constitution of 1776 is in *Am. Archives*, 5th ser. 1:1174–79.

John Hancock to George Washington

Sir,   Philadelphia 22d Augst. 1776
   Congress not having Come to a full Determination upon the Subject of your Letter by the Express, he is still Detain'd. I shall so soon as the Resolutions are perfected Dispatch him with them. Your favr. of 20th I have rec'd, & is before Congress with its Inclosures.
   I have now only to Inclose you several Resolves pass'd yesterday in Congress, to which beg Leave to Refer you.¹
   I have the honour to be, with all possible respect, Sir, Your most obedt servt.   John Hancock Presidt

[*P.S.*] The three Gentln. who Came from Virginia, for the apprehending of whom you issued a warrant, were taken at Eliza. Town, & deliver'd me yesterday by a party of the Light Horse, and are now under Guard, will be Examin'd this Day.²

RC (PHi).
¹ The "Subject" of Washington's "Letter by the Express" was the court-martial of Col. Donald Campbell. See Washington to Hancock, August 12, 1776, in Washington, *Writings* (Fitzpatrick), 5:419; and *Am. Archives*, 5th ser. 1:340, 358, 825. For the subsequent course of Campbell's case, which ended with his exoneration, see *JCC*, 6:882, 7:29, 45. Washington's letter to Hancock of August 20 and enclosures are in PCC, item 152, 2:447–58, and Washington, *Writings* (Fitzpatrick), 5:465–67. Congress' August 21 resolves dealt with the case of Bazil Bouderot, treatment of spies, pay for Washington's and cannon for Gates' forces, the continuance of Gen. Artemas Ward in Continental service, and the procurement of copper. *JCC*, 5:692–94.
² See *JCC*, 5:695.

Marine Committee to Esek Hopkins

Sir   In Marine Committee Philadelphia August 22nd 1776.
   As you are now about to return to Rhode Island where we Under-

stand the Alfred and Cabbot remain inactive, We think proper you should exert your Utmost endeavours in Conjunction with the commanders of those Vessels to get them equipped and Manned with all possible expedition, for a six Months Cruize.

We think a Most important Service may be performed by the Alfred, Columbus, Cabbot, and Hampden [1] by dispatching them for Newfoundland with orders to destroy the British Fishery there. They must make Prize of every British Ship or Vessel they meet with. They must seize and destroy their Fishing Boats and stages and make prisoners of their fishermen, or such of them as will not freely enter into our service; and as it is highly probable they may take more prizes than they can conveniently spare Men to bring into port, it may be proper in such case to destroy them. The season is now come when the Newfoundland Men begin to load their Fish Cargoes. Consequently no time must be lost, and if the Columbus is not in port when you reach Rhode Island, you'l dispatch the Alfred, Cabbot and Hampden immediately appointing such place of rendevouz and Such signals as will enable them to Meet again in Case of Seperation, and also enable the Columbus to follow and join them, and whenever she returns from her present Cruize, you must order her on this service giving the Commander of her a Copy of the instructions, Signals &c.

We doubt not there are Some British Ships of War on the Newfoundland station to protect their Fishery and of course our Commanders must act with Such caution as to avoid being taken themselves, but we hope this will not prevent a Spirited and resolute conduct in the execution of this expedition, which we flatter ourselves will in the event prove highly detrimental to our enemies—honourable and beneficial to the United States of America. These being the Objects we have in View we desire that your orders to the Commanders may be adapted in the best manner your knowledge and experience can devise to obtain the end proposed.

When this small Squadron have done the enemy as much mischief as they can in that quarter they must proceed into the Gulph of St Lawrence and there take Cruizing ground as may be Most likely to intercept the supplies of Indian goods and other stores that we suppose will be sent from England for Canada when they know that our Troops have evacuated that Country. There is another object well worthy of their Attention but we fear the acquisition of it is too uncertain to found A Cruize upon, we mean the Capture of the Hudsons Bay Ships which in their return must be very valueable. If the Captains should be of oppinion that by dividing their force they can accomplish both these services, we would submit that point to your and their determination. We have no doubt but they will take valuable prizes in the Gulph of St Lawrence if the Cruizing ground is well chosen, and they must Send their prizes for Such of our ports as they will be most likely to reach with safety. We deliver you herewith Some of the Marine Books, List of Continental Agents in every state, and Several of the printed declarations of Independance. They may do well to notify the inhabitants of the French Islands of St Pierre & Miquelon of this declaration and sound how the inhabitents stand effected towards us, assuring them the French Government favour our Cause and will probably become our Allies by treaty. Perhaps our Ships may find shelter and protection on these Islands if the enemy have Ships in that quarter too Strong for us.

Should this Fleet take any prizes whose Cargoes might be particularly usefull to the inhabitants of these States, they may do well to convoy Such into port, and if they gain any intelligence that the Commanders think important they Must dispatch one of the small vessells with the account to us, putting into the first port and Sending an express with it to the General or to us. You will instruct the commander of each vessel to write us by all opportunities of their proceedings and of the Occurrencies they meet with. They must make us Monthly returns of their Crews, of the Supplies made to them, of the provisions, and make Copies of their Log Books and Journals to be transmitted to us at their return. They must be carefull of their Ships, stores and materials, use their officers and Men in Such a Manner as will recommend the service and at the same time preserve strict discipline. They will no doubt from principles of humanity and generosity treat their prisoners with all the kindness and attention their respective Situations and circumstances will admit of and we hope their conduct will in all things be such as to Merit the continuance of our Confidence.

You will direct the commanders of each Vessel to be very exact in keeping a List of all persons on board that are intitled to prize Money Mentioning their Names, stations, & Shares, Copys of which they must furnish the Agent or Agents that receive the prizes in order that just & equitable distribution of Prize Money may in due time be made.

We also wish to have a full and just valuation of all the Cannon, Stores &c which you brought from Providence that have been appropriated to public use or that remain for that purpose, and we desire you would have the vessels you took and the property in them Libelled and tryed, in order that Such part as is condemned may be sold, the accounts Settled and distribution of the Prize Money made. We are sir, Your very Humble servts,

John Hancock	Geo. Read
Geo Walton	Robt Morris
Saml Huntington	Step Hopkins
Fras Lewis	Joseph Hewes

P.S. We deliver you herewith a Letter to Nathaniel Shaw junr. Esqr. of New London directing him to purchase the Armed Schooner You took in Your late Cruize. This Schooner Must be called the *Hopkins* and immediately fitted out as a Continental Cruizer and you are to add her to the Fleet destined against Newfoundland Fishery sending her away in Company with the Alfred &c. We deliver you herewith a blank Commission for the Captain and we choose the offer of it should be Made to Captain Chew of New Haven he being Strongly recommended by the Committee of that place, but if he refuses this appointment we hereby authorize you to put in a proper commander and fill this Commission with his Name. We also deliver you Some blank warrants which you will fill up with proper persons for the Master and other inferior officers for that Schooner.

Let it be an article of your instructions to all the Captains to be particularly carefull to Send all salt they may take to Some of these States as we expect it will be very Much Wanted. Should you think it adviseable to go upon the expidition to Newfoundland &c Your self You May do therein as you judge will be Most Serviceable to the Continent and hoist your Broad Pendant on board any of the Vessels you choose.[2]   John Hancock, For the Come.

RC (CSmH). In the hand of Timothy Matlack and signed by Hancock, Hewes, Hopkins, Huntington, Lewis, Morris, Read, and Walton. The postscript, which is also in Matlack's hand but signed only by Hancock, remains in the Hopkins Papers, RHi.

[1] This day the Marine Committee also wrote a letter to Capt. Hoysted Hacker, commander of the *Hampden*, instructing him to disregard his previous orders and place himself at the disposal of Commodore Hopkins. PCC, item 58, fol. 17; and *Am. Archives*, 5th ser. 1:1107.

[2] This day Francis Lewis of the Marine Committee wrote to Capt. Thomas Grenell: "I some time ago advised you that Congress had appointed you to the command of the largest of the frigates, called the *Congress*, now at Poughkeepsie, and desired you would furnish me with a list of such persons as you recommend for your commission and warrant officers, but am yet without your answer, so conclude my letter miscarried. Pray let me hear from you as soon as possible." *Journals of N.Y. Prov. Cong.*, 2:504. There is no record in the journals of when Grenell was first appointed commander of the *Congress*, nor has Lewis' letter to him announcing this appointment been found. But see *JCC*, 6:861. It may be of some interest to note that this day Congress appointed John Hodge to command the *Montgomery*, a frigate in New York which had previously been commanded by Grenell. See *JCC*, 5:696–97.

Marine Committee to Nathaniel Shaw, Jr.

Sir   Philadelphia Augt 22d 1776

Commodore Hopkins recommends the purchase of the armed Schooner his Fleet lately carried into New London as an adviseable measure for this committee to adopt and in hopes to promote the

Public Service thereby, we now request you will purchase said Schooner on the best terms in your power and assist the commodore to fit, equipp and man her with all possible expedition as a Continental Cruizer.[1] He is ordered to offer the command to Captain Chew of New London and we hope he may accept it as he is so well recommended by your Committee. You will supply this Vessel with all necessary Provisions and Stores for a Six Months Cruize providing the whole on the best terms and in due Time rendering us an account thereof. If you have not money sufficient for this purpose your drafts on us will be duely honored by Sir, Your very hble servants.

LB (DNA: PCC Miscellaneous Papers, Marine Committee Letter Book).
   [1] The schooner *Hawke* had been sold before this letter reached Shaw, the Continental prize agent in Connecticut. Morgan, *Naval Documents*, 6:639, 757.

Marine Committee to Nathaniel Shaw, Jr.

Sir   August 22nd 1776
   The Secret Committee have directed Mr Barnabas Deane of Whethersfeild Connecticut to deliver you sundry Articles he has imported On Continental Account which you are to receive for the use of the American Navy, granting Mr Deane a receipt for the whole in order to Answer the Accounts of said Secret Committee, but as Mr Deane is in want of some of those very articles as well as others for the Frigate built under his direction,[1] you are to supply any of these and assist him in procuring any other articles wanted for that Ship charging the same to his Account or to the Ships as you shall judge most proper. You are hereafter to render us an account of the expenditure of all Stores you receive or buy on Account of the Continent. The Salt you will keep for the purpose of putting up Pork the ensuing Season for the use of the Navy.
   We are sir, Your hble servants.

LB (DNA: PCC Miscellaneous Papers, Marine Committee Letter Book).
   [1] The Continental frigate *Trumbull*, which was launched at Chatham, Conn., early in September 1776. Morgan, *Naval Documents*, 6:654.

Robert Treat Paine to Henry Knox

My dear Sr,   Philada. Augt. 22d. 1776
   I have been hoping for some time to hear what progress Mr. Byers makes, & more perticularly what Success in working his Air Furnace with wood, as upon the success of that experiment will depend the place of erecting a new Furnace.

Congress have directed some six & twelve pounders to be cast, as also some 8 inch & 6 inch Howitzers & some Cohorn Mortars. They are wanted as soon as possible & therefore I must beg that the Experiment of working the Furnace with wood may be determined. In yr. last you desire to know where Mr. Byers is to get the Money to pay for the Copper he purchases. This matter was mentioned to Congress & they passed the inclosed Resolves by which you perceive you are impowered to draw upon the pay master General for such sums as may be wanted.[1] We desire you would give Such Orders for the security of the Copper as may be necessary. As to the price, Congress made no determination upon it, & all we can say is, to get it as cheap as you can. I should be glad to know what determination is had on the Congress Mortars. The above peices are wanted so soon, that I fear whether we can wait to build a furnace wch must Consume some time. When Mr. Byers was here I proposed to him to Consider the practicability of casting Cannon at the Blast Furnace on Rariton River where they smelt the Copper. It would save the trouble & time of building a new furnace, & as we expect to get considerable Copper at that Furnace, it may be very Convenient to cast the Cannon there. When Mr. Byers went from hence he was in the Stage & so could not go out of the Way to see that Furnace, but he proposed going from New York purposely for that business; if he can do it without his Works standing still, I think it will be proper for him to view the Furnace & determine whether he can speedily cast Cannon there & whether a stock of Charcoal can be immediately had. Pray let me hear from you on this subject. Meanwhile I rest your hble Sert,

RTP

FC (MHi).
[1] On August 21 Congress adopted resolutions on casting cannon and utilizing "the copper said to be at New London," and Knox was specifically authorized "to draw upon the paymaster general for money sufficient to pay for any quantity of copper that can be procured for the use of the United States." See *JCC*, 5:693–94.

Secret Committee to Thomas Mumford

Philada. August 22d. 1776

We have unanswered your favour of the 31st July & are well pleased to find you had recd more Powder. We hope the same good luck will attend you throughout and that in time we may receive the whole quantity safe. We have lately recd here 44 half barrells shipped by your Friends in St Eustatia per the Schooner Pluto, Cap Davis, by which we recd. a letter for you & sent it forward per Post not having time to write to you then. We now request that you will deliver any Salt you may have on hand to Nathl Shaw junr Esqr at New London as it will be wanted for the use of the Navy & send us his receipt for it. Its well you had recd the Powder from Govr Cooke & we remain, sir, Your obed Servants. By order of the Secret Committee,   Robt Morris, Chair Man

RC (Robert J. Sudderth, Jr., Lookout Mountain, Tenn., 1973). Written and signed by Robert Morris.

James Wilson to John Hancock

Sir   .   Amboy 22d August 1776
     A Number of Copies of the Resolutions of Congress, offering Rewards to the Foreign Troops who will desert the Service of Great Britain, have been transmitted here.[1] Permit me to express my Surprise that no Distinction is made between Officers and Privates. Several other Gentlemen—one of them a German, well acquainted with the Manners and Dispositions of his Countrymen—have signified their Concern on this Account. I am informed that a Colonel in the Hessian Army has given Intimations that he would willingly listen to Overtures. Perhaps it is not yet too late to offer additional Rewards to officers in Proportion to their Rank and Pay.[2] I am with much Esteem, Sir, Your very humble Servant,

                                                           James Wilson

RC (DNA: PCC, item 78, 23:301–4). Endorsed by Charles Thomson: "Letter from col Jas Wilson, 22d Aug. 1776. read 26. referred to Mr Jefferson, Mr Franklin, Mr J. Adams."

[1] On August 9 Wilson had been appointed, along with Thomas Jefferson and Richard Stockton, to a committee "to devise a plan for encouraging the Hessians, . . . sent to America for the purpose of subjugating these states, to quit that iniquitous service." In response to the committee's report, Congress on August 14 adopted resolutions declaring that "foreigners who shall leave the armies of his Britannic majesty" would receive 50 acres of land and a guarantee of protection in the free exercise of their religion and civil liberties. Congress then ordered the committee to have the resolutions translated into German and "take proper measures to have it communicated to the foreign troops," and added Benjamin Franklin to the committee, undoubtedly for the purpose expressed in the latter order. JCC, 5:640, 653–55.

[2] It is not known when or for what purpose Wilson had gone to Perth Amboy, but since he expressed "Surprise that no Distinction is made between Officers and Privates," he apparently had left Philadelphia before the committee had completed its work of translating and printing leaflets for distribution inside enemy lines. Wilson, who held a colonel's commission in the Cumberland County militia, may have gone to New Jersey to be with units of his troops that had been dispatched there as part of the flying camp established by Congress. It is known that John Dickinson and Thomas McKean had gone to New Jersey to be with their Pennsylvania battalions.
     In any event, in response to Wilson's letter, Congress immediately appointed a committee consisting of Franklin, Jefferson, and John Adams who reported

the very next day a resolution addressing the German mercenary officers serving with General Howe's forces at Staten Island. For Jefferson's draft of the committee's report, which Charles Thomson incorporated into his journal entry of August 27, see Jefferson, *Papers* (Boyd), 1:509–10; and *JCC*, 5:705, 707–8. A preamble to this report, in the hand of John Adams, which failed of adoption, is in the Jefferson Papers, DLC, and was printed by Worthington C. Ford in *JCC*, 5:655n. Ford, however, wrongly associated Adams' proposal with the resolutions of August 14, although the relationship between Adams' and Jefferson's drafts has since been properly explained in Jefferson, *Papers* (Boyd), 1:510n.

For a detailed discussion of the entire episode involving Congress' efforts to weaken General Howe's army by encouraging the desertion of German mercenaries, see Lyman H. Butterfield, "Psychological Warfare in 1776: The Jefferson-Franklin Plan to Cause Hessian Desertions," *Proceedings of the American Philosophical Society* 94 (June 1950): 233–41.

To Butterfield's excellent study of this confusing story, only one amendment is necessary. The writer of the present letter was indeed James Wilson, the Pennsylvania delegate who was also a member of the committee appointed on August 9. Burnett, who cited Force's *American Archives* as his source for this letter, mistakenly asserted that "this Col. James Wilson was not the delegate," and his assertion was understandably repeated by Butterfield. See Burnett, *Letters*, 2:63n.2; Butterfield, "Psychological Warfare," p. 237; and Jefferson, *Papers* (Boyd), 1:510n.

For additional information on Benjamin Franklin's role in this episode, see Franklin's letters to Thomas McKean of August 24 and to Horatio Gates of August 28, 1776.

Abraham Clark to John Adams

Dear Sir,   Eliza. Town Augst. 23d. 1776

Colo. Dayton, who with his battalion is Stationed at Fort Stanwix, informs me no Regimental Paymaster hath been apptd. to his battalion, and Genl Schuyler does not conceive himself Authorized to appoint one. Jonathan Dayton, a son of the Colo. is Recommended as a proper person for that Station, his father offers to become Security for his faithful discharge of the Office. Mr. Caldwell the Chaplain of that battalion is come down and informs me Genl. Schuyler would have appointed Dayton had he been Authorized, and offers to Recommend him to Congress if Necessary. The young mans Qualifications can be known from Dr. Witherspoon. If no just Objection appears against him, I wish a Commission may be sent to me for him.[1]

I remain in a Weak infirm State. We are daily Alarmed with News of an Attack on this Town but have hitherto escaped it. We hear the British Troops are busily employed hanging the Refractory among them. May their business increse. I am Dear Sir, Your Sincere Friend & Huml Servt.   Abra. Clark

RC (MHi).
[1] Congress appointed Jonathan Dayton regimental paymaster of Col. Elias Dayton's battalion on August 26. *JCC*, 5:701.

Marine Committee to John Baldwin

Sir
                                                        August 23d 1776
The Continental Schooner Wasp under your command being now
thoroughly repaired, well fitted, equipped and manned you are immediately to proceed in said Schooner on a Cruize against the enemies of these states. We deliver you herewith a marine Book by
which you will know who are our enemies and also how to conduct
yourself in conformity to the Continental Rules and Regulations.
You have likewise a List of the Agents in the several states to some
of whom you must address the Prizes you take.

We deliver you herewith a Letter for a Gentleman in Bermuda
which is of much consequence to America.[1] You are therefore to
proceed with the utmost expedition to Port Ellis at the East end of
that Island and deliver the said Letter as quickly as possible, receive
from him any others he may Send in return, and as you will then be
near the best Cruizing ground for West India Ships you may make
a Cruize about that Lattitude for such length of Time as your
Provisions will enable you to keep the sea, unless success should
tempt you to return much sooner with a good Prize. You must be
careful of the Schooner, her stores and Materials. Use your people
well but preserve strict discipline, treat prisoners, if any you make,
with humanity and in all things be duely attentive to the honor and
interest of America. If you can get any Seamen at Bermuda Ship
as many as you can accommodate and bring us the best Account
you can obtain of the State and condition of that Island, with
respect to Provisions, Numbers of Inhabitants, what Cannon, arms
&c they have there and enquire particularly after any British men
of war that have been there, that are there, or that are expected.
Should you be unfortunately taken either going to or after you leave
Bermuda be sure to destroy all Letters you may have for or from
that Island. Should you gain any intelligence you may think important you must quit all other pursuits to inform us thereof soon as
possible. Wishing you success, We are sir, Your hble servants.

LB (DNA: PCC Miscellaneous Papers, Marine Committee Letter Book). Addressed: "To Lieutenant John Baldwin commanding the Schooner Wasp."
    [1] This letter has not been found, but it may have been written to Henry
Tucker, a Bermuda merchant who had helped persuade Congress to relax its
restrictions on trade with Bermudians in 1775, and who was subsequently asked
by the Marine Committee to supply the Continental fleet with salt. See Thomas
Jefferson to St. George Tucker, June 10, 1775, note; and Marine Committee to
Thomas Godet and Henry Tucker, October 10, 1776.

John Adams to Daniel Hitchcock

Sir   Philadelphia August 24. 1776

Yours of the Twenty Second is before me.[1] You mention the Delicacy of appointing an officer of the Same State over another—and you put the Case of Coll Varnum and yourself. I have been a long Time puzzled to account for Varnums Standing on the List of Colonells before you, whom I know to be many Years older than that Gentn has been represented to me to be. I have heard this young Gentleman Spoken of in Raptures as a Genius, and from all I have heard I believe his Abilities and Accomplishments to be very good. But his Years are tender in Comparison of yours, and his Education is but equal at best, how happened it then that in Arranging of Collonells, you was placed after him, I am sure this has made a Puzzle in some Minds here which will continue. It may possibly prevent either of you from rising so soon, as one of you would have done, if this obstruction had not been in the way.

The Massachusetts Bay, your Native Country, continues to act the most odd, surprising and unaccountable Part, respecting officers. They have a most wonderfull Faculty of finding out Persons for Generals and Colonells of whom no Body ever heard before. Let me beg of you, in Confidence to give me your candid and explicit opinion, of the Massachusetts General and Field officers, and point out such as have any Education, Erudition, Sentiment, Reflection, Address or other Qualification or accomplishment excepting Honour and Valour for officers in high Rank. Who and What is General Fellows? Who and What is General Brickett? Who is Coll Holman, Cary, Smith? There is a brave Veteran gone as a Coll to Ticonderoga, who should have my Vote for a General sooner than an hundred of them, I mean Aaron Willard.

If there are any officers, young or old, among the Massachusetts Forces who have Genius, Spirit, Reflection, Science, Literature, and Breeding, do for the Lands sake, and the Armys sake, and the Province sake let me know their Names, Places of abodes and Characters.

Your Plan for New modelling the Army may be a good one, for what I know. But I will give you more for a Plan for new modelling Massachusetts officers. I am &c.

LB (MHi).

[1] Hitchcock's August 22 letter to Adams is in the Adams' Papers, MHi.

John Adams to William Tudor

Dear Sir　　　　　　　　　　　　　　Philadelphia August 24. 1776

Your Favours of 18 and 19 of August are before me.[1] I am much obliged to you for them, and am determined to pursue this Correspondence, untill I can obtain a perfect Knowledge of the Characters of our Field officers.

If the Coll quits the Regiment Austin will certainly be promoted, unless Some Stain can be fixed upon his Character, Since he has been in the Army. His Genius is equal to any one of his Age. His Education is not inferiour. So far I can Say of my own knowledge. If his Morals, his Honour, and his Discretion are equal there is not a Superiour Character of his Age in the Army. If I could Speak with as much Confidence of these as of those, I should not hesitate one Moment to propose him for the Command of a Regiment.

You mention a Major Lee in Glovers Regiment. I wish you had given me more of his Biography and Character. Captn. Jos. Lee the Son of Coll Jer. Lee, has so much Merit, that I think he ought to be promoted. I never heard of these two Gentlemen before. I mean of their being in the Army. Are they Men of Reflection? That is the Question. Honour, Spirit and Reflection are Sufficient to make very respectable officers, without extensive Genius, or deep Leisure, or great Literature. Yet all these are necessary to form the great Commander. You Say there are Several other young officers of Parts and Spirit in that Regiment, I wish you had mentioned their Names and Characters. You Say they will never "basely cringe." I hope not: but I also hope, that they will distinguish between Adulation and Politeness: between Servility and Complaisance: between Idolatry and Obedience. A manly, firm attachment to the General, as far as his Character and Conduct are good, is a Characteristic of a good officer, and absolutely necessary to establish Discipline in an Army.

I have a great Character of Lt Coll Shepherd and Major Brooks. I wish you would write me a History of their lives. I knew nothing of them. If Brooks is my old Friend Ned of Mistick, as Mr Hancock this Evening gave me some Reasons to suspect, and if he deserves the Character I have recd of him, as I doubt not he does, if he is not promoted before long it shall be because I have no Brains nor Resolution. I never untill this Evening Suspected that he was in the Army. Pray tell me what Regiment he is in.

The Articles of War, are all passed but one—that remains to be considered. But I fear they will not be made to take Place, yet.[2] Gentlemen are afraid the Militia, now in Such Numbers in the Army, will be disgusted and terrified with them. The General must quicken this Business, or I am afraid it will be very slow. Every Body seems convinced of the Necessity of them, yet many are afraid to venture the Experiment. I must intreat you to write me, by every Post. Let me intreat you, Mr Tudor, to exert yourself, among the young Gentlemen of your Acquaintance in the Army, to excite in them, an Ambition to excell: to inspire them, with that Sense of Honour, and Elevation of sentiment without which they must, and ought to remain undistinguished. Draw their attention to those Sciences, and those Branches of Literature, which are more immediately Subservient to the Art of War. Cant you excite in them a Thirst for military Knowledge? Make them inquisitive after the best Writers, curious to know, and ambitious to imitate the Lives and Actions of great Captains, ancient and modern. An officer, high in Rank, should be possessed of very extensive Knowledge of Science and Literature, Men and Things. A Citizen of a free Government, he should be Master of the Laws and Constitution, least he injure fundamentally those Rights which he professes to defend. He should have a keen Penetration and a deep Discernment of the Tempers, Natures, and Characters of Men. He should have an Activity, and Diligence, Superiour to all Fatigue. He should have a Patience and self Government, Superiour to all Flights and Transports of Passion. He should have a Candour & Moderation, above all Prejudices and Partialities. His Views should be large enough to comprehend the whole System of the Government and the Army, that he may accommodate his Plans and Measures to the best good, and the essential Movements of these great Machines. His Benevolence and Humanity, his Decency, Politeness and Civility, should ever predominate in his Breast. He should be possessed of a certain masterly order, Method, and Decision, Superiour to all Perplexity and Confusion in Business. There is in Such a Character, whenever and wherever it appears, a decisive Energy, which hurries away before it, all Difficulties, and leaves to the World of Mankind no Leisure or opportunity to do any Thing towards it, but Admire it.

There is nothing perhaps upon which the Character of a General so much depends, as the Talent of Writing Letters. The Duty of a constant Correspondence with the Sovereign, whether King or Congress, is inseperable from a Commander in any Department, and the Faculty of placing every Thing in the happiest Point of Light is as useful as any he can possess. I fear this is too much neglected by our young Gentlemen. I knew it is by you, who can write but will not.

Geography is of great Importance to a General. Our officers shd be perfect Masters of American Geography. Nothing is less understood. Sensible of this, Since I have belonged to the Board of War I have endeavoured to perswade my Colleagues of its Importance and We are making a Collection of all the Maps, extant, whether of all America or any Part of it, to be hung up in the office, so that Gentlemen may know of one Place in America where they may

Satisfy their Curiosity, or resolve any doubt. I should be obliged to you, if you would inquire at every Print sellers shop in New York, and of every Gentleman, curious in this way concerning American Maps, in the Whole or Part and send me an account of them. Mr Hazard is as likely to know as any Man, in New York. I should never find an End of Scribbling to you, if I had nothing else to do. I am, yours &c,   John Adams

RC (MHi).
[1] These letters are in the Adams Papers, MHi.
[2] The Articles of War were not adopted by Congress until September 20, 1776. *JCC*, 5:788–807. See also Edward Rutledge to Robert R. Livingston, August 19, 1776, note 4.

Benjamin Franklin to Thomas McKean

Dear Sir,   Philada. Augt. 24. 1776
   I heard your Letter read in Congress relating to the Disposition of the German Troops;[1] and understanding from Col. Ross, that they are canton'd on the Island opposite to the Jersey Shore, I send you herewith some of the Resolutions of the Congress translated into their Language, as possibly you may find some Opportunity of conveying them over the Water, to those People. Some of the Papers have Tobacco Marks on the Back, it being suppos'd by the Committee, that if a little Tobacco were put up in each as the Tobacconists use to do, and a Quantity made to fall into the Hands of that Soldiery, by being put into a Drift Canoe among some other little Things, it would be divided among them as Plunder before the Officers could know the Contents of the Paper & prevent it.[2] With great Esteem, I am, Sir, Your most obedt huml Servt.
                                                      B Franklin

[P.S.] ⟨*Inclos'd is the English Copy, wch. is requested to be return'd, it belonging to the Congress.*⟩ Mislaid.

RC (PHi). Addressed: "The honble. Colonel McKean of the Pennsylvania Forces, East Jersey."
   [1] Not found; McKean's letter is not mentioned in the journals. For information on McKean's activities and whereabouts during July–September 1776—while serving with his battalion of Pennsylvania Associators in New Jersey and attending the Delaware Convention at New Castle—see John M. Coleman, *Thomas McKean, Forgotten Leader of the Revolution* (Rockaway, N.J.: American Faculty Press, 1975), pp. 183–95; and Caesar Rodney to Thomas Rodney, August 21 and 28, 1776.
   [2] For the background of this scheme to encourage the desertion of German mercenaries from General Howe's army at Staten Island, see James Wilson to John Hancock, August 22, 1776. See also Franklin to Horatio Gates, August 28, 1776.

John Hancock to George Washington

Sir, Philada. August 24th. 1776

The late Conduct of Lord Drummond is as extraordinary, as his Motives are dark and mysterious.[1] To judge the most favourably of his Intentions, it should seem that an overweening Vanity has betrayed him into a criminal Breach of Honour. But whether his Views were upright, or intended only to mislead and deceive, cannot at present be a Matter of any Importance. In the mean Time, I have the Pleasure to acquaint you, that Congress highly approve of the Manner in which you have checked the officious & intemperate Zeal of his Lordship. Whether his Designs were hostile, or friendly, he equally merited the Reproof you have given him; and I hope for the future, he will be convinced, that it is highly imprudent to attract the Attention of the Public to a Character, which will only pass without Censure, when it passes without Notice.

The Congress having considered the Matter thoroughly are of Opinion to decline taking any public or farther Notice of his Lordship; or his Letters, and particularly as you have so fully expressed their Sentiments on the Subject in your Letter to him. It was the Consideration of this Point that induced Congress to detain the Express till now.

I have the Honour to be, with perfect Esteem and Regard, Sir, your most obedt. and very hble Sert.

John Hancock Presidt

RC (DLC). In the hand of Jacob Rush and signed by Hancock.

[1] Lord Drummond's "late Conduct" was his recent effort, undertaken with the consent of Lord Howe, to resume his role as mediator between Congress and Great Britain on the basis of the same "Plan of Accommodation" that he had presented to certain delegates in January 1776. Correspondence relating to this subject among Drummond, Howe, Washington, and Hancock is in Washington, *Writings* (Fitzpatrick), 5:449, 451–52, 490–92, and *Am. Archives*, 5th ser. 1:1025–28, 1158–59. Drummond's earlier attempts to effect a reconciliation are discussed in Lord Drummond's Notes, January 3–9? 1776, note 1.

Robert Treat Paine to Samuel and Daniel Hughes

Sr., Philada. Augt. 24 1776

Yours which I recd.[1] by the bearer I shewed to Govr. Hopkins & we were of opinion that at so short notice we could not determine the size & No. of each Cannon. The Opinion of Congress should be had, & there was not time for that, but I do not see that you need be in the least hindred for doubtless there will be wanted Cannon of all the sizes. If your preparations should be applied towards making Cannon of the largest sizes mentioned I believe it would be profitable; from the good Success you have had of making long 18 pounders I have great Expectations that you will furnish us with good 32 & 24 pounders. I believe the length you mention are right for battery Guns, they are 19 diameters. By the Question in yr letter I understand you to refer to Cannon to be made in the new furnaces you mean to build. If you expect to be able soon to make Cannon for Congress in the Furnace you now have (besides those you are about making for the Frigate) you will please to let us know it soon & we will give an answer to that particularly; I heartily wish you Success in this Undertaking, & am yr hble Sert,

RTP

P.S. If you write on this Subject, please to add these words to the Direction [of the Cannon Committee] [2] so that should I be absent it may be opened by the Comttee.

FC (MHi). Addressed: "To Saml. & Daniel Hughes at Annapolis."

[1] Daniel and Samuel Hughes' August 19, 1776, letter to Paine is in Morgan, *Naval Documents*, 6:236. Although Paine addressed his letter to Annapolis, their letter is datelined "Antietam Furnace." On July 19 Congress had authorized the cannon committee to contract with the Hughes brothers for 1,000 tons of cannon, and on July 22 it ordered payment of $8,000 to them. On September 30 Congress ordered another payment of $13,333 1/3. *JCC*, 5:593, 599, 835.

[2] Brackets in MS.

John Adams to Abigail Adams

Philadelphia August 25. 1776

The day before Yesterday and Yesterday, We expected Letters and Papers by the Post, but by some Accident, or Mismanagement of the Riders, no Post is arrived yet, which has been a great Disappointment to me. I watch, with longing Eyes for the Post, because you have been very good of late in writing by every one. I long to hear, that Charles is in as fair a Way, thro the Distemper as the rest of you.[1]

Poor Barrell is violently ill, in the next Chamber to mine, of an inflammatory Fever. I hear every Cough, Sigh, and Groan. His Fate hangs in a critical Suspence, the least Thing may turn the Scale against him. Miss Quincy is here, very humanely employed in nursing him. This Goodness does her Honour.

Mr. Paine has recovered of his illness, and by present Appearances, is in better Health than before. I hope it will not be my Fate to be sick here. Indeed I am not much afraid of these acute Disorders, mine are more chronical, nervous, and slow. I must have a Ride. I cannot make it do without it.

We are now approaching rapidly to the autumnal Æquinox, and

no great Blow has yet been struck, in the martial Way, by our Enemies nor by Us. If We should be blessed this Year, with a few Storms as happy as those which fell out last Year, in the Beginning of September, they will do much for Us. The British Fleet, where they now lie, have not an Harbour, so convenient, or safe, as they had last Year. Another Winter will do much for Us too. We shall have more and better Soldiers. We shall be better armed. We shall have a greater Force at Sea. We shall have more Trade. Our Artillery will be greatly increased, our Officers will have more Experience, and our Soldiers more Discipline—our Politicians more Courage and Confidence, and our Enemies less Hopes. Our American Commonwealths will be all compleatly form'd and organized, and every Thing, I hope, will go on, with greater Vigour.

After I had written thus far the Post came in and brought me, your Favour of the 14 of August. Nabby, by this Time, I conclude is well, and Charles I hope is broke out. Dont you recollect upon this occasion, Dr. Biles's Benediction to me, when I was innoculated? As you will see the Picquancy of it, now more than ever you could before, I will tell the Story.

After having been 10 or 11 days innoculated, I lay lolling on my Bed, in Major Cunninghams Chamber, under the Tree of Liberty, with half a Dozen young Fellows as lazy as my self, all waiting and wishing for Symptoms and Eruptions. All of a sudden, appeared at the Chamber Door, the reverend Doctor, with his rosy Face, many curled Wigg, and pontifical Air and Gate. I have been thinking, says he, that the Clergy of this Town, ought upon this Occasion, to adopt the Benediction of the Romish Clergy, and, when we enter the Apartments of the sick, to cry, in the foreign Pronunciation *"Pax tecum."* These Words are spoken by foreigners as the Dr. pronounced them *Pox take 'em.* One would think that Sir Isaac Newton's Discovery of the system of Gravitation did not require a deeper reach of Thought, than this frivolous Pun.

Your Plan of making our worthy Brother, Professor, would be very agreable to me.

Your Sentiments of the Importance of Education in Women, are exactly agreable to my own. Yet the Femmes Scavans, are contemptible Characters. So is that of a Pedant, universally, how much soever of a male he may be. In reading History you will generally observe, when you light upon a great Character, whether a General, a Statesman, or Philosopher, some female about him either in the Character of a Mother, Wife, or Sister, who has Knowledge and Ambition above the ordinary Level of Women, and that much of his Emminence is owing to her Precepts, Example, or Instigation, in some shape or other.

Let me mention an Example or two. Sempronius Gracchus, and Caius Gracchus, two great tho unfortunate Men, are said to have been instigated to their great Actions, by their Mother, who, in order to stimulate their Ambition, told them, that she was known in Rome by the Title of the Mother in Law of Scipio, not the Mother of the Gracchi. Thus she excited their Emulation, and put them upon reviving the old Project of an equal Division of the conquered Lands, (a genuine republican Measure, tho it had been too long neglected to be then practicable,) in order to make their Names as illustrious as Scipios.

The great Duke, who first excited the Portuguese to revolt from the Spanish Monarchy, was spurred on, to his great Enterprize by a most artfull, and ambitious Wife. And thus indeed you will find it very generally.

What Tale have you heard of Gerry? What Mistress is he courting?

RC (MHi). Adams, *Family Correspondence* (Butterfield), 2:108–10.
¹ Two days later Adams wrote a brief letter to Abigail again expressing his concern for their son Charles' health. Ibid., pp. 110–11.

John Adams to Joseph Hawley

Dear Sir   Philadelphia Aug. 25. 1776
It is so long since I had the Pleasure of Writing to you, or the Honour of receiving a Letter from You, that I have forgotten on which side the Ballance of the Account lies, at least which wrote the last Letter.¹ But Ceremonies of this Kind ought not to interrupt a free Communication of sentiments, in Times so critical and important as these.

We have been apt to flatter ourselves with gay Prospects of Happiness to the People, Prosperity to the state, and Glory to our Arms, from those free kinds of Government, which are to be erected in America.

And it is very true that no People ever had a finer opportunity to settle Things upon the best Foundations. But yet I fear that human Nature will be found to be the same in America as it has been in Europe, and that the true Principles of Liberty will not be sufficiently attended to.

Knowledge is among the most essential Foundations of Liberty. But is there not a Jealousy or an Envy taking Place among the Multitude of Men of Learning, and, a Wish to exclude them from the public Councils and from military Command? I could mention many Phenomena, in various Parts of these States, which indicate such a growing disposition. To what Cause Shall I attribute the Surprising Conduct of the Massachusetts Bay? How has it happened that such an illiterate Group of General and Field officers, have been thrust into public View by that Commonwealth which as it has an indisputable Superiority of Power to every other in America as well as of Experience and Skill in war, ought to have set an Example to her sisters, by sending into the Field her ablest Men. Men of the most Genius, Learning, Reflection, and Address. Instead of this, every Man you send into the Army as a General or a Coll, exhibits a Character, which nobody ever heard of before, or an awkward, illiterate, ill bred Man. Who is General Fellows? and who is General Brickett? Who is Coll Holman, Cary, Smith?

This Conduct is sinking the Character of the Province, into the lowest Contempt, and is injuring the service beyond description. Able officers are the soul of an Army. Good officers will make good soldiers, if you give them human Nature as a Material to work upon. But ignorant, unambitious, unfeeling, unprincipled officers will make bad soldiers of the best Men in the World.

I am ashamed and grieved to my inmost Soul, for the disgrace brought upon the Massachusetts, in not having half its Proportion of General officers. But there is not a Single Man among all our Collonells that I dare to recommend for a General officer, except Knox and Porter, and these are So low down in the List, that it is dangerous promoting them over the Heads of so many. If this is the Effect of popular Elections it is but a poor Pangyrick upon such Elections. I fear We shall find that popular Elections are not oftener determined, upon pure Principles of Merit, Virtue, and public Spirit, than the Nominations of a Court, if We dont take Care. I fear there is an infinity of Corruption in our Elections already crept in. All Kinds of Favour, Intrigue and Partiality in Elections are as real Corruption in my Mind, as Treats and Bribes. A popular Government is the worse Curse, to which human Nature can be devoted when it is thoroughly corrupted. Despotism is better. A Sober, conscientious Habit of electing for the public good alone must be introduced, and every Appearance of Interest, Favour, and Partiality, reprobated, or you will very soon make wise and honest Men wish for Monarchy again, nay you will make them introduce it into America.

There is another Particular, in which it is manifest that the Principles of Liberty have not sufficient Weight in Mens Minds, or are not well understood.

Equality of Representation in the Legislature is a first Principle of Liberty, and the Moment the least departure from such Equality takes Place, that Moment an Inroad is made upon Liberty. Yet this essential Principle is disregard[ed] in many Plans, in several of these Republicks. My County is to have an equal Voice altho some Counties are six times more numerous, and twelve times more wealthy. The same Iniquity will be established in Congress. R.I. will have an equal Weight with the Mass., the Delaware Government with Pensilvania and Georgia with Virginia.[2] Thus We are sowing the Seeds of Ignorance, Corruption, and Injustice, in the fairest Field of Liberty, that ever appeared upon Earth, even in the first attempts to cultivate it. You and I have very little to hope or expect for ourselves. But it is a poor Consolation, under the Cares of a whole Life Spent in the Vindication of the Principles of Liberty, to see them violated in the first formation of Government, erected by the People themselves on their own Authority, without the poisonous Interposition of Kings or Priests. I am with great affection your Friend & sert.

LB (MHi).

[1] For the most recent extant letter, see Adams to Hawley, November 25, 1775.
[2] Portions of the debates in Congress on the issue of representation are recorded in Adams' Notes of Debates, July 30 and August 1, 1776.

John Adams to Henry Knox

Dear Sir   Philadelphia August 25 1776
Your Favour of the 21 is before me.[1] I agree that we ought to have an hundred more of Mortars, Howitzers, and Field Pieces. And if I knew where to procure the Brass, I should be glad to promote the Manufacture of that Number. You say that Copper can be purchased at a little advanced Price. I wish I knew where and at what Price. We have contracted with a Gentleman in Maryland, for a large Quantity of Iron Cannon.[2]

Able officers are the Soul of an Army. Gentlemen of Sense and Knowledge, as well as valour, must be advanced. I wish you would give me in Confidence a List of the best officers from the Massachusetts, with their Characters. This may be delicate, but it will be safe. Pray write me the Characters of Coll Shepherd, Coll Henshaw, and Major Brooks. Does Austin merit Promotion, or not? I am much distressed for want of a List of all the Massachusetts officers, in their Ranks, as they now Stand. I have Sought it a long time but never could obtain it. Will you favour me with one. I am determined to find out the Characters of our officers, by Some means or other. If a Second Battallion of Artillery is formed, who are the officers of it? Would not Austin make a good Lt Coll of Artillery? Pray give me your Sentiments frankly, and candidly. We have been delicate too long. Our Country is too much interested, in this Subject. Men of Genius and Spirit, must be promoted, wherever they are. If you have no Lt Coll, who shall We put in that Place? I wish Austin was in the Artillery, because I knew him to have a Capacity equal to any Thing, and I conjecture he would turn his Thoughts to those Sciences, which an officer of Artillery ought to be Master of.

I am a constant Advocate for a regular Army, and the most masterly Discipline, because I know that without these We cannot reasonably hope to be a powerfull, a prosperous, or a free People, and therefore, I have been constantly labouring to obtain an handsome Encouragement for inlisting a permanent Body of Troops. But have not as yet prevailed, and indeed, I despair of ever Succeeding, unless the General, and the officers from the Southward, Should convince Gentlemen here; or unless two or three horrid Defeats should bring a more mellancholly Conviction, which I expect and believe will one day or other be the Case. I am, your humble Servant,   John Adams

RC (MHi).
[1] Knox's August 21 letter is in the Adams Papers, MHi.
[2] See also Robert Treat Paine to Samuel and Daniel Hughes, August 24, 1776.

Josiah Bartlett to Mary Bartlett

My Dear   Philadelphia Aug. 26th 1776
Yours of the 7th & 9th I Recd yesterday and am much pleased to hear you & the family are well and that there is a good prospect of a pretty plentiful Crop of the fruits of the Ground. May the Smiles of Heaven Continue to rest on us in Every other respect.
Last Saturday the Congress Did not Set, and I with the three Connecticut Delegats and Col. Floyd one of the New York Delegats, agreed to take a ride. We Crossed over Schuylkill river, and rid about fifteen miles to Chester on the river Deleware. We Dined there & then rode home a little before night; we had a pretty agreable ride. I Believe I have not rode so much before Since I Came here this last time. The weather here is very wet & muggy, quite Disagreable at present but hope it will soon be better as the fall Comes on. It is something Sickly here with Putrid fevers & something mortal. Remember my love to all the Children & tell Polly I Recd her letter with the Copy of verses for which I thank her. By the newspaper you will see what news we have here. We have just had news of the landing of the regulars on Long Island and of Some Skirmishes with them by some of our Souldiers.[1] I Expect soon to hear of a Considerable action.
Remember me to all friends. I Cant inform you that I am well, but hope it is nothing more than a great Cold. I am better today than I was yesterday. Saturday Evening had a Considerable ague fit and fever after it. Kept house yesterday, but have been able to attend Congress today, So hope I Shall be well again in a few days. I am, yours &c,   Josiah Bartlett

P.S. Have Col Greely & Mr Proctor provided any Bords for me as I Desired them for finishing my house; as I hope to be at home & Do something about it another year, God willing.

27th Holds better of my Cold.   J. B.

RC (NhHi).
¹ General Washington's August 23 letter to Hancock containing news of the British landing on Long Island was read in Congress this day. See *JCC*, 5:700; PCC, item 152, 2:483–86; and Washington, *Writings* (Fitzpatrick), 5:476–77.

John Hancock to Artemas Ward

Sir,   Philada. August 26th. 1776.

The Service in the Eastern Department requiring an Officer of Rank and Experience, and Colonel Whitcombe having declined accepting his Commission, the Congress have been induced, both from a Regard to your Merit while in the Army, and your Zeal and Attention since you left it, to request you will, if consistent with your Health, take the Command of the Forces in that Quarter.¹

As soon as Congress can fix on some Officer to relieve you, they will do it, and only desire you, in the mean Time, to continue in the Command until such appointment.

Your Readiness to comply with the Wishes of your Country, gives me the strongest Reason to believe, you will not resist their application at this Juncture.

I have the Honour to be, Sir, your most obedt. & very hble Servt.

John Hancock Presidt

[P.S.] Inclos'd you have sundry Resolutions of Congress to which I beg leave to Refer you.

RC (MHi). In the hand of Jacob Rush, with signature and postscript by Hancock.
¹ See *JCC*, 5:694; and Hancock to Ward, April 26, 1776, note 2. An August 8 letter from the Massachusetts Council to Hancock, urging that in the event of Ward's retirement "a General Officer may be directed to take the command of the troops here as soon as possible," is in *Am. Archives*, 5th ser. 1:859–60.

Thomas Jefferson to Edmund Pendleton

Dear Sir   Philadelphia. Aug. 26. 1776

Your's of the 10th. inst. came to hand about three days ago, the post having brought no mail with him the last week.¹ You seem to have misapprehended my proposition for the choice of a Senate. I had two things in view: to get the wisest men chosen, and to make them perfectly independent when chosen. I have ever observed that a choice by the people themselves is not generally distinguished for it's wisdom. This first secretion from them is usually crude and heterogeneous. But give to those so chosen by the people a second choice themselves, and they generally will chuse wise men. For this reason it was that I proposed the representatives (and not the people) should chuse the Senate, and thought I had notwithstanding that made the Senators (when chosen) perfectly independent of their electors. However I should have no objection to the mode of election proposed in the printed plan of your committee, to wit, that the people of each county should chuse twelve electors, who should meet those of the other counties in the same district and chuse a senator. I should prefer this too for another reason, that the upper as well as lower house should have an opportunity of superintending and judging of the situation of the whole state and be not all of one neighborhood as our upper house used to be. So much for the wisdom of the Senate. To make them independent, I had proposed that they should hold their places for nine years, and then go out (one third every three years) and be incapable for ever of being re-elected to that house. My idea was that if they might be re-elected, they would be casting their eyes forward to the period of election (however distant) and be currying favor with the electors, and consequently dependent on them. My reason for fixing them in office for a term of years rather than for life, was that they might have in idea that they were at a certain period to return into the mass of the people and become the governed instead of the governors which might still keep alive that regard to the public good that otherwise they might perhaps be induced by their independance to forget. Yet I could submit, tho' not so willingly to an appointment for life, or to any thing rather than a mere creation by and dependance on the people. I think the present mode of election objectionable because the larger county will be able to send and will always send a man (less fit perhaps) of their own county to the exclusion of a fitter who may chance to live in a smaller county. I wish experience may contradict my fears. That the Senate as well as lower [or shall I speak truth and call it upper] [2] house should hold no office of profit I am clear; but not that they should of necessity possess distinguished property. You have lived longer than I have and perhaps may have formed a different judgment on better grounds; but my observations do not enable me to say I think integrity the characteristic of wealth. In general I beleive the decisions of the people, in a body, will be more honest and more disinterested than those of wealthy men: and I can never doubt an attachment to his country in any man who has his family and peculium in it. Now as to the representative house which ought to be so constructed as to answer that character truly. I was for extending the right of suffrage (or in other words the rights of a citizen) to all who had a permanent intention of living in the country. Take what circumstances you please as evidence of this, either the having resided a certain time, or having a family, or having property, any or all of them. Whoever intends to live in a country must wish that country well, and has a natural right of assisting in the preservation of it. I think you cannot distinguish between such a person residing in the country and having no fixed property, and one residing in a township whom you say you would admit to a vote. The other point of equal representation I think capital and fundamental. I am glad you think an alteration may be attempted in that matter. The fantastical idea of virtue and the public good being a sufficient security to the state against the commission of crimes, which you say you have heard insisted on by some, I assure you was never mine. It is only the sanguinary hue of our penal laws which I meant to object to. Punishments I know are necessary, and I would provide them, strict and inflexible, but proportioned to the crime. Death might be inflicted for murther and perhaps for treason if you would take out of the description of treason all crimes which are not such in their nature. Rape, buggery &c. punish by castration. All other crimes by working on high roads, rivers, gallies &c. a certain time proportioned to the offence. But as this would be no punishment or change of condition to slaves (me miserum!) let them be sent to other countries. By these means we should be freed from the wickedness of the latter, and the former would be living monuments of public vengeance. Laws thus proportionate and mild should never be dispensed with. Let mercy be the character of the law-giver, but let the judge be a mere machine. The mercies of the law will be dispensed equally and impartially to every description of men; those of the judge, or of the executive power, will be the eccentric impulses of whimsical, capricious designing man. I am indebted to you for a topic to deny to the Pensylvania claim to a line 39 complete degrees from the equator. As an advocate I shall certainly insist on it; but I wish they would compromise by an extension of Mason & Dixon's line. They do not agree to the temporary line proposed by our assembly.[3]

We have assurance (not newspaper, but Official) that the French governors of the West Indies have received orders not only to furnish us with what we want but to protect our ships. They will convoy our vessels, they say, thro' the line of British cruisers. What you will see in the papers of Capt. Weeks is indubitably true.[4] The inhabitants of St. Pierre's went out in boats to see the promised battle, but the British captain chose not to shew. By our last letters from N. York the enemy had landed 8000 men on Long Island. On Friday a small party, about 40, of them were out maroding and had got some cattle in a barn. Some riflemen (with whom was our Jamieson) attacked them, took away the cattle, they retired as far as the house

of Judge Lifford where were their officer's quarters, they were
beaten thence also, and the house burnt by the riflemen. It is alwais
supposed you know that good execution was done. One officer was
killed and left with 9 guineas in his pocket, which shews they were
in a hurry; the swords and fusees of three other officers were found,
the owners supposed to be killed or wounded and carried away.[5]
On Saturday about 2000 of them attempted to march to Bedford.
Colo. Hans's [Edward Hand's?] battalion of 300 Pennsylvania riflemen having posted themselves in a cornfeild and a wood to advantage attacked them. The enemy had some of their Jagers with
them, who it seems are German riflemen used to the woods. General
Sullivan (who commands during the illness of Genl. Green) sent
some musquetry to support the riflemen. The enemy gave way and
were driven half a mile beyond their former station. Among the
dead left on the way, were three Jagers. Genl. Washington had sent
over 6 battalions to join Sullivan who had before three thousand,
some say and rightly I believe 6000; and had posted 5 battalions
more on the water side ready to join Sullivan if the enemy should
make that the field of trial, or to return to N. York if wanted there.
A general embarkation was certainly begun. 13 transports crouded
with men had fallen down to the narrows and others loading. So
that we expect every hour to hear of this great affair. Washington
by his last return had 23,000 men of whom however 5000 were sick.
Since this, Colo. Aylett just returned from there, tells us he has
received 16 New England battalions, so that we may certainly hope
he has 25,000 effective, which is about the strength of the enemy
probably, tho' we have never heard certainly that their last 5000,
are come, in which case I should think they have but 20,000. Washington discovers a confidence, which he usually does only on very
good grounds. He sais his men are high in spirits. Those ordered
to Long Island went with the eagerness of young men going to a
dance. A few more skirmishes would be an excellent preparative for
our people. Provisions on Staten Island were become so scarce that
a cow sold for t[en?] pounds, a sheep for ten dollars. They were
barreling up all the horse flesh they could get. Colo. Lee being not
yet come I am still here, and suppose I shall not get away till about
this day se'nnight. I shall see you in Williamsburgh the morning
of the Assembly. Adieu.   Th. J.

RC (MHi). Jefferson, *Papers* (Boyd), 1:503–6.
[1] For Pendleton's August 10 letter, see ibid., 1:488–91.
[2] Brackets in MS.
[3] See Virginia Delegates to the Speaker of the Pennsylvania Convention, July 15, 1776.
[4] A brief account of the July 27 engagement of Capt. Lambert Wickes' ship *Reprisal* and H.M. Sloop *Shark* near St. Pierre, Martinique, had appeared in the *Pennsylvania Evening Post* on August 22. For this and other accounts of the

confrontation and the subsequent response by French authorities, see Morgan, *Naval Documents*, 5:1263–66, 1277–79, 1317–18, 6:11–12, 26, 51–52, 77, 111.

[5] John Sullivan's August 23 report from Long Island was enclosed with Washington's August 24 letter to Congress. *Am. Archives*, 5th ser. 1:1136–37.

John Witherspoon to David Witherspoon

Dear David,   Philadelphia, Aug. 26, 1776.

Your letter of the 8th of August, I received yesterday by captain Stewart, and only this day, by post, that of July 22d. . . .[1] I am glad to perceive that you are endeavouring to make yourself master of the French: continue in it carefully, and be sure to read through, and be well acquainted with the dialogues and conversation phrases in the Grammar. You say you have not taught any yet. I am willing to understand this only of the French, for I hope you have not been wanting in teaching Latin in the school.[2] Make yourself as useful as possible to Mr. Smith, and perfect your classic learning.

It gives me great pleasure to see that the school increases so fast. I hope no pains will be spared to make the scholars as complete as possible. You ought to exercise them well in the grammar and syntax. It would be a great advantage, if they were kept some part of their time to writing and arithmetick. If among you, you can bring it about that the boys write their letters to their parents, neatly and sensibly, it will give them great pleasure. Many of them are not judges how far they profit in Latin and Greek; but if they write their letters well, they will perceive their improvement: and, on the contrary, if they write nothing home but blotted, ill-spelled nonsense, they will suppose they have learned nothing, though you take ever so much pains.

Your two letters which are now before me, please me better than any you have written. If you take pains, you will write a good hand. There are, however, some few oversights in point of spelling, which I hope you will guard against for the future. I think you will write better than either of your brothers. John is in the Hospital at New York, where they expect an attack every day. Some of the English troops are landed on Long Island: there has been a small scuffle with their advanced guard, in which we have had the better. I had also a letter from James lately, by which it appears probable that he will be at Princeton soon. The northern army at Ticonderoga, is now in a much more promising situation than heretofore. A treaty has been just concluded with the Indians at Fort Stanwix, which was read in Congress to-day, and by which they have promised a strict neutrality.[3] I am glad to hear that John Smith is studying divinity. His brother William has just passed his trials in New Castle Presbytery, and I hear has given great satisfaction. Mr. Smith, his father, is now gone to the camp at Amboy, and has carried Mrs. Smith with him to Princeton. I expect to see them both there at the end of this week. I was at Pequea, and preached there about a fortnight ago. . . .

The Philadelphia Associators, who went to the camp, have many of them behaved very badly. They were mutinous and disorderly; many went away without leave, and I believe they are now mostly dismissed. . . . Remember, my dear boy, to fear God, and serve him in sincerity and truth. Let this be your first and highest care, and accomplish yourself as much as possible for usefulness in life. . . .

I am, dear David, Your affectionate father,

Jno. Witherspoon.

MS not found; reprinted from *Christian Advocate* 2 (September 1824): 398–99.
[1] Suspension points in Tr, here and below.
[2] Hampden-Sidney Academy in Virginia.
[3] See Rhode Island Delegates to Nicholas Cooke, August 17, 1776, note 3.

John Adams to Joseph Palmer

Dear sir   Philadelphia August 27. 1776

Your Favour of July 1, ought not to have lain by me, so long unanswered.[1] But the old apology of Multiplicity of Avocations is Thread bare.

You Say you have been obliged to attend much upon the Fortifications. I am glad of it. I wish I could obtain Information what Fortifications have been erected, on the Islands in the Harbour, and on the Eminencies round it, of what Kind those Fortifications are, what Number of Cannon are mounted on them, what Number of Men are appointed to garrison them, and who are their officers. I am afraid that Boston Harbour is not yet impregnable. If it is not, it ought to be made so. Boston has not grown into favour with King George, Lord North or General Howe. It is no peculiar Spight against N. York, which has induced the Fleet and Army to invade it. It is no peculiar Friendship, Favour, or Partiality to Boston, which has induced them to leave it. Be upon your Guard. Hesitate at no Expence, no Toil, to fortify that Harbour against all its Enemies. You ought to suppose the whole British Empire to be your Enemy, and prepare your selves against its Malice and Revenge. How's Army must have Winter Quarters Somewhere, and will at all Hazards. They may try at Boston—there they lost their Honour. There they would fain regain it, if they could.

They have a hard Bone to pick, at N. York, according to present appearances. They are creeping on. Moments are now of Importance. They are landed on Long Island. If they attack our Forts in Columns they may carry them, but, if We do our Duty, they will loose the Worth of them, in Blood. A few days will disclose more of their Designs.

The Bearer, Mr Hare, is a Brother of the celebrated Porter Brewer of this City.[2] He wants to see the World. He means and will do no Harm. If you can shew him, any Part of the Curiosities of our Countries, you will oblige him, and me, your warmest Friend and Servant,   John Adams

RC (NNPM).
[1] Palmer's July 1 letter to Adams is in the Adams Papers, MHi.
[2] It is probable that Richard Hare was not the bearer of this letter after all, since Adams noted on a letter to Samuel Cooper written the following week that it was "Sent by Mr Hare." See Adams to Samuel Cooper, September 4, 1776.

Josiah Bartlett to William Whipple

Dear Sir,   Philadelphia August 27th 1776
Last week the articles of confederation were finished by the Committee of the whole House; they are again printed as now amended by the Committee and are delivered to the members in the same manner as before and are to undergo one operation through Congress more, before they are sent to the several States for confirmation. What alterations will be made in them I know not but am afraid none for the better. This will occasion such a delay that there is no probability it will be sent in time to be laid before our Assembly before your return here, so I would not have you wait for it but return as soon as convenient.[1] The new articles of War have passed Congress.[2] The plan of a T——y of foreign all——ce has passed in the Committee of the whole.[3] By the leave of Lord Howe the famous Lord Drummond has by a flag to General Washington, proposed Sundry articles as the basis of a negotiation, or conference (they are nearly the same as those proposed by Lord North—called Lord North's conciliatory propositions) and he requested leave of General Washington, for himself and one or two more to repair to this City to propose those terms, which he had the impudence to say would have been accepted by the Colonies a few months ago. The General did not think proper to give him leave to come here, but in his answer told him, he should send the papers to the Congress and wait their answer; he severely reprimanded Lord Drummond for his officiousness in meddling with the business, but especially for his going to the army under General Howe contrary to his parole of honor, which he gave when he was permitted to leave the Continent.

I need not tell you the Congress have not accepted the proposed
conference with his Lordship.[4] Lord Howe has wrote an answer to
Dr Franklin's letter to him which you saw. It is full of professions
of friendship for America, and of esteem and regard for the Doctor,
very polite but very artful.

By a letter from the Agent who was sent in the Reprisal, Capt
Weeks, to Martinico, he informs us, that the Governor (or General
as they call him) told him that he had lately received orders by a
frigate from France to give all possible assistance and protection
to the American vessels, and that he was ordered to send out some
ships of war to cruise round the Island for their defence, and that
the Same orders had been sent to the other French Islands; he also
told the Agent that if the American cruisers should bring any prizes
into the ports of Martinico he should not prevent their selling or
disposing of them as they should think proper (This is in confidence).[5]

We have just rec'd the account of the enemy landing on Long
Island: by the General's account our men are in good spirits, seem
firm and ready for action, from this and from some other circumstances, I hope I shall soon hear of the enemy's defeat and quitting
the country, never more to return as enemies, which will give the
greatest pleasure and satisfaction to Your friend & hble Serv.

Josiah Bartlett

P.S. Mr Wm Barril is sick with a fever. Dr. Rush says he is very
dangerous. Please to give my regards to our friend Col Langdon
as I have not time to write to him; tell him I have not recd his
letter last week as usual. I have rec'd your's of the 20th from Milford's. Yours ut sup.   J.B.

Tr (DLC).

[1] Both the first and second printed versions of the Articles of Confederation
are in *JCC,* 5:674–89. Bartlett's fears proved to be well-founded as Congress did
not approve a final text of the Articles of Confederation for transmittal to the
states until November 15, 1777. *JCC,* 9:928.

[2] Since Whipple's departure on August 12, Congress had twice debated the
Articles of War in the committee of the whole, but they were not completed and
approved until September 20, 1776. *JCC,* 5:652, 670, 788–807.

[3] This day Congress, having agreed to a plan of treaties in the committee of
the whole, referred the plan back to committee "in order to draw up instructions
pursuant to the amendments made by the committee of the whole." *JCC,* 5:709–
10.

[4] For further information on this second abortive Drummond "peace mission,"
see John Hancock to George Washington, August 24, 1776, note.

[5] Although agent William Bingham's letter to Congress has not survived, see
his August 5 letter to Silas Deane in *Collections of the Connecticut Historical
Society* 23 (1930): 31–34. See also comte d'Argout's account of his conversation
with Bingham about these subjects in his July 31 letter to the minister of
marine, in Morgan, *Naval Documents,* 5:1317–19.

John Hancock to George Washington

Sir   Tuesday 6 oClock PM Philada. 27 Augst. 1776
    I am this moment favd. with yours of yesterday's Date, which I
shall in the Morng Communicate to Congress.
    I inclose sundry Resolves of Congress to which beg leave to Refer
you,[1] & am with much Respect, Sir, Your most obed srt.,

                                                    John Hancock Prest

RC (NjP).
[1] Washington's letter to Hancock of August 26 is in PCC, item 152, 2:493–96,
and Washington, *Writings* (Fitzpatrick), 5:490–92. The "sundry Resolves," which
were passed by Congress on August 26 and 27, dealt with disabled American
soldiers and sailors and a plan for discouraging desertions among "'foreigners"
in the British army. *JCC*, 5:702–5, 707–8.

Francis Lewis to Elizabeth Gates

Dear Madam,   Phila. 27 Augt 1776.
    I was yesterday honored with your letter dated the 20th Inst
and happy to find you enjoyed your health.
    Your Son after a few days stay in this City went to Prince Town
where he is at present and in as perfect health as ever he enjoyed.
I conversed with Dr. Wetherspoon yesterday who informed me that
your son applyed closely to his Books and highly extolled his
Ability's. This he spoke sincerly and witho[ut] flattery. As I purpose
going in a few days to Eliza. Town shall have the pleasure of seeing
Bob and at my return shall advise you.
    I can assure you that Genl. Gates & the Army under his Command
at Ticonderoga are well and in high Spirits. We have frequent
advices from that Quarter thro' the medium of Genl. Washington.
There is little expectation of seeing Enemies upon the Lakes this
summer whatever may happen the Next. Genl. Gates Commands at
Ticonderoga. Genl. Schuyler is treating with the Indians at the
German Flatts. They will always be on seperate Commands, but we
are in pain for New York. I fear that City is devoted to distruction,
Ld & Genl How, Cornwallis, Clinton, & Dunmore upon Staten Island
with abt 26,000 Troops of which they landed 8 or 9000 last Friday
and by what we can learn intend in a day or two attackg New York.
I feel for the distress of my family who are still at WtStone [White-
stone] except Morgan who the next day after his return whom
[home] set off for Ticonderoga. His mother could not restrain him.
    We have abt. 20,000 Troop, say Militia, lining the Coast of East
Jersey from Powles Hook to Amboy and upwards of 30,000 on York
& Long Island. The fate of this Campaign a few days must determine.

I have not time at present to say more than that I am and ever shall be, Dr. Madam, yr. Sincere friend, & very H Servt,

F Lewis

P. S. It is said that Genl Carleton has drawn of[f] the Major part of his Army from the Neighbourhood of the lakes, & are filed off for Quebeck from which it is conjectured they are to be brougt round to reinforce Genl Howe as Genl. Bourgoine cannot penetrate the upper Country by the Lakes.

RC (NHi).

Marine Committee to William Stone

Sir   August 27th 1776

The Marine Committee have directed me to inform you that the Hornet Sloop is now returned from her Cruize, during which she has been extreamly leaky as Captain Hallock the Bearer hereof will inform you. The Committee have come to a resolution either to purchase the Sloop or deliver her up to you as they will not any longer hire her, but as the greatest part of the materials she now has on board belong to the Public they wou'd prefer buying her at the valuation to stripping her and when you consider that she will be a mere wreck when so stripped, and that the Hull is old and Schattered I should immagine you wou'd readily see that it is more your Interest to sell than to receive her back in such bad condition, as you will have the hire to this Time in addition to the price. You will upon the whole receive a great sum for her. I am Sir, Your hble servant,   Robert Morris

P.S. If you will not sell pray appoint some person to receive her.

LB (DNA: PCC Miscellaneous Papers, Marine Committee Letter Book). Addressed: "To Captain William Stone owner of the Sloop Hornet."

Robert Morris to John Bradford

[August 27, 1776]

I am now at the 27th August & fear being too late for Mr Merckle but my employment is so Constant I coud not help it. Shou'd he be gone pray forward the enclosed by the first good opportunity for France or if none such offers return it to me by Post under Cover, or if any Privateer going on a Cruize whose Captain you know & can depend on, give to him to put onboard the first Ship he Speaks

bound for France &c or to return it to you if he has no such opportunity. The Owners of the Privateer Hancock &c have applyed to us
not to send Money to Boston as they will pay in their Prize Money
and take drafts on us for it. Therefore you'l apply to their agents,
take money & give them drafts on us for the Cost of the Dispatch &
her Cargo. I am in haste, Dr sir, Your obedt Servt,

Robt Morris

RC (Donaldson, Lufkin & Jenrette, New York, N.Y., 1975). A continuation of
Morris to Bradford, August 16, 1776.

Robert Morris to John Bradford

Dear Sir   Philada. August 27th. 1776
   Our Worthy President having several times mentioned to me that
he had a very good Ship lying unemployed at Salem & that he has
also a quantity of Salt on hand, I have agreed to purchase the Ship
& as much Salt as she can take in without being too deep, but the
difficulty between us is how to fix the Price of this Ship & Salt,
neither of us desire any advantage of the other. I am Willing to
pay the Value of the Ship but no more & the Market price for the
Salt. The President desires no more than the real Value for them
according to the Prices in Boston. We have therefore mutually
agreed to referr the Matter to you & Mr. Bant (His Attorney) to
ascertain the Value & beg you will do it impartially either by your-
selves or by getting the assistance of such other good & honest
Judges as you may think proper and I will pay the President the
Amount of such Valuation. I must also request you will Employ an
Honest, Industrious, carefull Master, have the Vessell immediately
Loaded with the Salt & well fitted & manned & put onboard sufficient
Provisions & Stores for a Six months Voyage. You'l take bills of
Loading for the Salt Consigned to Carter Braxton Esqr near New
Castle, Virginia and order the Master to make the best of his way to
York River in Virginia where he must apply and put himself under
direction of said Colo. Braxton who will have a Cargo ready to put
onboard her. I cannot prescribe any terms for the Master, but beg
to have a carefull, Honest, Industrious Man, & the terms may be
such as will encourage him, without being too Extravagant for us.
He may ship the People to proceed for Virginia from thence to
France & back to some of the American States with an obligation
to Send them back to Boston if not discharged there.
   I am told Rum & Sugars are very cheap with you. If so you may
buy & Ship the value of a few hundred pounds onbd said Ship also
Consigned to Mr. Braxton, and for whatever you lay out in the
outfitt & Loading of this Vessell more than the President is to re-

ceive you'l please to draw on Willing, Morris & Co. Your bills shall be punctually paid and you'l have no difficulty in getting Money for them now that so many Prizes have been sent in, the proceeds of which are to be remitted this way. Recommending this business to your particular attention & leaving you to charge such Commission for the same as you shall judge right, I remain, Dr sir, Your very Obedt Servt.   Robt Morris

P.S. The Utmost Expedition is absolutely Necessary for there is not any British Cruizers in Chesapeak Bay at this time & probably none will be there untill something decissive happens at New York. Order the Capt to go well to the Eastward & not come in with the Land untill in the Lattitude of Cape Henry.

RC (InU).

Benjamin Rush to James McHenry

Dear sir,   Philadᵃ. August 27. 1776.
    The above resolution of Congress does you as much honor as if they had made you a director of a hospital.[1] I need not hint to you after this how unjust it will be in you to desert their Service especially at the present juncture. You will please to furnish Dr Morgan, Dr Stringer, and the other directors of the hospitals of the States with a copy of the above resolution. If there is at present a vacancy in any of their departments, you are authorised to demand a warrant for it. Wishing you my dear McHenry much health, honor & happiness I am with great regard your most Affectionate, humble, Servant,   B Rush

RC (DLC photostat).
[1] Rush wrote this letter beneath an August 26 resolution of Congress penned by Charles Thomson, which recommended that McHenry be appointed to the next "surgeon's birth" to fall vacant in any of the military hospitals of the United States. See JCC, 5:705. McHenry (1753–1816), who had served his medical apprenticeship with Rush, had been named surgeon of the Fifth Pennsylvania Battalion on August 10, a position he held until his capture at the fall of Fort Washington in November 1776. After his exchange in 1778 he secured an appointment as a secretary to General Washington, opening a new career outside medicine that led eventually to several elective and appointive public offices including three terms as delegate to Congress from Maryland, 1783–85. DAB.

Benjamin Franklin to John Adams

Sir   Augt 28. 1776
    The Bearer Mr Measam was a Merchant of good Reputation at Montreal; but having engag'd warmly in the American Cause, has

been obligd to abandon that Country, to the great Detriment of his Affairs. He was appointed by Gen. Wooster a Commissary of Stores there; and apprehending such an Officer to be at this time necessary in our Northern Army, he has apply'd to Congress for a Continuance in that Office.[1] I understand that his Memorial is referred to the Board of War. As I have had occasion to know Mr Measam as a good Accomptant, a Man of Method, and very correct in Business, I cannot but think that if such an Officer is wanting, he is extremely well qualify'd for the Employ, and as such beg leave to recommend him to the Favour of the Board. With great Respect, I have the Honour to be, Sir, Your most obedient, humble Servant,   B Franklin

RC (DNA: PCC, item 42).
    [1] In response to George Measam's petitions of August 7 and 26, 1776, Congress resolved on August 29 that he be continued in office. See *JCC*, 5:636, 700, 717. Measam's petitions are in *Am. Archives*, 5th ser. 1:725–26, 1157.

Benjamin Franklin to Horatio Gates

Dear Sir,   Philadelphia, 28 August, 1776.
    The Congress being advised, that there was a probability that the Hessians might be induced to quit the British service by offers of land, came to two resolves for this purpose, which, being translated into German and printed, are sent to Staten Island to be distributed, if practicable, among those people.[1] Some of them have tobacco marks on the back, that so tobacco being put up in them in small quantities, as the tobacconists use, and suffered to fall into the hands of these people, they might divide the papers as plunder, before their officers could come to the knowledge of the contents, and prevent their being read by the men. That was the first resolve. A second has since been made for the officers themselves. I am desired to send some of both sorts to you, that, if you find it practicable, you may convey them among the Germans that shall come against you.
    The Congress continue firmly united, and we begin to distress the enemy's trade very much; many valuable prizes being continually brought in. Arms and ammunition are also continually arriving, the French having resolved to permit the exportation to us, as they heartily wish us success; so that in another year we shall be well provided.
    As you may not have seen Dr. Price's excellent pamphlet, for writing which the city of London presented him a freedom in a gold box of fifty pounds' value, I send you one of them.[2]
    My last advices from England say, that the ministry have done

their utmost in fitting out this armament; and that, if it fails, they cannot find means next year to go on with the war. While I am writing comes an account, that the armies were engaged on Long Island, the event unknown, which throws us into anxious suspense. God grant success. I am, &c.   B. Franklin.

MS not found; reprinted from Benjamin Franklin, *The Works of Benjamin Franklin* . . . , ed. Jared Sparks, 10 vols. (Boston: Hilliard, Gray, and Co., 1836–40), 8:185–86.
[1] For the background of this effort to encourage the desertion of General Howe's German mercenaries and Franklin's activities as a member of the committee charged with translating and distributing leaflets inside enemy lines, see James Wilson to John Hancock, August 22, and Franklin to Thomas McKean, August 24, 1776.
[2] Richard Price, *Observations on the Nature of Civil Liberty*.

Benjamin Franklin to Anthony Wayne

Dear Sir,   Philada. Augt. 28, 1776

I have received two of your Favours which were immediately communicated to the Board of War,[1] who are a Committee of Congress appointed to take Care of every thing in this Department, and who will I make no doubt take the necessary Measures for Supplying your Wants. But as America is now in the Business of Providing for Armies, there must be for a time Deficiencies that are very inconvenient to the Troops, & which Experience only can bring us into the Mode of Preventing. I am pleas'd to find your People bear them with a Soldierly Spirit, and I hope they will soon be remedied.

A general Action is every day expected at New York. If the Enemy is beaten, it will probably be decisive as to them; for they can hardly produce such another Armament for another Campaign. But our growing Country can bear considerable Losses, & recover them, so that a Defeat on our part will not by any means occasion our giving up the Cause. Much depends on the Bravery of you who are posted at Ticonderoga. If you prevent the Junction of the two Armies, their Project for this Year will be broken, the Credit of the British Arms thro'out Europe and of the Ministry in England will be demolish'd & the Nation grow sick of the Contest.

I am much oblig'd by your Draft of the Situation of our Troops & of the Defences. I pray heartily for your Success, not doubting you will deserve it.

The greatest Unanimity continues in the Congress. The Convention of this Province is sitting, engag'd in framing a new Government. The greatest Part of our Militia are in New Jersey. Arms & Ammunition are daily arriving, the French Government having resolv'd to wink at the Supplying of us, So that in another Year our

People throughout the Continent will be both better arm'd & better disciplin'd, as most of them will have some Experience of a Camp Life & actual Service.

Present my best Respects to General Gates, and believe me, with sincere Esteem, Dear Sir, Your most obedient, humble Servant,

                                                                 B Franklin

RC (PHi).
[1] Not found.

John Hancock to George Weedon?

Sir,   Philada. August 28th 1776

The Congress being informed that you are on your March to New Jersey with Intention to pass through York Town & Philada., I have it in Charge to direct, that you continue your March from York Town by the nearest Route to New Jersey (avoiding Philada. on Acct. of the Small Pox) where on your Arrival you will execute such Orders as Genl. Washington shall think proper to give you.[1]

I am, Sir, your most obed. & very hble Servt.   J. H. Prest.

LB (DNA: PCC, item 12A). Addressed: "To Colo.
[1] See JCC, 5:711. Col. George Weedon was in command of the Third Virginia Battalion, although at the time this letter was written Hancock was uncertain about the identity of the Virginia unit that was on the march to New Jersey. This uncertainty stemmed from the fact that on August 22 Congress had read a letter from Gen. Andrew Lewis stating that he had ordered the First and Third Virginia Battalions to proceed to New Jersey—but saying that the third "may be expected before the other"—and describing Weedon as commander of the third only "for the present." PCC, item 159, fols. 246–47; Am. Archives, 5th ser. 1:1053–54; and JCC, 5:696. For evidence that this letter from Hancock was probably never delivered to Weedon, see Lancaster Committee to Hancock, August 30, 1776. PCC, item 69, fol. 223; and Am. Archives, 5th ser. 1:1230. In consequence of the battle of Long Island, however, Hancock on August 30 sent Weedon the following letter as "The Officer Comandg. the 3d Battn. of Va Troops." "You are Directed notwithstanding a former order to March to New Jersey & wait the orders of General Washington, to March your Battalion immediately on Receipt of this to New York, & inform the General of your Arrival." Roberts Collection, PHC. For the specific intelligence which led to this change in Weedon's earlier orders, see the letters to Hancock from Robert H. Harrison, August 27, from Hugh Mercer, August 28, and from Washington, August 29, which were read in Congress on August 29 and 30. PCC, item 152, 2:499–500, 503–6, item 159, fols. 178–79; Washington, Writings (Fitzpatrick), 5:494–97; Am. Archives, 5th ser. 1:1193–94; and JCC, 5:715, 718.

William Hooper to William Livingston

Dear Sir   Philadelphia August 28. 1776

I thank you for your kind favor which came to hand yesterday. Pray observe that this has a date.

You will see Hewes, Lynch & Rutledge in your Neighbourhood. You will conjecture that Congress has but little business when they can spare their members with so little pretence from the cause of *Necessity.*

Nothing new is stirring here. A Report is propagated and believed by some that a fleet of 12 Men of War is off these Capes, that they have landed 40 prisoners at the Capes for want of provisions to Support them on board.

We have had a late Arrival of Arms & Gunpowder & have expectations of large quantities very soon.

I cannot sufficiently express my horror at the Conduct of Col Zedwitz. There is something very particular & misterious in this matter. Pray find a moment & leisure to give me His history as far as it is material & the particulars which attended this infamous transaction—& what has been the result.[1] Ever remember me respectfully to your worthy family & permit me to subscribe myself, with sincere Esteem, Your Friend & Servant,   Wm Hooper

RC (MHi). Addressed: "To General Livingston, Elizabeth Town, New Jersey."
    [1] Livingston's reply to Hooper, dated August 29, disavowed personal knowledge of "the particulars of Colonel Zedwitz's crime" but went on to describe some of the wild rumors which were then current about it. *Am. Archives,* 5th ser. 1:1210. Lt. Col. Herman Zedwitz, a Prussian cavalary officer during the Seven Years War, had been wounded in the assault on Quebec while serving in the First New York Battalion. On August 24 he had written a letter to William Tryon, the royal governor of New York, falsely claiming that he had been asked by Washington to translate into German Congress' plan for encouraging desertions among Hessian mercenaries and offering to sell the British vital military intelligence about the Continental Army. This letter was intercepted before it reached Tryon, however, and in consequence Zedwitz was court-martialed, convicted, and cashiered from the army on August 26 for "attempting to treacherously correspond with, and give intelligence to the enemy." Ibid., pp. 1159–62. See also James Wilson to John Hancock, August 22, 1776; and Carl Van Doren, *Secret History of the American Revolution* (New York: Viking Press, 1941), pp. 15–17.

William Hooper to Jonathan Trumbull, Jr.

Dear Sir   Philadelphia August 28 1776
    I thank you for your very short Letter by the last post. Your Hurry shall plead your excuse in this Instance, pray do not transgress often, my mercy will be very soon exhausted.

    I have the pleasure to inform you that we have all the reason in the World to believe that France will soon take an active part in our favour. She has opened all her ports to our Merchandize—privateers & prizes, and has offered us Warlike stores in the Islands and every other Article which may tend to induce an intercourse with her.[1]

The Indians will soon be subdued in the Southern part of the Continent, the Southern Colonies have marched 3000 Men in the heart of the Cherokee Country & we shall be able soon to give you a good account of them.

Some Virginians & North Carolinians have marched against a party of Torries in Georgia. I apprehend Lee is at their Head, I wish not as he will be wanted in or about N York. Dear Jonathan! I glory in the North Carolinians. Without Cloaths, Tents, Waggons, they have marched in this extreme unhealthy Season without repining thousands of Miles to the inhospitable Clime of Georgia. Badly Armed, ill payed, still their Ardor in the Cause of liberty supersedes every convenience & private Comfort. May their Example annimate others. The Phila Associators have returned to their Homes—A Scandal to their Country. But the time limited for Service was out—poor pitiful Excuse to desert a post of honor & a post of danger in the Critical moment of Trial.

I wrote Bro. Jos. He inclosed my letter to Jack or yourself. I expected to have heard before this from you. I write in the Congress lobby & am called for in Congress; must therefore conclude this Scrawl. I beg a very particular account of the State of your northern Army & Navy.

Believe me to be, Yours Affectionately,   Wm Hooper

RC (CtHi). Addressed: "To Jonathan Trumbull esquire, Paymaster &c, Albany."
[1] See Josiah Bartlett to William Whipple, August 27, 1776, note 5.

Caesar Rodney to Thomas Rodney

Sir   Philada. Augst the 28th 1776
I have at last got from the Shoemaker and sent down by the Post Betsey's and Sally's Shoes. I don't know Which pair is Betseys or Which is Sally's. This they must find out themselves if they ever Come safe to hand. However I know they are verry dear—to wit 14/6 per pair.

I intended to Come down but have been prevailed on by the other delegates to stay and attend Congress during their absence, the business in Congress being important to each Colony (Especially ours). They proposed that the Convention Should Give the power of Voting for the Colony to one delegate, to prevent our Colony Suffering while they were imployed on other business. This I Consented to, being determined that the folly and ingratitude of the people Shall not divert my attention from the public Good. I have Seen Independence declared, and when I See this Campaign well Ended (as I hope it will) and Regular Government Established, then I intend to leave the public, and take the private path's of Life. Future

Generations will Honor those Names that are neglected by the present Race.

As soon as I Received the accounts from Kent and Newcastle of the Elections I Wrote to Mr McKean at Amboy and desired he would give imediate attendance at the Convention.[1] He got my Letter and in Consequence thereof Came to Philadelphia on Sunday Night last and set out Yesterday Morning verry Early to Newcastle. While he was here I mentioned to him the Circumstance of Vesting the power of Voteing (in Congress) in one delegate. He liked much to have the power in one, But was so aversed to and determined against the Convention takeing upon them, or Concerning with, the least Iota Except the barely frameing A plan of Government that he was of opinion he Should never Consent to their appointing delegates, or Even Altering their power, least they Should afterward be inclined to hold it out as a president for their takeing upon them some other Matters Which he thinks they would willingly be at. He say that for his part he is tired of attending the Congress, But is determined *they* Shall turn him nor no one Else out. That if they are determine to do these things by the Strength of their Majority He will Try the Strength of the Country with *them* Even at the risk of the Court House.

In the Opinion of many people the Convention of this province are makeing Such Strides as Will Effectually knock up both them and their plan.

When our Delegates Return, I am to go home for the Remainder the fall.

I am (by promise) to hear by Every opertunity how they go on at Newcastle. About ten thousand of the Enemy are Landed on Long Island. They have been Schirmishing Every day since, and We are Constantly looking for Something important.[2] Washington is in high Sperits, says they have over Stayed their time, that he is now Ready for them. The sooner the Better. Putnam Commands on Long-Island and has with him Major Genl. Sullivan, Brigr. Genl Lord Sterling and three other Briga[die]rs. Remember me kindly to my Relations & friends. I am Yrs.   Caesar Rodney

P.S. I Wrote to Coll Haslet, since the Battalion went to New-York But have not Yet got an Answer.[3] Therefore don't know how they are there.

RC (PHi).

[1] Not found.

[2] Information on the delegates' knowledge of the British invasion of Long Island on the eve of the New York campaign is also available in the diary of Robert Treat Paine. Thus Paine wrote on August 28: "Very Cool. Battle at Long Island N. York." On August 30: "Our Army retreated to New York." And on August 31: "News that Gen Washington had retreated from Long Island." Robert Treat Paine diary, MHi.

John Adams to William Tudor

Dear Sir.   Philadelphia August 29, 1776.

I Sett down now in the Character of a School Master, or a Fellow of a Colledge to give myself Airs, the Pedantry and Impertinence of which I have no doubt you will pardon, as the Precepts I am about to deliver are of such vast Importance, to the public, and so little practiced, altho they are so very easy, and natural.

You must be sensible that Intelligence is of the last Consequence to the Congress, to the Assemblies and to the Public at large; it ought therefore to be transmitted as quick and frequently, and with as much Exactness and Particularity as possible. In Time of War, the Letters from Generals, and other officers of the Army, are usually the Memorials, and Documents, from whence Annals are afterwards compiled and Histories composed. They cannot be too carefull therefore to transmit circumstantial Narratives of Facts, any more than for their own Safety, Success, and Glory, they can omit any Means of obtaining the most exact, particular and constant Information.

I have Suffered inexpressible Vexations upon many Occasions, when I have seen public Letters, containing vague Sketches, and imperfect Hints of Enterprises, and Movements both of Friends and Enemies.

When an officer setts down to write a Relation of a Skirmish, or a Battle I should think his first Care would be to ascertain and describe the Force of the Enemy—their Numbers—their Commanders—their Appointments—their Motions—the Situation of their Encampment—the Ground they occupied or were attempting to possess themselves of. In the next Place I should think he would tell you the Number of Men which he sent against the Enemy—the officer to whom he gave the Command, the other General officers under him—the Names of the Regiments which composed the Party—and then give you a Detail of the Marches and Countermarches, the Motions and Manœuvres of both Enemies and Friends during the Contention, the Result of the whole Transaction, on which Side Victory declared herself, and the Number of killed and wounded on each side—the Number of officers especially, and among them the most eminent by Name. All these Particulars together with the Loss or Acquisition of Arms, Ammunition, Baggage, ordinance and stores ought to be related with as much Precision, as the Writer can obtain.

Recollect the Letter of Coll Campbell lately taken Prisoner at Boston, relating the Circumstances of his Captivity—How clearly, and precisely he states his own Strength and that of his Enemy!

How minutely he remembers every Circumstance of the Engagement!

When Facts are related in this manner the Reader, the public, and Posterity are enabled to form a Judgment upon the whole, to decide what is the Consequence of the Event, to determine the Character and Conduct of Commanders and of Troops, to ascertain their Merit or Demerit. In short to pass just Reflection, to praise or blame with Propriety, to reward or punish with Justice.

Read the Relation of the Battle between Cataline, and his Adversaries, in Sallust. You See the Combatants—you feel the Ardor of the Battle—you see the Blood of the slain and you hear the wounded sigh and groan.

But if you read our American Relations of Battles and Sieges, in our News Papers, or in private Letters, or indeed in public official Letters, you see none of this Accuracy. You are left in Confusion and Uncertainty about every Thing. It may one day be your Fortune to be obliged to convey Information to the Public of the Course of the Events and Transactions of a War and whenever it is, I doubt not, it will be faithfully done. At present except by the Commander in Chief, and one or two others, it is done very Superficially, crudely and confusedly.

A General officer Should Spare no Pains to make himself Master of the Epistolary Style which is easy, natural, simple and familiar, and of the historical Style too, which is equally simple, altho a little more grave, solemn and noble. Xenophon, Cæsar, Wolf, Lee are all indebted for a very large share of their Fame, to their Pens.

The Strange Uncertainty in which we are Still involved concerning the late Skirmishes, upon Long Island, have given rise to the foregoing observations. My Friends have been a little negligent, in not writing me a Line, upon this occasion. I think We have Suffered in our Reputation for Generalship, in permitting the Enemy to Steal a March upon Us. Greens Sickness I conjecture has been the Cause of this. We have not been Sufficiently vigilant in obtaining Information of the Motions and Numbers of the Enemy after their landing on Long Island, in reconnoitering them and in keeping out advanced Guards and patrolling Parties. Our officers dont seem Sufficiently Sensible of the Importance of an observation of the King of Prussia, that Stratagem, Ambuscade, and Ambush are the Sublimest Chapter in the Art of War. Regular Forces are never Surprised. They are Masters of Rules, for guarding themselves in every Situation and Contingency. The old officers among them are full of Resources, Wiles, Artifices, and Strategems, to deceive, decoy, and over reach their Adversaries. We must oppose Art to Art. We must not disdain to learn of them. Fas est et ab Hoste doceri.

My Mind is more and more engaged with the Thoughts of the Importance of introducing into our Army officers of Parts and Ambition. Captain Lee has been constantly upon my Mind, ever

Since you mentioned him. His Fathers Merit and his own demand Promotion for him. Pray let me know who are Nixons Lt Coll and Major? Who are Learneds Lt Coll and Major? You Said there were other young officers of Parts and spirit in Glovers Regiment. Let me know the Name and Character of every one of them, I conjure you.

Have We not put too much to the Hazard in sending the greatest Part of the Army over to Long Island from whence there is no Retreat? Will not the Enemy by making regular Approaches upon us, be able to force Us, by Means of their Bombs and Carcasses, out of our Lines? [1]

LB (MHi).
[1] For the continuation of this letter, see Adams to Tudor, September 2, 1776.

William Hooper to William Livingston

Dear General   Philad. August 29. 1776
   The Bearer of this is Mr. Milles a Gentleman employed by the State of North Carolina to make inquiry after and employ manufacturers in the various branches of an Iron Work to proceed to North Carolina and be employed there. He goes to the Jersies with the expectation of finding some there as he has been told that several Iron Works in your State are discontinued and the Workmen out of Employ. I will esteem it a very particular favor if you will render him any Assistance in your power to accomplish the purpose of his Errand which is very interesting to our State.[1] Yours with Esteem,
                                                    Wm. Hooper

RC (MHi). Addressed: "General William Livingston, Elizabeth Town, New Jersey."
   [1] On August 2, James Milles had been commissioned by the North Carolina Council of Safety "to proceed to the Northern States there to Contract in behalf of this State with one or more persons well skilled in the Art of Casting Pig Iron, Cannon, Cannon Balls and hollow ware." N.C. Colonial Records, 10:693–94. For a report by Milles about iron manufacturing in North Carolina, dated July 3 and addressed to the council of safety, see ibid., pp. 647–50.

Francis Lewis to Jonathan Trumbull, Jr.

Sir,   Phila 29th Augt. 1776
   I have been duly favored with your letter of the 18th Inst. wherein you advise me that all the drafts I sent you were promised payment except mine on Walter Livingston Esqr. for £71.11 which I find he had paid to my son before my order came to his knowledge. You'l please to return me that Bill. And as I presume the other drafts have

long ere this been honored, I am daily applyed to by the Proprietor for an order for the money, which cannot be obtained without your Certificate of having received it there, the which I must desire you would immediately send me.

Upon the *Application* in your Letter, I moved Congress and obtained a Resolve for 500,000 dollars, to be Issued for your department.[1] Whenever I can render you any services here please to Command, Sir, Your very Humble Servt,   Fras. Lewis

RC (CtHi).
[1] See *JCC*, 5:659.

John Adams to Abigail Adams

Phil. Aug. 30. 1776

The two Armies, on Long Island have been shooting at each other, for this whole Week past, but We have no particular Account of the Advantages gained or Losses suffered, on either side.[1] The General and Officers have been so taken up, with their military Operations, that they have not been able to spare Time to give Us any very particular Information, and the Post which ought to come punctually every day, has been very irregular. I fear We have suffered a good deal.

Amidst all my Concern for the Army, my dear Charles is continually present to my Mind. I dont know what to think. A Load of variolous Matter, sufficient to stupify him for forty Eight Hours, and then to break out so thick, as to threaten a Confluence, I fear will be more than his delicate frame can support. Children of his Age, however, are often seen to bear a great deal. If I had foreseen, that he would have been seized so violently, I should have had no Heart to tell you the vain story of Mather Biles, as I did in my Letter of the 25th.

I have been obliged to hire a servant here, to attend me, untill another shall come for me, with my Horses. My Horses I want beyond Measure. I have never been once on Horse back, since I came here, and I suffer, in my Health, for Want of Exercise. Mr. Barrell is thought to be past recovery.

After I had written the above, my Servant came in from the Post Office, which he watches very diligently, and brought me yours of the 22d and if you knew how much Joy it gave me, your Benevolence would be satisfied. It has given me fine Spirits. I feel quite light. I did not know what fast Hold that little Pratler Charles had upon me before. Give my Love to my little Speckled Beauty, Nabby. Tell her I am glad she is like to have a few Pitts. She will not look the worse for them. If she does, she will learn to prize looks less, and

Ingenuity more. The best Way to prevent the Pitts from being lasting and conspicuous, is to keep her out of the sun for some time to
prevent her from tanning.

John and Tom, hardy fellows! I have hardly had occasion to feel
at all anxious about them.

L[incol]n is not appointed. Ward is requested to continue. I hope
he will.[2]

I am much pleased with your Spirit, in resolving to procure me
Horses your self and not to wait for a Method, which would be
more round about and uncertain. I think I have a Right and that it
is my duty, to take a little Respit and Relaxation. If my Life and
Health is of any Use to the Public, it is necessary for the Public
as well as for me, that I should take a little rest, in order to preserve
them. If they are of none, it is no matter how much rest, I take.

RC (MHi). Adams, *Family Correspondence* (Butterfield), 2:114–15.
    [1] On August 28, in a letter concerned chiefly with his family's health, Adams
had written to Abigail that "Every Moment grows more and more critical at
New York. We expect every Hour, News of serious Joy, or Sorrow. The two
Armies are very near each other at Long Island." Ibid., pp. 111–12.
    [2] See John Adams to Joseph Ward, August 20, note 3; and John Hancock to
Artemas Ward, August 26, 1776.

Samuel Huntington to Matthew Griswold, Eliphalet Dyer and William Pitkin

Gentlemen [1]   Philadelphia 30th August 1776
    As New York is now become the Scene of Action we are in con-
stant expectation of some Important events from that quarter. The
Landing of the British Troops on Long Island & the Skirmishes
which have hap[pe]ned there will doubtless be communicated to you
before this comes to hand, and propaly in a more particular manner
than I am able at present to relate. From the Situation I am placed
in cannot expect to give you any thing new relative to that Important
post, Saving that numbers of Troop from the State of Pensylvania,
Maryland, & Virginia are marching on with all possible expedition
to Join our Army there, & General Lee is ordered from S. Carolina
& soon expected in this City on his way to N. York.

We have Intilligence that the Indians in the Southern department
have Commenced Hostilities on the frontiers of the Carolinas &
Georgia. An expedition is forming from those States to march into
their Settlements & exterpate them unless they submit to reasonable
Terms of peace.

From the Middle and northern departments of Indians the accounts
are more favourable. A Treaty in the middle department is now

negotiating at Pittsburg & from the account of the Treaty which Colo. Butler held with the Indians met at Niagara this summer (a Copy of which we have receivd from an enterprizing person in what manner may not be made public at present) it appears the Chiefs & Sachems are determined to observe a Strict neutrality in the present war, so far as their Speaches can be relied upon. Col. Butler opened the Treaty by Inviting them to Join the Brittish Forces. He told them the Americans were mad & foolish, that they were weak, Boys, & women. They had no powder or ammunition. True they made a little but it was no better than dirt, & that if they would Join the Brittish forces they would soon drive the Americans into the Sea. Next morning the Indians by a Sachem replied you told us yesterday the Americans were mad &c but we say tis you are mad. They are wise for they advise us to be Still & quiet & let you & them fight it out which we Intend to do. If they have no powder, are weak, Boys & women, why do you want us to help you &c.[2]

By the late Treaty at the German flatts with our Commissioners the Indians engage to remain Neuter & to call home their young warriours which had been enticed as they Say to go into Canada & it Seems was without the Consent of their Sachems.[3]

Upon the whole Circumstances attending their conduct we have reason to hope the Indians in general in the Middle & Northern departments will remain Neuter unless some more unfavourable Events Should take place in our Armies & cause them to Change their minds which God prevent.

By a vessel arived here yesterday we are Informd from the Master, who lately sailed from this port for Cape Francois, that on his arrival there under American Colours, the curiosity of his flag drew Such numbers on board as almost Sunk his vessel. They enquired whence he came, what news &c. He told them he carried the flag of the Independant States of America, & gave them the declaration of Independance which they carried on Shore Soon after which the Govr Sent his Compliments to the Capt with permission to hoist his flag in that harbour. The Capt farther says that three days before he left the Cape, which is thirteen days Since, dispatches arrived from old France acquainting the Governor that Twenty Ships of war with a number of Troops were coming to that port in Consequence of which people were Set to work in repairing the barracks there to receive the Troops.

By authentic accounts from Martinique as late as the 3rd Instt. we are Advised the Commandant there had Just received Orders to protect all American vessels that came there, that an English Frigate chasing an American vessel into Port Royal came So near the fort they fired upon the Frigate & beat her off.[4]

I forgot to mention that we have procured two Companies to be raised and Stationed at Westmoreland to guard our Settlements there, they are Commanded by Capt Robert Durkee & Capt Strong on the Continental Establishment.

I have enjoyd as much health as could be expected with the fatigue of business during the Sultry Season in the Stagnate air of this City, Sometimes recollect with pleasing anxiety the fresh breeses of Litchfield in the Autumnal Circuit, & pant for the purer Air of my native land.

Pray excuse blots, incorrectness &c as the post is going & I write in haste, & be assured, I am Gentlemen with much Esteem, your humble Servt,   Saml Huntington

RC (CtY). Addressed: "Honble M. Griswold, E. Dyer & Wm Pitkin Esqrs."

[1] Griswold, Dyer, and Pitkin (1725–89) were members of the Connecticut Council of Safety, and it was probably in this connection that Huntington wrote to them jointly.

[2] For a discussion of the Indian conferences held at Niagara by British agent John Butler during May and June 1776, see Barbara Graymont, *The Iroquois in the American Revolution* (Syracuse: Syracuse University Press, 1972), pp. 94–101.

[3] General Schuyler's August 18 letter reporting on the German Flats conference, which was read in Congress on August 26, is in PCC, item 153, 2:285–87, and *Am. Archives*, 5th ser. 1:1030–31.

[4] See Thomas Jefferson to Edmund Pendleton, August 26, 1776, note 4.

Philip Livingston to Abraham Yates

Sir,   Phila. 30. Augt. 1776

Your favours datd. the 28th Came to hand by the post, who returned before we had any opportunity to Apply to Congress as you desired. The application was Imediately Agreed to & their resolve, to Employ the Blacksmiths, who are now Engaged in Building the frigates, for the purpose of obstructg. the Navigation of Hudsons River, is here inclosed.[1] We wish much to hear from You what is done in that Affair & what more is proposed to be done. The Advices from N. York respecting the Attack of the British Troops on our Army on Long-Island are very various & uncertain. We Could Wish to hear from you as often as time will permit. Our Anxiety as you may Easily judge is not small & particular accts. as often as possible would be very agreable. Many particulars that most Chiefly Concern Us, as Members of yr State & are more Interestg now than Ever, we are not Inf[orme]d of. We know you are much Engaged in Affairs of the Greatest Moment but perhaps one of yr Secretaries May find time to drop us a few Lines Every day or Two. A Considerable Numbr. of Troops have since Tuesday Marchd from hence to Amboy say Abt. three thousand & as many more will probably be dispatched within one week more. Mr. Lewis & Collo. Floyd beg to Assure You that they are as Well as the Subscriber, Sr., Your Most obedt. servant,   Phil. Livingston

RC (InU).
[1] The New York Convention's August 28 letter to the New York delegates is in *Am. Archives,* 5th ser. 1:1548. Congress' August 30 resolution granting the request of the convention's letter is in *JCC,* 5:720–21. Yates was president of the convention.

Josiah Bartlett to John Langdon

My Friend,   Philadelphia Septr. 1st 1776.
I am now to acknowledge thy favours of the 7th and 19th ulto. which are come to hand,[1] and ere this, you have rec'd by Col Whipple, every necessary both for fitting out the ship and for your conduct as Agent. Pray send her to sea as soon as possible that she may be doing something to distress our enemies and assist our friends.

By the enclosed papers, you will see what is the news current here. The affairs at New York seem at present to engross our chief attention. We have not had the particulars of the engagement last week on Long-Island, but believe it was very sharp and bloody. Generals Sullivan and Lord Sterling are prisoners to the enemy. I believe the enemy out-generalled our people, by decoying them out of their Intrenchments, and then surrounding them; but before this reaches you, you will have later accounts from our army and more particulars than I can inform you.

Sept 2d. This morning General Sullivan arrived here on his parole. He says he has a verbal message from Lord Howe to propose his being exchanged for General Prescott and Lord Sterling for General McDonald. He also says that Lord Howe is desirous to converse with some of the members of Congress, not as such (because he cannot acknowledge any such body) but as private gentlemen to see if they cant agree on some proposals for accommodation, and that he will meet them in any convenient place. These are verbal messages, and we have beside every reason to believe that Lord Howe has not and cannot in the nature of things have power to grant any terms that we can possibly accept; yet, as these reports are spread among the people by half Tories and those called moderate men, who (if it should be refused) would represent it that the Congress refused to hear his proposals and would add ten thousand lies of their own, on purpose to disaffect the common people especially at this very critical time—when I consider these things I am at a loss what is best to be done; however I hope we shall be directed to those measures that are best for the United States.[2]

I am Sir, your most obt,   Josiah Bartlett

P.S. Wm. Barrell is dead and buried.

Tr (DLC).

[1] An extract of Langdon's August 19 letter to Bartlett is in Morgan, *Naval Documents*, 6:229.

[2] John Sullivan, who was captured by the British during the battle of Long Island, was sent to Congress on parole by Lord Howe with a "verbal message"— a peace overture that threatened Congress' authority to speak for the united states—which he delivered on September 2. Perceiving the threat contained in Howe's maneuver, Congress requested that Sullivan submit his report in writing, which he did the following day. After extended debate, the delegates attempted to escape their dilemma by resolving on the fifth to send a "committee of their body to know whether he [Lord Howe] has any authority to treat with persons authorized by Congress for that purpose, in behalf of America, and what that authority is, and to hear such propositions as he shall think fit to make respecting the same." *JCC*, 5:723, 728, 730–31, 737. On September 4 Congress resolved to accept Howe's proposal to exchange Sullivan and William Alexander for Richard Prescott and Donald McDonald. *JCC*, 5:735. For further information on the conference with Lord Howe, see John Adams to Samuel Adams, September 8 and 14; and Henry Strachey's Notes on Lord Howe's Meeting with a Committee of Congress, September 11, 1776.

John Adams to William Tudor

Septr. 2. [1776]

So! The Fishers have Set a Seigne, and a whole School, a whole Shoal of Fish, have Swam into it, and been caught. The Fowlers have set a Net and a whole Flock of Pidgeons have alighted on the Bed, and the Net has been drawn over them. But the most insolent Thing of all, is sending one of those very Pidgeons,[1] as a Flatterer to Philadelphia, in order to decoy the great Flock of all. Did you ever see a Decoy duck, or a Decoy Beast?

Thank you for your last Letter.[2] There are a few Words in it, which contain a Hint of something, which, if Fact, has been industriously hidden from Us. "By the Action of last Tuesday, We are convinced that many of our Men are Cowards." I beg of you to explain this, in detail. Do you mean the Men who were in the Skirmish? those in the Lines on Long Island? or those in New York? Dont subscribe your Name. It shall be a secret. But I conjure you as you love your Country to let me know.[3]

LB (MHi). A continuation of Adams to Tudor, August 29, 1776.

[1] That is, John Sullivan, who brought Congress Lord Howe's proposal for a private conference with some delegates. See Josiah Bartlett to John Langdon, September 1, 1776; and Adams to James Warren, September 4, 1776.

[2] Tudor's August 29–31 letter to Adams is in the Adams Papers, MHi.

[3] For the continuation of this letter, see Adams to Tudor, September 20, 1776.

Josiah Bartlett to Nathaniel Folsom

My Dear Sir   Philadelphia Septembr 2nd 1776

I have Recd yours of the 14th Ulto with the acts of our Legislature inclosed, for which I thank you as it gives me particular Satisfaction to be informed of the Situation of affairs in our own State. I am fully Sensible of the great Difficulties we labor under, by the Soldiers being inlisted for Such Short periods, and that it would have been much better had they at first Recd a good bounty & been inlisted to Serve During the war, But you may recollect, the many and to appearance almost insuperable Difficulties that then lay in our way, no money, no magazines of provisions, no military Stores, no Government, in Short when I look back and Consider our Situation about 15 months ago, in Stead of wondering that we are in no better Situation than at present, I am Surprised we are in so good; who of us at that time Expected that the infatuation of Brittain would have forced us to the State we are now in; as Circumstances now are I think we ought by all means to be provided with a well Disciplined army to Serve during the war, and that they ought to be raised as Soon as possible.

I am Glad to hear that our powder mill is ready to be Set going; pray take particular Care that the powder is good; a Considerable Quantity made by one of the mills in this State appears not to have above half the force of good powder, and Does not Catch quick. The danger from bad powder in an Engagement is So great that the Congress have ordered that no powder Shall be Sent to the army but Such as have been well tried & approved by inspectors appointed for that purpose, and have Recommended it to the Several Legislatures to appoint inspectors to prove all the powder that is made or imported into their Respective States; a Copy I will Enclose if I Can procure one before the post Sets off. I will also inclose the order of Congress Concerning wounded & maimed Soldiers and Seamen.

The affairs at New York Seem at present almost wholly to Engross our attention; we have not had the full of the particulars of the action of the 27th ulto. on Long Island from the General; but by the best accounts we have obtained it appears that our people were Decoyed & Surrounded by the main Body of the Enemy and obliged to fight their way thro' or Surrender prisoners; It Seems there must have been Some very great neglect Either in not Sending out proper [guards] & parties to gain intelligence or they are not doing their Duty. Generals Sullivan & Lord Sterling are prisoners & I believe 6 or 700 others. The consequence has been the Evacuation of Long Island & Governors Island, of both which the Enemy are now in possession, a very unfortunate Begining of the Campain there. However it is not irreparable and I hope it will make both officers & Soldiers more Careful to keep proper guards & not Suffer themselves to be taken by Surprise any more.

After writing the above Genl Sullivan came to my Lodgings in this City and by his account the affair of Long Island was much as I had heard. He says he has two verbal messages from Lord Howe which he is per[mitted] on his parole to Come to Congress to propose. One is the Exchange of himself & Lord Sterling for Genls. Prescot & McDonald, the other is to propose a meeting with Some of the members of Congress (as private Gentlemen for he Can't acknowledge any such Body as Congress) to See if they Can't agree on Some propositions for an accommodation without further Bloodshed and Says he will meet at almost any place for the purpose. These are but verbal messages & I can Easily foresee great Difficulties that may arise let the Congress accept or refuse the proposed Conference. What the Congress will do is at present uncertain but hope they will be directed by the Supreme Disposer of all Events, to do in this & Every other affair before them what will be most Conducive to the Safety & Hapiness of these American States.[1] So wishes your friend and most obednt, Humble Servt,   Josiah Bartlett

RC (NN).
[1] For further information on John Sullivan's report to Congress, see Bartlett to John Langdon, September 1, 1776, note 2.

William Hooper to William Livingston

My dear Sir   September 2d 1776. Philadelphia
I thank you for your's of the 29th and sincerely sympathize with you in the trouble and sollicitude which attend you in your new department.[1] An Army raised (to use a Congress Cant) upon the spur of the occasion composed of Men who have no Idea of Subordination & when the officers have no security of being obeyed but from their orders being made to suit the taste of those to whom they are addressed, is such a motley system that it will require all your abilities to give it form and order and all your patience & philosophy to support the frequent disappointments which your best exertions will be subject to.

We have met a snarle in our armys reliniquishing Long Island. The measure was necessary perhaps when taken, as the preservation of the Army depended upon it, but was the Island incapable of being fortified, or was the whole of the last Summer too limited a time to accomplish it? or Have we no Engineers? The brave fellows who fell at Long Island from what I have heard deserved a better fate. Do we owe the misfortune to the overheated Zeal of young Officers or to what cause. I am apprehensive of the effects this disappointment may produce upon Luke Warm whigs, men too indolent to think for themselves, or too phlegmatick hitherto to have taken an active part. The Tories will assume a temporary Triumph, & there is a race of men who however otherways well disposed they may be, can not conflict—altho the contest was to purchase Liberty. Be it our endeavour as it is our duty to view the Hand of providence in every event & with resignation wait the day which is to give us reparation for the past & teach our Enemies that we fight the cause of heaven.

Zedwitz's affair is mysterious. How he could be criminal enough to merit being broke by a Court Martial (which I am told has been the case) when his charge was of so black a dye & yet not deserve death I confess I am at a loss to conjecture.

We expect Sullivant here every hour. We are told that he has a Message from Lord Howe to Congress. I fear the Arts and address of Lord Howe, who by all Accts is a Politician, a Soldier and a Gentleman, more than I dread the British Arms. Pray pick up every anecdote of the Long Island Affair—Deaths, Wounds, flight &c &c & direct a Sheet to a friend who esteems himself highly honoured with your Correspondence. I am affectionately, Yours &c,

Will Hooper

RC (MHi). Addressed: "General William Livingston, ⟨Elizabeth Town⟩ Prince Town, New Jersey."
[1] Livingston's August 29 letter to Hooper is in *Am. Archives,* 5th ser. 1:1210.

Marine Committee to Daniel Tillinghast

Sir September 2nd 1776

The Secret Committee of Congress have directed Mr Thomas Green of Providence in your State to put into your hands the following articles belonging to the Continent now in his possession for which you will please to give him a receipt.

330 Bolts of best Holland and Russia Duck
26¼ Casks of Powder
2 pair 4 lb Cannon
3 pair 3 lb Do.
4 pair Swivels
3 Casks leaden ball
21 Casks Sewing Twine
598 lb salt Petre
60 lb Brimstone
470 Bushels salt
50 half Johannes
1 Drum

You have underneath a Copy of a Resolve of Congress of the 30th Ulto ordering such part of the above Duck as is suitable for Tents to be made up and forwarded with all possible expedition to his

Excellency General Washington which we request you will immediately execute.[1] You will hold the rest of the articles ready for the future orders of this Committee, who are Sir, your hble Servants,

LB (DNA: PCC Miscellaneous Papers, Marine Committee Letter Book).
   [1] See *JCC*, 5:718. See also Washington, *Writings* (Fitzpatrick), 5:409, 435. Tillinghast was the Continental prize agent in Rhode Island.

Josiah Bartlett to William Whipple

Dear Sir,   Philadelphia Sept 3d 1776.
   By that time this reaches you, I expect you will be near ready to set out on your return to this City. Make all convenient haste. The Congress is at this time very thin. Col Lee is arrived here, but several others have taken leave of absence, among them Mr. Jefferson and Mr. Haywood.[1] The unhappy affair of the 27th on Long-Island has occasioned the evacuation of our works there and on Governor's Island. Our people were ensnared, and what vexes me, in a very careless manner.
   Yesterday, General Sullivan arrived at my lodgings, being on his parole. He says he has a verbal message to Congress to propose himself and Lord Sterling in exchange for Generals Prescott and McDonald. He also says that Lord Howe expressed himself very desirous of an accommodation with America, without any more bloodshed; that he was very willing to meet, at almost any place, a number of the members of Congress (as private gentlemen, for he could not own any such body as Congress) to try if they could make any proposals for an accommodation; that he said he had waited near two months longer in England than he should have otherwise done, to procure proper powers for a final accommodation, with which he said he was now vested, &c, and he allowed General Sullivan to come here to propose the aforesaid conference to Congress. What will be done in the affair by Congress I know not, but think there are difficulties on both sides. If the Congress should accept of the proposed conference, only on a verbal message, when at the same time Lord Howe declares he can consider them only as private gentlemen, especially when we are certain he can have no power to grant any terms we can possibly accept; this I fear will lessen the Congress in the eye of the public, and perhaps at this time intimidate people when they see us catching hold of so slender a thread to bring about a settlement. On the other hand, General Sullivan's arrival from Lord Howe with proposals of an accommodation, with 30 falsehoods in addition, are now spread over this City, and will soon be over the Continent, and if we should refuse the conference,

I fear the Tories, and moderate men, so called, will try to represent the Congress as obstinate, and so desirous of war and bloodshed that we would not so much as hear the proposals Lord Howe had to make, which they will represent (as they already do) to be highly advantageous for America, even that he would consent that we should be independent provided we would grant some advantages as to trade. Such an idea spread among the people, especially the soldiers at this time might be of the most fatal consequence. Whatever is done by Congress in the affair will I hope be ordered for the benefit of America.

Wm Barrell died on Sunday morning and was buried last evening. I am Sir your friend and most obt,   Josiah Bartlett

Tr (DLC).
[1] Heyward apparently did not leave for South Carolina until September 5. See Thomas Heyward to John Morgan, September 4, 1776.

John Hancock to Ebenezer Hancock

Sir   Philada. 3 Sepr. 1776
I have only time to Acknowledge the Receipt of your Letter with your return, & to inform you that 250,000 Dollars are order'd to be immediately Sent you. I Refer you to the above resolve,[1] & am, Your huml Servt,   John Hancock Prest

RC (MHi).
[1] Hancock wrote this letter beneath a resolve of July 31, 1776, directing the deputy paymaster in Massachusetts to pay "any militia which the general assembly of that state shall think proper to call in, to replace the continental troops ordered from thence." And on August 16 Congress ordered that Ebenezer Hancock be sent $250,000 "for the use of the army in the eastern department." *JCC*, 5:623, 660–61.

John Hancock to Certain Continental Officers

Sir,   Philada. Sepr. 3d. 1776.
The Congress having just received Information from Genl. Washington of the very great & superior Strength of the Enemy, and being convinced that they are determined to bend all their Force agt. New York in order, if possible, to penetrate into that, and the neighbouring States, have judged it absolutely necessary to augment our Troops in that Quarter. I have it in Command therefore to direct that immediately on the Receipt hereof, you order three [1] more Continental Battalions to march from Virginia [2] to reinforce the Army at New York.[3]

The critical State of our Affairs will not admit the least Delay in executing this Order. Suffer me therefore to press you to the greatest Expedition with that Earnestness so naturally suggested by the Importance of the Cause, altho I doubt not your own Ardor would be a sufficient Stimulus when called on by the Voice of Liberty and your Country.

I am, Sir, your most obed. & very hble Servt.

J. H. Prest.

LB (DNA: PCC, item 12A). Addressed: "To Genl. [Andrew] Lewis, Virginia, 3 Batt. Genl. [James] Moore, No. Carolina, two Battalions. Commanding officer of Continental Troops in Rhode Island, one Battalion."

[1] Or "two" or "one," according to recipient.

[2] Or "North Carolina" or "Rhode Island," according to recipient.

[3] For Congress' resolves of this date about reinforcing Washington with three Continental battalions from Virginia, two from North Carolina, and one from Rhode Island, see JCC, 5:733–34. In a letter to Hancock of September 2, Washington described his situation as "truly distressing" and confessed his "want of confidence, in the generality of the Troops." See PCC, item 152, 2:519–22, and Washington, Writings (Fitzpatrick), 6:4–7.

John Hancock to Certain States

Gentlemen,   Philada. Sepr. 3d. 1776

Our Enemies being determined to make a powerful Attack on New York and the States adjoining thereto; and having for this Purpose, collected their whole Force from every Part of the Continent, it is incumbent on the United States of America to take the most effectual Measures to defeat this deep laid Scheme against their Country.

The Congress have just received Information from General Washington of the very great & superior Strength of the Enemy; and if we consider the recent Change in the Situation of our Affairs at New York, we shall soon be convinced that Nothing will prove an adequate Remedy in our present Circumstances, but the most vigorous Exertions on our Part. I am therefore by Order of Congress to request you will immediately send all the Aid in your Power to our Army at New York.[1]

The State of our Affairs is so extremely critical, that Delay may be attended with fatal Consequences. Suffer me therefore to press you in the Name and by the Authority of your Country, to an immediate Compliance, and with all the Earnestness, so naturally suggested by the Importance of the Cause. Altho I doubt not your own Ardor would be a sufficient Stimulus when called on by the Voice of Liberty, yet my Anxiety is so great, I cannot refrain on the present Occasion from beseeching you to exert yourselves. Every Thing is at Stake—our Religion—our Liberty—the Peace & Happiness of Posterity—are the grand objects in Dispute; which, that we may be able to preserve & transmit to future Generations, is the constant and uninterrupted Wish of, Gentlemen, your most obedt. & very hble Servt.　　　　　　　　　　　　　　J. H. Prest.

LB (DNA: PCC, item 12A). A circular letter directed to the assemblies of Connecticut, Massachusetts, New Hampshire, and Rhode Island and the conventions of Delaware, Maryland, and Pennsylvania.

[1] See JCC, 5:734; and Washington, Writings (Fitzpatrick), 6:4–7. The RC of this letter to the Massachusetts Assembly contains a postscript in Hancock's hand referring to several enclosed "Resolutions of Congress." Hancock Papers, MWA. These "Resolutions" probably included those passed this day concerning Jeduthan Baldwin's appointment as a Continental engineer and sending a Massachusetts militia battalion to Rhode Island to replace a battalion of Continental troops simultaneously ordered to New York. See JCC, 5:732, 734.

John Hancock to George Washington

Sir,　　　　　　　　　　　　　　　　Philada. Sepr. 3d. 1776.

I do myself the Honour to enclose you sundry Resolves, by which you will perceive that Congress having taken your Letter of the 2d Inst. into Consideration, came to a Resolution, in a Committee of the whole House, that no Damage should be done to the City of New York.[1]

I have sent Expresses to order the Battalions up to Head Quarters agreeably to the Resolves herewith transmitted; & likewise to the several States to the Northward of Virginia to send all the Aid in their Power to the Army.

I have the Honour to be, with perfect Esteem & Regard, Sir, your most obed. & very hble Servant,　　　John Han[cock]

RC (DLC). In the hand of Jacob Rush and signed by Hancock.

[1] For these "sundry Resolves," see JCC 5:733–34. Washington and his officers subsequently misconstrued the resolve about avoiding damage to New York City to mean that Congress wanted the city held at all costs. However, after Washington had informed Congress of this interpretation, an additional resolve was passed on September 10 clearly stating that Congress did not intend that the army "should remain in that city a moment longer than [Washington] shall think it proper for the public service." See JCC, 5:749; Washington to Hancock, September 8, PCC, item 152, 2:531–37, and Washington, Writings (Fitzpatrick), 6:27–33; and Hancock to Washington, September 10, 1776.

Richard Henry Lee to John Page

My dear Sir,　　　　　　　　　　　Philadelphia 3d Septr. 1776.

I am concerned to find that the Governors health does not yet permit his attention to public business. Your anxiety no doubt is

great to hear how things go on at N. York. I will give you the best
account that Congress has been able to collect. Of our Troops about
6000 were stationed on Long Island under Command of Generals
Putnam, Sullivan and Lord Sterling. Of these, three guards of 800
men each were posted at the edge of a wood opposite the enemy
who with about 18,000 men were encamped on a plain below &
directly opposite these Guards. At 10 oClock in the night of the
25th [*i.e.* 26th] of Augt. Gen. Howe marched with 6000 men and
unperceived turned the left of our Guards and halted. Sometime
before day three large Columns under command of the Hessian
General, Lord Cornwallis, and Brigadier Gen. Grant marched to
the front and Right of our Guards with a view to attack and surround them at the same time. In the meantime Gen. Putnam received intelligence that the enemy were in motion and about break
of day ordered Gen. Sullivan & Lord Sterling to reenforce the Guard
with two Batallions and annoy the enemy in their march. Our
Officers having no knowledge of Gen. Howes march proceeded to
meet and engage the Corps under Cornwallis &c. These last by
their superior numbers had very soon outflanked, and in great degree surrounded our people. Thus they fought for some time, without advantage on either side, except that some of Cornwallis's
Troops & others had given way but were supported by reenforce-
ments, when they discovered Howe with a large body directly between them and their Lines. Environed on all sides with such
superiority of numbers they determined to fight their way thro, and
more than two thirds of them reached the Lines, three thousand
having been engaged and our loss in killed, wounded, and missing
not exceeding 7 or 800. The enemies loss in killed is certainly greater
than ours, but they have more prisoners, and on the whole our loss
of men is greater than theirs. Gen. Howe conceiving that our lines
were either abandoned or too much weakened marched boldly up
to them with his Corps, but they received so heavy and well directed
a fire that they retreated with great pricipitation. Generals Sullivan
and Lord Sterling are prisoners. We do not know of any Officer
among the enemy being killed of greater rank than Colo. Grant,
who is certainly among the Slain.

A Council of War having determined to evacuate Long Island as
no longer tenable, this dangerous service was effected on Friday
night last without loss, except two heavy Cannon which could not
be brought away and were spiked. Our Army, all now on the New
York side, and consisting when together of about 26,000 men are
in high spirits. The flying Camp increases daily. 'Twill presently
be 10,000 strong. Our enemies force, by the best accounts is about
23,000. We have so respectable a Marine force on Lake Champlain,
and so good an army on its borders that we are under no apprehentions from that quarter. In the W. Indies, every thing promises a

speedy rupture between France & G. Britain. They have certainly offered us their Ports to carry our Prizes into, and when Capt. Weeks in a Continental Ship of 16 six pounders lately drubbed Capt. Chapman in the Shark of 18 guns in sight of the people of Martinique and to their great joy, the Captain of our Vessel (suspecting Chapman was gone to Antigua for help) was offered by the Governor a Convoy of Frigates to see him on his way as far as he chose to take them.[1] All this looks well. It is amazing what fortunes are made here by Prizes. Small Privateers returning with large Sugar Ships &c. We all agree that it will be very wise and proper to order Lilly and Cocke at least to go Cruize in the way of the homeward bound West India Men.[2] A few of them will pay our Marine expences already incurred, and help us to build 10 or 12 large Sea Gallies to keep open the trade of our Bay. If you approve this plan, pray push it into immediate execution. The French harbors may receive them, or Chingotigue in the Eastern Shore, if our Bay should be shut up. Farewell dear Sir and believe me affectionately yours,   Richard Henry Lee

P.S. If you see our friend General Lee hasten him here, he is extremely wanted at N. York.

RC (MWA).
[1] For the July 27 engagement between the *Shark* and the Continental ship *Reprisal*, commanded by Lambert Wickes, see Thomas Jefferson to Edmund Pendleton, August 26, 1776, note 4.
[2] Thomas Lilly and James Cocke, commanders of Virginia naval vessels, had been ordered by the Virginia Council on August 6 to cruise against enemy ships in the vicinity of the York River. *Journals of the Council of the State of Virginia*, ed. H. R. McIlwaine, 3 vols. (Richmond: Virginia State Library, 1931–52), 1:109–10.

North Carolina Delegates to the North Carolina Council of Safety

Gentlemen   Philadelphia September 3. 1776
The present truly critical state of the Continental Army at New York has induced Congress to enter into the Resolve which this is intended to convey.[1] From the Newspapers aided with the Information which you will receive from our friend Mr Heyward you will learn that we have received a Check upon Long Island, our utmost exertions are immediately necessary to invigorate and give spirits to the Troops to the Eastward. As the fate of New York and all the Eastern Colonies in a great measure depends upon our success in that quarter & as this must work very powerful effects upon the Continent at large, We are well assured that a measure which puts it in your power to add two Reg'ts to our forces at a time when you

have no urgent occasion for them at home will meet your cordial approbation. Virginia is to march three Regiments with all possible expedition in addition to two which are now on the way & far advanced. We suppose that you will advise the filling up of the Regiments which you send hither to their compleat number out of the other Regiments & immediately order out recruiting parties to supply the places of those whom you may draw from the other Regiments. A large bounty sufficient to induce men to prefer a Soldier's to any other occupation must be given. The Exigincy is importunate. We must not be stopped by trifles.

If our Troops are to the Southward of North Carolina orders must immediately go for their return, & We doubt not every possible measure will be adopted to expedite their movements. Mr. Hewes will be with you shortly, to him we refer you for further particulars & for the Manner in which the Troops may be marched with the greatest ease & Expedition.

We are Gentlemen, With great Respect, Your obed. Serts,

> Wm Hooper
>
> Joseph Hewes
>
> John Penn

RC (Nc–Ar). Written by Hooper and signed by Hooper, Hewes, and Penn.

[1] For Congress' resolve of this date reinforcing Washington with two Continental battalions from North Carolina, see *JCC*, 5:733–34. However, after receiving an explanation that sending two battalions to New York would be "dangerous, if not impracticable," Congress decided on September 16 to allow North Carolina "to execute or suspend" this resolve as it saw fit. The council of safety subsequently decided not to carry out the September 3 resolve. See *JCC*, 5:761–62; *N.C. Colonial Records*, 10:878, 11:343–45; John Penn to the North Carolina Council of Safety, September 16; and North Carolina Delegates to the North Carolina Council of Safety, September 18, 1776.

John Adams to Abigail Adams

Wednesday Septr. 4. 1776

Mr. G[erry] arrived Yesterday, and brought me yours of August 17 and soon afterwards the Post came in, with yours of the 25 of Aug. Am happy to find you, in so good a Way, and am glad to learn that Horses and a Man are coming. I want them much. But our Affairs having taken a Turn at Long Island and New York, so much to our Disadvantage, I cannot see my Way clear, to return home so soon as I intended. I shall wait here, untill I see some more decisive Event, in our Favour or against Us. The General Court however will appoint some other Gentleman to relieve me, and my Man and Horses will come, and then I can ride a little in a Morning for my Health, and come home as soon as Circumstances will admit. I am obliged to General Lincoln for his Information, concerning the Fortifications, which I hope will be effectually attended to, as I am not clear, that Boston is yet secure from Invasion.

I hope, the Disasters at Long Island, and New York will not dispirit our People. The Ways of Providence are inscrutable. I have strong suspicions that these Disasters have saved Boston from another Invasion, which I think would have been attempted by the two gratefull Brothers, with their whole Fleet and Army, if they had not obtained Long Island.

RC (MHi). Adams, *Family Correspondence* (Butterfield), 2:117–18

John Adams to Samuel Cooper

Dear sir   Philadelphia Sept 4. 1776

Mr Hare, a Brother of Mr Robert Hare, the Porter Brewer in this City is bound to Boston. He has boarded sometime in the same House with me, and is very desirous of seeing the Town of Boston. He is travelling to Boston merely from the Curiosity of a Traveller, and meddles not with Politicks. He has an Inclination to see the public Buildings, your Church and the Chappell particularly. I should be much obliged to you if you would procure him the Sight of as many of the public Buildings in Town as you can conveniently.[1]

Our Generals I fear have made a Mistake in Retreating from Long Island. I fear they will retreat from the City of New York next. These are disagreable Events. I dont like these Measures. I wish there was more firmness. But let not these Things discourage. If they get Possession of New York, Long Island, and Staten Island, these are more Territory than their whole Army can defend, this year. They must keep their Force together. The instant they divide it they are ruined. They cannot march into the Country, for before they get Ten Miles into the Country they are surrounded or their Retreat cutt off. They cannot go up the North River to any purpose because a few Months will make Ice in it in which their Vessells cannot live. They must keep the most of their Ships in the Harbour of New York to defend their Army. I sometimes think, that Providence, against our own opinions and Inclinations has provided better for Us in this Instance than our own Wisdom would have done. Had the Enemies Fleet and Army been kept from Long Island, they must and would have made an Effort elsewhere for Winter Quarters. At Staten Island they could not have wintered. They must therefore have wintered at Boston, Rhode Island, or have gone to the Southward to Virginia, one of the Carolinas or

Georgia, and either of these Cases would, perhaps have been worse, for Us. The Panick, which is spread upon this occasion is weak and unmanly—it excites my shame, and Indignation. But it is wearing off. If our whole Army had been cutt to Pieces it would have been shameful to have been so intimidated, as some are or pretend to be. Congress I hope will stand firm. I am, my dear Sir, in all Conditions of affairs public and private, your Friend,   John Adams

LB (MHi). Endorsed: "Sent by Mr. Hare."

¹ Richard Hare also delivered a similar letter of this date from Adams to John Winthrop at Harvard College, who was asked to show Hare the college's "Library and Apparatus" as one of the sights suitable for "the Curiosity of a Traveller." *Collections of the Massachusetts Historical Society*, 5th ser. 4 (1878): 311.

John Adams to James Warren

Dear Sir   Philadelphia Septr. 4. 1776

It is in vain for me to think of telling you News, because you have direct Intelligence from Ticonderoga much sooner than I have, and from N. York sooner than I can transmit it to you.

Before this Time the Secretary has arrived,¹ and will give you all the Information you can wish, concerning the State of Things here. Mr G[erry] got in the day before yesterday, very well.

There has been a Change in our Affairs at New York. What Effects it will produce I cant pretend to foretell. I confess, I do not clearly foresee. Lord Howe is surrounded with disaffected American Machiavillians, Exiles from Boston and elsewhere, who are instigating him to mingle Art with Force. He has sent Sullivan here, upon his Parol, with the most insidious, 'tho ridiculous Messages which you can conceive. It has put Us rather in a delicate Situation, and gives Us much Trouble.² Before this day, no doubt you have appointed some other Persons to come here, and I shall embrace the first opportunity, after our Affairs shall get into a more settled Train to return. It is high Time, for me, I assure you: yet I will not go, while the present Fermentation lasts but Stay, and watch the Crisis, and like a good Phisician assist Nature in throwing off the morbific Matter.

The Bearer, Mr Hare, is a Brother of the Gentleman of the Same Name, in this City, who has made himself So famous by introducing the Brewing of Porter, into America. He wants to see our Country, Harvard Colledge, the Town of Boston &c. If you can help him to such a sight, I should be glad. Cant you agree with him to erect a Brewery of Porter in Mass. Your Barley and Water too, are preferable to any here.

Upon the Receipt of yours and Mrs. Temples Letters, I com-

municated the Contents of them to Congress, who appointed a
Committee to consider them, who reported that the Trees should
be paid for as Wood. The President, I suppose has communicated
the Resolution upon it, which agrees with the Report. I should
be glad to write Mrs Temple an account of this, but have not Time.
You will be So good as to let her know it. I answered her Letter
before her affair was determined.[3]

RC (MHi). In Adams' hand, though not signed.
[1] Samuel Adams.
[2] Adams' reaction to John Sullivan's delivery of Lord Howe's message to Congress was later graphically described by Benjamin Rush. "I sat next to him while Genl. Sullivan was delivering a request to Congress from Lord Howe for an interview with a committee of the House in their private capacities, after the defeat of the American Army on Long Island on the 26th of August 1776. Mr. Adams, under a sudden impression of the design, and dread of the consequences of the measure, whispered to me a wish 'that the first ball that had been fired on the day of the defeat of our army, had gone through his head.' When he rose to speak against the proposed interview, he called Genl. Sullivan 'a decoy duck, whom Lord Howe has sent among us to seduce us into a renunciation of our independance.'" Benjamin Rush, The Autobiography of Benjamin Rush, ed. George W. Corner (Princeton: Published for the American Philosophical Society by Princeton University Press, 1948), p. 140. For Adams' autobiographical account of this event, see Adams, Diary (Butterfield), 3:414–15.
[3] See Adams to Harriet Temple, August 21, 1776.

Thomas Heyward to John Morgan

Dear Sir   Philada. 4th Septr. 1776
     Pardon me for not acknowledging earlier the Receipt of your
several favours. I am sure you will not attribute my Neglect to
any Want of Respect or Esteem. A Mind deeply engaged in the
important Transactions of the present Day is not always capable
to discharge with Punctuality the Duties of private Friendship. This
I am persuaded you have frequently experienced & will make such
Allowance as I assure You my Situation requires.
     The Contents of your several Letters have been laid before the
Medical Committee & Congress have come into several Resolutions
which I imagine you must have received long before this time. I
wish they may answer the good Purposes intended by them & be
equally satisfactory to You & the Gentlemen in the different Departments.[1]
     Your Commands I shall always be glad to receive but it will for
sometime be out of my Power to execute any of them in Congress
as I purpose to set out for So. Carolina in the Morning.
     May the God of Heaven protect our General & his Army in this
great Day of Trial & Distress & may the virtuous Efforts of our brave

Countrymen be crowned with deserved Success. This is the most
ardent Wish of One who is with greatest Esteem, Dear Sir, Your
most obt., humble Servt,   Ths. Heyward Jun

RC (PHi). Addressed: "To John Morgan. M.D., Director General, New York."
    [1] In response to a June 18 memorial from Dr. Morgan, director general of hos-
pitals and physician in chief of the Continental Army, Congress had passed a
comprehensive set of resolutions on July 17 dealing with medical care for the
army and delineating Morgan's authority. See *JCC*, 5:460, 556, 568–71; PCC,
item 41, 6:3–6; and *Am. Archives*, 4th ser. 6:1714–15. Additional resolutions on
these points were also approved on August 20. *JCC*, 5:673.
    Two June–July 1776 letters from Morgan to Samuel Adams and other members
of the Medical Committee, of whom Heyward was one, are in John Morgan,
*A Vindication of His Public Character in the Stations of Director-General of the
Military Hospitals, and Physician in Chief of the American Army; Anno 1776*
(Boston: Powars and Willis, 1777), pp. 49–53, 67–71. Morgan also included in this
work brief extracts of an August 5 letter to him from Samuel Adams and one of
August 14 from Charles Thomson. The former reads: "I have received several
letters from you, which I should have sooner acknowledged, if I could have
found leisure. I took, however, the necessary steps, to have what you requested,
effected in Congress." The latter: "There is no man, Sir, acquainted with you,
who can doubt of your abilities. All the world bears witness to them, and the
learned in Europe, who must be allowed to be the best judges, have given ample
testimony, by the honours they have heaped upon you. While you exercise your
great talents, for the benefit of those entrusted to your care, your Country will
honour you, and posterity will do you justice; even though Dr. S[hippen], when
you chance to meet, should refuse to give you precedence." Ibid., pp. xxx, 71.
For a detailed account of Morgan's situation at this time, see Whitfield J. Bell,
Jr., *John Morgan: Continental Doctor* (Philadelphia: University of Pennsylvania
Press, 1965), pp. 182–96.

Caesar Rodney to George Read

Sir   Philada. Septr. the 4th 1776
    Inclosed you have a Resolution of Congress. One of these papers
was delivered to the Delegates of each Colony to be by them Transmitted to their several assemblies or Conventions that Order might
be taken therein.[1]
    I mentioned in my last [2] the arrival of General Sullivan and then
hinted the business of his Coming. The day I wrote you last he was
admitted in Congress and informed them that he had been on bord
the Eagle and there had private Conversation with Lord Howe.
The Substance of which was that his Lordship declared he had ample power (together with the General) to Settle matters between
Great Britain and the Colonies in Such manner as Should be for the
True Interest and benefit of both and to make such Settlement
permanent. That he wished for nothing more than to Converse
with General Washington or some one or more Members of Congress on that Head, but that there was a difficulty in the way which

prevent it, for that his Rank & Scituation was attended with that kind of delicacy. That he Could not treat with the Congress as Such, and had no doubt that the Congress from their Scituation lay under the same difficulty—therefore proposed his having Conversation of an Hour or two with some of the members as private Gentlemen. That he would meet them in that Carrector also where Ever they pleased. That he did not doubt by this Step matters might be put in a Train of Accommodation—if not that it would only be so much time Lost. That his Lordship further said he had stayed in England two months after he was otherwise Ready to Come on purpose to obtain those ample powers before mentioned, by which means the Declaration of Independency had taken place before his Arrival. There was other Conversation Such as that his Lordship thought this a fine Country, that he had many friends & Acquaintances here and that he should be pleased much to have an oppertunity to Ride thought [throughout] the Country to See them &c. You Sir may be desirous to know what Congress think of this Message delivered by Sullivan at the request of Lord Howe. To Satisfy your desire I think I may Venture to say that a verry great majority of the Members look on it as an Insult and believe a Resolution will pass that no proposals for the future be Received, Unless Reduced to writing and Signed [by] Some person who has authority to Treat with the Congress as an Assembly of the United Independent States of America, or to that Effect.

From Certain intelligence Recd. since I Wrote last Coll Haslet, Coll Smallwood and Coll Bedford were Setting on a Court-Martial in York at the time the Delawarers and Marylanders were Engaged with the Enemy. That those two Battalions fought as Bravely as Men Could possibly do. That the Marylanders lost 259 men missing, many of Whom were Killed. That it was owing cheifly to their being Seperated by which Means the Enemy got between them and oblidged them to fight in Small parties. The Delawares being well Trained kept and fought in a Compact Body the Whole Time, and when oblidged to retreat kept their Ranks and Entered the lines in that order, frequently while retreating obliged to fight their way through Bodies of the Enemy, Who had before make [sic] an attack on our lines, Where they were repulsed and were also retreating and Met each other. The Delawares in this retreat lost four or five Men, one or two killed and two or three drownd in Crossing a Creek. This would have been all their Loss, but unfortunately about the beginning of the Engagement had placed a Small party of observation at some distance with Whom they Could never again Join (the Enemy haveing Got between them) tho Frequently attempted. Greatest part of those were lost, either Killed or taken prisoners, but supposed Chiefly Killed. Upon the Whole the Delaware Battalion has now Missing thirty one including two officers to wit Lt.

Stuart and Lt. Harney. The Major had a Slight wound in the Knee. This is the Whole of the damage the[y] have Sustained. Captain Adams of Kent after fighting bravely a Considerable time was seized with a Most Violent Collick. He was sent off the Ground & a Soldier with him to Conduct him to our lines. In his way he had to Cross a deep Marsh in which when the Battalion Crossed they found him Just Expiring. They carried him over on boards, got him in the lines, and he is now well.

Our old friend Billy Livingston is appointed Governor of the Jersey. Stoggden [Stockton] Cheif-Justice. The other appointments not yet come to hand. I am Sir your Sincere Friend and Humble Servt.   Caesar Rodney

P.S. You'l Communicate the Matter Relative to Sullivan's Message to Mr. McKean.

RC (DeHi).
[1] It can not be determined at this point which resolution Rodney enclosed, but it may have been the August 26 resolution establishing regulations for the care of disabled soldiers and sailors. *JCC*, 5:702–5.
[2] Not found.

Thomas Stone to the Maryland Convention

Sir.   Phila. Sep. 4. 1776
    Inclosed I send You part of an Indian Speech which respects Maryland.[1] I have only time to inform the Convention that Assistance is extremely wanted at New York, and to express my Hope that the Exertions of that honourable Body will be in proportion to the Exigency of our affairs.

I am with great respect, sir, Yr most obt Sert,   T. Stone

RC (PU). Addressed: "To The Honorable Matthew Tilghman Esqr., President of the Convention of Maryland, Annapolis."
[1] For the enclosed "Indian Speech," see Benson J. Lossing, *The Life and Times of Philip Schuyler*, 2 vols. (1872; reprint ed., New York: Da Capo Press, 1973), 2:107–12. It apparently was enclosed by General Schuyler in his letter of August 18 to President Hancock, which was read in Congress on August 26. "Some of our best, and I believe real friends, the Oneidas and Ochquaques, complained that some Indians had been sent to Maryland," Schuyler explained, "to invite some Nanticokes that live in that Province to remove into the interior part of the country, and that neither those that were sent were suffered to return, or the others who they say incline to leave their present habitations, permitted to do it. We promised to lay the matter before Congress. . . . Please to give us some information on the subject." *Am. Archives*, 5th ser. 1:1031.
    The matter seems never to have been resolved. The Board of War directed another inquiry about the Nanticokes to the Maryland Council on November 8, to which a reply was returned the following week, but on November 30 Samuel Chase again requested that the council investigate the charges further. See Board

of War to the Maryland Council of Safety, November 8; and Samuel Chase to the Maryland Council of Safety, November 30, 1776.

John Adams to Abigail Adams

Philadelphia Septr. 5. 1776

Mr. Bass arrived this Day, with the joyfull News, that you were all well. By this Opportunity, I shall send you a Cannister of Green Tea, by Mr. Hare.

Before Mr. G[erry] went away from hence, I asked Mrs. Yard to send a Pound of Green Tea to you. She readily agreed. When I came home at Night I was told Mr. G. was gone. I asked Mrs. Y. if she had sent the Cannister? She said Yes and that Mr. G. under took to deliver it, with a great deal of Pleasure. From that Time I flattered my self, you would have the poor Relief of a dish of good Tea under all your Fatigues with the Children, and under all the disagreabble Circumstances attending the small Pox, and I never conceived a single doubt, that you had received it untill Mr. Gerrys Return. I asked him, accidentally, whether he delivered it, and he said Yes to Mr. S.A.'s Lady.[1] I was astonished. He misunderstood Mrs. Y intirely, for upon Inquiry she affirms she told him, it was for Mrs. J.A.

I was so vexed at this, that I have ordered another Cannister, and Mr. Hare has been kind enough to undertake to deliver it. How the Dispute will be settled I dont know. You must send a Card to Mrs. S.A., and let her know that the Cannister was intended for You, and she may send it you if she chooses, as it was charged to me. It is amazingly dear, nothing less than 40s. lawfull Money, a Pound.

I am rejoiced that my Horses are come. I shall now be able to take a ride. But it is uncertain, when I shall set off, for home. I will not go, at present. Affairs are too delicate and critical. The Panic may seize whom it will, it shall not seize me. I will stay here, untill the public Countenance is better, or much worse. It must and will be better. I think it is not now bad. Lyes by the Million will be told you. Dont believe any of them. There is no danger of the Communication being cutt off, between the northern and southern Colonies. I can go home, when I please, in spight of all the Fleet and Army of Great Britain.

RC (MHi). Adams, *Family Correspondence* (Butterfield), 2:119–20.
[1] That is, Mrs. Elizabeth Wells Adams, wife of Samuel Adams.

Secret Committee Minutes of Proceedings

Sepr. 5th. 1776

Come. met. Present Messrs. Morris, Hewes, Lee, Lewis, Livingston, Bartlett. Orderd That a letter be wrote to the Council of Safety of Maryland to supply the Frigate built at Baltimore with what powder may be wanted for proving Cannon & for other uses, out of that they borrowed from the Continent.[1] An Agreemt. with Messrs. Hewes & Smith of N. Carolina for importg. Arms, Ammunition & woollen & linen goods fit for Soldiers clothing & tents was signd by the Parties & an order on the Treasurer for 20,000 dlls in their favor.[2]

A Charter party for the Brigantine 2 Freinds, G. Meade & Co. Owners, was signd. by the Comee.[3] The Come. have agreed that Messrs. Hewes & Smith have liberty to ensure the vessels they charter in consequence of their Contract agt. the danger of the Seas as well as against Captures in case it be necessary, they receiving the usual premium for wch. they are to be accountable. Acct. of Josh. Gresgold for hawling powder &c was laid before the Come. amountg to £13.17.8 orderd to be pd. by Mr. Morris. Issued the following Drafts on the Treasurer, in favor of Andrew Lassal for 4536 dlls in full for 6804 lb. gunpowdr. purchasd from him at 5s. per lb. In favor of Chs. Lefevre for 216 dlls. in full for 324 lb Do. purchasd of him at Do. In favor of Capt. Ephraim Doane for 720 dlls in full for 1080 lb gunpowdr. purchased from him at Do. In favor of Willing & Morris & Co. for 153 6/90 dlls in full for freight of said duck for their ship Morris from Havre de Grace.[4] In favor of G. Meade & Co. for 2526 1/3 dlls being Amount of an Invoice of 700 brrs. shippd by them on board the Brigne Two Friends for Cape Francois on Contl. Accts. Do. in favor of J. Pringle for 158 36/90 dlls being the freight of 2376 lb G. Powder per the Brige. Pluto from St. Eustachia importd by Thos. Mumford Esqr. on continl. Acct.

MS (MH–H).

[1] See Secret Committee to the Maryland Council of Safety, September 13, 1776.

[2] For information on the fate of the sloop *James*, which was probably dispatched by Hewes and Smith pursuant to this contract, see Secret Committee Minutes of Proceedings, October 27, 1776.

[3] For the terms of this contract, see Secret Committee Minutes of Proceedings, August 15, 1776.

[4] See ibid., note 1.

John Witherspoon's Speech in Congress

Mr President, [September 5? 1776] [1]

The subject we are now upon, is felt and confessed by us all to be of the utmost consequence, and perhaps I may also say, of delicacy and difficulty. I have not been accustomed in such cases to make solemn professions of impartiality, and shall not do it now, because I will not suppose that there are any suspicions to the contrary in the minds of those who hear me. Besides the variety of opinions that have been formed and delivered upon it, seem to prove that we are giving our own proper judgment, without prejudice or influence; which I hope will lead to the discovery of what is most wise and expedient upon the whole.

As the deliberation arises from a message sent to us by Lord Howe, at least by his permission, I think it is of importance to attend with greater exactness to all the circumstances of that message, than has been done by any gentleman who has yet spoken on the subject. It comes from the commander in chief of the forces of the king of Great Britain, and one who is said to carry a commission to give peace to America.

From the conduct of the ministry at home, from the acts of parliament, and from Lord Howe's proclamation in conformity to both, it is plain, that absolute unconditional submission is what they require us to agree to, or mean to force us to. And from the most authentic private intelligence, the king has not laid aside his personal rancour; it is rather increasing every day. In these circumstances, Lord Howe has evidently a great desire to engage us in a treaty; and yet he has constantly avoided giving up the least punctilio on his side. He could never be induced to give General Washington his title. He plainly tells us he cannot treat with Congress as such; but he has allowed a prisoner of war to come and tell us he would be glad to see us as private gentlemen.

It has been said that this is no insult or disgrace to the Congress; that the point of honour is hard to be got over, in making the first advances. This, Sir, is mistaking the matter wholly. He has got over this point of honour; he has made the first overtures; he has told General Washington, by Colonel Putnam, that he wished that message to be considered as making the first step. His renewed attempts by Lord Drummond, and now by General Sullivan, point out to all the world that he has made the first step.[2] It will doubtless be related at home, and I am of opinion it is already written and boasted of to the ministry at home, that he has taken such a part. Therefore, any evil or condescension that can attend seeking peace first, has been submitted to by him. Yet has he uniformly avoided any circumstance that can imply that we are anything else but subjects of the king of Great Britain, in rebellion. Such a message as this, if in any degree intended as respectful to us, ought to have been secret; yet has it been open as the day. In short, such a message was unnecessary; for if he meant only to communicate his mind to the Congress by private gentlemen, he might have done that many ways, and it needed not to have been known either to the public or the Congress, till these private gentlemen came here on purpose to reveal it. These, then, are the circumstances which attend this message as it is now before us; and the question is, shall we comply with it in any degree, or not? Let us ask what benefit will be derived from it? There is none yet shewn to be possible. It has been admitted by every person without exception who has spoken, that we are not to admit a thought of giving up the independence we have so lately declared: and by the greatest part, if not the whole, that there is not the least reason to expect that any correspondence we can have with him will tend to peace. Yet I think, in the beginning of the debate, such reasonings were used as seemed to me only to conclude that we should grasp at it as a means of peace. We were told that it was easy for us to boast or be valiant here; but that our armies were running away before their enemies. I never loved boasting, neither here nor any where else. I look upon it as almost a certain forerunner of disgrace. I found my hope of success in this cause, not in the valour of Americans, or the cowardice of Britons, but upon the justice of the cause, and still more upon the nature of things. Britain has first injured and inflamed America to the highest degree; and now attempts, at the distance of three thousand miles, to carry on war with this whole country, and force it to absolute submission. If we take the whole events of the war since it commenced, we shall rather wonder at the uniformity of our success, than be surprised at some cross events. We have seen bravery as well as cowardice in this country; and there are no consequences of either that are probable, that can be worth mentioning as ascertaining the event of the contest.

Lord Howe speaks of a decisive blow not being yet struck; as if this cause depended upon one battle, which could not be avoided. Sir, this is a prodigious mistake. We may fight no battle at all for a long time, or may lose some battles, as was the case with the British themselves in the Scotch rebellion of 1745, and the cause notwithstanding be the same. I wish it were considered, that neither loss nor disgrace worth mentioning, has befallen us in the late engagement, nor comparable to what the British troops have often suffered. At the battle of Preston, Sir, they broke to pieces, and ran away like sheep, before a few highlanders. I myself saw them do the same thing at Falkirk, with very little difference, a small part only of the army making a stand, and in a few hours the whole retreating with precipitation before their enemies. Did that make any difference in the cause? Not in the least—so long as the body of the nation were determined, on principle, against the rebels. Nor would it have made any other difference, but in time, though they had got possession of London, which they might have easily done if they had understood their business; for the militia in England there gathered together, behaved fifty times worse than that of

America has done lately. They generally disbanded and ran off wholly as soon as the rebels came within ten or twenty miles of them. In short, Sir, from any thing that has happened, I see not the least reason for our attending to this delusive message. On the contrary, I think it is the very worst time that could be chosen for us; as it will be looked upon as the effect of fear, and diffuse the same spirit, in some degree, through different ranks of men.

The improbability of any thing arising from this conference, leading to a just and honourable peace, might be shewn by arguments too numerous to be even so much as named. But what I shall only mention is, that we are absolutely certain, from every circumstance, from all the proceedings at home, and Lord Howe's own explicit declaration in his letter to Dr Franklin, that he never will acknowledge the independence of the American States.[3]

I observed that one or two members said, in objection to the report of the board of war, that it was like a begging of the question, and making a preliminary of the whole subject in debate. Alas, Sir, this is a prodigious mistake. It was not only not the whole, but it was properly no subject of debate at all, till within these three months. We were contending for the restoration of certain privileges under the government of Great Britain, and we were praying for re-union with her. But in the beginning of July, with the universal approbation of all the states now united, we renounced this connection, and declared ourselves free and independent. Shall we bring this into question again? Is it not a preliminary? has it not been declared a preliminary by many gentlemen, who have yet given their opinion for a conference, while they have said they were determined on no account, and on no condition, to give up our independence? It is then a necessary preliminary—and it is quite a different thing from any punctilios of ceremony. If France and England were at war, and they were both desirous of peace, there might be some little difficulty as to who should make the first proposals; but if one of them should claim the other, as they did long ago, as a vassal or dependent subject, and should signify a desire to converse with the other, or some deputed by him, and propose him many privileges, so as to make him even better than before, I desire to know how such a proposal would be received? If we had been for ages an independent republic, we should feel this argument with all its force. That we do not feel it, shews that we have not yet acquired the whole ideas and habits of independence; from which I only infer, that every step taken in a correspondence as now proposed, will be a virtual or partial renunciation of that dignity so lately acquired.

I beg you would observe, Sir, that Lord Howe himself was fully sensible that the declaration of independence precluded any treaty, in the character in which he appeared; as he is said to have lamented that he had not arrived ten days sooner, before that declaration was made. Hence it appears, that entering into any correspondence with him in the manner now proposed, is actually giving up, or at least subjecting to a new consideration, the independence which we have declared. If I may be allowed to say it without offence, it seems to me that some members have unawares admitted this, though they are not sensible of it; for when they say that it is refusing to treat, unless the whole be granted us, they must mean that some part of that whole must be left to be discussed and obtained, or yielded, by the treaty.

But, Sir, many members of this house have either yielded, or at least supposed, that no desirable peace, or no real good, could be finally expected from this correspondence, which is wished to be set on foot; but they have considered it as necessary in the eye of the public, to satisfy them that we are always ready to hear any thing that will restore peace to the country. In this view it is considered as a sort of trial of skill between Lord Howe and us, in the political art. As I do truly believe, that many members of this house are determined by this circumstance, I shall consider it with some attention. With this view it will be necessary to distinguish the public in America into three great classes. 1. The tories, our secret enemies. 2. The whigs, the friends of independence, our sincere and hearty supporters. 3. The army, who must fight for us.

As to the first of them, I readily admit that they are earnest for our treating. They are exulting in the prospect of it; they are spreading innumerable lies to forward it. They are treating the whigs already with insult and insolence upon it. It has brought them from their lurking holes: they have taken liberty to say things in consequence of it, which they durst not have said before. In one word, if we set this negociation on foot, it will give new force and vigour to all their seditious machinations. But, Sir, shall their devices have any influence upon us at all? If they have at all, it should be to make us suspect that side of the question which they embrace. In cases where the expediency of a measure is doubtful, if I had an opportunity of knowing what my enemies wished me to do, I would not be easily induced to follow their advice.

As to the whigs and friends of independence, I am well persuaded that multitudes of them are already clear in their minds, that the conference should be utterly rejected; and to those who are in doubt about its nature, nothing more will be requisite, than a clear and full information of the state of the case, which I hope will be granted them.

As to the army, I cannot help being of opinion, that nothing will more effectually deaden the operations of war, than what is proposed. We do not ourselves expect any benefit from it, but they will. And they will possibly impute our conduct to fear and jealousy as to the issue of the cause; which will add to their present little discouragement, and produce a timorous and despondent spirit.[4]

MS not found; reprinted from John Witherspoon, *The Works of John Witherspoon . . .* , 9 vols. (Edinburgh: J. Ogle, 1815), 9:99–107, where it appears under the heading "Part of a Speech in Congress on the Conference proposed by Lord Howe."

[1] The finished quality of this speech indicates that Witherspoon probably delivered it on the day Congress decided to enter into talks with Lord Howe. *JCC*, 5:737.

[2] See *JCC*, 5:731; and Hancock to Washington, August 24, 1776.

[3] See the letters of June 20 and August 16 from Lord Howe to Franklin in Franklin, *Writings* (Smyth), 6:458, 462.

[4] In his autobiography Benjamin Rush gave this account of the debate on the issue of treating with Lord Howe:

"I took part in several debates; the first or second time I spoke was against a motion for a committee of Congress to meet Lord Howe in their private capacity to confer upon peace with Great Britain. On the same side of the question Jno. Adams, Dr. Witherspoon, and George Ross spoke with uncommon eloquence. The last of those gentlemen began his speech by asking what the conduct of George the 3rd would be, had Congress proposed to negociate with him as Elector of Hanover instead of King of Great Britain. He would spurn, and very properly spurn the insulting proposal. 'Let the American States,' said he, 'act in the same manner. We are bound to cherish the honour of our country which is now committed to our care. Nothing could dishonour the Sovereign of Britain that would not in equal circumstances dishonour us.' In the conclusion of my speech, I said that 'our country was far from being in a condition to make it necessary for us to humble ourselves at the feet of Great Britain. We had lost a battle, and a small island, but the city and State of New York were still in possession of their independance. But suppose that State had been conquered; suppose half the States in the Union had been conquered; nay, suppose all the States in the Union except one had been conquered, still let that one not renounce her independance; but I will go further: should this solitary state, the last repository of our freedom, be invaded, let her not survive her precious birthright, but in yielding to superiour force, let her last breath be spent in uttering the word *Independance*.' The speakers in favor of the motion were Ed. Rutledge, Thos. Lynch, Jno. [*i.e.* Thomas] Stone, and several others. One of them, in answer to the concluding sentence of my speech, said 'he would much rather live with *dependance* than die with *independance* upon his lips.' The motion was carried with some modification." Benjamin Rush, *The Autobiography of Benjamin Rush*, ed. George W. Corner (Princeton: Published for the American Philosophical Society by Princeton University Press, 1948), pp. 119–20.

John Adams to Abigail Adams

Fryday Septr. 6. 1776

This day, I think, has been the most remarkable of all. Sullivan came here from Lord Howe, five days ago with a Message that his Lordship desired a half an Hours Conversation with some of the Members of Congress, in their private Capacities. We have spent three or four days in debating whether We should take any Notice of it. I have, to the Utmost of my Abilities during the whole Time, opposed our taking any Notice of it. But at last it was determined by a Majority "that the Congress being the Representatives of the free and independent states of America, it was improper to appoint any of their Members to confer, in their private Characters with his Lordship. But they would appoint a Committee of their Body, to wait on him, to know whether he had Power, to treat with Congress upon Terms of Peace and to hear any Propositions, that his Lordship may think proper to make." [1]

When the Committee came to be ballotted for, Dr. Franklin and your humble servant were unanimously chosen. Coll. R. H. Lee and Mr. Rutledge had an equal Number: but upon a second Vote Mr. R. was chosen. I requested to be excused, but was desired to consider of it untill tomorrow. My Friends here Advise me to go. All the stanch and intrepid are very earnest with me to go, and the timid and wavering, if any such there are, agree in the request. So I believe I shall undertake the Journey.[2] I doubt whether his Lordship will see Us, but the same Committee will be directed to inquire into the State of the Army, at New York,[3] so that there will be Business enough, if his Lordship makes none. It would fill this Letter Book, to give you all the Arguments, for and against this Measure, if I had Liberty to attempt it. His Lordship seems to have been playing off a Number of Machiavillian Maneuvres, in order to throw upon Us the Odium of continuing this War. Those who had been Advocates for the Appointment of this Committee, are for opposing Maneuvre to Maneuvre, and are confident that the Consequence will be, that the Odium will fall upon him. However this may be, my Lesson is plain, to ask a few Questions, and take his Answers.

I can think of but one Reason for their putting me upon this Embassy, and that is this. An Idea has crept into many Minds here that his Lordship is such another as Mr. Hutchinson, and they may possibly think that a Man who has been accustomed to penetrate into the mazy Windings of Hutchinsons Heart, and the serpentine Wiles of his Head, may be tolerably qualified to converse with his Lordship.

Sunday Septr. 8.

Yesterdays Post brought me yours of Aug. 29. The Report you mention "that I was poisoned upon my Return at New York" I suppose will be thought to be a Prophecy, delivered by the Oracle in mystic Language, and meant that I should be politically or morally poisoned by Lord Howe. But the Prophecy shall be false.

RC (MHi). Adams, *Family Correspondence* (Butterfield), 2:120–21.

[1] For Congress' September 5 resolution, see *JCC*, 5:737.

[2] Secretary Thomson's entry pertaining to Adams' original request to be excused from serving on this committee was crossed out in the journals of Congress.

See *JCC*, 5:738. The vote on the selection of delegates to confer with Lord Howe is also described in Josiah Bartlett to William Whipple, September 10, 1776. Robert Treat Paine simply noted in his diary for September 6: "Agreed to Send Comittee to Ld. Howe." MHi.

³ From the evidence now available it seems clear that the committee neither received such directions nor made such an inquiry.

Elbridge Gerry to John Wendell

Dear sir   Philadelphia 6th Sepr. 1776

I have lately returned from a Journey to the Massa.¹ & have now an oppertunity of acknowledging the Receipt of your several Favours of June 12th & 25th, July 2d & 16th.

Our affairs in Canada wear a favourable Appearance, or rather at Ticonderoga & Crown Point; where by the last Return the Army were about thirteen thousand strong of wch. about 3000 were unfit for Duty. In addition to these, six other Regiments were on their March from Connecticut & Massachusetts & about four Regiments at other different Posts at New York. Things for the present are a little shattered by Means of the Retreat, but the Skirmish on Long Island has served to convince our Army that they are now able with the Regiments that are disciplined, to meet the Enemy on equal Terms. General Lee is ordered to reinforce them with several Regiments from the southward & one from Rhode Island, & with firm Conduct our Generals may yet baffle the Enemy. There is Reason to imagine that the Enemy have suffered more than our Army including the Captives, & Lord Howe has sent to Congress by General Sullivan a Desire of conferring with some members of it's Body in a private Capacity, not doubting that he can offer such Terms of peace as will be acceptable & proposing to treat with the Congress when the same are acceded to. But the whole is considered as an artifice to divide, by leading the people to suppose that his Lordship has used every Method for obtaining Peace while on our Part they have been rejected. To turn the Stratagem upon him Congress have resolved that being the Representatives of the independent States of America they cannot send a Committee but in their public Capacity, & that being every ready to listen to Terms of peace they will send a Committee to know his Lordships Power & proposals & to enquire what the Terms are which he has to offer to the Continent. The Committee are appointed, altho against the Mind of every Member from the State which I represent, as well as Rhode Island & Georgia who are apprehensive that the Appointment previous to his Lordships assurance that he will receive them will wear the appearance of an over great Desire for Peace which is neither consistent with Dignity or true Policy; & be construed as an Act of Timidity very discouraging to the States & animating to the Enemy.

But the Gentlemen on the other Side are very desirous of drawing out his Lordships proposals that if good they may be accepted & if bad exposed, which is a good Design if accomplished in a Way that will not disagreably affect the Continent. It is expected that the Committee will not be received; & if they are, any proposals wch his Lordship may offer that do not allow the States to be independent, will be without Hesitation rejected.

Since my Absence I find Mr Langdon has accepted the Agency, in Consequence of wch he will recommend the Vendue Master;[2] the Deputy Commissaries are appointed by the Commissary General, & the paymaster General provides his assistants. Mr. Trumbul You know fills the first place & Mr E Hancock is Dep[uty] G[eneral] for the eastern District.

I agree with You in your principles relative to persons filling places in the legislative Departments, that they ought in every other Respect to be *unplaced* & unpensioned, but in the Mode of effecting it We somewhat differ. The Situation of the Colonies differs from that of Britain, where the people have been under a feudal Government & with all the Success attending their Struggles for Liberty, have been only able to share power with the king in such a Way that they have been always in Danger of his engrossing it, which has finally proved to be the Case. By places, pensions & other Means wch you mention he has influenced the Elections & corrupted the Commons to give up the peoples property, & what is still more unhappy their Liberties. With the first he can keep in pay such a Number of Crown officers and Troops, that upon the least Appearance of an opposition to his Tyranny in Britain he has Notice of it wherever happening, & is enabled by his corrupt civil officers supported by the military to suppress every Measure that tends to serious opposition. In the Colonies the Case is widely different. The whole Power of Government are vested in the people; It is claimed by them & Congress have ratified it by recommending to them to form Constitutions of Government for themselves respectively. This being done, if their Legislatures conduct in the Way you mention it is very easy for Individuals to represent to their Towns & instruct their Representatives to make provission by Law that the persons holding the Power of Legislation & of appointing officers, shall themselves While having such Powers be disqualified to hold any other place or receive Pensions. This will put an effectual Stop to it, & in Order to make it general Circular Letters may be wrote by one Town to the others representing their Danger & inviting them to concur in their Measures. When any State shall be unable by these Means to remedy such Difficulties, It appears to me that the collective Body must have lost it's Vertue, & [Congress] (if it retains it's own) may then with propriety interfere [in the] Matter with the Recommendation You mention; but it would [be] now very unacceptable to the States. Indeed I cannot think it adviseable for the measures proposed above to be pursued untill an Issue happens to our present Difficulties, lest unhappy Divisions should take place. Representatives may nevertheless be changed without the Danger resulting from other Measures; & whenever the Electors of any State are alarmed at their Government & have Reason to think that by engrossing Places of Honor or Profit they have incapacitated themselves to govern, a new Choice will take place which must necessarily correct all that was amiss in the former Government.

The Conspiracies You mention are of the most dangerous Tendency, too much Care cannot be taken to comply as soon as possible wth the Recommendation of Congress for making Statutes of Treasons & when made for putting them into Execution. The Letter which You mention of Lord Chatham is a Forgery, as I always expected to find it. My Regards to Your Family & beleive me to be sir your assured Freind & hum ser,   E Gerry

RC (PPRF).
   [1] While at Hartford, Conn., en route to Philadelphia, Gerry had paused on August 24 to write a letter to Gen. Horatio Gates reporting bits of military intelligence he had picked up on his way through Connecticut. See *Am. Archives,* 5th ser. 1:1146–47.
   [2] For Wendell's interest in this office, see Gerry to John Wendell, June 11, 1776, note 3.

William Ellery to Nicholas Cooke

Sir.   Philadelphia September 7th 1776
   As Mr Hopkins expects the post will get to Providence before him he hath left with me the second and third [*bill*] of exchange drawn by Andrew Caldwell Treasurer upon Philip Moore, A Mercer, J Donnaldson and W Erskine Esqrs owners of the privateers Congress and Chance, New England, in favour of you and others, a committee for building the two frigates at Providence, for thirty seven thousand five hundred continental dollars, value received of Stephen Hopkins Esqr, and hath requested me to transmit to you one of the bills by the post and to keep the other. Agreeably to his request I now enclose you the second [*bill*] of Exchange; the first bill he hath with him and wish it may go safe.
   Mr Hopkins tells me he does not propose to return to Congress untill Spring, If ever. It is therefore necessary that an additional delegate should be immediately appointed, for otherwise the State of Rhode Island &c may be unrepresented, which might be attended with pernicious consequences to us. I may fall sick and not be able to attend Congress when some matter may be brought upon the Carpet which will immediately relate to our State; not to mention

that if two delegates were here they might have an opportunity to relax now and then from that constant attention which if one delegate only should be continued here he would be obliged to give, unless he should leave the State unrepresented in Congress, which I am determined not to do, let what will be the consequence; and a constant attendance on Congress for nine Months without any relaxation is too much even for a robust constitution. Beside it is necessary that motions should be made and supported in which case the advantage of having two on the same side is manifest. In causes of no great importance it is common to engage two lawyers and the vulgar observation that two heads are better than one is just. Can then the State of Rhode Island hesitate about immediately appointing an additional delegate? I am sure it cannot. I should be exceedingly glad that Gov Hopkins might return for he is well acquainted with the mode of conducting business and is well esteemed in Congress and I have reason to think from what hath passed that we should act in concert and harmony: but if he should conclude not to return it would be best that two should be immediately appointed; for matters of great consequence will be on the carpet. In the multitude of council is safety; and in that case the delegates might alternately visit home, brace up their relaxed minds and bodies by a journey and enjoying their native air, and thereby be better able to discharge the duties of their office. There is nothing against our State appointing three delegates but the expenses and if the amount of the allowance to the two delegates and their expenses for one year be summed up and compared with what would be the amount of the expence to the State of three delegates at five dollars per day I believe the difference will be found to be but trifling; but if it should be something considerable I am sure the benefits resulting to the State therefrom would compensate for any such additional expence. If a confederacy should hereafter take place a council of State would doubtless be appointed in which case our State would have only one delegate to support constantly. The other two if three should be appointed would be present only a small part of a year when the Congress should sit.[1] Mr Hopkins will acquaint you with the news and the state of our armies &c &c. So that I hope I shall be excused in not saying anything on those subjects.

The same reason will excuse my not writing to the Assembly by this post. I wrote a letter to send by the last post, but unluckily the post had set out before my letter reached the office. Congress have ordered one of our battalions to N York and its place to be supplied with a battallion of Militia from Massachusetts.[2] It was moved at first that both the battalions should be ordered thither. I opposed the motion to the best of my abilities, and think we have come off pretty well. I expect that if our affairs at N York should take an ill turn that the other battallion will be ordered from our

State; for it is the sentiment of Congress that the continental battalions should be drawn together, for that greater reliance is to be
placed in them than a Militia unaccustomed to discipline and the
hardships of a Camp: and indeed the liberties of this country in
my opinion cannot be established but by a large standing army.
Heartily wishing success to our cause and to you Sir and your family
health and prosperity I continue to be, with great respect, yours,

W Ellery

Tr (MH–H). William R. Staples, *Rhode Island in the Continental Congress,
1765–1790* (Providence: Providence Press Co., 1870), pp. 83–84.
   [1] The logic of Ellery's arguments in favor of an enlarged delegation evidently.
impressed the Rhode Island Assembly, which on October 28, 1776, chose Deputy
Governor William Bradford as the state's third delegate in Congress. Unfortunately, as Cooke subsequently informed Ellery, Bradford "declined the service."
See ibid., p. 103; and John R. Bartlett, ed., *Records of the Colony of Rhode
Island and Providence Plantations in New England,* 10 vols. (Providence: A.
Crawford Greene, 1856–65), 8:19.
   [2] See *JCC,* 5:734.

Samuel Huntington to Matthew Griswold, Eliphalet Dyer and William Pitkin

Gentlemen   Philadelphia 7th September 1776
   Since I had the honour to address you under the 30th of August
(which now comes by the same hand) we have the disagreable Intelligence of our Troops Evacuating Long Island, yet I hope no
serious heart will faint, as we are only Contending for our Just
rights on the Defensive, if we continue free & United we must secure
our rights & Liberties.
   Lord Howe hath manifested Repeatedly a desire to confer with
some members of Congress which has not been regarded, until he
sent General Sullivan with a Message to Congress Intimating his
delicate Situation, & desiring that he might confer with them tho,
at the same time saying he could not do it in that Capacity but that
he had large powers to enable him to Settle the Controversy &c.
The Congress rather Suppose this a finness to Create a belief in
the people that he is desirous for peace & we desire to protract the
war. However after mature consideration, Congress resolved as the
Representatives of the United Independant States of America, to
appoint a Committee to meet his Lordship if he pleases to know
what Authority he has to settle peace & hear his proposals that on
the one hand if he has any Authority & proposals that are Serious
they may know; & on the other if it be a finness the world make
[may] know it. This matter is not fully made public as yet but have

tho't proper to Communicate it to you thus early, the same is Communicated to Govr Trumbull.

The Committee appointed are Docr *Franklin, Mr. John Adams* & Edd Rutlidge.[1]

Remain Gentlemen with Esteem, your Humble Servt,

Saml Huntington

RC (CtY).

[1] Huntington also wrote a brief note to Jabez Huntington this day, requesting orders for the disposition of a sum of money he was to receive from Willing, Morris, & Co. on behalf of Capt. William Wattles. Samuel Huntington Papers, CtHi.

Caesar Rodney to George Read

Sir   Philadelphia Sepr. 7th 1776.

Since I wrote last three Letters directed to you have come to my hands. I imagine they are from New York and have sent them with this by the Newcastle Stage.

In my last Letter I gave you the Substance of Sullivans Message and what I then though would be the Determination of Congress thereon.[1] However the Matter (after three days debate) has in Some measure received a different determination. The Congress have refused Sending any of their members to Confer as private Gentlemen, but with a view to satisfie some disturbed minds out of Doors, rather than an Expectation of its bringing about Peace they have appointed a Committee of Congress to repair to New York with powers to Confer with Lord Howe, to know the Extent of his powers and the Terms he Shall propose. Genl. Sullivan was furnished with a Copy of this Resolution Certified, and Returned to Lord Howe Yesterday. You will See by this that if Lord Howe Receives the Committee thus Sent he acknowledges the Congress and of Course the Independency of the States, Which I am Convinced he will not do. Yet it may Tend to Convince the people at large that we are desirous of peace whenever it Can be had upon those principals.

There is no Material Change in affairs at New York, Except that a Great part of our Army are gone up to Kings–Bridge, among others the Delaware Battalion, and that Captain Wallace is gone up the East River with his Ship. She was fired on by the fort but not much if any hurt. She proceeded up till She got to a place Called Blackwells Island and Anchored. Our people there with two twelve pounders Oblidge her to Slip her Cable and get behind the Island. I am Sir Yr. most obedt, Humble Servt,   Caesar Rodney

P.S. How goes on your Convention?

RC (DeHi).

[1] See Rodney to George Read, September 4, 1776.

William Williams to Joseph Trumbull

My dear Sir   Philadel. 7 Sepr 1776

As You are the great Theater, on which the grand Tragedy is acting I wished to hear frequently from you tho I know I am in your Debt but I can most easily beleive your hands are full, & excuse your omission. I hope our Army are far from discouraged or dismayd, the Enemy are not invulnerable. They will defeat & confound them yet if our men hold their Spirits. To the Greif of Congress the Genl. has wrote several (they think) too gloomy Letters. Some speak with great Resolution.

After a most serious & long debate Congress have orderd three members, in their proper Character only, to wait on Ld Howe, in Consequence of his message by Gen. Sullivan to know if He has power to treat of Peace, what his Power is, & to hear his Propositions, if he please to receive them as such. If not the world will be satisfied there is no sincerity in his Professions. We are already. The Measure is an object of great Speculation & Anxiety. I hope no Ill can arise from it. Congress are greatly on their Guard you may rely. The whole will be published on Monday, & every one will be better able to judge of the Expediency of the Measure.

Howe wanted Them only as private Gent. but Congress wod only send as a Deputation of their Body, & He will act his Pleasure about receiving them.

I am dear Sir your affectionate Friend & brother,

W Williams

[P.S.] Have you heard any thing fr[om] Brother Jona &c. I hoped for a Letter eer now. There has been great Compla[int] to Congress, of Letters in that Departmt being playd fury with. They have given orders for better Regulations &c.

I mentioned the affair of Salt to the Presidt. He says he has laid all yr. & other Letters before Congress, & can give no Orders which they dont give but thinks as you must [provide?] Provisions, you most certainly may & ought to find the means to preserve it.

The Comte are Franklin, J Adams & Rutledge.

RC (Ct).

John Adams to Samuel Adams

Dear sir.   September 8. 1776

Tomorrow Morning Dr F., Mr. R. and your humble servant sett off, to see that rare Curiosity, Lord H. Dont imagine from this that a Panic has Spread to Philadelphia. By no Means. This is only Refinement in Policy. It has a deep, profound Reach, no doubt. So deep that you can not see to the Bottom of it, I dare Say. I am sure I can not. Dont however be concerned. When you See the whole, as you will eer long, you will not find it very bad. I will write you the Particulars, as soon as I shall be at Liberty, to do it.[1]

LB (MHi).

[1] Adams, Benjamin Franklin, and Edward Rutledge conferred with Lord Howe on Staten Island on September 11. Adams' autobiographical account contains more information on their trip to Staten Island than of the conference itself, but Adams does provide an anecdotal account of their first encounter with Lord Howe. "Lord How had sent over an Officer as an Hostage for our Security. I said to Dr. Franklin, it would be childish in Us to depend upon such a Pledge and insisted on taking him over with Us, and keeping our Surety on the same side of the Water with Us. My Colleagues exulted in the Proposition and agreed to it instantly. We told the Officer, if he held himself under our direction he must go back with Us. He bowed Assent, and We all embarked in his Lordships Barge. As We Approached the Shore his Lordship, observing Us, came down to the Waters Edge to receive Us, and looking at the Officer, he said, Gentlemen, you make me a very high Compliment, and you may depend upon it, I will consider it as the most sacred of Things. We walked up to the House between Lines of Guards of Grenadiers, looking as fierce as ten furies, and making all the Grimaces and Gestures and motions of their Musquets with Bayonets fixed, which I suppose military Ettiquette requires but which We neither understood nor regarded." Adams, *Diary* (Butterfield), 3:417–20. The only mention of the journey to Staten Island in Adams' diary is the terse entry for September 10: "Took with me to N.Y. 51 dollars and 5s. 8d. Pen. Currency in Change." Ibid., 2:250. For John's promised account of the conference, see Adams to Samuel Adams, September 14, 1776.

John Adams to James Warren

September 8. 1776

I am going tomorrow Morning on an Errand to Lord Howe not to beg a Pardon, I assure you, but to hear what he has to say. He sent Sullivan here to let us know that he wanted a Conversation with some Members of Congress. We are going to hear him, but as Congress have voted that they cannot Send Members to talk with him in their private Capacities but will send a Committee of their Body as Representatives of the free and independent States of America, I presume his Lordship cannot see Us, and I hope he will not, but if he should the whole will terminate in nothing. Some think it will occasion a delay of military operations, which they think We must want. I am not of this Mind. Some think it will clearly throw the odium of continuing this War, on his Lordship and his Master. I wish it may. Others think it will silence the Tories, and establish the timid Whigs. I wish this also. But dont expect it. But all these arguments and twenty others as weighty would not have convinced me of the Necessity, Propriety, or Utility of this Embassy, if Congress had not determined on it. I was totis Viribus against it, from first to last. But upon this occasion N.H., C[onnecticut] and even V[irginia] gave way. All sides agreed in sending me. The stanch and intrepid, I suppose, such as were Enemies to the Measure as well as myself, pushed for me, that as little Evil might come of it, as possible. Others agreed to vote for me in order to entice some of our Inflexibles to vote for the Measure. You will hear more of this Embassy—it will be famous enough.

Your Secretary will rip about this Measure, and well he may.[1] Nothing, I assure you but the unanimous Vote of Congress, the pressing Solicitations of the firmest Men in Congress and the particular Advice of my own Colleagues, at least of Mr Hancock and Mr Gerry would have induced me to have accepted this Trust.

RC (MHi). In Adams' hand, though not signed.

[1] Samuel Adams admitted in a September 30, 1776, letter to John that "I was indeed greatly 'concerned' for the Event of the proposed Conference with Lord Howe." The Adams Papers, MHi.

Benjamin Franklin to Lord Howe

My Lord   Philada. Sept. 8. 1776

I received your Favour of the 16th past.[1] I did not immediately answer it, because I found that my Corresponding with your Lordship was dislik'd by some Members of Congress. I hope now soon to have an Opportunity of discussing with you, vivâ voce, the Matters mention'd in it; as I am with Mr Adams & Mr Rutledge appointed to wait on your Lordship in consequence of a Desire you expresd in some Conversation with Gen. Sullivan, and of a Resolution of Congress made thereupon, which that Gentleman has probably before this time communicated to you.[2] We purpose to set out on our Journey to-morrow Morning, and to be at Amboy on Wednesday about 9 oClock, where we should be glad to meet a Line from your Lordship, appointing the Time and Place of Meeting. If it would be agreable to your Lordship, we apprehend that either at the House on Staten Island opposite to Amboy, or at the Governor's House in Amboy, we might be accommodated with a Room for the purpose.[3] With the greatest Esteem & Respect, I have the Honour to be, My Lord, &c

FC (PPAmP).

[1] See Franklin, *Writings* (Smyth), 6:462.

[2] See *JCC*, 5:737–38.

[3] For Lord Howe's response of September 10, see Franklin, *Writings* (Smyth), 6:464–65.

Benjamin Franklin to George Washington

Sir   Philada. Sept. 8. 1776

The Congress having appointed Mr. Adams, Mr Rutledge & myself, to meet Lord Howe, and hear what Propositions he may have to make,[1] we purpose setting out tomorrow, and to be at Perth Amboy on Wednesday morning, as you will see by the enclos'd, which you are requested immediately to forward to his Lordship;[2] and if an Answer comes to your hands, that you would send it to meet us at Amboy. What we have heard of the Badness of the Roads between that Place & New York, makes us wish to be spar'd that part of the Journey. With great Respect & esteem, I have the honour to be, Sir, Your Excy's. most obedt & most humble Servant,

B Franklin

RC (Facsimile, *Samuel T. Freeman &Co. Catalog*, November 18, 1924, illustration no. 107).

[1] See *JCC*, 5:737–38.

[2] See preceding entry.

John Hancock to George Washington

Sir,   Philada. Sepr. 8th. 1776. Sunday 6 oClock P.M.

I am this Minute honored with your Favour of the 6th Inst;[1] and am to acknowledge the Receipt of your several Favours to that Date.

The Congress, concurring with the Proposal of exchanging Generals Prescot & McDonald for Genls. Sullivan & Stirling have authorized the Board of War to send the two former to you for that Purpose, as soon as possible.[2]

In Consequence of the Message which Genl. Sullivan delivered to Congress from Lord Howe, respecting a Conference with some of their Members, they have, after great Debate, been induced to pass the first Resolution of the 5th of Sepr.; and have since appointed three Gentlemen on that Business, as you will observe by a subsequent Resolution, to which, without any Comment, I beg Leave to refer you.[3] But in Order to prevent similar Messages for the future, they have passed a Resolve directing the Mode in which all applications shall hereafter be made, either to Congress, or the Commander in Chief of the Army, and to which only any Attention is to be paid. I beg Leave to refer you to the Resolve itself, as the future Rule of your Conduct with Respect to every such verbal Application, until it shall be altered, or you shall hear further from Congress on the Subject.[4]

The List of Officers, who are Prisoners with the Enemy, which you mention as enclosed in your Favour of the 6th, it is probable, was thro Hurry omitted, as it has not come to Hand.

Before this reaches you, a Supply of Money will doubtless be arrived, it being now two Days since it was sent. Henceforth you will be more regularly supplied with that Article.

The Congress have ordered a large Stock of Cloth here to be immediately made up into Tents, and to be forwarded to you with all possible Dispatch. They have likewise ordered some Duck in the Eastern States to be made into Tents & sent you.

Tomorrow Morning I will lay your Letter before Congress and acquaint you immediately of the Result. Genl. Sullivan went from here two Days ago. The Committee to wait on Lord Howe will set out tomorrow Morning for New York.

The interesting State of our Affairs, and the Anxiety of Congress to hear from you as often as possible, will naturally suggest to you the Propriety of giving them all the Information in your Power, as often as your important Concerns will admit of it.

My most ardent and incessant Wishes attend you, that you may still rise superior to every Difficulty, and that your great & virtuous Exertions on Behalf of your Country, may be crowned with that Success, which from the Supreme Being's Love of Justice, and the Righteousness of our Cause, in Conjunction with our own Endeavours, it is not irrational to expect.

I am to request you will direct Major Hausacker to repair to this City as soon as possible to take the Command of the German Battalion, of which he is appointed Colonel, being extremely wanted.[5]

I have the Honour to be, with every Sentiment of Respect & Esteem, Sir, you most obed. & very hble Sert.

John Hancock Presidt

RC (DLC). In the hand of Jacob Rush and signed by Hancock.

[1] This letter is in PCC, item 152, 2:527–29, and Washington, *Writings* (Fitzpatrick), 6:22–24.

[2] See *JCC*, 5:735–36.

[3] See *JCC*, 5:738, 743.

[4] See *JCC*, 5:737.

[5] See *JCC*, 5:571, 734–35.

Lewis Morris to John Jay

My Dear friend   Phia Sepr 8 1776

I am very anxious about our Situation at N York, & should have gone off this day but Mr Lewis has taken flight towards that Place in quest of his family, that were on Long Island, and there remains only three of us.[1] I wish you would let me know how matters stand and at what Place our convention are. Genl Sullivan brought a message from Lord Howe to Congress in consequence of which they have Sent Doctor Franklin, John Adams and Ned Rutlege. I doubt in my own mind any good effect that it can have, as he was desirous to meet them in their private Characters. I will inclose you the resolve of Congress. Sullivan Says that L Howe Said he was ever against Taxing of us, and that they had no right to interfere with our internal Police, and that he was very sure America could not be conquered, and that it was a great pitty so brave a nation should be cutting one another to peices. Mr Linch yesterday asked me if you would part with your Chesnut Horse. I told him I did know I thought I had heard you Say once in this Place that if you did sel him you would have Seventy pounds. He beged of me to write to you and get your answer. Poor Mr Lawrence remains very unwell. He joins me in our best regards to you and all friends. Yours Most sincerely,   Lewis Morris

RC (NNC). Addressed: "To Coll. John Jay Esqr, New York. Favd. by E. Rutledge Esqr."
[1] A letter from Francis Lewis to Gov. William Livingston of New Jersey, written at New Brunswick on September 9 and defending Samuel Gouverneur, the "Clark of Morris County," against charges of being "unfriendly to the prosperity of America," is in the William Livingston Papers, MHi.

Josiah Bartlett to Mary Bartlett

My Dear   Philadelphia Septr 9th 1776
     I had not the pleasure of Receiving a letter from you by last Saturdays Post as usual but hope by the next to hear you are all well.
     I am Sorry to inform you that I am in a poor State of health, & have been so, for more than a fortnight; I have a bad Cough and a slow fever with a poor appetite for food and something of a purging. I have been vomited & purged & am taking sundry Medicines, which I hope will procure me relief if it is agreable to the will of God. I have been able to attend the Congress Every Day, tho Sometimes I have been obliged to leave it before it Broke up. When the weather permits, I ride out 3 or 4 & sometimes five or Six miles in a Day before or after Congress. I have Confined my self for food to hasty pudding (or as they Call it here mush) & milk for breakfast and Supper, & to Soop or fresh broth for Dinner, and shall omit nothing that I shall think likely to be serviceable to me. I think my asthma or Stuftness for breath is rather abated, and I hope (if it is for the best) I shall be able next post to inform you that I am better on all other accounts.
     Last week General Sullivan Came here on his Parole with two Messages from Lord Howe. One was for the Exchange of Genl Sullivan & Genl Sterling, for Genl Prescot & Genl McDonald which we

had taken from them; which the Congress have agreed to. The other
Message was to Desire that two or 3 of the members of Congress as
private Gentlemen would meet him at any time & place they should
think fit to see if they Could agree on any proposals for putting an
End to the war & Establishing peace between the two Countries. The
Congress have appointed 3 members to meet him, not as private
Gentlemen but as members of Congress, to Confer with him & Know
what he has to offer us as terms of peace and by what authority.

The Members appointed are Dr Franklin of this City, Mr John
Adams of the Massachusitts Bay & Mr Rutlidge of South Carolina.

Remember me to all friends, in a particular Manner to my Children, and hope neither you nor they will be too much Concerned
on my account. My Dear adieu: and when I write again I hope I
shall be able to inform you I am better in health.

Josiah Bartlett

RC (NhHi).

Josiah Bartlett to John Langdon

Dear Sir   Philadelphia Sept 9th 1776
Your's of the 26th ulto I have recd and delivered the enclosed to
Mr Hancock. I perceive you had not then rec'd mine of the 12th [1]
and am at a loss to guess the reason; I wrote by the post, expecting
it would come to your hand before the arrival of Col Whipple. His
arrival has no doubt settled all difficulties.

Yours by Commodore Manly I have not rec'd as yet. The Congress
have agreed to the exchange of Generals Prescot and McDonald for
Sullivan and Sterling; and agreeable to Lord Howe's request for an
interview with some of the members of Congress, they have appointed Dr Franklin, Mr J Adams and Mr E Rutlidge for that purpose, but not as private gentlemen, but as a Committee of Congress.
Whether or not he will receive them in that capacity is at present
uncertain. They set off this day for New York.[2]

Yesterday was sent in here by the Sachem, continental vessel, a
brig bound from Antigua to the British Army. She mounted six guns
and fought obstinately—killed 3 men on board the Sachem—her
loading said to be rum and sugar.

I hope before this, our State has appointed another Delegate in
your stead. Pray hurry them forward as fast as possible, as my very
bad state of health hinders often our State from being represented
in Congress, though I attend as much as possible.[3]

I am Sir your friend,   Josiah Bartlett

Tr (DLC).

[1] Not found.

[2] Robert Treat Paine noted the committee's departure this day in his diary: "Cmttee Sat off to Ld. Howe." MHi.

[3] Matthew Thornton was elected as a delegate to Congress on September 12, but he did not reach Philadelphia until November 4, 1776. *N.H. State Papers*, 8:333; and *JCC*, 6:920.

Josiah Bartlett to William Whipple

Dear Sir,   Philadelphia Sept 10th [1776]

The proposal of Lord Howe for the exchange of Generals Sullivan and Lord Sterling for Prescot and McDonald is accepted by the Congress. We have also agreed to send three of our members, not as private gentlemen but as a Committee of our body, to meet Lord Howe to know of him whether he has any terms of peace to propose, and what they are &c &c. Whether Lord Howe will meet them as a Committee of Congress is uncertain. The gentlemen appointed are Dr Franklin, Mr Adams and Mr Rutlidge. The two former had the unanimous vote of Congress and at the first vote there was a tye between Col R. H. Lee and Mr Rutlidge, but as Mr Lee had opposed the measur he declined being voted for, as he said he could not accept. The votes then were for Stogden [Stockton] and Rutlidge and the latter carried it. Nothing has since been done about the confederation as the Congress is pretty thin and hurried with other business.

I am sorry to hear you did not arrive at Boston till the 28th ult as I fear you will not return here so soon as I could wish and what makes me more anxious for your speedy return is my ill state of health which has hindered my constant attendance at Congress. I have for above a fortnight been troubled with a very severe cough and asthma and with a slow fever if not a hectic, and though I have attended the Congress every day, I have been often obliged to leave it long before it rose. I am loath that our Colony should be unrepresented and therefore hope you will return as speedily as possible. There is a report from the Board of War now before Congress for putting our army on a more respectable footing than at the present. The substance is that 84 regiments should be enlisted to serve during the war and to give as an encouragement 100 acres of land and dollars bounty to be proportioned to such State, who are to take care that it's quota is raised. The proportion set to our Colony is four regiments which is too much and shall try to get it altered if I am able to attend Congress when it comes on. This plan perhaps may be somewhat altered but will I am pretty sure be adopted in the main.[1] Quere—whether as this is like to be the case it is best for our State to do any thing at present about raising the regt. ordered in the

Spring for our own defence, and whether petitioning Congress to take into their pay our Colonial troops will not be best considering all circumstances. You'll excuse me as I am hardly able to write.
I am your friend &c. &c.   Josiah Bartlett

Tr (DLC).
[1] The "report from the Board of War" was undoubtedly one prepared in response to Congress' September 2 order "to prepare and bring in a plan of military operations for the next campaign." When the final report was adopted on September 16, New Hampshire was assigned a quota of three battalions; and a schedule of bounties for those enlisting for the duration of the war was established. *JCC*, 5:729, 762–63.

Benjamin Franklin to William Temple Franklin

Dear Grandson,[1]   Brunswick, Sept. 10, 1776
It is possible that a Line from Lord Howe may be left for me at your good Mother's, as I have appointed to be there to morrow˙ Morning, in order to meet a Notice from his Lordship relating to the Time & Place of a proposed Interview. If it should come there to-night, or very early in the Morning I could wish you would set ɔut with it on horseback so as to meet us on the Road not far from hence, that if N York should be the Place, we may not go so far out of our way as Amboy would be. Besides I should be glad to see you. My Love to your Mother. Mr Adams & Mr Rutledge are with me. If Amboy or the House opposite to us on Staten Island is to be the Place of a Meeting we shall want private Lodgings there. I am as ever, Your affectionate Grandfather,   B Franklin

[*P.S.*] If no Letter is come to your House enquire at Headquarters if any for me is come there: but do not mention from whom, or the Occasion.

RC (Facsimile, *American Art Association Catalog*, November 11, 1937, illustration no. 19).
[1] William Temple Franklin (ca. 1760–1823), who had come to America with his grandfather in May 1775 to be reunited with his father, William Franklin, governor of New Jersey, had been the object of a tug-of-war in 1775–76 between his father and his grandfather. The illegitimate son of an illegitimate son, Temple, as he was generally called, was only briefly reunited with his father before coming again under his grandfather's tutelage, as William remained estranged from the American cause and was finally arrested. For a time Temple provided a link between Franklin and his loyalist son, but William's determination to remain loyal to the crown ensured that Temple would follow the lead of his grandfather, with whom he cast his lot, embarking for Paris in October 1776 when Franklin was appointed commissioner to France. See Claude-Anne Lopez and Eugenia W. Herbert, *The Private Franklin, the Man and His Family* (New York: W. W. Norton & Co., 1975), chap. 17. A brief personal letter from Franklin to Temple of August 27, 1776, is in the Roberts Collection, PHC.

John Hancock to George Washington

Sir   Congress Chamr. 10 Sepr. 1776
    Your Letter of 8th Inst. is now under the Consideration of Congress; as soon as they have come to a Determination upon it the Results shall be transmitted you, in the meantime Congress, being apprehensive that their former Resolution of 3d Int. was not rightly understood, have directed me to Send you the foregoing, by which you will perceive that their wish is to preserve N York & leave the time of Evacuatg it to yor Judgment.[1] I beg leave to Refer you to the Resolve, not havg. time to add, but that I am, Sir, your very huml set,
                                           John Hancock P[resident]

RC (N).
    [1] See *JCC*, 5:733, 749; Washington, *Writings* (Fitzpatrick), 6:27–33; and Hancock to Washington, September 3, 1776, note.

Francis Hopkinson to Richard Smith

Sir;   Philadelphia 10th Sept. 1776.
    I received yours of the 7th inst. respecting a device for the Great-Seal of New Jersey, and shall pay all due attention to the service you had recommended to me. Dr Franklin is gone to New York, and Mr Rittenhouse is so entirely engaged in the Convention and Council of Safety that I have not seen him, nor do I expect he can spare time to attend to this matter. I will however mention it to him and to Dr Franklin on his return. I would recommend it to you to use some temporary seal for the commissions, etc., as it must be a considerable time before this can be executed, perhaps some months. You require six or seven devices as samples. You perhaps are not aware of the difficulty and expence attending such an exhibition. In order to draw a device for the engraver, a skilfull hand must be employed, as the whole accuracy and elegance of the execution depends on the correctness of the model. But if you mean only a verbal account of the device, this may be easily done. I have thought of one which I shall submit to your judgment. But it is first necessary to know whether you propose to have the seal *affixed* or *pendant;* if the latter, (which is most usual in Great-Seals) there must be two blocks; the one containing the arms of the State, and the other a device at pleasure. The arms I would recommend for the State of New Jersey should be, a Shield in the usual form, with *three Running deer,* and in a proper compartment, a *broken Crown and sceptre.* The shield to be supported by *Liberty* with her Cap and Staff, and *Ceres* with her Insignia. This to be the arms of the State, which will look better in the execution than in description. On the other block, or side of the

seal (if you will have it double) I would recommend a device suitable to this motto—*To your tents, oh Israel!* 10th Chapter of 2nd Chron. This refers to a passage in history very applicable to the present times. I wish to hear from you again. There is a gentleman here very ingenious in preparing models or drawings.[1] He has been employed in this way by Virginia and other States, and by the Congress for a gold medal. His charge will be £5, if a single seal; £10, if double; the drawing to be forwarded to you for approbation when compleat, which may be in about a week. I would observe the *running* deer are expressive of freedom, and characteristic of New Jersey.

I thank the Council and Assembly for the honour they have intended me. Shall always be happy to serve the State of New Jersey with my best abilities, but this appointment is unfortunately attended with some circumstances which make it necessary for me to take the advice of my friends on the occasion. Be assured, however, that whether I with gratitude accept, or from private reasons am under a necessity of declining this important charge, I shall be ever disposed to hold the Legislature of New Jersey in the highest respect, and to support, by every means in my power, their dignity and authority.[2] I have the honour to be, Your's and the Committee's most obt. humb sevt,   Fr. Hopkinson

Tr (NN).
[1] Pierre Eugène du Simitière.
[2] Hopkinson had been appointed an associate justice of the New Jersey Supreme Court by the New Jersey Council and Assembly on September 4. He had announced his intention to refuse this office in a September 7 letter to New Jersey Chief Justice John Hart which has not been found. See George E. Hastings, *The Life and Works of Francis Hopkinson* (Chicago: University of Chicago Press, 1926), pp. 216–17.

Richard Henry Lee's Proposed Instructions

[ante September 10, 1776] [1]

As the scarcity of Arms, artillery, and other military stores is so considerable, would it not be proper to instruct the Ambassador to France that he press for the immediate supply of 20, or 30 thousand stand of well fitted Muskets & Bayonets, a good supply of brass field pieces, Gunpowder &c. These to be sent under convoy, and the 13 States engaged for the payment. A few good Engineers would be greatly serviceable. It seems very clear that France means not to let N.A. sink in the present Contest, but distance and difficulty in giving true accounts of our condition may be the cause of opinions being entertained of our power to support the War on our own strength and resources longer than we can in fact do. Considering this may it not be proper for the Ambassador to press for the immediate and precise declaration of France, upon a suggestion that our reunion with G.B. may be greatly endangered by delay.

Should Spain be disinclined to our cause from an apprehension of danger to her South American dominions, cannot France be prevailed on at our request and assurances not to disturb theirs to Gurantee to that Crown her Territories there against any molestation from us.

Should not the Ambassador be instructed to give us the most speedy & effectual intelligence of his progress in this business, and of any other European intelligence that it may import us to know.

MS (PPAmP). In the hand of Richard Henry Lee. Endorsed by Lee: "Proposed addition to the instructions given the Commissioners going to France 1776 Octr. Agreed to."

[1] On August 27 the plan of foreign treaties was recommitted to committee. At the same time Richard Henry Lee and James Wilson were added to the committee, which was then ordered "to draw up instructions pursuant to the amendments made by the committee of the whole." Lee must have written this document before September 10, since these instructions were incorporated almost verbatim into the committee's report, which—according to Charles Thomson's endorsement—was "bro't in Septr. 10, 1776." The committee's report, with additional amendments by George Wythe and Lee, was approved on September 24 and served as the basic directions to the commissioners to France who were appointed on the 26th. See *JCC*, 5:709–10, 813–17, 827.

William Hooper to William Livingston

My dear Sir   [September 11, 1776] [1]

I congratulate you upon the honourable appointment which your Country hath called you to. I congratulate them upon the return of their reason, that they have found at length discernment enough to distinguish real merit, & virtue enough to reward it.[2]

I rejoiced that you approximate in your political Character, I wish you could find a little leisure to play the private Gentleman & pay us a visit here. Should that be impracticable, I will make an effort at least to meet you at Trenton. I had a letter from Duane this moment. Trop douloureux! Chere quam tristes! It is not a time to whine. I am of Montrose's Mind expressed in his pompous gingle.

Country & wounds demand supplies
More from Briareus hands than Argus eyes

& I would in the stile of the same poetick Herold speak forth my Country's wrongs "In trumpets sounds

I write his pungent wrongs in blood & wounds.

A little Interpolation of the Editor—but we Editors take liberties with our Authors.[3]

Immediately upon receiving yours of the 5th Instant. I rode out to Germantown to Bringhurst who is by far the best Carriage maker

in this province. In his Shop I found a single Chais that exactly
answers your description nearly finished. It was intended for one of
the honourable and heroick body of Philadelphia Associatiors but
Bringhurst from the promise of prompt pay from you & the improbability of getting it from the other, has suffered me to take it &
has most solemnly promised to finish it in the Course of next Week.
It will cost you £45 Penns. Currency. The materials are well seasoned
& the whole neat. If you have any Inclination to have your Crest or
Cypher upon it pray send me the former or direct the latter by the
first Oppty otherwise, I shall decorate it with a modest Urn, the tast
of the day. I consulted your brother's Crest, find it a Ship, too large
& tawdry for a Small carriage, therefore I will not adopt it without
your Orders.

I am, Dear sir, Yours with Esteem & Affection,

Will Hooper

[P.S.] Pardon me if I mistake the Address of the Govr of the Jersey.
Is it Excellency or Honour?

RC (MHi).
    ¹ This is undoubtedly the letter to which Hooper referred in his September 12
letter to Livingston when he mentioned that "I wrote you yesterday." See
Hooper to Livingston, September 12, 1776.
    ² Livingston had been elected governor of New Jersey on August 27.
    ³ For the correct reading of Montrose's verse, see *Poems of James Graham,
Marquis of Montrose (1612–50)*, ed. J. L. Weir (London: John Murray, 1938), p. 33.

Caesar Rodney to Thomas Rodney

Sir   Philadelphia Septr. 11th 1776
    I have no letter from you by this post, and indeed but seldom
have from Whence I Conclude you have either verry little to say for
yourselves or become verry Idle. As to One Mr. Killen (a former
Acquaintance of Mine) I have never heard but once of him Since the
late Storm Which happened in your part of the Country That
Blasted the Whig interest and laid prostrate many of the patriots.
If he too be fallen tell him he nobly fell in defence of his Country's
rights, and for his Comfort Virtue itself hath it's days of tryal. The
Israelites (the Chosen people of God) met with Crosses and disappointments in their Journey from the land [of] Bondage to that
of Liberty, But by a Steady perseverence and divine assistance they
at length possessed the promised Land. So that, that God, Who
Vieweth & Judgeth all things with Unerring Wisdom, Seeing the
Righteousness of his Cause (tho he permitteth Temporary Obstructions) Will one day (with a firm Reliance on him) Crown his Virtuous Endeavours with Success, and Cause the Modern Pharoah's

with their Hosts to be buried in the Sea of their Toryism, As he did the Antient Pharoah in the Red Sea. The Bulk of the people have been lead astray from a Virtuous persuit by the Art and Cunning of Wicked and designing men among You. He must undeceive and put them again in the right path. They are naturally honest and Mean Well, but are Weak and Credulous. And by so much as Wicked and designing men are more industrious than the Honest and Virtuous, are they lead to do that which is Evil, and to leave undone that which they ought to Do.

I have Recd two Letters from our friend Coll Haslet, since the Engagement on Long-Island, the last is dated at the heights near Kings-Bridge Where his Battalion and about 9000 others now are.[1] He is Well and desires to be kindly Remembered to you and Mr. Killen, who he terms the Barrister, and Says "I Condole with them Mightily in their present State of dejecting Dereliction." It is a long letter in which he Concludes with saying "We Expect every Moment Something important here, and hope in our next fight to be on more Equal terms and to give you a more pleasing account." It Seems Jack behaved Well and brought off his Colours like a Hero. The post before last I sent by Parke two pair of shoes, one for Betsey, the other for Sally, You have never told me Whether they Came to hand and it appears that Parke is about to decline Rideing. He did not go down the last time, but sent Robert the Old Rider. This I never knew till last evening when I perchance met him in the Street and Calling him to account for it he told me he had taken a Small house Somewhere in this town. That he meant to go into some small Trade and Could not say whether he should Continue to Ride or not, but believed he should not go down this time. I know not Parke's Circumstances, but as I imagined he might owe you Some Money, thought proper to give this information. Doctor Tilton wrote me a Letter from New York, in Which he inclosed me one for his Brother Mr. Nehemiah Tilton. I have Sent it by this Post (being the first Opertunity) and hope it will get safe to hand.

From What I can learn of the Convention at Newcastle, They will attempt nothing but Barely the framing A plan of Government, Except what may be necessary for the dispatching the flying Camp Battalion. Mr. Read lets me know that matters go on Slooly, and that the members of Kent & Sussex grow uneasy to get home. This is (I know) as it used to be with them.

I Suppose you have heard that General Sullivan has been with Congress on a Message from Lord Howe, and as it has occationed Various reports suppose you wou'd be Glad to know as of a truith the Sum and Substance of it. It is this. That Lord Howe told General Sullivan in Conversation, that he and his brother the General had full power to Treat, that he had stayed in England near two months after he was otherwise ready to come, for the purpose of Obtaining

Such ample powers, that he wished to Converse with General Wash-ing[ton], or rather in preference to that, with the Members of Con-gress on that head by which he thought Peace Interesting to both England and America might be had—but to bring about this Con-ference here was a difficulty—for that his Scituation was attended with that kind of delicacy he could not in the first instance Acknowl-edge the Congress—and on the other hand he had no doubt they were in the like Scituation. Therefore desired that Some of the Members might meet him where they Chose, as private Gentlemen, and that he on his part would meet them as Such. That if they Should Agree on Terms of accommodation, that then the Congress must be ack-nowledged or the Work Could not be Confirmed. Congress taking this matter into Consideration think little or nothing is to be Expected from it, but thinking it might Create a division among the people by the influence of the unfriendly to the Cause, thought it necessary to take the matter up, and determine on it in Such manner as might prevent the Scheme of his Lord–ship taking Effect. There-fore the Congress in the first place determined that it was Contrary to both their power and opinion to send members to Confer as private Gentlemen. They then proceeded to appoint a Committee of Con-gress to go and Confer with Lord Howe on the term of peace, Who are to report to Congress. Now you will see by this Method the Congress hold out to the people their Willingness to put an End to the War, Whenever it Can be done on principles of Liberty and Safety—and by this you will find that if Lord Howe Will treat with them (Which none of the Congress Expect) it is acknowledging the Congress in their independent State, and if that is done the Sooner the Better. I would Just observe that this Stroke Seems already to have baffled the Tories here. The Committee of three Set out the day before Yesterday. The proceedings of Congress Relative to these matters I believe will soon be published, till when let it remain with you, and your friends.[2] As I have no News Except such as you will find in the papers Shall Conclude with my Love and Compliments to my friends and acquaintances. I am Sir Yrs.

Caesar Rodney

RC (PHi).
[1] See John Haslet to Caesar Rodney, August 31 and September 4, 1776, in Rodney, *Letters* (Ryden), pp. 108–9, 111–13.
[2] On September 17 Congress ordered publication of an account of the confer-ence with Lord Howe. *JCC*, 5:765–66.

Edward Rutledge

Edward Rutledge to George Washington

Brunswick Wednesday [September 11, 1776]

My dear Sir   Evening 10 O'clock

Your Favour of this Morning is just put into my Hands. In Answer I must beg Leave to inform you that our Conferrence with Lord Howe has been attended with no immediate Advantages. He declared that he had no Powers to consider us as Independt. States, and we easily discover'd that were we still Dependt. we would have nothing to expect from those with which he is vested. He talk'd altogether in generals, that he came out here to consult, advise, & confer with Gentlemen of the greatest Influence in the Colonies about their Complaints, that the King would revise the Acts of Parliament & royal Instructions upon such Reports as should be made and appear'd to fix our Redress upon his Majesty's good Will & Pleasure. This kind of Conversation lasted for several Hours & as I have already said without any Effect. Our Reliance continues therefore to be (under God) on your Wisdom & Fortitude & that of your Forces. That you may be as successful as I know you are worthy is my most sincere wish. I saw Mrs. Washington the Evening before I left Philadelphia, she was well. I gave Mr. Griffin a Letter from her for you. The Gentlemen beg their Respects. God bless you my dear Sir. Your most affectionate Friend,   E. Rutledge

[P.S.] We wrote you about 2 Hours ago by the Post.[1]

RC (DLC).
[1] Not found.

Henry Strachey's Notes on Lord Howe's Meeting with a Committee of Congress

11th Septr 1776

Lord Howe received the Gentlemen on the Beach. Dr. Franklin introduced Mr. Adams and Mr. Rutledge. Lord Howe very politely expressed the Sense he entertained of the Confidence they had placed in him, by thus putting themselves in his hands.[1]

A general and immaterial Conversation from the Beach to the House—The Hessian Guard saluted, as they passed.

A cold dinner was on the Table—dined—the Hessian Colonel present—Immediately after dinner he retired.

Lord Howe informed them it was long since he had entertained an opinion that the Differences between the two Countries might be accommodated to the Satisfaction of both—that he was known to be a Well Wisher to America—particularly to the Province of Massa-

chusetts Bay, which had endeared itself to him by the very high
Honors it had bestowed upon the Memory of his eldest Brother [2]—
that his going out as Commissioner from the King had been early
mentioned, but that afterwards for some time, he had heard no more
of it—That an Idea had then arisen of sending several Commissioners, to which he had objected—that his Wish was to go out singly
and with a Civil Commission only, in which case, his Plan was to
have gone immediately to Philadelphia, that he had even objected to
his Brother's being in the Commission, from the Delicacy of the
Situation and his desire to take upon himself all the Reproach that
might be the Consequence of it—that it was however thought necessary that the General should be joined in the Commission (for
reasons which he explained) having their hands upon the Two
Services—and that he, Lord Howe, should also have the naval
Command, in which he had acquiesced—that he had hoped to reach
America before the Army had moved, and did not doubt but if their
Disposition had been the same as expressed in their Petition to the
King, he should have been able to have brought about an Accomo-
dation to the Satisfaction of both Countries—that he thought the
Petition was a sufficient Basis to confer upon—that it contained
Matter, which, with Candour & Discussion might be wrought into a
Plan of Permanency—that the Address to the People, which accompanied the Petition to His Majesty, tended to destroy the good Effects
that might otherwise have been hoped for from the Petition—that
he had however still flattered himself that upon the Grounds of the
Petition, he should be able to do some good [3]—that they themselves
had changed the ground since he left England by their Declaration
of Independency, which, if it could not be got over, precluded him
from all Treaty, as they must know, and he had explicitly said so in
his Letter to Dr. Franklin,[4] that he had not, nor did he expect ever
to have, Powers to consider the Colonies in the light of Independent
States—that they must also be sensible, that he could not confer with
them as a Congress—that he could not acknowledge that Body which
was not acknowledged by the King, whose Delegate he was, neither,
for the same reason, could he confer with these Gentlemen as a Committee of the Congress—that if they would not lay aside that Distinction, it would be improper for him to proceed—that he thought it an
unessential Form, which might for the present lie dormant—that they
must give him leave to consider them merely as Gentlemen of great
Ability, and Influence in the Country—and that they were now met
to converse together ⟨upon the Subject of Differences⟩, and to try if
any Outline could be drawn to put a stop to the Calamities of War,
and to bring forward some Plan that might be satisfactory both to
America and to England. He desired them to consider the Delicacy
of his Situation—the Reproach he was liable to, if he should be
understood by any step of his, to acknowledge, or to treat with, the

Congress—that he hoped they would not by any Implication commit him upon that Point—that he was rather going beyond his Powers in the present Meeting—[Dr. Franklin said You may depend upon our taking care of that, my Lord] That he thought the Idea of a Congress might easily be thrown out of the Question at present, for that if Matters could be so settled that the King's Government should be reestablished, the Congress would of course cease to exist, and if they meant such Accommodation, they must see how unnecessary & useless it was to stand upon that Form which they knew they were to give up upon the Restoration of legal Government.

Dr. Franklin said that His Lordship might consider the Gentlemen present in any view he thought proper—that they were also at liberty to consider themselves in their real Character—that there was no necessity on this occasion to distinguish between the Congress and Individuals—and that the Conversation might be held as amongst friends.

The Two other Gentlemen assented, in very few Words, to what the Doctor had said.

Lord Howe then proceeded—that on his Arrival in this Country he had thought it expedient to issue a Declaration, which they had done him the honor to comment upon [5]—that he had endeavored to couch it in such Terms as would be the least exceptionable—that he had concluded they must have judged he had not expressed in it all he had to say, though enough, he thought, to bring on a Discussion which might lead the way to Accommodation [6]—that their Declaration of Independency had since rendered him the more cautious of opening himself—that it was absolutely impossible for him to treat, or confer, upon that Ground, or to admit the Idea in the smallest degree—that he flattered himself if That were given up, their was still room for him to effect the King's Purposes—that His Majesty's most earnest desire was to make his American Subjects happy, to cause a Reform in whatever affected the Freedom of their Legislation, and to concur with his Parliament in the Redress of any real Grievances—that his Powers were, generally, to restore Peace and grant Pardons, to attend to Complaints & Representations, and to confer upon Means of establishing a Re-Union upon Terms honorable & advantageous to the Colonies as well as to Great Britain— that they knew We expected Aid from America—that the Dispute seemed to be only concerning the Mode of obtaining it.

[Doctor Franklin here said, *That* we never refused, upon *Requisition*.]

Lord Howe continued—that their Money was the smallest Consideration—that America could produce more solid Advantages to Great Britain—that it was her Commerce, her Strength, her Men, that we chiefly wanted.

[Here Dr. Franklin said with rather a sneering Laugh, Ay, my

Lord, we have a pretty considerable Manufactory of *Men*—alluding as it should seem to their numerous Army.[7]]

Lord Howe continued—it is desirable to put a stop to these ruinous Extremities, as well for the sake of our Country, as yours. When an American falls, England feels it. Is there no way of treading back this Step of Independency, and opening the door to a full discussion?

Lord Howe concluded with saying that having thus opened to them the general Purport of the Commission, and the King's Disposition to a permanent Peace, he must stop to hear what they might chuse to observe.

Dr. Franklin said he supposed His Lordship had seen the Resolution of the Congress which had sent them hither—that the Resolution contained the whole of their Commission—that if this Conversation was productive of no immediate good Effect, it might be of Service at a future time—that America had considered the Prohibitory Act as the Answer to her Petition to the King—Forces had been sent out, and Towns destroyed—that they could not expect Happiness now under the *Domination* of Great Britain—that all former Attachment was *obliterated*—that America could not return again to the Domination of Great Britain, and therefore imagined that Great Britain meant to rest it upon Force. The other Gentlemen will deliver their Sentiments.

Mr. Adams said that he had no objection to Lord Howe's considering him, on the present Occasion, merely as a private Gentleman, or in any Character except that of a British Subject [8]—that the Resolution of the Congress to declare the Independency was not taken up upon their own Authority—that they had been instructed so to do, by *all* the Colonies—and that it was not in their power to treat otherwise than as independent States. He mentioned warmly his own Determination not to depart from the Idea of Independency, and spoke in the common way of the Power of the Crown, which was comprehended in the Ideal Power of Lords & Commons.

Mr. Rutledge began by saying he had been one of the oldest Members of the Congress—that he had been one from the beginning—that he thought it was worth the Consideration of Great Britain whether she would not receive greater Advantages by an Alliance with the Colonies as independent States, than she had ever hitherto done—that she might still enjoy a *great Share* of the Commerce—that she would have their raw Materials for her Manufactures—that they could protect the West India Islands much more effectually and more easily than she can—that they could assist her in the Newfoundland Trade—that he was glad this Conversation had happened, as it would be the occasion of opening to Great Britain the Consideration of the Advantages she might derive from America by an Alliance with her as an independent State, before any thing is settled with other foreign Powers—that it was impossible the People should consent to come again under the English Government. He could answer for South Carolina—that Government had been very oppressive—that the Crown Officers had claimed Privilege and confined People upon pretence of a breach of Privilege—that they had at last taken the Government into their own hands—that the People were now settled and happy under that Government and would not (even if they, the Congress could desire it) return to the King's Government—

Mr. Rutledge mentioned (by way of Answer to Lord Howe's Remark upon that point) that their Petition to the King contained all which they thought was proper to be addressed to His Majesty,— that the other Matters which could not come under the head of a Petition and therefore could not with Propriety be inserted, were put into the Address to the People, which was only calculated to shew them the Importance of America to Great Britain—and that the Petition to King was by all of them meant to be respectful.[9]

Lord Howe said, that if such were their Sentitments, he could only lament it was not in his Power to bring about the Accommodation he wished—that he had not Authority, nor did he expect he ever should have, to treat with the Colonies as States independent of the Crown of Great Britain—and that he was sorry the Gentlemen had had the trouble of coming so far, to so little purpose—that if the Colonies would not give up the System of Independency, it was impossible for him to enter into any Negociation.

Dr. Franklin observed that it would take as much time for them to refer to, and get an answer from their Constituents, as it would the Commissioners to get fresh Instructions from home, which he supposed might be done in about 3 Months.

Lord Howe replied it was in vain to think of his receiving Instructions to treat upon that ground.

After a little Pause, Dr. Franklin suddenly said, well my Lord, as America is to expect nothing but upon ⟨total⟩ unconditional Submission, and Your Lordship has no Proposition to make us, give me leave to ask whether, if we should make Propositions to Great Britain (not that I know, or am authorized to say we shall) You would receive and transmit them.

Lord Howe interrupted the Doctor at the Word Submission—said that Great Britain did not require unconditional Submission, that he thought what he had already said to them, proved the contrary, and desired the Gentlemen would not go away with such an Idea.

Memdn. Perhaps Dr. Franklin meant Submission to the Crown, in opposition to their Principle of Independency.

Lord Howe said he did not know that he could avoid receiving

any Papers that might be put into his hands—seemed rather doubtful about the Propriety of transmitting home, but did not say that
he would decline it.[10]

MS (NN). These notes were made by Henry Strachey (1737–1810), an M.P. for
Bishop's Castle who served as secretary to the Howe brothers' peace commission
from 1776 to 1778. Alan Valentine, *The British Establishment, 1760–1784: An
Eighteenth-Century Biographical Dictionary*, 2 vols. (Norman: University of
Oklahoma Press, 1970), 2:832. The regular brackets in the text are also in the MS.
    [1] For the genesis of this meeting between Lord Howe and the committee of
Congress, see—in addition to the numerous comments on the subject in the
delegates' correspondence between September 1 and 10—*JCC*, 5:723, 728, 730–31,
737–38; and Josiah Bartlett to John Langdon, September 1, 1776, note 2. The
committee's own account of this conference, which was submitted to Congress
on September 17 and then ordered to be published, is in *JCC*, 5:765–66. Other
contemporary descriptions by American participants may be found in Edward
Rutledge to Washington, September 11, and to Robert R. Livingston, October 2,
as well as in John Adams to Samuel Adams, September 14, 1776. Almost three
decades later Adams also composed a particularly vivid account of this episode
in his autobiography. See Adams, *Diary* (Butterfield), 3:417–30. Finally Lord
Howe described his meeting with the committee in a letter to Lord George
Germain, secretary of state for American affairs, parts of which are worth quoting
here:
    "In the Evening of the same day [*i.e.* September 9], I received Information that
Doctor Franklin, Mr. (John) Adams, and Mr. Rutledge would meet me at any
appointed Place on the Morning of the 11th. General Howe's Presence being that
Day necessary with the Army, he could not accompany me to the Meeting,
which I appointed should be on Staten Island, opposite to the Town of Amboy.
    "I acquainted them that the King's Desire to restore the public Tranquillity,
and to render His American Subjects happy in a permanent Union with Great
Britain, had induced Him to constitute Commissioners upon the Spot, to remove
the Restrictions upon Trade and Intercourse, to dispense the Royal Clemency
to those who had been hurried away from their Allegiance, to receive Representations of Grievances, and to discuss the Means whereby that mutual Confidence and just Relation which ought to subsist between the Colonies and the
Parent State, might be restored and preserved. I also gave them to understand
that His Majesty was graciously disposed to a Revision of such of His Royal
Instructions as might have laid too much Restraint upon their Legislation, and
to concur in a Revisal of any of the Plantation Laws by which the Colonists
might be aggrieved; that the Commissioners were earnest on their Part to prevent
the farther Effusion of Blood, and to proceed upon all such Measures as might
expedite the Accomplishment of the Purposes of their Commission; that they
were willing to confer with any of His Majesty's Subjects, and to treat with
Delegates of the Colonies, legally chosen, upon all Matters relating to Grievances
and Regulations: But that, for very obvious Reasons, we could not enter into
any Treaty with their Congress, and much less proceed in any Conference or
Negociation, upon the inadmissible Ground of Independency; a Pretension which
the Commissioners had not, nor was it possible they ever should have, Authority
to acknowledge.
    "The Three Gentlemen were very explicit in their Opinions that the asso-
ciated Colonies would not accede to any Peace or Alliance, but as free and independent States; and they endeavored to prove that Great Britain would
derive more extensive and more durable Advantages from such an Alliance, than
from the Connection it was the object of the Commission to restore. Their
Arguments not meriting a serious Attention, the Conversation ended, and the

Gentlemen returned to Amboy." Lord Howe to Germain, September 20, 1776, PRO, C.O. 5, 177:38–40.

[2] Adams told the following anecdote about this remark in his autobiography: "Lord How was profuse in his Expressions of Gratitude to the State of Massachusetts, for erecting a marble Monument in Westminster Abbey to his Elder Brother Lord How who was killed in America in the last French War, saying 'he esteemed that Honour to his Family, *above all Things in this World.* That such was his gratitude and affection to this Country, on that Account, that he felt for America, as for a Brother, and if America should fall, he should feel and lament it, like the Loss of a Brother.' Dr. Franklin, with an easy Air and a collected Countenance, a Bow, a Smile and all that Naivetee which sometimes appeared in his Conversation and is often observed in his Writings, replied 'My Lord, We will do our Utmost Endeavours, to save your Lordship that mortification.' His Lordship appeared to feel this, with more Sensibility, than I could expect: but he only returned 'I suppose you will endeavour to give Us employment in Europe.' To this Observation, not a Word nor a look from which he could draw any Inference, escaped any of the Committee." Adams, *Diary* (Butterfield), 3:422.

[3] See the Olive Branch Petition and the second Address to the People of Great Britain, both adopted by Congress on July 8, 1775, in *JCC*, 2:158–61, 163–71.

[4] See Lord Howe to Franklin, August 16, 1776, in Franklin, *Writings* (Smyth), 5:462.

[5] Howe had sent a copy of his June 20 declaration "for restoring peace to his Majesty's Colonies" enclosed in a letter to Franklin of the same date with a July 12 postscript. *Am. Archives,* 4th ser. 6:1000–1002. Franklin had commented on both documents in Franklin to Lord Howe, July 20, 1776, and Congress had commented on the declaration in a published resolution of July 19. *JCC*, 5:592–93.

[6] After this clause Strachey first wrote and then deleted: "that He would so far communicate his Powers as to say generally that they were, to confer with any Persons upon the Subject of Peace and Rebellion—that the King was disposed."

[7] Alongside this paragraph Howe noted in the margin: "No—To their increasing population."

[8] In his autobiography Adams described an exchange with Howe to which this remark gave rise: "When his Lordship observed to Us, that he could not confer with Us as Members of Congress, or public Characters, but only as private Persons and British Subjects, Mr. John Adams answered somewhat quickly, 'Your Lordship may consider me, in what light you please; and indeed I should be willing to consider myself, for a few moments, in any Character which would be agreable to your Lordship, *except that of a British Subject.*' His Lordship at these Words turn'd to Dr. Franklin and Mr. Rutledge and said 'Mr. Adams is a decided Character:' with so much gravity and solemnity: that I now believe it meant more, than either of my Colleagues or myself understood at the time. In our report to Congress We supposed that the Commissioners, Lord and General Howe, had by their Commission Power to [except] from Pardon all that they should think proper. But I was informed in England, afterwards, that a Number were expressly excepted by Name from Pardon, by the privy Council, and that John Adams was one of them, and that this List of Exceptions was given as an Instruction to the two Howes, with their Commission." Adams, *Diary* (Butterfield), 3:422–23. The most recent authority on the subject mentions no exceptions to the Howe brothers' authority to grant pardons. Ira D. Gruber, *The Howe Brothers and the American Revolution* (New York: Atheneum, 1972), pp. 73–76.

[9] Rutledge also discussed the question of parliamentary authority over America with Howe. See John Adams to Samuel Adams, September 14, 1776.

[10] The committee's report to Congress describes the conclusion of its meeting

with Howe as follows: "His Lordship then saying that he was sorry to find, that
no accommodation was like to take place, put an end to the conference." *JCC*,
5:766.

Board of War to George Washington

Sir.   War Office Septr. 12th. 1776
   By Direction of Congress to the Board of War I have procured two
of the Philadelphia Light Horse to conduct the Generals Prescott &
Macdonald to your Excellency to be exchanged agreeable to the
Resolve of Congress for the Generals Sullivan & Lord Sterling.[1] I
have directed the Gentlemen of the Escort to stop short at some safe
Place on the Road & send off an Express to your Excellency for your
Directions in the Matter. The Generals are on their Parole not to
attempt an Escape or take any Step contrary to the Rules of War, but
to deliver themselves to your Excellency for your proper Disposal of
them until their Exchange can be effected.[2]
   I have the Honor to be, your obedt humble servt,
                                                 Richard Peters Secy

RC (DLC).
   [1] See *JCC*, 5:735. Sullivan was subsequently exchanged for Prescott, but, at the
insistence of General Howe, Lord Stirling was exchanged for Gov. Montfort
Browne of the Bahamas instead of General McDonald. Washington, *Writings*
(Fitzpatrick), 6:22, 23, 45, 74, 100, 117, 173, 183.
   [2] The Board of War also wrote brief letters to Washington on September 14
and 16. In the first Peters enclosed "a copy of the arrangement of Officers in the
old Virginia Regiments" and in the second a "Memorial of the Second Lieutenants
of the Virginia Regiments." Washington Papers, DLC; and *Am. Archives*, 5th
ser. 2:320–22, 348–49.

Elbridge Gerry to Joseph Trumbull

Dear sir   Philadelphia 12th Sepr 1776
   Colo Williams shewed me your Letter to him mentioning the
Situation of your Brother at Ticonderoga, in Consequence of wch
It was moved to Congress to appointment him D. Adjt. General & no
objection was offered. Mr. Lewis recommended by General Gates is
also appointed D. Quar. Master General.[1]
   The Difficulties which You mentioned as the Grounds of your
Resignation of the Commissaryship for the northern Department
being removed by Congress, will it is hoped induce You to renew
your Engagemt. therein.[2] Surely It is the Intention of Congress, that
the whole of the Commissary affairs shall be under your Direction,

& if Mr Levingston opposes, You will be supported in dismissing him. General Schuyler has nothing to do with your officers otherwise than to order where the Magazines shall be placed & the Quantity of provision to be procured or delivered. If he refuses to deliver Money You can easily receive a greater Sum from the N York Chest & Send it forward. 500,000 Dollars are I suppose arrived e'er this, & another Sum to the same amount is order'd to Mr Palfrey, whereby he will be able to supply You; & in such a Case I would remonstrate against G. Schuyler's Conduct in putting the Continent to the extra Expence of Sending forward the Money. I cannot conceive what his Intention is unless to put the northern Army which is now in good Order, in the same Confusion as has been heretofore experienced; but this will be prevented unless he is indulged by your giving up to his Schemes.

Congress seem now determined to have an Army of some Duration & to give sufficient Bounties for the purpose; I wish It had been sooner *acceded* to but We must move with the Waters.

The present Campaign will try the Resolution of Persons & discriminate pretenders from those who are fixed in good principles; I hope the latter will thro'out America exert themselves & prevent the former from disseminating their timid principles being sir with Esteem your very huml sert,   E Gerry

[*P.S.*] Your affairs will be attended to when the present Hurry is over.

[*P.S.*] Since writing the within, Letters from General Schuyler recommend the appointmt. of your Brother to the Office of D.A. General wch was previously complied wth. A Letter from Mr. Levingston contains his Resignation, wch was very agreable to some Members of Congress. One from South Carolina mentions several Engagements wth the Indians, in which the latter have been put to the Rout & several of their Towns & Cornfields laid Waste. One from Mr Deane in France mentioning great preparation by France & Spain wth an ostensible Design to attack Portugal, two Fleets are equipping by the former & one by the latter. The Reprisal is also arrived in the River wth two Tons of Powder & 450 stands of Arms from Martinico.

RC (Ct).
[1] John Trumbull was elected "deputy adjutant general of the army in the northern department, and Morgan Lewis, Esqr. was elected deputy quarter master general of said army." *JCC,* 5:753.
[2] Trumbull's ongoing jurisdictional conflict with Walter Livingston over the right to supply the armies on the lakes and at New York led both to submit letters of resignation, dated September 7, to President Hancock. *Am. Archives,* 5th ser. 2:213, 220–21. Trumbull's letter was read in Congress on September 11 and referred to a committee which reported to Congress the next day. Congress accepted the committee's resolution sustaining Trumbull's "right to direct the operations of his department" and expressing hope that this support would "induce his continuance in the office of commissary for both armies, at New York, and on the lakes." *JCC,* 5:750, 752–53.

This same committee, consisting of William Hooper, Richard Henry Lee, and Roger Sherman, was also directed "to enquire into the conduct of Mr. Livingston, deputy commissary general in the northern department." What is apparently their report on Livingston—two paragraphs of which are printed in *JCC*, 5:750n.2—recommended that the "Commissioners appointed to settle Accounts in the Northern Department be empowered and directed to enquire into the conduct of Walter Livingston." When Livingston's letter of resignation arrived on Sepetmber 13 it was referred to the Board of War and the next day Congress accepted Livingston's resignation. *JCC*, 5:750, 756, 758. See also Gerry to Joseph Trumbull, June 8, 18, 19, and 25; Gerry to John Adams and Samuel Adams, July 21; and Samuel Adams to Joseph Trumbull, August 3, 1776.

William Hooper to William Livingston

Dear Sir   Thursday Sept 12 1776
   Your's of the 11th Instant this moment came to my hands. I wrote you yesterday & have nothing since to add—except that your Brother [1] who has been a little indisposed is recovered & promises to accompany me to meet you at Bristol on Saturday the 21st, the Journey to Trenton being rather too far and the claims of Congress to our attendance rather too pressing to leave this City this Week. I am sorry that the Information we have received from Pittsburgh since Sunday leaves little doubt of our having an Indian War with the Wiandats, Delawares, & the other infernal Scoundrels on the back of this & Virginia.[2] I am, with Affection Yours,

                                                    Wm Hooper

RC (MHi).
   [1] Philip Livingston.
   [2] See *JCC*, 5:749, 752.

Robert Morris to Silas Deane

Sir   Philada. Septr. 12th. 1776
   You will receive herewith Copy of what I wrote You the 11th ulto. & by this Conveyance I remit the 2d bills of those setts mentioned in that letter. I have bought a considerable quantity of Tobacco but cannot get suitable Vessels to carry it. You cannot conceive the many disappointments we have met in this respect. However I expect a ship is now taking in about 400 hhds as I wrote two posts ago agreeing to the Owners terms and shall advise you more particularly in my next respecting this matter. I am sorry to tell you another Vessell bound from hence for Bourdeaux with a Cargo of flour &c has been taken and carried to N York with the Fleet. This was a fine New Brigt intended as a Packet between us; she had dispatches for You which were thrown overboard & sunk

by the Captain as were the Invoices &c of the Cargo. These unlucky accidents retard the remittances exceedingly, which is vexatious but cannot be helped. I hope your Credit has been sufficient to procure the Indn Goods & that they are on their way out, for they will be much wanted and we shall not give over remitting untill you are fully enabled to pay for them. I expect a Cargo of Rice & Indigo is now Shipping on this Account as orders have been given to that Effect but still the same difficulty about Vessells occurs in that quarter also. So many of the American Ships have been taken, lost, sold & employd abroad that they are now very scarce in every part of the Continent which I consider as a great misfortune, for ship building does not go on as formerly and this Want can only be supplyd by the arrival of Ships from Europe and by the Captures in which all the American Cruizers have been remarkably successful. Those who have engaged in Privateering are making large Fortunes in a most Rapid manner. I have not meddled in this business which I confess does not Square with my Principles for I have long had extensive Connections & Dealings with many Worthy Men in England & Coud not consent to take any part of their property because the Government have seized mine, which is the case in several instances.

The Trading plan recommended in my last is farr more eligible and if we have but luck in getting the Goods safe to America the Proffits will be sufficient to Content us all. I do therefore continue my recommendation of that plan and sincerely hope You & Tom [1] will be able to do something considerable therein for you may depend it will reward you beyond any other pursuit. If you can procure Insurances at any reasonable premium even at 50 per Cent (altho I dont think the Risque is really worth 15 per Cent) I think you had best to Charter two or three good Double Deck'd fast Sailing Vessells, ballast or Load them with Salt in the Hold and put onboard of each as many Dry Goods, say Woolens, Linins, Tin, Copper, Hosiery &c &c, as you can Conveniently obtain & let them proceed immediately for this place, Insuring the Value of the Cargoes on the best terms you can against the Risque of Capture by our Enemies as well as against all other Risques & dangers. I mean that you shou'd Charter French Vessells & by clearing them out for the Island of St. Piers & Miquelon they may sail along this Coast without being subject to Capture untill they come within three Leagues of the Land. You must take care that the Ships are sound, Strong & Staunch and that they are well fitted & Manned. Two suits of Sails and good Anchors & Cables they ought to have. Tell the Masters when they come on this Coast to venture in Close with the Land as our No. Westers in the Winter will keep them out a long time if they keep without Or in the Gulph Stream whereas if they come within it, nothing but an Easterly Wind can hurt them & those Winds do not prevail much in Winter. When they come in sight of our Light House they must hoist an Ensign at the Foretop Gall[an]t mast head and stand in for the Mouth of the Bay with it flying. If there is any Enemy or danger in the way, a Signal will be made at the Light House by shewing Colours there. If no danger they will not answer the Signal and the vessell may come boldly in to the mouth of the Bay or into Whore Kiln Road & send a Boat on shoar at Lewis Town for a Pilot. In short I think there is very little danger in all this matter for the Men of Warr cannot keep the Coast & we will not let them Harbour here in the Winter Season. You shou'd Charter the Vessells out here & back again, so that you may afford them a good Freight & we will load them back with Wheat, flour, Tobacco, Rice, Indigo, Bees Wax &c to pay for the Cost of the Cargoe You Ship by them. Besides these Vessells I wou'd have you begin sending out Goods Constantly to Martinico, *St. Eustatia* & Cape Francois but the first & last are safest for the present & I suppose will continue so, unless the French become parties in our Warr which I think very likely and then the Dutch Islands must engross our attention. At St. Eustatia Mr. Cornelius Stevenson and at Curracoa Mr Isaac Governeur will receive & forward Goods for us, at Cape Francois Mr. Stephen Ceronio, at St. Nicholas Mole Mr. John Dupuy, at Martinico Wm Bingham Esqr who has already written you some letters & with whom I expect you will support a Constant Correspondence both Political & Commercial. He is a Young Gent of good Education, Family & Fortune. His Correspondence has yet a good deal of the Fancifull Young man in it, but experience will cure him of this and upon the whole I think he has abilitys & Merit both in the Political & Commercial line. You will inform him soon as you can whether Insurances can be effected on Goods & Vessells from the French Island to this Continent and on what terms, indeed we expect to hear from you pretty regularly through that Channell.

I wou'd make you some remittances in advance toward the purchase of the Goods I recommend your Shipping but having already engaged pretty extensively in that way with Mr. Ross & others who have not the advantage of a Publick Character to recommend them, I am obliged to remit them what bills I can Collect on my House's private Account in order to support their pursuits, and it is not necessary with you because I have no doubt but Tom & you together will be able to establish the needfull credit, that once obtained you may depend I will punctually enable you to support it by making ample & speedy remittances and when freed from other engagements I shall have no objection to lodge Funds for ready Money purchases. I have had some doubts in my own mind whether it will be best for Tom to attend to Political pursuits, or to fix him as a merchant in some one of the French Ports. I believe it will be in my Power to do well by him in either way but particularly in the latter which is the most Independant & on that account the most Honorable Station according to my Mind. Yet if he has Talent to become usefull in a Publick character I shou'd have no objections and will therefore leave the matter open untill I hear from him & you on the Subject. Your Candid opinion on this and all other matters relative to him I shall be very thankfull for. In the meantime I mean to direct some Cargoes of this Country produce to be Consigned to him or his order that if he inclines to sit down as a Merchant he may begin immediately. If otherways he can put them into proper hands for Sale &c.

Since my last Genl Howe & his army have taken possession of Long Island leaving about 4 or 5000 Men on Staten Island where they first landed. We had some Works & about 6000 Men on Long Isld. when the Enemy landed with 20 thousand. A Skirmish very soon followed the landing there. About 3000 of our Men went out of the lines to take possession of some Hills & high Lands, but the Enemy out General'd us and surrounded our People with four times their Number. However they purchased the honor of the day at a very dear rate for our Folks drew up, gave them Battle & two different times broke & routed double their Number in fair Maneuvering & Platoons firing in the open Field, but in the end superiour Numbers & Superiour Generalship prevailed. We lost about 7 to 800 Men in Killed, Wounded & Prisoners. The Enemies loss was farr greater as they acknowledge in Killed & Wounded, but not so in Prisoners for we only took one party a Lieutt & 30 men. Sullivan commanded in this affair & was well seconded by Ld Stirling who behaved Nobly indeed. They are both Prisoners as are several Cols., Lt Cols. & other officers. In short such Victorys as these alarm our Enemies & will be their ruin. We have evacuated Long Island & must do the same by N York which is not tenable against their Ships. For my part I wish our Men & Stores were all removed to Kings bridge where we must sooner or later take post & make the great stand. We are no ways dismayed at the Force of the Enemy but have full hopes of getting the better of them in the long run altho they seem very formidable at present. Our Army on the Lakes is now very Strong and we seem perfectly secure in that quarter for the present. I find I must write you another letter by this Conveyance which will not sail so soon as I expected & for the present shall only add that I am very truely, Dr sir, Your Friend & Servt.   Robt Morris

RC (CtHi).
[1] Morris' half brother, Thomas Morris. Morris wrote another letter this day, which was intercepted at sea, in which he mentioned transactions that he expected Thomas to explore involving the Lisbon operations of the London merchant James Burn. Thomas, Morris reported to Burn, had just gone to France, and "as we wish to make some proposals to Mr. John Green & Mr. John Robertson

which we think may be of mutual advantage both to them & us, especially if
they are in Lisbon, We have directed him to write both to you & them on the
subject and you'l please to consider what comes from him the same light as if
it were from us, desiring them to do the same. We write to your Lisbon house
respecting our dependancys in their hands not doubting but they will duely
attend to our orders." Willing, Morris & Co. to James Burn, September 12, 1776,
PRO, C.O. 5, 38:214–15.

Caesar Rodney to John Haslet

Dear Sir   Philadelphia Sepr. 12th 1776
   I have been favoured with two Letters from you, one dated at
New York, the Other at Kings Bridge,[1] in both of which you desired I would Communicate to my friends your Scituation after
the Engagement from whom Misses Haslet might hear it. Imagining it might be a Considerable time before the News woud Get to
her in that way, and that in the meantime She would be verry uneasy, therefore I wrote a Letter to her immediately on the Rect
of your first, in which I let her know the whole affair and Sent
it by a safe hand.
   I am happy that I have it in my power to Congratulate you on
the Bravery your Battalion has Shewn in the late Action, and the
great Honor the Officers and Men have Acquired by it. They are
much Spoken of here and I have been often Complimented in behalf of the Government on their account. They deserve much of
their Country, and (as an Individual) have my most hearty Thanks.
I am Extreemly Sorry for poor Stuart and the other brave Lads
that fell, tho in the Bed of Honor. Must Confess I don't like your
present Scituation, yet hope the best. The Justice of our Cause, and
the bravery of our Troops may do Wonders.
   In your last Letter you Seem to Show some Uneasiness least there
Should be Some Change in the delegates. I believe you may be
Easy on that head. In the first place I imagine They would not
venture to Risque the making Such an Uproar in the Government
as the turning me out probably wou'd make, and in the Next the
undesigning Patriotick part are determined to protest against their
doing any thing but that of framing a plan of Government. In Mr.
Reads last letter to me is the following paragraff. "Our business
has been delayed in Convention by the death of Mrs. Thompson,
the Sister of Mr. McKean, who was buried this day. Mr. McKean's
Eldest son lies dangerously ill at Mr. Thompson's house, and I
know not when he can attend. A Committee of Ten is Employed
in the Drafting a Declaration of Rights, the rest of the Members
from Kent & Sussex are getting impatient, Doctr. Ridgely is Returned Home Sick. Such is the Scituation of Matters Here." When
Mr. Read went to Newcastle he prevailed on me to stay in Con-

gress, and that he would get the Convention to give a power to one Member to Act so that our Government might be Represented by me alone till the Convention Should Rise. I mentioned this to Mr. McKean who directly declared they should make no appointment of Delegates, nor even alter the powers Given them, least they (meaning the Convention) should plead that as a president for going into some other appointments, which they were not authorised to do by their Choice. Therefore Upon the Whole I don't imagine they will attempt any Change. But sir whether they do or not, I do not purpose Continuing here longer than till the other Gentlemen Return; I have made a verry Great Sacrifice of my property to the Cause, Government never paid me above half what I have necessarily Expended even when my friends were at the Helm. What may I Expect from these? They would see me Serve without a Shilling. You know they wou'd, because you know they like not either me or the Cause.[2]

General Dagworthy, Mr. Clowes and Mr. Peery were here, and say the Tory plan for leaving me out of the Convention was, first to put me at the head of their Ticket to shew their approbation of me, after which they put another person in my Stead, and assigned as a Reason for it, that it was now a Critical time. That it was absolutely necessary We should keep up our Representation in the Congress. That they wished I might not be laid under the necessity of leaving the Congress at a time so Interesting which I must Do if Chose in Convention &c. These Gentlemen then said that the Inhabitants of Newcastle County had not Considered to the Matter in that light for they had chose both their delegates. In Answer to this, it was said they, the people of Newcastle, had done verry wrong &c. By Such little Cunning are the people to be Cajoled. I saw a Man from Mispillion who left there a day or two before my letter Could have reached it, who told me that yours and Captain Adams's families were well, but they were in Much distress for the Delawares who (from all accots. they had Received) were at least two thirds Cut off, that almost all the officers were killed particularly you. He told me the people were Generally distressed haveing most of them some friend or Relation in the Battalion. My letter I am Sure has set that Matter Right.

I wrote above a week ago to Mr. Montgomery the Chaplain, not knowing then whether you were among the Dead or living. Should be Glad to know whether the letter got Safe [to] hand.[3] Be pleased to Enquire of him and let me know in your next which I hope will be soon. Make my compliments to Doctr. Tilton, and tell him I forwarded his Brothers letter. That you may have a happy deliverance, and your Battalion be Crowned (if possible) with still more Honor in every Combat is the Sincere wish of Sir, Yr. Real Friend & Humble Servt.   Caesar Rodney

P.S. I Remembered you as desired to Messers Killen & Rodney

RC (DeHi).
[1] John Haslet's letters of August 31 and September 4 to Rodney are in Rodney, *Letters* (Ryden), pp. 108–9, 111–13.
[2] Rodney left Congress early the following month and did not return. See Rodney to John Haslet, October 6, 1776.
[3] Not found.

Secret Committee Minutes of Proceedings

Sepr. 12. 1776.

Come. met. Present, Messrs. Morris, Hewes, Col. Lee, & Mr. Bartlett. Js. Marsh applys for extraordinary Pilotage of the ship Olive Branch up and down the river. Agreed to allow him £9 for sd service for wch. gave an order on Mr. Morris. Issued follg. drafts on the Treasurer. In favor of G. Meade & Co. for 1466 2/3 dlls being value of their sloop Fanny chartered & insured by this Come. & since lost by barratry of the Seamen.[1] In favor of Meredith & Clymer for 2143 1/3 dlls being value of their ship Peggy taken by the Orpheus man of war as appears by protest.[2] (N.B. This Order was cancelled & another drawn April 18, 1777.)

MS (MH–H).
[1] For additional information on this contract and the condemnation of the sloop *Fanny* in Nova Scotia, see Secret Committee Minutes of Proceedings, May 2, 1776; and Morgan, *Naval Documents*, 5:1121–22, 6:277.
[2] For a contract with Meredith & Clymer for the sloop *Peggy*, see Secret Committee Minutes of Proceedings, June 13, 1776.

Virginia Delegates to a Committee of the Pennsylvania Convention

[September 12, 1776] [1]

The Virginia Delegates have received the proposal for establishing a Temporary Boundary between the States of Virginia and Pennsylvania, and for answer, say, their power is ended; having been expressly limited to the line already proposed to the honorable Convention of the State of Pennsylvania as a temporary boundary.[2]

That they will without delay transmit the proposal of the honorable Committee to the Governor and Council of the Commonwealth of Virginia, in order to its being laid before the General Assembly that meets early in October next; and in the mean time they wish that the influence of both Governments may be exerted to preserve

friendship and peace between the people of both States on the
controverted Boundary.   Signed   Thomas Nelson Jun.

Richard Henry Lee

Francis Lightfoot Lee

Tr (James S. Copley Library, La Jolla, Calif., 1974). In the hand of Richard
Henry Lee.

[1] This date is taken from the minutes of the proceedings of the Pennsylvania
Convention of July–September 1776, where the document was entered with the
business transacted on September 14. See *Am. Archives*, 5th ser. 2:42.

[2] On July 15 the Virginia delegates had transmitted to the Pennsylvania Convention a resolution of the Virginia Convention proposing a temporary boundary
between the two states. For the counterproposal offered by a committee of the
Pennsylvania Convention, to which this memorandum is a reply, see ibid., pp.
41–42. See also Virginia Delegates to the Speaker of the Pennsylvania Convention,
July 15, 1776.

Lewis Morris to Lewis Morris, Jr.

Dear Lewis [1]   Phia Sepr 13 1776
This will be handed you by Mr. Mitchel who goes for N York;
from what I have heard he will meet you on the road. I am so
much taken up in Congress at present about Indian Affairs that I
cannot leave the town and we have only a representation for our
state in congress.[2] I just this moment heard of a number of the
enemys troops being landed on Montrasuers Island.[3] I hope my
Dear Boy you have got every thing Valuable from Morrisania, that
is all the stock and movables. As for the wheat, hay, flax, oats &c
I do not expect it. These are Shocking times. But we shall I make
not the least dou't soon have the French to revenge our Cause and
make these raskals pay four fold. Keep up your Mothers Spirits.
She is a good woman and deserves a better fate. I would write you
more but it is uncertain whether this will be delivered or not.
Therefore shall conclude with wishing a happy Sight of you all.
From your Affe Father,   Lewis Morris

RC (MeHi).

[1] Maj. Lewis Morris, Jr., the delegate's eldest son, served as an aide-de-camp
to Gen. John Sullivan from August 1776 to November 1779. F. B. Heitman, *Historical Register of Officers of the Continental Army* . . . (Washington, D. C.,
1892), p. 301. Letters of September 6 and 11 from the younger Morris to his
father, describing the dangers threatening the family estate of Morrisania, are in
NYHS Collections 8 (1875): 440–44.

[2] Morris was a member of the committee on Indian affairs.

[3] This day Congress received Washington's September 11 letter to Hancock
containing news of the British capture of Montresor's Island "in the Mouth of
Harlem River," close by Morrisania. See *JCC*, 5:755; PCC, item 152, 2:543–46;
and Washington, *Writings* (Fitzpatrick), 6:44–46.

Caesar Rodney to George Read

Dear Sir,   Philadelphia, September 13th. 1776.

The whole of your time must certainly be engaged in the affairs of the Convention or I should have heard from you more frequently. I have wrote you three letters since you went to New Castle, but whether you have received more than one of them I cannot say. However this letter is proof I am not discouraged as yet.

The people here have been, for several days, fully employed in forming conjectures with respect to the conference between the Commissioners of Congress and Lord Howe. They have been various—some Lord Howe has full powers, and if we have not peace it is the fault of Congress—others there is no doubt but they will finally settle matters, and the armies be disbanded—others again are cursed if they believe he has any powers at all. However, this business is put an end to by the return of the Committee, who report that having sent a letter to Lord Howe, by Express, to acquaint him of their coming, they proceeded to Amboy, where they arrived on Tuesday evening, and there, the same evening, received a letter from Lord Howe, in answer to theirs, letting them know that he would meet them, on Wednesday, at a house on Staten Island, opposite Amboy—that his Lordship the next day sent his boat for them, with a flag, and met them himself at the waterside, and in a very polite manner conducted them up to the house, where he had a dinner, and plenty of good wine for them—and that after dinner they had a conference, which, with the time they were dining, was about three hours. Upon the whole it seems his Lordship has no power to make a peace, or even to order a cessation of arms—that he had a power to confer with any person or persons whatsoever to hear what they had to offer, and report to his majesty, but that previous to any thing else we must return to and acknowledge obedience to his majesty. This being done, he did not doubt, on his representing matters home, but that the several acts of parliament and instructions might and would be revised, and many of our greivances removed. The whole proceedings of the Committee, Sullivan's message, and everything relating to it will be published on Monday or Tuesday.[1]

One Mr. Duff, a young man, called on me for a commission as a Doctor's Assistant, in our battalion, of the "flying camp." Should be glad you would let me know immediately when and how he was appointed, and whether he ought to have a commission. They are to march on Tuesday, if possible, and if there be propriety in giving him a commission I could wish he had it, as it would be of great service in case of his being a prisoner.

We have letters, dated in July last, from our Connecticut freind in Paris.[2] There's a change of ministry in France, and he is the greatest man in the world, except Lord North, and has as great a levee as he has. This is a secret.

I don't recollect anything else worth communicating just now except that I am, Sir, your humble servant,

Caesar Rodney

Tr (NN).
  [1] See *JCC*, 5:765–66; and Evans, *Am. Bibliography*, no. 15168.
  [2] That is Silas Deane. Deane's July 30, 1776, covering letter to Robert Morris with several enclosures is in *NYHS Collections* 19 (1886): 143–70.

Secret Committee to the Maryland Council of Safety

Gentn.   Philada. Septr. 13th. 1776

We have been applyed to for a supply of Powder for the Continental Frigate built at Baltimore which shou'd have been ordered down there, but as we understand you have a considerable quantity at that place & as there is some Powder due to the Continent from your State, We request the favour of you to supply Messrs. Wm Lux, Saml Purviance & David Stewart with four Tons & a half of Gun Powder for the use of the said Frigate & for Proving Her Canon &c and hereafter we will repay you in powder the ballance that will then become due to your State or supply you with more Shou'd it become necessary. Your Complyance with this request will save time & charges.[1] It will also oblige the Secret Committee of Congress of which we are a Quorum & We remain, Gentn, Your obedt hble servts,   Robert Morris   B Franklin

Richard Henry Lee   Josiah Bartlett

RC (MHi photostat). Written by Morris and signed by Morris, Bartlett, Franklin, and Lee.
  [1] For the Maryland Council of Safety's reply, see *Md. Archives*, 12:305–6.

William Williams to Joseph Trumbull

Dear Sir   Philadel. Sepr. 13 1776

I recd yours of the 7th. I had wrote you the same day by Mr. Halsey, but about nothing. You will see by the Copys &c gone from the Presidt to you I trust that Congress will not give you up as Commisa for the nothern Department.[1] Many of them greatly resent the Conduct of the Gent. who has so interferd with you & there are appearances of many other things agst him, which begin to work, & will I beleive force his downfall, but things are not fully ripe yet nor can they possibly be attended to now. He had lately written a very long Epistle to inforce the necessity & expedience, the bestness & Cheapness &c of supplying the nothern Army by a Contract with somebody there. It was hastily read thro in the House, & not the lest further notice taken of it. I presume he will not interpose in your departmt. again, tho I know He has paid but little attention to his orders in many things.

We yesterday moved the appointment of a D. Adjt Genl. for that Army, & with no great Difficulty carried the appointmt of your Bror. Jno. to that office. Nothing is added about the rank & Pay, but on motion & Enquiry I found it to be an establishment already made, of a Colo. & there was no need of it. I trust the Prest has forwarded the Comisn. Morgan Lewis was also appointed D. Qr. Masr. Genl for the same Department.

Our Affairs are truly in a critical Situation, but far I hope from desperate. My trust & hope is in a merciful & just God, who with one Volition of his Will can change their appearance. I fear we shall be chastized for our Sins, but not forsaken I trust & firmly believe. But most certainly it becomes all to humble Themselves deeply before Him, repent of our Sins & most earnestly to supplicate his Favor. He will be known in the Judgements he executes. He has a Controversie with His People, & will certainly accomplish his Design in it. We must bend or break.

No Means for our defence & Safety must be omitted & may God grant Our Officers & Soldiers, great Wisdom, understanding, Courage & Resolution. Our Enemies are not invulnerable, & one severe trimming must amazingly dishearten & unnerve them. We have every thing to fight for, that is valuable & good. They have nothing but their pay & to establish the greatest of political & moral Evil. They cannot, will not be always prospered. Every thing shod be done, & doubless is, to inspire the Men with the greatest Intrepidity & by all acco They f'ot bravely on L. Island.

The Enemy doubtless intend to surround you, & I see not why they cant go beyond you, go as far as you will, & attempt to cut off your Supplies.

Our Officers are far more acquainted with their movements & Intentions than I & will doubtless take the best Measures. We just hear They are possessd of Montorzour or &c Island, against Harlem. I have no Doubt Congress will reward their Services.

Are now busie in planing &c for forming a new & permanent Army. Will 20 dols. bounty & 100 acres of Land at the Close sufficiently operate upon N Engld. Men to engage for 5 years. Tho I pretend not to say such a thing will be carried if attempted, indeed I much fear it, but I wish I had the best opinions &c &c about it, soon as possible.

I am dear Sir with undissembled & strong Affection, your Friend & Bror,   Wm. Williams

[*P.S.*] I am grieved & confounded at the Conduct of some of our Militia & ———. Have found the same Accos are given in other Letters, but They add they have enow left to fight &c.

Mr Huntington has several Times expresd his Wonder that you have wholly done writing him, that he continued a Correspondence with you whenever he had anything worth communicating. I really think it might be well, & that He is truly Friendly to You & He has weight in Congress, & ever on the right side. His Passions are not, nor can be warm.

I have excused it by yr exceeding hurry of Business &c.

RC (CtHi).
[1] See Elbridge Gerry to Joseph Trumbull, September 12, note 2; and John Hancock to Joseph Trumbull, September 16, 1776.

William Williams to Joseph Trumbull

Dr Sir   Sepr 13. P.M. [1776]
Since writing my Letter, I found at the House unexpectedly that our Comtee were last night returned from their interview with Lord Howe. The sum & substance of their Report is, that having sent a previous message to him he agreed to receive Them on Staten Island at a house opposite Amboy. He accordingly sent over a Barge Wednisd. morning. They went in without Ceremony. H. met Them on their Landing, complimented them on the Honor they did by their unlimited Confidence that they placed in Him, by puting Themselves so intirely in his Power &c, waited on Them to the House, entertained them most politely, & with a cold Collation &c introduced the Subject by informing Them how He first came to give his Attention to this American Dispute, viz the passing the Boston Port Bill awakened & alarmed his grateful remembrance & attention to that Town & Province which had been impressed on Him from the high Respect & Honor They had done his Brother &c & from that Time he attended to the American Affairs &c.

He was urged to come over, had an ardent Desire to Settle the Controversie amicably &c.

Being asked if He had Powers to settle it, He owned He had no other than to confer with Congress Members, but not as such, or any other Gent. whom they called Rebels (This it seems took him his two months to obtain) & to move & urge Them to their Duty &c & to declare them in the Kings Peace. He had no power to treat with Them as Members of Congress, & no Terms or Proposals to make to any, without a full return to their Alleigance as an indispensible Preliminary. When that shod be come into his Majesty wod certainly cause the greivous Acts of Parliament to be revised

& if it shod appear just & fit, his Majesty wod obtain such reasonable Relaxation as He shod think just and right, or to that purpose. This is the substance as I can recollect. So that on the whole He appears to have no kind of Power but what is contained in the Act of Parliamt. save on[l]y a Libery of personal Conference with the Rebels as well as the Friends of Governmt.

This is what was expected by almost every one who were for sending them. Indeed there is less daubing & Pretentions of Power, & much less plausible pretentions & assurances of relaxation & generous fair Treatment &c &c than was expected. He says Genl Sullivan mistook him, in saying he offerd that Parliament wod give up the Idea of Taxation & governg. our internal Police &c.

Thus, it is conceived one great point is gained, is to strike the Torys dumb, or rather to defeat & kill the impressions they were makeing & wod have made on many Friendly but credulous Minds by their confident & undaunted assertions, that Ld H. was vested with full & ample Powers to Settle the Controversie on the most equitable Terms & Such as wod give perfect Satisfaction to all America except the turbulent & haughty, who wishd to continue the War, for their own Honor & Emolument, & was disposed & ardently desirous to do so.

His Ld. Ship expresd his great Pain & Regret for the unhappy Consequences to America of their refusal to submit &c & was told America wod use great Endeavours to save those Consequences safe & save him that Pain.

The whole affair will I trust be published, in a few days. The Comte desired till Monday to draw up & lay in their Report in Writing.[1] I have wrote our Govr. all but this Result.[2] I wish you cod immediately sent him this or a Copy of it, as I can not write him now, & fear my Letters may miscarry. Your Friend &c

RC (CtHi).
[1] See *JCC*, 5:755, 765–66.
[2] Not found.

John Adams to Abigail Adams

Philadelphia Saturday Septr. 14. 1776
Yesterday Morning I returned with Dr. F. and Mr. R. from Staten Island where We met L[ord] H[owe] and had about three Hours Conversation with him. The Result of this Interview, will do no disservice to Us. It is now plain that his L[ordshi]p has no Power, but what is given him in the Act of P[arliament]. His Commission authorises him to grant Pardons upon Submission, and to converse, confer, consult and advise with such Persons as he may

think proper, upon American Grievances, upon the Instructions to Governors and the Acts of Parliament, and if any Errors should be found to have crept in, his Majesty and the Ministry were willing they should be rectified.

I found yours of 31 of Aug. and 2d of September. I now congratulate you on your Return home with the Children. Am sorry to find you anxious on Account of idle Reports. Dont regard them. I think our Friends are to blame to mention such silly Stories to you. What good do they expect to do by it?

My Ride has been of Service to me. We were absent but four days. It was an agreable Excursion. His L[ordshi]p is about fifty Years of Age. He is a well bred Man, but his Address is not so irresistable, as it has been represented. I could name you many Americans, in your own Neighbourhood, whose Art, Address, and Abilities are greatly superiour. His head is rather confused, I think.

When I shall return I cant say. I expect now, every day, fresh Hands from Watertown.

RC (MHi). Adams, *Family Correspondence* (Butterfield), 2:124.

John Adams to Samuel Adams

Septr. 14. 1776 [1]

In a few Lines of the 8th instant, I promised you, a more particular account of the Conference.[2] On Monday the Comtee. sett off from Philadelphia, and reached Brunswick on Tuesday night. Wednesday Morning proceeded to Amboy, and from thence to Staten Island where they met the Lord Howe, by whom they were politely received and entertained. His Ldship opened the Conference, by giving Us, an account of the Motive which first induced him to attend to the dispute with America, which he Said was the Honour which had been done to his Family, by the Massachusetts Bay, which he prized very highly, from whence I concluded in my own Mind, that his Lordship had not attended to the Controversy earlier than the Port Bill and Charter Bill, and consequently must have a very inadequate Idea of the Nature, as well as of the Rise and Progress of the Contest.

His Lordship then observed that he had requested this Interview that he might Satisfy himself, whether there was any Probability, that America would return to her Allegiance: but he must observe to Us, that he could not acknowledge Us as Members of Congress, or a Commitee of that Body, but that he only desired this Conversation with us, as private Gentlemen, in hopes that it might prepare the Way, for the Peoples returning to their Allegiance and to an Accommodation of the Disputes between the two Countries. That he had no Power to treat with us, as independent States, or in any other Character, than as British Subjects and private Gentlemen. But that upon our acknowledging ourselves to be British subjects, he had Power to *consult* with Us.

That the Act of Parliament had given Power to the King, upon certain Conditions, of declaring the Colonies to be at Peace, and his Commission gave him Power to *confer, advise* and *consult* with any Number or description of Persons concerning the Complaints of the People in America. That the King and Ministry had very good dispositions to redress the grievances of the People and reform the Errors of Administration in America. That his Commission gave him Power to converse with any Persons whatever in America, concerning the former Instructions to Governors, and the Acts of Parliament complained of. That the King and Ministry were very willing to have all these revised and reconsidered, and if any Errors had crept in, if they could be pointed out, were very willing they should be rectified.

Mr R[utledge] mentioned to his Lordship, what G[eneral] Sullivan had said, that his Lordship told him he would set the Act of Parliament wholly aside, and that Parliament had no Right to tax America, or meddle with her internal Polity. His Lordship answered Mr R. that G. Sullivan had misunderstood him, and extended his Words much beyond their Import.

His Lordship gave us, a long account of his Negociations, in order to obtain Powers Sufficiently ample for his purpose. He said, He told them (the Ministry I suppose he meant) that those Persons whom you call Rebells, are the most proper to confer with of any, because they are the Persons who complain of Grievances. The others, those who are not in Arms and are not according to your Ideas in Rebellion, have no Complaints or Grievances. They are Satisfied, and therefore it would be to no Purpose to converse with them. So that his Lordship said He would not accept the Command, or Commission untill he had full Power to confer with any Persons whom he should think proper, who had the most abilities and Influences. But having obtained these Powers, he intended to have gone directly to Philadelphia, not to have treated with Congress as such, or to have acknowledged that Body, but to have consulted with Gentlemen of that Body in their private Capacities, upon the subject in his Commission.

His Lordship did not incline to give us any further account of his Powers, or to make any other Propositions to us, in one Capacity or another, than those which are contained in substance in the foregoing Lines.

I have the Pleasure to assure you that there was no disagreement in opinion among the Members of the Committee upon any one Point. They were perfectly united in Sentiment and Language, as they are in the Result of the whole, which is that his Lordships Powers are fully expressed in the act of Parliament, and that his Commission contains no other Authority than that of granting Pardons, with such Exceptions as the Commissioners shall think proper to make, and of declaring America, or any Part of it, to be at Peace, upon Submission, and of enquiring into the State of America, of any Persons with whom they might think proper to confer, advise, converse, and consult, even although they should be officers of the Army or Members of Congress, and then representing the Result of their Enquiries to the Ministry, who, after all, might or might not, at their pleasure, make any alterations in the former Instructions to Governors, or propose in Parliament any alteration in the acts complained of.

The whole affair of the Commission appears to me, as it ever did, to be a Bubble, an Ambuscade, a mere insidious Manœuvre, calculated only to decoy and deceive, and it is so gross, that they must have a wretched opinion of our Generalship to Suppose that we can fall into it.

The Committee assured his Lordship, that they had no authority to wait upon him, or to treat, or converse with him, in any other Character but that of a Committee of Congress, and as Members of independent states. That the Vote which was their Commission, clearly ascertained their character. That the Declaration which had been made of Independence was the Result of long and cool deliberation. That it was made by Congress after long and great Reluctance, in obedience to the positive Instructions of their Constituents, every assembly upon the Continent having instructed their Delegates to this Purpose, and since the Declaration has been made and published, it has been solemnly ratified and confirmed by the assemblies, so that neither this Committee nor that Congress which sent it here, have authority to treat in any other Character than as independent States. One of the Comte., Dr. F. assured his Lordship that in his private opinion America would not again come under the domination of G.B. and therefore it was the duty of every good Man, on both sides the water, to promote Peace, and an acknowledgment of American Independence, and a Treaty of Friendship and alliance between the two Countries. Another of the Comtee., Mr. J. A., assured his Lordship that in his private opinion America would never treat in any other Character than as independent States. The other Member, Mr. R., concurred in the same opinion. His Lordship said he had no powers nor instructions upon that subject; it was entirely new. Mr. R. observed to his Lordship that most of the Colonies had Submitted for two years to live without Government, and to all the Inconveniences of Anarchy, in hopes of Reconciliation, but now had instituted Governments. Mr. J. A. observed that all the Colonies had gone compleatly through a Revolution. That they had taken all authority from the officers of the Crown, and had appointed officers of their own, which his Lordship might easily conceive had cost great Struggles, and that they could not easily go back; and that Americans had too much understanding not to know that after such a declaration as they had made, the Government of G.B. never would have any Confidence in them, or could govern them again but by force of Arms.

RC (NN). In Adams' hand, though not signed.

[1] Edmund C. Burnett, who took this letter from Charles Francis Adams' edition of *The Works of John Adams*, also reprinted it under the date September 17, 1776, which Charles Francis had erroneously assigned to it. Burnett, *Letters*, 2:91–93.

[2] For another eyewitness account, see Henry Strachey's Notes on Lord Howe's Meeting with a Committee of Congress, September 11, 1776.

Josiah Bartlett to William Whipple

Dear Sir,   Philadelphia, Septr. [14?] 1776 [1]

I have not rec'd a line from you since your's of the 20th ulto. from Milford. I have wrote to you every week since you left this City, which I hope are come safe to your hand, But shall not write you after this, as I expect you will be on your return here by the time you receive this, or soon after. I hope our Legislature has appointed another Delegate to return with you that I may return home immediately on your arrival and try whether a change of air will be serviceable to my health, which is very much altered since you left me, tho' I am now rather better than I was last week. I shall be under some difficulty about procuring a horse and waiter to attend me on my return unless you and your colleague will agree to deliver up one of your's to me for that purpose on your arrival, and keep but one to wait on you both here. If you shall not agree to that, I have wrote to Mrs. Bartlett to procure (if she can) a man and horse, and send with you here, to accompany me back, as I think it will be much cheaper & better than to hire here. Pray inform Mrs. Bartlett of your determination that she may know what to do.

Last Wednesday our Committee met Lord Howe on Staten Island where they eat and drank together; he treated them with free civility & politeness, and after about 3 hours conversation they took their leave of each other. His Lordship's conversation was full of his friendship for America particularly the town of Boston for their respect to the memory of his brother. He said that the ravaging and destroying America would give him great pain and uneasiness. Dr. Franklin replied that *we* should take proper and he hoped effective care to prevent his Lordship's feelings on that account.

On the whole all the terms he had to propose was that we first of all lay down our arms and return to our alligiance, and then he said the King and Parliament would consider the acts we formally complained of, and if they judged it proper would alter or amend them. They told him that General Sullivan said, that his Lordship in conversation told him that the King and Parliament would give up the right of taxation and of intermeddleing with the internal police of the Colonies and desired to know what authority he had to say it. Lord Howe replied that Gen. Sullivan must certainly have misunderstood him, as he had no right to say any such thing, nor did he believe the Parliament would give up those claims. The Committee are about to publish the whole affair, which I hope will stop the mouths of the weak and credulous who have had great hope of peace from the supposed great powers intrusted with Lord Howe as a Commissioner for that purpose.[2]

Capt. Weeks in the Reprisal is returned from Martinico which he left the 26th ulto.; he has brought 4 or 500 muskets, some powder, &c., &c. The affair of the Reprisal and the Shark man of war in the Harbor of St. Piers in Martinico, occasioned the British Admiral Young to send to the French General, informing him that the Capt. of the Shark would have taken the pirate ship commanded by Capt. Weeks if it had not been for the French forts protecting him, and he in the name of his Brittanic Majesty demanded that she should be forthwith seized and delivered up into his hands, or otherwise his protecting not only the trading ships of rebels, but their ships of war would be deemed a breach of the peace between the two nations, and that on his refusal he should immediately send a man of war to acquaint his Britannic Majesty of the circumstances, &c., &c.

The French General in answer told Admiral Young that he had been misinformed concerning the affair, that the forts did not interfere, but that the Shark, after engaging the American vessel for some time, thought proper to quit her and shear off, and that the forts did not fire on the Shark till after she had quitted the Reprisal and was attempting, as they suspected, to seize an unarmed vessel that was then within reach of their cannon; that Capt. Weeks has put himself under his most Christian Majesty's protection, and that he should not deliver him up, or suffer him to be injured while there. That if the Admiral had been well acquainted with him (the General) he would never have made such a demand of him, that he should immediately send an account of the affair to the King his Master to whom alone he was answerable for his conduct, &c., &c. This is the substance as near as I can remember. I have seen authentic copies of both.

The affair of the confederation rests at present. The Committee of the whole, have agreed that ninety regiments shall be enlisted for five years if not sooner discharged by Congress; the affair of bounty is not yet settled; the proposal of giving lands as a part of the bounty has boggled us, however it will be got over in a few days I believe, and sent forward. The great difficulty of raising men for so long a period made me think it my duty to prevent more being required of our State, than their just proportion by numbers, and by producing the return of our number of inhabitants. I have got the proportion to be fixed at 3 instead of 4 regiments for our State to see raised and completed for that term.[3]

Mr. Wythe is come to Congress.[4]

My very poor state of health makes it uncertain whether I may not be obliged to leave Congress before your return; if it should happen so, I should be very glad to meet you on the road and would therefore propose your coming the upper road to Hartford if you can conveniently. I am Sir, your friend and most humble Servant,   Josiah Bartlett.

Tr (DLC).
[1] This letter was probably written shortly after the arrival of Capt. Lambert Wickes off Philadelphia on September 13 and before Bartlett's September 16 letters to his wife Mary and to John Langdon. Morgan, *Naval Documents*, 6:824. Bartlett's comments on formal actions of Congress which occurred after the date of this letter were probably based on decisions made by Congress in the committee of the whole.
[2] See *JCC*, 5:765–66.
[3] See Bartlett to Whipple, September 10, 1776, note.
[4] Wythe apparently had just arrived in Philadelphia. Although the credentials of the Virginia delegates were presented to Congress on August 28, Wythe did not sign the September 12 letter of the Virginia delegates to a committee of the Pennsylvania Convention. *JCC*, 5:712.

William Ellery to Nicholas Cooke

Sir,   Philadelphia Sept. 14th 1776

Agreeably to the Resolution of the State of Rhode Island &c. My Colleague and I made Application to Congress, and received an Order on the Treasury for One hundred and twenty thousand Dollars.[1] Out of that Sum I have received Seven hundred Dollars, partly to procure &c a Monument for the late Honble Samuel Ward Esqr., and partly for my own Use; for the whole of which I promised to be responsible to said State. I should not have taken any of the Money to my own Use could I have been supplied from Home without Risque; but as the Chance of a Loss may soon be great, and indeed the Communication by the North River may be intercepted, and it will make no great Difference to the State whether two hundred Dollars are advanced to One of their Delegates or not I hope my Conduct in this Instance will not be blamed.

By a Resolve of Congress there is ordered a Paymaster for each Battalion in the Continental Service.[2] I know not whom to recommend as Paymaster to the Battalion ordered to New York: Nor do I know whom to recommend as Surgeon to it. I shall recommend a Paymaster and Surgeon for the Battalion that shall remain at Newport when it shall be known which of the Battalions hath march'd to N. York. At present it is to me uncertain; for the President first required the Commanding Officer to order One of the Battalions to N. York, and afterwards, when it was known that the Field Officers were not commissionated, they were ordered by Congress to be commissionated, agreeable to the Recommendation of the Assembly, and the Second, Col. Lippit's, Battalion is ordered to march to N. York provided the first should not have marched before the Arrival of the last Direction of Congress.[3]

I should be glad to know when the Battalions and Artillery Company raised in our Colony were inlisted and for what Time; and what the whole Number of our Militia was before the War commenced: And also the Number of white, black, and Indian Inhabitants of our State.

I hope the Genl. Assembly will not neglect to appoint an additional Delegate at their first Session after the Receipt of this. The Reasons for such an Appointment I suggested in a private Letter to your Honour and have not Time now to mention to them.[4] Indeed so many, so obvious and so cogent are they, that they will readily offer themselves to every Member and induce them to come into this necessary Measure. I could wish that a certain Sum by the Day might be speedily fixed upon for the Delegates of our State; for it is very troublesome and disagreeable to keep an Account of every Expence which accrues, and a lumping Account I imagine would not be satisfactory to the Assembly.

A considerable Number of the Enemy have landed at Montrozer's Island, which lies at the Mouth of Harlem River, and it is supposed that they mean to land at Harlem or Maurisania or both.

Capt.——— Weeks in a Continental armed Ship hath arrived here from Martinico and imported Two Tons of Powder and four hundred and fifty small Arms and some coarse Goods.

The Northern Army is so respectable that we are not afraid of Irruption into our States by the Lakes, and I hope We shall be able to maintain our Posts at and near New York, if Genl. Washington should think proper to keep any Troops in that City.

I heartily congratulate our State upon the Success of our Privateers,[5] and wishing that I may have the Pleasure of congratulating them very soon upon a Victory over our haughty implacable Enemies I continue to be with great Respect, Yr Honor's most Obedient, Humble Servant,   W Ellery

RC (R–Ar).

¹ On this point, see Rhode Island Delegates to Nicholas Cooke, August 17, 1776, note 5.

² Passed on June 25, 1776. See *JCC*, 5:479.

³ See *JCC*, 5:472. Congress chose the field officers for these two Rhode Island battalions in accordance with the recommendations made by Governor Cooke in his August 27 letter to the Rhode Island delegates. See William R. Staples, *Rhode Island in the Continental Congress, 1765–1790* (Providence: Providence Press Co., 1870), p. 82.

⁴ See Ellery to Nicholas Cooke, September 7, 1776.

⁵ On this point, see Cooke's August 13 letter to the Rhode Island delegates in Staples, *Rhode Island in the Continental Congress*, pp. 81–82.

Arthur Middleton to William Henry Drayton

Dear Drayton   Philadelphia Septemr. 14th. 1776.

This comes to you by Sea; an Oppertunity I have just heard of, & tho' it is doubtfull whether it will ever reach you, I cannot avoid making the Attempt meerly to acknowledge the receipt of your Two favours (by the Express) of the 11th & 15th of the last month; I most heartily thank you for the Contents, & will endeavour not to be behind hand with so excellent a Correspondent, tho' I must confess to you I am so much taken up with matters of one kind or other, that I cannot promise much; I will however endeavour now & then to work double Tides & let you hear from me. Every Article in your's shall have it's proper weight, with me, & you may depend upon it, that every thing that can be done shall be done by me (which God knows is very little) for I trust, & I think I need not tell you so, I have the good of my Country at heart, & only lament that it is not in my power to render her that Service I could wish & she deserves.

You must only look upon this as a Line by accident, I hope to have an Opporty. by Land in a few days, & will particularize. Between you & I, the General seems to be an odd fish & I am glad you are about to get rid of him. The moment I heard of the Augustine Business, I set it down as a whimsical affair, if not a sacrifice, I pray God it may prove neither. The predatory intention is to me shocking. We should carefully avoid debauching the minds of that Class of people; instead of that noble Spirit which should animate the Soldiers of a free State, let us beware of encouraging a Spirit of a different Kind & of converting them into a Band of robbers egg'd on by avaricious Views; when that is the Case, adieu to all Liberty, peace, & happiness.¹ I bewail from my heart the fate of that poor fellow Salvador; what I feel for him gives me some Idea of what I must experience, should any dear Connection, or intimate Friend receive an untimely stroke; the Time seems to be approaching when many of those strokes must be suffer'd, it therefore behoves us my Friend to prepare for them, & we cannot do it better than by putting our Trust in the Allmighty, & endeavouring to deserve well in our several Stations. Thomson's Rank has been this day given him.[2]

I have great hopes that the Indian Expedition will turn out much to our advantage; especially if N C & Virginia cooperate *properly* of which I cannot help doubting. Our Country has lately supplied us here with great & agreeable news; I dare not flatter you with hopes of having any from this Quarter, at least I see no prospect of it just now; we must do our best, & hope for the best. I should rejoice that the winter is near, were I not apprehensive the Enemy would return to you with that favourable Season. You must be sensible of that probability, & I rely upon the wisdom, diligence & Spirit of my Countrymen, & trust they will arm themselves at all points for the reception of them; we will strive to get you all possible aid, but let me entreat you to put most dependance upon yourselves, for it is with a mixture of pleasure & of grief that I tell you there are none like to yourselves. Above all things for God's sake take care, let the Expence or Labour be what it may, to obstruct all the Channels up to your Town, & compell the men of war to lie before the Forts, & aim at silenceing them, if they will attack you. This, & this alone, can in my opinion save you. A large reinforcement of men, except such as you can get from N Carolina, you must not Expect; *stationary* armies from these northern parts, for (Intre nous, they will not *stand*) are not to be had. O my Friend, if you did but know what I daily suffer you would heartily pity me! I hope I shall be indulged with leave to come home as soon as my Time is out. I sigh for it daily; I envy Heyward, who set out the 5th Instant; I look upon myself as an Exile & my only Consolation is that I am obeying the orders of my Country, & when I cease to be obedient I shall no longer deserve Life. Bad News travels fast. You will have heard that we have retreated from Long Island, & are only Tenants at sufferance of N York, which must be shortly abandon'd. Our Troops got into a Scrape, we have lost all together near 1000 (mostly prisoners) it is *said* the Enemy had 500 kill'd. We want *Generals,* we want *Soldiers*—militia will not do. We are now endeavourg to new modell & increase the army. Congress have sent to know what *powers* Ld. Howe has—answer he has *none*—we must fight it out. I am far from *despairing;* our *workmen* are indifferent, our *materials* indifferent, but our Cause is good, & we must in the *End* be victorious, tho' not without *rubs.* Make what you can out of this, & expect more from me very soon. Remember me affectionately to all & believe me till Death, affectly your's.

[*P.S.*] The Committee of Congress went as repres[entative]s of *free & Independt.* States. C.C.P. will give you the partic[ular]s; he has them from E.R.[3]

RC (NjR: Elsie O. and Philip D. Sang deposit). In Middleton's hand, though not signed.
    [1] For a brief account of Gen. Charles Lee's projected expedition against St. Augustine, see John R. Alden, *General Charles Lee: Traitor or Patriot?* (Baton Rouge: Louisiana State University Press, 1951), pp. 131–32. Concerning Congress' decision to recall Lee to Philadelphia for consultation, see John Hancock to Charles Lee, August 8, 1776.
    [2] On this point, see *JCC*, 5:461–62, 760.
    [3] Apparently a reference to a letter from Edward Rutledge to Charles Cotesworth Pinckney which has not been found.

Benjamin Rush to Julia Rush

My dear Julia,   Philada. Septemr. 14. 1776.

Our commissioners returned yesterday, After having Spent 3 hours with Lord Howe. They reported to Congress that the whole of his Lordship's powers extended no further than to confer with people of influence in America upon the Subject of our greivances, and if it should appear that any *material* errors had crept into the instructions given to Governors, or into the American Acts of parliament, the King & his ministers promise to use their influence with parliament to have them *Altered*. But he added further that he had no power to make even such a proposition to the colonies Untill they first returned to their Allegiance. In the course of the interview many clever things were said on both sides. When his Lordship asked in what capacity he was to receive them, Mr. Adams said "in any capacity your Lordship pleases except in that of *british Subjects*." His Lordship said that nothing would mortify him more than to witness the fall of America, and that he would weep for her as for a brother. "I hope (said Dr Franklin) your Lordship will be saved that mortification. America is able to take care of herself."

Adeiu my dear girl. My extreme hurry continues. I was called up and obliged to go out last night. I am just now sent for to visit a family four miles in the country. What shall I do for horse—carriage—and William? Betsey is hunting a barbar. My prentices are as irregular in their attendance upon the shop as ever. What a pretty figure will a life of 40 or 50 years with a fine agreeable wife spent in this manner make in the history of a man? Oh! dear! The Romans educated slaves only to the profession of physic for 600 years. A wise nation! and a most suitable employment for slaves!

Much love to everybody. Yours—yours,   B Rush

P.S. I borrowed Mr Walton's carriage to go into the country, but was obliged to wait three hours for it beyond the time I expected it. Judge how I felt! Nothing new since morning.

RC (CtY).

Willing, Morris & Co. to William Bingham

Philada. Septr. 14th. 1776. "Your several favours of the 2d, 15th & 26th August have come duely to hand. . . . The observations you make on the different modes of Conducting a Commerce between Europe & this Continent through the Islands of Martinico & St Lucia are very proper. They are what have frequently occurred to us, but do not remove the only difficulty we have to encounter, which is the establishing proper Funds in Europe as a foundation to Trade on. Our Produce is bulky & little value in it requires large Ships for the Transportation, large Ships are much exposed to Capture and indeed we have not many of them left, so that you see us encircled with difficultys in this respect. For this reason, & for this reason chiefly we like the Idea of your agreeing with some Good French House in the Island to Import certain quantitys of Goods as for his own Account to be delivered over to you on arrival at a Certain advance." Discusses several options Bingham can consider in planning future transactions.

"You will doubtless have learned that West India property is now liable to Confiscation as well as British, Consequently your plan in that respect will not do. So long as the French remain in Peace it is probable that French Papers may prove the best Cover, especially in your Seas."

"Mr. John Ross of this City is now in Europe and will ship out Goods by various ways for us, our Thos. Morris is with Mr Deane at Paris; they may probably do the same. We depend on Your care in forwarding & receiving any Goods that may come for us." [1]

RC (DLC). In the hand of Robert Morris.

[1] For the complete text of this lengthy letter, see Morgan, *Naval Documents,* 6:824–28. Robert Morris, writing in behalf of his firm and discussing a wide range of commercial topics in which they were jointly interested, directed several letters to Bingham during the fall of 1776. His letters of September 24, 27, and October 20 can also be consulted in the *Naval Documents,* 6:977, 1026–27, 1337–39. In addition, there are similar, unpublished letters to Bingham of November 8 and December 3 and 6, as well as one to Richard Harrison and Bingham of November 7, 1776, in the collections of Morris Papers and Bingham Papers at DLC.

Another letter written by Morris during this period in behalf of Willing, Morris & Co., illustrating the scale of operations in which he continued to be involved while serving in Congress and carrying a heavy load as a member of the Committee of Secret Correspondence, Marine Committee, and Secret Committee, is that of September 30, 1776, to the Maryland Council of Safety, ibid., p. 1070.

James Wilson to John Montgomery and Jasper Yates

Dear Gentlemen   Woodstock 14th September 1776

Your interesting Dispatches by Mr. Girty have been received, and been attended to by the Committee for Indian Affairs, and by Congress. The Result you will learn by the Resolutions transmitted to you by Mr. Boyd.[1] What the Convention has done or proposes to do I cannot yet inform you of; but presume they will give every Assistance in their Power.[2] The Congress, you will observe, have strengthened your Hands as far as they could by Ammunition and the Regiment in their Service. I think it peculiarly fortunate that you are at Pittsburgh in this very critical Season.

It is probable that you have heard before this Time of the Action on Long Island and of the Retreat of our Troops from it. There was certainly a Defect somewhere with Regard to Vigilance. Had a proper Look-out been kept, it is impossible that eleven thousand of the Enemy could have got between our Troops engaged and the Lines, without being discovered before they could have cut off their Retreat. Our Men, in general, behaved with remarkable Spirit. We have lost a great Number, that were made Prisoners. But the Loss of the Enemy in killed and wounded is, according to all Accounts, superior to ours. The Hessians, it is said, behaved with great Inhumanity. They even knocked on the Head the Men that were lying wounded on the Field of Battle.

After the Action, the Retreat from the Island became, I believe, absolutely necessary. It was performed in a very masterly Manner, and without any Loss. Even the Field Officers in our own Camp did not know what was the Design of the Movements. Col. Shee's and Col. Magaw's Regiments covered the Retreat; and were for half an Hour, the only Troops on the Island, with above twenty thousand of the Enemy within a very short Distance of them. By the Possession of Long Island, Genl Howe has gained the important Advantage of being able now to supply his Troops with fresh Provisions.

All the late Movements on the Side of the Enemy indicate an Intention to surround the Island, on which the City of New York stands, and hem in our Army upon it. Should they accomplish this Design, the Consequences must be very disagreeable to us. General Washington must either surrender, or fight at a Disadvantage; and with inferior Numbers. But I hope they will not succeed in their Views; for I have the best Reason to believe that General Washington has, before this Time, retired above Kingsbridge, and I expect to hear the Accounts of it every Hour. Inconveniences will, without Doubt, always attend a retreating Army; but amidst surrounding Difficulties it is Prudence to make Choice of the least. A Retreat may have a Tendency to dispirit our Troops, and may prevent our acquiring that brilliant Figure, which a State would always wish to support in the Opinion of the World. But Fabius became glorious cunctando. A Defeat, in our present Situation, would produce the most disastrous Effects. We have Men enough to recruit an Army; but Arms and Ammunition and Artillery and other military Stores, which would be lost in an unsuccessful Engagement, we could not, by any Means, replace during the present Campaign. By Delay the Enemy will suffer more than we shall.

Our Affairs in the Northern Army begin to wear a very smiling Aspect.[3] Our Army at Ticonderoga is numerous, in high Spirits, and in good Order. Our Naval Force on Lake Champlain is very respectable, and much superior to that of the Enemy.

I wish I could say that the Militia of this State, who have marched into New Jersey, have conducted themselves unexceptionably in every Respect. They have not, on any Occasion, discovered Want of Spirit, as far as I have been able to learn both at the Camp, and since I left it. But it has been impossible to introduce any Kind of regular Discipline among them. A Number of them, particularly those from Philadelphia, shewed an intemperate Desire of returning Home. However, they gain much by a Comparison with those from some other States. Two thirds of the Militia of Connecticut, though they came much later into the Field than ours, have already run Home without the General's Leave.

Our Convention is still sitting. What they have been about during Part of their Session, and what their Spirit is, will, in some Measure, appear to you from their Plan of government published for Consideration. This and the News papers Mr Boyd will carry up to you.

The Germans, particularly in Berks County, are becoming totally unreasonable and ungovernable. They are jealous and violent to the last Degree. Mr Yeates's Brother in Law Major Burd commanded a Detachment of the flying Camp, furnished from Reading and the Neighbourhood, in the late Action on Long Island. He behaved with great Propriety and Spirit, and has gained much Honour. But, with other brave Men, was obliged to surrender himself and his Party Prisoners of War. What do you think the People in Reading have said of the Matter? That he was an Englishman, and sold to the Enemy the Men under his Command. The Rewards that the best of Services sometimes receive! I am told the Women in Reading have entered into a Confederacy against high Caps as infallible Evidences of Toryism.

Lord Howe, about ten Days ago, sent a verbal Message to Congress by General Sullivan, who was made a Prisoner on Long Island, desiring a Conference with some of its Members in their private Characters, and that he would meet them in his. This Message occasioned much Speculation. His Lordship said he had ample Powers, and he professed the strongest Inclination to accomodate the Differences between Great Britain and the Colonies. Some regarded this Message as an Artifice to draw the Congress into a dangerous Train of Negociations, divert the Attention of the Troops and the public from the War, and turn it upon delusive Prospects of Peace. They therefore thought it highly improper to consent to a Conference. Others thought it an Artifice of a different Kind; and that Lord Howe, by the Earnestness which he professed for an Accomodation, meant if a Conference should not be agreed to by Congress, to throw the Odium of Continuing the War upon their Shoulders, and remove it from those of his Masters. They were of Opinion that, by consenting to a Conference, his Lordships own Battery would be turned upon himself; for that it would be found, upon Enquiry, that instead of having ample Powers, he had no Power to grant any Conditions of a Peace. The Congress agreed to a Conference, but could not, with any Propriety, send their Members in a private Character. Dr Franklin, Mr John Adams and Mr Rutledge were the Members chosen. They had a Conversation with Lord Howe; and the Result justifies the Opinion of those, who were in Favour of it. The Particulars I will transmit to you by the next Opportunity. It is enough at present to observe, that the Commissioners, as far as we can learn, have no Power to offer any Terms whatever. It extends only to confering, consulting and receiving Submissions.

This Letter has already bored you: I will conclude it after mentioning a Matter respecting Mr. Devereux Smith. You know his Merits and his Sufferings. The Gentlemen who are from Virginia will surely not be unwilling to give their Consent to his Removal to any Place more agreeable to him than Pittsburgh is. You will be good enough to make the Application to them. I would make it in Congress; but think better if it can be done in this Way. I would write to Mr Smith; but have no more Paper here. Make my Compliments to him; and to all the other Gentlemen, my Friends, that are with you. I am, Dear Gentlemen, Yours very sincerely,

James Wilson

RC (DLC).

[1] For Congress' resolutions of September 12, 1776, which were apparently sent by John Boyd, paymaster of Col. Aeneas Mackay's battalion raised for the defense of the western frontiers, see *JCC*, 5:752.

[2] For action taken by the Pennsylvania Convention on September 19 and 20 in response to information received from Montgomery and Yeates on the danger of Indian war in the region of Fort Pitt, see *Am. Archives*, 5th ser. 2:46–47.

[3] Wilson had written to Montgomery the week before to reassure him that despite the misfortunes suffered by the army in Canada there was no reason to fear for the safety of Montgomery's son, who had been with the Sixth Pennsylvania Battalion. Wilson to John Montgomery, September 7, 1776, Montgomery Papers. ICHi.

Francis Lightfoot Lee to Landon Carter

My dear Col.   Philadelphia Sepr. 15. 1776

I acknowledge myself greatly indebted to your goodness, for which, tho' I despair of ever making full returns, yet I shall endeavour to show my gratitude by such partial payments, as my time & abilities will admit of.

I cannot think the apprehensions of our Council, without foundation; for whether the Enemy is successfull or not at N. York, there is reason to believe they will make some attempt upon some of the southern states and we know that our people, upon the least removal of danger, are too apt to relapse into supineness & inattention. We find from experience that regulars only can effectually be opposed to the British troops; therefore we are collecting our regular batallions to resist the efforts of the Enemy at N. York and if any sudden attack shou'd be made upon any state, we must depend upon the Militia to impede their progress, untill they can be opposed by some regular troops.

The Militia is not only ineffectual, but beyond measure expensive. Such a number of regulars will therefore be raised for the next campaign, that we shall not have recourse to the militia, but upon extraordinary occasions. Six new Regiments will be raised in Virginia.

You have no doubt, before this, been inform'd that our Generals upon finding Long Island not tenable, have quitted it, after a smart engagement between a party of between 2 & 3000 of our men, & the greater part of the Enemy's Army in which tho we were outgeneral'd, yet the troops behaved so exceedingly well, that Howe has been very cautious in all his movements since. All of which indicate his intention of geting upon the back of our Army, & with their shiping on the front & each side cut off all communication with the Country, in which case we must either fight to a disadvantage or surrender for want of provisions. Our Genl. is taking measures to prevent this; for which purpose the City of N. York, must be evacuated; which is by no means tenable, if the Enemy chuse to direct their efforts agst. it. As the Court of G.B. has ever accompanied Violence with deception, Ld Howe their agent since his arrival, has constantly endeavour'd to make the people believe that he has great powers & earnestly wish'd for peace; & at length carried the matter so far as to desire a conference with some members of Congress in their private capacities. The Congress to show they were not averse to peace, sent a Comtee. of their body to confer with him. They had the honor of three hours conversation with his LdShip & return'd here last Fryday. He acknowledged he had no power to suspend the operations of war, or to offer any terms; but said he had waited two months in England to prevail with the Ministry to empower him to *converse* & *confer* with Gentn. of influence in America, that he was sure of the good intentions of the King & the Ministry; & if we woud return to our allegiance, they wou'd revise the late instructions to Govrs. & the Acts of Parliament, & if there was any thing in them that appear'd unreasonable to *them,* he did not doubt but they wou'd make them easy. The whole affair will soon be publish'd by Congress, which I will send to my friends in Richmond & I shall be glad of Your remarks. All well at Ticonderogo.

Every advice from all parts of the French dominions give us hopes of a speedy rupture with G.B. That event will make us somewhat easy. My best respects to the Ladies & my friend Mr. Carter.[1]

Believe me, my dear Col. yr. afft. & oblig'd friend,

Francis Lightfoot Lee

RC (ViHi).

[1] On the basis of notes Carter made on the verso of this letter, it would appear that Lee also wrote him another letter on the 17th which has not survived. Carter was apparently attempting to establish the exact date of the battle at Harlem Heights, N.Y., by analyzing conflicting accounts he had received. The pertinent section of his notes reads as follows: "Colo. F. Lees 2 letters 15 & 17. As NY is 100 miles from Philadelphia he could not hear of it nor mention it. His letter 17. says day before Yesterday a firing heard at NY. It might be some commencing manœuvere for the enemys landing their men." This reference by Lee to "firing heard at NY" was repeated in his letter of the 17th to Thomas Jefferson and undoubtedly referred to the British bombardment and landing at Kip's Bay, N.Y., on the 15th.

Richard Henry Lee to Patrick Henry

Dear Sir: Philadelphia, 15th Sept., 1776.

I am happy to hear of your returning health and hope you will long enjoy it. We still continue here in anxious suspense about the event of things at N. York. Since the removal of our troops from Long Island nothing of consequence hath happened, but the enemy show by their motions a design to land their army above ours, on the tongue of land upon which stands the city of N. York. Their design being foreseen, I hope it may be prevented, if the large frequent desertions of the militia do not weaken us too much. The enemies' force is very considerable, it being by the best accounts about 24,000 men, besides their Canada army which is about 7,000, opposed by 13,000 of our people under the command of Gen. Gates, who with a superior marine force on lake Champlain, appears not to be apprehensive of injury from that quarter this campaign. Lord Howe's great powers to do us good have lately been bared to public view, as you will see by the Congress publication of a conversation between his Lordship and a commitee of their body lately on Staten

Island. The tories are almost driven out of their last holds, but still they say "Lord Howe could not be expected to produce his powers, when such strong independents as Franklin & Adams were sent to him." These men will not be right, tho' one should rise from the dead to set them so. The conduct of the militia has been so insufferably bad, that we find it impossible to support the war by their means, and therefore a powerful army of regular troops must be obtained, or all will be lost. It seems to be the opinion that each State should furnish a number of Batallions proportionate to its strength, appoint all the officers from the Colonel downwards, and the whole be paid by the Continent. Letters from Bourdeaux the last of June, inform us of the greatest preperation for war in France and Spain. From the French W. Indies we have the same accounts, and the strongest assurance and acts of friendship imaginable shown to N. America. I verily believe that all the submissions, art and management of G. Britain cannot much longer prevent a war with France. When we consider the water accessibility of our country, it is most clear that no defence can avail us so much as a Marine one— and of all sea force practicable to us, that of Gallies is the cheapest and the best. I wish therefore most earnestly that my Countrymen, at their next meeting of General Assembly, may early direct the immediate building of 10 or 12 large sea Gallies, upon the plan of these large ones now building here by Congress, to carry two 32 pounders in the bow, two in the stern, and 10 six pounders on the sides, to row with 40 oars, and be manned with an hundred men. These placed between the Middle ground and Cape Charles, near to a fine harbour in the Eastern shore, will secure our Bay against everything but line of battle ships, keep open our trade, and secure our shores better than 50,000 men. An able Builder here advises them to be ship-rigged. Besides the great security these Vessels will yield, they will be a fine nursery for seamen so much wanted by us. If the forge and foundry on James River be well attended to, we may easily and quickly be furnished with plenty of Cannon. I pray you, sir, to consider this matter, for I am sure if it be viewed in the light that I think it may be seen in, the plan will be adopted, and pushed with vigor into execution. At present, two or three Sloops of war can stop up our Bay, harrass our shores, and greatly distress our country, when with the Gallies I have described, it would not be safe for twice as many line of battle ships to attempt it, and utterly impossible for smaller vessels to effect it.

The committee that waited on L. Howe have not returned their written report, and therefore it is not yet published, but the verbal report was, substantially, that his Lordship had no power at all but to grant pardon and prosecute the war.

I am, with much esteem, dear Sir, your affectionate and obedient Servant,   Richard Henry Lee

MS not found; reprinted from William Wirt Henry, *Patrick Henry, Life, Correspondence and Speeches*, 3 vols. (New York: Charles Scribner's Sons, 1891), 3:10–11.

John Adams to Abigail Adams

Monday Septr. 16. 1776

The Postmaster at N. York, in a Panick, about a fortnight ago fled to Dobbs's Ferry, about 30 Miles above N.Y. upon Hudsons River, which has thrown the Office into disorder, and interrupted the Communication so much that I have not received a Line of yours, since that dated the Second of September. Nor have I received a News Paper, or any other Letter from Boston since that date. The same Cause, it is probable has disturbed the Conveyance, to the Eastward, and prevented you from receiving Letters regularly, from me.

One of the Horses, which has been sent me, is very low in flesh. I must wait, some time, I fear for him to recruit.

No new Delegates come yet. I hope to see some in a few days.

We have good News from France and the French West Indies. There is great Reason to think they will not always remain inactive.

You commanded me to write every Post, and I obey altho I have nothing in Particular to say, only that I am as usual, not worse in Health, nor yet well, but ever Yours.

RC (MHi). Adams, *Family Correspondence* (Butterfield), 2:126.

Josiah Bartlett to Mary Bartlett

My Dear   Philadelphia Septr 16th 1776

I am now better than when I wrote you last week; My Cough Still Continues bad, and if I had a Colleague here I should Set out for home in hopes that Change of air might be serviceable to me, but I am loath to leave our Colony unrepresented in Congress, and shall try to remain here till the return of Col Whipple, when I shall immediately return if able & nothing Extraordinary hinder. I shall be in want of a man & horse to attend me home. I Expect that our Legislature has appointed another Delegate in the room of Capt Langdon, and that Whipple & he will Set out for this place Soon after the receipt of My letter to him of this Date. I have proposed to him to let me have one of their horses & servants to return with me immediately on their arrival here. I hope they will agree to it, but if not, I have Desired Col Whipple to inform you, so that you may hire a Good Strong Horse & man to Come here with Col Whipple & to return with me; if you Can hire a horse & man for that purpose

I shall be glad, provided I Cant have one of Col Whipples; if you Cannot hire one I must hire here in the best manner I am able.[1]

As my health is very precarious I may possibly think it not Safe to Continue here till my Colleagues return but absolutely necessary to try a Change of air sooner. If that should be the Case I should be glad to meet the man you shall send (if you send any) and for that reason would have him Come the upper road as it is Called thro Marlborough & Worcester to Hartford & New Haven in Connecticut, which way I shall go if I return before their arrival here. I hope I shall not be obliged to, but am not Certain how it may be.

I have not had the pleasure to hear from you Since yours of the 19th of August which I Recd above a fortnight ago. However I Suppose it is owing to an interruption of the Posts and that you have very likely been Disappointed in receiving my letters as often as I have of receiving yours, Tho I have not failed to write to you once Every week at least.

I hope I shall have a letter from you next post & hear that you & the family are will.

The weather here is now very warm which Disagrees with me more than Cooler weather. I Remember my Love to Lieut Pearson & all friends in particular my own family. I am, yours &c,

Josiah Bartlett

P.S. I send this one Day sooner than Commonly so Cant send the Tuesdays newspaper.[2]

RC (NhHi).
[1] See Bartlett to William Whipple, September 14, 1776.
[2] Bartlett wrote another letter to Mary on September 17, but failing to send it "as I expected" added a long postscript on the 23d. Upon both occasions Bartlett returned to the subjects of his plan to start home from Philadelphia when William Whipple returned from New Hampshire and his ill health, which continued to keep him from attending to congressional business full time. "I hope I am rather better on most accounts," he wrote on the 17th. "I have never omitted being at Congress every Day tho I am often obliged to leave it before it adjourns." Watt Collection, NhHi.

Josiah Bartlett to John Langdon

Dear Sir,   Philadelphia Sept 16th 1776
I have not had the pleasure of receiving but one letter from New Hampshire for some time. I fear there is some stoppage in the post and that my friends in New Hampshire find it as difficult to get letters from this place as I from them.

The Congress have passed a new order concerning the posts which will I hope put them in a better situation.[1] Yours by Capt Roche I have just rec'd and if it is in my power to serve him, will do it, depending on your recommendation, but at present know of no place open for him.

The Secret Committee are in want of proper goods to export to an European market, such as potash, dry fish, bees wax &c. &c. and they have desired me to write home to New Hampshire to know whether any quantity sufficient to load a vessel or two can be procured; if so, they would give some body a contract for that purpose. Please to make enquiry, and inform me if such things can be procured and sent from our State. It will be an advantage both to the public and to individuals. I have wrote to some others to make the same enquiry.

As to news we have nothing very material here and must beg leave to refer you to my letter to Col Whipple for what I have to send. I suppose you have formally resigned your seat in Congress and another is appointed in your stead. Pray send them forward with all expedition as my ill state of health will I fear prevent my attending Congress till they arrive here.

I am Sir, your sincere friend and humble servant,

Josiah Bartlett

Tr (DLC).
[1] For the August 30 resolutions reorganizing the post office, see *JCC*, 5:719–20.

Elbridge Gerry to Joseph Trumbull

Dear Sir,   Philadelphia Sepr 16th 1776

I have only Time to advise You that General Schuyler finds himself so uneasy at the Northward from the Reflections of the people that he proposes to resign from which We have Reason to hope that Harmony will ensue.[1] The Army is to consist the ensuing Year of eighty eight full Batalions to be inlisted for the War, the officers to have Bounties of Land, the Men one hundred Acres each & twenty Dollars.[2] The Express is Waiting. My Respects to all Friends & believe me to be yours sincerely,   E Gerry

RC (Ct).
[1] In a September 9 letter to President Hancock, which was read in Congress this day, Schuyler had announced his intention to resign and to demand an inquiry "to evince how unjustly my character has suffered." PCC, item 153, 2:364; *Am. Archives*, 5th ser. 2:263; and *JCC*, 5:760. His actual resignation was sent in a September 14 letter to Hancock which was read in Congress on September 23. *Am. Archives*, 5th ser. 2:333–34; and *JCC*, 5:809. For Congress' subsequent refusal to accept Schuyler's resignation, see Edward Rutledge to Robert R. Livingston, September 23, 1776, note 2.

Edmund C. Burnett printed Gerry's letter of September 16 under the date September 26, 1776, mistakenly linking it to Schuyler's letter of September 14 rather than that of the ninth. Burnett, *Letters*, 2:103. Although Gerry's numerals are not carefully formed, his letter is clearly concerned with Congress' proceedings of September 16; and on September 26 Gerry was at New York. See Gerry to Thomas Gerry, September 26, 1776.

[2] See *JCC*, 5:762–63.

John Hancock to Joseph Trumbull

Sir,   Philada. Septr 16th. 1776.

I have the pleasure to enclose you a Resolution of Congress relative to your Department, by which you will perceive that your Letter and the Papers transmitted therewith, have been under their Consideration, that it is the Expectation of Congress your Difficulties will be thereby removed.[1]

Since passing this Resolve, your Brother Mr. John Trumbull has been appointed by Congress Deputy Adjutant Genl. of the Army in the Northern Department, and Mr. Livingston's Resignation as Deputy Commissary, has been accepted, agreeably to his Request.[2]

The Honour and Reputation with which you have hitherto executed the arduous and extensive Business of your Office, and the Satisfaction you have afforded the Public, convince me that you will still continue to render your Country all the Services in your Power, and by no Means decline your present Employment.

Your Bills on me to this Date have been duely honoured.

I am, Sir, with Respect, your most obed Ser,

John Hancock Presidt

RC (Ct). In the hand of Jacob Rush and signed by Hancock.

[1] For the context of Congress' September 12 resolution reaffirming "the commissary general's right to direct the operations of his department, both as contractor and issuer of provisions," see Elbridge Gerry to Joseph Trumbull, September 12, 1776, note 2.

[2] See *JCC*, 5:753, 758.

John Hancock to George Washington

Sir,   Philada. Sepr. 16th. 1776.

The Congress having at different Times passed sundry Resolves relative to a Variety of Subjects, I do myself the Honour to enclose you a Copy of the same, as necessary for your Information & Direction.[1]

The Resolve of the 12th respecting Colonel Trumbull, will I trust be satisfactory, & prove the Means of his continuing in an office of such Importance to the Army, and which he has hitherto discharged with the greatest Fidelity & Success.

I have the Honour to be, with perfect Esteem & Respect, Sir, your most obed. & very hble Ser.   John Hancock Presidt

RC (DLC). In the hand of Jacob Rush and signed by Hancock.
[1] For the "sundry Resolves" on military affairs passed by Congress on September
10, 12, and 14, see *JCC*, 5:749, 752-54, 757-58.

Richard Henry Lee to Samuel Purviance, Jr.

Dear Sir,   Philadelphia 16th Septr. 1776
    Since your brother left this City, Mr. Nicholson has been con-
firmed first Lieutenant of the Washington, and his worthy brother
may be assured that in settling the rank of the Captains his merit
will not be forgotten.[1] It is not probable that the Frigates will sail in
fleets for some time; and therefore tis likely that no higher appointment than that of Captain will soon take place. It will be highly
proper for Captain Nicholson to hasten on the Virginia (for that is
most certainly the name of the Baltimore Frigate) as quick as possible. Her great obstruction, I fear, will be Anchors. However, we hope
that will be removed eer long, as measures have been taken to procure them.
    You will shortly see published the conference of our Members with
Lord Howe on Staten Island, in which you will find that his Lordships much talked of powers, are no more than to *confer* & *converse*
with Gentlemen of influence, and to prosecute the war! We anxiously
expect here, the issue of a long Cannonade at York, and another
lately on Lake Champlain.
    I am Sir Your most humble Servant,

                                        Richard Henry Lee

RC (MdHi).
    [1] John Nicholson had been appointed 2nd lieutenant of the frigate *Washington*
on August 22. When the Marine Committee's report was approved on October
10, Capt. James Nicholson was ranked first among captains of the Continental
Navy. *JCC*, 5:697, 6:861. See also William J. Fowler, "James Nicholson and the
Continental Frigate Virginia," *American Neptune* 34 (April 1974): 135-41.

Robert Treat Paine's Diary

                                        [September 16, 1776]
Very Cool day. Try'd appeal to Congress.[1]

MS (MHi).
    [1] Paine was a member of a committee appointed by Congress on September 9
"to hear the parties on the appeal against the verdict and sentence of condemnation passed against the schooner *Thistle* and her cargo." The *Thistle*,
after clearing Pensacola, had been captured by the privateer *Congress* and brought
into Philadelphia, where she was condemned on July 1, 1776, by the Admiralty
Court of Pennsylvania. On September 17 the congressional committee of appeal

reversed the condemnation decision against the *Thistle*, and on September 25 Congress granted the schooner and its master, Charles Roberts, a 60-day passport and safe conduct. See *JCC*, 5:631, 647, 702, 741, 747, 807, 908; and Morgan, *Naval Documents*, 5:73, 401, 857, 6:1408.

John Penn to the North Carolina Council of Safety

Dear Sir   Philaa. Septr. 16. 1776

I wrote to you by Thomas Hayward esqr.[1] one of the Delegates of So. Carolina that General Howe was in possession of Long Island as also the manner in which we left it. General Sullivan who was made a prisoner on that occasion was sent here lately by Lord Howe with a message that his Lordship was very desirous to converse with some of the members of Congress as private Gentn. and that he would meet them as Mr. Howe, that he had great power from the King to negotiate a peace, tho we were pursuaded that he only intended to throw the odium of carrying on the war on the Congress. Having no reason to believe that he had any such authority yet to counteract his design Doctr. Franklin, John Adams & Edwd. Rutledge esqrs. were directed to meet his Lordship not as private Gentn. but as a Committee of Congress to know of him what his powers were if any he had to treat with the Congress on the subject of peace.

The Gentn. had a Conference with Lord Howe who owned that he had no terms to offer to America and was not at liberty to treat with any set of men who were Representatives of the People, that he had a right to converse with Individuals & represent to the King the substance of what passed. I hope this will have a good effect as it will satisfie the people at large that we have no alternative for our safety but our spirit as Soldiers.

The Congress have left the sending two Battalions from No. Carolina with General Moore to New York altogether to the Council of Safety.[2] I would not advise the sending them at any rate as it is too late in the year. I suppose General Washington will remove from New York into King's bridge so that the enemy will take possession of the Town, this will be of no great consequence as it is nearly an Island & we shall be able to confine them in it.

The Army under General Gates were recovering their health and spirits, we have also a considerable Fleet on lake Champlain.

The last letters we had from Martinique mention that there is great reason to expect a war between France & England will break out soon in consequence of the protection given to our Vessels.

I wish the Council of Safety would signifie their pleasure to your delegates about our being at the next Convention at Halifax, indeed my Friend we shall have very little to do in Congress of any great importance untill we know what reception the Confideration plan will meet with in the different states. Hooper as well as myself would be glad to come, it is what has been done in these States, do leave it to us to determine. You may depend we will not leave the Congress if any thing of Consequence should require us to stay. I am, Dear Sir, Your mo. obt. Sevt.   John Penn

[*P.S.*] Perhaps it would be better to direct that we should come.

Since we are to raise such a number of Battalions would it be prudent to stop the officers of the neighbourg. states from inlisting any more men in No. Carolina untill we have compleated our Quota? J.P.

Since writing the above I hear General Washington has removed from New York so that Lord Howe I suppose is there; it was prudent or otherwise he might have been surrounded.   J.P.

RC (Nc–Ar).
[1] Not found.
[2] See North Carolina Delegates to the North Carolina Council of Safety, September 3, 1776.

Benjamin Rush to Jacques Barbeu-Dubourg

My dear Sir,   Philada September 16th. 1776.

I write this letter at a venture. I wish it may reach you, but I shall not complain if it falls into the hands of our enemies. It shall contain nothing but facts.

The campaign was opened in this country on the 27th of last month on Long Island in the neighbourhood of New York. 3000 American troops opposed 10,000 British & Hessian troops for six hours. At last our people were obliged to give way with the loss of about 1000 men killed & taken prisoners. The Enemy had 500 men killed & wounded in the action. Our troops behaved like veterans. One brigade sustained three heavy fires in an open field without moving. When the word of command to "fire" was given, the enemy gave way, and a total rout was expected, but alas, their numbers supplied their want of ⟨courage⟩ order, and our men were surrounded and cut to pieces or taken. The enemy soon after this victory gained possession of Long Island by means of their ships, and as the heights on this Island command New York, our troops are preparing to evacuate it. Genl Howe's army will probably winter there. The disaffected people begin to flock to his standard. We hope in a few months to oblige them to decamp with [their] new masters, for Genl. Washington has it in his power to prevent their penetrating more than 10 or 11 miles into the country around New York. Our army consists at present of 30,000 men: 20,000 at New York, & 10,000 at Ticonderoga under the command of Genl. Gates. As we expect 20,000 Russians to reinforce Genl. Howe next spring, we are about to encrease our army to 60,000. They will suffer much from the want of woolens unless soon supplied by our good friends the subjects of the king of France.

New governments are instituted in all the states, founded on the authority of the people. They all differ in some particulars, but they all agree in having their legislative officers chosen *annually* and in establishing a rotation of power.

My Countrymen have done me the honor of making me a member of the congress. I can therefore from authority assure you that a *fixed determination* still prevails in that body to establish the liberties of America or to perish in their ruins. No difficulties discourage us, no losses depress us. We look only to heaven and France for succour, being resolved if we are subdued that our last breath shall be "Independance upon the court of Britain." Lord Howe sent a message to us a few days ago requesting a conference with some members of the congress. Dr. Franklin, Mr. Jno. Adams, and Mr. Rutledge were ordered to wait upon his Lordship. He talked much of his powers to accommodate the dispute between Britain & America, but said he could offer nothing & promise nothing till we returned to our Allegiance. Here the negotiation ended. All America disdains such propositions. I must here mention an anecdote in honor of Mr. Adams. When his Lordship asked in what capacity he was to receive the gentlemen of the congress, Mr. Adams told him "in any capacity his Lordship pleased except in that of BRITISH SUBJECTS." This illustrious patriot has not his superior, scarcely his equal, for Abilities & virtue on the whole continent of America.

A confederation is now forming between the united States. Each State is to have an equal vote, but no question relative to peace & war or other important matters is to be determined by less than 9 states. The States are to confer no titles, and no American is to hold any post under the States who accepts of a title from any foreign power. No delegate is to set in congress more than three years in seven. A counsel of State consisting of one delegate from each state is to do business during the recess of the congress. This business is always to be only of an executive nature.

We have nearly finished a treaty which we expect soon to offer to your court through the hands of Mr. Dean—& perhaps of Dr. Franklin. The common toasts in Philada. now are: "His most christian majesty," and "a speedy Alliance between the king of France & the united States."

My wife joins in compts. to your dear M. Dubourg, with, my dear friend, yours most sincerely.

P.S. The Baron Wotke [Woedtke] dishonored your recommendation. He died a few weeks ago at Ticonderoga with the effects of hard drinking. The Chevalier Kormorvan behaves well. Five French officers arrived here yesterday from Martinique with strong recommendations from the govr. of that Island.

RC (Archives du ministère des affaires étrangères: Correspondance politique, Etats-Unis, 1). In the hand of Benjamin Rush, though not signed. Reproduced as document no. 584 in Benjamin Franklin Stevens, comp., *B. F. Stevens's Facsimiles of Manuscripts in European Archives Relating to America, 1773–1783*, 2107 facsim. in 24 portfolios (London, 1889–95); and enclosed with Dubourg's letter of December 16, 1776, to Vergennes, Stevens' no. 602.

Secret Committee to Horatio Gates

Sir   In Secret Committee, Philada. Septr. 16th. 1776
By orders of Congress we have dispatched in Sundry Waggons Fifteen Tons of Powder, Twenty thousand Gun Flints, Ten Tons of lead & one hundred Rheams of Cartridge Paper for the use of the army under your Command and hope the same will arrive safe & in good time.[1] We have the honor to remain, sir, Your very obedt. Servants. By order of the Committee,

Robt Morris Chair Man

RC (NHi). Written and signed by Robert Morris.
[1] Gates' September 5 letter to General Schuyler, in which he had requested this ammunition, and Schuyler's September 8 letter to Congress repeating the request, are in *Am. Archives*, 5th ser. 2:185, 246–47. See also *JCC*, 5:756, 758.

Secret Committee to the Pennsylvania Council of Safety

Gentn.   Philada. Septr. 16. 1776.
We are directed by Congress to apply to your Honorable Board for a supply of Thirty five Thousand Gun Flints, Twenty thousand whereof for the Northern Army & ten thousand for Indian Treaty at Pittsburg. As your Commissary Mr. Towers or Colo. Matlack have plenty of Flints belonging to this State, we request an order for the delivery of the above quantitys which are to be charged to the Congress.[1]
By order of the Secret Committee, I have the honor to be Gentn., Your Obed. hble servt.   Robt. Morris, Chair Man

Tr (PHarH).
[1] *JCC*, 5:752, 758. The Pennsylvania Council of Safety directed Timothy Matlack to fulfill this request this day. *Am. Archives*, 5th ser. 2:67.

Joseph Hewes to Samuel Purviance, Jr.

Dr Sir   Philada. 17th Sepr. 1776
   Agreeable to my Promise to your brother I now send a printed
Article for Seamen.[1] You will observe the wages allowed to able
Seamen is eight dollars per month, ordinary Seamen & Landsmen
Six dollars & two thirds of a dollar per month. I am respectfully,
Dear Sir, Your mo Obed Servant,   Joseph Hewes

RC (MdHi).
[1] Not found.

Francis Lightfoot Lee to Thomas Jefferson

Dear Sir,   Philadelphia Sepr. 17. 1776
   Our affairs at N. York have not much alter'd since your departure,
the Militia of the eastern states have mostly left it, & probably improved the Army. The Enemy having by every motion shewn a
design to get above our troops, Genl. Washington is busy in removing his stores from the City, & collecting his forces at & about King's
bridge, but we fear he has been interrupted by the Enemy, as a very
heavy firing was heard there on Sunday last.[1]
   Genl. Gates in his last Letter says, there was just then heard a
heavy cannonade upon the Lake, from whence he judged, our fleet
under the command of Genl. Arnold, was engaged with the Enemy,
on their way to Crownpoint. We therefore expect every moment to
hear of some considerable Actions at both places. All our advices
from the Indians, indicate a general war with them. I hope our
people will have done the business of the southern Indians, that they
may be ready to chastise those of the west.
   The week before last Ld. Howe sent Genl. Sullivan to Congress
with a message, that he was very sollicitous for peace, that he had
great powers, that tho he cou'd not at present acknowlege the Congress, yet he wished to confer with some of the members, as private
Gentlemen. This message made a great noise without doors, & it was
fear'd wou'd have a bad effect upon our Military operations. The
Congress fully apprized of the perfidy & villainous designs of these
Ministerial Agents; yet willing to convince our people that they are
not averse to peace; sent him in answer That being the representatives of free & independant States, they cou'd not allow their Members to confer with him in their private capacities; but wou'd send a
Committee of their body to know his powers & his terms. The Committee met his Ld.ship last Wednesday on Staten Island, & had the
honor to dine upon plate with him, & a three hour's conversation,
the substance of which was: that he had waited 2 months in England

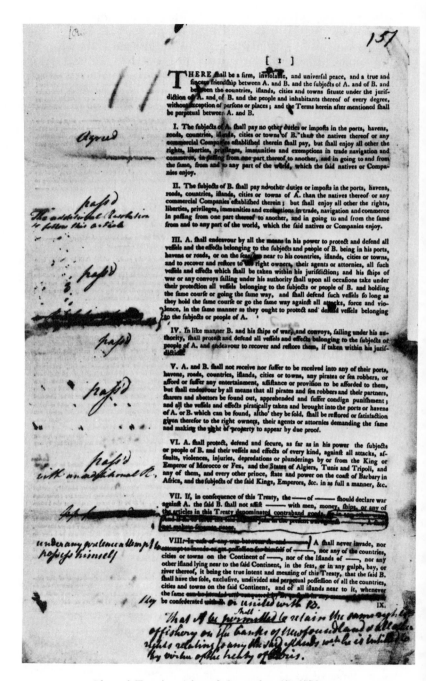

[1]

THERE shall be a firm, inviolable, and universal peace, and a true and sincere friendship between A. and B. and the subjects of A. and of B. and between the countries, islands, cities and towns situate under the jurisdiction of A. and of B. and the people and inhabitants thereof of every degree, without exception of persons or places; and the Terms herein after mentioned shall be perpetual between A. and B.

I. The subjects of A. shall pay no other duties or imposts in the ports, havens, roads, countries, islands, cities or towns of B. than the natives thereof or any commercial Companies established therein shall pay, but shall enjoy all other the rights, liberties, privileges, immunities and exemptions in trade navigation and commerce, in passing from one part thereof to another, and in going to and from the same, from and to any part of the world, which the said natives or Companies enjoy.

II. The subjects of B. shall pay no other duties or imposts in the ports, havens, roads, countries, islands, cities or towns of A. than the natives thereof or any commercial Companies established therein shall pay, but shall enjoy all other the rights, liberties, privileges, immunities and exemptions in trade, navigation and commerce in passing from one part thereof to another, and in going to and from the same from and to any part of the world, which the said natives or Companies enjoy.

III. A. shall endeavour by all the means in his power to protect and defend all vessels and the effects belonging to the subjects and people of B. being in his ports, havens or roads, or on the seas near to his countries, islands, cities or towns, and to recover and restore to the right owners, their agents or attorneys, all such vessels and effects which shall be taken within his jurisdiction; and his ships of war or any convoys sailing under his authority shall upon all occasions take under their protection all vessels belonging to the subjects or people of B. and holding the same course or going the same way, and shall defend such vessels so long as they hold the same course or go the same way against all attacks, force and violence, in the same manner as they ought to protect and defend vessels belonging to the subjects or people of A.

IV. In like manner B. and his ships of war, and convoys, sailing under his authority, shall protect and defend all vessels and effects belonging to the subjects or people of A. and endeavour to recover and restore them, if taken within his jurisdiction.

V. A. and B. shall not receive nor suffer to be received into any of their ports, havens, roads, countries, islands, cities or towns, any pirates or sea robbers, or afford or suffer any entertainment, assistance or provision to be afforded to them, but shall endeavour by all means that all pirates and sea robbers and their partners, sharers and abettors be found out, apprehended and suffer condign punishment; and all the vessels and effects piratically taken and brought into the ports or havens of A. or B. which can be found, altho' they be sold, shall be restored or satisfaction given therefor to the right owners, their agents or attornies demanding the same and making the right of property to appear by due proof.

VI. A. shall protect, defend and secure, as far as in his power the subjects or people of B. and their vessels and effects of every kind, against all attacks, assaults, violences, injuries, depredations or plunderings by or from the King or Emperor of Morocco or Fez, and the States of Algiers, Tunis and Tripoli, and any of them, and every other prince, state and power on the coast of Barbary in Africa, and the subjects of the said Kings, Emperors, &c. in as full a manner, &c.

VII. If, in consequence of this Treaty, the —— of —— should declare war against A. the said B. shall not assist —— with men, money, ships, or any of the articles in this Treaty denominated contraband goods ——

VIII. —— A. shall never invade, nor —— nor any of the countries, cities or towns on the Continent of ——, nor of the Islands of ——, nor any other island lying near to the said Continent, in the seas, or in any gulph, bay, or river thereof, it being the true intent and meaning of this Treaty, that the said B. shall have the sole, exclusive, undivided and perpetual possession of all the countries, cities and towns on the said Continent, and of all islands near to it, whenever the same —— be confederated with —— or united with B.

IX.

Plan of Treaties, Adopted September 17, 1776

to prevail with the Ministry to empower him to *confer* & *converse* with some Gentlemen of influence in America. That he was sure of the good intentions of the King & the Ministry; and if we wou'd return to our allegiance, they wou'd revise the late instructions to Govrs. & Acts of Parliament; & *if* there was anything in them which appear'd to *them* unreasonable, he did not doubt, but they wou'd make them easy. That he had no power to suspend the operations of war, or to offer any terms. The tories are struck dumb, but I fear it will have a bad effect upon our foreign negotiations; as it will show too great an eagerness in us, to make up with G.B.

This whole transaction will be soon published by Congress, which the next post will bring you, & I hope the Accts. of our glorious Victories.

I am Dear Sir, Yr. afft. friend & hble Servant,

Francis Lightfoot Lee

[*P.S.*] During the conversation Ld. Howe said it wou'd make him very uneasy to see America plunder'd & laid waste. Doctr. Franklin assured his Ldship we were taking the most effectual measures to save him that uneasiness.

RC (PHi). Jefferson, *Papers* (Boyd), 1:520–21.

[1] Undoubtedly a reference to the British bombardment and landing at Kip's Bay on September 15. See also Arthur Middleton to William Henry Drayton, September 18, 1776, note 1.

Thomas Nelson to John Page

My Dear Page   Philada Sepr 18th [*i.e.* 17th] 1776 [1]

I was extreamly sorry to find your Last Letter that you had had a return of your old complaint. You should retire a little from business; for I find, myself, who am stronger than you, that I am almost overdone with such constant attendance upon the business of Congress, either in Committee or the House, and if the affair at N York was favourably determin'd, I should return to Virginia for a little time.[2] There was a very heavy firing heard on the 16th Instant [3] by some persons travelling thro' the Jerseys, but we have had nothing certain from Camp since. It is probable that something has been attempted by the British Troops, as they had made dispositions to surround our Men upon New York Island, which it is to be wish'd they may not effect, as by that means, our whole Army would be pounded. Measures have been taken to prevent it. We have been grossly deceiv'd with respect to the assistance we should have from the eastward upon an emergency, not but that each of these States have a great many Troops in the Service, but it was imagin'd in case of an invasion that the whole of them, able to bear arms, would have march'd down to the Seacoasts, but they have got the privateering scheme in their Heads by which they can make Fortunes & they will not inlist to fight for 1/6 per day. We are about to raise several more Battallions in the different States—six more in Virginia, in the whole to have about 90 Battalions of Regulars, which ought to have been done before, so as to have had them now in the field.[4]

The Congress determind yesterday that Commissioners should be appointed, to audit the Continental Accounts, in the Southern department and they are to proceed to day to the appointment of them.[5] The Virginia Accounts, that were transmitted to us some time ago, are to be referrd to them, but in the meantime the State is to have money advanced to it upon account. Were the Accounts to be immediately settled, there would be nothing due to Virginia; but a Balance against her, admitting the whole to be allowed, for there has been a grant to that State of 65,000 Dollars & the Balance upon the account is only 63,484; but then you have still a further demand for the two first Regiments, which we were told, could not be sent with the Accounts, and a very considerable Sum must be due for raising the last seven Regiments & maintaining Prisoners, which must be paid by Congress, so that altho the Commissioners may not settle the Accounts of the whole, so soon as you will want the money, yet you may have part of it advanced by application to Congress, who will not admit of any settlements, but by persons of their own appointment.

I am with sincere esteem, Your obedt Servt,

Thos Nelson Jr.

RC (NN).

[1] Although Nelson clearly dated this letter September 18 and mentions "heavy firing heard on the 16th Instant by some persons travelling thro' the Jerseys," his second paragraph reference to the appointment of commissioners for auditing accounts in the southern states suggests that he wrote it on the 17th. See notes 3, and 5 below.

[2] Despite the tense situation in New York, Nelson apparently decided by the end of the week to return home, for his account with the commonwealth of Virginia included a claim for attendance in Congress "from Aug. 11th till Sepr 21st, 41 days." Nelson attended the October session of the Virginia legislature, but his respite from congressional duties was brief. According to his account he resumed attendance at Congress "from 10th Novr 76 till the 20 Jany, 71 Days." Emmet Collection, NN. For a brief discussion of Nelson's activities while in Virginia, see Emory G. Evans, *Thomas Nelson of Yorktown* (Williamsburg: Colonial Williamsburg Foundation, 1975), pp. 61–62.

[3] If Nelson actually wrote this letter on September 17 instead of the 18th, this reference may pertain to a report of heavy firing heard on the 15th rather than the 16th. In this context, it is instructive to note that Francis Lightfoot Lee in a September 17 letter to Jefferson mentioned that "very heavy firing was heard . . . on Sunday [*i.e. the 15th*] last." See preceding entry.

[4] According to the resolve of September 16, Virginia's quota under the new enlistment for a standing army was 15 battalions, but the 9 battalions already raised were considered as part of that quota. See *JCC*, 5:762; and John Hancock to the States, September 24, 1776.

⁵Although the journals for September 16 indicated that commissioners for settling Virginia's Continental accounts were to be appointed on the 17th, they were not selected until November 6. See *JCC*, 5:761, 6:930.

Caesar Rodney to Thomas Rodney

Sir   Philadelphia Sepr. the 17th 1776

Knowing that Small Veshells were in Great demand here at present, and knowing also that the Sloop Could not be so interesting to keep as to Sell at Such a time, had determined to write you (previous to the Receipt of Your letter) to Send her up here immediately for the purpose of having her Sold. Am Glad to find You are in the Same mind with me and therefore that you would not delay a Single moment in Sending her after the Receipt of this because it is uncertain how long this demand will Continue, however am Convinced from the reason of the thing Arising from Certain Circumstances, the demand cannot hold Long. John Bell has Sold both his for more than a hundred pounds more than he Ever thought of asking—in Short more than they Cost him at first. Therefore dont neglect to Send her imediately. Theophilus Parke is here, but is afraid to go back to Kent least his Creditors there Should fall upon him; Bullin with my Assistance will Get his Mare, by which he will be pretty Safe. Parke has Volentarily appeared before me, and Got his deposition taken, which I have inclosed; if it Should be of any Service to his just Creditors they are wellcome to my trouble. But if the Deposition be true am Surprised that Loockerman Should Claim the whole of two years Rent.[1]

Our Committee have returned, have Seen and Conversed with Lord Howe, have found out that he had no more or other powers than at first Contained in his declaration. This point was only to prove what they knew before, purely for the Satisfaction of the Tories. Shall forward John's letter to Kings-Bridge. No news from Camp that is important but Expect some Every Moment.[2] What will you Do now for Want of a Post rider? I am Yours &c,

                                                        Caesar Rodney

RC (CSmH).
[1] For Thomas' replies on these issues, see his letters to Caesar of September 19, 22, and 23, 1776, in Rodney, *Letters* (Ryden), pp. 124–28.
[2] This day Robert Treat Paine noted in his diary the arrival of a report of the evacuation of New York. "News came of the Evacuation of N. York, last Sunday." MHi.

Virginia Delegates to Patrick Henry

Sir,   Philadelphia Septr. 17th. 1776
We have the honor to inclose you the answer of Pennsylvania to
the proposed temporary boundary between the Commonwealth of
Virginia and this State and also our reply to the same.[1] We need
not observe to your Excellency on the manner in which the question is begged by this answer supposing that our Cession of the
Charter'd bounds of Pennsylvania, gives an exclusive right to this
country of saying where those bounds shall extend to.
That the line proposed by the answer is a proper one, seems very
problematical, and is likely to produce as great expence as running
the true one; and therefore we submit it, whether 'twill not be
best to run the true line at this time, which will quiet all disputes
on this subject forever.
We beg leave to refer you to Mr. Jefferson, lately returned to
Virginia, who has conversed much with the Philosopher Rittenhouse
on this subject.
We are, with much respect, your Excellencies most obedient and
very humble servants,   G. Wythe

                                          Richard Henry Lee

                                          Francis Lightfoot Lee

RC (MH-H). Written by Richard Henry Lee and signed by Francis Lightfoot
Lee, Richard Henry Lee, and George Wythe.
[1] See Virginia Delegates to a Committee of the Pennsylvania Convention, September 12, 1776.

Arthur Middleton to William Henry Drayton

My dear Drayton   Philadelphia Septembr. 18th 1776.
The inclosed Letter, or scrawl, I meant should come to you by
Sea, but as the Sloop slip'd away sooner than I expected, I embrace an opportunity of inclosing it with a few papers, by a Land
Conveyance (Mr. Weereat of Georgia). I desire you will look upon
these only as loose Sheets, containing a few Sentences in gratitude for the Notice you have taken of me, & not as Answers to
your *long Letter*, which require a full & determined Consideration, & which you shall have as soon as Time and Opportunity
will permit. The inclos'd Newspapers will give you some *Traits*
of our late Transactions, & present Circumstances; you will form
your own Judgments upon them, & if you please, let me have
them. Entre nous we seem to be getting into a pretty pickle, how
we are to get out of it is the difficulty; the Scripture tells us of
the Wise men of the East; that Text must now be alter'd into the
Cunning men, & it will come nearer the Truth; I dont recollect

that it mentions anything of the *Brave men* of *the East,* & therefore
we are not to believe them such; their late behaviour has prov'd
them not to be so—2 whole Brigades have run in a most shamefull manner, which has occasion'd us to loose a great deal of Baggage, & many of our heavy Cannon.[1]

N. York belongs to the Enemy; what the Consequences will be
is very uncertain. The North either cannot or does not seem inclin'd
to defend itself, you must therefore put your whole Confidence
in yourselves & your Neighbours of North Carolina—for God's sake
as soon as possible obstruct all the water Channels up to your Town,
upon this, in my opinion your Security must Depend in a great
measure, as the Enemy will no doubt send a large Force to the So.
as soon as they have got themselves properly fixed in New York.
We yesterday got Cols. Gadsden & Moultrie *Generalled;* Lee I suppose will not return to you.[2]

I close this in haste, let me hear from you often & believe me
with Truth, Your truly affect.   A.M.

P.S. What is become of Charles? my Love to him, & to all Friends.

MS not found; reprinted from *South Carolina Historical and Genealogical Maga-
zine,* 27 (July 1926): 142–43. Addressed: "To the Honble William Henry Drayton,
Esq., Chief Justice of South Carolina. By favour of Mr. Weereat of Georgia,
Q.D.C."

[1] On the previous day Congress had received Washington's September 16 letter
to Hancock describing the landing of British troops at Kip's Bay on Manhattan
and the resultant failure of a number of state and Continental units from Connecticut and Massachusetts to hold their positions against them. See *JCC,* 5:779;
PCC, item 152, 2:555–57; and Washington, *Writings* (Fitzpatrick), 6:57–59.

[2] Gadsden and Moultrie were actually promoted on September 16. *JCC,* 5:761.

North Carolina Delegates to the
North Carolina Council of Safety

Gentlemen   Philadelphia Sept. 18. 1776

We wrote the honourable the Council of Safety by Mr. Heyward
who left this sometime since. We then inclosed you a Resolve of
the Continental Congress directing Brigadier General Moore with
two of the Continental battalions which were raised in the State of
North Carolina to proceed to New York with all possible expedition. A further Revision of that Subject together with some private
information by letters of the present state of our Country have induced your delegates to obtain an alteration of that Resolve; from
which it will appear that the movement of our Troops is now left
to the discretion of your honourable Body and considering that
you are now engaged in a War with the savages on your frontiers,
and have nothing to expect from the disposition of the late insurgents but hostilities as soon as their fears have so far subsided as

not to restrain them from such attempts, we are induced to hope that you will retain within yourselves the Regular troops as they seem to be absolutely necessary for our own security.[1] And it may be viewed almost as a certainty that General Howe instead of keeping his Army in Winter Quarters idle will make a formidable diversion in a Southern Climate which will call forth your utmost exertions to oppose with success.

We need say nothing to you who have so well considered and digested the matters to induce you to compleat to their full number the Continental Battalions which have been raised in our state. The inclosed System agreed upon by Congress for the modelling a new Army holds forth such encouragement that we flatter ourselves you will find no difficulty in carrying into execution that part of the plan which has been allotted to your share.[2] The Bounty proposed is liberal, and aided with the stimulus which every honest American does or ought to feel effectually to establish the liberties of America upon a sure and solid basis we hope to have an opportunity soon to congratulate you, that it has obtained for you an additional force which will effectually baffle the future efforts of our Enemies.

You will observe that in addition to the six Regiments already raised by you, you are impowered to raise three more. Should you think yourselves inadequate to so large a number you will as early as possible represent such your Incapacity to Congress who will no doubt make such alteration as will suit your Circumstances, tho We hope that you will find no difficulty in complying with this Resolve to the full as you will no doubt be often called upon hereafter to aid the Weakness of South Carolina and Georgia and the calling forth the militia is so expensive and burdensome that it ought as much as possible to be avoided.[3]

Would it not be advisable to draw your scattered troops together as soon as possible that they may be ready to cooperate as soon as their whole strength may be required to oppose the Enemy. We fear the effects of a Southern Climate upon those which General Lee has led to Georgia. What may be his views we cannot ascertain but surely the Object ought to be of the last necessity to justify a measure which must, even without an opposition from an enemy, involve the loss of so many brave men from the Inclemency of the season, fatigue & our Troops being almost naked.

We shall write you very fully by Mr. Hewes who leaves this in a few days. In the mean time We beg leave to subscribe ourselves with all possible respect, Gentlemen, Your most Obed Huml Servts,

Wm Hooper

Joseph Hewes

John Penn

RC (Nc–Ar). Written by Hooper and signed by Hooper, Hewes, and Penn. *N.C. Colonial Records*, 10:804–6. RC damaged; missing words supplied from Tr.

[1] See North Carolina Delegates to the North Carolina Council of Safety, September 3, 1776.

[2] See *JCC*, 5:762–63.

[3] The North Carolina Provincial Congress agreed to raise three new Continental battalions on November 26, 1776. *N.C. Colonial Records*, 10:941.

North Carolina Delegates to the North Carolina Council of Safety

Gentlemen   [September 18, 1776] [1]

This will be handed to you by our worthy Colleague Mr Hewes who after a long and diligent attendance in congress, and the different committees of which he has been member is now upon his return home. From the large share of naval & mercantile business which has been allotted to his Attention by Congress, his health has been much injured, we wish his Journey may tend to restore it & that he may enjoy in his recess from publick employment much happiness among his Country men who it has been his unwearied endeavour to serve while he has been in publick trust.

Mr Hewes will inform you by letter or in person of the state of our publick affairs, of the situation of our Army at New York and whatever else that has occurred in this quarter which may immediately or in its consequences operate importantly upon the State of North Carolina. The Check which the American Arms have lately received on Long Island reflects no dishonor upon those who bore them. The Struggle was bravely maintained by our young Soldiery and to a want of Generalship in some of our inferiour Officers is to be ascribed the necessity we have been under of relinquishing so important a Post. To the honor of 3000 Troops which we had that day upon the Island it will be remembered that they opposed, fought and for many hours maintained their ground against the Enemys whole force which at the least on that day outnumberd them by 12,000. They cut their Way thro the main body & marked their retreat with the blood of great numbers of the Enemy who we are well assured lost in killed more than fell on our side. From the Enemys obtaining possession of some advantageous heights on the Island our works were commanded by them and were no longer tenable. Under these Circumstances Genl Washington thought it prudent to draw all his Strength to New York. This retreat was effected without any loss to us and in a manner which reflects great Credit upon the Military Abilities of our commanding officer. Unfortunately for us New York being accessible to the Enemys Ships, and lying much lower than Long Island was exposed to all the Enemys Batteries without a possibility of injuring them in return. This rendered the City a post which from the nature of things & the manner in which in all probability the Enemy would conduct their operations could not long be a place of Safety for our Army. Our General foresaw the difficulty & bestowed the utmost endeavours which human prudence could suggest to provide a safe retreat for his Troops & to prevent our Stores falling into the Enemys hands. The first has been effected without loss, the latter in a great measure. The difficulty of removing heavy Cannon was a great obstacle to the perfect accomplishment of this. The General is now at the hights about 9 miles from New York with his Army posted advantageously. Should the Enemy attack him there We hope he will give a good account of them. Thus we have given you a general view of our military matters that you may not be alarmed with false rumors & that you may be furnished with materials to confute the misrepresentations of wicked men who are already pluming themselves with this small success and striving to dispirit the good friends of America by falsehood and exaggeration.

Sept. 19. In obedience to your orders We have directed the several parts of Brownriggs Essay upon making Salt by Sun Evaporation or by Culinary fire to be extracted and published so far as they would apply to the Circumstances of our State and afford information which might be useful to those who may attempt the manufacture of Salt in No Carolina.[2] The pamphlets have been printed with as much Œconomy as possible that there being no occasion for a parsimonious distribution of them, they might fall into many hands and induce great numbers to try and experiment upon which so much at present depends & in which success is so easily attainable.

The Salt pans are engaged tho it has cost us much trouble to prevail upon any one to undertake them. The Blacksmiths here have such full employment in the common routine of their trade that they are averse to any Work which takes them the least out of the common course. The man who is now at work upon the pans has engaged to finish them in four Weeks. We have some doubts whether he will not claim the allowance of an additional Week. He shall not want frequent Applications from us to stimulate him to be expeditious as we know the urgent necessity which you are under for them. By this or the next Opportunity we think it would be proper that you should direct in what manner they should be transported to you, by Water or by land. The Congress have directed a packet to ply between this & our State; should you approve of that mode of conveyance it shall be embraced, as Waggonage will be very expensive. We will send you the weight & size of the pans as nearly as they can be ascertained before they are finished that you may prepare proper works to receive them. The Pamphlets directing the mode of Salt making go in the Congress packet boat to Edenton which sails in a few days; from thence they will immediately be sent to you or where you shall order them.

The military books which you ordered went with the Gunpowder except 14 Volumes which we send packed up with the Salt pamphlets, these are entitled the Field Engineer; It is thought a performance of great merit and from the favourable reception it has met with here among Gentlemen in the military line we have been induced to send a few copies of them to you as practical Engineering is but little understood amongst us and it is a science both in theory and practice essentially necessary to the conducting this war with success.

We hear with great satisfaction of your Intentions to carry on the Iron Works upon deep river upon an extensive plan, which shall comprehend not only the manufacture of military stores but family utensils which we shall not be able to procure elsewhere but at a great expence. The design is great and if carried liberally into execution will not only be attended with great advantages to ourselves, but will make us importantly useful to our southern neighbours to whom nature has not furnished the means for similar undertakings. We have given every possible assistance to Mr Milles while he has been here to make his journey hither successfull and to comply with the views of your honbl body. We regret that our endeavours have not met that success which our Industry and exertions seem to entitle them to. We have yet been able to procure only one Workman, and he is ignorant of the casting of Cannon. Mr Milles in his way home has some expectations of procuring a German who has the reputation of being skilled in the latter branch, if he is so fortunate We shall congratulate you upon the consequences of his embassy. We have yet been able to procure no patterns for casting pots without which the work cannot proceed. We are flattered with the expectation of Mr Milles finding a set at Lancaster, if he gets them he must pay a great price as we are told that they are the only set now for sale in this State. We should not do justice to Mr Milles if we did not assure you that he has been extremely assiduous to comply with the Intentions which you had in sending him here. From the best Judgment we can form of his Abilities as well as the Observation of others He is well qualified to superintend the Works you propose to erect and seems to have the undertaking very near his heart. Indeed he has done every thing here that you could expect from the utmost fidelity, skill and Industry. The Zeal with which all the Iron Works are prosecuted here leaves very little opportunity to prevail on Workmen to go abroad when their Services are so well rewarded at home. We have bought a Waggon and two horses to transport the man he has employed & his baggage & the Patterns.[3] You will learn the Expence from Mr. Hewes, and we doubt not the articles will sell with you at least for what they cost. Should that be the case our views will be answered which are to consult all possible Œconomy in this as in every other matter committed to our care.[4]

RC (Nc–Ar). Written by Hooper and signed by Hooper and Penn.

[1] Hooper wrote this letter over a period of several days extending to September 26. The concluding paragraph of the preceding entry and this letter's continuation on September 19 suggest that he began writing it on the 18th.

[2] See North Carolina Council of Safety to the North Carolina Delegates, July 7, 1776, in *N.C. State Records,* 11:308–9.

[3] For additional information about James Milles, see William Hooper to William Livingston, August 29, 1776, note.

[4] In a continuation of the present letter written on September 24, Hooper noted: "Mr Milles left this yesterday. He takes with him one Ball who has undertaken to cast pots and other open Ware for us. Milles on his way in the neighbourhood of Lancaster expects to procure a Cannon. There he takes up the patterns. We have advanced him 100 dollars which we beg you to note in your settlement with him."

For the continuation of this letter, see North Carolina Delegates to the North Carolina Council of Safety, September 26, 1776.

Robert Treat Paine to Peter Grubb

Sr,[1]   Philaa. Septr. 18th. 1776

By Capt Joy I understand you have at last made some 12 pounders, but I fear they are heavier than they ought to be; those made by Col. Bird weigh but 27 cwt & some under.

You have drawn on the Committee for £1500, it is not sent because the matter is not understood, we can't suppose you want such a sum to carry on the works, & you certainly don't desire the Cannon should be paid for before they are delivered; the sum you draw for is the value of the Guns already made, & as the Contract was made with your Brother Col. Curtis Grubb (tho' you may be equally interested with him) yet I should like to hear from him before so large a sum was paid, however I have sent you by Capt Danl. Joy one thousand Dollars.[2] I mentioned to Congress your Inclination to have some of the Prisoners from Lancaster to work for you, but it was supposed the Committee of Lancaster would Object to it. I hope you will make all Expedition in making the Cannon & getting them down, for they are much wanted. The Cannon must be proved with two shott or they will never be put on board the ships.

I am yr hble Servt,   R T Paine

RC (DLC). Addressed: "To Peter Grubb Esq at Cornwal Furnace."

[1] Peter Grubb was colonel of the eighth battalion of Lancaster militia and

joint owner, with his brother Curtis, of the Cornwall iron furnace at Lancaster. Alexander Harris, *A Biographical History of Lancaster County* (Lancaster, Pa.: E. Barr & Co., 1872), pp. 251–52.

² See Paine to Curtis Grubb, September 20, 1776.

Caesar Rodney to Thomas McKean and George Read

Gentmn.   Philadelphia Sepr. 18th 1776

I have sent my Servant to you with the following disagreable inteligence. By letter from General Washington to Congress, we Are informed that General Howe with About 6 or 7 thousand of his Troops took possession of New-York on Sunday last. We are not so much Astonished that he Should get possession of New York (because we have Expected it for Some time past) As at the Scandelous behaviour of our Troops that were placed to defend the post Where the enemy Landed, Who run away from their lines & breastwork, in a most dastardly manner when not more then Sixty were Landed to oppose them. You must know that the main Body of the Enemy have been for time past placed on the Long-Island side opposite the mouth of Harlem Creek or River, and had Erected Several Batteries there, That played on ours at Horns-hook on the New-York island Side of the Harlem. A part of this main Body of the Enemy had also taken possession of Montisure's Island Situated at the mouth of Harlem and is divided from Morriseny on the East Side of Harlem and Harlem point on the west side, by a water not so wide as Schuylkill ferry. At one or both of these places it was and is Expected they would attempt a Landing. General Washington therefore fixed his Head Quarters on the Heights of Harlem (as they are Called) on the York Island Side of the Creek and posted General Miflin with his Brigade consisting of Shee's, Magaw's, Haslets and Some other Battalions on the heights of Morriseny. He had also placed on the Heights near Kings-Bridge five or Six thousand to Support either the main Army or Mifflins detachment as the Case might Require. The General finding that two forty Gun Ships, two Frigates and one Twenty had Come up the East River, and Come to an Anchor opposite Turtle Bay, which is four Miles above the City, and three miles or thereabout below head Quarters, placed Brigadier General Parsons with his Brigade and some Connecticut Militia, in the whole near three thousand there, to defend that post, at least till they Could be supported by the main Body or a detachment from it. General Putnam with about Three Thousand were left in the City to defend it in the best manner he Could till the Stores Should all be Removed in Which they had been Employ[ed] for Several days before and would have Compleated in one more.

From all I Can collect This was the Situation of Affairs on Sunday Morning, When the Ships before mentioned began a verry heavy Firing at Turtle-Bay to Scour the Country previous to their landing the Troops, but hurt no Body that I can hear of. When the Firing ceased their Troops began to Land and ours to Run as if the Devil was in them, in Spite of all the Genel. Could do. They never fired one Gun. General Washington having discovered their intention to Land at that place, and haveing properly disposed of his Troops in case of an Attempt in either or both the other places, ordered a Reinforcement and set out there himself. However before he got to the place, met our people running in Every direction. He Endeavoured by persuation, Threats &c to get them back, but all to no purpose. In Short they run till they left the General to Shift for himself. General Putnam who was in New-York with his people, hearing What had happened made the best of his way for head Quarters least he should be kooped up, fought his way Through the Enemys lines, brought his men to Camp with the Loss of only three of four as said. It Seems not one of the men who run from the place of the Enemy's landing was from this Side the North River—all New-England men. General Washington Writes he is Advantageously situated at present, and if attacked Should be more than a Match for the Enemy if their numbers were even More than they are, provided his men would fight, which is more to be wished than Expected. I have wrote on this Subject till I am in an Ill Humour, and my only Comfort is that by the time you have read it you'l be as Angry as I am.

I have inclosed Mr. McKean's order on the Trustees of Newcastle thinking it might be wanting. I am Gentmn., Your Most Obedt., Humble Servt.   Caesar Rodney

P.S.   My boy will return tomorrow morning.

RC (DeHi).

Benjamin Rush to Julia Rush

My dearest Julia,   Wednesday Eveng. [September 18–25? 1776] [1]
I begin to sicken for your company. What will become of me a fortnight thence? But I will not as formerly tear you from Morven. I flatter myself that you will soon be infected with home sickness & that you will tease me in less than a fortnight to send Wm. for you.

Our Affairs in New York ⟨grow worse & worse⟩ wear a melancholly aspect in the eyes of most people. You witness for me that I have for a long time not only expected, but *wished* that Genl. Howe might gain possession of New York. I have seen molasses wasted on a board on purpose to collect together & destroy all the flies of a house. In like manner I believe Genl. Howe will attract all the tories of New York & the adjacent states to his army where they will ripen as the tories of Boston did for banishment & destruction. The continent in the mean while will be purged of those rascals whose idleness or perfidy have brought most of our present calamities upon us. But further, I think we stood in need of a frown from heaven. I should have suspected that our cause had not been owned as a divine one, if we had prospered without it. It is, you know, thro' difficulties & tryals that states as well as individuals are trained up to glory & happiness. My faith is now stronger than ever. I begin to hear with pleasure an outcry among some people that there is no dependance to be had upon the arm of flesh. But the worst is not over. We must be bro't lower. I predict a defeat, or another disgraceful retreat. We stand in need of it. We must all be taught that "Salvation is not to be hoped from the hills, nor from the multitude of the Mountains," before we can expect to prevail over our enemies. Adieu my dearest angel. Mrs Stamper joins in love to you & your Mama with, yrs,   B Rush

P.S. I shall write again if possible by the post.

RC (CtY).
[1] Rush's reference to the "melancholly aspect" of "our affairs in New York" suggests that he wrote this letter shortly after the September 15 evacuation of New York, and when in a mood similar to that expressed in his letter to Anthony Wayne of September 24, 1776. September 18 and 25 were Wednesdays.

Benjamin Franklin to William Temple Franklin

Dear Billy   Philada Sept. 19. 1776

I received yours of the 16th, in which you propose going to your Father, if I have no Objection. I have consider'd the matter, and cannot approve of your taking such a Journey at this time, especially alone, for many reasons, which I have not time to write. I am persuaded, that if your Mother should write a sealed Letter to her Husband, and enclose it under Cover to Govr. Trumbull of Connecticut, acquainting him that it contains nothing but what relates to her private Family Concerns, and requesting him to forward or deliver it, (opening it first if he should think fit) he would cause it to be deliver'd safe without opening. I hope you do not feel any Reluctance in returning to your Studies. This is the Time of Life in which you are to lay the Foundations of your future Improvement, and of your Importance among Men. If this Season is neglected, it will be like cutting off the Spring from the Year.

Your Aunt had the Carelessness to send the Bundle containing your Wastecoat, undirected, by Prichard. He forgot where he was to leave it, & with his usual Stupidity carried it to your House & brought it away again without asking a Question about it till he came home. He has also brought away the Razor Case you lent to Mr Adams. We shall send both when there is *another* Opportunity; for one has since been miss'd, that of Mr Bache, who intended calling to see Mrs Franklin. There seems to be a kind of Fatality attending the Conveyance of your things between Amboy & Philadelphia. Benny had written as I told you, but his Letter it seems was not sent. It was thought to be too full of Pothooks & Hangers, and so unintelligible by the dividing Words in the Middle, and joining Ends of some to Beginnings of others, that if it had fallen into the Hands of some Committee it might have given them too much Trouble to decypher it, on a Suspicion of its containing Treason, especially as directed to a Tory House. He is now diligent in learning to write better, that he may arrive at the Honour of Corresponding with his Aunt after you leave her. Mr & Mrs. Green went from hence on Monday, on their Return. I wish they may be in time to cross the North River safely at some of the upper Ferries. My Love to your good Mama, & Respects to her Friends in the Family. Your Aunts join in best Wishes, with, Your affectionate Grandfather,   B Franklin

[*P.S.*] They desire I would express more particularly their Love to Mrs Franklin.

RC (PPAmP). Addressed: "Mr. William Temple Franklin, at Mrs. Franklin's, Perth Amboy. B Free Franklin."

John Adams to William Tudor

Septr. 20. [1776]
We have so many Reports here of the infamous Cowardice of the New England Troops especially of Fellows's and Parsons's Brigades in running away in Spight of their two Generals and General Wash. too, that I am ashamed of my Country. Pray let me know the Truth and whether there is less Courage in the Northern than Southern Troops. The Report of Fellows's and Parsons's Brigades is confirmed by the Generals Letter.[1]

RC (MHi). A continuation of Adams to Tudor, September 2, 1776.
[1] See Arthur Middleton to William Henry Drayton, September 18, 1776, note 1.

Board of War to George Washington

Sir   War Office Septr. 20th. 1776

This will be handed you by four French Gentlemen who arrived from Martinique well recommended & they have accordingly been appointed by Congress Officers in the Army of the United States. The first *Monsr. Marquis de Malmidy* is appointed Major by Brevet, *Monsr. Jean Louis Imbert* is an Engineer & goes without any particular Appointment to be employed in that Capacity in Order to shew to your Excellency his Abilities that you may judge of his Qualifications. Monsr *Christian de Colerus* is appointed to the Rank & Pay of Major by Brevet & Monsr. Jean *Louis de Vernejout* is appointed a Captain by Brevet. They are ordered to wait on you for Directions as to the Duty they are to execute.[1]

I have the Honour to be, your obedt humble Servt,
Richard Peters Secy Bd War

RC (DLC).
[1] See *JCC*, 5:783–84; and the postscript to Benjamin Rush to Jacques Barbeu-Dubourg, September 16, 1776.

Marine Committee to John Young

Sir   September 20th 1776

The Sloop Independence of which you are appointed Commander being now laden, compleatly fitted, armed, victualled and manned, you are to proceed with said Sloop and Cargo for the Island of Martinico putting into Fort Royal or St Piers just as the winds and other circumstances point out for the best. On your arrival at either place you must enquire for Mr William Bingham our resident in that Island. Should he be at the place where you put in, deliver to him the sundry dispatches now committed to your care. Should he be at any other part of the Island you will send an express to inform him of your arrival, & that you have such dispatches which you are directed to deliver into his own hands. He will then repair to you immediately and you must comply with his orders by landing the Cargo wherever he may direct. You must also consult with him and be advised by Mr Bingham in all things that respects the Interest or honor of the united states in the concerns of their sloop under your command. If you put into Fort Royal and Mr Bingham is not there, you must wait on the general and inform him you belong to the United States of America, ask the liberty of the Port and protection during your stay there. If you put into St Piers and dont find Mr Bingham wait on the Governor and Intendant observing the same conduct. If Mr Bingham is present he will direct what you are to do on these points. You are to consider the French and all nations but Great Britain as the Friends of these united states and conduct yourself towards them accordingly and during your Stay in any French Ports be particularly attentive to the behaviour and prudent conduct of your people. You are to receive on board the Sloop any arms, ammunition or other goods Mr Bingham may order. Receive from him also his dispatches and then proceed back for this Port. You are to consider that we are anxious for you to make an expeditious voyage, notwithstanding which as you are well armed and manned and the Sloop sails fast, we do not forbid you chasing such Vessels either going or coming as you think may become your Prizes. For this purpose you have a Commission, a book containing the Resolves of Congress respecting Prizes which you must strictly conform to, and a list of the Continental agents to some of whom you must Address any Prize you take. Should Mr Bingham find it necessary to detain you any time, and he and you should think it adviseable to make a Short cruize during that Time, we do not forbid it, but take care not to fall into the enemys hands. It is an Object with us that you should pick up and bring home with you as many Seamen as possible, the more the better, and you may enter all you get on the same pay and terms of those you carry out.

You must sling our dispatches to Mr Bingham, and on your return, his to us, with a weight sufficient to sink them and always keep them ready to be thrown over board should you unfortunately be taken for you must not let these Packets fall into the enemies hands on any Account. You are to afford releife or assistance to any of the subjects of the united States that want it if in your power, unless proof should appear that they are inimical to their Country and its cause. You are authorized to take, burn, Sink or destroy the vessels and property of all British Subjects except those residing in Bermuda and New Providence, but we recommend humanity and politness to be inseperable companions of the officers in the Continental Service. It is necessary you should be careful of the Sloop, her materials and Stores, diligent in the discharge of your own duty and careful to make your officers and men perform theirs, Strict in discipline but attentive to render the service agreeable to all concerned in it.

We expect you will be frugal in expences and on your return furnish us with duplicates of your Log book and Journal giving also a Satisfactory account of your voyage, and when you approach this coast, keep a good look out as you may expect many of the enemies Ships will be Cruizing for plunder. If you cannot get in here you may push for any of the Inlets or other place of safety the nearer to this the better.

We are Sir, Your hble servants.

LB (DNA: PCC Miscellaneous Papers, Marine Committee Letter Book).

Maryland Delegates to the
Maryland Council of Safety

Gent.   Phila. 20th Septr. 1776. Friday

Capt. Watkins waits on you by our Advice with a Return of his Company by which it appears he has now here only thirty seven effective privates and indeed several of that Number appear to us not really effective. The Men complained of not being furnished with Blankets and Cloathing according to the Engagemts. made with them, and f[rom this] Ground as Capt. Watkins alledges the p[resent] Discontent of the men originated. We have no Certainty of getting the Cloathing though our Endeavours shall be continued. The Officers have procured the Blankets. Lieut. Lang goes to Worcester to endeavour to get the Deserters to return to their Duty under an Assurance which we have presumed to give that on their immediate Return the past shall be forgiven. Capt. Watkins and his Men we are sorry to inform you are on very ill Terms. The Capt. had beat some of them. He says he had great Cause; they say he had none. Some of the Men have said nothing shall induce them to continue in the Company under Capt. Watkins. We shall endeavour to keep the Remnant of the Company together under the Care of the third Lieutt. until your Orders can interpose for though our Inquiry seems to us to be necessary it cannot be had here; if the Independt. companies should be regimented or even if the Soldiers Cloaths can be got perhaps Order may be restored in the Company.

We have a Letter of the 15 Instant from Capt. Thomas from whence it appears our Sick have not such Care taken of them as they ought. We wish if it is in your power to send a skilful and attentive person who should have the immediate Care of the Independt. Companies you would do so. We have requested Dr Bond to recommend such a one that we may propose him to Congress for this Service but from the Doctors Answer we almost despair of finding a suitable person here.

By a Letter from Genl Washington of the 18 Inst. we had a little Brush on Monday in which the Enemy had about 100 killed and wounded. Our Loss was considerably less. Report had much exaggerated our Advantage. Majr. Leach [Leitch] of the Virginians is wounded though it is hoped he will recover. Some of Richardsons and Griffiths Battalions were in the Action and behaved well.

Colo. Richardson told W[illiam] P[aca] that he lodged in the same House as Capt. Watkins, that he is addicted to Drink, and his Appearance at several Times we have seen him bespeaks it. Perhaps Colo. Richardson wd. not choose that what he said should be mentioned to Capt. Watkins.[1] We are Gent., Your most obedt. Servts.,   Ths. Johnson Junr   Saml. Chase

                Wm Paca   T. Stone

[*P.S.*] By a Letter this Minute received from Gen. Washington dated the 19th, We are informed that he expects a general attack on his Lines.[2]

RC (MdAA). Written by Johnson and signed by Johnson, Chase, Paca, and Stone, with postscript by Stone.

[1] Despite the difficulties involving Capt. Thomas Watkins related by the delegates and a subsequent suggestion by Stone that he be dismissed from the service, the captain continued in command of his company. For the council's response to the present letter, see *Md. Archives*, 12:304–5. See also Thomas Stone to the Maryland Council of Safety, September 30, 1776.

[2] This day Johnson also wrote a second letter to the council inquiring about the disposition of a shipment of powder which had recently arrived with a cargo shipped by Richard Harrison from Martinique for Willing, Morris & Co. Johnson's letter and the council's response are in *Md. Archives*, 12:291, 304–5.

Robert Treat Paine to Curtis Grubb

Sr.,   Philada. Septr. 20. 1776.

    Your Brother Mr. Peter Grubb the other day drew an Order on the Cannon Comittee for £1500 & sent it by Capt. Daniel Joy who tells me that they had cast 27 12-pounders & were going on successfully, but as none of the Guns were sent down & I did not know your inclination about paying so large a Sum, I concluded not to send it, but understanding by Mr. Joy that the Clerk of the Furnace had told him that some money was wanting I sent one thousand dollars on the Orders. I wish I know your mind on the matter & whether you would have any more money paid.[1] I wish likewise you would write me what you think to be a sufficient proof for Cannon for you know it is of the last importance that they should not burst on board the ships, & unless they are sufficiently proved the sailors will be shy of them. We have wanted the Cannon more than they are worth but I am now in hopes they will be made to answer both our Expectations.

    Wishing you health & Success I am,   RTP

FC (MHi). Addressed: "To Col. Curtis Grubb at the Flying Camp."

[1] See Paine to Peter Grubb, September 18, 1776; and Daniel Joy to Paine, September 10, 1776, in Morgan, *Naval Documents*, 6:773–74.

Robert Treat Paine to Jonathan Trumbull, Sr.

Sr.   Philada. Septr. 20. 1776

The Congress have directed me to write to you respecting the practicability of Casting heavy Cannon at Salisbury furnace & to desire yr. opinion concerning the same.¹ The Occasion of this Resolve was that Congress were informed that the ore wch. is worked at that furnace is of the best quality for casting Cannon & that this appears by the Cannon already Cast there, that the furnace is not large enough to Cast Cannon heavier than 12 pounders; that the furnace & beds of ore belonged to a Mr. Richard Smith late of Boston an absconding Tory & that the State of Connecticut had taken it into the possession of Government & had sett it to work in making Cannon, & Congress being desirous that heavier Cannon should be made at a place convenient to Supply the middle & Eastern Colonies they directed this Consultation to be had.

As this furnace is in the Care of yr. State it is necessary to address you on the subject which I think you will not consider as troublesome when the advantage of establishing a Manufacture of heavy Cannon in so convenient a scituation occurs to yr. mind. The grand Question is how it can be done, previous to the answering which I think it will be necessary to be fully ascertained that the ore is as good in quality for making Cannon as has been supposed, that there is a sufficiency of it, that Coal may be had in the neighbourhood & that the stream of Water is sufficient for the purpose. This being the case, I suppose that in order to cast heavy Cannon another Stack must be built adjoining to the one that now is, so that both together may have mettal sufficient in fusion at once to cast a 32 pounder or even larger by tapping both at once, but who shall erect the new furnace & carry on the works? If the place was now private property the owner might undertake it, but whether yr. State will undertake it themselves or allow any body to do it I dont know. I think if some person who understands the business should be found to undertake it with the permission of yr. State it would be profitable to him; for I suppose Congress would engage to take a large no. of heavy Cannon at such a price as wd. be advantagious to him. Messrs. Hughes of Maryland Who have made exceeding good long 18 pdrs. wch. have stood the highest proof has Contracted with Congress to build another Stack & make 1000 Tons of Cannon from 32 lb. downwards as Congress may direct for, £36 Pen. Curr. per Ton, but if the War should be pushed hard upon us it may be very difficult getting Any of these Guns into N England, the advantages of which I need not mention. It is therefore I think incumbent on us to exert our selves to effect this valuable manufacture. I have so little knowledge of the manner in which the furnace has been carried on lately (tho' I have taken pains to acquire it) that I can make no particular proposals about it. Perhaps the Person who has had the management wd. undertake it; whatever is done this Season must be done soon; & a particular Answer as soon as you conveniently can will be very agreable.

The maintaining the post at the highlands is of the utmost importance to the united States in general & to N England in particular in order for which Cannon are still wanted. It is said that 18 pounders are cast at the furnace. I am desired by the Committee on the highland affairs to request of you to inform us of this fact & if there be any such whether they can be removed for those forts. I am &c,   RTP

FC (MHi).
  [1] For Congress' instructions to Paine this day, see *JCC*, 5:807. Governor Trumbull's October 25 response is in Morgan, *Naval Documents*, 6:1271–72.

Secret Committee Minutes of Proceedings

Sepr. 20. 1776

Come. met. Present, Morris, Hewes, Lewis, Bartlett. Agreed to pay Mr. Jonn. Hudson the valuation of his ship Molly, taken by Ld. Dunmore & retaken on her passage to Burmuda, by the Andrew Doria, Capt. Biddle, & sent for Rhode Isld. valuation or sum insurd on Charter party £5000. Also agreed to pay his Acct. for Expences, incurrd by said ship being taken by the Otter & retaken by Ship Defence of Maryland amount £159.8—

£5159.8 Equal to Dollars 13755 36/90
deduct what is already paid him .. 2133 30/90
leaving due 11625   6/90, for which drew an order on the Treasurer.[1]

Mr. Benjamin Gibbs appeared before the Come. & represented that the Ship Aurora, Capt. Getshuis, is taken & carried into Gibralter, for the truth of wch. he refers to a Letter from Messrs. Livingston & Trumbull of that place to Messrs. Willg., Morris & Co. wch. they confirm to be the case. Agreed to pay Mr. Gibbs £3500 the valuation as per Chartr. party he givg. a receit for the money bindg. him to refund it if the ship should not be condemnd as a prize, of wch. however there is no hopes. Therefore issued an order on the Treasurer for 9333 1/3 dlls in favor of Mr. Gibbs.[2] Mr. Oswell Eve producd his acct. for manufacturing powdr. to this time amountg to 13157 lb with the Comy's receit for that quantity wch. at half cost of Casks amounts to £405.11, deduct already pd. him £200, balance £205.11, equal to Dlls 548 12/90 for wch. sum we this day issued an order on the Treasurer in favor said Oswell Eve being in full to this time. Agreed That Mr. Morris be desird to buy up quantities of tobo. here, in Maryld., Virga. & N. Carolina & of Indigo & Rice in S. Carolina & Georgia. Agreed that Mr. Morris be desird to write to the Continental Agents in Connecticut & Rhode Island to get 600 tents made up with all possible expedition & send them as fast as made to Genl. Washington.

MS (MH–H).
  [1] For additional information on Jonathan Hudson's contract with the committee, see Secret Committee Minutes of Proceedings, May 25, 1776.
  [2] For Gibbs' contract with the committee, see Secret Committee Minutes of Proceedings, March 4, 1776.

Secret Committee to William Bingham

Sir   Philada. Septemr. 20th 1776
    You will find inclosed herein Invoice and bill of Loading for
hhds of Tobacco and   Tons barr Iron which we have Shipped
on board the Sloop Independance, John Young Master, for Martinico Consigned to your order for Sale on accot of the United States of America. You will please to have this Cargo sold to the best advantage and Credit the Secret Committee for the Neat proceeds. We hope the Brigt Cornelia & Molly, Capt Lockhard, arrived Safe, and that you will have placed the Neat proceeds of that Cargoe also at our Credit. The two Sloops were very unfortunate adventures.
    You will charge the Cost of the Arms and powder you Sent by the Reprisal, Capt Wickes, to this Committee but if you apply any part of our Consignments to making the needfull Supplies for the Reprisal, Independance or any other Continental Vessell, you Must Remit us drafts on the Marine Committee for amount of such and if you make any to private Ships we charter and Send to your address, then Remit us the Captains drafts on the Owners for Such Amount, and if you apply any part to pay your Own expences or other necessary charges Relating to the business of the Committee of Secret Correspondence Send us your drafts on them for such amount. By this means we can keep perfect accots. and each department will answer for its proper disbursements.
    We inclose you herein a List of Medicines which we are ordered to import for the Continental Service. Pray collect any part you can get in the West Indies and send them here Soon as possible, and at the same time send a Copy of the List forward to Mr. Thomas Morris and desire him to order the full quantity from Europe to your care which you'l forward as soon as they arrive. We request you to send us all the good Arms & Gunlocks, Powder, Gun Flints, Salt petre, Sulphur, Sail Cloth, Blankets, or other Woolin goods

you can possibly get, by return of the Sloop Independance & we Shall keep making you further Remittances to enable your paying for whatever you buy in the Service of these States. With the best wishes for your health and Success, We remain sir, Your very hble Servants,   Robt Morris   Fras Lewis

                              Richard Henry Lee   Josiah Bartlett

                                                          Phil. Livingston

Copy.

FC (PHi). In a clerical hand and signed by Bartlett, Lee, Lewis, Livingston, and Morris.

William Williams to Jonathan Trumbull, Sr.

Hond & Dear Sir   Philadel. 20th Sepr. 1776
    It will undoubtedly be needless for me to give You any account of the Evacuation of N York by our army on Sab. Day the 15th, of most of our heavy Cannon falling into the hands of our Enemies &c, as it will be communicated to you by my Bror. Comissa., many ways ee'r this can reach your Hand. This Event unhappy & distressing as it is has been foreseen & known ever since the quitting of Long Island, & had been determined by the Genl. & his Council; Congress had been made fully accquainted with & assented to it as absolutely necessary, & directed that it shod not be destroyed by Us on leaving it. These Events however, & signal advantage gained by our oppressors, & the Distress to which our Army & Country are & must be subjected in Consequence of them, are loud speaking Testimonies of the Displeasure & Anger of almighty God against a sinful People, louder than sevenfold Thunder. Is it possible that the most obdurate & stupid of the Children of America shod not hear & tremble? God has surely a Controversie with this People, & He is most certainly able to manage it & He will accomplish his Designs, & bring Us to Repentance & Reformation, or destroy Us. We must bend or break. The ways of his Providence are dark & deep but they are holy, wise, & just & altogether right, tho our feeble Understandings comprehend them not, & tho his Chastisements are severe & dreadful, They are dictated by unbounded Wisdom & Love. They have a meaning of awful & kind Import. Turn unto me for why will ye die O Sons of America. We have thought God was for Us & had given many & signal Instances of His Power & Mercy in our Favor, & had greatly frowned upon & disappointed our Enemies & verily it has been so, but have we repented & given Him the Glory? Verily no. His Hand seems to be turned & stretched out against Us, & strong is his Hand & high is his right Hand. He

can & will accomplish all his Pleasure. It is God who has blunted
the Weapons of our warfare, that has turned the Counsels of wise
Men into Foolishness, that has thus far blasted & disappointed our
Hopes, & made Us flee before our Enemies, & given them Possession of our Strong Holds. Trouble does not spring out of the dust
nor rise out of the Ground. I have always thot this was a just &
righteous Cause in which We are engaged. I remain unshaken in
that firm persuasion, & that God wod sooner or later vindicate &
support it, I believe so still, but I believe this People must first be
brot to know & Acknowledge the righteousness of his Judgment, &
their own exceeding Sinfulness & Guilt, & be deeply humbled under
his mighty hand, & look & cry to & trust in Him for all their Help
& Salvation but in the Use & Exertion of all the Strength He has
given Us. Surely We have seen enough to convince Us of all this, &
then why are We not convinced, why is not every Soul humbled
under the mighty hand of God, repenting & mourning For its Sins &
putting away the evil of his Doings, & looking to Him that smites
Us by humble, earnest & fervent Prayer & Supplication day & Night.
Why are not the dear Children of God (surely there are many, tho
the Scorn & Insult of our Enemies) beseiging the Throne of Grace,
sighing & crying for their own Sins & back slidings & for all the
abominations that are done in the Land, & saying spare, spare thy
People O Lord & give not thine Heritage to Reproach. Let not the
Vine which thy right Hand has planted here be rooted up & destroyed, let not thy Churches be wasted & devoured, let not virtue &
the remains of Religion be torn down & trampled in the Dust, Let
not thy Name be blasphemed, nor our insulting wicked Foes say
where is your God, nor the profane world that there is no God
that rules the world & regardeth the Right, that vindicateth the
just & the righteous Cause. I know that God can vindicate his own
Name & Honor without our Help, & out of the Stones raise up
Children to Abraham, & it is amazing Folly & Madness to cry the
Temple, the Temple of the Lord, & trust in that while We remain
an incorrigible People. But Such Things are what God wod have
Us learn & practice while his Judgments are abroad in the Land, &
with such like Arguments fill our Mouths, & pour out our Souls
before Him. Are any? Are not all? in N England especially, who
have any Interest in Heaven, crying, beging & intreating for the out
pouring of blessed Spirit of God upon the Land, tis a most grievous
& distressing Consideration that God is pleased so to withhold the
blessed Influences & operations thereof, without which We shall
remain stupid forever. Therefore with redoubled fervency of ardent
Prayer & Supplication, shod every Soul that has one Sparck of Heav-
enly Fire kindle it to a fervent Heat & expanded Blaze.

O New England, O my dear native Land, how does my Soul
Love thee. Be Instructed therefore lest Gods Soul depart from thee,

lest thou be like Corazin & Bethsaida in Condemnation as thou
hast been in Privileges, lest He make thee as Admah & set thee as
Zeboim. Are the Ministers of the Gospel alive & awake & lifting up
their Voices like a trumpet & sounding the Alarm of the Almightys
Anger & Wrath ready to burst on the defenseless Heads of a guilty
People? Are they warning the wicked of their infinite Danger, animating & arousing them to Consideration? Are they with ardent
Zeal & Fervour animating & enlivening the languid Graces of the
Godly, exciting & leading them to fervent Prayer, sighing & crying
for their own Declensions & Luke warmness in Religion & for the
Sins & Iniquities of the Land, praying, beging & intreating with un-
ceasing & as it were resistless Importunity for the copious Effusions
of the Blessed Spirit upon all orders & degrees of People & refusing
to let God go, without an Answer of Peace, & in the midst of
Wrath to remember Mercy, & not give up this his Heritage to Reproach nor blast the blooming Hopes & Prospects of this infant
Country, the Asylum of Liberty & Relegion?

Strange that Mankind shod need such alarming Providences to
produce such an Effect. It is no more than to act like reasonable
Creatures, to possess a Spirit & Temper that will add a thousand
fold sweetness & pleasure to all the Enjoyments of this World, to
exchange the Slavery of the Devil, that accursed Enemy of our
Souls, for the Service of God & the Liberty of his Children, to do
justly, to love Mercy & walk humbly with our God, to answer the
sole end of our Creation, to secure a Peace here infinitely better
than the World can give, & an Eternity of Peace & Happiness in the
World to come. But still more strange if possible, & astonishing is
it that They Shod disregard the Voice of the most high, remain
thoughtless & stupid under the dreadful Tokens of his Anger &
the awful Judgments of his Hand, by Sickness & by the Sword
of our unnatural & enraged Enemies threatening to depopulate the
Land & drench the Plains with the Blood of its Inhabitants, leaving
the weeping Widows, helpless Orphans & the all that survive the
shocking Carnage & subsequent Masacre to drag out their Lives in
Want, Wretchedness & miserable Bondage & all this aggravated
with the certain Prospect of leaving this dreadful Curse intailed on
all Posterity.

A thorough Repentance & Reformation, without all peradven-
ture will appease the Anger of a holy & just God, avert these amazing Calamities, secure Liberty & Happiness to this & all succeeding
Ages & eternal Felicity & Glory to all the Subjects of it. If such
Considerations & Motives wont awaken a[ll] to serious Though-
fulness & Attention, I know n[ot] what will, but the Voice of the
Arch Angel & the Trump[et] of God.

I am hond & dear Sir most affectionately your dutiful Son &
Servant.   Wm Williams

P.S. You will not think proper to communicate this Letter to the Assembly. I am anxious beyond the power of Language to describe, of contributing something to the Good & Salvation, temporal & eternal, of my Countrymen. (Hope I have not been totally useless here.) If you shod think this may have any tendency, to awake our sleepy People & be of no disadvantage, I am willing it shod be printed &, for no other possible reason, leaving out such of the begining as may be a clue to guess the author or where He is, & with the description or Signature of a Letter from a Gent of Connecticut, now in a different Colony.[1]

May God in great Mercy preserve your Health, & long continue your valuable & important Life. With kindest Remembrance to my dear Wife & Friends.   W W

RC (Ct).
[1] A slightly edited version of the main body of this letter appeared in the October 14, 1776, issue of the *Connecticut Courant and Hartford Weekly Intelligencer* under the heading: "Extract of a letter from a gentlemen of Connecticut, now in a distant State."

John Adams to Abigail Adams

Septr. 21. 1776

Yours of Septr. 9 I have received. Septr. 5 I sent you another Cannister by Mr. Hare. I have only Time to tell you I am not worse in Health than I have been. Where are your new Delegates? None arrived here yet. Our People are as lazy and slothfull, as Congress.[1]

LB (MHi). Adams, *Family Correspondence* (Butterfield), 2:130.
[1] For the inaction of the Massachusetts General Court, see Adams to John Avery, July 25, 1776, note 1. Seven delegates were elected by Joint ballot of the council and house of representatives on November 15 and commissioned on December 10, 1776. But James Lovell did not appear in Congress until February 4, 1777. See Minutes of the Massachusetts Council, DLC (ESR); and *JCC*, 7:85.

Samuel Chase to Horatio Gates

Dear Sir   Philadelphia Septr. 21st. 1776

I came from Annapolis ten Days ago, and have the pleasure to inform You that your Lady was well at Frederick Town a few Days before, as Mr Beatty informed Me. I wrote to Mrs. Gates and enclosed her your Letter to Me.

I readily make Peace with you,[1] and shall wait with Patience 'till I see you for a full Explanation. I could not but be mortified at your Censure, because I both respect and esteem You.

I wish You would by Letter inform Me of your Suspicions and disclose the secret Springs which You suppose have influenced Men and Measures in your Department. It is not Curiosity but an earnest Desire to hunt out the Villain and to drag him before the awful Tribunal of the public that urges Me to know the Mystery.

Our affairs here wear a very unfavourable Aspect. You have been undoubtedly informed of the Battle on Long Island. On this Day week, the Enemy landed a Body of forces at Turtle Bay (after a severe Cannonade from their ships in the East River to scour the County, and to cover their Landing). Our Troops posted in Lines thrown up to oppose their Landing abandoned them at the first appearance of the Enemy, in the utmost precipitation and Confusion. Two Brigades commanded by Generals Parsons and Fellows were ordered to support them, they also fled in every Direction, without firing a single Shot, notwithstanding the Exertions of their Generals to form them, and oh disgraceful on the appearance of only about 60 or 70 of the Enemy! By this infamous Conduct We lost a great part of our Baggage and most of our heavy Cannon which had been left at N York. Our Army retreated & possessed themselves of the Heights of Harlem, Our Head Quarters at Roger Morris's House. On Monday last the Enemy appeared in the plains 2 1/2 Miles from the Heights—about 400 under Genl Leslie. A Skirmish began between them and a Party of volunteers from several New England Regimts. commanded by Colo. Knolton. Our people were supported by Companies from a Virginia Battalion and from two Militia Maryland Regiments. The Enemy were obliged to retreat with the Loss of about 100 killed & prisoners. Colo. Knolton, a brave officer, was killed. Major Leitch of Maryland was wounded & despaired of. The Enemies main Army is now encamped between 7 & 8 Mile Stones. Gen. Howes head Quarters at one Mr. Apthorps. On the 19th Gen. Washington writes that he expects from the Movements of the Enemy a general attack. I greatly fear the Event.

If Gen. Schuyler is with you make Me most respectfully remembered to him, also to Generals Arnold and Saint Clair.[2] Adieu. Your Affectionate and Obedt Servant,   Saml. Chase

[*P.S.*] Congress have resolved to raise 88 Battalions of regular forces to be enlisted during the War. Would it had been done last Year.

RC (NHi).
    [1] See Chase to Horatio Gates, August 9, 1776.
    [2] In his last letter to Gates, written from Annapolis, Chase had offered the following observation on Arthur St. Clair. "The same good opinion of Colonel Saint Clair which induced Me to recommend him to your Notice, compelled Me to urge his promotion and for which I stayed in Congress beyond my Time limitted for my Return here." Chase to Gates, September 8, 1776, Gates Papers, NHi.

Committee of Secret Correspondence to William Bingham

Sir,   Philadelphia September 21st 1776

Your several letters of the 4th, 15th and 26th August to this Committee have been duely received with the several enclosures & the whole have been laid before the Congress. We can therefore communicate that satisfaction which we dare say it must afford you to know that you have so far obtained the approbation of that August Body.

It is not necessary that we should enter into minute replys to the Contents of your letters, therefore we shall only notice such parts as seem to require it.

Captain Wickes behaviour meets the approbation of his country and fortune seems to have had an Eye to his merit when she conducted his three prizes safely in.[1] You made a very proper use of his engagement, by your question to the General and it is extreamly satisfactory, that our prizes may be carried into and protected in the French ports, but hitherto the Congress have not thought proper to intrust blank Commissions beyond Sea's, Neither can their Resolve for bringing prizes into some of these States for Condemnation be dispensed with. These matters are now under consideration of a Committee and should any alteration take place you Shall be informed of it.

We are bound to return thanks to his Excellency the General for the information he Authorized you to give us as mentioned in your letter of the 4th and particularly for his disposition to Favour Our Commerce in Port and protect it at Sea and likewise for that concern he expressed at not having it in his power to assist us with the Arms and powder we requested.[2] You will therefore signify to His Excellency that this Committee entertain the warmest sentiments of esteem and respect for his person and character, and of gratitude for His Favourable attention to the concerns of our much injured Country, that we request the continuance of his Friendship and hope during your residence at Martinico there will be many opportunities of benefiting by His Favourable disposition—particularly in countenancing you in the purchase and exportation of Arms, Ammunition and Clothing.

We are not surprized that Admiral Young's letter shou'd alter the Generals sentiments respecting Convoys, but we esteem much his Spirited answer to the Admiral which may probably be productive of some alteration.[3] We like well your proposal for a Constant intercourse by Packets, and the Sloop Independance, Capt Young, is now sent on that service in which we hope she will be Successfull and continue. More of the like kind shall follow and probably this may be found the best method of supporting our intercourse with Europe, and as these Vessels are properly Commissioned we cannot see any impropriety in fitting out Tenders with Coppies of their Commissions provided the Commanding officer of those Tenders are really officers belonging to the vessel whose Commissions they bear, but the prizes must be sent to America for condemnation (unless the Cargoes are perishable) and in such case if properly certifyed it might be best to make sale of them.

We thank you for Mr. Prices Pamphlet [4] and wish you woud write to Mr Deane & Mr. Morris to contrive you a Constant and ample supply of the English, Irish, & French News papers, Political publications &c. We Send you by this opportunity the Journals of Congress as far as published and the news Papers to this time. We received the Arms & Powder by the Reprisal; they came seasonably, and we wish there had been more of them. The Secret Committee will Supply you with Funds for the payments for these and more.

Since the arrival of Ld. Howe and Gen. Howe in the Neighbourhood of New York with their Forces, they have been rather too Strong for our people to cope with, and consequently have succeeded in their interprizes, which however have not been of that importance that they will probably to the World. They have been ten or twelve weeks with a powerfull Fleet & are well provided and appointed with every thing necessary and what have they done? They have got possession of three small Islands on the Coast of America, these were hardly disputed with them and yet if every Acre of American teritory is to cost them in the same proportion the Conquest woud ruin all Europe. Our Army are now collected to a point and are Strongly entrenched on New York Island and at Kingsbridge, so that in fact Mr Howe is hemmed in as he was at Boston, except that he has more Elbow Room and a powerfull Fleet commanding an extensive Inland Navigation. Our Northern Army are Strongly posted at Tyconderago and expect they will be able to keep Mr Burgoyne from Crossing the Lakes this Campaigne.

We are worse off for Woolen Cloathing for our Army than any other matter, and you must exert your utmost industry to buy and send us every thing of that kind you can meet with in Martinico or any of the Neighbouring Islands. We have gone into this detail of our present situation that you may have a just Idea of it and be able to make proper representations to the General and inhabitants of Martinico.

We recommended the French officers that came with Captain Wickes to Congress, and the board of war have provided for them to their Satisfaction. On this Subject your remarks have been very proper. Officers unacquainted with our Language cannot be Usefull, therefore we do not wish to encourage such to come amongst us. At the same time men of Merit and abilities will always meet with Suitable encouragement. You must therefore pursue the line you set out in, give general discouragement to those that apply and recommend none but such as the General will pledge his word for, and you may even intimate to him that if too many come over the Congress will not know what to do with them.[5]

RC (CtY). In a clerical hand, and signed by Franklin and Morris. Morris' draft of this letter is in PCC, item 37.

[1] For Capt. Lambert Wickes' encounter with H.M. Sloop *Shark,* see Thomas Jefferson to Edmund Pendleton, August 26, 1776, note 4.

[2] General d'Argout's offer to favor "the interest of the Insurgents as much as it would be within my power" was immediately overruled by the French minister of marine, Gabriel de Sartine. See Morgan, *Naval Documents,* 5:1317–19, 6:583–84.

[3] For British Admiral James Young's strongly worded protest and General d'Argout's response, see ibid., 6:51–52, 111.

[4] Richard Price's *Observations on the Nature of Civil Liberty.*

[5] For the continuation of this letter, see Committee of Secret Correspondence to Bingham, October 1, 1776.

William Ellery to Nicholas Cooke

Sir,   Philadelphia Sept. 21st. 1776

Congress have ordered a New Army to be raised to consist of Eighty eight Battalions, each State to furnish as follows—New Hampshire three, Massachusetts Fifteen, Rhode Island &c Two, Connecticut Eight, New York Four, New Jersey Four, Pennsylvania Twelve, Lower Counties One, Maryland Eight, Virginia Fifteen, North Carolina Nine, South Carolina Six and Georgia One, to serve during the War; and to encourage a speedy Inlistment have ordered a Bounty of Twenty Dollars for each Soldier that shall inlist, and a Grant of Land &c &c. The Resolve of Congress respecting the new Army, & the new Articles of war will be transmitted to you; but as it is possible they may not reach you so soon as a Letter by the Post, I have therefore been more particular than I should have otherwise been.[1]

The State of Massachusetts Bay have ordered every Fifth Man to march to reinforce the Army near New York, from all their Towns except Those which from their Situation are exposed to the Enemy, and from which the Battalion is to be composed that is to supply the Place of the Continental Battalion ordered from Newport to New York. I wish they may arrive at Camp before a decisive Battle is fought. You have heard without Doubt of a Skirmish between a Party of our Troops and a Party of the Enemy, and that our Troops drove them repeatedly from their Ground and forced them to retreat. It was the Intention of Genl. Washington to have served the Enemy as they did Us at Long Island. He ordered a Party to attack them in Front, while another Party should march round and attack them in the Rear; but it so happen'd that they attacked them in Flank. However our Men behaved like Heroes, killed about 20 or 30, and wounded three Times that Number, according to an account given by a Deserter. Our Loss would have been trifling if We had not lost Col. Knowlton of Connecticut, who was a brave officer. We had but a few Men killed and a few slightly wounded.[2]

Although this Action in itself consider'd is but of little Moment; yet considering the Spirit it hath infused into our Army it may be attended with the most happy Consequences.

The Enemy have moved Eight large Ships up the North River against our Encampment, and are moving some heavy Cannon towards it; so that Genl. Washington expects soon to be cannonaded in Front and Flank. He is determined to keep his Post so long as he can with Prudence.[3] We have had nothing lately from the Northern Army, when We have I will communicate it, if it can be done with Honour.

I could wish to know whether any of the Hemp purchased for the Continental Ships in Providence hath been apply'd to making rigging for Privateers; and whether any Number of Soldiers have quitted the Battalions in our State and been received on board the Privateers. Such a Story hath been told to many Members of Congress, and hath been thrown in my Teeth. I should be extremely sorry if any of the Hemp so purchased hath been misapplied and that our Merchants should have connived at the Soldiery enlisting on Board their Privateers; for, to say nothing of the Injustice of such Conduct, it might be exceedingly injurious to our little State. I can't beleive there is any Truth in this Story but should be glad to have Authority to say that it is false.

I take the Liberty to inclose two Letters directed to Govr. Hopkins; which came by the last Post which please to send to Him. I should not have taken this Freedom; but I have not Time to write Him. I am with great Respect, Yr Honor's most obedient, humble Servant, Wm Ellery

RC (R–Ar).
[1] See *JCC,* 5:762–63.
[2] See Washington, *Writings* (Fitzpatrick), 6:67–70.
[3] See ibid., p. 73.

Francis Lewis to Nathaniel Shaw, Jr.

Dear Sir   Phila. 21 Septmr. 1776

I have your favor of the 11 Septmr. and am pleased to find you can procure seed sufficient to compleat the lading of Cap Kennedys ship, & that you would give her all the possible dispatch in your power.[1]

I am also glad to hear Capt Exceen with the Brigt Friendship is at your Port with 6 or 700 bus[hels] salt. If you can prevail upon him to come round with his salt either to this place or Virginia (where the Coast is intirely clear from Cruizers as Vessells arive here daily) we would from either place give his Vessell an extraordinary good freight out again and allow him for his extra time and still hold his Vessell insured by the Congress. Should this be objected to (which I hope will not be the case as the Vessell can earn nothing now) endeavor to get his Vessell discharged at New London, & let me know the result.

I am, Sir, Your very Humble Servt,   Fras Lewis

P.S. Pray let the Flaxseed be well cleaned.

RC (CtY).
[1] This letter to Lewis from Shaw, the Continental prize agent in Connecticut, is in Morgan, *Naval Documents*, 6:781. In it Shaw mentions an August 24 letter from Lewis which has not been found. See also New York Delegates to Augustine Lawrence and Samuel Tuder, October 21, 1776, note 3.

Marine Committee to Thomas Cushing

Sir,   In Marine Committee, Philadelphia Septem. 21, 1776

In consequence of a letter from the president of Massachusetts Bay dated the 13 Instant to the President of the Congress which was by Congress referrd to this Committee; we have determined to Comply with the wishes of your assembly by Ordering the Frigate Commanded by Capt. McNeill and that by Captain Thompson of New Hampshire to be fitted immediately and proceed on a Cruize on your Coast in hopes of taking the Milford Frigate or of drawing her or any other Enemy away from those Seas.[1]

We therefore authorize you to accept the Profferd assistance of the said assembly or any Committee they appoint to assist in fitting, equipping, arming & manning that Frigate. You are also to Accept their offer of Twenty four nine Pounders (cannon) and to Co-operate with them in getting this ship to sea with the utmost Expedition, and we agree to reimburse the state of Massachusetts Bay for all Just & necessary Expences they incurr in Effecting this Business. We shall in due time also cause this Cannon to be returned unless they think proper to make Sale of them for the use of this ship and in that case we woud choose to purchase them provided they are good guns quite suitable for the service.

You will please to purchase a proper number of Swivell Guns, good musketts, Blunderbusses, cutlasses, Pikes & other arms & instruments suitable for this ship. You will apply to your state for powder, Ball, muskett shott, other military stores to be paid or returned by the Congress and in short as this ship will instantly go into Danger we hope nothing will be neglected that ought to be done in fitting & manning her.

We are very sincerely, Your most obedient Servants,

<table>
<tr><td>John Hancock</td><td>Richard Henry Lee</td></tr>
<tr><td>Robt Morris</td><td>Samuel Huntington</td></tr>
<tr><td>Joseph Hewes</td><td>Samuel Chase</td></tr>
<tr><td></td><td>Josiah Bartlett</td></tr>
</table>

P.S. If Mr Langdon applys to you, Mr Bradford or to your state for assistance in fitting out the frigate under his care we hope it will be granted & we shall reimburse all Just Expences & Charges. The intended Enterprize shoud be Kept as secret as possible.[2]

Tr (MHi). Endorsed: "The above is a True Coppy. Thomas Cushing Junr."

[1] James Bowdoin's September 13 letter to John Hancock is in *Am. Archives,* 5th ser. 2:315. Cushing was currently in charge of the construction of Continental frigates at Newburyport, Mass. Morgan, *Naval Documents,* 5:448. He subsequently informed the Marine Committee that he was doing his best to get the frigate *Boston,* commanded by Capt. Hector McNeill, ready for sea "but must beg leave to remind your Honors that I have not yet received the Commissions for the Officers and they will not Care to go to Sea till they are possessed of them least they should be deem'd Pirates." See Cushing to the Marine Committee, October 7, 1776, ibid., 6:1146–47.

[2] On September 25 Stephen Hopkins, a member of the Marine Committee who was then in Providence, wrote the following letter to Gen. Artemas Ward, the Continental commander at Boston: "Being informed that their is a quantity of Eighteen pound shott now at Boston belonging to the Continent, a number of large Anchors &c. and as a part of those Articles are wanted for the equipping of the two ships of War here, desire you will deliver to Mr John Innis Clarke the Bearer Nine hundred of the shott, one anchor, also two Magazine Lanthorns. Your Complyance with the above will greatly forward the General Service and Oblige Your Friend in behalf of the Marine Comtee." James S. Copley Library, La Jolla, Cal.

A few days later Hopkins, who was still in Providence, wrote a letter requesting John Adams to use his influence as chairman of the Board of War to procure the release of "a strange groupe of about fourteen Prisoners" Hopkins had recently encountered in New Jersey while on his way back to Rhode Island. Hopkins to Adams, October 1, 1776, PCC, item 78, 11:101; and Morgan. *Naval Documents,* 6:1080.

Marine Committee to John Langdon

Sir   September 21. 1776.

The Assembly of Massachusets Bay having represented the necessity and utillity of fitting out with all possible expedition One of the Frigates built in that State and that under your direction, to

Cruize on your Coasts, in order to take or drive off the enemy that
now infest them, and having offered their Assistance to equipp
and Man these Ships, and also handed us the Copy of a Vote or
resolve of your honorable Assembly to the same purport, We have
determined to comply with their wishes, so far as depends on us,
and have this day given the necessary orders to Mr. Cushing, Captain McNeill and Captain Bradford for getting their Ship ready.[1]

We are therefore to request that you will exert your utmost endeavours to have the frigate under your care compleated immediately. You will accept the assistance of your Assembly or the
Committee they appoint for that purpose. You may either purchase
or borrow suitable Cannon, Swivels, Blunderbusses, Muskets, Pistols,
Cutlasses, Pikes, Ball, Shott, Powder &c &c. You May apply to the
State of Massachusets, to the Honble Mr. Cushing or to any of the
Continental Agents in the neighbouring States for materials or
other assistance you stand in need of and this Committee on behalf
of the United States will pay all just equitable Charges that you or
any of them incur in effecting this business, so that we hope Captain
Thompson will soon be able to join Captain McNeill in this enterprize which ought to be kept as secret as possible.[2]

We are, Sir, Your freinds &c &c

LB (DNA: PCC Miscellaneous Papers, Marine Committee Letter Book).
[1] For the Marine Committee's brief letter of this date to John Bradford, the
Continental prize agent in Massachusetts, instructing him to assist Thomas
Cushing and Capt. Hector McNeill in getting the frigate *Boston* ready for sea,
see PCC Miscellaneous Papers, Marine Committee Letter Book, fol. 22; and
Paullin, *Marine Committee Letters*, 1:11–12.
[2] Langdon, Continental prize agent in New Hampshire, subsequently informed John Hancock that he would be unable to send the frigate *Raleigh* out
to sea because of a shortage of cannon in New Hampshire. See Langdon to
Hancock, October 8, 1776, in Morgan, *Naval Documents*, 6:1158–59.

Marine Committee to Thomas Thompson

Sir   September 21st. 1776
The assembly of New Hampshire and Massachusetts having offered
their assistance in equipping, arming and manning the Frigate
under your command [1] we have accepted their kind offers and hope
in consequence thereof, you will soon be ready for sea. We expect
the same will be the case with the Frigate commanded by Captain
McNeill of Massachusetts and our design is that you should join
Company soon as possible and cruize in concert.

We are informed the Millford Frigate now infests the Coast of
those States and does much Injury to their commerce. It is our
duty to prevent the continuance of this soon as we can, and as the

two Frigates mentioned will be an overmatch for the Millford or any single Frigate of the enemy, you are to join Captain McNeill and go in Search of that or any of the enemies Ships in those seas that you can cope with, and we hope in due Time that you have taken destroyed or drove off the said enemy. The Rank betwixt you and Captain McNeill is not yet established. You are therefore to act in concert and consult each other in all things that relate to the good of the service, to the safety and preservation of your Ships or the Interest and honor of the United States of America. The Continental Agents in any State you put into will supply provisions or any necessarys that may be wanted. To some of them you are to address your Prizes, and you must advise the Committee of your proceedings as opportunitys occur. You are also to furnish us in due Time with Copies of your Log Book and Journal, and advise us of any important intelligence that may come to your knowledge.[2]

With the best wishes for your Success, We are sir, Your hble servants.[3]

LB (DNA: PCC Miscellaneous Papers, Marine Committee Letter Book).
[1] Captain Thompson was commander of the Continental frigate *Raleigh*.
[2] This day the Marine Committee sent virtually the same letter to Capt. Hector McNeill, commander of the frigate *Boston*. PCC Miscellaneous Papers, Marine Committee Letter Book, fols. 23–24; and Paullin, *Marine Committee Letters*, 1:14–15.
[3] The Marine Committee also sent brief letters this day to Capt. Isaiah Robinson of the brig *Andrew Doria* and to Capt. Lambert Wickes of the brig *Reprisal*, instructing them to "take in provisions and Stores for two Months and get ready for Sea with the Utmost expedition." See PCC Miscellaneous Papers, Marine Committee Letter Book, fol. 25; and Morgan, *Naval Documents*, 6:936.

John Adams to Abigail Adams

22 Sept. 1776

We have at last agreed upon a Plan, for forming a regular Army. We have offered 20 dollars, and 100 Acres of Land to every Man, who will inlist, during the war.[1] And a new sett of Articles of War are agreed on.[2] I will send you, if I can a Copy of these Resolutions and Regulations.

I am at a Loss what to write. News We have not. Congress seems to be forgotten by the Armies. We are most unfaithfully served in the Post Office, as well as many other Offices, civil and military.

Unfaithfullness in public Stations, is deeply criminal. But there is no Encouragement to be faithful. Neither Profit, nor Honour, nor Applause is acquired by faithfullness. But I know by what. There is too much Corruption, even in this infant Age of our Republic. Virtue is not in Fashion. Vice is not infamous.[3]

RC (MHi). Adams, *Family Correspondence* (Butterfield), 2:131.

[1] The plan for the army was embodied in resolutions adopted by Congress on September 16 and ordered published on September 20, 1776. *JCC,* 5:762–63, 807. In his autobiography, Adams asserted that "The Articles of War and the Institution of the Army during the War, were all my Work," measures that emerged from the Board of War under Adams' chairmanship. Adams, *Diary* (Butterfield), 3:434–35.

[2] The Articles of War, as agreed to by Congress on September 20 after long debate, are in *JCC,* 5:788–807. For passages in Adams' autobiography pertaining to the Articles of War, see Adams, *Diary* (Butterfield), 3:392, 409–10, 433–34.

[3] For the continuation of this letter, see Adams to Abigail Adams, October 1, 1776.

Benjamin Franklin to William Temple Franklin

Dear Grandson,   Philada. Sept. 22. 1776

You are mistaken in imagining that I am apprehensive of your carrying dangerous Intelligence to your Father; for while he remains where he is, he could make no use of it were you to know & acquaint him with all that passes. You would have been more in the right if you could have suspected me of a little tender Concern for your Welfare, on Acct of the Length of the Journey, your Youth and Inexperience, the Number of Sick returning on that Road with the Infectious Camp Distemper, which makes the Beds unsafe, together with the Loss of Time in your Studies, of which I fear you begin to grow tired. To send you on such a Journey merely to avoid the being oblig'd to Govr Trumbull for so small a Favour as the forwarding a Letter, seems to me inconsistent with your Mothers usual Prudence. I rather think the Project takes its rise from your own Inclination to a Ramble, & Disinclination for Returning to College, join'd with a Desire I do not blame of seeing a Father you have so much Reason to love.

They send to me from the Office for my Letter, so I cannot add more than to acquaint you, I shall by next post if desired send several Frank'd Covers directed to Govr Trumbull, for Mrs F. to use as she has occasion. I write to him in the first now sent,[1] to introduce her Request. She may desire her Husband to send his Letters to her under Cover to me: It will make but 2 Days add. The Family is well & join in Love to her & you.[2]

Your affectionate Grandfather,   B Franklin

RC (PPAmP).

[1] Not found.

[2] Franklin hurried off the following brief note to Temple a few days later: "I hope you will return hither [*i.e.,* Philadelphia] immediately, & that your Mother will make no Objection to it, something offering here that will be much to your Advantage if you are not out of the Way." Franklin to William Temple Franklin, September 28, 1776, Franklin Papers, PPAmP.

Caesar Rodney to Thomas Rodney

Sir,   Philada. Sepr. 22d 1776.

I am Glad you are Sending the Sloop up to Sell, and hope you'l not delay doing it, least some of the Men of War now at New York should be thought no longer Necessary there, and be sent to our Capes. A Circumstance of this Sort would inevitably knock up the Sale of all kind of Veshells, for it is the trade they are now pushing that keeps up the demand for them, and the men of War Coming to the Cape would put an End to that trade. Super-fine Flower is now at 18 Shillings and Rising as Brown tells me, tho' when I Sold Could Get no more than 13/6. It is What they Call light packed, or Seven Quarter that brings this price. I Should have no Objection to Your Sending the Schooner Also. But am Doubtfull shee is too Flat and therefore would not answer the purpose of foreign trade and of Course not sell well. If the Sloop is not Come away before you Get this Letter, would advise you to get John Bell to Come in her. He has been dealing in that way and would be of Great[use?] to me in Selling her here. But if shee is Come away And you Should Conclude to Send the Schooner pray Get him to Come in her. I had Some Convention [Conversation?] with Bell while in Town, and he promised to Call on You Concerning the Sale of them. I don't know what you do for News now since Your Post has fell through. I have Recd no Letter from Colonel Haslet for eight or ten days past, But Received one from a Worthy Gentleman of my Acquaintance dated the 16th Instant, Wherein he Says "Yesterday a Most Inglorious day! The British Troops Landed on New York Island, from Long Island, at a place Called Turtle Bay about five miles above New York City, when the Appearance of only a few of them made two or three Regiments of Americans Retreat. Retreat did I say, it ought to be *Run away* notwithstanding all the Solicitations, prayers and I might say tears of General Washington. These were not Southern Troops. Our people had a few Hours before, Evacuated New York. The Enemy then took possession of it, and all the Lower End of the Island. A line was immediately thrown up, about Eight Miles from New York Across from East to North River. The Enemy possessing the West and We the East part up to Kings–Bridge, and the Pensylvanians and Delaware Encampment is on the East side of the Bridge, under the Command of General Mifflin. This far for Bad News. This Morning I was Spectator to a Most Glorious Scene. The Enemy Advanced to An Eminence, about a Mile from our Lines. The Maryland and Virginia Troops were Ordered by General Washington to disposses them, and with undaunted Bravery they Marched up. When a Smart Engagement Ensued, Fresh Troops were Poured in upon both Sides, The Contest Obstinate, and Long. Finely our Heroes forced them from three different Grounds, at which they Retreated leaving behind them three field-pieces, and many Slain. In the number of our Killed, which does not amount to ten, We Count Some officers of distinction, Particularly one Colonel Knowlton of Connecticut Who Commanded and Who had Infinitely more than Roman Bravery. As I was there only Accidentally And came away as soon as the Action was over Can't give you particulars. The Delaware Battalion were not Engaged. Colo. Haslet has been for some time and Still is Unwell. Some of the Other Officers have Laboured Under what the New England Men Call the *Camp Difficulty*, but are Getting Better."

Our people are not yet Returnd from Newcastle. I Shall Come home in a Short time after their Return whether appointed a Delegate or not—in short, shall stay no longer than those Veshells if they Come up may detain me. Remember me to my friends &c. Yrs.

Caesar Rodney

RC (PHi).

Josiah Bartlett to John Langdon

Dear Sir,   Philadelphia, Sept 23d 1776.

Yours by Capt Manly I have received and should have been glad of affording him any assistance in my power, but unluckily they (the Marine Committee) commonly meet in the evening, when I am not able to attend them on account of my health. The latter end of last week Capt Roche called on me and told me Capt Manly was taken very sick. I have not heard from him since so hope he is better. I hope Col Whipple and your successor as a delegate are now setting off for this city to relieve me. I am very anxious to have them here as some very important affairs are before the Congress and my health will not permit my constant attendance, and I am loath to be absent as you know the voice of a single Colony is often very important.[1] I shall not write to Col Whipple as I think he must be on his journey before this reaches you. I am sorry our affairs at New York have succeeded so badly. We want a regular well disciplined army and more experienced Generals. A regular standing army we must have at all events against another year. You will see the plan the Congress has laid for effecting it. The conduct of some of the New England soldiers this year has afforded me great pain, though I believe some of the disaffected this way, have represented their conduct worse than it deserved, yet the affair at the Cedars, and of some at New York, are not to be excused.

I have this moment received Col Whipple's letter of the 10th inst wherein he recommends Hopley Yeaton for a Lt of your ship, in the room of Mr. Wheelright, and some other marine affairs which

I shall lay before the Marine Committee and try to procure the orders he mentions, tho at present I cannot meet with them in the evening as I am at present troubled with a fever fit every evening; however, I will do the best I can in the affair.

Col Whipple informs me the Colony had not then appointed another Delegate in your stead. I hope the Colonel has set off without him and the other may be appointed and follow after as soon as convenient. I hope you will soon have the Raleigh fit for sea; I will try to procure orders for her and one of the Newbury ships to take the Millford frigate, which it seems is a great plague to the Northern States. Prepare her as soon as possible for the business.

I am dear Sir, you sincere friend,   Josiah Bartlett.

Tr (DLC).
[1] Bartlett's health continued to plague him until about mid-October. Two days after writing this letter to Langdon, he wrote to his wife explaining that he was "half addleheaded with the fever" and unable to attend Congress. "I am now in bed," he continued, "& just sit up to write you this line by Mr. Cox. I have for some time fatigued my mind with the thoughts of getting home & had agreed for a sulky to purchase & was making preparation for setting out before the weather grew cold; but Providence has put a stop to it at least for the present and I am determined to rest satisfied with the allotments of Providence who I firmly believe orders all things for the best." Thomas F. Madigan, *Autograph Album* 1 (April 1934), p. 24, item 16.

Robert Morris to John Jay

Dear Sir   Philada. Septr. 23d. 1776

Tho your express delivered me your favour[1] last Wednesday or Thursday yet I did not receive the letter from Mr Deane untill this day and shall now send after the Express that he may Convey this safe to your hands. Shou'd he be gone I must find some other safe conveyance. You will find enclosed both Mr. D——ne's letters as you desired and I shall thank you for the Copy of the Invisible part.[2] He had Communicated so much of this Secret to me, before his departure, as to let me know he had fixed with you a mode of writing that wou'd be invisible to the rest of the World; he also promised to ask you to make a full Communication to me, but in this use your pleasure. The Secret so farr as I do or shall know it, will remain so to all other persons. It appears clear to me that we may very soon Involve all Europe in a Warr by managing properly the apparent forwardness of the Court of France. Its a horrid consideration that our own Safety shou'd call on us to involve other Nations in the Calamities of warr. Can this be morally right or have morality & Policy nothing to do with each other? Perhaps it may not be good Policy to investigate the Question at this time. I will therefore only ask you whether General Howe will give us time to cause a diversion favourable to us in Europe, I confess as things now appear to me the prospect is gloomy Indeed. Therefore if you can administer Comfort do it. Why are we so long deprived of your abilitys in Congress? Perhaps they are more usefully exerted where you are. That may be the case, but such Men as you, in times like these, shou'd be every where. I am with true sentiments of respect & esteem, Dr Sir, Your obedt Hble servt.

Robt Morris

RC (NNC).

¹ Jay's letter to Morris of September 15, 1776, is in Jay, *Papers* (Morris), 1:315–16.

² Jay had explained how he had received letters of June 23, 1776, from Silas Deane to both himself and Morris and had asked Morris to return the latter, which Jay had already forwarded before discovering that he should have examined it first. Jay and Deane had developed a system for transmitting messages with invisible ink before Deane had gone to France, and Deane had sent an invisible message in halves in the two letters. Only Jay knew the technique for applying the "counterpart" to the invisible ink, and therefore he needed to develop Morris' half to complete the secret message.

In 1935 several documents from a collection of Jay's papers were made available by Frank Monaghan of Yale University to Lodewyk Bendikson of the Henry E. Huntington Library, who made a study of the documents with ultraviolet and infrared radiation techniques. The results of that study were published in Lodewyk Bendikson, "The Restoration of Obliterated Passages and of Secret Writing in Diplomatic Missives," *Franco-American Review* 1 (Winter 1937): 240–56. For the text of Jay's transcription of Deane's invisible June 23 message as well as others not published elsewhere dated June 11 and 20 and December 2, 1776, see pp. 248–53.

Although the documents analyzed by Bendikson cannot now be located, the Robert Morris Papers, DLC, contain a "duplicate" of Deane's June 23 letter to Morris. The duplicate also includes the section in invisible ink, but it cannot be read with currently available techniques because, unlike the manuscripts analyzed by Bendikson, Deane's duplicate has undergone preservation treatment and is silked.

For the origins of the technique Deane used to write his invisible messages, which was improved by Jay's brother the physician Sir James Jay, see Victor Hugo Paltsits, "The Use of Invisible Ink for Secret Writing during the American Revolution," *New York Public Library Bulletin* 39 (May 1935): 361–64.

For Jay's October 6, 1776, response to Morris explaining a few difficulties he had with illegible passages in Deane's letter, see John Jay, *The Correspondence and Public Papers of John Jay*, ed. Henry P. Johnston, 4 vols. (New York: G.P. Putnam's Sons, 1890–93), 1:85–89.

North Carolina Delegates to the North Carolina Council of Safety

Gentlemen   Philadelphia Sept 23. 1776

We wrote you very lately by Mr Werryat of Georgia, & shall write you very fully by Mr Hewes in a few days.

This goes by Mr Milles who returns to acquaint you with the

result of his agency.[1] We regret with him that it has not been accompanied with the successes you had reason to expect from it. Nothing was wanting on his part that the most earnest zeal to serve you could prompt, & we have cooperated with our best endeavours to carry his designs into execution. But such is the demand for Workmen in every branch of the Iron Manufactury & the Wages so very extravagantly high that men who have any pretensions to skill in the business cannot be prevailed upon to leave home. We have been under the necessity to purchase a light Waggon and two horses to remove the man whom he has employed together with the Patterns of Pots which we have been so fortunate as to procure tho at a great price, as they were the only ones to be sold in the province of Pennsylvania.

We have advanced 100 dollars to Mr Milles for which he will be accountable to you. We have been induced to this from an expectation that on his way out he may meet some Workmen who may answer his purpose & to whom it may be necessary to pay something in hand to induce to accompany him to Carolina.

We are Gentlemen, With great Respect, Your Obed. Humble Serts,

Will Hooper

Joseph Hewes

John Penn

[*P.S.*] Inclosed is the Expence of the Waggon & Horses.

RC (Nc–Ar). Written by Hooper and signed by Hooper, Hewes, and Penn. *N.C. Colonial Records*, 10:806–7. RC damaged; missing words supplied from Tr.
   [1] On this point, see William Hooper to William Livingston, August 29, 1776, note.

Edward Rutledge to Robert R. Livingston

My dr. Livingston,   Philada. Sept. 23d. 1776.

I have been so much upon the going that for some Weeks past it has been impossible for me to put Pen to Paper. The Hurry is however past away in a Degree & I snatch a Moment's Leisure to request that you or Jay or both of you will immediately on receipt of this set off for this Place. Little less than the *Salvation* of your Colony may depend on your Presence. I would tell you a great deal, had I Time, or were it not possible that this might fall into Hands inimical to us & our Cause. If I have Leisure I shall write to Jay to desire his Attendance, if not make my Love to him, tell him how I esteem him, & how much I long to see him.[1] By a Letter received this Day from Schuyler he informs us that he is no longer a

Major Genl. in our Service, but that he will attend his Duty in
Congress in a Fortnight from the Date of his Letter. I wish he was
now here. You know as well as I do, that the Rascals who took
much Liberty with the Character of that Gentleman would not
venture to look him in the Face. I admire his Wisdom; it was the
only Step which he could take to recover & establish his Reputation. If it is in your way to write him let him know how agreeable
his presence will be in Congress to all who wish well to our Affairs.
Let me repeat it; you cannot render as much Service to your Country in any other way whatever as by coming to us immediately &
bringing with you Jay & Schuyler.[2] I shall go from hence for Carolina within a Month. I wish to see Matters put upon a better Foot
than they now are, & to contribute as far as my Abilities can carry
me, towards rendering your Country free & happy. Don't take my
Silence amiss, but let me hear from you soon. God bless you. Yours
Sincerely & affectionately,   E Rutledge

RC (NHpR: Livingston-Redmond Collection deposit). Addressed: "To Robert R.
Livingston Esquire at the Congress of New York, to be forwarded to him
wherever he may be in New York."
  [1] Jay and Livingston were too involved in local New York political affairs to
return to Congress at this time. See Robert R. Livingston to Rutledge, October
10, Miscellaneous Manuscripts, DLC; and John Jay to Rutledge, October 11,
1776, Am. Archives, 5th ser. 2:998–99.
  [2] Infuriated by criticisms of his performance as commander of the northern
army and aroused by allegations of corruption in the provisioning of his men,
General Schuyler submitted his resignation in a letter written to Hancock on
September 14, which was read in Congress on September 23 and referred to the
Board of War. Although a number of New England delegates, who had been
especially critical of Schuyler's military strategy, were confident that the general's
resignation would be accepted, this confidence was misplaced. Even before
Schuyler's letter reached Congress, opposition to his resignation had been expressed by the Albany Committee of Correspondence and the New York Convention. The convention in particular had adopted a series of resolves on September 20 calling for Schuyler's continuance in office and had written a letter
to the New York delegates warning that "General Schuyler's resignation will not
only be highly prejudicial to the common cause of America, by the loss of an
able and vigilant officer . . . but will be productive of internal jealousy and discontent, at a period when union and harmony are necessary for our preservation."
Congress referred these resolves to a committee consisting of William Hooper,
Thomas McKean, and Edward Rutledge on September 27. The convention's
intervention, when combined with the critical military situation then existing
in both northern and southern New York, led Congress on October 2 to approve
a resolution drawn up by Rutledge rejecting Schuyler's resignation and promising
the appointment of a committee "to enquire fully into his conduct, which, they
trust, will establish his reputation in the opinion of all good men." See JCC,
5:809, 831, 841; PCC, item 67, 1:332, item 153, 2:368–71; Am. Archives, 5th ser.
2:333–34, 703–4, 707–10; William Williams to Joseph Trumbull, September 26;
Philip Livingston to the New York Convention, September 28; Edward Rutledge
to Robert R. Livingston, October 2; and John Hancock to Philip Schuyler, October 4, 1776. See also Jonathan G. Rossie, The Politics of Command in the
American Revolution (Syracuse: Syracuse University Press, 1975), pp. 110–29.

Richard Stockton to William Livingston

Sir,   Philada. Septr. 23d. 1776
   Last evening I recd. your's of 19th instant inclosing a packet for
the President of the Congress. It was opened early this morning,
and referred to the Board of War. I have, as you requested, urged
the necessity of a speedy determination of this matter, and shall
not fail of giving it all necessary attention. As soon as the report
comes in, and Congress have determined thereon, I will transmit
their resolution.[1] I have the honor to be, Sir, Your most obedt. and
very hl Servt.   Richd Stockton

RC (MHi).
   [1] Livingston's letter of September 19 to the New Jersey delegates, forwarding
an application for payment of New Jersey militiamen "in the Service of the
Continent," is in the William Livingston Papers, MHi. For Congress' handling
of this issue, see Francis Hopkinson to William Livingston, October 16, 1776, note.

John Hancock to the States

Gentlemen,   Philada. Sept. 24th. 1776.
   You will perceive by the enclosed Resolves, which I have the
Honour to forward, in obedience to the Commands of Congress,
that they have come to a Determination to augment our Army,
and to engage the Troops to serve during the Continuance of the
War. As an Inducement to enlist on these Terms, the Congress
have agreed to give, besides a Bounty of twenty Dollars, a Hundred
Acres of Land to each Soldier, and in Case he should fall in Battle,
they have resolved, that his Children, or other Representatives, shall
succeed to such Land.[1]
   The many ill Consequences arising from a short and limited
Inlistment of Troops, are too obvious to be mentioned. In general
give me Leave to observe, that to make Men well acquainted with
the Duties of a Soldier requires Time; and to bring them under
proper Subordination and Discipline, not only requires Time, but
has always been a Work of much Difficulty. We have had frequent
Experience that Men of a few Days Standing will not look forward;
but as the Time of their Discharge approaches, grow careless of
their Arms, Ammunition &c and impatient of all Restraint. The
Consequence of which is, the latter Part of the Time for which the
Soldier was engaged, is spent in undoing what the greatest Pains
had been taken to inculcate at first. Need I add to this, that the Fall
of the late Genl. Montgomery before Quebeck is undoubtedly to be
ascribed to the limited Time for which the Troops were engaged;
whose Impatience to return Home compelled him to make the At-

tack contrary to the Conviction of his own Judgment. This Fact alone
furnishes a striking Argument of the Danger and Impropriety of
sending Troops into the Field under any Restriction as to the Time
of their Inlistment. The noblest Enterprize may be left unfinished
by Troops in such a Predicament, or abandoned at the very Moment Success must have crowned the Attempt.

The heavy & enormous Expences consequent upon calling forth
the Militia, the Delay attending their Motions, and the Difficulty
of keeping them in Camp, render it extremely improper to place
our whole Dependance upon them. Experience hath uniformly convinced us of this, some of the Militia having actually deserted the
Camp at the very Moment their Services were most wanted. In the
mean Time, the Strength of the British Army which is great, is
rendered much more formidable by the superior Order and Regularity which prevail in it.

Under these Circumstances and in this Situation of our Affairs
it is evident, that the only Means left us of preserving our Liberties,
is the Measure which the Congress have now adopted, and which I
am ordered most earnestly to recommend to you to carry into immediate Effect. Without a well disciplined Army we can never expect Success against veteran Troops; and it is totally impossible
we should ever have a well disciplined Army, unless our Troops are
engaged to serve during the War. To attain therefore this most
desirable End, I am to request you will at once, and without a
Moment's Delay, bend all your Attention to raise your Quota of
the American Army. The Times call for the greatest Dispatch &
Vigour of Conduct. When the bloody Standard of Tyranny is erected
in a Land of Liberty, no good Man, no Friend of his Country, can
possibly remain an inactive Spectator of her Fall. Display therefore,
I most ardently entreat you, that Virtue which alone can save her
on this Occasion. Let us convince our Enemies, that as we entered
into the present Contest for the Defence of our Liberties, so we
are resolved, with the firmest Reliance on Heaven for the Justice
of our Cause, never to relinquish it, but rather to perish in the
Ruins of it. If we do but remain firm, if we are not dismayed at the
little Shocks of Fortune, and are determined at all Hazards that we
will be free, I am persuaded, under the gracious Smiles of Providence, assisted by our most strenuous Endeavours, we shall finally
succeed agreeably to our Wishes; and thereby establish the Independence, the Happiness, and the Glory of the United States of
America.

As the Troops now in Service belonging to the several States,
will be considered as Part of their Quota in the American Army,
you will please to take such Steps as you judge necessary to ascertain
what Number of the Troops, as well as what officers, will engage
to serve during the War. I send by this Express, blank Commissions

to be filled with such as you shall please to appoint. I also forward a Number of the Rules and Articles of War as altered by Congress, and just published. I have the Honour to be, Gentlemen, your most obed. & very hble Servt.   J. H. Presidt.

LB (DNA: PCC, item 12A).
¹ See *JCC*, 5:762–63, 781, 788. These resolves may have been sent to South Carolina with a letter from Edward Rutledge to his brother John, the chief executive of the state, of which only an extract has been found. "The Congress are resolved to raise eighty-eight battalions to continue during the war. We mean to re-inlist all those who are now engaged if they will serve. It is not intended by the Resolutions that you should raise six battalions over and above what you now have, but that they should be re-inlisted to serve during the war." William E. Hemphill et al., eds., *Journals of the General Assembly and House of Representatives, 1776–1780* (Columbia: University of South Carolina Press, 1970), p. 131.

John Hancock to George Washington

Sir,   Philada. Septr. 24th. 1776.

You will perceive by the enclosed Resolves of Congress, which I have the Honour to forward, that they have come to a Determination to augment our Army, & to engage the Troops to serve during the Continuance of the War. As an Inducement to enlist on these Terms, the Congress have agreed to give, besides a Bounty of twenty Dollars, a Hundred Acres of Land to each Soldier; and in Case he should lose his Life in Battle they have resolved that his Children, or other Representatives shall succeed to such Grant.¹

It is unnecessary to repeat to you the numberless ill Consequences resulting from the limited Inlistment of Troops. The untimely Death of General Montgomery alone, independent of other Arguments, is a stricking Proof of the Danger and Impropriety of sending Troops into the Field, under any Restriction as to the Time of their Service. The noblest Enterprize may be left unfinished by Soldiers in such a Predicament, or abandoned the very Moment Success must have crowned the Attempt. Your own Experience has long since convinced you, that without a well disciplined Army we cannot rationally expect Success against veteran Troops; and that it is totally impossible we should ever have a well disciplined Army, unless our Troops are engaged to serve during the War. The Congress therefore, impressed with these, & other Reasons, and fully convinced, that our Militia is inadequate to the Duty expected of them have adopted the enclosed Resolves, which I am persuaded will afford you Pleasure, as the only Means left to defend our Country in its present critical Situation. I have wrote to all the States, and forwarded a Copy of the printed Resolves herewith transmitted, and urged them in the most pressing Language to comply in the fullest Manner with the Requisition of Congress.

As the Troops now in Service belonging to the several States will be considered as Part of their Quota in the American Army, it will be necessary to ascertain what Number of the Troops, as well as what Officers will engage to serve during the War. For this Purpose I have wrote to the States, and forwarded blank Commissions for all such Officers, and others whom they shall appoint agreeably to the enclosed Resolves.

The Articles of War as first adopted by Congress being exploded, I send you sundry Copies of those, which they have instituted in their Room.[2]

I enclose you also sundry other Resolves, to which I beg Leave to request your Attention.[3]

As the Committee of Congress will confer with you on the State of the Army, to them I beg Leave to refer you, and am with every Sentiment of Esteem & Respect, Sir, your most obedient and very hble Sevt.   John Hancock Presidt

RC (DLC). In the hand of Jacob Rush and signed by Hancock.
[1] See *JCC*, 5:762–63; and Washington, *Writings* (Fitzpatrick), 6:4–7.
[2] See *JCC*, 5:788–807.
[3] These consisted of numerous resolves on military affairs passed by Congress on September 16, 18, 19, 20, and 23. See *JCC*, 5:761, 780–81, 783–84, 808, 810–11.

Lewis Morris to the New York Convention

Sir   Philadelphia Septemr 24 1776

I had the honor to receive your Letter accompanying the Resolve of Congress relative to my returne to resume the command of my Brigade. At a time when the State to which I belong is invaded, and particularly as I am honored with a military command, I esteem it my duty to account for my absence.

Since my arrival at Philadelphia the State of N York has had no more than a representation in Congress, and as the Gentlemen of the Committee for Indian affairs were mostly out of Town, the whole of that necessary business has Devolved upon me. My family have been Obliged to desert their home and meeting with them in this place, altogether unprovided, I have been under the necessity of delaying the time of my Stay untill I could fix them in some situation where they could be accommodated. The distress of my Family on this occasion made it my particular duty to attend to them, and which I flatter myself will be justifiable upon every principle of justice.

The Situation of my Brigade I was convinced was well known to

Lewis Morris

the Convention. I apprehended that not more than a Colls Command was left in it, and as such did not think my presence was so absolutely necessary. I have thought that the existance of such a Brigade, in which were so many disaffected persons, was dangerous to the cause, as well as to my own Life. But being desirous to participate in the virtuous opposition to the British Tyrant, I had determined as soon as possible to join Genl Washington, and contribute my assistance to him, prompted in the first instance by a Love to my Country, and in the next place the preservation of my property, being thoroughly convinced that unless we conquer, I am ruined. However in obedience to the commands of Convention, I shall prepare with all possible expedition to set out for West Chester, and will endeavour to execute any orders they may be pleased to give to the utmost of my ability.[1]

I have the honor to Subscribe myself, Sir Your Obliged and Obet. Huml Servt,   Lewis Morris

RC (NN).

[1] Noting that as a result of the absence of Morris, a brigadier general in the New York militia, "the Militia of Westchester County are not so properly arranged and managed as they ought to be at this critical juncture," the convention on September 16 had ordered him to return to his command. In answer to the present letter, the convention reaffirmed this order on October 8, although by then Morris had already left Philadelphia. On January 9, 1777, the New York Committee of Safety ordered him to be paid "two hundred and eleven pounds four shillings . . . for his attendance as a Delegate of this State in Continental Congress, to the fourth day of October last, as per his account delivered in this day." See Am. Archives, 5th ser. 2:693, 3:231–32; and Journals of N.Y. Prov. Cong., 1:766.

New York Delegates to the New York Committee of Safety

Gentlemen   Phila. 24 Sepr. 1776

We recd. your lett. of the 9th Sepr. with Sundry Inclosures which were laid before Congress, who have Come to Several resolutions A Copy of which we Send here inclosed.[1] You will See that 3 Tons of powdr. was directd. to be delivd. at New Windsor to be sent to the forts, but that will not be done as the Waggons with the 15 Tons referred to In the resolution went by Way of Minisink. The five Tons we Shall forward Immediately. We obtained an Order from Congress for 6700 dollr. to be laid out in Arms for yr. State which we Shall purchase when we have an opportunity.[2] None are more to be had here, but parcells frequently Arrive, if You Shd have occasion for the Money for a More pressing purpose you will please to Acquaint us. We wrote you the 30 Augt. which we hope Came to hand. The En-

couragement Now given by Congress, will we hope Enable You to
raise 4 Compleat Battalions as Speedily as possible. We referr you to
the Presidents Lettr. on that head.³ 4 Battalions is All that is required of N. York Including those Already raised.⁴ Inclosed are
Sundry news papers. We Could wish to hear from you at Least once a
week which seems to be more necessary now than Ever.

Brookland on Long Island is Burnt as well as the City of N. York
Without doubt on purpose. This Acct. we have from Mr. Blanchard
of Elizth. Town. We Are Gent., Your Most Obedt Servants,

                                                    Phil. Livingston

                                                    Wm. Floyd

                                                    Lewis Morris

RC (PHi). Written by Livingston and signed by Livingston, Floyd, and Morris.
  ¹ The committee of safety's September 9 letter to the New York delegates, dealing with "the great importance of the posts in the Highlands," had been referred,
with enclosures, to a committee of Congress on September 20. Congress had then
considered this committee's report on September 23 and adopted a series of
resolves about the defense of the Highlands. See *JCC,* 5:808, 810–11; PCC, item 67,
1:268–97; and *Am. Archives,* 5th ser. 2:260–63.
  ² See *JCC,* 5:807.
  ³ See John Hancock to the States, this date.
  ⁴ The committee of safety finally agreed to raise four new Continental battalions in New York on November 22, 1776. See *Am. Archives,* 5th ser. 3:218, 271–
72, 312–15.

Benjamin Rush to Anthony Wayne

My dear sir,   Philada Septemr 24th. 1776.
I have not been unmindful of you since we parted. No man
rejoiced more than I did in hearing of your gallant behaviour at the
Three Rivers, and General Sullivan can witness for me that when
He repeated any anecdote that related to our Army in Canada in
which your name was mentioned with respect, I felt, and Showed
the same Satisfaction that I should have done had he been lavishing
encomiums upon a brother.

You will hear before this reaches you that the command of
General Sinclair's regiment was given to Col. Wood. I lament with
you Col. Allen's resignation, and loss to our army, but I beleive
you have been misinformed as to his motives in that transaction.
His family suffered no indignities in this State but such as they in
some degree merited by their opposition to the institution of a new
goverment and the declaration of independance. I have constantly
made great allowances for gentlemen of moderate sentiments, and
still class several of them among the worthiest of my friends, but I

think it no breach of charity to suppose that a family so much affected in power, and property as the one above mentioned were actuated only by low and interested motives.

My Seat in Congress has subjected me to many cares to which I was a stranger when my whole business consisted in reading, writing & feeling pulses. I am obliged daily to hear the most melancholly Accounts of the distresses of our troops from wants of every kind. I have felt a large share of the pain & shame brought upon our arms by the desertion of Long Island, and evacuation of New York. The military Spirit of our countrymen seems to have subsided in that part of the continent, and a torpor seems likewise to have seized upon the citizens of America in general. I apprehend we have over-rated the public virtue of our country. If this is the case, let us not repine at misfortunes. They are necessary to the growth & existence of patriotism. History shows us that states like individuals have arisen to importance only when their foundations were laid in difficulties & Adversity. We received so many pledges during the last Campaign of the favor and protection of heaven that it would seem a Species of infidelity to doubt our Success in the issue of the present controversy.

A convention have at last formed a goverment for our State. Herewith I send you a copy of it.[1] It is tho't by many people to be rather too much upon the democratical Order, for liberty is as apt to degenerate into licenciousness, as power is to become arbitrary. Restraints therefore are as necessary in the former as the latter case.

Had the governor & counsel in the new constitution of Pennsylvania possessed a negative upon the proceedings of the assembly the goverment would have derived safety, wisdom & dignity from it. But we hope the counsel of Censors will remedy this defect at the expiration of seven years.

My present Situation requires that I should possess a thorough knowledge of the State of the Armies of the continent. Let me beg of you therefore to furnish me every week (if possible) with the history of every material occurrence in the northern department. Tell me all your wants whether they relate to provisions, cloathing, tents, ammunition or medicines. I could wish you would go further and inform me what officers, and what brigades, or regiments stand highest with you for courage, conduct, and military discipline. Duty & inclination will prompt me to do every thing in my power to remedy abuses, correct delays, and reward merit of every kind in the army.

My Compts. await Genl Gates, and Genl. St Clair. Tell the latter that I have done nothing since I took my seat in congress with greater pleasure than giving my Vote for making him a Brigadr., and I wish for nothing more than to do the same justice to the merit of my friend Col. Wayne. Inter Nos—an Attention in you to

Genl Gates may facilitate this matter if it should soon come before congress.

Adieu my dear Anthony. God bless you! & bring you back in Safety to our native province in which I hope to spend many days with you in the enjoyment of that freedom for which we are both making sacrifices in the cabinet & field. Yours sincerely,

B Rush

RC (PHi). Addressed: "Col. Anthony Wayne of the 4th Pennsylvania Regem. at Ticonderoga."

[1] According to the minutes of the proceedings of the Pennsylvania Convention, the new frame of government was not finally agreed to until September 27. The text of the Pennsylvania constitution was entered on the minutes the following day. See *Am. Archives*, 5th ser. 2:48–59.

Secret Committee to William Bingham

Sir   Philada. Septr. 24th. 1776

We have Shipped 1000 bbls flour onboard the Ship Betsey, Capt Wm. Stevens, for your address on Account & Risque of the United States of America agreable to the enclosed Invoice & bill of Loading.[1] The Captn has liberty either to go into St Lucia or Martinico just as winds or other Circumstances may serve. You will therefore receive this flour at either place and cause it to be sold to the best advantage, pay the freight as per bill of Loading & place the net proceeds to the Credit of this Committee. We hope the Brigt Cornelia & Molly, Capt Lockhard, arrived safe & delivered her Cargo in good order. If so you will no doubt have paid for the Muskets & Powder you remitted by Cap Wickes, out of that Cargo, but if it did not arrive you will have to pay for them out of the present one, or from that of the Sloop Independance also Sent to your address.

You must dispatch this Ship back as expeditiously as possible and if the Sloop Independance does not arrive whilst she is there you may remit us back in her the Value of £1500 to £2000, in Good blankets and other Woolen Goods suitable for Soldiers, with some more Muskets, Powder, Gun Flints, Salt Petre, Sulphur &c just as you can obtain them to the best advantage observing that we now want Cloathing for our Troops beyond any other Articles. Shou'd the Sloop Independance arrive safe, You may then remit the less Value in the Ship because we deem the Sloop a safer conveyance but still we wou'd have some Goods by each, The Value proportioned to the Effects you have in hand unless you can obtain Credit & then you may increase it one half. We are sir, Your hble servants,

Robt Morris	Joseph Hewes
Josiah Bartlett	Tho M:Kean
Phil. Livingston	Richard Henry Lee

RC (PHi). Written by Morris and signed by Morris, Bartlett, Hewes, Lee, Livingston, and McKean.

[1] This day Robert Morris also wrote a brief note on behalf of the Secret Committee to the Pennsylvania Council of Safety requesting their permission for a pilot to carry the *Betsey* down Delaware Bay. Signers Collection, InU; and *Pa. Archives*, 1st ser. 5:28.

John Adams to James Warren

Dr sir   Septr. 25. 1776 [1]

This Express carries a new Plan of an Army. I hope the Gen. Ct. without one Moments delay will Send Commissions to whole Corps of their officers, either by Expresses or Committees to New York and Ticonderoga that as many Men may be inlisted without delay as possible. It may be best to send a Committee with full Powers to each Place. There is no Time to be lost. I inclose you a Sett of Articles as lately amended.[2] Discipline I hope will be introduced at last. I am,   John Adams

RC (MHi).

[1] This day Adams also wrote a brief letter to his wife Abigail. "I have only Time to say, by Mr. Taylor, that I am not worse than I have been—that however, I think, the G Ct might have sent somebody here, before now—and that it will not be many days before I shall sett off. I shall wait for the Completion of a few Things and then go—perhaps in a Week or ten days." Adams, *Family Correspondence* (Butterfield), 2:134.

[2] For the "new Plan of an Army" and the "Articles as lately amended," see Adams to Abigail Adams, September 22, 1776, notes 1 and 2.

William Hooper to Robert R. Livingston

Dear Sir [1]   Philada. Sept 25. 1776

I Thank you for your very obliging letter of the 9th of this Instant. I take my pen in hand rather to prove my own punctuality than because I have anything that is important enough to intrude among the many weighty matters which press upon your attention. We anxiously wait the important consequences which two such numerous armies brought in contact may produce. Genl Howe supported with Officers & Men inured to service—found with every species of Military stores which can make them formidable; determined, and desperate some of them from the disgrace which attended their retreat from Boston & anxious to restore the honour of the British Arms—to conflict with an army of new troops—ill found—ill cloathed—headed by officers who supposing they have every other merit have no pretensions to experience—& unhappily for us I fear that past events may have a future effect & some of our turgid friends may not feel *bould* when it is necessary that they should.

We have been alarmed with an account of the City of New York having been in flames several days past & that the greatest part of it has been consumed. Some accounts attribute this Calamity to Genl Howe's orders while others with greater probability ascribe it to accident or the ungovernable Brutality to those Men monsters the Hessians. General Howe in full possession surely would not be mad enough to burn his house over his own head.

The Congress have ordered 88 Regiments to be raised for the next Year's service to continue during the War. I wish this may save the dreadful Consequences of short Enlistments or calling forth the Militia upon Exigencies. Were we to persist in the method hitherto pursued the Contest would be of short duration. Our Treasury would soon discover its weakness.

Juniper Lees Express arrived here last night.[2] He left Lee at Georgia, the Congress Express within a day & half ride of him. Possibly Lee may be here in a day or two. The weight is too great for any one man, the conduct of the American Army without any to lean upon for advice.

Adieu. I scrawl this amidst the confusion of tongues—at the Treasury board. Your's truly,   Wm Hooper

RC (Facsimile, Lawrence H. Leder, ed., *The Genesis of American Freedom, 1765–1795*, Waltham, Mass.: Brandeis University, 1961, plate 9).

[1] Recipient identified in *American Art Association Catalog* (January 25, 1918), items 16–17, where an extract of Livingston's October 26 reply to Hooper is also printed.

[2] This day Congress read letters from Gen. Charles Lee to Hancock of August 24 and to the Board of War of August 27. See *JCC*, 5:818. See also PCC, item 158, 1:79; and *NYHS Collections* 5 (1872): 239, 241–45, in which the letter to Hancock is dated August 23.

Robert Treat Paine to Samuel Phillips, Jr.

Sr.[1]   Philada. Septr. 25th. 1776.

Mr. Gerry delivered me a letter you sent by Major Cox;[2] I have been a long time anxious to know the state of Gun Powder manufacture in our Government and have wrote repeatedly without being able to get any satisfactory information. We have had great success in making saltpetre, but without great Care it will be all spoilt in making into Gunpowder. There have been some great instances here of miserable trash turn'd out for Gunpowder, which occasioned the Congress to appoint a Committee to enquire into the defect and procure a remedy. . . .[3]

. . . .I am exceeding glad to find you turning yr. attention to this very important Manufacture. I hope you will not only make improvements in yr. own Works but communicate Knowledge to the other Powder makers and do what lays in yr Power to promote the manufacture of good Powder for it must be a most cruel Vexation in *the day of decision for Liberty or Slavery* to have the Scale turn against us meerly thro' the defect of our own Powder. This matter has lain as a Burthen on my mind and has caused me to apply great attention to this manufacture. . . .

Congress have passed some resolves to prevent the bad manufacture of Powder and also the importation of bad Powder, (for much Powder which has been imported from abroad has proved exceed bad) and have recommended inspectors to be appointed to prove all Powder. This matter should be carefully attended to. Majr. Cox will describe to you the machine by which we made most of our Experiments. You will excuse the freedom I take in addressing you thus freely when you consider the real importance of the subject. I wish the Inhabitants of the United States were more intent upon providing and manufacturing the Means of defence, than making Governments witht. providing for the means of their Support. Wishing you Success in yr. noble Efforts to promote that best Good of yr Country, its defence from powerful Enemies, I part your most hble Servt,   R T Paine

MS not found; reprinted from Burnett, *Letters*, 2:101. Endorsed: "Mr. Paine to S. P. Eve [?] on Gun powder."

    [1] Although it now seems clear that Paine wrote this letter to Samuel Phillips, Jr. (1752–1802), Burnett, interpreting a transcribed endorsement, ventured to identify the recipient as "S.P. Eve [?]." An Andover, Mass., merchant and mill-owner, Phillips manufactured gunpowder from 1776 to 1796, except for a period after his mill exploded in 1778. He served in the general court from 1775 to 1801, and in 1776 served on a committee to supervise and encourage the manufacture of saltpetre. Shipton, *Harvard Graduates*, 17:593–605.

    [2] In his September 11 letter to Elbridge Gerry, Phillips had requested information on the manufacture of saltpetre and gunpowder. Paine Papers, MHi.

    [3] Elipses in Tr here and below.

Caesar Rodney to Thomas Rodney

Sir,   Philada. Sepr. 25th 1776

That the New England men placed to defend the Landing place Behaved in a Most Dastardly, Cowardly Scandelous Manner is Most Certain. But that Courage is not always to be found the Same Even in the Same person is Equally true, and Verryfied in those verry same Men. For Some of them the day following were in the other Engagement and behaved with great Bravery, As did the whole Body Engaged; You have Some Account of the Skirmish in the papers, therefore Shall refer you to them and a Letter I wrote by Wilds & Kirkley. I saw Carsons but not till this morning, When he told me some person by the name of Jones from Mifflins Cross-Roads had set out from below since he did and having got here before him with Subscription papers Signed by Some people below went to the Several printing offices before he did and Engaged the packets to Carry down as a post in the place of Parke. After I saw Bradford, the [Eldest?], and telling him what accounts I had from below, and what Carsons himself had said, they said they would let Carson have the papers for the Gentlemen of Dover and ElseWhere Except those who suscribed to the other. I suppose the Subscribers will Settle the matter between them, when they go down. I doubt whether you will get any powder & shott. The Schooner is not arrived that I know of and you have made no Mention of the Sloop but Sent the Schooner before you heard what my opinion was about selling her. I wrote you Concerning them both by Kirkly. My Penn is Confounded Bad, I am too blind to mend it, and Captain Passley who mends and makes them for me is gone out, therefore must Bid you farewell,

Caesar Rodney

P.S. The Convention is dissolved, made a plan of Government it seems and ordered an Election at a Short day.[1] Querry do these late opponents intend Calmly to submit, or try again to Rally? I am Sorry for Mr. Killen's Illness.

R (NN).

[1] In a letter of September 19, 1776, Thomas McKean had informed Rodney that the Delaware Convention had completed a constitution and set election day for October 21, 1776. Rodney, *Letters* (Ryden), pp. 123–24.

John Adams to William Tudor

Dear Sir   Philadelphia Sepr. 26th. 1776

Your obliging Favours of Sepr. 6th from New York & that of the 23d from the Plains of Haerlem are now before me.[1]

The Picture you draw of the Army, & the Disorders which prevail in it is shocking, but I believe it is just. But We often find in the variegated Scenes of human Life, that much good grows out of great Evil. A few Disgraces & Defeats have done more towards convincing the Congress, than the Rhetorick of many months assisted by frequent Letters from the General & many other of you belonging to the Army, was able to effect.

Before this Time You have been informed that the Articles of War are passed & printed, & a new Plan for a permanent & regular Army, is adopted. I wish it may have Success. Pray give me your Opinion of it.

The late Events at New York have almost overcome my utmost Patience. I can bear the Conflagration of Towns, any, almost any

Thing else, public or private better than Disgrace. The Cowardice of New England Men is an unexpected Discovery to me & I confess has put my Philosophy to the Trial. If I had heard that Parsons's & Fellows's Brigades had been cut to Peices, & had my Father, my Brother, & my Son, been among the Slain, I sincerely believe upon a cool Examination of my own Heart it would not have given me so much Grief as the Shamefull Flight of the 15th Inst.[2] I hope that God will forgive the guilty in the next World, but should any Question concerning this Transaction come into any Place where I have a Voice, I should think it my Duty, to be inexorable in this. We have none of the Particulars, but I conclude that such detestible Behaviour of whole Brigades could not have happened without the worst Examples in some Officers of Rank. These if any Such there are, shall never want my Voice for sending them to another World. If the best Friend I have should prove to be one of them, I should think myself guilty of his Crime & that I deserved his Punishment, if I interposed one Word between him & Death.

I lament the Fall of the young Hero Henley, but I wish you had been more particular in your Narration of the Enterprize which proved so glorious & so fatal to him. You are much mistaken in your apprehension that we are minutely informed of such Events. We suffer great Anxiety & the Publick many Misfortunes for want of Information from those of you who are so capable of giving it. The Post Office which has been in Fault is now beginning to do it's Duty. Don't you neglect yours.

My young Friend, I pity the Situation of the General because it is a difficult, a dangerous and a most important one. I make it my Rule to cover all Imperfections in the Generals & other officers of inferior Rank, & to make full & ample allowances for all their Virtues, Merits & Services.

I recollect that Polybius, who was as great a Judge of War as any one of his Age, was loud in his Praises of the Roman Troops. He never imputed any Defeat to the Fault of the Men but universally to the Folly & Incapacity of their Commanders. Our Generals & Officers must learn the same Justice & Policy. General Imputations of Cowardice & Impatience of Discipline, to the Men, are false, or if true, it is the Fault of the Officers. It is owing to their Ignorance, Incapacity & Indolence. And farther if it was true, concealing is the Way to cure it, not publishing it. The frequent Surprizes by which our Men & Officers are taken in the most palpable Traps, convince me that there is a Dearth of Genius among them.

There never was perhaps a Crisis in which a Coincidence of Circumstances afforded a fairer Opportunity to some great Mind to shew & exert itself. And perhaps there is not in all Antiquity, if there is in universal History, an Example more apposite to our

Situation than that of Thebes, or a Character more deserving of Imitation than that of Epaminondas.

The Bœotians were remarkable even to a Proverb for their Dullness, & untill the age of Epaminondas made no Figure in War. By the Peace of Antalcidas the Honour & Interest of Greece was prostituted to the Pride of Sparta. The Thebans were compelled to accede to that Treaty although it deprived them of the Dominion of Bœotia, & the Spartans by tampering with a perfidious Aristocratick Faction at last got Possession of their Citadel & reduced the Thebans to unconditional Subjugation. From this wretched State both of foreign & domestic Slavery, they were delivered by the Virtue & Ability of Epaminondas, & raised to Power superior to the other Grecian States.

The honest Citizens, enraged to see their Country thus cheated into Servitude, determined to set her free. The Project was well laid, & boldly executed by Pelopidas who entered the City with a small Number of resolute Men in Disguise, destroyed Leontidas & Archias the two Traytors & Tyrants & with the Assistance of Epaminondas & his Friends, together with a Body of Athenians, regained the Citadel.

The Spartans hearing of this Revolution, entered the Territories of the Thebans with a powerfull army to take Vengance of the Rebels & reduce the City to its former Subjection. The timorous Athenians dreading the formidable Power of Sparta, renounced all Friendship for the Thebans, & punished with great Severity such of their Citizens, as favoured them. The Thebans destitute of Friends & deserted by their Allies, appeared to the rest of the World to be devoted to inevitable Destruction. In such a desperate Conjuncture of Affairs the Genius & Virtue of two great Men shewn forth to the astonishment of all Mankind.

But what Means did they use? Their Men were raw Militia, fresh Recruits, new raised Citizens & Husbandmen, inexperienced, undisciplined, unused to Subordination, having been born & educated under the most democratical Government & what is worse from a natural Habitude, not very adroit at learning any Thing.

They begun by training their Men, inspiring them with a Contempt & Hatred of Servitude, & the noble Resolution of dying in Defence of the Liberty & Glory of their Country. They judged it rash to hazard a decisive Battle, with their new raised Militia against the best Troops in Greece, but chose rather to harass the Spartans with frequent Skirmishes, to instruct their Men in military Discipline & the Manœuvres of War. The Minds of their Soldiers were thus animated with the Desire of Glory & their Bodies hardened to the Fatigues of War. Whilst they gained Experience, Confidence & Courage by daily Rencounters.

Those great Generals like all other great Generals in similar

Circumstances, never engaging presumptuously, but carefully watching for favourable opportunities, let loose the Thebans like young Hounds upon their Enemies & rendered them alert & brave, by tasting the Sweets of Victory. By bringing them off in Safety they made them fond of the Sport, & eager to engage in the most dangerous Enterprizes. By this skillfull Conduct they brought their Forces to defeat the Spartans at Platea, Thespia, Tenagra [Tanagra] & Tegyra.

These Actions were only Preludes to the decisive Battle of Leuctra; for flushed with those Successes the Thebans dreaded no Enemy however superior in Number. Greece saw with astonishment the Spartans defeated by inferior Numbers of Men, who had always been held in Contempt. This Train of Successes elated the Thebans, but only enraged the Spartans. They negotiated a Peace with Athens & all the other Greecian States, & Thebes was devoted to Spartan Revenge. The largest Army they ever sent into the Field entered Bœotia, but Epaminondas with six thousand Men only, by his admirable Disposition of them, & their Bravery, engaged & defeated three Times the Number, & soon after marched to the Gates of Sparta, & exhibited to that haughty People a Sight they had never before beheld.

Excuse my reminding you of this Peice of Greecian History. I wish all of You who are in the Army & are Scholars would frequently contemplate the great Spirits of former Ages, & while your generous Souls catch Fire at the recital of illustrious Actions, would assiduously imitate the great Examples.

Believe me to be as usual, Yours,   John Adams

Tr (MHi).
[1] Tudor's September 6 and 23 letters to Adams are in the Adams Papers, MHi.
[2] The precipitous retreat of the New England troops at Kip's Bay on September 15 is described in George Washington to John Hancock, September 16, 1776, Washington, *Writings* (Fitzpatrick), 6:57–59.

Elbridge Gerry to Thomas Gerry

Dear Brother   New York 26th Sepr 1776
    I inclose You an Order on Mr Miller D. Commissary at Boston from the Commissary General for four thousand Quintals mercha[ntable . . .] Fish, if so much can be spared And a sufficient Quantity reserved for supplyg. abt. two thousand Men at Boston untill next Spring, which at 1 [lb?] per Week will be but about five hundred Quintals. The Quantity which I take is to be culled, & You are to have the Choice from all the barrells, in which You will take the Fish that can be transported to Vessels with the least

Expence provided the Qualities are equal. I shall be glad to have it shipped on board two good Vessels without delay, & will give a War Freight According to the Regulation adopted in the County of Essex last War, or the owner shall be allowed another in the Continental Service for Hire of the Vessel Insurance &c, but I think it best to fix the Freight on Delivery in Europe.

I suppose your Vessels will take the Whole, & one will be wanted to bring Home the Effects which shall be allowed the same Freight Home as out, the other can take a Cargo of Salt on your own Account. If Brother J Gerry's Vessel is in port I should be glad to give her a Freight out of the Quantity aforesaid & if not or You should have but one Vessel in port Mr. Devereux's may have a Freight, if You find her fit for the Business. Your Expences & such a part of the Carting as does not belong to the owner is to be paid by me.

Pray inform me as soon as may be of your proceedings, the Quantity taken, the Quality, the usual Freight, the place to load & Expences of Transportation &c, how long before it will be shipped, how much each Vessel takes & the owners, the Masters Names &c that I may send the necessary papers to dispatch the Vessels. I shall be glad to receive the Whole Account of Expences as soon as possible.

I have spoke to Colo Trumbull for a place for Mr Devereux when a Vacancy shall offer & he will give Notice accordingly.

Pray inform what is done in the other Matters between us, whether the Interest is vested in privateers & if not whether You have agreable to my Desire invested it in Sugar.

I am here upon a Committee for enquiring into the State of the Army & reportg a plan for supplying its Wants.[1] Have therefore not a Moments Time more to spare than to advise that every thing is right both foreign & Domestic excepting in this Department which I hope will be recovered soon. Nothing shall be wanting in My power to effect it. Love to Brothers, Sisters, Friends & Connections & believe me to be, your sincere Friend & Brother,

E Gerry

RC (MHi).

[1] On September 20 Gerry had been appointed, with Francis Lewis and Roger Sherman, to a committee "to repair to head quarters, near New York, to enquire into the state of the army, and the best means of supplying their wants." After about four days of meetings, the committee returned to Philadelphia and submitted a report to Congress on October 3. See JCC, 5:808, 842–44.

The following document pertaining to the work of the committee—captioned "Queries to be made at Head Quarters" and filed under the date September 20–27, 1776—is located in the Washington Papers, DLC. It is in a clerical hand and arranged in a double column format, with answers to the first two "Queries" appearing in the second column.

"1st. What Numbers of Troops are at present in the Army upon the Establish-

ment to the 1st of December or for a longer Time. Answered: by the Return
delivered the Committee from Congress.

"2d. Whether those numbers are sufficient, & if not what augmentation will be
necessary. [Answered:] The Number of men to oppose the Enemy should be
Forty Thousand exclusive of the Complement voted for the Flying Camp.

"3d. To be informed by the General officers the properest method for well
Officering and recruiting the Army upon the new Establishment.

"4th. To be informed what Articles are now & have been wanting in the
Commissary Genls. Departmt. & if any what the defect is owing to.

"5th. To be informed what deficiencies now are in the Commissary of Stores
Department, and the Cause thereof.

"6th. The same queries into the deficiencies of the Quartr. Mastr. Genl's. Department & the cause thereof.

"7th. The same in the Paymaster Genl's. Departmt. & the cause.

"8th. The same in the Artillery Stores & Laboratory Departmts.

"9th. The same as to the Waggon Masters Department & what number of
Waggons may be at all times necessary for the use of each Regiment.

"10th. The same enquiry into the Director General of the Hospitals Department.

"11th. The same with respect to Clothing the Army and whether a proper
Officer be not necessary to Superintend that Branch.

"12th. To know the present State of the Army with respect to discipline and
if any Deficiency, the best method for rectifying the same."

William Hooper to Samuel Johnston

Philadelphia, Sept 26th, 1776.

This, my Dear Sir, is truly confidential. Were it not that my
friend Hewes is to be the bearer, I should not trust out of my own
hands a letter which may be attended with unhappy consequences
should it fall into the power of any one disposed to make an
unfriendly use of it. I have waited impatiently for our publick
affairs to take a favourable turn to the Eastward before I set down
to delineate to you the state of them. I have waited to little purpose; every day gives a blacker tinge to the picture, and I assume
my pen at this stage of them, least I should be induced hereafter to
turn from the prospect with abhorrence and be averse to trouble you
upon so unpleasing a contemplation. You will feel yourself little
obliged to me even now that I draw off your attention from the
endearing concerns of private and domestick life, from the recesses
of rural and philosophic retirement, to fix it upon scenes that charac-
terise human nature in its most depraved state, and almost tempt a
man to arraign providence that he has been cast into being at a time
when private & political Vice is at a Crisis & the measure of Iniquity
full and overflowing. But, Dear Sir, It becomes our duty to see
things as they are, divested of all disguise, and when the happiness
of the present age and of Millions yet unborn depends upon a
reformation of them, we ought to spare no pains to effect so desirable a purpose. I know it to be very unpolite to dwell upon his

losses to a man who is unlucky, but when you play so deep a hazard as at present, you ought not to be kept in Ignorance how the Game runs.

After the constant employment of the American Army during a whole summer in fortifying Long Island and New York, General Howe landed with his Army on the former, and being opposed with a handful of our troops, whose bravery did honour to the glorious cause they fought for, with greatly superior numbers Howe bore down all resistance, and after having killed and wounded many and taken near 1000 prisoners, retired to his Encampment now enlarged by that part of the Island of which he had dispossessed our friends. Our men now confined to their lines were thought unequal to the defence of them; the Enemy possessed of Heights which our Troops with all their opportunities had neglected to fortify, had the entire Command. Our General wisely ordered a retreat, which was conducted without any loss but that of our honor. New York received us in our retreat, but from what you know of its situation, not to hold us long. We retired with the loss of great part of our Stores in sight of a victorious Enemy, abandoning their works which had been reared at an immense expense without any use but to stand as monuments of the absurdities which must ever attend a War conducted with raw, undisciplined Troops in the field and want of political experience in the Cabinet. Would I could draw a veil of oblivion over what ensued. The Enemy attempted to land a body of Troops near Haerlem where we had two Brigades of Eastern forces stationed. Our men made way for them as soon as their arrival was announced. They saw, they fled, not a single man faced his Enemy or fired his Gun. Our brave General flew to the scene of Action, but not a man would follow him. With prayers, entreaties, nay tears, he endeavoured to cause them to rally. At one time sixty of the Enemy, separated from the main body, had the pleasure of pursuing two compleat Brigades of New England Heroes. Where then had fled "That spirit of freedom which animated them? Where were then the Yeomanry of a Country, Men of property, not mere mercenaries, who fight the cause of freedom, and will succeed or perish with it." Mere words of puff *vox et praeterea nil.*

Washington is now at Col. Roger Morris's advantageously posted, His army however in a condition far from pleasing. The scarcity of clothes of all kinds prevents their being cloathed and covered as the season requires. Near 4000 of them are now sick, which is but small compared with them who have been returned formerly in that state. He has had an immense deal of trouble with the Militia, who from real or feigned sickness have been a constant burden to the army without any use whatsoever. Of 13 battalions of Connecticut Militia all but 700 deserted, and these he dismissed to save such a burdensome Expence, without any benefit resulting from it.

I am sorry to find that my Countrymen [1] are become a byword among the nations—Eastern Prowess—Nation poorly—Camp Difficulty are standing terms of reproach and dishonour—they suffer in the comparison with the troops to the Southward of Hudson's River who have to a man behaved well and born the whole brunt on Long Island—and that for which the Eastern troops must be damned to eternal fame—they have plundered friends and foes without discrimination. When I commend the Southern Troops I except the Philadelphia City Militia who Poltroon like deserted their station, not being able to bear the absence of the Muskets.

All this is in a great measure to be ascribed to the present footing upon which our army has been enlisted. The Enlistments have been so short that they were scarce on the field before it was time to disband them. They acquired no military knowledge from Experience. Their service was too short to establish subordination and discipline amongst them.

Another great grievance has been the want of proper officers to command. The scantiness of pay or some other cause has drawn few Gentlemen into commands; Offices have been chiefly distributed amongst men to the Eastward who aimed at nothing but popularity in the army and knew that nothing would so effectually secure it as condescension and equality. Judge what would be the privates when such were the officers. I am told that they have even stimulated their men to desertion to find an excuse to follow them, and the Regimental Surgeons have taken bribes to certify sickness in order to exempt soldiers from Duty. It is a fact that a Connecticut Militia Brigadier induced his whole Brigade to run away and then most bravely run away himself.

In a word I begin to believe that patriotism among the common soldiery is a bubble and that pay well and hang well are the grand secrets to make an army—that this is a mere machine, that ought never to think, or act but when acted upon; that it requires skilfull artificers or officers, to wind up and conduct its movements, for when left to itself it will soon run down or go into irregularities which must produce confusion and ruin to itself. If once a soldier is suffered to think for himself or reason upon the propriety of the commands of his Officers—farewell to suddenness and decision in execution. These are the imperfections of our present army. The inclosed will shew you the method which we have adopted to remedy them.[2]

Thus we stand alike and contrasted—Washington brave, Howe brave. Howe Experienced, Washington not. Howes' army disciplined, orderly, satisfied, well found with everything. Washington's, raw troops, disorderly, discontented and wanting almost every thing necessary for cloathing, and very many for defence & the term of Enlistment nearly expired. Don't start from the picture. It is taken strictly from the original, and far from exciting despair it ought rather to rouse us from our Lethargy and induce us to remedy

the Evils while in our power for yet they are so. By way of
back shade to the painting I would inform you that a few days ago
a detachment from the Enemy took possession of our works at Paulus
Hook, the guard we had there retired and left them a bloodless
conquest. Hewes will inform you that we lately had some advantage in a skirmish with the Enemy. That perhaps has served to
keep together our present Army.

Our privateers have been successful. I will not say anything of our
Continental Ships lest I should infringe upon Hewes' department. I
fear that the want of Men & Cannon will prove an insuperable
obstacle to their Movements.

To what accident it is to be ascribed I know not but since Howe
got possession of York above one-third of the City has been consumed by fire. It is reported, I know not with what truth, that
Howe who is obliged now and then to condescend to humour the
Hessians gave them one day to rejoice & riot & that in the heat of
their festivity they made a Bonfire of the City. So says Rumour.
Others with less probability ascribe it to our forces who were 9 Miles
distant from it at the time.

The Successes of Howe have given a strange Spring to Toryism;
men who have hitherto lurked in silence and neutrality, seem willing to take a side in opposition to the liberties of their Country.
Toryism is a Strange Weed, the growth of a barren soil whose vege-
tation is not progressive, but is indebted for a sudden Existence to
the Sunshine of prosperity and perishes as soon as that leaves it,
having nothing radical in itself or the soil from which it springs to
continue its existence longer.

You have seen the constitution of Pennsylvania—*Humano capite
cervix equinna juncte*—the motley mixture of limited monarchy,
and an execrable democracy—a Beast without a head. The Mob
made a second branch of Legislation—Laws subjected to their
revisal in order to refine them, a Washing in ordure by way of
purification. Taverns and dram shops are the councils to which
the laws of this State are to be referred for approbation before they
possess a binding Influence. No man to be an Assemblyman unless
he believes in God. Is Irreligion then the flourishing growth of
Pennsylvania and is Atheism a weed that thrives there? Sure this
insinuates as much. It is a melancholy consideration, that publick
proceedings now are in a great measure the histories of those concerned in them—and popularity—Interest—Office, are the strong
outlines which mark the production—in this Instance they all work
powerfully. I shall lament that any prepossession should have taken
place in Carolina in favor of the wisdom in politicks of this State;
or that the name which authenticates the public Acts of Convention
should have any weight to give such a plan a currency. It is truly
the Excrement of expiring Genius & political Phrenzy. It has
made more Tories than Lord North; deserves more Imprecations

than the Devil and all his Angels. It will shake the very being of this once flourishing Country.

But I am at the Bottom of my page, I have performed all I promised & have given you a Tale—piteous truly piteous, and will now leave you to indulge all the luxury of melancholy & distress for our bleeding Country. Do not however imagine that I rather delineate the history of my own mind than a state of facts as they are unwarped by Gloomy fancy. Do not mistake me, my spirits have not failed me—I do not look upon present ills as incurable, I never considered the path to liberty as strewed with roses. She keeps her Temple upon the highest Pinnacles on Earth; they who would enter with sincerity and pure devotion, must climb over Rocks & frightful precipices covered with thorns & weeds; these miscarriages will be frequent & how many thousand must perish in the pursuit, but the prize is worth all the fatigue and hazard, and the adventurer when at his Journey's end will look down with pleasure on the difficulties he has surmounted, & with triumph count the glorious wounds that have purchased to him and posterity the invaluable blessing. Thus I sport in the field of Metaphor, more at ease than I till now thought myself capable of. It is the standard which every man at the present day should bring himself to, and were I to choose a motto for a Modern Whig—It should be—"Whatever is, is right"—& on the reverse *"Nil desperandum."* May you and yours ever feel those blessings which are the result of genuine goodness of heart, and may the misfortunes of the public never intrude themselves upon your domestick peace.

When I began this scrawl I intended it only for you. I have been led into a train of scribbling which has not left me a moment to write to the man whom I love and esteem, Mr Iredell. In supreme confidence give him a sight of this and beg his rememberance of Me. To Your & his family pray offer my most respectful Compliments & believe me to be with Unaltered Esteem & Affection, Your Friend,

William Hooper.

Reprinted from *N.C. Colonial Records,* 10:815–20. Only the eighth page of the RC of this letter has been found. Nc–Ar.

[1] Hooper had been born and raised in Massachusetts.
[2] See *JCC,* 5:788–807.

North Carolina Delegates to the North Carolina Council of Safety

[September] 26th [1776]

Yesterday Evening we applied to the man employed to make the Salt pans. He notwithstanding his most solemn engagements to Us has not yet begun them. We feel ourselves much hurt by this disappointment but must submit with patience to the caprice of the Blacksmith as he is the only person in the City who will undertake this Business. We shall not cease to stimulate him to his duty if the most pressing importunity will avail anything.

We inclose you herewith the plan for raising the new Army, from which you will observe what proportion of strength the Continent expects to derive from the state of North Carolina in the next ensuing year.[1] We shall perhaps meet some difficulty in accomplishing the whole of what is required of us but considering the great advantages which must result to us in point of local provincial security and defence against our Enemies in case we should effect it, I doubt not our utmost indeavours will be exerted for this desirable purpose. To possess within ourselves a strength competent for our defence without calling upon our neighbours, will give us an Independence and self Importance which must rank us high in the scale of the States. It will save us the necessity of drawing forth the militia, to a service peculiarly burdensome to men, the subsistence of whose families and of the state at large depends upon their continuance at their homes and the Cultivation of their lands. It will give Circulation to the vast quantity of paper currency which we have amongst us, and which without this will become a dead weight upon us, a medium infinitely beyond the Exigincies of Trade and commerce, checked as they are within our State. This is not all; the Farmer will find a ready sale for his Commodities and so many craving mouths will go far to consume the great quantities of provisions which would otherwise perish on the hands of the Planters. It will give occupation to many who in the present Stagnation of trade would be without Employment and from being Idle might become disorderly and dangerous to society—but to comprehend in one a thousand substantial goods which will be produced by it, It will lodge amongst us, or give us a Credit with the Treasury of the united States for a large sum which will tend to assist us in the discharge of that immense load of debt which this struggle for our liberties hath already and must hereafter cost us. We beg pardon for dwelling upon a subject which you have already anticipated, We feel so forcibly the prudence of the measure we urge, that our earnest wishes for the happiness of our state have perhaps led us beyond the rules of strict propriety.

We cannot conclude this matter of Military Arrangements without hinting to you the great probability there is that Lord Howe will attempt a descent upon some part of Your State during the winter Season. The happy temperature of our Climate at that season of the year is exceedingly well calculated for a Campaign without endangering their health when otherways in an Eastern State they must be idle in Winter quarters, expensive to Britain & without any Employment. From General Howes large Army He can spare a very considerable force. His Object during Winter will in the Eastern Colonies be only to secure the Conquests which he has made, and with Works to defend him & the necessity our army must be under to go into Winter quarters, a part of his Army will be fully competent to that purpose. The Southern Colonies are a tempting morsel to them, & they have not forgot their disgraceful expedition at Charlestown and no doubt will strain every nerve to retrieve their Honour. This calls for our most serious attention that in this day of leisure and safety nothing may be unessayed which may tend hereafter to repel the Efforts of our unrelenting Enemies. Batteries where they can be erected to advantage, Obstructions in rivers which nature has made most accessible to shipping, works thrown up at defiles and narrow passes, Redoubts, Block houses & many other preparations familiar to military Gentlemen would be a proper employment for our Soldiery while an Enemy is at a distance and render him less formidable when near us. We need say nothing more inducing an attention to these concerns, than that if General Howe should get a firm footing in Carolina and be able to establish there again the Government of Britain, It would affect the Continent at large and go far to the Subjugation of America & the total ruin of our Cause.

We shall send Cloathing for the Soldiers as soon as Waggons and Horses can be procured. We think the Risque too great by Water, as in case of a Capture or Loss they could not be replaced from the present scarcity of materials. We refer you for the matters which we have omitted to our friend Mr Hewes & beg leave to subscribe ourselves with great respect, Your Obedt Humble Servants,

Wm Hooper

John Penn

P.S. We wrote you by Mr Heyward, Mr Wyrriott & Milles, since which Genl Washington has had a Skirmish with the Enemy, defeated them, drove them from their ground & killed, wounded & taken about 80 or 90. This tho trifling in itself will We hope be important in its consequences as it has given great Spirits to our Soldiery.[2] Yours &c.

RC (Nc–Ar). A continuation of North Carolina Delegates to the North Carolina Council of Safety, September 18, 1776.

[1] See *JCC*, 5:761–62.

[2] For Washington's letter to President Hancock of September 18 describing a skirmish at Harlem Plains, see Washington, *Writings* (Fitzpatrick), 6:67–70.

Secret Committee Minutes of Proceedings

Sepr. 26. 1776

Come. met. Present Messrs. Morris, Hewes, Col. Lee, Livingston & McKean. A Charter party for the Ship Betsey, Wm. Stevens Mas-

ter, was signd by the Come. Orderd That Mr. Morris employ a
proper person to go to N. England to charter vessals to proceed
from thence to Chesapeake Bay, there to load with tobo. now purchasg. on acct. of the Continent. Issued the followg. drafts on the
Treasurer. In Favr. of G. Meade & Co. for 4434 17/90 dlls being
amount of an Invoice of 1000 barrels flour purchasd by them &
shippd on board the ship Betsey, Wm. Stevens Mr., for St. Lucia
or Martinico on Contl. Acct. Consignd to Mr. Wm. Bingham
Mercht. there. In favr. Jh. Hewes Esqr. for 2000 dlls part paymt.
of the freight of his Brige. Fanny, Capn. Tokeley, now under
Charter party to this Come.[1] In favor of Robert Morris Esqr. for
40,000 dlls advanced him to pay for produce now purchasg. on Contl.
Acct. Order on Col. Timy. Matlack to deliver G. Losch 4 Casks Salt
petre to be manufacturd into powdr.

MS (MH–H).
[1] For information on the troubles that beset the *Fanny* before she finally sailed
for France, see Joseph Hewes to William Tokeley, May 18, 1776, note.

William Williams to Joseph Trumbull

Dear Sir   Philadel. 26 Sepr 1776
    I recd yours of the 19th. Have you recd mine containg. an ex-
tempore Accot. of the Nego[tiatio]n with Ld Howe.[1] Congress
have directed You to purchase Salt & put up Provisions as You
shall judge necessary for next years army.[2] Trust You have recd
it from the Presidt. They have alarming Accos. from the No. Army
that the Sick have nothing but bread & meat, not so much as Ind.
meal nor any kind of Vegetable &c & the Sick perish for want &c &
have sent a Comte of Mr Stocton & Clymer to enquire into all the
Circumstances of that Army in order to make Them as comfortable
as possible, & the Idea of a Contract for that Departmt. is received &
adopted & the Comte are instructed to endeavor to make one, upon
Schylers Plan, of which They have a Copy. Suppose it will ease You
of a heavy Burden. Three wod have been sent but they cod not find
a 3d man, two had been sucessively chosen & begd off, & then it was
concluded to send but the two.[3] Tis also said the Jersey Troops
have nothing but bread & meat & that none of the Troops have
their full rations, & that there is jobbing & cheating, tho nobody
directly blames you & surely you have powerful Friends & Supporters but there is great uneasiness that yr Deputies or somebody
grossly fails &c. Tis very possible they may soon be for enterg. into
a Contract for the York Army & have you continue Comissary. They
say tis his business only to issue & be a Check upon the Contractor.
I tell Them if They make a Contract then You ought by all means

to have the offer of it, & they yes by all means. What relates to the Y[ork] [4] army is only out of Doors talk, & I cant say it will be any thing else, but very likely it may, tho nothing yet moved.

If it shod be the Case shod be glad to know Your mind about contracting &c. I trust the Comte. will see you on the road, to get what advice & assistance They can from You. I think Mr Clymer is a very good sort of a Man, & Mr. Stocton is not bad. I forgot whether I told You Gen. Schuyler had resigned.[5] It has not been acted upon but I imagine it will be accepted, but am sensible it will cause great heart burning in many members, & they will curse N Engld. as having by malicious Clamors forced him to it &c &c. The Measures are taken for formg a new Army as you will have seen, & learnd per Mr Sherman[6] &c; also I hope it will succeed, wish to know how it is relished in the Army. It is of the last importance to have it succeed. As I have but a moments Time cant look over your Letter to know whether I shod have mentioned any thing more which you hint at. You will let me hear what you can get Time for &c.

I am dear Sir, your most sincere & affece. Friend & Servt.

[*P.S.*] Complimts to Mr. Sherman &c.[7]

RC (Ct). In the hand of William Williams, though not signed.

[1] See Williams' second letter to Joseph Trumbull of September 13.

[2] See *JCC*, 5:825.

[3] On September 25 Congress approved instructions for a committee to be sent to Ticonderoga to assess the state of the northern department and on the 26th appointed Richard Stockton and George Clymer to undertake the mission. *JCC*, 5:822–23, 828. General Schuyler's August 25 proposal for supplying the northern army by contract and the committee's November 27 report, which rejected this plan and recommended continuing supply by the commissary general, are in *Am. Archives*, 5th ser. 1:1151–53, 3:1584–85. For other aspects of the committee's mission, see John Hancock to Philip Schuyler, September 27, 1776, note 4.

[4] That is, New York.

[5] See Edward Rutledge to Robert R. Livingston, September 23, 1776, note 2.

[6] On September 20 Roger Sherman had been appointed to a committee to inquire into the state of the army near New York and was apparently absent from Congress September 21–30. See *JCC*, 5:808, 838, 842.

[7] For the continuation of this letter, see Williams to Joseph Trumbull, September 28, 1776.

Elbridge Gerry to Horatio Gates

My dear sir   Kingsbridge 27th Sepr 1776

Being here with a Committee of Congress for enquiring into the State of the Army, I take the Oppertunity of informing You by Mr Trumbull that We are endeav[orin]g to new model the Army in every Respect where necessary. Congress have resolved to establish eighty eight full Batalions for the War & the Assemblies are to appoint the Regimental Officers, in doing which if some extra Measures are not adopted We shall have such a Corps of Officers as the Army have been hitherto incumbered with. I have desired General Washington to furnish the Committee with a List of such officers in the Army here as he is desirous of having again engaged in the Service with the States to wch. they belong, & the General thinks it will be necessary to obtain the same from the northern Army. The use We intend to make of this is to send it with a Member of Congress to the Assembly of each respective State who is to be ordered to impress the Necessity of appointing Gentlemen of Education to military offices as a Measure absolutely necessary for saving the Country & to urge the assemblies to apportion the Men on the Terms & raise them by recruiting or draughting in Readiness for reinforcing or forming the Camps by the 1st Decr. next. We have obtained Colo Moylan's Resignation & General Miflin comes again into the office of Q.M.G. Many other Measures will be reported wch I think will put Things on a good Footing. I suppose you will hear of the Retreat from N York e'er this is at Headq. & of the Fire wch has consumed about one Quarter of the City, & remain sir in great Haste, your assured Friend & very hum sert,

E Gerry

[*P.S.*] Pray direct the List to me at Philadelphia without Delay. The Men are to have a Bounty of twenty Dollars & 100 Acres Land each at the End of the War—the officers Land in proportion.[1]

RC (NHi).
[1] On the next day Gerry wrote another letter from Kingsbridge in a similar vein. "The congress have ordered me here with two other gentlemen, to enquire into the state of the army and report a plan for supplying its wants. We have attended the business very closely with all the general officers three days, and shall return with all expedition.

"The situation of the camp affairs I dislike, but doubt not we shall soon bring them right. Resolution and perseverance will carry men through difficulties, which at first view look insurmountable, and I hope Americans will ever keep this in mind as an animating consideration under disappointments, which naturally happen in war.

"We have been fortunate enough to procure the resignation of the former quarter-master-general, whose department was in an exceeding bad way, and have prevailed on general Mifflin to resume it. This has given affairs new life. Our plan is to reinforce the army, adopt more effectual means for clothing it; to hasten the new levies; to procure better officers, and have an instructer of the first abilities for the officers of each brigade; to establish a laboratory under the direction of a board of ordnance; to regulate the hospital *de novo* that better care may be taken of the sick; and various other minor improvements. The general aspect of our affairs has nothing that ought to discourage us; and the misfortunes of the army should lead us to make greater exertions." Gerry to Unknown, September 28, 1776, extracted in Austin, *Life of Gerry*, 1:214–15.

For evidence that this letter may have been directed to James Warren, speaker

of the Massachusetts House of Representatives, see Gerry to Samuel Adams,
October 4, 1776, note 4.

John Hancock to Horatio Gates

Sir,   Philadelphia 27th Sept. 1776
    I have the Honour to enclose you Sundry Resolves of Congress,
to which I must Refer your Attention. They relate to a variety of
Subjects as you will percieve; and are extremely necessary for your
Information, and the Direction of your future Conduct.[1]
    The Congress having resolved to Raise eighty eight Battalions
of Continental Troops, are Anxious to promote discipline and
Subordination in their army as much as Possible. For this Purpose,
they have Repeald the System of military Law they at first Adopted,
& Instituted in its Room a more Severe and Rigorous one, as better
Calculated to Introduce Obediance and Regularity among the
Troops. It is also the determination of Congress that an Attention
to these things will be the best method of Attaining Promotion, and
will be the most Effectual means of Recommending the Officers in
the Army of the United States to their notice. Without a Well disciplined Army it is impossible to Expect Success against veteran
Troops, you will therefore give Orders to all the Officers under
your Command to have the Troops daily Traind & to enure them
to the most examplary discipline. The Congress having appointed
a Committee to Repair to Ticonderoga to devise ways & means of
Providing the Nothern Army with Provisions, Medicines, & Other
Necessarys, have chosen Mr Stockden & Mr. Clymer, who will begin
their Journey on Monday next. To them therefore I beg leave to
refer you for further Particulars on this Subject & am, with Great
Respect & Esteem, Sir, your most Obedt. & very Hum. Servant,
                                        J. H. Presid.

LB (DNA: PCC, item 12A).
    [1] For the resolves which Hancock probably sent Gates, see *JCC*, 5:758, 762–63,
784, 788–807, 822–23.

John Hancock to Philip Schuyler

Sir   Philadelphia Sept 27th 1776
    I have the honor to enclose you sundry Resolves which are so
explicit that I need only request your attention to them.
    You will perceive that Congress have come to a determination to
augment our Army to 88 Battalions & to ingage the Troops to serve
during the continuance of the war, Being thoroughly convinced by

repeated instances that the short & limited Enlistment of troops has been the source of much mischief to the service.[1] In order that these troops may be better disciplined the Congress have abolished the system of Rules & articles for the government of the Army which they at first instituted & have adopted a new one, sundry copies of which I inclose you.[2]

It is also their determination that the strictest discipline should be kept up in the Army, that the soldiers should be daily trained & practised in their different Manœvres. An attention to these things you will observe by the inclosed Resolves will be the likeliest way to attain promotion & will be the surest recommendation to their notice.[3]

The committee of Congress to confer with you on the State of the army &c will set out tomorrow or next day for Ticonderoga.[4] To them I beg leave to refer you & am with every sentiment of esteem & regard, Sir, yours &c,   J H Presid.

P.S. The attention of Congress has been so much taken up by our affairs at New York that I have not time to reply to your several Letters but hope I shall have leisure to do it by the next conveyance & that congress will soon determine on the subject of them. They are now in the hands of a Special Committee.

Tr (MH-H). LB (DNA: PCC, item 12A).
[1] See JCC, 5:762–63. In the LB this sentence ends with the phrase: "and that our Militia is inadequate to the Duty expected of them."
[2] See JCC, 5:788–807.
[3] See JCC, 5:784.
[4] On September 25 Congress, moved by "alarming Accos. from the No. Army that the Sick have nothing but bread & meat, not so much as Ind. meal nor any kind of Vegetable &c & the Sick perish for want &c.," approved instructions for a committee to "be immediately sent to Ticonderoga" and on the following day appointed George Clymer and Richard Stockton to the committee. Clymer and Stockton set out on their mission several days later. On their way to northern New York they stopped at Kingsbridge and conferred with Commissary General Joseph Trumbull on October 5 and 6. Later in the month they consulted with General Schuyler at Albany and Saratoga, inspected the general hospital at Fort George, and conferred with General Gates at Ticonderoga. On their return to Albany early in November they met with Robert R. Livingston and Walter Livingston, the recently resigned deputy commissary of the northern army, and rejected a contract for supplying this force that was offered by the Livingstons.
Clymer and Stockton returned to Philadelphia and presented a report on the state of the northern army on November 27 in which they declared that "at present" it would be impractical to supply this force by private contract, made several suggestions for improving medical care for the sick and wounded, and brought a number of the army's other needs to Congress' attention. They also submitted supporting letters and memoranda from Gates and Schuyler setting forth the requirements of the northern army in even greater detail. Congress referred all of this material to a new "committee on the affairs of the northern army" and on the basis of its reports passed resolves on November 28 and 29 and December 28 that on the whole closely followed the recommendations of the original committee and the two generals. In addition to the letters of Clymer

and Stockton printed in this volume, see also PCC, item 21, fols. 73–75, 79–82, 85–95, 103–6; *Am. Archives*, 5th ser. 1:151–53, 2:920, 1299, 3:592, 1584–89; *JCC*, 5:822–23, 828, 6:985, 988–89, 990–91, 1013, 1037, 1047–48; and William Williams to Joseph Trumbull, September 26, 1776. Letters from Robert R. Livingston and Walter Livingston to Philip Schuyler of October 27, 1776, discussing issues raised by the committee at that time, are in the Schuyler Papers, NN.

Robert Treat Paine was apparently referring to Clymer and Stockton when he noted in his diary on September 28: "Pleasant. Field deputys set out for Camp." MHi.

Richard Henry Lee to Thomas Jefferson

Dear Sir   Philadelphia 27th Septr. 1776

I should have written to you before now if I had not been uncertain about finding you at home, as the distance was great, and the meeting of our Assembly approaching. All the material events that have happened since you left us are to be found related pretty faithfully in the public papers, which I suppose are regularly conveyed to you.

The plan of foreign treaty is just finished, and yourself, with Doctor Franklin, and Mr. Deane now in France, are the Trustees to execute this all important business.[1] The great abilities and unshaken virtue, necessary for the execution of what the safety of America does so capitally rest upon, has directed the Congress in their choice; and tho ambition may have no influence in this case, yet that distinguished love for your country that has marked your life, will determine you here. In my judgement, the most emminent services that the greatest of her sons can do America will not more essentially serve her and honor themselves, than a successful negotiation with France. With this country, every thing depends upon it, and if we may form a judgement of what is at a distance, the dispositions of that Court are friendly in a high degree, and want only to be properly acted upon, to be wrought into fixt attachment and essential good. We find ourselves greatly endangered by the Armament at present here, but what will be our situation the next campaign, when the present force shall be increas[ed] by the addition of 20 or 30 thousand Russians with a larg[e] body of British and Irish troops? I fear the power of America will fail in the mighty struggle And the barbarous hand of despotism will extirpate libe[rty] and virtue from this our native land; placing in th[eir] stead slavery, vice, ignorance, and ruin. Already these foes of human kind have opened their Courts of Justice (as they call them) on Long Island, and the first frui[ts] of their tender mercies, are confiscation of estates, and condemnation of Whigs to perpetual imprisonment.

The idea of Congress is, that yourself and Dr. Frank[lin] should go in different Ships. The Doctor, I suppose, will sail from hence, and if it is your pleasure, on[e] of our Armed Vessels will meet you in any River in Virginia that you choose.

I am, with singular esteem, dear Sir, your affectionate friend and obedient Servant, Richard Henry Lee

RC (DLC). Jefferson, *Papers* (Boyd), 1:522–23.
[1] The plan of foreign treaties had been approved on September 17 and commissioners to France appointed on the 26th. See *JCC*, 5:768, 827; and John Hancock to Jefferson, September 30, 1776.

Secret Committee to John Ross

Sir [1]   Philada. Septr. 27th. 1776

As several of the vessells by which we have heretofore ordered out blankets & cloathing for the use of the Publick have unfortunately been taken, We think it prudent to give fresh orders in hopes the Goods may yet reach America in time to be very serviceable. We therefore request of you to purchase on the very best terms in your power immediately on the receipt of this letter: Ten Thousand Striped blankets, Thirty Thousand Yards of 6/4 broad cloth, brown & blue Colours from 3/ to 6/ stg per yd., Three Thousand yards different Colors for Facings at about 4/ stg per yd., One Thousand pieces of Duffields or some such Cloth at about 90/. We will immediately set about making you remittances to pay for these Goods, therefore you may either employ any money already in your hands on Publick acct in this purchase or pledge your Credit for speedy Payments, as we are making large purchases of Rice, Indico, Tobacco &c for immediate Exportation and the approaching Season will give us fair opportunitys of getting these Goods to market whereas we have been much hampered during the Summer by the Cruizers on our Coast. You will buy these Goods where ever you can soonest get them, Great Britain & Ireland excepted, and you may send them out by any good Vessell belonging to America, but if none such offers immediately, you may Charter a Foreign Vessell to take them & proceed for this Coast immediately with orders to get into the first place of Safety she possibly can in these united States of America. Whatever terms you fix shall be Complyed with, depending that you will have them as moderate as possible and we will load the Vessell back to Europe immediately. If any difficulty occurrs about getting these Goods out to America direct, you may then ship them out to Wm. Bingham Esqr. at Martinico, to Mr. Cornelius Stevenson at St. Eustatia, Mr. Isaac Hicks, Governeur at Curracoa or to Mr. Stephen Ceronio at Cape Francois with orders for them to forward them to us with all possible dispatch by different Conveyances. We beg your utmost attention & dilligence in the execution of this order. The Goods are extreamly wanted & you must not loose one Moment of time. You may rest assured of soon being enabled to pay for them & we remain Sir, Your most hble servants,

B Franklin	Richard Henry Lee
Robt Morris	Fras. Lewis
	Phil. Livingston

RC (NNPM). Written by Morris and signed by Morris, Franklin, Lee, Lewis, and Livingston.

[1] John Ross (1726–1800), Philadelphia merchant, had gone to Europe in the spring of 1776 to contract for military supplies both on private and public accounts. *Appleton's Cyclopaedia of American Biography*; and Morgan, *Naval Documents*, 4:580.

New York Delegates to the New York Convention

Gentlemen   Phila. Septr. 28th. 1776.

We received your letter, desiring us to apply to Congress for the loan of a sum of money. We have applied accordingly, and obtained an order on the treasury for $100,000, which will certainly be sent you by Thursday next.[1]

Your resolutions respecting Genl. Schuyler we have laid before Congress, and they have appointed a committee to consider them, who have promised us to report on Monday next. The committee is to our wishes, vizt: Mr. Rutledge, Mr. Hooper and Mr. McKean. As soon as their report is agreed to, it shall be forwarded for your information. It will, without question, be satisfactory.

We are, gentlemen, Your mo. obt. servants,

Phil. Livingston.

MS not found; reprinted from *Journals of N.Y. Prov. Cong.*, 1:656. Addressed: "Abm. Yates Esqr. Prest. of the Convention of the State of New-York."

[1] See *JCC*, 5:830. For the convention's September 20 letter to Hancock, together with enclosed accounts and resolutions supporting its request that "the honourable Congress . . . advance to this State one hundred thousand dollars in consideration of the vast expense to which we are exposed, and the impracticability . . . of emitting bills of credit with a despatch suitable to the urgency of our publick affairs," see PCC, item 68, 1:298–306; and *Am. Archives*, 5th ser. 2:417–20.

William Williams to Joseph Trumbull

September 28, 1776

Sat. 28. I have unluckily lost 2 days, in the conveyance of this, by a misinformation, about the Posts going out on Thursday. I said Gen. Schuys. Resigna. wod probably be accepted, but I trust I was mistaken.[1] I did not forsee what Maneuvre wod take place; the N. York Convention have sent a warm & spirited Remonstrance agst. acceptg it representg the Consequences of it as fatal & total destruction &c &c &c in the most pressing Terms & unanimous they say. It is possible some body wrote to them to procure this. His Friends here blaze away on the same side, & have got a Comte. to consider the remonstrance & to report, & no doubt what the report will be. His Friends are so many & fierce, that I doubt not those who wod willingly accept it, must give way to such a Torrent in his Favr. for the sake of Peace here.

RC (Ct). A continuation of Williams to Joseph Trumbull, September 26, 1776.
  [1] See Edward Rutledge to Robert R. Livingston, September 23, 1776, note 2.

John Adams to Henry Knox

Dear Sir.   Philadelphia Septr. 29. 1776
    This Evening I had the Pleasure of yours of the 25th.[1] I have only to ask you whether it would be agreable to you to have Austin made your Lt Coll.? Let me know sincerely, for I will never propose it without your Approbation.
    I agree with you that there is nothing of the vast in the Characters of the Enemies General, or Admiral. But I differ in opinion from you, when you think, that if there had been, they would have annihilated your Army. It is very true that a Silly Panick has been spread in your Army, and from thence come to Philadelphia. But Hannibal spread as great a Panick once at Rome, without daring to attempt to take advantage of it. If he had his own Army would have been annihilated—and he knew it. A Panic, in an Army, when pushed to Desperation becomes Heroism.
    However, I despise that Panic and those who have been infected with it, and I could almost consent that the good old Roman fashion of Decimation should be Introduced. The Legion which run away, had the Name of every Man in it, put into a Box and then drawn out, and every tenth Man was put to death. The Terror of this Uncertainty whose Lot it would be to die, restrained the whole in the Time of danger from indulging their Fears.
    Pray tell me, Coll Knox, does every Man to the Southward of Hudsons River behave like an Hero and every Man to the Northward of it like a Poltroon or not. The Rumours, Reports, and Letters which come here upon every occasion represent the New England Troops as Cowards running away perpetually, and the Southern Troops as standing bravely. I wish I could know whether it is true. I want to know for the Government of my own Conduct, because if the New Englandmen are a Pack of Cowards, I would resign my Place in Congress where I should not choose to represent

Poltroons and remove to some Southern Colony, where I could enjoy the Society of Heroes, and have a Chance of learning Sometime or other, to be Part of an Hero myself. I must say that your *amiable* General gives too much occasion for these Reports by his Letters, in which he ⟨is *eternally throwing some slur or other upon*⟩ often mentions things to the Disadvantage of some Part of New England, but ⟨never one Word⟩ Seldom any Thing of the Kind about any other Part of the Continent.

You complain of the popular Plan of raising the new Army. But if you make the Plan, as unpopular as you please, you will not mend the Matter. If you leave the appointment of officers to the General, or to the Congress, it will not be so well done, as if left to the assemblies. The true Cause of the Want of good officers in the Army is not because the appointment is left to the assemblies, but because such officers in sufficient Numbers are not in America. Without Materials the best Workman can do nothing. Time, Study and Experience alone must make a sufficient Number of able officers.

I wish We had a military Accademy, and should be obliged to you for a plan of such an Institution. The Expence would be a Trifle, no object at all with me.

Oct. 1. This day I had the Honour of making a Motion for the appointment of a Committee to consider of a Plan for the Establishment of a military Academy in the Army. The Comtee was appointed and your ser[van]t was one.[2] Write me your sentiments upon the subject.

LB (MHi).
[1] Knox's September 25 letter to Adams is in the Adams Papers, MHi.
[2] See *JCC*, 5:838. Although this committee apparently made no report, the report of the committee sent to inquire into the state of the army at New York, which was submitted to Congress on October 3, contained a resolution proposing "That the Board of War be directed to prepare a plan for establishing a continental Laboratory and a military Academy." *JCC*, 5:844n, 860. The proposed resolution was not adopted, but for Adams' remarks on the need to train officers see Adams, *Diary* (Butterfield), 3:436, 445–46.

Samuel Chase to John Dickinson

My Dear Sir   Philadelphia Septr. 29th. 1776 Sunday Morning
It is my very earnest Desire and anxious Wish that you would come to Annapolis.[1] I am satisfied you could render very great and essential Service to our State. However I will not press you to grant that to my importunate Sollictation which you think you can refuse to a whole province.

I beg the favor of you to enclose your Remarks on our draft of Government and Bill of Rights (together with the Bill of Rights) by Tuesdays Post.[2]

I wish you every Blessing in this Life and I am, with the greatest
Sincerity, Your Affectionate and Obedient Servant,

Saml. Chase

RC (PHi).
¹ Chase wrote this letter just before returning to Annapolis to resume his seat
in the Maryland Convention. See Thomas Stone to the Maryland Council of
Safety, September 30, 1776.
² For Dickinson's copy of *The Constitution and Form of Government proposed
for the Consideration of the Delegates of Maryland*, probably the one Chase enclosed in this letter, see *A Rising People: The Founding of the United States,
1765 to 1789* (Philadelphia: American Philosophical Society, 1976), p. 227.
In a letter dated only "Fryday Morn." but undoubtedly written on October 4,
Chase wrote another letter to Dickinson from Annapolis thanking him for his
"Letter and Remarks." "I see the propriety of your Amendments. I am afraid
the popular Errors will prevail. Congress have requested a full Representation
as soon as possible. We shall endeavor to postpone the Consideration of our
form of Government, but I doubt if We shall succeed. A Distemper of Governing
has seised all Ranks of Men. . . . What do you mean in saying 'I am told our
Friend, C—— courts popularity too assiduously'? I guess it was introduced only
to make way for your Observations on that Subject. Mr. Caroll suspects he has
been misrepresented to you.
"General Lee crossed from hence over the Bay this Morning.
"Jubeo Te bene valere." Samuel Chase to John Dickinson, [October 4? 1776].
R. R. Logan Collection, PHi.
In his next letter to Dickinson, dated October 19, Chase again thanked Dickin-
son for his "Thoughts on this Subject" and acknowledged that he had circulated
Dickinson's letter among friends. Ibid.
In view of his previous relationship with John Adams and his impatience with
those who had counseled against independence, Chase's relationship with Dickinson at this time is an interesting one. After serving as a member of the Maryland
Convention that had just drafted a new constitution and declaration of rights,
Chase found Dickinson's political philosophy much more congenial upon his
return to Philadelphia in mid-September. Under attack from many of his own
constituents, and recently scarred in a number of bruising battles for political
control in Maryland, Chase sought to enlist Dickinson's support in the struggle
against the radicals over the state's new constitution. In one respect, the situations faced by Dickinson in Pennsylvania and Chase in Maryland were remarkably
similar, because the states almost simultaneously adopted new constitutions. But
the similarity ended at this point, since Pennsylvania subsequently adopted a new
government that was easily the most radical in the new nation, while Maryland's
was the most conservative. For a discussion of the political situation Chase faced
during this volatile period, see Ronald Hoffman, *A Spirit of Dissension: Eco-
nomics, Politics, and the Revolution in Maryland* (Baltimore: Johns Hopkins
University Press, 1973), pp. 169–83.

Benjamin Rush to Anthony Wayne

Dear sir,   Philada Septemr 29. 1776

I did myself the pleasure of acknowledging the receipt of your
favor by Capt. Todd in a long letter which I dispatched a few
days ago by one of the expresses bound to Ticonderoga.¹ Since that
time Col. Shea has resigned the command of the 3rd Pennsylvania
regiment, by which means you are now the first Colonel in the

Service of this State. The late resolution of congress for encreasing our army to 60,000 men will necessarily call for a number of new Brigadiers, and the proportion which Pennsylvania will send into the field will give her a right to demand one or two more for her Share. Merit like yours will weigh heavily with the congress, but it must be held up in a pointed light to their view. Col. Magaw tho' a younger Officer than you being near the congress, & having one or two eloquent friends in the house may perhaps be held up in colours that may injure your more just pretensions to promotion.

Upon this Acct. I beg leave to suggest to you that your friends in congress (among whom I desire to be classed) will derive great support from a few words in your favor from General Gates. You must not omit improving this hint to your advantage. And in every thing relative to this matter I beg you will command my services. I should not have suggested these ideas to you, had I not more than once seen the most emminent military merit neglected in our promotions, from ignorance in the congress, or from the want of proper recommendations.

The bearer Mr Stockton is my father in law—a most zealous & faithful servant of the States. He commands the vote of New Jersey. I therefore beg (for your sake as well as my own) your particular Attention to him.

With best compts. to Genl. Gates, Genl. St Clair, Col. Erwin, Col. Johnson, Capt. Frazer [2] & such other of the officers at Ticonderoga as I have the pleasure of being acquainted with I am dear sir yours sincerely,   B Rush

P.S. I have this day seen a prisoner belonging to the 23rd regiment taken by our people near New York. I was much pleased with the fashion of his hair. It was cut Short all round by Genl Howe's orders. Count Saxe recommended this fashion in his memoirs. It saves time & trouble & prevents lice. It moreover prevents a Soldier from suffering from rain which often keeps the hair wet for hours Afterwards. Suppose you introduce it in your regiment? If you begin with yourself, every private as well as officer must follow your example.

RC (PHi).
[1] Undoubtedly Rush's letter to Wayne of September 24, 1776.
[2] Apparently the last three officers to whom Rush refers here were James Irvine, Francis Johnston, and Persifor Frazer.

Josiah Bartlett to John Langdon

Dear Sir   Philadelphia, Sept. 30th, 1776.
Last Saturday I rec'd yours of the 14th inst. and am very sorry for your bad success in procuring guns for the frigate; you say you

have mentioned the affair to the President, and I hope some order will be taken about it, but what I know not.[1] I have not been able to attend either the Marine or Secret Committee for some time past and Congress but little. It is now above five weeks since I have been troubled with a severe cough, slow fever, profuse sweats and loss of appetite, except for light food. By the advice of my friends and physicians I design to leave this City in a few days and try to move homeward in hopes a change of air, moderate exercise and a recess from business may assist in restoring my health. Mr. Hancock has offered me a seat in his carriage, which I shall accept, as it is impossible for me to return on horseback in my present state of health. I rec'd Col. Whipple's letter of the 15th,[2] where he informs me he expects to set out for this place about the 10th of October. I hope he will set off before that time, when he comes to be informed by my letters of my bad state of health and the necessity there is of a Delegate here. There is no news here more than you will see in the public prints.

I am your friend,   Josiah Bartlett.

Tr (DLC).

[1] Langdon's September 14 letter to Bartlett is in Morgan, *Naval Documents*, 6:816–17. For Congress' action on the cannon at Providence, R.I., see Marine Committee to Langdon, October 9, 1776.

[2] An extract from William Whipple's September 15 letter to Bartlett, which is in the Gratz Collection, PHi, is in Morgan, *Naval Documents*, 6:831.

John Hancock to Thomas Jefferson

Sir   Philadelphia Septr. 30th. 1776.

The Congress having appointed you to fill a most important and honorable Department, it is with particular Pleasure I congratulate you on the Occasion.

By the enclosed Resolves you will percieve, that Doctor Franklin, Mr. Deane, and yourself, are chosen Commissioners at the Court of France, to negotiate such Business as the Congress shall entrust you with. For this Purpose, Letters of Credence, and Instructions will be delivered to Doctor Franklin, and Duplicates forwarded to you and Mr. Deane. You will therefore, be pleased to acquaint me, by the Return of the Express, who brings you this, at what Time and Place it will be most convenient for you to embark, in Order that a Vessel may be sent to take you on Board. A suitable Vessel, will, in the mean Time, be provided here for the Accommodation of Doctor Franklin, it being judged most prudent, that you should sail in different Ships.[1]

As it is fully in your Power, so I am persuaded it is the favorite Wish of your Heart, to promote the Interest and Happiness of your Country; and that you will, in particular, render her the great Services which she so fondly expects from you on this Occasion. With the warmest Wishes for your Health, and a safe and speedy Passage, I have the Honour to be, with every Sentiment of Esteem, Sir Your most obed. & very hble Servt.,

John Hancock, Presidt.

RC (MHi). Jefferson, *Papers* (Boyd), 1:523–24.

[1] In response to the news of his appointment as a commissioner to France, Jefferson regretfully informed Hancock on October 11 that "circumstances very peculiar in the situation of my family, such as neither permit me to leave nor to carry it, compel me to ask leave to decline a service so honourable and at the same time so important to the American cause." Congress acceded to Jefferson's request to be relieved of this appointment and on October 22 chose Arthur Lee in his place. See ibid., 1:524; and *JCC*, 5:827–28, 879, 897.

Thomas Stone to the Maryland Council of Safety

Gent.   Phila. Sep. 30th. 1776, Tuesday [1]

Your Letter of the 27th to the Delegates of Maryland was delivered to Me yesterday.[2] Capt. Watkins did not leave this city so soon as I expected he would do, I fear nothing will do with him but Dismission. I have procured Clothes for his Company & have directed Lt. Grace, who at present commands, to have every thing got ready for them as soon as possible. Every thing here is very dear, but I thought it better to pay high, than keep the Soldiers doing Nothing or send them naked to Camp. I have heard nothing of the Powder you mention, my Col[leagu]es I presume attended to that Matter. Messrs Chase & Paca left this on Sunday & I shall sett out on Thursday if my State of Body will permit tho this I much doubt being at present much indisposed. The two adverse Armies remain in Statu quo. Genl Miflin who is in Town sais our Army is getting into better order & he hopes will be able to sustain any Attack the Enimy may make. Doctr Brown arrived here the Day after my Letter to him was sent, but has been very ill ever since. Surgeons are much wanted in Camp but where proper ones will be procured I know not.[3] I am with great Esteem, Gent., Yr most obt Sert,   T Stone

RC (PHi).

[1] Since September 30, 1776, was a Monday, Stone may have misdated this letter.

[2] See *Md. Archives*, 12:304–5.

[3] A few days later Stone sent a brief letter to the president of the Maryland Convention recommending "Mr. Hopkins, a Young Gentleman of great Merit who wishes to enter into the Service in some Office among the Maryland Troops. He went a volunteer to Quebec where he behaved as I am informed very well, he was also in the Engagement on Long Island and showed great Spirit & Readiness." Thomas Stone to Matthew Tilghman, October 11, 1776, Gratz Collection, PHi.

William Williams to Jabez Huntington

Hond & dear Sir   [Philadelphia September 30, 1776]

I recd your Favor of the 7th a few days since & thank you for it, have nothing material to give you in Return. Congress are pressed with an exceeding Load of Business, I wish They wod sit more hours to attend it, but it is indeed extreemly fatiguing & exhausts the Spirits. Since the Affairs of N. York have happend, there has been no Time to attend to the Confederation, having passed the Comte it is redrafted & lies for Congress. Maryland solemnly protest They will never agree to it. Their capital objection is that it does not limit the Claims of Virginia, by whom they shall be swallowed up &c. If We were rid of our foreign cruel oppressors, that wod give me little concern. The Enemy have lately got Possession of Powles Hook on Jersey side,[1] it seems to have been deserted by Us, & that it will be no advantage to Them but only serves to divide their Force. It is thot by many that our Army is in a better Situation in one Body & out of the reach of the Ships, than they were or cod be while They had so many Posts to defend & accessible by Land & Sea, & as it obliges them in their Station to divide their Army & renders their Ships in a manner useless, if We are not wanting to our Selves, it must puzzle them extreemly to steer their Course. All was in statu quo the last we heard, but doubtless Howe is meditating some important blow. I sent the Issue of the Negotiation to the Govr. I think it will be happy, nothing but the attempt wod have satisfied many, & silenced those who wished to divide Us. He is instructed to talk much & thro out indeterminate words & Seems specious & fair. I think He greatly faild in his Politics, but will not say for him what He might have said. It must confirm every one that nothing can be Expected but total Destruction or absolute Submission, if in the power of their Hands. Mr ————————[2] was sent by the Secret Comte only for Intelligence & to promote Commerce. They have a Letter from him containing very little of importance, he had not then reached his Place of Residence. The French are certainly strongly inclined in our Favor, but they are consummate Politicians. Sev[era]l Ships of Fr. & Spain are arrived in their West Indies to protect our trade, we have it in a Letter from an Agent there, as well as News Papers. Am glad to hear the poor long Islanders are geting off, tis said They are called upon to swear Alleigance & then forced to take up Arms. Am concerned for our Army's winter Quarters, & Cloathing. Hope the last Militia will do better than the first. The Genll. says they have no Tents or Camp Kettles &c which distresses him beyond measure, it must be true for I know we have them not. The most bitter reproaches are thrown out against their late Conduct, & which I hope are groundless, but surely there can be no dependance on Militia; all are deeply convinced of it, it is of the last importance that a permanent Army shod be established. There is no looking back, the prospect forward is exceedingly better & more hopeful. I hope no one is at all discouraged. It was not to be conceivd that We shod establish Liberty & Freedom for ever, without some trouble & Distress indeed, the Enemy have attained as yet far less than might have been feard, from such immense preparation & Expence, tis scarce possible to believe the Nation can bear it much longer. If We are distresd, so are They. We have a noble Prize in View, while nothing but infernal Rage dictates the measures of our Enemies. It is said there is great bickering between the German & English Troops, but this is uncertain.

Nothing is wanting on our Side but the repentance & Reformation of the Land. The great & mercifull God seems to hold his uplifted Hand suspended & loth to strike the Blow, & waiting for our amendment, to say look to Me for why will ye die, my Children of America. He that can do most to promote this blessed work will do the most important & essential Good to his Friends & to his Country.

Strange that a sick Man shod be loth to apply a Remedy pleasant & sweet to the Taste, kind in its opperation, & sovereign in its Effect.

We are sending a Comte to the nothern Army to indeavor to supply their Wants. We hear They are distresd. Will it not be best for Us to send a proper Person there also, with Commissions &c to inlist Men upon the new Regulation.

Have not heard of Niles's 2d Prize, fear She is lost.[3]

The Loss of so many of our dear Countrymen, peirces my Heart with anguish. Do not their Friends pity Them & will They not destroy the Weapons of their Destruction; They are slain by the Sword, the Sins of their own Country.

If our Assembly rechose their Delegates, I hope They will be guided by Wisdom & Prudence.[4] I must say that Mr Sherman from his early acquaintance, his good sense, Judgment, Steadiness & inflexible Integrity, has acquired much Respect & is an exceeding valuable Member, & so is Mr Huntington & truly judicious, upright & worthy the Trust in Spight of that awful Contempt of Religion & Goodness too visible &c. Integrity & Virtue does & will Command Respect. For my part I neither expect nor wish to remain here, the Burden is exceeding great, but in this Critical time the acquaintance the others have with the men & Connection of affairs, is very usefull. It is of very great Importance that whoever attends here shod be Men of Uprightness & Integrity, inflexibly resolved to pursue & serve the great Cause, insensible to motives of Ambition, Interest & any other Applause than that of a good

Conscience. If all the Members were & had been of that Image I am sure our Affairs wod have been in a better Situation. If one House shod be intrigued into any thing different, I hope the Firmness of the Other may not fail. Your Candor will not mistake Me, I am not putting in a Word for myself, the Burden is too great to be covetable. I long to be at Home, & hope to see You eer the Assembly rises, but my Pains cod not be eased by Change of Place, nor till the Wounds of my Country are healed, & why are they not when the forreign Balm is at hand.

If our Assembly shod think it necessary by a formal act to establish or reestablish Government I hope Wisdom & Integrity will guide them. Our form is just what our Fathers chose & is a most excellent one & under which We have enjoyed great Tranquillity, & the least alteration wod be dangerous. It is an unhappy Truth that People in general do not know their own happiness. No Form adopted by any of the Colonies is comparable to ours. This Convention according to the prejudices in favor of the former Plan under the Penn's have excluded any Legislative Council (they never had any but a privy or advisory Council of their own chusing) & a very bad form in many respects. If We are to make any formal Establishment, I believe this is the best Time on many accounts.

I cod wish an early acknowledgmt. or approbation of the Decision of Independancy had been made, our Life depends on supporting it but am not certain tis best, now, to say any thing about it in a public way.

Congress has become extreemly thin in this alarming Time & are passing a Resolve to recall their Members, recommending it to all the States to keep a full Representation here.[5] This Convention (as I just learn) are sending three Gent. to camp, to exert Their influence, for reinlisting their Quota of the Army. This confirms me in the hint I before gave of such a Step to be taken by Us & shod think it necessary to consult the Genll. &c about officers, there is great Complaint of their deficiency & the Safety & Success of the Army depends greatly upon Them.[6] The premiums are to be paid by the paymasters. Money will be sent for the purpose to N. York, but it is necessary some shod be in the hands of Recruiting officers in the Country, but no particular provision is made for that as yet.

But I have tired your Patience & will add no more but my kindest Compliments to Col. H. if yet at home, & that I am with great esteem, affection & Regard, your most Sincere unworthy Friend & very humble Servant,   Wm Williams

[P.S.] I hope to see you at N. Haven, & wod bespeak part of your Bed. I did not like my Former, at our House.[7]

RC (NjR, Elsie O. and Philip D. Sang deposit, 1972).

[1] Gen. Nathanael Greene's September 23 letter to Washington, reporting the British occupation of Paulus Hook, was read in Congress on September 25 and is in Greene, *Papers* (Showman), 1:302–3.

[2] Silas Deane.

[3] Robert Niles, captain of the Connecticut navy schooner *Spy*, had recently returned from a cruise on which he had captured two prizes, one of which was retaken by the British. See Morgan, *Naval Documents*, 6:680, 804, 925.

[4] At the October 1776 session of the Connecticut General Assembly Samuel Huntington, Roger Sherman, Oliver Wolcott, and William Williams were reappointed delegates and Eliphalet Dyer and Richard Law were added to the delegation, any of three of whom were to serve at the same time. *JCC*, 7:11–12.

[5] See *JCC*, 5:837; and John Hancock to Certain States, October 2, 1776.

[6] For measures adopted by the Connecticut General Assembly to encourage enlistment in the standing army, see *Am. Archives*, 5th ser. 3:451; and *A Historical Collection, From Official Records, Files, &c., of the Part Sustained by Connecticut, during the War of the Revolution*, comp. Royal R. Hinman (Hartford: E. Gleason, 1842), pp. 234, 240.

[7] This day Williams also wrote a long letter to his wife, dilating on his gratitude for the health and safety of his family and the necessity for "repentance & Reformation . . . to Save our Army & Country from Destruction" and explaining his determination to return home "before the cold Season comes on, whether Mr. Wolcott relieves me or not." Williams Papers, CtHi.

Although Wolcott returned to Philadelphia the following day, both Roger Sherman and Samuel Huntington returned home to Connecticut before Williams finally set out from Philadelphia on November 13. See Oliver Wolcott's letters to Laura Wolcott of October 1 and 8, to Samuel Adams, November 16, and to Matthew Griswold, November 18, 1776; and Roger Sherman's Memoranda Book, DLC.

John Adams to Abigail Adams

October 1, 1776

Since I wrote the foregoing Lines, I have not been able to find Time to write you a Line. Altho I cannot write you, so often as I wish, you are never out of my Thoughts. I am repining at my hard Lot, in being torn from you, much oftener than I ought.

I have often mentioned to you, the Multiplicity of my Engagements, and have been once exposed to the Ridicule and Censure of the World for mentioning the great Importance of the Business which lay upon me, and if this Letter should ever see the Light, it would be again imputed to Vanity, that I mention to you, how busy I am. But I must repeat it by Way of Apology for not writing you oftener. From four O Clock in the Morning untill ten at Night, I have not a single Moment, which I can call my own. I will not say that I expect to run distracted, to grow melancholly, to drop in an Apoplexy, or fall into a Consumption. But I do say, it is little less than a Miracle, that one or other of these Misfortunes has not befallen me before now.

Your Favours of September 15, 20, and 23d are now before me.

Every Line from you gives me inexpressible Pleasure. But it is a great Grief to me, that I can write no oftener to you.

There is one Thing which excites my utmost Indignation and Contempt, I mean the Brutality, with which People talk to you, of my Death. I beg you would openly affront every Man, Woman or Child, for the future who mentions any such Thing to you, except your Relations, and Friends whose Affections you cannot doubt. I expect it of all my Friends, that they resent, as Affronts to me, every Repetition of such Reports.

I shall inclose to you, Governor Livingstons Speech, the most elegant and masterly, ever made in America.[1]

Depend upon it, the Enemy cannot cutt off the Communication. I can come home when I will. They have N. York—and this is their Ne Plus Ultra.

RC (MHi). Adams, *Family Correspondence* (Butterfield), 2:131–32. A continuation of Adams to Abigail Adams, September 22, 1776.

[1] William Livingston's first gubernatorial address to the New Jersey legislature, which was delivered on September 11, was printed in the *Pennsylvania Gazette*, October 1, 1776, and is in *Am. Archives*, 5th ser. 2:288–89.

John Adams to Thomas Edwards

Mr Edwards.   Philadelphia Octr. 1. 1776

I duely received your favour of August 23d, and I wish I could have answered it before now.[1] And even now it would give me more Pleasure, if I could answer it, more to your Satisfaction.

The Continental Agent, I believe has applied to Mr Lowell, to file Libells against Prizes, and it would not be proper for me to interfere in this Matter, both because Mr Lowells Character at the Bar, denotes him to be a very Suitable Person, and because the Agents Business lies within the marine Department, at the Head of which is Mr Hancock, and I have nothing in particular to do with it.

Whether a Deputy Judge Advocate is wanted at Boston I dont know, but Congress will not be at the Expence of appointing one unless the Necessity of it should be represented by the Commanding officer, who, I suppose is General Ward. In Short Sir, I dont know of any Place into which I can be instrumental of introducing you, But if you know of any, and will mention it, I will do you any Service, which I can with Propriety as it always gives me Pleasure, to assist any young Gentleman, who has an Inclination and a Capacity, to serve his fellow Men. I am your Friend & humble Servant,   John Adams

LB (MHi).

[1] Thomas Edwards (1753–1806), Boston lawyer and former Braintree school-

teacher, became a lieutenant colonel of the Sixteenth Massachusetts Regiment in 1777, deputy judge advocate of the Continental Army in 1780, and judge advocate in 1782. Shipton, *Harvard Graduates*, 17:507–10. Edwards' August 23 letter to Adams is in the Adams Papers, MHi.

John Adams to Daniel Hitchcock

Dear Sir   Philadelphia October 1. 1776 Tuesday

Yours of September the 9th was duely recd, but has not yet been answered.[1]

The Measure of a Standing Army is, at length, resolved on. You have seen the Plan. How do you like it? I wish it was liable to fewer Exceptions, but We must be content to crawl into the right way, by degrees. This was the best that we could obtain at present.

I am extreamly Sorry, to learn that the Troops have been disheartened. But This Despondency of Spirit, was the natural Effect, of the Retreats you have made one after another. When the Men Saw your General officers taken in a Trap upon Long Island, and the Army obliged to abandon that important Post, in Consequence of that Ambuscade, and the City of New York evacuated in Consequence of the Retreat from Long Island, the finest Army in the world would have been seized, in similar Circumstances, with more or less of a Panick. But your Men will now recover their Spirits in a short Time.

There is a way of introducing Discipline into the most irregular Army, and of inspiring Courage into the most pusillanimous Collection of Men.

Your Army, Sir, give me leave to say, has been ill managed, in two most Essential Points. The first is in neglecting to train your Regiments and Brigades to the manual Exercises and Maneuvres. Nothing inspires the Men with military Pride and Ambition (for even the Men must have Ambition) like calling them together every day, and making them appear as well as they can. By living much together and moving in Concert, they acquire a Confidence in themselves and in each other. By being exposed to the Inspection and observations of each other they become ambitious of appearing as clean and neat as they can, which as well as the Exercise preserves their Health and hardens their Bodies against diseases. But instead of these martial, manly and elegant Exercises, they have been kept constantly at work in digging Trenches in the Earth— which keeps them constantly dirty, and not having Wifes, Mothers, Sisters, or Daughters as they used to have at home to take Care of them and keep them clean, they gradually loose their Perspiration and their Health.

Another Particular which is absolutely necessary to introduce military Ardour into a new raised Army has been totally neglected. Such an Army should be governed with Caution and Circumspection I agree. It should Act chiefly upon the defensive and no decisive Battle should be hazarded. But still an Enterprizing spirit should be encouraged, favourable opportunities should be watched, and Parties should be ordered out upon little Excursions, and Expeditions, and in this Manner, officers and Men should be permitted to acquire fame and Honour in the Army, which will soon give them a real Fondness for fighting. They will have the Spirit. But instead of this, every spark of an enterprizing spirit, in the Army, seems to have been carefully extinguished.

Our inevitable Destruction will be the consequence if these Faults are not amended. I rejoiced to hear of the Attempt upon Montresors Island. But am vexed and mortified at its shamefull Issue. But I am more humiliated Still to learn that the Enterprize was not renewed. If there had been officers or Men who would have undertaken the Expedition a second time, a third, or a fiftieth time I would have had that Island, if it had cost me half my army. Pray inform me what officers and Men were sent upon that Attempt. It is Said there was shamefull Cowardice. If any officer was guilty of it, I sincerely hope he will be punished with Death. This most infamous and detestable Crime must never be forgiven in an officer. Punishments as well as Rewards will be necessary to Government, as long as Fear, as well as Hope, is a natural Passion, in the human Breast.

LB (MHi).
[1] Hitchcock's September 9 letter to Adams is in the Adams Papers, MHi.
[2] According to a note he penned to Henry Knox, Adams this day made a personal effort to mend some of the faults discussed here by moving "the appointment of a Committee to consider of a Plan for the Establishment of a military Academy in the Army." See Adams to Henry Knox, September 29, 1776, note 2.

Committee of Secret Correspondence Statement

[October 1, 1776]

[Mr. Thomas Story, who had been sent by the committee of secret correspondence, December 13, 1775, to France, Holland, and England, reported verbally as follows:] [1]

"On my leaving London, Arthur Lee Esqr. requested me to inform the Committee of Correspondence that he has had several conferences with the French Embassador, who had communicated the same to the French Court; that in consequence thereof the Duke De Vergennes had sent a Gentleman to Mr. Lee who informed him that the French Court could not think of entering into a War with England, but that they would assist America by sending from Holland this Fall £200,000 Sterling worth of Arms and Ammunition to St. Eustatius, Martinico, or Cape Francois; that application was to be made to the Governors or Commandants of those Places by inquiring for Mons. Hortalez and that on Persons properly authorized applying, the above Articles would be delivered to them." [2]

Philada. October 1st. 1776.

The above intelligence was Communicated to the Subscribers being the only two Members of the Committee of Secret Correspondence now in this City and on Considering the Nature & importance of it, We agree in opinion that it is our indispensable duty to keep it Secret even from Congress for the following reasons.

First. Shou'd it get to the ears of our Enemies at New York they wou'd undoubtedly take measures to intercept the Supplies & thereby deprive us not only of these Succours but of Others expected by the same route.

Second. As the Court of France have taken Measures to Negotiate this loan and Succour in the most cautious & Secret Manner, shou'd we divulge it immediately, we may not only loose the present benefit, but also render that Court Cautious of any further Connection with such unguarded People & prevent their granting other Loans & assistance that we Stand in need of & have directed Mr Dean to ask of them—for it appears from all our Intelligence they are not disposed to Enter into an immediate War with Britain altho disposed to Support us in our Contest with them. We therefore think it our duty to Cultivate their favourable disposition toward us, draw from them all the support we can & in the end their private Aid must assist us to establish Peace or inevitably draw them in as Parties to the War.

Third. We find by Fatal Experience the Congress Consists of too many Members to keep Secrets, as none cou'd be more Strongly enjoined than the present Embassy to France, notwithstanding which, Mr. Morris was this day asked by Mr. Reese Meredith [3] whether Doctor Franklin & others were really going Ambassadors to France, which plainly proves that this Committee ought to keep this Secret if Secrecy is required.

Fourthly. We are also of opinion that it is *unnecessary* to inform Congress of this Intelligence at present because Mr Morris belongs to all the Committees that can properly be employed in receiving & importing the expected Supplys from Martinico, St. Eustatia or Cape Francois and will immediately influence the necessary measures for that purpose. Indeed we have already authorized Wm Bingham Esqr. to supply at Martinico & St Eustatia for what comes there & remit part by the Armed Sloop Independance Capt Young promising to send others for the rest. [4] Mr Morris will apply to the Marine Committee to send other armed Vessells after her

& also to Cape Francois (without Communicating this advice) in Consequence private Intelligence lately recd that Arms, ammunition & Cloathing can now be procured at those places.

But shou'd any unexpected misfortune befall the States of America so as to depress the Spirits of the Congress, it is our opinion that on any event of that kind, Mr. Morris (if Doctr. Franklin shou'd be absent) shou'd communicate this Important matter to Congress, otherwise keep it untill part of or the whole Supplys arrive, unless other events happen to render the Communication of it more proper than it appears to be at this time.[5]

B Franklin

Robt Morris

Communicated to me the 11th October 1776 and I concur heartily in the measure.   Richard Henry Lee

Communicated to me the 10th [i.e. 11th] of October 1776 and I do also sincerely approve of the Measure.[6]   Wm Hooper

MS (DNA: PCC, item 78). Written by Morris, signed by Franklin and Morris, and endorsed and signed by Lee and Hooper. Tr (DNA: PCC, item 133). In the hand of Robert Morris.

[1] This introductory sentence does not appear in the two extant manuscript copies of this document. It was first printed in this form in the April 1, 1828, Committee of Foreign Affairs report on the claim of the heirs of Caron de Beaumarchais for $1 million and was printed from "a paper which was before the Committee of Claims in 1808." U.S. Congress, House Committee on Foreign Affairs, 20th Cong., 1st sess., 1828, H. Rept. 220, pp. 19–20. It appears as an integral part of the document which follows in Wharton, *Diplomatic Correspondence*, 2:151–52, and Burnett, *Letters*, 2:110–11.

[2] In addition to this verbal report from Arthur Lee, Story also delivered to the committee several items from C. W. F. Dumas, Congress' agent at The Hague. It cannot now be determined precisely what Dumas had sent to the committee, but the best evidence available on this point is contained in the following brief acknowledgment Franklin wrote to Dumas this day. "I have just time to acknowledge the Receipt of your two Packets, A & B, with the Pamphlets enclos'd, the Contents of which are very satisfactory. You will hear from me more fully in a little time. . . . We have a great Force brought against us here, but continue firm." Beinecke Library, CtY. Packets "A & B" were apparently Dumas' letters of April 30–May 9, and May 14–June 6, 1776, which are in PCC, item 93, fols. 18–28, 36–41, translations of which are in Wharton, *Diplomatic Correspondence*, 2:85–89, 90–92. The second of these letters is clearly designated "B," but since the first bears no similar identification mark, its identity as "A" can only be conjectured. "The Pamphlets enclos'd" have not been identified.

[3] A Philadelphia merchant.

[4] See Committee of Secret Correspondence to William Bingham, this date.

[5] President Hancock formally certified that Franklin and Morris were authorized to carry on the activities of the Committee of Secret Correspondence in a certificate of October 1, 1776. "I do hereby Certify that Benjamin Franklin ⟨Richard Henry Lee, William Hooper⟩ and Robert Morris Esqrs. delegates in Congress from Pennsylvania have been duely appointed Members of the Honorable Committee of Secret Correspondence, and that they are fully empowered to

direct all matters in their department on behalf of the United States of America, the other Members of Said Committee being now absent.

"I do also Certify that the delivery of Arms, ammunition, Specie or other Stores, to them or their Order on behalf of the Congress, is and will be acknowledged as Valid and binding on the United States of America." Continental Congress Miscellany, DLC.

Lee's and Hooper's names were subsequently inserted between the lines, perhaps after they were appointed to the committee on October 11, 1776. An attempt to erase their names was only partially successful.

There is no evidence in the journals to indicate that Hancock penned this certificate in consequence of any official action by Congress.

⁶ Hooper apparently made the simple error of writing "10th" for "11th" when he added his endorsement to the document. Hooper, Lee, and John Witherspoon were added to the committee on October 11. *JCC*, 6:867. There is no evidence indicating why Witherspoon did not subsequently add his endorsement to the statement or why Hancock failed to include him in the certificate of authorization quoted in the preceding footnote.

Committee of Secret Correspondence to William Bingham

[October 1, 1776]

We are now at the 1st of October and have heard from Mr Deane after his arrival at Bourdeaux. His last letter is dated the 23d June when he was just setting out for Paris. We have later than his. In consequence of which we desire you to enquire of the General and Governor whither they have received any Arms or ammunition from Monsr. Hortalez with directions to deliver the same to any person properly authorized by Congress to receive them. If they have, we hereby authorize you to receive the Same, giving you receipts on behalf of the United States of America. If none Such are Arrived enquire if they have any advice of Such and request they will make known to you when they do arrive.

We desire you to make the like application to the Governor of St. Eustatia,¹ but proceed cautiously in this business. We think you Should go there yourself in a French Vessel or if that might be unsafe or make a Noise, get Mr. Richard Harrison or Some person in whose prudence you can confide. Let the first question be, whether His Excellency has received any advices from Monsr. Hortalez. If the answer be in the negative, tell him he will receive letters from such a person and that those advices have reference to you; therefore request the favour of being immediately made acquainted when they come to hand when you will wait on him or Send a proper person in your Stead. If the Answer be in the affirmative then enquire if His Excellency has received any thing beside advice from Monsr. Hortalez and if he has, inform him you are empowered to receive the Same from him agreeable to the directions sent with the Goods. We beleive you had best proceed in the same cautious manner at Martinico and open no more of this business than circumstances Shall make absolutely necessary. We also enjoin you to the Stricktest secrecy and herewith enclose you two Seperate letters [2] as your proper Authority for receiving any goods or money Mr Hortalez our Agent in Europe may Remit. It was intended that Capt Young Should deliver you this letter but as we have some important dispatches to send to M Deane, we have concluded to send Mr Wm Hodge junr. the bearer hereof with the same in order that he may deliver them with his own hands. You'l plese to shew Mr Hodge proper attention and assist him to the utmost of your power in procuring him a passage immediately from Martinico to France in a good Ship. If any Men of War or packet Should be going, make application to the General to recommend Mr Hodge to the Commander, also to the Governor or commander of the port where he goes to in France, to give him Support and assistance from thence to Paris with the best dispatch. If Mr Hodge Should want money for his expences supply him and transmit us his Receipts for the Same. You will serve your Country by forwarding Mr Hodge without delay, but you need not mention to the General how urgent we are on this point, unless you find it will promote his dispatch.

We learn from Many Quarters that a Fleet of twenty Sail of the line are fitting out at Brest & Toulon. Shou'd they come out to the West Indies and be destined to commit Hostilities against the British Trade or Territorys, they have a fair opportunity to Strike a Capital Stroke at New York where they have upwards of 400 Sail of Ships Guarded only by two Sixty four Gun Ships, two fiftys and Six Fortys, the rest are all Frigates &c. Twenty Sail of the line wou'd take their whole Fleet with ease & then we cou'd as easily manage their Army.

We had Ommitted above to desire that you Should send back in the Sloop Independance, Captain Young, a proportion of the Arms, ammunition, Money or other Stores you May receive either at Martinico or St. Eustatia from Monsr. Hortalez, taking bills of loading for the same deliverable to us or our order and if the quantity you receive should be considerable you May send by Captain Young about the value of Three or four Thousand pounds Sterling observing that we want muskets and woolen Cloathing most immediately. We shall send more Armed vessels after Capt Young to bring away the Remainder of what you may receive or buy, and are, Sir, Your Obedt hble Servants,

B Franklin

Robt Morris

RC (CtY). A continuation of Committee of Secret Correspondonce to Bingham, September 21, 1776.

[1] Johannes de Graaff. For an account of the role of St. Eustatius as a trading mecca during the American Revolution, see J. Franklin Jameson, "St. Eustatius

in the American Revolution," *American Historical Review* 8 (July 1903): 683–708.

² The Committee of Secret Correspondence wrote another brief letter to Bingham this date, directing him to contact General d'Argout about the delivery in Martinique of arms and ammunition from France.

"Having received advice that our Agent Monsr. Hortalez is dispatching Sundry Articles wanted for the Service of the United States of America to Martinico recommended to the care of his Excellency the General or the Governor and Intendant there, to be by them delivered to whoever Shall be properly authorized by Congress to receive the Same, We hereby request that you will make application for all Arms, ammunition, Money, cloathing or other Articles, that may arrive in Martinico with the above directions, and you are hereby empowered to receive and Grant Receipts for the same on behalf of the United States of America, or to Sign Certificates or any other writing that may be required purporting the delivery thereof to you as Agent for the Congress." RC (PPAmP). FC (PCC, item 37, fol. 45).

The second enclosure almost certainly was John Hancock's October 1 certificate, authorizing Franklin and Morris to "direct all matters" for the committee, which is quoted in the Committee of Secret Correspondence Statement, this date, note 5.

Both of these enclosures are contained in the same file copy in PCC, item 37, fols. 45–46.

Committee of Secret Correspondence to Silas Deane

Dear Sir,   Philadelphia October 1st 1776

Mr. Morris has communicated to us the Substance of your letters to him down to the 23rd June when you was near setting out for Paris.¹ We hope your reception there has been equal to your expectation and our wishes. Indeed we have no reason to doubt it considering the countenance we have met with amongst the French Islands and their seaports in Europe. It woud be very agreeable and usefull to hear from you just now in order to form more certain of the designs of the French Court respecting us and our Contest, especially as we learn by various ways they are fitting out a considerable Squadron at Brest and Toulon.² What a noble Stroke they might now strike at New York. Twenty Sail of the line woud take the whole Fleet there consisting of between 4 & 500 Sail of Men [of] War, Transports, Stores, Ships and prizes. Was that piece of business once effected by a French Fleet we wou'd engage to give them a very good account of Genl. Howe's army in a short time, but alas we fear the Court of France will let slip the glorious opportunity and go to war by halves as we have done. We say go to war because we are of the opinion they must take part in the war sooner or later and the longer they are about it, the worse terms will they come in upon. We doubt not you will obtain from England a regular account of the proceedings of Ld Howe and his Brother and we suppose the General's military opperations will be ushered into the world with an eclat beyond their true merits; or at least, the conduct of our people and their present Situation will be misrepresented as ten times worse than the reality. We shall therefore State

these things to you as they really are. The Fleet under Ld. Howe
you know is vastly Superior to any thing we have in the Navy way;
consequently where ever Ships can move they must command;
therefore it was long foreseen that we cou'd not hold either Long
Island or New York. Nevertheless as our fortifications were chiefly
built with Axes and Spades the time and trouble in raising them
was not mispent, for it must have been oweing to those works that
they remained several weeks at Staten Island without making any
attempt. The first they did make was on Long Island where they
landed 20,000 Men or upwards. At this time we had our Army consisting of not more than 20,000 Effective men Stationed at Kings
bridge, New York and on Long Island; 6 to 7000 was the whole
of our Force on the latter and about 3000 of them commanded
by Genl Sullivan & Ld Stirling turned out of the Lines took possession of some heights and intended to annoy the Enemy in their
approaches. They however out General'd us, and got a body of
5000 Men between our people and the Lines, so that we were
Surrounded and of course came off second best, but they purchased
the Victory dear and many such wou'd be their ruin. Sullivan, Ld.
Stirling and many other officers fell into their hands, these with
privates amounted to from 800 to 1000 Men in killed, wounded &
taken Prisoners. They lost a greater number in killed and wounded
but we took but a few prisoners as you may suppose. Genl. Howe
then laid a Trap in which he fully expected to have caught every
man we had on that Island, but Genl. Washington saw and frustrated his design by an unexpected and well conducted retreat across
the Sound. This retreat is spoke of on both sides as a Master Stroke.

The Enemy immediately marched up a large Body of Men opposite to Hell Gate. Our people threw up entrenchments on York
Island to oppose their landing, but Shame to say it, on the day of
Tryal two Brigades behaved infamously and cou'd not be Stopped
by the intreatys or Threats of the General who came up in the
Midst of their flight. It had been previously determined to abandon
New York and most of our Cannon and Military Stores were removed from thence in time. The Enemy took possession of the
city and incamped on the plains of Harlem. Our side occupy
the Heights of Harlem, Kings bridge and Mount Washington
where they have made Lines as Strong as can be. In this Situation
they had a Skirmish between about 1000 to 1200 Men on each Side
in which we gained greatly the advantage, beat them off the Feild
and took three Feild pieces from them, having killed and wounded
Considerable Numbers of their men. Since then the city of New
York has been on Fire and its said one fifth or one sixth of it is
reduced to Ashes. The Enemy charged some stragglers of our people
that happened to be in New York with having set the City on
Fire designedly and took that occasion as we are told to exercise
some inhuman Crueltys on those poor Wretches that were in their

power. They will no doubt endeavour to throw the odium of Such a Measure on Us, but in this they will fail, for Genl. Washington previous to the evacuation of that City whilst it was in his power to do as he pleased with it, desired to know the sense of Congress respecting the destruction of the City as many officers had given it as their opinion it would be an adviseable measure, but Congress Resolved that it should be evacuated and left unhurt as they had no doubt of being able to take it back at a future day. This will convince all the world we had no desire to burn Towns or destroy Citys but that we left such Meritorious works to grace the History of our Enemies.

Upon the whole our Army near New York are not sufficiently strong to Cope with Genl. Howe in the open Feild. They have therefore entrenched themselves and act on the defensive. They want better Arms, better Tents and more Cloathing than they now have, or is in our power at this time to Supply them with, consequently we cannot recruit or increase that Army under these discouragements. Men cannot chearfully enter a Service where they have the prospect of facing a powerfull Enemy and encountering the inclemency of a hard, cold Winter, without covering at the same time. These are discouraging circumstances but we must encounter them with double dillegence and we still have hopes to procure Cloathing partly by Importation, partly by Capture, and chiefly by purchasing all that can be found on the Continent. If France means to befreind us or wishes us well, they Shou'd send us succours in good Muskets, Blankets, Cloaths, Coatings and proper Stuff for Tents, also in ammunition, but not like the Venetians wait untill we are beat and then send assistance. We are willing to pay for them, and shall be able soon as we can Safely export our Tobacco & other valuable produce.

Our Northern Army is Strong, well intrenched, in an advantageous Post at Tyconderoga which can only be taken from them by Storm as it cannot be approached in a regular manner on account of the Situation. We are also formidable in the Lakes, in Galleys, Boats & Gondolas under command of your freind Arnold, and that Army is better provided than the others so that we do not seem to apprehend any danger in that quarter at present. The Southern States are for the present in peace and quietness except some interruptions from the Indians who were instigated thereto by Mr. Stewart the Superintendant and other Agents from our Enemies. However they have not any cause to rejoice in their machinations as yet, for the Carolinians and Virginians have attacked and beat them Several times, destroyed several of their Towns & Corn Feilds and made them repent sorely what they have done, so that we have little to apprehend on account of Indians.

The Only Source of uneasiness, amongst us arises from the Number of Tories we find in every State. They are more Numerous

than formerly & Speak more openly but Tories are now of various
kinds and various principles, some are so from real attachment to
Britain, some from interested Views, many, very many from fear
of the British Force, some because they are dissatisfied with the
General Measures of Congress, more because they disapprove of the
Men in power & the measures in their respective States, but these
different passions, veiws and expectations are so combined in their
Consequences that the parties affected by them, either withhold
their assistance or oppose our operations and if America falls it
will be oweing to Such divisions more than the force of our
Enemies. However there is much to be done before America can
be lost and if France will but join us in time there is no danger
but America will soon be established an Independant Empire and
France drawing from her the principal part of those sources of
Wealth & power that formerly flowed into Great Britain will immediately become the greatest power in Europe. We have given you
as just a Picture of our present Situation as we can draw in the
Compass of a Letter in order that you may be well informed, but
you will only impart such circumstances, as you may think prudent.

Our Frigates are fine Vessels, but we meet with difficulty in procuring Guns and Anchors. Our people are but young in casting the
former, and we want Coals to make the latter; however these difficulties we shall surmount and are bent on building some Line of
Battle Ships immediately. The Success in privateering and encouragement given by the Merchants will inevitably bring Seamen
Amongst us. This, with the measures that will be adopted to
encourage the breeding of Seamen amongst ourselves will in a few
Years make us respectable on the Ocean. Surely France cannot be
so blind to her own Interest as to neglect this Glorious opportunity
of destroying the power and humbling the pride of her Natural
and our declared enemy.

We make no doubt you have been made acquainted with the
Negotiations of Monsr. Hortalez,[3] and in consequence thereof we
conclude that you will be at no loss to obtain the Supplies of Goods
wanted for a particular department, notwithstanding we know that
the greatest part of those Remittances that were intended you have
been intercepted by One means or other. It is unfortunate and
much to be regretted that those remittances have had such Ill fate,
but we hope you have obtained the goods on Credit, and you
may depend that Remittances will be continued until all your
engagements are discharged.

Cloathing and Tents are so much Wanted for our Armys that we
intreat you to apply immediately to the Court of France for a Loan
of Money Sufficient to dispatch immediately very considerable quantities of Stuff fit for Tents, & of Coarse Cloths, Coatings, Stockings,
and such other comfortable necessarys for any Army as you can
readily judge will be proper.

You will get these goods sent out direct in French Vessels, or to their Islands where we can Send for them, but if you cou'd prevail on the Court of France to send out Men of War with them it wou'd be most acceptable.

Whatever engagements you make for payment of the Cost of Such Cloathing and Necessarys the Congress will order Sufficient Remittances to fullfill the Same but in our circumstances it requires time to accomplish them.

You'l Observe the Secret Committee have given orders to Mr. Thomas Morris to procure Sundry Articles and dispatch them immediately,[4] and if you succeed in the negotiation of a loan from the Court for this purpose you may employ him or act in Conjunction with him, to procure and dispatch those Articles ordered by them and Such others as you Shall judge Necessary and the Remittances to be made him will serve to refund the Loan. Should the Court decline this matter perhaps the Farmers General may be induced to advance the Money or Stake their Credit, for the Sake of securing the Tobacco the Secret Committee will Remit to Europe. These things we throw out as hints and Shall only further observe that you cannot render your injured Country more essential service at this time than by procuring these Supplies immediately.

We are told our vigilant enemies have demanded of the Courts of France, Spain, and Portugal to deliver up the American Ships in their Ports, and to forbid their having any further intercourse with them, that the Court of Portugal has complyed so far as to order our Ships away on ten days Notice—That France & Spain gave evasive Answers. This is private uncertain intelligence, but we think you will do well, to intimate to the Ministers of those Nations, that first impressions are lasting, that the time has been when they stood much in need of American Supplies, that such time may come again, that altho we are Stiled Rebels by Britain, yet our Friendship may hereafter be of the utmost importance to those powers particularly that possess American Colonies, and that injuries now done us will not be easilly effaced. These hints and arguments you'l offer as the Suggestions of your own mind and endeavour to influence them by Interest or fear from taking any part against us. On the contrary as it is evidently their Interest to encourage our Commerce, so we hope you'l be able to influence them by One Means or other to protect and Licence it in the utmost extent. We Shall not take up more of your time at present but remain, Sir, Your very hble Servants,   B Franklin

                                                Robt Morris

RC (MH–H). In a clerical hand and signed by Franklin and Morris.

[1] See Robert Morris to John Jay, September 23, 1776, note 2.

[2] Louis XVI had given orders on April 22, 1776, to outfit 20 ships of the line and a "proportionate number of frigates" in Toulon and Brest. But these were destined for convoying merchant ships carrying arms to America rather than

offensive action. Jonathan R. Dull, *The French Navy and American Independence* (Princeton: Princeton University Press, 1975), pp. 52–65.

³ Pierre Augustin Caron de Beaumarchais (1732–99), playwright and French secret agent, who had performed several delicate and discreet tasks for Louis XV and Louis XVI. His performance of these services and personal connections with Vergennes led the French court to direct him to explore ways for providing secret aid to the United States. Beaumarchais had originally contacted Arthur Lee in London and alerted him to the formation of Hortalez & Cie as a mercantile firm to conceal a million livres tournois in aid from France. See Hortalez & Cie to Mary Johnston [*i.e.* Arthur Lee], June 6 and 12, 1776, Wharton, *Diplomatic Correspondence*, 2:97; and Pierre Augustin Caron de Beaumarchais, *Beaumarchais Correspondence*, ed. Brian N. Morton (Paris: A. G. Nizet, 1962–), 2:219–20.

When Deane arrived in France he was almost immediately contacted by Beaumarchais, who transferred his working relationship from Lee to Deane.

For their initial work together forwarding supplies to America, see the July 1776 Beaumarchais–Deane correspondence in *NYHS Collections* 19 (1886): 144–46, 153–66.

⁴ See Robert Morris to Silas Deane, August 7, 1776, note 2.

Marine Committee to Thomas Albertson

Sir   October 1. 1776

The Continental Schooner Muskieto under your Command being well fitted and manned you are to set sail for Occracock in North Carolina and proceed up with said Schooner to Edenton. On your arrival there put into the post office any letters you carry with you, and the Military Stores and other goods you have on board deliver to Messrs. Hewes & Smith Merchants at that place. Those Gentn. are to lade you back, therefore you must loose no time in discharging and getting the Vessell ready for the reception of Naval Stores or any other goods which they may want you to put on board, which you are to receive to the full lading of your vessel. You are to apply to the Convention or any other Public body at that place for any dispatches they may want to send by you, and as soon as you have received your Cargo and dispatches from Messrs. Hewes & Smith you are to set sail for this place, proceeding with caution to avoid being taken by the enemy. Should you find our Bay shut up by the Men of war and that you cannot get in by the Cape May Channel, bear away for some of the Inlets and write to us when you get in.

You are to be careful of the Schooner, her materials and Stores and we expect you will be diligent and attentive to the execution of your business. We are Sir, Your hble servants.

P.S. You must make the utmost dispatch from Carolina & take care not to waste any Powder. Should you be taken, throw all Letters & Papers over board Slung to a shott to Sink them.

LB (DNA: PCC Miscellaneous Papers, Marine Committee Letter Book). Addressed: "To Lieutenant Thomas Albertson of the Continental Schooner Muskieto."

Robert Treat Paine to Samuel and Daniel Hughes

Gentlemen,   Philada. Octr. [1,] 1776[1]

I recd. yrs. by Mr. David Gillispe & laid the same before Congress, who have Ordered the Sum of £5000 to [be] paid you in full expectation of reaping the benefit of the Contract. The Treasurer has paid the money to Mr. David Gillispe agreable to your desire in your Letter but it is very proper you should sign the inclosed receipt & send it soon as may be.[2] Mr. Gillispe says you intend to build only one stack at the new place & expect to cast 32 pounders from it. I trust you will consider well whether one hearth will hold Mettle enough in proper order to cast so large a Gun with certainty, for the congress will depend much on having those large cannon. I understood you intended to build two stacks close together.

I am glad to hear you have cast all the Frigate Guns & hope you will get them down as soon as possible. Mr. Gillispe tells me you were to blow out immediately. I am sorry you did not continue casting 12 pounders. If you are not blown out when this meets you & can continue to cast 12 pounders you will much serve the cause & would have you keep on & let us know it & we will tell you how many. Wishing you Success I am yrs &c.

FC (MHi).
[1] The date assigned this letter is derived from the supposition that Paine wrote it soon after Congress ordered the payment of £5000 to the Hughes brothers on September 30, which is the reason he composed it. JCC, 5:835.
[2] At the bottom of the letter, Paine drafted the following "enclosed receipt": "Recd. of Michael Hillegas Esqr. Treasurer to the United States of America   Dollars &   agreable to an Order of Congress of the 30th of Sept. last to be paid in Cannon to the Congress, according to our Contract with them or in failure thereof the same sum to be repaid them by the time mentioned in said Contract for the delivery of the last Cannon."

Secret Committee to the Maryland Council of Safety

Gentn.   In Secret Committee Philada. Octr. 1st. 1776

Publick Bodys shou'd be equaly cautious of taking offence as of giving it, because mischiefs are very apt to arise therefrom & generally before a remedy can be applyed. You have taken amiss the refusal of fourteen p[iece]s Canvass wanted for your Colonial Vessells & had information that 2000 ps had been imported in one Vessell hence.[1] These are your premises & the Facts are as follow. It was not this Committee that refused you the Canvass for we had agreable to orders of Congress delivered the whole to the Marine Committee & that whole consisted of about 600 ps instead of 2000, but it was not possible the marine Committee cou'd spare you a single Bolt, because the Congress had but a day or two before your application ordered all the light Duck & other Stuff then in the Publick stores or that cou'd be bought in the City to be made into Tents and sent immediately to Genl. Washington.[2] The Marine Committee remonstrated against this measure alledging that none of the Continental Vessells cou'd be sent out if this Canvass was taken from them. No matter they were told the Soldiers shou'd have Tents if they stripped the Yards of those Continental Frigates & Cruizers that had sails made up, & in Consequence of this measure which nothing but the extreame necessity of our Army coud justify, We have now a parcell of fine Vessells lying here useless at a time they might have been most advantageously employed. Therefore Judge you, whether that Committee or the Congress itself cou'd have justifyed sparing you the Canvass you wanted. You may depend Gentn that as just grounds are ever meant to be given by Congress or any of its Committees for Complaints like yours We are all embarked in a Cause that requires our utmost united exertions to carry us through, and be assured that you can always command our utmost aid and assistance when it can possibly be extended, consistent with the general Welfare. For & on behalf of the Secret Committee, I have the honor to be, Gentn, Your most obedient & very hble Servant,   Robt Morris

RC (MdAA). Written and signed by Robert Morris.
    [1] For the Maryland Council's September 25 complaint at being refused "so trifling a quantity of Canvass," to which Morris is responding, see *Md. Archives*, 12:305–6.
    [2] See *JCC*, 5:735.

Richard Stockton to Robert Treat Paine

Dear Sir,   Morven Octr. 1st. 1776
    I have presented the Resolve of Congress respecting the purchase of Cloathing for the Army to the Legislature of this State, agreeably to the determination of our Committee;[1] and they are much disposed to exert themselves in so important a Service, without the least delay. They propose to take a recess for a few weeks in order the more effectually to execute the business. This morning one of the members called upon me with the inclosed resolves

which I transmit to the Committee of Congress by two persons who go express at the expence of this State. The assembly are clearly of opinion that the Articles will be purchased 25 per Cent cheaper if they have the Cash in hand. The House seemed to think that I ought to draw on the President; but that power is properly vested in the Committee of Congress, and not in an individual member. If the Committee should approve of the mode, and the sum mentioned, they will I doubt not immediately draw on the President for the money that no time may be lost. The Assembly continue to sit now, only for the return of their messengers with the money, which will be proportionately distributed among the members of the several Counties. I wait Mr Clymer's arrival here, which I expect this evening and expect to proceed on for Ticonderoga tomorrow morning.[2] I am Sir, your most obedt. hb Servant,

Richd. Stockton

RC (MHi). Addressed: "The Honl. Mr. Paine, Chairman of the Committee of Congress for &c &c."

[1] Paine was the chairman and Stockton a member of the committee on clothing appointed on September 25. JCC, 5:822. Congress' resolution of the same date authorizing each member of this committee to employ "proper persons" in his state to purchase "blankets and woolens . . . [and] all other necessary cloathing for the soldiers" is in JCC, 5:821. On October 1 the New Jersey Assembly resolved that it would be "proper to appoint the Representatives in Council and Assembly of this State in their respective Counties" to carry out this resolution and sent Jonathan Baldwin and William C. Houston to obtain $30,000 from Congress for this purpose. There is no mention of this matter in the journals, but Baldwin and Houston must have been successful in their mission because one week later the assembly decided to reimburse them "for their Trouble and Expenses in bringing the Money from the Continental Congress." See Votes and Proceedings of the General Assembly of the State of New Jersey (Burlington: Isaac Collins, 1777), pp. 26, 28–29, 40.

[2] See John Hancock to Philip Schuyler, September 27, 1776, note 4.

Oliver Wolcott to Laura Wolcott

My Dear,   Philadelpa 1 Octo. 1776

This morning I arrived safe to this City with as much Health as when I left Home tho a little fatueged with a long Journey. I went by the Way of the Fishkill as I expected to find Mr. Hallet and Broome there, but Mr. Broome was gone to N Haven, and Mr. Hallet to the Jerseys. I found Mr. Miller in the Jerseys tho I was oblidged to go out of my Way for him with whom I have fully settled my Acco. but Mr. Hallet and Hazard were gone to the Eastward but I have paid Mrs. Hallet £340.0.6 N York Currency and have her Receipt therefor, which same I think settles that Acco. Mr. Hallet it is said will be at Philadelpa in about a Month when I hope finally to Close that Matter. My Search for these Gentlemen prevented my going by Elisabethtown but since learn that if I had I should not have Accomplished any Thing. I believe I shall as well be able to Obtain a carriage a few miles out of this city where Business of that Kind is carried on to great Perfection. Every Thing here is rising in its Price as I am informed tho' I have been but little abroad. I have called at sundry Book sellers to get those Books which Oliver Wants but have not been able to find them. If they can be had I will send them to him. I have sent some Camphire and Rubard by Thompson.

As to News have nothing of consequence to Write upon. The Report of the Interview which the Deputation from Congress had with Lord Howe you will see, and a kind of Manifesto which he has lately published.[1] He is tho't to be insidiously Attempting to raise a Division, but it will probably be altogether ineffectual. There are none of the Kings Ships in this River neither has there been for some time, so that some considerable Trade has been bro't in here. Wishing you and the Family all Health and Happiness and that God would ever make you the objects of his gracious care, I subscribe myself most affectionately your's,   Oliver Wolcott

P.S. Have paid Thomson fifty three shillings and four pence for his pocket Expences home, which he will adjust.

RC (CtHi).
  [1] By Lord Howe's "Manifesto," Wolcott undoubtedly meant the joint declaration issued by the Howe brothers on September 19 indicating their desire to discuss means of reconciliation with all colonists and asserting the king's willingness to revise royal orders and acts of Parliament that had been found objectionable. The declaration is in *Am. Archives*, 5th ser. 2:398. For a discussion of how it was received, see Ira D. Gruber, *The Howe Brothers and the American Revolution*, (New York: Atheneum, 1972), p. 125.

John Adams to Samuel H. Parsons

My dear Sir   Philadelphia Octr 2d. 1776. Wednesday
    Your Letter from Long Island of the 29 of August, has not been answered.[1] I was very much obliged to you for it, because it contained Intelligence of a Transaction about which we were left much in the dark at that Time and indeed to this Hour, are not so well informed as we should be.

    I think, Sir, that the Enemy, by landing upon that Island put it compleatly in our Power to have broke their Plans for this Campaign and to have defended New York. But there are strong Marks of Negligence, Indolence, Presumption, and Incapacity on our Side by which Scandalous Attributes we lost that Island wholly, and Manhattans Island nearly. I am happy to hear your Behaviour commended.[2] But, sir, it is manifest that our officers were not acquainted with the Ground, that they had never reconnoitred the Enemy, that they had neither Spies, Sentries, nor Guards, placed as they ought to have been, and that they had been Shamefully remiss in obtaining Intelligence of the Numbers, and Motions of the Enemy, as well as of the Nature of the Ground.

I have read somewhere or other that "A Commander who is Surprised in the Night, though guilty of an egregious Fault, may yet plead something in Excuse; but, in Point of Discipline, for a general to be surprised by an Enemy, just under his Nose, in open day, and caught in a state of wanton security, from an overweening Presumption of his own Strength, is a Crime of so capital a Nature as to admit, neither of Alleviation, nor Pardon." Ancient Generals have been nailed to Gibbetts, alive, for such Crimes. E. W. Montagues Reflections on the Rise and fall of the ancient Republicks. p. 203.

Be this as it may, I think the Enemy have reached their Ne Plus, for this year. ⟨Yet I hope that your Army will continually harrass them with skirmishes, on Long Island, and wherever you can come at them.⟩

I have drawn this Conclusion from the Example of Hannibal, whose Conquest changed the face and Fortune of the war. According to Montesquieu, so long as he kept his whole Army together, he always defeated the Romans; but when he was obliged to put Garrisons into Cities, to defend his allies, to besiege Strong holds, or prevent their being besieged, he then found himself too weak, and lost a great Part of his Army, by Piece meal. "Conquests are easily made, because We atchieve them with our whole Force: they are retained with difficulty, because We defend them with only a Part of our Forces."

Howe with his whole Army, could easily take Possession of Staten Island where there was nothing to oppose him. With the Same Army, he found no great difficulty in getting Long Island, where even his Talent at Strategem which is very far from eminent, was superiour to the Capacity of his Antagonist. After this, it was easy to take New York, which was wisely abandoned to him. But, sir the Case is altered. A Garrison is left at Staten Island, another at Long Island, a little one at Montresors Island, another at Paulus Hook, a large Body in the City of New York and a larger still to man the Lines across the Island between the Seventh and Eighth Mile Stone. After Such a Division and Distribution of his Forces, I think he has nearly reached the End of his Tether, for this year.

The Enemies Forces are now in a situation peculiarly happy for Us to take advantage of. If an enterprising Spirit should be indulged and encouraged by your Commander in little Expeditions to Staten Island, Long Island, Montresors Island, and elsewhere, you would gradually form your Soldiers for great Exploits and you would weaken, harrass, and dispirit your Enemy.

Thus you see I Scribble my opinions with great assurance upon subjects which I understand not. If they are right, it is well, if wrong they will not mislead you.

LB (MHi).

[1] Parsons' August 29 letter to Adams is in the Adams Papers, MHi.

[2] In a September 16 letter to President Hancock, Washington had commended Generals Parsons and John Fellows for their "exertions" in attempting to rally their brigades at Kip's Bay. Washington, *Writings* (Fitzpatrick), 6:58.

Committee of Secret Correspondence to Silas Deane

Sir   Philada. October 2d. 1776

We have this day received from the Honorable Congress of Delegates of the United States of America the important papers that accompany this letter being,

first, a Treaty of Commerce & Alliance between the Court of France & these States.[1]

second, Instructions to their Commissioners relative to the said Treaty.[2]

lastly, A commission whereby you will see that Doctr. Franklin, The Honorable Thos. Jefferson Esqr & yourself are appointed Commissioners for Negotiating said Treaty at the Court of France.

These papers speak for themselves & need no Strictures or remarks from us, neither is it our business to make any. You will observe, that in case of the absence or disability of any one or two of the Commissioners the other has full Power to Act.

We therefore think it proper to inform You that Doctr Franklin & Mr. Jefferson will take Passage with all Speed, but it is necessary that their appointment on this business remain a profound Secret and we do not choose even to trust this paper with their rout. Suffice it therefore, that you expect them soon after this reaches your hands, but by different conveyances. And if you do not see some evident advantage will arise by Communicating this Commission to the French Ministry immediately, We give it as our opinion You had best suspend it, untill the arrival of one or both these Gentlemen, because you will then benefit of each others advice & abilities, and we apprehend their arrival will give additional Importance to the Embassy.

But should you be of opinion that delay will be in the least degree injurious to our Country or its Cause, You must by all means use your own discretion in this matter, wherein we are not authorised to instruct or advise; we only offer our own thoughts on the Subject. Shou'd you think proper to disclose this Commission to the

Ministers of France, enjoin the Stricktest Secrecy respecting the Names, or rather insist that it be not made known to any Persons, but those whose office and employments entitle them to the communication that any others are joined with you in it because if that Circumstance reaches England, before their arrival it will evidently endanger their Persons. The Congress have ordered the Secret Committee to lodge Ten thousand Pounds Sterling in France subject to the drafts or orders of the Commissioners for their support, and you may depend that remittances will be made for that purpose with all possible dilligence. We can also inform you, that you may expect instructions for forming Treaties with other Nations. Consequently you will Cultivate a good understanding with all the Foreign Ministers. We have Committed these Important dispatches to the care of Mr. Wm. Hodge junr who we hope will in due time have the pleasure to deliver them in person.[3] He knows nothing more of their Contents, than that they are Important and in case of Capture his orders are to sink them in the Sea. This Young Gentlemans Character, Family, & alertness in the Publick Service, all entitle him to your Notice. He is also charged with some business from the Secret Committee wherein your Countenance & assistance may be usefull. You will no doubt extend it to him and also engage Mr. Morris's exertions therein.

You will please to advance Mr. Hodge the Value of One hundred & fifty pounds Sterling for his Expences & transmit us his receipt for the same. We most fervently pray for a successfull negotiation & are, with the utmost attention & regard, Dear Sir, Your affectionate Friends & obedient hble Servants,   B Franklin

Robt Morris

P.S. Mr Hodge has some instructions from the Secret Committee which he will lay before you & if the Negotiation of Monsr Hortalez respecting Arms & Ammunition has been Conducted with Success it will be needless for Mr Hodge to make Contracts for those Articles.[4] You will know how that matter is and direct Mr Hodge accordingly, and if you shoud think it of more Consequence to send him immediately back here with dispatches than to employ him in the business that Committee have proposed he will obey your orders & Mr Morris may do the other.

RC (PHC). Written by Morris and signed by Franklin and Morris.

[1] The Plan of Treaties, which Congress had adopted on September 17, 1776, is in *JCC*, 5:768–78.

[2] Although the enclosed copy of the "Instructions to their Commissioners relative to the said Treaty" has not been found, this is undoubtedly a reference to the instructions adopted by Congress on September 24, 1776. *JCC*, 5:813–17.

[3] See Committee of Secret Correspondence to William Hodge, October 3, 1776.

[4] See Secret Committee to William Hodge, October 3, 1776.

John Hancock to Certain States

Gentlemen,   Philada. Octr. 2d. 1776.

The many and just Complaints of the Insufficiency of the Surgeons and their Mates to discharge their Duty in a proper Manner, have induced Congress to pass the enclosed Resolves, recommending it to the several States, to appoint some skilful Physicians as Examiners, without whose Approbation, no Surgeon or Surgeon's Mate, shall receive a Commission either in the Army or Navy.[1]

The Congress being at present deeply engaged in Matters of the utmost Importance to the Welfare of America, have judged it absolutely necessary, that there should be a full Representation of the several States as soon as possible. For this End, I am to request, in Obedience to their Commands, you will immediately take proper Measures to comply with the enclosed Resolve,[2] in Order that the United States may be fully represented in Congress, and the Sentiments of America be the better known, upon those interesting Subjects that lie before them. I shall therefore only once more request your Compliance with this Requisition of Congress—and have the Honour to be, Gentlemen, your most obed. & very hble Servt.

John Hancock Presidt

RC (R–Ar). In the hand of Jacob Rush and signed by Hancock. LB (DNA: PCC, item 12A). Addressed: "Assembly of New Hampshire. Massachusetts Bay. Rhode Island. Connecticut. New York. New Jersey." Except for the omission of the first paragraph, Hancock sent the same letter this day to Maryland, Virginia, North Carolina, South Carolina, and Georgia. PCC, item 12A; and *Am. Archives*, 5th ser. 2:838.

[1] Congress passed these medical resolutions in response to Washington's insistence that Continental surgeons should undergo a regular examination. See *JCC*, 5:836–37; and Washington to Hancock, September 24, 1776, Washington, *Writings* (Fitzpatrick), 6:106–16.

[2] See *JCC*, 5:837. Edward Rutledge persuaded Congress to pass this resolution about "full Representation" for a number of reasons which he explained in his letter to Robert R. Livingston of October 2, printed below.

John Hancock to George Washington

Sir,   Philada. Octr. 2d. 1776.

The Bearer Major Ross calling on Me previous to his setting out for Head Quarters, I have only Time to enclose you sundry Resolves, and to inform you, that I shall write you fully by General Mifflin.[1] In the Interim I have the Honour to be, with the greatest Esteem and Respect, Sir, your most hble Ser.

John Hancock Presidt

RC (DLC). In the hand of Jacob Rush and signed by Hancock.

[1] Hancock sent Washington a variety of resolutions pertaining to the army

which were passed by Congress between September 25 and October 1. *JCC*, 5:819–25, 829–30, 831–32, 836–37, 838.

On October 3 Hancock also sent Commissary General Joseph Trumbull a brief note requesting his "greatest Attention" to an enclosed resolve of Congress, which was probably Congress' September 25 resolve directing Trumbull to procure salt and provisions "for the next campaign." PCC, item 12A; *Am. Archives*, 5th ser. 2:851; and *JCC*, 5:825.

Richard Henry Lee to William Lee

Philadelphia October the 2d. 1776

As I have but now been made acquainted with this opportunity that is just departing, you will therefore excuse my not gratifying your curiosity so fully as it might wish, and the same reason will be an apology for my considering this letter as written both to you & your acquaintance in the Temple.[1] Early preparations had been made to receive the force coming against America as you will perceive by the manner in which that force has been received. The Troops ready in Virginia & North Carolina, with the united alertness of those States (for so they are now called) to meet Gen. Clinton, occasioned him to go with his whole force against Charles Town in South Carolina, where his landing was prevented, and Sr. Peter Parkers fleet beaten and repulsed as you will see in the inclosed paper, which is a very authentic account. Thus defeated and disappointed they returned to join Lord & Gen. Howe then before New York. Lord Dunmore, after having figured most contemptibly in Virginia for some time, was at length compelled by hunger, disease, and fear, to retire to N. York likewise. You will see herein a printed true account of the last attack made on him and the consequences. The small pox having raged with pestilential fury and universality, leaving not above one in ten of the American Army unattackt in Canada, in that state the British troops &c. arrived in that Country. It is realy not surprising that the former retreated to the east side of Lake Champlain, but it is most astonishing that they effected their retreat with little or no loss. The American strength on that Lake is at this time so great both by land and water that they rest secure against any attempts from Gens. Carleton and Burgoyn. When the whole Fleet and Army were collected before New York, the British Troops had been for some time in possession of Staten Island, they landed the greatest part of their Army on Long Island, where they had not been long, before an engagement happened between 3000 of the American troops and (as the best accounts here agree) at least 18,000 of the regulars, which ended in the loss of about 1000 Men taken, killed, & wounded of the Americans, who made few prisoners, but who slaughtered of their enemies many more than were killed of their own people. It being very evident that Long Island and the City of N. York were not to be defended against a potent land army & sea force acting in conjunction, both these places were in their turns evacuated, and the American Army retreated to their present post on the heights of Haerlem about 8 or 10 miles above the City and on the same Tongue of land upon which the Town stands. This is a very strong post by nature and strongly fortified by Art. 30,000 men are there placed to prevent the further progress of Mr. Howe, and to this time he has been effectually prevented. A thousand men under command of Brigr. Gen. Leslie lately attempted some of Gen. Washingtons Outposts, and was beaten off with the loss of about 400 killed & wounded. Thus things remain this 2d of October. The British Army have Connecticut on their right where they do not incline to go, Gen Washington with 30,000 men on the heights of Haerlem in their Front, and on their left the Jersies in which an army of Observation is posted either to prevent penetration that way or to aid Gen. Washington occasionally. The N. river is so obstructed that Vessels cannot go above thè heights of Haerlem, and these obstructions are covered by 50 pieces of heavy Cannon placed on the heights. This you may depend upon it is a true state of things at present, and you will readily see how poor a compensation it promises for the expence of 12 millions this Campaign, and the loss of America forever. You may remember that I wrote you my opinion 14 months ago, that if the Ministry pushed the war another year this would be the consequence, and facts seem to authenticate my judgment. The manner in which the last petition of the Congress, was treated and the last speech to Parliament alarmed the people here, but when the Army and Fleet destined against America was made known, the eyes of all Men were opened, the blind saw, the timid became determin'd, and all joined in commanding the Congress to declare the Colonies Free & Independant States which they did, as you will see among the inclosures. A very trifling few indeed, amazingly few excepted, saw that it was no longer optional in America to be connected with G.B. on Constitutional terms, but that this Country was reduced to the Alternative of Slavery or Independency, and they hesitated not to choose the latter. In most of the States new and regular Governments are established. The Legislature in most consists of two branches, the third being confined to the executive line. Since Lord Howes arrival he has not mended matters in the way of treaty. The Americans say the insidious nothings that he proposes is adding insult to injury. You will see by one of the inclosures how his plan was bared to public view by a conference he had with a Committee of Congress, that, it would seem, had been sent on purpose to expose to the World that nothing but Subduction was ever intended. We understand the Hessians carry it with a high hand over the British Troops who are obliged to truckle on every occasion! The number of Prizes taken by the American Cruisers is wonderful. At least 6000 hhds of Sugar and a world of other Goods are already safe in these Ports, and the American force by Sea daily increasing. I do realy think, that if a great Statesman with proper powers were to arise in England, he would endeavor to save his Country by immediately acknowledging the independence of North America and forming with these States an advantageous Treaty of Commerce. Shortly it may be too late.

A new Stewart is placed at Green Spring in the room of Fauntleroy who is removed. A Mr. Ellis of Hanover, extremely well recommended for sobriety, honesty, skill & diligence is appointed. An Acquaintance of yours would be happy if two in the North could be contrived to him, provided every thing relative to learning is not likely to go on well. Adieu.

[*P.S.*] One fourth of the City of New York has been burnt since it fell into the hands of the B. forces.

In great haste.

RC (PRO: C.O. 5, 40). In the hand of Richard Henry Lee, though not signed.

¹ This indirect reference to Arthur Lee and the reference in the concluding paragraph to "Green Spring," William Lee's Virginia estate, constitute the evidence for identifying William Lee as the intended recipient of this intercepted letter.

Caesar Rodney to Thomas Rodney

Sir   Philada. Octr. the 2d 1776

I Recd your Letter Yesterday About three OClock in the Afternoon per post.¹ Luke who set out from the Creeks mouth on Monday Morning Arrived here Yesterday afternoon About One OClock, but did not Call on me till the Evening. However this Could be no fault of his, Unless it been pleased God to have Endowed him more Understanding, for I realy believe (as he says) that he had been hunting from the Minute he Came and Could not find me, or the House where I lodged. If he had been Lucky Enough to have blundered on the House he wou'd have found me as I happened to be at home all that afternoon. This turned out to be the Case at Last, for Stalking Along the Street, he saw Moses Standing my Door, which relieved him. I Shall Sell the Veshell as soon, and for as Good a price as possible. Mr. Read is not Yet Come up. However I Shall Set out for Kent on Saturday or Sunday at furthest, whether he Comes or Not. Yesterday I Recd a Letter from Doctor Tilton. The officers are in pretty Good Health, Except Coll Haslet who has been Unwell with the flux for a Considerable time past but Getting better. One Paragraft in the Old Mans Letters is Verry full of the Great Honor obtained by the Delaware Battalion in the affair of Long Island, from the Unparralelled Bravery they shewed in View of all the Generals & troops within the Lines, Who alternately Praised and Pittied them. By General Howe's Return of the prisoners to Congress, Lieutt. Stuart & Lieutt. Harney are both Alive and Well.

General Mifflin Came to town the day before yesterday. He brought Letters from General Washington informing Congress that Mr. Moyland the Quarter-Master-General had Resigned his Commission as unable to Conduct the business for so many Troops. That in Consequence thereof, the General Says he had prevailed on General Mifflin to Accept Confident that there was not another man in the Army who Could Carry on the business upon the present large plan. Under these Circumstances Mifflin has with reluctance Accepted.[2] General Mifflin says Our Army is Numerous, Mending fast as to their Sickness, in high Sperits, well fortifyed and wish for nothing more than a General Engagement. There is Seldom a day but some prize or some French trading Veshell Comes into this Port. Some days two or three. I hope the Children will Get better of their sickness soon—and Am Glad Sally is better. I am with love to you all, yrs &c,   Caesar Rodney

RC (MHi).
[1] Not found.
[2] The Committee of Congress sent to confer with General Washington at New York near the end of September apparently also participated in obtaining Stephen Moylan's resignation and his replacement by Thomas Mifflin. See Elbridge Gerry to Horatio Gates, September 27, 1776. Congress accepted Moylan's resignation and appointed Mifflin in his place on October 1, 1776. *JCC*, 5:838.

Edward Rutledge to Robert R. Livingston

My dear Robert   Philadelphia Octr. 2d. 1776

The Day before I received your Last Favour, I wrote you a few Lines requesting that you, Jay & Schuyler would immediately come hither upon Business of great Importance.[1] Since which we have received a Letter from your Convention relative to the Last Gentleman, whose Fate has been hard indeed. However, his spirited Conduct & the Support which your Body seem determined to give him will I trust have a proper Effect upon Congress, & make him respectful even in the Eyes of his Enemies. The enclosed Resolution (which I drew & which passed the House unanimously) will justify the Conjecture.[2] It will be a farther Satisfaction to you to know that upon the Receipt of your Conventions Letter, when some of us took the opportunity of applauding his (P's) Conduct in high Terms, no Man could be found to say any Thing against him. Let him not imagine from this, that the Members are all his Friends, this is not to be expected, nor do I know that it is to be desired, the Esteem of the honest part of the Community, & the Approbation of his own Conduct must content him. I wished much to have had him in Congress before I quitted; he would have been very useful in the war-Office, but his Presence at Albany & its Neighbourhood, will (now that he is possessed of the Confidence of Congress) be so very beneficial to your State that I shall be satisfied with his staying away. I concur with you in thinking that our Ships would be more Advantageously employed in the Hands of private Adventures, than in those of the Congress; for the Star of the East has not lost its Influence.[3] And how is it possible to expect that it should when the Eastern Colonies are always, & your State, the Lower Counties & Maryland seldom or ever represented. To put us upon an equal Footing, to give Consequence to our Proceedings, & vigor to our operations, I moved Congress yesterday & they accordingly directed all absent Members to attend.[4] Our Confederation has been neglected for many Weeks because the States have been unrepresented, Necessity requires that it be immediately past. If I am not much mistaken the Salvation of your State depends upon some thing being soon done in this Business.[5] We have great Reason to think that the Quakers have determined to refuse our Continental Currency. If they make a point of it, we must make a point of hanging them, which will bring on a storm that will take the Wisdom of all our wise Men to direct. If the Troops under Washington should be defeated, I am satisfied this Country will be on the Brink of a Revolt, nothing will prevent it, but a great deal more Firmness than we at present possess. With such a Prospect is it not absolutely necessary that your State should be represented by Men who can & will think & think deeply too? Is this the Case? If it is not should not the Evil be got rid of as soon as possible. I think it should—& I am sure you must think with me. Indeed I am convinced that you would render your State more essential Services by attending in Congress than you can by riding about the Country in counteracting the Schemes of Tories. I have much Compassion for your Poor & will assist you in any Plan for their Relief—but come & propose it & bring Jay with you. I must forego the pleasure of telling you what past between Lord Howe & your humble Servant—it is too long for the Compass of a Letter.[6] Delay was my Object. I wish we could have procrastinated better until we could have procured more assistance from the Southward; I think the thing was possible. However my Scheme did not take—tho' we had the good Fortune to throw into New York between 3 & 4000 Maryland & Virginia Troops from the Time of Sulivan's leaving Ld. Howe to our Interview. I shall write to Govr Morris tomorrow. Remember me to him & Jay: Adieu my Friend. Yours most affectionately,   E. Rutledge

P.S. I have no time to correct & write this over—therefore take it as it is & make it out as well as you can.

RC (DLC).
[1] See Rutledge to Robert R. Livingston, September 23, 1776.

² See Congress' resolution of this date rejecting General Schuyler's resignation from his command of the northern army. *JCC*, 5:841. See also Rutledge to Livingston, September 23, 1776, note 2.

³ Livingston also discussed this issue in a September 27 letter to Rutledge. Morgan, *Naval Documents*, 6:1023.

⁴ See *JCC*, 5:837.

⁵ In response to a previous complaint by Rutledge about Congress' failure to approve the Articles of Confederation, which was apparently made in a letter to Livingston that has not been found, Livingston had been moved to write: "I am sorry for what you say of the confederation. It is necessary some thing should be done on it. What is the great obstacle to its passage? Representation?" Livingston to Rutledge, September 27, 1776, Miscellaneous Manuscripts, DLC.

⁶ On this point see Rutledge to Washington, September 11, 1776. This meeting with Lord Howe had led Livingston to note: "I am persuaded there is no rock on which we are so likely to split as negotiation. You cant think the speculatibn it occationed here. Duane seriously insisted that Lord Howe had great *powers* & that some thing of the last importance call'd you over—while I who know enough of human nature to believe that even great characters are sometimes influenced by familiar motives attributed your jaunt to curiosity covered by ostensible reasons." Livingston to Rutledge, September 27, 1776, Miscellaneous Manuscripts, DLC.

James Smith to Eleanor Smith

My dear,   Philada. 2d Octr 1776

Your agreable favour of 20th of last Month Came to hand, & I should have answered it sooner but I expected to have been home about this time. The Convention did not end untill last Saturday. I am now eased of much trouble & fatigue having Nothing to do but attend Congress. I believe I might have been appointed to go to the Army as a Commissioner on business of importance, but your too tender feelings for me prevented my accepting that Comission. As many of the Members of Congress are gone on Publick business to the Army & other places I Cannot be spared, at least untill Mr Wilson returns which will be the end of this Week. New Comissions are now settling for the whole Army to Continue during the War, & anxious as I am to be with you & the Children yet it woud be unpardonable in me not to stay & put in a good word for some of my Acquaintances in the Army to get them promoted. Last Saturday I dined at Mr. Dickinsons House in the Country. He Enquired very kindly about you & the young Ladies, his Wife is decent & not disagreable. Same day Arrived here Genl Thompson & all the Prisoners from Canada.¹ Monday Genl. Mifflin Came to Town from our Camp Near New York, I dined with him & Mr Hancock. He says the English lost much more men, Monday was two Weeks,² than our People thought. Some of the Deserters say it was a second Bunkers Hill affair to the English, they keep very Close quarters since, & dont seem fond of looking our Army in the face. Genl

Mifflin is in high Spirits & returns tomorrow. He says the Army are now all in good Spirits, & since I have seen him it has much raised my spirits, for I Confess before I had my doubts & fears, but am now fully relieved. When you are in a Chiding humour at my stay, think me employed in getting some worthy man Advanced in the Army or getting some Prisoner exchanged who now pines in Captivity but such objects as those & others of still higher importance employ my time & thoughts. Col Shee of this City has resigned his Comission & Come to Town from Genl Washington Army. 'Tis said his Wife's Fears & prayers induced him to this Step. He was a Gallant Officer & brave man & friend to Liberty. If this step should blast his fame in the opinion of the World, & hurt his Peace of Mind, how very unhappy has her Womanish tenderness made him.

I remain, dear Nelly, your affecte. Husband,   Jas Smith

[*P.S.*] I have not time to read this Letter over, so that 'tis a question if you Can.

RC (N).
[1] For a list of the American officers who had arrived with Gen. William Thompson at Elizabethtown, N.J., from Quebec, on September 26, see *Am. Archives*, 5th ser. 2:588.
[2] The battle of Harlem Heights occurred on Monday, September 16.

Committee of Secret Correspondence to William Hodge

Sir,   Philada, October 3d 1776

We Commit to your care sundry dispatches delivered you herewith, & you are immediately to repair onboard the Sloop Independance, John Young Commander, now waighting for you between this & Rheedy Island. This Sloop will carry you & said dispatches with the utmost Expedition to the Island of Martinico, where you must apply to Wm. Bingham Esqr. delivering to him all the letters & Packages directed for him. This Gentn. will assist in procuring you an immediate Passage from thence to some port in France onbd. a French Vessel. Choose a good one if you have a Choice, & a Man of War or Packet in preference to a Merchantman. The General of Martinico will give you a letter to the Commander of the Port you sail for, requesting him to grant you a Passport, & to expedite you immediately to Paris. On your arrival there you must find out Silas Deane Esqr. and Mr. Thos. Morris, & deliver to each the letters & Packages directed for them. If you arrive at Nantes apply to Mr. John Danl. Schweighauser. At Bourdeaux to Messrs. Saml. & Jno. Hans Delap. At Havre de Grace to Mr. Andw. Limozin. At Dunkirk to Messrs. P. Stival & Son in the name of Willing, Morris & Co. to furnish you with the Address of Mr. Deane & Mr. Morris at Parris, as it will be well known to them all, & they will also render you any other Services you may Stand in need of.[1] Should you go to Paris without previously finding out the Address of these Gentn, Apply to Messrs.   Bankers in Paris who can direct you to Mr. Deane.

The Letters & Packets directed for him & Thos. Morris, you are to consider as dispatches of the utmost Importance. You must never Suffer them to be out of your possession one Moment untill you deliver them safe with untouched Seals to those two Gentlemen, unless you shoud unfortunately be taken & in that case you must throw them over board, always keeping them ready Slung with a Weight to Sink them if that Measure Should be necessary, & for your faithful discharge of this trust, you are answerable to your God, Your Country & to us that have reposed this Confidence in you. We have desired Mr. Bingham to supply you with what Money you want at Martinico, & to transmit us your receipts for the Amot. Mr. Deane will supply you with any sum not Exceeding One Hundred & fifty Pounds Sterlg. in France. You will keep an account of your Expences, which will be paid by the Congress, who will also Compensate you Generously hereafter for your time, trouble & Risque in this Voyage. Should Mr. Deane think proper to send you immediately back with dispatches for us, you will no doubt take charge of them, & proceed according to his Instructions. You must Cautiously avoid letting any person whatever know what is your Business or that you have the least Connection with Publick business. We wish you a Safe & Successfull Voyage & are Sir, Your Obedt. hbl. Servts.

FC (DNA: PCC, item 37).

[1] The Committee of Secret Correspondence this day also wrote a general letter of introduction for Hodge's use, which was addressed to the merchants named at the four ports listed here. *Am. Archives*, 5th ser. 2:851–52.

Marine Committee to
Joseph Hewes and Robert Smith

Gentlemen,[1]   October 3d 1776

You will receive this from Lieutenant Thomas Albertson commander of the Schooner Muskeeto now employed in the Continental service as an advice Boat. She carries but few Letters this voyage but what there are must be put in the post office, and the same price charged for carriage as if they had gone from hence by Land, which you will please to see done. Mr Hewes having fitted this Schooner himself before he left this, you will take care to receive the Cargo which consists altogether of Continental Stores sent for the use of the Continental Troops in your State and deliver the same to the proper officers granting Lieutenant Albertson a receipt for what he delivers and you'l please also to supply him with what money may be absolutely necessary to defray the charges and expences of his Vessel but no more, taking his accountable receipts for what you pay him, One of which you'l transmit by the Vessel. We desire you to ship back by this Vessel One hundred barrels Cool Tar, two tons tawlow [tallow?] in barrels, and twelve barrels Rosin, for the use of our Navy. If the Schooner will carry more put it on board, if not so much, you must leave out a little of each. We beg you will despatch Mr. Albertson back immediately, don't allow him to stay on any account. If he wants a few Men pray assist him in getting them, and your drafts on the Chairman of the Marine Committee for the Cost of the goods ordered & of the Schooners disbursements will be duely honored. We are sir, Your very hble servants

P. S. You have enclosed a Manifest of the Cargo and Mr Hewes must allow a handsome freight for his goods which you'l Credit in the Schooners Accounts.

LB (DNA: PCC Miscellaneous Papers, Marine Committee Letter Book).
[1] Hewes and Smith were partners in an Edenton, N.C., mercantile firm. See Joseph Hewes and Robert Smith to a London Mercantile Firm, July 31, 1775.

Secret Committee Minutes of Proceedings

Octr. 3d. 1776

Come. met. Present Messrs. Morris, Lewis, R. H. Lee, & Mr. Livingston. Letters were wrote to the follg. persons for the purpose of procurg. Supplies of Arms, Ammunition, Clothg. & other Necessaries for the Army: To Jn. Danl. Schweighauser Merchts. Nantes, Saml. & Frans. [John] Hans Delaps Merchts. Bourdeaux, Andrew Limozin Mercht. Havre de Grace, P. Stival & Sons merchts Dunkirk, Estienne Cathalan Mercht. Marseilles, John Ross of Philada. now in Europe, Thoms. Morris, of Philada., now in Europe, Wm. Bingham Esqr. Martinico.[1] Agreed that Mr. Morris write to his correspondt. at St. Eustatia to purchase all the blankets he can for use of the Army.

Come. met. Present Messrs. Morris, R. H. Lee, Lewis, Livingston, Bartlett. Order on the Com[missar]y to deliver to Messrs. Wharton & Falconer 100 lb Salt petre for the use of the Ships of war. A Letter was written to J. Bradford Esqr. ordering him to purchase a prize ship from Honduras now at Boston (London with Mahagony & Logwood) or any others that may be brought in there with the same cargo, on public Acct. wch. he is to dispatch for Amsterdam consignd to J. Ph. Merckle Esqr. Mercht. there, with directions to sell the Cargoes & the vessels also, if a good price can be obtaind. If not, he is to load them back with salt for this Contnt. & credit this Come. for the nett proceeds of the Cargoes.[2]

MS (MH–H).

[1] Most of these letters have not been found, but on the next day Robert Morris did write the following letter to William Bingham on behalf of the Secret Committee: "You have herein a Memorandum from the Commissioners of the Continental Store of Sundry Articles wanted for our Navy. If You can send the whole or any part back by the Sloop Independance do, but if you can not get them send forward the List & the Files to Mr. Thomas Morris with this letter requesting him to Ship them soon as possible & charge the amt to the Secret Committee." Gratz Collection, PHi; PCC Miscellaneous Papers, Marine Committee Letter Book, fol. 26.

[2] The Secret Committee's letter to John Bradford has not been found; but for additional information on the committee's dealings with Johann Philip Merkle, see Secret Committee Minutes of Proceedings, June 27, 1776, note 1.

Secret Committee to William Hodge

Sir   Philadelphia Octr. 3d 1776

We deliver you herewith Copies of the Letters & Credentials you had from us when you sailed on your late unfortunate voyage, the originals whereof we understand you destroyed on being taken by the Orpheus man of War.[1] We have since that time taken other measures for procuring Arms and Ammunition which probably may have succeeded, therefore we request you will lay these Copies and this letter before Silas Deane esqr. at Paris and follow such advice and directions as he may give respecting Arms and Ammunition, but with respect to the Cutters we approve much of that Plan and wish it to be executed and even enlarged.[2] We therefore propose that you should consult with Mr Deane and Mr Thomas Morris on this subject, and if you find it will be in your power to procure Seamen and obtain liberty to Arm and fit out vessels in France, Spain, or Holland, that you should if possible buy a Frigate of 20 to 40 Guns, have her compleatly fitted, armed and manned, putting in a gentleman of unexceptionable good character, being also an able Seaman to command her for which purpose we give you herewith a blank Commission to be filled up with his and the Ships name which may be the Surprize. The Captain and you may appoint the other Officers necessary for this Ship giving to each a Certificate shewing his Station. When this Ship is compleated you must give Orders to the Captain signed by Mr Deane to cruize in the Channel against the enemies of the United States of America, making Prizes of all such British property as he can meet with. He may send his prizes into such Ports in France as may be most convenient, and you will there demand protection for them, or rather let Mr Deane demand this and also liberty to make sale of such goods as he, Mr Morris and yourself may think best to sell there. Direct the Captain to take out any dry goods he finds on board his Prizes into his own Ship, and when by this means he has got a considerable quantity on board, let him come away for this Coast, and get into the first place of safety he can in the United States of America. The Captain must before he goes, give bond duly to observe all the Rules and Regulations of Congress and herewith we deliver you a blank bond, with a book of those Rules and a List of the Continental agents. Any prize that he sends into France you must send forward from thence to some of these States, unless Mr Deane, Mr Morris & yourself agree it is more for the Public good to sell in France, and if you sell them there apply the Neat proceeds to pay the Debts you Contract in this business. Besides this Ship, we approve also of the Two Cutters as mentioned in our former Letters. You may Arm, fit and man them and dispatch them hither soon as possible, either with Arms, Ammunition, or such Other goods as Mr Deane and Mr. Morris may recommend or provide. We deliver you Commissions &c. for these Vessels also, and recommend you to be very attentive to the choice of Captains. They should all be good Seamen, men of good character and principles, strongly attached to this Country and its cause, and prefer Americans thus deserving to any Other Country. If such Americans are not to be found, seek for good men of other Countries that have been here or have connections amongst us. We know that there are many such in Europe that woud be glad of the employ. The Ship must make but a Short Cruize in the Channel and a Short one will do the business for she will daily meet Prizes, but if she is long there they will have men of War in quest of her. We hope you'l meet with some fine fast sailing Ship for this purpose, and be able to purchase & fit her on reasonable Terms. We shall desire Mr Deane and Mr Morris to join you in the necessary assurances to those you deal with of being faithfully reimbursed & we again repeat that we shall make remittances in the produce of this Country for that purpose. We will also make you a proper Compensation for your trouble and services hereafter when they can be better Ascertained. Therefore wishing you success we remain, sir, Your hble servants.

P.S. It is absolutely necessary that you observe the utmost secrecy in All this business, and make use of every Cloak or Cover you can think of to hide the real design.

Tr (DNA: PCC, item 37).
  [1] See Secret Committee to William Hodge, May 30, 1776.
  [2] See *JCC*, 5:846.

John Adams to Abigail Adams

Philadelphia Octr: 4th: 1776
I am seated, in a large Library Room, with Eight Gentlemen round about me, all engaged in Conversation. Amidst these Interruptions, how shall I make it out to write a Letter? [1]

The first day of October, the day appointed by the Charter of Pensilvania for the annual Election of Representatives, has passed away, and two Counties only have chosen Members, Bucks and Chester.

The Assembly is therefore dead, and the Convention is dissolved. A new Convention is to be chosen, the Beginning of November.

The Proceedings of the late Convention are not well liked, by the best of the Whiggs. Their Constitution is reprobated and the Oath with which they have endeavoured to prop it, by obliging every Man to swear that he will not add to, or diminish from or any Way alter that Constitution, before he can vote, is execrated.

We live in the Age of political Experiments. Among many that will fail some, I hope will succeed. But Pensilvania will be divided and weakend, and rendered much less vigorous in the Cause, by the wretched Ideas of Government, which prevail, in the Minds of many People in it.

RC (MHi). Adams, *Family Correspondence* (Butterfield), 2:137-38).

[1] Earlier in the day, Adams had written a brief note to Abigail. After complaining that he had no time to write, he concluded: "When I shall come home I dont know. But this you may depend on, I can come when I will. The Communication is open and will remain so. It cannot be cutt off.

"The General Court have not appointed any one in my stead. I expected they would—but whether they do or not I shall come home, before long." Ibid., p. 137.

Elbridge Gerry to Samuel Adams

My dear sir   Philadelphia Octr 4th 1776
The post just going out affords me Time only to acknowledge the Receipt of your agreable Favour of Sepr 23d[1] & to inclose You part of an old paper containing the Report of the Committee that Conferred wth Lord Howe which I have not yet discovered in your News papers, also the Pennsylvania constitution to be lodged with the Speaker, after you have perused it for the Use of the Committee on that Business, & Copies of two Letters from your old Friend in L——.

With Respect to the two affairs which You allude to the C—— is not finished, the other is & persons appointed to carry it into Execution.[2] *Doctr F*—— & *Mr J*—— of Virginia are well & We have had late Accounts from *Mr. D*—— of Connecticut.[3] The plan which You desire to have a Copy of would be no Ways useful at present, as It must undergo great Alterations.

With Respect to the Camp I wrote a Line from Harlem Heights to the Speaker last Week & beg Leave to refer You thereto from want of Time to repeat the purport;[4] the Ground which the army are now possess'd of is allowed by all to be very advantageous, & I hope We shall retain it. Great Delays have taken place in the marine Department. I am sure it is high Time to adopt a plan for a Board of Admiralty that can be obliged to attend the Business.

I wrote Major Hawley a Line relative to the Comme. & desired him to communicate it to my worthy Friend.[5] I wish he may have done it. General Lee is hourly expected. An Engagement is looked for at Ticonderoga. The Indian Queen Department are firm without effeminacy or the least Disposition for Wavering. Some others have the Disorders mentioned in Mr J Adams *famous* Letters.[6] I remain in great Haste sir Your assured Friend & hum sert,

E Gerry

[P.S.] We hope to see you soon.[7]

RC (Justin Turner, Los Angeles, Calif., 1971).

[1] Samuel Adams' September 23 letter to Gerry is in William V. Wells, *The Life and Public Services of Samuel Adams . . .*, 3 vols. (Boston: Little, Brown, & Co., 1865), 2:447-48.

[2] Gerry is referring to the Articles of Confederation and the Plan of Foreign Treaties.

[3] Although the wording is purposely vague, Gerry intended to inform Adams that Benjamin Franklin, Thomas Jefferson, and Silas Deane had been appointed commissioners to France. *JCC*, 5:827. For references to Deane's dispatches, see Robert Morris to Silas Deane, October 4, 1776.

[4] Not found, but for an extract that may have come from this letter, see Gerry to Horatio Gates, September 27, 1776, note.

[5] Not found.

[6] That is, John Adams' July 24, 1775, letters to James Warren and Abigail Adams.

[7] This day Gerry also wrote a letter to his brother Thomas, primarily to discuss information pertaining to the Gerry family's commercial affairs. He also reported that "The Commissary General has desired me to Let Mr Miller the Deputy Commissary at Boston have what Salt is left in Mr Harris Hands & that for Cash on the Delivery by which means he will be able to deliver You the proceeds of that likewise & enable You to make the payment mentioned to Mr. Gill." And he concluded: "Nothing new at New York, Things remaining by advices this Day much as they were. General Lee is daily Expected. At Ticonderoga the Enemy are expected." Gerry Papers, MHi.

John Hancock to Philip Schuyler

Sir,   Philada. Octr. 4th. 1776

It is with the greatest Pleasure I transmit the enclosed Resolve, in which you will perceive that the Congress have fully expressed their Sense of your past Conduct, and their Determination to do your Character that Justice which you have a Right to expect from them.

At the same Time, Congress can not give their Consent to your re-
tireing from the Army in its present Situation. Such a Step would
give your Enemies Occasion to exult, as they *might* suppose, you
were induced to take it, from an Apprehension of the Truth and
Reality of their Charges against you.[1]

The unmerited Reproaches of Ignorance and mistaken Zeal, are
infinitely overballanced by the Satisfaction arising from a conscious
Integrity. As long therefore as you can wrap yourself in your Inno-
cence, I flatter myself you will not pay so great a Regard to the
Calumnies of your Enemies, as to deprive your Country of any
Services, which you may have it in your Power to render her. I have
the Honour to be with the greatest Esteem & Respect, Sir, your most
obed. & very hble Servt.   J. H. Presid.

LB (DNA: PCC, item 12A).
[1] See *JCC*, 5:840; and Edward Rutledge to Robert R. Livingston, September 23,
1776, note 2.

John Hancock to George Washington

Sir,   Philada. Octr. 4th. 1776
The enclosed Resolves will inform you of the Steps the Congress
are taking to provide for the Army.[1] They are so explicit that I need
only refer your Attention to them—and indeed this is all I have
Time to do at present. By General Mifflin who will set out tomorrow
or next Day, I shall do myself the Pleasure to write you fully. I have
the Honour to be, with the greatest Esteem, Sir, your most obed. &
very hble Sert.   John Hancock Presidt

[*P.S.*] Inclos'd you have Col Shepard's Commission.[2] The Vacancy
of Col. in room of the late Col. Stephenson is order'd to be kept for
Mr Morgan, agreeable to yor Recommendation.[3]

RC (DLC). In the hand of Jacob Rush, with signature and postscript by Hancock.
[1] In addition to the resolutions on supplies for the Continental Army, which
were passed by Congress on October 2, Hancock also sent Washington resolutions
of the same date about William Shepard's promotion and Congress' refusal to
accept General Schuyler's resignation. *JCC*, 5:839-41.
[2] See *JCC*, 5:839. For William Shepard's petition for permission to resign his
commission and Washington's recommendation that Shepard be given command
of the Third Continental Regiment, see *Am. Archives*, 5th ser. 2:603-4.
[3] Congress made no mention in the journals of its intention to make Daniel
Morgan colonel of the Eleventh Virginia Regiment because, as Washington had
explained to Hancock, Morgan's "acceptance of a commission under his present
circumstances, might be construed a violation of his Engagement" to his British
captors not to bear arms again until he had been exchanged. See Washington,
Writings (Fitzpatrick), 6:128; and Don Higginbotham, *Daniel Morgan: Revolutionary Rifleman* (Chapel Hill: University of North Carolina Press, 1961), pp. 53-56.

Robert Morris to Silas Deane

Dear Sir   Philada. October 4th. 1776

I have received since my letter of the 12th Ulto. your favour of the
23d June[1] and am extremely Concerned to find most of the bills that
you carried or have been remitted to you have been noted and likely
that some of them will be protested. There is great reason to believe
Ministerial influence is used to prevent the payment of many bills in
London. Indeed I am informed by a Gentn now here that he knew
it to be the case with respect to some of my Houses drafts. They first
prevaild to have them protested & then circulated a report that the
Sum was ten times as much as the reality. This I suppose to hurt our
Credit with others for they had information we were transacting
business for the Congress, however if they do us no greater Injury
than that I shall be happy having already taken up & paid all such
drafts as have come back. The Amot hitherto is not above £2000 Stg
& We have not £4000 depending but it now seems a matter of doubt
whether any bills will be paid or whether they will Seize on the
property of Individuals. If they do that we must make Reprizals
here and in the mean time we shall use our utmost endeavours to
lodge sufficient Effects in Europe to make good yours & all other
engagements on Account of the Publick. Therefore be not dismayed
if they dont arrive as fast as you cou'd wish, make allowances for the
Power of our Enemy by Sea & the disappoinments that must inevitably happen thereby. Consider the great Value we have to remit &
how Bulky most Commodities of this Country are. These and other
Circumstances must prevent that punctuality we cou'd wish but all
that can be done shall be done. I am happy to find my Recommendations have had the desired effect & that you have been so well received as farr as you had gone to the 23d June & hope we shall soon
hear of your further progress. Such parts of your letters as ought shall
be Communicated to the Committee or to Congress whenever necessary. The dispatches that go by this Conveyance will probably open
your Views in the Political line. I have therefore determined to push
my Brother in the Commercial. The Secret Committee have sent him
a large order by this Conveyance and directed me to make him Consignments. I hope he will meet with your advice & assistance whenever necessary and I doubt not he will before this time have
recommended himself to you for I think he has a good Heart & clear
Head. I expect also that he has been & will be usefull to you in many
respects. I think you shou'd at all events procure a loan of Money
either from the Government or the Farmers General to pay for the
Goods ordered which may be repaid out of the remittances to be
made. I also wish you wou'd assist in procuring Insurances against
all Risques, including those of British Men of Warr & Cruizers &c.
I recommend Mr. Ross also to your Services & assistance if you fall in

with him. I need not say any thing to you on Political Subjects, you'l have enough of that from other quarters. I will however tell you that your Interest is well supported in Congress & if you have any Enemies there they are not from the middle or Southern States.

You may depend that I shall ever be mindfull of you whilst I hold a Seat in the Publick Councils & ever after in my private Capacity being with sincere regard & esteem, Dr. sir, Your obedt hble servt,   Robt Morris

RC (CtHi).
[1] For Deane's letter to Morris of June 23, 1776, see Robert Morris to John Jay, September 23, 1776, note 2.

John Adams to James Warren

Octr. 5. 1776

Yours of September 19 came duely to Hand.[1] You have raised every fifth Man to march to New York. But to what Purpose should you send forth your Thousands and Tens of Thousands of Men, if they are all to run away from the Enemy when they come in Sight of them? If whole Brigades, officers and Men are to run away, as Fellows's and Parsons's did on the fifteenth of September, throwing away their Arms, Cloaths, Knapsacks and other Things that they might be the lighter and run the faster, what avail your Numbers? All the Events of this War together have not inflamed my Breast with such a Complication of Passions, as the many late Examples of such dastardly, infamous, rascally Behaviour. It is a serious affair, Coll Warren, think of it as you will. You have certainly promoted a Multitude of Creatures who are totally unworthy of the Commissions they hold. The least that your House can do is to appoint a Committee instantly to inquire into the Conduct of your officers and to discard without favour or affection, all who have dishonoured themselves and their Country.

Lincoln I hope will do better.

I am glad you have thought of Cannon, Musquets and Lead and I hope that Sulphur is not forgotten. But I should have been better pleased if I could have learned more particularily what you have done. Cannon and Arms are of infinite Importance. They ought not to be neglected a Single Moment, and no Expense should be Spared, to insure them in sufficient Quantities. Salt is growing here very scarce and dear, and what We shall do for want of it, I know not. The Cannon Foundries in Maryland, Pensilvania and Connecticutt begin to perform very well. But the great Things must be done by the Massachusetts, if by any body.

I am very sorry that the General Court have arisen without choosing a Delegate in my Room. Of what Materials do they think that I am made? However they may do as they please, I will go home. If I were happier at Philadelphia than at home, as some People are, I would stay here with as stupid a Patience as they. But I am not. Besides, the melancholly Scenes which have afflicted my family ever Since I have been here, would have induced Persons who cared more about me than the Reptiles of the Dust, to have relieved me, at least for a Time. But I find if I will do the Drudgery, my family may perish with their good Will. The Members of both Houses are very happy I find with their Honours and offices, and Profit, and very willing that I should be sacrificed to protect them in the Enjoyment of them. If they expect that their Delegates here should drudge till they are stupid or distracted, and their families starve in the mean Time, they must look out for Men of fortune, who can afford it, and Men of stronger Bodies and minds too than mine, to bear it.

The Frolic to Lord Howe you have seen e'er now. It has done no Harm.[2]

LB (MHi). Endorsed by Adams: "Not Sent, nor fit to be Sent."
   [1] Warren's September 19 letter to Adams is in *Warren-Adams Letters*, 1:273–74.
   [2] For Adams' brief letter to his wife this day, see Adams, *Family Correspondence* (Butterfield), 2:138–39.

William Ellery to Nicholas Cooke

Sir,   Philadelphia Octr. 5th. 1776.
   I received a Letter from Mr Ward of the 17th of September, which informed Me that your Honour & your Lady were inoculated and were expected to break out in a Day or Two. I most sincerely hope that when this reaches you, you will be intirely recovered from the Small Pox.

Since my last, Congress have entered into sundry Resolves which respect the several United States, and which will be communicated to you so soon as the Multiplicity of Business in which the President is engaged will admit of it; But as they may not reach our State so soon as the Post, it may not be improper to give you the Heads of them.

It is recommended to the Legislatures of the United States to appoint Gentn. in their respective States skillful in Physick & Surgery to examine those who offers to serve as Surgeons or Surgeon's Mates in the Army and Navy, and that no Surgeons or Mates shall hereafter receive a Commission or Warrant to act as such in the Army or Navy who shall not produce a Certificate from some or one of the Examiners so to be appointed to prove that he is qualified to execute the office.[1]

A Loan Office is to be established in each of the United States, and a Comme. to superintend such officers to be appointed by the States respectively. The Sum proposed to be hired is Five Millions of Continental Dollars and the Commissioners are to receive One Eighth per Cent in Lieu of all Demands for their Services. Certificates with the Resolve will be transmitted to our State when the Certificates are printed.[2]

It is Resolved that the President be desired to write Letters to the Conventions & Assemblies of the respective States, requesting that Measures be taken to cause as speedily as possible a full Representation of the States in Congress.[3] I would beg Leave here just to mention in Addition to what I have said in a former Letter that there is not a State that sends less than Three Delegates to represent it in Congress.

Congress too have recommended it to the several Legislatures in the United States to confine the Price of such Articles as the Quarter Master General may want to a reasonable Sum by an Act of the Legislature.[4]

The Committee who were appointed to inspect the State of the Army &c at Haerlem have returned and represented Things in a more favorable Light than We had used to view them. Methods are taking that the Army shall be better disciplined and provided in every Respect than it hath been. Although We have some good officers in some of the principal Departments; yet in others there is great Want of Skill and Abilities. The Quarter Master General Moylan was perswaded by the Committee to resign and Brigadier Genl. Mifflin to accept that office with the Rank and Pay of Brigadier General.

This Appointment will give great Satisfaction to the Army; for Gen. Mifflin is not only well acquainted with the Business of the Office, but he hath Spirit and Activity to execute it in a proper Manner.

The Officers of the Army in general are not equal to their Appointments and from hence it is that our Soldiery is disorderly and undisciplined. It is therefore recommended by Congress to the several States in officering the new Army, that they pay a particular Regard to Merit and Qualifications in their Appointments.[5] It is agreed on all Hands that our Men will make good Soldiers when they have good Officers. I hope the Genl. Assembly will be as ready and active in raising the new Levies as they were in dispatching the Continental Battalion to New York. The Time for raising the new Levies is short, and it is of the last Importance that they should be ready to supply the Places of the Troops that may quit the Service when the Time of their Inlistments shall expire. The Enemy if they should have such an Opportunity as they had last Fall will without Doubt improve it.

By Letters from G. Washington recd. yesterday Things at our Camp in Harlem remained as they were; and by some inclosed

Letters from Henry B. Livingston Captn. of a Company which have been employed on Long Island to bring off Inhabitants and Stock it appeared that he had brot off a Number of Families and a considerable Quantity of Stock and Grain. That the Enemy were collecting all the Stock and Grain they could and levying Companies there. In which Business Brigr. Genl. Oliver De Lancey is very active. Capt. Livingston having heard that One Richard Miller a Tory of Distinction had raised a Company of Men and that he was about to join them, posted his Men so advantageously for intercepting him that they came across him, & ordered him to stop, which he refusing and attempting to escape they shot him dead on the Spot.[6]

Letters were also received the same day from the Northern Army from Genls. Schuyler & Gates & Arnold, some of them inclosing Accounts from Deserters respecting the Enemy's Army & Navy.[7] By One of the Accounts it appears that their Army was sickly; That they had plundered and otherwise abused the Canadians so that but few had joined them, and that fifty of the British Troops had agreed to desert, but were unluckily discovered. From what I am able to collect the Enemy's Naval Force is equal if not superior to ours; but there Land Force not superior if equal. Genl. Arnold was at the Island Le Motte when he wrote, and intended to place his Fleet advantageously for Attack & Retreat. Our Army was still sickly, and in Want of cloathing, especially of Shoes & Stockings.

Congress have sent a Committee to Ticonderoga to inspect the State of the Army &c &c. When they return I will communicate such Part of their Report as I may be at Liberty to disclose.

We have nothing New from the Southward. The Papers have already informed that We have burned a Number of the Lower Towns of the Indians & an Expedition is formed for destroying their Upper Towns. General Lee is not arrived. Genl. Green to the Joy of the Army hath recovered his Health. I have nothing more to add at present but that I am with the sincerest Regard your Honor's & the State's Friends and humble Servant,   William Ellery

RC (R-Ar).
  [1] See *JCC*, 5:836–37.
  [2] *JCC*, 5:845–46.
  [3] *JCC*, 5:837.
  [4] *JCC*, 5:840.
  [5] Although Congress did not actually pass a resolution to this effect until October 8, it was undoubtedly already under consideration by the committee dealing with Washington's letters to Hancock of September 24 and 25. See *JCC*, 5:830, 836, 853, 855–56; and Washington, *Writings* (Fitzpatrick), 6:106–18.
  [6] Washington's letter to Hancock of October 2–3 is in PCC, item 152, 3:87–90, and Washington, *Writings* (Fitzpatrick), 6:148–51. The enclosed letter of Col. Henry Beekman Livingston and the orders of Brig. Gen. Oliver De Lancey, a loyalist officer, are in PCC, item 152, 3:91–102, and *Am. Archives*, 5th ser. 2:504–6.
  [7] These letters are in PCC, item 153, 2:382–415, and *Am. Archives*, 5th ser. 2:481, 530–32.

Caesar Rodney to John Haslet

Philada. Octr. the 6th 1776.

It is now a long time Since my Eyes have been blest with the Sight of one of your Letters, I hear you have been Ill of Flux, fever &c for which I am Extreemly Sorry, but hope not so bad as to have been the Cause of your not Writeing—I believe You are under some difficulty by the Irregularity of the Post—However hope you will soon mend, both of your Illness and disposition to Write me.

If Health and Weather permits, I Set out This day for Kent, and don't Intend to return to Congress soon again, at least not in the present Reign.[1] My Domestick business will Employ me all the remaining part of this fall, let matters turn out hereafter as they may. On weighing and duely Considering the matter I thought it best and safest for your Interest (in Case any accident Should happen to you) to keep in my Custody the Vouchers and other papers you left with me Rather than place them in the Treasury, unless They Could have been passed and filed imediately, which Could not be done without you—I shall Carry them home with me, Where they Shall Be Secure and Subject to your Order, or in Case of Your Death (Which God forbid) to the order of Such person or persons as You Shall intrust with Your Affairs. They are now printing in the papers of this City the plan of the Delaware Government, therefore if you are fortunate Enough Ever to Get those papers you'l be blest with a Sight of the Plans and will have an oppertunity to pass your opinion of it—but whether you like it or not You are bound to Swallow it—for they have Ordered an Election to be held on the 21st day of this Month for the filling it up with men, and for Your further Comfort will have it in their power (I Dare say) with Such men as they Shall Think proper to point out. In this State, in the Counties of Chester, Bucks & one other they have held Elections for Assemblymen, Sheriffs, Coroners &c. and Signd Returns Regularly to the Governor as usual. The Sheriff of Chester Came up here with his return but the Committee of Safety hearing of it apprehended him, and he is now (as the Quakers say) under deallings. I Suppose by this time you have seen the plan published by Congress for Establishing an Army, By this Plan You'l find a bounty of twenty Dollars and one hundred acres of Land to Each Soldier that will Enter. There is also a Bounty in Land to the officers. You will no doubt wonder that the Congress have not Raised the pay of the Officers. I Confess it is Strange that they have not—But depend on it (between you and I) their pay will be raised verry soon, and verry Considerably too. This for your private Satisfaction therefore not to be mentioned Yet.[2] Your private Satisfaction: Did I say? in this I may be wrong not knowing whether you may find yourself dispossed to Enter the List during the War; or whether if you Were so inclined, as the Congress

Have left it to the Several Assemblies to appoint all the officers Except General officers, You'd have any Chance in the nomination Even if you deserved it ten times as much more as I think you Do. However time will inform us more of These Matters. The Whigs of our Government Seem to have given up all pretentions by their Conduct, They are not satisfied with Great numbers of them having necessarily gone to the Camp, but many others have wantonly Gone, as if for no good Reason but to be out of the way. They are Such as might be of Service at Home, and Cannot possibly be of any there—I mean Mark McCall, Gordon, Vandike, Griffin &c. who I Suppose you have by this time seen. They did Tell me they wou'd be back by the fair, whether they will or not I Can't Say. Pray make my Compliments to the officers of your Battalion.

P.S. Don't Suppose from what I have said, they have left me out of Congress. they have not.

MS not found; reprinted from Rodney, *Letters* (Ryden), pp. 133–35.

[1] Although Rodney was not reelected by the new state assembly on November 8, 1776, he was later elected several times but never returned to Congress. John A. Munroe, *Federalist Delaware, 1775–1815* (New Brunswick: Rutgers University Press, 1954), pp. 266–67.

Writing to an unidentified friend in Philadelphia a few weeks later, Rodney openly conceded his reluctance to return to Congress. At the same time he discussed some "Laughable Reflections" that suggest he often managed to enjoy himself while in Philadelphia.

"I am in a better state of Health than When I left Philadelphia, and Tho' Verry Much Engaged in business, have many, not only pleasing, but Laughable Reflections; Among Others the happyness my Good Landlady must feel in my being so far removed from the Backgammon Tables which so often interrupted her Evening Repose. Yet I think She bore it with as much patience as most new married ladies possible Could. Pray make my Compliments to her and Miss Sukey, and let not Sally be forgot. It is thought by many that Sally is apt to discover too much warmth of Temper, it may be so. But I have allways found her Candid, Honest, Sensible and Oblidging, and therefore a favourite. She will (I have no doubt) with the addition of a few years, under so good a manager as She has, make a verry fine woman. If it Should be my misfortune to be Oblidged to leave home and attend Congress, I Shall be with you." Rodney to [John Capley?], November 3, 1776, Emmet Collection, NN.

[2] Officers' pay was raised on October 7. *JCC*, 5:853.

John Adams to Abigail Adams

Octr. 7th. 1776

I have been here, untill I am stupified. If I set down to write even to you, I am at a Loss what to write.

We expect General Lee, in Town every Hour, He dined at Wilmington Yesterday. His Appearance at Head Quarters on the Heights of Ha'arlem, would give a flow of Spirits to our Army, there. Some Officer of his Spirit and Experience, seems to be wanted.

The Quarter Master Generals Department, the Adjutant Generals Department, and the Surgion Generals Department, have for sometime past, been in great Confusion. The Army have suffered, in their Baggage, Discipline and Health, from those Causes.

RC (MHi). Adams, *Family Correspondence* (Butterfield), 2:139.

Josiah Bartlett to John Langdon

Dear sir   Philadelphia Octobr 7th. 1776

As I have not been able for some time to attend the marine Committe, I last Saturday took the liberty to show Mr Morrice[1] your letters Concerning the Conduct of the Providence Committe about Guns and soon found Mr. Hancock thro the multiplicity of Business had not laid the affair before the Marine Committe. Mr Morrice resented their Conduct extremely and Desired liberty to lay the letter before Congress but as I was uncertain but some bad Effect might arise from laying it before the whole Congress I Declined it. He then Desired liberty to lay it before the marine Committe to which I Consented. He said he would do his utmost that your ship should have them Guns at Providence and without paying that Enormous price for them. I am in hopes them guns will be ordered for your ship & one of theirs ordered to wait till guns can be sent from here where they are contracted for at 35 & 40 pound this money per tun.[2]

I Believe (inter nos) your letters to the President concerning marine affairs have not been laid before the committe nor much attention been paid them. The great & important Business in which he is constantly Employed and the almost immense number of letters which he is constantly receiving on the most interesting subjects makes it impossible for him to attend to them all and lesser matters must be neglected. I sincerely wish he did not belong to the marine Committe but would confine himself to the affairs of Congress which is Business abundantly sufficient to employ the time of any one human being.

I was Disappointed of seting out last week as I Expected and as I am in hopes I am some better than I have been I Believe I shall try to tarry here till Col. Whipples arrival which I think I may Expect in 12 or 14 days from this time according to his letter of the 23d ulto.[3]

As for news we have none at this time. How long we shall be without any I Cant Say as by the last accounts from Ticonderoga they were dayly looking for Burgoine up the lake and it seems Genl Howe is preparing to attack our Camp at Harleam. God grant we may have better fortune than we had at the attack on Long Island. The Enemy are now in Possession of Stratton Island, Long Island,

Governors Island, the City of New York & Powles's hook. I pray God they have now reached their Ultimatum and that from this time their power may Decline. I am your very hearty friend,

Josiah Bartlett

RC (PHi).

¹ That is, Robert Morris.

² For further information on the Marine Committee's response to Langdon's frustrated efforts to secure cannons, see Marine Committee to John Langdon, October 9, 1776; and Morgan, *Naval Documents,* 6:815–16.

³ In a letter to his wife this date, Bartlett made substantially the same observation, adding a few comments about his health during the past few days. Watt Collection, NhHi.

Committee on Clothing to the New York Convention

Gentlemen   Philadelphia October 7th. 1776.

The Committee Appointed to Carry into Execution, the Inclosed Resolve,¹ can think of no method So proper for the State of New York as to apply to the Convention, and for that purpose we do Send you ten thousand dollars, and desire you to appoint proper persons in the Several Districts to Execute the Same; and if upon trial you find that more Cloathing may be had than this money will purchase you may have more by applying to this Committee.

Rob Treat Paine	G. Wythe
Josiah Bartlett	Arthur Middleton
William Ellery	Wm. Floyd
Wm. Williams	Lyman Hall
	Geo. Ross

RC (NN). Written by Floyd and signed by Floyd, Bartlett, Ellery, Hall, Middleton, Paine, Ross, Williams, and Wythe.

¹ The committee on clothing, which was appointed on September 25, not only sent the convention a resolution of that date about the purchase of "blankets and woolens fit for soldiers' cloaths . . . [and] all other necessary cloathing for the soldiers," but also one of June 19 on the same general subject. *JCC,* 5:466–67, 820–22; and *Am. Archives,* 5th ser. 3:248.

New York Delegates to the New York Convention

Gentlemen.   Phila. 7th October, 1776.

Mr. Livingston wrote you a few lines the 28th September, acquainting you that we had obtained a vote of Congress on the Treasurer for One hundred thousand dollars, which it was not in our power to send you before this time.[1] Inclosed you have Mr. Hunter's receipt for the same. The gentlemen who Carry this Money are of the Lighthorse of this city, and of respectable Characters; we request you will pay attention to them as such.

The Committee of Congress to whom your papers respecting Genl. Schuyler were committed, have reported, we hope to your satisfaction.[2]

Mr. Rutledge informs us that he had transmitted a Copy to Robt. R. Livingston, Esqr. and a certified Copy shall be sent you per post, which will probably come to your hands before this letter.

On the 5th inst. we were going to move Congress, That they would direct Genl. Washington to propose to Genl. Howe, the Exchange of Brigadier-Genl. Woodhull for Brigd. Genl. McDonald, when a Pennsylvania newspaper of same date was handed to us, by which it would appear that Brigadier-Genl. Woodhull had taken such a part as would put it out of our power to move for his exchange; should be glad you would inform us if there be any truth in this conjecture, and direct us as to our conduct therein.[3]

We are respectfully, gentlemen, Your very humble Servts.

Fra. Lewis

Phil. Livingston

Wm. Floyd

Journals of N. Y. Prov. Cong., 2:320–21. RC (N). Written by Lewis and signed by Lewis, Floyd, and Livingston. RC damaged.

[1] See Philip Livingston to the New York Convention, September 28, 1776.

[2] See Edward Rutledge to Robert R. Livingston, September 23, 1776, note 2.

[3] The October 5 issue of the *Pennsylvania Ledger* printed copies of four orders which had been issued by Oliver De Lancey, a loyalist brigadier general, to some of his subordinates on Long Island between September 1 and 11. These orders are also in *Am. Archives*, 5th ser. 2:505–6. One of them, dated September 1, seemed to indicate that Nathaniel Woodhull, a brigadier general of New York militia, sometime president of the New York Convention, and brother-in-law of William Floyd, had reaffirmed his allegiance to the king and offered to surrender Suffolk County to the British. Since then Woodhull, who had been wounded and taken prisoner by the British at the battle of Long Island, had died on September 20. That Woodhull did in fact desert the patriot cause after his capture by the British is the contention of Willam H. W. Sabine, *Murder, 1776 & Washington's Policy of Silence* (New York: Theo. Gaus' Sons, Inc., 1973).

James Smith to Eleanor Smith

My dear Wife   Philada. Octr 7th 1776

Mr Kennedy promised me to Call at York. I cou'd not omit so good an oppertunity of Writing tho' I have nothing worth troubling you with since my last by Mr Eday which I hope Came safe to hand. Yesterday I dined with Geo. Campble & Helen in the   [1]—They much vexed at not seeing you & lay all the blame on me. About half an hour agoe Genl Lee arrived here. He has long been wished for at the Camp. I hope his arrival there will give our Army such new Spirits as may enable them to give Genl How's Army a drubbing but I ask pardon for troubling you with News, as you are not fond of it but I coud not help mentioning Genl Lee's arrival as I wished so ardently for it myself & I am Confident he will be better than 10,000 men to our Army. Mr. Wilson is not yet returned from Carlisle. I expect leave to come home after his Arrival but not before. I am in good health & Spirits & live mostly at my own little house as the People here Call it. Give Pegsy & Betsy & George & Jim each a buss for me. I write this in Congress Chamber not having time to go to my lodging. My respects to all Friends, & am, dear Ellen, Your loving & affecte. Spouse,   Jas Smith

[*P.S.*] Mr Hancock Calls me to the other room. Adieu. J.S.

RC (NN).
[1] Apparently Smith simply failed to complete his thought. The manuscript is not significantly damaged.

William Williams to Joseph Trumbull

Dear Sir   Philadela. 7 Octr. 1776
   I recd your favr of the 1st Inst. & observe the Contents. Have also shewn it to my Colleagues, & Mr G. & H.[1] but have not had Time to consult much upon it. I think tis not best to move the matter you insist on without a previous Consultation, & finding our Strength, when I will attempt. We have a Club once a week, but am not certain They are all fit to be consulted in this matter. I truly fear what will be the result of the motion in the House. Am not without hopes of Success, but am extreemly unwilling you shod leave the Service. There are strange Mortals in Con[gres]s be assured, tis hard to say what some of Them aim at, but easie to say a number invariably hate & persecute every N Engld Man, & can embroil Matters exceedingly. I expect to leave Them soon as Mr Sherman returns or before. It will be pleasure to me to get away & it wod give me inexpressible Satisfaction to leave the great Affairs of America in better Hands, but these are dangerous hints. The Salvation of the Country depends on the Character of Congress. Excellent Men there are also, & the great Affairs generally are well determined tho some times with great Altercation. I hope to see You in abt a fortnight. The Affair of Salt We have moved, & not without opposition (from its being wanted for the Navy) have got a Resolve that the Continental Agents deliver You on Order what they have &c.[2] The moment I cod I desired the Presit to Sent You the Copy &c as I have frequently

done before. He assured me he wod but always seems to be half offended that I shod doubt his Care in all those Things. He says he has sent the other order for purchasing &c.

Have nothing lately of the Scolding about the Vegetables. This Militiae are got back to their dens, & pamperd their Guts, & are perhaps more easie. This Province have a fixed hatred of N.E. & every thing that belongs to it, but Money, & that is all the God they worship. I fully agree their Troops have done more mischief than ever they did or will do good. Have heard nothing said about a Contract at N York, & I think there will not, at least till the Comte returns from Ty. I shall not be unmindful of your affair, but I dread the Clamour to be raised by it. I know so perfectly the rancor of some against You as of N. E. & an honest Man & the pleasure They wod have to get rid of you, & give yr birth to a southern or middle Colony man. The Distress & Confusion of the Army in Consequence of it wod give me great pain. Congress have refused Schylers Resigna & sent him high Compliments & assurances of their great esteem, & resentmt of malicious Clamours &c &c. In a Lettr. late from him he expresses his surprise that he shod be forbid to interfere in yr supplies &c, says he has interfered no more than he thot the Good of the service required, & that he will forever do. I beleive if Genl. Washington shod write so contemptuous a Letter, he wod come near to be broke,[3] but if Schyr shod damn the Congress & the Cause it wod not be resisted by some. Such Letters as this must be burnt. I have no Time to add but that I am with much affection & good Will, yr affece Frd. & Bror.[4]   W. Williams

[*P.S.*] Do you know any thing abt my Kinsman, Col Wards adjutant.

RC (CtHi).

[1] Probably Elbridge Gerry and William Hooper. See Gerry to Joseph Trumbull, October 22, 1776.

[2] *JCC*, 5:849.

[3] Suggestions that Washington was not universally admired in Congress are rare in the correspondence of the delegates at this early date, but Benjamin Harrison's October 10 letter to Robert Morris from Williamsburg contains a similar hint. "I fear the force of what you say respecting our Worthy General, I have long seen some Dark design against him, and have been on the Watch to prevent it. I know he has many Friends in Congress who will also strive in his Favor, but I fear the ways of the wicked are so Dark and intricate that they will at. last prevail. If they do, from that moment the American Cause will droop it's Head, and in a very short time be lost. We must not give over our attempts to save him. I say we, because I am again coming amongst you, my Country has made full reperation for the Injury done me, and have Honourd me beyond my Expectations." Etting Old Congress Collection, PHi. See, however, John Adams to Henry Knox, September 29, 1776, for evidence that the general's frequent criticism of New England troops had already begun to irritate northern delegates. Harrison's comment on the "full reperation" made to him is a reference to the fact that he had just been returned to Congress by the Virginia House of Delegates to fill the position recently vacated by Jefferson.

[4] This day Williams also wrote a letter to his wife's uncle Ichabod Robinson

urging a reconciliation between Robinson and his brother-in-law Gov. Jonathan Trumbull. "I think it my Duty to God & to you," Williams explained, "& I know it is in Sincerest Friendship, permit me I say the kindest Intention, to ask you whether you can think it right & justifie it to God & yr own Conscience, to live in such an habitual Privation, prejudice & bitterness towd yr Frd & Bror. Gov Trumbull, a Gent. who has treated you with great kindness with paternal as well as fraternal affection & good Will in yr early Life, & still is & never was other than your sincere & affece Friend, a Frd of his Country eminently so & a Frd of Mankd. & more than all these, I have no doubt a Friend of God & in the same temper toward yr most valuable & excellt Sistr." Williams Papers, CtHi.

George Wythe to John Page

Sir,   Philadelphia, 7 Oct. 1776

Before I received your letter of the 27th of last month, I had written one to you, which will go with this.[1] To what it contains I can add nothing on the subject of the seal but that I fear it will not be soon finished, and that when it is, I will forward it to you.[2] By this time, I presume you have been informed of what passed at the conference between Lord Howe and the triumviri from hence, the report of it being published in print. Whatever might have been the motives for that legation, I am apprehensive the evil consequences you mention may result from it.

Some of the same men who retreated from New York (for what you heard is true) next day in a skirmish behaved very gallantly, and gained some advantage. It would have been greater, if the reverse of their former conduct had not prevented it; too much ardor and eagerness, with a desire to repair their honour, urging them to attack earlier than was intended. Major Leitch, in this action wounded with no less than three balls, was thought to be in a way to recover; but I am told he died last week.[3] I understand by a general officer from head-quarters that our army, advantageously posted on the heighths of Haerlem, are not dispirited, but wish for a general engagement; those who suffered disgrace at New York attributing their flight to some officers who accompanied them in their flight, if they did not set the example. It will give me pleasure to receive a letter from you at any time. Wishing you better health, with every other felicity, I take leave to subscribe myself your friend,   G Wythe

[P.S.] General Lee is here on his way to head-quarters.

RC (NjHi). Addressed: "Hon. Mr Page."

[1] Not found.

[2] Pursuant to the request of John Page, Thomas Jefferson had engaged Pierre Eugène Du Simitière to engrave a state seal for Virginia. See Thomas Jefferson to John Page, July 30, 1776.

[3] For Washington's report of the September 16 skirmish on the plains of Harlem in which Maj. Andrew Leitch of the Third Virginia Regiment received a fatal wound, see Washington, Writings (Fitzpatrick), 6:67–69.

John Adams to Abigail Adams

Oct. 8. 76

I ought to acknowledge with Gratitude, your constant Kindness in Writing to me, by every Post. Your favour of Septr. 29 came by the last. I wish it had been in my Power, to have returned your Civilities with the same Punctuality, but it has not.

Long before this you have received Letters from me, and Newspapers containing a full Account of the Negociation. The Communication is still open and the Post Riders now do their Duty and will continue to do so.

I assure you, We are as much at a Loss, about Affairs at New York, as you are. In general, our Generals were out generalled on Long Island, and Sullivan and Stirling with 1000 Men were made Prisoners, in Consequence of which, several other unfortunate Circumstances, a Council of War thought it prudent to retreat from that Island, and Governors Island and then from New York. They are now posted at Haarlem about 10 or 11 Miles from the City. They left behind them some Provisions, some Cannon and some Baggage.

Wherever the Men of War have approached, our Militia have most manfully turned their backs and run away, Officers and Men, like sturdy fellows—and their panicks have sometimes seized the regular Regiments.

One little skirmish on Montresors Island, ended with the Loss of the brave Major Henley, and the disgrace of the rest of the Party. Another Skirmish, which might indeed be called an Action, ended in the defeat and shamefull flight of the Enemy, with the Loss of the brave Coll. Knowlton on our Part. The Enemy have Possession of Paulus Hook and Bergen Point, Places on the Jersey side of the North River.

By this Time their Force is so divided between Staten Island, Long Island, New York, Paulus Hook and Bergen Point, that, I think they will do no great Matter more this fall, unless the Expiration of the Term of Inlistment of our Army, should disband it. If our new Inlistments fill up, for Soldiers during the War, We shall do well enough. Every Body must encourage this.

You are told that a Regiment of Yorkers behaved ill, and it may be true, but I can tell you that several Regiments of Massachusetts Men have behaved ill, too.

The Spirit of Venality, you mention, is the most dreadfull and alarming Enemy, that America has to oppose. It is as rapacious and insatiable as the Grave. We are in the Fæce Romuli, non Republica Platonis. This predominant Avarice will ruin America, if she is ever ruined. If God almighty does not interpose by his Grace to controul this universal Idolatry to the Mammon of Unrighteousness, We shall be given up to the Chastisements of his Judgments. I am ashamed of the Age I live in.

You surprise me with your Account of the Prayers in publick for an Abdicated King, a Pretender to the Crown. Nothing of that Kind is heard in this Place, or any other Part of the Continent, but New York and the Place you mention. This Practice is Treason against the State and cannot be long tolerated.

I lament the Loss of Soper, as an honest, and usefull Member of Society.

Dont leave off writing to me—I write as often as I can.

I am glad Master John has an office so usefull to his Mamma and Pappa, as that of Post rider.

RC (MHi). Adams, *Family Correspondence* (Butterfield), 2:139–41.

Elbridge Gerry to Joseph Trumbull

Dear sir   Philadelphia 8th Octr 1776

I have just recd your Favours of 3d & 7th Instt., & am at a Loss to know what is meant by "supplying the Army by Contract." I have never heard a proposal of the Kind made in Congress; if such a plan has been agitated It was in my absence. The Committee exerted themselves to return to Congress & make their report. It has now been under Consideration four Days & the part that respects your powers contains sufficient provission for your purposes, but has not yet been considered. I suppose the Congress will have no objection to making You a generous Allowance for your services when the Matter can be properly agitated, but a Multiplicity of Business & not an apprehension that the Measure cannot be carryed, has prevented a Determination of it before this. It will be proposed when several Important Matters are finished, & I hope to your Satisfaction. If not & You resign, It is probable to me that Congress will supply the Army by Contract. For my own part I have sacrificed Ease & Interest to the Libertys of America, & am fully convinced that unless a general Determination prevails to establish it at every Expense & Hazard, Slavery & inevitable Ruin must be the Consequence. I could wish therefore that a Determination had taken place in your Mind to have sustained the Office of Commissary General without annexing the Conditions mentioned, since Congress must exercise an unbiassed Judgment in determining the Quantum meruit of all their officers or surrender the purse strings of the Continent to those who are employed in its Services—a Measure that would soon end in the ruin of all. I am the more desirous of this as your Friend would not be the less attentive to your Merits, & as Your present plan may end in the Introduction of an officer to succeed you who may dissatisfy the Army, yea cause it to be disbanded, & risk the loosing America. These are my Sentiments on the Matter but shall nevertheless endeavour to have your Affair properly regulated & the most generous allowances made for your services.[1] My Complimts to Colo Cortland & the Ladies & believe Me to be sir your very humble Sert,   E Gerry

P.S. The officers pay is raised 50 per Cent but this to be communicated but to a few Friends untill the report relative to the Men is considered.[2] General Lee is arrived. The Cherokees have had a severe drubbing, abt 300 killed, 75 of wch. are scalped & great Numbers put to Flight leaving their Towns to be burnt & Corn Fields destroyed. I am just informed that while We were at N York the Ticonderoga Committee had power to supply the army by Contract, & inclose a Letter Which pray examine & forward per 1st Oppertunity.

RC (CtHi).
[1] The commissary department was not reorganized until June 10, 1777. *JCC*, 8:433–48, 469–70. See also Gerry to Joseph Trumbull, October 22, 1776, note 4.
[2] Congress had just taken this action on October 7. *JCC*, 5:853.

Robert Morris to John Bradford

Dear Sir   Philada. October 8th. 1776
   I am indebted for several of your favours from the 26 August to 30th Septr.[1] but you must excuse my want of punctuality in this Correspondance and I am sure you will do it when you know that I am not master of my own time. If I was you shou'd never have cause to complain for want of a letter. The Anxiety you expressed to have the Brigt Dispatch sent away always gave me pleasure because it convinced me you had the Public Interest at heart and if that was truely the case with all Concerned we shou'd make a good Figure. The delay of Mr Merckle & other dispatches does not lie at my door, but theres no getting Committees & Public body's to move quick. Poor Merckle was very unfortunate in his Journey but I am glad he has got away at last with such a fair prospect of going safe. I have written you a letter from the Secret Committee respecting the Bay Ships [2] and hope you'l be able to make some cheap purchases—and the modes pointed out will I hope supply you with money but as yet I dont hear of your drafts for the Cost of the Dispatch & her Cargo. The Money is waiting for them. I approve much of the purchase you have made of a schooner for my Virginia plan & hope you will succeed in getting the Salt, Rum & Sugar. These Articles as well as the Vessell are exceedingly wanted in Virginia and I hope you have sent the Vessell away, that Coast is now clear of Cruizers but theres no knowing how long it may remain so & I wou'd have her dispatched at once Insured or not. Your drafts for this Vessell & Cargo will also meet punctual honor, and you may be assured I have a proper sense of your attention to my Concerns & wish we cou'd fall on some plan

to make this renewal of our acquaintance produce mutual benefit in the Commercial line. What think you of buying up in your State all such Prize Goods (not perishable) as sell Cheap & laying them by awhile, this years Fares must be nearly over & its a long time to the next Crop of West India Produce, beside I suppose measures will be taken to prevent our drawing so large a share of it. If you approve of this plan I will join you in a purchase to the extent of £20 to £30,000 Lawfull Money to be laid out (only) in articles that are sold cheap & will bear keeping and we may either bring them here or to any other State where most wanted in the Winter or resell them with you if an adequate advance of Price tempts us thereto, you to be allowed a Com[ission] of 2 ½ percent on the purchase & whoever sells them to draw the like Commission on the Sale. If you approve of this plan you may commence the Execution immediately one half or one third on your own Account & the rest for me, & my Friends. Your drafts on me on this Account shall be paid and you'l advise me particularly of what You buy, the Quantities & prices &c. You'l observe by this the unlimited Confidence I place in you & I am sure it will be fully answered by the most honorable Conduct in this affair.

If you can buy Tortoise shell, Elephants Teeth, Sassaparilla & Furrs cheap buy all you can lay your hands on, on such terms and I will procure you either Public or private orders for them and in the mean time you may avail yourself of the means pointed out by the Secret Committee to make any of those payments until Funds are provided and I dont know but I shall Cause money to be sent you for this purpose. You'l observe I propose your Charging 2 ½ per cent Coms. We have all our business in peaceable times done for that Coms. in the Neighbouring States, but as in the present instance I mean to have others Concerned in what you do, it is my design that they shou'd pay you 2 ½ per cent & me 2 ½ per cent for our trouble in the matter and if it be agreable to you to charge 5 per cent on such orders as I shall procure You & credit me for one half thereof it will be a further inducement to turn my Views Your way, altho Friendship alone wou'd prompt me to throw what Coms. I can in your way. You'l please to answer me on this point immediately because I have much in my power or under my influence both Public & private and my desire and design is to serve justly & faithfully every interest I am connected with, & at the same time as I take the trouble my Friends cant begrudge paying so small a consideration as now proposed both for your trouble & mine.

We have not so many Privateers from this Port neither have such a Number of Prizes been sent in as you have to the Eastward so that we remain in great want of many of the very Articles you abound with, consequently good hits may be made in the way I have proposed. Many of our People being sensible of this have gone into the

New England Governmts. to purchase, but I shou'd suppose a Resident as you are will have greatly the advantage of them. I believe I shall send to the Eastward one or two Captains to purchase Vessells & shall take the liberty to address them to you if they go so farr as Boston. My time is so much engrossed by Public business that I have but little left to employ in speculation, therefore I shall be glad to hear from you on the Subject of Private Concerns as your opinions will have great weight with me. What is the Meaning that our Continental Cruizers are less successful than Privateers. I want them to send You in some good Prizes that will supply you with Funds & afford you good Commissions.

I am with great regard, Dear Sir, Your obedt hble servt.

Robt Morris

P.S. My Brother Mr. Thos. Morris is now in France and will do business as a mercht there during the present troubles. He was brought up in our Counting House, has been in most parts of Europe, Speaks & writes French & Spanish as fluently as English and is very Capable of transacting business to the best advantage. I have wrote him not to sit down in any one Port, but to fix with the best House at each place to execute any orders he receives & divide with him the Coms. He will visit every Port in France & learn where every kind of business can be done best. Therefore Consignments he can direct to the properest Ports for sale, orders for Goods he will send to those places where they are Manufactured, all which I mention that you or your Friends may avail of his services. Letters addressed to him under Cover of Mr. John Danl. Schweighauser at Nantes, Messrs. Saml. & Jno Hans Delap at Bourdeaux, Mr. Andw Limozin at Havre de Grace or Messrs. P. Stival & Son at Dunkirk will readily find him.   R Morris

P.S. Pray how sells the best pickt particular London Madeira wine taken onboard the West India Men? I immagine they are as likely to sell very cheap as any article whatever, if you can buy those of the very best quality for £40 Lawful Money or less per pipe pray purchase Ten Pipes & lay them by for my future orders.

RC (CtY: Pequot Library deposit).
[1] For letters of Bradford to Morris dated September 5 and 23, 1776, see Morgan, *Naval Documents*, 6:690–91, 953.
[2] Not found.

Oliver Wolcott to Laura Wolcott

My Dear,   Philadelpa. 8 Octo. 1776
    I Wrote to you by A. Thompson which I think you likely have recd. Nothing Material has since Occurred, except an Acco. of some

Advantages obtained against the Cherokees, and an Expectation that We shall be able to Subdue those Savages. The Congress have agreed to establish an Army during the Warr to consist of 88 Battalions of 720 Men each exclusive of Field and Staff Officers eight of which are to be raised in Connecticut, out of the Forces now in service and others. Genl Lee came into Town yesterday and goes immediately to N York.

I have taken Lodgings at Mrs Duncans my former Quarters where the Air and Water are good. My own Health by the Blessing of God is better tho' I have for a few days been troubled as tho I had the Flux, which I have amongst my other military Advantages catched by lying on a Bed which I remember stink terribly, or else it is owing to an opening Persperation, which I am sensible I have suffered much for the Want of. I have not yet got Oliver his Books, but I have bought a Carriage and I find my Horse goes well in it, tho he is bad for the saddle. Mr. Huntington says he has wrote me Two Letters, one some time ago, which he directed to be left at N Haven P Office. Oliver Will enquire wheither any Letters are there for me directed to Litchfd. and send them to you. I shall Write often to you, and hope to have frequent Returns. May you injoy Health and be free from Anxiety. The aspect of publick affairs is the same, I wish that God in his Providence would bring this Country into a State of Peace safe and equitable, but I fear this happy Period is pritty remote.

A People suffered to be invoulved in the Calamities of War, is I think a certain Symptom of the great Displeasure of the Almighty. Yet I think We have no Reason to dispair of our Cause tho' it is Attended with many Perplexities. God can and I trust Will bring order out of this Confusion. Mr. Sherman goes home for a short Visit, upon his Return Mr. Williams will probably go home. I shall likely continue here till the Expiration of my Delegation, I think it is not likely that I shall be reappointed, and if not I think I shall without Anxiety Acquese in the Dispensation. I am Very sure that I can never injoy equal Pleasure in any Society as with my own Family. I have for a pritty while led a Solicitous Life; if Others are Ambitious of it I shall not quarrel if their Inclination is indulged. My Love to my Children and Freinds. That God may preserve you and them in his Protection is the devout Wish of him who is most affectionately yours, Oliver Wolcott

P.S. I believe I mentioned in my last that Ld. Howe had published a kind of Manefesto, I was credibly informed so, but as I have not yet seen it the Acco. ought to be regarded as a Mistake.[1]

RC (CtHi).
[1] See Wolcott to Laura Wolcott, October 1, 1776, note.

Elbridge Gerry to Horatio Gates

Dear Sir,   Philadelphia Octr. 9th. 1776

I wrote you about 10 days ago from the Camp at Harlem & since my return to this City, find that the Committee of Congress to enquire into the state of your affairs a Tyconderoga are empowered to make Contracts for supplying your Army.[1] What gave rise to this matter I have not yet learnt, but it counteracts a measure of having it supplied by the commissary General, which has alone proved salutary in that department. I suspect it originates from Tory influence, and that if any alteration is made, the Committee not Knowing or being intimately acquainted with the Characters of the persons who are desirous of the place, will introduce a person that will put the Northern Army in the same ruinous situation heretofore experienced. For God's sake then use your influence to prevent new schemes at this critical juncture, if no great inconveniences are felt from the present mode of supplies.

General Lee leaves this City for New York this morning. The Cherokees are driven from all their settlements near the Carolinas & our army has penetrated the Country as far as Overhills. 300 were killed in a late engagement, 75 of which were scalped. Things at New York in *statu quo*. In haste, I remain, dear Sir, Your very humble servant,   Elbridge Gerry

Tr (MH–H).

[1] The instructions for the committee sent to Ticonderoga, which consisted of George Clymer and Richard Stockton, are in *JCC*, 5:822–23, 828.

John Hancock to Certain States

Gentlemen,   Philada. Octr. 9th. 1776

The enclosed Resolves, which I transmit in obedience to the Commands of Congress, will inform you of the ample Provision they have made for the Support of both officer & Soldier, who shall enter into the Service during the War. The Pay of the former is considerably increased, and the latter is to receive annually a compleat Suit of Cloaths, or in Lieu thereof, the Sum of twenty Dollars, should he provide the Suit for himself. This additional Encouragement besides the twenty Dollars Bounty, and one Hundred Acres of Land formerly granted, the Congress expect will be the Means of engaging the Troops to serve during the War. For this Purpose also, I am to request you will appoint a Comee. or Committees to repair immediately to the Army, to induce such of the Troops as have been raised by your State, to enlist during the War, and to appoint Officers for the same.[1]

The Congress, for very obvious Reasons, are extremely anxious to keep the Army together. The dangerous Consequences of their breaking up, and the Difficulty of forming a new one, are inconceiveable. Were this Barrier once removed, military Power would quickly spread Desolation and Ruin over the Face of our Country. The Importance, and indeed the absolute Necessity of filling up the Army, of providing for the Troops, and engaging them to serve during the War, is so apparent, and has been so frequently urged, that I shall only request your Attention to the Resolves of Congress on this Subject; and beseech you, by that Love you have for your Country, her Rights, and Liberties to exert yourselves to carry them speedily and effectually into Execution, as the only Means of preserving her in this her critical and alarming Situation.

I have the Honour to be, Gentlemen, your most obed. & very hble Servt.   J. H. Presidt.

[*P.S.*] The printed Resolves herewith inclosed, relative to the establishing of Loan offices in the respective States, for the Purpose of borrowing Money on Continental Security, & the Regulations with Regard to the same, I beg Leave to recommend to your immediate Notice & Attention, & that you will take the proper Steps to comply with them.[2]

LB (DNA: PCC, item 12A). Addressed to New Hampshire, Massachusetts, Rhode Island, Connecticut, New York, and New Jersey. Hancock also sent the same letter to Maryland and Virginia on October 12. Red Books, MdAA; and Munn Collection, NNF.

[1] For the "enclosed Resolves," which were passed by Congress on October 7 and 8, see *JCC*, 5:853–56. The resolves about raises in officers' pay and clothing allowances for noncommissioned officers and soldiers were prompted by Washington's September 24 letter to Hancock. Washington, *Writings* (Fitzpatrick), 6:106–16.

[2] See *JCC*, 5:845–46, 849–50.

John Hancock to George Washington

Sir,   Philada. Octr. 9th. 1776.

The enclosed Resolves, which I do myself the Honour to forward, will inform you of the ample Provision the Congress have made for the Support of both Officer and Soldier who shall enter into the Service during the War. The Pay of the former is considerably increased, and the latter is to receive annually a compleat Suit of Cloaths, or in Lieu thereof, the Sum of twenty Dollars, should he provide the Suit for himself. This additional Encouragement, besides the twenty Dollars Bounty and fifty Acres of Land formerly granted, the Congress expect, will be the Means (if any Thing can) of engaging the Troops during the War.[1]

The Importance, and indeed the absolute Necessity of filling up the Army, of providing for the Troops, and engaging them during the War, having induced Congress to come to the enclosed Resolves, in obedience to their Commands, I am preparing to forward them with all possible Expedition to the several States.

Your Letters to the 5th of October have been duely received and laid before Congress. I shall immediately transmit all such Resolves which may hereafter be passed, any Ways relatives to your Department, or necessary for your information.

I have the Honour to be, with every Sentiment of Respect & Esteem, Sir, your most obed. & very hble Servt.

John Hancock Presidt

[*P.S.*] The several Resolves go to the States this day by Express.

RC (DLC). In the hand of Jacob Rush, with signature and postscript by Hancock.
   [1] See Hancock to Certain States, this date, note 1.

Marine Committee to Stephen Hopkins

Sir   October 9th. 1776

We have received from John Langdon Esquire of Portsmouth New Hampshire such an extraordinary Account of the conduct of the Committee you appointed to Superintend the building of two Frigates in Providence, that we cannot forbear transmitting you a Copy of his Letter.[1] The respect we all entertain for you and the Justice due to them induces us to do this, at the same time we impart to you that common sense says many things respecting them which Mr Langdon does not touch upon. We do not however pretend to condemn them either on his or her report, but when they exhibit an account of their proceedings we shall expect these things to be cleared up to the satisfaction of the Commitee or of Congress. We have ordered them to supply Mr Langdon with a Set of those Cannon that have been paid for, and as we find the demands of the owners of your Furnace are so extravagant, we now request that you will desire them to give in the terms on which they will cast another Set in lieu thereof to be ready in time for the Frigates at Providence. If they persist in these extravagant demands we shall supply them either from Hughes' works in Maryland or from this State, as we shall soon be able to spare sufficient from either place and no consideration shall induce us to submit to such extortion as was attempted with Mr. Langdon. We hope Sir, that your attachment to the general Interests of America, Your regard to the character of your State and your Freinds employed therein and your influence in that State will all combine to have those abuses rectified that have given rise to reflections and complaints if any such abuses have really taken place in the management of Marine Affairs. We hope for an immediate answer respecting the terms of Casting more Cannon & are, Sir, Your very hble servants

LB (DNA: PCC Miscellaneous Papers, Marine Committee Letter Book).
   [1] Langdon's difficulties with the Rhode Island Frigate Committee are described

at length in his September 14 letter to Josiah Bartlett. See Morgan, *Naval Documents*, 6:815–16.

Marine Committee to John Langdon

Sir   October 9th 1776.

Your freind Mr Bartlett having laid before this board your Letter to him of the 14th Ultimo respecting the conduct of the Committee at Providence Rhode Island,[1] on your applying to them for Cannon for the Raleigh, this Conduct appears to us in the most extraordinary point of light, but as it is unbecoming of public Bodies to condemn the conduct of any before they are heard in their own defense, We have wrote them of this date telling the points of which you complain and ordering them to deliver you a compleat set of the Continental Cannon in their possession those that are most suitable for the Raleigh and farther we have directed them to deliver you Shot or any other Continental Stores they have, if you think them necessary to expedite the Sailing of that Ship. We have also requested them to afford you any assistance in their power in transporting the cannon and Stores safe and soon to Portsmouth. We may not omit telling you that we have thought it only common justice to send Governor Hopkins a Copy of your Letter As the Committee were all of his appointment. We have said that deeming you a Gentleman of honor we doubt not but you will support the charge made against them, and under that beliefe we think it is justly your due and return you thanks for the information given us, as well as for your apparent solicitude for the public good. We have determined to have the Frigates inspected, and report made thereon. Before we close we must request your utmost exertions to get the Raleigh out to Sea, and the Captains and other officers Commissions will now go forward immediately.

We are sir, Your obedt & hble servants

LB (DNA: PCC Miscellaneous Papers, Marine Committee Letter Book).
[1] Langdon's September 14 letter to Josiah Bartlett is in Morgan, *Naval Documents*, 6:815–16. For Langdon's reply to the present letter, see ibid., 7:31.

Marine Committee to the Rhode Island Frigate Committee

Gentlemen   October 9th. 1776

We have been presented with a Letter from John Langdon Esquire Continental Agent at Portsmouth in New Hampshire to Josiah Bartlett Esquire a member of Congress, giving a very extraordinary account of your proceedings in respect to the Canon cast in your State for the use of the Continental Frigates. He says that the frigates at Providence cannot be ready to go to sea for two or three months, and the frigate at New Hampshire waits only for Cannon, which under One pretence or other you have refused to supply him with altho they are lying useless in Rhode Island, and another Set might be cast in time for your ships. He represents your refusal of his reasonable request as having its foundation partly in interested motives and partly in Jealousy of the New Hampshire Ship being at Sea before yours.

We cannot pretend to judge of the propriety of his observations, having only heard One side, but if the representation he has made be a just one, We shall think the Continental Interest was much misplaced when put into the hands of those who are capable of acting from such Motives against the public good. You'l observe we do pretend to decide on your conduct, because we are willing to hear your defence of it. Mr Langdon is a Gentleman of character and puts his name to what he writes, therefore we suppose he will be ready to make good his charge, however it is not our present purpose to inquire into your conduct at this time, but to inform you that we have sent Mr Langdon Orders to call on You again for a Set of Cannon suitable for the New Hampshire Frigate, & as we understand those Cannon are paid for out of the Moneys you have received and drawn for, We now direct and insist that a Compleat set of the Cannon most suitable for that Ship be immediately delivered to the said John Langdon Esquire or to his order for the use of the Continental Frigate the Raleigh now at Portsmouth, and we request that you will render him or his Agents all the assistance in your power in transporting the said Cannon to Portsmouth in the most safe and expeditious manner.[1] Mr Langdon has said nothing about Shot or other stores, but as it is our business to consider and attend to the Continental Interest at large abstracted from Jarring Interest or Jealousey of one State against another we likewise desire you may Supply Mr Langdon with Shott or any other Stores you have provided for the Continental service provided he wants them to expedite the Sailing of the Raleigh which is now under Orders for immediate service. We also inform you that we shall send an Agent[2] to inspect the state of the Frigates built under your direction that we may include them in our intended report to Congress.

We are Gentlemen, Your obedt servants

LB (DNA: PCC Miscellaneous Papers, Marine Committee Letter Book). Addressed: "To the Committee for building Continental Frigates at Providence."

[1] The committee's order was written this day in the form of a separate letter to the frigate committee and reads as follows: "We the Subscribers Members of the Marine Committee of Congress being duely authorized to give such directions as may conduce to the Service of the United States of America in all things relative to this department, are now of opinion that a Compleat Set of the Cannon you have had Cast for the Continental Service ought to be applied to the immediate use of the Raleigh Frigate and therefore do order and direct that you deliver

a Sufficient number of the most suitable Cannon for that Ship to John Langdon Esquire or to his Agent employed for the purpose of receiving and forwarding the same to Portsmouth, and for so doing this shall be your warrant." PCC Miscellaneous Papers, Marine Committee Letter Book, fols. 28–29; and Paullin, *Marine Committee Letters,* 1:23–24. Four days later this order was drastically modified. See Marine Committee to the Rhode Island Frigate Committee, October 13, 1776.

    [2] This agent was Capt. Nathaniel Falconer of the Pennsylvania Navy. A letter of this date from the Marine Committee instructing him "to repair to Providence in Rhode Island and there view, examine and inspect two frigates lately built & now lying at that place" is in PCC Miscellaneous Papers, Marine Committee Letter Book, fol. 29, and Paullin, *Marine Committee Letters,* 1:24–25.

Secret Committee to the Massachusetts Council

Gentn.   In Secret Committee. Philadelphia, Octor. 9th. 1776
    Mr. Gerry one of the Delegates from your State having Informed the Congress that the Ten Tons of Salt Petere sent from hence last Winter to be Manufactured into Powder, remains to this day untouched & that the Quantity of this Article now made in Massachusetts rendered that Supply Unnecessary, the Congress thought proper to pass an Order that this Committee should give immediate directions to have the said Ten Tons of Salt Petre sent from your State to Mr. John R Livingston's Powder Mills Situated at or near Pougkeepsie, on the North River Near York Government, as we find it Convenient to keep those Mills constantly employed.[1] They lying between our two Armies are Convenient to Deliver Powder to the Order of the Commanding Generals, and in Obedience to the said Order of Congress we now request the favour of Your Honorable Board to Cause the said Salt Petre to be Immediately sent Away to Mr. Livingston in the Most expeditious & safe Manner. The Charges attending its removal, he will pay. Your Complyance with this request will serve the Public & Oblige, Honorable Gentlemen, Your most Obdt. Servants,

Robt. Morris	Francis Lewis
Richd. H. Lee	Josiah Bartlett

Tr (M–Ar).
    [1] See *JCC,* 5:854. On November 4, 1776, a committee of the Massachusetts General Court reported to the council that the ten tons of saltpetre would be transported to Livingston's mill. Massachusetts Council Minutes, pp. 129–30. DLC(ESR).

Marine Committee to Thomas Godet and Henry Tucker

Gentlemen   October 10th 1776
    We have occasion for a quantity of Salt to cure beef & Pork the ensuing season for the use of our fleet and dont care to buy up what

arrives here transiently as the people are much in want of that article, and would murmer were it to be bought off their hands. We therefore request that you will immediately on receipt of this letter Charter five or Six good fast sailing large Sloops, schooners or Brigantines, and either load them with Salt at Bermudas or send them to Turks Island for it, just as you may find safest and best. Send one of them to Edenton in North Carolina consigned to Messrs. Hewes & Smith, One to Baltimore in Maryland consigned to our order; & the others here addressed to us. Perhaps it may be most prudent to load part in Bermudas and part in Turks Island but our great Object is to get the Salt soon and safe here.

You will Charter these Vessels on the best terms in your power by the month or otherways, have them valued and we agree to insure them for so long as they remain in our Service, and if the terms are reasonable that may probably be a long time. You'l buy the salt as cheap as you can and give them the utmost dispatch or it will be too late for our purpose. We must depend on you to advance the money for the cost of the Salt until we can reimburse you, which shall be done by returning some of these Vessels to you with Cargoes of Provisions and probably a Convoy with them. Should any of the Vessels be taken or lost we will either pay for them in Provisions or undoubted good bills on Europe or the West Indies as may best suit the Owners. We hope you will be able to comply with these orders immediately for which we shall allow you a reasonable Commission. Interest for the advance of your Money and Commissions on the Goods we shall consign you hereafter and for your security we pledge you the faith and Credit of the United States of America being so authorized to do by the Honorable the Continental Congress of which we are members and are Gentlemen, Your very hble servants

P.S. If you cannot send Six send as many vessels as you can short of that Number.

LB (DNA: PCC Miscellaneous Papers, Marine Committee Letter Book). Addressed: "To Messrs. Henry Tucker & Thomas Godet of Somerset, Bermuda."

Marine Committee to Esek Hopkins

Sir,　　　　　　　　　　　　　　　　　　　　October 10th 1776

We learned some time ago with much concern that the expedition we had planned for you to execute woud prove abortive;[1] as the ships had gone out a Cruizing under the Sanction of Governor Trumbulls recommendation, with which we cannot be well satisfied, Altho in this instance we are disposed to pass it by in silence being well convinced both he and the several Captains meant to perform service at a time the Ships were idle. Supposing therefore that you will have been obliged to lay aside the expedition to Newfoundland We now direct that you immediately collect the Alfred, Columbus, Cabbot & Hampden, take them under your command and proceed for Cape Fear in North Carolina where you will find the following Ships of war:

The Falcon of 18 Guns
The Scorpion of 16 Guns &
the Cruizer of 8 Guns & a number of valuable prizes said to be 40 or 50 in Number, and other vessels under their protection the whole of which you will make prize of with ease. We understand they have erected a kind of a fort on Bald head at the entrance of Cape Fear River but it being only manned with a few people from these Ships we expect you will easily reduce it and put the same in possession of the State of North Carolina or dismantle it as may appear best. When you have performed this Service you had best deliver to the Continental Agents there such of your prizes as may sell well or be useful in North Carolina; others you may Convoy into Virginia or this place for we don't recommend your remaining at North Carolina for fear of being blocked up there; perhaps you will receive advice that will render it eligible to proceed farther Southward to rout the enemies ships at South Carolina and Georgia and if that is practicable you have not only our approbation but our Orders for the Attempt.

We hope, Sir, you will not loose one single moment after receipt of this Letter but proceed instantly on this expedition. We are Sir, Your hble servants.

P.S. Should the Cabbot be still on a Cruize or if returned cannot be ready to proceed upon the Above expedition as early as one of the frigates lately launched at Rhode Island, you will proceed with the latter in lieu of the Cabot as soon as she can be prepared for the Sea or you may take both the Cabot and frigate if to be done without delay. We wish your plan for manning this fleet from the State of Rhode Island may prove effectual, and we do in the warmest manner urge you to omit nothing on your part which may tend to promote so important a purpose and which we have most earnestly at heart. The Commissions for the officers of the frigates will be forwarded immediately.[2]

LB (DNA: PCC Miscellaneous Papers, Marine Committee Letter Book).
[1] See Marine Committee to Esek Hopkins, August 22, 1776. Commodore Hopkins' November 3 reply to the committee's present letter is in Morgan, *Naval Documents*, 7:27–28.
[2] The postscript of this letter, signed by eight members of the committee and endorsed by Hopkins' son, is in the Hopkins Papers, RHi. The members signing the postscript were Josiah Bartlett, William Ellery, John Hancock, William Hooper, Richard Henry Lee, Thomas McKean, Arthur Middleton, and Robert

Morris. The endorsement reads: "Just Recd. Honourd sir Have Taken the Liberty to open it and Find That it Should be Forwarded Immediately. Have Sealed and Dispatch it. Our Ship is all Ready but maning. Your Dutifull Son, J. B. Hopkins."

William Williams to Joseph Trumbull

Dear Sir   Philadelphia Octo. 10 1776

I inclose You a Resolution, brot in among others, by the New York Comte & yesterday pasd, not without opposition.[1] I suppose however the President has sent it, but not being certain, & knowing it of importance, think it my Duty to inform you of it, lest it shod escape Him.

There was also a Resolve pasd same Time that for the preservation of the Health &c of the army, the Comissa. Genl. be directed to purchase & have suffecient Quantitys of Indian Meal & Vegetables, or to that purpose. It was a good deal urged, that the Words Pease, Beens &c shod be inserted, but it was said they were included in Vegetables, & it pasd as drawn.

I shod suppose you cannot employ a better Person to import Salt than Colo Jaz Huntington, & perhaps He alone is quite sufficient.

The affair you mention is not yet moved &c. Our Club meets this Evening. I intend to sound them, & prepare the Matter as well & soon may be.

You have doubtless heard of a addition of 50 per Cent made to the Wages of the officers from Colo to Ensn, Adj, Quar. Mastr.[2] Adjuts stand as established a little before, viz the Pay & Rations of a Capt & rank of 1st Leiuts. Since that, on an exceeding, most laborious & warmly spirited Debate that ever I was Witness to, they have added, an annual Suit of Cloaths to the non Com. officers & Soldiers to the value & amount of twenty Dollars, & the man procuring a Certificate from his Capt that He is provided with the enumerated Articles will be entitled to the 20 Dols in Cash. This is the very utmost that can possibly be obtained & certainly is as much as can be reasonably wished or desired, & I am sure it is a very large & sufficient Encouragemt, & as much as it is possible for the Continent to support. New England pressed it to the utmost of their Power & were but just able to carry it, but they wod not wish to add another farthing.

To save great Delay & Inconvenience, a Resolve is also pasd recomending it all the States from this to N. H. inclusive forthwith to send a Comtee or Deputies to each of the Camps, to appoint all the officers &c & to consult the Genl Officers abt it & promote & appoint such as have recomended them selves by their good Conduct & espcially their Attention to Discipline &c. The Express with these

Resolves goes eastward this Day. The additional Bounty to the Soldiers cod never have been carried but by a Letter, from Gen Washingn recomendg & inforcing the reasonableness & absolute Necessity of it in Terms moving pathatic, rational & nervous, exceedly so, which came in not an hour before the same question wod have been irreversibly negatived.[3]

I hope things will be assured happily. We have many Difficulties to encounter, but our Encouragements are very great. Let Us trust in God alone, & earnestly look to him for his Blessing & Protection.

I am Dr Sir your most Affecte Friend & Brother,

Wm Williams

[*P.S.*] I wish you wod caution Col Dyer &c abt whom they send for a Comte to settle the officers. It must be soon if ever the Assembly is setting.[4]

RC (CtHi).
[1] Undoubtedly the resolution empowering the commissary general to employ persons to import salt, which had been recommended by the committee on the state of the army at New York. *JCC*, 6:859.
[2] See *JCC*, 5:853.
[3] The resolves recommending that state committees be sent to the camps and establishing a clothing bounty were passed in Congress on October 8. *JCC*, 5:854–55. Washington's October 4 letter, which was read on the eighth, is in PCC, item 152, 3:103–9, and Washington, *Writings* (Fitzpatrick), 6:152–56.
[4] For the composition of the committee appointed by the Connecticut Assembly for this purpose, see *A Historical Collection, from Official Records, Files, &c., of the Part Sustained by Connecticut, during the War of the Revolution*, comp. Royal R. Hinman (Hartford: E. Gleason, 1842), p. 240.

John Adams to Abigail Adams

Philadelphia Octr. 11. 1776

I suppose your Ladyship has been in the Twitters, for some Time past, because you have not received a Letter by every Post, as you used to do. But I am coming to make my Apology in Person. I, Yesterday asked and obtained Leave of Absence. It will take me till next Monday, to get ready, to finish off a few Remnants of public Business, and to put my private Affairs in proper Order. On the 14th day of October, I shall get away, perhaps. But I don't expect to reach Home, in less than a fortnight, perhaps not in three Weeks, as I shall be obliged to make stops by the Way.[1]

RC (MHi). Adams, *Family Correspondence* (Butterfield), 2:141.
[1] The journals do not record any vote on Adams' "leave of Absence," but according to his diary he left Philadelphia on October 13. Adams, *Diary* (Butterfield), 2:251.

Committee on Clothing to Nicholas Cooke

Sir,   Philadelphia Oct. 11th. 1776
Congress being earnestly engaged to make the best Provision in their Power for cloathing the Troops particularly those who enlist into the new Army, have passed the inclosed Resolve; [1] And the Committee being of Opinion that the Assembly of your State can direct the Execution of this Matter more effectually than they can, request you to apply to the Assembly of your State to appoint the most suitable Persons to transact this Business with all possible Dispatch, and upon letting us know what Sums of Money you may be able to lay out it shall be sent you.[2]

We are with great Respect Your Honours most obedient humble Servants,

Rob Treat Paine	Jno Witherspoon
Wm. Williams	John Penn
G. Wythe	Josiah Bartlett
Lyman Hall	T. Stone
	Wm Ellery

RC (R–Ar). Written by Ellery and signed by Ellery, Bartlett, Hall, Paine, Penn, Stone, Williams, Witherspoon, and Wythe. Addressed: "To The Honorable Nicholas Cooke Esqr., Governor of the State of Rhode–Island and Providence–Plantations."

[1] See *JCC*, 5:820–21.

[2] On October 10 the committee on clothing had sent the same letter to the Massachusetts General Court. American Revolution Letterbook, M–Ar.

William Ellery to Nicholas Cooke

Sir,   Philadelphia Oct. 11th. 1776.
The President of Congress hath sent you, by Express, all the Resolves which have passed since my last, which he had in Charge to communicate to you. You will receive by this Post a Letter from the Committee to procure Cloathing for the Army inclosing Two Resolves of Congress on that Subject. I hope the Genl. Assembly will take effectual Care that our Quota of new Levies shall be in the Field in Season, well equipped at all Points and well officered: and that suitable Persons in each County be appointed to collect Cloathing immediately, agreeable to the Request of the aforesaid Committee.

A naval Expedition is on Foot, which if carried into Execution will be very advantageous to the United States, and to the Officers and Seamen in the Navy. If the Cabot should not be in Port the

Marine Committee have ordered that One of the Frigates should be employed in it. Commodore Hopkins in a Letter to that Committee hath informed them, that One of the Frigates could soon be got ready, and intimated that he could mann her with Draughts from our Troops. I hope that the Genl. Assembly will countenance this Measure, and give every other Assistance in their Power to forward the sailing of the Fleet.[1]

On the 6th Instant G[enera]l Lee arrived here, and on the 8th sat out for the Camp on the Heights of Harlem. He brings the good News, that the Carolinians had utterly defeated the Cherokee Tribe of Indians, had burnt their Towns, killed 250 of their Warriours, got 75 Scalps, and that the Remainder of that Tribe had fled to the Mississippi. This Expedition, the Sickliness of the Troops, and the strong Garrison at Augustine had prevented an attempt upon East-Florida. That the Garrison at Augustine consisted of 1800 German & 1000 Brith. Troops. That the Sphinx and Raven were at Georgia, and that the Govt. of the State had ordered all the Stock on the Islands on that Coast to be moved off, to prevent its falling into the Hands of the Enemy. The Scorpion, Falcon & Cruiser are at Cape Fear.

The Committee have not returned from Ticonderoga. By the last Accounts from thence, They expected to be attacked very soon and were preparing to give the Enemy a proper Reception.

I saw General Mifflin lately and he informed that in the Fight, the Day after the Enemy took Possession of New York, by the best Account he could get and from the Appearance of the Field of Battle, they lost between four and five hundred killed and wounded, and that We lost about 100 killed and wounded. In the first Part of this Account David Hopkins, Son of the Minister in Newport, who saw the Fight agrees with the General, but says that he saw our killed and wounded and that they were much short of that Number. They both Two agree that some of our Men who had behaved shamefully the Day before, fought gallantly then, and that with equal Numbers We drove the Enemy from the Field. I believe they think the Americans will fight notwithstanding we have retreated and retreated. Genl. Washington as I am told played off a pretty Manœuvre the other Day. Determined to remove the Grain and the Furniture of the Houses from Harlem, he drew out into the Field a Party of 1700. The Enemy turned out as many. They approached within 300 yds. and looked at each other. While they were thus opposed Front to Front, our Waggons carried off the Grain and Furniture. When this was accomplished both Parties retired within their Lines. It is said that our Men preserved very good Faces. It would be of Use to draw out our Men in Battle Array frequently, to let them look the Enemy in the Face, and have frequent Skirmishes with them.

Genl. Washington in a Letter of the 8th Instant inform'd Congress that 2 forty Gun, and One Twenty Gun Ship with some Tenders had passed the Cheveaux de Frise, and Fort Washington without Interruption or Damage and were between the latter and Fort Constitution. How the Cheveaux de frise came to be insufficient I know not; but I am afraid that the Enemy's Ships will cut off the Communication by the North River.[2]

Thus, Sir, I have given you all the News I can recollect, with a few Observations. I wish I had more, I mean good News to communicate; for it would give me great Pleasure to gratify the Assembly. Whenever I shall receive any Intelligence that is well authenticated and I can be at Liberty to transmit it, you may depend upon having it. I continue to be with great Respect, Your Honor's and the States sincere Friend and humble Servant,   Wm Ellery

RC (R–Ar).
[1] See Marine Committee to Esek Hopkins, October 10, 1776. See also Esek Hopkins to the Marine Committee, September 30, 1776, in Morgan, *Naval Documents*, 6:1055–56. Ellery became a member of the Marine Committee on October 11, replacing fellow Rhode Island delegate Stephen Hopkins. *JCC*, 6:869.
[2] This letter is in PCC, item 152, 3:139–42, and Washington, *Writings* (Fitzpatrick), 6:182–85.

Richard Henry Lee to Samuel Purviance, Jr.

Dear Sir,   Philadelphia 11th October 1776
Among the inconveniences of this busy scene, I esteem it not the least, to be so often prevented from acknowledging the favors of my friends sooner than I do. It has been owing to much business that your letter of the 27th has not received an answer before now. I have the pleasure to acquaint you that in ranking the Captains of our Continental Ships, the Congress have placed Captain Nicholson at the head, he being the first Captain.[1] I wish it were in my power to give you a satisfactory answer about the building another Frigate.[2] Hitherto nothing has been determined on this subject, the Committee having been prevented by an infinite multiplicity of other business; and to the same cause has it owing that no orders have been sent concerning the Frigate Virginia. I have no doubt but that another Frigate will soon be directed, and that the Builder of greatest merit will be prefer'd. It would give me the greatest pleasure to hear that the Virginia was ready for Sea, and I am happy in being satisfied that the Managers of this business in Baltimore will not loose a moment in effecting so salutary a work. I suppose a want of Anchors will be the greatest obstruction, as I take it for granted no time will be lost in getting the guns down from Mr. Hughes's works, and having the Carriages made. I shall be glad to have an exact

state of the Frigate & what she wants to complete her. I refer you to the papers for news and am Sir Your most obedient Servant,

Richard Henry Lee

RC (MdHi).
  [1] See *JCC*, 6:861.
  [2] See Lee to Purviance, November 24, 1776.

Benjamin Rush to the Pennsylvania Council of Safety

Sir,   Friday [October 11, 1776]
The congress have ordered the board of war to confer with a committee of the council of Safety of Pennsylvania (agreeable to their request) upon the propriety of having a few battallions Stationed in or near this city.[1] The board of war will set this morning at 9 oClock at the War Office at which time & place they expect the pleasure of meeting your committee. I beg leave to inform the council that such information was given yesterday in Congress respecting the designs of our enemies against this city, as makes the delay of a single day, or even an hour dangerous. I have the honor to be sir with great respect your most humble servant.   B. Rush

RC (PHi). Addressed: "The Honble. Thomas Wharton Esqr., President of the Council of Safety."
  [1] For Congress' resolution of October 10 on this subject, see *JCC*, 6:863.

Marine Committee to the New York Convention

Gentlemen   October 9th [*i.e.* 12] 1776 [1]
Having received information that some of the enemies Ships of war and Tenders have passed the obstructions laid in Hudsons River, and got above the same, we are very anxious for the fate of the Frigates now building in your State. We therefore earnestly desire to direct your close attention to some probable means of securing the said Ships; either by launching them immediately, if possible, and removing them to some place of greater Safety, or by such other Methods as your wisdom shall devise.

With great respect, We are Gentn, Your very hble servants

LB (DNA: PCC Miscellaneous Papers, Marine Committee Letter Book).
  [1] There are compelling reasons for believing that this letter—although clearly dated October 9 and located in the Marine Committee letterbook before other letters composed on October 10—was actually written on October 12. The "enemies Ships" mentioned below did not sail up the Hudson past American "obstructions" until October 9, and Congress did not learn of this event until October 11.

JCC, 6:866; and Washington, *Writings* (Fitzpatrick), 6:184. Furthermore, on October 19 the New York Committee of Safety, which was sitting in place of the convention, received a letter from the Marine Committee "dated the 12th instant . . . relative to the safety of the Continental ships building at Poughkeepsie," a description perfectly fitting this letter dated October 9 in the Marine Committee letterbook. *Am. Archives*, 5th ser. 3:259.

For the reaction in New York to this letter, see ibid., pp. 259, 275; and Morgan, *Naval Documents*, 6:1435.

Marine Committee to Nathaniel Falconer

Sir   October 13th 1776.

We are in great want of Coals to make anchors and other Smith work for the frigates here, and as you are going on public business into the states of Connecticut, Rhode Island, Massachusets & New Hampshire you may probably meet with some Coals fit for Smiths use, that have been or may be taken on board some of the Prizes sent into those places.[1] Should that happen we request you will purchase as many as will load two schooners or sloops and send them to us immediately. For this purpose we desire you will buy two fast Sailing Marblehead schooners or Sloops that will sail and carry well, buy them cheap as possible and if you get coals send them here directly. If you get the Schooners but cannot get the Coals, then put some salt, Sugars, or rum on board as much in value as you think will pay for a load of Coals for each at about 2/ per bushel and dispatch them with the same immediately for James's River Virginia consigned to the Honble Benjamin Harrison Esqr. inclosing him an Invoice of the Goods you send and advising him to sell those goods and load the Vessel with coals immediately dispatching the same to us.

You will take care to procure active good Masters, Mates and Men, and manage the whole to the best advantage for the public and as you have this and other business to transact we deliver you herewith Four thousand Dollars for which you are to account on your return. We also give you letters of Credit & recommendation to the Continental Agents in each State and a warrant authorizing you to Survey the Continental Frigates at Rhode Island, [2] but since this was agreed to, we have heard those frigates are compleated and ready for the sea which we hope may be true.

We are sir, Your very hble servants

LB (DNA: PCC Miscellaneous Papers, Marine Committee Letter Book).

[1] See Marine Committee to the Rhode Island Frigate Committee, October 9, 1776, note 2.

[2] For the Marine Committee's brief circular letter of this date to the Continental prize agents in New England, requesting them to provide assistance to Falconer if called upon, see PCC Miscellaneous Papers, Marine Committee Letter Book, fol. 33; and Paullin, *Marine Committee Letters*, 1:32.

Marine Committee to John Langdon

Sir   October 13th. 1776

Since sending you our order of the 9th instant we are well informed that the Frigates at Rhode Island are ready for sea and if that is really the case it would be improper to strip them of the Cannon to send them to you.[1] We have now wrote the Committee to keep their Cannon if their Ships are actually fit for service, for we did not mean by the former order to give a preference, it was our design only to prevent the Guns from lying useless there when you wanted them but we desire them to tell us whether they will not cast another set and on what terms.

We are Sir, Your hble servants

LB (DNA: PCC Miscellaneous Papers, Marine Committee Letter Book).
[1] See the Marine Committee's letters to Langdon and to the Rhode Island Frigate Committee, October 9, 1776.

Marine Committee to the
Rhode Island Frigate Committee

Gentlemen   October 13th 1776

We fear our Orders of the 9th Instant for sending a Set of Cannon from your State to New Hampshire may not be so proper as we thought them at the time of Signing, because we are since informed through several Channels [the frigates] are quite or very near fit for the Sea, which is a very different Account from that which caused us to send that order.[1] Therefore to prevent inconvenience or disadvantage to the public Service we dispatch this immediately after the other and desire you may not forward the said Cannon to Portsmouth if your Ships are actually ready for service, for our view is only to get such of the frigates as are ready into action, and it matters not to us whether it be yours or the New Hampshire frigate that goes first, but you will still answer what we have said to Governor Hopkins respecting Cannon. We are Gentlemen, Your hble servants

LB (DNA: PCC Miscellaneous Papers, Marine Committee Letter Book).
[1] See Marine Committee to the Rhode Island Frigate Committee, October 9, 1776.

Secret Committee Minutes of Proceedings

Octr. 13. 1776.

Come. met. Present Messrs. Morris, Col. Lee, Lewis, McKean, Livingston, Bartlett. The Come. agreable to orders of Congress[1] having taken into consideration how to make the best disposition of

the Cargo lately arrived at Providence R.I. in the Brige. Happy
Return, Capt. Gid[eo]n Crawford, think proper to report that in
their opinion it will [be] most for the benefit of the public service to
enclose a copy of the Invoice of the Cloths & blankets to Genl. Mifflin
with an order to Messrs Brownes of R. Island, to deliver the whole to
his order, & that it be recommended to the sd. Q.M. General to have
the Cloths immediately made up for the Soldiers either in R.I.,
Connecticut or by the Taylors in the Army, as may be thought best
by Genl. Washington & himself.

That Messrs. Browns be directed to deliver to the Contl. Agent at
R. Island the remaing. part of the Cargo with orders to apply the
lead, bullets, flints, muskets & powder, to the use of the Contl.
frigates & Cruisers, or such part thereof, as may be wanted for that
service, & the rest to remain for future orders.

That sd. Agent be directed to buy as much good fat beef & pork,
as can be cured by the Salt in his possession for the use of the Army
& navy.

That sd. Agent be directed to forward the Sulphur of sd Cargo, &
5 tons Saltpetre formerly sent by Congress, from Philadela. to Rhode
Island, from thence to the powdr. Mills of Messrs. Livingston &
Wisner, on the N. River, State of N. York, to be manufacturd into
powdr. for the Continental Service.[2]

The Come. have agreed with Tho. Yorke for the hire of his Brign
Hetty, at 6. 10. per ton & to insure sd. vessel for the voyage valued
at £1300 curry.

MS (MH–H).
    [1] See JCC, 6:866.
    [2] Although the committee wrote letters to the Browns and to General Mifflin
this day, this report was not actually approved by Congress until October 15.
JCC, 6:878–79.

Secret Committee to Nicholas and John Brown

Gentlemen   In Secret Committee. Philada. October 13th 1776
    Your favour of the 1st instant[1] afforded us much pleasure but we
hope you have not delivered any of the Goods as you mentioned, for
this Congress will order a distribution as they think most for the
publick Service. It is their Orders that you deliver the whole of the
Cloths and Blankets to the order of Brigdr. Genl. Mifflin the Qr
Master General for the use of the Army, and you'l please to comply
therewith transmitting us the Receipts of his Agents for what you
deliver. Should he direct the Cloth or any part of it to be made up at
your place we hope he will have your assistance or Mr Tillinghasts

if asked, and we will write you further respecting the other goods very Soon, being Sir, Your Obedt Servts,

        Robt Morris   Tho M:Kean

        Josiah Bartlett   Richard Henry Lee

RC (RPJCB). In a clerical hand and signed by Bartlett, Lee, McKean, and Morris.
    [1] The Browns' October 1 letter to the Secret Committee is in Morgan, *Naval Documents*, 6:1078–79.

Secret Committee to Thomas Mifflin

Sir,   In Secret Committee Philada. October 13th 1776
    We have the pleasure to inclose you herein an Invoice of Some Cloths and Blankets lately imported into Rhode Island on Continental account and the Congress have directed the whole to be applyed to the use of the Army, wherefore we also inclose herein an Order to Messrs. Nicholas & John Brown in whose care they are to deliver them to your Order.
    It is recommended to you by Congress to have the Cloths made up immediately into Soldiers Cloaths and you will consider whether it may be best to have them made in Rhode Island & Connecticut or by the Taylors in the Army or whether it may be best to employ all the Taylors at each place. We expect you can get Thread, Buttons, &c at Rh. Island, Connecticut or New York Government, respecting which you'l give the needfull Orders. Be pleased to lay these papers before his Excellency and consult him thereon. Colo Moylan Sometime Since wrote Us that 1200 Tents were wanting for the Army, [1] we ordered 600 from hence by Mr Mease and 600 from Danl Tillinghast Esqr. Continental Agent at Rhode Island and Nath Shaw junr. Esqr. Agent at New London. The later had not much of the Materials but the other had. If they are not come to Camp you'l write for them, and we hope it will not be long before we give you considerable Supplys of Cloathing, Tents, Arms and Ammunition, our prospects of obtaining in plenty being greatly Mended, which you'l please to communicate to the General with our warmest wishes for his and your Success & happiness. Very respectfully We remain, Sir, Your Obedt Servts,

        Robt Morris   Tho M:Kean

        Josiah Bartlett   Richard Henry Lee

RC (DLC). In a clerical hand, and signed by Bartlett, Lee, McKean, and Morris.
    [1] Stephen Moylan's September 6 letter to President Hancock in in *Am. Archives*, 5th ser. 2:197.

Richard Stockton to Benjamin Rush

My dear Sir,   Albany Octr. 13th 1776
   We arrived here the night before last, after a very fatiguing
journey, over the worst roads I ever passed in my life.[1] We tho't it
indispensibly necessary to the execution of the business, with which
we were intrusted, to see Mr Trumbull the Commissary Genl. and
therefore we took Head Quarters in our way, and spent an evening
and morning in conversation with the Commissary; from whom we
recd. much information. Yesterday we spent chiefly with Genl.
Schuyler and we hope that from the additional lights we shall receive
from him, Genl. Gates, and an actual inspection into the state of the
nothern Army, we shall be able to answer the reasonable expectations of Congress, and the public in this laborious service. In this
place we have met with a return of Provisions at Ticonderoga & Fort
George made the 28th of last month, and are happy in finding that
they are much better supplied with the smaller necessaries of *indian
meal, molasses* &c than we feared. They have also already had several
hundred Sheep driven up, and more are on the way. The return I
have mentioned as on 28th of Septr. is said to be sufficient for 40 days
from that time. The accts. from Genl Gates, just recd. here, are very
favorable; and his force upon the Lake is said to be superior to the
Enemy, notwithstanding what has been reported as from our officers
lately arrived with you from Canada. The Article most immediately
necessary for this Army is *cloathing*; and I hope that the Committee
of Congress lately appointed for purchasing Cloathing in the several
states will suffer no time to be lost in executing this very important
business. Shoes and Stockings shou'd first be procured, and I flatter
myself that if nearly the same mode should be adopted in the other
states, as that I was enabled to set on foot in New Jersey, it would be
found the most efficacious.[2] The building of Barracks for the Nothern Army must be immediately set about. Genl. Schuyler mentioned
Nails as the principal article which would be wanting. I have suggested to him the substitute of *half inch white oak pins* with which
I know a good House was built in New Jersey. He has fallen in with
the Idea very fully, and is determined to make the experiment. I am
perswaded that if Nails could be purchased (which is not the case)
yet the enormous price which must be given for them will make *pins*
infinitely the most eligible, as I am perfectly assured that they will
answer, and save the Continent many thousand of pounds. I am
much used to building, and think myself as good a judge as any man.
You will have recd. eer this, an acct. of three of the Enemies Ships
having again passed up the North river our *Chevaux de frise* notwithstanding. I greatly fear their landing above our Army; in which
case the numerous Tories in the county of Dutchess in this Province,
will join them. Notwithstanding my great fatigue I am, thank God,

in good health. We propose to sett off in the morning for Saratoga and from thence to Ticonderoga, where we expect to be by the middle of the week. The ground is hard frozen here this morning. My love to my dear Julia, and be assured of the constant affection of your's forever,   Richd Stockton

RC (MdHi: William Middendorf deposit, 1972).
[1] See John Hancock to Philip Schuyler, September 27, 1776, note 4.
[2] See Stockton to Robert Treat Paine, October 1, 1776, note 1.

Josiah Bartlett to John Langdon

Dear Sir,   Philadelphia Oct 15th 1776.

As I rec'd no letter from Col Whipple or you last week, I am in hopes he is on the road here and will bring your letter with him. I wait with some impatience for his return as it is very hard for one delegate to constantly attend Congress and the several Committees where one delegate is appointed from each State, especially if unwell, as has been my case for some time past; however I am now much better and hope to be able to ride home in a short time on horse back.[1]

Yesterday the Committee appointed to hear the appeal from the Maritime Court in New Hampshire concerning the Elizabeth made their report which was accepted; they have reversed the sentence of our Court and have ordered a salvage of one tenth part to be paid by the Claimants as she did not come under the order of Congress of November and December last. Afterwards the Congress by a vote gave up to the said claimants their share of the said tenth, so that they will have but one twentieth part to pay, beside the costs.[2]

The same Committee have had Mr. Sheafe's petition under their consideration but have made no report. By what I have conversed with them, I believe they will not think themselves authorized to do anything in that affair as there is no appeal from the Court to the Congress and the opposite party not present to be heard in the case and nothing but the Petition without anything more before them. They all say the case appears to be hard but know not how to remedy it without more proofs than they have at present and without the opposite party being heard and the case brought properly before them.[3]

Before this reaches you, you will see the several Orders of the Marine Committee about guns for your ship and the reason of those orders. The rank of the Captains is settled. Capt Thompson is the Sixth. Capt Manly is uneasy at his being the 3d and has desired leave to Resign; whether his resignation will be accepted or his rank altered I am uncertain.[4]

Captains Manly and Roche are got pretty hearty again as to their health. As to news you will see what is passing here by the inclosed paper. By letters from France of the 3d of August we have some favorable advices.

In haste my Friends. Adieu.   Josiah Bartlett

Tr (DLC).

[1] Bartlett reported substantially the same news in a letter to his wife, Mary, this date. "I find I gain Strength, so that if I have no relapse I hope I shall be able in about a fortnight to set out for home provided my Colleagues arrive here soon." Watt Collection, NhHi.

[2] This report is in *JCC*, 6:870–73. See also, *JCC*, 5:835.

[3] Jacob Sheafe's petition had been referred on October 5 to the same committee that heard the case of the *Elizabeth*, but there is no record in the journals that any further action was taken. *JCC*, 5:848.

[4] For the seniority list of Continental Navy captains, adopted on October 10, see *JCC*, 6:861.

Board of War to George Washington

Sir   War Office October 15th. 1776

The Board of War have endeavoured to form an exact Acct. of Ordinance Stores, in the several Departments, as well as of those in the Magazine under their immediate Notice here. But from the Want of accurate Returns they have not yet been enabled to accomplish their Design. If these Returns were made monthly the Board would be enabled in some degree to anticipate the Wants of Ammunition in the Army and keep up the supply as far as may be in their Power. I have it in Direction to request your Excellency will order a Return to be forthwith made of all Ordinance Stores in your Department and that you would be pleased to direct as exact Returns to be made monthly as the situation of the Army will admit.[1] As well as Accounts of the Men, as to their Numbers and Capacity to do Duty, Returns should, if possible, be made of their Arms & Accoutriments & also of the Rations drawn from the Commissary of Provisions as it has been said that Regiments not half full draw their Rations as if they were complete; with how much justice this has been said cannot be clearly known but if monthly Returns were made from the Commissaries Office of the Rations drawn by each Regiment, the Returns from the Adjutant General would shew whether they had exceeded in their Number of Rations what they were justly ent'tled to. A List of the Army is making out wherein at one View every thing relating will be seen. But the Fluctuating State of the Army has prevented that Accuracy which it is hoped will be shewn in the Military Affairs of the Continent when they shall, by the new Establishment, be put upon a more permanent, & of Course a more respectable Footing.

I have the Honour to be with the greatest Respect, Your very obedt, humble Servant,   Richard Peters Secy

RC (DLC). In a clerical hand and signed by Peters.

[1] "In respect to your requisition for an immediate return of ordnance stores," Washington's secretary, Robert H. Harrison, wrote the Board on October 22, "his Excellency says it cannot possibly be compiled with in the present unsettled state of the army." *Am. Archives*, 5th ser. 2:1187.

For another document pertaining to an issue that came before the board periodically, the management of prisoners of war, see also ibid., p. 956.

William Floyd to the
New York Committee of Safety

Gentlemen   Head Quarters at Harlem. October 15, 1776

Inclosed I Send you Some Resolves of Congress, with a news paper agreable to your Desire.[1] I yesterday Sent you by Mr. Wisner ten thousand Dollars for the purpose of paying for the Blankets and Cloathing to be purchased in this State; all which I hope will come Safe to hand.[2]

I am now going to try to get off Some of my Effects from the Island if it is possible and Shall be absent from Congress a few Days. I beg you would Excuse me as it is the first time I have absented my Self; But it happens at a time when no Important matter was like to Come before us.[3]

I am Gentlemen with the greatest Esteem, Your most Obedt. Servt.   Wm Floyd

RC (N).

[1] These "Resolves" have not been identified. However, on October 11 Floyd had written a letter to the committee of safety from Washington's headquarters at Harlem "enclosing two Resolutions of Congress, the one relating to General Schuyler, the other respecting Clothing for the Troops." *Am. Archives*, 5th ser. 3:244. This letter has not been found, but for the resolves in question see *JCC*, 5:841, 855. The "news paper" which Floyd sent to the committee was probably the October 5 issue of the *Pennsylvania Ledger*, on the significance of which see New York Delegates to the New York Convention, October 7, 1776, note 3.

[2] See the letter of October 7 from the committee on clothing, of which Floyd was a member, to the New York Convention, printed above.

[3] Evidently Floyd was occupied for the remainder of this month in helping his family to move from their Suffolk County home to Connecticut in order to escape the British occupation of Long Island. William Q. Maxwell, *A Portrait of William Floyd, Long Islander* (Setauket, N.Y.: Society for the Preservation of Long Island Antiquities, 1956), pp. 20–21. Floyd's account with the New York Convention shows that he was paid $676 "for Expenses in attending the Continental Congress from 23 of April 1776 to the 8 October 1776 Inclusive" and $140 for the period "from 14 Novr. 1776 to the 18 Decr 1776 Inclusive." See William Floyd, Account with the New York Convention, April 30, 1777, Emmet Collection, NN. A business letter from Floyd to Peter Lyon of Virginia, written in Philadelphia on November 18 and dealing with "the Administration on the

Northward estate of Mr. Smith," is in the possession of Ronald von Klaussen (state of Florida, 1976).

Benjamin Franklin to Robert Erskine

Sir   Philade. Oct. 16. 76
    I should sooner have acknowledged your Favour of Aug. 16 containing the Drawing of your Chevaux de Frise,[1] but that I have been so extreamly occupy'd as to be oblig'd to postpone writing to many of my Correspondents.
    Please to accept my Thanks for the Communication of your Contrivance, which I am persuaded will answer the Purpose where ever the Bottom is so hard as to prevent the Points being press'd into the Ground by the passing Ship before the Resistance shall become great enough to force the upper Points thro' her Bottom. The Ground being soft in our Channel, we were oblig'd to fix our pointed Beams to a Floor, in the Chevaux we plac'd there during the Summer of the preceding Year. That Floor gives them so firm a Stand, that all the Vessels which thro' Inadvertance have run upon them, have had such Breaches made in their Bottoms as immediately sunk them. One was a large Ship.
    I am, Sir, with great Esteem, Your most obedt., humble Servant,
                                                                    B Franklin

RC (PPAmP).
    [1] Erskine's letter and enclosed drawing, which explained his proposal for building "Marine Chevaux de Frise" consisting of Beams "12 or 15 inches square" and 32 feet long capable of obstructing navigation in river channels up to seven fathoms deep, are in the Franklin Papers, PPAmP. Erskine (1735–80), Scottish geographer, hydraulic engineer, and fellow of the Royal Society, had emigrated to New Jersey in 1771 to represent investors interested in developing iron mines in Passaic County. Sympathetic with the American cause, he became a captain in the Bergen County militia in 1775, and in July 1777 was appointed "geographer and surveyor of the roads" in the Continental Army. *DAB*; and *JCC*, 8:580.

Francis Hopkinson to William Livingston

Dear sir,   Philada 16th Octr 1776
    Agreeable to your Desire I have taken the first Opportunity of forwarding to your Exᵣellency the inclosed Resolves of Congress. I shall move Congress to replenish the Pay Masters Chest to enable him to answer the Draughts which will be made on him in Consequence of the said Resolves.[1]
    With great Respect, I have the Honour to be, Your Excellency's most obedient humble servt.   F. Hopkinson

RC (MHi).
¹ See *JCC*, 6:874–75. The New Jersey delegates secured the passage of these resolves concerning pay for the New Jersey militia in response to Governor Livingston's letter to them of September 19, 1776. William Livingston Papers, MHi.

Elbridge Gerry to Joseph Trumbull

Dear sir   Philadelphia 17th Octr 1776
    I recd your Favours of the 9th & 11th Instant & find by the Journals that the Continental Agents are as follows: John Langdon Esqr. of Portsmouth, John Bradford Boston, Daniel Tillinghast for Rhode [*Island*] but I think John Brown of Providence is Agent for that State, Nathaniel Shaw Jr. for Connecticut & Jacobus Vanzantz for New York.¹ The Resolve for impowering You to import Salt is past & You will probably receive it e'er this.² I agree with You that it is absurd to supply One Army with & the other without a Contract; my Suspicions are confirmed relative to the Rise of a certain Committee, ³ while We were on the Business of the Army. I hope however that the plan will not be carryed. Congress have sent to all the Assemblies for a fuller Representation & on their Return I hope your allowance will be settled. I am glad You discontinue the Thought of giving up your office; such practices in so important a Department may ruin the Cause before We are aware of it. If this should reach You in Connecticut pray give my best Respects to Governor Trumbull, Colo Dyer &c & believe me to be your assured Friend & serv,   E Gerry

RC (CtHi).
    ¹ For the list of Continental prize agents, except for John Brown, who appears not to have received such an appointment, see *JCC*, 4:301, 5:478.
    ² This resolve was passed on October 9. *JCC*, 6:859.
    ³ Perhaps the committee appointed to go to Ticonderoga. See Gerry to Horatio Gates, October 9, 1776.

Marine Committee to John Langdon

Sir   In Marine Committee. Philadelphia October 17th 1776
    Capt. John Roche having laid his plan before Congress they have referred the same to this Committee with power to carry it into Execution, and as we are of opinion the publick Service of America will be promoted by it We hereby authorize and require you to have built with the utmost Expedition a Brigantine calculated for a Vessell of War a fast Sailer and of strong Construction to carry Eighteen Six Pounders and about 120 Men.¹ As both Capt. Roche

and you are well acquainted with Warlike Vessells we think it best to leave the dimensions to be fixed by you with the advice of the Carpenters &ca. We Expect this business will be conducted on the best terms for the Publick Interest and that you will not lose one Moments time untill compleated. You will take proper Measures for procuring Guns and all other Stores necessary and Capt. Roche will attend and assist in this Business. Inform us from time to time what occurs as necessary for us to be acquainted with in this business, and in proper Season we shall direct further what is to be done. You are to pay for this Vessell out of the Continental Share of Prize Money in your Hands.

We are Sir, Your Hb'le Servants,

John Hancock	Wm Ellery
Robt Morris	Saml Huntington
Geo Walton	Richard Henry Lee
Fras. Hopkinson	Will Hooper

RC (MdAN). In a clerical hand and signed by Ellery, Hancock, Hooper, Hopkinson, Huntington, Lee, Morris, and Walton.

[1] See *JCC*, 6:881. Roche was a "Gentleman" from the "West Indies" who had been serving since 1775 as first lieutenant of the *Lynch*, a schooner in Washington's navy, and who had come to Philadelphia with recommendations to several delegates from Langdon. The "plan" Roche submitted to Congress led to the construction of the Continental sloop *Ranger*. See Morgan, *Naval Documents*, 6:161–62, 1051; and Executive Committee to John Hancock, January 25, 1777, note. Langdon's November 6 response to the present letter is in Morgan, *Naval Documents*, 7:58–59.

Marine Committee to Isaiah Robinson

Sir   October 17th 1776

The Honorable the Congress having ordered that you should make a voyage under direction of the Secret Committee therefore you will receive their Instructions and comply with them. Those fulfilled, you must give us notice that we may again direct your further proceedings, and during your present voyage we expect you will transmit us any useful or important intelligence that comes to your knowledge—that you take good care of the Andrea Doria, her Stores, provisions and materials, that you maintain proper discipline amongst your officers & men at the same time useing them well. We dare say you will treat all such as become your prisoners with tenderness and humanity and on your return lodge Coppies of your log book & Journal in this Office.[1] We are sir, Your most hble servants

LB (DNA: PCC Miscellaneous Papers, Marine Committee Letter Book). Addressed: "Captain Isaiah Robinson of the Brig. Andrea Doria."

[1] The Marine Committee wrote similar letters to Capt. William Hallock of the brig *Lexington* and to Capt. James Robinson of the sloop *Sachem* on October

18. See PCC Miscellaneous Papers, Marine Committee Letter Book, fol. 35; and Paullin, *Marine Committee Letters*, 1:35–36. For the intended destinations of all three vessels, see Secret Committee Minutes of Proceedings, October 18, 1776.

Oliver Wolcott to Laura Wolcott

Philadelphia 17t Octo. 1776. Reports that he still has not recovered his health. "Nothing Material has occurred since my last, all Eyes are turned to N York to see the Events of the Military Operations in that Country. I have a pretty while inclined to the Opinion that Howe would not bring on a decisive Battle. His Design I think of ruining this Country is in a more dilatory Way, and which he imagines will give a greater Probability of success. But I trust and beleive that God will defeat him in his Expectations.

"The Congress have agreed to borrow five Million Dollars for three years at an annual Interest of four per cent.[1] I think they will probably adopt some further Measures, for raising Money.

"Pensylvania is thrown into a good deal of Division on Acco. of the N[ew] Form of Government which you may have seen, as established by their Convention. The Constitution I think is quite imperfect and I beleive will not be adopted. This is Matter of joy to all Torys, whose Spirit of Iniquity now works I suppose everywhere, with uncommon Zeal."

RC (CtHi).
[1] See the resolves of October 3. *JCC*, 5:845–46.

Marine Committee to the Continental Prize Agents

(Circular)

Sir   October 18th 1776

Herein you will find two Resolves of the Continental Congress of which we have the honor to be members, whereby you'l observe you are ordered to Account with us from time to time for the Continental Share of all Prizes received and sold by you as Agent and to pay the amount thereof to our order.[1] In obedience to this Resolve we think proper to lay it down as a Rule, that you State your accounts every three Months crediting therein the Continental Share of every Prize whose accounts can be settled and included within that quarter of a year, and that you add thereto a Schedule containing an exact account of all the prizes that then remain in your care whose accounts are unsettled, and we desire that you will constantly remit us undoubted good bills on this place as you can meet with them which will save the trouble and risque of sending money. In taking drafts prefer those of the Continental Agents, Paymasters & Commissarys to any other provided they are drawn on the President of Congress, this Committee or any other public Board for public Service. Next to these undoubted good private Bills but none others. When neither One or the Other can be met with, inform us and of the sums you have, that we may give particular orders respecting the remittance or application thereof.

By the other Resolve you will find yourself under orders of Congress to make a just distribution amongst the officers and men concerned in taking each Prize as soon after the Sales as possible agreeable to the Rules and Regulations made by Congress in this respect, and it is our duty to see this punctually complied with as the Service has already suffered by delay—therefore you will always make the said distribution soon as can be after the Sale and transmit us duplicates of the accounts and your proceedings therein. We shall allow all your just expenditures on Account of the Continent to be charged against their share of the Prize Money but those charges must be supported by vouchers. We are Sir, Your very hble servants

LB (DNA: PCC Miscellaneous Papers, Marine Committee Letter Book). Addressed: "To John Langdon Esqr. Continental Agent, Portsmouth, New Hampshire. John Bradford Esqr., Boston, Massachusetts. Daniel Tillinghast Esqr., Providence, Rhode Island. Nathl. Shaw jr. Esqr., New London, Connecticut. Jacobus Vantzantz Esqr., New York. John Nixon & John Maxwell Nesbitt Esqrs., Philada., Pennsylvania. William Lux Esqr., Baltimore, Maryland. John Teazwell Esqr., Williamsburg, Virginia. Robert Smith Esqr., Edenton, No. Carolina. Richard Ellis esqr., Newbern, No. Carolina. Corneilus Harnet esqr., Wilmington, No. Carolina. Livinus Clarkson & John Dorsius esqrs., Chs. Town, So. Carolina. John Wereat Esqr., Savannah, Georgia."

[1] See *JCC*, 6:882–83.

Marine Committee to
George Washington's Prize Agents

(Circular)

Sir   October 18th 1776.

We have the honor to inclose herein a Resolve of the Continental Congress of which we are members whereby you will see we are empowered to order a proper and just distribution of all Prizes taken by the Cruizers Genl Washington caused to be fitted out on Continental Account, and also that we are authorized or rather ordered to receive from the Agents who received and sold the said Prizes, the Continental share thereof, [1] and as we find you have been employed as an Agent in this business, we desire that you will immediately send us an Account of the Prizes that have been put under your care, with Coppies of the decrees of the Court of Admiralty, Inventories of Ships and Cargoes with Copys of the Accounts Sales properly

Authenticated, an Account Current for each Prize wherein you Credit the Neat Proceeds, and charge the share appertaining to the officers and Crews who were interested in the Capture and also the Continental Share agreeable to the Rules and Regulations laid down by Congress and a General Account Current wherein you will credit the Continent for their share in every Prize and charge for all such Remittances as you make to us in consequence of these orders as well as for any other just charge you have to make against them. We desire that you will remit to this Board whatever moneys you have in hand arising from the Continental Share of the Prizes put under your management, and as there are many persons gone from hence to purchase prize goods, you may procure drafts on this place from undoubted safe good men which will save the trouble and risque of sending the money, or you may pay it in to the Continental paymaster at Boston Ebenezer Hancock Esqr. and transmit us his draft on the President of Congress, or the Honorable Thomas Cushing Esqr., John Bradford Esqr of Boston or John Langdon Esqr. of New Hampshire have occasion for money on our Account. Their drafts on ourselves will be good and the sooner you make these Remittances and render the Accounts the better. We must also enjoin you to make an immediate division and distribution of that share of Prizes that appertains to the officers and Crews that took them, agreeable to and in strict conformity with the Rules and Regulations of Congress, and that you transmit as soon as can be duplicates of those Accounts as it is our duty to see this business perfected, otherways the maritime service of America will suffer greatly, by the discouragements arising from delays in the payment of Prize money &c. Where any part of the Prizes have been applyed to Continental use, that part must be valued and included at the valuation in the new account of Sales—if applyed to the use of yours or any other State, they must pay the valuation and that be includes in the Acct. Sales. Expecting your complyance with an answer to this Letter We remain sirs, Your Obedient servants

LB (DNA: PCC Miscellaneous Papers, Marine Committee Letter Book). Addressed: "To William Bartlett Esqr. in Beverly. William Watson Esqr. in Plymouth. John Wentworth Esqr. in Plymouth. Wintrop Serjint in Cape Anne. Messrs. Bartlet & Glover in Lynn, Marble Head and Boston. John Bradford Esqr., Boston."

[1] See *JCC*, 6:882–83.

Secret Committee Minutes of Proceedings

Octr. 18, 1776.

Comme met. Present, Mr. Morris, Col. Lee, Messrs. Lewis, Livingston & Bartlett. The follg. letters were wrote & signed by the Come.[1] To Mr. Thos. Morris,[2] now in France, appointg. him general Agent for transactg. the business of this Comme. in Europe. Another Letter to Thomas Morris respectg. the Cargo of the Ship Success, Capt. James Anderson, that now goes consignd to him for sale, on Acct. of the Continent. To Messrs. Plearne & Penet & Co. at Nantes.

Congress have orderd the Marine Come. to put the followg. vessels under the direction of this Come. for this voyage: Brig Andrew Doria, Capt. Josa. [Isaiah] Robinson, Lexington, Capt. Wm. Hallock, Sloop Sachem, Capt. Js. Robinson. Resd. that the follg arrangemt. be made of them, for the purpose of procurg. Supplies for the Army &c: Andrew Doria for St Eustatia, Lexington for Cape Francois, Sachem for Martinico. With orders to the Agents at the different ports to purchase & ship by them all the woollen manufactures, Arms & Ammunition, they can procure with the effects they have on hand or on the credit of these States & shou'd they procure more than the Armd vessels can bring back, then to hire or buy other vessels suitable to bring sd. Articles to America.[3] Agreed That £50 be allowd & paid Mr. Jams. Sterret for services done by his Son Andw. deceased—as Clerk to this Come.

MS (MH–H).

[1] Not found.

[2] A footnote in the copyist's hand keyed at this point reads: "and Partner with his Brother, the Chairman of the Comme. A. Lee." For information on similar footnoted comments pertaining to Robert Morris found in this copy of the committee's "journal," see Secret Committee Minutes of Proceedings, August 8, 1776, note 2.

[3] For a further explanation of why these vessels were being sent to the West Indies, see Committee of Secret Correspondence Statement, October 1, 1776. See also Marine Committee to Isaiah Robinson, October 17; and Secret Committee to William Bingham, October 21, 1776. By mid-January 1777 all three vessels had returned with military supplies. See Robert Morris to John Hancock, December 23, 1776; and Morgan, *Naval Documents*, 7:862, 972.

Secret Committee to Andrew Limozin

Sir   Philada. October 18th 1776

We hope you will in due time receive this by the hands of Capt Thos. Kennedy of the Ship Mary which is now loaden at New London with wheat in the Hold & Flaxseed between Decks.[1] This Cargo is addressed to Mr. Thos. Morris of Philadelphia, but now in France or to his assigns, and as your House is strongly recommended to us by Messrs. Willing, Morris & Compy as very solid, active & well attached to the Interest of this Country, we have desired the said Mr. Thos. Morris to give you the preferrance of our business at Havre de Grace which there is little doubt but he will comply with. We therefore direct Nathl. Shaw Junr Esqr our agent at New London to inclose this letter with the Invoice & bills of Loading for the said Cargo to you and on the Ships arrival you will please to advise Mr. Morris immediately of the Ships arrival & the Contents of the Cargo,

which you will receive out of the Ship with all possible expedition
& shou'd the wheat bear a good price you may proceed in the Sale
of it without waiting an answer from Mr Morris. On the Contrary
if yours be a loosing Market you must keep it untill you hear from
or see him. With respect to the Flaxseed we apprehend it will be
absolutely necessary that you wait his advice & opinion on that
article which we suppose to be a new one from America to your part
of the World, but in Ireland where they have had long experience
of it, they prefer American Seed to that of any other Country and
on tryal your People will find it so. If any Irish Traders are with
you they will soon buy it up on being informed it is not only
American seed, but also from Connecticut which is recokened
amongst the best. You will please to Consult with Mr. Morris as to
the Sales of this Cargo unless you can Sell it to good Proffit & then
you need not wait but you are to Account with him for the Net
proceeds of the Whole Cargo & as the Ship is Chartered to bring out
a Cargo freight Free he will direct you what Goods to ship back by
her, but shou'd you not hear from him in time you may load her
with Coals for Smiths use as we know such can generally be had at
your place or failing thereof you must procure her a Cargo of Salt
at yours or some other Port and pay for what you ship out of the
Net proceeds, then acct with Mr Morris for the ballance, but if he
directs you to ship other & more Valuable Commodities he will
Acct. with you for the same. We beg you will give this Ship all
possible dispatch & render the Captain such assistance as he stands
in need of. You will probably have many Consignments from us &
We are sir, Your obedt hbl servts,

Robt Morris	Josiah Bartlett
Fras. Lewis	Richard Henry Lee
Tho M:Kean	Phil. Livingston

P.S. By Charter party the Freight is to be paid by us at New York
upon our receiving advice of the Cargo being delivered at Havre De
Grace according to Bill Lading, we therefore desire you to supply the
Captain with what money he may want to defray the necessary
expences of his Vessell & transmit us his receipt for the same.

R.M.

F.L.

R.H.L.

RC (CtY). Written by Morris and signed by Morris, Bartlett, Lee, Lewis, Livingston, and McKean. Postscript written by Lewis, except last eight words added by Morris.
¹ The *Mary* was not permitted to sail because of fears that she would be captured by British ships. Her cargo of wheat was eventually landed for use by the Continental Army. See Morgan, *Naval Documents*, 7:155, 169, 220–21, 251–52, 385, 402, 1103.

Josiah Bartlett to John Langdon

Dear Sir   Philadelphia October 19th 1776
   This will be handed you by Capt. Roche who has at length
finished his Business here and got orders for you to Build another
Ship as you will see by the letter from the Marine Committe to
you.[1] After I wrote you last Tuesday I Recd yours of the 30th ulto.
and Desired the Clerk of the Secret & Marine Committee to take out
from the Books the Sums of money you have Recd of Each of those
Committes. The Sum you have Recd of the Secret Committe is
Twenty five Thousand Dollars but the Clerk was so Engaged he
could not give me the other account at this time, will try to Send it
you next week. I Mentioned in the Marine Comitte that you were
Desirous to Know whither you were to allow any Passenger or seaman on board any of the prizes their adventures or private property
more than the wages to the seamen agreable to the resolve of Congress; they informed me they had not given any orders about it, and
that it was not in their power to give any orders Different from the
resolves of Congress yet it seemed to be the Desire of the Committee
that such Passengers & seamen as behaved themselves Decently Should
be Dealt well by, and not Striped of Every thing that might be taken
from them by the rules of war.
   As for news I have none at present to Communicate. We have had
no Certain accounts from our Camp at Harleam Since the 13th.
There are some flying accounts but Capt Roche as he passes that way
will be able to give you a true account of our affairs there. A great
number of foreigners Especially French officers[2] are Daily almost
arriving here & requesting to be employed in our Army, many of
whom are well recommended.
   Col. Whipple is not arrived here yet. I shall look for him every
day now till I see him when I shall return home and after your
example enjoy the pleasure of residing in my own Country in future.
Remember me to all friends and be assured that I am, your affectionate friend,   Josiah Bartlett.

P.S. I am much better in health than I was for four or five weeks.

RC (Facsimile, *Robert F. Batchelder Autographs*, catalog 15, item 74). Tr (DLC).
   [1] See Marine Committee to John Langdon, October 17, 1776.
   [2] Remainder of text taken from Tr.

North Carolina Delegates to the
North Carolina Council of Safety

Gentlemen   Oct 19th 1776 Phila
   This goes with four Waggons charged with different Articles,
agreeable to Invoices inclosed, for the State of North Carolina.[1] The

necessities of our army at Ticonderoga when the Winter makes such early advances, the pressing demands of General Washington from New York with the scarcity of Cloathing here will explain to you the reason of this provision having been so long delayed.

We have agreeable to your advice thought it prudent to purchase rather than hire Waggons and Teams and have been particular in the choice of the horses that you may incur as little loss as possible in the sale of them if you should not think proper to reserve them for continental use. The Waggons are well calculated for our roads as in selecting them we have had an eye principally to make them useful to our troops in their movements, as they are light and not constructed upon so heavy a plan as those made use of in the Eastern states. The prices of the Horses and Waggons are high but considering the vast demand for them for publick use is not excessive.

The proceedings of the Continental Congress since September must be very necessary to assist your deliberations at the next convention. We have therefore sent you 12 Copies of them. You will observe the Apology which the Bookseller makes for packing other Articles with them, as they are such as will be useful to the state, or if not may be sold without loss we have tho't proper to forward them.

As the Waggons will proceed very slowly we shall make use of the post or some conveyance which will reach you before this to write you upon the state of publick affairs and whatever else we may deem interesting to North Carolina.

We are Gentlemen, with great Respect, Your Obed Sevts.

Wm Hooper

[P.S.] We send 200 Copies of the Articles of War.

RC (Nc-Ar). Written and signed by Hooper. Endorsed: "Letter from the Delegates at Phila. October 19th. 1776 containing Invoices for Cloathing &ca."
[1] For the "Invoices inclosed," see N.C. Colonial Records, 10:851–54.

Edward Rutledge to Robert R. Livingston

Philadelphia Octr 19th. 1776

Indeed my dear Robert I feel exceedingly distressed for the unhappy Situation of your Country and readily concur with you in thinking that until it shall be changed for the better you cannot leave it with that Reputation which your Friends must wish you ever to retain. But I must press upon you the necessity of having your State represented in Congress by Men whose Judgment may be depended upon. I wished to have had either Jay or yourself if not both, but since that is impossible cannot you obtain a Resolution from your Convention empowering any two, or one (if two be not present) to represent your State. I know this will appear at first view to be placing too much Confidence in an individual, but it is what has been and now is done by every other State on the Continent, Maryland, Virginia & the Lower Counties (if they can be called a State) excepted. Were you represented, you might frequently prevent Mischief or do good; & as Things are circumstanced it would be impossible for you to do any Injury were your Powers committed to any Hands. This you will readily see when I tell you that the 4 Eastern Colonies & Virginia are always present, and Maryland, the Lower Counties & New York seldom or ever. What has become of General Morris I cannot think.[1] He left us near three weeks since from some Hints which his Friends here took the Liberty of giving him, and declared he would never return until he had conquer'd. Should he be worse than his word & pay us another Visit, I'll answer for him that he will not stay here above two days to rest himself. Indeed I much doubt whether he will be able to call those Days of rest, for I will immediately make a Party to plague his very heart out. Philadelphia shall not be a place of Safety for him I assure you. We all understood him, that he had been sent to Congress by your Convention upon Business of Importance to your State & for a long while wonder'd that he did not disclose it, his Errand remains a Secret to this Hour. I am amazed at Governeur![2] Good God what will mankind come to! Is it not possible to awake him to a sense of his Duty? Has he no one Virtue left that can plead in favour of an oppressed & bleeding Country? Has he no Friendship for those who are standing so opposed as you & Jay are to the attacks of open and secret Enemies? One would think he would find a solid Satisfaction in acting and even suffering with such Men in such a Cause. Does he desire to live for ever in Obscurity, or would he prefer being "dam'd to ever Lasting Fame," to a Life devoted to his Country? Tis a hard case indeed my dear Robert that the Burthen should be cast upon the Sholders of a few—but the Honour will bear a just proportion to the Trouble, & the Reflection of having deserved well of the Community will elevate you I trust beyond the reach of Affliction. I am sorry I cannot explain to you a Passage in my last Letter—that must be left to a better Moment.[3] You may rest satisfied as to the Exertions of the South; & you and your Country may depend upon me as long as I have a shilling or a nerve. They can never be serviceable to better Men than my Friends of New York, nor employed in a better Cause than that in which my Friends are engaged. I wish to God that Hudson's River ran on the other Side of your State & then our Exertions would be more effectual.

I feel for Schuyler's ill usage—but I hope his Love for his Country will silence his Resentment, at least for the present. It was impossible to prevent the Resolutions going as they did & it will I am afraid be long so until Colonies are more regularly represented.[4] I can say nothing as to my own Return to Carolina. It depends upon Circumstances over which I have no Influence. My Intention some time ago was to leave this City about the tenth or 15th Instant, but judging it improper to leave Congress until our Affairs were put in better order than they were at the Time fixed on for my Departure, I have continued to act. Indeed so many Members have moved off in this Day of Danger that I thought it incumbent upon me to stay, lest as you say my Departure might be attributed to unworthy Motives. This is doubly distressing, & you will confess it, when I tell you that Mrs. Rutledge's Situation requires her being at Home amongst her Friends. Your Brother should have been long since appointed to the Command of Clynton's Regiment, but Mr. Phil. Livingston thinking the Congress had no Right to fill up Vacancies after their Resolution of the 16th of Sepr. & that it wd. be interfering in the internal Polity of the State I did not press the Matter, But got the inclosed Resolution pass'd in order to preserve to him his proper Rank.[5] I shall not leave this *before* the 10th of next Month. I am called off & cannot add anything more than that I am what I always shall be yr. most affectionate Friend.   E. Rutledge

P.S. I wish you wd. tell me what you mean when you say that the No. River might be stopt by sinking Blocks. How is it to be done.[6] Remember me to Jay. I shall write him tomorrow.

RC (NHi).

[1] See Lewis Morris to the New York Convention, September 24, 1776, note.

[2] A reference to Gouverneur Morris' absence from the New York Convention, which Morris himself ascribed to "a series of accidents too trifling for recital." *Am. Archives,* 5th ser. 2:1023–24. Rutledge was responding to the harsh appraisal of Morris' behavior contained in Livingston's letter to Rutledge of October 10. Miscellaneous Manuscripts, DLC.

[3] Livingston was disturbed by a passage in Rutledge's October 2 letter to him, which, in Livingston's words, "gives us reasons to imagine that some are ungenerous enough to take advantage of the distresses of this state." Livingston to Rutledge, October 10, 1776, Miscellaneous Manuscripts, DLC.

[4] Schuyler was irritated by Congress' September 25 resolutions creating a committee to journey to Ticonderoga and "consult with the commanding officer in the northern department," because, for reasons that are still difficult to fathom, he persuaded himself that Congress intended this committee to meet only with General Gates. See *JCC,* 5:822–23; and *Am. Archives,* 5th ser. 2:921–22. See also Jonathan G. Rossie, *The Politics of Command in the American Revolution* (Syracuse: Syracuse University Press, 1975), pp. 129–31.

[5] Rutledge is probably referring to the October 10 resolution calling for the making out of new commissions for such Continental officers "who have been appointed in the places of others resigning and promoted." *JCC,* 6:864. On September 16 Congress had resolved that "the appointment of all officers, and filling up vanancies, (except general officers) be left to the governments of the several states." *JCC,* 5:763. See also Livingston to Rutledge, September 27, 1776, Miscellaneous Manuscripts, DLC. In an editorial note to Rutledge's letter, Burnett confused Henry Brockholst Livingston, the son of former New Jersey delegate William Livingston, with Henry Beekman Livingston, the brother of Robert R. Livingston. Burnett, *Letters,* 2:126n.3.

Committee to Ticonderoga to General Gates

Sir: Saratoga, October 20, 1776.

Having been appointed by Congress as a Committee to examine into and transact certain matters relative to the army in the Northern department, and having spent several days with General *Schuyler*, at *Albany* and this place, in execution of part of our commission, we were about to proceed to *Ticonderoga;* but being informed by the General of the great probability of our army being now attacked by the enemy, or that such an event might be hourly expected, we have concluded to wait here until we shall have the pleasure of hearing from you. If the enemy have not yet made their attack, and you think it probable that we may be able to reach *Ticonderoga*, and have an opportunity of conversing with you and the other principal officers of your army, and to inspect into its present state before that event may happen, we shall immediately, upon being advised by you, proceed on our journey.[1]

With great respect, we are, sir, your most obedient and very humble servants,   Rich'd Stockton,

Geo. Clymer.

Reprinted from *Am. Archives*, 5th ser. 2:1142.
[1] Gates wrote to the committee on October 24 advising them to remain at Saratoga until they received further notice. They apparently set out for Ticonderoga on the 30th. See Committee to Ticonderoga to John Hancock, October 26 and November 10, 1776; and *Am. Archives*, 5th ser. 2:1299.

Committee of Secret Correspondence to William Bingham

Sir,   Philadelphia October 21st 1776

We send you herewith a Copy of what we wrote you the 1st Inst. per the Sloop Independance, Capt Young, and hope some of the articles that were to be forwarded to your Island or St. Eustatia by Monsr. Hortalez have arrived. In that case you will apply for, receive and Ship them by these opportunities of our Continental Cruizers, which are Sent for that purpose, and also to bring back such woolen Goods as can be procured agreeable to the Orders of the Secret Committee.

You'l observe this goes by the Sachem, Captain Robinson, to Martinico, a Copy of it we send by the Armed Brigt. Andrea Doria,

Capt Isaiah Robinson,[1] to St Eustatia where he values an Mr Samuel Curson Mercht., and if you have made application to the Governor there in consequence of our former letter, you must renew it now and give orders for some of the articles to be Remitted by the Andrea Doria, or the vessel that is to Sail under her Convoy, and we think you had best Send us by every good conveyance both from St. Eustatia & Martinico a part of these Supplies. We are Sir, Your obedt Servts,   B Franklin

Robt Morris

RC (PPAmP). In a clerical hand and signed by Franklin and Morris.
[1] See Committee of Secret Correspondence to Bingham, October 23, 1776.

Francis Lewis to John Hodge

Sir.[1]   Philadelphia, 21st October, 1776
    I have received your letter of the 18th instant. In answer thereto relative to the ship Montgomery, we have lately wrote to the Convention for the State of New-York leaving it to them to give direction in what manner to dispose of the ships at Poughkeepsie;[2] they are now convened at the Fishkills. If they should find it practicable to get these ships out this year, Congress are disposed to have them fitted and manned with all expedition, but in this you must consult the Convention and superintendents. If there should be a probability of getting the ships out, you should furnish us with a list of such officers as yourself with the gentlemen of the Convention shall recommend.
    You may apply to the Treasurer, Mr. Denning, or draw upon me here for what money you may be in want of for your present supplies on account of your sloop freight.
    I am, sir, yr. very humble servt.   Fra. Lewis

MS not found; reprinted from *Journals of N.Y. Prov. Cong.*, 2:340.
[1] Hodge had been appointed captain of the Continental frigate *Montgomery* on August 22, 1776.
[2] See Marine Committee to the New York Convention, October 9, 1776.

New York Delegates to Augustine Lawrence and Samuel Tuder

Gentlemen.   Philadelphia, 21st October, 1776
    Your letter of the 7th inst. advising that the ships Congress and Montgomery were nearly ready for launching, was received.[1] You will observe the above names are now to be given to those ships. We

are, at this distance, at a loss to direct their destination. The marine committee have therefore wrote to the Convention for the State of New-York, now at the Fishkills, requesting that they would give you proper directions relative to the launching and otherwise disposing of those ships with their stores, so as to preserve them in the best manner you can from being destroyed.[2] You are therefore to correspond with the said Convention for that purpose.

Your humble servants,   Fra. Lewis

Phil. Livingston

MS not found; reprinted from *Journals of N.Y. Prov. Cong.*, 2:340–41.
[1] Lawrence and Tuder were in charge of the construction of these frigates at Poughkeepsie. Morgan, *Naval Documents*, 5:1102, 6:872–73.
[2] See Marine Committee to the New York Convention, October 9, 1776.

Robert Treat Paine's Diary

October 21, 1776

Fair. News of the defeat of Genl Arnolds fleet on Lake Champlain. Wrote to Col. Grubb, Col Bird & Capt. Joy abt. proving Cannon by Capt. Alexander.[1]

MS (MHi).
[1] None of these letters have been found, but on the proving of cannon, see Paine to Jonathan Trumbull, October 25, 1776.

Edward Rutledge to the Pennsylvania Council of Safety

Dr Sir,   [October 21, 1776] [1]

The Congress have directed the Board of War to apply to the Council of Safety of this State for the *Loan* of such Cartridges as they can conveniently part with, & have farther ordered that the Board of War forward the same in Light Waggons immediately, that is to day, to General Green at Fort Lee, for the use of the Army under General Washington. Some persons must be employed to make up a large Quantity of Powder into Cartriges. Think of what can be done as to Salt.

The Congress have ordered that all the Powder in the public Magazines be kept for public use; therefore Mr B. McClenaghan cannot be supplied.

Your obd. Servt.   E Rutledge

FC (DNA: PCC, item 78).
[1] Rutledge, a member of the Board of War, most likely wrote this letter on October 21, the day the resolves mentioned in it were passed by Congress. *JCC*, 6:890.

Secret Committee to William Bingham

Sir   In Secret Committee. Philada. October 21st. 1776
    You have herewith a Copy of a letter we wrote you the 20th Ulto.
by the Sloop Independance, Capt Young, which we hope may arrive
safe as well as the Ship Betsey, Capt Stevens, and they will furnish
you with some Funds in addition to what you received by the Brigt.
Cornelia & Molly, Cap Lockard, which is safely returned & by her
we received your favour of the 24th Ulto., the Contents whereof are
very agreable. The Mollasses you remitted us sold high but we shou'd
have preferred more Powder, Muskets &c. We send this by the Continental armed Sloop Sachem commanded by Capt. James Robinson
who we hope will have the pleasure to deliver it in due time. This
Vessell we have dispatched for the sole purpose of bringing back
such a supply of Blankets, Coarse Cloths, Coatings, Flannells &
other Woolen Goods suitable for Winter Wear as you can procure
in Martinico. They are already much wanted & will be more so,
therefore we earnestly entreat You to exert your utmost interest to
procure on the best terms you possibly can a large supply of all the
above Articles. You may apply what Funds you are already possessed
of toward the payment for them & be assured that we shall Continue
our remittances untill you discharge every debt you Contract on the
Publick Account. We must press you to dispatch Capt Robinson
with as much of these Goods as he can take in immediately & if you
can procure more than he can carry You will please to Charter or
buy a Suitable Vessell to bring the Surplus under his Convoy but
both must be dispatched immediately. We have sent another Vessell
to St Eustatia & one to the Cape on the like errands & our want of
these Goods is so great that many Ships load cou'd be dispensed
with, therefore send all you possibly can. You will supply Capt
Robinson what may be necessary for the Sloops Expences & send his
draft for the Amount on the Marine Committee. We must not be
disapointed of these Goods, therefore you must pledge the Credit of
the United States pretty freely and we will leave nothing in our
power undone to send you supplys but Vessells are Scarce at present.
If you charter one or more & send with Goods, Mollasses, Coffee,
Sugar &c we will load them all back with flour & Tobacco &c. You
shall soon hear from us again being sir, Your obedt hbl servts,

Robt Morris	Fra. Lewis
Richard Henry Lee	Josiah Bartlett
	Phil. Livingston

RC (PHi). Written by Morris and signed by Morris, Bartlett, Lee, Lewis, and
Livingston.

Board of War to Nathanael Greene

Sir,   War Office Philadelphia Oct. 22d 1776

The Congress having done the Board of War the Honour of referring to them your Letter for Consideration and execution, we beg leave to inform you that we have order'd two hundred thousand Cartridges to be instantly forwarded you; Light Waggons have been got and are fitting ready, and you will receive the above supply by tomorrow evening, or the next morning. We have employd persons to make up a quantity for the use of the Army, which shall be forwarded to your care as soon as a proper number shall be compleated.[1] We cannot however but wish that General Washington could procure such supplies of Ammunition as he may want, from the Eastern States, there being very little in this City, from whence alone every Demand to the Southward of Hudsons River must be answered. Every assistance however, that can be, shall be afforded you, as well as his Excellency the General, from this Office.

We have given Orders about the purchase of Salt, the result of which you shall hear so soon as we can write satisfactorily. With every wish for your success & Honour, We sir are your very Obed., humble Servts. By Order of the Board of War.

                                                        Edward Rutledge

Tr (DLC).
[1] These actions were taken in response to General Greene's October 20 letter to President Hancock, which was read in Congress on the 21st. See *JCC*, 6:890; PCC, item 155, 1:11–12; and Greene, *Papers* (Showman), 1:318–19.

Elbridge Gerry to Joseph Trumbull

Dear sir   Philadelphia Octr 22. 1776

Since my last your Friend Mr. W——[1] in Consequence of an Order of Congress directing the Board of War to consider an Application of Mr. Harrison Deputy paymaster General for the Southern Department & of your Brother for the northern that their Salaries may be augmented, moved that the Board may at the Same Time consider the Salary of the Commissary General & report an augmentation.[2] I confess that I was not less puzled than surprized at this injudicious Measure, taken previous to a Consultation of your Friends in Congress, at an unfavourable Time, & proposing the Consideration of this Matter for Gentlemen whose Sentiments would in all probability be against it. Had the Motion not been seconded, It might have been passed over without prejudice, untill a favorable Opportunity should offer for looking into the Reasonableness of your Expectations; but Mr. H——[3] adopting it from friendly

Motives produced an opposition that at once prevented a Committment. Nothing remains to be done but your stating in a Petition to Congress the principles upon wch. You ground your Request for an augmentation & praying for the Same; if this is done with Reason & Coolness & Supported by the Opinion of the General who has spoken in Favour of the Measure, I have no Doubt that It will be favourably recd.[4] As the Salary which You now have, compared with others of the Staf, is very large, Congress will expect to have it demonstrated that the Army is better supplyed & at less Expence in the present Mode than It would probably be by Contract; & with respect to the Method of paying the Commissary It must be left with Congress without any proposals in the petition for this purpose.

I could wish that your Friend aforesd. had not medled with the Matter, as his observations on it have only served to injure the Cause; but that cannot be now remedied.

This is a critical Time for our affairs at Ticonderoga as well as New York; may God support & prosper them. I remain with Esteem your Friend & humble serv,   E Gerry

RC (CtHi).
[1] Undoubtedly William Williams. See Williams to Joesph Trumbull, October 7 and 10, 1776.
[2] There is no mention in the journals of this issue.
[3] Gerry probably meant William Hooper. See Gerry to Joseph Trumbull, December 7, 1776.
[4] Although Trumbull's petition for an augmentation in salary was referred to the Board of Treasury on November 18, 1776, the question was set aside until July 1777 when it was revived in the board. At that time the commissary department had recently been reorganized, and Trumbull declined the post of commissary general of purchases under the new system but continued for a time under the old arrangement at Congress' request. See JCC, 6:958, 8:620; Gerry to Joseph Trumbull, July 9, 1777; and Trumbull's letter to President Hancock, July 19, 1777, in PCC, item 78, 22:259.

Francis Hopkinson to William Livingston

Sir,   Philadelphia Octr. 22d. 1776.
I am directed by the Honble The Marine Committee (of which I am a Member) to transmit you the enclosed Papers respecting the Schooner Betsy and her Cargo, lately stranded on the Jersey Shore near Shrewsbury, requesting that you would be so good as to take Charge of the said Schooner and Cargo, and order the same to be disposed of in the best Manner for their Security, until the Owners in Boston shall make proper application for the Recovery of their Property. For this Purpose, you are further requested to give Notice to the said Owners of the Disposition of the said Vessel and Cargo, and call upon them to make their Claim.[1]

I have the Honour to be, with great Respect and Esteem, Sir, your very hble Servt.   Fras. Hopkinson

RC (MHi). In the hand of Jacob Rush and signed by Hopkinson.

[1] The case of the *Betsy* is discussed in Gen. Hugh Mercer's October 17 letter to President Hancock, which was read in Congress on October 21 and was presumably one of the "enclosed Papers" sent to Governor Livingston. See PCC, item 159, fols. 194–97; and *Am. Archives*, 5th ser. 2:1093. See also Morgan, *Naval Documents*, 6:1019, 1391. In response to Hopkinson's letter, Livingston noted that "as I have not the Honour to be acquainted with the Power & authorities of the [*Marine*] Committee respecting Vessels stranded on the Jersey Shore, it is impossible for me to know what Authority . . . they are capable of conferring upon me." Livingston to Hopkinson, October 28, 1776, William Livingston Papers, MHi.

Richard Henry Lee to Unknown

Dear Sir,   Phila. 22d Octr. 1776

Accept my thanks for your favor of the 1st which I received by this post only. The inclosed paper will give you all the military news that yesterday arrived to Congress.[1] Our enemies have been amazingly industrious (as I think wickedness ever is) in Canada, coming out, contrary to all expectation, with 4 times our Marine force on Lake Champlain. The consequence was as you will see, our people bravely maintained the unequal contest, conducting themselves with a valor that has extorted applause even from their enemies, and which certainly deserved a better fortune. Carleton is now Master of the water, but we do not discover any great advantage that will result to him from that possession for this Campaign, as we have an Army equal to his at Ticonderoga, and the Season is fast approaching when no operations can be conducted on Lake Champlain, at least by means of Vessels. The Generals Washington & Howe are maneuvering on the ground above Kings bridge, each endeavoring to out flank the other. In the course of these operations, a few days since, two opposite Brigades met each other, when a very hot contest arose between the enemy and these New England Batallions, and which ended by driving the British Troops back to their main body. The General says, "our Men behaved with great coolness and intrepidity." Private letters say we lost 30 men and the enemy 150 at the least. Gen. Mercer informs us that 150 Sail of Ships came in to the enemy from Sea last Saturday. That the whole power of Great Britain is now exerted against us is most certain, and that it behooves us to strain every nerve in every part of America to oppose them is equally clear; or else Slavery the most ignominious will surely be our lot. We must Cast Cannon, make powder, build Ships and Forts, and raise Armies with unremitting zeal and industry. Cannot we be as brave and industrious in the cause of liberty & virtue, as they are in Vice and the establishment of human Slavery? Let us lay aside

every private consideration, and press the war with force and union.
We shall do every thing in our power to procure foreign assistance,
and I think a general war in Europe is not far off. May Heaven
prosper your righteous consultations and give success to the virtuous
cause of America. Farewell.   Richard Henry Lee

RC ((OClWHi).
[1] For the various letters containing military intelligence that were read in
Congress on October 21, see *JCC*, 6:889–91. Benedict Arnold's October 12 letter
to General Gates describing the October 11 engagement between the Lake Champlain fleets and Robert H. Harrison's letter to President Hancock reporting the
October 18 skirmish at East Chester, N.Y., are in *Am. Archives*, 5th ser.
2:1038–39, 1137–38.

Benjamin Rush to Thomas Morris

Philadelphia, 22 October 1776

I wrote you[1] a few days ago and gave you a particular account of
the state of our affairs. This letter will be conveyed to you by our
illustrious fellow countryman Doctor Franklin, who goes to your
court as ambassador of the United States. I refer you to him for
information on the situation of our military and civil affairs. I will
tell you that General and Lord Howe are confined to New York
island, and that our army, commanded by General Washington and
General Lee, is well posted and in good spirits about seven miles
from New York.

I will add only an anecdote that does honor to the bearer of this
letter. I had the honor of sitting near him in Congress at the time
when he was appointed to set out at once for your court; and in reply
to the compliment I paid him, he observed to me: "I have only a few
years to live, and I am resolved to devote them to the work that my
fellow citizens deem proper for me; or speaking as old-clothes dealers
do of a remnant of goods, 'You shall have me for what you please.' "

Since writing you this, we learn that our fleet has been defeated
and that Burgoyne is marching on Ticonderoga. General Arnold
commanded on the Lakes and has conducted himself like a hero.
Like Francis I, he has lost all save honor and the honor of the States.

We expect news every moment of a general action between
General Washington and General Howe. God grant us success equal
to the justice of our cause!

Reprinted from Rush, *Letters* (Butterfield), 1:118.
[1] Identification of the author and recipient of this letter rests upon the endorsement found on the MS and the anecdote about Franklin contained in the
second paragraph of the letter. Butterfield's text is a retranslation of the MS in
the Archives du ministère des affaires etrangères, Correspondance politique,
Etats-Unis, 1:263, which he described as a "copy in French, without signature
and in an unknown hand." It is endorsed: "Va avec la lettre de Franklin à

Morris. Bush [Rush?] à Morris. Traduite de l'anglais. Interceptée." The Franklin anecdote is also found in Benjamin Rush, *The Autobiography of Benjamin Rush,* ed. George W. Corner (Princeton: Published for the American Philosophical Society by Princeton University Press, 1948), p. 149.

"La lettre de Franklin à Morris" is Franklin's letter to Thomas Morris of December 4, 1776, which he wrote from Auray in Brittany just after reaching France. At the same time he also wrote a letter to Silas Deane announcing his arrival at Quiberon Bay and one to Jacques Barbeu-Dubourg asking him to forward the letters to Morris and Deane, which he was sending "under your cover." Whether they were sent to Vergennes by Dubourg is not known, but French translations of all three letters, along with a December 10 letter of "W.L." [William Lee] to Dubourg, are now in the Archives du ministère des affaires etrangères. It is known that Dubourg sent Vergennes Benjamin Rush's letter to Dubourg of September 16, 1776, printed above, although the French extract of that letter is in a hand different from that of the other four documents. See Archives du ministère des affaires etrangères, Correspondance politique, Etats-Unis, 1:292–95; and (for English retranslations of the three Franklin letters) Franklin, *Writings* (Smyth), 6:469–73.

Committee of Secret Correspondence to William Bingham

Sir   Philada. October 23d. 1776
   We have wrote you already by this Conveyance of the Brigt Andw Doria to St Eustatia which we deam safer than the Sachem as she sails faster & is of more Force.[1] Therefore we now enclose you some very Important dispatches for Mr Dean & request you will forward them by the very first good Conveyance advising us hereafter the Vessell & Masters name by which they go & also of their arrival when you hear it. We are sir, Your Obedt Servants,

B Franklin	Richard Henry Lee
Robt Morris	Wm Hooper
	Jno Witherspoon

RC (PHi). Written by Morris and signed by Morris, Franklin, Hooper, Lee, and Witherspoon.
[1] See Committee of Secret Correspondence to Bingham, October 21, 1776.

Committee of Secret Correspondence to Stephen Ceronio

In Committee of Secret Correspondence.
Sir   Philada. October 23d 1776
   The Inclosed[1] letter was wrote and Signed before we had an opporty to transmit it and having now so good a conveyance as this Brigt Lexington we transmit the Same to you as an official Letter

from the Committee of Secret Correspondance which you'l observe is distinct from the Secret Committee with whom you also correspond. By this letter you'l find we expect Some Arms, ammunition, money or Cloathing may be Sent out by Our Agents Monsr. Hortalez to the Governor at Cape François, with orders for the delivery of them to whoever may be properly impowered by Congress to receive the same. That power is granted to you, and you'l please to apply to the Governor with our respectful Compts., desire to know if he has received Such supply. If he has produce the letter to him, if he has not, then request he will inform you when such Supplies do Arrive or any advice respecting them.[2] When you receive the Goods in consequence of this appointment, Ship a quantity of them by the Lexington if they are ready, if not you may Charter suitable French vessels to bring them here dividing them into as many Bottoms and Sending an assortment consisting of part of every article you receive. In short you must transmit the whole to us in the Safest and most expeditious manner you can Contrive, Consigning to this Committee for the Use and on Accot of the United States of America. We are sir yr Obt Serts.   B.F.

RM

FC (PCC, item 37).

[1] At this point an asterisk was inserted, keyed to the following note which appeared at the end of the letter: "a letter similar to that written to Mr. Bingham Octr. 1st, only substituting Cape Francois for Martinique & St. Eustatius." This letter has been quoted in note 2 to the committee's letter to William Bingham of October 1 above.

[2] Ceronio also contacted Spanish officials, apparently suggesting that he would be willing to provide reports on American affairs in exchange for the right to trade at Havana and other ports in the Spanish West Indies. The marquis de la Torre, governor at Havana, quickly sent an agent to Ceronio with instructions to get the reports but to avoid commitments on trade. The Spanish agent, Antonio Raffelin, met with Ceronio on March 19, 1777, and sent a highly favorable account to Governor Torre. The plan was endorsed by the Spanish king on June 29, 1777, but a year later Spanish officials were still seeking their first report. Kathryn Abbey, "Efforts of Spain to Maintain Sources of Information in the British Colonies before 1779," *Mississippi Valley Historical Review* 15 (June 1928): 61–62.

Committee of Secret Correspondence to Silas Deane

Sir   Philada. Octr. 23d. 1776

We have already wrote you two letters of this date by different Conveyances, the present we send by the Andrew Doria, Isaiah Robinson Esqr. Commander, for St Eustatia from whence it will be sent to Wm Bingham Esqr. at Martinico and by him be transmitted to you in a French Bottom.[1] You will find enclosed Two Resolves of Congress passed yesterday, from one of them you will learn that Thomas Jefferson Esqr. declined going to France & that Arthur Lee Esqr. of London is Elected to serve as a Commissioner in his stead. You will therefore contrive to give him immediate Notice to repair to you & then deliver him that resolve & the inclosed letter.[2] By the other Resolve you will see that Congress direct you to procure Eight Line of Battle Ships either by Hire or purchase.[3] We hope you will meet immediate success in this application and that you may be able to influence the Courts of France & Spain to send a large Fleet at their own Expense to Act in Concert with these Ships, which shou'd be expedited immediately with directions to the Commander to make the first Port he can with safety in these States preferring this, if Winds & Weather favour him. And he must also have instructions to Subject himself totally to the orders of Congress, after he arrives.

We are Sir, Your hble Servants,

Signed by.　　B Franklin　　　　Richd Henry Lee

Rt. Morris　　　　Wm Hooper

Dr Witherspoon

Tr (PHC). Endorsed by Robert Morris: "A true Copy from the original by Robt Morris."

[1] The committee's "two letters of this date," enclosing duplicate and triplicate copies of the proposed treaty of alliance with France and instructions to the American commissioners in France for negotiating additional treaties with other powers in Europe, are in *NYHS Collections* 19 (1886): 333–34. In order to get this package of letters to Deane, the committee sent them through William Bingham at Martinique and Stephen Ceronio at Cape François, Saint-Domingue, to the Bordeaux merchants Samuel and John Delap. The committee's October 23 letter to Ceronio, asking him to forward the packet to the Delaps, and their letter to the Delaps asking to forward it to Deane, are in PCC, item 37, fols. 71–72, and *Am. Archives,* 5th ser. 2:1198. See also Committee of Secret Correspondence to Deane, October 24, 1776.

[2] See Committee of Secret Correspondence to Arthur Lee, this date.

[3] *JCC,* 6:895–96. Despite these instructions from Congress the American commissioners in France were never able to procure and outfit more than a few small ships of war in France, among them John Paul Jones' *Bonhomme Richard.* See Jonathan R. Dull, *The French Navy and American Independence* (Princeton: Princeton University Press, 1975), pp. 75–80, 158n.

Committee of Secret Correspondence to Arthur Lee

Sir　　　　　　　　　　　　　Philadelphia October 23d 1776

By this conveyance we transmit to Silas Deane Esq. a Resolve of the Honble the Continental Congress of Delegates from the Thirteen United States of America, whereby you are appointed one of their

Commissioners for negotiating a treaty of alliance, Amity and Commerce with the Court of France, and also for negotiating Treaties with other Nations agreable to certain plans and instructions of Congress, which we have transmitted by various conveyances to Mr Deane another of the Commissioners.[1] We have requested him to give you immediate notice to join him, and on your meeting to deliver this letter and lay before you all the Papers and instructions, also to deliver you the Resolve whereby you are appointed. We flatter ourselves from the assurances of your Friends here, that you will chearfully undertake this important business & that our Country will greatly benefit of those abilities and that attachment you have already manifested in Sundry important Services, which at a proper period, shall be made known to those you woud wish.

This Committee will think it proper to address all their despatches unto Mr. Deane untill they have certain advice that his Colleagues have joined him, but the communication of them will be the Same as if addressed to the whole.

We remain with much Esteem and regard, Sir, Your most obedt hble Servts.   Rob Morris

B Franklin

RC (CtY). In a clerical hand, and signed by Franklin and Morris.

[1] See *JCC*, 6:897. Lee, who had been acting as an overseas agent for Congress since early 1776, had been collaborating with France's agent Beaumarchais in laying the groundwork for shipping French military supplies to America. See Committee of Secret Correspondence to Arthur Lee, December 12, 1775; and to Silas Deane, October 1, 1776, note 3. Lee accepted his appointment as commissioner to the French court on December 31, 1776, referring to a now missing letter of October 31 from the Committee of Secret Correspondence. Lee's letter reflects the tension between Deane and himself that became increasingly important in future years. "The politics of Europe are in a state of trembling hestitation. It is in consequence of this that I find the promises that were made me by the French agent in London, and which I stated to you by Mr. Storey and others, have not been entirely fulfilled. The changing of the mode of conveying what was promised was settled with Mr. Deane, whom Mr. Hortalez found here on his return, and with whom all the arrangements were afterwards made. I hope you will have received some of the supplies long before this reaches you. Infinitely short as they are of what was promised in quantity, quality, and time, I trust they will be of very material service in the operation of the next campaign." Wharton, *Diplomatic Correspondence*, 2:242.

John Hancock to Philip Schuyler

Sir,   Philada. Octr. 23d. 1776.

I have the Honour to transmit herewith sundry Resolutions of Congress, to which I must request your Attention. They relate to a Variety of Subjects, and are absolutely necessary for your Information & Direction.[1]

Being at present extremely engaged in forwarding Dispatches to General Washington, I have only Time to add, that I am with Sentiments of perfect Esteem, Sir, your most obed. & very hble Sert.

J. H. Prest.

LB (DNA: PCC, item 12A).

¹ Although most of these "Resolutions" cannot be identified with certainty, one of them was an October 14 resolve declaring that "the allowance to officers of 1 1/3 dollars for enlisting soldiers be not extended or given on the reinlistment of the soldiers in camp." Schuyler immediately objected to this on the grounds that henceforth "the recruiting officers will not be able to give their recruiting Sergeants any money to treat with those whom they attempt to enlist," and consequently Congress repealed it on November 7. See *JCC*, 6:874, 932; and *Am. Archives*, 5th ser. 2:1296.

Marine Committee to Esek Hopkins

Sir   In Marine Committee Philadelphia October 23d. 1776

Since our last to you we are informed that the Galatia a New 20 Gun Ship with the Nautilus of 16 Guns are gone to Cruize of[f] the Capes of Virginia. These Ships you will endeavour to fall in with and take or destroy in your way to Cape Fear. We are also informed that the Raven of 20 Guns & the Sphynx of 16 have quitted Georgia and South Carolina but where gone we know not. You may take with you to the Southward both the Rhode Island Frigates as well as the Cabbot if they are ready, and we write to North Carolina to have two fine Brigantines belonging to that State in readiness to join you. They have 16 Guns each and near 100 men. You had best send one of your Fleet into Occracock Inlet for them as they are in there. We understand the Sloop Providence, Capt Jones, has put into Rhode Island, you may add him to your Fleet and then you'l be very Strong. As this Service to the southward is of much publick importance, we expect from your Zeal and Attachment to the Interest of the United States that you proceed on and execute this Service with all possible vigor and dispatch.¹ Wishing you health and Success we are Sir, Your humble Servants,

Richard Henry Lee	Fras. Hopkinson
Fras. Lewis	John Hancock
	Robt Morris

P.S. We are informed that two British Ships of War passed the other day along the Jersey Shore Steering Southward. We know not whether to cruize off the mouth of Delaware or to join the Southern Ships. But we deem it highly proper that you provide yourself with a very quick sailing Tender commanded by a spirited, sensible and skilful man to precede your Fleet and bring you intelligence of the number force and situation of the Enemies Ships. It might not be amiss for you to remain a short time within the Capes of Virginia until the Tender should reconnoitre & inform you of the State of things at Cape Fear.   John Hancock   Fras. Lewis

Robt Morris   Fras. Hopkinson

Richard Henry Lee   Will Hooper

RC (CSmH). In the hand of Timothy Matlack and signed by Hancock, Hopkinson, Lee, Lewis, and Morris. The postscript, written by Hooper and signed by Hooper, Hancock, Hopkinson, Lee, Lewis, and Morris, is in the Hopkins Papers, RHi.

[1] Commodore Hopkins' November 24 reply to this letter is in Morgan, *Naval Documents*, 7:277.

Marine Committee to John Manley, Hector McNeill, and Thomas Thompson

Gentlemen   October 23d 1776

We expect the Continental frigates Hancock, Boston and Raleigh under your respective commands are either now ready for the Sea, or shortly will be so. You are hereby directed to Act in concert and Cruize together, for the following purposes, and on the following Stations. Your first object must be to inform yourselves in the best manner possible if any of the British men of War are Cruizing in the bay of Boston or off the Coast of Massachusetts, and all such you are to endeavour with your utmost force to take, sink, or destroy.[1] Having effected this service you are to proceed together towards Rhode Island, and there make prize of or destroy any of the enemies Ships of war that may be found Cruizing off the Harbour or Coast of Rhode Island. The Prizes you make are to be sent into the nearest Port. When you arrive at Rhode Island if Commodore Hopkins should not be already sailed on his Southern expedition, and the two frigates built in that State should not be ready for the Sea, in that case you are to join Commodore Hopkins, and proceed with him on the said expedition producing those orders to him to justify the measure. But if the Rhode Island frigates should be ready for the sea there will be no occasion for you or either of you to go Southward. And you will then proceed taking with you any Continental Vessel that may be at Rhode Island and ready if Commodore Hopkins should be sailed before you come there, and proceed to Cruize against the enemies Ships & Vessels that may be found of[f] the Coast between the Harbour of Newport and the Banks of Newfoundland.

We have no doubt from your zeal and attachment to the cause of America, that you will execute this service with all possible dispatch and vigor, and so bid you heartily farewell.

LB (DNA: PCC Miscellaneous Papers, Marine Committee Letter Book).
¹ Congress took this action only after the Massachusetts General Court had threatened to withhold state aid for the completion of the frigates unless the *Hancock* was used to protect Massachusetts coastal waters. See James Bowdoin to John Hancock, September 23, 1776, in Morgan, *Naval Documents,* 6:953, and PCC, item 65, 1:113–17; and *JCC,* 5:848, 6:882.

Marine Committee to the North Carolina Council of Safety

Gentlemen [October 23, 1776]

We have ordered Commodore Hopkins immediately to proceed to Cape Fear in the state of North Carolina with the following Vessells under his command viz.

The Alfred of 30 Guns
Columbus . . . . . 28 do
Cabot . . . . 16 do
Hampden . . . . 16 do
Providence . . . . 10 do

Continental } Warren . . . . 32 do } if these two last mentioned
Frigates } Providence . . . . 28 do } can be made ready in season.

The Object of this expedition is to take or destroy the Brittish men of War in the River of Cape Fear, or any others cruizing upon the southern coasts with a view to distress the trade of your's and the neighbouring states. Strong as the Commodore may be with the force which accompanies him from Rhode Island, yet as we wish to put as little as possible to the hazard but to pursue this measure with the fullest confidence of success we request that you would upon the earliest intimation of Commodore Hopkins being off your coast dispatch the two provincial Armed Vessels and any others which may be under your control to join him and cooperate in this important expedition in the event of which your state is particularly and essentially interested. You will therefore hold your Vessels in perfect readiness to comply with this requisition.

We beg leave to hint to you the necessity of providing skilful pilots for conducting the Commodore that he may suffer no delay or run any risque from his Ignorance of the Coast of No Carolina.

As the success of this Attempt depends much upon the Secrecy with which it may be conducted we need say nothing to urge you to the strict Observance of this Injunction.

We are Gentlemen, Your very hume Servts,

John Hancock	Josiah Bartlett
Robt Morris	Fras. Hopkinson
Richard Henry Lee	Fras. Lewis
	Will Hooper

FC (MdAN). Written by Hooper and signed by Hooper, Bartlett, Hancock, Hopkinson, Lee, Lewis, and Morris. LB (DNA: PCC Miscellaneous Papers, Marine Committee Letter Book). Recipient and date taken from LB. The LB is clearly addressed "To the Governor & Council of North Carolina," but the signed FC is simply directed to "The Council of Safety & Committees of   ," suggesting that this was a circular letter which was also sent to several North Carolina local committees.

Robert Morris to Silas Deane

Dear Sir   Philada. October 23d. 1776

Herewith you have Copies of what I wrote you the 12th Septr & 4th October both of which I confirm & not having had the pleasure to hear from you since, I do not intend to take up much of your time of Politicks. I shall not write as you will gain ample information in another way.

The Secret Committee finding it impossible to make remittances fast enough to support the Credit of all their Contracts in the way they cou'd wish have determined to employ my Brother as a Superintending Agent over all their European Concerns and have given him ample instructions for the purpose & as they now make all their Consignments to his order, he is instructed amongst other things to make up to you what you have other ways received short of the forty thousand pounds Sterling for the purchase of Indian Goods, but if you have bought these Goods on Credit as We expect you have you must Stretch that Credit untill he gets pretty strong handed, which I hope will be 'ere long if we have tolerable luck, for I have bought a great deal of Valueable produce for the purpose.

Tom must fix with the best Houses at every Port in France or in most Foreign parts of Europe to transact the business for him, & I expect they will agree to charge only the customary Coms. on Sales & returns and allow him a share of it but be this as it may he must fix the best People for his Agents. He must employ such Bankers in Paris as you best approve of, he must direct all the Cargoes to the best Markets and order our Goods from the Cheapest & best places and in short I expect he will exert himself to the utmost to render us faithful & Effectual Services. I hope my Dr. Sir you will be attentive to his Conduct and if need there be, spur him up to a dilligent, honest & faithful discharge of his Duty. I have also recommended a good deal of Private business to him in full dependance that he will apply his whole time & attention to business for in that line I have determined to push his future Fortunes. If you & he have engaged in the plans I recommended they must undoubtedly turn out well, especially if you make Insurances & T. Morris will have effects in hand to pay our Share of such Concerns, as we have directed him to settle all our Accounts in England where much more Money is due to us than from us—and I hope he will pay all the ballances we owe & recover those due to us.

I have advice from Mr. Langdon of Portsmouth that Capt Palmer is arrived there but he threw over the Packet of letters he had from you & indeed all his letters expecting to be taken by a Man of War from which he had a hairs breadth escape. I intend writing you more at large than I can spare time to do at present. Be assured that I am with perfect esteem & regard Dr sir Your affectionate hble Servant, Robt Morris

RC (CtHi).

Board of War to George Washington

Sir. War Office Octr. 24th. 1776

The Board of War have directed me to enclose you the Plan they intended to present to Congress for preventing Abuses in Regiments or Companies receiving more Rations than they are entitled to; an Evil which has been complained of perhaps with too much Foundation.

It frequently happens that sick Soldiers are either left behind at Posts or Places thro' which their Regiments or Companies are marching, or they are sent to Hospitals at a Distance from their Corps. These unhappy People, or some of them, are often thought incurable & discharged by the Director or Surgeon of the Hospital as unfit for Service, & turned out to beg their Subsistence to their Homes, or Places of their former residence, altho' they may have Pay due to them sufficient to support them. This not only raises Compassion & from this Motive should be remedied, but is extremely detrimental to the Service, by deterring others from enlisting. The Board therefore have thought that the Soldiers, so discharged, should have it in their Power to receive their Pay in whatever Part of the States they may be & have accordingly formed a Plan to enable them to do it, & request your Excellency's Advice on both these Subjects.[1]

With the greatest Respect, I have the Honour to be, your obedt humble Servt, Richard Peters Secy

RC (DLC).

[1] The "Plan" discussed by Peters is in the Washington Papers, DLC, and *Am. Archives*, 5th ser. 2:1211. Washington's secretary subsequently informed Congress that the general considered the proposal "for preventing more rations being drawn than may be due, well calculated to answer the end," but that the portions "respecting the sick seems to him not entirely perfect." See Robert H. Harrison to John Hancock, November 4, 1776, in *Am. Archives*, 5th ser. 3:509–10. The plan was put into effect by a resolution adopted by Congress on November 19, after the proposal relating to the sick had been modified to meet Washington's objections. *JCC*, 6:965–66.

Board of War to George Washington

Sir   War Office Octr. 24th. 1776

By Order of the Board of War I have the Honour to inform your Excellency that the Congress have this Day given them directions to order the two Virginia Regiments now at Chester, immediately to Trentown, there to wait your Excellency's Commands; and at the same time to acquaint you of the Situation of the People of this State, that having as comprehensive a View of the State of Affairs as possible you may make such Disposition as the good of the Service may require.[1]

The Council of Safety of this State requested some days since a Conference with this Board in Order to lay before it, a Representation of their Situation and Expectations.[2] In the course of this Conference it appeared very clearly, that they were in a most defenceless Condition, that they had no works upon the River except one Fort unfinished, that the Militia of this City are inactive and languid to the last Degree & to close their distress a number of the People of this Place were disaffected. Indeed they went so far as to say that in their Judgment a large Party might be found to espouse openly the Cause of the Enemy should our Affairs run retrograde at New York. As your Excellency, however, must know more of your own Strength and your own intended Operations than Congress possibly can, & as it is of the greatest importance that you should be Supported at all Events General Stephens with the Virginia Forces will take Post at Trentown in Order to Obey such Commands as you may be pleased to give him.

I have the Honour to be, Your Excellency's most Obed. & very Humble Servant,   Richard Peters Secy

RC (DLC). In a clerical hand and signed by Peters.
[1] See *JCC*, 6:901. See also Robert H. Harrison to John Hancock, November 4, 1776, in *Am. Archives*, 5th ser. 3:509–10.
[2] For the Pennsylvania Council of Safety's October 16 representation to the Board of War, see ibid., 2:88.

Committee of Secret Correspondence to the Commissioners at Paris

Gentlemen   Philada. October 24th. 1776

The Congress having Committed to our charge & Management their Ship of War called the Reprisal Commanded by Lambert Wickes Esqr. carrying Sixteen Six pounders & about one hundred & twenty Men, We have allotted her to carry Doctor Franklin to France and directed Capt Wickes to proceed for the Port of Nantes where the Doctor will land & from thence proceed to Paris, & he will either carry with him or send forward this letter by express as to him may then appear best. The Reprisal is a fast sailing Ship and Capt. Wickes has already done honor in Action to the American Flagg. We have therefore ordered him to land at Nantes some Indico he has onboard, take in any refreshments, Stores, Provisions or other necessarys he may want and immediately to proceed on a Cruize against our Enemies, and we think he will not be long before he meets with a sufficient Number of Prizes.[1] We have directed him to send them into such of the French Ports as are most Convenient addressing them at Dunkirk to Messrs. P. Stival & Son, at Havre de Grace to Mr. Andw Limozin, at Bourdeaux to Messrs. Saml & J. H. Delap, at Nantes to Messrs. Pliarne, Penet & Compy and at any other Ports in France to such persons as you may appoint to receive them. When he finishes his Cruize he will call in at Nantes or Bourdeaux or Brest for your orders & advices which we beg you will have ready for him lodged at those places. In Consequence of this plan for the Reprisals Cruize we desire you to make immediate application to the Court of France to Grant the Protection of their Ports to American Men of War & their Prizes.[2] Shew them that British Men of War under Sanction of an Act of Parliament are daily Capturing American Ships & Cargoes. Shew them the Resolves of Congress for making Reprisals on British & West India property & that our Continental Men of War and numerous private Ships of War are most successfully employed in executing those Resolutions of the Congress. Shew them the Justice & equity of this proceeding, and surely they cannot, they will not refuse the protection of their Ports to American Ships of War, Privateers & their Prizes. If your application on this head is crowned with Success, try another which it is their interest to grant, that is to obtain leave to make Sale of those Prizes & their Cargoes or any part thereof that may be suitable for that Country. If you succeed in this also, you must appoint some person to Act as judge of the Admiralty who shoud give the Bond prescribed for those Judges to determine in all Cases agreable to the Rules & Regulations of Congress, and for this purpose we will Report to Congress some Resolves Vesting you with Authority to make such appointment and Authorizing such judge to Condemn without a jury as required here.[3] If these Resolves are agreed to by Congress they shall be immediately transmitted to you. If they are not that plan must drop and the Prizes must all proceed for America for Condemnation. You can in the mean time consult the Ministers whether they will permit such Courts in France and in the French West India Islands. If protection is granted to our Cruizers & their Prizes you will immediately procure proper orders to be sent to the officers of all their Ports on this Subject, and write yourselves to those Houses we have Named at the several Ports that the Prizes are to remain for Cap Wickes further orders, also lodge such orders with proper persons at the other Ports in France. On the Contrary if The Prizes are not to be protected in their Ports then give immediate Notice to all those Houses & proper persons at the other Ports, to furnish the Prizes that Cap Wickes of the Reprisal may send into their port with any necessarys the Prize Master may judge they stand in need of and to order him immediately to make the best of his way with the Prize to the first safe Port he can make in the United States of America. Lodge advice also for Cap Wickes at Bourdeaux, Brest & Nantes whether his Prizes are to be protected in Port or not & whether or not any sales will be permitted. If they are protected he can take his own time to Collect & bring them Home under his own Convoy. If any Sale is permitted, he can sell perishable Commodities & Vessells unfit for so long a Voyage as to this Coast. If no protection for Prizes they will be come away by your orders & need not stay for his, and If they deny Protection to our Cruizers themselves, he will only remain in Port for your advices and to obtain such supplys as may be necessary. We have recommended Cap Wickes to take onboard his own Ship as many Valuable Commodities as he can if he is successfull, but shou'd he be unsuccessfull in Cruizing then Messrs. Pliarne & Co may put some Goods onboard when he is coming away. You will readily see the Tendancy these measures have, and as their consequences may be very important so we hope your attention to them will be immediate & Constant whilst necessary. Capt. Wickes is a Worthy Man. As such we recommend him & shou'd he have the misfortune to be taken or meet with any other misfortune we hope you will adopt measures for his relief. He will treat Prisoners with Humanity and we are Convinced his Conduct will do honour to his appointment. We have the honor to be, Gentn., Your most obedt and most hble Servants,

Robt Morris	Jno Witherspoon
Richard Henry Lee	Will Hooper

RC (PPAmP). Written by Morris, and signed by Morris, Hooper, Lee, and Witherspoon.

[1] See Committee of Secret Correspondence to Lambert Wickes, this date.

[2] The American commissioners at Paris did not have to await an opportunity to deal with the disposal of American prizes, because when Captain Wickes delivered this letter he brought into port two British ships captured en route to France. Wickes promptly disposed of the prizes to French merchants and left the commissioners to explain his actions to French officials. Subsequently American ship captains and the commissioners generally obtained the unofficial cooperation of French merchants and government officials in permitting American privateers to so use French ports despite the fact that the practice violated provisions of the 1713 Treaty of Utrecht. The practical effect of such French cooperation was to permit Americans to enjoy the latitude Congress sought in this instruction to the commissioners at Paris. At times French officials simply feigned ignorance of American practices when confronted by British protests and on occasion,

when pressed further, ordered American ships and prizes out-of-port while permitting delays for refitting.

Issues arising from the arrival of American privateers in French ports nevertheless produced a crisis in Anglo-French relations the following summer when American privateers operating in St. George's Channel returned to France with 18 prizes. Thus in late August, in response to the repeated protests of the British ambassador, Lord Stormont, the comte de Vergennes finally ordered Wickes' squadron to depart and issued new instructions prohibiting the use of French ports by American privateers. Designed to prevent the outbreak of war with Britain prematurely, this action, coupled with the sailing of the *Reprisal* and *Lexington* from St. Malo and Morlaix in September, enabled France to postpone a rupture with Britain and to maintain her neutral stance until 1778.

For additional information on this issue, see Jonathan R. Dull, *The French Navy and American Independence* (Princeton: Princeton University Press, 1975), pp. 75–83; and William Bell Clark, *Lambert Wickes Sea Raider and Diplomat* (New Haven: Yale University Press, 1932) pp. 98–348. The American commissioner's correspondence with Congress and with Vergennes on this issue can be followed in Wharton, *Diplomatic Correspondence*, 2:283–90, 296–98, 322–27, 364–66, 375–82, 388–91.

³ The committee apparently failed to obtain such a resolve, and Congress did not authorize the commissioners to appoint a person "to act as judge of the Admiralty." As Silas Deane subsequently reported: "The prizes are sold without condemnation, and consequently to a great loss." See Deane to Robert Morris, August 23, 1776, Wharton, *Diplomatic Correspondence*, 2:381. For the article pertaining to privateers in the treaty of amity and commerce later negotiated with France, see *JCC*, 11:434.

Committee of Secret Correspondence to Silas Deane

Dear Sir   Philada. October 24th. 1776

We embrace this opportunity of your Worthy Colleague & our mutual good Friend Docr. Franklin to transmit you Copies of our letters of the 1st Octr.¹ by the Sloop Independance, Cap Young, to Martinico from whence they wou'd be carried to you by Mr. Wm Hodge junr sent in said Sloop for that purpose. Those letters contained a Commission from the Congress appointing Doctr. Franklin, Thos Jefferson Esqr. & yourself Commissioners on behalf of the United States of America to Negotiate a Treaty of Alliance, Amity & Peace with the Court of France, a plan of that Treaty, Instructions from Congress relative thereto, Form of Passports for the Ships of each Nation &c. We consider those papers as of the utmost consequence & hope they will arrive safe. Yesterday we wrote you a few lines enclosing additional Instructions from Congress to their Commissioners authorizing them to Treat with other Nations, also Two Resolves of Congress by one of which you wou'd see that Thos. Jefferson Esqr declined his appointment & that Arthur Lee Esqr was appointed in his stead, to whom we enclosed a letter, Copy whereof goes herewith. By the other the Commissioners are directed to hire or buy Eight Line of Battle Ships for the American Service. These papers were sent under Cover to Wm Bingham Esqr our Resident at Martinico with orders to forward them immediately. We wrote you another letter yesterday covering duplicates of all the papers & letters mentioned herein and sent it by the armed Brigt Lexington, Wm Hallock Esqr Commander, to Mr Stephen Ceronio our Resident at Cape Francois with directions to forward the same to Messrs Saml & J. Hans Delap Merchts at Bourdeaux who are requested to send the Packet from thences by Express to you, and Doctor Franklin carrys with him Triplicates of all these publick papers. We have been thus particular in mentioning them & the Conveyances by which they are sent that you may know when the whole are received & we desire you to be equally pointed in advising us thereof for we shall be anxious to hear of their getting safe & shall be very uneasy if we dont hear this in due time, for they ought not on any Account to fall into the hands of our Enemies.

Since Mr. Dickinson & Colo. Harrison were out of Congress & Doctr Franklin appointed one of the Commissioners at the Court of France, the Congress have filled up the Vacancys in this Committee & the Members now are Mr. Jay, Mr. Johnston, Mr Morris, Colo Richd Henry Lee, Mr Wm Hooper & Doctr. John Witherspoon which we mention for your information. We shall Continue to address all our advices & dispatches to you only, untill informed that the other Commissioners have joined you but you will Communicate the letters to them as if directed to the whole & we depend on you to notify Doctr Lee of his appointment using the utmost precaution in the method of doing it, or his person may be endangered. We suppose it may be best to have the letter enclosed by the Ministers of France to their Ambassador in England with proper Cautions respecting the delivery of it. Doctr. Franklin being the bearer of this letter, it is totally unnecessary for us to enter into any detail of what is passing here or to convey any Political remarks, he being possessed of every knowledge necessary for your information will communicate very fully every thing you can wish to know. Therefore wishing you a happy meeting with him & a successfull issue to your labours in the Service of your Country we remain with perfect esteem & regard, Dear Sir, Your affectionate Friends & Obedt hble Servants,

Robt Morris	Jno Witherspoon
Richard Henry Lee	Will Hooper

RC (PHi). Written by Morris, and signed by Morris, Hooper, Lee, and Witherspoon.

[1] Apparently the committee's letters to Deane of October 1 and 2. The appearance of the RC indicates that Morris originally left the date blank and that "1st Octr." was added later with a different pen and probably by one of the other signers of the letter.

Committee of Secret Correspondence to Charles William Frederic Dumas

Philada. October 24 [1776]

Our worthy Friend Doctor Franklin being indefatigueable in the Service of his Country and few men so qualify'd to be usefull to the Community of which he is a member, You will not be surprized that the Unanimous Voice of the Congress of Delegates from the United States of America has called upon him to Visit the Court of France in the Character of one of their Commissioners for Negotiating a Treaty of Alliance &c with that Nation. He is the bearer of this letter and on his arrival will forward it. To him we refer you for information as to the Political state of this Country, our design in addressing you at this time being only to Continue that Correspondence which he has opened & conducted hitherto with you on our behalf. We request to hear from you frequently and if you make use of the Cypher, The Doctor has communicatted the knowledge of it to one of our Members. Your letters Via St Eustatia directed to the Committee of Secret Correspondance, then put under a Cover to Mr. Robert Morris Merchant in Philadelphia & that letter under Cover to Mr. Cornelius Stevenson or Mr. Henricus Godet Merchts at St Eustatia or under Cover to Mr. Isaac Governeur Mercht of Curracoa will Certainly come safe & if you can send with them regular supplys of the English and other News papers you will add to the obligation. The expence of procurring them shall be reimbursed together with any other charges and a reasonable allowance for your time & trouble in this agency. The members of this Committee, Stiled the Committee of Secret Correspondance, are John Jay Esqr., Thos. Johnston Esqr., Robt Morris Esqr., Colo Richd Henry Lee, Wm Hooper Esqr & the Revd Doctr John Witherspoon, and as Vacancys happen by Deaths or absence the Congress fill them up with New Members which we Mention for your information & with great respect & Esteem remain, sir, Your most obedt hble servts.

                Robt Morris   Jno Witherspoon

                Richard Henry Lee   Will Hooper

RC (CtY). Written by Morris, and signed by Morris, Hooper, Lee, and Witherspoon.

Committee of Secret Correspondence to Lambert Wickes

Sir.   Philada. October 24th 1776

The Honorable Congress having thought proper to Submit the Ship Reprisal under your command to our direction for the present voyage or Cruize, you are to be governed by the following orders.

The Honorable Doctor Franklin being appointed by Congress one of their Commissioners for negotiating some publick business at the Court of France, You are to receive him and his Suite on board the Reprisal as passengers whom it is your duty and we dare say it will be your inclination to treat with the greatest respect and attention and your best endeavours will not be wanting to make their time onboard the ship perfectly agreeable.[1]

When they are on board you are to proceed with the utmost dilligence for the port of Nantes in France where they will land and there you will deliver their baggage &c. It is of more importance that you get safe and soon to France than any prizes are that you cou'd take, therefore you are not to delay time on this outward passage for the Sake of Cruizing, but if you are beset with Contrary winds or during the passage be So circumstanced that Doctor Franklin may approve of your speaking any Vessels you see, do therein as he shall direct.

We understand the Secret Committee have put on board the Reprisal a quantity of Indigo. This you must land at Nantes immediately on your arrival and deliver it to their order and they have directed their Agents to Supply you immediately with what ever refreshments or necessarys you may stand in need of. We deem it Essential to the Success & Safety of your Ship that you Make a very Short Stay in the River of Nantes. It is equally so that you keep totally Secret where you are bound from thence or what your business. These things promised, we take it for granted your Stay will not exceed more than two or three days, and that you will rather dispose people to think you are returning back here again but you are directly to proceed on a Cruize against our Enemies. You have the Resolves of Congress by which you will know who they are. By them you will know what Ships you are authorized to make prize of and the Resolves of Congress must be the Rule of your Conduct. We think you had best proceed directly on the Coast of England up the channell before they can have any Notice of you, and we judge every day if not every hour you are there will give you opportunity of making prizes; you will Always have some of the French ports at hand either to send in your prizes or to run into yourself if chased by Superior force. Doctor Franklin will make application at the Court of France for the protection of their ports to the Reprisal and her prizes and we hope he will be successfull therein. However we propose as follows. Should you take one or two valuable prizes with woolen or linen goods on board, or Such Cargoes as you Know us to be in immediate want of, that you dispatch them immediately under the command of trusty officers and Men for this port. If you meet other vessels partly loaden with such goods that you take as many of them on board your own Ship as you conveniently can, and that you Send all the other prizes you take, immediately into Some of the ports of France with orders to Apply at Dunkirk to Messrs. P. Stival

& Son Merchants, at Havre De Grace to Mr. Andrew Limozin Mercht., at Bourdeaux to Messrs. Saml & J. Hans Delap Merchts., at Nantes to Messrs. Pliarne Penet & Co.; at any other port to apply to the Commander thereof for protection untill he receives orders from his Court on the Subject, and with these orders will also come instructions from Dr. Franklin, Silas Deane Esqr. & Dr. Lee or some of them which he Must obey. You may direct all the prize Masters to wait in port for your further orders provided the above Gentlemen wrote that they will be protected, but if that protection is not granted they must then apply to our Agents for such Supplies, as are Necessary, and push away immediately for this Continent making the first safe port they Can. We are convinced you will treat all prisoners with humanity but we think you had best land them in France whenever they are too numerous on board your Ship to prevent giving alarms in England, for You may depend they will have Cruizers out after you soon as they hear of your being there. We expect therefore you will make but a Short Cruize, especially as every day Must immediately throw plenty of English vessels in your way. Perhaps off Falmouth you might meet with a Lisbon Packet, and whatever Specie you collect take it onboard and carry it into France, where you may deliver or pay the same to the order of Doctor Franklin, Mr Deane &c, or to Mr. Thos Morris on his order as agent for the Secret Committee of Congress, and the Congress will pay here yours and the peoples Shares of Such money, as well as their Shares of any prizes or parts of Prizes that [may] be sold there and the Money applyed to publick use. When you are about to quite your Cruize it may be well to send any prisoners you then have on Shore and make them believe you are coming direct for America, or going round into St George channell to Cruize for Bristol ships just as you think may be most likely to gain Credit, clear your Ship of them and then Run of[f] into Bourdeaux, Brest or Nantes, just as may be most convenient. You will find letters from our Commissioners at Paris with Messrs. Delap at Bourdeaux. Messrs. Pliarne Penet & Co at Nantes or Some proper person at Brest, advising you the success of their application and if they tell you the Prizes are to be protected, you can then write to the Prize Masters and either collect and bring them home under your Convoy or order them to proceed seperately as you shall then judge best. If protections was not to be given, they will come away of Course, and in that case we think you should put your Ship in good order, advise the Commissioners and Mr. Thomas Morris that [you] only wait for their dispatches. If you have Room on board the Ship receive any goods Mr. Morris or they may order, and when you have received their dispatches make the best of your way back to this place or any other port of Safety in these States, bringing with you any prizes you can take by the way. Should the Court of France grant free protection for our Cruizers and prizes in their ports, we think you may do better in Europe than here, respecting which consult with and be governed by the advice of our Said Commissioners at the Court of Paris, and if prizes are allowed to be sold there consign all you take to the order of Mr. Thomas Morris, who has correspondents in every port of France and will take care that Justice is done in the Management of [it]. Your Stay in Europe must depend on the advice of the Commissioners and your Cruizes should always be quick as you can be soon in and out. Keep your Ship well Manned, fitted and provided, and let old England see how they like to have an active Enemy at their own Door, they have sent Fire and Sword to ours. You know we want Seamen here, therefore encourage all you meet with both at Sea and on shore to enter our Service and send or bring as many of them to these States as possible. You must by all opportunitys inform us of your proceedings, and communicate all the usefull or important intelligence that comes to your Knowledge. A Spirited active conduct in this enterprize will recommend you to all America and you have our best wishes for your Success and honor being very Sincerely Sir, Yr. Friends and humbl Servts.[2]

FC (DNA: PCC, item 37).

[1] Captain Wickes left Marcus Hook, Pa., on October 27, arriving in France on November 30, 1776. For an account of this voyage and his subsequent exploits in European waters, see William Bell Clark, *Lambert Wickes Sea Raider and Diplomat* (New Haven: Yale University Press, 1932). See also Secret Committee to Thomas Morris, October 25, 1776.

[2] This day Wickes also received the following directive from the Marine Committee. "The honble Congress of the United States of America have directed us to commit the Reprisal under your command to the management of the Committee of Secret Correspondence for the present voyage or Cruize, you are therefore to receive and obey the orders of that Committee. To us however you are to communicate such occurrences as ought to be known by those who superintend the American Navy." PCC, item 37, fol. 83; and *Am. Archives,* 5th ser. 2:1213.

John Hancock to Thomas Cushing

Dear Sir   Philada. 24th Octor. 1776. 11 oClock Night

Our incessant Attention to the Affairs of the Northern Army & Genl Washington's (& my Duty you know) with my present Engagedness to that Service prevents my writing more, than just to Inclose you the Resolve of Congress respectg the other Frigate, which you will Exert yourself to Compleat as soon as possible.[1] Pray lay it before the Assembly, & Apologize to them for my not writing them by this, but will by the Express which I shall Dispatch in 48 hours with Manley's Instructions [2] & your Money & the other Commisss. The Warrants you have Inclos'd, what you do not use you will keep for future purposes. The Inclos'd Letters please to Seal & Deliver.

The Inclos'd Commisss. please to forward; the Commisss. for the
Lieuts. &c will go by the Express. I was loth to Detain Capt Manley.[3]
You will Set him about getting the men & let the Capts. of Marines
fill their Comps.; their Coms. will go by the Express. I shall send
them all in blank for you to fill up. I am almost worn out, my Duty
is Constant, I have hardly time for necessary Rest. Manly is second
officer on the List; The Members determine the Rank.[4] Can I do any
thing agreeable for you, let me know & I will not be wanting. I must
Close. God bless you. I am yours sincerely,

John Hancock

RC (MHi).
[1] See Congress' October 16 resolve about making the frigate *Hancock* "ready
for sea immediately." *JCC*, 6:882.
[2] See Marine Committee to John Manley, Hector McNeill, and Thomas Thompson, October 23, 1776.
[3] Capt. John Manley had come to Philadelphia in a successful effort to help
persuade Congress to reverse the decision of the maritime court of New Hampshire in the case of the brig *Elizabeth*, which had been captured by Manley and
other Continental naval officers in April 1776. See *JCC*, 5:835, 6:870–73; and
Morgan, *Naval Documents*, 5:1033–34, 6:177, 246–48, 302, 368–69, 675, 772. See
also Josiah Bartlett to John Langdon, October 15, 1776.
[4] See *JCC*, 6:861.

John Hancock to George Washington

Sir,   Philada. Octr. 24th 1776.
   I have only Time to forward the enclosed Resolves.[1] The Cart-
tridges are on the Way, and I hope will arrive in Season. The
Congress will be attentive to all your Requests. With Sentiments of
Esteem, and every Wish in your Favour, I have the Honour to be,
Sir, your most obed & very hble Servt.

John Hancock Prest.

RC (DLC). In the hand of Jacob Rush and signed by Hancock.
[1] Hancock sent Washington a variety of resolves on military affairs passed
by Congress between October 14 and 23. See *JCC*, 6:873–74, 878–79, 880–81,
888, 889–94, 897–98.

George Ross to the
Lancaster County Committee of Safety

Gent   Philada. 24th Octr. 1776
   Pardon my once more writing to you on the Subject of our publick
Affairs. I mean not to direct, trusting in the Affection you have for
the Libertys of our Country which can never be safe but under a
free & Good Government. Believe me that my first wish is that my

country be free and that in every station they please to place me I will to the best of my Judgmt. do my utmost to serve them.

Whatever may be the result of the determinations of the County of Lancaster [1] I wish they may be communicated with expedition to the Neighbouring Countys. Accept of the affecte. regards of, Gent, yor. Obligd Hble Servt.[2]   Geo. Ross

RC (DLC).
[1] The subject of this vague letter was undoubtedly the proposed Pennsylvania constitution which had been drawn up in convention at Philadelphia the preceding month. Although the instrument was not submitted to the people for ratification, a vigorous effort was made to subvert it by preventing the organization of a new government under the forms prescribed by the convention. In a previous letter, which has not been found, Ross had transmitted to the Lancaster Committee a number of resolves "respecting the proceedings of the late Convention," which the committee had printed and distributed (in both English and German) in preparation for a public meeting to be held on October 25. At that time, representatives from the various Lancaster County precincts "passed in the affirmative" a motion to adopt "the Constitution of the Commonwealth of Pennsylvania, as established by the late General Convention," ensuring that the county would cooperate in implementing the new government. *Am. Archives,* 5th ser. 2:1155–57.
[2] This day Ross also wrote the following brief letter to the Pennsylvania Committee of Safety. "I am requested by a Committee of Congress to inform you that Mr. Lewis Guyon will be able to render essential Service to the States if he can have liberty to go to New York. And as he is in your Service he wants your permission which it is hoped you will grant on behalf of the Committee." Fogg Collection, MeHi.

Benjamin Franklin to Samuel Cooper [1]

[October 25, 1776] [2]

Being once more ordered to *Europe,* and to embark this day, I write this line, &c.

As to our publick affairs, I hope our people will keep up their courage. I have no doubt of their finally succeeding by the blessing of God, nor have I any doubt that so good a cause will fail of that blessing. It is computed that we have already taken a million sterling from the enemy. They must soon be sick of their piratical project. No time should be lost in fortifying three or four posts on our extended coast as strong as art and expense can make them. Nothing will give us greater weight and importance in the eyes of the commercial States, than a conviction that we can annoy, on occasion, their trade, and carry our prizes into safe harbours; and whatever expense we are at in such fortifying, will be soon repaid by the encouragement and success of privateering.

Reprinted from *Am. Archives,* 5th ser. 2:1245. Captioned: "Extract of a letter from Dr. Franklin to D. C., dated Philadelphia, October 25, 1776." Endorsed:

Benjamin Franklin

"In Council, November 20, 1776: Read and sent down. John Avery, Deputy Secretary [*of the Massachusetts Council*]."

¹ This letter was undoubtedly directed to Dr. Cooper—identified as "D.C." in the extract submitted to the Massachusetts Council—who subsequently acknowledged a farewell letter from Franklin of this date. Dr. Samuel Cooper to Benjamin Franklin, February 27, 1777, Franklin Papers, PPAmP.

² This day Franklin also wrote another letter upon the occasion of his imminent departure for France, primarily to procure a settlement of his accounts as Georgia's agent in London before his return to America in May 1775. "Being just about to embark for Europe," Franklin wrote, "I take the Liberty of troubling you with my Acct. and requesting you would be so good as to procure an Adjustment of it from your Government, and remit the Sum you receive to my Son-in-law, Richard Bache, Secretary of the General Post Office Residing in this Place, whose Receipt shall be a Discharge.

"I congratulate you on the Success against the Cherokees; I hope it will tend to the Security of your Frontiers. I hope your Health is re-establish'd. If on the other side the Water I can in anything render you either Service or Pleasure, be so good as to command freely, Dear Sir, Your obliged Friend & most obedt Servant, B. Franklin." Guild Library Collection, MHi.

Although the letter's recipient is not identified on the surviving document, Franklin's previous correspondence as Georgia's agent was conducted chiefly with Dr. Noble Wimberly Jones. Franklin's references to "the Security of your Frontiers" and "your Health" were undoubtedly responses to Jones' comments on Indian massacres and his own recent illness in Jones' letter to Franklin of July 11, 1776, which is in the Franklin Papers, PU.

Robert Treat Paine to Jonathan Trumbull, Sr.

Sr,   Philada. Octr. 25th. 1776

I have recd. yrs. of 15th Curet. & with great pleasure hear of the Success of the Cannon foundary at Salisbury.¹ I have been informed that not one has burst in proving. If the proof be sufficient this is remarkable Success & will pay for transporting Coal a great distance. You will give me Leave to be particular on the Subject of proving the Cannon as it has fallen under my inspection here. When we first Contracted for Cannon in this State we did not determine the proof but only that they should be sufficient, for at that time there were so many Opinions what was the Woolwich proof ² that we left it unsettled, but we since find that for 18 pounders & downwards they are the weight of the Ball in powder, two Balls & three hard Wadds & Kram a 2d Charge of ⅔ wt of Ball, 2 Balls & 3 Wadds because the first Charge may crack the gun tho not [. . .] & accordingly Messrs Hughes & Co of Maryland have proved all the Cannon they have made in that manner being 20 long 18 pdrs. for that state & the 12 pdrs. for the Frigate building there, & they are said to be exceeding good Guns & they have contracted for that proof for all the Guns they are to make for Congress. The Cannon that have been made here have been proved with ¾ wt of the Ball in powder, 3 Balls & 3 hard Wadds & Kram a 2d charge of ⅔ & 2 shott & 3 wadds which I take to be as good a proof as the other because the severity of the proof consists in the resistance the powder meets in passing thro the [barrel?]; But many of the Cannon made here have burst under this operation. You say the Guns made at yr. Furnace were proved with a double quantity of powder & Shott. I do not surmise that this is not a Sufficient proof, but as it is indeterminate I wish you to be ascertained precisely what it is. Some reckon $\frac{1}{3}$ the wt of the ball a proper charge for Action wch I believe to be the practice & that will make the proof $\frac{2}{3}$ & 2 balls wch. I do not think Sufficient beside 3 hard Wadds & considerable addition. Another thing that requires attention is the quality of the powder, a great deal made in this State & also some imported is exceeding poor. It has been said that some made with you has been bad, but if the Resolves of Congress respecting the Inspectors of Gunpowder be attended to I hope that difficulty will be soon cured; you will excuse my Freedom on this subject when you consider of what importance it is that the Guns should be Sound for Should any burst on board a Ship it might destroy many lives, occasion the loss of the Ship & discourage the service. We hope soon to hear that a convenient place is found for erecting a Stack sufficient for heavy Cannon. Perhaps they will never be more wanted than Next summer, & there are few matters that require more immediate attention.[3]

FC (MHi).

[1] Trumbull's October 15 letter to Paine is in Morgan, *Naval Documents*, 6:1271–72.

[2] A reference to the standards required at the royal foundry at Woolwich.

[3] This day the Marine Committee also wrote to Trumbull, directing him "to provide Sixty four Cannon for the use of the Frigate building in New Hampshire, and one of those in the Massachusetts Bay," and authorizing the transfer of cannon to the New Hampshire frigate from the Connecticut frigate, if the latter "not be in equal forwardness." See ibid., pp. 1415–16.

Secret Committee to Thomas Morris

Sir: [October 25, 1776]

You will receive herewith a copy of our letter of the 16th instant,[1] whereby you are appointed our agent to superintend all our business in *Europe*. This goes by the Continental ship-of-war called the *Reprisal, Lambert Weeks,* commander.

The value of this indigo is particularly intended to the lodged with your banker in *Paris*, for the use and subject to the order of Dr. *Franklin, Silas Deane,* and *Arthur Lee,* &c.

The *Reprisal,* Captain *Weeks,* will make but a short stay at *Nantes,* as she will immediately proceed on a cruise, and if fortunate, some of the prizes may probably be sent into some of the ports of

France. The Commissioners will apply at Court for the liberty and protection of their ports. If this should be granted, it's probable that they may also permit the sale of prizes there, and in such case, the prizes, or such parts of their cargoes as are to be sold in *France*, will be put under your direction. You must take care that every thing is disposed of to the best advantage, apply the proceeds to the payments we have ordered you to make on account of the publick, and render us very exact accounts of what you credit us in this way, and a particular account of sales of each prize. Should Captain *Weeks* take any specie, he will pay it to you or the Commissioner, or to their or your order for the same purpose, and you must grant him receipts for the same, expressing that you receive it for the use of the *United States of America*, and that he is to be repaid by Congress.[2]

MS not found; extract reprinted from *Am. Archives*, 5th ser. 2:1237.

[1] Not found.

[2] The following extract, also dated October 25 and endorsed "per Wickes," was probably taken from the same letter. "We have chartered and are now loading a fine Ship in Virginia called the Aurora, the master not yet fixed. She will carry upwards of 400 Hhds. of Tobacco and be dispatched soon as possible for Nantes consigned to your Order. You may insure this Tobacco valuing it at £10 Sterling per hhd. not exceeding 15 per Cent Premium. We have also chartered and are loading a New Ship at Baltimore, name nor Master yet fixed. She will carry 5 to 600 hhds. Tobacco also for Nantes consigned to your order on which we wish for Insurance valuing the Tobacco as above. We have bought large quantities of Tobacco and are trying to get ships to carry it. Some are engaged, but we must trust to future opportunities to write for insurance." PCC, item 19, 4:303. For Congress' request for assistance from Virginia in dispatching the Aurora, see *JCC*, 5:850–51; and John Hancock to Patrick Henry, November 12, 1776.

Samuel Adams to Samuel Mather

My dear Sir [1]   Philada Octob 26 1776

On the evening of the 24th Instant I arrivd in good health in this City. I give you this Information in Compliance with my word, and flattering myself that I shall very soon be favored with a Letter from you. I will promise to give you hereafter as much Intelligence as the Secrecy to which I am in honour bound will allow.

I met with Nothing disagreeable in my journey, saving my being prevented from passing through the direct Road in East Chester, the Enemy having taken Possession of the Ground there. Our Army is extended in several Encampments from Kings Bridge to White Plains which is 12 or 15 Miles Northward, commanded by the Generals Lord Sterling, Bell (of Maryland) Lincoln, McDougal, Lee, Heath & Putnam. I mention them, I think, in the order as they are posted from the Plains to the Bridge. The Generals Head Quarters are now at Valentine Hill about the Center of the Encampment. The Army is in high Spirits and wish for Action. There have been several Skirmishes; one on Fryday the 18th in which the Massachusetts Regiment commanded by Coll Glover distinguished their Bravery and they have receivd the Thanks of the General. In this Rencounter the Enemy sustaind a considerable Loss, it is said not less than 700 Men. Another on the Night of the 21st. The infamous Major Rogers with about 400 Tories of Long Island, having advanced toward Mareneck on the Main, was defeated by a Party of ours with the Loss of 36 Prisoners besides killed & wounded. This valiant Hero was the first off the Feild. Such Skirmishes, if successful on our Part, will give Spirit to our Soldiers and fit them for more important and decisive Action, which I confess I impatiently wish for. I have said that our Soldiers are in high Spirits; I add that so far as I can learn the Character of the General officers of the Enemy's Army, we at least equal them in this Instance. We have an excellent Commissary & Quarter Master General, officers of great Importance. Mifflin, who servd so much to our Advantage in the latter of these Employments, has condescended to take it again though he had been promoted to the Rank & Pay of a Brigadier General. The Enemy is posted in a rough hilly Country, the Advantages of which Americans have convinced them they know how to improve. Under all these Circumstances I should think that the sooner a General Battle was brot on, the better; but I am no Judge in military Matters.

An interesting Affair, about which a Circle of Friends whom I had the Pleasure of meeting at Dr Chauncys, is finishd, I think, agreably to their wishes. I can only add at present that I am with the most cordial Esteem, Sir your assured Friend, & very humble Servant,

S A

RC (PHi). Addressed: "The Revd. Dr. Samuel Mather Boston."

[1] Samuel Mather (1706–85), son of Cotton Mather, was a Boston minister. Although Thomas Hutchinson was his brother-in-law, Mather was a staunch patriot and Whig propagandist. Shipton, *Harvard Graduates*, 7:216–38.

Board of War to the Maryland Council of Safety

Gentlemen   War Office Octr. 26th. 1776

I am directed by the Board of War in Answer to your Letter of the 18th instant to inform you that it is their Opinion & they request you will direct that the Rifle Company mentioned in your Letter be immediately marched to Philadelphia, if Cloathes cannot be provided for them where they are which would be much the best, as Cloathing of all Sorts is extremely difficult to be had at Philadelphia & Blanketts are not to be procured at any Rate.[1] They might be armed & accoutred, but might lie here a very considerable Time before Cloathes & Blanketts could be furnished. You will therefore be pleased to endeavour at supplying them with Blanketts & whatever other Necessaries can be had your Way as this State is much drained of all Articles required by the Army. If Musketts were given them instead of Rifles the Service would be more benefitted, as there is a Superabundance of Riflemen in the Army. Were it in the Power of the Congress to supply Musketts they would speedily reduce the Number of Rifles & replace them with the former, as they are more easily kept in order, can be fired oftner & have the Advantage of Bayonetts.

I have the Honour to be, your very obedt Servt,

Richard Peters, Secy

RC (MdAA).

[1] The council of safety's October 18 letter to the board, dealing with the "want of both guns and blankets" for "a rifle Company on the Continental Establishment . . . raised in Harford County" is in *Md. Archives*, 12:365.

Abraham Clark to Elias Dayton

Eliza. Town Octor. 26. 1776. It is long since I recd. a Letter from you, and longer since I wrote to you. The last I recd was by Mr. Caldwell. I had then just returned from Phila. much indisposed and was Elected into the Assembly, which, tho' very infirm I Attended for About ten days & returned home Sick where I have remained ever since with my self and most of my family much indisposed.[1] We are all got tolerable Well except my wife who hath the 3d day Ague, and one of my younger Children I lost. I purpose next Monday to return again to Phila. where I can remain but two Weeks when Our Assembly will Meet again, when I purpose to Sue for a dismission from Congress finding it too hard to Attend there & at the Assembly, between both of which I could not expect to spend much of my Time at home. Public News I Suppose you know as much of as I do from my long Confinement." Recapitulates recent military developments and concludes: "I hear Genl. Schuyler lately wrote to the Congress requesting to resign his Commission, upon a Supposition they meant to cast an Oblique Censure on him by Approving Gen. Wosters Conduct in Canada; concluding there must be a fault some where, and if not in Genl. Woster it would Naturally fall on him. His Conclusion was ill founded as the Congress when they cleared Genl. Woster of Misconduct never thought of laying it on Genl. Schuyler, but imputed the Miscarriage there to the Short Time the Soldiers had inlisted for, the Small pox getting into the Army, the want of hard money to purchase Provisions in Canada, and the almost impossibility of transporting any quantity there in the Winter." [2]

RC (MeHi).

[1] Clark had also discussed the state of his health in two letters to John Hart,

the speaker of the New Jersey Assembly, written from Elizabethtown. In the first, dated September 17, he stated: "At my return home I found my family down with the bloody Flux. One I have buried, Another is Dangerously ill, the others appear upon the recovery. My indisposition remains. I was by it confined to my house, & till yesterday I remained a stranger to my disorder which Appears to be the jaundice. My exceeding Languid state gives me no hopes of being able to Attend my duty with you soon." Southard Hay Collection, CtY. In the second, dated September 28, he observed: "I think it my duty to inform you that I yet remain in a weak, Languid state tho' I am in hopes my disorder is upon the Remove, but were I in health the weak and dangerous State two of my Children are in would not suffer me to leave home." *A Catalogue of Autograph Letters and Documents Relating to the Declaration of Independence and the Revolutionary War* (Philadelphia: Rosenbach Co., 1926), no. 8, item 30.

² Schuyler formally complained about Congress' August 17 resolve exonerating Wooster of misconduct during the Canadian campaign in an October 23 letter to Hancock, which was read in Congress on November 4. PCC, item 153, 2:463–66; and *Am. Archives,* 5th ser. 2:1205–6. See also *JCC,* 5:664–65.

Committee to Ticonderoga to John Hancock

Sir,   Saratoga Octr. 26th 1776

In execution of the Commission with which we were charged by Congress, we proceeded, with as much expedition as the nature of the service would permit, to Albany; having taken Head Quarters in our way, and thereby obtained all the information which could be given us by Mr Trumbul, your Commissary General. At Albany we spent two days with General Schuyler, and then proceeded in company with him, to this place. On our way, we received information by Express, of our Fleet having been attacked on Lake Champlain; and the next day of it's total defeat. We were nevertheless about to proceed on to Tyonderoga, but were advised by Genl. Schuyler, that in all probability our Army would be attacked by the Enemy, before we could possibly reach that place; or if otherwise, yet that Genl. Gates his attention would be so totally taken up in preparing to receive the Enemy, that we could do no business with him. We therefore concluded to suspend our journey to Tyonderoga for a few days, untill we might have some further Accounts from Genl. Gates; and in the meantime, we gave our attention to the Barracks to be erected in this place, and in considering the application of two Gentn. respecting the contract for supplying the Army.¹ Happily Genl. Schuyler's precaution & diligence as to the Barracks had left us little more to do, but to go with him and mark out the ground where they were to be erected. He had prepared the most of the Timber before we arrived, and they are now raising, and will be ready in good time. Other Barracks will be built at Fort Edward and elsewhere. Nails are exceedingly wanted, and if any could be procured at Philada. they should be sent immediately. After having gotten thro' the business which had arisen at this place, and having sent on a letter to Genl. Gates for speedy information from him, we set out for Fort George, in order to inspect the State of the Hospital at that place.

The chief of the sick from Tyonderoga are sent there, as being a much more healthy & convenient situation: and we are happy in being able to inform Congress that the Building is convenient & comfortable, that the Director Genl. has lately received a large supply of the most capital medicines, and that they are now furnished with a sufficient quantity of fresh mutton and Indian meal. They yet want Beding, and some other matters which we shall state upon our return: we shall endeavour to procure some straw (a very scarce article here) which is much needed at the Hospital. At the close of our business at Fort George, we received a letter from Genl. Gates, advising us not to pursue our journey to Tyonderoga, but to remain at Saratoga, until further advise from him. We are just returned here from Fort George, and shall wait a few days to hear further from Genl. Gates. In the mean time, we shall be pursuing the other parts of our instructions, which can be executed here.

Genl. Schuyler has taken every possible step in order to keep open the communication from hence to Tyonderoga, that the Army may not want supplies. Considerable bodies of the militia are daily going up: yet we heard, the last evening, that the Savages had appeared between the upper End of Lake George & Tyonderoga, and had, on the day we left Fort-George, taken two and killed & scalped one of our people going to Tyonderoga. An Express comes in this moment, who brings a letter from the commanding officer at Fort George, informing that a party of the Enemy had made their appearance and fired on some of our people who were crossing Lake George. Genl. Schuyler yet doubts of this fact.

We shall attend, with all possible diligence, to the remaining business committed to us by Congress; and for our own sake, as well as the public interest, return as soon as may be. With the greatest esteem & respect, we have the honor to be, Sir, Your most obedient and very humble Servants,   Richd. Stockton

Geo. Clymer

RC (DNA: PCC, item 78). Written by Stockton and signed by Stockton and Clymer. Endorsed: "read 4 Novr. 1776."

[1] Robert R. Livingston and Walter Livingston. See John Hancock to Philip Schuyler, September 27, 1776, note 4.

William Ellery to Nicholas Cooke

Sir,   Philadelphia Oct. 26th 1776

Since my last Congress have received the disagreeable Intelligence of the Destruction of our Fleet on Lake Champlain. The Enemy were vastly superior to Us in the Number and Size of their armed Vessells, and in the Number of Men and Weight of Metal. Genl.

Arnold was obliged to give Way to superior Force; but he did not do it until he had sustained the Shock, many Glasses, in Two Engagements, nor until several of his Gondaloes were sunk, his Schooner forced on Shore, and the Remainder of his Fleet were so shattered that it was impossible for him to fight any longer; in this Situation he ran the Congress ashore, and least She should fall into the Hands of the Enemy burnt her; and with about 200 Men, he had collected, got safe to Crown Point.

Congress have appointed a Committee of Intelligence to select and publish such Intelligence as Congress shall receive from Time to Time, and it shall be proper to publish.[1]

That Committee have, in this Week's Papers, published an Account of the Sea-Fight on the Lake; but omitted some Particulars which I have mentioned.[2] They have also given the Publick such Intelligence as hath been received from the army in the middle Department. I inclosed a News-Paper, which contained those Accounts, in a Letter to my Brother Christo[pher],[3] which went by Express yesterday Morning and desired him to convey the Paper to your Honor immediately upon his receiving it. By the same Express you will receive a Letter from the Committee of Cloathing, inclosing a Resolve of Congress respecting the Blankets and coarse Goods taken and imported into our State in a Prize Store-Ship bound to Quebec.[4] It is not meant that this Resolve should supersede the Resolve lately sent to your Honour by the same Committee.[5] With all the Cloathing than can be collected in the several States, and imported, We shall not I am afraid have more than sufficient to cloath our Armies. Hang well and pay well is a good military Maxim. In paying well I presume Cloathing and Food is involved, otherwise they ought to be subjoined. The former, Congress attended to in their last Articles of War, and I hope their Resolutions respecting the latter will be carried into Execution by those to whom the Execution thereof hath been committed.

I should have wrote to your Honour by the Express to the State of Massachusetts; but had not Time and I chose to wait until the Post should arrive hoping to get something new to communicate. There hath been no Post this Week. By private Accounts it seems that the Enemy are intrenching at New Rochell, and that Genl. Washington determined not to be outflanked, hath extended his Army from Kingsbridge to White Plains. I expect to hear, by the first Express from the Northern Army, that there hath been a Battle. From the Army in the Middle Department I expect to hear of nothing but Skirmishes, unless Burgoyne should penetrate through our northern Army, and form a Junction with Howe which, considering the strong Posts and the Number of that Army I cannot imagine, for Genls Washington & Howe move with great Caution, and will not come to a general Battle unless One or the other can gain some great Advantage of Ground, or outflank, or play off some capital Manœuvre.

I could wish to have it in my Power, through your Honour, to give the State an early Account of every material Article of Intelligence; but as the Arrival of the Post is uncertain, and he goes out very soon after he comes in I am obliged frequently to close my Letters before he arrives, or loose the Opportunity of writing by him. At this critical Period, when We have so much at Stake, every Friend to his Country is anxious to know every Thing that takes Place. Sensible of this, Congress, as I have already mentioned, have appointed a Committee of Intelligence, whose Publications may be relied on; and if the Accounts which Congress receives from the Armies are but particular, the Public will be gratified so soon as Posts can convey the News-Papers to the different States.

I hope the Genl. Assembly have or will soon appoint an Additional Delegate. Congress is so very thin that I am obliged to observe a constant wearisome Punctuality in Attendance. I do therefore, as well as on Account of the late Recommendation to the States of a full Representation, earnestly desire that the new Delegate may be here as soon as possible.

It is long since I have received any Letter from the Government, and I have received no Information at all respecting several Matters about which I requested it. I should be glad to know whether the Militia from the Massachusetts have arrived in our State; whether the Militia of our State is yet muster'd and equipped that was to supply the Place of Col. Richmond's Battalion, and whether that Battalion hath marched to join the Army under G[enera]l Washington. I imagin from some Advertisements I have seen in the Newport Mercury that it is still in Newport. If it should not have marched, I hope it will remain there until Congress or Genl. Washington shall have given Orders for its Removal; and that our Militia may be equipped and hold themselves in Readiness to march to any Part of our State or of the neighbouring States that may be attacked. I vehemently suspect that the Commodiousness of our Bay, the Stock on Rhode Island and along our Coast will allure and the Irritation which the great Success of our Privateers must have excited in the Breasts of our Enemies will urge them to pay Us a Visit. This is my private, humble Opinion. It is prudent to be always on our guard and prepared for the worst. The Wisdom of the Genl. Assembly and Council of Safety will suggest to them the best Measures to be pursued for our Security, and their Spirit and Activity will urge the Pursuit and Execution thereof. Heartily wishing the Happiness and Prosperity of the State I have the Honour to represent, that of the United States of America and that of your Honour, I continue to be with great Respect your Honor's most Obedient, humble Servant,   Wm Ellery

P.S. Since I wrote the foregoing the President read in Congress a Letter from Genl. Mifflin to a Gent. in this Town dated at Fort Washington Oct. 23,[6] in which he says, if my Memory serves Me, that by Two Deserters from the Enemy's York Lines, it appeared that in the Engagement of last Friday Week We killed and wounded Eight Hundred of the Enemy—That We had only 1500 of our Men engaged and only 3000 in that Quarter, while the Enemy's whole Force at and near the Spot was 8000—That last Monday some of our Troops came across Major Rogers with a Party of Long-Island Militia Rangers, killed a Number of them and took 36 of Them Prisoners, sixty odd fine Muskets and a Number of Blankets—That Two of our Battalions ambushed a Body of Hessians and drove them. Genl. Mifflin saw our Troops discharge Three Vollies at them which doubtless did Execution; after which the Armies annoyed each other with a Cannonade, in which a Ball from One of our Cannon killed the Sentry who stood at the Door of Genl. Howes Tent, enter'd it and shattered One of his (Genl Howe's) Legs so that his Life was despaired of. This Account the Genl. says was bro't by a Deserter who said that he heard his Capt. relate it. That Col. Livingston with Two Regiments had gone from Fairfield to the East End of Long-Island and that the Enemy had sent thither Two Battalions to oppose them and that he heard that Livingston had taken and sent over to Connecticut some of the Enemy's Cattle— That the Main Body of the Enemy was at New Rochelle—That our Army out flanked them and that if they moved, so as to quit the Cover of their shipping a Battle would probably ensue, That the Events of War were uncertain, but that our Troops were in good Spirits, and he did not doubt in Case of a Battle they would be successful. The President would not permit Me to copy the Letter, so that I may have made some Mistakes. The Substance I am confident is right.   W E

RC (R–Ar).
   [1] See *JCC*, 6:886.
   [2] This "account" is also in Morgan, *Naval Documents*, 6:1388–91.
   [3] This letter has not been found.
   [4] See Committee on Clothing to Nicholas Cooke, October 11, 1776.
   [5] See *JCC*, 6:897.
   [6] This letter is printed under the heading "Extract of a Letter from a General Officer" in *Am. Archives*, 5th ser. 2:1202–3.

William Hooper to the
North Carolina Provincial Convention

Honoured Sir   Philadelphia, Oct 26 1776
   I beg leave through you to address the honourable the Congress of the state of North Carolina and to explain to them the motives

which induce my stay here at a time when the return of their delegates may be considered as an act of duty which they owe to those
who constituted them. A desire to be present at that interesting
period which is in a great measure to decide upon the portion of
happiness which Carolina is to enjoy in its state of independency,
weighs powerfully with me. And tho' my country may not have
thought proper to have called me as a colonial delegate to assist in
her councils in framing a system of Government for her future
regulation, yet I most earnestly wish to be with you, altho I should
be only an inactive spectator of the Game in which every member
of the state risques so great a Stake. That man must possess a more
than stoical Apathy who can be indifferent to the event of deliberations which is to involve the rule of conduct which is to be prescribed to him, and under the influence of which he is destined to
spend the remainder of his days & be happy or miserable in proportion as the spirit of the government shall be adapted to those whom
it is intended to control. Another motive which has a powerful
influence with me is the insight which in the course of the business
of the Continental Congress one necessarily obtains of the condition
of the Continent at large and the possibility of applying this experimental knowledge to the benefit of our own state. Were I upon the
spot in this respect I might be made perhaps convenient, tho only
as the vehicle of useful Intelligence. I might explain to you the
measures of the Continental Congress so far as they concern our state
and contribute my mite to aid the purposes for which they are
intended. My private connections have a large share in my inclinations. A family seated in that part of the state whither Lord Howe
will no doubt direct the first efforts of his winter campaign excite
an anxiety that I am too much of the man not to feel in the most
sensible manner, and earnestly wish to snatch them from impending
danger.

These are considerations which one would imagine could scarce
be overballanced by any private or publick duty. The case is otherways—and from an obligation superiour to them all I am induced
for the present not to accede to them.

The necessary absence of my two very worthy Colleagues from the
Continental Congress leaves the representation of the state of
Carolina with me singly. At this critical period when the fate of
American liberty may depend upon the full and perfect exertions of
America on a sudden, when the energy of this Congress must be felt
thro all the parts of this extended Continent, Representation should
be as large as possible least the united Councils of America should
loose their weight from the fewness of those who are concerned in
them. Thus circumstanced to leave the seat of our state vacant would
be a gross violation of the sacred trust which you have reposed in
me and might be considered by America as a dishonourable deser-

tion of her in the day of danger. The honour of North Carolina is concerned and with me that supersedes every other consideration.

We have a large army in the neighbourhood of New York and Gen Howe with a formidable one to oppose it. The maneuvres of our Enemies indicate a design to bring on an action. The armies have continued for 6 days within a mile of each other, skirmishing at the extremities; this must soon communicate to the center and the action become general. What will be the event Heaven alone knows. Success is so often the result of unforseen accidents that the most experienced never count with confidence. Our hopes are indeed sanguine. Our General stands high in the opinion of those who know him, as the soldier, the Citizen, the Man his character is great. Lee is with him and is an able assistant, and we have very many other officers who would do honour to any Corps in Europe. Our men are in high spirits, zealous for action, leaving the event to him who has most miraculously fought for us on former occasions. We trust we shall succeed, but the contrary is possible, as such this congress means to provide for such an event, if it does not happen our precautions will have been useless & this is the worst epithet they will merit. Should we be defeated at New York it is absolutely necessary that a full congress should be upon the spot to counteract the uses which the Tories may make of it to dispirit our friends, to encourage the disaffected and bring our glorious cause into disrepute. Men who have made observations on the History of past ages, or studied the nature of things are convinced that uninterrupted success is not the portion of man however meritorious his cause, but others who think superficially or are too lazy to think at all, Men who have weak nerves, or like the Cappadocians chose rather to be slaves than freemen, despising the habit of thinking for themselves, these and such as these are governed by the event of the day, and if they do not run on in a continued tide of success, they lift up their hands in despair and give over all for lost; these unhappily are the bulk of mankind, it is the history of Human nature not of any particular place. Such exist here. To prevent the consequences of such ill grounded terrors, which when once set afloat spread like a contagion, it becomes the duty of the continental delegates by no conduct of theirs to give occasion to the weak or wicked, to draw insinuations from their conduct that may encourage such a spirit. This furnishes another reason, if another was necessary to explain the motives of my continuance here.

With respect to the state of publick affairs in this part of the Continent I beg leave to refer you to Mr Hewes & Mr Penn, satisfying myself with making some observations which necessarily arise out of the facts, and which may not occur to you at your distance from the Scene of Action. The successes which General Howe has obtained on Long Island and New York have been magnified into such importance that one would imagine that they proved a total incapacity on our part to resist him & must necessarily involve the ruin of our cause. Strange Infatuation. What are the mighty feats that the utmost exertions of Great Britain by sea and land, aided with all the auxiliaries that Germany would credit them with, collected into a focus in the center of America, performed. They have taken possession of Long Island and York Island. The first they purchased at the expence of 1000 men after a well fought battle which with 3000 men we maintained against twice that number, & where success even then determined in their favor by a superiour stroke of experimental Generalship. Were we disgraced here? No! We retired in a manner that would have honoured a Roman General, and they took possession of their dear bought purchase, with nothing to boast but that from their Shipping they might have cut off our communication with our main army and prevented us a supply of provisions. Have they any extraordinary merit in the acquisition of New York? Believe me they have none. This place was long ago thought incapable of defence against Shipping, and an experienced Engineer who some time ago was sent out for the express purpose of fortifying it declared that it was impossible to make it formidable. It required more men than we could spare to make it tenable, and as we had many other posts to which as well as to this, the Enemy had access with their shipping, It was tho't prudent to abandon it and concenter our force where the Enemies Ships could not annoy them. Have the Enemy notwithstanding this advanced into the Country? No! They keep close to their shipping and with all their advances have not yet marched a mile into our Country. The trouble (for that was all, the work being done by the soldiers when otherwise they would have been idle saving the greatest part of the Expence) of erecting Batteries was well bestowed. It has retarded the Enemies operations, advanced a Summer Campaign into the Month of November, distressed them for food, and gives us oppertunities to arm and accoutre & cloath our own Army and furnish them with the means of defence. Staten Island has seen British Troops fly before us. The 16th on Haerlem plains it is believed they lost near 1000 in killed and wounded, & we held possession of the field. Last Week They left 150 dead near Frog point to grace the success of Genl Glover. Deserters say they lost above 500 in killed & Wounded & a Skirmish at Rochele last Week thinned them of 30 or 40 men. How stands the ballance? Britain surely has not much to boast? The Officers of the British Troops called Long Island a second Bunker Hill Affair and I believe it proved so to them.

Altho this Skirmishing immediately decides nothing of importance yet as it accustoms our troops to the sound of Musquetry, it is of essential service to them. Many men have courage by mechanism, & fighting may by frequent practice become so habitual as to constitute part of a mans pleasure.

The Affair on the lakes is a matter of real importance, & the success which the British troops have obtained must for some time give them the command of the entrance into Canada, but it is a victory which they have obtained not at the expence of American honour. The Contest was maintained on our side with a bravery that would have graced the page of Roman history. Success decided in favour of vastly superiour members and strength, Britain fought on the Water her national Element against the infant efforts of America in the formation of naval strength. It is a fact which they confess that we did all that men could do. When in a future period justice shall be done to Arnold who commanded, Posterity will lament that such amazing fortitude should have been attended with such undeserved ill fortune. I flatter myself that should they make an Attack upon Ticonderoga Genl Gates will give a good account of them. He has 9000 effective men in good spirits, reinforced by a large body of Militia who consider this pass as the key to the Eastern Colonies and are determined not to cede it but with their lives. Mr Penn will inform the Convention of any other matters of publick import as well as of a report which prevails and is believed of Genl Howe being wounded by a cannon shot in the Leg.

Before I close this letter I beg leave to hint a few things for the consideration of your honourable body. You will give them attention in proportion to their merit, and pardon my presumption in offering them from the motive which influences me; which is a sincere wish to promote the publick good and even at this distance contribute my mite to aid the useful purposes for which you are assembled.

The first and most important object which will engage your deliberations will be the formation of a constitution of Government under which yourselves and posterity are to be happy or miserable. As the happiness of society ought to be the end and aim of all Government, & that is most promoted by assimilating it to the tempers, pursuits, Customs, & Inclinations of those who are to be ruled, in the plan proposed for the future regulation of their conduct I doubt not much regard will be paid to the prevalance of habit, & that system adopted which will remedy the defects of the police under which we have lately lived, without such a violent deviation as may tend to produce a convulsion from unnecessary alteration. I am well assured that the British Constitution in its purity (for what is at present stiled the British Constitution is an apostate) was a system that approached as near to perfection as any could within the compass of human Abilities. The powers of the Crown are perhaps too independent of the people, and tho' upon fundamental principles, derived from and subject to Revocation, Yet from being long exercised, to an inattentive people they assume the appearance of being the inherent right of sovereignty, and subjects are so dazzled or dismayed with the Blaze of Majesty as not to dare to question the source from which power is derived. Hence it is necessary that recurrence should often be had to original principles to prevent those evils which in a course of years must creep in and vitiate every human institution and by insensible gradations at length steal upon the Understanding as part of the original System. To these pure, genuine, unadulterated principles I sincerely wish we may, in our present state untramelled by any rule but that of right have recourse. Let us consider the people at large as the source from which all power is to be derived, & that whatever restraints may be imposed upon them, if they have not their happiness as their only aim, are the fetters of tyranny and the badges of Slavery. Rulers must be conceived as the Creatures of the people, made for their use accountable to them, and subject to removal as soon as they act inconsistent with the purposes for which they were formed. With this for a Basis, if we will divest ourselves of theoretical or practical prejudices except as they arise from knowlege founded on experience we shall find little difficulty in adopting a frame of Government which will be stable and lasting. The Constitution of Britain had for its object the union of the three grand qualities of virtue, wisdom and power as the Characteristicks of perfect Government. From the people at large the first of these was most to be expected, the second from a selected few whom superiour Talents or better opportunities for Improvement had raised into a second Class, and the latter from some one whom variety of Circumstances may have placed in a singular and conspicuous point of view, and to whom Heaven had given talents to make him the choice of the people to intrust with powers for sudden and decisive execution. The middle class like the hand which holds a pair of scales balancing between the *One* & the *many* and impartially casting weight against the scale that preponderates in order to preserve that equality which is the essence of a mixed Monarchy & is called the ballance of power. Might not this or something like this serve as a Model for us? A Single branch of Legislation is a many headed Monster which without any check must soon defeat the very purposes for which it was created, and its members become a Tyranny dreadful in proportion to the numbers which compose it, and possessed of power uncontrolled would soon exercise it to put themselves free from the restraint of those who made them; and to make their own political existence perpetual. The consultations of large bodies are likewise less correct and perfect than those where a few only are concerned, the people at large have generally just Objects in their pursuit but often fall short in the means made use of to obtain them. A Warmth of Zeal may lead them into errors which a more cool dispassionate enquiry may discover and rectify. This points out the necessity of another branch of legislation at least, which may be a refinement of the first choice of the people at large selected for their Wisdom, remarkable Integrity, or that weight which arises from property and gives Independence and Impartiality to the human Mind. For my own part I once thought it would be wise to adopt a double check as in the British Constitution but from the Abuses which power in the hand of an Individual is liable to, & the unreasonableness that an individual should abrogate at pleasure the acts of the Representatives of the people, refined by a second body whom we may call for fashion sake Counsellors & as they are a kind of barrier for the people's rights against the encroachments of their delegates, I am now convinced that a third branch of Legislation is at least Unnecessary. But for the sake of Execution We must have a Magistrate solely executive and with the aid of his Council (I mean a Privy Council) let him have such executive powers as may give energy to Government.

Pennsylvania adopted the visionary system of a single branch, the people soon saw the Monster the Convention had framed for them with horror & with one accord stifled it [in] its cradle before it had begun its outrages.

The Constitution of Delaware has in my opinion great merit. From this with the Plans of South Carolina and the Jersey may be framed a System that may make North Carolina happy to endless ages. I admire no part of the Delaware plan more than the appointing Judges during good behaviour. Limit their political existence and make them dependent upon the suffrages of the people; that instant you corrupt the Channels of publick Justice. Rhode Island furnishes an example too dreadful to imitate. Pardon me if I have trespassed too far. My Zeal for the happiness of my Country at a period when it is in a manner to be decided upon has hurried me beyond the bounds of propriety. Happy should I be could I consistent with my duty to you contribute my mite to raising the glorious structure, but if that cannot be, God grant that I may with transport hail your handy work when compleated, built upon the foundation of pure genuine liberty and upon those principles upon which the happiness of human society depends.

I cannot but most earnestly press upon you the necessity of fortifying the harbours of Carolina into which the Enemy have access, their Absence gives you ample opportunity at present for that purpose, the only objection must arise from a scarcity of battering Cannon; Some you have which might be made useful and it is impossible to apply them more beneficially than as I propose. If the Enemy could be kept out of Cape Fear River, where else could they land? What a security for our own & the shipping of those who may wish to carry on trade with us. It might be accomplished by drawing the regular troops together at the Entrance of Cape Fear and having a great number of hands to perfect the Work immediately. Could not Cannon be borrowed from South Carolina, You will soon be in a Condition to repay them from your Iron Works, the vast advantages which would result from this measure to the Continent at large would no doubt induce ⟨the Congress⟩ South Carolina to aid you in the Attempt. At any rate is it not a Subject worthy the appointment of a Committee instantly. If you resolve upon it Send an express to me & I will endeavour to procure an Engineer to superintend the Works.[1]

Your Iron Works deserve your most strenuous exertions. Mr Milles who has been sent hither by the Council of Safety will inform you of what he has with the Assistance of your delegates accomplished. I think him sensible; I wish you may have the benefit of his abilities in carrying this most excellent plan into Execution. It will be expensive, but when we consider the Work as a Cannon foundery and manufacture of Shot and other implements of War and that upon a proper supply of these our salvation as a free people must in a great measure depend, when we reflect that Husbandry, manufactures, the very means of our subsistence must depend upon internal supplies of iron tools, implements and Utensils, our trade with Britain being altogether interrupted and elsewhere in a great measure, The expence, I say under such Circumstances ought not to weigh even as a feather. Since Milles left this an ingenious Man in the process of Cannon casting has applied to us. Should you think prudent to employ him I must have very early notice of your Intentions.

The delegates from North Carolina have exerted their utmost endeavours to procure Salt pans in obedience to the Council of Safety. They have been deluded with false promises from time to time and at length have been told that the demand at home for Plate Iron is such that they cannot spare any to go abroad. We must rely at present upon Frederick & soon I hope upon our own Works at Deep River.

Can any thing be more necessary than fitting up our own Regiments immediately. The plans which the delegates from your state have sent to you shew the advantageous terms which are offered, & the additional resolve inclosed relative to Cloathing makes proposals which I think must be irresistible and tend immediately to compleat your Military allotment.[2]

By Waggons which left this last Sunday We have sent you what Cloathing can from this at present be procured—some copies of the proceedings of Congress to May—some medicines & Articles of War. The Horses & Waggons are purchased for our State. The Invoice of the whole together with the Expences of the Books & Teams are with the Waggoner, if I have time before Mr Penn leaves this I will send Copies of the whole, rectifying an Error in the Commissary of Waggons Account, He having charged some trifle less than what he was entitled to.

I am, Gentlemen, With the Greatest Respect, Your most Obedt, most Obliged Humble Sert,   Will Hooper

[P.S.] I send the plans of Gov't of several states.

RC (Nc–Ar).
[1] See Hooper to the North Carolina Provincial Convention, October 29, 1776.
[2] See *JCC*, 5:855.

William Hooper to the
North Carolina Provincial Convention

Honoured Sir   Oct 26 1776 Philadelphia
By favour of Mr Penn I inclose you Copies of the several bills of parcels which go by Waggons which in all probability will arrive about the Time this reaches you.[1]
The Waggons & Horses are purchased for the State of North Carolina I therefore send you a very particular account of the several prices & descriptions of the Horses. The Letters & papers which the Waggoners upon their Arrival will hand you will explain this transaction more fully. Permit me in the Meantime to subscribe myself with great Respect, Sir, Yours & the Convention's Most Obed Hum Sert,   Wm Hooper

RC (Nc–Ar).
[1] For these enclosures, see *N.C. Colonial Records*, 10:851–57.

William Hooper to the
North Carolina Provincial Convention

Sir   [October 26–28? 1776] [1]
As the printed Journals of the Continental Congress which have been lately forwarded to you by your delegates come down no lower than the Month of May, I do myself the honour by Mr Penn to transmit you some resolves which have passed in congress since that period. You will find several of them particularly interesting to our state and necessary in some measure to produce that uniformity of conduct in military arrangements which it is proper shd pervade the whole Continent.
Among the rest you will observe a resolve relative the Carolina prisoners confined here from whence it will appear that they are left entirely to the discretion of your Convention to dispose of them as you think proper. I have the fullest confidence that you will extend every Indulgence to them which you can consistent with the security of the Continent at large & the particular safety of Your own State.[2]
I am, Sir, Your's & the Conventions Obedt Humble Sert,
                                        Wm Hooper

P.S. You will observe the supplemental Resolve of Congress offering Cloathing in addition to the Bounty of Land & Money already offered for the encouragement of Soldiers to enlist in the New Army.[3]

RC (Nc–Ar).
[1] Hooper undoubtedly wrote this letter after October 20, when the printed journals of Congress had been forwarded to North Carolina, and before his letter

to the provincial convention of October 29, 1776, which was also to be delivered
by John Penn. Because Hooper first mentioned Penn's plan to leave Philadelphia
in a letter dated October 26, it is likely he also wrote this one about the same
time. The immediate recipient of this letter cannot be identified, but there can
be no doubt that it was intended for and actually received by the provincial
convention.

² See *JCC*, 6:885–86; and Hooper to the North Carolina Provincial Convention,
November 1, 1776.

³ See *JCC*, 5:855.

New York Delegates to the New York Convention

Gentlemen.   Philadelphia 26th October, 1776.
    As the State of New-York has not been represented in Congress
for several weeks past, (Mr. P. Livingston with myself being their
only Delegates at present here,) we are requested by Congress to
apply to you, sirs, for a full representation. Therefore hope you will
speedily send us one other member, that we may be enabled to give
our vote for that State which we have been sent here to represent.¹
    We are, respectfully, gentlemen, Your very humble servts.
                        Fra. Lewis, for self and Ph. Livingston.

MS not found; reprinted from *Journals of N.Y. Prov. Cong.*, 2:232.
    ¹ On November 5 the New York Committee of Safety directed a letter to James
Duane asking him to "prepare to attend at Congress." *Am. Archives*, 5th ser.
3:286. However, Duane did not in fact return to Congress until April 17, 1777.

William Whipple to Joshua Brackett

My Dear Sir   Philad. 26th Octor 1776
    I came through the army last Monday & found them in good
spirits & much pleas'd at the arrival of Genl Lee. You have ere this
heard of the Enemy's landing at East-Chester. They have got as far as
New Rochel which is about 6 Miles Eastward of Kings Bridge. There
have been several Skirmishes in which we have always had the
advantage. I was obliged to go a little out of the old Road to avoid
the Enemy who were posted as above & found our army had out
Flank'd them. Our main Body now extends from Kings Bridge to
White Plain about 15 Miles, Posted very advantagiously as they say,
& I doubt not we shall give a good accot. of them. The plan seems
to be to draw them farther into the Country. I must refer you to Mr.
Langdon for a description of the ground which is very advantagious
for us. The News from the Lakes is not so good as I cod. wish, However we shall be all right soon. You have often appear'd anxious

about F——n A——ce.[1] Make your self easy about that matter. Proper steps are taken, to set all matters right. It is the duty of every friend to his country to exert himself to encourage the inlisting the New Army. Was that compleated I shod think all our Difficulties at an end, Your very affecte Friend &c,   W W

[*P.S.*] The Ministerial Committee desir'd me to send them a Parson. When I arriv'd at N. Haven Mr Dwight the Gen[tlema]n on whose assistance I relyed was gone out of town & my Company was unwilling [to] delay any time on the Road so that it has not been in my power to do any thing in that Matter.

RC (MHi).
    [1] That is, a foreign alliance.

William Whipple to John Langdon

My Dear Sir,   Philadelphia 26th Oct 1776.
    I arrived here the 24th. The Committee [1] have not met since my arrival but have mentioned your demand to some of the members. There is no doubt but I shall be in cash to honor your drafts whenever they appear. There is no prospect of cannon from this place, however, I have some hopes from another quarter viz. Connecticut. The circumstances are these. The cannon are made for the Trumbell in that State and there is no prospect of her being provided with other necessaries. The Committee have wrote to Govr. Trumbell to procure cannon for two ships and in the mean time to send those made for the Trumbell to you.[2] From the known Disposition of that gentleman to promote the public good I have great hopes you will be supplied from that quarter. Orders are gone to Providence to supply you with canvass for a second suit of sails.[3] I don't know but you'll have a wrangle on your hands with the Providence gentry. However my boy I'll stand by you as long as I can. The ships here are not so forward as I expected to find them; only three of them are launched. The rank of the Captains in the naval service was established before I arrived. I find Thompson is the 6th on the list—had I been here I certainly would have had him higher. However considering the train after him, I think it pretty well. For want of time must refer you to Col. Bartlett for news &c.[4]
    In haste as you see, Your affectionate friend & humble servt.
                                        Wm Whipple.

Tr (DLC).
    [1] That is, the Marine Committee.
    [2] See Robert Treat Paine to Jonathan Trumbull, Sr., October 25, 1776, note 3.
    [3] See Marine Committee to Daniel Tillinghast, October 30, 1776.
    [4] This day Josiah Bartlett noted in his travel diary: "October 26. Set out [fro]m Philadelphia for N Hampshire." Bartlett Papers (Nh).

Oliver Wolcott to Samuel Lyman

Sir,   Philidelpa. 26 Octr. 1776

I sit down to Write to you, rather to give you a Mark of my Regard for you than that I have any Thing of Consequence to Communicate. The publick Attention is greatly turned to Observe the Movements at N York and Ticonderoga, from which Places something important is soon expected but whatever they may be you may receive as early an Information as I can. The Period is Very interesting, but hope soon that something decisive will appear in our favour. May that God who presides Over human Events grant a prosperous Issue to our Undertakings. I have not heard a Word from any of my Freinds at Litchfield since I left them. I hope they do not forget me, I beleive they do not, tho I have for some time expected at least a Letter from you.[1] I do not injoy good Health tho I am much better than I have been lately—and hope before long that I may be favoured with established Health. Mr. Sherman went home on my coming here, his Return is dayly expected. Mr. Huntington goes home on his Return as he is not well. Williams will douptless continue here, and have a farther Appointment for that Purpose.

Nothing New from the Southward. Present my kindest Regards to my Freinds and be Assured that I am, sir, your Freind and most humble Servant,   Oliver Wolcott

RC (Ronald von Klaussen, state of Florida, 1976).
[1] Wolcott also wrote a brief letter to his wife, Laura, this day, complaining that he had not heard from her since he had left home. Wolcott Papers, CtHi.

William Hooper to Joseph Hewes

My dear Friends   October 27, 1776. Philadelphia

Mr. Penn having come to a determination to leave this City immediately and to attend the Convention in North Carolina, nothing is left to my choice but to submit with patience to the allotment which it necessarily makes of me and not to murmur at a disappointment which it was not in my power to prevent. You well know that I had it in contemplation to have been present at the framing a constitution for the future Government of our Colony, and as I am likely to spend my days under the influence of it, it may be naturally supposed that I do not feel myself altogether indifferent to what may be the result of the publick deliberations on this important subject. Superficial as my knowledge may be of the theoretical principles of Government, yet from an intimate observation of the late experiments which have been made in several states, I profess myself not a mere noviciate in the practical line, and think I have profited somewhat from the Blunders of others. This mite I should be happy to contribute, trifling as it is it would serve as an evidence of the goodness of my intentions. The present situation of my family in a part of the country to which I have the fullest confidence that General Howe will transfer part of his force as soon as the Winter begins excites my most anxious sollicitude for their future security and an earnest desire that I could afford them my personal assistance to remove them at a greater distance from the impending horrors of War.

But I have still a duty superiour to all these, which supersedes every tie of private affection, and every connection in publick life that is not essential to the salvation of the liberties of America. Yes! We are upon the verge of that important moment which tho it may not decide, yet must have a very important influence upon the state of these colonies in the future struggle for their liberties. Genl Washington at the head of an Army of 25,000, Howe perhaps with a number not inferiour to him, at half a mile distance from each other, and in expectation every instant of a general action, when the stakes they fight for are the liberties of millions living and unborn, is an Idea almost too vast for comprehension. In firm reliance upon that being whose almighty fiat disposes the fate of Empires I wait the results. I took an early share in this controversy & when it was believed that it might have been decided without the effusion of human blood. I will not desert it when the conflict is grown serious; and am prepared to meet its most formidable approaches and resign myself to my fate however severe, if this can in the least contribute to the happiness of those who sent me hither. What may be the consequence of an engagement at New York it is impossible to foretell, the success of War is often the effect of casualty where bravery or conduct have little share in the decision. And should we be unfortunate, it will be necessary that this Congress should have all its powers in their full energy. We cannot be always successful yet a series of good fortune is apt to blind us against the possibility of a reverse, and in proportion to our elevation we become depressed with a sudden stroke of Adversity. This event we must conceive possible and therefore as the trustees of the liberties of America we must be prepared to meet the worst, and be upon the spot to counteract the effect which it may have upon those of weak minds and to prevent dispiritedness from becoming contagious. It will be necessary also to check the career of our enemies by immediate exertions, and to locate a success which otherwise might extend its pernicious consequences, thro'ought America. God grant that these precautions may be unnecessary; at least they are prudent. And in justice to my constituents in respect to the sacred trust they have reposed in me I cannot leave them unrepresented at a time perhaps when the fate of America may turn upon a single vote. My private feelings shall never weigh

against this publick duty, & I will never be unfaithful to them whatever torture I may thereby inflict upon myself. Yet My friends, Is
there not a possibility that I may be e'er long relieved, soon enough
perhaps to congratulate the convention before they disperse, upon
the prudent establishment which they may have formed for the regulation of our state. Could the number of delegates in Congress be
increased to five the service would be much less irksome, three might
always attend, and the other two relieve them occasionally.[1] This
might be done with little or no additional expence to the State by
dividing the sum now given or that with a small addition amongst
the five, who from their short absence from home, and greater opportunity to attend to their own private affairs, may without injustice to
themselves serve the publick for much less than the delegates receive
at present. Think not that in this arrangement, I have the most
distant view to myself, I solemnly assure you that I have not. A
Choice is soon to take place, and without the least regret will I
resign my seat to whomsoever my country shall appoint to fill it. In
accepting the trust originally my end and aim was the publick good.
I have held, I yet hold it from that principle only. I will lay it down
with Joy to anyone whom my Country may direct to assume it,
conscious that many may be found with better capacities and as good
inclinations to serve the common Cause. The vast expence which
attends living in this City has notwithstanding the great liberality of
my Constituents prevented it from being a post of profit. The Honour
is surely amply recompensed by the fatigue which attends it. At the
Treasury board from 8 oClock AM till 12 at noon, in Congress till
4 PM, and in Marine Committee often till ten at night, with the business of the secret Committee of Correspondence to fill up the
moments which I have not otherways disposed of. Judge what time I
can call my own or what I can give to the Amusement of myself or
my Friends. However I repine not, I never thought that the road to
liberty was strewed with roses; thorns & thick briars are the growth
of it & happy he who has virtue and perseverance to surmount the
obstacles. The reward in value exceeds infinitely the labour which
may attend the procuring it.

I know not whether I have a seat in your Convention. Should my
friends in any of the Counties have thought proper to prefer me to
that honour, I shall feel the most sincere gratitude for such a mark
of their respect. I am aware of the intentions of my friends in Wake
and ⟨Chowan⟩ Perquimans County, and have some reason to believe
that I have been named in New Hanover, to these or any of these the
reasons I have assigned for my stay here will I am well assured serve
as a sufficient apology; if they have intended to make use of my poor
abilities; that I am not upon the spot to exert them.

Mr Penn will inform you of the check which we have received at
the lakes, it is unfortunate but not dishonourable, it was a well con-

tested field & even our enemies do us the justice to confess that they never saw examples of more determined heroism. Every moment we expect an attack at Ticonderoga. We shall I hope & trust play a winning game and repair our late loss. What an eventful period! My doubts have greatly vanished as to Eastern courage. Give them good officers, I am now convinced that they will not dishonour them or our Cause.

I inclose you the Constitutions of several states for the speculation of yourself and friends. That of Pennsylvania which came into the world when Mr. Hewes was here, has since made its solemn exit in this City. The People at large have met, arraigned the proceedings of the last convention, resolved that they have exceeded the powers with which they were intrusted and disclaim obedience to any acts of theirs. The Monster which they called a Government has expired with the political existence of those who created it, and Cannon & Matlack with some other factious demagogues have slunk into their pristine obscurity—but unhappily not till this measure had given general dissatisfaction and like leaven in the political mass had caused a general fermentation, & like a contagion diffused its baneful effects far & near. It made more tories than the whole treasury of Britain could have done in the same space of time. Its subversion will I hope in a great measure work a cure of the evil. This presents an example of the ill effects of a single branch of legislature, & points out Rocks which I hope no other state will split upon. The Constitution of the Jersies has its full Energy and gives general satisfaction. That of Delaware is much commended. They are determined to adopt in this one as nearly similar as possible to the old one, abolishing little else but the regal & proprietary powers and deriving all power from the people.

Adieu, I have much to write & but little time to do it in, this must serve as the communication of my sentiments to several of my friends to whom my good friend Mr Hewes may think proper to disclose it. Mr Skinner & the Messrs Harveys, Mr Rand & my Wake friends will please to consider themselves as addressed by the letter & Mr Hewes will to them, Mr Johnston & Maclaine & Gen Jones save me the necessity of any further apologies. I have had an attack of a bilious Cholic a few days ago, I still feel the effects of it in a relaxation which I must so far indulge as not to trespass longer upon your Patience than to conclude myself Gentlemen, with great respect, Your Obedt Hum Sert,   Will Hooper

[P.S.] Remember me kindly to Col Caswell. Show him this.

RC (CSmH). Addressed: "To Joseph Hewes esquire. In his Absence to Samuel Johnston esqr at Halifax. By favor of Mr. Penn."
    [1] When the North Carolina Provincial Congress selected new delegates on December 20, 1776, it ignored Hooper's advice to enlarge the state's delegation

and again appointed only three men to represent the state in Congress. *N.C. Colonial Records*, 10:977–78.

Richard Henry Lee to George Washington

Dear Sir,   Philadelphia 27th October 1776

I congratulate you sincerely on the several advantages your Troops have lately gained over the enemy, for tho each has been but small, yet in the whole they are considerable, and will certainly have the effect of inspiriting our army, whilst it wastes and discourages the other. May the great Dispenser of justice to Mankind put it in your power before this campaign ends, to give these foes to human kind, the stroke, their wicked intentions entitles them to. 'Tis amazing with what force, and infamous perseverance the Devils of despotism with their corrupted Agents pursue the purpose of enslaving this great Continent! Their system of policy has been evident for sometime past. They mean to keep their own people in G.B. quiet, and the other powers of Europe still for this campaign, by an infinite number of falsehoods touching the progress of their arms, and the consequent probable submission of the colonies, whilst they endeavor by an extraordinary exertion of force to put things realy into such a situation this year, as to terrify foreigners from interfering, and encourage with hope their own deluded people. Pursuing this idea, Europe will be made to ring with sounding accounts of their immense successes in Canada and at New York, when in fact, considering the greatness of their force both by sea and land with the amazing expence these will create, what they have done is meer nothing. But should fortune favor us so, as that any considerable impression could be made on Gen. Howes army this Campaign, the high hopes they have raised, and the numberless lies they have told will disgrace and ruin them with the whole world.

I have the pleasure to assure you the train is so la[id] that we have the fairest prospect of being soon supplied and copiously too, with military stores of all kind and with clothing fit for the soldiers. Immediately to be sure we are much pressed for want of the latter, but if we can brush thro this crisis, we shall be secure. The French court has given us so many unequivocal proofs of their friendship, that I can entertain no doubt of their full exertions in our favor, and as little that a war between them and G.B. is not far distant. I sincerely wish you health sir, and that you may be happy in the success you are so eminently intitled to. I am with, perfect esteem, dear Sir your most affectionate and obedient servant,

                                         Richard Henry Lee

RC (DLC).

Robert Morris to Horatio Gates

Dear Sir   Philada. October 27th. 1776

I find by your letter of the 5th Inst. you had not received one of my letters wrote in Answer to one of yours. I kept no Copy of it which you'l say is unusual for a merchant. I acknowledge it and only plead in excuse, that I did not write to you in that Character. The letter for Mrs. Gates is gone forward by Post as I cou'd not meet any other Conveyance altho I kept it here some days in expectation of one. Mr. Johnston and indeed all the Maryland Delegates are at home forming a Constitution. This seems to be the present business of all America, except the Army, it is the fruits of a certain premature declaration which you know I always opposed. My opposition was founded on the evil consequences I foresaw or thought I foresaw and the present State of Several Colonies justifys my apprehensions. We are disputing about Liberties, Priviledges, Posts, & places at the very time we ought to have nothing in View but the securing those objects, & placing them on such a footing as to make them worth Contending for amongst ourselves hereafter but instead of that the Vigour of this & several other States is lost in Intestine division, and, unless this spirit of Contention is checked by some means or other, I fear it will have banefull influence on the general measures of America.

I am not one of those Testy Politicians that run resty when my own plans are not adopted, for I think it the duty of a good Citizen to follow when he cannot lead, & happy wou'd it be for America if all her Inhabitants wou'd adopt this Maxim, and make it an invariable Rule during this great Contest for the Minority on every question to Submit to & cooperate with the Majority; but alas this cannot be. It is not to be expected from Human Nature. We must take Men as we find them, and do the best we can. You tell me the Congress are bad Correspondents, and I fear you have too much truth on your side. Was you here I cou'd explain this in a Tete a Tete but I have neither time nor inclination to commit that explanation to paper. You may depend there is no intentional Neglect or Slight meant to you or the department You Act in. It is deemed of the utmost importance, and all the Members of Congress wish that & every other department was duly attended to, but the Fact is they have too many objects & retain too much executive business in their own hands for their Members to effect with that vigor & dispatch that is necessary.

You say I must tell you good News. I will if you will repay me in kind for of late we have had nothing but very bad News from both our Armys. We expect daily to hear of your being attacked & have sanguine hopes of a Vigorous and successfull defence on your part—much depends on it. If you keep your Ground I think Genl. Washington will keep his and if both do this for the present Fall & ensuing Winter, the Good News I mean to tell you will be verified.

It is, that the French are undoubtedly disposed to assist us in this Contest, and I have little doubt but they will take part in the War next Summer. Indeed it seems to me impossible but all Europe will be involved in War and, if so, Great Britain will have her hands full and probably be glad to render justice & reparation to the Country she has so much injured.

Nothing do I wish for more than a Peace on terms honorable & beneficial to both Country's and I am convinced it is more consistent with the Interest of Great Britain to acknowledge our Independancy & enter into Commercial Treatys with us than to persist in attempting to reduce us to unconditional Submission. I hope we shall never be reduced to vile situation whilst a true Friend of America & freedom exists. Life will not be worth having & it is better to perish by the Sword than drag out the remaining days in misery & scorn; but I hope Heaven has better things in store for the Votaries of so just a Cause. I am Dr. Sir Yours affectionately,   Robt Morris

RC (NHi).

Secret Committee Minutes of Proceedings

Octr. 27. 1776

The Come. met. Present Messrs. Morris, Col. Lee, & Lewis. A letter wrote by the chairman to J. Langdon Esqr. dated 25 was read & approvd of by the Come.[1] Issued the follg. Drafts on the Treasurer in favor of Barnabas Deane for 1774 2/16 dlls being in full for the balance of Silas & Barnabas Deane's Accots as appears by an acct. currt. renderd by them dated 25 June last. In favor of sd. Bs. Deane for 1800 dlls being the Sum insurd by Silas & Bs. Deane, on the Schooner Rose charterd & insurd by them in consequence of contract with this Come., sd. vessel being taken by the Enemy, as appears by a protest dated 12 instant. In favor of Ami Gibbs owner of the Ship Nancy & Sukey for 4168 2/3 dlls, being in full of the balance due to her for the freight of sd. ship as per charter-party on a voyage to Barcelona, Marsailles & from thence back to this place. A charter-party for the ship Success, Capt. Jams. Anderson, was signd by the Come. By sundry letters receivd it appears that a sloop calld the James loaded with tobacco & staves, by Messrs Hewes & Smith of N. Carolina by order of this Come. per acct of the Continent has been capturd by the Enemy & recapturd & carried into Salem in New England. Orderd that Mr. Morris write to the Contl. Agent at Boston,[2] to claim sd. sloop for the Continent & to settle with the Recapturers for their salvage & afterwards, that he provide sd. Sloop with proper Necessaries & dispatch her with her Cargo for Nantes, in France provided she is fit for that voyage, & that Capt. Willis [Gillis] the Master, will agree to the same. If not She must proceed to

Martinico, Hispaniola or to the Mole the place She was first charterd for. A letter was likewise orderd to be wrote to the Come. of Salem to assist sd. Agent in this business.

MS (MH–H).
¹ Not found.
² The committee's letter to John Bradford has not been found, but for Bradford's November 26 letter to the committee regarding the *James*, see Morgan, *Naval Documents*, 7:291.

John Hancock to Jacob Duche

Sir,   Philada. Octr. 28th. 1776.
I do myself the Pleasure, in the Name of the Congress, and by their Direction, to return you the Thanks of that House for the devout and acceptable Manner in which you discharged your Duty during the Time you officiated as Chaplain to it.

In Obedience to their Commands I send the enclosed one Hundred and fifty Dollars, which they have ordered me to present to you as an Acknowledgment for your Services.¹

With sincere Wishes for your Health and Happiness, I am, Sir, your most hble Ser.   J. H. Presidt.

LB (DNA: PCC, item 12A).
¹ See *JCC*, 6:886–87. Duché wrote a letter to Hancock on October 29, asking him to apply this $150 to the relief of the widows and orphans of Pennsylvania officers who have "fallen in battle." PCC, item 78, 7:75; *Am. Archives*, 5th ser. 2:1280; and *JCC*, 6:911. On the back of Duché's letter Hancock wrote this note: "Nov. 7. Wrote the Council of Safety of Penna & Sent them that 150 Dolls to be dispos'd of agreeable to the request of Mr Duché & the Resolve of Congress of Octo. 30th. 1776." Hancock's letter to the council of safety has not been found. For information about Duché's appointment as chaplain of Congress, see Hancock to Duché, July 9, 1776.

John Hancock to George Washington

Sir,   Philada. Monday Eveng. 11 O'Clock, 28th Octor. 1776
This moment Dodd the Express from the State of Massachusetts, who Took your Dispatches to Congress on Saturday last, arriv'd at my house, and informs me that this Day about 12 oClock he put up at one Bissinett's a publick house in Bristol, where he open'd his Bundle to deliver a Letter to be forwarded over the Ferry to Mrs. Reed, & leaving his Bundle in the Barr Room, while he Stept out, on his return the whole of his Letters were carried off, & no person could give any Accott. of them, and after Enquiring and getting all

the Assistance he could to Endeavour the obtaing them, their Searches were fruitless, & he is here without a single Letter. As your Letters may be of the utmost Consequence, & the Enemy may derive great advantages from the knowledge of their Contents (as I have no Doubt but they will soon be in possession of them) I have Judg'd it proper without waiting for the Meeting of Congress in the Morning to Dispatch this Express to you, to give you this Intelligence, that you may as far as possible Guard against the Movements the Enemy may make in Consequence of the Intelligence they may gain by the possession of those Letters, and that you may Take such Steps as this Accident may Suggest to you from the particulars of your Letters as necessary to Counteract the attempts of the Enemy. I however hope that your Letters, should they fall into their hands, will not afford them much Comfort, nor give them any great Prospects of advantages, tho' I shall be unhappy untill I know the Contents, & Beg by the Return of this Express you will send me a Copy of them as it will be a great Relief to Congress to Receive the earliest Accott.[1]

I shall early in the Morng. Send to Bristol & have a strict Scrutiny made, & Recover the Letters if possible, or Detect the persons who Rob'd the mail.

You will Excuse this hasty Letter, & wrote in great agitation & hurry, as I would not lose a moment in Sending it off.

I am with the utmost Respect & Esteem, Sir, Your most obedt hume set,   John Hancock, Presidt

RC (DLC).

[1] On November 1 Robert H. Harrison, Washington's secretary, informed Hancock that "Had the express been charged with no other letter [than Harrison's October 25 letter to Hancock], the loss would not have been attended with any material injury to us or advantage to the enemy . . . but there were others from his Excellency, of a very interesting nature, the miscarriage of which gives him much concern. . . . Besides his Excellency's letters, the most material of which was to Mr. Rutledge, there were five or six more from the gentlemen of his family." PCC, item 152, 2:193–94; and *Am. Archives*, 5th ser. 3:464–65. Harrison's October 25 letter (evidently a later copy supplied by the secretary) is in PCC, item 152, 3:181–83, and *Am. Archives*, 5th ser. 2:1239–40. For Congress' inconclusive investigation into the theft of these letters, see *JCC*, 6:907, 915, 968–69, 985, 1026. See also James Wilson to William Livingston, March 28, 1777.

Richard Stockton to Abraham Clark

Dear Sir: Saratoga, October 28, 1776.

Before I left *Philadelphia* Congress appointed a committee, consisting of one member from each State, to devise ways and means for furnishing the army with clothing, &c. As the member appointed for *New-Jersey,* I laid the resolution before our Legislature, then sitting at *Princeton,* and recommended to them the great importance of their appointing persons in every County. They were pleased to take up the matter with that zeal which the nature of it required, and determined to take a recess that they might, in their own persons, the more effectually and speedily execute the business. I hope, therefore, that already a considerable quantity of shoes and stockings at least, may be provided, and that you will take immediate order for the sending a parcel to our regiments who are in this quarter.[1] Colonel *Dayton's* regiment is ordered from *Fort Stanwix* to *Tyconderoga.* The Colonel and Major *Barber* came here last evening, and the regiment is now within a few miles of this place, marching with cheerfulness, but great part of the men barefooted and barelegged. My heart melts with compassion for my brave countrymen who are thus venturing their lives in the publick service, and yet are so distressed. There is not a single shoe or stocking to be had in this part of the world, or I would ride a hundred miles through the woods and purchase them with my own money; for you'll consider that the weather here must be very different from that in *New-Jersey:* it is very cold now I assure you. For God's sake, my dear sir, upon the receipt of this, collect all the shoes and stockings you can, and send them off for *Albany* in light wagons; a couple of two-horse wagons will bring a great many, which may be distributed among our several regiments who will be all together at *Tyconderoga* in a few days. If any breeches and waistcoats be ready, send them along; but do not wait for them if the shoes and stockings are ready and the others not.

We have despatches from General *Gates* this morning, informing that he hourly expects to be attacked by the enemy; but our works are very strong, and a boom thrown across the water from *Tyconderoga* to *Mount Independence,* to prevent the enemy's shipping from getting below us.[2] Therefore, I trust, with the blessing of Almighty God, that we shall disappoint their wicked and sanguinary purposes. But shall the brave troops from *New-Jersey* stand in the lines half-leg deep in snow, without shoes or stockings? God forbid! I shall empty my portmanteau of the stockings I have for my own use on this journey, excepting a pair to take me home; but this is a drop of water in the ocean.

In the utmost haste, I am, with much esteem, dear sir, your most obedient, humble servant,   Rich'd Stockton.

MS not found; reprinted from *Am. Archives,* 5th ser. 2:1274–75.

[1] On November 16 the New Jersey Assembly appointed a committee "to provide Ways and Means to send the Shoes and Stockings, and such other Articles as are in Readiness to be sent, to the northern Army, agreeable to a Request in a Letter from the Honourable *Richard Stockton,* Esqr. one of the Delegates of the Continental Congress." See *Votes and Proceedings of the General Assembly of the State of New Jersey* (Burlington: Isaac Collins, 1777), p. 41. Clark was a member of the assembly as well as a delegate to Congress.

[2] See Horatio Gates to Phillip Schuyler, October 24, 1776, in *Am. Archives,* 5th ser. 2:1257–58.

William Hooper to the
North Carolina Provincial Convention

Honoured Sir   Philadelphia Oct 29. 1776

By my worthy Colleague Mr Penn, I do myself the honour to transmit a resolution of the continental Congress which bears immediate relation to the State of North Carolina. The Congress having been informed that the Armed vessels belonging to the Enemy have lately quitted the River of Cape Fear, and have proceeded to the Northward, have bestowed their thoughts upon the practicability of fortifying that entrance into your state, and excluding the British Men of War.[1] The importance of such a measure must weigh as powerfully with you as with them, & I am well assured that nothing will be wanting on your part to carry it into Execution with all possible dispatch. As this is the only Port in the State of North Carolina, into which the Enemies can introduce ships of any considerable force, should they be prevented here, we shall have nothing to fear from any forces which they may send against us in the insuing Winter. The Harbour of Cape Fear will furnish a secure receptacle for our own trading Vessels and those of foreigners who from this Advantage may be induced to prefer ours to the ports of other states. The privateers of the several states, as well as the Continental armed Vessels will carry any prizes which they make to the Southward, into No Carolina when they are apprized of the protection which they and their Captures will receive, and by these means we shall be supplied with the many articles of which we now feel the most pressing necessity. We are aware of the scarcity of heavy Cannon in your state & have therefore procured a recommendation to you to apply to South Carolina to aid you in that respect. We flatter ourselves that it may produce the effect we wish, as it will be nothing but a reciprocal Civility and what North Carolina is well entitled to for the ready and ample succour afforded to South Carolina when in imminent danger from its Enemies. Our own Guns small as they are may be made useful and I know not how more essentially. The Continental Troops will be employed in this service, & the Expence arising from the hire of negroes to perform the most laborious part of the operation will be considerable, but must appear contemptible when weighed against the publick emolument which will result from it.

You will observe that this is to be executed at the Expence of your own particular state; a recommendation of a similar kind went to South Carolina, in consequence of which they have erected very great & very expensive fortifications at their own cost.[2] It becomes Œconomy in you to bear this Expence yourself, rather than by making it Continental, expose yourself to pay your proportion of the large fortifications which have been or may hereafter be erected in the Eastern States. Your proportion only of the Connecticut forts would amount to as much as the whole of these proposed for your colonial security. In this case therefore It will be political (at least for us) to suffer each state to bear its own burdens.

Should the Convention think it proper to apply to the Continenl Congress for the Assistance of an Engineer to execute this proposal, I shall upon being informed thereof immediately take the proper steps to procure one and send him on.

I am, Sir, With great Respect to your self & the Convention, Your's & their most Obedt, Humble Servant,   Will Hooper

RC (Nc–Ar). Addressed: "The Honourable The President of the Convention of North Carolina."
    [1] See JCC, 6:908.
    [2] Doubtless a reference to Congress' November 4, 1775, resolve on the defense of Charleston. JCC, 3:326.

Marine Committee to Esek Hopkins

Sir   In Marine Committee Philadelphia October 30th 1776

We have received Such intelligence as Satisfies us that Enemies Ships and vessels have all quitted Georgia, and the Carolinas, which renders it unnecessary for you to pursue the expeditions formerly directed to these States, But as we have Still reason to Suppose that the Galatia and Nautilus are Cruizing of[f] the Capes of Virginia we desire you will proceed thither with all possible dispatch, and endeavour to fall in with these Ships, and take, Sink, or destroy them.

If when you are on that Station you Shall be informed that any of the Enemies Ships of War have returned to the Carolinas, or Georgia, you are in that case to go in Search of them and effectually remove them.

Having finished this business, you are to return and Cruize for and endeavour to intercept the Store and provision Vessels coming from Europe to the Enemies army at New York.

We expect you will give this Committee information by every opportunity of your proceedings and what success you may meet with in the above enterprizes. We wish you Success and are Sir, Your most hble Servts.   Fras. Lewis   Geo Walton

                         Wm. Whipple   John Hancock

                         Will Hooper   Robt Morris

                                              Richard Henry Lee

RC (Facsimile, American Art Association Catalog, December 7, 1921, item 314). In the hand of Timothy Matlack and signed by Hancock, Hooper, Lee, Lewis, Morris, Walton, and Whipple.

Marine Committee to Daniel Tillinghast

Sir   October 30th 1776

As heavy duck is wanted for the New Hampshire frigate which cannot be procured in that State, we desire you will without delay send forward to John Langdon Esq. Eighty Bolts of heavy duck of that quantity belonging to the Continent is in your possession or in the possession of any other person in your State. You will also supply Mr Langdon and Messrs. Silas & Barnabas Deane with any Continental stores that they may apply to you for, for the use of the Frigates Raleigh and Trumbull.[1]

Lieutenant McDougal of the Brig Andrea Doria has accounted for the expenditure of £45 you advanced him to defray his travelling expences together with seven of the people belonging to said Brigt from your State to this place, therefore we think proper to direct that you deduct that Sum from the Sales of the prize which they brought in and put under your care.

We are sir, Your very hble servants

LB (DNA: PCC Miscellaneous Papers, Marine Committee Letter Book).
[1] This day the Marine Committee also wrote a brief letter to Nathaniel Shaw, Jr., the Continental prize agent in Connecticut, instructing him "to deliver Mr. Barnabas Deane any Continental Stores in your possession which he may want for the use of the Frigate Trumbull now fitting out in your State." American Revolution Papers, CtHi.

John Witherspoon to Horatio Gates

Sir   Princeton Octr 30. 1776

It is not long since I heard from Mrs. Gates & your Son who went home the beginning of Vacation. I expect her here with him in about 10 Days when the College session begins. I have the pleasure of assuring you that he has in all respects behaved in the most unexceptionable Manner & acquitted himself well at Examination for Admission into College so that I hope you will have much pleasure in him.

I send this by my Son who finds he can do nothing in the present Situation of Affairs upon his Farm & therefore is desirous of going into the Army.[1] It is his own particular Desire to be with you. He can easily get a Commission in the New Levies of this Province but if he could be appointed Aide de Camp to any of the Generals I think it could be a happy Introduction and as he is young, vigorous & active I hope he would acquit himself with fidelity & Credit in that Service. I have given him a Letter to Col. Maxwell[2] just new appointed a Brigadier General but do chiefly depend on Your friendship & Advice to him which he will certainly follow.

It gave me much Concern that you had not an immediate & fully satisfying Answer to your Letter to Congress relating to the dissolving the Court Martial.[3] There was a full & ample report brought in upon it by the board of War but it was postponed after some Debate for a little & many things being thrust in that seemed to require immediate Dispatch it was some time before it was brought in again and the second time when it was just about to be almost unanimously agreed to by the Artful Management of some who wanted a little Alteration made it was postponed again by the Demand of a paper which was not at hand, & since that time your Friends thought it not worthwhile to resume it. I must however assure You that by far the greatest part of the Congress has a very high Sense of your importance & Services in a particular Manner for discouraging to the utmost of your power Colonial Jealousies & Distinctions.

I have written to General Maxwell that he is indebted to you for a very honourable Mention of him in your letter to Congress which was read at the last promotion of General Officers when he could certainly have been promoted but for some of his friends here.[4]

We have heard with Concern the Destruction of our fleet upon the Lake, but it is satisfying to think that they behaved so well. I heartily pray that God almighty may Crown you with Success in your present critical Situation & most important Charge. I have given all the attention in my power to the supply & Interest of the Northern Army & Shall continue to do so. Wishing you all happiness, I am Sir your most obedt humble Servant,   Jno Witherspoon

RC (NHi).

[1] This day Witherspoon also sent a letter of recommendation with his son James to General Schuyler, a facsimile of which is in *Parke-Bernet Galleries Catalog*, no. 2569 (May 16, 1967), item 69. James Witherspoon (1751–77), who subsequently became a major in the Continental Army and an aide-de-camp to Gen. William Maxwell, was killed at the battle of Germantown in October 1777. Varnum L. Collins, *President Witherspoon: A Biography*, 2 vols. (Princeton: Princeton University Press, 1925), 2:31n.23.

[2] Not found.

[3] Gates described the reasons for the dissolution of the court-martial of Col. Moses Hazen in a September 2 letter to Hancock, which was read in Congress on September 16. See PCC, item 154, 1:59–60; and *Am. Archives*, 5th ser. 1:1267–68. For a recent discussion of this episode see Allan S. Everest, *Moses Hazen and the Canadian Refugees in the American Revolution* (Syracuse: Syracuse University Press, 1976), pp. 44–45.

[4] In an August 28 memorial to Congress Maxwell had criticized the promotion of Arthur St. Clair, an officer with less military experience than himself. *Am. Archives*, 5th ser. 1:1203; and *JCC*, 5:641. The day before St. Clair's promotion, Congress had read a letter from Gates, but, contrary to Witherspoon's recollection, it did not mention Maxwell; and in fact before Maxwell's own promotion on October 23, there is no reference to him in any of Gates' letters to Congress. PCC, item 154, 1:19–22; and *Am. Archives*, 5th ser. 1:649.

Secret Committee Minutes of Proceedings

Ocr. 31st. 1776

Come. met. Prest. Messrs. Morris, Lee, Lewis & Livingston. Letters were wrote to Messrs. Pliarne, Penet & Co, Nantes; Mr. Ths. Morris per Ship Mary & Elizabeth, Capt. Young, for Nantes whose Cargo goes consignd to Mr. Morris on Acct. of the Continent. To Capt. Peter Young giving him Instructs. To J. Bradford Esqr. Conl. Agent Boston. To the Come. of Salem, N. England.[1]

Robert Briges producd an acct. for the hire of his Brige. Cornelia & Molly who has performd her voyage agreable to charter-party. 3¾ at £180 currency per month is £675. Orderd that Mr Morris pay the same out of the nett proceeds of that vessels cargo wch. he is likewise orderd to receive. The Come. have agreed with Stewart & Jackson Owners of the ship Cyrus to charter sd. vessel for a voyage to Nantes & back to this place, on the follg. terms—Three guineas per hhd. freight for tobo., 7/6 per bbl. flour—& if she loads Salt back 2/ per busll. The Come. to insure the vessel valued at £6000 curry.

Order on the Treasurer in favor of J. Nixon & Co. for 9856 9/90 dlls being amount of a parcel of Indigo purchased from them & now in possession of the Chairmn. of this Come. to be exported by him for Acct of the Contt. 3576 lb nett at 10/. Order on Tim. Matlack in favr. of G. Losch for all the Contl. Salt petre under his care & to make return of quantity & weight.

MS (MH-H).
[1] Only the committee's letter to the Salem committee has been found.

Secret Committee to the Salem Committee

In Secret Committee of Congress.
Gentlemen   Philadelphia [October 31, 1776] [1]

By the inclosed Letters from the C[ommittee] of Edenton in North Carolina and from Robt Sm[ith] Esqr. of that place, which came to our hands only yeste[rday] we learn't the fate of the Sloop James, Capt. Gillis, [which] was chartered and loaded by our orders on Account of the United States of America. We think it our duty to return you thanks for your attention to this matter and at the Same time request the Favor of your assistance in getting the Salvage adjusted and the Sloop dispatched on her voyage, but we cannot tresspass on you to do this business intirely. We have wrote by this Post to John Bradford Esqr. Continental Agent desiring him to do the needfull,[2] and that you will afford him any assistance he may Stand in Need of.

We are with great respect, Gentlemen, Your very hble Servts,

Robt Morris

Phil. Livingston

Richard Henry Lee

RC (MeHi). In a clerical hand and signed by Lee, Livingston, and Morris. Addressed: "To Barth. Putnam, Saml. Ward, Benja. Goodhue, & Jos. Sprague, Esqrs., The Committee of Salem, N. England."

[1] This letter was apparently dated October 31, 1776, and was written pursuant to a committee order of the 27th. See Secret Committee Minutes of Proceedings, October 27 and 31, 1776.

[2] Not found.

Propositions for Peace

[October ? 1776]

Sketch of Propositions for a peace: 1776

There shall be a perpetual peace between Great Britain and the United States of America on the following conditions:

Great Britain shall renounce and disclaim all pretence of right or authority to govern in any of the United States of America.

To prevent those occasions of misunderstanding which are apt to arise where the territories of different powers border on each other through the bad conduct of frontier inhabitants on both sides, Britain shall cede to the united States the provinces or Colonies of Quebec, St John's, Nova Scotia, Bermuda, East and West Florida, and the Bahama islands, with all their adjoining and intermediate territories now claimed by her.

In return for this Cession, the United States shall pay to Great Britain the sum of . . . . Sterling in annual payments, that is to say . . . . . per annum for and during the term of . . . . . years.

And shall moreover grant a free trade to all British subjects throughout the United States and the ceaded Colonies, And shall guarantee to Great Britain the Possession of her islands in the West Indies.

Motives for proposing a peace at this time.

1. The having such propositions in charge, will by the Law of nations, be some protection to the Commissioners or Ambassadors if they should be taken.

2. As the news of our declared independence will tend to unite in Britain all parties against us, so our offering peace with commerce and payments of money, will tend to divide them again. For peace is as necessary to them as to us: our commerce is wanted by

their merchants and manufacturers, who will therefore incline to the accommodation, even though the monopoly is not continued, since it can be easily made appear their *share* of our growing trade, will soon be greater than the *whole* has been heretofore. Then for the landed interest, who wish an alleviation of taxes, it is demonstrable by figures that if we should agree to pay suppose ten millions in one hundred years, viz £100,000 per annum for that term, it would being faithfully employed [as] a sinking fund more than pay off all their present national debt. It is besides a prevailing opinion in England, that they must in the nature of things sooner or later lose the Colonies, and may think they had better be without the government of them, so that the Proposition will on that account have more supporters and fewer opposers.

3. As the having such propositions to make; or any powers to treat of peace, will furnish a pretence for BF's going to England, where he has many friends and acquaintances, particularly among the best writers and ablest speakers in both Houses of Parliament, he thinks he shall be able when there if the terms are not accepted, to work up such a division of sentiments in the nation as greatly to weaken its exertions against the United States and lessen its credit in foreign countries.

4. The knowledge of there being powers given to the Commissioners to treat with England, may have some effect in facilitating and expediting the proposed treaty with France.

5. It is worth our while to offer such a sum for the countries to be ceded, since the vacant lands will in time sell for a great part of what we shall give, if not more; and if we are to obtain them by conquest, after perhaps a long war, they will probably cost us more than that sum. It is absolutely necessary for us to have them for our own security, and though the sum may seem large to the present generation, in less than half the term, it will be to the whole United States, a mere trifle.

MS (DLC). In an unidentified hand. The MS is among the papers Benjamin Franklin left to his grandson William Temple Franklin, but otherwise Franklin's connection with the document is conjectural. Temple is the source of the tradition that Franklin drafted it. When he published his memoirs on his grandfather, Temple introduced the document with a brief, one-paragraph statement, and following the "Sketch" he added a two-paragraph note, which is also found at the foot of the last page of the MS. Temple's explanation is as follows.

"Previous to Dr. Franklin's departure [*for France*], he conceived it would be advisable, on many accounts, to be the bearer of propositions for peace with Great Britain; and with this view he drew up, and submitted to the secret committee of congress, the following paper [*the "Sketch" follows*].

"It is uncertain to what extent this Plan was adopted by Congress. The Propositions were certainly not such as the British Ministry would have listen'd to a Moment, at that period of the Revolutionary War, whatever they might have been disposed to have done in a more advanced state of it.

"It is possible, however, that this or some other Proposals for Peace with

Great Britain may have been furnish'd to Dr. Franklin by the Secret Committee of Congress, to serve him in some Measure as a Protection in Case of his Capture at Sea; of which there was at that time the most imminent Danger."

William Temple Franklin, *Memoirs of the Life and Writings of Benjamin Franklin . . .*, (Philadelphia: T. S. Manning, 1818), pp. 372–75.

In the note to the document appearing in his edition of Franklin's works, Sparks seems merely to have taken his information from Temple; and Smyth simply reprinted Sparks' note when he published the document. Benjamin Franklin, *The Works of Benjamin Franklin*, ed. Jared Sparks, 10 vols (Boston: Hilliard, Gray, and Co., 1836–40), 5:113; Franklin, *Writings* (Smyth), 6:452.

No contemporary evidence has been found, however, to confirm that the document originated with Franklin or was discussed in the Committee of Secret Correspondence or in Congress.

William Hooper to Joseph Hewes

My dear Hewes   November 1. 1776

I thank you for your friendly Attention to me on your way from this to Carolina. I acknowledge the receipt of two letters from you, one from Maryland, the other from Williamsburgh.

I refer you for the state of this city to Mr Penn. He has a pretty general acquaintance here and can inform you of any material changes which have taken place since you left this. The circle of my acquaintance you know is much confined, it becomes more so every day. A man whose appointment is for the express purpose of supporting the liberties of America, with a very ill grace associates with those who are constantly employed in decrying and attempting to bring into contempt the measures of Congress. And believe me Dear Hewes, it flows from me like my heart's blood (but this is not a time to palliate). The growth of Tories exceeds all comprehension. It is a weed that lately discovers itself in soils where I the least expected it. But the least success on our part will instantly extinguish it.

The Council of Safety is become a poor, vapid set of insignificant beings, is rather the pageantry than the reality of power. They have made a most violent effort to confine a man in jail for refusing the Continental Currency, and after a week's struggle have stropped him. I expect to hear in a few days that they have taken him out again, for there is nothing too absurd for their fears or Ignorance to effect.[1]

On the 29th Instant Howe's Army made a grand movement in three Columns in the front of our Army & when it was expected that they would attack in our Center, they made a sudden Wheel to our right and brought up their cannon and began a violent and incessant fire upon a party of 1500 Men which were stationed upon a hill by G Washington and were beginning to throw up lines. Our Men sustained their whole fire for a considerable time when being overcome by superiour Numbers they gave way and retreated in good order to our Main body. What we lost is uncertain in killed, wounded & missing: perhaps 500, the Enemy not less. Smallwoods, Ritzemas, Haslets, Webbs, & McDougals Regts maintained the unequal conflict. McDougal commanded. The Battalions of Smallwood & Ritzema suffered most. Smallwood is wounded in the Arm & Hip but not mortally, it is said that Haslet also is wounded slightly. Every moment a General Action is expected. Col Magaw is at Mount Washington with Cadwallader's, late Shee's, battalion, and also his own. For good reasons (I suppose) we have left Kingsbridge.[2]

We are in perfect ignorance of what has passed at Ticonderoga since the battle on the lake. The Tories say Ti. is taken, ergo I do not believe it.

One of the frigates, Biddle's, will have 14 Guns onboard on Monday and will be ready in every thing, men excepted, in a fortnight. The additional encouragement to Seamen in the continental Service by which they are put on a footing with Privaters & have the whole property of armed Vessels which belong'd to his British Majesty will soon make up that defeciency.[3]

The Effingham, Barrys Ship, & the Repulse, a Galley, were launched yesterday. She is I think the finest Vessell of the whole.

The Guns cast here turn out very ill. They split; full one half of them.

Privateering is attended with amazing success in New England. Not a day passes without a fresh acquisition. They took a Vessell not long ago with 1600 pieces of woolen on board. The Soldiers may bless God for that. Also an armed vessell of 16 Guns—& the Privateer which took the latter was left in pursuit of a three decker with Sugars mounting 20 Guns & by a private letter we are informed that the last was taken and on her way into Newbury port.

The Portsmouth, Newbery & Providence Frigates are out. We shall soon hear of some mischief they have done—at least I hope so.

They will have a violent struggle here about their Constitution. Cannon & Matlack have still some influence left amongst the people. Dickinson, Rush & McKean at the head of the other party think they possess a superiour influence & shall be able to effect their purpose. I confess I have some doubts about the Matter. Time will decide. If Matlack prevails farewell to this Country. Cannon declines all accommodation of terms. He says publickly that their motley system of Govt shall be supported or they will shed rivers of blood. A foolish vaunt which I think proves him desperate.[4]

I have wrote letters to the Convention; pray hand them to the President when you think it contains a pretty full representation. I have wrote of matters which I have most seriously at heart. For Heavens sake attend to them or the Jig is up. I beg your Care of all the letters, papers & packets which go by this. Adieu. By Roger

Main who leaves this in a few days I will again write you. Remember me to my dear friend S Johnston. Shew him this. The next week will be the great, the important week; as soon as any Events turn up of real consequence I will write you or him. Notice me kindly to Col Skinner & My good friends the Harveys & Mr Iredell. Your's Affectionately, most sincerely,   W Hooper

RC (MH–H).
    [1] Hooper is apparently referring to the Pennsylvania Council of Safety's condemnation of John Baldwin, a cordwainer. *Am. Archives,* 5th ser. 2:98.
    [2] Congress received word of most of these military developments in an October 29 letter to Hancock from Robert H. Harrison, Washington's secretary, which was read on October 31. See PCC, item 152, 3:185–86; *Am. Archives,* 5th ser. 2:1282; and *JCC,* 6:914. See also *Am. Archives,* 5th ser. 2:1284.
    [3] Congress had passed a resolution granting these concessions on October 30. *JCC,* 6:913.
    [4] For further comments by Hooper on political developments in Pennsylvania, see his letters of November 5 and 6 to Hewes and to Hewes and Samuel Johnston.

William Hooper to the
North Carolina Convention

Sir,   Philadelphia November 1, 1776
    I take the freedom thro' you to communicate to the Honourable the Convention the memorial of several of the prisoners from North Carolina now confined in the Goal of this City. Their confinement tho accompanied with every circumstance of humanity which the publick security will admit of must however as the Winter advances become more irksome from a scarcity of Cloathing, an inconvenience which at this time it will be very difficult to relieve. I shall not take the freedom to intrude my opinion upon the Convention, I may be permitted to say that I lament that conduct which has drawn upon them the resentment of their injured Coun[try.] I feel sincerely for their distressed families, and earnestly wish that they may be restored to their homes as soon as such a measure can take place without hazarding the safety of North Carolina.[1] I am, Sir, With great respect, Your's & the Convention's Most Obedt Humble Ser,   Will Hooper

RC (Nc–Ar).
    [1] On October 17 Congress had resolved that North Carolina loyalists who had been captured at the battle of Moores' Creek Bridge in February 1776 and subsequently sent to Philadelphia should "be permitted to return to their families, if the convention of that state shall be of opinion they may do so, without danger to that or any other of the United States." *JCC,* 6:885–86. A petition to the North Carolina Convention from sixteen of these prisoners, dated October 31 and asking for permission to return home, is in *N.C. Colonial*

Records, 10:888–89. The convention received this petition on November 19 and decided to take it into consideration at a later date, but there is no record of any subsequent action on it in the convention's journal. Ibid., p. 925.

Marine Committee to Elisha Warner

Sir   November 1, 1776.

You are to proceed with the Continental Sloop Fly now under your command for the Coast of Shrewsberry in New Jersey and take such stations along the Jersey shore as will enable you to see every vessel that goes in or out of Sandy Hook. We immagine there must be Transports, Store Ships and provision vessels daily arriving or expected to arrive at that place for supplying our enemies with provisions and other Stores, and the design of your present Cruize is to intercept as many of those vessels and supplies as you possibly can.

You have got or may get a good coasting Pilot so that you may run close in shore or into Toms River or any other River, Inlet or Harbour in the Jerseys whenever you are chased or endangered by vessels of a superior force. Therefore you will keep an especial good look out for all vessels inward or outward bound and whenever you discover any give chase, make prize of as many as possible, and as fast as you take 'em send them for this port, unless you hear men of war take station at our Capes, and in that case send them into Toms River, Egg Harbour or any other safe place, and fast as your people arrive here we will send them or others over land to Tom's River or Shrewsberry from whence you can take them on board again, therefore you must keep this Station and pursue this business as long as possible unless we send you other orders.

You must be careful not to let any British frigate get between you and the land, and then there's no danger for they cannot pursue you in shore, and they have no boats or Tenders that can take you, besides the Country people will assist in driving them off shore if they should attempt to follow you in. The Schooner Wasp commanded by Lieutenant Baldwin goes round on the same service. You must act in Concert, Consult the best stations and best method of Cruizing, and be sure to pursue your Object the taking of provision Vessels, store Ships and Transports with the utmost vigor and vigillence, and altho we recommend your taking good care of your Vessel and people, yet we should deem it more praise worthy in an officer to loose his vessel in a bold enterprize than to loose a good Prize by too timid a Conduct. As fast as you make prisoners you may send them in the Jerseys, and deliver them to the Continental officers to be sent here or confined in New Jersey, but if Seamen send them here unless they enter. Use your officers and men well, and do the same by your prisoners. Let us hear from you as often as necessary. Wishing you success, We are sir, Your very hble servants

LB (DNA: PCC Miscellaneous Papers, Marine Committee Letter Book). Addressed: "To Captain Elisha Warner of the Sloop Fly." Endorsed: "Similar Instructions to the foregoing were given Lt. Baldwin Commanding the Schooner Wasp."

Benjamin Rush to the Pennsylvania Council of Safety

Sir,　　　　　　　　　　　　　　　　　　　Friday [November 1, 1776]

In consequence of the letter from Mr Fisher to the counsel of Safety of Pensylvania being laid before Congress, the congress resolved that the board of war should immediately order a part of a Virginia regiment now on the Eastern Shore of Maryland to march to Dover there to wait for such orders as the future Accounts they shall receive from the Sussex tories shall render necessary.[1]

I have the honor to be sir, your most humble Servant,[2]

B. Rush

RC (DLC). Addressed: "The Honble President of the Counsel of Safety of Pennsylvania."

[1] For Congress' November 1 resolution ordering "four companies of the Virginia battalion on the eastern shore" to Dover, see *JCC*, 6:917. For Henry Fisher's letter to the Pennsylvania Council of Safety, dated "Lewes, October 25th, 1776," see *Pa. Archives*, 1st ser. 5:53–55. See also Robert Morris to George Read, November 6, 1776.

[2] The preceding day Rush had forwarded another document to the Council of Safety—"The Petition of Ezekiel Letts, late Lieutenant in Col. Wayne's Battalion"—with the following endorsement. "I have had the pleasure of knowing Mr. Letts for several years, and beg leave to recommend him as a prudent, sensible, worthy man, & warmly attached to the American cause." Ibid., pp. 57–58.

John Hancock to Barnabas Deane

Sir　　　　　　　　　　　　　　　　　　　Philada. Novr 2d. 1776

Inclos'd you have the Comissions for the Officers of the Frigate in the State of Connecticutt call'd the Trumbull.[1] You will perceive the Lieutens. Commissions are not fill'd. I did not know but some alteration might have taken place, tho' we have only the Names of the first & second Lieuts. Vizt. Jonathan Maltbay 1st Lieut. & David Phipps 2d Lieut. If they agree to go, you will then please to fill them up with their Names, & you with the Capt. & Mr Huntingdon appoint the 3d Lieut., or if the others decline you will in the same manner proceed to appoint others in their stead.

You have also Blank Warrants to be fill'd with proper officers to be Appointed in the same manner. You will return to me a List of the Names of all the officers both Commission & Warrant as soon as possible after they are fix'd. You have also Inclos'd the Books, & some new Regulations.[2] I Refer you to your Brother [*Simeon Deane*] who takes Charge of this for every other Instruction relative to the Frigate.

I wish you happy & am with Respect, Sir, Your very hum set,
John Hancock Prest

[*P.S.*] You have Blank Commisss. for Marine officers, which are to be appointed in same manner as mention'd before; of these you will also return a List. Take care of the spare Warrants & Commisss.; either Return them to me or destroy them. I think there has been neither Capt. nor Lieutenants for the Compa. of Marines appointed, that you must appoint the whole.

RC (CtHi).
[1] These officers had been appointed by Congress on August 22, *JCC*, 5:696–97. Deane, a Wethersfield, Conn., merchant and brother of former delegate Silas Deane, had been in charge of the construction of the *Trumbull*, which was launched early in September 1776. See Marine Committee to Nathaniel Shaw, Jr., August 22, 1776.
[2] These may have been the resolutions on marine affairs passed by Congress on October 29 and 30. *JCC*, 6:909, 913.

John Hancock to Thomas Cushing

Dr Sir   Philada. 3d Novr. 1776

By Capt. Manly I Sent you the Warrants for the Officers.[1] I now Inclose you the Commisss. for the Officers of the Ships & of Marines. I have not fill'd in the Names, you will therefore please to fill in the Names of such as have been already Appointed, but in case they Decline you will fill them with such as you & the Captn. & Mr Agent Bradford shall Judge proper. As it will not answer to Delay, you will Send me a List of all the Officers to these Ships as soon as compleat. Inclos'd are Capt. Manly's orders open for your perusal,[2] do hurry them on as fast as possible. Inclos'd you have some new regulations respectg Prizes. The Inclos'd Letters please to order to be Deliver'd. You will Remember that Mr Palmer, Brown, Thompson &c have been Appointed. The Money will come as soon as it is safe for an Express to Travel with it, which I hope will be in a day or two. We are now at a very critical moment, God grant us Success.

I Beg you will please immediately on Rec[eip]t of this to Inform our Honable Assembly that the Dispatches they Sent by Dod the

Express were all Stole from him at Bristol last Tuesday 20 miles from this City.[3] He had also Dispatches from Genl Washington, all which are no doubt by this time in the possession of Genl How. We are very uneasy to know the Contents of the Dispatches from the Assembly. The Express Says he had a large Packet from them. He cannot well Account for the Loss of them, he is in Confinement. The original Express was taken Sick at Hartford & Sent his Brother on. I intreat you to Request the Assembly to order Copies of their Dispatches immediately to be forwarded, as it will be a great Relief to Congress to receive early Advice. Do Apologize to the Assembly for my not writing them by this, it is now late at Night & tho' Sunday I have been the whole Day busily employ'd at my Pen. This goes by a Connecticutt Gentn. who promises to forward it to you.

I will Send your Money the first Opening, when I shall write you fully.

If any thing else be needful for the Ships let me know by Express, if no other way, but I think I have sent you every thing necessary.

Adieu. God Bless you. I am very truly, Your Obedt sert,

John Hancock

RC (MHi).
[1] See Hancock to Cushing, October 24, 1776.
[2] See Marine Committee to John Manley, Hector McNeill, and Thomas Thompson, October 23, 1776.
[3] On this point, see also Hancock to Washington, October 28, 1776.

John Hancock to John Langdon

Sir   Philada. November 3d. 1776

My constant attention to the Business of Congress has prevented my writing you so often as I could have wish'd.

I have forwarded the Commission for Capt Thompson;[1] and now Inclose you the Commisss. for the Lieuts. of the Raleigh, & for the officers of Marines. You will please to fill them with the Names of such Persons as have been already Appointed, or in case any of them decline you will with Capt. Thompson Appoint such Persons as you Judge proper, & return to me a List of the Commissions & Warrant Officers as soon as Compleat. I inclose you some New regulations respectg prizes,[2] & a few Warrants lest Col Whipple should not have Carried you a sufficiency. You will be careful of the spare Warrants & either Send them to me or destroy them. The necessary orders respectg the Cruize of the Ships go by this Conveyance to Capt Manly, who will Send them to Capt Thompson.[3]

I shall write you by an Express soon, I improve this Oppory. by

Mr Dean late on Sunday Eveng. & hope will Reach you, tho' the Rout is doubtfull.

I wish you happy & am, Your very huml Servt,

John Hancock Prest.

RC (Universiteitsbibliotheek van Amsterdam).
  [1] See JCC, 6:861.
  [2] See JCC, 6:913.
  [3] See Marine Committee to John Manley, Hector McNeill, and Thomas Thompson, October 23, 1776.

Richard Henry Lee to Thomas Jefferson

Dear Sir   Philadelphia 3d. Novr. 1776

As I have received no answer to the letter I wrote you by the Express from Congress I conclude it has miscarried.[1] I heared with much regret that you had declined both the voyage, and your seat in Congress. No Man feels more deeply than I do, the love of, and the loss of, private enjoyments; but let attention to these be universal, and we are gone, beyond redemption lost in the deep perdition of slavery. By every account from lake Champlain we had reason to think ourselves in no danger on that water for this Campaign. Nor did Gen. Arnold seem to apprehend any until he was defeated by an enemy four times as strong as himself.[2] This Officer, fiery, hot and impetuous, but without discretion, never thought of informing himself how the enemy went on, and he had no idea of retiring when he saw them coming, tho so much superior to his force! Since his defeat, our people evacuated Crown point, and joined their whole strength at Ticonderoga. We do not hear the enemy have thought proper to visit them there, and the Season must now stop operations on the Lake. On the [borders of] the Sound it has been a war of skirmishes, in which I [think we] have gained 5 out of 6. Never was a Ship more mauled [than] a Frigate that lately attempted Fort Washington, she had [26] eighteen pounders thro her and most of the guns double s[hotted.] At the same time an attack on the same place by land w[as] repelled, but the day following the enemy gained an emine[nce] from our people near the white plains, on the sound, about 10 miles above Kingsbridge. The loss on our part in killed, wounded, and Missing, between 3 and 400, the enemies loss considerable but numbers not fixt. Our troops fought well and retired in order before a much superior force. This was McDougals brigade consisting of York, Maryland, and I believe some Eastern Troops.[3] In a skirmish the next day We learn the enemy were defeated. By London papers middle of August it seems quite probable that the quarrel between Spain and Portugal with

the manoeuvres of the Russian fleet, will produce events in Europe
of great importance to our cause.

I have been informed that very malignant and very scandalous
hints and innuendo's concerning me have been uttered in the house.
From the justice of the House I should expect they would not suffer
the character of an absent perso[n] (and one in their service) to be
reviled by any slande[rous] tongue whatever. When I am present,
I shall be perfect[ly] satisfied with the justice I am able to do
myself. From your candor Sir, and knowledge of my political
mo[ve]ments I hope such mistatings as may happen in y[our] presence will be rectified.[4]

Among the various difficulties that press our Country, I know of
none greater than the want of Ships and Seamen. Perhaps a good
basis for remedying the latter might be an alteration of the Act of
Assembly for binding out Orphan and poor Children, and direct
that, for some time at least, the whole of such children should be
bound to the Sea. Without safe Ports to build ships in, and give
protection to foreign Vessels, our trade must long lang[uish.] Would
it not be proper therefore, to make Portsmouth and Norfolk immediately as strong as Cannon can render them, by adding to the
guns already [there] as many from York as will answer the purpo[ses.
Gen.] Stephen tells me that the works he laid out at [Ports]mouth
will put (if properly gunned) that [pla]ce in a state of security from
any Seaforce [tha]t can come against it. The Cannon are of no use
at York, experience proving incontestibly, that Ships will pass any
fort or Battery with ease, when favored by wind and tide. The
quantity of seasoned timber said to be in the neighborhood of Norfolk would furn[ish] a number of fine Vessels, whether for fighting
or for commerce. I think the large Sea gallies that carry such a
number of men for war and for the navigatio[n] part of the Vessel,
are well contrived for the defence of our bay and for raising seamen
quickly. I sent our Navy board a draught of the large gallies building here by order of Congress.[5] It seems to me, that for the different
purposes of battery and Ships our Country could well employ a
thousand Cannon. How very important is it that the Cannon foundery on James river should be pushed on with all possible vigor and
attention. I understand Mr. Ballantine manages some part of these
works, if so, my fears are that very little may be expected. He will
talk amazingly, promise most fairly, but do nothing to purpose. This
I fancy has been the case with a variety of that Gentlemans undertakings, but such conduct, in the Cannon business, will ruin us.
I am very uneasy, I own, on this account. Let us have Cannon,
Small Arms, gun powder, and industry; we shall be secure. But it
is in vain to have good systems of Government and good Laws, if
we are exposed to the ravage of the Sword, without means of re-
sisting. This winter will be an age to us if rightly employed. Let

us get strong in Vessels, Troops, and proper fortifications in proper places. Let us import plenty of military stores, soldiers, cloathing, and Sail cloth for tents, shipping &c. I do not think our armed Vessels can be so well [em]ployed in any other business as in m[aking] two or three trips to the French and Dutch Islands for these necessaries, carrying Tobacco and fine flour to purchase them.

I am with much esteem dear Sir, affectionately yours,

Richard Henry Lee

P.S. Let every method be essayed to get the valuable old papers that Colo. Richard Bland was possessed of.[6]   R.H.L.

RC (DLC). Jefferson, *Papers* (Boyd), 1:589–91.

[1] See Lee to Jefferson, September 27, 1776.

[2] General Arnold's October 15 letter to General Schuyler describing the defeat of his Lake Champlain fleet on the 13th is in *Am. Archives*, 5th ser. 2:1079–80.

[3] For contemporary accounts of the October 27 cannonading of the British frigates *Repulse* and *Pearl* and the battle at White Plains on the 28th, see ibid., 1271, 1282, 1284–85, 1311–13; and Morgan, *Naval Documents*, 6:1428–30, 7:36–37.

[4] For discussion of the accusations made by Lee's enemies in Virginia and efforts to prevent his reelection as a delegate to Congress, see Richard Henry Lee to Patrick Henry, May 26, 1777; Oliver Perry Chitwood, *Richard Henry Lee, Statesman of the Revolution* (Morgantown: West Virginia University Library, 1967), pp. 136–42; and Jefferson, *Papers* (Boyd), 2:15–18.

[5] In a November 8 letter to Lee, the Virginia Navy Board thanked him for this drawing, which he had sent with an October 22 letter that has not been found. See Morgan, *Naval Documents*, 7:91.

[6] Jefferson later purchased part of Richard Bland's library containing valuable early records of Virginia. Jefferson, *Papers* (Boyd), 1:591.

Robert Treat Paine to James Byers

Sr.   Philada. Novr. 3d. 1776

I was in hopes to have wrote to you before this time on the business of casting brass Cannon as we consulted when you was last here. I have waited to see the Process of the Air Furnace here with Wood but they have never tryed it wholly with wood & not till lately have made Any Castings, but it seems to be much more certain that Wood will Answer. I have but lately been able to find out that the owner of the Air furnace in the Common will not let it & therefore there must be a further Consultation about the best place to build one. I therefore desire you as soon as possible to come to Philada. & bring with you an exact Account of how much Copper & Tin you have got & where it is & inquire whether you can get any more,[1] & before you come Consider & Settle in your mind whether the Air Furnace at New Ark can be used for this business & whether it will be Sufficiently Safe from the Enemy & whether Wood can be got there & whether the furnace can be built if it will do. If this will not do, you will think of some suitable place to erect an Air Furnace & be at this place as soon as you can. If any thing hinders you from coming immediately pray write me word of it.

FC (MHi). Addressed: "To Mr. James Byers, brass Founder, late of N York. To the Care of Archibald Camble Tavern Keeper at Hackensack."

[1] When Byers arrived in Philadelphia, he complained to Paine that his copper supplier would not release the copper because it had not been paid for as agreed. Accordingly Paine wrote to the unidentified vendor and chided him for ignoring the public welfare. "You cannot suppose there was any design in keeping you out of the Money. The Continual Military Engagements of Col Knox I am satisfied must have occasioned his ommission of it (tho I have not heard his acct of the matter) but you must be sensible the Copper was as really sold as any thing ever was & the only reason it was not taken away was because the affair of New York would not admit of its being worked up there, & there was no preparation to work it up any where else, but I never suspected the Copper was not paid for or that there would be any difficulty about the delivery of it. The disappointment & damage to the Public in not having this Copper would be so great that I am sure you will not obstruct the public Works by a dispute of this kind." Paine to Unknown, November 22, 1776, Paine Papers, MHi. See also Henry Knox to Paine, September 25, 1776, ibid.

John Hancock to the Maryland Convention

Gentlemen,   Philada. Novr. 4th. 1776.

I am particularly instructed by Congress to inform you, that the Resolutions of your House, to pay ten Dollars in Lieu of the Hundred Acres of Land determined by Congress to be given to such non-commissioned Officers and Soldiers as shall inlist to serve during the War, will, in the opinion of Congress, prove extremely detrimental to these States, if carried into Execution, as it will, in all Probability, induce such Soldiers as are to compose the Remainder of the Levies, to require an equal Sum from the United States; and by refusing until their Demands shall be complied with, compel the Congress to the immediate Payment of an additional Bounty, far beyond what is reasonable.[1]

The Congress are so entirely satisfied with the Propriety of offering Land to the Soldiery as an Inducement to enlist in the Service, that they cannot rescind the Resolve they passed for that Purpose; and are moreover of Opinion, that the Faith of Congress which they have plighted (by Virtue of the Power with which they were vested) must be obligatory upon their Constituents; that no one State, can by its own Act, be released therefrom, and that the Interest of the United States, would be deeply and injuriously affected, should the Congress at this Time consent to a Compromise between any State, and the Forces to be raised by such State.

From the Resolves of your House it should seem that you apprehended your State would be obliged in their individual Capacity to make good the Bounty of Land hereafter to be given to the Soldiery, whereas it was the Intention of Congress to provide such Land at the Expence of the United States.

I have it therefore in Charge from Congress to request that you will reconsider your Resolves on this Subject, and give such Instructions to your Commissioners appointed to repair to the Camp, as will enable them to carry into Execution, the Views of Congress; and also to inform you, that the Paymaster General has been furnished with a Sum of Money for the Purpose of paying the Bounty of twenty Dollars ordered by Congress to such Soldiers as shall inlist to serve the United States during the War.

I have the Honour to be with much Esteem, Gentlemen, your most obedt. and very hble Ser.   John Hancock Presidt.

[*P.S.*] Colonel William Smallwood was appointed a Brigadier General by Congress Octr. 23d.[2]

RC (MdAA). In the hand of Jacob Rush and signed by Hancock. The first four paragraphs of this letter are taken almost verbatim from the October 30 report of the committee "to whom were referred the resolutions of the convention of Maryland." *JCC,* 6:912–13.

[1] On October 9 the Maryland Convention resolved that it could not comply with some September 16 resolutions of Congress offering a bounty of $20 and 100 acres of land to noncommissioned officers and privates who enlisted for the duration of the war, because "there are no lands belonging solely and exclusively to this State [*and*] the purchase of lands might eventually involve this State in an expense exceeding its abilities," and decided instead to give such men an additional $10 bounty in lieu of land. These and other resolves, having been presented to Congress on October 23 by four commissioners appointed by the convention to encourage enlistments among Maryland soldiers, were referred to a committee whose report was submitted and approved on October 30. *JCC,* 6:898, 912–13; and *Am. Archives,* 5th ser. 3:116, 120–21. Even before then one of the Maryland commissioners, Benjamin Rumsey, had vividly described initial congressional reaction to the convention's resolves:

"I arrived here on Saturday Evening last but my Colleagues did not all arrive before last Monday. On Tuesday we laid the Resolves of Convention before the Congress and on Wednesday about one oClock two of their Members informed us that the mode proposed by our Convention of substituting the Gift of ten Dollars in Lieu of the hundred Acres of Land would prove in the opinion of Congress extremely prejudicial to the united States as it would subject them all to the same Advance, an Expence in their Apprehension too great to be borne and wch to use their own Expressions would break the Back of all North America. They represented that Land might be bought for three Dollars per hundred that the Soldiery had already extorted from the State greater Wages than could well be borne. They further requested to know if we would proceed to attempt the Inlistment of the men with the twenty Dollars Bounty without promising the ten Dollars which Congress were not inclinable to grant at present but had appointed a Committee to draw up a Letter to the Convention of Maryld on the Subject of their Resolves setting forth their Reasons for not furnishing us with money and dissuading them from that mode of raising men.

"We informed the Gentlemen our Province had no Land solely, that an Expectation was formed by the People of our State that what was conquered from an Enemy at the joint Expence of Blood and Treasure of the whole should become their joint property but as Claims had been set up opposite to our Ideas of natural Justice it became wise people rather to prepare for the worst by giving ten Dollars now than trust to the mercy of a few Venders from whom they would be obliged to purchase (having pledged their Honour) at any price, the Case of all Monopolies; that we had limited Orders from our Convention a special Authority under which we must act and not deviate; that if their Letter to our Convention could be wrote in any reasonable Time we would await the Event and return or advance as we should be by them ordered.

"They also observed that the State of Maryland shewed a Disposition to separate by their Resolves from the united States, that the Resolves ran in the Stile of we would not. We remarked in Reply that the Terms made use of were *ought not* and the two Reasons that appeared in the Resolves themselves were first that the mode of Calculation was unequal and the second that it was out of our power to comply not having the Lands solely and exclusively and yet notwithstanding Injustice was done us and we had not the Lands &c We had as a State resolved to raise the men requested by Congress which together with our former Zeal in the Cause evinced our Attachment to it and ought in our opinion to have excused us from such an Imputation. Thus ended the Discourse and it is now Thursday Evening and no Lre wrote that we know of. I shall wait upon a Gentleman of the Congress tomorrow for the Lre to go by the Post and we intend to write to the Convention." Benjamin Rumsey to James Tilghman, October 24, 1776, *Md. Archives*, 12:397–400.

For further developments in this affair, see Hancock to the Maryland Commissioners, November 13, 1776. Maryland's position in this dispute is analyzed more fully in Merrill Jensen, *The Articles of Confederation: An Interpretation of the Social-Constitutional History of the American Revolution, 1774–1781* (Madison: University of Wisconsin Press, 1940), pp. 155–57.

² See *JCC*, 6:898.

Richard Henry Lee to John Page

Dear Sir,   Philadelphia Novr. 4th 1776

I am much concerned to hear of your illness but I hope the bracing season that is approaching will restore you to health and vigor.

I have not a doubt about the wisdom of your opinion that our military should precede our civil arrangements. Unless we are sure of enjoying them to what purpose do we plague ourselves about wise governments or good laws? The worst of all governments and the greatest of all abuses await us, unless we make the most timely and adequate provisions of fortifications, armed vessels, Cannon, small arms, ammunition, and Troops. Until these are in a proper way, all other provisions are vain illusions. A similar mistake is at this moment doing immense injury to the cause of America in this State, which is totally enervated and lost in political controversy. The enemies of freedom see this, and encourage it everywhere. I wish Portsmouth & Norfolk were speedily made impregnable by removing Cannon thither from whereever it can be got, and then our Ship building may be safely and quickly carried on. Gen. Stephen says that those places may, on the plan he has laid down, with a few more guns than are now there, be made secure. I pray you Sir to recommend strenuously the most vigorous attention to the Cannon Foundery on James river. Let nothing suffice but the most diligent and faithful execution of that business. The various factories of small arms deserve the encouragement and attention. The powder mills & Salt petre works I hope are not neglected. Let every nerve be strained this winter to procure Arms, ammunition, and Soldiers clothing from the foreign Islands. Before the Spring I should suppose our armed Vessels may make two or three trips apiece with produce out and Stores in. You will want a great deal of Sail cloth for your Gallies and for Soldiers Tents.

The enemy still keep the borders of the Sound and seem not willing to quit the protection of their Ships. In the 6 last skirmishes we have beaten them 5 times, and the one they gained was with loss at least equal to ours. One of their frigates that lately attempted fort Constitution was towed away after having slipped her Cable under a severe mauling. She was hulled 26 times by an 18 pounder. I verily believe we shall ketch the three ships of war that some time ago went up the North river, as their return seems now impracticable, and that river freezes in the winter. Our army is in good spirits and do not wish to avoid a general engagement.

I am, with great regard, dear Sir your most affectionate and obedient servant. Richard Henry Lee

RC (NjR, Elsie O. and Philip D. Sang deposit, 1972).

John Hancock to George Washington

Sir, Philada. Novr. 5th. 1776.

The Congress, apprehensive that Commissioners from some of the States for the Purpose of appointing Officers in the Army under the new Establishment, may not have arrived at the Camp, and at the same Time fully and deeply impressed with the Necessity of recruiting the Army to its full Complement, have passed the enclosed Resolves, authorizing you to grant Warrants to such Officers as you shall think proper, provided there are no Commissioners from the State to which such Officers belong.[1]

As it is of the greatest Consequence that the Militia now in Service should not leave the Camp at this Crisis, it is the Desire of Congress that you will take such Steps as you shall judge best for attaining this End; and that in particular you should for that Pur-

pose write to such of the States as have any Militia in the Government of New York requesting their Assistance in the Business.

The Commissions for such Officers as you shall please to appoint
by Warrant in Consequence of the enclosed Resolves, shall be forwarded as soon as possible.

The Resolves herewith transmitted, I am to inform you, do not
extend to the Maryland Troops, as the Commissioners from that
State are on their Way to Head Quarters to appoint Officers agreeably to the former Resolves of Congress. You will therefore be
pleased to suspend any appointment of Officers for that State, until
you shall hear further from Congress, or until the arrival of those
Gentlemen shall make it unnecessary.[2]

The enclosed Commission of Brigadier General you will please to
have delivered to Genl. Smallwood.[3]

With every Sentiment of Esteem & Respect, I am Sir your very
hble Set.   John Hancock Presidt.

[P.S.] I send some Commissions, & shall send others immediately.
Mr Harrisons Letters to 3rd Inst. are come to hand.

RC (DLC). In the hand of Jacob Rush, with signature and last sentence of
postscript by Hancock.
[1] See JCC, 6:920–21.
[2] See Hancock to the Maryland Convention, November 4, 1776, note 1.
[3] See JCC, 6:898.

William Hooper to Joseph Hewes

Philadelphia November 5th 1776

This, my dear Hewes, is truly confidential and intended for the
perusal of yourself & my friend Samuel Johnston only. I refer you
to Penn and the Gentleman who bears this for a state of political
and military occurrences so far as they have fallen under their Observation, and whatever may have escaped them you will learn
particularly from newspapers. I have no inclination to transcribe
when you can so easily have recourse to originals.

What may be the event of an engagement betwixt Genl. Howe
and Genl. Washington I am not bold enough to pronounce, it is
known only to the Lord of hosts. Should we succeed I think the
stroke will be decisive with respect to Britain. Should we be defeated, judge yourself what effects it will operate upon the tempers
of the Inhabitants of America. It may discourage the future Enlistment of an army and leave us unprepared to meet the efforts of
Great Britain in the Spring. We shall under the best of Circum-

stances find difficulty enough to reinlist our Army, without Blankets, without cloathing in an extreme cold country, without a probability of these difficulties being suddenly removed, Men will not easily be tempted to persevere in a service where they are to purchase honour at so dear a rate. The Enlistment of 9/10ths of our Army will expire before the last day of December, of great part of them in the middle of November & of very many in the beginning of December. The greatest number that are enlisted for a longer time and will be at the command of the Cont. in the beginning of January will not be above 2000, a handful to conflict with 25000 British troops. I find to my sincere mortification that no measures have yet taken place for recruiting in Camp. This has been entrusted to the respective states and has succeeded as I expected, What is everybodys is nobodys business.[1] The day which the Continental Congress gave out of its own power the officering of the new army induced a Solecism in the military which I fear will produce the most important ill consequences to the common cause. Military Abilities will not be the test for promotion. Popular talents, abject condescension to leading men in Assemblies, venality and corruption will become the road to Military honours. What effects this measure will have in the eastern Governments you can anticipate. Our Troops will no longer look to the Continental Congress as the power which is to direct their movements, they will consider themselves as the Creatures of the respective Assemblies, constituted for provincial purposes, and distinguished interests, when called upon to act in conjunction with other troops, they will consult the State they *belong* to for the propriety of the measure, which will be ready enough to assume the power proposed & exercise it to the prejudice of that uniformity and unanimity upon which the Salvation of America must depend. I tremble for the consequences of it. Already such a hatred to the Eastern troops exists in the Southern Corps, that it requires the utmost exertions of the Genl. Officers to prevent its breaking out into acts of violence and occasioning a general schism in the Army.

You know in part the depreciation of the continental currency, it is an evil which has now grown to such a height that the most unthinking of our friends begin to be seriously apprehensive of the effects which it may produce upon our future opposition. The first cause of this might have been innocent. French Traders having received in exchange for their Cargoes more than their vessels could carry off by way of returns have taken the residue in Continental money and as this could be of no use to them at home, they have been driven to the necessity of exchanging it to a very great disadvantage to themselves, for Gold, to those who preferred their own private Interest at the risque of every ill consequence it might have upon the credit of the Continental Money. The Tories have

taken the hint & with Israel Pemberton at their head openly and
avowedly decry the Currency and refuse to take it in payment of
their debts. The prejudice is becoming general & timid whigs are
catching the infection. I have heard that half Joes have lately sold
for six pounds. This is striking radically at our struggle and unless
vigorous & immediate steps are taken to cure the evil we are a
ruined Country. The Council of Safety here are the mere pageantry
not the reality of what they should be. Instead of striking a bold
stroke and making an example of some character of consequence,
they seize only the small fry and let Characters of importance escape
with Impunity. A Poor Shoemaker has felt their resentment while
men of fortune every day commit the same offences and triumph
in their baseness. The Continental Congress cannot interfere lest
they should violate the rights of the state and break in upon its
internal policy. This points to you the immediate necessity of providing in every state laws and ordinances to secure the Credit of
colonial & Continental Currency against Counterfeiting, or depreciation from other Causes.

Nothing lately from France. As to any measures taken by Congress
for foreign Alliances I refer you to Mr Penn. I will not trust a
thought on this subject to paper least it should by any accident
miscarry.

Genl. Washington is now at White Plains near New Rochelle
with about 20,000 men. Col. Magaw at Mount Washington with
1000. Green at fort Lee & Mercer at Amboy together have about
6000. 2 Virginia Regiments are at Trenton—the German battalion
here. The Enemy are in possession of Kings bridge. Our Army are
in good Spirits.

I have just recd. a letter from Rob. R. Livingston at Albany, I
have from him that Carlton with his Army are at Crown Point.
Gates with his at Ticon are in good Spirits. We have lately received
thro Schuyler a Supply of 6 Weeks provision in that Garrison so
that we are well off in that respect.[2]

This is Election day for the City and County of Philad, the
Altercation is like to be warm, Matlack & Cannon for the convention and the oath to be taken by Electors—Dickinson & his friends
against it. The issue is yet uncertain tho' I believe & wish that the
latter may succeed.

Adieu for the present, Yr

[P.S.] Pray deliver the several letters which I have addressed to the
Convention as soon as they are pretty generally assembled.

RC (Hayes Collection, NcU microfilm). Tr (Nc–Ar).
    [1] See Congress' September 16 resolution on this issue in *JCC*, 5:763.
    [2] Remainder of letter taken from Tr.

Secret Committee to Nathaniel Shaw, Jr.

Sir   Philadelphia Novr. 5th. 1776
   The Inclosed Letter was sent up from the Council of Safety of
Maryland with some others to us, it came by a Brig arrived there
from Martinique and was enclosed under Cover to your Friends
Messr. Thomas & Isaac Wharton who gave it back that we might
forward it to you free of Postage.[1] In the Brig at Maryland is also
arrived 133 bbs. & 20 Casks of Powder for you which we suppose to
be on Continental Account, and shall give the Board of War an
Order to receive the same, but if we are mistaken & this should be
private property you will set us right and we will either pay you
powder or Money for it.
   We are sir your Hb servts. For & on behalf of the Secret Committee, Signed,   Robert Morris, Chairman

[P.S.] The within mentioned Powder is marked in the Bill Lading,
as follows—
   LI   60 Barrels
   MP 16 do.
   AR 18 do.
   LC 39 do. 20 Keggs
   Bill Lading Dated St. Pierre, Martinico 9th Septr 1776. Signed
John Martin.
   On Accot. Nathl. Shaw Junr. to the Address of Messrs. Thos. &
Isaac Wharton.

Tr (CtY).
   [1] A transcript of the enclosed October 12 letters from William Constant, Jr., of
Pointe-a-Pitre, Guadeloupe, which informed Shaw that Constant had sent 12,950
pounds of powder to Fort Royal, Martinique, for shipment by Capt. John Martin,
is in the Shaw Papers, CtY.

Samuel Adams to James Warren

My dear Sir   Philada. Nov 6 1776
   I just now receivd your obliging Letter of the 24 of Octobr by
the Post. I am exceedingly pleasd with the patriotick Spirit which
prevails in our Genl Assembly. Indeed it does them great Honor.
I hope the Increase of Pay will be confind to the Militia to induce
them to continue in the Army till a full Inlistment of our Quota
for a new Army shall be compleated on the Encouragement offerd
by Congress which I have found since I left you is increasd by a
Suit of Cloaths annually. Congress could not account for the Delay
of the Assemblies to send Committees to the Camp agreable to their

Recommendation but by your Letter I am led to believe that the Answer of our Assembly was among those letters which were lately stolen from an Express on the Road. The Necessity of immediate Application to the important Business of inlisting a new Army inducd Congress to direct the Commander in Cheif to give orders for that Purpose even though the Committees should not have arrivd. I am glad however that your Committee is gone to Head Quarters, for I am perswaded they will be very usefull.[1] I hear with Pleasure that you have appointed a Committee of War.[2] It has ever appeard to me to be necessary and it must be attended with happy Effects. While we are taking such Measures as I trust will be effectuall to put a Stop to and totally defeat the Designs of the open Invaders of our Rights, are we not too inatentive to the Machinations of our secret & perhaps more inveterate Enemies? Beleive me, it is my opinion that of the two, the Latter are by far the more dangerous. I hope you have not many of these among you, Some I know you have. Measures are taking here to suppress them.[3]

RC (MHi).
[1] The Massachusetts General Court actually appointed two committees to appoint field officers and reenlist troops—one for the camp at New York City and the other for the army at Ticonderoga. The former consisted of Timothy Danielson, George Partridge, Josiah Sartel, Jonathan Gardner, and Seth Washburn; the latter of Abraham Watson, Nathaniel Leonard, Jacob Davis, Elisha Cranston, and William Page. Massachusetts Council Minutes, October 16, 1776, pp. 32–33. DLC(ESR). For the ensuing difficulties related to the committee at the New York camp and to Massachusetts' decision to pay a bounty to soldiers extending their term of service, see Samuel Adams to James Warren, November 9, 1776. The Massachusetts resolve of October 24 granting the soldiers a temporary bounty of 20 shillings a month is in *Am. Archives*, 5th ser. 3:409.
[2] A Board of War was established by the Massachusetts General Court on October 26, 1776. The original slate of members was appointed on October 30, but following several resignations, five new members, including James Warren, were appointed on November 16. Massachusetts Council Minutes, pp. 109, 187. DLC (ESR).
[3] For the continuation of this letter, see Adams to Warren, November 9, 1776.

William Hooper to
Joseph Hewes and Samuel Johnston

Philadelphia November 6th [1776]
My dear friends, for this is addressed both to you and Mr Johnston, I thank you for your kind favours by Mr. Bondfield, who this moment called me out of Congress, and as Capt Maclaine is unexpectedly delayed, it gives me an opportunity to acknowledge the obligations I am under to you, for your friendly attention. Mr

Maclaine has two large packages inclosing letters for you both, as well as many of my other friends whom I imagine he will find at the Convention. There you will find the causes of my detention here and other Circumstances which I think it unnecessary to repeat.

The Constitution of Pennsylvania, so far as it affects the City and County of Philadelphia, expired yesterday in the State house yard. Dickinson, Rob Morris, Christian Saml Morris, Clymer, Shubler [Shubert], Parker were elected and now ride triumphant upon the ruins of the Constitution (which Mr. Johnston thinks I condemn too freely) and upon the Characters of Matlack & Cannon who are now consigned to insignificance as they merit.

Two fine frigates are afloat from Rhode Island. 32 prizes lately carried in there—a few days ago into Salem a Turkey Ship taken in the British Channel, the Invoice of her Cargoe amounts in first Cost to 36,000 Sterling.

All well at Ticonderoga the 27th of October. Carleton at Crown Point. Schuyler in a letter this moment says that we are well supplied with provisions and there is some doubt whether Carleton will come further on. We are formidable at Tyonderoga.[1]

This moment arrived 12 Waldeckers & 8 British prisoners sent hither by Genl Washington.

I must conclude. I am called to my duty in Congress. Yours truly, W H

[*P.S.*] Mr R Morris wrote Mr Hewes two letters by post which will explain the nature of the Capture of the Tobacco Vessels.[2]

No change lately as to Genl Washington.

RC (Nc–Ar).
[1] Schuyler's October 30 letter to Hancock is in PCC, item 153, 2:471–76, and *Am. Archives*, 5th ser. 2:1296–97.
[2] These two letters have not been found. Hooper also wrote a letter this day to Gov. William Livingston of New Jersey, discussing, among other things, a November 5 resolve of Congress relating to that state. This letter, which is badly damaged, is located in the William Livingston Papers, MHi. See also *JCC*, 6:925–26; and John Hancock to William Livingston, November 7, 1776.

William Hooper to the North Carolina Convention

Sir   Philadelphia November 6th 1776

By a letter which the Congress have this moment received from their Genls Secretary at New York no change of any consequence has taken place since I last wrote you.[1]

By a letter received at the same time from General Schuyler we are informed that General Carleton with his Army are at Crown Point. General Gates is at Tionderoga with a formidable army, every hour receiving reinforcements of men and supplies of provisions from Albany and the Eastern states. Schuyler is of opinion that should the Enemy attack Tyonderoga (and from the accounts of two deserters he has great reason to think that they soon will) we shall be able to give a good account of them & that should they be able (which he does not much apprehend) to compel us to retreat from Tyonderoga, he rests confident that he shall be able to confine him to the lakes this Winter & before next Spring. I hope we shall be able to stop his progress effectually.

A Vessell this day arrived from the Southward met with several armed Ships and brigs and from the course they steared he imagined they were bound to Virginia.

A large Turkey ship the original Invoice of whose Cargoe amounted to £36000 Sterling is arrived at Salem taken by a Massachusetts privateer commanded by Captain Forrester.

The above facts may afford some Amusement to the Honourable the convention. I beg leave therefore thro you to communicate the same to them.

I am, Sir, with great Respect, Your's & the Convention's most Obedt Humble Servant,   Will Hooper

RC (Nc–Ar).
[1] Robert H. Harrison's letter to Hancock of November 3 is in PCC, item 152, 3:201, and *Am. Archives*, 5th ser. 3:493.

William Hooper to the
North Carolina Convention

Sir   Philadelphia Novr 6th 1776
By some accident I omitted to inclose the Bill of Cloathing in the letter which it was intended to accompany & herewith you will receive it. Nothing very material has occurred with respect to our Armies since I wrote you. As to the successes we have had in some small skirmishes with the Enemy I refer you to the late papers which I send to our Mr Hewes. Our Garrison were well and in good spirits at Tionderoga the 24th, Carleton with his Army at Crown Point 15 miles from them.

I am Sir, With great Respect, Your Obed Hum Ser,
                                                    Will Hooper

[P.S.] By this Opportunity I send you a Collection of the late news papers for the amusement of yourself & the Members of the Convention.

RC (Nc–Ar).

Robert Morris to George Read

Dear Sir   Philada Novr 6th. 1776

You will not wonder that I shoud be obliged to answer your favour of the 4th in a great hurry after detaining the bearer some time before I cou'd even sit down to write.

It seems there is some foundation for the report you heard [1] altho not Strictly true. I was not in Congress when Doctr Rush brought the Account from the Council of Safety but am told he moved for some Continental Troops being ordered down, which was opposed by several Members on the very principles you wou'd wish and finally the Motion was rejected, but as a Virginia Regiment was ordered up from the Eastern Shoar they were directed to halt at Dover for the further orders of Congress on the supposition that your Government wou'd apply for them if they sho'd think it necessary. This I believe to be the true state of Facts & as my Sentiments on this subject are totally with you I am ready to obey your Commands or do any thing you desire, if in my power, being very Sincerely, Dr. sir, Your obedt hble servt,   Robt Morris

RC (DeHi).

[1] Read had written to Morris from Newcastle: "A Report prevails here this Morning that Congress have ordered 4 Companies of one of the Virginia Battalions to Lewis Town on some intelligence supposed to have been transmitted to the Council of Safety of your Province by Harry Fisher. Upon inquiry I find that Mr. Rush, Secry. to the President, told the Under-Sheriff of this County so yesterday morning. I must own that I can hardly believe that Congress wou'd take A Step of this kind upon any Application other than from the Legislative or Executive bodies of this State, and more especially as the Congress must know that the General Assembly is now sitting at New Castle who it is presumed are the best Judges of the Necessity or propriety of such a Measure—but if the fact is so, take the most speedy way to prevent it's being carried into Execution, otherwise it may be Attended with bad consequences as I well know the Legislature of this State, which hath all the powers of Government at present, will look upon it as an ill timed interference with their internal affairs and without the least Grounds for such a Measure. Harry Fisher *may be* Qualified for the Post assigned him by your Council of Safety and they may give him Credit in that line but they and all others ought to be careful of giving Credit to his information of the Political Conduct or Sentiments of the People of Sussex or any other County in this Government. It was the heighth of imprudence in Congress to have ordered Col. Miles's Battalion there last Summer, but in this they were imposed upon by other Characters who may feel the effects 'ere long. The insult must not be repeated." George Read to Robert Morris, November 4, 1776, Gratz Collection, PHi.

For the episode to which Read is here referring, see Benjamin Rush to the Pennsylvania Council of Safety, November 1, 1776. For Read's reference to Congress' imprudence in having ordered "Col. Miles's Battalion there last Summer," see *JCC*, 5:436; and John Hancock's letters of June 13, 1776, to Thomas McKean and to the Pennsylvania Council of Safety.

George Ross to the
Lancaster Committee of Safety

Gent   [November 6, 1776]
I have the pleasure of informing you that I have now hopes of seeing a happy Constitution Setled for our distracted State. The City of Philada. have exerted themselves as has also the County and have by a Vast Majority carried the Election against the Supporters of the Convention. The whole Tory interest was in favour of the Convention In expectation of Embarrasing our State under a Governmt. Weak but yet Arbitrary but they have failed.[1]
I wish for the Honor of Lancaster County they may have Acted with the same Spirit & propriety. I am sure of their Affection for the Cause but fear they have been guided more by passion than Judgmt. I hope they will pardon my Apprehensions. They Arise from the best of Motives, my sincere wishes for the happiness of my Country, which is intituled to all the services in my Power to Afford her and which I will ever give. I am with Sincere regard, Your Friend & Hble Servt.,   Geo. Ross

[*P.S.*] By a letter this day from Genl. Schuyler Congress is informed our Army at Ticonderoga is in a prosperous State & well Supplyed with Provisions. Genl. Carlton is at Crown Point & if he makes an Attack we have good hopes he will meet with a Severe Repulse.
Genl. Washingtons Army in health & Spirits. He sent us this day 22 prisoners—10 of them Waldeckers.

Philada County	City Assembly
Jno Dickinson	John Bayard
Robt Knox	Jos. Parker
Isaac Hughes	Rob Morris
Fred. Antis	Geo. Clymer
Thos Potts	Sam Morris Junr
Geo. Grey	Mick Shubert
——————————	No Counsellor
No Counsellor	

RC (DLC).
[1] For a discussion of the movement in Philadelphia to frustrate implementation of the new Pennsylvania Constitution, to which Ross had contributed as a member of the convention that had recently framed it, see J. Paul Selsam, *The Pennsylvania Constitution of 1776* (Philadelphia: University of Pennsylvania

Press, 1936), pp. 226–30. The election to which Ross refers—the results of which he listed in his postscript—was held on November 5.

See also John N. Shaeffer, "Public Consideration of the 1776 Pennsylvania Constitution," *PMHB* 98 (October 1974): 415–37.

Edward Rutledge to Philip Schuyler

Dear Sir   November 6th. 1776

The Part which I have taken in Congress relative to your Character and Conduct, has I trust, been such as the Measures which you have adopted, and the Principles by which they were directed will fully justify.[1] That you have sustain'd for a length of Time an uncommon Load of Calumny is alas! too true; but tho' your Friends were much mortified to find that they were unable effectually to oppose the Torrent, yet they felt some Consolation in reflecting that the Day would come when you would appear in your true Character; I mean in the Character of a firm and disinterested Patriot. I congratulate you upon the Prospect of its Approach, and wish that I could hold my Seat in Congress until I could see you in Philadelphia, and contribute my Assistance to do Justice to your Reputation.[2] But a Desire of returning to my native Home from which I have been absent for more than Eighteen Months will deprive me of that Satisfaction. You however will suffer nothing from my Absence, as I am convinc'd you will receive ample Justice from those whose Duty it is to Administer it. I am exceeding Glad to find that you have a Prospect of keeping Carlton to the Lakes at all Events. Much is to be done this Winter & much will be done if you attend Congress as soon as you conveniently can, lay your Plans with the House, & return to execute what a large Majority of us think no one can execute so well as yourself. With every Sentiment of Esteem & every Wish for your Honour & Happiness I am, dr. Sir, Yours most Sincerely,   E. Rutledge

RC (MH–H).

[1] See Rutledge to Robert R. Livingston, September 23, 1776, note 2.

[2] In a letter to President Hancock which was read in Congress this day, Schuyler had announced his intention of coming to Philadelphia at the earliest possible moment. *Am. Archives*, 5th ser. 2:1296–97.

William Williams to Jonathan Trumbull, Jr.

Dear Sir   Philadelphia Nov 6. 1776

Contrary to my Expectations & Wishes I am yet detained here but expect Mr Shermans return every day & hour & then I propose to Set homeward.[1] Mr Huntington is also gone home unwell.[2] We know not the Situation of Affairs near N York as the passage of the river is interrupted as high as Peepskill. The Armys by the last Acct seemed to be near each other, & something decicive dayly expected. Let all Eyes & Hearts be to God &c.

The special Occasion of my writing is to mention an affair yesterd. under Considera[tion], viz a Petn of one Maj Cary [3] setting forth that he with a Body of men marchd to Canada after the fall of G[eneral] Montgomery &c, that He has never been able to obtain any Pay by reason that Gen. Schuyler forbid it, he knows not why & the men greatly disaffected & prejudiced agst the Service, & praying to be allowed their Wages &c. (I suppose in the same situation with Col Warner).[4] Much dispute was about it & finally all that cod be obtained was to refer it to the Comisrs of Accos at Albany to examine & make Report. It was suggested the probable reason was, His men went into Inoculution contrary to order &c & that was alledged as a sufficient Reason to cut them off &c & that Crime if one in the Circumstances, was treated with impolitic Severity I think to say no more.

I am greatly concerned that it will have a very ill Effect & disaffect Men to the Nothern Service. The destresing feelings of the men under the certain prospect of taking & dying with that Disease &c in my opinion pleads strongly in their Excuse, & in such Cases allowances ought to be made & Faults winked at, especially when the men are so much wanted &c. Things appear in a very different light to me than to some here &c.

I know not the man in the present Case nor where He is from, but for the reasons hinted at &c I earnestly wish You to interpose every good office in your Power with the Genl & the Comisrs & whoever can influence in the affair, that the men may be incouraged & paid, & the same with Respect to Col Warner, but know not when nor in what Situation he is in now. It seems to me of great importance, even tho they deserved nothing that they shod not be discouraged at this junction.

I have heard nothing from home since the 7th Octo., I suppose because They daily expected me to return, but I have been strangely kept here for one reason after another & may be yet longer, but hope not many days.[5]

We are at great uncertainty about Genl Gates situation, & whether he is or like to be attacked but cant expect a Letter from you before I hope to be gone. All Things are in the hands of our exquisitely wise & good God. May every Soul be induced to repent & seek Him with all their heart & entreat his favor for this distressed Land. I am with great Affection your Friend & Bror,

W Williams

RC (CtHi).
[1] In his account with Connecticut, Williams' claim—"To my Service attending Congress from July 22d to Novemr. 21st, 123 days at 18s"—undoubtedly included

travel time, for according to Oliver Wolcott, Williams left Philadelphia on November 13. Revolutionary War Collection, Ct. See Oliver Wolcott to Samuel Adams, November 16, and to Matthew Griswold, November 18, 1776.

[2] The exact date of Samuel Huntington's departure has not been determined. Since his claim with Connecticut for "services attending Congress from Jany. 1st 1776 to November 7th, 312 days at 18s" apparently included travel time, he probably left Philadelphia near the end of October. Revolutionary War Collection, Ct.

[3] Jeremiah Cady. On December 12 General Schuyler ordered Paymaster Trumbull to pay Cady and his men. See *JCC*, 6:927; and Burnett, *Letters*, 2:142n.3.

[4] For Seth Warner's petition for back pay, see *Am. Archives*, 5th ser. 2:884.

[5] Among Williams' duties was his membership on the committee on clothing, in which capacity he had written the committee's brief letter of November 4 to President Hancock requesting him "to pay to the Delegates of the State of Connecticut the sum of Twenty thousand Dollars, to be by Them improved to purchase Cloathing for the Soldiers in the Service of the united States." The letter was signed by Williams, William Ellery, Lyman Hall, Arthur Middleton, Robert Treat Paine, George Ross, and George Wythe. PCC, item 58, fols. 409–10.

William Ellery to William Vernon

Sir,[1]   Novr. 7th. 1776.

I have laid the Abstract of the Account of Losses sustained by the Inhabitants of our State by the ministerial Fleet stationed formerly in Newport, before the Comm[itt]ee appointed by Congress to collect such Accounts. The Sufferers have nothing to expect from this Quarter, The Design of the Resolve of Congress having been answered another Way. The Intention of Congress was by collecting such Accounts to show to the World the Provocations and Injuries they had sustained from Britain, to vindicate their Conduct; and if a Reconciliation should take Place to endeavour at a Compensation for such Losses; but if there were any Prospects of this Sort they have utterly vanished.[2] If We succeed in the glorious Struggle in which We are engaged, and establish our Independency, perhaps the forfeited Estates in our Commonwealth may be apply'd to the Purposes of compensating the Sufferers. If they should, they will be no great Loosers in the End; and this ought to be a Motive particularly with them to exert themselves in the present War.

Your Son was so good as to visit and take a Breakfast with Me when he was here just before his Graduation. He told me that you had given him the Offer of continuing at College another Year. I recommended it and encouraged him to embrace and improve this Opportunity to cultivate the Study of natural Philosophy and the Mathematicks, and to learn the French Language, which possibly may turn out to be more than a bare Accomplishment. George Hazard was with him in a miserable Plight, without Money, Cloaths or Health. He had indulged his volatile Cast too far, left College and been in the Army at Long Island, where he was taken sick, was bro't off in that State when the Island was evacuated, and lost all his Cloaths. He was in a most humble repenting Situation, said that he would again live at College, if it would receive him and his Father would permit it. The College will receive him, and I hope his Father will give him an Opportunity to complete his Education.

Congress publish every Article of Intelligence which they receive and think suitable to publish, therefore give me Leave to refer you to the News-Papers for Intelligence. If any thing should occur before I close this Letter, which is wrote per Saltum as I can catch Time, I will give it to you. I should be glad to know what is the Office of Commissioners of the Navy, and that you would point it out particularly; unless you can refer Me to some Author who particularly describes. The Conduct of the Affairs of a Navy as well as those of an Army We are yet to learn. We are still unacquainted with the systematical Management of them, although We have made considerable Progress in the latter. It is the Duty of every Friend to his Country to throw his Knowledge into the common Stock. I know you are well skilled in Commerce and I believe you are acquainted with the System of the British Navy, and I am sure of your Disposition to do every Service to the Cause of Liberty in your Power.[3]

MS not found; reprinted from *Publications of the Rhode Island Historical Society,* 8 (January 1901): 200–201.

[1] William Vernon (1719–1806), a Newport, R.I., merchant who was married to the niece of Ellery's brother Christopher, became one of the commissioners of the Navy Board in Boston in May 1777. *DAB;* and "Papers of William Vernon and the Navy Board, 1776–1794," *Publications of the Rhode Island Historical Society* 8 (January 1901): 198–99.

[2] See *JCC,* 3:298–99; and Committee on Hostilities to Nathaniel Woodhull, October 19, and to James Warren, October 24, 1775.

[3] For the continuation of this letter, see Ellery to Vernon, November 11, 1776.

John Hancock to William Livingston

Sir,   Philada. Novr. 7th. 1776.

I have it in Charge from Congress to request you will send immediately two Companies of Militia to guard the Salt Works near Toms River, and likewise order one Company to be stationed at or near Shre[wsbury] to intercept and put a Stop to the Intelligence said to be carrying on between the Town and Lord Howe's Fleet.[1] The said Companies are to consist of fifty Men each.

I have the Honour to be, with great Respect, Sir, your most obedt. and very hble Servt.   John Hancock Presidt

RC (MHi). In the hand of Jacob Rush and signed by Hancock.

[1] See *JCC,* 6:925–26.

Virginia Delegates to Patrick Henry?

Honorable Sir,[1]   Philadelphia, 7 Nov. 1776.

Congress judging it best that the accounts of one state be settled by persons of some other, have appointed three auditors of North Carolina, for Virginia, as you will see by the inclosed resolution.[2] We are, Honble Sir, Your obedient servants,

G Wythe	Benj Harrison
Richard Henry Lee	Francis Lightfoot Lee

RC (PHi). Written by Wythe and signed by Wythe, Harrison, F. L. Lee, and R. H. Lee.

[1] Although the recipient is not identified, this brief transmittal letter was probably intended for Gov. Patrick Henry.

[2] See *JCC*, 6:930.

William Whipple to John Langdon

My Dear Sir,   Philadelphia 7th Novr. 1776.

My last was by the schooner Betsey by whom through your favor I shipped 12 barrels flour. I now take the liberty to inclose James Miller's receipt for the same, have desired Mrs. W. to settle the freight with you and shall also desire to apologize for the trouble I give you. I have got an order on the Treasury and shall honor your drafts whenever they appear. I mentioned by Col. Bartlett how matters stood respecting the guns and cannot help flattering myself you'll have them from Connecticut.[1] The furnaces here have been very unfortunate. The guns that were brought down before I left this place last Augt. have been tried a second time and many of them would not stand the proof, so that there is not guns in this City for one ship.

The President tells me has forwarded the Commissions for the officers. It happened unlucky for the officers of the Raleigh that the rank was established before my arrival; had not that have been the case, I am inclined to think they would have been higher on the list. However their merit I am in no doubt will recommend them to promotion. The Marine Committee have rec'd a letter from the Committee of Providence in answer to one sent them in consequence of what you wrote Col. Bartlet,[2] a copy of which, also a copy of one from Governor Hopkins (who is now at Providence) I shall procure and transmit and leave you to comment on them. In the meantime I'll undertake to defend you against calumny.

I have just rec'd. your favor of the 21st ulto. Your giving up to Capt. Plance his small adventure is in my opinion very right, but by some hints that have been dropped am inclined to think that some gentlemen suppose you have exceeded your power. Capt. Bowden I find has preferred a Petition which is referred to a Committee. I have a letter from Col Wentworth on the subject, which I shall answer in a day or two. I heartily wish there may be some method adopted whereby that Gentleman may be relieved but must confess am doubtful of the success of his petition, for a public body to break their own general rules may be attended with evil consequences. However I shall do all in my power to have this matter determined as speedily as possible, and shall use my endeavours to serve Capt Bowden so far as (in my opinion) is consistent with the public good.[3] I have no news to tell you. Accounts from abroad are very favorable, hope to have it in my power to transmit you some pleasing intelligence shortly, in the meantime I wish effectual measures may be taken to procure clothing for the army. Congress pass Resolves and send them abroad, but gentlemen even those who compose public bodies suffer their attention to be so much engrossed by their private interest that the public concerns of the utmost importance are neglected notwithstanding their own and their country's salvation is at stake. Our army are in good spirits, but can it be expected that that will be the case long, when they are almost naked? Congress have been disappointed in some goods that was expected some time ago. Perhaps they will still arrive, no doubt some will. In the meantime it has been recommended to the several states to make all the provision they can, but I don't see that such recommendation has any effect. I have wrote very freely, but hope you'll make a prudent use of it. I by no means would discourage; my desire is to animate everyone to exert himself in the glorious cause in which America is engaged. For my own part I have not a doubt of success in the end, but my wish is to put a speedy end to slaughter and devastation which already is great, but must be still greater if the war continues, which nothing will prevent but the utmost exertions of the Friends to Liberty and humanity. Such exertions, under the smile of Heaven, will restore peace to and establish happiness in this Western world.

Our last accounts from the army is favorable. Gen. Lee in a private letter to a friend says that Howe has but two moves more in which we shall checkmate him. I must leave the explanation of this to those who understand the game of chess. A report is just arrived that many Hessians had deserted—if this proves true it's a favorable circumstance. Great pains have been taken to persuade those people that they would be massacred if they fell into the hands of the Americans. Those that have been taken are very agreeably disappointed and say that if their countrymen were undeceived, there would be a general revolt. Some measures have been taken for this purpose and perhaps with effect. Enclosed you have some late Resolutions of Congress respecting the Navy.[4] Some further proposals are before Congress, which I expect will be soon taken up. Present my regards wherever due, and be assured of the best wishes of your friend, &c.[5]   Wm Whipple

Tr (DLC).
[1] On the issue of supplying cannon for the New Hampshire-built frigate, see Whipple to Langdon, October 26, 1776.
[2] See Marine Committee to the Rhode Island Frigate Committee, October 9 and 13, 1776.
[3] Langdon's October 21 letter to Whipple is in Morgan, *Naval Documents*, 6:1346. The petition of Lawrence Bowden, a captured British shipmaster, was read in Congress on November 9 and referred to the Marine Committee, but apparently no further action was taken. For additional information on Bowden's court-martial for mutiny and his subsequent release, see ibid., 6:1398, 7:233–34, 1067, 1273; and *JCC*, 6:939.
[4] Probably the resolves of November 6 and 7 authorizing the appointment of three men at salaries of $1500 per annum "to execute the business of the navy, under the direction of the Marine Committee." *JCC*, 6:929, 933.
[5] For the continuation of this letter, see Whipple to Langdon, November 10, 1776.

Board of War to the
Maryland Council of Safety

Honourable Gentlemen.   War office Novr 8th 1776.
    General Schuyler is very desirous of having an answer to his Letters respecting the Nanticoke Indians. The six Nations repeatedly complain that those of that Nation who were left in Maryland are detained there contrary to their Inclinations.[1] This Idea, tho' not founded in Truth creates much uneasiness and is constantly held up by the Indians in their conferences with the General. Congress have before written to your State on the Subject [2] on which I have now the Honour of addressing you by order of the Board of War, but have not been favoured with an Answer, which I have it in command to request you will now be pleased to give that it may be transmitted to General Schuyler, and he may thereby be enabled to satisfy the minds of the Indians on this subject.
    With the greatest Respect I have the Honour to be your most obedt hble Servt,   Richard Peters Secy

P. S. The Board have received an acct of Prisoners of war in your State, and would be obliged to you for a list of the officers of Continental troops raised in your State, their ranks & Dates of commission & also the number of privates.[3]

Reprinted from *Md. Archives*, 12:429–30.
[1] On November 15 the council of safety wrote to the board that "upon the strictest enquiry" they could not find "that any Indians of the Six Nations are

detained in Maryland contrary to their inclinations." Ibid., p. 447; and PCC, item 70, fol. 85. Schuyler's letters to Hancock on the subject of the Nanticokes, written on August 18 and September 14, 1776, are in *Am. Archives*, 5th ser. 1:1030–31, 2:333–34. See also Samuel Chase to the Maryland Council of Safety, November 30, 1776.

² Apparently a reference to Thomas Stone to the Maryland Convention, September 4, 1776.

³ The council of safety sent the board such a "list" along with its November 15 letter. *Md. Archives*, 12:447.

Board of War to George Washington

Sir   War Office Novr. 8th. 1776

Mr. Lewis (a Brother Delegate) has given Congress Information that Application had been made to your Excellency by a Flag from Genl. Howe to permit Mrs. Watts & Mrs. Barrow the Pay Masters Wife to go to their Husbands in New York and at the same Time requested Congress to assist him with their Authority to obtain the Release of his Lady whom the Enemy would not permit to come out. The House having refer'd the Matter to the Board of War, we beg Leave to represent to your Excellency the Propriety of obtaining Mrs. Lewis & Mrs. Robinson her Daughter with her Chil-. dren in exchange for Mrs. Watts & Mrs. Barrow; and, if you have not already permitted those Ladies to go into York or give Genl. Howe a Promise to that effect, that you will make the Release of our Ladies, if we may be allowed the expression, a necessary requisite. Indeed should you have complied with Genl. How's Request, we submit it to your Excellency whether Mrs. Lewis & Mrs. Robinson may not be asked for in Return. We do not imagine that you will be refused, but should you, we must recur to the unhappy Expedient of with-holding in future every simular Indulgence to those Ladies in our Power, who may desire to visit their Connections in the Army.[1]

We are very sorry that our Enemies have compelled us to resolve upon any Thing which looks like severity, or indeed to lay any Restraint upon the fair Sex, but tho' we cannot approve the Practice, we shall be obliged to follow the Example of his Britannic Majesty's Commanders. We have the Honour to be with the most perfect Esteem, Your very obedt Servants,

Benja Harrison

James Wilson

Edward Rutledge

P.S. Should Mrs. Watts & Mrs. Barrow carry in their Baggage, Mrs. Lewis and Mrs. Robinson must have the same Indulgence. Perhaps

if the Ladies cannot be exchanged upon the above Terms Mrs.
Lewis may be exchanged for Mrs. Kempe.   B H
                                                      J.W.
                                                      E.R.

RC (DLC). In a clerical hand and signed by Harrison, Rutledge, and Wilson.
   [1] See *JCC*, 6:936. Washington's November 15 reply to the board is in Washington, *Writings* (Fitzpatrick), 6:283–84.

John Hancock to Artemas Ward

Sir,   Philada. Novr. 8th. 1776.
   I do myself the Pleasure of forwarding the enclosed Resolve, by
which you will be informed that Congress, in Consideration of your
keeping the Command in the Eastern Department, have come to a
Determination to allow you the Pay of a Major General commanding in a seperate Department, from the Time of your Resignation,
until a suitable Person can be appointed in your Stead, or the
Matter shall be otherwise ordered by Congress.[1]
   Wishing you all possible Health and Happiness, I am with Sentiments of Esteem, Sir, your most obed. and very hble sert.
                                            John Hancock Presidt

RC (MHi). In the hand of Jacob Rush and signed by Hancock.
   [1] See *JCC*, 6:931.

William Hooper to the
North Carolina Convention

Sir   Philadelphia Novr 8th 1776
   I take the earliest Opportunity to communicate to you a piece
of information which I have lately received & which is truly interesting to the Southern States. A Deserter from General Howes
army who has lately arrived in this City, upon his examination says
that the cause of his desertion was as follows: "That General Howe
was planning an expedition against the Southern Colonies, that
Draughts for that purpose were immediately to be made from the
Army at large, that he was apprehensive that it might fall to his
lot to be selected, that he was to the Southward last fall and
suffered so much from drinking bad Water, and from musquetoes
& flies, that he would rather go to the Devil than make another
expedition thither." [1] What tends to corroborate this report, is that
a large fleet of Transports is now lying at Red Hook in readiness

to take in troops and proceed to Sea. They give out that these are intended for Rhode Island, meaning thereby to put us off our guard that we may become a more easy prey to them. The Convention will pay the respect to this information which they may think it merits & take such measures to prevent the designs of their Enemies as they in their wisdom shall think best. I beg my most respectful Compliments to the Members of the Convention and am, Sir, With great regard, Your's & their most Obedient, Humble Servant,   Will Hooper

RC (Nc–Ar).
[1] Soon afterward Congress received a letter from Washington stating that he would not be surprised if Howe "sends a detachment to the Southward, for the purpose of making a Winter's Campaign." Washington, *Writings* (Fitzpatrick), 6:249. In fact the British did not undertake another Southern campaign until 1778.

Philip Livingston to George Clinton

Dr Sir   Phila. 8 Novr [1776]
    Inclosed are three letters directed to you. I have not recd. a line from you, which I have Most sincerely wished for. Do let Me hear from You. I have not one friend in the Army that thinks it worth while to drop me a Single Lettr. Pray desire Genl McDougall to write me once a week or once a fortnight.
    I see by the News Papers that Govr Tryon is Exhibiting at N. York. I hope He Will not Make any Considerable party. I Mean I hope the Tories will not be Very Numerous there, which wd give him Spirits & indeed I beleive Sowing intestine divisions Among us is their Chief dependence. Our Accts. from Europe are favorable & I make No doubt but Every thing will go right at Last. *Our State must Suffer greatly & that only that the Tories May be Protected.* I hope they will not be forgot. I am, Dr Sr, Yours &c,
                                        Phil Livingston

RC (ICHi).

William Whipple to Josiah Bartlett

My Dear Sir,   Philaa 8th. Nov. 1776
    Our Colleage arriv'd the 3d inst.[1] He crossed the River several miles above Dobb's ferry by which means I suppose you Miss'd him. He complains much of the Roads & I believe justly. He was Inoculated Yesterday, but attends Congress. Nothing meterial has happen'd since your departure. Some private Letters from Genl Lee of Yesterdays date are very incouraging. If you pass'd through

the Army, you must be sensible of the want of Cloathing & as you know what was done in Congress respecting that matter no doubt you'll use your influence to draw the attention of the Executive Power of our state to that Subject. I find the Genl. Court of the Massachusetts have increas'd the pay of their Soldiers & have sent a committee to camp to inlist the men, but Genl. Washington wod not consent to their giving out Orders till the matter was lay'd before Congress. One of the Gentn arriv'd Yesterday. What will be done in the affair I know not. We really have a Choice of Difficulties which I am in no doubt we shall get over, but the thing is to make advantages of those difficulties. The Massachuts. have increas'd the pay of their Soldiers to 10 Dols. per Month for the new army. If that shod be come into, the charge of the army will be so great that it will discourage many & undoubtedly will cause some heartburnings in a certain assembly. On the other hand, if the matter has taken air among the Soldiers & shod not be agree'd to there is great danger that we shall have no Army. This affair is referr'd to a Committee who I suppose will report tomorrow. Shall be able to give you a more perticular accot. of the matter in my next. In the meantime I hope every measure is & will be taken to raise our Proportion & as many more as possible.[2]

I shod have speculated this side down but have a most violent head ake which has increas'd within a few Minutes to such a degree that it deprives me of the power of thinking. Must therefore bid you Adieu. Yours &c,   W Whipple

9th Just receiv'd advice that the Enemy had retreated from Crown Point & expect an express every hour that will give the perticulars.[3] Genl. Howe has suddenly remov'd from White Plains it is conjectur'd with a design to cross the North River. 4000 of our army have cross'd above him ready to attack him on this side.

RC (NhD).
[1] Matthew Thornton presented his credentials to Congress on November 4. JCC, 6:920.
[2] On this question, see Samuel Adams to James Warren, November 9, 1776, note.
[3] The journals do not indicate how this information was transmitted to Congress. Gen. Horatio Gates' November 5 letter to Hancock "advising the retreat of General Carleton from Crown Point" was not received and read in Congress until November 15. JCC, 6:951; and Am. Archives, 5th ser. 3:526–27.

Samuel Adams to James Warren

Novr 9th [1776]

Mr Partridge arrivd in this City the last Evening, having been dispatchd by your Committee at Genl Washingtons Head Quarters who have consulted with the General concerning the Augmentation made by our Assembly of the Pay of the Troops to be raisd by our State.[1] The General advisd them to lay the Matter before Congress. We intend to bring it on this day. I have strong Doubt whether it will succeed here. Men must be prevaild upon to inlist at some Rate or other, and I think it must be confessd that our State have shewn a laudable Zeal for the publick Service. But if the other States which are to have Troops in the Army should not consent to give the same Encouragement it may cause great uneasiness among them. I am the more ready to beleive it will not be well receivd in Congress because a proposal made not long ago by the Maryland Convention for them to offer to their Men Ten Dollars in Lieu of the 100 Acres of Land was rejected.

Novr 11. On Saturday last Congress considerd the Business on which Mr Partridge is here. A Comte was appointed who have this day reported against your Resolution and the Report is agreed to, but as the Resolution must be known to the Soldiers it has greatly embarrassd us. A Motion was made to limit the Duration of the Inlistments which after Debate was postpond and is to be determind tomorrow. If the present Encouragement offerd by Congress is continued only for a limited Time of three or four years it certainly would be very great. I will inform you further of this Affair tomorrow.

Novr 12th. The Motion I yesterday mentiond has been this Day considerd, and Congress have resolvd upon an Alternative; that is, so far to reconsider their former resolution as to admit of Inlistments for three years, with the Bounty of 20 Dollars & the Suit of Cloaths annually, or during the War with the Addition of the 100 Acres of Land; and our Committee is desired not to offer the further Encouragement of 20s. You will have a Copy of this Resolution sent to you by the President. Would it not be proper to send immediate Instructions to your Committee at the several Camps to settle the Affair of Officers and exert themselves in the most important Business of procuring a new Army. I am affectionately yours,   S A

RC (MHi). A continuation of Adams to Warren, November 6, 1776.

[1] George Partridge (1740–1828), who later served in Congress, was one of the Massachusetts committee sent to reenlist Bay State troops in the Continental Army and appoint regimental officers for the army at New York. When General Washington refused to allow Massachusetts to offer higher monthly pay than authorized by Congress, the committee chairman, Gen. Timothy Danielson, sent Partridge to Philadelphia to argue their cause. But despite the efforts of Partridge and the Massachusetts delegates, Congress on November 12 ordered Massachusetts to pay no more than the authorized amount to reenlist its soldiers in New York. Shipton, *Harvard Graduates*, 15:282–85; and *JCC*, 6:936–37, 940, 944–45. For Timothy Danielson's November 3 letter to John Hancock and other related letters and documents, see *Am. Archives*, 5th ser. 3:494–96, 521–22, 711–14. Adams' fellow Massachusetts delegate Robert Treat Paine simply noted in his

diary for November 9: "Mr. Partridge to Town, one of the Commissioners from Mass govermt to appoint officers in Army." MHi.

John Hancock to Philip Schuyler

Sir,   Philada. Novr. 9th. 1776

You will perceive from the enclosed Resolve, that Congress having reconsidered their Vote of the 14th of Octr. have agreed to give the former Allowance of one Dollar and one Third of a Dollar to the Officers on the Reinlistment of every Soldier in the Camp. The compleating the Army being at present an Object of the utmost Importance, the Congress are desirous of adopting every Means in their Power, to induce the Officers to fill up their respective Companies, as soon as possible.[1]

The Situation of the Northern Army being at this Juncture extremely critical, and your Services in that Department of the highest Use and Importance, the Congress, wish for a Continuance of your Influence & Abilities on Behalf of your Country. They have however, agreeable to your Request, consented that you should repair to this City, whenever in your opinion, the Service will admit of your Absence.[2]

Altho Congress have repeatedly applied to Maryland on the Subject of the Nanticoke Indians without Effect, yet are they determined to make another application, the Result of which shall be immediately transmitted to you.[3]

I do myself the Pleasure to forward blank Commissions agreeably to the inclosed Resolves, and am to request, you will fill them up according to the Ranks and Times of Service of the officers, making in Col. Elmore's Regiment, such Arrangements as you shall think proper.[4]

I have the Honour to be, with every Sentiment of Esteem & Respect, Sir, your most obed. & very hble Sert.   J. H.

Novr. 13. Congress have had sundry Resolves from Massch. Bay laid before them increasing the Pay of their Troops beyond what Congress had given. The enclosed Resolves will inform you that this Measure was disapproved of by Congress, who have agreed that the Troops may be enlisted during the War, or for three years as shall be most agreeable to them.[5]

LB (DNA: PCC, item 12A).
[1] See *JCC*, 6:932; and Hancock to Schuyler, October 23, 1776, note.
[2] See *JCC*, 6:932.
[3] See *JCC*, 6:932-33; and Board of War to the Maryland Council of Safety, November 8, 1776.
[4] See *JCC*, 6:932.
[5] See *JCC*, 6:944-45; and Samuel Adams to James Warren, November 9, 1776, note.

John Hancock to George Washington

Sir,   Philada. Novr. 9th. 1776

You will perceive from the enclosed Resolve, that Congress having reconsidered their Vote of the 14th of Octr., have agreed to give the former Allowance of one Dollar & one Third of a Dollar to the Officers on the Reinlistment of every Soldier in the Camp. The compleating the Army being at present an Object of the utmost Importance, the Congress are desirous of adopting every Means in their Power, to induce the Officers to fill up their respective Companies, as soon as possible.[1]

You will please to take the most effectual Steps for punishing in an exemplary Manner, as far as the Articles of War will admit, all Deserters from the Army at this Time of Trial and Danger. The Baseness of those Officers and Soldiers who can turn their Backs upon their Country in her present Situation, merits the severest Chastisement.[2]

The enclosed Letter from Col. Miles to Mr. Wister of this City, I am directed by Congress to transmit to you, that you may take such Steps relative to the Exchange of the Gentlemen therein mentioned, as you may judge proper.[3]

Mr. Partridge, one of the Committee from the State of Massachusetts Bay, having laid before Congress sundry Resolves of that State concerning the Pay of their Troops beyond what the Congress had given, they have come to a Resolution disapproving of that Measure; and have agreed that the Troops in the American Army may be enlisted for three years, or during the War, as shall be most agreeable to them, subject to the Terms mentioned in the enclosed Resolves.[4]

I have the Honour to be with every Sentiment of Esteem & Respect, Sir, your most obed & very hble Sert.

                                                    John Hancock Presidt

RC (DLC). In the hand of Jacob Rush and signed by Hancock.
[1] See JCC, 6:874, 932.
[2] See JCC, 6:933.
[3] In this letter Col. Samuel Miles of Pennsylvania, who had been captured at the battle of Long Island, proposed that he be exchanged for John Foxcroft, the royal postmaster in New York who apparently had been sent to Philadelphia by that state's council of safety. Washington authorized Miles to make this proposal to General Howe, but he was pessimistic about the colonel's chances for success "as by the Terms of our Cartel, Officers of equal Rank are only to be proposed for each other," and in fact Miles was not exchanged until 1778. JCC, 6:933; and Washington, Writings (Fitzpatrick), 6:294n.58, 308.

Foxcroft, who was then in Philadelphia, had submitted a letter to Congress on October 15, requesting permission to return to his wife and family in New York. Congress granted his request on the same day. Foxcroft's letter, which ordinarily would be in PCC, is located instead among the papers of Elias Boudinot (later commissary of prisoners), at DLC. It is endorsed by Secretary Thomson: "Letter from John Foxcroft praying leave to go to New York. Read in Congress Octr. 15. 1776. Leave granted, he giving his parole to the board of war & not setting out on his Journey before next week." Immediately below Thomson's endorsement is the following notation in the hand of Edward Rutledge, a member of the Board of War: "Mr. Foxcroft to give a Parole not to disclose any thing which may have come to his Knowledge respecting the political State of Affairs of this or any other Colony. And further to return as soon as he can conveniently bring off his Family." See also *JCC*, 6:875–76.

⁴ This paragraph must have been written on November 12, the day Congress passed the "enclosed Resolves" referred to by Hancock. See *JCC*, 6:944–45; and Samuel Adams to James Warren, this date, note.

William Hooper to the North Carolina Convention

Sir   Philadelphia Nov 9th 1776

I inclose to you and beg you would communicate to the Convention a petition from John Smith of Anson Country [County] praying to be relieved from his present confinement & to be restored to his afflicted Family and friends. His age, Indisposition, sincere contrition for the past, and engagements for his future conduct plead warmly in his behalf, and have so far interested me in his petition as to induce me to wish that if you should entertain the same sentiments of him which I do, the Journey of his Son hither and back again may not be without effect.¹

I am, With great Respect, Sir, Your's & the Convention's Most Obed Humble Sert.²   Will Hooper

RC (Nc–Ar).

¹ Smith was a loyalist soldier who had been captured at the battle of Moore's Creek Bridge in February 1776 and subsequently sent to Philadelphia. His petition to the convention, dated November 9, is in *N.C. Colonial Records*, 10:900–901. It was referred to the convention's committee of inquiry on November 25, but no further action on it appears in the convention's journal. Ibid., p. 936.

² This day Hooper also sent the convention "a plan of the present Seat of War in America. The topical & very particular description of the places where anything interesting has happened," he went on to explain, "will no doubt afford you much Amusement, & put it in your power to read with much greater satisfaction the accounts you receive of the military in New York & its vicinities." Secretary of State Papers, Nc–Ar. The enclosure has not been identified, but it was undoubtedly the same item Richard Henry Lee sent to a friend the following day. See the postscript to Richard Henry Lee to Robert Carter, November 10, 1776.

Francis Lightfoot Lee to Landon Carter

My dear Colonel,   Philadelphia Novr. 9th. 1776

Mr. Dye having been hurried away a day or two sooner than he expected, prevented my writing to you by him. He will not probably be with you sooner than this, as Mr. Colston sets off early tomorrow morning.

I have been so entirely engaged in politics, that I found myself very badly qualified for the business you was pleased to put into my hands; indeed I presently found that Dye wou'd manage it much better than I cou'd; engaged as I was with other business. I therefore desired him to sell your tobo. with the rest, & settle the Accts. with you. I do not think you will suffer by it, bad as the venture has turned out. It wou'd give me pain, if I was not sure you will beleive that it was not want of inclination that prevented my doing the business myself. I have sent you nothing but the medicines, being desirous that you shou'd judge for yourself; after having received full information from Mr. Dye, as to the price of goods here. If you determine to have the other things, Mrs. Lee & myself will purchase them upon the first notice, and I expect there will be many opportunities to Poto. or Rapa.

The exorbitant high prices of good is occasion'd in a great measure by the artifices of the wealthy tories cheifly in this State, in order to distress the Army & people, and to depreciate the Cont. Cury. Congress cannot with propriety interfere in this business; as the states now have powers competent to prevent the evil. The mischief has been pointed out, & the states requested to apply a remedy; but unhappily the rage of making regulations for future ages is gone forth, & little attention is paid to immediate defence; while our Enemies, open & concealed, are exerting every nerve to put a speedy end to our political existence. What a fine fund of ridicule, will our fine systems afford to our Victorious adversaries! I entirely agree with your Author, as to the impropriety of Overseers mustering. It woud be well enough to make them keep their arms in good order. However these young hands must run wild a little at first.

You was in the right not to be alarm'd all is well in Congress; only the members grow weary, go off & leave us too thin; which obliged us to call for them. There are some, my dear Col. who wish the Congress to be divided & contemptible; as that cant be accomplished, the next thing is to make the world think it is so. These endeavors affect me only as the public good is concern'd. Your sentiments with respect to the same persons continuing long in high offices, have my full approbation, & therefore tho, I hope, not in the least intoxicated, but most confoundedly tired, I shall next spring beg leave to retire to Virginia, and shall then have the pleasure of laying my conduct before you, as one of my constituents, over a bowl of your good brandy toddy.

Congress made no observations on the report of the Committee to Ld. Howe,[1] thinking it better to leave the plain facts to the judgment of the people. This was not my opinion, & allways hoped some private hand wou'd have done it, but alass! *Constitutions* employ every pen. I have not yet been able to meet with Doctr. Bond, when I do, shall confer upon the subject of your Letter, & let you know the results. The two mighty British armies are not likely to effect much in the State of N. York this year; when we heard last from Ticonderoga, Carlton was at Crown Point, uncertain whether he wou'd retire into Canada, or make an attempt upon Ticonderoga; if the latter, Gates thinks he can drub him. As to Genl. Howe, after long attempting to get by our Army & penetrate into the Country, we this moment learn by express from Genl. W. that he decamped the other night with precipitation, & is making his way toward the City of N. York. The Genl. is uncertain what the Enemy means to do next, but thinks he will either cross the North River & endeavor to come thro' the Jerseys to this City; or will move to the Southward. If his Ships prevent our Army from crossing the North river, we shall be in a bad pickle. I hope the Southern states will be able to keep him at bay, till they are reinforced. But your Convention must really give a truce to every consideration, but warlike preparations. Tis vain to sow the feild, unless it is fenced against the spoiler. Our best respects to our friends of Sabine Hall. I am with much esteem Dear Col., Yr. afft. hble Sevt.   Francis Lightfoot Lee

[*P.S.*] Inclosed is the apothecary's bill for the medicines. I recd. £14 from Dye.

RC (NN).
¹ See *JCC*, 5:765–66.

Samuel Adams to Artemas Ward

My dear Sir   Philada Novr 10th 1776
    Early after my Arrival in this City, I made mention in Congress of the Affair we were talking of when I last saw you in Boston, and upon a Motion obtaind an order that you should receive the Pay of a Major General *commanding in a seperate Department* from the 26th of April being the Day on which Congress dischargd you of your Trust agreeable to your Request, until another shod be appointed to command in your Stead or it shall be otherwise orderd. The Pay of a Major General, you know, is one hundred and Sixty Dollars per month, and while he commands in a seperate Department it is double that Sum. If shall not have receivd the before mentioned letter from the President before this reaches you, you will soon after, and then you will conduct your self accordingly.¹ I am with cordial Esteem, Your Friend & very humble Servt,
                                                    Saml Adams

RC (DLC photostat).
¹ Congress took this action on November 7. See *JCC*, 6:931; and John Hancock to Artemas Ward, November 8, 1776.

Committee to Ticonderoga to John Hancock

Sir,   Albany Novr. 10th 1776 ¹
   We did ourselves the honor of writing you on the 26th of last month from Saratoga; and after waiting, in vain, a few days, in expectation of advice from Genl. Gates, agreeably to his letter to us of the 24th we thought it our duty, nevertheless, to proceed on to Tyonderoga. We continued there during the first two days in hourly expectation of sharing in the glory of our Army in a successful opposition to the attack of Genl. Carlton: but we were disappointed— and instead thereof, had the pleasure of knowing that he had totally evacuated Crown Point. Of this great event, you will have received authentic accounts before this can reach you. We returned here the morning before the last, and this morning we received from Genl. Gates the inclosed letter, together with some dispatches for ourselves—the letter he requested might be immediately forwarded to you by express. We are acquainted with the contents of it, and had a conference with the Commissioners from the Massachusetts Bay, in company with Genl. Gates before we left Tyonderoga. We did not fail to represent to them, in the strongest terms, our apprehensions of the fatal consequences of the measure adopted by their General Court; and advised them, by all means, to suspend the declaration of their powers untill Congress shou'd be advised of this extraordinary step. We left them apparently undetermined; and as to what has followed Genl. Gates's letter will fully inform you.² Having gone thro' the business committed to us by Congress, as far as it has been in our power, we propose to set out to morrow on our return, if the weather shall permit. In the meantime, with the greatest respect, we have the honor to be, Sir, Your most obedient and most humble Servants,   Richd. Stockton

                                                    Geo Clymer

P.S. This moment fresh accts. from Genl. Gates inform us,³ that he had sent Boats *40 miles* down Lake Champlain, and no appearance of the Enemy.⁴

RC (DNA: PCC, item 78). Written by Stockton and signed by Stockton and Clymer. Read in Congress on November 18. *JCC*, 6:957.
¹ This day Clymer and Stockton also wrote a letter to Commissary General Joseph Trumbull, complaining that his deputies at Albany and Ticonderoga had been disposing of hides at a fraction of their value and ordering him to direct them to stop the practice immediately. PCC, item 21, fols. 109–10; and *Am.*

Archives, 5th ser. 3:1588–89. They submitted this letter to Congress on November 27 along with their final report on the state of the northern army.

² Gates' November 7 letter to the committee is in *Am. Archives*, 5th ser. 3:592. Enclosed in it was a November 6 letter from Gates to Hancock complaining of the actions of the Connecticut and Massachusetts assemblies in offering additional money to new recruits "over and above the very great bounty allowed by Congress." Ibid., pp. 549–50. Congress had already dealt with this problem in a different context before Gates' letter reached Philadelphia. See *JCC*, 6:944–45; and Samuel Adams to James Warren, November 9, 1776, note. Gates also sent the committee a "List of the wants of the Northern Army" that was submitted to Congress with the committee's final report on November 27. PCC, item 21, fols. 81–82; and *Am. Archives*, 5th ser. 3:1585.

³ See Gates to Schuyler, November 8, 1776, in *Am. Archives*, 5th ser. 3:607.

⁴ Upon his return to New Jersey, Stockton submitted a claim of £150 to the state legislature on December 2 for "his attendance as a Member of the general Congress from 25th June to 21st Novr., 150 days at 20s per day." Richard Stockton, Account, Signers of the Declaration of Independence Collection, N.

William Ellery to Nicholas Cooke

Sir   Philadelphia Novr. 10th 1776.

Although nothing remarkable hath occurred since my last; yet as it is my Duty to write frequently I take up my Pen to avoid the Imputation of Neglect.

Our Army in the middle Department have moved four Miles, to some Heights beyond White Plains. In a private Letter I am told Genl. Lee hath wrote that the Enemy had but two Moves more to make before it would be check Mate, alluding to the Game of Chess. There have been several Skirmishes within 3 Weeks past in all which We have been successful excepting that of last Monday Fortnight, and in that, although We lost the Ground, yet the Loss of the Enemy was three Times as great as ours. By the best Account I can collect We lost only about 100 killed and wounded. I have conversed with a Gentleman who was a Spectator of the Fight. He says that our Men behaved with great Firmness and Spirit, that they frequently repulsed the Enemy, who repeatedly reinforced their Detachment from the main Body, which was within a Quarter of a Mile of the Place of Action, and so compelled our Men to retreat, which was done in good Order, and without the Loss of their Arms or Field Peices. He further said that our Musketry was more frequently discharged than but our Field Peices not so often as those of the Enemy. We have again routed Major Rogers with his rebel Band; and should have taken Twenty of the Enemy's Light Horse if our Men had not been too eager. A few more Skirmishes with a Battle now and then would learn our Troops, coolness, Obedience, and Discipline. I do not expect a general Battle this Campaign. The Generals seem to be determined not to put any Thing to a Risk. If there should be, barring Accidents, We shall beat the Enemy.

Our last Accounts from the Northern Army say, that Carlton was at Crown-Point and that if he should attack our Troops that We should repel him, and at the worst confine him to the Lakes. Our Armies are well supply'd with Provisions but they want Cloathing. I hope that your Honour and the Genl. Assembly will expeditiously execute what hath been recommended & requested of you & them by Congress, respecting the Article of Cloathing and that Care will be taken that our Two Battalions be raised and equipped in Season. Congress have lately passed a Resolve empowering Gl. Washington to appoint Officers, where any of the States had not Commrs. on the Spot at the Time that he should receive the Resolves, the Time for which a great Part of the Army was inlisted being so near expiring as not to admit of any longer Delay.[1]

I should be very happy to receive a Letter now and then from my Constituents with the Information I have and may request. I received a Letter, from your Honour I imagin by the Contents, without a Signature, and am glad to find that the Report was as I suspected groundless and scandalous. An Œmulation among the respective States who shall do most in the glorious Cause in which We are engaged is highly commendable, and would be beneficial; but if it should degenerate into Jealousies, Suspicions and Calumny it might be dangerous.

Your Honour will see in the late Papers an Extract of a Letter dated at Fort Lee giving an Account that Six Gentn. who had escaped from the Enemy's Fleet informed that 70 Transports with 3000 Troops were destined for our State. The News Paper doth not mention from what Letter the Extract was made, it was taken from a Letter of Major Genl. Greene.[2] I don't think We are in any Danger at present. Hereafter when their Army shall go into Winter Quarters the Enemy may have Men to spare for that Purpose. It would be well however to be upon our Guard, to let our Apprehensions be known to the neighbouring Sister States, and to request them to stand prepared to assist Us whenever We may be invaded. If an Attack should be made on Rhode Island I am afraid that some who have subscribed the Test Act would immediately discover that they did not think themselves bound by their Subscriptions, and that those who have refused to subscribe and have received Indulgences would not on that Account be less forward to join and assist the Invaders. We ought to guard against our internal as well as external Enemies, and if we can, put it out of their Power to injure Us. I hope I shall be pardoned for giving these Hints, and I don't doubt it when it is considered that I have been urged to it, by a sacred Regard to the State I have the honour to represent, and to the United States of America.

I continue to be with the sincerest Respect your Honour's, and the Republick of Rhode Island &c, Friend and humble Servant,

Wm Ellery

P.S. As I am obliged to write in haste I hope Blurrs, Blots and Inaccuracies will be overlooked.   W E

RC (R–Ar).
    [1] See *JCC*, 6:920–21.
    [2] Greene's October 31 letter to General Washington is in Greene, *Papers* (Showman), 1:328–29.

Richard Henry Lee to Robert Carter

Dear Sir,   Philadelphia Novr. 10. 1776

I have been the less solicitous about writing to you and my other Westmoreland friends as I know you get the Packet from hence weekly which brings you the news of this place the day that every post quits it. We have hitherto seen the mighty land and sea force of our enemies capable of effecting very little indeed of that great business which brought it here. Three Islands, their only acquisition yet, being a very inconsiderable part of this large Northern Continent. As for Canada, it was the small pox, not their arms, that procured them it. And the whole is but a miserable compensation for 12 millions the expence of the Campaign and 2 millions more of value in prizes made by our Cruizers. Should they be obliged to close the Campaign thus, they will fall under the contempt of all Europe, after the extravagant boast they have made of reducing the whole Continent this summer. Various have been the manœuvres of the two armies, and many smart skirmishes have ensued in which we have beaten them five out of six. Gen Lee writes me that "Mr. Howe has but two moves left, and I expect we shall checkmate him in both." By an Express just arrived from Gen. Washington we are informed that Gen. Howe having vainly strived to outflank him, did on Thursday night last decamp with his whole army and precipitately retreated during the night towards the North river & Kingsbridge as if returning to the City of New York.[1] Various are the conjectures concerning this Manœuvre. Some think he is going into Winter quarters, some that he intends Southward, and some that his destination is for this City. Few are of the first opinion, more of the second, and most of the last. The reasons already suggested in this letter make it not probable that after such potent efforts they shd. go to Sleep having done so little. Nor does there appear object great enough (unless it be Charles Town) to the Southward for such a force. However we ought to be laying up Magazines of provisions and getting our people in the best readiness. This City & Province are great objects. No government here at present, many Tories, and too much languor. The enemy know this, However, they will not get here easily. To come by water will puzzle them amazingly,

and if thro the Jersies, we have 5 or 6000 men there already and
Gen. Washington's Army will follow on their rear. What will be
the issue of this movement of the enemy a few days will discover.
At present, it is evidently disgraceful to them. They were pursued
by parties of our men but they had got too far, except some Waggons
and a few strollers that were taken. We have taken every proper measure to secure the French Court in our interest, and I shall think it
among the strangest events that have happened if occurrences cast
not up soon in Europe that will lighten our burthen. We have had
a fair trial of skill between our rifle men and the Hessian Chassuers
in which we fairly beat them. Numbers were equal, the Hessians
had 10 or 12 killed and some made prisoners, the rest fled. The price
of every thing has risen so here that we can scarcely live. Wood
40s a Chord, Beef 11d per lb & Hay £10 a Ton. Mrs. Lee presents
her compliments to Mrs. Carter in which I beg to join.

I am dear Sir affectionately, yours,

Richard Henry Lee

P.S. I have sent you the best Map of the Seat of War that is published here.

RC (InU). Addressed: "Honorable Robert Carter esquire, in Westmorland
County, Virginia. Favored by—⟨Mr. Coulston⟩ Mr. Brockenbrough."
    ¹ According to Washington's November 6 letter to Hancock—which was read
on November 11 and is in PCC, item 152, 3:213–15, and Washington, *Writings*
(Fitzpatrick), 6:248–50—this maneuver by General Howe occurred on Monday
evening and Tuesday, November 4–5.

William Whipple to John Langdon

10 Nov. [1776]

Genl. Howe (not liking the situation of our Army) removed very
suddenly in the night from White Plains, where he has been encamped, this movement was a matter of great speculation in our
Army, but from the observations made on his motions it was con-
jected that he intended to cross over to New Jersey. Gen. Washington has detached about 4000 under command of Gen. Putman over
the River, above him, in order to give him a proper reception on
this side. Advice is just arrived that the Enemy had retreated from
Crown Point—the Particulars of this affair is hourly expected by
Express thats on the road.

Tr (DLC). A continuation of Whipple to Langdon, November 7, 1776.

Board of War to the
Pennsylvania Council of Safety

Gentlemen,   November 11th. [1776] 12 o'clock at Noon
    The Congress having come to the inclosed Resolution,[1] and the
Situation of Affairs requiring, in our Opinion, the utmost Dispatch,
we beg Leave to request that you will immediately appoint a Committee of your honourable Board to meet us at the War Office
as soon as possible.
    We are with Respect, your very obedt. servts.

Benj Harrison   Edward Rutledge

James Wilson   Francis Lightfoot Lee

RC (NN). Written by Rutledge and signed by Rutledge, Harrison, Lee, and
Wilson.
    [1] See *JCC*, 6:940. The minutes of the council of safety do not indicate the
council's response to this request.

William Ellery to William Vernon

[November 11, 1776]
    Novr. 10th [*i.e.* 11th].[1] We are informed this Morning by Express
from G. Washington [2] that the Army under Genl. Howe had broke
up their Encampment and on the 5th of this Month had retreated
towards Kingsbridge, but whether it was only a Feint and that he
meant by making a sudden Wheel to out flank and surround our
Army was uncertain, that he had sent off Detachments to harass
them in their Retreat and watch their Motions. That if it was a
Manoeuvre he should send a Body of his Men over to the Jersey
to prevent the Enemy's getting Foot there. That our Loss in the
skirmish of Monday fortnight was not great, that the Enemy had
lost 400 killed and wounded, and among them Col. Carr of the 35th.
That by Advices the Enemy meant to invest Fort Washington. That
70 Transports with 3000 Men were at Redhook, and that it was
said that they were destined for Rhode-Island; but that for various
Reasons he did not believe it and particularly mentioned that the
Season of the Year was against it. That it was more probable that
they were destined for the Southward, where they might carry on
some Expedition during the Winter. Genl. Mercer in a Letter of
the 8th Instant writes that had recd. a Letter from Gl. Greene at
Fort Lee informing him that about 10,000 of the Enemy had appeared opposite Dob's Ferry and that he imagined they meant to
cross the North River &c.[3] Mr. Lovell who at length is released from
his Captivity in a Letter to a Member of Congress dated at Fort

Lee Novr 8th writes that the first of this Instant or the Day before Orders were Issued to get into complete Readiness, Transports for 15,000 (Mr. Lovell was then on board a Ship in the Fleet). What the Destination of this Body is, is unknown. Some Conjecture they are bound to this City, some that they are bound further to the Southward. I rather think that they are destined for this Place. Time will discover whether Mr. Howes Decampment was a Feint or not, whether the Information of Mr Lovell was well founded and what the Destination of the British Troops. I imagin Rhode-Island is not an Object sufficient to engage the Attention of Mr. Howe at this Time. To be sure it would not require so great a Force as 15,000 Men to subdue it. Genl. Mifflin hath wrote to a Friend here that the Comm[itt]ee of Albany had wrote to the Convention of New York that Carleton evacuated Crown Point the 28th of October and had repassed the Lake, and had retreated with his whole Army to Quebec. G. Mifflin's Letter is dated at Peeks-Kiln Novr. 10th.[4]

Novr. 11th [i.e. 12th]. This last Article is premature; for Congress hath this Moment recd a Letter from G. Gates by which it appears that Carlton was at Crown Point with his Army.[5]

I would be obliged to you if you would send an Extract of this Letter, to wit, of the News from Novr. 10th to Genl. Mifflin's premature Account to Govr Cooke mentioning that you sent it by my Request, and that my Letter to him was in the Post Office when this was wrote otherwise I should not have taken this Way to have conveyed to him. I am Yrs,   W.E.

MS not found; reprinted from *Publications of the Rhode Island Historical Society* 8 (January 1901), 201–3. A continuation of Ellery to Vernon, November 7, 1776.

[1] The notes that follow contain evidence that Ellery continued this portion of his letter no earlier than November 11.

[2] Washington's letter to Hancock of November 6, which was received by Congress on November 11, is in PCC, item 152, 3:213–15, and Washington, *Writings* (Fitzpatrick), 6:248–50.

[3] Mercer's letter to the Board of War, which did not reach Congress until November 11, is in *Am. Archives,* 5th ser. 3:600–601.

[4] A November 10 letter from Mifflin to President Hancock, which contains the same intelligence but was not read in Congress until November 12, is in PCC, item 161, 1:1; and *Am. Archives,* 5th ser. 3:634.

[5] See Gates' October 31 letter to Schuyler, which was forwarded to Congress by Washington and received there on November 12, in *Am. Archives,* 5th ser. 2:1314–15.

Elbridge Gerry to Joseph Trumbull

Dear sir   Philadelphia 11th Novr 1776
I have not recd a Line from You since your leaving the Camp, & have only to inform You that having engaged to order back the

proceeds of the Fish in one of the Vessels that carries it to Market I am apprehensive that it will prevent the Secret Committee from taking it for the Continent, as they are desirous of having it remitted. Indeed I Am not sanguine upon making it continental, since the military Stores will otherwise be imported into & for the Use of the eastern States. I tho't it necessary to mention this on account of what I wrote You before, altho I do not expect that It will make any Difference in your computing the price. I shall be glad to know what it cost in Ster[ling] when You have an Opportunity & remain sir your Friend & hum Sert,   E Gerry

P.S. I think it a good Time to bring on your affair & wish you had sent the petition.[1]

RC (CtHi).
[1] See Gerry to Joseph Trumbull, October 22, 1776, note 4.

Elbridge Gerry to John Wendell

Dear sir   Philadelphia 11th Novr 1776
    I recd your Favours of the 20th & 27th Octr. & have layed before Congress Capt Bodens petition, in Consequence of which it committed to the Marine Committee. Colo Whipple being a Member of that Comee & well acquainted with the Circumstances will undoubtedly take proper Measures for rightly conducting the Matter; I have likewise shewn to him & Mr. Ellery your Letter on the Subject.[1]
    The Want of public Virtue which You mention in your Letter, is too apparent to admit of a Doubt; & it is greatly to be regretted when We consider that without it a people cannot long preserve their Liberties. I know of no Way to recover or support it, but by virtuous Legislatives continental & Colonial, who will make it an invariable Rule of their Conduct to promote to Office no person that is destitute of this important Qualification. This cannot be expected in the present convulsed State of Things, since a Measure of this kind would I fear deprive Us of the Services of many interested Advocates for the Cause of Liberty, both in the civil & military Department, at a Time when they are greatly wanted. It would likewise be but an indifferent Requital to such Friends of Freedom to remove them from their Offices altho gained by espousing the Cause of their Country by venal Motives when perhaps in a more pacific State of Affairs they may submit to be ostensibly virtuous, knowing It to be an indispensable Condition of their holding public office & thus by Habit become really so. The Soldiers thro'out America have not been so well provided for, as every Friend to the

Army could wish, owing partly to a Scarcity of some articles & partly to a Multiplicity of Business; but I beleive that every State as well as Congress are fully convinced of the Necessity of paying a particular Regard to this part of their Concern. Medicines are sent in sufficient Quantities for the Army at Tionderoga, & by a late Letter from the Commissioners We are informed that comfortable provission is made for the Sick.[2] They have good Houses, fresh provissions &c & only wanted Straw. The Army were Healthy & in Expectation of an Engagement. The Sutlers have by all Accounts been exceedingly extortionate & Congress are now making provision for rectifying this Matter.[3] A Resolve has lately passed Congress for preventing Monopolies & if the States do not make effectual provission the people should call on them for this purpose.[4] The Currency is a most important object, but if provission is made to pay all Interest on the Loan office Certificates in Specie & the possessor is at Liberty to receive continental Currency for the principal when his Certificate becomes due or continue it on Interest untill the Continent shall redeem it in Specie, I think It must immediately appreciate to its Original Value; & this is now under the Consideration of Congress.

I beleive You may with great Reason look for a general War in Europe; every Information favours the Expectation, & It is acknowledged on all Hands that now is the Time for France & Spain to destroy the Balance of power which has been heretofore said to be preserved in Europe, but considered by them as preponderating against them. As to a Reconciliation with Britain it can never take place; We must be totally independant of them or a ruined people; this was never the Wishes of Congress but the Choice of a corrupt Court.

General Howe's sudden Retreat occasions much Speculation. He undoubtedly intends to land on the Jersey Shore & if he comes this Way I hope You will hear a good Account of him. Time must convince the Continent of the true Character of the people of each State but I cannot think they will any where be backward in Defence. On the whole our Difficulties are great, but the State is never to be dispaired of. Had the southern States been in the politics of the eastern, We should have declared Independence last Winter & received a great Advantage therefrom, but this being omitted We must make the best of it. My Regards to Miss Sally & your Family & believe me to be sir your assured Friend & ser,

E. Gerry

RC (PHi).
  [1] For Capt. Lawrence Bowden's petition, see William Whipple to John Langdon, November 7, 1776, note 3; and *JCC*, 6:939.
  [2] See Committee to Ticonderoga to John Hancock, October 26, 1776.
  [3] Gerry had proposed restrictions on sutlers and was subsequently appointed a

member of the committee to consider his own motions. The committee reported on November 9, but Congress took no further action on the report. *JCC*, 6:935, 937–39. For the provisions of the Articles of War pertaining to sutlers, see *JCC*, 5:794.

⁴ See *JCC*, 6:906, 915–16, 980–81.

Richard Henry Lee to William Aylett

Dear Sir,   Philadelphia 11th Novr. 1776

I have but a minute to write you and therefore you will not be surprized if I am not so full as you could wish. Your letter received at 3 oClock today and the post going out in the morning has afforded no opportunity of consulting the board of war who are this evening in consultation with the Council of Safety about the means of defending this City against a visit from the enemy, who after finding their efforts against Gen. Washingtons army vain, have precipitately in the night returned towards N. York. There, we are well informed, they have ordered Transports to be got in immediate readiness to receive 16,000 men. This City is supposed to be their object, where indeed we are very defenceless, yet they will be opposed in their attempt. I have inclosed you a true copy of the Continental ration from the Journal which still remains the same.¹ As the number of Batallions asked from Virginia are 15, it is clearly my opinion that you cannot err in laying up provisions for 15 complete Batallions, taking care your engagements are so made that if all these regiments are not stationed in Virginia the provisions may without increase of price be removed to where they may be wanted. And this precaution will be the more necessary if you should contract by the ration. Salt is not to be had here, and so you must do the best you can where you are. No doubt can be entertained but that you may advance prudently to Contractors taking bond with proper security.

It is now a week since more than 100,000 dollars were sent off to the Paymaster in Virginia.

I am, with sincere esteem, dear Sir affectionately yours,

Richard Henry Lee

P.S. I shall lay your Accounts before the Board of Treasury and will inform you by next post when they desire your attendance with Vouchers. Gen Carleton has returned to Canada with his whole force.

This comes by a Express just arrived.

RC (Vi).

¹ William Aylett had been appointed deputy commissary general in Virginia on April 27, 1776. Regulations regarding his department had been approved on October 21. See *JCC*, 4:315, 6:891–92.

Marine Committee to Elisha Warner

Sir   November 11th 1776

We have received intelligence that our enemies at New York are about to embarque 15000 Men on board their Transports, but where they are bound remains to be found out. The station assigned you makes it probable that we may best discover their destination by your means for it will be impossible this fleet of Transports can get out of Sandy Hook without your seeing them; and we particularly direct you to take such station as will prevent a probability of their passing you unseen. The Wasp must act in conjunction with you, and for that purpose you will concert with Lieutenant Baldwin what is best to be done and give him orders Accordingly. When you discover this fleet watch their motions and the moment they get out to Sea and shape their course send your boat on Shore with a Letter to be dispatched by express informing us what course they steer, how many sail they consist of if you can ascertain their numbers and how many Ships of war attend them. We expect this Letter will be sent off to you by Mr. James Searle who is at Shrewsberry and he will either receive your letters and send them off to us by express or get some proper person to do it. If this fleet steer to the Southward either the Fly or Wasp which ever sails fastest must preceede the fleet, keeping in shore and ahead of them, and if you find they are bound into the Capes of Delaware, run into some of the Inlets on the Jersey Shore, and send one of your officers or some proper person to us instantly with an Account thereof. The dullest sailer of the Fly or Wasp must follow after this fleet and watch their motions, and when ever you make discovery of their destination so as to know it with certainty put in for the Land and send us the information by Express. Thus you must watch this fleet one before and the other after them until you can inform us where they are bound. Should they go for Cheseapeak Bay, put into some of the Inlets on the Coast and give advice to the Council of Safety of Virginia and Maryland by express. If they go for North Carolina, South Carolina or Georgia observe the same conduct, and if they go to the Northward do the like. In short we think you may by a Spirited execution of these orders prevent them from coming by Surprize on any part of this Continent, and be assured you cannot recommend yourself more effectually to our freindship. If you could find an opportunity of attacking and taking one of the fleet on their coming out it might be the means of giving us ample intelligence, in such case send all the papers and prisoners here expeditiously.[1]

We are sir, Your hble servants

LB (DNA: PCC Miscellaneous Papers, Marine Committee Letter Book).

[1] Elisha Warner was commander of the Continental sloop *Fly*. *JCC*, 6:861. In the course of carrying out her mission the *Fly* was severely damaged in an encounter with the British, leading the Marine Committee to write Warner on November 29: "We have sent Doctor Smith to take charge of the wounded men belonging to the Fly, and since the Vessel is no longer in condition for prosecuting her Cruize, you are to return with her into this Port as quickly as you can, bringing with you the wounded men, and the Surgeon now sent to take care of them." PCC Miscellaneous Papers, Marine Committee Letter Book, fol. 47; and Paullin, *Marine Committee Letters*, 1:56–57.

George Wythe to Thomas Jefferson

11 Nov. 1776

The resolutions describing treasons are inclosed.[1] The report for ascertaining the value of coins, &c. remains in the same state of repose as you left it in,[2] among several others that are, as the president says, not acted upon. I gave Col. Harrison an extract of that part of your letter which related to him, and asked him what answer I should make? He told me he would do what you desired so soon as he could. The enemy's army we are credibly informed have left their camp at Whiteplains and retreated towards Newyork. I just now hear that Carleton, on the 28th of last month evacuated Crown point, and is retiring to Quebec. Tell the speaker[3] I will endeavour soon to discharge my arrears to him. Adieu.

RC (DLC). Jefferson, *Papers* (Boyd), 1:597–98.
[1] Probably the resolves of June 24, which Jefferson may have requested in connection with his recent appointment to a committee to draft a treason statute for Virginia. *JCC*, 5:475–76.
[2] Jefferson's notes and his revised report on the value of gold and silver coins that had been tabled on September 2 are in Jefferson, *Papers* (Boyd), 1:511–18.
[3] Edmund Pendleton.

John Hancock to Patrick Henry

Sir,   Philada. Novr. 12th. 1776.
The Secret Committee of Congress having chartered and loaded in the State of Virginia, the Aurora, on Account of the Continent, and the Voyage on which she is bound being a most important one, I have it in Charge from Congress to request, you will give all the Assistance in your Power to expedite her Sailing, by issuing such Orders as you shall judge proper, for manning and dispatching her with the greatest Expedition.[1]
I have the Honour to be with the utmost Esteem, Sir, your most obedt. and very hble Sert.   J. H. Presidt.

LB (DNA: PCC, item 12A). Addressed: "His Excellcy. Govr. Henry, Virginia."
[1] Congress had originally instructed Hancock to write this letter on October 7. *JCC*, 5:850–51. See also Secret Committee to Thomas Morris, October 25, 1776, note 2.

John Hancock to William Livingston

Sir,   Philada. Novr. 12th. 1776.
    I am directed by Congress to transmit you the enclosed Resolve, and to request your Attention to it.[1] The dangerous Intercourse between our Enemies in New York and Staten Island, and the internal Enemies of America in Different Parts of New Jersey, calls for the immediate Interposition of Government to suppress it. You will therefore be pleased, in Conjunction with your Council & Assembly, to take such Measures for this End, as you shall judge most expedient.
    I have the Honour to be, with the utmost Esteem, Sir, your most obed. & very hble Sert.   J. H. Presidt.

LB (DNA: PCC, item 12A).
[1] See Congress' November 9 resolution on the communication of intelligence to the British "from Elizabethtown, Newark and the parts adjacent." *JCC*, 6:939.

Edward Rutledge to Michael Hillegas?

                                                        [November 12? 1776] [1]
    If Mr. Peters has not already sent forward the 50,000 Dollars ordered by Congress some Day last Week (Friday I think) you will be pleased to comply with Mr Dallams Request & have it sent to him immediately. The Order for the money was sent to the Treasury.
                                                                E. Rutledge

RC (PHi).
[1] Rutledge wrote this note at the foot of a November 10 letter to John Hancock from Richard Dallam, the deputy paymaster general of the flying camp, who stated that he was "out of Cash" and requested "a supply as soon as possible—As the demands on me are very pressing." Congress, which received this letter on November 12, had already ordered $50,000 to be sent to Dallam three days earlier. *JCC*, 6:937, 940. Rutledge's note was apparently intended for the Continental treasurer, Michael Hillegas.

Matthew Thornton to Meshech Weare

Hond Sir,   Philadelphia Novr. 12th 1776.
    The 3d Instant we arived Safe in this City, & the 8th innoculated for the Small Pox. I have Attended the Congress every day yet. The

ferries over North River ware so Obstructed by the enemie we ware Obliged to Cross at a place called Peekskill whare I see Col. Tash, who used me Exceeding well. This day the Congress was informed by his Excellency General Washington that the Enemie Decampt from White Plains, & ware Landing on the Jursie shore, & he was taking every precaution, to prevent them from penetrating into the Country.[1] By a letter from General Gates, Dated the 31st of Octr., the enemie a few days before, appear'd in Order of Battle, & on his preparing to Receive them Return'd to their Camp. For better, & further information, & news I must Refere you to the News papers, & you wont find more falshood in them then is passing through this City.

Before my arrival the Honble. Col. Bartlet was Set off, & I had not the pleasure to meet him, the Honble. Col. Whipple is well. Please to take the trouble to present my Compliments, to every member of the Honourable Council, & House & Except the Same from him who has the Honour to be your most Obedient Hble Sert.,

Matthew Thornton

N.B. No Danger by this letter.

RC (MeHi).
[1] General Washington's November 9 letter to President Hancock, which was read this day in Congress, is in PCC, item 152, 3:219, and Washington, *Writings* (Fitzpatrick), 6:261–62. *JCC*, 6:944.

John Hancock to the Maryland Commissioners

Gentlemen   Philada. Novr. 13th. 1776

In Consequence of a Letter to Congress this day Rec'd from The Honl. Convention of Maryland, inclosing sundry Resolutions of that Body relative to the Raising their Quota of the New Levies, I have it in Charge to furnish you with the Resolutions of Congress pass'd yesterday admitting the New Levies to inlist for three years, & at the same time to inform you that if the Inhabitants of the State of Maryland will Inlist to serve during the continuance of the present war, they already have the Faith of the United States of America pledged for the Land to be granted to such Soldiers.[1] The Resolutions Referr'd to, you have inclos'd, & contain the Sense of Congress as to the mode of the new Inlistments.[2]

I am with Esteem, Gentn., Your very hum servt.

J H Pt.

LB (DNA: PCC, item 12A). Addressed: "Honl Commissioners from Maryland, for Appointg officers & promotg Inlistmts. in the Army at Camp."
[1] See *JCC* 6:944–45, 947. The Maryland Convention's November 10 letter to Hancock and enclosed resolves about the grant of lands to soldiers who enlisted

for the duration of the war are in PCC, item 70, fols. 75–84, and *Am. Archives*, 5th ser. 3:627–28. See also Hancock to the Maryland Convention, November 4, note 1; and Samuel Adams to James Warren, November 9, 1776, note.

² Congress' action in this matter created almost as many problems for the Maryland commissioners as it solved. See Benjamin Rumsey to the Maryland Council of Safety, this date.

John Hancock to the Massachusetts Assembly

Gentlemen,   Philadelphia 13th Novr. 1776

Agreeable to my Promise to Mr. Patridge I now inclose you the Resolutions of Congress in consequence of your Application, whereby you will perceive it is their Desire that you would not inlist the Men on the Additional pay offer'd by the Assembly of Massachusetts. They have however Agreed that the Men be inlisted for three years under the former incouragement, excpt the one hundrd Acres of Land which is not to be given to any but those who inlist during the War. I beg leave to Refer you to the Resolutions Inclos'd, and hope you will not find much difficulty in obtaining the Men, I know your best exertions will not be wanting.[1]

I am so exceedingly Engag'd that I can't Add, but that I am with great Esteem, Gentlemen, Your most Obedt. Servt.

John Hancock

[*P.S.*] I shall be exceeding Glad to hear of your Success in Inlisting, & when your Leisure will admit shall be oblig'd for a Line.

I shall be much oblig'd to you to forward the Inclos'd Letter to General Ward.[2]

RC (M–Ar).
[1] See *JCC*, 6:944–45; and Samuel Adams to James Warren, November 9, 1776, note.
[2] See Hancock to Artemas Ward, November 8, 1776.

Benjamin Rumsey to the Maryland Council of Safety

Sir   Philada. 13th. Novr. 1776

Congress have this Day given an Answer to the Resolutions of our State [1] which being an intire new One We have dispatched it to the proper place to be considered.[2] They resolve that the Troops may be inlisted for three Years and a Bounty of twenty Dollars only be given or during the War and One hundred Acres of Land be added to the Bounty. They will not specify where the Land lies belonging to the United States.

Our Instructions run that they are to be inlisted during the War, of Course when our State accedes to it we can proceed. Congress has got rid of the Difficulty with Respect to the Land and has not closed in with either of the Propositions made by our State nor receded intirely from their own Resolutions.

But if they have escaped they embarrass Us. What can We do with our Regulars? They are inlisted during the War: Must we inlist them again in the Service of the States for three years? I imagine our State will not incline to do so, if they do we ought to have Instructions on that Head.[3]

King brought only One of the Bundles of Commissions up, there are not more than enough for four Battallions, there are five of the flying Camp and two of the Regulars. The German and Rifle Companies will make the eighth, surely then you have not sent Commisssions enough. I should be obliged to you to send up a Copy also of the Resolves of Congress relative to the raising the eighty eight Battallions as We have not got it and would be as little troublesome as possible to the Congress.

Four Thousand of our Troops under General Putnam have crossed the North River to reinforce Genl. Green who has six Thousand under his Command to prevent the Enemy's plundering the Jerseys or penetrating to this place and I suppose they will be followed by a more considerable Number if the Enemy pass that River.

Very little of the Transactions of Convention have transpired here, You are exceedingly concise on that head. You tell me they are still engaged about the Constitution. I should naturally have concluded they were so but pray what Sort of a Constitution have they framed? how far monarchical, aristocratick or democratick? how far a Mixture? how Balanced each power? It is a Matter of great Importance to a Subject of a State that Power should be well and equally balanced. I am Sir, Your most humble Servt.

Benjamin Rumsey

[P.S.] If we stay much longer here the flying Camp will come near Us or to Us.[4]

RC (MdAA). Although Rumsey was elected a delegate to Congress on November 10, he wrote this letter in his capacity as a commissioner appointed on October 9 by the Maryland Convention to assist in raising the state's new quota of troops. It was undoubtedly directed to the president of the Maryland Council of Safety, Daniel of St. Thomas Jenifer.

[1] See John Hancock to the Maryland Commissioners, this day.

[2] The commissioners' November 14 letter to Matthew Tilghman, president of the Maryland Convention, enclosing Congress' resolutions of November 12, is in the Red Books, MdAA, and Am. Archives, 5th ser. 3:673.

[3] The Maryland Council of Safety's response of November 17 to this letter is in Md. Archives, 12:454.

[4] For a second letter Rumsey wrote this day to Jenifer, on the subject of prospects for obtaining 50 reams of paper for Maryland, see ibid., p. 443.

Secret Committee Minutes of Proceedings

Novr. 13, 1776.

Come. met. Present Messrs. Morris, Lee, Lewis, Livingston. Charter party for ship Mary & Elizabeth was signd by the Come. Order on Mr. Morris in favor of Ths. McKean for the use of Mr. Js. Sterret for 133 1/3 dlls being for 6 months service of his son Andrew Sterret dec[ease]d as Clerk to the Come. A letter to Messrs. Levinus Clarkson & J. Dorsius of Chs. town S. Carolina authorising them to charter & purchase vessels & load them with the produce of that State on acct. of the Continent.[1]

MS (MH–H).
[1] Not found, but see Marine Committee to Levinus Clarkson and John Dorsius, November 17, and Secret Committee to William Bingham, November 22, 1776.

Secret Committee to the Pennsylvania Council of Safety

Gentn   In Secret Committee of Congress. Philada. Novr. 13th. 1776
As this Committee is charged with the management of the Commerce carried on for the Continental Service, We think it our duty to represent to your Board the Necessity there is for an Armed Vessell of some kind to be stationed at Cape May for the protection of the Trade to & from this Port. At present there is none of the Continental armed Vessells fit or ready for this Service, being all employed on other important pursuits, besides it has been judged the proper object of every State on this Continent to protect their own Ports to the utmost of their Power. We understand You have a large Galley intended to Cruize in the Bay. If this Vessell is ordered down to Cape May immediately she may render Important Service to the private Trade of this port as well as to the Continental interest, and if any thing in the power of this or the Marine Committee is wanted to compleat your Galley depend on a ready Concurrence with Your desires.[1] We have the honor to be, Gentn, Your obedt hble servts,

Robt. Morris   Richard Henry Lee

Phil. Livingston   Fras. Lewis

P.S. Mr Bridges informs us his Brige Cornelia & Molly is detained for want of a Pilot. The Continent are interested & We wish for her dispatch.

RC (PHi). Written by Morris and signed by Morris, Lee, Lewis, and Livingston.
[1] In response to this request, the Pennsylvania Council of Safety on November 18 ordered Capt. John Rice of the Pennsylvania row galley Convention down to Cape May. Pa. Council Minutes, 11:8–9.

Samuel Adams to Elizabeth Adams

My dear Betsy   Philada Novr 14th 1776

I wrote you within a Day or two after my Arrival here by an Express. I cannot say that I was not disappointed in not receiving a line from you by the last Post, as I thought I had Reason to expect. While I am absent from you I am continually anxious to know the State of your Health. I must therefore beg you to write to me often. I have not for many years enjoyd a greater Share of that invalueable Blessing than I have since I left Boston. I beleive the Journey on Horseback has been greatly beneficial to me.

We have lately received Intelligence from the Northern Army of certain Movements of the Enemy in that Quarter, of which you will see an Account in the inclosd News Paper. This day we have further Intelligence that they have totally abandoned Crown Point & retreated into Canada.[1] We have also just receivd a Letter from a Gentleman living on the Sea Coast of New Jersey informing us that near 100 Sail of the Enemies Ships with two Frigates & a fifty Gun Ship were seen steering to the Eastward. It is supposed they are bound to England. We had before heard that the whole Force of the Enemy had marchd unexpectedly & precipitately into the City of New York. This Evening an Express is come in from General Green who commands on this Side the North River in the Jerseys with Advice that ten thousand of the Enemies Troops were embarkd, and that it was given out that they were destind to South Carolina.[2] This may be a Feint. Possibly they may be coming to this City, which in my opinion is rather to be desired, because the People of this State are more numerous than that of South Carolina. In either Case however I dare say that a good Account will be given of them. It is said that Lord Dunmore is to take the Command. If this be true, it looks as if they were going to Virginia. Be it as it may, the withdrawing so great a Part of these Troops from New York, it is hoped, will make it an easy Matter for our Army to conquer the Remainder.

It has not been usual for me to write to you of War or Politicks— but I know how deeply you have always interested your self in the Welfare of our Country and I am disposed to gratify your Curiosity. Besides you will hope that from these Movements of our Enemies a Communication between Boston and Philadelphia will be more safe and we may the more frequently hear from each other.[3]

RC (NN).
[1] Probably Horatio Gates' November 5 letter to John Hancock, which was read in Congress on November 15, 1776. *JCC*, 6:951; *Am. Archives*, 5th ser. 3:526.
[2] Nathanael Greene's November 12 letter to John Hancock is in Greene, *Papers* (Showman), 1:348–49.
[3] For the continuation of this letter, see Adams to Elizabeth Adams, November 17, 1776.

Board of War to the Pennsylvania Associators

Gentlemen,   War-Office, November 14th, 1776.

Congress have received Intelligence that a Fleet of the Enemy, consisting of several hundred Sail, were yesterday discovered near Sandy-Hook, steering to the Southward.[1] It is highly probable that their Destination is for Delaware and the City of Philadelphia. It is needless to observe that the utmost Vigour and despatch are necessary to counteract the Designs of the Enemy, and defend this City, the Preservation of which is of very great Importance to the general Cause. Congress have directed us to cooperate with the Council of Safety of this State in concerting Measures proper on the present Emergency; and have invested us with their full Power to carry such Measures into Execution. In Discharge of the Trust committed to us, we think it our Duty to recommend it to you, in the warmest and most earnest Manner, immediately to put yourselves in Array and march by Companies and Parts of Companies as you can be ready, with the utmost Expedition to this City. Its Safety and the Interest of the United States point out the Necessity of your strongest Exertions.

General Washington, at the Head of a considerable Part of his Army, is advancing Southward; but, notwithstanding all the Dispatch he can possibly make, the Enemy may arrive before him. If they shall be opposed, with proper Spirit and sufficient Numbers, at their first Approach, there is the greatest Reason to expect that their Views will finally be defeated; and they will experience, to their Cost and Disgrace, that on no Part of the Continent they can make an Impression. They have been already obliged to abandon Crown-Point and retire into Canada.

It is vain to hope for Lenity from your inveterate Foes. Their tender Mercies are Cruelty. The Property of those who have acted as their Friends is not safer than that of those whom they consider as their Enemies. Devastation of every Kind marks their Footsteps.

Congress will do every thing in their Power to strengthen you. Expresses for this Purpose are already sent off to the neighbouring States.

Every Thing dear to Freemen is now at Stake. The freemen of Pennsylvania will undoubtedly discover the Spirit and Zeal, which their Country expects and their critical Situation demands.

Benjamin Harrison.   Edward Rutledge.

James Wilson.   Francis Lightfoot Lee.

Attest: Richard Peters, Secretary

Reprinted from John Dunlap broadside, Philadelphia, 1776, Evans, *Am. Bibliography*, No. 15192.

¹ This day Congress received a letter of the 13th from James Searle, written from Long Branch, N.J., reporting the movements of the British fleet and stating that "at present about one hundred sail appear round the Hook; and appear to be standing to the Southward, wind at northwest." *Am. Archives,* 5th ser. 3:669; and *JCC,* 6:950–51. But on the following day Congress was relieved to learn from Searle that Philadelphia was in no immediate danger since he had seen the fleet, as William Ellery later explained, "bear away . . . and sail Eastward until they sunk below his horizon." See William Ellery's second letter of November 16 to Nicholas Cooke; and Board of War to the Pennsylvania Council of Safety, November 15, 1776.

Board of War to George Washington

Sir   War Office Novr 14th. 1776.

The Congress having received Information that a considerable part of the Enemy's Fleet had sailed from Sandy Hook to the Southward, & judging that immediate Steps were necessary to be taken for the preservation and Defence of this City, were pleased to vest us with all their powers to effect this important Business. As Genl. Mifflin has a considerable Influence in this place, the Board judge it for the Interest of the Service that he be immediately order'd to this City, where his Exertions we doubt not will turn out to the Advantage of our Cause. Your Excellency will therefore be pleased to give him Directions upon the Subject as soon as possible; provided you shall be of Opinion that he cannot be more usefully employ'd in any other place, which we beg Leave to submit to you. If the Enemy should find their Way to this part of the Continent we doubt not that your Excellency will yield us every possible Assistance. With every Sentiment of Esteem we have the Honour to be your Excellency's most obedt. & very hble Serts.

Benja Harrison   E. Rutledge

James Wilson   Francis Lightfoot Lee

RC (DLC). Written by Rutledge and signed by Rutledge, Harrison, Lee, and Wilson.

John Hancock to Certain States

Gentlemen,   Philada. Novr. 14th. 1776.

The enclosed Letter from Mr. Searle a Gentleman of Honour, and a Friend to the Cause of America, containing the most important Intelligence, I am commanded by Congress to forward to you with the utmost Expedition.¹ The uncertain Destination of the Fleet therein mentioned, makes it absolutely necessary that you should be informed of their Sailing, that you may make any Preparation in your Power to defend yourselves in Case of an Attack. I most ardently entreat your Attention & Exertion on the present Occasion, & have the Honour to be Gentlemen, your most obed. & very hble Svt.[2]   J H Presidt.

[P.S.][3] By an Express just recd. Genl. Carlton has retreated, with all his Forces, to Quebec.

LB (DNA: PCC, item 12A). Addressed: "Assembly of Delaware. Convention of Maryland. Assembly of Virginia. Convention of North Carolina. Assembly of South Carolina."

[1] See JCC, 6:950–51. The abbreviated version of James Searle's November 13 letter, which Hancock apparently sent to all these states, is in Am. Archives, 5th ser. 3:669.

[2] This day Hancock sent another circular letter—nearly the same as this letter to the states—to Washington, Gov. William Livingston of New Jersey, and the commanding officer in New Jersey. PCC, item 12A; and Am. Archives, 5th ser. 3:669. At the same time he sent these three men copies of the full text of Searle's letter. Ibid., pp. 369-70.

[3] Postscript taken from Hancock's letter to North Carolina, Secretary of State Papers, Nc–Ar.

William Hooper to the
North Carolina Convention

Gentlemen   Philadelphia Novr 14th 1776

We have this moment received Intelligence from the Jersies that 100 of the Enemies Ships have been seen of[f] the Coast of Shrewsbury steering Southward. They probably intend for this place, however as it is possible they may intend farther Southward, the Congress have thought proper to dispatch an express to you that you may hold yourselves in immediate readiness to oppose any attempts against your state, or to render assistance to your Neighbours.

A Careful look out should be kept along the Sea coast, that we may be apprized of their movements and not taken napping. As your defence & that of South Carolina must consist chiefly in Militia, You will take measures that they hold thmselves in perfect readiness to march when and wherever the Convention shall think fit to order them. We are making every possible preparation to oppose any designs they may have against this place & with the blessing of God I confide shall be able to disappoint them. I am, Gentlemen, With the greatest Respect, Your Obedt Humble Servant,

Will Hooper

RC (Nc–Ar).

Marine Committee to John Wereat

Sir   November 14th 1776

By the recommendation of George Walton Esqr. one of your Delegates in Congress we have appointed you Continental Agent in the State of Georgia.[1] In that Station it will fall to your share to supply all Continental Cruizers or other vessels in the Continental service with provisions, Stores and necessarys, to assist the Captains and officers in what ever may be needful, to advance them monies, give them advice, and in all things take care of the Interests of the United States. If any Prizes are sent into Georgia by the Continental Cruizers you are to receive them, libel and prosecute to condemnation, then make public Sale of vessels, Cargoes, and all effects that are condemned; and for your guidance we send you a pamphlet containing the Rules and Regulations in these respects, and we shall also send you at a future day Coppies of our official letters to all our Agents along the Continent.

You will receive this by an advice boat belonging to the Continent called the Georgia Packet, intended to be an advice Boat between your State and Congress.[2] She has been loaden this voyage by your Delegates with stores for your State, and we expect you will Credit us a handsome freight for the same. We desire you may receive these goods with dispatch and as the secret Committee of Congress order a Cargo back we hope you will use equal dispatch in shipping it. Lieutenant Buck who commands this schooner is ordered to put all the Letters he carrys into the Post office and we desire you will inform the postmaster he is to charge the same postage as if they had come by land, for we expect in this way to raise some thing towards defraying the expence of these packets in future altho at present the Letters will be very few. You will please to advertize for Letters back by this packet, and as soon as you can dispatch this Schooner back for this post. You will keep a regular account of your disbursements for this schooner and if any balance arises in your favour we will pay your drafts on us for the Amount.

We hope you will not suffer Captain Buck to loose any time nor Stand in need of any assistance that you can afford him.

We are sir, Your hble servants

LB (DNA: PCC Miscellaneous Papers, Marine Committee Letter Book).

[1] John Wereat (ca. 1730–98), a lawyer in St. Andrews Parish, Ga., subsequently served as president of the Georgia Executive Council, chief justice of the Georgia Superior Court, and president of the federal ratifying convention in Georgia. William J. Northen, ed., *Men of Mark in Georgia*, 7 vols. (Atlanta: A. B. Caldwell, 1907–12), 1:342–44.

[2] For the Marine Committee's letter of instruction of this date to Lt. Isaac Buck, commander of the *Georgia Packet,* see PCC Miscellaneous Papers, Marine Committee Letter Book, fol. 45; and Paullin, *Marine Committee Letters,* 1:54–55.

James Wilson to the
Pennsylvania Council of Safety

Gentlemen   14th Novr. 1776

The enclosed Letter from Mr Blaine was laid before Congress. They directed an Application to be made to you for the Salt mentioned in it. The Bearer, who is a Waggoner employed by Mr Blaine, waits upon you for a Load. I hope it will be in your Power to furnish one. I am, Gentlemen, Your very humble Servant,

James Wilson

RC (PHi).

John Witherspoon to William Livingston

Sir   Philadelphia Nov 14. 1776

The inclosed Letter delivered to me this Morning in Congress has been so long on its Way that perhaps Mr Stockton is himself at home by this time.[1] Yet I thought it necessary that you should receive it by Express & lay it before the Assembly who will do upon it what appears to them necessary.

I also take Leave to inform you & by you the Council & Assembly that this Moment Congress has received an Express that ships are turning out from the Hook & steering Southward. The former Intelligence which you can inform them of will enable them to determine what use they should make of this. Expresses are sent to the Southern Governments & every means is using in this City to prepare for its Defence in Case the Enemy should intend here. The ships come out steady but 100 were seen two of them large Yesterday afternoon when the Express left Long Branch. It is the opinion of intelligent Persons that you should immediately send a Body of Militia to the fort at Billingsport in Delaware lest they should send a Detachment against it. As soon as further Intelligence comes the Assembly shall be made acquainted with it and I doubt not the most vigorous Exertions will be made as most here seem to think the Design is against this important Place.[2]

I am sir your most obedt humble Servant,

Jno Witherspoon

RC (Nj).

[1] Perhaps a reference to Richard Stockton to Abraham Clark, October 28, 1776.

[2] On the following day Witherspoon wrote a letter to his son David, "at Hampden Sydney, Prince Edward County, Virginia," dealing strictly with family affairs. Gratz Collection, PHi. There are also letters from Witherspoon to David dated October 3 and 25—the first written in French and the second in Latin— urging him to be diligent in his studies and his teaching at the Hampden-Sidney Academy, in the *Christian Advocate* 2 (September 1824): 399–400.

Board of War to the
Pennsylvania Council of Safety

Gentlemen   Philadelphia War Office November 15. 1776.

As every Reason to suppose that the British Armament intend for this Place is now removed, the Board of War are of Opinion that the Directions to the Militia to march to this City should be countermanded.[1] You will therefore be pleased to give such Orders upon the Subject as to your honourable Board shall appear necessary, & you'll be so good as to advise us therewith as soon as convenient.[2]

We are Gentlemen, with Respect your most obedt. humble Servts.

Benja Harrison

Edward Rutledge

RC (PHi). Written by Rutledge and signed by Rutledge and Harrison.

[1] See Board of War to the Pennsylvania Associators, November 14, 1776.

[2] This day the Board of War also directed the committee of safety of Lancaster, Pa., to inquire into reports that prisoners on parole were "procuring and conveying intelligence secretly . . . [and] spreading false rumours" and to "Confine any British prisoner who is found speaking on any political subject relative to the dispute between Great Britain and the United States, spreading false news, speaking in derogation or otherwise injuring the credit of the Continental currency." *Am. Archives*, 5th ser. 3:698.

John Hancock to Certain States

Gentlemen,   Philada. Novr. 15th. 1776

Since dispatching the Express yesterday, with Intelligence that a Fleet of above a Hundred Vessels had left New York, the Congress have received a Letter from Genl. Green containing further Accounts; a Copy of which in Obedience to their Commands I now enclose.[1]

It appears from this Information that Lord Dunmore is to take the Command of a Fleet bound for the Southward, said to be for South Carolina. But as it is by no Means certain against which of the Southern States, the Expedition is designed, it is highly necessary you should be on your Guard. I shall not detain the Express, only to add that you will make such Use of this Intelligence as the Importance of it requires.

I have the Honour to be, Gentlemen, your most obed, & very hble Ser.   J. H. Presidt.

[P.S.] Since the foregoing Congress have pass'd a Resolve, respectg. the Disposition of the Troops in North Carolina which I inclose, & to which I Beg Leave to Refer you as also to the Resolve respecting the Inlistments.[2]

LB (DNA: PCC, item 12A). Addressed: "Convention of Maryland. Assembly of Virginia. Convention of N. Carolina. Convention of S. Carolina."

[1] Nathanael Greene's November 12 letter to Hancock is in PCC, item 155, 1:19–20, and Greene, *Papers* (Showman), 1:348–49. In response Hancock wrote this day to Greene: "I Rec'd your Letter of 12th Inst by Express, which I laid before Congress & in Consequence of your Intelligence have Dispatch'd an Express to Virginia & South Carolina, acquainting them with the Reports, that they may be prepar'd in case the Enemy should Visit that quarter. Please to give me the earliest Advice of the Movements of the Enemy." Greene, *Papers* (Showman), 1:350.

[2] Congress had passed the resolve about "Inlistments" on November 12; the resolve concerning "Troops in North Carolina" was adopted November 16. *JCC*, 6:945, 956–57. For the background of the latter, see William Hooper to the North Carolina Convention, November 16, 1776.

The RC of Hancock's letter to the Maryland Convention contains this addition to the postscript: "Please to forward the Dispatches to the Southward by a fresh Express to Williamsburg, & I have requested the Gov. to forward them from thence by another hand." Red Books, MdAA.

John Hancock to Certain States

Gentlemen,   Philada. Novr. 15th. 1776.

In Consequence of sundry Votes of the Assembly of Massachusetts Bay being laid before Congress, they have come to the enclosed Resolves; wherein you will perceive they have disapproved of the Measure of increasing, in any one State, the Bounty given by Congress on the Reinlistment of the Troops, as having a manifest Tendency to lay the Foundation of Discontent in the Army. They have however, upon revising the Resolution of the 16th of Sepr., agreed to engage for three years, such of the Soldiers as may decline enlisting during the Continuance of the War.[1]

In the present Exigency of our Affairs, every Measure should be adopted that will assist in filling up the Army, the compleating of which is an object of the utmost Importance. The Congress have therefore determined that those Troops who will engage for three years, shall be entitled to receive the same Bounty and Pay, with those who enlist during the War, except the one Hundred Acres of Land, which are to be given only to those who will enlist without Limitation of Time.

As the Resolves of Congress for raising eighty eight Battalions for the Defence of the American States was positive that they should be engaged during the War, General Washington in a Conference with Mr. Partridge, did not think himself at Liberty to consent to the Troops being inlisted on any other Terms, until the Sense of Congress could be obtained in the Matter. (N.B. The foregoing Paragraph was inserted only in the Letter to the Massachusetts Bay.)

It being a Matter of the highest Importance, that you should be informed of the Resolves herewith transmitted as soon as possible, in

Order that the Service may not be injured by any of the Soldiers declining to engage during the War, who would otherwise be willing to enlist for a limited Time, I have forwarded the enclosed by Express—and have the Honour to be, Gentlemen, your most obed. & very hble Serv.   J. H. Presidt.

LB (DNA: PCC, item 12A). Addressed to the assemblies of New Hampshire, Massachusetts, Rhode Island, and Connecticut.
¹ See *JCC*, 6:944–45.

William Hooper to Joseph Hewes and John Penn

My dear Friends   Philadelphia Nov 15 1776
I refer you to my letter to the Convention for the cause of this Express. I am happy that at this important Crisis you are upon the spot. Nothing will I am sure be wanting on your part to Stimulate the exertions of our countrymen and make such an application of the force of our State as will most effectually repel our Enemies. I beg leave to press upon the necessity of driving our back from the Sea, as the Enemy are but Scantily Supplied with provisions.
I refer you to the newspapers for any late maneuvers of the Enemy or your own troops, and congratulate sincerely upon the retreat of [*Carleton?*] from Crownpoint into Canada.
I shall write by Mr. Walker who leaves this on Monday. Pray forward the inclosed with all possible Expedition, it concerns the removal of my family to a place of safety & is therefore truly interesting to your, Affectionate,   Will Hooper

Tr (Nc–Ar). Recipients identified as "Joseph Hewes & John Penn, at Halifax."

William Hooper to the North Carolina Convention

Gentlemen   Philadelphia Novr 15. 1776
By an express which was dispatched to the Southern states yesterday, I suggested to you the probability that a large body of forces had embarked and part of them had sail'd from N York for this place or the Carolinas. Since yesterday by a letter from General Greene who commands at Fort Lee we have further information upon this subject. He says that by a Gentleman of undoubted veracity and warm attachment to the American Cause who is just from New York he has obtained Intelligence that the enemy are now embarking ten thousand men which are destined for an Expedition against South Carolina, that Ld Dunmore is to proceed with them

and have the Command. This information has induced Congress to
send dispatches to your & the other Southern states, that you may
take measures immediately to counteract the design of the Enemy.
I cannot imagine that the Enemy, infatuated as their Councils have
hitherto been, are yet so far lost to every Idea of propriety as to entrust such an important Command to Ld Dunmore. He no doubt
with Gov Martin & Ld William Campbell will go in the fleet, and
give every assistance they may be capable of but Clinton I imagine
will conduct the land forces.

I cannot take upon me to direct what measures it will be prudent
for you to pursue. Whether Virginia, North or South Carolina will
be the first object it is yet impossible to decide. It would become you
to hold all the Militia and regular troops of your state in readiness
to repel the British troops whether they should attempt to land upon
your own coast or whether it should be necessary to afford Succour
to South Carolina or Virginia. Upon this important occasion when
the fate of our Southern Country is perhaps to be decided and those
liberties which we have been long gloriously struggling for are to be
fixed upon a permanent foundation or lost forever I trust in God no
man will deny his Aid, but that all as one man will step forth to
meet the foes of America to liberty to Heaven, for our's is the cause
of God.

I have ordered three tons of Gunpowder to Charlestown by an
armed Vessell bound thither.[1] She will probably sail in the course of
the next Week. I will apprize you of it as soon as it takes place &
if you have not a plentiful supply upon hand of that article you can
have recourse then to supply yourself. Should you have occasion for
more let me have your commands seasonably as at present our Magazines are tolerably full.

I enclose you the last newspapers from which you will perceive
General Washingtons late operations, as well as the sudden retreat
of General Sir Guy Carleton from Tionderoga. I sincerely congratulate you upon the latter as an event of much Importance to these
states & Am, Gentlemen, With the greatest respect, Your most
Obedient, Humble Servant,   Will Hooper

RC (Nc–Ar).
[1] See JCC, 6:952.

William Hooper to the
North Carolina Convention

Sir   Philadelphia, Nov 15, 1776.
I omitted to mention in the letter which I have closed and
accompanies this, that the Enemy are scant of provisions & may have

some dependance upon the Cattle on the Sea Coast of the southern States for a supply. In that Case you will perhaps think it prudent to drive back the Stock from the low Country as soon as possible. Horses are much an Object with them for their Waggons—& therefore must be kept out of their way. It may be worth while to spend a thought upon a mode of securing our Negroes, and preventing any Communication between the Enemy & any who may be disaffected amongst you whether of the late Insurgents or others.

I am, Gentlemen, With great Respect, Your Obed Serv,

Will Hooper

RC (Nc–Ar).

Secret Committee to Nicholas Cooke

Sir   In Secret Committee of Congress. Philada. Novr. 15th 1776

We received a letter last week from Capt. Samuel Smith junr. Commander of the Ship Hancock & Adams belonging to Mr. Blair McClenachan of this City informing us of his arrival with that Ship and Cargo at the port of Bedford in Massachusetts. His letter is dated the 19th instant and he Says that in Latitude 38.29 and Longitude 65.23 he fell in with the Game Cock Privateer of Rhode Island Commanded by Capt Timothy Pierce of Providence, who brought him too, examined his papers and finally determined to make Prize of his Ship and cargo, under pretence of her having two or three Sets of Papers, and accordingly he put a prize Master and men onboard the Ship taking out Captain Smith, his officers and men, also Some passengers, but Capt Smith after intreating him for thirteen hours got Liberty to go onboard his Ship again and was Sent in with her to the Port of Bedford where he now is. We Chartered this Ship in Feby last to perform a Voyage from hence to Lisbon thence to France and back to this Port on account and risque of the United States (then Colonies) of America.[1] The Ship had the voyage before narrowly escaped being Seized in Ireland in Consequence of an attempt to take in Gun Powder to be brought hither and Mr. McClenachans Friends found it necessary to take out a New Register for her there in order to screen her from the intended Seizure. When we Chartered her this Irish Register was deemed a fortunate circumstance as the Restraining Act of Parliament was not then known to us, and having her cleared from the Custom house here for Falmouth Under that Register, with Bills, Loading Invoice and letters suited thereto, it was presumed wou'd carry her clear of Seizure by British Men of War Should any of them meet her on the outward passage. Our Instructions to Captain Smith are dated the 22nd Feby 1776 & recapitulate all these Circumstances, after which they direct him peremtorily to proceed for Lisbon and there deliver his Cargo to Messrs. Pasley & Co. of that place, unless they direct him to a better Market, after which he was ordered to proceed to Nantes and receive from our Agent a Cargo of Arms, ammunition and other Goods or Merchandize and then to return to this Port with that Cargo on Accot. of the United Colonies. It seems that when Captain Smith first fell in with the Game Cock he feared She was his Enemy as no Letters of Marque were granted by Congress when he departed from hence, he therefore on his first examination produced to Capt Peirce only his Irish Register and Shipping Paper, but when he Saw the Commission Signed by Mr Hancock he then produced All his Papers and amongst the Rest our Orders to Captain Smith which must have fully and clearly explained to any man of Common Sense and Common honesty the Nature of the Voyage, and if the love of Plunder had not prevailed over every other consideration Capt Peirce would have released the Ship, especially as there were on board Four French Gentlemen and their Domesticks, two of whom We suppose to be officers, and two Manufacturers with their people whom we wrote for by order of Congress, and there can be little doubt but they would make Capt Peirce Sensible that this ship was in the Continental Service. In Short we have laid this matter before Congress and Capt Peirces Conduct is judged to be extreamly Criminal, but it is a just and commendable Maxim not to condemn any Man unheard and the Congress passed on this occasion the Resolve of which you will [find] a Copy inclosed.[2] Now Sir, it is our duty to inform You, that the public Service is exceedingly injured by this transaction, for every article of this Ships Cargo (which belongs to the Continent) is and has been much wanted for some time past. If Capt. Peirce had not interupted the Ships voyage She would in all probabillity been Safe in this port some weeks Since, and the Several articles before now have been with the Army, instead of which they are now onboard Ship at a Port distant from the Army, and the delay, danger, and expence of transporting them will be very Great.[3] Indeed the public are also insurers on the Ship and obliged to deliver her to the owner in this Port at their Risque. We cannot help mentioning that this is the Second or third instance of the Kind, and unless Such practices are discouraged in the beginning there is no knowing what lengths the Privateers may go, in short it is laying the foundation for breaking the union of America and opening the door to prey upon each other. We do therefore most earnestly intreat you, to order the Strictest Scrutiny into the Conduct of this same Capt Peirce, discover what reasons he can offer in his justification, and if they are not satisfactory we shall order him to be prosecuted for the penalty of his Bond and sued for damages. We observe by a Copy of his letter to his Owners he acknowledges Capt Smiths orders were signed by Some Members of Congress, but he objects that they are interlined with different hand Writing and different Ink and without any Seal or permit from the President, but all this will not avail, he must give much Stronger reasons than these or those he calls a *Foible* before he will be justifyed in the Eyes of the Publick. We think it of the utmost importance to check this improper Itch for Plunder, and hope You will exert yourself in Support of So Salutary a measure.

We have the honor to remain, Your Honors Most obedt & most hble servts,   Robt Morris   Phil. Livingston

Richard Henry Lee   Fra. Lewis

RC (R–Ar). In a clerical hand and signed by Lee, Lewis, Livingston, and Morris.
[1] See Secret Committee Minutes of Proceedings, February 23, 1776.
[2] See *JCC*, 6:943, 949–50.
[3] For orders regarding the delivery of the cargo, see *JCC*, 6:952–53; and Board of War to George Washington, November 18, 1776.

Samuel Adams to James Warren

My dear Sir   Philada Novr 16th 1776
I have already wrote to you by this Conveyance. The Express having been delayd till this Time affords me an opportunity of congratulating you and my other Friends on the Retreat of General Carleton with his whole Force from Crown Point into Canada, an Account of which we had the day before yesterday in a Letter from General Gates. Yesterday we had a Letter from a Gentleman living on the Sea Coasts of New Jersey acquainting us that near 100 Sail of the Enemies Transports with a 50 or 60 Gun Ship & two Frigates were seen coming from Sandy Hook & steering Eastward. We had also a Letter from Genl Green who informs that he had Intelligence by a Gentleman of good Credit who came from Staten Island that Ten Thousand of the Enemies Troops were embarqed, and it was given out that they were destind to South Carolina. It is said that Lord Dunmore is to take the Command, from whence one would suppose they are bound to Virginia. Some think they are coming to this City, which I confess as an American I would chuse. The People here are preparing to give them a proper Reception. Wherever they may make the Attack, I flatter my self a good Account will be given of them. If so great a Part of the Enemies Army is withdrawn from New York may we not reasonably expect that the Remainder will be easily conquerd this Winter. I am earnestly sollicitous that they may have a handsome Drubbing. We must not however suffer any flattering Prospect to abate our Zeal in procuring a Sufficient Army. We know not what Game our Enemies may play. There is no Reason to believe they will quit their darling Plan of Subduing if possible the

New England States. We ought therefore to be very vigilant & active. An Army we must keep up. A Plan is now in Agitation to prevent the Soldiers being abusd by the Extortion of Sutlers.

Nov 17th. I know not what detains this Express, but he is still here, which affords me an opportunity of informing you that we have this day recd a Letter from Genl Gates. Your advancd Pay to the Soldiers is as disagreable to him as it is to Genl Washington & for the same Reason.[1]

Pray write to me by every Opportunity & beleive me to be your Friend.

RC (MHi). In Adams' hand, though not signed.
[1] Horatio Gates' November 6 letter to John Hancock, which was read in Congress on November 18, is in PCC, item 154, 1:117–19, and *Am. Archives*, 5th ser. 3:549–50. See also Adams to Warren, November 9, 1776, note 1.

William Ellery to Nicholas Cooke

Sir,   Philadelphia Novr. 16th 1776

I congratulate you on Carleton's Retreat from Crown Point to Canada and on Genl. Howes retiring towards York Island of both which you will see a particular Account in the News Papers. These Events will I hope be attended with beneficial Consequences to Us. The Retreat of the former will afford G. Washington an Opportunity to make a large Draught from the Northern Army, to fill up the Deficiencies which may be made by any of our Troops quitting the Service at the Expiration of the Time of their Inlistments, or to be made Use of as the Service may require. Beside as it is a manifest Acknowledgment of our Strength it will doubtless give Spirits to our Troops, and may encourage them to reinlist. By this Express you will probably receive a Resolve which Congress have been forced into by the additional Bounty and Pay which have been offered by some of the New England States, and the additional Bounty which hath been offered in One of them.[1] This Measure is condemned by many Members of Congress, and by our General. It will they say necessitate the other States to do the same, which will greatly enhance the continental Debt and Expence; or we must have an Army doing the same Services for different Rewards which would occasion Jealousies, Envyings and Discord among the Soldiers to the great Injury of the public Service. As We have only offered an Additional Bounty We are less culpable in the Estimation of those who condemn the Deviation from the Original Resolve than any of the Transgressors. It is now in the Option of Soldiers to inlist for Three years without the Grant of Land, or during the War with it. This Alternative with the retiring of the Enemy will I hope answer the Purpose.

Thursday last a Gent. of Credit in the Jersey informed Congress, by Letter, that the preceeding Morning he saw about 100 Sail of Ships standing out from the Hook to the Southward with the Wind at North West. Yesterday he came to this City and acquainted Congress that he saw the Fleet bear away, after he had wrote, and sail Eastward until they sunk below his Horizon; That they were headed by Two Frigates and their Rear was guarded by a large Ship. By a Letter from Genl. Greene dated the 12th of this Instant at Fort Lee, which came to hand yesterday we are informed that a Gentleman, who had escaped the Day before from Staten Island, told him that there was a Fleet of Transports of about 100 Sail lying at the watering Place on Long or Staten Island bound to England, and that his Informant further said that, by a Person who had lately come from N. York to Staten Island, he was advised that Ten Thousand Men under the Command of Ld Dunmore was soon to embark for So. Carolina. The first Part of this Intelligence so exactly tallies with the Account of the Jersey Gentleman that I believe that the Fleet he saw was the same with that mentioned by G. Green's Informant, and that it was bound to England. The latter Part of the Account seems to Me improbable; because I can't conceive that they can spare so many Men for a Southern Expedition, much less can I believe that so large a Body would be put under the Command of his Lordship. Imagining that Genl. [Howe] intended to cross the North River with his Army, Genl Washington [has] sent a large Reinforcement into the Jersey; but whether the Enemy mean to go into Winter Quarters or to come this Way, or what their Design is, is unknown. Genl. Washington cannot indulge the Idea that Mr. Howe will finish the Campaign without attempting to do something more than he hath done. The News We had of the sailing of the before mentioned Fleet to the Southward, and some other Intelligence induced an Opinion that the Enemy intended to attempt the Possession of this City; and thereupon the Committee of Safety published and distributed a Hand-Bill through Town & Country requesting the Inhabitants to arm and prepare themselves to defend the City. The Account of the Number of the Fleet was exaggerated beyond the Intelligence and beyond all Credibility. What Effect this inflated Hand-Bill had on the People I don't know, for the next Morning they countermanded their Request.

I see by the News-Papers that the Assembly had risen; but do not see that an Additional Delegate is appointed. I am afraid that this Matter hath been postponed; if it hath been give me Leave Sir, once more to intreat that the next Session an Appointment may be made, and a Salary fixed of a certain Sum by the Day. I also earnestly desire that I may have the Information I have some Time since requested. I should be glad to know what Sum of Paper Money We have emitted, when the several Emissions were made, for what

Periods and what Interest. The sooner I receive the much desired Information the better. I continue to be with the sincerest Regard your Honors and my Country's Friend and humble Servant,

William Ellery

P.S. Mr. W. Hooper One of the Delegates for No. Carolina frequently writes to his Brother in Law Mr. Clarke, and may mention some News that I may not know or recollect.[2]

RC (R–Ar).

[1] See *JCC*, 6:944–45. This issue led to a mildly amusing poetical exchange between Ellery and George Wythe of Virginia. Wythe, assuming the title of "A member of the antinovanglian faction to W.E.," initiated the exchange with this verse:

"To works of supererogation
By others, some owe their salvation.
To what the good yankees are doing
Their duty beyond, we owe ruin!"

To these lines, which he subtitled "Epigram by the ingenious George Wythe Esqr," Ellery added this explanation: "In the two first Lines the Author alludes to the Roman Catholicks. In the two last to the Additional Pay, and Bounty given to the Soldiers by the Eastern States." Then, not to be outdone by his colleague from Virginia, he composed the following lines and entitled them "A Novanglian to G.W.":

"As by Works supererogatory
Rom. Caths. are saved from Purgatory;
So by what the yankees good are doing
Buckskins will save from utter Ruin."

Both these poems are in the Mellen Chamberlain Collection, MB.

[2] None of William Hooper's letters to Thomas Clark has been found.

William Ellery to Nicholas Cooke

Sir,   Philadelphia Novr. 16th 1776

I should be glad to be informed immediately whether Two Frigates can be built in Providence to be launched about the same Time the next as the other were the last Spring; and whether the same Committee would undertake again to collect Materials, and undertake the Building of them &c.[1]

I could wish to serve the State I belong to; but in Order to [do] this your Honor is sensible that I ought to have every necessary Information. I have thrown this upon a distinct Peice of Paper, because I did not think it would be proper in a Letter to the State. Please to present my Regards to Govr. Hopkins & the Secretary, and believe me to be, Yrs sincerely & respectfully,   Willm Ellery

RC (R–Ar).

[1] Cooke informed Ellery that the Rhode Island Frigate Committee had refused to undertake this task because of a shortage of building materials and the high cost of labor. William R. Staples, *Rhode Island in the Continental Congress, 1765–1790* (Providence: Providence Press Co., 1870), p. 104.

John Hancock to George Washington

Sir,   Philada. Novr. 16th. 1776.

Since my last Nothing material has occurred here, nor have I any Thing in Charge from Congress, except to request you will negotiate an Exchange of the Hessian Prisoners at Elizabeth Town under the Care of Mr. Ludwick as soon as possible.[1] They have been treated in such a Manner during their Stay in this City, that it is apprehended their going back among their Countrymen will be attended with some good Consequences.

Your Favour of the 11th of Novr. came duely to Hand and was laid before Congress.[2]

I have the Honour to be, with the most perfect Esteem & Respect, Sir, your most obed. & very hble Sert.[3]

John Hancock Presidt

RC (DLC). In the hand of Jacob Rush and signed by Hancock.

[1] See *JCC*, 6:955.

[2] This letter is in PCC, item 152, 3:245–47, and Washington, *Writings* (Fitzpatrick), 6:271–73.

[3] Hancock also wrote a letter this day to Thomas Cushing which has not been found, but for some indication of its contents see Cushing's December 16 reply in Morgan, *Naval Documents*, 7:492–93.

William Hooper to Joseph Hewes

My dear Hewes   [November 16? 1776][1]

I intended to have postponed writing to you till Monday but as the Express is unexpectedly detained till this afternoon I make use of it as it will move more expeditiously than Mr. Walker.

I lament the late changes in your Convention. To what strange infatuation has been owing the removal of Mr Johnston from your Councils. At a time when the Abilities of the first Characters in the State are necessary to give you a Constitution which will secure happiness, Life, liberty & property to the Inhabitants, you have deprived yourself of the most able head in North Carolina and as good a heart as God ever made. Is it become criminal then to stretch forth the hand of compassion, & shed the tear of pity upon suffering weakness. Is not liberty the same to one Class of beings as to another, or are a few of us Gods Elect who have a right to think & act as we please, without suffering any others to step within the pale of our Privileges. I confess there are few incidents which have taken place since my entrance into publick life which have given me equal distress. Past services seem to be no security for future preferment & a life far exhausted in promoting the publick good is to close under the greatest Example of Ingratitude that ever marked a people. In dust and ashes may they attone for it, to God & to my friend, & the friend of his Country.[2]

Your Convention will in all probability be soon drawn off from Constitution making to provide for the defense of our Country. Troops are certainly embarking for some one of the Southward states; which is uncertain, tho the Report is that Chastown is their Object. I believe it true, and wish that every possible exertion may be made to render them Assistance. The Enemys Attempts will be sudden. I therefore wish that any Strength which you may exert to support yourselves or defend your Neighbours may be in such a state as that they may be seasonably upon the spot to oppose any attempts which the Enemy may make upon yourselves or South Carolina. The Station will for the present I suppose be at Boundary House on little River where Our troops I mean the regulars will be aware of the Enemys movements and prepared to meet them whenever they shew a design to land whether in South or North Carolina. Accompanying this and inclosed in a letter to our Convention I send a Resolve of Congress, from which you will learn that the Congress have consented that whatever militia we may embody as far as 5000 are to be at the Continental Expence.[3] If General Moore has begun works at the mouth of Cape Fear river, His situation is perhaps as convenient where he is as elsewhere but should the Convention think proper to move him farther Southward the Militia will supply his place and compleat what he has begun. Would you believe it and yet what can surprize you upon that Score, Ge——y this day moved for leave to enlarge the bounty of the Masstts recruits.[4] Not satisfied with having been the occasion of altering the original plan of the new Army as devised by congress they are still attempting to have their hands deeper in our pockets, with a pretty excuse, that they would pay it themselves. Paltry subterfuge. Must it not have gone thro' the levies of all the states & the Continent pay it in the end. It met the opposition it deserved, and my blood still boils with a resentment that language will not find curses to express. I am wearied of Bloodsuckers. I care not how soon I am relieved from them.

Now for your own department. A House of rendezvous is opened. Biddle has all his Guns on board & by the latter end of this Week will be ready for Sea. The other Ships will be prepared as soon as possible and proceed upon business. The Congress have appointed Nixon & Wharton Commissioners to execute the orders of the marine Committee & compleat any Shipping begun or to be begun in Philadelphia, a third will next Week be named to assist them.[5] Things go on swimmingly now in the marine way. On Tuesday next We take up the propriety of building more men of War and some of larger force. Shall I undertake one for North Carolina? [6]

I refer you to the Newspapers for Genl. Washingtons and Howes movements, the people here have been horridly frightened. The Council of Safety a set of water Gruel Sons of B——s told the people a damned Lie "that they had certain information that 100 Ships had left Sandy Hook for this City." [7] The people at first believed & trembled, the tories grinned. Rumour trumpeted it for a day. Searle from Shrewsbury from whom the report originated was mistaken. The transports seen were empty bound for England. I can with pleasure however assure you that upon this Alarm all ranks of people, Quakers & Tories excepted, declared their readiness to turn out as soon as matters were ascertained.

The Conduct of the Hessians amidst all our troubles affords us some amusement. They have played fury with the Tories in New York and the Neighbourhood of [. . . .] At White Plains Genl Washington found many in abject wretchedness who had by the Enemy been stripped of every thing. They spared neither men, Women or Children. Their General Heister says it is their way of warring, and cant be help't. Howe says he has nothing to do with them but in General orders. A Hessian chasing a Turkey cock the other day. The turkey cackled—ay, ay, says the Hessian mocking him, You tory. No matter, good for Hesse—you Rebel! They are much dissatisfied with the service. They threaten to desert and will I fancy soon in great numbers. We kill many of them; those we take prisoners will not go back again but insist upon enlisting. Some of them are very likely fellows. The Waldeckers are small. The Tories are treated with great Contempt by the Regulars. Mr. Lewis's Son lately amongst them was told by the Officers who escorted him that they despised them as much as we do & have no dependance upon them but thought them a rascally set of Cowards. Courtlandt Skinners Battalion is reduced to 37 men. So much for this tittle tattle.

Pray hasten by every means in your power the recruiting Service amongst you; we shall have difficulty enough this way to encounter. Urge the Convention to apply for Genl. Washington for the Southern department if the Enemy go that Way. In my next I will tell you why or Rutledge will; he leaves this on Thursday. You will judge this Scrawl is not for everybodys perusal, but When Mr Johnston knows that 9 Colonies compose a Congress, that 9 only are here & I one of them, that every moment I am out of Congress belongs to Marine, Treasury, or Secret Committee, He will take this as you must a letter in Confidence and addressed to both of you. The time that this cost me is stolen from one duty to give to another.   **Yours affectionately.**

Pray forward the inclosed as soon as possible to my brother. Your friends here are well. Tom Wharton is a Tory of the first magnitude and is too apt to forget the peaceful doctrines of Quakerism, that the only master which he has is his master in Heaven. He has a strong penchant to his old friend King George, and disbelieves everything that augurs favourably of the pretensions of America to support her dear Independence. *Petty* & his Sister are well &c.

I have had a violent attack of my old bilious complaint & am indebted for this attempt to be merry rather to a Spasm of the Guts than any sprightly flow of my Animal Spirits. I note Situations & Circumstances. Believe me to be your's & your's Affectionately,

Will Hooper

[*P.S.*] By this Oppty I forward a Letter from your Bror.

Your friends the Portuguese have interdicted us from any Commerce with them & stiled us Rebels—for which they are a set of fools.[8] What fine picking amongst their Southern Cargoes as soon as we can justify a declaration of war against them—that I hope & believe will be soon.

RC (DLC photostat).

[1] A comparison of this letter with the one Hooper wrote to the North Carolina Convention on November 16 strongly suggests that both were composed on the same day. Burnett conjectured that the last five paragraphs and postscript of this letter were written sometime after the 16th because "It does not appear, for instance, that on the 16th the incorrectness of Searle's information had yet been discovered." In fact Congress had learned as early as November 15 that Searle's intelligence was in error. See Burnett, *Letters,* 2:155n.2; and Board of War to the Pennsylvania Associators, November 14, 1776, note.

[2] Samuel Johnston had not been elected to the North Carolina Provincial Congress which met at Halifax from November 12 to December 23, 1776, and drew up North Carolina's first state constitution.

[3] See *JCC,* 6:956–57.

[4] Elbridge Gerry's motion is not recorded in the journals.

[5] Francis Hopkinson was appointed the third commissioner on November 18. See Francis Hopkinson to John Hart?, November 19, 1776.

[6] Congress agreed to build nine new Continental ships of varying sizes on November 20, but none of them were to be constructed in North Carolina. *JCC,* 6:970.

[7] The Council of Safety had received this "information" from Congress. See Board of War to the Pennsylvania Associators, November 14, 1776.

[8] The king of Portugal had declared Portuguese ports closed to American shipping in an edict issued on July 4, 1776. *Am. Archives,* 4th ser. 6:1255.

William Hooper to the North Carolina Convention

Sir   Philadelphia November 16 1776

When I closed my letters last evening, I did not imagine that it would be necessary for me to write any thing further upon the motives which induced the Congress to send the Express who is the bearer of this. The Representation of the delegates of South Carolina, stating the weakness of that colony & its incompetency to its own defence, if attacked by a formidable force of the Enemy, its reliance upon North Carolina for that succour which it had little reason to expect from any other source, their Apprehensions that an attack was immediately intended by General Howe upon Charlestown, have induced Congress to pass a resolve which this incloses, and have detained the express to give an Opportunity to communicate it to your honourable body.[1]

The Congress of North Carolina are well aware that should the Enemy succeed in an attempt upon Charlestown and obtain possession of that metropolis, it would operate very important Consequences with respect to the neighbouring Colonies in their future struggle. As that place might from the advantages of Nature be easily fortified on the land side, & with a fleet commanded every where else, a small force would be competent to the defence of it, and an enemy once in possession would obtain a permanent lodgment there. It would become an Asylum for the disaffected from all parts of the Southern states, by which means the enemy will be enabled to fill up those deficiencies which Nature or the chance of war may produce in their forces. It will at the same time furnish them with a safe commodious Harbour for their Shipping from whence they may be sent occasionally to distress their neighbours or find safety themselves when pressed by their Enemies, or the inclemency of the Weather. The Inhabitants of the Western Counties of North Carolina may see the importance of South Carolina being kept secure from the introduction of the Enemy in another but not less important point of view; the intercourse which they have had with the town of Charlestown marks it as an object of much importance to them. I will not be as positive; for I judge perhaps upon more superficial grounds; as General Armstrong, but I will not pronounce him wrong, when he says, that the Battles of our State will be fought in So Carolina or Virginia & that in one or the other No Carolina will be saved or subdued.

North Carolina at an early period in this contest disclosed a spirit, a determined resolution, a strength which raised it from an obscurity to a distinction which it now respectably holds in the list of the united states. Its intestine foes were soon taught the weight of its collective powers, and their opposition sunk into insignificance and contempt. Their Crimes have produced an abject contrition, and some of them are humbled so low as to merit rather pity than resentment. From within ourselves then little is to be feared, and from the situation of our Country in that part where a foreign Enemy is to make its advances at first, they must hazard more than the importance of the Object would justify. Sudden landing for the sake of Water, depredations of Cattle or negroes will be all which they will attempt and scouting parties may be so employed to harrass them as to prevent this being long a business of pleasure to them.

Virginia has, or the Inhabitants of that state, expressing themselves by their delegates imagine they have much to apprehend in case the Enemy should attempt to obtain a footing amongst them. This depends much upon their own exertions. True it is from the great number of Water courses which pervade that Country, the enemy from their Shipping may harrass them by small indecisive encounters but I am confident that nothing upon a large scale, when Success will determine any thing important as to the common cause will be attempted there. For these reasons I conclude that the Enemy will shape their course immediately to Charlestown, & well aware to what causes they owed their disappointments in the former attempt, will go with a formidable army not less than 10,000 & without spending any part of their Strength in a conflict with Sullivans or other Batteries, will endeavour to pass them with a fair Wind and invest the town before it is prepared to give them a proper reception, or possibly may land at a distance and advance under cover of occasional temporary Works.

This points out strongly the necessity of their having a force at or near Charlestown to make a sudden effort to repel the first attempts of the Enemy, a delay might defeat the whole, and a force be inadequate to remove them from a lodgment made when a third of it might, if seasonably applied have prevented their obtaining it at first. The Continental Congress have therefore thought proper to recommend that the Continental Troops under Genl Moore should be stationed where they may be in a capacity to be suddenly and most effectually useful to South Carolina, and at the same time not at such a distance from ourselves, as to be incapable of rendering No Carolina Assistance in case the Enemy should be infatuated enough to attempt to penetrate it. This measure recommended by Congress will I doubt not obtain your approbation, yet as the full and perfect security of North Carolina is a first and important object to me the representative of it, I did not think myself at liberty to consent to any arrangement which might weaken our internal resources without a competent substitute in lieu of them. This induced my application that the Militia which we might have occasion to call forth should be at the Continental Expence which from the justice of it obtained their assent. If you have begun any works at Cape Fear River or elsewhere, you will now have the means of compleating them, and have a force on hand to assist your Neighbours in So Carolina or Virginia; and the State of North Carolina may perhaps be remembred hereafter with gratitude as have given salvation to one or both of them. I have promised much for my dear Countrymen upon this occasion, not more than I am well assured they will perform. I know the hardships they have encountered, the difficulties under which they labour at present, but when they consider the prize they contend for is liberty to themselves & to posterity, to avoid the galling yoke of Abject Slavery now & to latest ages, all they suffer or can suffer will weigh but as a feather against a world when they contemplate things as they are.

Circumstanced as matters are, should you have occasion for stores of any kind which this place supplies I beg to know your wants immediately that, upon the Arrival of the packet from Edenton they may be dispatched to you. We expect her every moment and are much surprized that she has not appeared before this.

Inclosed you have another resolve which the necessity of recruiting an Army immediately to the Eastward has rendered proper. Congress tho well convinced of the utility of enlisting men *during the war*, as it would tend to prevent the frequent calls for bounty upon new enlistments, and obviate the difficulties which result from troops leaving Camp when their services are most essential, and when perhaps the fate of America might depend upon their stay, that we might have an army inured to service and discipline, thought proper to direct them to be raised during the War. An application from the state of the Mass[achuse]tts accompanied with information that Connecticut and Rhode Island were pursuing similar and equally improper means to compleat their levies, finding that these states urged as an excuse for their extraordinary bounties, the insurmountable difficulties which they met with in recruiting Men during the War, suggesting that Soldiers complained of such an engagement as a contract for perpetual servitude. The Cont. Congress thought proper to relax & shorten the terms of Enlistment, agreeable to the Resolve which I send you herewith & which the above will fully explain.[2]

Nothing in addition to what this & my many preceeding letters contain occurs to me as necessary at present to be subjoined. I have already far trespassed upon the patience & the momentous employment of that honourable Assembly in which you preside, & for which I seek my excuse in their candor which will I flatter myself attribute it to a belief on my part that I am in the way of my duty. I am, Sir, With great Respect, Your's & the Convention's Most Obedient, Humble Servant, Will Hooper

RC (Nc–Ar).
[1] See *JCC*, 6:956–57.
[2] See *JCC*, 6:944–45.

Secret Committee Minutes of Proceedings

Nov. 16th. 1776

Come. met. Present Messrs. Morris, Lee, Lewis, Livingston. Acct. of Robt. Brige's amountg. to £84, was laid before the Come. for the passage of 9 Frenchmen from Martinique in his Brige Cornelia & Molly who were put on board by Mr. Bingham Agt. for this Come. as a politic measure to screen the vessel from capture by the Enemy, as She was insurd by the Contint.[1] Orderd that the Sum be pd. by Mr. Morris. An Acct. of Robt. Morris Esqr. for 216 lb powdr. at 5s per lb amt £54 deliverd the Commissy. per receit was laid before the Come. Orderd that Mr. Morris charge the same to Acct. of the Come. Agreed that Mr. Morris receive the Cargo brought into this place by Capt. Ord from the Missisippi & that he deliver to Mr. Js. Mease, any part thereof that may be wanted for the use of the Army;[2] the remaindr. to be disposed of by public sale & pay the freight of the whole out of the nett proceeds & credit this Come. with the balance. Resd. that Mr. Morris pay to Capt. Ord fifty pounds as a reward from this Come. for his faithful & good conduct in transactg. their business.

MS (MH–H).
[1] See Secret Committee Minutes of Proceedings, July 11 and October 31, 1776.
[2] For Oliver Pollock's October 10 letter regarding George Ord's voyage to New Orleans, see Morgan, *Naval Documents*, 6:1210.

William Whipple to Josiah Bartlett

My Dear Sir,   Philadelphia 16th Novr. 1776
    The Sudden & freequent movments of the Armies renders it impossible to give a just accot of their Scituation. Howe has Retreated from White Plains, by the last accots was encamped on the Bank of the River below Dobbs's ferry & by the disposition of his army it is judg'd intends making a desent on New-Jersey. In order to counteract him, part of Genl Washington Army (about 4 or 5000) have crossed the River above him & are now on this side ready to receive him. They are continually Skirmishing in small parties, in which we always have the advantage. By some accots from deserters it is conjectured by some that a large detachment say 10,000 will go to South Carolina. I wish it may be true; let them divide if they dare. A fleet of about 100 sail left Sandy Hook last Wednesday supposed to be bound for Europe.
    A Committee from the Massachusetts Genl Court arriv'd at the Camp about a fortnight ago to Commission the Officers &c. As that Genl Court had raised the pay of their Soldiers 20s per month the Genl. choose the Matter should be layed before Congress before they proceeded to business. Accordingly one of Committee came here. This affair has perplext congress exceedingly. All the Southern states think the Incouragement to the Soldiers much too great before & if this committee are permitted to follow their Instructions the pay of the whole army must be raised, this by no means could

be consented to. Congress have therefore revoked their Resolution for Inlisting the army during the war, & recommend the inlistment for three years only, as you'll see by the Resolution transmitted by the President. I Heartily wish this may have the desired effect, I really think they (the Massachusetts) were very wrong in raising the Monthly pay. If they supposed the encouragment given by Congress insufficient why could they not have increased the Bounty, or have persued some measure, that would not have effected the whole Army. This affair has caused more perplexity & uneasiness then any thing that has happen'd in my time.[1]

One vessel has arriv'd here from France since your departure with arms & amunition only, several others will soon follow her, with such articles as are at this time more wanted. Harrison is arriv'd from Verginia. There has been a new Election in Delaware. McKean & Rodney are left out & the Farmer [2] is elected instead of one of them, but he has not yet taken his seat. Our Colleague is as well as can be expected, the operation of the small pox has kept him two days from Congress.[3] I hope he will be able to attend in a few days. Please to present my most Respectful Regards to Col. Weare, Dr. Thompson, the Genl. &c &c &c. I will trouble either of them with a letter when ever they'll give me an opportunity. I want very much to hear from you, perticularly as to your health, tho' I am in no doubt the Northern air & a *sight of Your Family* will do great things. I hear a great number of Torys are sent into our state from that of New-York. I hope proper care will be taken of them, as well as those in and of our state. What think you of transporting them. This I wod like exceedingly, but then I'm puzle'd for a place bad Enough to send them to. Scotland indeed might do, but the difficulty is, how to keep them there, but to be serious, I think some very spirited Measure must be speedily taken with those people & I know of none that will answer the purpose so effectually as clearing the United states of them by some means or other. I can think of but two ways of effecting this, that is death or transportation, & Humanity inclines me to the latter. Indeed we had better send them to the Enemys army then let them continue among us. On the whole I dont know but this wod be a good peice of policy, to send not only the avow'd Torys but all those who are not active in their Countrys Cause with their Families, to Lord Howe, and let him make the most of them.

I have run on to a much greater length then I expected to, when I took up my pen by which means I shall loose the benefit of a Sermon, this forenoon, which I shod charge to your accot. If I thought you could possibly reap any benifit from this lengthey Scrawl but as that cannot be the case, I must put up with the loss & bid you Adieu, assureing you that I am very Sincerely, Yours,

                         Wm Whipple

RC (InU).

[1] See Samuel Adams to James Warren, November 9, 1776, note.

[2] John Dickinson.

[3] Matthew Thornton had had himself inoculated upon his arrival in Philadelphia on November 3.

William Whipple to John Langdon

My Dear Sir,   Philadelphia 16th Novr 1776

I have been about two months and six days from Portsmouth and have rec'd *one short letter* from my professed friend, J. Langdon Esq. Pray Sir, do you know that Gentleman. If you do, please to present my regards to him and tell him, I shall always be ready to execute any of his commands in my way, but that I by no means expect he will give himself the trouble of writing unless it is on a subject that immediately concerns himself, for as all mankind was created merely for their own benefit, why should one man concern himself about the advantage or disadvantage that may arise to another. It's true the word friendship is often used, but there is no substantial meaning to it in this refined age; it's quite an old fashioned word; nothing is now meant by it but that I will readily gratify the person I call my friend, provided I thereby can obtain any real advantage to myself. What think you of this matter? Dont you think that this is the modern acceptation of the word friendship? I know you think with me that it is, but at the same time your *general* conduct convinces me that your sentiments are not so far modernized as not to be actuated by the true principles of friendship, and to convince you that I am actuated by the same principle, I now enclose you the copies of the letters from Providence mentioned in my last. I don't mean by sending these letters to excite resentment, but to put it in your power when an opportunity offers to vindicate yourself. Whenever the person for whom I profess a friendship is treated in a manner that appears to me injurious to his character, I esteem it an indispensable duty to vindicate him. Is that all? No, I must do more. I must let him know by whom and in what manner he has been traduced in order that he may know who are his enemies and in what manner to guard against them. This ever has been and ever shall be my conduct towards the person for whom I profess a friendship.

You have here enclosed the late Resolutions of Congress so far as they have gone respecting the Navy. I hope for some farther alterations, but you know things of this sort must be done by degrees. The encouragement now given to officers and men in the navy are in my opinion as great as they can possibly expect, and I hope will be to their entire satisfaction.[1]

It is impossible to give you an idea of the situation of the Armies, they being in perpetual motion. Our people always have the advantage in skirmishes. That being the case, it is undoubtedly for our interest not to come to a general battle, which in my opinion will be avoided. A considerable fleet about 100 sail left Sandy Hook last Wednesday, it's supposed they are empty transports for Europe. A ship arrived from France a few days since with arms & ammunition only. Several others were to sail in a few days after her with other articles. God send them safe. Give me leave to congratulate on Carlton's retreat from Crown Point. What a glorious Campaign those Boasters have made, I think it will make a grand figure in the annals of Britain.

This goes by an express who sets off tomorrow morning. I shall keep it open that if anything should turn up worth communicating will give it you. In the meantime be assured that I am your Sincere friend and humble servant,   Wm Whipple

Tr (DLC).
[1] The resolutions of November 15 that set the pay for naval personnel are in *JCC*, 6:953–55.

Oliver Wolcott to Samuel Adams

Sir,[1]   Philidelpa. 16t Nov. 1776
Your kind favr of the 21t Ult came to hand and for which I thank you. This together with a Letter from Mr. Adams are the only ones I have recd. since I have been here, but as by the Return of the British Army to N York and Carlton to Canada the Communication will be kept fully open so that probably in future no Interuption will be given to the Post I hope I may hear more frequently from my Freinds.

Nothing in special has occured since my last Letters. An Expedition is supposd to be forming by the Enemy, Many Think agt. this City, in Consequence of which Expectation, all the associators are ordered to it. I think it is more probably they will go farther South, I think, to the Carolinas or Georgia.

Some Very Considerable Success has been had agt. the Cherokees, a number of their Towns have been burnt, so that it is hopd. these Savages will be thoroly quelld.

To establish a New Army is of infinite moment and Demands every attention to have Accomplished. Many Difficulties will attend it but I hope they will all be Surmounted. It is an established Opinion here and amongst all the Officers of the Army, that the pay of it must be uniform. An Army it is said under different pay cannot Subsist together, and that for any colony to Vary in this Circumstance is totally to Subvert a continental Regulation, which if it can be done, it is in Vain to make any—for if the Veiws of a particular Colony were answered, and a new & general Regulation took place in Consequence of it, another Colony might Vary from that, and so render every Regulation ineffectual.

At present I am alone from Connecticut. Messrs. Sherman and Huntington went home some time ago, and Col Williams the 13th inst. I expect Mr. Sherman will soon Return. I think Mr. Williams might as well have tarryed at the present, as to have come here at all, as there have not since the 1st of this month been but nine colonies represented, the lowest Number necessary to make a Congress, so that my failure of attendance would intirely put a stop to all Business, but for some Reason I will not conjecture what, he was determined and has gone home.[2] I beleive more Colonies will soon be in. N York Wants one more member for a Representation who is hourly expected, Delaware and Maryland Members are settling their Government, Georgia Representation expired the 1 of this month and their members are Waiting for New Powers. I perceive by a Philidelpa. paper Published therein under the N Haven Head, that the former Connecticut Members are re-elected with Mr. Law.[3] Whether they are all to attend, or some of us to supply Vacancies I have not heard, and indeed nothing more about it, than what I saw in that Paper.

I will Endeavour while here to be even with you in the Letter Writing Way but if at any Time I should fail I hope it will be no Discouragement to your perseverance, only I Wish that it might be a little quickened. My best Regards to my Freinds. I am sir, your most Obedient, humble Servant,   Oliver Wolcott

RC (Paul Francis Webster, Beverly Hills, Calif., 1974).

[1] Probably Samuel Adams (1703?–88), a Litchfield, Conn., lawyer and father of the judge and delegate Andrew Adams. George C. Woodruff, *A Genealogical Register of the Inhabitants of the Town of Litchfield, Conn.* (Hartford: The Case, Lockwood & Brainard Company, 1900), p. 5.

[2] For Wolcott's further comment on Williams' departure, see Wolcott to Laura Wolcott, November 24, 1776.

[3] Both Eliphalet Dyer and Richard Law had been added to the Connecticut delegation, joining Samuel Huntington, Roger Sherman, William Williams, and Wolcott, with any three of the six to serve at the same time. See *JCC,* 7:11. In his November 21 letter to the Connecticut Assembly Eliphalet Dyer requested permission not to serve because of "my late Decline of Health" and "the present particular Situation of my Affairs Occasioned principally by my long & almost Continual Absence for Years past from my family, on the Service of the publick." Revolutionary War Collection, Ct. However, he did return to Congress in June 1777.

Oliver Wolcott to Laura Wolcott

My Dear   Philidelpa 16t Nov. 1776
I Wrote you a Letter the 12 instant by Col Williams, which I
trust you will soon receive as he set out for home the Next Morning.[1] Nothing New has occured since that but what you will be
informed of before this comes to you or by my Letter to Mr Lyman.
We had the happy News of Carlton going back to Canada the 14t.
This I hope will give Peace for the present to the Northward, tho
if he had been heartily drubbed before he set out it would have
been Well, but Nobody but himself is to blame in that it was not
done, and God be Thanked that the Affair has turn'd out so favourably.
I find myself in a tolerable State of Health, and I hope that it
is dayly growing more confirmed. I mean to Attend to it, and shall
regulate my Conduct accordingly. I think myself pritty free from
the Jaundice, and by Care I am satisfied shall prevent it returning
upon Me.
I have some Books for Oliver but I do not know when I shall
be able to send them to him. Traders for some time have failed
coming from Connecticut to this Place, but I think it is probable
they will be here again soon.
I wish frequently to hear from you. I think none of my Freinds
would fail Writing every Oppertunity if it were but Two Words.
They Wait till they can find some long political Subject to Write
upon but that is not Necessary amongst Friends.
I Wish you to take Care of your Health, which I well know is
Very necessary for you to do. Nothing could give me more Satisfaction, than that my Condition in Life would permit Me to live
with my Family, but We must follow the guidance of divine Provi-
dence, to whose Protection I commit you and our Children. My
Regards to Mr. and Mrs Reeve and my other Freinds and Kindred.
Love to my Children. I am yours with the tenderest affection,
                                              Oliver Wolcott

RC (CtHi).
[1] Wolcott's letter of the 12th "by Col Williams who is returning home,"
which was primarily concerned with Wolcott's health, is in the Wolcott Papers,
CtHi.

Samuel Adams to Elizabeth Adams

                                              Novr 17th [1776]
I wish you would acquaint your Brother Sammy that General
Mifflin is now Quartermaster General in the Room of Coll Moylan—

that when I was at Head Quarters I mentioned to the General the Treatment your Brother had met with.[1] He told me that he would have him state the Matter to him in Writing and that he would endeavor to have Justice done to him. The Letter your Brother formerly wrote to me I left at Boston. If he will give me a full Account of the Matter in another Letter, I will State it to General Mifflin, but the Circumstances of things are such at present that I would not have him depend upon it being immediately attended to. I will however do all in my Power to serve him.

Our Friend Mr Lovel is at last exchangd.[2] We received a Letter from him two or three days ago. Probably before this reaches you he will have arrivd at Boston. Pray remember me to my Daughter, Sister Polly with the rest of my Family & Friends, and be assured that I am most sincerely & affectionately, Your,　　　S A

RC (NN). A continuation of Adams to Elizabeth Adams, November 14, 1776.
[1] That is, Samuel Wells.
[2] For further information on the complicated exchange of James Lovell, see John Hancock to George Washington, January 6, 1776, note 1.

Marine Committee to
Levinus Clarkson and John Dorsius

Gentlemen　　　　　　　　　　　　　　　　November 17th 1776

Upon the recommendation of your freinds here we have appointed you Continental Agents in the State of South Carolina. As such you are to supply any of the Ships or Cruizers with whatever Provisions, Stores or necessarys they may be in want of when they put into or arrive in any of your ports. If repairs are necessary we depend on you to employ the best Tradesmen and see that the business is done with dispatch. You will in short do all things in this department that you think will serve the Continent and promote the service of the Navy and you must send us proper Certificates Signed by the Captain or principle officer of each Ship or Vessel of your expenditure and your drafts on this board for the amount will be duely honored. It is a Standing order to all our men of war and Cruizers to send their prizes address to the Continental Agents at the ports where they arrive. If any such come into South Carolina, you must receive the same into your charge, prosecute them in the Admiralty to condemnation, make the sale of them at Public vendue, pay all charges justly attending each Prize, and credit us for such part as appertains to the Continent agreeable to the Rules and Regulations of Congress, a book of which shall be sent you. The shares belonging to the officers and Crews of the Captors you must divide amongst them agreeable to the said Rules and Regulations, and to do this justly and equitably the Commanders must furnish you with compleat and certified list of the officers and men intitled to a Share of each prize and the share or shares they are respectively intitled to, and you are to pay all persons concerned their shares as soon after Sale is made as you possibly can, and return to this Board duplicates of all your accounts and proceedings.

We are Gentlemen, Your very hble servants

LB (DNA: PCC Miscellaneous Papers, Marine Committee Letter Book).

John Witherspoon to Benjamin Rush

Dr Sir   Princeton Nov 17. 1776

On coming home here I found a Letter from a very good friend in the State of Massachusetts which I thought of so much Consequence that I send an extract from it to you but for a certain reason or rather on Acct of a certain Expression in it I conceal his Name.[1] My son [2] without knowing any thing of that Letter confirmed it in every part as to the Sick. Oh the want of public Spirit & detestable selfishness in some Persons. I hope you will make a prudent if any use at all of it. Perhaps you may guess the Author; if so do not express it to any one. D[octor] M[organ] seems very unfit for his Charge & seems set upon nothing but making Money. The Bearer will more fully inform you.[3]

If John wants a Set of Instruments please to direct & assist him. I am glad to find by all Accts from different hands that he has been pretty active. As soon after the Trustees meeting as the Business of the College will permit I propose to return being anxious for the public Cause. I am with compliments to Mrs Rush, Sir your &c,

Jno Witherspoon

P.S. Please Show the Extract to Col. Lee.

RC (CtY).

[1] Witherspoon's Massachusetts correspondent has not been identified, but see Elbridge Gerry to Unknown, November 27, 1776.

[2] John Witherspoon, Jr. (1757–95?), was a medical student who served under Dr. John Morgan at the general hospital in New York in July and August 1776. Varnum L. Collins, President Witherspoon: A Biography, 2 vols. (Princeton, N.J.: Princeton University Press, 1925), 2:49n.35.

[3] For some indication of the growing disenchantment with Dr. Morgan, culminating in his abrupt dismissal as director general and physician in chief of the Continental Army on January 9, 1777, see John Hancock to John Morgan and William Shippen, December 1, 1776; and Samuel Adams to John Adams, January 9, 1777.

Board of War to George Washington

Sir   War Office 18th Novr. 1776
   The Hancock and Adams, loaded from France with military
Stores and other Articles for the Use of the Continent, was taken
by a Rhode Island Privateer, and carried into the Port of Dartmouth in New England. The Muskets, Powder, Lead and Gunflints
are to be delivered, by Virtue of the enclos'd Resolution of Congress, to the Order of this Board. We have wrote to the Committee
of Bedford, in whose District Dartmouth Lies, to deliver to your
Order such of the before-mentioned Articles as you shall direct.[1] We
have the Honour to be, with great Esteem, Sir, Your very humble
Servants,   Benja Harrison

                                                     James Wilson

                                                     Francis Lightfoot Lee

RC (DLC). Written by Wilson and signed by Wilson, Harrison, and Lee.
   [1] See *JCC*, 6:952–53. On November 30 Washington informed the board that
in view of the uncertain military situation "I would advise, that you give directions to have the whole Cargo removed from Dartmouth to some secure
place in the Neighbourhood of Philadelphia, and there deposited till call'd
for." Washington, *Writings* (Fitzpatrick), 6:316–17. The board's letter to the
Bedford committee has not been found.

Robert Treat Paine's Diary

                                                     November 18, 1776
   Fair. Heard that Fort Washington surrendered on Saturday last.[1]

MS (MHi).
   [1] News of the fall of Fort Washington was brought by George Washington's
November 16 letter to President Hancock, which was read in Congress on November 19. See *JCC*, 6:963; and Washington, *Writings* (Fitzpatrick), 6:284–87.

Charles Thomson to the
Pennsylvania Council of Safety

Gentlemen,   [ca. November 18, 1776]
   The bearer[1] has a scheme to propose of fire rafts for burning
Vessels. I have, therefore, referred him to you for examination of
his plans.   Chas. Thomson.

Reprinted from *Pa. Archives*, 1st ser. 5:68.
   [1] Apparently Jacob Giesling of Reading, Pa. He had been recommended to
Thomson by James Read of Reading, who explained in a November 16 letter to

Thomson that Giesling "has something of the utmost moment to the Service of the States to communicate to Congress." Instead of introducing him to Congress, however, Thomson sent him to the council of safety with this brief introduction and Read's letter. On November 21 the council ordered payment of £10 "in favour of Jacob Kisling . . . for services rendered to the State, in producing a Model for a Fire-Ship." See ibid.; and *Pa. Council Minutes*, 11:11.

Oliver Wolcott to Matthew Griswold

Sir,   Philidelpa. 18 Nov. 1776

The establishing the New Army is a Subject of the most interesting Nature, and I fear will be attended with much Dificulty, notwithstanding all the Encouragement Offerd the men for inlisting. The Service the People have been calld to has been hard. They have suffered much for the Want of Many Things, and have been too much exposed to the Oppressions of Harpys who for Triffles have stript them of their Wages. These Evils I hope in future will in a good Measure be remedied, as the Men are to be cloathed, and it is now the Deliberation of Congress how they shall be regularly and in the cheapest Manner supplyed in the suttling Way,[1] and I hope also the Medical Department will undergo a Reform of Men at least, if not of Measures, that not so much complaint which I fear has been too well grounded, may be heard respecting the Conduct of that Department. But after all that can be done I still fear that the inlisting Business will go on slowly and sorry I am that the late Encouragement for that purpose was not earlier made. Congress Apprehend this Matter may become more embarrassed by what the Massachusetts have done in raising the pay, and which I now understand has been adopted by Connecticut.[2] It is the opinion of Gentlemen here, and so of Genl. Washington and of all the other Genl. Officers, that no Army can subsist together under different continental pay, and also, if the Massachusetts Plan had been adopted by Congress (and which would entrench an Expence which it is tho't We are not well able to bear) they could not be certain that any Other plan would take Effect, if particular States might at their pleasure offer Troops other pay. In a Word they say that such Conduct must immediately Subvert any continental Regulation for this purpose, and if therefore permitted it would be altogether ineffectual to make any military Establishment whatsoever.

One of the Gentlemen of Massachusetts, appointed to assist in providing their Quota, was sent by Genl. Washington here before he entered on the Business of his appointment.[3] You will perceive that the Measure Adopted by Massachusetts has been reprobated by Congress. The Gentleman has gone back with this Errand to Genl. Washington where I understand the Gentlemen from Connecticut are upon this Business. I think it is Very unhappy that the Massachusetts took this step, without advice. R. Island I understand has offered their men a large additional Bounty which may be much less Mischeivous, as it is but a temporary Business, and Whether Connecticut will not be finally oblidged to take some such step I cannot say, tho I know many Gentlemen here and I beleive a considerable majority will equally reprobate this measure as the Other, and if it is done it must be certainly at the Colony's Expence. Such a Thing has been mentioned in Congress, but it gave many Gentlemen much offence, as they Said that every other State must be oblidged to do the like. I mention these Dificulties, hoping that the Wisdom of the Colony will be able to Obviate them, tho' to me they are too perplexing to point out any particular Way in which it can be done. But it is certain We must have an Army Otherwise We shall be reduced to the most unhappy Condition. A Lottery is agreed upon by Congress, that With the Loan Office may Effect something considerable to reduce the Currency, but yet I think something more extensive must Very Shortly be adopted to establish the Finances.[4] You will hear sooner than I can inform you that an offer is made to the men to inlist for three years, with the same Encouragements as before exclusive of Land Reward. At present the Congress are pritty thin, there have not been but nine Colonies represented in Congress since the first of this month, which is the lowest Number necessary to make one. N York will this day be added, and Delaware and Maryland, who have been lately attending to the affairs of their Government will be here in a few days. Georgia members are Waiting for new Powers which will be probably soon recd.[5] At present there is none with me from Connecticut. Col Williams returned the 13th, but I expect Mr. Sherman here dayly.

No Material news from the Southward, and as to the eastern affairs you can receive no Information from me. There is a Strong perswation that an Expedition will be made to S Carolina, but this matter yet rests in Conjecture only. The Conduct of the Enemy just now Appears to be a little misterious but time will Very soon discover their Intentions.

To Morrow the assembly of Pensilvania meet. The People here are Very unhappily divided about their Constitution. The City and County of Philadelphia have chosen members to prevent its taking effect, the Other Counties tho generally much divided have chose it is said members of contrary Sentiments. What the Result will be is uncertain, but it is rather tho't they will act upon the new Establishment. Government is extremely Wanted here, and these Contentions and Discussions are therefore Very unhappy, but I hope they will subside.

The Quakers may not be expected to take any open Active part in any political matter in these Times, but their secret Influence I fear is to Embarrass our measures. They dread to lose that Predominancy which they have heretofore held. The Proprietary Interest are governed by the same Considerations.

My Health at present seems to be in some measure established, tho' I have been quite ill since I have been here, but as I have for some time past endeavoured as farr as my circumstances would Admit to Obtain a radical cure of those sundry Disorders which for a long time have troubled me, I hope I have nearly Obtained a radical cure of them, tho I could Wish on this acco. as well as others that I had some Assistance in the Colony Representation, but this I beleive I shall have by Mr. Sherman in a few days. My best Regards to my Sister and your Family, and be assured that I am, Sir, with esteem, your most Obedient, humble Servant,   Oliver Wolcott

RC (CtY).
¹ The committee to establish regulations for sutlers, to which Wolcott had been appointed on November 8, submitted their report on the ninth. *JCC*, 6:935, 937–39. See also Elbridge Gerry to John Wendell, November 11, 1776, note 3.

² For the Connecticut Assembly's resolution for increasing the pay of noncommissioned officers and soldiers, see *Am. Archives*, 5th ser. 3:451.

³ George Partridge. See Samuel Adams to James Warren, November 9, 1776, note.

⁴ See *JCC*, 6:917, 955–56, 959–62.

⁵ For the credentials of the Maryland and Delaware delegates, which were presented on November 19 and December 2, respectively, see *JCC*, 6:962, 1000. On Georgia's representation, see Georgia Delgates to John Hancock, December 10, 1776.

George Wythe to Thomas Jefferson

GW to TJ   Philadelphia, 18 November. 1776.
Whenever you and the speaker think I should return to Virginia to engage in the part which shall be assigned to me in revising the laws, I shall attend you.¹ As to the time and place of meeting and my share in this work, I can accommodate myself to the appointment, and be content with the allotment my colleagues shall make. In the mean time, I purpose to abide here, if the enemy do not drive me away; an event some think not improbable. What to think of it myself I know not: especially if a report we heard today, 'that the garrison in fort Washington, consisting of 2,000 men, surrendered themselves prisoners, at the first summons,' be confirmed. Are the judges in chancery, whilst they are on the circuits, to hear cases in equity? If not, are forty days in the year sufficient for that business? I suppose not.² I will inquire tomorrow by whom the regimental paymasters are to be appointed; and if I have time before the departure of the post, will let you know: if by congress your recommendation of Mr. Moore shall be remember[ed.] The journals shall also be sent to you, if they can be procured. The conveniency

George Wythe

of my house servants and furniture to you and Mrs. Jefferson adds
not a little to their value in my estimation. Our best respects to the
lady. Be so kind as let me know if our general assembly hath agreed
to give any additional bounty to the noncommissioned officers and
soldiers of the new levies more than what congress had offered. The
eastern states, or some of them, by doing a thing of that kind, have
much embarrassed us. I understood by the person employed to draw
the figures for our great seal that you intended to propose an alteration in those on the reverse.[3] I wish you would propose it; for though
I had something to do in designing them, I do not like them. Let me
know of the alteration, if any; and send a neat impression made by
the old seal. It will be useful to the workman. Adieu.

My compliments to Mr. Page. I wrote to him several weeks since,
and desired him to send me an impression made by the old seal—
that I received no answer I attribute to his ill health. I wish it better.

This morning (19 Nov.) we hear fort Washington was not taken
last Sunday morning the day after the garrison was supposed to have
surrendered by the report mentioned above; but it seems it is invested.

RC (DLC). Jefferson, *Papers* (Boyd), 1:603–4.

[1] Wythe, Jefferson, and Speaker Edmund Pendleton were all members of a
committee that had been appointed by the Virginia House of Delegates on
November 5 to revise the laws of the commonwealth. William W. Hening, *The
Statutes at Large; Being a Collection of All the Laws of Virginia* (Richmond:
J. & G. Cochran, 1821), 9:175–77. Wythe also wrote a brief note to Pendleton this
day indicating that he was ready to return whenever called by his colleagues "to
assist in revising the laws." Emmet Collection, NN. It is not known exactly when
Wythe left Congress, but he probably remained at least until the December 12
adjournment to Baltimore.

[2] For further discussion of Jefferson's proposals for judicial reform, which were
currently under consideration in the Virginia House of Delegates, see Jefferson,
Papers (Boyd), 1:605–7.

[3] See Thomas Jefferson to John Page, July 30, 1776.

Board of War to George Washington

Sir   War Office Novr. 19th. 1776

I am directed by the Board of War to inform your Excellency that
they have given Orders for the immediate Collection of all the
Prisoners in New Jersey, Pennsilvania, and those in the more
Southern States.[1] They are to be sent to Fort Lee agreeable to your
Excellencies Desire, but a considerable Time will elapse before the
Whole can possibly arrive.[2] There are a great number in Virginia
whose Journey will be long. But perhaps it may be better that their
Arrivals at Fort Lee should happen at different Times lest their too
great Numbers might be disadvantageous. It would be much better

if your Excellency could be furnished with Lists of all the Prisoners that you might at one View be enabled to settle the arrangement of the Exchange; but altho frequent Attempts have been made by the Board to obtain such Lists from the several States their endeavours have hitherto been for the most part ineffectual. Such Accts. of Prisoners as are in the possession of the Board shall be sent imperfect as they are. Measures are taken to restore Major Stuarts Servant Peter Jack.[3] He was permitted to go to Princetown with Doctr. Witherspoon who has been wrote to on the Subject [4] and desired to send the Man to your Excellency at Hackinsack. Many Prisoners have been desirous to enlist and some have been accepted in our Service. Is it your Opinion that these People should return? or will it not be dangerous for them so to do? [5] The Enemy have enlisted great Numbers of our People who were Prisoners & it is but Justice that we should retaliate. Offers however from Prisoners to engage in our Service have in General been refused.

I have the Honour to be with the greatest Respect, your very obedt & most humble Servt,   Richard Peters Secy

P.S. An Officer from Camp informs that Fort Lee is about being evacuated. If so your Excellency will no Doubt alter the Place of Destination of the Prisoners.

RC (DLC). In a clerical hand, with signature and postscript by Peters.

[1] For Washington's recent suggestions on an exchange of prisoners, see his November 14 letter to President Hancock, Washington, *Writings* (Fitzpatrick), 6:282–84. For Peters' letters to Pennsylvania and Maryland, this date, see *Am. Archives*, 5th ser. 3:778; and *Md. Archives*, 12:456.

[2] On November 23 the board wrote Washington that in view of the reported evacuation of Fort Lee they had ordered these prisoners to "be sent to Brunswick" instead. Washington Papers, DLC; and *Am. Archives*, 5th ser. 3:820.

[3] On this point, see *Am. Archives*, 5th ser. 3:676–78; and Washington, *Writings* (Fitzpatrick), 6:284.

[4] Not found.

[5] "As to the propriety of inlisting prisoners of War," Washington wrote to the board on November 22, "I would just observe, that in my opinion, it is neither consistent with the Rules of War, nor politic, nor can I think that because our Enemies have committed an unjustifiable action by inticing and in some instances intimidating our men into their service, we ought to follow their Example." Washington, *Writings* (Fitzpatrick), 6:317.

Samuel Chase to the Maryland Council of Safety

Gentlemen,   Philadelphia. Nov 19th. 1776
I arrived here yesterday afternoon. I have seen our Commissioners. Congress in Answer to the three Propositions from our State for Raising our Quota have given a Copy of a Resolve,[1] relative to the

Massachusetts Bay, who it I am informed, offered 30s a Month extra for the privates, in which Congress agree to give 20 Dollars bounty to each Soldier who will inlist for three Years. Our Commissioners are much distressed.

On Saturday last Genl. Howe with his whole army surrounded fort Washington. We had 2000 Men in the fort. There were two Lines outside of the fort. A large Body of our Men marched out to the *further* Lines, & sustained the attack with great Bravery untill a party of the Enemy entered [. . .] within the first Line: on the back of our Troops. Our forces then retreated into the fort and soon afterwards surrendered. It seems agreed here, that the fort was injudiciously defended, & not with the Bravery that might have been expected from the officer (Col Magaw) who commanded, & the Troops which consist of Magaws & Cadwalladers Battalions, & a party of the flying Camp, chiefly Pennsylvanians. If the fort had held out 'till the Evening, Genl. Washington had Expectations of bringing off the Men. However 2000 Men could not, I suppose, withstand an Army of at least five Times their Numbers. Thus we have lost two thousand of our best Troops, & some of our best officers, with provisions & stores for 4 Months.

Be pleased to send Me the form of Govt. when published. I write this in Congress. Your obedt. Servant,   Saml. Chase

RC (MdAA).
[1] See *JCC*, 5:944–45.

William Hooper to Joseph Hewes

Dear Hewes   [November 19? 1776] [1]
In your letter to your Brother you ask "what is become of Hooper." I answer, Here he is the Packhorse of North Carolina, carrying his burden in congress all day and varying it only by taking it upon Committees all the Evening. In a word I am fatigued almost to death. 9 Colonies you know are required to compose a Congress. Neither Georgia, Maryland, Delaware or New York have been for some time past represented so that your humble Servant is compelled to a constant unremitting attendance. I never in my life felt myself so perfectly exculpated from the Sin of Omission, I am at a loss to conceive how I have found time to write so many publick & private letters, amongst the latter before this you are convinced that I have not been unmindful of you.

I refer you to newspapers for the state of publick Intelligence. Fort Washington has fallen into the Enemy's hands, but without disgrace to the American Arms. It was a well contested prize on our part & Great Britain when she counts her dead & wounded will have no cause to triumph. It is however a disappointment as we have lost stores of considerable consequence, but this in the course of War must be expected for uniform success never was & never will be the portion of man, & we have little pretensions to deserving liberty if small defeats discourage us in the glorious pursuit.

From the many difficulties which attend the raising an Army here and to the Eastward I cannot too earnestly press upon you the necessity of forwarding by every possible method the recruiting Service. The Bounty & pay are both enormous & I hope will secure us success in recruiting & to the Southward tho the Eastern Gentry are not yet satisfied & wish to screw us up a few pegs higher—but they will be disappointed for in my opinion matters are now come to this. Give way to the extortion of the Army & you part with the property of the Continent to them and become Slaves to their Avarice & Caprice. Disband your Army & you are Slaves to a British Tyrant. Your Slavery differs only in the name of the Superiour, if I am a Slave let me have one rather than 60,000 Masters. However these Gentry will soon I hope be brought to reason & we shall have a formidable force on reasonable Terms.

It is absolutely necessary that you should have a press established amongst you for the publication of a newspaper, you suffer in your significance with other states from the want of such a Channell of Communication, and your own people are kept in ignorance of what passes abroad; & the political papers which tend to explain the Controversy and confirm them in the Justice and necessity of the Opposition in which they are engaged. I would propose that the Convention immediately order the delegates to employ a printer here and send him properly accoutred to Carolina to carry on the Work.

Albertson has not yet arrived here.[2] I wish no accident has happened to him. Upon his return I will endeavour to procure a quantity of Military Stores, I mean Shot & Powder & send it by him. We have plenty of both & may afford to run the risque of the Sea rather than pay the horrid Expence of Waggonage.

Pray cast your thoughts to the encouragement of the Iron Works & Salt making. The Salvation of Carolina depends upon it. I cannot get Salt pans here, therefore you must look elsewhere for them.

• I lament the clashing exertions of Genl Moore & General Ashe, I tremble lest they should so far counteract the publick Service as to produce the most dreadful consequences. I wish General Moore would sollicit to come this way. I am averse to urging it lest it should disgust him but sure I am a Command here would be less irksome to him & then Congress might order some officer there who might be more agreeable to the people. I love Moore & wish him happy & think I could not serve him better than by bringing him to the Eastward.

Pray request the Convention to write me fully of what they wish to have accomplished here within the compass of my abilities & not leave me to guess at a meaning. If it can be prevented I wish you could avoid a demand for a large Sum on the Contl Treasury for a while at least. It runs a little low just now but will soon I hope by Lottery & Loan Office, both of which are established by Congress, will be up again. As to settling the publick Accounts Gentlemen in Carolina are employed to adjust those in Virginia so vice versa. Adieu. I am at the bottom of my Sheet. Love to Penn. Yours Affectionately,   Wm Hooper

RC (MH–H).
[1] Since Congress did not receive official notice of the fall of Fort Washington until November 19, it is unlikely that Hooper wrote this letter before then. *JCC,* 6:963; and Washington, *Writings* (Fitzpatrick), 6:284–87. Burnett, who omitted the paragraph relating to Fort Washington in his edition, conjecturally dated this letter November 8 but failed to explain why. Burnett, *Letters,* 2:146–47.
[2] See Marine Committee to Thomas Albertson, October 1, 1776.

Francis Hopkinson to the New Jersey Assembly

Sir,   Philada. 19th. Novr. 1776
Congress having thought proper to honour me with an appointment inconsistent with my Seat in the House, & which will necessarily occasion my Removal from Jersey, I am under a Necessity of resigning my Delegation from the State of Jersey, & of requesting your Honourable House to appoint some other Person to take my Place as speedily as possible, otherwise your State will not be represented in Congress, there being at present no other Delegate here from Jersey but myself.[1]
I am fully sensible of the Honour New Jersey hath done me in committing so high a Trust to my Charge, I can only say that I have endeavoured to discharge that Trust to the best of my Abilities, & shall upon all Occasions be happy in seizing every Opportunity of shewing my Zeal for the Honour & Advantage of the State of New Jersey.
I beg my most respectful Regards to your Honourable House & am, Your most obedient, Humble servant,
                                                        Fras Hopkinson

P.S. The Loan Office Certificates being now almost ready for Emission, it is hoped your House will immediately appoint the officer for your State & forward his Name to Congress, that proper Advertisements of the opening of this office may be forthwith made.

RC (NjFrHi).
[1] On November 18 Congress made Hopkinson a member of a naval board in Philadelphia which had been created 12 days earlier "to execute the business of

the navy, under the direction of the Marine Committee." *JCC*, 6:929, 958. As a result, the New Jersey General Assembly left Hopkinson out of the new delegation chosen on November 30. See *JCC*, 6:1002.

Hopkinson also wrote a brief letter this day to Gov. William Livingston requesting permission to resign from Congress. William Livingston Papers, MHi.

Robert Treat Paine's Diary

November 19, 1776

Fair. I went in Co. with a Comttee of Council of Safety, Genl. Armstrong & Genl. Roche Fermoi & some other French Engineers to the Forts down the River.[1]

MS (MHi).
[1] Paine was not a member of either the Board of War or the Marine Committee, the two standing committees recently concerned with the defense of Philadelphia and environs. He probably undertook this trip as a consequence of his chairmanship of the Cannon Committee. See *JCC*, 6:951, 1064.

Elbridge Gerry to John Morgan

Sir [1]   Philada. Novr 20. 1776

With respect to regimental Hospitals, I cannot but think them an unnecessary and dangerous Institution, for upon every removal of such regiments, these Hospitals are a dead Weight, & must be removed, or exposed to the Enemy. The latter you will agree is by no means adviseable, and the removing such Hospitals is attended with Hardships to the diseased, and prevents them from an early recovery.

As to regimental Surgeons, being otherwise wholly useless, I have always supposed that they were never intended to answer any other Purpose, in time of War, than to cure in Camp, slight Wounds & diseases, by which the Patients were not confined, and to attend the regiments in time of Action, to dress the wounded Soldiers, untill they can be removed to the General Hospital.[2]

E Gerry

I received your favour of the 7 Inst. with Respect to the meaning of the Resolve (viz of Octor. 9) ordering the *Directors* to take Care of the sick of the Army,[3] as they may be on the East or West Side of the River, it appears to me to be this; that whatever sick of the army shall happen to be on the East side, they shall be under the Care of *yourself,* and the others under Direction of Dr. Shippen. *Your Medicines & Surgeons are undoubtedly under your own Command.*

E. Gerry.

Tr (DNA: PCC, item 63). This entry consists of two extracts from a Gerry letter quoted in Morgan's manuscript "Vindication," dated February 1, 1779, which

Morgan prepared for a committee of Congress appointed on September 18, 1778, to consider his defense against charges that had led to his dismissal from office in January 1777. See *JCC*, 7:24, 8:626, 12:925, 1259. The extracts are in two different hands and are quoted in widely different contexts of Morgan's defense.

[1] For a discussion of the events surrounding Morgan's dismissal as "director general and physician in chief of the American hospital," see Whitfield J. Bell, Jr., *John Morgan, Continental Doctor* (Philadelphia: University of Pennsylvania Press, 1965), pp. 178–239. See also Thomas Heyward to John Morgan, September 4; and John Hancock to John Morgan and William Shippen, Jr., December 1, 1776, note.

[2] The preceding paragraphs appear on folio 189 of Morgan's "Vindication." The following extract, which Morgan quoted to illustrate "the Intention of Congress with Regard to the Hospital Stores," is taken from fols. 257–58. It seems likely that in Gerry's original letter the following paragraph actually preceded the other two extracted by Morgan.

[3] Morgan's November 7 letter to Gerry is in the Hopkinson Papers, PHi, and John Morgan, *A Vindication of His Public Character in the Station of Director-General of the Military Hospitals, and Physician in Chief to the American Army: Anno 1776* (Boston: Powars and Willis, 1777), p. 140.

John Hancock to Certain States

Gentlemen,   Philada. Novr. 20th. 1776.

I have it in Charge from Congress to forward the enclosed Resolves, and to request your Attention to them.[1] From their great Importance in carrying on the War against our Enemies, I am persuaded you will take immediate Measures for complying with them in the most effectual Manner.

You will perceive, from the Vote of Congress, herewith transmitted, the Sense of that Body with Regard to the Necessity of furnishing the Troops for the new Army, as soon as possible.

As our Enemies will no Doubt take the Field early in the Spring, it becomes us to be prepared to meet them; and for this End, to exert ourselves the approaching Winter, to compleat the Army agreeable to the new Establishment.

I have the Honour to be, Gentlemen, Your most obed. & very hble Servt.   J. H. Presidt.

LB (DNA: PCC, item 12A). Addressed: "To the States of New Hampshire, Massachusetts Bay, Rhode Island, Connecticut, Delaware, Maryland, Virginia, North Carolina, South Carolina, Georgia."

[1] These were Congress' November 19 resolutions on supply, magazines, and recruitment. *JCC*, 6:966. Apparently Hancock also sent the states a November 21 resolution on recruitment. *JCC*, 6:971. The RC of this letter to the Delaware Assembly, which is clearly dated November 20, contains this postscript: "Resolves of the 19th & 21st Novr enclosed." *Parke-Bernet Galleries Catalog*, no. 2569 (May 16, 1967), item 8. See also *Am. Archives*, 5th ser. 3:777. Hancock sent substantially the same letter this day to the New Jersey Assembly and the New York Convention. PCC, item 12A; and *Am. Archives*, 5th ser. 3:776. He also sent the first paragraph of the letter printed here to the Pennsylvania Council of Safety this day. PCC, item 12A; and *Am. Archives*, 5th ser. 3:776.

Robert Treat Paine to Daniel and Samuel Hughes

Gentlemen   Philada. Novr. 20. 1776

I have before me yrs. of the 12th Currt. & as you incline to make 12 p[ou]nd[er]s & under before you make any larger ones, you are desired to make 52 12 pndrs. & 20 9 pndrs. & to make them 18 diameters long & let them be as light as will be consistent with their bearing proof. I think our Cannon made in America have generally been too much banded abt. the Neck. You are also desired to cast 40 four pndrs. & 20 three pndrs. & let them be made about the same Number of Diameters. You are desired to get these Guns done as soon as possible & transport them to Baltimore. As to the heavier Cannon they will be wanted quite as soon as you can make them & we hope you will not neglect to make every Preparation to make them as soon as possible. There are in this Government some exceeding fine Guns which they got made in England last War. The 18 pndrs. are 9 ft. long from the base ring to the muzzle & wt. 40 & 41 cwt. 24pdrs are also 9 ft. long & wt. [49.2 cwt?] & the 32 pdrs. are 9 ft. long. These seem to be approved dimensions & if you can make as good ones it will be happy for us both. You may make preparation for Numbers of these sizes; the particular number you may be informed of seasonably enough. Give me Leave to mention that Mr. Hillegas saith he has not recd. the Receipt which I desired you to send him for the Sum of money sent you by Mr. Gallispe. In my Letter by him was inclosed the form of the Rect. wch. you'll please to sign & send either to the Treasurer or to me. Wishing you success I am

FC (MHi). Addressed: "To Messrs. Danl & Saml Hughes at Antietam Furnace Maryland."

Board of War to the
Pennsylvania Council of Safety

                                                            War Office,
Gentlemen   2 o'clock P.M. Thursday. [November 21, 1776]

I did myself the Honour of writing you about two Hours since informing your honourable Body that the Members of this Board were very ready to confer & co-operate with you in any Measures you should think necessary for the Defence of this State. The Congress having vested us with all their Powers we beg Leave to repeat that we are and shall be ready at all Times to meet a Committee from your Board to consult upon such Steps as may require our joint Exertions. Should you be inclined to hold a Conference you will be pleased to signify the same to Gentlemen, Your most obedt. Sevts.[1] By order of the Board of War.   E Rutledge

RC (NN). Endorsed: "War Office, 21 Novr. 1776."
¹ The board's first letter of this date to the council of safety has not been found. Congress had passed resolutions authorizing the board to confer with the council of safety about the defense of Philadelphia on November 11 and 14. *JCC*, 6:940, 950. There is no record of any conference between these two bodies on this subject, but see also Committee of Congress to William Livingston and to George Read, November 25, 1776.

Samuel Chase to the Maryland Council of Safety

Gentlemen,   Philada. Novr. 21st. 1776. Thursday Evening.
Congress have not received any further particulars of the Loss of Fort Washington, than the accounts published Novr. 19th. Capt. Ramsay arrived here this afternoon. I am informed by Dr. Rush, that he relates the affair in this Manner (from Colonel Cadwallader, who is released by the Enemy without any Parole, on the Request of General Prescott, for the Civilities & attendance of his father, the Doctor, on the general when a prisoner in this City). That fort Washington could not contain any thing near the Number of our Troops ordered for its Defence. That there were two Lines thrown up, the first at a considerable Distance from the fort, the second (and by far the strongest and capable of holding all the Garrison) much nearer to the fort. Our Troops were posted chiefly in the first Lines and were there attacked by the British Troops. At this Time a large Body of Hessians crossed Harlem River and landed within the second Lines, there not being any Lines, Breastworks or forces to oppose them. As soon as this Movement of the Enemy was discovered a Body was sent to oppose them. Of the British Troops there were only 40 privates & one Captain killed. Of the Hessians there were 200 privates killed, and 27 officers killed & wounded. Of our Troops *only* 30 privates, and a Colonel Baxter, and a Captain Miller, of Pennsylvania, killed. 2,200 of our Troops are prisoners. The fort was victualed for three Months, & amply supplied with Cannon and all military stores. If this account be true, we have again blundered. Our Loss is certainly very great. Dr. Rush says that Genl. Washington is abandoning fort Lee.
All is well at Tionderoga. I have this Evening received an exact account of the Enemies naval force on Lake Champlane.

1 Ship	16 Guns
1 Snow	16 Do.
1 Schooner	14 Do.
1 Do.	12 Do.
1 Do.	12 Do.
1 Sloop	10 Do.
1 Do.	10 Do. Bomb Ketch

1 large floating Battery, 24—18 pounders
20 Gondolas of 1 Gun each 12 & 18 pounders
15 Batteaus for boarding 1 Gun in each 3 pounder.
Manned with 1000 Men.

I have seen your opinion to our Commissioners that they should proceed and inlist our Troops for three Years.[1] I am apprehensive You do not see the opinion and object of Congress in its fullest Extent. The Congress will agree that Maryland may raise her Troops for three Years but have declared, & now hold, our State bound to contribute her proportion of the Expence attending the procuring of Lands for the officers & Soldiers furnished by other States for the War. We have proposed & urged in Congress, that the Question as to the procuring Lands at the Expence of the United States, and our claim that the back Lands acquired from the Crown of G.B. in the present War should be a common Stock for the benefit of the united States, and should remain open for the Determination of some future Congress. We have proposed that any State which may raise its Quota for the War, & gives a bounty in Lieu of Land should imdemnify the united States from any Claim from their officers & Soldiers who received an allowance in Lieu of Land, and that such State should not be chargeable to the united States for any part of the Expences attending the procuring of Lands for the officers & Soldiers of the other States who shall furnish Troops for the War. Both these propositions have been rejected. This Day a Resolve passed, that each State be at liberty to inlist for the War or three Years.[2] What our Commissioners will do I know not, nor can I advise them. I am amazed at the obstinancy of Congress.

The Paper for our Money is shipped this Day. Mr. Paca arrived this Morning so that We are now represented, but if Mr. Rumsey shod. go to Camp, We shall soon be without a Representation.

I am, Gent., with Respect & Regard, Your Most obedt. Servt.,

Saml. Chase

RC (MdAA).
[1] For this opinion, see the council of safety's November 17 letter to the commissioners, *Md. Archives*, 12:454.
[2] See *JCC*, 6:971.

John Hancock to George Washington

Sir,   Philada. Novr. 21t. 1776

I have the Honour to transmit the enclosed Resolves, in Obedience to the Commands of Congress. They are so explicit, that I shall only request your Attention to them.

You will percieve from the Vote of Congress, the Sense of that Body with Regard to the Necessity of furnishing the Troops for the new Army, as soon as possible; a Copy of which I have forwarded to the respective States agreeably to the Orders of Congress. I have also written to the States southward of Pennsylvania, inclusively, urging them to lay up Magazines of military Stores and Salt Provisions, for the Use of the Army & Militia, in Case it should be necessary to call them into the Field the approaching Winter.[1]

As our Enemies will doubtless open the Campaign early in the Spring, it is absolutely necessary we should prepare for them, and exert ourselves to fill up the Army agreeably to the new Establishment.

The Congress, to remove every Objection, and in Hopes of forwarding the recruiting Service, have resolved that the Troops may be engaged for three years, without presenting enlisting Rolls, both for that Term, and during the Continuance of the War, as ordered by a former Resolution.[2]

I have the Honour to be, with every Sentiment of Esteem, & Regard, Sir, your most obed. & very hble Serv.

John Hancock Presid.

[P.S.] The Inclos'd Letter from Mrs. Graydon for her Son, I should esteem a favr. you would order to be Convey'd if any Oppory.

RC (DLC). In the hand of Jacob Rush, with signature and postscript by Hancock.
[1] See *JCC*, 6:966, 971; and Hancock to Certain States, November 20, 1776. No separate letter from Hancock "to the States southward of Pennsylvania" on the subject of "Magazines of military Stores and Salt Provisions" has been found.
[2] See *JCC*, 6:944–45.

John Witherspoon to Richard Stockton

Sir   Princeton Novr 21. 1776

I beg the favour of you when at Philadelphia to lose as little time as possible in getting some orders given about the Sick in passing through this Town. I spoke to John Hill two Days ago who promised to take Care of them provided some Money was sent up for the Necessary Expences. I gave him reason to think that would be done & perhaps it would be best to give some money into Mr Kelseys hands to supply John Hill as it is needed. Whether it should be done in this Way or the Appointment immediately of a deputy quarter master to stay here I leave you but the Case is clamant & affecting & very well known to you. I have left some little Affairs to friends in Philadelphia for which I may perhaps be in a Day or two next week but cannot be certain.

There was sent to me this Day the inclosed List of medicines ordered for tending the Sick which if they are furnished it seems Dr Bainbridge whom I did not see has offered his assistance.[1] You

may do in this as you think best but nursing & attendance &
shelter to them are absolutely necessary. Wishing you a good Journey, I am, Dr Sir your most obedt, humble servant,

                                                   Jno Witherspoon

RC (DNA: PCC, item 78).
[1] This list is in PCC, item 78, 23:323.

Robert Treat Paine's Diary

                                                   November 22, 1776
    Rainy day. Heard that Fort Lee was abandoned by us & taken
possession of by the Enemy on Wednesday last.[1]

MS (MHi).
[1] Paine may have heard of Fort Lee's abandonment through the November 21
letter of Thomas Mifflin mentioned in Samuel Chase to the Maryland Council
of Safety, November 23, 1776. Confirmation arrived the 23d when General
Washington's November 19–21 letter to President Hancock was read in Congress.
See *JCC*, 6:975; and Washington, *Writings* (Fitzpatrick), 6:292–96.

Secret Committee Minutes of Proceedings

                                                   Novr. 22. 1776
    The Come. met. Present Messrs. Morris, Lee, Lewis, Whipple,
who is appointd. a member of this Come.[1] Order on the treasurer in
favr. of J. Brown for the use of J.H. Norton, for 16666 2/3 dlls
to pay for tobo. purchasd. by him in Virgia. for Acot. of the Contint.
(to be chargd Mr. Morris). Letter to Wm. Lux Esqr.[2] Contl. Agt.
at Baltimore in Maryld. inclosg. a bill of Loadg. for 29 brrls, 378
half brrls & 48 qur. barls. powdr. on board the Success, Capt.
Hill, orderg. him to receive the same, & to deliver it to the order
of the board of war. Note this powdr. was importd by Tho. Mumford Esqr. on public Acot. in consequence of his Contract.

MS (MH–H).
[1] William Whipple had been appointed in the room of Josiah Bartlett on
November 20. *JCC*, 6:968.
[2] Not found.

Secret Committee to William Bingham

Sir   In Secret Committee Philada. Novr. 22d. 1776
    We hope you may in due time receive this letter by Capt Stevens
of the Continental Schooner Lewis, which goes from hence to Carolina where we have directed her to be loaden with Rice & Indico

for your address. We hope she may arrive safe & deliver you a valuable Cargo, the Rice you will sell of course, but it is not likely the Indico will sell to advantage at Martinico & if that shou'd be the case you will please to reship it onbd. the first good French Vessel in which you can obtain freight for old France & Consign it to the order of Mr. Thos. Morris at whatever Port it goes to. Write him to make the best Sale he can of it, to Credit us for the net proceeds and apply the money to such uses as we have ordered, or may order. You must also Credit us for the net proceeds of what you sell in Martinico & apply the money to the uses we have directed or such as we may hereafter direct. Shou'd the West Indias be so Crowded with British Cruizers that you think it dangerous for this little thing to remain in those Seas, you may in that case Ship a quantity of Powder, Lead, or Bullets & Arms onboard her. Consign them to the Continental Agents at Charles Town or if he cannot get in there to the Continental agent in Georgia, John Wereat Esqr is agent in the latter State & Messrs. Levinus Clarkson & John Dorsius in the other. Tell them to keep those articles for Continental Service & they will receive orders respecting them from the Board of War or from us. To us you must send duplicate Invoices &c & charge us for the Cost. We are sir Your obed Servants

Fra Lewis	Richard Henry Lee
Robt Morris	Wm. Whipple

[*P.S.*] If you send the Schooner back with arms and ammunition write to the agents to reload her to you with another Cargo of Rice & Indico and then in the Spring you may send her here with arms &c.

RC (NN). Written by Morris and signed by Morris, Lee, Lewis, and Whipple.

Samuel Chase to the Maryland Council of Safety

Gentlemen   Philada. Nov. 23d. 1776, Saturday

Since I wrote you on yesterday[1] I saw a Letter from General Mifflin from Elizabeth Town dated the 21st Inst. in which he writes that the Enemy crossed the North River below Dobbes ferry in 400 Boats, and stole a March to fort Lee, which the Garrison evacuated leaving all their Artillery, Cannon, Stores, provisions and their Baggage.[2] We have not heard from the Army since the Generals Letter of the 19th. The alarm of a fleet sailing from New York with Troops is without any foundation. About 150 Transport & Store Ships sailed under Convoy of Commodore Shuldam in the Bristol, & two frigates, and are supposed to be bound to Ireland for provisions. This Information comes from General Mercer.

On yesterday I procured a State of our Treasury—as [of] a few days ago:

                                                          Dollars
        Emitted 20,000,000
        Expended 16,817,737
        In Treasury 3,182,263

This is for your private Information, & not to be made public.

The Congress have resolved to encrease their Navy—two frigates of 36 Guns are to be built in our State.

Many of the Congress, some true Friends, are uneasy at the Powers to the Delegates of Maryland, they are apprehensive, if made known, they will reach Lord Howe, and encourage him, and if the Courts of Europe should see them, it would prevent a foreign alliance. Some Reasons are given to countenance this opinion. I do not see why they should be published in the Journall. The powers relate to Peace & War, and can be of no Service to the public. I wish You would consider this Subject.[3]

In eight Days the Enlistment of the far greater part of our Army expires. I greatly doubt if We shall be able to prevail on the Troops to enter into the Service. I have some Hopes of obtaining our Wish from Congress. Our Commissioners will proceed on tomorrow I believe. However whether they do or not is a Secret. I am, Gent., with Respect & Regard, Your obedt. Servt.,   Saml. Chase

RC (MdAA).
    [1] For Chase's brief letter of November 22, which deals entirely with military subjects, see *Md. Archives*, 12:473.
    [2] Thomas Mifflin's letter to Robert Morris, dated "Elisabeth Town, 21 Novr. 1776, 8 O'Clock A.M.," is at the James S. Copley Library, La Jolla, Calif.
    [3] For the delegates' credentials, which had been presented to Congress on November 19, see *JCC*, 6:962. The Maryland Convention had authorized the Maryland delegates to concur with the other states "in forming a Confederation, and in making foreign Alliances; provided that such Confederation, when formed, be not binding upon this State without the Assent of the General Assembly." The prospect that individual states would determine what congressional decisions they would or would not honor threatened Congress' authority to speak with one voice for the United States, leading delegates to fear that the Howes would exploit Maryland's action to undermine American unity and that France would be reluctant to negotiate an alliance if individual states might subsequently withhold their assent from treaties negotiated by commissioners appointed by Congress. The delegates' credentials would be made public with the forthcoming publication of the proceedings of the recently adjourned Maryland Convention.
    For the council of safety's response to this and Chase's two preceding letters of November 21 and 22, see *Md. Archives*, 12:490–91. See also Matthew Tilghman to the Maryland Council of Safety, December 3, 1776, note.

John Hancock to the
Pennsylvania Council of Safety

Gentn.   Novr. 23. 1776

The foregoing Extract I Send you by Desire of Congress, & is the whole Information Congress are possess'd of relative to the Designs of the Enemy.[1]

I am Gentn, Your very huml Servt.   John Hancock Prst

RC (InU).
[1] Hancock sent the council of safety an extract of a November 20 letter from Gen. Hugh Mercer, the commander of the flying camp, stating that "the enemy intend to reduce Fort Lee, and then to march through the Jerseys to attack the city of Philadelphia." See JCC, 6:971; and Am. Archives, 5th ser. 3:778–79. For the council's response to this intelligence, see Am. Archives, 5th ser. 3:196.

Richard Henry Lee to Unknown

Philadelphia, 23rd November, 1776. ". . . You may observe by the letter accompanying this, that I had paid my respects to you some time ago, but Mr. Coulston disappointed me in not calling for my letter.[1] The enemy have been lately amazingly active on the banks of the North river, both forts Washington & Lee having become theirs. We have not had the particulars of either from authority, but you will see by the paper that they have paid a good price for the former, and report says our troops had evacuated the latter before they came up, but had not time to remove their stores. Indeed it had been determined to abandon Fort Lee as no longer useful after Mount Washington was lost. It is most clear, upon every view of things, that Gen. Howe must exert every nerve to effect something more than he has yet done with a land and marine force that all Europe had been taught to believe would in one Campaign crush America. Our enemies must become the laughing stock of Europe and the contempt even of their own nation if much, very much more than has yet been done is not expected before they go into winter quarters. Upon these principles it is said Gen. Howe proposes to endeavor to get to this City thro the Jersies—I think he will find this a difficult & dangerous enterprize—But I should have very little objections to his plundering the Quakers, if we can get the public stores removed, because they have taken such true pains to get him & his Hessians here. . . .

"The late proceedings of Portugal will probably produce a rupture between us & them. This foolish Court, that cannot injure us, that has every thing to loose on the water, dependent in Commerce, and cannot gain by war, has shut its ports to us, and, as some suppose, confiscated our Vessels.[2] If this last is done, it will not be long before we hear of some Brazelemen being brought into our ports. . . ."

Extract reprinted from Samuel T. Freeman & Co. Catalog. *The Frederick S. Peck Collection of American Historical Autographs* (May 13, 1947), pp. 11–12.

[1] Although Samuel T. Freeman & Co. suggested Landon Carter as the probable recipient of this letter, his nephew Robert Carter of Nomini Hall, Westmoreland County, may have been the actual recipient, since Lee originally expected that his November 10 letter to Robert Carter would be delivered by "Mr. Coulston." See Richard Henry Lee to Robert Carter, November 10, 1776, document note.

[2] See William Hooper to Joseph Hewes, November 16, 1776, note 8; and *JCC*, 6:1035–36.

Edward Rutledge to Robert R. Livingston

My dear Robert   Philada. Novr 23. 1776.

The Movements of the Enemy being entirely changed, and having great Reason to believe that ten thousand of General Howe's Army will in a few Days bend their Way to South Carolina I have determined to proceed to my native Home with all possible Expedition; to render my Country that Assistance in the Field which she will have a Right to expect. The Reverse of our Affairs within the few Days last past, should have taught us, had we been ignorant of it, that the Fortune of War is precarious indeed! As I mean to share every Danger in common with my Countrymen, & as the Number of the Enemy will be vastly superior to any Force which we shall be able to bring against them, it is far from being improbable that we shall never meet again; be this however as it may, I could not think of quitting Philadelphia before I had given you my best Wishes for every Happiness which human Nature is capable of receiving. May you enjoy a large portion of domestic Comfort, and public Esteem, & may you be able to establish the Independency of these States upon a firm & lasting Foundation!

As the Enemy have removed their Forces into Canada & every Reason to fear a junction of the two Armies, or an Attack from the North is now at an End, I wish you would immediately prevail upon Schuyler to come down to Congress. After embracing the first opportunity which may offer to clear up his Character, he will proceed to explain to the House the Steps which are necessary for preventing Carlton from making any Impression from Canada; & having obtained full powers for that purpose let him return to his Command to carry those Measures into Execution. By all Means obstruct the Navigation of Hudson's River, it surely may be done by the Forts in the Highlands. If it is not your Country will be lost, if it is, it will be safe. Pray establish in your own State as soon as possible a good Government. Let the Executive be strong, & set the Machine in Motion immediately. Can't you fall upon Ways and Means to clear your Country of Tories. 'Tis of vast Importance and if done at all must be done· this Winter. As soon as it can be conveniently done, you or Jay must attend Congress. I think one of you should accompany Schuyler. I have much more to say to you, but have not Time, nor have I leisure to correct this. Take it therefore & make it out as well as you can. Let me hear from you when you can find Time. Middleton or Hancock will forward any Letter directed to their Care & I shall be always happy to receive it. Adieu my dear Robert & believe me to be, your affectionate Friend.

Edward Rutledge

RC (James S. Copley Library, La Jolla, Calif.).

Secret Committee Minutes of Proceedings

Novr. 23d [1776]

Order on the Treasurer in favr. of Alexandr. Gillon for 8000 dlls in part paymt. for powdr. he deliverd the Board of War.

Come. met. Present Messrs. Morris, Lee, Whipple, Lewis. Resd. that the Contl. Agents to the Eastward be authorized to purchase ten good ships on public Acct. Six of wch. are to be sent into Cheseapeake Bay & the rest to S. Carolina there to load with tobo. & Rice, wch. is purchasd on Contl. Acct. A charter party for the Brig Cornelia & Molly was signd by the Come. Issued the followg. drafts on the Treasurer. In favor of Messrs. Abraham Livingston & Wm Turnbull for 20,000 dlls advanced them to purchase clothing for the Army in the Eastern States, where this Come. has sent them for this purpose. In favor of John R. Livingston Esqr. for 1250 dlls pd. him in part of his Acct. for manufacturing powder at his Mills in the State of N. York.[1]

MS (MH–H).
[1] The following paragraph appears at the end of this entry: "At this point the Congress being alarmed at the near approach of the Enemy to this City, removd to Baltimore where the Committee transacted the followg. business."
Apparently the committee did not keep a minute book while Congress was meeting in Baltimore, for the next entry in the Journal of the Secret Committee is Robert Morris' summary of transactions carried out during Congress' tenure there. See Summary of Secret Committee Proceedings, March 6, 1777.

John Hancock to George Washington

Sir,   Philada. Novr. 24th. 1776.

You will perceive from the enclosed Resolves, the Steps which Congress have thought proper to take in the present critical State of our Affairs.[1]

In Order to give you all possible Assistance in keeping the Army together at this Juncture, the Congress have appointed a Committee to repair to Head Quarters to co-opperate with you in the Business. They will set out tomorrow Morning; at which Time, the blank Commissions, ordered to be sent by the enclosed Resolve, shall be forwarded.[2]

You will please to order, from the Northern Department, such of the Troops as were raised in Pennsylvania & New Jersey, to join the Army immediately under your Command. Should there be a Necessity of supplying their Places, the Eastern States are to be applied to for that Purpose.

The Congress being desirous of exchanging Mr. Franklin for General Thompson, you will please to propose the Matter to Genl. Howe agreeably to the enclosed Resolve.[3] I have the Honour to be, with every Sentiment of Esteem & Respect, Sir, your most obed. and very hble Servt.   John Hancock Prest.

[*P.S.*] Your favr. of 21st is rec'd & laid before Congress.[4]

The Comee appointed to devise Measures for reinforcing you,[5] have taken sundry Steps for that End, of which the Comee. that sets out tomorrow will inform you, and make you fully acquainted with Particulars.

The Bearer hereof will proceed immediately to Genl. Schuyler with Dispatches, and will convey any Commands from you to the Northern Department.

RC (DLC). In the hand of Jacob Rush, with signature and first paragraph of postscript by Hancock.

[1] Hancock sent Washington an assortment of resolves passed between November 19 and 22, dealing with commissary returns, sick pay, military magazines, state troop quotas, officers' commissions, the appointment of a committee to consult with the general, the storage of hides and tallow, reinforcements, and the exchange of Gov. William Franklin. See *JCC*, 6:965–66, 972–74, 977.

[2] Little is known about the work of this committee, which consisted of William Paca, George Ross, and John Witherspoon. On about November 26 it appointed an assistant quartermaster and a commissary "to provide for a number of sick, and to take care of stores sent to Princeton," and later that month it conferred with Washington. When the committee returned to Congress is not known, but on January 18, 1777, Congress ordered the payment of $8,690.90 "To George Ross, Esq. for the expenses of himself, Dr. Witherspoon, and Mr. Paca, a committee of Congress, sent to New Jersey; and for cash he paid to Mr. Jacob Hier, for keeping an express horse at Princetown." See *JCC*, 6:973, 986, 7:48; and George Ross to James Wilson, November 26 and 28, 1776.

[3] See also Hancock to Washington, December 4, 1776.

[4] This letter is in PCC, item 152, 3:265–68; and Washington, *Writings* (Fitzpatrick), 6:292–96.

[5] See Committee of Congress to William Livingston, November 25, 1776, note.

Richard Henry Lee to Samuel Purviance, Jr.

Dear Sir,[1]   Philadelphia 24th Novr. 1776

You have imputed to the right cause my not answering your former letter sooner, it was indeed multiplicity of business.

Very long before your recommendation of Mr. Plunket came to hand, a Capt. Disney had been appointed Capt. of Marines on board the Virginia, upon the recommendation of Mr. Stone.

The Congress have determined to build in Maryland two Frigates of 36 guns each, and I make no doubt but that one at least of these will be built at Baltimore.[2] I suppose, when the Committee meets on Tuesday next, that directions concerning the building the new ships will issue to the respective States. Not a word has been yet said in Congress touching a quarrel with Portugal, no[r] will any such thing happen, I imagine, unless they should confiscate any of our Vessels.

It will give us much pleasure to hear that Capt. Nicholson is ready for sea, and I think we can furnish him from hence with one such Anchor as you mention. Capt. Biddles frigate Randolph of 32 guns is now completely ready except that she wants Men, which want we hope to remedy when the Vessels, daily expected, arrive. The Virginia & the Randolph cruising together, might bring us in some of the enemies scattering frigates that now go about, very badly manned, injuring our trade extremely. I wish therefore, that every effort were strained to get the Virginia ready. Our enemies army has been pretty busy since they retreated from the White Plains. Already they have got possession both of Mount Washington and Fort Lee, and they talk, or the Tories talk for them, strongly of their aiming at this City. I fancy they will find some difficulty, and not a little danger in the accomplishment of this part of their plan.

My compliments, if you please, to the reverend Mr. Allison, and my other friends in Baltimore.

If the Tories do not mend their manners, be more modest, and less noisy, they will shortly be haled over the coals in such a manner as will make this country too hot to hold them.

I am Sir your most obedient humble servant,

Richard Henry Lee

List of new Ships to be immediately undertaken

N. Hampshire	One Ship of	74 guns
Massachusetts	1 do.	Do. & 1 of 36 guns
Pennsylvania	1 do.	do. 1 of 18 do.
Maryland	2 do.	36 guns each
Virginia	2 do.	do. do. do.

P.S. Novr. 25. 1776. I thank you for your favor of the 22d. with its inclosures, and will answer your letter by next post, not being able now to do it with proper effect. I know we want Vessels both on Charter & to purchase in Virga. & Maryland. But more of this hereafter. Gen. Howe seems intent on this city.   R. H. Lee

RC (MdHi).
¹ Although originally addressed by Lee "General Stephen at Amboy in New Jersey," Lee subsequently carefully lined out these words. The content of the letter and Purviance's response clearly establish the identity of the recipient. For Purviance's response, dated November 29, see Morgan, *Naval Documents*, 7:326–28.
² See *JCC*, 6:970.

Benjamin Rumsey to the
Maryland Council of Safety

Sir   Philada. 24 Novr. 1776
We have continued in this place untill this Day in which We shall set off for the Camp not being able to proceed before neither under the Letter nor Spirit of our Commission.¹

Our Convention had certainly two capital Objects in View that as the Congress had engaged the Faith of the United States to furnish the Soldiery with the Bounty of Lands which they were to purchase it followed by Implication that the united States had None belonging to them in Common but must purchase of particular States who claimed a Monopoly in them and of Course might ruin those States who had None. Her View then was to have these Lands declared a common Stock as being purchased (if ever purchased) by the joint Blood and Treasure of the Confederacy or find no Land to her Ruin.

The first Satisfaction She received on this Head was that She might inlist for three Year and give the 20 Doll. Bounty, but must give the Soldiers the Alternative to inlist during the War on the first Conditions—Opening two Rolls for the Purpose.

This not pleasing they Resolve again that the Commissioners may proceed to inlist for three Years upon one Roll alone keeping it always in View that it was better to inlist during the War if it did not retard the Service.

This Resolution keeping up the first Bone of Contention the Land and by Implication that the States had none still not answering Expectation, The Congress further resolved that any Resolutions that had passed should neither operate to weaken or strengthen the Claim of the United States or any of them to any Back Lands by which this point that has given such Uneasiness in our Province will be saved & be discussed hereafter in our future Confederacy.

The Second point they had in View was the point of Taxation which they thought unequal being rated on Slaves as well as Whites.

This has been expressly named as the Mode as to 6 Millions of Dollars. As to 14 more the same Declaration is made as in the Article of Land that the proportion of sinking it shall be adjusted hereafter on each State and that Nothing heretofore done shall strengthen or weaken such Enquiry or Questions.

Our Province having in some Measure obtained a Satisfaction on those two Heads Nothing now remains but to consider whether the Convention having impowered Us to proceed and inlist for and during the War on the 20 Dollars We can go on the Terms of three Years and the same Bounty being for a less Term and in this point we are pretty generally agreed to depart from the Letter to preserve the Spirit.

Fort Lee has followed the same Fate as Fort Washington except that our Powder and Men with two 12 Pounders escaped. We lost 1000 Barrells of Flour & 300 Tents, better than 400 of the Maryland Troops were taken in and about Fort Washington where Major Price writes our Brother Commissioner's Son fell as well as Colo. Williams of the Rifle Battallion bravely fighting in his Country's Cause.

I am greatly surprised that these Britons are so bent on surprising and that we should be so often so Surprised in Long Island, York Island, White Plains, Fort Washington and now Fort Lee; 'tho' the Enemy crossed at Dobbs Ferry they became not visible 'till within Sight of the Fort. In Short there are so many of them that I shall be all Wonder and Surprise or learn in the Poets Phrase Nil admirari.

I am Sir, Your most humble Servt.,   Benjamin Rumsey

[P.S.] I am afraid You have not sent Commissions enough. Wrote in the Midst of Company.

RC (MdAA). Addressed: "The Honble Daniel of St. Thomas Jenifer Esqr. at Annapolis."

[1] Rumsey clearly wrote this letter in his capacity as one of the commissioners appointed by the Maryland Convention to promote the enlistment of Maryland troops. He did not attend Congress until December 12, although he had been elected a delegate on November 10 and was regarded by his fellow delegates as one of the members of the Maryland delegation. He had been in Philadelphia since October 19 conferring and negotiating over terms to be offered troops recruited into the Maryland Continental battalions; after mid-November it is pointless to attempt to establish precisely under what authority he was operating at particular moments. See JCC, 6:962; John Hancock to the Maryland Convention, November 4, note 1; Samuel Chase to the Maryland Council of Safety, November 23; and Benjamin Rumsey to John Hall?, December 19, 1776.

Edward Rutledge to John Jay

My dear Jay   Philada. Novr. 24th. 1776.

I expected long e'er this to have been seated quietly at home; but the Progress which the Enemy had made and seem'd likely to make into your Country, Induced me to suspend My Resolution which I came to several Months ago, and assist with the whole of my Power (little enough God knows) a State which appear'd to be marked for Destruction. The Storm however has past over you; & tho' I have Reason to dread its bursting upon the Heads of my Countrymen I cannot but most sincerely congratulate you upon the Event. I wish you may improve the Time, and if you concur with me in Sentiment it will be improved in the following manner. Let Schuyler whose Reputation has been deeply wounded by the Malevolence of party Spirit immediately repair to Congress, & after establishing himself in the good opinion of his Countrymen, by a fair & open Enquiry into his Conduct, concert with the House such a Plan as he shall think will effectually secure *all* the upper Country of New York against the Attacks of the Enemy, which Plan being agreed to by the House, give him full Powers to effect it, & send him off with all possible Dispatch to carry it into Execution. Let Steps be taken to place *real* Obstructions in the North River at least in that part of it which can be commanded by Fort Montgomery & the other Fort in the High Lands. If these things be done & that soon, your Country I think will be safe, provided you establish a good Government, with a strong Executive. A pure Democracy may possibly do when patriotism is the ruling Passion, but when a State abounds in Rascals (as is the case with too many at this day) you must suppress a little of that Popular Spirit, vest the executive powers of Government in an individual that they may have Vigor, & let them be as ample as is consistent with the great Outline of Freedom. As several of the Reasons which operated against you, or Livingstons quitting your State are now removed, I think you would be of vast Service in Congress. You know that Body possesses its Share of human Weakness, & that it is not impossible for the Members of that House to have their Attention engrossed by Subjects which might as well be postponed for the present, whilst such as require Dispatch have been, I had almost said, neglected. This may be the case with the Measures which should be taken for the Defence of your State. It is therefore your Interest & your Duty, if you are not prevented by some superior public Concern, to attend the House, & that soon; you have a Right to demand their attention, & I think they will give you early Assistance.

Every Intelligence from New York for the last ten Days convinces me that the Enemy are preparing to attack my State with a large Body of Troops. I shall take the Wings of the morning & hasten to my native home; where I shall endeavour to render my Country more Service in the Field that I have been able to render her in the Cabinet. I have therefore very little time to write, & have to lengthen this Letter. I could not however think of quitting this part of the Continent without writing you what appeared to me of Consequence, especially when I consider that it is probable, or at least possible, that this may be the last time I may have it in my power to give you any Evidence of my Affection. I shall add no more than that you have my best Wishes for your Happiness & that if I fall in the Defence of my Country, it will alleviate my Misfortune to think that it is in support of the best of Causes, & that I am esteem'd by one of the best of Men. God bless you. Adieu my Friend. Yours Sincerely.   E. Rutledge

RC (NNC).

Oliver Wolcott to Laura Wolcott

My Dear,   Philidelpa 24t Novr. 1776
    I Wrote to you the 12 inst by Col Williams which you have probably recd. On the 16t I put a Letter for you into the Post office, also one to Mr Adams and Lyman which I hope will go safe.[1] Mr Lyman favour of the 16 has come to hand, by which I had the Pleasure of being informed of your and Family's Wellfare. By the Blessing of God I am well, and think I have obtained a radical Cure of those bilious disorders which have for so long a time troubled me. Nothing but perserverance in a Course of Medicine will free a Person from those Disorders when they are once pretty deeply rooted.
    The Loss of Fort Lee you have or will hear of. The Enemy have now a free Passage up the N River—whether they will improve it this Season to endeavour to get Possession of the highlands or Make an attempt for this City, or perform any Other Enterprize Time must discover.
    I have been alone in the Connecticut Delegation since Col Williams went home. Mr Sherman is dayly expected, but I suppose he finds a good deal of Dificullty in executing his Business which he was employed in by the Colony, with the Army.[2]
    Unless Col Williams tho't the present times less difficult, than when his Presence here was first tho't to be so Very essential I can assign no Reason why he went off, except what he himself gave, which was that he did not know wheither he should do any good if he staid. A most puzzling Question, and which probably will be a Matter of ever lasting Doupt—but the true Reason of his Re-

turn was, that he did not know any particular personal or Family Interest to induce him to tarry longer.

My Kindest Love to my Children and Friends and be assured that I am yours, with the sincerest affection,   Oliver Wolcott

P.S. I know not Wheither it is expected by the Colony that I should soon Return or not. I Saw Sometime ago in a Philidelpa Paper that the former Connecticut Delegates were reelected with the Addition of Mr Law. This is all that I have heard, indeed I have about as much Intelligence from Asia as from Connecticut, but however I suppose I shall hear more about it before January. In hast.

RC (CtHi).
  ¹ Wolcott's letter to Samuel Lyman has not been found.
  ² At the October session of the Connecticut Assembly Roger Sherman had been appointed to a committee charged with reorganizing the Connecticut regiments at Washington's headquarters. *A Historical Collection, from Official Records, Files, &c., of the Part Sustained by Connecticut, during the War of the Revolution,* comp. Royal R. Hinman (Hartford: E. Gleason, 1842), p. 240.

Committee of Congress to William Livingston

Sir,   Philada. 25th Novr. 1776

When Congress took into their Consideration the probable Views of General Howe, the Strength of his Army, the Insufficiency of the Numbers under General Washington, and the Danger of an almost total Dissolution of our Army between the Discharge of the Men now in Service, and the Inlistment of others, they found it indispensably necessary that Application should be made to the States on this Side of Hudson's River nearest the Scene of War, immediately to call forth their Militia or a part of them, in order to reinforce Gen. Washington. Congress have done Us the Honor of appointing Us a Committee to devise and execute the Means most effectual for this Purpose. In the Resolutions transmitted to you herewith,¹ you will see what we consider as the most expeditious, the least burthensome, and the most efficacious Mode of obtaining real Aid from the Militia. We are far however from intending that the Plan we have laid down, should preclude the State of New Jersey from adopting any other, which their superior Knowledge of their own Situation and Circumstances may point out as most agreeable and effectual. Whatever Sums of Money you may want for carrying on this necessary and important Service, will be paid to your Order at the continental Treasury in this City. We have much Dependance on the vigorous Exertions of New Jersey.

Since the Committee agreed to the Resolutions before mentioned, Congress have received farther Intelligence from General Mifflin

265

IN CONGRESS,
NOVEMBER 23, 1776.

RESOLVED, That a Committee of Five be appointed, with full powers to devise and execute measures for effectually reinforcing General Washington, and obstructing the progress of General Howe's army, and that they proceed immediately on this business.

THE members chosen, Mr. WILSON, Mr. SMITH, Mr. CHASE, Mr. CLYMER, and Mr. STOCKDEN.

JOHN HANCOCK, PRESIDENT.

THE Committee before mentioned have come to the following Resolutions—

RESOLVED, That it be recommended to the Commanding Officers of the several battalions of Associators in Pennsylvania immediately to call together the battalions respectively under their command; and to select out of each battalion one company, or, if possible, two companies of Volunteers.

THAT each company consist of seventy-six privates, one Drummer, one Fifer, four Corporals, and four Serjeants, under the command of a Captain, two Lieutenants, and one Ensign.

THAT the field officers of each battalion, or such of them as shall be present, with the approbation and concurrence of the Volunteers, appoint the commissioned and non-commissioned officers of each company.

THAT the companies be engaged in the service of the United States till the tenth day of March next, unless sooner discharged by Congress; and be entitled to a pair of shoes and stockings, and to the same rations and the same monthly pay with the other troops on the Continental Establishment, to commence from the time of their enrolment.

THAT the form of the enrolment be as follows: I——hereby promise and engage to enter into the service of the United States, and to serve them till the tenth day of March next, unless sooner discharged by Congress; and to observe and obey the orders of Congress, and the orders of the Generals and Officers set over me by them.

THAT in order to supply the companies with arms, accoutrements, and other necessaries, the field officers of each battalion, or any of them, be empowered and directed to purchase, and, if they cannot purchase, to impress arms, cartouch-boxes, blankets, shoes, stockings, and other necessaries for the use of the said companies.

THAT the articles impressed be appraised by persons to be appointed by the field officers or any of them for that purpose.

THAT the field officers or any of them give certificates of the value of the articles so purchased or appraised, which certificates shall be deemed sufficient vouchers to the persons to whom they shall be given, or to their assigns, for the respective sums therein mentioned, and shall be paid at the Continental Treasury.

THAT the Captains march their companies with the utmost expedition, and join the army under General Washington.

THAT the Council of Safety of Pennsylvania be empowered and directed to form the said companies into battalions; and to adopt such farther measures as they may find necessary for the march and equipment of the said companies; and particularly to collect, in the city of Philadelphia and its neighbourhood, blankets and other necessaries for their use, and to seize such articles, paying the value of them, if they cannot otherwise be procured.

THAT one month's pay be advanced to each Volunteer upon his enrolment; and that the Council of Safety be supplied with money for this purpose.

THAT the Council of Safety be requested to forward by express the foregoing Resolutions to the Commanding Officers of the several battalions of the State of Pennsylvania.

PHILADELPHIA,
November 24, 1776.

JAMES WILSON,
GEORGE CLYMER,
JAMES SMITH,
SAMUEL CHASE.

IN COUNCIL OF SAFETY,
PHILADELPHIA, *November* 24, 1776.

SIR,

GENERAL HOWE, after having reduced Fort Washington, and obtained possession of Fort Lee, is now directing his operations against New-Jersey. There is much reason to believe that his views extend to the city of Philadelphia. The forces in New-Jersey may be insufficient to oppose his progress: It is therefore indispensably requisite for the preservation of this State, and the support of the general cause, that troops be immediately raised to re-inforce General Washington. The measures adopted for this purpose you will learn from the resolutions enclosed. In this time of danger it is unnecessary to use arguments with freemen, who are determined never to lose that character but with their lives. We have entire confidence, that you and the battalion under your command, will, upon this occasion, give the strongest proofs of vigour and patriotism.

A JUDICIOUS choice of the officers will do honour to the volunteers, and produce essential advantages to the service, for it is our opinion that the volunteers ought to have the election of them, and we recommend to you the utmost circumspection and care, not only in the persons you may recommend to them, but also in the manner of doing it.—As this Council can only have in view the interest of the whole, you may safely assure the people of our care and attention in the appointment of the field officers, so as, at the same time, to forward the service, and, as much as possible, to give satisfaction to the people.

A PAY-MASTER will be appointed for each battalion, and the volunteers may depend on having their pay regularly.—The Colonel or Commanding Officer ought to muster each company and send a certificate thereof to this Board.

MONEY is forwarded to   in order to advance the month's pay—to him you will please to apply for what money will be necessary in your battalion for that purpose.   *By Order of the Council,*

DAVID RITTENHOUSE, VICE PRESIDENT.

To the Colonel or Commanding Officer of the   Battalion of

Committee of Congress Resolves, November 24, 1776

upon which they have requested that *all* the Militia of the Counties of Pennsylvania nearest to Delaware should be called forth. We submit the Propriety of adopting similar Measures in New Jersey.

We are Sir with the greatest Regard, Your most obedt hum Servants,   James Wilson

Geo Clymer

Samuel Chase

RC (NHi). Written by Clymer and signed by Clymer, Chase, and Wilson.

[1] On November 23 Congress appointed Samuel Chase, George Clymer, James Smith, Richard Stockton, and James Wilson as a committee "to devise and execute measures for effectually reinforcing General Washington, and obstructing the progress of General Howe's army." Accordingly, the committee met the following day with the members of the Pennsylvania Assembly and Council of Safety that were immediately available, after which they issued a series of resolutions for mobilizing the militia and distributed them as a broadside to the commanding officers of the various battalions of Pennsylvania associators. For these resolutions, which carried the force of congressional resolves and embodied a Continental fiscal commitment but were never entered on the journals, see illustration. They were accompanied by an order by the Pennsylvania Council of Safety and were reprinted in several newspapers. See also *JCC*, 6:975–76; PCC, item 69, fol. 265; and *Pa. Council Minutes*, 11:14.

Committee of Congress to George Read

Sir   Philada. Novr. 25th. 1776

The enclosed Resolutions will inform You of the Steps adopted in this State for the immediate reinforcement of the Army under the command of General Washington.[1] We wish for Assistance from the State of Delaware, & cannot doubt their alacrity in furnishing every Aid in their Power, in this Hour of common Danger.

We know not to whom our Application ought to be made but we earnestly intreat your Influence & Exertions with the proper Authority of your State to send a speedy Assistance of 500 Volunteers if possible, on the same Terms & Times of Service with the Volunteers from this State. We are Sir, with great Regard, Your most obedt. hum Servs,   James Wilson

Copy   Geo Clymer

Saml Chase

Tr (Facsimile, *Parke-Bernet Galleries Catalog*, May 16, 1967, item 8).

[1] For these resolutions, see the note to the committee's letter in the preceding entry and accompanying illustration. The writer of the present letter used an asterisk to note, at the foot of the document, that the enclosures were "published in all the Newspapers."

Richard Henry Lee to John Page?

Dear Sir,[1]   Philadelphia 25th Novr. 1776

I am greatly concerned that the necessity of immediate and principal attention to our military securities should be overlookt for any other consideration whatever. However I hope the most complete regard will be paid to this business before the Assembly disperses. Portsmouth is an Object of capital concern and deserves a constant and a powerful guard in my opinion, since it presents so fine and convenient a harbour for our Vessels to retire to if pursued, and at the same time so convenient for building. No object I think deserves our attention more than Ships and Seamen, and therefore every encouragement should be given to building the former and raising & bringing in the latter. Gen. Howes success against the forts Washington and Lee has so raised his hopes as to have turned his eyes upon this City, and here he is said to intend his next visit by marching his army thro the Jerseys, where Gen. Washington has at present, not quite 6000 men to oppose him. Much alarm has taken place here on this account, but I hope it will rouse such a spirit as must compel the Tyrants troops to go quickly into Winter quarters. It is certainly very necessary for their mighty force, from which the immediate conquest of all N. America was confidently affirmed, to do a great deal more than they have done to prevent them & their Master from falling under the contempt of Europe. We are just furnished with a prize ship sent in here by a small Continental Cruiser freighted with 13,000 silver dollars and some other merchandise.

I hope our manufacturers have not lost sight of Salt Petre and Gun powder. I wish to be Independent indeed, not of G.B. only, but of the whole world. Therefore Cannon, Small Arms, Saltpetre, Gunpowder & discipline should be our objects.

We hear from N. York that Ld. Dunmore has certainly sailed for England, but not before he had so conducted himself that no Officer would speak to him or keep company with him.

Farewell dear Sir, be healthy & happy,

Richard Henry Lee

RC (MH–H).

[1] Although the recipient's identity has been taken from the inside address, "Honbe John Page," which was obviously added at a latter date by an unknown hand, comparison of this letter with Lee's November 4 letter to Page suggests that both were directed to the same person. In a December 6 letter to Lee, Edmund Pendleton acknowledged receipt of "your obliging favor of the 25th of November," but the content of Pendleton's letter indicates only that Richard Henry wrote another letter this date which has not been found. Edmund Pendleton, *The Letters and Papers of Edmund Pendleton, 1734–1803*, ed. David J. Mays, 2 vols. (Charlottesville: University Press of Virginia, 1967), 1:203–4.

Samuel Chase to the
Maryland Council of Safety

Gentlemen,   Philadelphia Novr. 26th. 1776 Tuesday Morning

In my last I expressed some Hopes of prevailing on Congress to give our State some Satisfaction as to the back Lands, and the Mode by which the Proportion of the Expences of the War was to be paid by each State. In this Expectation I was delayed & disappointed for two Days, by Mr. Jenifers mentioning that our Commissioners had your orders to proceed. By an obstinate perseverance the enclosed Resolve was obtained last Saturday;[1] on Sunday afternoon our Commissioners left this City. On yesterday the Commissioners from Congress, of which Mr. Paca is one, also sett off for the Camps. Much depends on their Success.

The Reduction of fort Washington and easy Possession obtained of fort Lee has greatly encouraged General Howe, and probably induced him to carry on the Campain much longer than he would otherwise have done. There is great Reason to beleive his Views extend to this City. On Sunday Evening General Mifflin arrived in this City. Our Army, under the Command of General Washington in the Jerseys are about 6,000, of which the Service of about 1500 expires on Sunday next. General Lee has about 11000 effectives on the west Side of North River, of which the Enlistment of about 3000 expires on the same Day. The Enemy have about 21,000 effectives. They can spare about 16,000 & leave a sufficient Garrison to maintain New York. Genl. Howe has 6,000 in the Jerseys opposite to Newark. In this State it is proposed to call out all the Militia of four Countys & this City immediately for Six Weeks. Chester, Bucks, Northampton and Philadelphia Counties are the nearest to the Jerseys, & it is also proposed to call out a Company of Volunteers from each Battalion in this state to enroll 'till 10th March next.

The preservation of this State & the Jerseys and, in great Measure, the common Safety will depend on the Success of this Requisition.

New Jersey is also called on for Aid, Delaware is solicitted, and if our State could afford any assistance in Time an application would also be made to her.

If the present Cloud should be happily dispersed, the new Levies will be the first object of your attention. We can neither prosecute the War, nor obtain honorable Terms of Peace without an Army. The Enlistment will be only for three years, on the bounty of 20 Dollars, and the annual Cloathing, or the 20 Dollars in Lieu thereof.[2] By the Resolves of Congress, I am informed, the recruiting officers are intitled to 10s for each man inlisted & passed, and 10s per week for provisions till the Recruits arrive to some Place where they can be furnished by the Continental Commissaries.[3]

We have certain Intelligence that a Number of Ships, of the smallest Draught of Water, sufficient to carry 10,000 Troops, are now lying ready in the North River, with Fascines on their Sides. The Destination of this fleet is uncertain, some conjecture to land a Body of Troops at South Amboy, which is very probable, if this City is the object with Mr. Howe. Others guess Virginia or South Carolina. The latter is the most suspicious because if they succeed against Charles Town, they can pass the Winter there. A few Days will releive Us from Conjecture.

I submit to You the Propriety of ordering the Artillery Companies at Baltimore Town & Annapolis, be exercised daily if the Weather will permit, & at least three Times a Week. Practice alone can make Artillerists. In our Army, we destroy as many of our own People as of the Enemy.

Your Letter of the 22d I received by yesterdays Post.[4] We have paid for the Paper, there are not 400 Dollars in Mr Paca's Hands. Would it not be proper to transmit the account agt. Congress, or by some Means lodge Money here to exchange our Money.

I am, Gentn., with Respect, your obedt. Servt.,

Saml Chase

[P.S.] I delivered the Resolves relative to Virginia to the Delegates of that State.

RC (MdAA).
    [1] See JCC, 6:978.
    [2] For Congress' resolves on this subject of September 16, October 8, and November 21, see JCC, 5:762-63, 855, 6:971.
    [3] See JCC, 4:63-64, 341.
    [4] Md. Archives, 12:471-72.

Elbridge Gerry to James Warren

November 26, 1776 [1]

I have lately ordered three Cargoes of Fish to be Shipped for the purpose of importing military Stores, one half of which I shall resign on my own Account & the other half reserve untill you can have an Opportunity of Communicating the matter to the honerable assembly & informing me whether it is wanted for the State. The Secret Committee were desirous of having the whole to make Remittances for articles which they had ordered, but this I declined . . .[2] Should Measures be not adopted before this reaches you for importing any of the military Stores recommended by Congress, I suppose the Small Concern mentioned above will be considered as very inadequate, & knowing the difficulty in the eastern States to obtain articles for Exportation I have enquired into the prices of produce in the Southern Governments. . . . the late Events at New York relative to Forts Washington & Lee must be known before this reaches you; I wish they may be forgot as there appeared to me Want of Generalship. I have the pleasure to alleviate this by informing you that the Disposition of the Court of France is exceedingly favourable, Such proofs were given of this so long ago as June last (but lately discovered to Congress), as were not expected; I am not at liberty to say more on this matter at present.[3] A Mr. Chamberlain who will probably bring the Money, has given some Relation of his Discoveries relative to the manufacturing of Field pieces of Wrought Iron, and other Military Improvements; I have desired him to open the matter to the Assembly and if his Accounts correspond with Facts think he merits their assistance.

MS not found; reprinted from A. S. W. Rosenbach, *The History of America in Documents*, 3 vols. (Philadelphia: The Rosenbach Co., 1949), 1:85, item 285; and *George D. Smith Autograph Letters* (New York: 898 items, n.d.), item 291.

[1] Although Burnett printed a brief extract of this letter from a transcript obtained from Stan V. Henkels and tentatively identified the recipient as Joseph Trumbull, it seems clear that James Warren was the recipient. Its content leaves little doubt that it was this document Gerry had in mind when, two days later, he referred Warren to "what I wrote you by Mr. Chamberlain," and when in February he described to the Massachusetts Board of War "the proposals made in my letter to General Warren from Philadelphia the 26th November." See Burnett, *Letters*, 2:164–65, 173; Gerry to James Warren, November 28, 1776; and Gerry to the Massachusetts Board of War, February 2, 1777.

A letter Gerry wrote to Joseph Trumbull this day is mentioned in his December 7 letter to Trumbull, a reference that led Burnett to suggest Trumbull as the recipient of the document printed here, but that letter has not been found.

[2] Elipses in Tr, here and below.

[3] Remainder of entry taken from George D. Smith catalog.

John Hancock to George Washington

Sir,   Philada. Novr. 26th. 1776.

In Consequence of your Dispatches by Genl. Mifflin, who arrived here on Sunday Evening, the Congress, the next Day, came to the enclosed Resolves, which I do myself the Honour of forwarding in Obedience to their Commands. They will inform you of the Steps taken to reinforce your Army at this Juncture.[1]

The Urgency of Affairs, will, I trust, induce the Militia to exert themselves in a proper Manner on this Occasion; as it is extremely evident that Nothing but such an Exertion will be effectual in our present Situation.

The Congress have ordered General Mifflin to stay in this City, until you shall require his Attendance at Head Quarters, being well convinced that his Influence, which is very considerable over the Associators of this Place, will be employed to spirit them on to the most vigorous Measures.[2] I have the Honour to be with every Sentiment of Esteem & Respect, Sir, your most obed. & very hble Servt.

John Hancock Presidt

RC (DLC). In the hand of Jacob Rush and signed by Hancock.

[1] For these resolves, see *JCC*, 6:979–80. For Washington's November 23 letter, which Mifflin had delivered the 24th, see PCC, item 152, 3:269–73; Washington, *Writings* (Fitzpatrick), 6:303–4; and *Am. Archives*, 5th ser. 3:822.

[2] See *JCC*, 6:980.

George Ross to James Wilson

Dear Willson   Prince Town Nov. 26th. 1776

The distress of our Soldiers who I have met almost naked and hardly able to walk or rather wade through the mud has given infinite pain but I shudder to tell you that they fall dead on the road with their packs on their backs or are found accidentally perishing in hay lofts. There has indeed been too much Inattention to the sick. Pray God forgive the negligence wherever it may be.

We have done somewhat to remidy the Evil for which referr you to our letter to Congress.[1]

You shall hear from me by every opportunity. My love to Mrs. Turner & Juliana and to my Polly if you see her. I am, yrs. Affectly.

Geo. Ross

RC (PHi).

[1] Ross, William Paca, and John Witherspoon had been appointed on November 22 a committee to consult with General Washington at headquarters on measures for augmenting and stabilizing the army. "Our letter to Congress" is undoubtedly the one received on November 27, to which Congress responded by approving the committee's appointment of "an assistant quarter master and commissary, to provide for a number of sick, and to take care of stores sent to Princeton." See *JCC*, 6:973, 986. The letter has not been found.

Elbridge Gerry to Unknown

Sir [1]   Philadelphia 27th Novr 1776

In Answer to your Favour of the 15th I am most concerned to hear that Medicines are wanted for the Army; this has been the Complaint of the northern Army untill of late a full supply has been sent them. Doctor Hall a Member of Congress & of the Medical Committee has been mentioned to Doctor Foster as a proper Gentleman to be consulted on the Measure, & will undoubtedly take Care & remedy the Difficulty.

With respect to Subdirectors I think it not improbable that they will be necessary; & that You may stand Candidate when Congress shall think proper to make an Establishment, It may be convenient to have a Recommendation from the Director, in which I think the Names of the five or six Gentlemen who have officiated as hospital Surgeons should be mentioned. I have conferred with Doctor Foster & he will communicate the substance of the Interview. I remain sir in Haste your Friend & hum ser,

E Gerry

RC (CtY).

[1] Although the intended recipient of this letter cannot be positively identified, it is possible that Gerry directed it to John Warren. Warren (1753–1815), a brother of the slain revolutionary leader Joseph Warren and a Salem, Mass., physician who was currently surgeon general of the Continental hospital at Hackensack, N.J., subsequently wrote a letter to Gerry in which he discussed the reorganization of the medical department and mentioned the possibility of his appointment as an "Assistant Director." John Warren to Elbridge Gerry, February 26, 1777, RG 27, PHarH. Later in the war Warren served as senior surgeon of the Continental hospital in Boston. Shipton, *Harvard Graduates*, 17:655–69.

Francis Lewis to the New York Convention

Gentlemen   Phila. 27th Novr. 1776.

Upon the information given to the marine committee by Capt. Patrick Dennis, of the then state of the frigates built at Poughkeepsie, the said committee desired me to inform you that it was their opinion, those ships being launched should as soon as possible be sent up to Esopus creek, to be there laid up for the winter, as there appears at present no prospect of bringing them into service for this year. And it is their opinion that a lieutenant of marines be appointed, with orders given him to immediately enlist thirty marines to guard those frigates during winter, and that all such stores that are remaining, together with those belonging to such vessels as were ordered to be sunk in the North and East rivers, be also put under the care of said lieutenant of marines.

That Capt. Dennis, who has at present the custody of all the rigging, &c. belonging to the vessels so sunk, be directed to deliver the same to said lieutenant, furnishing him with an inventory of the particulars; a copy thereof to be signed by the lieutenant, and transmitted to the marine committee, who apprehend the stores aforesaid will be this winter wanted by Genl. Schuyler.

In regard to the destination of the frigates for the winter, if you see any likelihood of their being brought into use, they are submitted entirely to your direction. Upon your nominating the lieutenant, his commission will be sent up to you as you, are more immediately upon the spot. In regard to the frigates, the marine

committee refers it to your judgment to direct what may be necessary to be done with them, and desires you would advise them thereof.[1]
I am respectfully, sirs, Your very hble. servt.   F. Lewis.

MS not found; reprinted from *Journals of N.Y. Prov. Cong.*, 1:730.
[1] For the convention's December 4 resolves respecting the frigates at Pough-keepsie and December 5 reply to Lewis, see *Am. Archives*, 5th ser. 3:355, 357.

Elbridge Gerry to James Warren

Dear Sir [1]   Philadelphia 28th. Nov. 1776
In addition to what I wrote you by Mr. Chamberlain give me leave to inform you that I shall order such a part of the amount of the Schooner Rockingham & Cargo as may be saved by Mess. Gardoque & Sons, to be remitted in Military Stores if the Honorable Assembly approve thereof.[2] I shall be glad to know their sentiments on the matter [3] & remain, Sir, Yours Sincerely,   E Gerry

Tr (DLC).
[1] Although the copyist who made this transcript wrote "Hon James Bowdoin Esq" for the inside address, the recipient is clearly James Warren. The printed journals of the Massachusetts House of Representatives note that on December 24, 1776—the date this letter was first read in the House—"A letter from Elbridge Gerry to Mr. Speaker Warren read and committed to Mr. Gardner, Mr. Perry and Judge Cushing." Massachusetts House Journal, December 24, 1776, p. 198. DLC (ESR).
[2] For "what I wrote you by Mr. Chamberlain," see Gerry to James Warren, November 26, 1776.
[3] On December 30, 1776, the general court recommended that the proceeds of the *Rockingham* be "vested in Military Stores." Massachusetts General Court Resolves, Force Papers, DLC. However, the Massachusetts Board of War subsequently requested that the proceeds of the *Rockingham* be invested in "Duck, Cordage, and Blankets" rather than military stores, a decision the board communicated to Gerry on January 14, 1777. Morgan, *Naval Documents*, 7:949–50. See also Gerry to the Massachusetts Board of War, February 2, 1777.

George Ross to James Wilson

Dear Wilson   Eliza. Town 28th Novr. 1776
I met the Genl. this morning retreating from Newark to this Place with about 2000 Men at Most and another division of not quite that Number are expected in half an hour. They continue their March through this place to Brunswick where we are again to make a Stand in hopes of a reinforcemt. The Enemy are now at Newark & about 8000 Strong and tis Supposed intend for Philada. I hope we shall rouse from our Lethergy & play the part of men who merit freedom. We have it in our power if we will exert our

whole Force at this crisis. Tis not a time to trifle for our scituation
is aut Caesar aut Nullus. My best respects to the Presidt. & Gent.
of Congress but can say nothing more than what I have now said to
you.[1] Love to all Friends &c. Yors. affectly.,   Geo. Ross

RC (PHi).
  [1] John Witherspoon, who with Ross and William Paca had been sent to consult
with General Washington at headquarters on defense measures, wrote the following, mutilated letter to William Livingston the next day asking him "to communicate what I learned" to the New Jersey Council and Assembly.
  "The General found his Army altogether insufficient to face the Enemy & com-
plains that they are continuously going away. He proposes to make some Stand at
[Brunswick, but] I do not think he has any Expectation of be[ing able to hold his]
ground long there. . . . It is his Opinion that the Enemy mean to penetrate
through this State to Philadelphia & therefore it will be necessary that we exert
ourselves to the utmost. If the Army had not been in Motion upon their Retreat
I should have endeavoured to assist in getting those of our State to reinlist & if
they continue at Brunswick will [return?] there for that purpose. If there is no
prospect of being [helpful] in that way I shall return immediately to Philadelphia
& call upon you on my way thither." Witherspoon to William Livingston,
November 29, 1776, Livingston Papers, MHi.

William Whipple to Meshech Weare

Sir   Philadelphia 28th Nov 1776
   Inclos'd you have a Resolution which Congress wish may be
executed as soon as possible. What quantity can be procured in New
Hampshire you are a much better judge of, then I can be but I
am sure the army will dispence with all that can be obtained. I
could wish to be informed of the success of the Resolution transmitted you sometime ago, for procuring Cloathing.[1]
   I hope every exertion will be use'd to furnish the Soldiers with
these necessary articles.
   Col. Bartlett can inform you of the state of the army when he
pass'd through it since which I have no reason to think there has
been any alteration for the better with respect to Cloathing. The
disposition that the state that I have the Honour to represent, has
hitherrto discovered leaves me no room to doubt that proper measures will be persued to effect these purposes, as well as compleating
Her Quota of the new Army.
   Genl. Howe is on this side Hudsons River with 8 or 10,000 men.
Its thot by some that he intends to march this way, if so I flatter
myself we shall give a good accot. of him, as proper dispositions
are makeing for his reception.
   Accots from abroad are very favorable, 'tho of such a nature that
I am not at Liberty to Communicate them. We have nothing to do
but keep a Sufficient Army in the field to oppose that of the Enemy

one Campaign more; and its over with them. I am with every Sentiment of Respect, Your Most Obt Sert,   Wm. Whipple

P.S. My Colleague [2] is now confin'd with the small Pox but is on the recovery & I Expect will be out in a very few days.

RC (Nh–Ar).
[1] The November 27 resolve calling on the New England states to procure 10,000 pairs of shoes and stockings for Washington's army. *JCC*, 6:984. On December 16, Meshech Weare responded that if the Congress would forward money "Very considerable Quantities of Shoes, Leather-Breeches, and some other Articles Can be procured here." *N.H. State Papers*, 8:420.
[2] Matthew Thornton.

Samuel Adams to Elizabeth Adams

My dear Betsy   Philadelphia Novr 29 1776
    I take this opportunity by Mr Chamberlain to acquaint you that I am in good health & Spirits. This Intelligence, I flatter myself, will not be disagreable to you. I have not receivd a line from you since I left Boston which gives me Reason to suspect that your Letters may have fallen into wrong hands. Traveling, it seems, is of late become somewhat dangerous; should this be intercepted and be seen by the two Brothers, they will have an opportunity of knowing that I am still most firmly attached to the best Cause that virtuous Men contend for, and that I am animated with the full Perswasion that righteous Heaven will support the Americans if they persevere in their manly Struggles for their Liberty. I have no Reason to suspect the Virtue of the Generality of my Countrymen. There are indeed Poltroons & Trayters everywhere. I do not therefore think it strange that some such Characters are to be found in this City—but the Indignation of the People kindles at the expected approach of the Enemies Army, and every proper Measure is taking to meet them on the Road and stop their wild Career. I am told that Lord Howe has lately issued a Proclamation offering a general Pardon with the Exception of only four Persons viz Dr Franklin, Coll Richard Henry Lee, Mr John Adams & myself.[1] I am not certain of the Truth of this Report. If it be a Fact I am greatly oblig'd to his Lordship for the flattering opinion he has given me of myself as being a Person obnoxious to those who are desolating a once happy Country for the sake of extinguishing the remaining Lamp of Liberty, and for the singular Honor he does me in ranking me with Men so eminently patriotick.
    I hope you will write to me by every opportunity. Pay my due Respects to my Family and Friends and be assured that I am most affectionately, your,   S Adams

RC (NN).

¹ The rumor Adams had heard was inaccurate. No such proclamation had been issued, and under the terms of the proclamation the Howe brothers published the following day, no one was ineligible for the new offer of pardon. See *Am. Archives*, 5th ser. 3:927–28; and Ira D. Gruber, *The Howe Brothers and the American Revolution* (New York: Atheneum, 1972), pp. 172–73.

Samuel Adams to James Warren

My dear Sir,   Philad Nov 29 1776

I inclose a Resolve passd in Congress and attested by the Secretary which I doubt not the Honbe House of Representatives will duly regard.¹ Indeed I am in hopes your Committee for providing Cloathing &c for the Army have already in a great Measure answerd the Request. You will have heard of the Situation of the Armies before this will reach you. A Part of the Enemy have got on this Side of Hudsons River, but I dare say you will have a good Account of them. I am more chagrind at the Disgrace than the Loss we have met with by the Surrender of Forts Washington & Lee. They should not have cost the Enemy less than thousands of their Troops. After all, what have the mighty Victors gaind? A few Miles of Ground at the Expence of many Millions of their Treasure & the Effusion of much of their Blood. But we must stop their Career. This I am satisfied can & will be done. Mr. Gerry writes to you by this opportunity ² therefore I need not add more than that I am very affectionately, Yours,   S. Adams

[*P.S.*] Pray deliver the inclosd, if your Leisure will admit, with your own hand.

RC (MB).

¹ The November 27 resolve asking the New England states to supply 10,000 pairs of shoes and stockings. *JCC*, 6:984.

² See Elbridge Gerry to James Warren, November 28, 1776.

William Hooper to Joseph Hewes

Dear Hewes   [November 29, 1776] ¹

If no other duty pressed upon me but that which I owe to private personal friendship, I should not hesitate a moment whether to write you or to be silent. The latter most surely would be my choice. I have no inclination to narrate affliction or to make you the hearer of it, but a duty of a superiour nature presses upon me & when I consider you as the representative of a very considerable part of that Continent whose most important stake is upon the verge of being cast, cast forever to slavery or freedom, that we are embarked together in the same bottom and must together take the fate of the Ship sink or swim, I should be wanting in the catalogue of moral virtues if I did not give you the truth without a cover of Gauze if disguize it.

An exhausted Treasury—An Army which in ten days will be reduced to 1500—Genl Howe pressing on with 15000 (another Cypher) —ours dispirited, naked, defeated—his victorious & pursuing all their Advantages with the insult & triumph of Success—New Jersey languid in forwarding militia to the requisitions of Gnl Washington —Pennsylvania refusing it altogether—All our Stores & Magazines here—4 fine frigates &c & &c & &c. What must be the consequence? Here—Certain Ruin. New England skulks within her own bounds. The Middle Colonies shrink into insignificance, & the Southern Colonies from their own Virtue must decide the Contests. I believe sincerely that the Virtue of the whole Continent has fled to the Southward. Oh clasp her, nourish her until she bless us. Many days will not elapse before Howe is here. I feel my self more resigned than I conceived was possible. I have done my best, Heaven expects no more. Washington again and again has asked the Militia from this. Not a man moves, the excuses are various. "The Constitution is not settled," "we have not chosen our officers," "Salt has been unequally distributed," thus seeking every flimsy pretence to fly from danger & from duty.

The Congress, the Council of Safety, Mifflin who is now here for that purpose have endeavoured to rouse them from their Lethargy— but it is a torper from which they never will awake but in bondage. We do not deserve to be saved, We have not virtue to merit it. With my attention in and out of Congress my health is much impaired, & I now write under the pain of tormenting Earach & lingering fever the result of want of Exercise, and of too close application. The people here are vastly comforted with 7 days of Rainy Weather which we have had as it must retard Gen Howes progress thro' the Jersies. Heaven they say fights for them, well that it does for they attempt nothing for themselves. If Salvation comes to them it is the superabundant unmerited grace of God which gives to Sinners infinitely more than they can *ask or think*. Howe is advancing. He has taken possession of Hackensack Town. G. Washington is at Passyunk, With 3000 men, the rest of his force in different parts of the Jerseys. Lee is crossing Hudson with 2000 to join him (if he can). I'll close the gloomy picture, when you hear of me again I know not where I will be. I mean to stay here while there is the most distant hope of being useful. I have long ago lost sight of myself. I feel, I deeply feel for my Country. I do not despair if Carolina is not Corrupt as this. Under all Circumstances I am your friend.

RC (Nc–Ar). In Hooper's hand, though not signed.
[1] Internal evidence suggests that Hooper could not have written this letter

before November 25, the day General Washington's letter of the 23d was read in Congress; and the second part of Hooper's statement in his December 1 letter to Hewes that "I wrote you yesterday and the day before" is almost certainly a reference to the present letter. See *JCC*, 6:979; Washington, *Writings* (Fitzpatrick), 6:303–4; and Hooper to Hewes, December 1, 1776.

Oliver Wolcott to Timothy Edwards

Sir,   Philidelphia 29t Novr 1776

Your kind Favour of last May after a Very slow Conveyance came to Hand, and which ought to have been earlier Acknowledged, had not a Variety of Circumstances prevented. I should probably have Attended with you at the Indian Conferance in July had my Health permitted.[1] You were I understand long detained upon this Necessary Business. I Wish the Indian Virtue may not by any success of our Enemys be bro't to a severe Tryal. Their Conduct doubtless ought to be most carefully attended to, and We shall be happy, since the Foe has an Open Communication into their Country by the Lakes, if We shall be able to keep them in a State of Neutrality. We have the Oneida, I take it, well in our Interest together with their particular Connexions—and sorry I am to find it so difficult a Matter to perswade some Gentlemen of the Importance of supporting our Friends amongst them. Cashula is now here, with a Deligation from the Shawanese and Mingoes, they have not yet delivered any thing publickly but I understand their Professions will be Friendly.[2] The Friendship of the Wyondots is not to be relyed upon.

Congress does not allow the Commissioners any Thing more than their Expences. For my Service I intend to Apply to our Assembly for pay, which I hope they will allow, for as the Commissioners are almost from every State I do not know why they may not be paid by them. Any Monies which may be Wanted for the Northern Department will be sent upon application of the Commissioners, perhaps the Ten Thousand Dollars sent last summer may have answered the necessary Expenditures. Last April I was directed by Congress to Conferr with Col Francis respecting some Indians then in this City. I waited upon him the first Time I had seen him the three proceeding Months I had been here tho' I Went every day by his House. He was Very Complesant and said he knew I had been appointed to attend Congress but had never heard that I had been in the City. After the Business was over, I tho't it best to Mention to him the bringing the Susquehannah Affair into the late Treaty so that he might not be able to say that I had been with him, but had not Honor enough to say a Word to him upon the Subject.[3] I told him that he had doutless been informed, that an Enquiry had been made, how the Susquehannah Business had been introduced into the late Indian Conferance. He said he had never been informed of it which to me after all my Acquaintance with this Gentlemen was surprizing. I then told him the affair particularly. He became Very angry, recriminated with great Severity upon the Commissioners, upon Genl. Schyler in particular, called it an ex Parte Affair &c. I let him know that the Matter had been conducted with great Honor and Propriety and that as I might be suspected of some Partiality as belonging to Connecticut, I had declined going into the Examination myself, but left the Matter to those whose Impartiality and Integrity could not be suspected. This was the Substance of every Thing that passed between him and Me at that time. I did not imagine I had been guilty of any Disrespect to the Commissioners or had with Impropriety mentioned the affair. Nothing but a mere Point of Honor induced me to say a Word to him upon the Subject. Sometime after he delivered an Open Letter to Me, the Copy of which I Enclose,[4] I felt much Chagrined at it, and told Francis that I never had blamed the Commissioners for what they had done and that I would now inform him if he could be under any misapprehension that in my opinion if they had neglected an Enquiry they would have been guilty of a criminal omission and that I never Signified a Lisp to him more than that I did not take the Examination, but that I did most cordially approve of what they had done, and that he never had the least Reason from any Thing I ever said to him to doupt of it. This was the Substance of what passed at this Time. Sometime after he put in a Memorial to Congress, setting forth as tho' I had been guilty of Maltreating him and the Commissioners and moved for an Enquiry, which I most heartily seconded. A Committee was Appointed of such Gentlemen as he certainly could have no Objection against. Fulmer and one of the Onondagas, who with with Col Francis the Evening referred to in the Report, when this Matter was first agitated by Col Francis was then in Town. Fulmer reaserted his former Testimony.[5] The Onondago was Examined, who said that a White Man was the Occasion of the matter being mentioned. He was asked who he was, he said he did not come there to talk about Lands and declined giving any further Acco. Col Francis was present during the Enquiry. I desired the Committee fully to Investigate the Subject of Col Francis Memorial, but contrary to my Expectation they never proceeded farther with it, but made Report that they did not find the Facts Stated in the Memorial. I have as Short as I could given you the Hystory of this Affair which you may probably have heard something of from another Qua[r]ter. So concious as I am myself of my own Innocency, I could not but Wonder that Col Francis Letter should make so much Impression upon Genl. Schyler Mind as it appeared to have done. I meant before now to have Wrote him upon the Subject, but for the general Reasons which have prevented me from answered your Favour earlier has hindered me I cannot think it a Crime to have mentioned the affair to Col Francis as I have no Apprehension that the Commissioners meant to keep the matter secret. If they did, I have been ignorantly faulty.

I Was sorry to be informed by you of the unhappy State of your County. In these unhappy Times ignorant and ambitious Men are too apt, by a great apparent Zeal, to acquire an Importance which they are but little intituled to, and every Necessitous Man will join the Wicked Designs of these Men in suppressing Justice. But their Influence being founded in Delusion must be temporary only, and a People will soon recover a Love of order and Justice, so that I hope the personal Injuries which you now sustain will be but of a short Duration, and that you will be repaid by such a Reward, as a good Man ought to expect, who maintains his Integrity in the Hour of severe Tryal and Adversity.

For News refer you to Mr Sergeant. My best Compliments to your Lady, and Gentlemen of my Acquaintance in your Town. I am sir, your most Obedient, humble Servant,   Oliver Wolcott

RC (NN).
[1] Both Wolcott and Timothy Edwards (1738–1813), a Stockbridge, Mass., judge, were Indian commissioners for the northern department. *Appleton's Cyclopaedia of American Biography;* and *JCC,* 2:183.
[2] The Indians visited Congress on December 5, 7, and 9. *JCC,* 6:1006, 1010–11, 1013. For an account of their first appearance in Congress, see Benjamin Rush's Notes of Proceedings in Congress, December 5, 1776.
[3] For further information about the Indian commissioners dispute with their colleague Turbutt Francis, see Oliver Wolcott to Philip Schuyler, January 22, 1776, note 2.
[4] Probably Turbutt Francis' April 23 letter to Philip Schuyler and Volkert P. Douw. See *Susquehannah Co. Papers,* 7:11–12.
[5] For a later deposition by Thomas Fulmer summarizing this entire affair, see ibid., pp. 26–28.

Samuel Chase to the Maryland Council of Safety

Gentlemen,   Philadelphia Novr. 30th. 1776. Saturday Morning
By a Resolve of Congress of the 12th of October 1775, "each Captain & other commissioned officer, while in the recruiting Service of this Continent, or on their March to join the Army shall be allowed two Dollars & two thirds per Week *for their Subsistance;* and that the Men who enlist shall each of them, whilst in Quarters, be allowed one Dollar per week, & one Dollar & one third of a Dollar, when on their March, to join the Army for the same Purpose."

The Resolves enclosed will shew the allowance by Congress for Recruiting. I have given you this Trouble on a Presumption, that the allowances by Congress were unknown at the Time recruiting orders issued in our State.

I am desired by Congress to call your immediate attention to their Request some Time ago to our Convention, to make Enquiry of some Nanticoak Indians,[1] which the Six Nations alledge came into our State, & have not since been heard of, & they express fears for their Safety. Be pleased to enquire of Mr Duvall for the Letter from Congress on this Subject, & take effectual Measures for a speedy Enquiry. I should imagine the Committee of Dorset County could make the proper Enquiry.

Congress have not heard from General Washington since the 27th when he was at New ark. Young Bradford writes that our Army left New Ark on 28th in the Morning, and were at Brunswick yesterday.

I am, Gentn., with Respect, Your Most obedt. Servt.,

Saml. Chase

[*P.S.*] The enclosed Letter was delivd. to Me open.

Our Troops are perishing for the want of Shoes & Stockings, can't You send some for the Use of our forces?

RC (PHi).
    [1] For the background of this request, see Thomas Stone to Matthew Tilghman, September 4, 1776, note. For the council's December 6th response, in which they explained that "we have wrote General Hooper and desired him to make a particular Enquiry . . . [*and*] shall write more fully when we hear from Brigadier Hooper," see *Md. Archives*, 12:502, 510. No record of Henry Hooper's response to the council has been found.

William Hooper to Joseph Hewes

November 30th [1776]

You are before this informed that the surrender of fort Lee soon followed that of Fort Washington. The Enemy advanced to and took possession of Hackinsack Town. There they remained till the day before yesterday, when they moved on to Newark which our Army abandoned to them. G. Washington proceeded to Elisabeth Town where he did not long continue but proceeded with his whole force to Brunswick. There he means to make a stand, if the province of Jersey or of Pennsylvania will afford him any succours by their Militia. This State is in a Lethargy. Jersey is little better. Before this day week I expect to hear that the Enemy are at Burlington, for no person here seems more interested to oppose the Enemy than if they existed in the moon, except those whose Power of Swallowing depends upon the Event, I mean the Congress. Washington has about 6000 with him, but alas this night the Enlistment of one half of them expires & they will go home! The Enemy know this from an intercepted letter & are preparing to advantage themselves of the Misfortune. Cornwallis it is said commands on this side of Hudson River. His army may be about 6000. He is now at Eliz Town, will no doubt advance to Amboy. There a number of Transports whose destination has been long a matter of Speculation will probably join them, or rather the Enemy from these Ships will land at South Amboy & penetrate up Raritan River to Brunswick while Cornwallis with his Brigades will attempt to force a passage at some other place thereby to distract and divide our little army. Where the Eastern Army is, or how employed God only knows. Lee is with them & may possibly hereafter explain their Movements. Oh how I feel for Washington that best of men. The difficulties which he has now to encounter are beyond the power of language to describe but to be unfortunate is to be wrong & there are men, you know who, who are villains enough to brand him. There are some long faces here, & the Hero from M——d who disavowed his Allegiance to G.B. 6 months ago & frightend poor parson Zubly home shakes in his shoes, now talks of accommodation, Conciliation, reconciliation, Peace on honourable terms. This man had the impudence to call those tories who talked thus when the Scheme was practicable & when I thought & when I still think that if America could have had her terms, it was the best bargain she could have made. I hate such puffing. Such as these if America falls have ruined her by giving vain hopes, & lying without Compunction or restraint.[1]

Still this City might be saved if the Inhabitants of Jersey & Pennsylvania would move. Mifflin came here to try his powers, a few are dragged in to follow him, their motions I fear will be very slow, and *retrogade* some of them.

We have heard that an attack is begun in the Highlands upon Fort Montg[omer]y, we yet have not the Event. In Lat. 32, Long. 70, A man just arrived at Baltimore saw 160 large Vessells steering S.W. & W.S.W. Were these intended for Chas town, you know before this. It is suspected that they are a fleet which Burgoyne with Men is carrying to the Southward. Rise my dear Carolina Men—Rise to a Man. To the Southern Provinces is reserved for aught I know the glorious task of rescuing America from Slavery here & hereafter. Pray compleat your new Enlistments, Succour your Sister S Carolina. From whence I shall write you next I know not. Perhaps from this—perhaps Lancaster—perhaps Baltimore—Perhaps Heaven. Was it not for my family, I could wish the latter. Adieu. This Letter is confidential—to you, Penn, & J[ohnsto]n.

RC (Nc–Ar). In Hooper's hand, though not signed.

[1] These cryptic comments about Samuel Chase add not only to an understanding of the evolution of his views in the autumn of 1776 but also provide con-

firmation of the key role he played in bringing about Georgia delegate John Zubly's sudden departure from Congress in November 1775. See John Zubly to Archibald Bulloch and John Houston, November 10, 1775, note 1.

John Hancock to
John Morgan and William Shippen, Jr.

Sir,   Philada. Decr. 1t. 1776.

The enclosed Resolve of Congress, relative to your Duty, and the Department in which you are to exercise it, I have it in Charge from Congress to transmit to you as the Rule of your Conduct.[1]

I have the Honour to be, Sir, your most obed. & very hble Ser.

J. H. Presid.

LB (DNA: PCC, item 12A).
[1] On October 9 Congress had ordered Dr. Morgan to "provide and superintend a hospital . . . for the army posted on the east side of Hudson's river" and Dr. Shippen to do likewise "for the army, in the state of New Jersey." This order blurred the lines of responsibility between Morgan, the director general and physician in chief of the Continental Army, and Shippen, the director of the hospital for the flying camp in New Jersey, and led Shippen to claim independence of Morgan's authority in that state. Shippen presented his case in a letter to Hancock that was read on November 12; and on November 28 Congress resolved "That Dr. Morgan take care of such sick and wounded of the army of the United States, as are on the east side of Hudson's river, and that Dr. Shippen take care of such of the said sick and wounded as are on the west side of Hudson's river." With Washington's army then in New Jersey, this resolution, as a biographer of Morgan has noted, put Shippen "effectively in control of the Medical Department" and foreshadowed Morgan's dismissal from office on January 9, 1777. See JCC, 6:940, 983, 989; PCC, item 78, 20:67–68, 73, 75–76; Am. Archives, 5th ser. 3:463–64, 509, 618; Washington, Writings (Fitzpatrick), 6:239; and Whitfield J. Bell, Jr., John Morgan: Continental Doctor (Philadelphia: University of Pennsylvania Press, 1965), pp. 197–205.

John Hancock to George Washington

Sir,   Philada. Decr. 1t. 1776.

Your Favour of the 30th Novr. was duely received; in Consequence of which, as the Contents were of the utmost Importance, I thought proper to call the Congress together; whose Resolutions of this Day, I now do myself the Honour to inclose.[1]

Considering the very critical Situation of our Affairs, the Congress have agreed that you may order into the Jerseys, the Troops who are at present on the East Side of Hudson's River, if it should be your Opinion, the public Service will receive any Benefit from such a Movement.[2]

You will please to direct that the Cloathing, as fast as it arrives

John Morgan

at Head Quarters or at any of the Camps, should be given to those Soldiers who stand most in Need of them.

The Secret Committee will order one or two Persons to set out immediately to the Eastern States, to see that the Cloathing & Stores which have been purchased in that Quarter, be sent to the Army with all possible Dispatch.[3]

I have the Honour to be, with Sentiments of perfect Esteem & Respect, Sir, your most obed. & very hble Servt.

John Hancock Prest.

RC (DLC). In the hand of Jacob Rush and signed by Hancock.

[1] Washington's November 30 letter to Hancock, announcing that his army had retreated from Newark to Brunswick and was in desperate need of reinforcements, is in PCC, item 152, 3:279–80, and Washington, *Writings* (Fitzpatrick), 6:314–16. For the resolves passed this day in response to it, during a rare Sunday session, see *JCC*, 6:997–98.

[2] See Washington, *Writings* (Fitzpatrick), 6:323.

[3] See Secret Committee to the Massachusetts Assembly, December 4, 1776. On December 2 Hancock also wrote a brief note to Governor Cooke of Rhode Island in which he stated: "The Inclos'd Resolutions I transmitt by order of Congress, your Attachment to the common Cause & great Zeal to promote the Service renders any further Recommendation unnecessary." Samuel T. Freeman & Co. Catalog, *The Frederick S. Peck Collection of American Historical Autographs* (February 17, 1947), p. 11. One of these enclosures was probably the December 1 resolve on the purchase of "cloathing and stores" in "the eastern states." *JCC*, 6:997. The others have not been identified.

William Hooper to Joseph Hewes

Dear Hewes   Philadelphia Decr. 1. 1776.

I wrote you yesterday and the day before. This is intended to close the packet by Bondfield who proposes to leave this early to morrow morning. This is Sunday, the Congress is now setting, you will conclude that matters are growing very critical. Your conclusions will be just. By a letter from General Washington this day received We find that he is at Brunswick with about 4000 Men; before night I fear this number will be much reduced. By the Capture of Ft Lee & Washington they have lost Tents, Blankets & Baggage; of course they are half naked & greatly dispirited. Cornwallis is at Eliz. Town & part of his troops about 5 miles on this side. We have ordered Housacker's German Battalion & such of the City Associators as can be prevailed upon to leave this to march immediately under the Command of Genl Mifflin.[1] Very few of the Jersey Militia have turned out, few or none here. From the difficulty of getting men for our frigates We have formed Artillery Companies amounting in the whole to about 400 under Command of Barry & Reid & other of the Masters of the Vessells who with 12 field pieces march this day to join Genl Washington. The Enemy are pressing on to this City. Heaven knows we are very ill prepared to receive them. Yours truly,   Wm Hooper

[*P.S.*] You will perhaps think that it will not be prudent to shew this letter to everybody.[2]

RC (PHi).
   [1] See *JCC*, 6:997.
   [2] For the continuation of this letter, see Hooper to Hewes, December 3, 1776.

Richard Henry Lee to James Maxwell

Sir,   Philadelphia 1t Decr. 1776
   The Congress having resolved immediately to undertake the building of two Ships of War of 36 guns each in Virginia, I am directed by the Marine Committee to apply to some proper person in that State to superintend the business.[1] You Sir have been recommended so strongly to me by Gen. Stephen and others, as a person of great fitness for this business; and not doubting but that you may comply with this, altho you are the same way employed by our Government, I do in the name of that Committee request you will, taking the advice of the Navy board in Virginia, determine on the most safe, and in other respects most fit place or places to put these ships upon the Stocks at.[2] Safety against the enemy is a very necessary object, and proper water for Launching. Convenience for getting proper timber you will consider. I suppose it will be no objection if both these Vessels are put upon the Stocks at the same place but in determining on the place or places, not private or local but public considerations alone are to govern. A Master Builder with 4 or 6 Workmen will soon go from hence to Virginia for this business, and I have no doubt a sufficiency of other workmen will be to be had in that state to carry on the work briskly. The Builder desires that the Trees may be immediately felled whilst the Sap is down, that a quantity of Locust Trunnels be split $1\frac{1}{2}$ inches, and in length from 18 to 30 inches. That Sawyers be employed to get up plank (white oak) of $3\frac{1}{2}$ inches. These things and whatever else may be immediately necessary for the right pursuit of this business you will take care to have done, and your drafts for the expence created by the same, on the Chairman of the Marine Committee of Congress, shall be duely honored. One or more Associates will be joined with you in this Agency, but for the present you will singly do what is necessary, and for your trouble you will be liberally compensated by Congress. The Board of Assistants are directed to prepare a proper draught of these Ships which shall be forwarded

to you when ready. Let me have your answer to this letter by return of Post.

I am Sir you most humble servant,

Richard Henry Lee

P.S. The Builder tells me that Cedar, Locust, Pitch Pine, or Wild Cherrytree, will be the proper Timber for upper works.

RC (C. Stribling Snodgrass, Leesburg, Va., 1973).
[1] See the November 20 resolve in *JCC*, 6:970.
[2] James Maxwell, (1735–95), of Norfolk, Va., was a captain in the Virginia navy, commissioner of the Virginia navy board, and superintendent of the Virginia navy yard. William Maxwell, "My Mother," *The Lower Norfolk County Virginia Antiquary* 3 (1901): 46n. Upon Maxwell's recommendation, the Virginia navy board ordered the Continental frigates to be built at Gosport. Morgan, *Naval Documents*, 7:1065–66.

Benjamin Rush to John Dickinson

My dear sir,   Philada. Decemr 1st. 1776.

While I disapprove most heartily of the coalition of parties in the Assembly I cannot help lamenting that you have left the house upon the Account of it. The members from Westmorland & Bedford will turn the scale in our favor as soon as they come to town, and we shall [have] a convention, and a consistant legislature in spite of all their cunning & malice. For the present it becomes us to unite heart & hand in repelling the common enemy. The eyes of the whole city are fixed upon you. We expect, we are sure you will head your battalion. All our hopes of your future Usefulness in our state depend upon it. Mr. Howe cannot mean to winter in Philadelphia, Unless he is invited here by the slender opposition Genl Washington now makes against him. A body of 10,000 militia will certainly terrify him into Winter Quarters. The safety of the continent depends upon the part Pensylvania will take upon this occasion. The whole state of Pensylvania will be influenced by the city of Philada. and the city *waits* only to see what part you will take upon the Occasion.[1] Excuse the liberty I have taken of suggesting these hints, and believe me to be with the most sincere regard your most Affectionate, humble servant,

Benja Rush

RC (PHi). Addressed: "John Dickinson Esqr. at Fairhill."
[1] Although Dickinson served with his battalion of the Pennsylvania militia in New Jersey during July and August, he had resigned his colonelcy of the first battalion at the end of September when Pennsylvania promoted two brigadiers over him. He had already withdrawn from the political arena following his failure to win reelection as a delegate to Congress from Pennsylvania on July 20, 1776, and although elected a delegate by the Delaware Assembly on November 8, he did not return to Congress until April 1779. During the autumn of 1776

he spent most of his time at his Fairhill estate, limiting his political activity to
writing sporadically in opposition to the new Pennsylvania constitution and refusing to take the seat to which he had been elected in the first assembly convened
under that instrument of government. On December 10, at the continued approach of British troops and almost simultaneously with the general evacuation
of Philadelphia by Congress and most active whig leaders, Dickinson retired
with his family to his estate in Kent, near Dover, Delaware. See Charles J. Stillé,
The Life and Times of John Dickinson, 1732–1808 (1891; reprint ed., New York:
Burt Franklin, 1969), pp. 201–15, 383–93.

William Hooper to Joseph Hewes

Philadelphia Decr. 3. [1776]
The Enemy move rapidly this way. On Sunday 7 oClock p.m.
they advanced in sight of Brunswick.[1] Our little Army reduced to
about 3000 by the Expiration of Enlistments upon their arrival at
the fording place kept up a Cannonade till our Men were paraded,
the effect was nothing. It was impossible with such a handful to
make a stand against this superiour force. Gen Washington retreated, is before this at Trenton, intends immediately to cross the
River where Putman has been providing boats for them. The Associators here come out very slowly, I fear they will be too late to be
very useful.

Dear Hewes, I have been much indisposed, my Constitution is
not equal to the fatigue I undergo. I have had my share of it. I beg
that the Convention would send on some one to relieve me. I cannot bear a longer absence from my family. I think myself neglected. Where is Penn? I give this notice that I may not be culpable
in case the State of No Carolina should not soon send me relief.
Yours truly,   Wm Hooper

RC (PHi). A continuation of Hooper to Hewes, December 1, 1776.
[1] Robert Treat Paine made the following entry in his diary under the date
December 2: "Alarmed with the approach of Genl Howes forces commanded
by Genl Cornwallis to Brunswick." MHi.

Richard Henry Lee to Patrick Henry

Dear Sir,   Philadelphia 3 Decr. 1776
The present moment is critical in the American war. The enemy
have taken vigorous advantage of the space between the old and
the new inlistments, and have rushed like a Torrent thru the
Jersies, our little army of no more than 5000 men under the command of Genl. Washington, being compelled to retreat rapidly
before them. The object is this City, and they were on Sunday last

at Brunswick, about 60 miles off in the Jersies. The Associators are at length alarmed and turning out to reenforce the General, but they move rather slower that the important stake demands. We hear that Gen. Lee has crossed North river and is following quickly after the enemy, but we are not sure that his numbers are sufficient for anything decisive. However, if the people here have any title to the freedom they claim, Mr. Howe will not be gratified with the possession of this City. And if he gained 20 such Cities, still he would be short of gaining the point meditated over America. You remember Sir, we told them from the beginning, that we lookt on our Cities & Sea Coasts as devoted to destruction, but that ample resources were still left for a numerous, brave, and free people to contend with.

Our latest accounts from the French W. Indies tell us that war between G.B. & France & Spain is inevitable and must be immediate.

I hope our winter councils will be every where devoted solely to the purpose of carrying on a vigorous, active, and early Campaign. For this purpose the recruiting Officers in all quarters should be often called upon by the respective governments to know how they go on, and to urge them to a quick and effectual execution of the business. Everything my dear Sir, depends upon the new Levies being nearly ready. Colo. Charles Harrison leaves this place today, with 250,000 dollars under his care for the use of our forces in Virginia, and for paying the bounties. Your recommendation of this Gentlemen, seconded by his real merit, has procured him the command of a Regiment of Artillery to be raised in Virginia, Congress having resolved to keep the Artillery & Engineers departments under immediate Continental inspection.[1] The other day we dispatched for the Head of Elk to the care of Mr. Hollingsworth there, the Arms taken from our Soldiers here that better might be put in their hands. They are between 7 & 8 hundred in number and may be had from thence when you are pleased to send for them. With some repair they will do tolerably for the new Levies.

I am extremely pleased to hear that you have recovered your health. May it long continue good. I am, with great regard, dear Sir Your most affectionate and obedient,

Richard Henry Lee

[P.S.] Business and alarm press so constantly that we have scarce one moment to spare.

RC (ViStrR).
[1] See *JCC*, 6:981, 983, 995.

Matthew Tilghman to the
Maryland Council of Safety

Gent.   Phila. Decr. 3. 1776

Mr. Hanson & Mr Chamberlaine arrived here last Night after I believe a very fruitless Journey to the Camp which they found on the retreat & is now no doubt at Trenton being left by our Gent. on the road thither O'Sunday Night.

By the best Information our General cou'd get the Enemy are between 6 & 7 thousand, his Army now not more than 3 thousand. If any considerable reinforcement can be sent from Hence, He intends to make a Stand at Trenton in Case the Enemy come forward which it is generally thought they will Tho' Genl. Chamberlaine thinks they will not.

The German Battalion are nearly ready to March from Hence and every Measure is taking to Spirit up the Mil[iti]a to move, shoud the Enemy move forward with any degree of Speed, I greatly fear our reinforcements will not be in Time. A little Time will open their Designs. If we dont hear to day of their coming forward from Brunswick, of which they must have possessed themselves o'Sunday Eveng. after the retreat of our Army, I shall be inclined to think their Aim is not at this place. Where Genl. Lee is, seems not to be well known. Tis Said Genl Sinclair is on his Mar[ch] with about 1500 Men. We had a report indeed yesterday which for a time gained Credit that Lee & Sinclair were joined with an Army of 10 or 15000 Men but it dwindled before Night into almost Nothing. Such is the present Situation of our Affairs. It is bad eno', but may be worse, a few Days will determine & afford us either a small respit or greatly add to the distress & Confusion of this place.

I am, Gentlemen, with great respect, Yr. mo. Obedt Servant,

Mat. Tilghman

[*P.S.*] I can't see how the Council or the delegates to Congress can suppress any part of the proceedings of Convention.[1]

RC (MdAA).

[1] In a letter of November 23, Samuel Chase had lamented that the state convention's instructions to the Maryland delegates contained reservations on consenting to a confederation, which "if made known, they will reach Lord Howe, and encourage him, and if the courts of Europe should see them, it would prevent a foreign alliance." When the council responded to Chase's letter, it was unprepared to send additional instructions although "very desirous of doing any thing that might be offered to the common cause, or tend to satisfy the minds of our Friends in Congress." Before reaching a decision on publication of the delegates' instructions, the council explained, "we wish to hear from you on the subject, and in the mean time we will consider what is best to be done, and wait for a full board and until we hear further from you." See Samuel Chase to the Maryland Council of Safety, November 23, 1776, note 3; and *Md. Archives*, 12:491.

Samuel Adams to James Warren

My dear Sir   Philad[elphia December 4, 1776]
   I receivd your obliging Letter [. . .] by Mr Brown.[1] It affords me
singular pleasure to be informd that our Assembly is now sitting in
Boston. It has ever been my opinion that the publick Business can
be done with more Dispatch there than elsewhere. "You have appointed a Committee of War," "with very extensive Powers," and
"appropriated to their Disposition £200,000 to purchase every thing
necessary to carry on the War with Vigour the next year."[2] I am
heartily rejoycd to hear this. I hope the Committee are Men of
Business and will make a good Use of the Power and Monies they
are entrusted with. Let me tell you that every Nerve must be
straind to resist the British Tyrant, who in Despair of availing
himself of his own Strength which lately he so much prided himself in, is now summoning the Powers of Earth & Hell to subjugate
America. The Lamp of Liberty burns there & there only. He sees
it, and is impatient even to Madness to extinguish it. It is our
Duty, at all Hazards to prevent it. But I am sensible I need not
write to *you* in this Stile. You and the rest of my Countrymen have
hitherto done and I have no Doubt will continue to do your Duty
in Defence of a Cause as interesting to Mankind. It is with inexpressible Pleasure that I reflect, that the mercenary Forces of the
Tyrant have for two years in vain attempted to penetrate the Eastern
Colonies. *There,* our Enemies themselves and those who even hate
us, acknowledge that the Rights of Men have been defended with
Bravery. And did not South Carolina nobly withstand the Efforts
of Tyranny & defeat them. She did. Virginia too & North Carolina
have in their Turns acted with a Spirit becoming the Character of
Americans. But what will be said of Pennsylvania & the Jerseys?
Have they not disgracd themselves by standing the idle Spectators
while the Enemy overran a great Part of their Country? They have
seen our Army, unfortunately seperated by the river, retreating to
Hakinsack—to Newark—to Elisabeth Town, Woodbridge, Brunswick & Princeton. The [. . .] is about 40 miles from this [. . . .] The
enemy's Army by the last Accounts were within an 60 Miles March
to this place. If they were as near Boston, would not our hardy
Countrymen cut them all to Pieces or take them Prisoners. But by
the unaccountable Stupor which seems to have pervaded these States,
The Enemy have gaind a Tryumph, which they did not themselves
expect—A Tryumph indeed! Without a Victory—without one
Laurel to boast of—For Bunkers Hill they fought & bled. They lost
their bravest officers, and we wishd them twenty such Victories. But
the People of the Jersys have sufferd them to run thro' their Country without the Risque of even a private soldier. They expended
their Ammunition at the Trees and Bushes as they marchd. But I

hear the Sound of a Drum. The People of Pennsylvania say of themselves that they are usually slow in determining, but vigorous in executing. I hope we shall find both Parts of this Predication to be just. They say they are now determind; and promise to bring General Howe to a hearty Repentance for venturing his Troops so near them. I have the Pleasure to tell you that within a few days past they have made a spirited Appearance. In Spite of Quakers, Proprietarians, timid Whigs, Tories, Pettit Maitres & Trimmers, there are a sufficient Number in Arms resolvd to defend their Country. Many are now on the March. Heaven grant they may be the honorable Instruments to retrieve the Reputation of their Countrymen and reduce Britain to a contemptible Figure at the End of this Campaign.

I am glad to hear that our harbor looks so brilliant. *I hope it is fortified against every Attempt of the Enemy the next Spring.* In your Letter you ask me two very important Questions. I dare not repeat them.[3] With regard to *the last* you will understand what I mean when I say Let not your Mind be any more troubled about it. I am in good health & Spirits. Adieu.

RC (MHi). In Adams' hand, though not signed. Endorsed: "Decr. 4. 1776." William V. Wells, *The Life and Public Services of Samuel Adams* . . . , 3 vols. (Boston: Little, Brown, and Co., 1865), 2:452–54. RC damaged; missing words supplied from Tr.

[1] See James Warren's November 18 letter to Samuel Adams in *Warren-Adams Letters*, 2:440–41.

[2] For the appointment of the Massachusetts Board of War, see Samuel Adams to James Warren, November 6, 1776, note 2.

[3] Warren had asked Adams: "Where is your Confederation. Are your Embassadors gone, etc., etc." *Warren-Adams*, 2:441.

William Ellery to Nicholas Cooke

Sir,   Philadelphia Decr. 4th 1776.

It is long since I received a Letter from the Assembly notwithstanding my repeated Requests. I should rejoice by the Return of the Express, who will take the Charge of this, to receive the Information I have desired. I am uninformed with Regard to the Force actually muster'd in the Colony for its Defence, and what Number the Militia, now employed in that Service, consists of. Whether We have any Powder Mills agoing, what Quantity of Money our State hath issued, at what Periods the several Emissions are redeemable, and what Interest is allowed on any of them? Whether any Cloathing hath been purchased for the Army and sent forward, &c &c &c. In short I know nothing about the affairs of our State but what I collect from the private Letters and News Papers, which I now and then receive. In Addition to the Information before prayed for I

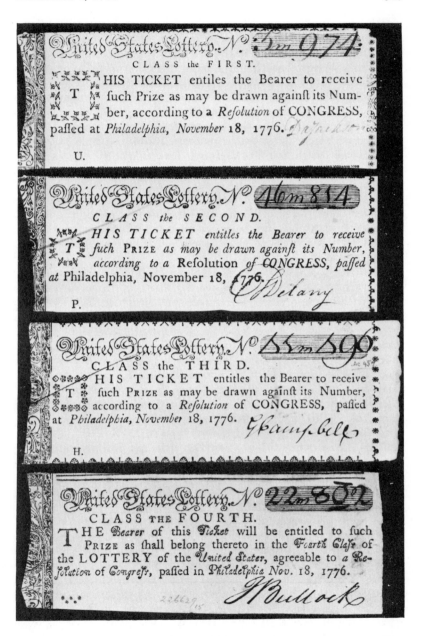

Lottery Tickets

could wish to know whether the Assembly have appointed a Commissioner of the Loan-Office for our State.[1] Certificates will soon be ready to be transmitted to the several States, and it is a Matter of great Importance that Commrs should be appointed to exchange them with those who may be disposed to let Money on Loan. Please to advise Me what Sum you think may be hired in our State. I hope the Loan Office & State Lottery will be encouraged in the respective United States; for upon the Success thereof, very much depends the Supply of the Treasury in such a Manner as will check the Depretiation of the public Medium. Tickets will in a short Time be transmitted by the Managers of the Lottery to Agents appointed by them in the several States, and I think the Lottery is so well calculated that with the Countenance which may be given to it by the States the Tickets will soon be purchased. Every Step ought to be taken that can be taken to retard, to put a full Stop to the Career of Depretiation otherwise such Floods of Money must issue as can never be sunk.[2]

The Prices of all the Necessaries of Life, by the Depretiation, owing very much to the great Quantity of Paper Money in Circulation, by the Limitation of Commerce, and by a vile sordid Practice of monopolizing, which some wealthy Men here have got into, have been raised within a year or Two, One hundred per Cent. I hope that the Necessaries of Life have not arisen in their Value, in the same rapid and extravagant Manner in our State; if they have the Poor especially must be in a most deplorable Situation. I am told that the Genll. Assembly at their Novr. Session fixed the Salary of their Delegates at four Dollars a Day.[3] I believe they did not at that Time think of the enhanced Price of every Article of Living since the first Congress; otherwise they must have known that four Dollars a Day now, were not equal to the three Dollars which were allowed them then, and untill the Session referred to, exclusive of their Expences; and I think would not have fixed their Salary at less than five Dollars a Day, which was the Sum I had mentioned in my Letters. I hope the General Assembly will reconsider their Resolve. If Three Dollars were not inadequate to the Service of the Delegates, exclusive of Expences, in the first Congress, most certainly four Dollars, which will not purchase now more than Two would then, cannot be adequate, and beside this, out of these four Dollars, the Delegates must pay their Expences, which let them be as frugal as they can will amount to a very large Sum, and leave nothing behind as a Reward for their Service.

I should be extremely glad that the Additional Delegate who may be appointed this Decr. Session might proceed as soon as possible. I have scracely had a Minute for Relaxation since Govr. Hopkins returned Home. I am obliged to attend Committees Morning and Evening, and Congress from 10' until 3 every Day, Sundays sometimes not excepted. Such constant Attention without any Opportunity for Exercise is too much for Humanity.

Since the Enemy took Possession of Fort Lee, our little Army under Genl. Washington have been constantly on the Retreat. He is now at Trenton with the main Body, having left at Prince-Town Two Brigades under Genl. Stirling. The Associators of this State are turning out to reinforce him, and stop the further Progress of the Enemy. By a Letter from G.W. of the 3d Instant dated at Trenton he informs that the Enemy had not passed the Rariton to Brunswick the 2d at 9 o'Clock in the Morning, but that there was an Account that a Fleet of upwards of 100 Sail were turning out at the Hook last Sunday. Some suppose that they were destined for this River, and that the Enemy mean to attack this Place both by Sea and Land. I believe they will not be able to pass the Delaware with an Army, and I should think they would not attempt the River with their Ships at this Season, for although the Weather is now warm, yet We may expect a Frost every Day.

I hope that our Battalions will be raised in Season, and that We shall be able to bring a large Army into the Field the next Spring; otherwise they will be able to carry Fire and Sword into our States, in which Case the private Property which hath been so fortunately amassed by privateering in some of the Eastern States, as well as other Property, will be destroyed. We should take Care to preserve what We collect; and the Preservation of our Property, our Wives & Children, our Lives and Liberties depends upon our being able to face the Enemy in the Spring with a respectable Army. I said in the first Part of this Letter that you would receive this by Express, you will receive it by Commissioners appointed by the Secret Committee to collect and transmit to the Army the Cloathing collected by the several States, and to make further Purchases of Cloathing. They will not return till they have visited each of the Eastern States. Give me Leave Sir to expect an Answer by the very first safe Opportunity. I continue to be with the utmost Respect, Your Honor's most obedient, humble Servant,

William Ellery

P.S. Since I wrote the above I am told that the Number of Loan-Office Certificates will be sent off to Morrow to our State. I write in Congress and find I have wrote on a dirty Table. I have not Time to copy. Your Honor I hope will excuse every Imperfection.

W E

RC (R–Ar).

[1] Governor Cooke had already provided the answers to many of these questions in a November 30 letter to Ellery that had obviously not yet reached Philadelphia. William R. Staples, *Rhode Island in the Continental Congress, 1765–1790* (Providence: Providence Press Co., 1870), pp. 101–4.

[2] For various resolves on the lottery passed between November 18 and 30, see

JCC, 6:959–61, 963–64, 993–94. On December 5 Congress postponed the opening drawing of the lottery from March 1 to April 10, 1777. *JCC*, 6:1007. For the troubled history of the lottery voted by Congress on November 18, see Lucius Wilmerding, Jr., "The United States Lottery," *New-York Historical Society Quarterly* 47 (1963): 5–39. The drawing of the first class of tickets did not actually take place until May 1778, or 14 months after the March 1, 1777, date originally set, and the drawing for the fourth class of tickets was not held until April 1782. Congress did not finally conclude the business of the lottery until it adopted on December 21, 1872, a resolve authorizing the commissioners for settling accounts to "receive lottery tickets as vouchers for the prizes which may have been drawn . . . at . . . the rate of one dollar in specie for every forty dollars of such prizes." *JCC*, 23:824.

[3] No such act was passed in Rhode Island at this time. Staples, *Rhode Island in the Continental Congress*, pp. 106–7.

John Hancock to George Washington

Sir,   Philada. Decr. 4th. 1776.

The Congress apprehending that, in the present State of the Army, and Situation of our Affairs, an Exchange of Governor Franklin might be prejudicial, and attended with some bad Consequences, have been induced to come to the above Resolution, which I transmit by their Directions.[1]

I have the Honour to be, with the utmost Esteem & Respect, Sir, your most obed Sert.   John Hancock Prest.

[*P.S.*] Your favr. of 3d Inst. just came to hand.[2]

RC (DLC). In the hand of Jacob Rush, with signature and postscript by Hancock.

[1] See *JCC*, 6:1004. See also Hancock to Washington, November 24, 1776. Hancock also sent Washington another December 3 resolve about having "the prisoners, now at Bristol, removed from thence back into the country." *JCC*, 6:1002.

[2] This letter is in PCC, item 152, 3:303–4, and Washington, *Writings* (Fitzpatrick), 6:324–26.

Robert Morris to William Bingham

Dear Sir   Philada. Decemr. 4th 1776

This will be delivered to you by Capt. Geo. Ord[1] who takes his passage with Monsr. Cotiney de Prejent in the Ship Esperance for Guadaloupe. He is a worthy, Active, Industrious, Honest Man in whom you may safely repose Confidence, at least such is the Character he has hitherto borne & such is my good opinion of him.

Under this opinion, from Mr. Prejents solicitations, and from a desire to comply with your request as mentioned in your letter of the 1st October to me, I have procured a Commission for Captain Ord to Command a Privateer and send him with it in order that you may purchase, fit & Man a suitable Vessell for this purpose under his Command. I propose that this Privateer shou'd be a Stout, good, & fast sailing Vessell quite fit for the purpose, a Ship, Brigt, Sloop or Schooner just as you can best suit yourself. I think she shoud have 12 to 16, six or four Pounders & 100 to 150 Men if to be got, and be well fitted & provided in every respect. She may be bought, fitted & sent out on a Cruize with all possible expedition the sooner the better, and I leave the Choice of the Vessell & all other Circumstances to you, Mr. Prejent & Capt Ord, as also the Cruizing Ground, altho I think good business may be done amongst the Outward bound West India Men by Cruizing to Windward of Barbados where is also the Track for Guinea Men. I propose this Privateer to be one third on your Acct., one third on Acct of Mr. Prejent & one third on my account, and If the Esperance arrives safe Mr. Prejent & you will have sufficient Value to accomplish this business. If she does not arrive you will otherways receive sufficient Remittances to pay for your & my part. You must observe I have not hitherto had any Concern in privateering & even at this day my Partner Mr Willing objects possitively to any Concern. Therefore this has no Connection with the business of my House but is totally distinct & on my own Account. You will charge me for my part the Cost & Outfit & Credit me for my third the Net proceeds of all Prizes &c. You may use the Effects of W,M & Co to pay for my third but I hope that amot. will soon be Reimbursed by some good Prizes, if not, I will repay them the Amot. here. I have not imparted my concern in this plan to any person and shall Copy this letter myself to prevent its being Known, therefore I request you will never mention the least Tittle about the matter to any person nor in any letter but private ones to myself. You must know I had determined not to be Concerned in privateering but having had several Vessells taken from me & otherways lost a great deal of my property by this War, I conceive myself perfectly justifiable in the Eyes of God & Man to seek what I have lost from those that have plundered me. I recommend a Stout Privateer because I can imagine the British Ships will now come out very generally Armed, and little will be done by small ones. I have delivered Capt. Ord the Rules & Instructions of Congress and request that both he & you will closely abide by them, indeed I have given Bond that you shou'd do so. I think however that you may sell negroes, perishable Commodities & other Articles suitable for the Islands in Martinico if the General will give you leave without waiting a formal Condemnation in any of these States, but I think you had best send the Vessells & such parts of their Cargoes as are suited to the Continent to some part of it for Condemnation & Sale, & when you take out a Cargo or any part of it from a Prize you might Ship Salt or Mollasses, Rum &c in lieu thereof. You'l Consign to Mr. John Dorsius in Charles Town, to Messrs Hewes & Smith at Occracock North Carolina, to Benj. Harrison junr. Esqr. in Virginia, to Mr. David Stewart at Baltimore, to us on this Coast, to Mr. Nathl Shaw junr. at New London, Mr. Danl Tillinghast at Rhode Island, John Bradford Esqr, Continental agent at Boston or any port in Massachusetts or to John Langdon C. agent in New Hampshire. I forgot to Mention Benjn. Wereat Esqr. in Georgia, however I wou'd always have you prefer sending to Charles Town & this place whilst they remain ours, indeed If you hear this place falls into the hands of the Enemy it may probably be best to keep the whole of the Prizes in your own hands.[2]

We have been much alarmed for some days past for the safety of this City & are not yet intirely relieved of our apprehensions on Acct of the unfortunate change in our affairs since the reduction of Fort Washington. The Enemy landed a Body of 8 to 10,000 Men in the Jerseys with a large Train of Artillery, and after forcing Genl. Washington with between 4 & 5000 Men to evacuate Fort Lee, they have continued their March as far as N Brunswick in the Jerseys where they now are & obliged Genl. Washington to Retreat before them to Prince Town & Trentown. He is at the latter place with about 3000 Men, Ld Stirling at the other with 1000 to 1500 Men, but if the Enemy come on they will be obliged to Cross Delaware for Safety as they are not a Force to make a stand before the Enemy. In this Retreat we have lost many usefull Stores, Provisions & I fear Artillery, and You may suppose the alarm & confusion here as it was generally believed they intended for this City. Thus you have one side of the Picture. I hope the other may be better. Our associators had been much disgusted with their Service in the Flying Camp & their Spirit had gone to sleep. They were called upon but did not rouse, untill within this two days when they began to Conceive their danger was real & they are now turning out with a Spirit becoming Free Men. This day & tomorrow the whole Militia of this City & Suburbs March to join Genl Washington. The Country will follow the example of the City. The Jerseys are in Motion and Genl. Lee has Crossed the North River with Considerable Force & is on the March towards the Enemy, so that I expect they will now be driven into Winter quarters. More I do not promise myself at this time as their Artillery is extreamly formidable & we have but little to oppose it. Our affairs are amazingly altered for the worse. Within a few Weeks however I hope the exertions of Congress this Winter will put them in a Respectable posture before the Spring.

I am in daily hopes of hearing from you by Capt. Young. The Committee will not have time to write by this Conveyance. I am Dr Sir with much regard Your Friend & Servant,

Robt. Morris

P.S. I expect Mr. Prejent will be very useful in buying, fitting &
manning the Privateer.[3] You must however get as many Anglo
Americans as possible for Officers & Men and be sure that no Prize
is detained unless clearly British or British-West India property.

R.M.

RC (TxU).
[1] With this letter Morris included a second one to Bingham, which was simply
a brief letter of recommendation for Captain Ord. Robert Morris to William
Bingham, December 4, 1776, Gratz Collection, PHi.
[2] An extract of this letter, consisting of the remainder of the document except
for the postscript, was printed in *NYHS Collections* 19 (1887): 408–9 and identified as a letter to Silas Deane dated December 6, 1776.
[3] For information on the great success of Prejent's subsequent privateering ventures, see Robert C. Alberts, *The Golden Voyage: The Life and Times of William
Bingham, 1752–1804* (Boston: Houghton Mifflin Co., 1969), pp. 52–56.

New York Delegates to the New York Convention

Gent.   Phila. 4 Decembr. 1776
    We recd. Mr. McKessons lettr dated the 25 of November. We have
according to your request applied to Congress for leave for our
State to raise Anothr. Battalion to be Commanded by Collo DuBois
which is Agreed to & a Resolve to that Purpose is inclosed as Also a
Resolve for Imploying 5 Aid Majors at the Expence of our State.
Blank Coms. for Both the Battalion & Aid Majors are herewith Sent.
There are 45 blanks a few More than the Number wanted to Serve
in Case some Might be Spoild in filling up. The rank of the Officers
of the 5 Battalions is with you to Settle. The Congress does not
Interfere under the New Arrangement, in the rank of Officers Appointed by the Several States.[1]
    Genl. Washington is At Trenton with his Army. Genl. Cornwallis
at Brunswick. This City has been in Great Confusion for Some
days, Their Consternation was Great from an apprehention that the
Enemy wd. March on to this place, but they have now in a Great
Measure recovered their Spirits & are marchg out in Considerable
Numbers to Join Genl. Washington & in A few days our Army
will be Strong Enough to face the Enemy. We have no Acct. Where
our Troops under Genl. Lee are at present but are in hopes, if they
are on their march as is Said, that Cornwallis will not proceed any
farther this way too Speedily. If he delays a very few days longer
there is Nothing to fear from him. We Are, Gent., Your Most obedt.
servants,   Phil. Livingston

                                                   Fras. Lewis

                                                   Wm. Floyd

RC (NN). Written by Livingston and signed by Livingston, Floyd, and Lewis.

¹ Congress passed these resolves on November 30. *JCC*, 6:994. A November 23 letter from the New York Committee of Safety to Hancock on the subject of raising an additional Continental battalion in New York is in *Am. Archives*, 5th ser. 3:317–18.

Secret Committee to the Massachusetts Assembly

In Secret Committee of Congress   Philada. Decr. 4th. 1776
Gentn.

A Committee of Congress was appointed the 25th Septr. last to procure Cloathing in all the States on this Continent for the use of our Army & we find they wrote to you on the 10th Octr. requesting the favour of you to employ proper persons to purchase what cou'd be obtained in your State.¹ To this letter they have not recd any answer, and the Congress being very anxious & impatient to have this important business duely attended to & executed have directed us to send one or more trusty persons into the Eastern States to Collect what has been bought & to make such further purchases of suitable Articles as they can accomplish.² We have engaged Messrs. Abm. Livingston and Wm. Turnbull bearers hereof to go upon this Service. You will be pleased to direct them to the persons who have made purchases on Continental acct by order, & let the Goods be delivered to these Gentlemen or their order. We have also by direction of Congress authorized them to make further purchases & must beg the favour of your advice & assistance to them in the prosecution of that business or that you will desire your Committee to give them such assistance. We have judged it dangerous to send a large Sum of money with them at this time on acct of the situation of our Enemy, neither cou'd we well judge what Sum might be sufficient, therefore we request you will order them to be supplyed out of your Publick Treasury if needfull. Their drafts on this Committee for the Amount shall be paid, & if desired the money shall be sent by express.³ Your Zeal to serve the general Cause on all occasions makes us satisfyed of your Concurrence with our desires & we remain with the utmost respect Gentn., Your most Obedt & most hble servts,   Robt. Morris   Richard Henry Lee

           Phil. Livingston   Wm. Whipple

                              Fras. Lewis

RC (PPRF). Written by Morris and signed by Morris, Lee, Lewis, Livingston, and Whipple.

¹ See Committee on Clothing to Nicholas Cooke, October 11, 1776, note 2.

² See the resolve of December 1, *JCC*, 6:997. On December 5 the Massachusetts General Court voted £7,000 for the purchase of clothing and on January 10, 1777, it authorized an additional £4,000 to be used for that purpose. Minutes of the Massachusetts Council, pp. 287, 452–53, DLC(ESR).

³ The Secret Committee wrote a similar letter to Nicholas Cooke this day, introducing Livingston and Turnbull and requesting Cooke's "advice and Assistance to these Gentn. in the prosecution of their business' in Rhode Island. Red Series, R–Ar.

Robert Treat Paine's Diary

December 5, 1776

Fair fine Weather. Heard that the Enemy were only 6,000 strong & had not cross'd the Rariton & that Genl. Washington was return'd to Prince Town.

MS (MHi).

Robert Treat Paine to Samuel and Robert Purviance

Sir   Philadelphia Decr. 5. 1776

The Bearer Mr. Henry Stevenson is upon a Journey to Maryland in order to purchase a quantity of Pigg Iron for the Use of the State of Massa. Bay. As its uncertain what Monies he may want on this Occasion we have thought it best that he should take with him a Letter of Credit from us, he being impowered by the Assembly of Massa. Bay to draw on us for the Amount of two hundred Tons of Pigg Iron. We therefore request of you to give him what assistance he may want in purchasing & shipping any quantity of Pigg Iron he may incline to purchase to the above amount & his Draughts on us Shall be paid on Sight.

FC (MHi). Addressed: "Messr. Saml & Robt Purviance Merchts. at Baltimore." Endorsed: "Messrs Purviance, Phila. Dec. 5, 1776. letters of Credit for Agent of Massa. Bay."

Benjamin Rush's Notes on Proceedings in Congress

[December 5? 1776] ¹

A number of Indian chiefs came from Fort Pitt (where a treaty had been held with them by commissioners appointed by congress) came to Philada in Novr 1776. They were all introduced to the congress. They took each member by the hand, and afterwards sat down. One of them (after a pause of 10 minutes) rose up and addressed the congress in the following words.

"Brothers. We received your commissioners at the little counsel fire at Fort Pitt. We wiped the sweat from their bodies. We cleansed the dirt from their ankles. We pulled the thorns from [their] feet. We took their staffs from their hands, and leaned them agt the tree of peace, we took their belts from their waists, and conducted them to the seats of peace." [2]

MS (PPL). In the hand of Benjamin Rush.

[1] These notes appear in a small booklet of miscellaneous notes, sandwiched between a discussion of the American people (divided into five classes according to their political opinons) and notes dated April 8, 1777, speculating on General Howe's designs and General Washington's probable responses. The bulk of the material contained in the notebook was published by S. Weir Mitchell, "Historical Notes of Dr. Benjamin Rush, 1777," *PMHB* 27 (April 1903): 129–50. For additional notes taken from this booklet, see Benjamin Rush's Notes of Debates, February 4, 10, 14, 19, 20, and 26, 1777.

Although the section printed here bears no identifying information, Rush's reference to the arrival of an Indian delegation "in Novr 1776" and entries in the journals pertaining to the appearance of Indians in Congress on December 5, 7, and 9 suggest that the remarks he recorded were those delivered on the fifth. See *JCC*, 6:1003, 1006, 1010–11, 1013.

[2] Rush also discussed this episode in his autobiography, where he recorded this speech in a sligʻ. ly revised form. In the MS printed here, Rush inserted superscript numerals "2" and "1" before the sentences beginning "We wiped" and "We took their Staffs," perhaps indicating an intent to transpose the passages when he transferred them to his autobiography. No such transposition was made in the latter version, however, which has been published as follows:

"During my attendance in Congress in Philadelphia I had the pleasure of being present at an interview between some chiefs of the Six Nations and Congress in their hall in the State House. After a pause of about ten minutes one of the chiefs rose from his seat, and pointing to the Sun said 'The business of this day will end well. Yonder Sun rose clear this morning. The great Spirit is propitious to us. Brothers, we received the commissioners you sent us at the little council fire at Pittsburgh. We wiped the sweat from their bodies. We cleaned the dust from their legs. We pulled the thorns from their feet. We took their staffs from their hands, and placed them against the tree of peace. We took their belts from their waists, and afterwards conducted them to the seats of peace.' In retiring, they all shook hands with every member of Congress." Benjamin Rush, *The Autobiography of Benjamin Rush*, ed. George W. Corner (Princeton: Published for the American Philosophical Society by Princeton University Press, 1948), pp. 121–22.

Oliver Wolcott to Laura Wolcott

My Dear,   Philidelpha. 5th Decr 1776

I Wrote to you the 16 and 24t last which I hope you have recd. My Letter of the 12t Col Williams tells me he delivered and I most Sincerely rejoiced to be informed by him that you was then well.

By the Blessing of God I am in Health, and which now appears to be as much confirmed to Me, as it has been at any time the year past. No Delegates are yet come from Connecticut, tho I am informed Mr. Huntington will soo'ι Return. I have sent Martin Philosophy for Oliver which will be left at Col Porter's at Salisbury.

As to News Nothing Material from the Southward. What the affairs are to the Eastward of us, you will probably be informed of, earlier than I can give you. At present Part of Howe's Army under Cornwallis are advancd as farr as Rariton. Genl. Washington and his Army are at Trenton and Princtown. Wheither the Enemy will in good earnest Attempt to Possess themselves of this City a few days will discover.

It has been a long time since the eastern Post has been here. Letters for the future during the unsettled state of Affairs will go by private Hands, but as the Course from hince to Boston will be thro Litchfield, hope I may pretty frequently have Opportunities of Writing to you. I have at Times been a little impatient that my Freinds have not oftener and more particularly Wrote to Me. The Tyes of affection especially for my Own Family, together with a Desire to know how matters go on in Connecticut strongly induce me to Wish for their Correspondence, but I am sensible of the Dificulty of Correspondence and therefore do not impute their omission to the Want of Freindship and indeed Care ought to be taken in forwarding Letters that they do not fall into the Hands of the Enemy which has too often been the case. I have recd None from Litchfield except Two from Mr Lyman and one from Mr Adams.

I Wish you to take care of your Health and that it would please God to grant you and the Family his chocest Blessings. I am your's with the most inviolable affection,   Oliver Wolcott

P.S. The Militia of Pensylvania are going forward to Stem the Progress of the Foe, should they attempt to proceed.

RC (CtHi).

Samuel Adams to James Warren

My dear Sir   Philadelpa Decr 6th 1776

I wrote to you two days ago by a Captn Potes. This will be delivered to you by Mr Livingston who is employed by a Committee of Congress to repair to the Eastern States to purchase Cloathing for the Army. I inclosd to you not long ago a Resolve of Congress relating to Shoes & Stockings which it is supposd can be procured in very considerable Quantities in those States. I then mentioned to you my hopes that your Committee had collected a good Stock of Cloaths.[1] I had venturd almost to assure Congress that this had been done. There is a Fatality attends the Post notwithstanding all that has been done to regulate it, so that we can seldom get Intelligence from our Constituents, while the Gentlemen of other States have Advice from theirs, either by Post or Express at least every Week. Would you believe it, we had but one Post from the Eastward since my last Arrival here on the 24th of October. I wish we could hear often from you. Much is to be done this Winter to prepare for the ensuing Spring. The Enemy, it is now said, are in retreating order from Brunswick.

By the last Accounts from the Northward we are informd that the Ice begins to make on the Lakes. A few choice Friends have conceivd it very practicable when the Enemies Vessels are closd in the Ice, to destroy them by burning. Could this be done, it woud exceedingly distress the Enemy and confound them. I confess I am enthusiastical in this Matter. I wish you could consult *a few* concerning it. If it is a Proposal worth your Notice, and I hardly doubt you will think it so, it must be communicated to a very few. I should think it would be best set on foot & executed by the New England People and I daresay there are trusty Men in our State who thoroughly understand such kind of Business. Sat Verbum Sapienti. Think seriously of it. Adieu.

RC (MHi). In Adams' hand, though not signed.
[1] For further discussion about the collection of clothing and supplies, see Samuel Adams to James Warren, November 29; and Secret Committee to the Massachusetts Assembly, December 4, 1776.

Robert Treat Paine to David Cobb

My dear Sir,   Philada. Decr. 6th. 1776
I have not heard from you a long time, owing I suppose to your unsettled state of Body which I understand has been vibrating between Boston & Taunton till I find you have at last decided in favour of the latter.[1] I can assure you that the Expectation of your Removing from Taunton gave me much uneasiness & if ever I am able to spend my days there it will be an Addition to any happiness that you are with me. Our public affairs have been exceedingly agitated Since I wrote you last. The loss of Fort Washington made way for that of Fort Lee & the dissolution of our army hapning at the same time threw us into a most disagreable Scituation. The interception of an Express gave the Enemy full assurance of what they must have had Some Knowledge of before, the State of our Army, & they took the Advantage of it; in two days after their possession of Fort Lee on the 20th ult Where we lost much Baggage & the Chief of our battering Cannon, they march'd to Hackensack a pretty Town, from thence to Newark driving Genl. Washing-

ton before them with his 3 or 4,000 men, thence to Elizabeth Town by the 24th. Genl. Washington Supposed by the best Information he could get that they were 10 or 12,000 Strong marching With a large Body of Horse in front & very large train of Artillery. We began to be Apprehensive they intended for Philada. & Congress satt all Sunday Decr. 1 in determining proper measures on the Occasion. I will not describe to you the Scituation of the City. The prospect was really alarming; we could not fairly calculate a force Sufficient to defend the City on so sudden a Call. Genl. Lee was on t'other Side of Hudson's River, no help could be expected from Tionderoga, but to work we went. The Associators of the City were drawn forth & abt. 3000 with an addition of Artillery march'd. The Country Associators were called upon but there was no expectation of Sudden assistance from them. As the Week came on we had repeated Advices from the General of the unopposd approach of the Enemy headed by General Cornwallis. On Monday We were informed by the Genl. that they were arrived at Brunswick & that he was retreating to the West Side of Delaware River 30 miles from Phila. Brunswick is 60 miles from Philada. & stands upon a Wide River that is fordable at Low Water. They had not crossed the River & Genl. Washington exchanged some Cannon Shot with them before he retreated & we since find they lost some men & an officer. It was now a very rainy season & the Marching thro all this Country exceeding mirey. We sent many Continental Stores into the Country & great numbers of People are moving. The shops have not been opened since Sunday. There was a real Apprehension that we should be routed. I need not tell you what our Calculations were on the expectation of loosing this City. I had Called in my accounts & prepared matters for a regular retreat, but on Thursday we found the Enemy had not crossed the Rariton, i.e. Brunswic River, & by An Officer of my acquaintance whom Genl. Washington had sent with a Flag to escort a Prisoner to the Enemy in Exchange & who tarried two days with them. I learn many particulars of them, that they were abt. 6,000 Strong, abt 40 Light Horse, that they left no troops at the places they marched thro, & were surprised to find Newark & Eliza Town evacuated by its Inhabitants, that they knew the State of our Army which induced them to make the Excursion. The Inhabitants of Prince Town & Trenton which lay between Brunswick & the Enemy are evacuated. The people left them on Sunday Night with Pannic & Precipitation, While the Enemy were as much afraid of approaching as *they* were that they should. Thus stands the matter this day, & we have no Apprehensions the Enemy will proceed further for, as I should have told you, we heard yesterday that Genl Lee with a large Body of Men was close in the rear of the Enemy. Our Apprehensions now are from an Embarkation of Six thousand men which we have pretty certain intelligence of. When we first heard it We expected it was designed for an Attack on Philada. by Water while the first Party penetrated by Land, but we are now apprehensive for So. Carolina, Virginia, some say Newport. The Enemy are in Possession of a very large & valuable part of N Jersey & the remaining part is greatly distressed by his Approach, but I hope this affair will rouse them from that lethargy which Occasioned this excursion, for had their militia been alert & resolute & given Genl Washington the support they might have done, these Evils had not happened, but stupidity & carelessness have been the Lord of our ascendants this last month. Tis to no purpose to scold, let us carefully ascertain our past Errors & amend them.[2]

FC (MHi).

[1] David Cobb (1748–1830), Paine's brother-in-law, was a physician who had just returned to Taunton, Mass., after trying to establish a practice in Boston. He served as a lieutenant colonel and colonel in the Continental Army, 1777–83, and later was elected to the United States Congress. Shipton, *Harvard Graduates*, 16:337–51.

[2] For the continuation of this letter, see Paine to Cobb, December 8, 1776.

George Read to Gertrude Read

My dear Gitty   Philada. the 6th Decr. 1776

Attendance Night & Morning at Committees and all day at Congress puts it out of my power to write you so frequently as I ought & have had Opportunities but I have no chance of A Moment but when I retire out of Congress to the Comittee room where I now am to write to any person. However be assured that if any[thing] very material occurs you shall hear it. Genl. Washington in his Letter of yesterday mentions the Enemy's being at Brunswick & Ld. Sterling with 2 Brigades consisting 1200 Men including the Delaware Battalion at Princetown abot. 15 Miles a part—that Genl. Mercer has marched back from Trenton to Prince Town 1200 more as A Reinforcemt. & Genl. Washington is to follow this day.[1] Genl. Lee is somewhere in the Neighbourhood but where particularly or what force is not precisely known. The German Battalion belonging to the Continent with the City Militia have Marched from here supposed more than 3000. I have little doubt that the Progress of the British Army will be stopped if no more. The Troops belonging to Flying Camp whose times of Inlistment had expired left the General in whole Brigades, particularly Jersey & Maryland—as also to Paterson's Batta. They wod. [not] serve an Hour longer, so that this City is filled with returning Soldiers tho never more wanted in the field. The Delegates of Maryland with Genl Mifflin harangued a great Number perhaps 6 or 700 of them in the State House Yard yester-

day with Success and it is expected a great part will return for a
Month. Polly Bird is come to Town tho I have not seen her. Mark
says she has given over all thought of going to parson Thompson's.
Gitty Gurney told as I came by to Congress that she had thoughts
still of going down to you. She is presently engaged in preparing
their House in Town for Messrs. Tilghman & Carrol of Maryland
who are to go into it. Bedford came to Town Tuesday Evening &
is mending. Tom Read marched last Evening. Jemmy goes this Evening, his Company went yesterday. Genl. [. . .] is still with us. I am
satisfied you will not be disturbed in your Quarters this Season,
therefore make yourself easy and kiss our little ones. I know not
when I may See you. I cannot stir for the Non Attendance of our
Representatn. for times past has been severely animadverted upon
since my return. I am yors. most affectely,   Geo. Read

RC (DeHi).
[1] General Washington's December 5 letter to President Hancock, which was read
in Congress this date, is in PCC, item 152, 3:317–19, and Washington, *Writings*
(Fitzpatrick), 6:330–33.

John Witherspoon to the
Pennsylvania Council of Safety

Sir   Philadelphia Dec 6. 1776
    Agreable to the Conversation I had with you this Evening I have
conversed fully & explicitly with Mr Ingram [1] who has given me
entire Satisfaction & therefore I am willing to be bound for him
to any Amount that the Council of Safety shall think proper that he
shall not henceforth correspond with, give Intelligence to or in any
Ways assist or abet the Enemies of American Liberty & that he shall
proceed directly from this place to Virginia where this Obligation he
is laid under may be made known to any that the Council may
think proper. I am Sir your most obed, humble servant,
                                    Jno Witherspoon

RC (N). Addressed: "To Captain Blewer to be Communicated to the Council of
Safety of Pennsylvania." Endorsed: "Agreed to in Council & Mr. Ingram discharged
accordingly. Decr. 7. 1776." Joseph Blewer was a member of the Pennsylvania
Council of Safety.
[1] This was probably James Ingram, a Virginia loyalist who moved to Maryland
in 1777 and then to England. Lorenzo Sabine, *Biographical Sketches of Loyalists
of the American Revolution with an Historical Essay*, 2 vols. (Boston: Little,
Brown and Co., 1864), 1:566. There is no mention of Ingram in the council of
safety's official proceedings.

Charles Carroll, Barrister to the
Maryland Council of Safety

Dear Sir [1]   Philada. Decr 7t 1776

As Soon as I Saw Mr Morriss in Congress I made enquiry about the Powder but he Could not Recollect any Circumstance Relating to it. I Gave Him the Memor[andum] & He Promised to Give Me an answer but Such Has been the Hurry and Confusion that he Has not had time to advert to it Since. We now tho in My opinion far from being entirely Secure begin to be a little More Composed. By the Last Letters the Enemy were still at Brunswick and General Washington had left Trentown and Had advanced to Prince Town tho With very Little addition to His force, as the Jersey Militia Had not Moved, and I am sure He Could not Have been Join'd by above 1200 from this state. General Lee has Crossed the North River and is Marching with a body of forces the Number Uncertain but said to be ten Thousand to His assistance and there is another Body Moving from Ticonderoga. Should the Enemy Continue inactive they May Reach us in Time to Prevent their advancing further & save this City. We have Certain advices of an Embarkation of 6000 Troops at N Y, but their Destination not Known, and We Likewise Hear that General Howe is himself Coming to Brunswick to Erect the Kings Standard and Regain the submission of that Province. Should that be the Case and the Reduction of that Province his only object, should He stop there any Time and that fleet not be destind against this City He will Have Lost in My apprehension the finest opportunity a General Ever Had of Possessing himself of this Important Place and thereby Plucking up the War by the Roots. However Eight or Ten Days will Shew his Designs. The Inactivity of the People here was so Great & their Disinclination to Stir to oppose the Enemy so apparent that We Were forced to offer Clothing to some of our flying Camp Troops here that Will amount to about four Pounds per Man to Induce them to return & Join the Army for one Month only and to Engage that our Province will be at the Expence should the Congress Refuse it, Wch surely they will not. How many We may get to return I Know not as from what they have Sufferd they do not seem to have Much appetite for the Service. We have at Present 12 states represented in Congress but Many of them by one Person only so that we are Thin in Number. If the Situation of Mr Stones family be such that He Can Leave it we should have Much Pleasure in seeing him & I Must Request you will write to Mr Johnson to Join us.[2] The Arrival of Conway Gives me real satisfaction as it Contributes to your Reputations for Dilligence and attention to the Public Service in as it is Really of Much value at this Time to our State. Pray Remember me to Vice President & all your Brothers of the Council. Let Me know your News & how you Proceed in Executing your new form of Govnt, & believe me to be, Sincerely and obediently yours,

Chas Carroll

[P.S.] Money Flies Here Like Wildfire. My Colleagues are Crying out with one Voice for a Supply. Do not forget us. Lee has Certainly Crossed the North River with between 7 & 10 thousand Men & General Washington is advancing towards the Enemy. He left Princetown yesterday Mor[nin]g.

RC (PHi).

[1] This letter was undoubtedly written to Daniel of St. Thomas Jenifer, president of the Maryland Council of Safety. Carroll's comments on "Mr. Stone's family" and the delegates' need for money seem to have been elicited by the council's letter to the delegates of November 29. See Md. Archives, 12:490–91.

[2] On December 12 the council of safety sent brief letters to Thomas Stone and to Thomas Johnson requesting that they return to Congress. Ibid., pp. 524–25.

Elbridge Gerry to Joseph Trumbull

Dear Sir   Philadelphia 7th Decr 1776

I wrote You the 26th Novr touching several Matters mentioned in the Letters received from You before that Time, & am informed by General Mifflin that he forwarded two of my Letters.[1] You will therein find my Sentiments relative to a Contract, & the present Improbability there is that any will take place. You will also see that your Petition is referred to the Treasury; [2] that Congress have impowered You to import Rice from the southern States, & that I have recommended your immediate Application in strong Terms for Liberty to import Flower.[3] I find You place great Confidence in a certain southern Friend,[4] had he Voted with Us in this Instance, It had prevented the Necessity of a second Application, but this he rarely omits to avoid. Mention is likewise made of the Fish purchased of You to import military Stores, that the Quality was greatly reduced by age, insomuch that it must be sent to the West Indies instead of Europe as was first intended, & You was desired when Oppertunity offers to send a Bill thereof. I have nothing at this Time to say in answer to your Favour of the 26th Novr as I suppose You know the Circumstances of our military Movements; unless to suggest the Expediency & Necessity of your establishing Magazines in such interior parts of the Country, as cannot be penetrated by the Enemy without great Misfortunes on the Side of the States. I remain sir with much Esteem your sincere Friend & huml ser,

E Gerry

RC (Ct).

[1] Not found, but see Gerry's letters to Trumbull of October 22 and November 11, 1776.

[2] Trumbull's petition for an increase in salary was referred to the Board of Treasury on November 18, 1776. *JCC*, 6:958. But for further discussion of its disposition see Gerry to Joseph Trumbull, October 22, 1776.

[3] On November 28 Congress had authorized Trumbull to import rice from the southern states, and on December 26 it approved similar authorization for importing flour. *JCC*, 6:989, 1040–41; and Gerry to Trumbull, December 26, 1776.

[4] Probably William Hooper.

William Paca to the
Maryland Council of Safety

Gentn.   Saturday 7 Dec. 1776.

Congress is of Opinion that the order from the Board of War extends only to such Prisoners as are natives of Great Britain and Soldiers from thence in the present War and therefore the Prisoners from Carolina and Residents there lately taken in Arms against us are not comprehended and are still to be detained.[1] As to the two Gentlemen taken by Capt Cooke whether they be Prisoners or not is a Matter our State must decide and not Congress.[2] I am told by the Delegates to the Eastward that Persons in such Predicaments are let at Liberty but the property taken is confiscated; but this is not a general Rule. Circumstances often require them to be prisoners: you must therefore (I speak my own Opinion only) exercise your discretion in the present Case.

The Enemy is still at Brunswic: Genl. Washington has faced about and is moving towards them with the reinforcements from this State. Genl. Lee has crossed the River as we are informed with about 12000 men and we are now also informed that Genl. St. Clair with about 1200 Men left New Windsor last Friday Week so that by this time we hope the Enemy will find themselves between two Fires and Heaven grant they may be well roasted.

Great Complaints have been made by the Privates of our flying Camp of neglect & want of Pay. I am afraid our officers have not been so careful & industrious in making out their Rolls as they ought to have been. We are doing all we can to get them their money which indeed has been long ago ready for them and only detained from the want of the officers Rolls. Our poor Sick were much distressed till they came to this City: here every necessary is found them & the best Care taken of them. We have declined no Trouble to have these poor Creatures comfortably provided for.[3]

Yr. hb. Sert.,   W Paca.

RC (MdAA).

[1] There is no indication in the journals of Congress that a formal determination

William Paca

had been made on this point. For the "Order from the Board of War" that is here
at issue, see Board of War to the Pennsylvania Council of Safety, November 19,
1776; and *Md. Archives*, 12:456, 486.

² "The two Gentlemen taken" were undoubtedly the passengers on board a vessel
captured by Capt. George Cook of the Maryland ship *Defence* discussed in his
letters to the council of safety of October 4, 1776. Their status apparently came
up at this time in consequence of the preparation of responses to the Board of
War's "Order" mentioned in note 1 above. Despite Paca's explanation here that
"our State must decide and not Congress," the council again referred the matter
to their delegates on December 27. Chase apparently resolved the case to the
council's satisfaction when he subsequently explained that "the Georgia delegates
object to the discharge of the Gentlemen, whose cases you referred to Congress."
See *Md. Archives*, 12:319–20, 555–56, 16:62–63; and Samuel Chase to the Maryland
Council of Safety, January 3 and 19? 1777.

³ Two days later Matthew Tilghman, Samuel Chase, and Charles Carroll, Barrister, asked the Maryland commissioners to "advance to Lieutenant Harwood as
much Money as will defray the Expence of conveying our Sick to Maryland."
According to the receipt appended to the bottom of this letter, Thomas Harwood
received $260 the same day. Maryland Delegates to "The Commissioners of Mary-
land," December 9, 1776, manuscript collection of Mr. Ronald von Klaussen.

Robert Treat Paine's Diary

December 7, 1776

I had an Interview with Sachems & Warriors of Delaware, Shaw-
nese & Mingo Tribes of Indians.¹

MS (MHi).
¹ See Benjamin Rush's Notes of Proceedings in Congress, December 5, 1776. John
Hancock's address to the Indians which was delivered this day is in *JCC*, 6:1011.

Robert Treat Paine to Daniel and Samuel Hughes

Gentlemen   Philada Decr. 7. 1776

I yesterday recd. yours by Melchor Saladin & immediately procured the within discharge he brought with a John Haine & said that
after your Letter was [. . .] you sent a verbal Message desiring that
he might likewise be discharged & put into your Service. He was
so positive that I gave Credit to him & hope it is right, I shall
direct them to make the best of their way to you. I understand by
them that your new furnace is built & ready for blast. I hope you
will take every precaution to prevent miscarriages. When you consider the importance of your undertaking to the public as well as
to your Selves, you will not wonder of my importunity with you
to attend critically to the quality of the metal. So large a proportion
of the Guns made in the Furnaces here have failed in proving that
I am satisfied of the truth of what Mr. Mathews told me that the

great art of making Cannon was the getting the metal to a due temper. What should be the reason that Iron when Cast into a thin Pot or Kettle shall be fine & close grained & very Strong & tough, & yet when Cast from the same furnace & the same Sort of Ore into a large Cannon it is coarse & open grained & brittle. I think it Shews that some further preparation is wanting for Iron cast into a large body than a small one. Stone lime is found to be a great refiner of Iron, I suppose it is generally used at the furnace, or rather the Lime Stone is used. Mr. Wm. Henry of Lancaster is of Opinion & I think with good reason that the Burnt Lime should be put in rather than the Stone, because before the Lime Stone is burnt so as to operate on the Iron the ore is melted & gone off. But the Lime operates immediately in absorbing the sulphur [. . .] & other [heterogeneous?] matter. He is also of opinion that the quantity put in is never Sufficient. Some experiments he has tryed of the Effects of Lime in toughening Iron are very Satisfactory. I dont undertake to direct or instruct you in yr business but if I should drop a hint to yr. advantage you will not take it amiss. I wish a thorough tryal was made of the Advantage of putting in very large quantities of Lime into the furnace. I really believe you would find your [. . .] it. Yrs., RTP

FC (MHi). Addresed: "To Danl & Saml Hughes at Antietam Furnace. Per Melchor Saladin."

John Hancock to James Wilson

Dear Sir: Sunday Eveg [December 8, 1776]

The instant your messenger came in, an Express arrived from the Genl. & bro't the Inclos'd Letter. The General dates his Letter this Day at Mr Berkley's Sommerset,[1] he has cross'd the Delaware with his whole Army, which he writes was 3500 before the German Battaln & Pennsylva Militia came in & they about 2000; he begs more force, as he thinks undoubtedly Philada is their object. He had heard nothing of Genl Lee, wonders much at his slow movements. We must Exert ourselves now. I hope you will be early at Congress & let us do what we can. We must save the Country.

I am hurried. Adieu, Yours sincerely,   J. Hancock

Tr (PSC). Endorsed by Burton A. Konkle: "Original in Papers of Herbert Morris, Esq. of Phila., which formerly belonged to his father, the late Galloway C. Morris of Lake George, N.Y."

[1] Washington's December 8 letter to President Hancock is in PCC, item 152, 3:327–28, Washington, *Writings* (Fitzpatrick), 6:335–37.

Robert Treat Paine to David Cobb

Sunday 8th [December 1776]
Congress were called this morning on advice that Genl Howe had joined Genl Cornwallis with a Reinforcement & was marching on to Princetown.[1] This Maneuvre induces me to think that the Expedition is agt. Philada.[2]

Monday 9th
Yesterday Genl. Washington crossed the Delaware & the Enemy arrived at Trenton on the East side of it (close quarters for Congress) 30 miles from Philada, fine road. Congress resolved if they were obliged to remove to go to Baltimore in Maryland 100 miles from hence. I have got leave to return home but shall here a while longer unless we are routed.[3]

I have this day recd. yrs. of Novr. 23rd per Post, in wch. I have the assurance of yr settlement at Taunton; I doubt whether I shall see you by Christmass as you desire, but nothing cou'd hinder me but attention to important matters. Let my Wife see this Letter.

FC (MHi). A continuation of Paine to Cobb, December 6, 1776.
[1] Paine made a similar entry in his diary for this date. "Advice that Genl Howe had joined Ld. Cornwallis & was marching on to Princetown. Congress satt. P.M. I had Mr. Montgomery at Dr. Swans." MHi. The journals do not record this emergency session of Congress. *JCC*, 6:1012.
[2] This day Thomas McKean also wrote a brief letter to his wife containing a similar report and instructing her "to take a house at Newark as soon as you can." "We have received today undoubted intelligence that our enemies are advancing towards Philadelphia, General How by the way of Bound brook (nine miles from Brunswick up the Rariton) at the head of one column, and Lord Cornwallis at the head of the other, the two columns containing, it is said, the whole army, except Garrisons for the forts they have taken, and amounting (some say) to twenty thousand men, others think twelve thousand. . . . A Fleet has actually sailed from New-York, and every one believes for our river; the enemy seem determined to be here before Christmas, and the weather and every thing hitherto seems to be in their favor, but I flatter myself, they will meet with a check ere long." McKean to Sarah McKean, December 8, 1776, McKean Papers, PHi.
[3] There is no mention in the journals of Congress granting permission to Paine to return home, although according to his diary he did leave for Massachusetts on December 11. See Samuel Adams to James Warren, December 12, 1776, note.

Samuel Adams to Elizabeth Adams

My dear Betsy   Philadelphia Decr 9 1776
My last by Mr Pliarne I hope you will have receivd before this reaches you. I am still in good Health and Spirits, although the Enemy is within Forty Miles of this City. I do not regret the Part I have taken in a Cause so just and interresting to Mankind. I must

confess it chagrins me greatly to find it so illy suported by the People of Pennsylvania and the Jerseys. They seem to me to be determined to give it up—but I trust that my dear New England will maintain it at the Expence of every thing dear to them in this Life. They know how to prize their Liberties. May Heaven bless them! It is not yet determind to what place to adjourn the Congress, if it should be necessary to move. Wherever I may be, I shall write to you by every opportunity. Mr Brown who carries this Letter will give you a particular Account of the Circumstances of things here—to him I refer you. Pray remember me to my Daughter, Sister Polly, the rest of my Family & Friends. I hope the Life of our valuable Friend Mrs March will yet be spared. She is indeed a good Woman. Tell my worthy Neighbor Mr Preston, that I rejoyce to hear of his honorable Appointment. I hope & beleive he will use his office well. I wish to have a Letter from you. You cannot imagine how highly I prize such a Favor. My daily Prayer is for your Safety, & Happiness in this Life & a better. Adieu, my dear. You cannot doubt the sincere & most cordial Affection of your,[1]   S A.

RC (NN).
[1] For the continuation of this letter, see Adams to Elizabeth Adams, December 11, 1776.

Matthew Thornton to Meshech Weare

Sir   Philadelphia Decr. 9th 1776
    Please to pay to John Langdon Esqr on order Three Hundred Dollars it being for value receiv'd here of William Whipple and charge the same to my accot with the State of New Hampshire, for which Sum I have drawn two orders of the same Tenor & date one of which being paid the other to be void. Your most obt. Sert,
                                             Matthew Thornton

RC (PPRF). Written by William Whipple and signed by Thornton.

William Ellery to Nicholas Cooke

Sir,   Philadelphia Decr. 10th 1776
    Since the Enemy took Possession of Fort Lee Genl. Washington with the Division under his immediate Command hath been constantly retreating, until they have at Length passed the Delaware and I suppose mean to make a Stand on the Banks of the River opposite to Trenton. To prevent their being hemmed in at Hakinsack they passed the River of that Name and the River Posaick, and

retired to Newark. The Enemy advanced, and upon their Approach, our Army, being insufficient to withstand them, retreated to Woodbridge. The Enemy followed. From thence our Army marched to Brunswick. The British Army soon appeared on the Side of the Rariton opposite to that Town. A Cannonade ensued but without any Hurt on either Side saving the killing of an Hessian Officer by one of our Cannon Shot. As the River is fordable it would not do to continue there. Our Troops decamped and marched to Prince Town, where Genl. Washington left a Body of 1200 Men under Lord Stirling, and with the Rest moved to Trenton; and sent over the Delaware his principal Stores to secure them from the Enemy. After this was effected he sent a Reinforcement to Ld Stirling, and hoping that he should be joined by the Militia of the Jersey and this State, and by Genl. Lee who it was said with his Division had passed the North River and was advancing to join him, intended to make a Stand at Princetown; but by a strange Dilatoriness and the Confusion which took Place in the Jersey on the Enemy's penetrating their State, and the Lukewarmness, not to give it a worse Name, of this, the Enemy had approached Prince Town before a sufficient Number of Militia from these States had joined Gl. Washington to enable him to make an effectual Stand there. He therefore retreated to Trenton and crossed the River with his Army last Saturday Night. On Sunday the Enemy appeared at Trenton and a Cannonade ensued as at Brunswick. Yesterday Genls. Putnam & Mifflin came to Town, and inform that the Enemy had disappeared from Trenton but they could [not] tell whither they were gone. I imagin We shall soon see them in that Part of the Jersey opposite this City and perhaps hear the Thunder of their Cannon and Mortars, and feel the Effects of Shot and Bombs. We don't hear of a Fleet yet in the Delaware which I have for some Time expected. I imagin the Enemy durst not venture it, for fear they shall have Ice as well as Cheveaux de frise to encounter.

I hope We shall be able to keep them out of this State, and We should be able to do it, if the Country would exert Themselves with a Tenth Part of the Spirit which the City hath manifested on this Occasion, or if Genl. Lee should join G. Washington with five or six thousand Men which I most devoutly wish for and ex[pect]. Where he is or what Delays his coming is unknown.

I find by a private Letter from Newport, for I have had [no] Intelligence of a higher Nature for a long Time, that Genl. Lee had wrote to our State that he thought that the Embarkation at New York was intended for Rhode Island,[1] and that this Intelligence had thrown the Town of Newport into great Confusion and that the Inhabitants were all upon the Wing. We have heard of Transports being prepared to receive Troops various Ways and for six Weeks past and sometimes that Troops were really embarked, and some-

The REPRESENTATIVES of the UNITED STATES of *America*, in CONGRESS assembled,

To the PEOPLE in general, and particularly to the Inhabitants of *Pennsylvania*, and the adjacent STATES.

FRIENDS and BRETHREN,

WE think it our Duty to address a few Words of Exhortation to you in this important Crisis. You are not unacquainted with the History of the Rise and Progress of this War. A Plan was carried on by the British Ministry for several Years in a systematic Manner to enslave you to that Kingdom. After various Attempts in an artful and insidious Manner to bring into Practice the laying you under Tribute, they at last openly and decisively asserted their Right of making Laws to bind you in *all Cases whatsoever*.

Opposition was made to these Encroachments by earnest and humble Petitions from every Legislature on the Continent, and more than once by the Congress representing the whole. These were treated with the utmost Contempt. Acts of the most unjust and oppressive Nature were passed and carried into Execution, such as exempting the Soldiers charged with Murder in America from a legal Trial, and ordering them to be carried to Britain for certain Absolution, as also directing Prisoners taken at Sea to be entered on board their Ships, and obliged either to kill their own Friends or fall themselves by their Hands. We only mention these from among the many oppressive Acts of Parliament as Proofs to what horrid Injustice the Love of Dominion will sometimes carry Societies as well as Men. At the same Time to shew how insensible they will be to the Sufferings of others, you may see by the Preambles to the Acts and Addresses to the King, that they constantly extol their own Lenity in those very Proceedings which filled this whole Continent with Resentment and Horror.

To crown the whole, they have waged War with us in the most cruel and unrelenting Manner, employing not only the Force of the British Nation but hiring foreign Mercenaries, who, without Feeling, indulge themselves in Rapine and Bloodshed. The Spirit indeed of the Army in general is but too well determined, by their inhuman Treatment of those who have unhappily fallen into their Hands.

It is well known to you, that at the universal Desire of the People, and with the hearty Approbation of every Province, the Congress declared the United States free and independent; a Measure not only just, but which had become absolutely necessary. It would have been impossible to have resisted the formidable Force destined against us last Spring, while we confessed ourselves the Subjects of that State against which we had taken Arms. Besides, after repeated Trials, no Terms could be obtained but Pardon, upon absolute Submission, which every public Body in America had rejected with Disdain.

Resistance has now been made with a Spirit and Resolution becoming a free People, and with a Degree of Success hitherto which could scarce have been expected. The Enemy have been expelled from the northern Provinces where they at first had Possession, and have been repulsed in their Attempt upon the southern by the undaunted Valour of the Inhabitants. Our Success at Sea, in the Capture of the Enemies Ships, has been astonishing. They have been compelled to retreat before the northern Army. Notwithstanding the Difficulty and Uncertainty at first of our being supplied with Ammunition and military Stores, those we have now in Abundance, and by some late Arrivals and Captures there is an immediate Prospect of sufficient Clothing for the Army.

What we have particularly in View, in this Address, is not only to promote Unanimity and Vigour through the whole States, but to excite the Inhabitants of *Pennsylvania*, *New Jersey*, and the adjacent States to an immediate and spirited Exertion in Opposition to the Army that now threatens to take Possession of this City. You know that during the whole Campaign they have been checked in their Progress, and have not till within these two Weeks ventured above ten Miles from their Shipping. Their present Advances are owing not to any capital Defeat, or a Want of Valour in the Army that opposed them, but to a sudden Diminution of its Numbers from the Expiration of those short Enlistments which, to take the People, were at first adopted. Many have already joined the Army to supply the Deficiency, and we call in the most earnest Manner on all the Friends of Liberty to exert themselves without Delay in this pressing Emergency. In every other Part your Arms have been successful, and in other Respects our sacred Cause is in the most promising Situation. We think it proper to inform and assure you that essential Services have been already rendered us by foreign States, and we have received the most positive Assurances of further Aid. Let us not then be wanting to ourselves. Even a short Resistance will probably be effectual, as General LEE is advancing with a strong Reinforcement, and his Troops in high Spirits.

What Pity is it then that the rich and populous City of *Philadelphia* should fall into the Enemy's Hands, or that we should not lay hold of the Opportunity of destroying their principal Army now removed from the Ships of War, in which their greatest Strength lies.

It is certainly needless to multiply Arguments in such a Situation. All that is valuable to us as Men and Freemen is at Stake. It does not admit of a Question, what would be the Effect of our finally failing. Even the boasted Commissioners for giving Peace to America have not offered, and do not now offer any Terms but Pardon on absolute Submission. And though (blessed be God) even the Loss of *Philadelphia* would not be the Loss of the Cause—Yet while it can be saved, let us not, in the Close of the Campaign, afford them such Ground of Triumph; but give a Check to their Progress, and convince our Friends, in the distant Parts, that ONE SPIRIT ANIMATES THE WHOLE.

Confiding in your Fidelity and Zeal in a Contest the most illustrious and important, and firmly trusting in the good Providence of God, we wish you Happiness and Success.

Given at Philadelphia, December 10, 1776.

By order of Congress,

JOHN HANCOCK, *President*.

Address to the People of America, Adopted December 10, 1776

times that they have sailed for So. Carolina or Rhode Island; but I can't find that they have ever embarked any Troops, nor do I think they will for either of those Places while they pursue such high Game and mean to secure the Posts & Places they have and may possess. They have not Men enough to spare at present nor do I think they will have them this Winter for any distant Expedition. However as I have often said it is wise and prudent to be on our Guard.

Capt. Garzia who will hand you this Letter cannot wait a Moment longer which obliges to close abruptly.

I am with great Respect your Honor's most Obedient humble Servant,   Wm Ellery

RC (R–Ar).
[1] See *NYHS Collections*, 5 (1872): 277–78, 300.

Georgia Delegates to John Hancock

Sir,   10th Decr. 1776.

We have received accounts of our reappointment to represent the state of Georgia in Congress; and will be ready to take our seats in a day or two.[1] In the meantime we request an order on the Treasury for two thousand dollars on account of the state we are appointed to represent.[2]

We are, Sir, your most Obedient Servants,   Lyman Hall

Geo Walton

RC (DNA: PCC, item 78). Written by Walton and signed by Walton and Hall.
[1] Although Hall and Walton had remained in Philadelphia, Georgia had not been represented in Congress since their terms expired on November 2. Walton attended Congress on December 12, but Georgia credentials were not read until Congress convened in Baltimore on December 20. See *JCC*, 6:1025, 1028.
[2] See *JCC*, 6:1017.

Marine Committee to Elisha Hinman

Sir   In Marine Committee, Philada. Decemr 10th 1776

We expect this will find the vessel under your Command in readiness for Service and therefore you are hereby directed to proceed to Sea with all possible dispatch and in a Cruize of Six Weeks or two Months to intercept as many of the Store Ships and Supply vessels going to the Enemy at New York as you may fall in with. You will in this Cruize do as much injury to the Enemy and service to the United States as it may be in your power to accomplish.

When this Cruize is finished you will return to the most convenient port in the United States, and if no further Orders are there lodged for you from this Board, you will proceed on a New Cruize for the Purpose above mentioned. We are persuaded it is not necessary to recommend to you the practice of humanity to those whom the fortune of war may make your prisoners.[1]

We expect to hear from you by every opportunity and wishing you Success We are sir, Your very hble Servts.

William Ellery	Fras. Lewis
Robt Morris	Wm Whipple
	Richard Henry Lee

RC (DNDAR). In the hand of Timothy Matlack and signed by Ellery, Lee, Lewis, Morris, and Whipple. Addressed: "To Capt Hinman of the Brigt Cabbot, Rhode Island."

[1] This day the Marine Committee sent the same letter to John Paul Jones. PCC, item 58, fol. 179; and *Am. Archives*, 5th ser. 3:1148.

Marine Committee to Esek Hopkins

Sir   In Marine Committee. Philada. Decemr 10th 1776

We have ordered the Captains of the Armed vessels now at Rhode Island Severally to proceed to Sea with all possible dispatch and to cruize for the Enemies Store Ships & Supply Vessels going to New York.

You Sir will exert yourself to have these orders carried into execution as Quickly as possible.

We are sir, Your hble Servts.

William Ellery	Fras. Lewis
Robt Morris	Wm. Whipple
	Richard Henry Lee

RC (RHi). Written by Morris and signed by Morris, Ellery, Lee, Lewis, and Whipple. Addressed: "To Commodore Esek Hopkins, Providence, Rhode Island."

Marine Committee to John Langdon

Sir   Philada. Decemr. 10th 1776

We have of this date ordered Capt Thompson of the Raliegh Frigate to proceed to Sea with all possible dispatch.[1]

We therefore request that you will advance what money may be necessary to have this business Speedily executed, and render us an Account thereof which shall be passed to your Credit. You will also

make us A Return of the men on board at the time of her departure.[2]
We are Sir, Your hble Serts.

Fras. Lewis   Robt Morris

Wm. Whipple   Richard Henry Lee

Wm Ellery

RC (Capt. J. G. M. Stone, Annapolis, Md., 1973). Written by Morris and signed by Morris, Ellery, Lee, Lewis, and Whipple.

[1] Not found.

[2] Langdon's January 22, 1777, reply to this letter is in Morgan, *Naval Documents*, 7:1011–13. For Langdon's accounts with the "Marine & Secret Committees," see ibid., pp. 635–36, under the conjectural date of December 31, 1776.

Robert Treat Paine's Diary

December 10, 1776

Cold day. Froze last night. Congress prepared to move to Baltimore agreeable to the vote of yesterday. I put a Box of 8 bottles of port Wine on board Schooner Defiance, Eliphalet Williams Master, to carry to Dighton. I packt up my things. Genl. Washington crossed the Delaware at Trenton last Friday & Genl Howe follow'd him to Trenton that night.[1] The Associators of Philada. are mustering to reinforce Genl. Washington, & the inhabitants of Philada. are moving out their Effects.

MS (MHi).

[1] Washington actually carried out this crossing on Saturday, December 7.

Samuel Adams to Elizabeth Adams

Decr 11 [1776]

Since writing the Above I have receivd your Letter of the 9th of Nove, for which I am much obligd to you. If this City should be *surrenderd*, I should by no means dispair of our Cause. It is a righteous Cause and I am fully perswaded righteous Heaven will succeed it. Congress will adjourn to Baltimore in Maryland, about 120 Miles from this place, when Necessity requires it and not before. It is agreed to appoint a Day of Prayer, & a Come will bring in a Resolution for that purpose This day.[1] I wish we were a more religious People. That Heaven may bless you here & hereafter is the most ardent Prayer of, my dear, most cordially, your,

Saml Adams

RC (NN). A continuation of Adams to Elizabeth Adams, December 9, 1776.

¹ The resolution for a day of prayer and fasting was passed later this day. *JCC*, 6:1022.

Samuel Chase to James Nicholson

Sir,¹   Philada. Decr. 11 [1776], Wednesday M[orning]
It has been reported that You was coming up to this City with a Body of Seamen and Marines. One of the frigates is ready for the Sea. The other three may be soon ready for a short Voyage, if Men ⟨& Guns⟩ could be procured. You would render essential Service, if you could immediately come up with a Body of Seamen ⟨and Marines. If you could get a clever, diligent & trusty officer, with a sufficient Number of Sailors & Men to bring up the Guns of your frigate and the Defense⟩ and an attempt might be made to bring round all the frigates here to Baltimore Town. It cannot be doubted the Council of Safety would lend the ⟨Guns and⟩ Hands belonging to the [Defenc]e for this every important Service. You will send an Express to the Council of Safety. Not one Moment is to be lost.² I write this by the order of Congress.

We were informed yesterday Morning that the Enemy were at Burlington Monday [eveni]ng. We have certain Intelligence just now, that the Enemy were not there last Night. It is reported & Beleived, that some of their light Horse were seven Miles above that place on Monday. Not one of the Enemy are on the west Side of the Delaware. It is beleived the main Body of general Howes Army is at Maidenhead, about Six Miles to the East of Trenton. General Lee with between 5 & 6000 Men was at Morriss Town last Sunday Evening. He will join General Washington, who is with his army opposite Trenton. The Congress will not quit this City but in the last Extremity. To prevent false Reports, publish the above.

Inform Mr Purviance that Mrs. Hancock will sett off this Day.

Let it be known, that Arms are furnished to our Militia. Let the want of them be no Excuse.

Your obedt. Servant,   Saml. Chase

RC (MdAA). Addressed: "Captain James Nicholson, Baltimore Town, Maryland."
¹ James Nicholson, formerly captain of the Maryland ship *Defence*, was appointed in June 1776 captain of the Continental frigate *Virginia* constructed at Baltimore. See Morgan, *Naval Documents*, 3:754, 5:497, 956; and *JCC*, 5:423.
² For the response to this request, see *Md. Archives*, 12:521, 529–31. Chase apparently also sent an appeal this day to the Baltimore Committee of Safety for small craft to be employed in the removal of public stores, prisoners, and the sick from Philadelphia to Baltimore via the Head of Elk, in consequence of which the committee transmitted the same appeal to the Annapolis Committee of Safety. See ibid., pp. 524, 530–31.
In addition, Chase also sent a letter to Allen Quynn, messenger to the Maryland

Council of Safety, requesting the council's assistance in this effort, and President Hancock sent a verbal message via Col. Thomas Ewing, commander of a battalion of Maryland militia with the flying camp, requisitioning militia from four Maryland counties to assist in Philadelphia's defense. However, the decision to send appeals to Maryland by such indirect means, rather than directly to the Maryland Council of Safety, was regarded as an improper and inefficient practice and drew the following protest from the council to its delegates in Congress. "We have not received a script of a Pen either from Congress, our Delegates, or any one of them, relative to the assistance mentioned to Colo. Ewing, Mr Quynn or Captn Nicholson and we cannot help observing to you that applying to individuals who necessarily must apply to the Council of Safety from whom their power must be deputed before they can act is losing of time to say nothing of the want of respect to a Body of men with whom the Executive Powers of the State are entrusted." Ibid., p. 531.

For further evidence that some of the informal steps taken to communicate with various Maryland officials during this unsettled period were resented by members of the convention and the council of safety, see also John Hancock to the Frederick County Committee, December 21, 1776, note 2.

Francis Lightfoot Lee to Walter Jones

My dear friend   Philadelphia Decr. 11. 1776
I have but a moment to thank you for your late letters, & to inform you that I think there is crude Sal Ammoniac among my medicines. This I am pretty certain of but if I shou'd be mistaken, make them send to Chantilly where my bror. says there is plenty. We are all here in confusion, short inlistments has allmost ruined us. Our Army having disbanded before a new one was raised, has enabled Genl. Howe to make considerable progress this way. If the weather dont stop him I hardly think the people will. There is little spirit & [. . .] Virtue among them in these middle Colonies. Remember me to all friends. Adieu my Friend.

Francis Lightfoot Lee

RC (DLC). Addressed: "To Doctor Walter Jones, Richmond County, Virginia."

Richard Henry Lee's Proposed Resolution

[December 11? 1776] [1]
Congress being informed that Monsr. Weibert a French Gentleman and a   Colonel in the Continental service who was lately made prisoner in Fort Washington has been committed to Close confinement contrary to the usage of civilized [nations] where no improper conduct hath marked the character of captive Officers, Resolved that Gen. Washington be directed to send a flag to General Howe and remonstrate against this severe treatment of Colonel Weibert and desiring to know of General Howe whether he means

to enlarge Colo. Weibert on his parole, or whether the United States are to consider this [as the] established mode for the treatmt of Officers on both sides whom the fortune of war shall place in captivity.

MS (ViU).
[1] Although there is no record of such a resolution in the journals, Lee probably drafted this undated resolve shortly before December 12. On that day General Putnam sent Lt. Col. Antoine Felix Wuibert's commission to Washington, noting that "for want of which I am credibly informed he is confined in the provost guard in New-York"; and Washington immediately dispatched a letter to Gen. William Howe protesting Wuibert's treatment. See *Am. Archives*, 5th ser. 3:1180, 1187; and *JCC*, 5:477, 480–81, 656.

Charles Thomson to George Washington

Sir,   [December 11, 1776]
The president being necessarily engaged with his family, I have the honour to inform you that your letter of the 10th was duly received & laid before Congress, and to transmit you a resolution of Congress passed this day.[1]
I am Sir, Your obedient humble servant,

Chas. Thomson

RC (DLC).
[1] Washington's December 10 letter to Hancock is in PCC, item 152, 3:335, and Washington, *Writings* (Fitzpatrick), 6:342. Secretary Thomson sent Washington a December 11 resolve calling upon him to publish a general order contradicting the "false and malicious report . . . spread by the enemies of America that the Congress was about to disperse." *JCC*, 6:1023. However, Washington refused to comply with the resolve, considering "it a matter that may be as well disregarded, and that the removal or staying of Congress, depending entirely upon events should not have been the Subject of a Resolve." Washington, *Writings* (Fitzpatrick), 6:353–54. The offending resolve was later erased from the journals.

Oliver Wolcott to Laura Wolcott

My Dear   Philidelphia 11 Decr 1776
I Wrote to you the 5 by the Way of Salisbury, and sent by the same hand Martin's Philosophy for Oliver. I now send you 6 Vol of Sterne's Works and Gulliver's Travells for Frederic. I did not Read Sternes Sentiments with so much Pleasure as I expected.

As to News, Washington with his Army &c have passd. the River at Trenton. The Enemy are now at that Place said to be about 12,000 and that a Reinforcement is to follow them. Genl. Lee with another Reinforcement is coming on to join Washington. The

Militia are all gone out of this City. They are also coming in from the Country and I hope they will be able to prevent the Enemy from gaining Possession of this City. People have for some Days been removing their Familys and effects from this Place, which has occasioned a prodigious hurry amongst them.

A large Naval Armament together with a Land Force has by this Time probably Arrived from France to their West Indies, and I think it probable that a War will pretty soon commence between France and G. Britain. If the Enemy should drive us out of this City (which I do not really expect) you will soon hear to what Place I shall go. By the Blessing of God I am well. Take care of your Health. My Love to my Children and Freinds. I am yours with the most inviolate affection.   Oliver Wolcott

[*P.S.*] Mr Lymans favr of the 23d last I have recd. He mentions one as sent by Mr Sherman which never came to hand.

RC (CtHi).

Samuel Adams to James Warren

My dear sir,   Philadelphia Decr 12 1776

As I keep no Copies of my Letters, you must excuse me if I sometimes make Repetitions. I recollect that in my last I gave you some Account of the Movements of the two Armies. The Enemy have advanced as far as Trenton, thirty Miles from this City, and this Evening we are informd that a body of about 400 Hessians are got to Burlington about 17 miles distance on the opposite Side of the Delaware. Nothing can exceed the Lethargy that has seizd the People of this State & the Jerseys. Our Friends who belong to those States are unwilling to have it imputed to Disaffection and indeed I am unwilling myself to attribute it to so shameful a Cause. Non Resistance is the professed Principle of Quakers, but the Religion of many of them is to get money & sleep as the vulgar Phrase is, in a whole Skin. The Interest of the Proprietor is at Antipodes with that of America, at least I suppose he thinks so—and though he is apparently inactive, there are many Engines which he can secretly set to work. These are no doubt partly the Causes of the Evil. Besides there are many Tories here who have been for months past exciting a violent Contest among the well affected about their new form of Government on purpose to imbitter their Spirits & divert their Attention from the great Cause. But the foundation of all was laid Months ago through the Folly, I will not say a harsher word of that excellent, superlatively wise and great Patriot D[ickinson], who from the 10th of Septr 1774 to the 4th of July 1776 has been urging upon every Individual & Body of Men over whom he had any influence, the Necessity of making Terms of Accommodation with Great Britain. With this he has poisond the Minds of the People, the Effect of which is a total Stagnation of the Power of Resentment, the utter Loss of every manly Sentiment of Liberty & Virtue. I give up this City & State for lost until recoverd by other Americans. Our Cause however will be supported. It is the Cause of God & Men, and virtuous Men by the Smiles of Heaven will bring it to a happy Issue. Our Army is reducd to an handful & I suppose by the last of this Month will be reducd to Nothing—and Some of the *Friends* think the Congress will soon be taken napping. There are, I am well assured, Materials on this great Continent to make as good an Army if not a better Congress. There are indeed some Members of that respectable body whose understanding and true Patriotism I revere. May God prosper them and increase their Number. Where are your new Members? I greatly applaude your Choice of them. Mr J[ohn] A[dams] I hope is on the Road. We never wanted him more. Mr P[aine] has this day left the Congress having leave after laboring in the Service Sixteen Months without Cessation.[1] I wish him safe with his Family. We seldom hear from N England—One Post perhaps in a month! I am told that Soldiers inlist there very briskly. I wish I could have an Assurance of it from you. Have you provided a good Stock of Cloathing, I have venturd almost positively to assert that you have. It would be a Satisfaction to me to be Authorizd by you to assert it. Britain will strain every Nerve to subjugate America the next year. She will call wicked Men & Devils to her Aid. Remember that New England is the Object of her Fury. She hates her for the very Reason for which virtuous Men even adore her. Are you enough on your Guard? Is Boston sufficiently fortified? For your Comfort I will tell you that in my opinion our Affairs abroad wear a promising Aspect. I wish I could be more explicit—but I conjure you not to depend too much upon foreign Aid. Let America exert her own Strength. Let her depend upon Gods Blessing, and He who cannot be indifferent to her righteous Cause will even work Miracles if necessary to carry her thro this glorious Conflict, and establish her feet upon a Rock. Adieu my Friend, the Clock strikes Twelve.

RC (MHi). In Adams' hand, though not signed.

[1] Robert Treat Paine recorded his departure in his December 11 diary entry: "Delivered my Trunk (containing books, & papers &c that I could not bring home) to Mr. Hancock to be carried in his Waggon to Baltimore & sent from thence to me by Land or water. Small snow last night & this morning. Raw cold air. At 11 oClock set out for home, Dined at Wilke's Tavern, Abington 12 1/2 m, thence to Bogards 16m. Lodged. Small Snow tonight." MHi.

Board of War to Robert Towers

Mr. Towers   War Office. [December 12? 1776]
    You are to receive from the Maryland Troops late of the flying
Camp all their Arms and Accoutrements giving to the respective
Captains or Officers Receipts for the same and return a List of the
Arms and Accoutrements You receive to this Board.[1]
                                                            Benja Harrison
True Copy.

Tr (MdAA). In the hand of Benjamin Rumsey.
    [1] This letter was apparently an outgrowth of a December 12 resolve "That the
arms, ammunition and cloathing, in or near the city of Philadelphia, be put under
the direction of General Putnam; and that Mr. J. Mease, Mr. Towers, and all
other persons having continent stores in care, make immediate return of the same
to General Putnam." JCC, 6:1026. Towers was commissary of stores for Pennsylvania's state forces and a Continental gunpowder inspector. JCC, 5:714.
    Another letter illustrating the variety of mundane details delegates became im-
mersed in during this critical period is a December 10 note from the Board of
War (written by James Wilson but signed by Benjamin Harrison) to the Pennsylvania Council of Safety involving a determination of which company of Pennsylvania militia should be assigned duty "guarding the Powder Mills and Magazine
belonging to Congress." The board's note was simply to "request the Council of
Safety to do whatever they think most proper concerning the Matter." Gratz Collection, PHi.

Elbridge Gerry to Unknown

Dear Sir   Philadelphia Decr 12th 1776
    The parsimony of some Gentlemen having prevented Congress
from offering in June last the Bounty lately offered to the Soldiers
for reinlisting, a Resolution past for giving them ten Dollars to
inlist for three Years. It has had the Effect that was then predicted,
the Continent is at this Time not provided with a sufficient Force
to check their progress thro' the Jersies. To promote this Mistake
some capital Errors have taken place in the Camp relative to continuing a Garrison in Fort Washington & being surprized at Fort
Lee. And the Militia of these States are altogether lifeless, Phila-
delphians excepted. The Enemy are now at Burlington eighteen
Miles above this place, on the other Side the Delaware. General
Washington is at Bristol a Town on the River opposite the post of
the Enemy with about 5 or 6000 Men, General Lee may Joyn him in
a Day or two with about 5000 more. The Enemy are said to be from
10 to 15000 strong. I think it would be no Misfortune to the Continent if they should take it in their Heads to surprize the City
which has not at present two hundred Men in it, & the Congress
with it, if the Continent would then be attentive to send new

Members & *Men of Business*. I believe this will [ac]cord with the Opinion of a certain Friend of ours in Massachusetts. Mr Pain having been absent from the *pleasures of domestic Life* for a considerable Time, left this place Yesterday on his Return to his Family. Mr Adams is well & joyns in Regards to Yourself & all Friends with Sir your sincere Friend & hum serv,   E Gerry

P.S. The Enemy are said to be provided with forty flat Bottom Boats. If they should by this unlucky Circumstance of our Army obtain Philadelphia & *even all the middle Colonies,* I think with manly Exertions We may soon recover them. N England & New York are able of themselves to keep them at Bay untill assistance comes from Europe, which I cannot doubt of.

RC (MHi).

New England Delegates to George Washington

Sir   Philadelphia Decr 12 1776
   We are this Moment informd by a Gentleman who is Brother of Collo Griffen and has lately been at New York, that a Body of ten thousand of the Enemies Troops are actually arrivd at Rhode Island.
   As Congress is now adjournd to Baltimore in Maryland, and the President and the Board of War are not in Town, we think it our Duty to send you this Intelligence; and as there is no General Officer in that Department, we refer it to your Consideration whether the Service does not absolutely require that one be immediately sent, to take the Command of Troops to be raisd there, to repel the Progress of the Enemy.
   If Major General Green or Gates, who are greatly belovd in that Part of America, with a suitable Number of Brigadiers, could be spared for this Service, it might be attended with another Advantage, that of facilitating the new Inlistments.[1]
   We intreat your Attention to this important Matter and are with very great Respect, Your Excellcys very humble Servants,

Samuel Adams   William Ellery

Elbridge Gerry   Wm. Whipple

RC (MH–H). Written by Adams and signed by Adams, Ellery, Gerry, and Whipple. Writing later to the governor of Rhode Island, Ellery explained that this letter was written at his instigation. See Ellery to Nicholas Cooke, December 24, 1776.
   [1] General Washington ordered Gen. Benedict Arnold and Gen. Joseph Spencer to Rhode Island. Washington to John Hancock, December 20, 1776, Washington, *Writings* (Fitzpatrick), 6:407–8.

Charles Thomson to George Washington

Sir,   Philada Decr. 12. 1776

The president being still necessarily engaged with his family I have the honour to inform you that your letter of yesterday was recd. & laid before Congress. I enclose you sundry resolutions passed this day[1] and am, Sr., Your obedient humble Serv,

Chas Thomson

RC (DLC).

[1] Washington's December 11 letter to Hancock is in PCC, item 152, 3:339–40; and Washington, *Writings* (Fitzpatrick), 6:349–51. Secretary Thomson sent Washington resolves about the use of frigates to defend Philadelphia, the establishment of a cavalry regiment under the command of Elisha Sheldon, the defense of Philadelphia, the decision to move Congress to Baltimore, and the grant to Washington "of full power to order and direct all things relative to the department, and to the operations of war." *JCC*, 6:1024–27.

Robert Morris to John Hancock

Sir   Philada Decemr 13th. 1776

The enclosed letter from the General[1] was delivered to me open by Mr Walton who judged it prudent to examine the Contents before it went forward & in which I concur with him as it was probable some service might result to this place from their being known & I flatter myself that essential service will be rendered to the Continent thereby. As soon as I saw this authentic Account of the Enemy's design to Cross Delaware above the Falls, I waited on Genl. Putnam & proposed that the Frigate Randolph & Sloop Hornet shou'd be sent to Sea immediately as it was plain to me they wou'd be of no use here & I had received certain advice that there was not any British Men of War in our Bay. The General very readily Consented & I have this afternoon given Capt. Biddle & Capt Nicholson their Instructions signed by me on behalf of the Marine Committee.[2] They will depart early in the Morning and I entertain the most sanguine hopes of their escape. The Hornet goes for Carolina with the Shot, but part of the flour was landed previous to this new determination. I have presumed to go one step farther in this Navy business and flatter myself I shall be entitled to the approbation of Congress whether I meet it or not, for my intentions are good and I procure myself much trouble with the sole view of serving the Cause. On Viewing the Frigate Delaware, I thought it possible to get her away before Genl Howe cou'd get here. I have therefore set about it stoutly. A number of People scarce as they now are here, are at work on her, the sails will be bent, anchors to the Bows, stores onbd. and every thing in some forwardness tomorrow. I have sent an Express to the General[3] informing him of my design & Requesting him to send down Capt Alexander, his Officers & such Seamen as are willing to go with him & if it is possible to get her away I shall order her to Baltimore under your own care. If I fail in this attempt you only add a little Expence of labour to the loss, for the Ship may in that case be destroyed, however if Genl. Howe will give me but a few days more & Ld Howe keep away his Myrmidons I shall have the pleasure to dispatch the Randolph, Hornet, Delaware, Security, Fly & a large Ship loaden with Tobacco all which you may deem as saved from the Flames. The removal of Congress has left me much other business, I am paying your Debts at least those of the Marine Committee & directing fifty necessary things to be done and with Genl. Howes permission shall be glad to finish the business you wou'd wish to have done here, but if Mr Howe advances I shall push off & leave him to finish the business in his own way. I am told there is a letter in Town that mentions Genl Clintons arrival at Rhode Island & that he took Peaceable possession of it, as all the Inhabitants to a Man abandoned the Island, but tell Mr. Ellery I have not seen this letter nor will I vouch for its authenticity. You will please to receive enclosed some pleasing letters for the Marine Committee & with perfect esteem & respect I remain, Sir, Yours & the Congresses most obedient, & most hble Servant, Robt Morris

RC (DNA: PCC, item 137).

[1] For Washington's December 12 letter to Hancock, see Washington, *Writings* (Fitzpatrick), 6:353–56.

[2] See Morgan, *Naval Documents*, 7:476–77.

[3] Not found; but for Washington's December 14 response, reporting that he was enclosing Morris' letter to Col. John Cadwalader "with direction for Capt. Alexander with his officers and a sufficient number of men to proceed to Phila. without delay in order to carry the Frigate out of your River before the opportunity is lost," see Washington, *Writings* (Fitzpatrick), 6:375.

Oliver Wolcott to Laura Wolcott

My Dear,   Philidelphia 13t Decr. 1776

I Wrote to you the 11t and 5t inst by the Bearer of which I have sent Martin's Philosophy for Oliver and Gulliver's Travells for Frederic, and six Vol of Sterne's Works for yourself or for any to whom they might be agreable. I also Wrote to you the 24t and 16t ult. which I hope you have recd. Mr Lyman's favour of the 23d last has come to hand. He mentions one which he sent by Mr. Sherman which I have not recd. I was happy in being told by him of your Wellfare and that of the Familys and I doupt not but that you will receive an equal Pleasure in being told that I am Very

Well, I think as much so as I have been at any time the year past. A Favour for which may I possess the most gratefull Sentiments to that God who gives every Blessing.

The 11t in the Evening the Enemy to wit a Detachment of them took Possession of Burlington about 20 Miles from this City on the Jersey Shore, the Rest of their Army are at Trenton and upon the Banks of the River above it. Their Number are uncertain but are computed about Twelve Thousand and as their Designs are undouptedly to gain Possession of this City, the Congress upon the advice of Genl. Putman and Mifflin who are now here to provide for the Protection of the Places as Well as from the Result of their own opinion have adjourned themselves to Baltimore in Maryland, a Place about 110 miles from this City, as it was judged that the Council of America ought not to Sit in a Place liable to be interrupted by the rude Disorder of Arms—so that I am this moment going forward for that Place. Wheither the Enemy will suceed in their cruel Designs against this City must be left to time to Discover. Congress have ordered the Genl to Defend it to the last extremity and God grant that he may be successful in his exertions.

Whatever Events may take Place the American Cause will be supported to the last; and I trust in God that it will succeed. The Grecian, Roman and Dutch States were in their Infancy reduced to the greatest Distress infinitely beyond what We have yet experienced. The God Who governs the Universe and who holds Empires in his Hand Can with the least Effort of his Will grant us all that Security, Opulence and Power, which they have injoyed. The present Scene it is true Appears somewhat gloomy but the Natural or more obvious Cause seems to be owing to the Term of Enlistment of the Army being expired. I hope We may have a most respectable one before long established. The Business of War is the Result of Experience.

It is probable that France before long will involve G. Brittain in a War, who by unhappy Experience may learn the Folly of attempting to Inslave a People who by the Tyes of Consanguinity and affection ever were desirous of promoting her truest Happiness. Genl Howe has lately published a Proclamation abusing the Congress of having Sinister Designs upon the People, has offered to such as will accept of Pardon upon an unlimited Submission, royal Forgiveness.[1] But who is base enough to Wish to have a precarious Case dependent upon the Caprice of Power, unsustained by any Laws and governed by the Wild and dangerous Thirst of Avarice and Ambition.

The Pleasure of Writing to you may not be so frequent as it has been, but I shall omit no Oppertunity which I think safe, for that Purpose. All Conveyances for the present will probably be thro Litchfield which go to the Eastward, and even that Rout I fear will not be altogether safe. But as the Communication by Expresses will be attempted as well as by private Hands I hope my Freinds will not be remiss in Writing to Me. Letters of your own you may easily beleive will be pecurliarly agreable. No Gentleman from Connecticut are arrived since I last Wrote to you upon this Head. Majr Elisha Sheldon is here and well, and is appointed by Congress to raise a Regiment of Horse in Connecticut.[2] He tells me Cap. Seymour is well. My best Love to my Children and Freinds. May the Almighty ever keep you and them in his Protection. I am, your's, with the tenderest and most inviolable Affection.

Oliver Wolcott

P.S. I have in my Letters noted all such as I have recd. from Litchfield.

RC (CtHi).
[1] See Samuel Adams to Elizabeth Adams, November 29, 1776, note.
[2] See *JCC*, 6:1025.

Marine Committee to William Bingham

Sir   December 14th 1776

We expect this will be delivered to you by John Nicholson Esqr. who commands the Hornet Sloop of war belonging to the Continent.[1] She will carry you some Rice and Indigo by order of the Secret Committee which you'l please to receive expeditiously. As this sloop touches at Carolina before she sails for the West Indies it is uncertain when you may see, therefore our orders must be discretionary, and when she arrives if you [have] any advices or any goods to send that you think of importance to these States, you may dispatch Capt. Nicholson therewith immediately. Should this not be the case you may assist him to procure more men and let him go a cruizing during the winter Months only dispatching him so as to be here by the beginning of April. If our Trade in the Islands is interrupted by any privateers or Tenders that this Sloop can match they should be her Object. If there be none such she may cruize where there is the best chance of good Prizes.

If Captain Nicholson is lucky enough to send any in to you, sell such parts as are suited for the Islands consumption, but be careful what you sell is the property of none but British subjects not resident in Bermuda or New Providence. Whatever you sell render regular accounts of it. Make the seamen &c necessary advances and transmit us their receipts with the accots., sales &c for what you sell that just distribution may be made on their return. If Captain Nicholson meets with any Canon more suitable for the Hornet than those on board, assist him in buying and getting them mounted. Supply him with money and necessaries he may want for the service his receipts will be your vouchers and your drafts on us will be paid.

When you dispatch him for the Continent he will take on board any goods you have to ship. We are sir, Your very hble servants

LB (DNA: PCC Miscellaneous Papers, Marine Committee Letter Book).
[1] Nicholson was unable to leave Philadelphia until the middle of February 1777. Morgan, *Naval Documents*, 7:1215, 1296.

Robert Morris to John Dorsius

Sir   Philada. Decr. 14th. 1776
You have herein a Copy of what I wrote you by Capt Nicholson in the Hornet.[1] This goes by the Brigt. Friendship, Capt. Exeen, which is to be loaded on Continental acct. but if you can Ship the Value of a few hundred Pounds Stg by her in Skins, furrs, Indico, Tobacco or Rice of Acct. of W[illing] & M[orris] & Co I think it will be a good Conveyance & shall be glad you do it.

I am still in doubt respecting the fate of this City. Genl. Howe finds it difficult to cross Delaware & may possibly be forced to desist. God send he may. I am Sir [&c.]   Robt. Morris

Tr (William Bell Clark transcript, from Bank of North America Papers, PHi).
[1] Not found.

Robert Morris to John Hancock

Sir   Philada. Decr. 14th. 1776
I wrote you last night & enclosed a letter from the General & several other letters, then expecting to send that letter by Mr Walton this morning, but that Gentn having just now delivered me another open letter from the General dated yesterday at Trenton Falls [1] I do myself the Honor to enclose it herein & as Mr Walton does not set of[f] so soon as he intended I have sent out after an express, but have some expectation that Colo Jenifer will be the bearer of both these letters as I understand he is just going off for Baltimore they will certainly go in half an hour by one or the other. As our Enemies are still kept at Bay on the other side Delaware I cannot help flattering myself with the expectation of some favourable event that will save this City. I shall certainly remain here as long as I can with safety & during my stay the Congress may depend on my utmost exertions for the Publick service. The

Randolph & Hornet are gone down this morning. We are at Work on the Delaware & a chartered Brigt, Capt Exeen, sails in an hour. If they give us time I shall attempt to get the Washington Frigate into a place of safety.

I have the honor to remain, sir, Your Obedt hble servt.

Robt Morris

RC (DNA: PCC, item 137).
[1] For Washington's December 13 letter to Hancock, see Washington, *Writings* (Fitzpatrick), 6:363–65.

Robert Morris to the Committee of Secret Correspondence

Gentn   Philada. Decr. 16th. 1776

Since I wrote the President this morning, a young Gentn came up from Chincoteague where he had landed out of the Sloop Independance (Capt Young) belonging to the Continent. This sloop was from Martinico bound hither but was chased into that place by a large Frigate. The Sloop has onboard a quantity of Blankets, Coarse Cloths & near 1000 Muskets, which I will take care of. Capt Young staid behind sick & she is now Commanded by Lieutt Robinson who had no paper to write on but sent up word he wou'd push round for this place soon as he cou'd. The Goods are what was ordered by the Secret Committee & the Andw Doria will bring a good Cargo from St Eustatia where she is arrived. The Sachem is also arrived at Martinico, but no News yet from Monsr. Hortalez.

You have enclosed the letters from Mr Bingham & Mr Dean,[1] the latter complaining as I have long expected he woud for want of advices & Remittances. In short if the Congress mean to succeed in this Contest they must pay good Executive Men to do their business as it ought to be & not lavish milions away by their own mismanagement. I say mismanagemt because no Men living can attend the daily deliberations of Congress & do executive parts of business at the same time. I do aver here will be more money lost, totally lost, in Horses, Waggons, Cattle &c &c for want of sufficient numbers of proper persons to look after them, than wou'd have paid all the Salarys *Payne* ever did or ever will grumble at. Mr Deane has had a hard situation. I foretold it long since & unless you employ some man of Talents to Collect materials & keep the Commissioners abroad Constantly informed of what is passing here, You never will have that Consequence nor your agents that Dignity they ought to have. I shou'd be glad you wou'd return me these letters or Copies of them &c. I will reply from hence. They have been with me but a few minutes & I will not keep the express any

longer as I expect you are hungry as Hawkes after news from France.
I cannot keep a Copy of this, but in haste remain very sincerely,
Gentn, Your devoted hble servt.   Robt Morris

RC (DNA: PCC, item 137).
  [1] See Morris to Silas Deane, December 20, 1776, note 1.

Robert Morris to John Hancock

Sir   Philada. Decemr. 16th 1776
   The enclosed letter from Genl. Wooster was delivered to me by
Mr Walton,[1] it contradicts the report respecting Rhode Island
mentioned in my last & I am glad of it, but it still appears as if that
was Mr Clintons object. I take the liberty to enclose you a letter
I received yesterday from Colo Cadwallader & am truely sorry to
add that the intelligence respecting Genl. Lee comes confirmed
through another channell with several circumstances that stagger
my faith, altho I was yesterday very unwilling to give Credit to Mr
Symes & Capt Murrays storys.[2] The person who came to Town last
night has been examined by the Council of Safety, who as I am told
beleive his Account. Being out of Town yesterday I have not seen
any of them or him, therefore am not master of all the particulars,
but see reports that some of the Tories have given notice to the
Enemy that the General lodged at a certain House 5 Miles distant
from his Army. In consequence, a party of Light Horse about 50
Surrounded the House at day break. The Genl. had an aid de Camp
& ten Men with him. They defended themselves in the House for
two hours, when the Men offered to Surrender, alledging that the
General was not there they answered they knew he was in that
House & if he did not immediately surrender himself, they woud
burn the House & him in it. In short the Genl was obliged to appear
& he promised to Surrender on Condition they woud treat him like
an officer & a Gentn. The moment they got him they mounted him
on a Horse & Galloped off with him not even allowing him time
to get his Hat, nor did they take any of his party but left them to
do as they pleased. The Aid de Camp is wounded. These are the
only particulars that I have heard & I do not pretend to Vouch for
the truth of them but pray Heaven the whole may be a fiction. The
loss of Genl Lee at this time is in itself a severe Stroke, and the
effect it will have on the Spirits of our Shattered Army will add
greatly to it.
   The Express I sent to Genl. Washington is returned & brings
me a letter from him of the 14th at night,[3] he was then some miles
beyond Coriells Ferry, but says nothing to me respecting the military operations. The enclosed letter for Messr. Adams, Gerry, Ellery

& Whipple comes under cover & Mr. Peters has desired me to send the letter from the Governor of Virginia.

The sudden departure of the Congress from this place seems to be a matter of much speculatiori & People who judge by events think they have been too precipitate. Be that as it may, many things are thrown into great confusion by it, and I find ample employment in applying remedies wherever I can. The unfinished business of the Marine & Secret Committees I intend to confine myself to, but I hear so many complaints & see so much confusion from other quarters that I am obliged to advise in things not committed to me. Circumstanced as our affairs now are I conceive it better to take libertys & assume some powers than to let the general interest suffer. Much money is wanted for the Publick Service & it must be Sent up immediately, as the Militia of our Country are at length turning out & call for the advance. The lower parts of New Jersey are also in motion & they want Money. The Troops returned from Canada call aloud for their pay & they should have it instantly as they very generally promise to reinlist when they have spent what is due to them.

Mr. Smith the loan officer is not here or I believe it woud be in my power to procure a good deal of money through that channell, on his return I will assist all in my power. I suppose Congress will not determine on a hasty return to this place nor do I think it adviseable untill the Enemy are actually gone into Winter Quarters for a severe Frost may in a few hours enable them to Cross Delaware above the Falls, so that if they remain in that Neighbourhood you cou'd here be subject to perpetual alarms. At the same time it may be depended on, that great inconveniences will arise daily in every department during your absence. To remedy this as much as possible I think a Committee shoud be sent here with such powers as Congress may Judge proper in order that they may regulate the business of the Continent necessary to be done here.[4] There is the greatest Scene of confusion in the management of the Continental Horses, Wagons, & Expresses that ever was exhibited. It was bad enough before Congress departed but is ten times worse now & Jacob Hiltziemer a very honest man will run mad soon, if not properly assisted or relieved in this department.[5] In short the Committee you send shoud have full powers to do whatever may be necessary to put every department on a Systematic footing. Mr. Clymer, Mr Walton & myself will bestir ourselves & advise or assist in such things as we think absolutely necessary untill you appoint a Committee & as the Board of War did not leave any orders for their Secy we have desired him to stay & assist us untill he receives Orders. We hope the Board will excuse us for taking this liberty as Mr. Peters will be usefull here.[6] The Committee must have the Command of Money to answer Various purposes as the calls for it

are loud, large & constant. Shou'd the Enemy retire to Brunswick or
New York it may & I believe will be best for Congress to return
as soon as that is certain. Upon the appearance of their retiring I
have detained the Cruizers intended to turn inward bound Vessells
from our Capes & shall not send them unless the scene changes
again & it shou'd be evident this City must fall into their hands.
Capt Alexander is come down from Camp and we are at work on
the Delaware but if the Enemy go back I will attempt the getting
her regularly fitted for Sea. I have dispatched the Ship Loaden with
Tobacco for France but in the present situation of things it did not
seem eligible to write on Political subjects to any of our agents
there. If Fortune will once more smile on us I will find opportunities to communicate the glad Tidings. You will please to receive
herewith Sundry French letters lately brought here by Monsr
Coleaux who will visit you in Baltimore in due time. As I did not
recollect any members of Congress that are perfect masters of the
French I put them in the hands of Paul Fooks, the Sworn Inter-
preter & his translations go with the originals. I also send herewith
some letters to the Marine Committee particularly a very pleasing
one from Capt Jones of the Alfred. I have sent to Genl. Putnam to
inform him of this Express & am now expecting his Dispatches.

The Papers & Books of the Marine Committee, Secret Committee
& Committee of Correspondence I sent to Christeen with a proper
person to take care of them so they are convenient either for this
place or Baltimore. I shall take the liberty to address you whenever
occurrances require it & with sincere regard remain, sir, Your
obedt hble servt.   Robt Morris

RC (DNA: PCC, item 137).
    ¹ For Gen. David Wooster's December 8 letter to President Hancock, which was
reported to a committee of Congress on December 20, see *Am. Archives*, 5th ser.
3:1129.
    ² For Col. John Cadwalader's December 15 letter to Morris reporting the news
of General Lee's capture, see ibid., pp. 1230–31.
    ³ See Washington, *Writings* (Fitzpatrick), 6:375.
    ⁴ For Congress' response to this recommendation, which led to the appointment
on December 21 of Morris, George Clymer, and George Walton as a committee
"to execute such continental business as may be proper and necessary to be done
at Philadelphia," see *JCC*, 6:1032.
    ⁵ Morris returned to this subject again in the Executive Committee's first letter
to John Hancock of January 10, 1777.
    ⁶ Congress ignored this suggestion and directed Richard Peters "to repair to
Baltimore as soon as possible." See *JCC*, 6:1033; and Hancock to Robert Morris,
December 23, 1776.

Robert Morris to John Hancock

Sir   Philada Decemr 17th. 1776

Mr Walton, Mr Clymer & myself thought it advisable to open the enclosed letter last night that we might judge if the expence of another express shou'd be incurred or detain it for the Post, which we concluded to do as I had wrote you the unfortunate Fate of Genl. Lee before. I am sorry to inform you that the Roebuck & Falcon Men of War are in Delaware Bay & two Bomb Ketches said to be in the offing. On rect. of this News (which is certain) I hired a Pilot Boat & sent her with a letter to Capt Biddle & all the other Vessells outward bound, desiring them to stop or come back, so that my labours appear to be lost & sorry I am for the disappointment, however its likely the first smart NoWester may give us an opening to push them out. I have just heard that a party or partys of the Enemie were yesterday at Morris Town & Haddonfield in the Jerseys opposite to this & distant about 7 to 9 Miles. What their Views are I cannot say, but by the appearance of the Men of War below & the Bomb Ketches being said to have sailed from N York it woud seem as if these party's meant to make their way to Red Bank, erect Works to command the Chevaux de Frize & then to come up with the Ships. This however is meer matter of speculation. Colo Griffin is I understand gone over with about 800 Men but I fear he will not be Strong enough for them.[1]

I have the honor to be very respectfully, sir Your Obedt hble servt,   Robt Morris

RC (DNA: PCC, item 137).

[1] This day Morris also sent the following message to Gen. William Heath. "Since I saw you I am informed that a person in New York who had an opportunity of being acquainted with the motions of the Enemy, had advised a friend, to move her effects from Fish Kill to some place of safety. I am not at liberty to mention names, but make no doubt that such message was sent, and that the person sending might be acquainted with their motions. This I understand was before any movement of your Division." Washington Papers, DLC.

For another letter Morris wrote this day, to James Martin and pertaining to the consignment of goods on board the *Independence* at Chincoteague, see Morgan, *Naval Documents*, 7:505.

Samuel Chase to William Paca?

                                    Annapolis December 18th. 1776

My Dear Sir [1]   Wednesday Evening

I am just arrived in this City. I am very desirous of staying a few Days with my Family, but if this State is not represented without Me, or if my Attendance can render the least Service I will instantly come up. I imagine Mr. Tilghman, Mr. Carroll, & Mr.

Rumsey are with You. I am anxious to hear the last Intelligence from the General and the City of Philadelphia. Be pleased to favor Me with a Line.

I do not know of any House in Baltimore Town in which the Congress can sit, in this City they can be furnished with an elegant Room. I know Baltimore Town to be a most disagreeable place in Winter. I beleive the Members could be as well, if not better accomodated here.[2]

I am, Sir, Your Affectionate & obedt. Servt.

Saml Chase

RC (NN).

[1] Apparently William Paca. Chase obviously directed this letter to one of his fellow Maryland delegates, and of those who had recently attended Congress in Philadelphia only Paca is not mentioned below.

[2] A few days later while still at Annapolis, Chase wrote to Gen. John Sullivan in response to a letter he had received just before leaving Philadelphia. "I perfectly agree with You," Chase explained, "as to the impropriety of our military System. The several States will forever be influenced by local attachments, & I am convinced the Nomination to office will, in many Instances, be very injudicious. If we expect to succeed in the present war, we must change our Mode of Conduct. The Business of the Congress must be placed in different Hands. Distinct & precise Departments ought to be established, & a Gentleman of the Military must be of the Board of War." Chase to Sullivan, December 24, 1776, Sullivan Papers, NhHi; and *Am. Archives*, 5th ser. 3:1395.

Benjamin Harrison to the
Maryland Council of Safety

Sir. Baltimore Decr. 18. 1776

The Express delivered your Favor of the 16th this morning at 9 oClock.[1] Your great Willingness to serve the Common Cause shall never induce me to insist on any Thing that may be prejudicial to the State of Maryland, particularly when I see no great Injury can arise to America. The Step you have taken in sending up the armed Vessel will I hope fully answer my purpose.

Capt. Martin is ordered to proceed on his Voyage, which I hope will be attended with all the Success you can expect.[2]

I have the Honor to be your's and the Council of Safety's most obedt. humble Servt.

FC (DNA: PCC, item 37). Addressed: "Daniel of St. Thomas Jenifer Esqr."

[1] Probably the Maryland Council's letter of December 17 to Harrison, reporting that Capt. William Patterson had been ordered to the Head of Elk to assist in removing public stores to Baltimore. *Md. Archives*, 12:534. See also Samuel Chase to James Nicholson, December 11, 1776, note 2.

[2] John Martin, captain of the Maryland state brig *Friendship*, was preparing another voyage to Martinque to procure war stores for the state. *Md. Archives*, 12:541–42. See also Harrison the Maryland Council of Safety, December 25, 1776.

Richard Henry Lee to Patrick Henry

Baltimore, December 18th, 1776.

The movements of the enemy's army in the Jerseys, by which the neighborhood of Philadelphia had become the seat of war, determined Congress to adjourn from thence to this town, where publick business will be entered on the 20 instant, unless a sufficient number of members should be assembled to begin sooner. At this place the publick business can be conducted with more deliberation and undisturbed attention, than could be the case in a city subject to perpetual alarm, and that had necessarily been made a place of arms.[1] The propriety of this measure was strongly enforced by the continental Generals Putnam and Mifflin, who commanded in Philadelphia, and who gave it as their opinion, that, although they did not consider the town as liable to fall into the enemy's hands but by surprise, yet that possibility rendered it improper for Congress to continue there.

So long as the American Army kept together the enemy's progress was extremely limited, but they knew and seized the opportunity of coming forward, which was occasioned by the greater part of the army dispersing in consequence of short enlistments; and this indeed was a plan early founded on hopes of accommodation, and for the greater ease of the people.

When a new Army is assembled, the enemy must again narrow their bounds, and this demonstrates the necessity of every State exerting every means to bring the new levies into the field with all possible expedition. It is the only sure means of placing America on the ground where every good man would wish to see it.

The British army is at present stationed along the Delaware from above Trenton, on the Jersey side, to Burlington, about 20 miles above Philadelphia. General Washington, with near 6000 men, is on the river side, opposite to Trenton; and the gondolas, with other armed vessels, are stationed from Philadelphia to Trenton, to prevent the passage of the Delaware. General Lee, with about 5000 men, remains on the enemy's rear, a little to the westward of their line of march through the Jerseys.

In this State, if the country associators of Pennsylvania, and from this neighborhood, reinforce the General with a few thousands, so as to enable him to press the enemy's front, it may turn out a happy circumstance that they have been encouraged to leave their ships so far behind.

We have good reason to expect a general war in Europe soon, and we have such proof of the friendship of France, as to leave little doubt of the willingness of that country to assist us.

The enclosed handbill will sufficiently instruct the Americans what treatment they are to expect from the cruel disturbers of their

peace, and evince the necessity of the most speedy and manly exertions to drive these foes of the human race from this continent.[2]
I am, &c.,   Richard Henry Lee.

MS not found; reprinted from William Wirt Henry, *Patrick Henry, Life, Correspondence and Speeches*, 3 vols. (New York: Charles Scribner's Sons, 1891), 3:33–35.
  [1] For further information on the meeting place and activities of Congress while in Baltimore, see Edith R. Bevan, "The Continental Congress in Baltimore, Dec. 20, 1776 to Feb. 27, 1777," *Md. Hist. Magazine* 42 (March 1947): 21–28.
  [2] For the handbill from Buck's County, N.J., describing "scenes of desolation and outrage" resulting from the march of British and Hessian troops through New Jersey, see W. W. Henry, *Patrick Henry*, 3:35–36; and Evans, *Am. Bibliography*, no. 15037.

George Ross to the
Lancaster Committee of Safety

Gentlemen   Reading 18th Decr. 1776
  General Mifflin at the Request of Congress will be at Lancaster on Saturday to devise with you & the Associators the best Mode of calling forth the Strength of the Country & on consulting with him This Morning I wrote a circular Letter of which the inclosed is a Copy [1] & have sent Expresses to Cols Grubb, Greenwalt, Burd, Green & Galbreath as we thought the Notice this Way would be earlier than to have troubled you to have sent them from Lanc[aste]r. You will I doubt not procure the Attendance of the Officers & Privates from the other Parts of the Country to meet on Saturday & if you please may send my Letter or conduct the Matter in any Manner you think proper.
  I am with Esteem, Gentlemen, yrs. &c,   Geo. Ross

RC (DLC). In a clerical hand, with place and dateline and signature by Ross.
  [1] For Ross' circular letter to the eleven battalions of the Lancaster County militia, see *Am. Archives*, 5th ser. 3:1273. His letter to Col. James Burd is in the Chamberlain Collection, MB.

Samuel Adams to Elizabeth Adams

My dear Betsy   Baltimore in Maryland Dec 19th 1776
  The Day before yesterday I arrivd in this Place which is One hundred Miles from Philadelphia. The Congress had resolvd to adjourn here when it should become absolutely necessary and not before. This sudden Removal may perhaps be wonderd at by some of my Friends, but it was not without the Advice of Generals Putnam & Mifflin, who were at Philadelphia to take Measures for its Preservation from the Enemy. For my own part, I had been used

to allarms in my own Country, and did not see the Necessity of removing so soon, but I suppose I misjudgd because it was otherwise ruled. It must be confessd that deliberative Bodies should not sit in Places of Confusion. This was heightned by an unaccountable Backwardness in the People of the Jerseys & Pennsylvania to defend their Country and crush their Enemies when I am satisfied it was in their Power to do it. The British as well as Hessian officers have severely chastisd them for their Folly. We are told that such savage Tragedies have been acted by them without Respect to Age or Sex as have equaled the most barbarous Ages & Nations of the World. Sorry I am that the People so long refusd to hearken to the repeated Calls of their Country. They have already deeply staind the Honor of America, and they must surely be as unfeeling as Rocks if they do not rise with Indignation and revenge the shocking Injuries done to their Wives and Daughters. Great Britain has taught us what to expect from Submission to its Power. No People ever more tamely surrenderd than of that Part of the Jerseys through which the Enemy marchd. No opposition was made—And yet the grossest Insults have been offerd to them, and the rude Soldiery have been sufferd to perpetrate Deeds more horrid than Murder. If Heaven punishes Communities for their Vices, how sore must be the Punishment of that Community who think the Rights of human Nature not worth struggling for and patiently submit to Tyranny. I will rely upon it that New England will never incur the Curse of Heaven, for neglecting to defend her Liberties. I pray God to increase their Virtue and make them happy in the full and quiet Possession of those Liberties they have ever so highly prizd. *Your* Wellfare, my dear, is ever near my heart. Remember me to my Daughter, Sister Polly & the rest of my Family and friends. I am in high Health & Spirits. Let me hear from you often. Adieu,

S A

[*P.S.*] Mr Hancock is just now arrivd with his family—all in good health.

RC (NN).

Benjamin Rumsey to John Hall?

Sir [1]   Joppa 19th Decr. 1776

Engaged in the Commission and the Business thereof in which we met with great Difficulties & Interruption I never attended Congress till this Day Week and should not then as the Business remained unfinished had I not heard Mr. Tilghman and Mr. Carroll had gone Home and left the Province unrepresented.[2]

When I got into Congress where I came determind to stay 'till
the last Extremity, altho exceeding inconvenient to me, I found that
Congress had two or three Days before that determined by the
Advice of their Generals to remove from thence to Baltimore, Upon
a presumption that the Enemy being possessed of the Jersey above
by marching Parties opposite the City might make a push in the
Night in Conjunction with the Tories and seise the Persons of the
Congress, and this might have been done with great Facility as the
City Militia had all marched to join General Washington.

The Enemy are posted on the Banks of the Delaware at Trentown
and from thence have pushed their parties as low as Burlington and
as high as Penny Town. They are commanded by General Howe
who has with him it is supposed the whole Brittish Force that can
be spared from their Conquests and are thought to amount to about
thirteen Thousand Men.

General Washington had not when we came away above 5000
Men with the Junction of the Militia posted on the opposite Banks
with forty Peices of Cannon. Genl. Lee was posted about 25 Miles
in the Rear of the British Army at a place called Chattam about 3
miles from Morris Town with a large Body of Forces composed of a
Detachment from the Northern Army Troops returning from Ticonderoga and encreasing daily with the Jersey Militia Numbers unknown to me but between 5000 and 12,000 from whence he has
positive Orders to march and join Genl Washington very injudiciously in my Opinion but the Slowness of the coming in of the
Militia in the State of Pennsylvania possibly may justify the Measure.

If the Militia would join Genl. Washington in such Numbers as
to make him strong enough in Front to prevent the Enemy's crossing Delaware and taking Philada. Lee by strong Detachments may
cut off all their Supplies and destroy the British Army without
striking a Blow or if they decamp expose them to two fires in Front
and Rear.

My Colleagues Colo. Contee and Mr. Hanson have just parted
from me after finishing our Business as far as we could to lay before
your Honours and this in some Measure will account to you for my
not writing.

I understood that as the Pennsylvania Militia rather moved slow
the Congress had come into a Resolution to request the Militia of
our State to march to the Assistance of Genl. Washington. I understood too Col. Ewing undertook voluntarily to bring them up and
rode away without any written Orders; my Intelligence was from
One of the Officers of our Army. You know Colo. Ewing (I presume the Congress do) and eer this or at their first setting at Baltimore You will receive a written Requisition.

I heard Mr. Chase tell Mr. Robt. Morris that all our sick, the

Baggage of the Congress and even Mr. Morris's Effects which are pretty considerable would be removed with Ease as he had wrote for Vessells to transport them but none were at the Head of Elk as I came by, at least they pressed Colo. Aquila Halls Vessell for that purpose. How Mr. Chase has transacted this whether in a public or private Capacity I cant tell, he can best answer it.

I had just received Orders from the Brigr. Genl. to give my Battallion Notice to hold itself in Readiness (If I am yet a Colo. which I doubt of from Report) and in Letters to the Officers was communicating that Intelligence when the Express brought to me your Letter directed here by the honorable John Hancock Esqr. on his Way to Baltimore. I much approve of your giving the Militia Notice to hold themselves in Readiness but I now tell you that will be totally useless without more, that they are without Arms, Blanketts many of them & Baggage Waggons with a numerous &ca. that ought to be supplied them before or on their March, and that they ought really to be better supplied than other Troops especially at this severe Season. I have advertised the 8th Battallion that if I am still their Colo. I will with the greatest alacrity do myself the Honour to march at their Head if the Province is represented without me.

A Doubt may arise with You respecting the Reason of the Tardiness of Pennsylvania. You know great Part of Philada., Bucks and Chester are Tories and the Councill of Safety of Pennsylvania have cried Wolf, Wolf two or three Times falsly to the back Counties and now the Wolf is really come they think it still a false Alarm. They are distracted too abt. the State of their Governmt., People being of various Opinions about it.

I have opened Mr. Presidents Letter [3] but shall seal and send it by Express to Baltimore to Mr. Chase who I expect by this Time is there. Seamen were much wanted and your Orders in sending the Seamen will be very agreeable to Congress. For if Philadelphia should ever be taken by some Coup de Main of the Enemy, wch. by the by a well manned Frigate will render much more difficult, there being no Ships of the Enemy in Delaware Bay, the Frigates and a great Quantity of Stores may be saved thereby.

You are also requested by me to inform Mr. President that it has not been either with my privity, Consent or Knowledge that Individuals have been applied to, that I am exceedingly sensible it rather tends to delay Business and that he and the whole Board I hope will acquit me of any Design in being Wanting in Respect to the cheif executive Power in the State, the Dignity of which I was always strenuous in supporting while I had the Honour of Seat there and still am 'tho I have not thot I am ⟨besides my Love for my Country⟩, added to other Motives, actuated by a Friendship and Esteem for the Individuals of that Board that will always induce me to treat them with the Utmost Respect, Esteem and Regard.

I am Sir, Your most humble Servt.   Benjamin Rumsey

RC (MdHi).

[1] Perhaps John Hall, vice president of the Maryland Council of Safety. Rumsey obviously directed this letter to a member of the council of safety and in the course of it twice mentions "Mr. President," Daniel of St. Thomas Jenifer.

[2] Matthew Tilghman and Charles Carroll, Barrister, are known to have been in Philadelphia as late as December 9, the day they and Samuel Chase requested money for the removal of sick troops to Maryland. Tilghman apparently left soon afterward, leaving only Chase and William Paca to represent Maryland, which until February 15, 1777, required the presence of three delegates to cast the state's vote in Congress. See William Paca to the Maryland Council of Safety, December 7, 1776, note 3; and JCC, 7:111.

[3] Probably the council's December 15 letter to the Maryland delegates. See Md. Archives, 12:530–31.

Robert Morris to Silas Deane

Dear Sir   Phila. Decr. 20th. 1776

With a heavy heart I sit down to write to you at this time as the unfortunate case of American Affairs at this period leave [no] room for joy in the mind of a true friend to this Country. I am now the only Member of Congress in this City unless Mr Walton of Georgia & Mr Clymer my Colleague still remain, which I am not sure of. I cannot pretend to give you a regular detail of our manyfold Misfortune because my Books & Papers are all gone into the Country as is my Family. But these unfortunate Events commenced with the loss of Fort Washington by the reduction of which the Enemy made about 2700 prisoners, & at this critical time, they by Treachery, Bribery or accident intercepted some dispatches from Gen Washington to Congress, also some of the Generals private Letters, particularly one to Ned Rutlidge in which he had fully laid open the unfortunate situation he was then involved in by the curs'd short inlistments of our army, for the times of most of them expired on the first of Decr. & the rest on the 1st of Jan., when the whole army would leave him, as they had undergone great fatigue during the whole Campaigne, had suffer'd amazingly by sickness and the approach of Winter added an appearance of starving for want of cloaths. All these things he stated fully & the Enemy became possessed of a most authentic account of his real situation. They determined to take advantage of it, and before Genl Washn had time to make any new arrangements at Fort Lee, on the west side of the North River to which he had cross'd with about 8000, a large body of Troops landed above & another below him, so that he was near being inclosed

with a Force vastly Superior. In this situation he had nothing left
for it but to retire directly off the neck of Land on which that
Fort Stands, leaving behind him considerable Baggage & Stores
with most of our large Cannon & Mortars. He retreated to Hackensack & was there in hopes of making a stand untill the militia of
the Country should come to his assitance, but the vigilence of the
enemy did not give him time for this. They pursued and he retreated all the way thro' the Jerseys to Trenton & from thence
they forced him across the Delewar, where he still remains to oppose their passage across the River. Lord Cornwallis commanded
the British Forces in the Jerseys untill they reach'd Brunswick
when Genl Howe join'd them with reinforcements determined
to make his way to this City without futher loss of time. You
may be sure the Militia of N Jersey & this State were call'd upon
to turn out & defend their Country in this Hour of distress. Alass
our internal Enemies had by various arts & means frighten'd many,
disaffected others & caused a general langoor to prevail over the
minds of almost all men, not before actually engaged in the war.
Many are also exceedingly disaffected with the Constitutions form'd
for their respective States, so that from one cause or other no Jersey
Militia turn'd out to oppose the march of an Enemy thro the heart
of their Country, and it was with the utmost difficulty the associators of this City could be prevail'd on to march agt them. At length
however it has been effected. They have been up with the Gen'l
about two weeks & the example at length is like to produce its
effect in the Country, as they are now pretty generally on their
march towards Trenton. During Genl Washingtons retreat thro'
the Jerseys he wrote for Genl Lee who was left to command on the
East Side of the N River with about 10 to 11 thousand men most
of whose inlistments are now expired or near it. He obeyed the
Summons, & brot with about 3000 men. With those he follow'd
the Enemys rear, but was obliged to make slow marches as his
people were in great want of shoes, stockings, & other necessaries
which he was obliged to collect from the Tories in the neibourhood
of his Rout. After he had pass'd a place call'd Chatham near
Elizh Town, he lodged at a Farm House. Last night was a Week
some treacherous Villain gave notice to the Enemy & the General's
ill fate or some other cause I am not acquainted with delay'd him
there untill near 10 oClo on Friday Morning his army having
march'd & their rear about 3 miles from him, when he was surprized by about 70 light horse who made prisoner of & imm[ediatel]y
bore him off in Triumph. This is an event much to be lamented. I
sincerely pity Lee & I feel for the loss my Country sustains. His
abilities had frequently been immensely useful—the want of them
will be severely felt. The Command of this party devolved on Genl
Sullivan who contined his Rout, fell in with Genl Gates with 500

men returning from the Lakes, and both join'd Genl Washton. yesterday. This junction is what we have long impatiently wish'd for, but still I fear our Force is not equal to the Task before them, & unless that Task is perform'd Phila. nay I may say Pensa must fall. The Task I mean is to drive the Enemy out of N. Jersey for at present they occupy Brunswick, Prince Town, Trenton, Penny Town, Bordenton, Burlington, Morris Town, Mount Holly & Hardonfield, having their main Body about Prince Town & strong detachments in all the other places—it is supposed with a design of attacking this City whenever they can cross the Delewar on Ice, for they have only been kept from it by our sending up the Gondoloes & brot off or destroy'd all the boats along the Jersey Shore. You will think the Enemy are now in a Situation for us to attack their scatter'd parties, & cut them off. This we think too & are preparing to do it but it will be a work of extreme difficulty to get at them. They have excellent intelligence of all our motions—we can hardly come at any certainty about theirs—for Lord Howe & Genl Howe issued a proclamation on the 30th Novr offering pardon to all who should submit within 60 days & subscribe a Declaration that they will not hereafter bear arms agt the Kings Troops nor encourage others to do it. This has had a wonderful effect, and all Jersey or far the greater part of it, is suposed to have made their Submission and subscribed the declaration required. Those who do so, of Course become our most inveterate enemies, they have the means of Conveying inteligence & they avail themselves of it. In this perplexing Situation of things the Congress were informed this Day week that an advanced party of Hessians & Highlanders had taken possession of Burlington, that they were pushing for Coopers Ferry oposite the City and it was thought had the means of Crossing the River; here was no troops to oppose them, our whole force both by Land and water was above. It was therefore deemed unsafe for the Congress to remain here & absolutely necessary that they should be in a place of safety where they could deliberate Cooly & freely without interuption & late Saturday they adjourned to Baltimore where they are now Sitting. This City was for ten Days the meerest Scene of Distress that you can Conceive. Everybody but Quakers were removing their Families & effects and now it Looks dismal & Melancoly. The Quakers & their families pretty generally Remain, the other Inhabitants are principally Sick Soldiers, some few effective ones under General Putnam who is come here to throw up Lines & prepare for the defence of the place if Genl. Washington Should be forced to Retreat heither. You may be sure I have my full Share of trouble on this occasion but having got my family & Books removed to a place of Safety my mind is more at ease and my time is now given up to the Public although I have many thousand Pounds worth of effects here without any prospect of saving them. We are told the British troops are kept from plunder but the Hessians & other foreigners looking upon that as the Right of War plunder wherever they go from both whigs & tories without distinction & horid devastations they have made on Long Island. New York Island, white plains, & New Jerseys being the only parts they have yet set foot on, should they get this fine City, they will be satiated if the Ruin of thousands worthy Citizens can Satisfy their avarice. This is not the only part of the Continent that now feels the weight of their Resentment. Genl. Clinton with from 3 to 6000 men has invaded Rhode Island and it is said has taken possession of it, whether he will make any attempt on the Main during this Severe inclement season I do not know but if he does I hope he may find Cause to repent it. I must add to this Gloomy Picture one Circumstance more distressing than all the rest because it threatens instant & total Ruin to the american Cause unless Some radical Cure is aplied & that speedily. I mean the Depreciation of the Continental Curency, the enormous Pay of our army the immense expence at which they are suplied with Provisions, cloathing & other necessarys and in short the extravagance that has prevailed in most departments of the public Service have Called forth prodigious emissions of Paper money both Continental and Colonial. Our internal Enemies, who alas are numerous & rich have always been undermining its value by various artifices and now that our distresses are wrought to a Pitch by the Success and near approach of the Enemy they speak plainer & many peremtorily refuse to take it at any rate. Those that do receive it, do it with fear & trembling and you may Judge of its value even amongst these when I tell you that £250 Continental money or 666 2/3 Dollars is given for a Bill of Exchange of £100 Sterling, 16 Dollars for a half Johannes, two paper Dollars for one of Silver, 3 Dollars for a pair of shoes, 12 dollars for a hat, 1/12 dollar for a pound of Butter & so on. A Common Labourer ask two Dollars a day for his Work & Idles half his time. All this amounts to real depreciation of the money. The War must be Carried on at an Expence proportioned to this Value which must inevitably call for immense emissions & of Course Still farther depreciations must ensue. This can only be prevented by borowing in the money now in Circulation. The attempt is made & I hope will Succeed, by loan of Lottery. The present troubles interupts those measures here & as yet I am not informed how they go on in other States—but something more is necessary—force must be inevitably employed & I dread to See that day. We have already Calamities sufficient for any Country and the measure will be up when one part of the American People are obliged to dragoon another at the same time that they are oposing a more powerfull external foe. For my part I see but two Chances for relief—one is from you. If the Court of France open their Eyes to their own Interest and think the Comerce of North America will Compensate them for the Expence & Evil of a War with Brittain, they may readily create a diversion & afford us Succours that will Change the fate of affairs but they must do it Soon. Our Situation is critical & does not admit of Delay. I dont mean by this, that instant Submission must ensue if they do not directly afford us relief—but there is a great difference between the Benefits they will derive from a Comercial Connection with this Country in full health & Vigour & what they can possibly expect after it is exausted by repeated efforts during the precarious process of a tedious War during which its Cities will be destroyed, the Country Ravaged, the inhabitants reduced in Numbers, plundered of their property and unable to reap the Luxuriant produces of the finest Soil in the World. Neither can they after a tedious delay in negociation expect that Vigourous assistance from us in prosecuting the War, that they may be assured of, if they Join us in the Infancy. If they Join us generously in the day of our distress without attempting undue advantages because we are so, they will find a gratefull people to promote their future glory & interest with unabating Zeal and from my Knowledge of the Commerce of this Country with Europe I dare assert that whatever European Power possesses the presumption of it, must of Consequence become the Richest & most potent in Europe. But alas should time be Lost in tedious negociations & succours be withheld, America must sue for peace from her opressors. Our people knew not the hardships & Calamities of War when they so boldly dared Brittain to arms. Every man was then a bold Patriot, felt himself equal to the Contest and seemed to wish for an opportunity of evincing his prowess, but now when we are fairly engaged, when Death & Ruin stare us in the face and when nothing but the most intrepid Courage can rescue us from Contempt & disgrace, sorry I am to Say it, many of those who were foremost in Noise, Shrink coward like from the Danger and are begging pardon without striking a Blow. This however is not general but dejection of spirits is an epidemical desease and unless Some fortunate event or other gives a turn to the disorder, in time it may prevail through out the Community. No event would give that turn so soon as a Declaration of War on the part of France against Great Brittain and I am sure if they lose this golden oportunity they will never have such another. You will doubtless be Surprized that we have not made better progress with our Navy, because you are unacquainted with the many dificulties & Causes of delay that have encountered us. The want of Sea Coal for our Anchor Smiths has been a great Bar to our progress, the disapointments in our first attempts to Cast Cannons has been another, but above all we have been hindered by the Constant calling out of our Militia in a manner that did not admit of the necessary tradesmen being exempted. You will wonder at this, it would be a long Story to unfold the reasons, therefore suffice that it is so. Doctr. Franklin can inform you many particulars respecting the Flying Camp & on that will account for it, therefore I shall give you the present state of our Navy according to the best of my knowledge at this time.

The Frigate in New Hampshire is a very fine ship compleated in every particular, but the want of Cannon which was to have been Cast in Rhode Island, but the Spirit of Privateering has prevailed so eminently there that they have Sacrificed every other pursuit to it both publick & private as I am informed & we have ordered the Guns cast in Connecticut for that Frigate to be sent to Portsmouth. As soon as they arrive the Raleigh will be manned & sail on a Cruise.

At Boston they have also two fine Frigates, the Boston of 24 guns I expect is at sea before this time commanded by Captn. McNeil a very clever fellow. The other is nearly ready, commanded by Capn. Manly.

At Rhode Island was built the two Worst frigates as I have been informed, by those that have Seen the whole, these two are compleatly fitted & was partly manned when we last heard from them, so that I hope they are now at Sea.

At Conecticut the Frigate is said to be a fine Ship but she cannot get to sea this winter for want of Cordage & other Stores. At New York two very fine Frigates are blocked up by the Enemy and halled into Esopus Creek for Safety.

At this place we have four very fine ships. One of them the Randolph, Capt. Biddle, of 26 twelve pounders will I hope go to Sea in Company with this Letter. Another the Delawar, Captn. Alexander, is geting ready & hope will get out this Winter. The other two wants Guns, anchors & Men. At Baltimore is a fine frigate now only waiting for an anchor & Men. Besides these we have in Service, the Alfred, Columbus & Reprisal, ships from 16 to 24 Guns, the Brigts. Cabot, Camden, Andrew Dorria & Lexington of 12 to 16 Guns, the Sloops Providence, Hornet, Fly, Independance, Sachem & Schooners Wasp, Musquito & Georgia Pacquet all in actual service, and they have great Success in taking valuable Prizes as indeed have numbers of Privateers from all parts of America. We have besides, two very fine Rowe Galleys built here of 90 feet keel but they are not yet rigged, and it has lately been determined by Congress to build Some Line of Battle Ships & at all events to push forward & pay the utmost attention to an American Navy. The greatest Encouragement is given to Seamen which ought to be made known throughout Europe. Their pay in our Navy is 8 Dollars per Month with the best Chance of Prize Money that Men Ever had & liberty of Discharges after every Cruise if they chuse it. In the Merchant Service they now get from 30 to 40 Dollars per Month and this Leads me to the State of our Comerce. In the Eastern States they are so intent on privatering that they mind little else. However there is some Exportation of produce from thence & as to imports they are the best Suplied of any part of America, having been more Surprizingly Successfull in Captures. New York being in the hands of the Enemy we have nothing to say to it and the produce of New Jersey will be totally consumed by their army and ours. In this State we had last season the worst Crop of Wheat ever known both as to Quantity and Quality. This being our Staple Comodity & stores prohibited our Merchants have been led to purchase much Tobaco in Maryld. & Virginia and their Ships are employed in the export of this Article with some flour, Boards, Beeswax [. . . .] We have a good many Imports but fast as goods arrive they are bought up for the Army or for the use of Neighbouring States and therefore continue to bear high prices. The Value of ships has risen in the same enormous proportion with every thing else & ships that were deemed worth £1000 twelve Months ago now sell for £3000 or upwards. Every article belonging to them is also excessive Dear, hard to be got & the insolence and dificulty of Seamen is beyond bearing. In Maryland, Virginia, South Carolina & Georgia they have plenty of valuable produce on hand but no Ships to Carry it away & constant Cruizers all along the Coast makes it very dangerous to send Ships from one port to another, so that look which way you will, you find us surounded with dificulties in the Land service, in the Sea service & in our Comerce. Agriculture and Mechanicks have their Impediments by the enlisting of Soldiers & frequent Calls on the Militia. In short nothing but the most arduous exertions & Virtuous Conduct in the Leaders Seconded by a Spirited behaviour in the Army and a patient indurance of hardships by the people in General, can long suport the Contest. Therefore the Court of France should strike at once as they will reap an immediate harvest. They may sell their manufactures for any price they please to ask, they will get in payment tobaco, Rice, Indigo, Deer Skins, furs, wheat, flour, Iron, Bees Wax, Lumber, fish, oil, whale Bone, Pot & pearl ashes and various other articles and if they please here is an ample field to employ their shipping & raise seamen for their Navy, but they must put in for this treasure now or never. I will not enter into any detail of our Conduct in Congress, but you may depend on this that so Long as that respectable body persist in the attempt to execute as well as to deliberate on their business it never will be done as it ought & this has been urged many & many a time by myself & others but some of them dont Like to part with power or to pay others for doing what they cannot do themselves.

I have your favour of the 30th Sepr. to myself now before me. The Letter by the same Conveyance from Martinico under cover of

Mr. Bingham I sent down to the Committee at Baltimore [1] & wrote them my mind on the Justice of your Complaints for want of intelligence. I had often told it to them before. You Know well I was not put in that Commitee to Carry on the Correspondence, but to find out the Conveyances, however I have been obliged to write all the Letters that have been wrote for some time past but as Colol. Lee, Mr. Hooper & the Revd. Dr. Weatherspoon are now added to the Committee, I shall excuse myself from that task altho I have thought it proper to give you a just state of our affairs at this time because I do supose the Comitee will not be got fairly in their Geers at Baltimore yet while & when they do it is probable they may not be fond of laying things before you so fully as I have done. Some of us are of very sanguine Complexions and are too apt to flater ourselves that Things are not so bad as they appear to be or that they will soon mend &c. Now my notion is that you Gentlemn. Commissioners should be fairly & fully informed of the true state of affairs that you may make a proper use of that knowledge keeping secret what ought to be so & promulgating what should be known. You will shew this scrawl to Doctr. Franklin for whose safe arrival my best wishes have often gone forth and I embrace this opportunity of assuring him of the High Respect & Esteem I entertain for him. I also beg my Comps to Mr. Lee if he is with you, tell him I have the Commission in which he is nominated already to send but it is gone into the Country with my papers or I would send it by this Conveyance.

My own affairs necessarily detained me here after the departure of Congress and it is well I staid as I am obliged to set many things right that would otherways be in the greatest Confusion, indeed I find my presence so very necessary that I shall remain here untill the Enemy drive me away. I am Dr Sir &c   R.M.[2]

Tr (MH–H). Two variant copies of this letter (one of which is in the hand of Edward Bancroft), from the Auckland MSS, British Museum, are reproduced in Benjamin Franklin Stevens, comp., *B. F. Stevens's Facsimiles of Manuscripts in European Archives Relating to America, 1773–1783*, 2107 facsim. in 24 portfolios (London: Photographed and printed by Malby & Sons, 1889–95), nos. 1396, 1397. Of the first, Stevens noted: "This copy is believed to have been made from Arthur Lee's papers and transmitted from Berlin by Mr. [Hugh] Elliot in July 1777." It was undoubtedly made from the Tr reproduced here from the Lee Papers, MH–H. The same letter, minus only the opening sentence, dated December 21 and directed to the commissioners at Paris, is in Jared Sparks, ed., *The Diplomatic Correspondence of the American Revolution*, 12 vols. (Boston: N. Hale & Gray & Bowen: 1829–30), 1:233–46. The texts reprinted in Burnett, *Letters*, Wharton, *Diplomatic Correspondence*, and *Am. Archives* are taken from Sparks.

[1] For Deane's September 30 letter to Morris and October 1 letter to the Committee of Secret Correspondence, see Sparks, *Diplomatic Correspondence*, 1:41–48. Bingham's letter has not been found.

[2] For the continuation of this letter, see Morris to Deane, January 8, 1777.

628   DECEMBER 20, 1776

Benjamin Rush to Richard Henry Lee

My dear sir,   Philada Decemr. 20. 1776

An officer (German by birth) who has served in Russia & Hanover several campaigns called upon me a few hours ago, and after producing certificates &c that he *now* holds a captains commission under the Empress of Russia gave me the following information in confidence. He says that he is personally acquainted with many of the Hessian Officers & privates now in How's Army—that as they serve for pay only, he thinks the bounty, pay & cloathing offered by Congress so much above what they now enjoy that if they were properly tendered to them they would serve us with more chearfulness than the king of Britain. He offers to go in person into How's army at the risk of his life, and is sanguine eno' to think he could immediately bring off 200 recruits with him. He demands continental money only to pay the bounties. If he fails, he will return the money. He very justly objected to taking gold or silver as it might be useful to them in How's camp. I submit these hints to your consideration. I am bound to inform you that the Captain (who from his certificates is a Baron) appears very modest, and possesses the manners & address of a gentleman. He added in the course of our conversation that we had many warm friends in Russia, & that a majority of the nation expressed a dislike at the tho'ts of being employed to fight against us. He thinks there is no probability of any troops being procured from that quarter next Summer. If you think the above scheme practicable, please to mention it in congress. I am at a loss what to advise in the affair. At any rate communicate your opinion or the determination of congress to Mr. Philip Boehm in Philada. who will communicate it to the Baron. If he is encouraged he will wait upon Congress & receive his instructions from them.[1]

We are much blamed by the whigs and ridiculed by the tories for leaving Philada so suddenly. All the back counties of Philada are in Motion. Several hundreds of the miltia join Gen Washington daily.[2] Mr Galloway & three of the Allen family have received absolution at Trenton. Gen Putnam sent a guard to apprehend Mr Dick——n yesterday; you will soon hear of the cause of it.[3] He has escaped. I refer you to Mr Saml Purviance for particulars. I have a thousand things to say to you. Vigor, firmness & decisive measures are more necessary than ever. Dispute less & do more in congress or we are undone. Compts to your brother & the worthy members of the weekly club. I am on my way to Bristol, being summoned to attend the Philada Militia for a few weeks.[4] Yours sincerely,

                                              Benja Rush

P.S. I need not suggest to you the necessity of Secrecy if the Baron's Scheme is adopted.

RC (PPAmP).

[1] There is no record indicating that Congress responded to this offer.

[2] The three following sentences were omitted from previously published versions of this letter. Lee's grandson deleted them when he published his grandfather's correspondence in 1825, and Peter Force subsequently reprinted the younger Lee's text. See Richard H. Lee, *Memoir of the Life of Richard Henry Lee . . .*, 2 vols. (Philadelphia: H. C. Carey and I. Lea, 1825), 2:159–60; and *Am. Archives*, 5th ser. 3:1308.

[3] Rush somewhat clarified this reference to the threatened arrest of John Dickinson in a letter to Lee the next day when he explained that Gen. Israel Putnam had threatened to confine persons who refused to accept Continental money in payment of debt. Dickinson had come under suspicion because his letter of December 14 to his brother, Gen. Philemon Dickinson, advising against receiving Continental paper money, had been intercepted by the Pennsylvania Council of Safety and made public. For the letter and Dickinson's personal explanation of the episode, see Charles J. Stillé, *The Life and Times of John Dickinson, 1732–1808* (1891; reprint ed., New York: Burt Franklin, 1969), pp. 400–406. See also *Am. Archives*, 5th ser. 3:1254–55; and Rush to Richard Henry Lee, December 21, 1776.

[4] After the adjournment of Congress on December 12, Rush had arranged for his family's safety with a relative in Maryland and volunteered to serve with Gen. John Cadwalader's brigade of Philadelphia Associators in the defense of the city. He subsequently tended the troops engaged in the Trenton-Princeton campaign until mid-January and did not go to Baltimore until January 23 or 24.

During the interval Rush wrote several letters to Lee—at least six between January 6 and 15 in addition to this letter and those of December 21, 25, and 30 printed below—sending intelligence and giving advice on what must be done to preserve America from ruin. See Rush, *Letters* (Butterfield), 1:124–30; and *PMHB*, 78 (January 1954): 15–18.

Years later Rush described his activities during this period at considerable length in his autobiography. See Benjamin Rush, *The Autobiography of Benjamin Rush*, ed. George W. Corner (Princeton: Published for the American Philosophical Society by Princeton University Press, 1948), pp. 124–30.

Committee of Secret Correspondence to the Commissioners at Paris

Honourable Gentlemen   Baltimore in Maryland Decr 21 1776 [1]

After expressing our hopes that this will find you all three safely fixed at Paris we proceed with pleasure to acknowledge the Receipt of Mr Deane's Letter of the first of October.[2] When we reflect on the Character & views of the Court of London it ceases to be a Wonder that the British Ambassader & all other British Agents should employ every Means that tended to prevent European Powers but France more especially from giving America Aid in this War. Prospects of Accommodation it is well known would effectually prevent foreign Interferences and therefore without one

serious Design of accommodating on any Principles but the absolute Submission of America the delusive Idea of Conciliation hath
been industriously Suggested on both sides the Water that under
cover of this dividing & Aid withholding Prospect the vast British
Force sent to America might have the fairest Chance of succeeding.
And this Policy hath in fact done considerable Injury to the United
States as we shall presently shew by a just Detail of this Campaign
for it is not yet ended.

You know Gentlemen that at the Moment a potent Land and
marine force was preparing to be sent here an Act was passed for
appointing Commissioners whom too many expected were to give
peace to America. As therefore the War might be soon concluded
so were our military Arrangements accommodated & the Troops
taken into service the last spring consisting of regular Corps and
Bodies of Militia were all engaged for short Periods. With these
the Campaign began in various parts of N. America. Dr. Franklin
is so well acquainted with the Progress of the War in Canada
previous to his Departure that we need only observe the Campaign
has ended as favourably for us in that Quarter as we could reasonably expect. The Enemy having been able to pierce no further
than Crown Point after a Short Stay & reconnoitring General
Gates' Army at Ticonderoga thought proper to recross the Lake
and leave us in quiet Possession of these Passes. General Gates
having left a proper force at Ticonderoga and on the Communication retired with the rest of his Troops. New York and its
Neighbourhood not being defensible by an army singly against a
strong land and sea force acting in Conjunction was of necessity
yeilded to the Enemy after some Contest General Washington retiring until the Situation of the Country above Kingsbridge no
longer enabled the Enemy to receive Aid from their ships. General
Howe having stopped here and General Carlton at Crown Point
effectually disappointed the great Object of joining the two Armies.
The latter as we have said returning to Canada & the former retreating from the White Plains towards N. York gave us a favourable
Prospect of seeing a happy End put to this dangerous Campaign.
However many Causes have concurred in producing an unlucky
Reverse of fortune. The Nature of the Country, the uncommon
fineness of the Weather even to this day and above all the short
Enlistments which gave the soldiery an Opportunity of going home
tired as they were with the Operations of an active Summer. When
General Howe retreated from the White Plains he halted his whole
Army on the N. River between Dobbs's Ferry and Kingsbridge where
he remained for some time. Having effected so little of the great
Business that brought him here and the Season allowing him
time for it most Men were of Opinion that the next Attempt would
be to get Possession of Philadelphia by a March through the

Jerseys whilst a Fleet should be sent up the Delaware to facilitate the Enterprize. To guard against such a Manoeuvre Gen Washington crossed the North River with all the Battalions that had been raised to the westward of it leaving General Lee with the eastern Troops to guard the pass of the highlands on Hudsons River. In this situation of things Mr Howe made a sudden Attack on Fort Washington with the greatest Part of his Army & carried it with a Considerable Loss: here he made near 3000 of our Men Prisoners. By this Event it became unnecessary longer to hold Fort Lee or Fort Constitution as it was formerly called which is on the west side of the N. River nearly opposite to Fort Washington. It had therefore been determined to abandon Fort Lee but before the Stores could be all removed the Enemy came suddenly upon it and the Garrison retreated leaving some of their Baggage & Stores behind. About this Time General Howe became possessed of a Letter (by the Agency of some wicked Person who contrived to get it from the Express) written by General Washington to the Board of War in which he had given an exact account when the Time of Service of all our Battalions would expire & his apprehensions that the Men would not reinlist without first going home to see their families and friends. Possessed of this Intelligence the Opportunity was carefully watched & a vigorous Impression actually made at the very Crisis when our Army in the Jersies was reduced to 3000 men by the retiring of Numbers and the Sickness of others and before our Militia could in this extensive Country be brought up to supply their Places. The Enemy marched rapidly on through the Jersies while our feeble Army was obliged to retreat from Post to Post until it crossed the Delaware at Trenton where about 2500 Militia from the City of Philadelphia joined the General. Since General Howes Arrival on the Borders of the Delaware various Manoeuvres & Stratagems have been practiced to effect a Passage over the River but they have hitherto failed. General Washingtons small Army is placed along the west side of Delaware from above the Corrells Ferry to within 14 Miles of Philadelphia which with the Gondolas, one Frigate of 32 Guns & other Armed vessels in the River above the Cheveaux de Frise cover the Passage of it. General Lee who had crossed the North River with as many of the eastern Troops as could be spared from the Defence of the Highlands (either to join General Washington or to act on the Enemies Rear as occasion might point out) was the other Day unfortunately surprised & made Prisoner by a party of 70 light horse who found him in a house a few miles in the Rear of his army with his Domestics only. This Loss though great will in some Degree be repaired for the present by General Gates who we understand had joined the Army commanded by Genl Lee & who we have reason to think has by this time effected a junction of his force with that of Genl Washington.

As the Militia are marching from various quarters to reinforce the General if the Enemy do not quickly accomplish their wishes of possessing Philadelphia We hope not only to save that City but to see Genl Howe retreat as fast as he advanced through the Jersies. General Clinton with a fleet on which it is said he carried 8000 men has gone from New York through the Sound some suppose for Rhode Island but neither his Distination nor its Consequences are yet certainly known to us. Thus Gentlemen we have given you a true Detail of the Progress and present State of our Affairs which although not in so good a Posture as they were two months ago are by no means in so bad a Way as the Emissaries of the British Court will undoubtedly represent them. If the great Land and Sea force with which we have been attacked be compared with the feeble state in which the Commencement of this War found us with Respect to Military Stores of all kinds, Soldiers Cloathing, Navy & regular force and if the infinite Art be considered with which Great Britain hath endeavored to prevent our getting these Necessaries from foreign parts which has in part prevailed the wonder will rather be that our Enemies have made so little progress than that they have made so much.

All views of Accommodation with Great Britain but on Principles of Peace as independent States and in a manner perfectly consistent with the Treaties our Commissioners may make with foreign States being totally at an End since the Declaration of Independence & the Embassy to the Court of France Congress have directed the raising of 94 Battalions of Infantry with some Cavalry. Thirteen Frigates from 24 to 36 Guns are already launched and fitting and two ships of the Line with five more Frigates are ordered to be put on the Stocks. We hear the Levies are going on well in the different States. Until the New Army is Collected the militia must curb the Enemies Progress. The very considerable Force that Great Britain has already in N. America, the Possibility of recruiting it here within their own Quarters by force and fraud together, added to the Reinforcements that may be sent from Europe and the difficulty of finding Funds in the present depressed State of American Commerce, all conspire to prove incontestibly that if France desires to preclude the Possibility of North America being ever reunited with Great Britain now is the favourable moment for establishing the Glory, Strength and Commercial Greatness of the former Kingdom by the Ruin of her ancient Rival. A decided part now taken by the Court of Versailles and a vigorous Engagement in the War in Union with North America would with Ease sacrifice the fleet and Army of Great Britain at this time cheifly collected about New York. The inevitable Consequence would be the quick Reduction of the British Islands in the West Indies already bared of Defence by the Removal of their Troops to this Continent. For Reasons herein assigned Gentlemen You will readily discern how all-important it is to the security of American Independence that France should enter the War as soon as may be and how necessary it is if it be possible to procure from her the Line of Battle Ships you were desired in your Instructions to obtain for us the speedy arrival of which here in the present State of things might decide the Contest at one Stroke.

We shall pay proper Attention to what Mr Deane writes concerning Dr Williamson & Mr Hopkins and we think the ill Treatment this Country and Mr Deane have received from these Men strongly suggests the necessity of invincible Reserve with Persons coming to France as Americans and Friends to America whom the most impregnable Proofs have not removed all Doubt about. The British Recall of their Mediterranean Passes is an Object of great Consequence and may require much Intercession with the Court of France to prevent the Mischeifs that may be derived to American Commerce therefrom. But this subject has been already touched upon in your Instructions on the Sixth Article of the Treaty proposed to be made with France. As all affairs relative to the Conduct of Commerce and Remittances pass through another Department we beg leave to refer you to the Secret Committee & Mr Thomas Morris their Agent in France for every Information on these Subjects.

The Neighbourhood of Philadelphia having by the Enemies movements become the Seat of War it was judged proper that Congress should adjourn to this Town where the public Business may be attended to with the undisturbed Deliberation that its Importance demands. The Congress was accordingly opened here on the 20th Inst.

As it is more than probable that the Conference with Lord Howe on Staten Island may be misrepresented to the Injury of these States we do ourselves the pleasure to inclose you an authenticated Account of that whole Business which the Possibility of Doctor Franklins not arriving renders proper.[3] This step was taken to unmask his Lordship and evince to the World that he did not possess powers which for the purpose of Delusion & division it had been suggested he did.

Mr Deanes Proposition of Loan is accepted by Congress and they have desired two millions Sterling to be obtained if possible.[4] The Necessity of keeping up the Credit of our Paper Currency and the Variety of important uses that may be made on this Money have induced Congress to go so far as 6 Per Cent but the Interest is heavy and it is hoped you may be able to do the Business on much easier Terms. The Resolves of Congress on this subject are inclosed and Your earliest Attention to them is desired that we may know as soon as possible the Event of this Application.

Another Resolve of Congress inclosed will shew you that Congress approve of armed Vessels being fitted out by you on continental Account provided the Court of France dislike not the Measure and blank Commissions for this Purpose will be sent you by the next Opportunity. Private Ships of War or Privateers can not be admitted where you are because the Securities necessary in such Cases to prevent irregular Practices cannot be given by the Owners and Commanders of such Privateers.[5] Another Resolve of Congress which we have the honour to inclose you directs the Conduct to be pursued with Regard to Portugal.[6]

We have nothing further to add at present but to request that you will omit no good Oppertunity of informing us how you succeed in your mission, what Events take place in Europe by which these States may be affected and that you continue us in regular succession some of the best London, French & Dutch Newspapers with any valuable political Publications that may concern North America.

We have the Honour to be Gentlemen with great Respect & Esteem your most obedient and very humble Servants,

      Benja. Harrison   Will Hooper

      Richard Henry Lee   Jno Witherspoon

                  Robert Morris, at Philada.

P.S. The American Captures of British vessels at Sea have not been less Numerous or less valuable than before Dr Franklin left us. The value of these Captures have been esteemed at two Millions.[7]

RC (NN). In a clerical hand, and signed by Harrison, Hooper, Lee, Morris, and Witherspoon. Duplicate RCs are at PHC, PPAmP, and ViU; and an intercepted dispatch is in the Auckland MSS, British Museum. For Lee's draft of this letter, see Richard Henry Lee, *The Letters of Richard Henry Lee*, ed. James C. Ballagh, 2 vols. (New York: Macmillan Co., 1911–14), 1:231–40.

[1] Although dated December 21, it is clear that this letter was written over a period of several days, since two of the resolves discussed were not passed by Congress until December 23, 1776. It was forwarded to Morris for signature on the 25th. See Benjamin Harrison to Robert Morris, December 25, 1776.

[2] Silas Deane's October 1 letter to the committee is in Wharton, *Diplomatic Correspondence*, 2:153–57.

[3] The report of the committee of Congress that met with Lord Howe was published by order of Congress in the fall of 1776. See Evans, *Am. Bibliography*, no. 15168.

[4] In his October 1 letter, Deane had said: "I have no doubt but I can obtain a loan for the Colonies if empowered, and on very favorable terms. I have already sounded on the subject, and will be more explicit hereafter, both as to my proposals, for I can go no further, and the answers I may receive." See Wharton, *Diplomatic Correspondence*, 2:157; and *JCC*, 6:1036–37.

[5] On December 23 Congress directed the committee to inform the commissioners that they were authorized "to arm and fit for war any number of vessels not exceeding six, at the expence of the United States, to war upon British property, and that commissions and warrants be for this purpose sent to the Commissioners, provided the Commissioners be well satisfied this measure will not be disagreeable to the court of France." *JCC*, 6:1036.

[6] On December 23 Congress directed the committee to inform the commissioners "that Congress have received no advices concerning the proceedings of Portugal but what they have seen in the news papers, the authenticity of which may be doubtful. That Congress desire exact information from the Commissioners, whether any American vessels have been prohibited entering, or have been confiscated, in the dominions of Portugal, and on what principles.

"That they be directed to remonstrate in the firmest tone with the Portugese Ambassador on these subjects, so soon as they shall have well informed themselves of the facts above mentioned." *JCC*, 6:1035–36.

[7] For lists of some of the British ships captured and brought into American ports, see Morgan, *Naval Documents*, 7:642–47, 809–10, 1273–74; and *Am. Archives*, 5th ser. 3:1527–30.

John Hancock to the Frederick County Committee

Gentlemen,   Baltimore Decr. 21t 1776.

I was duely honored with your Favour of the 19th. inst which I immediately communicated to Congress, who highly approve your Zeal and Activity for the Promotion of the American Cause. In Consequence of your Letter, the Congress passed the foregoing Resolution; & by this opportunity I forward you the Eighteen Thousand Dollars, which you will please to apply agreeably to the Terms of the Resolve; and will please also to transmit to Genl. Washington a particular State of the Payments to the several Militia.[1] In Confidence that you will expedite the March of the Militia as early as possible, I add not, but that I am with every Sentiment of Esteem, Gentlemen, your most obed. & very hble Servt.[2]

J H. Presidt.

LB (DNA: PCC, item 12A).

[1] The Frederick County Committee's December 19 letter to Hancock and accompanying resolves, promising to send militia reinforcements to Washington in compliance with a December 9 resolve of Congress, are in PCC, item 70, fols. 97–102, and *Am. Archives*, 5th ser. 3:1288–89. See also *JCC*, 6:1015–16. Congress' December 21 resolve granting the committee $18,000 "for the use of the militia of the counties of Frederic, Washington, and Montgomery, who march to reinforce General Washington," is in *JCC*, 6:1033.

[2] Around this time, Hancock—apparently prompted by a December 20 resolve that was later erased from the journals—wrote the following note to the Maryland Convention at the foot of a page containing a copy of a December 9 resolve calling upon four Maryland county committees—including the one from Frederick—to send military assistance to Philadelphia:

"No material News.

"The Application to those Counties was made as the most Expeditious way of obtaing. it. I shall address your Council of Safety by order of Congress assigning the Reasons why the application was not directly made to them." Red Books, MdAA.

This document is endorsed: "Not recd till 4 Jany 1777." For further references, see *JCC*, 6:1015, 1029; *Am. Archives*, 5th ser. 3:1396–97; and *Md. Archives*, 12:529–31, 540.

Robert Morris to John Hancock

Sir   Philada. Decr. 21st 1776

The Express that carrys you this letter has just called on me, saying that he came from the Convention of New York. I thought it prudent to open the letter and know whether the business it respected cou'd be done here or whether it must be sent forward & finding it must go forward I only detain him to make this apology & to inform you that the Sloop Independance Commanded by Lt Robinson (Capt Young being left behind sick) pushed out from Chincoteague where she first put in, and notwithstanding she was chased by Six of the Enemys Cruizers at our Capes, She got safe up here & is now landing the Cargo. I have determined to send 856 Blankets that came in her, to Genl. Washington and have informed him they were imported for the use of the New Recruits, but as the Inclemency of the weather and the exceeding severe duty of the Troops now with him entitle them to every comfort we can afford I submit to him whether to make use of them for their use or not.

The Cloths I will deliver to Mr. Mease with orders to have them made up fast as possible. 919 Muskets shall be delivered to Mr. Commissary Towers to wait the orders of Genl. Washington or of the Board of War and I hope one or other of them will send orders soon as possible.[1]

The Council of safety want money & have sent an express for a Supply. I have borrowed sufficient for the Marine department altho the Disbursements are considerable. Capt Biddle will get more Seamen than we expected. The Delaware is getting ready and I have ordered the Fly, Capt Warner, down the Bay to watch the Enemies Ships & bring us word if they should quit that Station. I have sent an express across the Jerseys to Capt Baldwin of the Wasp to Cruize outward of them to give Notice to inward bound Ships,[2] and have Stationed the Hornet, Capt Nicholson, (who attempted to get out to Sea but coud not) in Christeen Creeks Mouth to act in Conjunction with a large Galley of this State in defence of that Creek as there are many valuable Stores up it. I shall get the Sloop Independance hove down & some little damage she recd at Chincoteague repaired & then send her also to watch the Enemys Ships. There are a large number of Waggons in the City and as I fear Genl. Howe does not yet give up his plan of getting possession of it this Winter I will order a good part of the Salt Provisions now in the Commissarys care to be carried up to Lancaster as we certainly ought to have inland Magazines of Provisions and of military Stores, but I long to hear from you that I may judge whether Congress approve of these things which I have undertaken for the sake of serving my Country. Mr. Smith is not yet returned and am very sorry for it as I do think a good deal of Money might have been borrowed by this time. I am very fearfull that this bad Weather will sicken the associators & break up our Campaign whatever may be its effect on the Enemy. There are some Prisoners onboard the Enemies Ships at our Capes that have wrote up to me to procure their release, amongst the rest Capt Morgan of the Bermuda sloop that carried Mr Deane to France who was returning here with dispatches & some Goods and was unfortunately taken near Cape May. I will send a letter for Capt Hammond of the Roebuck open to Henry Fisher at Lewis Town to be sent of[f] by a Flag,[3] in which I shall assure him that we have suffered great numbers of Masters, [Mates?] & Men belonging to merchant ships taken by our Cruizers to depart, without thinking of detaining them for an exchange & recommend his releasing these People or he will oblige us to alter that part of our Conduct, as this is Striktly true in a number of instances that have come under my Notice I hope Congress will approve the design.

I am with great Regard & Esteem, sir, Your obedt hble servt.

Robt Morris

RC (DNA: PCC, item 137).
[1] For Washington's response, see his December 22 letter to Morris in Washington, *Writings* (Fitzpatrick), 6:420–21.
[2] Not found.
[3] Not found; but for Capt. Andrew Snape Hamond's response, see *Morgan, Naval Documents*, 7:629.

Robert Morris to the Pennsylvania Council of Safety

Gentn   Philada. Decr. 21st. 1776

Cap Alexander of the Delaware Frigate informs me, that some few of the Tradesmen now at Camp are absolutely necessary to put his ship in a Condition to push down the Bay when the Enemies ships retire. I think it will promote the Publick service very much to order them down immediately.[1] I have sent down a Sloop to watch the Men of War & doubt not we shall find an opportunity of gitting these ships to Sea. Cap Alexander will furnish the Council with the names of the Tradesmen wanted & I submit to your determination being, Gentn, Your Obedt Servt.   Robt Morris

RC (NN).
[1] Morris had written the following note to the council of safety on the same subject the day before. "I have some hopes of getting the Frigate Delaware away during the Winter & wish to have Mr. Warwick Hale the Boat builder detained from Camp to finish her Boats & if one of his hands cou'd be ordered down it wou'd be very useful." Society Collection, PHi.

Robert Morris to George Washington

Sir   Philada. Decemr. 21st. 1776

Notwithstanding there are several British Men of War cruising in our Bay, the Continental Sloop Independance Commanded by Lieutt Robinson has pushed through & got up here yesterday afternoon. There is onboard 856 Blankets which were intended with many others now expected in, for the use of the new enlistments, but the inclement weather and the severe duty the Troops now under your Command have to perform Induces me to think these Blankets shou'd be applyed to their use in this matter. However you will please to Judge & act as you see fit, for I shall send them to the Camp for your orders so soon as the Weather will permit them to be landed.[1] There is also arrived in this Sloop a quantity of Cloths which I shall put into the hands of Mr Mease Commissary to have made up immediately. There is also 919 Muskets onboard. These I suppose you do not want, and I will send them out of Town to the other Stores unless you signify a desire for any other application of them. I have the pleasure to inform you that Mr Deane in his letters of the 30th Septr. recd by this Sloop says he *looks* upon a French War as inevitable. He expects to furnish us with ample supplys for 30 thousand Men & a noble train of Artillery, mortars &c so that, if you can but drive our Enemies back to New York for this Winter, we may hope for much better things next Spring than we have experienced of late.

I find my presence so necessary here in several departments that I shall stay as long as I can with safety, but as I am possessed of Publick papers that must never fall into the hands of the Enemy I shou'd be glad of a line from you whenever you think it wou'd be best for me to retire, and if you have any Commands here in which I can be serviceable, be assured of my ready attention. Your several dispatches to Congress have passed through my hands & I have informed them fully of such things as have come to my knowledge respecting Publick matters.

Poor Lee. I pity him exceedingly & feel much for the publick loss in him. Shou'd you hear any thing of the Treatment he meets with I shou'd thank you or Mr. Tilghman for a line on that Subject. I fear he will meet with insupportable Insults & if so his situation must be worse than that of the Damn'd. I have been told to day that you are preparing to Cross into the Jerseys. I hope it may be true & promise myself Joyfull tidings from Your expedition. You have my sincere prayers for Success as nothing wou'd give me greater pleasure than to hear of such occurrences as your exalted merit deserves.

I have the honor to remain, Your Excellencys Most Obedt hble servt,
                                                            Robt Morris

RC (DLC).
[1] For a photocopy of Morris' second letter to Washington this date, which simply covered an invoice and receipt for the 856 blankets mentioned here, see Washington, *Writings* (Fitzpatrick), 6:362–63.

Benjamin Rush to Richard Henry Lee

Dear Sir,   Near Bristol Decemr 21 1776

Wherever I go I bear in my mind the small Share of the weight of our dear countrys happiness which the State of Pensylvania hath committed to my care. I wish sometimes to throw my mite into the councils of the congress, but as this is impossible for the present I beg leave to suggest such things as have occurred to me in my passage thro' Philada to this place, and submit it to your good sense to make any use of them you may think proper.

I need not inform you of the general disposition of the people in & near Philada to refuse continental money upon the late prospect of Genl Howe's getting possession of the city. Genl Putnam's threatning to confine such people as refused it, and declaring the debt for which the money was offered to be void produced only a temporary remedy against the evil. People who had goods refused to sell them— and men who had money out at interest either refused to give up bonds or kept out of the way when continental money was offered for them. The legislatures of America look up to Congress for a remedy equal to the danger of the disease. Suppose you recommend to every state to make a law not only to forfit the debt for which our money is offered, but to *fine* the person who refuses it *severely*. This will be more effectual than imprisonment which from becoming so common for tory practices has now lost its infamy. The punishment in this case strikes directly at that principle in human nature which is the source of the contempt in which our money has fallen. I mean avarice and a want of public Spirit. Pray dont let this matter be neglected. Our salvation hangs upon it. I tremble every time I think of the danger of the further progress of the refusal of our money.

Connected with the above subject is the state of our loan office. If possible let the resolutions for the emmision of five millions of dollars be *concealed*. I hope it will be the last resolution of that kind that will appear on our journals. If it is not the whole continent must complain of our injustice in allowing only 4 per Cent for the money now deposited in the loan office, unless we can give *positive* assurances that we shall pay it in hard money.

I have learnt from many people and among Others from two New England officers that the 4 Eastern states will find great difficulty in raising their quota of men owing to that excessive rage for privateering which now prevails among them. Many of the continental troops now in our service pant for the expiration of their enlistments in order that they may partake of the Spoils of the West Indies. At a moderate computation there are now not less than 10,000 men belonging to New England on board privateers. New England and the Continent can not spare them. They have a right at this juncture to their services and their blood.[1] Suppose they were all now called home. Suppose Commissions were refused to private ships of war for [. . .] months, Suppose even the trade of the [. . .] was monopolized by the Congress [for the?] same space of time. Would it not [. . .] fill our army with soldiers, & [our navy?] with Seamen? It would be a Substitu[te to] pressing, and would secure to individuals the freedom of their wills. It must be done. We cannot fill our army without it. We must have an army. The fate of America must be decided by an Army. It must consist of 70, or 80,000 men, and they must all be fit for the field before the first day of May next.

Since the captivity of Gen Lee a distrust has crept in among the troops of the abilities of some of our general officers high in command. They expect nothing now from heaven taught & book taught Generals. I hope in our next promotions, we shall disregard seniority. Stevens musi be made a Major General. He has genius as well as knowledge. Mercer must not be neglected. He has the confidence of the troops. Adieu. Yours,   Benja Rush

P.S. Congress must take up the affair of our money *wholly:* It is a national concern. Legislatures are too distant—too languid—and in many states too incompletely formed for that purpose.

RC (PPAmP).
[1] Previously published texts of this letter do not contain the six following sentences. Words missing as a result of a tear along the margin of the manuscript are indicated here with ellipses in brackets. Cf. Rush, *Letters* (Butterfield), 1:121; and *Am. Archives*, 5th ser. 3:1513.

Elbridge Gerry to James Warren?

Dear Sir[1]   Baltimore Decr 23d 1776
My last was dated at Philadelphia, since which Congress have adjourned to this place. It was in Consequence of the Opinion of Generals Putnam & Mifflin given in Congress that it was unsafe to continue the Session any longer in the City, as the near approach of the Enemy rendered it liable to be surprized at a Time when there were not above one hundred Troops under their Command to defend it. The Eastern Members were not pleased with the proposal,

as they did not conceive the necessity of adopting it & tho't it improper to be carried further from the scene of Action & their own State. However I hope it will finally have a good Effect, as there are no Tories here to diffuse their poisonous & destructive principles to the weak & wavering.

You will undoubtedly hear of the Captivity of General Lee & may probably be at a Loss to account for it. I Confess myself in such a predicament, & that for some Time past I have been in a state of Suspence. Time will instruct us further on the Matter & may Remove every Suspicion unfavorable to his Character.

We have heard of the Transports sailing for Rhode Island & Mr Adams, Colo Whipple & Mr Ellery & others joined in a Letter which we sent to General Washington desiring him to order General Gates or Green to repair to that place & take Command of the Militia that might be raised to defend the Country.[2] A suitable Number of Brigadiers We also recommended to be sent, & the General writes us for answer that he has ordered Generals Spencer & Arnold to command & join our forces there, & that General Wooster is in Connecticut, Which is not complying with our Request. We shall propose it to Congress & in the Interim it may be well to order General Lincoln to be added to the List.

I think there is a prospect of checking the progress of the Enemy in the Jersies very soon, as the Militia are in Motion in the middle Colonies & will very generally turn out. General Mifflin is riding thro Pennsylvania & rendering great Service in Spiriting his Countrymen. There will be very soon a Junction of Lee's Army with General Washington, & if they act with Spirit (which I think it high Time to adopt) the Enemy must retreat to their Kennel in New York.

Some persons whose Sincerity has been for some Time suspected, are said to have gone over to the Enemy, amongst the Rest Andrew Allen the Kings attorney in Pennsylvania lately left out of Congress on Account of his disapproved Conduct. Mr Dickison the Farmer, We are informed Has wrote to his Brother General Dickinson desiring him to resign & make Terms for himself & *Connections*, & that Judge Stockton of the Jersies who was also a Member of Congress has sued for pardon. I wish every timid Whig or pretended Whig in America would pursue the same plan, as their weak & ineffectual system of politics has been the Cause of every Misfortune that we have suffered. Mr Purviance of this place informs me that Dickinson has secreted himself since his Letter was intercepted, & that Diligent Search is making after him, as his Brother in Philadelphia wrote him a few Days since.

The Gentleman who will deliver You this Alex. [Rose] from Charlestown, South Carolina, & with his Friend Capt Abely worthy your Acquaintance.[3] I wish he may be introduced to [4]

RC (DLC photostat). In the hand of Elbridge Gerry.

[1] Although the recipient of this letter can not be identified positively, James Warren, in a letter to Gerry of January 15, 1777, acknowledged having just received a letter "by Mr. Rose." Alexander Rose, Gerry explains below, was the bearer of this letter. C. Harvey Gardiner, *A Study in Dissent, the Warren-Gerry Correspondence, 1776–1792* (Carbondale, Ill.: Southern Illinois Press, 1968), p. 52. In the absence of additional evidence, any attribution must remain conjectural, but Gerry is also known to have written to Warren with great regularity, and the content of the document indicates that it was directed to a political ally and intimate acquaintance.

[2] See New England Delegates to George Washington, December 12, 1776.

[3] Gerry also wrote a brief letter of introduction for Rose to Joseph Trumbull, this date: "This will be delivered You by Alexander Rose Esq. of Charlestown in South Carolina, who with his Friend Capt. Abely are on a Tour thro the eastern Governments. Give me Leave to recommend them to Your Acquaintance as Gentlemen of established Character & firm Friends to the Cause of America, & to desire that You will make their Journey thro Your Government agreable, by a Line to such of your Friends therein as are on the Road leading to Boston. I shall take an early Oppertunity of writing You on other Matters." Joseph Trumbull Papers, CtHi.

Rose also carried with him a similar letter of introduction written by William Whipple to John Langdon, this date. See *Am. Archives,* 5th ser. 3:1369.

[4] Remainder of MS missing.

John Hancock to Robert Morris

Sir,   Baltimore Decr. 23d. 1776

Your Several Favours of the 13th, 14th, 16th, and 17th inst have been duely recd. in the Order of their respective Dates, and laid before Congress. In Consequence of which, I am directed to transmit you the enclosed Resolves.

The Intelligence of Genl. Lee's being taken Prisoner is really alarming in the present State of our Army; and I am afraid his Loss will be severely felt, as he was, in a great Measure, the Idol of the Officers, and possessed still more the Confidence of the Soldiery. As the Fortune of War has made him a Prisoner, the United States are bound by every Tie of Justice and Generosity to afford him all the Relief in their Power. They have accordingly resolved that one Hundred Half Johannes should be sent to Genl. Washington for the Use of Genl. Lee, should it be found practicable to convey Money to him; which the Congress deem a Matter of so much Importance that they have ordered a Flag to be sent to Genl. Howe to know whether he will permit it or not. I am however directed by Congress to request that you will lodge for this Purpose the above mentioned Sum in the Hands of Genl. Washington.[1]

The Congress concurring in Opinion with you, that a Committee should be appointed in the City of Philada. to take Care of the public Interest, and at the same Time highly approving of the Zeal and Attention you have particularly discovered to the Welfare of your Country since their Departure from that City, have nominated

Mr. Clymer, Mr. Walton, and yourself to execute such Continental Business as it may be necessary to transact in Philadelphia. They have also directed that two Hundred Thousand Dollars be immediately sent to the Commissary in Pennsylvania, subject to your Draughts, and to be applied as you may judge proper. Should this Sum prove insufficient, you are empowered to draw on the Loan Office for any additional Sum you may think necessary for public Purposes.[2]

The enclosed Resolves will inform you, that Congress highly approve of the Conduct of yourself, Mr. Walton, and Mr. Clymer in the Care you have taken of public Business; and particularly of the Attention *you* have shewn, and the Plan *you* have laid for preserving the Continental Frigates.[3]

Be pleased to acquaint Mr. Peters, that he is directed by the Board of War to repair to Baltimore as soon as possible, where his Services are judged absolutely necessary by Congress.[4]

I have the Honour to be, with very great Respect, Sir, your most obed. & very hble Servt. John Hancock Prest.

[*P.S.*] Pray forward the Inclos'd to the General by Express.[5]

RC (DNA: PCC, item 58). In the hand of Jacob Rush, with signature and postscript by Hancock.

[1] See *JCC*, 6:1029.
[2] See *JCC*, 6:1032.
[3] Ibid.
[4] See *JCC*, 6:1033.
[5] See Hancock to Washington, this date.

John Hancock to George Washington

Sir, Baltimore Decr. 23d. 1776.

I do myself the Honour to acknowledge the Receipt of your several Favours of the 12th, 13th, and 15th inst. in the Order of their respective Dates, and to inform you that they were duely laid before Congress.[1]

As Genl. Lee by the Fortune of War, has become a Prisoner in the Hands of our Enemies, the Congress are anxious to afford him all the Relief in their Power during his Confinement. They have therefore resolved that a Flag be immediately sent to Genl. Howe to know in what Manner Genl. Lee is treated; and have directed Mr. R. Morris (to whom I have written on the Occasion) to forward to you for his Use, one Hundred Half Johannes. The United States from every Principle of Justice and Generosity, are bound to render the Situation of that Gentleman as easy as possible during his Captivity. His Loss must be extremely regretted by every Friend to this Country.[2]

The Congress, upon reconsidering the Vote of the 11th inst. have come to a Resolution expressing their Approbation of your Conduct in declining to publish it in general Orders.[3] They also approve of your sending General Armstrong to Pennsylvania, and Genl. Smalwood to Maryland to stimulate the People to exert themselves on this Occasion.[4] I have the Pleasure to acquaint you that the Militia in the upper Parts of Maryland are in Motion, and seem at last sensible of the Danger which threatens them.

The Multiplicity of Business which the Congress left unfinished at the Time of their Departure from Philada. has induced them to appoint a Committee of three Gentlemen with full Powers to perfect the Business in such Manner as they shall judge proper.[5]

You will please to pay the Militia who reinforce your Army, in the same Manner as you pay your other Troops, and on their Discharge allow them a Penny per Mile to bear their Expences on the Way to their respective Homes.[6]

The enclosed Resolves of Congress, I transmit by their Order, and beg Leave to request your Attention to them.

I have the Honour to be, with the utmost Esteem and Respect, Sir, your most obedt. & very hble Servt.

John Hancock Presidt

RC (DLC). In the hand of Jacob Rush and signed by Hancock.

[1] These letters are in PCC, item 152, 3:343–45, 351–52, 355, and Washington, *Writings* (Fitzpatrick), 6:353–56, 363–65, 378–79.

[2] For Congress' December 20 resolution on General Lee, see *JCC*, 6:1029. The following draft of this resolve, in the hand of Richard Henry Lee, is in the Lee Family Papers, ViU. "Resolved that General Washington be directed to send a flag to General Howe and to request of him, as the fortune of war hath made Major General Lee his prisoner, that he cause that Gentleman to be treated with the civility due to his rank, and to his emminent personal merit. Taking General Lees parole as has been the humane practice of both Parties since the commencement of this war, where no improper conduct hath marked the character of captive Officers during their Captivity. Also to know of General How if permission will be granted to send General Lee such supplies of money as may be necessary to support him during his confinement in a manner suitable to his rank in the Continental service."

[3] See *JCC*, 6:1031. This resolve was later erased from the journals. See also Charles Thomson to Washington, December 11, 1776, note.

[4] See *JCC*, 6:1031–32.

[5] *JCC*, 6:1032.

[6] *JCC*, 6:1034.

Robert Morris to John Hancock

Sir   Philada Decr. 23d. 1776

I have the pleasure to inform you that the Continental Fleet in this Port is encreased by the arrival of the Andrew Doria, Capt

Isaiah Robison, from St Eustatia which place she left the beginning of this month & next day fell in with a British Sloop of War of 12 Guns which she took after a very obstinate engagement in which the Andrew Doria had two men killed, some wounded, the main mast shot through & some other damage. The Sloop had many Men wounded, Three Shot through her Mast, her sails shot to pieces & much damage done to her. This is one of the Sloops the Lds. of the Admiralty ordered Admiral Gayton to fit out at Jamaica, & Mr. Jones who commanded her has the Kings Commission as master & Commander. He defended her obstinately & is certainly a brave man. I will desire the Council of Safety to take his Parole & send him to some safe Place. Capt Robinson manned this Prize & ordered her in for this Port. He also took a Snow from Jam[aic]a Loaden with Mahogony & Logwood and ordered her for this Port but it is next to an impossibility for them to get in, nothing but the fast sailing of the Andrew Doria & the extream vigilance of the Captain brought her safe past the Enemies Ships, one of which lies in the Cape May Channell.

The Cargo onbd this Brigt. Consists of 208 Dozen pair of Woolen Stockings, 106 Dozn. pair of Worsted Stockings, 215 Sailors Jackets, 23 Great Coats, 50 ps. Dutch Plains, 30 ps. 900 yds Flannell, 45 ps. blue, Brown & white Cloth, 463 Blankets, 218 ps. $\frac{7}{8}$ Linens Contg 6795 Dutch Ells, 496 Muskets, 326 pair of Pistols, 100 bbls Powder & 14101 lb of Lead, for acct. of the Continent. I recd a letter last night from Genl. Washington by Colo. Moylan, requesting me to hurry Mr. Mease to have Soldiers Cloaths made up with all possible dilligence. He says Muskets are not wanted there but that comfortable Cloathing is exceedingly wanted. Colo. Moylan advises by all means to send up the Stockings & great Coats now arrived, which I think to do, but shall tell the Genl. they were intended for the New Levies and leave him to dispose of them, as he may think most beneficial to the Service. The Linnens, Plains & Cloths I will deliver to Mr Mease with orders to have them made up, but he will find much difficulty as all the Taylors or near all, are at the Camp & the Council of Safety dare not order them down for fear the rest will follow. The Blankets shall also go to the General to be disposed of as he may think proper. The Pistols, Muskets, Powder & Lead I think had best be sent to Lancaster but wish to hear from the Board of War in answer to what I wrote before on this Subject. The Sailors Jackets must be put onboard the Fleet being much wanted there. I propose that Captn. Robinson shou'd put all the Seamen Prisoners onboard the Randolph, Cap Biddle, & that the latter shou'd Compell them to do duty whether they enter or not, only following the example set us by the British act of Parliament.

Mr Davis Bevan of this City was taken about five weeks ago coming into our Capes & carried to New York from thence brought round in the Roebuck and suffered to land at Cape Henlopin under a promise to return. He told me that he heard Capt Hammond & other Officers say they are now determined to put a total stop to our Trade. Six Frigates were sent to cruize of[f] Georgia & Carolina, Six of[f] the Capes of Virginia & six of[f] our Capes. They have fixed signals & stations so as to keep a compleat line along the Coast and are determined to keep these Stations throughout the Winter if possible. He says only part of the Troops sent to Rhode Island are to remain there. The remainder are going for Carolina. Bevan is an intelligent Man & had an opportunity of hearing and learning these things from Ld Howes under Secretary or Clerk with whom he ingratiated himself & was employed in writing for him onbd the Eagle. I have sent Mr Bevan down with the letter mentioned in my last to Capt Hammond and I hope it will procure the discharge of Capt Morgan and the Prisoners onboard that Fleet. The Schooner Wasp Commanded by Lieutt. Baldwin has brought into Egg Harbour a Schooner loaded with Indian Corn & oats bound from the Lower Countys to New York. He has sent up the Master & five or six others Prisoners here. They had been onboard the Falcon Man of War, Capt Linzee, & subscribed the oaths of allegiance, Certificates of which were found on them. I sent these Papers to the Council of safety who Committed the Men to Goal, as there is no Judge of the Admiralty in the Jerseys & Judge Ross is at Lancaster. I think it adviseable to send Waggons to Egg Harbour for the Corn & Oats to feed the Continental Horses in this City. These articles are very scarce here & will bear the Carriage, but I will Consult Genl. Putnam and the Waggon Master on this subject. As to the Vessell I am of opinion it wou'd be best to sell her without waiting for Condemnation as the Proofs of her Guilt are clear & incontestable and she lies in too much danger to wait patiently for the usual forms, however Congress or the Marine Committee will please to give a possitive order what must be done in this respect. Baldwin had retaken a French Schooner that had been taken going out of our Capes by one of the Men of War cruizing there. He was bringing her into Egg Harbour when a Fleet of 15 Sail hove in sight, two of which were two Deckers. One or two Frigates and an Armed Brigt pursued him so close that he was obliged to abandon his Prize & get into the inlet fast as he cou'd. This happened last Wednesday. Being short of Provisions he intends coming in here and I wish he may escape the Enemy.

You will perceive Sir, that our Fleet will be pretty Numerous here altho their Force but small compared to the Dangers that surround them. I have conversed with several of the Captains & formed a plan for their getting safe out to Sea & taking such merchantmen with them as may be ready. They approve the plan and I hope will execute it, but we must have time to get ready & they must act with great Vigilance & Spirit to affect it. Upon this occasion I cannot help saying that I am very uneasy, as I am neither instructed what to do nor vested with proper Powers to act as may appear best, I must therefore request that Congress or the Marine Committee will either instruct me pointedly what to do, or give me proper authority to act for the best for the object is important and if misfortunes happen which is very probable it wou'd be hard that I shou'd hereafter be blamed when the event is known, for measures that appear previously to be well calculated for the Publick Good. The vessels to be got out are the Randolph, Delaware, Andrew Doria, Independence, Hornet, Fly, & Musquito with many Valuable Merchantmen. The Lexington, Sachem & Wasp may be hourly expected in if they escape the Enemy. Sailors are scarce, Tradesmen at the Camp, and a kind of stupor seems to have seized every body that ought to give us assistance, so that it is inconceivable how slowly all work goes on & with how much difficulty we can get any thing done. I have applyed to the Council of Safety to order down some Tradesmen to finish the Delaware if possible, they wish but fear to Comply and if they do not she must after all remain here. Genl. Washington desires me to remain here as long as possible & promises to give me notice of any immediate danger. He thinks the Enemy are only waiting two events & when they happen, they will prosecute their designs against this City, that is, for Ice to cross the River & for the 1st Jany when most of his Army will disband & he says you might as well attempt to stop the Winds from blowing or the Sun in its diurnal as stop them from going when their time is up. Genl Sullivan brought him about 2000 men, Genl Gates about 600 & his whole Force now Consists of about 5000 men besides the City Militia. Its true the Country Militia are coming in, but I suppose as many will leave him the 1st Jany as will join before that time & if so it will not be possible for him to save this City out of the hands of the Enemy after they cross the Delaware. On this view of things, I think we ought to hazard every thing to get the Ships out & I shall advise Mr Mease, Mr Tod & all others that have Continental Stores to be prepared for removing them.

It is very mortifying to me when I am obliged to tell you disagreable things, but I am compelled to inform Congress that the Continental Currency keeps loosing its Credit, many People refuse openly & avowedly to receive it, and several Citizens that retired into the Country must have starved if their own private Credit had not procured them the common necessarys of life, when nothing cou'd be got for Your Money. Some effectual remedy shou'd be speedily applyed to this evil or the Game will be up. Mr. Commissary Wharton has told the General that the Mills refuse to Grind for him either from disafection or dislike to the Money. Be that as it may the consequences are terrible, for I do Suppose the Army will not consent to Starve. At present I dont recollect any thing to add to this letter but as other occurrences happen I shall give you the trouble of more letters. I think it is time that Mr Pluckrose the Express I sent down with letters to you last Tuesday shou'd return, unless detained for some purpose of Congress. By him I sent a Number of French letters &c.

    I am with great respect, sir, Your obedt Servant,

Robt Morris

P.S. I am informed by Mr Moylan that Colo. Guyon (I think that is the name) was taken Prisoner with Genl Lee. He is the Colo. that came over in the Hancock & Adams, Capt Smith, from Nantes.

RC (DNA: PCC, item 137).

Robert Morris to George Washington

Sir   Philada. Decr. 23d. 1776
    I had the honor to receive your obliging favour of Yesterday by Colo Moylan.[1] The Contents give a most mellancholly aspect to our affairs and I wish to Heaven it may be in our power to retrieve them. It is useless at this period to examine into the causes of our present unhappy Situation, unless that examination wou'd be productive of a cure for the evils that surround us. In fact those causes have long been known to such as wou'd open their Eyes. The very consequences of them was often foretold & the measures execrated by some of the best Friends of America but in vain. An obstinate partiality to the habits & Customs of one part of this Continent has predominated in the Publick Councils, and too little attention been paid to others. To Criminate the Authors of our errors wou'd not avail, but we cannot see ruin staring us in the Face without thinking of them. It has been my fate to make an *ineffectual* opposition to all short enlistments, to Colonial appointment of Officers and to many other measures that I thought pregnant with mischiefs, but these things either suited the genius & habbits or Squared with the interests of some States that had sufficient influence to prevail and nothing is now left but to extricate ourselves from the difficulties in which we are involved if we can. Let us try our utmost, man can do no more. I shall Urge Mr Mease to go on as briskly as possible with the Cloathing, but its impossible for him to make much progress as most of the Taylors are at the Camp. The Muskets & other Stores shall be sent out of the City, and such papers as I can spare shall be sent away. The Fleet has always been my particular care & at this time I am exceedingly anxious for its safety, but the difficulty of getting anything done is inconceivable. Most of the

Tradesmen necessary to finish the Delaware are at Camp. I have applyed to the Council of Safety to order some few of them down & altho they wish yet they fear to do it, least the rest should follow. I have now under my care the Randolph & Delaware Frigates, the Brigt Andrew Doria, Sloops Hornet, Independance, Fly & Schooner Musquito, all Continental Armed Vessells, beside several valuable Merchantmen, all which I wish to get out to Sea & think it might be effected if every man concerned wou'd exert himself in his department. I try to give them Spirits & invigorate their exertions all in my power. The Enemy have Six Sail Cruizing about our Capes and keep a special look out. Notwithstanding this, The Brigt Andrew Doria, Capt Isaiah Robison, passed through them & got safe up this day. She left St Eustatia the beginning of this month & on the passage took a Sloop of Twelve Guns fitted out by Admiral Gayton at Jamaica agreable to orders of the Lords of the Admiralty. She also took a Snow from Jam[aic]a & ordered both Prizes in here, but its most likely they will be retaken. Before I quit this Subject permit me to observe that there is a Lieutt Josiah of our Navy Prisoner & now at New York, and we have Prisoner at York Town in this State a Lieutt Boger of their Navy. I coud wish an exchange between them coud be effected. There is also a Doctr Hodge, Surgeon to Colo Cadwalladers Battalion of Pensylvanians, now Prisoner in New York a Young Man of much Merit & his abilities in'his Profession woud render him very usefull coud he be exchanged.

The Sloop taken by the Andw Doria was commanded by a Mr. Jones who has the Kings Commission as master & Commander. He behaved bravely & I am told he says Ld Howe will be desirous to redeem him. I suppose his Rank to be equal to a Major or Lt Colo which I mention that your Excellency may advert to it, if you wish for an Exchange of any particular officer of Merit of that Rank. This Brigt was sent by the Secret Committee for Cloathing & Stores & has brought in the following cargo:

   208 Dozen pair of Woolen Stockings
   106 Dozen pair of Worsted do
   215 Sailors Jackets
    23 Great Coats
    50 ps Dutch plains
    30 ps 900 yds Flannell
    45 ps blue, brown & white Cloth
   463 Blankets
   218 ps $\frac{7}{8}$ Linen
   496 Muskets
   326 pair Pistols
   200 half barrells Powder
14101 lb. Lead

I have enumerated these articles that you may judge what part is wanted for your Army and your orders shall be complied with. I shall only observe these Imports were intended for the new Levies but circumstanced as you are I think you shou'd judge solely of the propriety of applying them to our present exigencye. The Brigt Lexington and Sloop Sachem may be hourly looked for with further supplys also sundry Merchantmen but I dread their approach to our Capes. They took a French Snow in sight of the Andrew Doria who protected her as long as it was possible.

I am fearfull Genl Lee may suffer for want of money if the Resentment of British officers runs as high as they have threatned, therefore to prevent present distress I inclose herewith a set of Exchange drawn by the late Governor Edens Secretary Mr. Smith on Messrs. Thos Eden & Co for one hundred Pounds Sterling which I beg you will convey by a Flag to Genl Lee with an assurance of a further supply whenever he wants it. I have endorsed the bills & flatter myself that many Gentlemen now in New York to whom I am known will advance the General the Money upon them. I have no doubt but this matter may be so managed as that Genl. Lee will certainly get these bills & the Money for them without putting you to much inconvenience & with the utmost esteem I remain, Dear sir, your most Obedient servt.   Robt Morris

P.S. Having sent my Stores out of Town this is the best paper I can Command at present.

Decr. 24th.

Not meeting any Conveyance for this letter yesterday, I have since obtained the enclosed bill drawn by Capt Duncan, Mr Nicol & Hugh Fraser Lieutt of the Royal Highland Emigrants for £116.9.3 Sterling in favr of Alexr Inglis Esqr for amot. of supplys to them in Charles Town. It is drawn on Major Small & I dare say will be paid, therefore I think it a preferable remittance to Genl Lee than bills on London and hope you will Convey it to him immediately.

                                                 R M

RC (DLC).
[1] See Washington, *Writings* (Fitzpatrick), 6:420–21.

Secret Committee to Robert Morris

Sir,   Baltimore December the 23d. 1776

We have received your favor of the 18th covering the Invoice of Cargo by the Independance.[1] 'Tis a valuable Cargo, and we hope Mr. Martin will arrive in time to prevent the danger that may be derived from its being again committed to the Ocean. Should Lieutenant Robinson not have left Chingoteague before the goods are stopped, we shall take proper care of them, and any advance that Mr. Martin may make in consequence of your directions therein shall be punctually repaid on demand.[2] We highly approve the directions you have given the Independance and the other Vessels, they are wisely calculated to save our inward bound Ships. As you have been so kind as undertake the unfinished business of the Secret Committee, we wish you would in the name of that body write by the first, and by many opportunities if you have time, for the Brass field pieces and the Cavalry accoutrements that Congress have directed us to import. The war cannot be successfully carried on without them, and they ought to be here early in the spring. It will be very lucky if Capt. Weeks should not be come away before these things are ready to come in him, or would it not be proper to send the Andrew Doria or Lexington immediately away for them on the return of either from the West Indies? Mr. Deane desires the Committee of Secret correspondence would commission him to send us a quantity of Sail Duck which he says may be procured on good terms from the North, & he also writes about 14 or 20 thousand hhds of Tobacco being sent to France. The Committee have referred him to the secret Committee and to Mr. Thomas Morris for satisfaction on these points.[3] We approve the importation of Duck and the Tobacco remittance, and we shall be obliged to you for writing both these Gentlemen on the above mentioned subjects. Medicines for the Army we were ordered to import, it is a necessary business, and demands that repeated copies of the orders for them should be sent.

We much wish to have your company and assistance here, but we are fully sensible of the important services you are performing at Philadelphia.

God grant the enemy may fail in their scheme against your City. The Militia promise to turn out well from hence to your assistance. The Committee of Frederick promise 1200 from thence & 2 or 3 Batallions from the counties of Washington & Montgomerie, besides what may be expected from Baltimore, Cecil, & Hartford. If they come not too late we shall be happy.

We are, with great esteem, Sir, your most obedient and very humble servants   Richard Henry Lee

Wm Whipple

RC (MdBJ–G). Written by Lee and signed by Lee and Whipple.

[1] Not found; but for Morris' instructions to James Martin regarding the disposition of goods on the *Independence* belonging to Willing, Morris & Co., see Morgan, *Naval Documents*, 7:505.

[2] According to Morris' December 21 letter to John Hancock, James Robertson had already brought the *Independence* safely into Philadelphia.

³ Deane made these requests in his October 1 letter to the Committee of Secret Correspondence. Wharton, *Diplomatic Correspondence*, 2:153–57. See also Committee of Secret Correspondence to the Commissioners at Paris, December 21, 1776.

William Whipple to Josiah Bartlett

My Dear Sir   Baltimore 23 Decr. 1776

The many Misfortunes that have attended the American arms since you left Philaa. have undoubtedly reach'd you. The loss of fort Washington has been the Source of all these misfortunes. As the Success of the Enemy there gave them incouragemt to persue victory, so it struck our troops with a panic that spred through the Country, & this unluckely happen'd at the time when the inlistment of the greatest part of the Army expired. However the People of Pensilvania are now turning out with spirit, great numbers have already join'd Genl Washington, the people of Maryland are also turning out. The Jersey Men are by this time fully convic'd of their errors, for the Ravages committed by the Enemy in their way through that state is really shocking to Humanity. They spared neither Age nor sex, whig nor tory. The Brutal vengence of an abandon'd Soldiry was exercis'd on all with out distinction. Thus we see what is to be expected from those worse then savages, but if they shod gain footing in New England we are to expect, if possible, greater cruelties then New Jersey has experienced. The whole vengence of the most abandon'd of the Human Race will be exercis'd on that Country. It therefore behoves us with the utmost assiduity to raise a sufficient force to oppose them. I have not heard a word from New Hampshire for more then a month past, but I hope the new leavies are nearly compleated. I expect there will be another Regiment required of our state as the prevailing opinion is that the Army must be augmented on the new establishment. Congress adjournd from Philaa. the 11th inst. & meet here the 20, are now doing business with more spirit then they have for some time past. I hope the air of this place which is much purer then that of Philaa. will brace up the weak nerves. I think it already has that affect.

The Sechem is arriv'd at Philaa. with about 1000 stand of arms & a considerable quantity of Blankets & other woolens. A letter from Mr. D—— of 1st Octor. gives very incouraging accot.¹ I wish to communicate them to you, but am not at Liberty. The British Court are trying every art in their power with every Court in Europe but can not get any Satisfaction from F[rance] or S[pain]. To use the words of a Correspondent, "A genl war in Europe seems unavoidable."

The Fortress at Ticonderoga is left exceedingly weak & the time that the few troops that are there is nearly expir'd so that if that place is not very soon reinforced there is great danger of loosing it. No time shod be lost in geting a sufficient Garrison at that important post.

How does taxing go on? Do you raise much money in that way? The People certainly were never so well able to pay a large tax as at this time. Who shall we get for a Brigadier Genl. I wish Genl. Folsom wod take the Commision. Genl. Lee I suppose you have heard is taken. This is a loss to us but I hope not so great a loss as People in general immagine. Before I conclude this I wod just remind you that I have not receiv'd a line from you since you left Philaa. Wishing that I may soon have that Pleasure for the present bid you Adieu & am with Great Respect Your Most Hume Srt,

Wm. Whipple

RC (NhD).
[1] Silas Deane's October 1 letter to the Committee of Secret Correspondence is in Wharton, *Diplomatic Correspondence*, 2:153–57.

William Ellery to Nicholas Cooke

Sir, Baltimore Decr. 25th [*i.e.* 24] 1776 [1]
I did myself the Honor of writing to you by Capt. Garzia the 10th Instant; since which nothing new hath taken Place, that I know of, in the Army excepting the Capture of Genl. Lee by a Party of the Enemy's Light Horse on the 13th. By some Fatality, as Genl. Sullivan in a Letter to Congress expresses himself,[2] Genl. Lee with his Family took Lodging in a Farm House about Three Miles distant from the Army under his Command. Some Tories informed the Enemy of his Situation. They sent off 70 Light Horse to take him, who surrounded and attacked the House. The Genl. with his Family made a manly Resistance, but were finally obliged to submit, and the poor Genl. was carried away captive. A Fatality strange indeed for some Time past hath seemed to attend our Affairs. The Loss of Fort Washington, where 2600 of our Men were captivated in an inglorious Manner, The Loss of Fort Lee by Surprize, with a great Quantity of Stores, and the Capture of the General who was honoured by his Name being given to that Fort, & in Short all our Affairs have in a strange Manner proceeded. I hope in God better Fortune will attend our future Operations. Genl. Howe's Army by our last Advices had extended itself along the Delaware towards the North principally, with an apparent Design to pass the River. Genl. Washington had posted his Army along the River so as to obstruct their Passage. Some of the Militia of Pennsylvania, the Lower Counties and Maryland are about to reinforce and some have actually reinforced his Army; and Genl. Sullivan on whom

the Command of the Division, late under the Command of the unhappy Lee, is devolved, was on the 13th of this Month marching to join him. When they join they will together make a respectable Army, sufficient to prevent Howe's entering Pennsylvania. Indeed the Armies must before this have formed a Junction; if Genl. Sullivan's Division hath not been repulsed by Genl. Howe. We expect to hear from Philadelphia every Moment; if any thing New shall arrive before I am obliged to close my Letter. You have doubtless before this heard of the Removal of Congress to this Place. This is the first Opportunity I have had and this is circuitous (via Boston) to inform you of it. The Enemy was so near, and Affairs in the City in such Confusion, that it was improper and unsafe to continue there, and for Reasons too long for a Letter Baltimore was fixed upon as the most suitable Place for holding Congress in for the present. I should like the Place well enough if it was less distant from the Army, less dirty and less expensive. It is long since I have heard from my Constituents. What is doing and how Matters stand in our State I know no more than an Inhabitant of the Moon; although it would be beneficial to have every necessary Information seasonably.

We have an Account that a Fleet with Eight or Ten Thousand Men have gone to Newport, and that the Island was evacuated by the Inhabitants, but that the Enemy had not landed. By a Letter from Genl. Wooster to Congress, of the Eighth of this Instant, We are informed that the Fleet on the Sixth were off New London.[3] If it be true that so large a Force hath gone to Rhode-Island something more is intended in my Opinion than the bare taking the Town of Newport for Winter Quarters. I suspect that they mean to take Possession of Providence, and from thence penetrate into the Massachusetts-Bay. If they attack Providence it will be by Land. They will pass up the Bay to Warwick Neck perhaps, there Land and march to the Town. There ought to be a good Redoubt at Warwick Point, to check their landing, and give Time for Troops to be arranged to oppose their Progress. I think that this Division of the Enemy's Army affords Us a fine Opportunity to make an efficacious Stroke on them. As soon as I had Notice, that I thought I could depend upon I immediately proposed to the New England Delegates to write to Genl. Washington informing him that a Fleet with a large Body of Troops under Clinton had sailed for Rhode-Island, and desiring him to send Genls Gates or Green with such Brigr. Genls as could be spared to take the Command and Direction of the Troops that might be raised in New England to repell the Enemy from the Island; or oppose their making any Inroads into the Country. It was agreed to, and a Letter wrote.[4] The Genl. told Us in Answer that he had received previous Notice, and had sent Orders to Genls Arnold and Spencer who were then at Albany to repair to New-England and take the Command of the yeomanry that should muster on that Occasion. I hope that the Militia will universally turn out and not suffer the Enemy to enter and ravage our State as they have done the Jersy. I hope that they will turn out in such Numbers as to be able to give an effectual Blow to the Enemy in our Quarter. If the Army under Clinton should receive a mortal Wound from the brave New-Englanders it would in my Opinion bring the War to a speedy Close; whereas if this Opportunity, of the Division of the British Army, should be neglected or not improved, the War in all Probability will be protracted to a great Length, if not speedily issued in our Destruction, in the Destruction of all We hold dear: For We have good Reason to think that a Reinforcement of Twenty thousand Men will be sent over next Spring. By a Letter from an unknown, but I suppose a good Hand, read in Congress this Day, it appears that the Court of London had attempted and were attempting by every Means they could devise to procure Aid from every Power in Europe, or to induce them to a Neutrality; and the Writer of the Letter gave it as his Opinion that what they could collect in Germany together with Recruits raised in England, Scotland and Ireland would amount to about that Number, and that Russia would not furnish them with any Men.[5] From hence the Necessity appears that we should act in every Quarter this Winter with the Spirit of Men contending for an invaluable Prize. By Expresses from Philadelphia received this Day it seems that the Militia of that State begin to rouze themselves, and are collecting very fast to reinforce Genl. Washington.[6] I have some hopes that Howe will be drove out off the Jersey this Winter; if this should take Place, and the New-England States should give Clinton a round Drubbing, We then need not Fear what Britain with all her Mercenaries should attempt. There are brave, enterprizing Spirits in Providence. They burned a Gaspee. They may burn the British Fleet. I hope they will make the Trial and every Effort to destroy both Fleet and Army. I imagin that there are a Number of Seamen in Port, belonging to the Navy of the United States as well as Privateers. These Men I should think could be easily induced to enterprize any thing. They are brave and well know that if the British Fleet is suffered to remain in our Bay there will be an End to privateering, by which they have made immense Gain. What I have wrote on this Head goes on a Supposition, that a Fleet with a large Body of Troops is at Rhode-Island, and flows from that warm Regard I have for the State of Rhode-Island and the glorious Cause in which We are embarked. In this Cause I am willing to exert and have exerted my best abilities; for this I have suffered great Anxiety, have left Wife and Children and the sweetest & closest Connections in Life. Where my Wife and Children are I know not. I hope they have escaped from Rhode-Island, and are not fallen into the Hands of the Enemy. If they should have been so unhappy, I hope that the State will interfere in their Behalf and procure their Release.

I wish that an additional Delegate may have been chosen, and that he may have set off for Congress. If it should not have been done I hope it will be speedily done, and that an Addition might be made to the Salary already voted; and I believe that the Assembly will not think Me mercenary, nor an Addition unnecessary when they are informed that I am obliged to give Six Dollars a Week for Boarding myself, and that every article of living is doubled within a year or Two. I ask no more of the State than sufficient to give me a decent Support while I am in its Service, and I know the Generosity of my Constituents too well to doubt of their Dispositions to do what is right in this instance. To that Generosity and good Disposition I readily submit this Matter, and am with the sincerest Regard their, and your Honor's Friend & humble Servant,   William Ellery

RC (R–Ar).

[1] In a passage below Ellery mentions a letter "read in Congress this day," although Congress did not meet on December 25; and in a subsequent letter to Governor Cooke he mentions "my last of the 24th of this Instant," which must refer to the present letter. See Ellery to Nicholas Cooke, November 31, 1776.

[2] Sullivan's December 13 letter about Lee's capture was actually written to Washington, who forwarded it to Congress. See *Am. Archives*, 5th ser. 3:1232; and *JCC*, 6:1028.

[3] This letter, which was read in Congress on December 20, is in PCC, item 161, 2:325, and *Am. Archives*, 5th ser. 3:1129.

[4] See New England Delegates to George Washington, December 12, 1776.

[5] There is no mention of this letter in the journals.

[6] See the Pennsylvania Council of Safety to Hancock, December 20, *Am. Archives*, 5th ser. 3:1308–9; and Robert Morris to Hancock, December 21, 1776.

Richard Henry Lee to Robert Morris

Dear Sir,   Baltimore 24th Decr. 1776

The following extract of a letter from London dated 21st of September last I send for your future government. "The Americans seem strangely infatuated, for notwithstanding the repeated perfidy they have experienced from the Scotch & the bitter hatred every one of that nation, in all parts of the world, bear to the American cause, some how or other that people are parties concerned in all the trade that the Americans carry on to parts of Europe, in consequence of which the B. Ministry have an accurate accot. of every Vessel that arrives in every Port of Europe from America with the particulars of her returns and they know also of every Vessel that loads in Europe for America. This is accomplished principally by the means of the house of Hope & Co. in Amsterdam (all of them Scotchmen) who have the most extensive correspondence of any power in Europe & have been employed these two years to give the British Ministry information of whatever is done in any of the European Ports relative to America. Besides the Scotchmen & Tories in London seem to be the only persons in whom the Merchants of America at present place confidence by which means two Ships have been lately stopt by the Magistracy of Hamburgh that were loading there, as is supposed on account of Messrs. Willing & Morris & Co. in Philadelphia.

"The bills with which their Cargos were to be purchased, were remitted for negotiation to some Scotch House in London, & it is imagined thro that Channel information was given of the real destination of the Vessels, th' the property appears to be British & the Vessels were said publickly to be bound to Madeira. However upon this information, the British resident there, Mr. Matthias applied to the Magistracy of Hamburgh, who have stoped the Vessel, & some say, have imprisoned the Masters. You know that Hamburg is a very small independent State that *must* at all times comply with the requisitions of the strong European Powers in order to preserve their independence.

"It is said that a plan is formed with France to supply that Country with Tobo. from America, should this be the case, they, vizt. the Americans will no doubt take care to send there, only such kind of Tobo. as the French have been accustomed to receive, otherwise the general trade in that Comodity will hereafter be much injured, if not totally ruined." I do not write you this on a supposition that you have meddled with these treacherous people, but to put you on your guard against those who mean our Ruin.[1]

I am with much esteem Sir your most obedient Servant,

Richard Henry Lee

In great haste

RC (James S. Copley Library, La Jolla, Calif., 1974).
[1] For Morris' reply, see Morris to Lee, December 27, 1776.

Robert Morris to John Bradford

Dear Sir   Philada Decemr. 24th. 1776 [1]

I have just received your favours of the 28th Novr. & 5th Decr. By the first it appears to me that you had written some letters that have never come to hand for I know nothing about the ship loaded with Staves in *a particular manner* nor have I heard any thing of the others you say were to be sold in the course of a month. I suppose the letters in which these things have been mentioned must have fallen into the Enemys hands. The bill you have drawn for acct of the Schooner Wolfe & Cargo shall be paid when presented and I am very glad you have drawn it as I wished the matter settled before I left this Town; if I shou'd be obliged to leave it. You must undoubtedly have heard of our unhappy situation here. The Enemy have marched unmolested through New Jersey with an avowed design of taking possession of this City, & yet the militia or rather associatiors both of that & this State cannot be prevailed on to turn out in that general & Spirited manner that People shou'd do on such an Occasion. Their backwardness does not proceed from want of Spirit, but from a dissatisfaction that is but too general both there & here, with the Constitutions formed for their future Governments, with many of the People now in power, with the Scarcity & high price of Salt and many other Articles. The Tories & dissafected People amongst us take advantage of the present confusion, work on the fears of the timid, incite the Jealousies of the Suspicious and in short one way or other prevent the Force of the Country from being exerted in this day of Tryal.

I am now at the 26th Decr. & have the pleasure to tell you the associatiors are coming down from the back parts of this State. Those from the City have been with Genl Washington for some time & I begin to have hopes that Philada may be preserved from the hands of our Enemies. The loss of it would be the most fatal blow that America cou'd receive as our artificers & manufacturers have proved a Constant Magazine of Necessarys for the Army, Navy & all the other States.

The Congress adjourned about a fortnight ago to Baltimore in Maryland. At that time I sent away my Family, Books, papers and a considerable Value in Effects but having still a great deal left here I am unwilling to depart untill it becomes absolutely necessary for personal Safety, especially as I find myself very usefull in adjusting a deal of Publick business that the Congress left unfinished. I mention these things to shew you that I have not with me the Copies of the former letters I wrote you, nor any other of your letters than the two acknowledged in the beginning of this. I cannot help regretting very much that your answer to my letter of the 8th Octr never Came to hand, for it was in that letter of the 8th if I remember right that I proposed Speculating in Prize Goods &c. Your reply therefore wou'd have been very usefull & for want of it I am much at a loss what to say on that Subject.[2]

RC (MeHi).
[1] This day Morris also wrote brief letters to the Maryland Council of Safety and to the Pennsylvania Council of Safety. For the former, pertaining to the payment of a bill of exchange involved in a shipment to the West Indies, see *Md. Archives*, 12:552. For the latter, which was transmitted by Capt. Isaiah Robinson and

directed the Pennsylvania Council to take the parole of Lt. William Jones, late commander of H. M. Sloop *Racehorse,* whom Robinson had recently taken prisoner, see Morgan, *Naval Documents,* 7:592.

² For the continuation of this letter, see Morris to Bradford, January 12, 1777.

William Whipple to John Langdon

My Dear Sir,   Baltimore, 24th Dec 1776

My last from Philadelphia I think was a day or two before Congress adjourned from that place which was the 11th inst. They meet here the 20th and are now doing business with spirit. The near approach of the Enemy to that City struck such a panic in all orders of people there except Tories (of which you know there are not a small number) that the contagion seized the nerves of some members of C—— which caused a removal to this place which I assure you was much against my inclination; however, I hope its all for the best. The main body of the enemy advanced as far as Trenton and a party of 500 to 1000 visited Burlington. Whether any of them remain at the last mentioned place We have not had any late accounts but by the last account they remained at Trenton and at some places farther up the river. Our army, by the loss at Fort Washington and the expiration of inlistments were reduced to a handfull, by no means sufficient to make a stand against the enemy before they reached the Deleware. Gen Washington was there joined by some militia from Philadelphia. His army is daily increased by militia, besides he has been lately joined by the division lately commanded by General Lee, also by a body of troops from Ticonderoga under command of Gen Gates, so that they are now pretty strong and I think (if they have got rid of the panic that seized them at the time they lost Fort Washington) they may still give a good account of Howe's army and be amply revenged for the brutal cruelties and worse than Savage ravages committed by those infernal instruments of Tyranny for the consolation of the Tories these Barbarians seek their vengeance indiscriminately on Whig and Tory. Notwithstanding all this, some are so infatuated as to go and sue for pardon among which are three of the Allens, viz. Andrew, John & Wm. Thus as far as my head will permit me I have given you a state of the army in this quarter. I should be very happy if I could hear the levies for the new army were completed in the Eastern States. I expect there will be a still further requisition, it is absolutely necessary that we should have a very formidable army in the field immediately. I hope every friend of America in the several States will forward this business with every possible exertion.

The accounts from France which are down to October are very

favorable. I wish for the consolation of my friends I was at liberty to communicate them, but circumstances will not admit of it; but I can say this much in the words of a correspondent, "a General War in Europe seems unavoidable." [1] A vessel is arrived at Philadelphia with about 1000 stand of arms, a considerable parcel of blankets and other woolens and other valuable articles.

We have not had a Marine Board since we arrived here, nor have I been able to get the dimensions of the ship that is to be built in N.H. but I hope the business of collecting timber &c. is going on. So soon as the Committee meets, I intend to procure orders for two or three small vessels say of 60 or 80 tons to be sent here for iron. They can take in iron sufficient to ballast them and fill up with flour. I am in no doubt of obtaining this order, therefore wish you would procure those vessels immediately. Many articles may be sent here that would pay a good freight of which I shall furnish you with a list in my next. Iron and flour may be had here much cheaper than at Philadelphia. I am with every sentiment of esteem your most ob. servt,   Wm Whipple

Tr (DLC).

[1] This quotation is from Silas Deane's September 17 letter to Robert Morris. Wharton, *Diplomatic Correspondence*, 2:148.

Samuel Adams to James Warren

My dear Sir   Baltimore in Maryld Decr 25. [17]76

Although I have been continually writing to you, I have had the Pleasure of receiving only one Letter from you since I left New England.[1]

The Congress is here, scituated conveniently enough and doing Business. You will ask how we came here. I own I did not see the Necessity of removing so soon; but I must conclude that I misjudgd, because it was otherwise ruled, not indeed till the opinions of Putnam & Mifflin, then at Philadelphia had been taken. The Truth is, the Enemy were within seventeen Miles of us, and it was apprehended by some, that the People of Pennsylvania, influenced by Fear, Folly or Treachery, would have surrenderd their Capital to appease the Anger of the two Brothers, and atone for their Crime in suffering it to remain so long the Seat of Rebellion. We are now informd that they have at length bestirrd themselves, and that hundreds are flocking daily to General Washingtons Camp. So if our Army are as expeditious in pursuing as they have been in retreating, we may hope they will take the Enemy all Prisoners before they will be able to reach the Borders of Hudsons River.

We yesterday receivd a Letter from General Schuyler, which has occasiond the passing a Resolution, forwarded to you, as I suppose, by this opportunity.[2] The General says he is informd that the Levies are making in the Eastern States very tardily. I hope he has been misinformd. It is certainly of the greatest Importance that New England in a particular Manner should be very active in preparing to meet the Enemy early in the Spring. The British Tyrant will not quit his darling Object of subduing that Country. The Intent of the Enemy seems to me to be to attack it on all sides. Howes Troops have penetrated this Way, I believe, farther than his Instructions or Intentions. I flatter myself they will be driven back to New York. If so, he will winter there. Carleton, unless he is prevented by an immediate Exertion from New England, will most certainly possess himself of Tyonderoga as soon as the Lake Champlain shall be frozen hard enough to transport his Army. Clinton, it is said is gone to Rhode Island with 8 or 10 thousand to make Winter Quarters there. The infamous Behavior of the People of Jersey & Pennsylvania will give fresh Spirit to the British Court, and afford a further Pretence to apply for Troops to every Power in Europe where they can have any Prospect of Success. Some additional Force they will most probably obtain. Russia has already been applied to. Their whole Force will be pourd into New England, for they take it for granted that having once subdued those stubborn States, the rest will give up without a Struggle. They will take occasion from what has happend in Jersey to inculcate this opinion. How necessary is it then for our Countrymen to strain every Nerve to defeat their Design. The Time is short. Let this be the only Subject of our Thought and Consultation. Our Affairs in France I think, wear a promising Aspect. Let us do our Duty and defend the fair Inheritance which our Fathers have left us—our pious forefathers who mindful of Posterity fought and bled that they might transmit to them the Blessing of Liberty.

When we first heard at Philadelphia of Clintons having saild to Rhode Island, Mr Gerry & myself joynd with Coll Whipple of New Hampshire & Mr Ellery of Rhode Island in a Letter to General Washington, and proposd to him the sending of General Gates or Green with a suitable Number of Brigadiers to take the Command in the Eastern Department. In his Answer which we receivd in this Place he tells us he has orderd Major General Spencer & Brigadier General Arnold to repair thither, who, he hopes may be sufficient to head the Yeomanry of that Country and repel the Enemy in their Attempts to gain the Possession of that part of the Continent. He adds that he will if possible send some other Brigadier & says General Wooster is also at hand.[3]

I wrote to you soon after my Arrival in Philadelphia and inclosd a Resolution of Congress relative to the procuring of Cloathing in New England for the Army.[4] In another Letter I suggested to you a Hint which I think of great Importance if the Measure proposd be practicable.[5] I hope both these Letters were duly receivd by you. I am expecting Mr J A and my other worthy Colleagues from Boston. We want them much. You cannot, my dear Sir, do me a greater Kindness than by writing to me. I suffer greatly through Want of Intelligence from N. E. I pray you therefore let your Letters to me be very frequent. Believe me to be most cordially, your Friend,

S Adams

[*P.S.*] By a late Letter from London written by a Gentleman upon whose Intelligence I greatly rely, a Treaty is on foot with Russia to furnish Britain with twenty or thirty thousand troops. Levies are making with all possible Industry in Germany and in Britain & Ireland from whence it is expected that 20,000 will be raisd. It is indeed to be supposd that as usual a great Appearance will be made on Paper than they will realize. But let us consider that they realizd the last year in America 35,000, and do without Doubt recruit the Numbers they lose, because they are able to do it, we then may set down their actual Force in America by May or June next at least 55 and probably 60,000.

We have the pleasure of hearing that a valueable Prize is arrivd at Boston, among the rest of her Cargo 10,000 Suits of Cloaths! [6] A most fortunate Prize to us, especially as she is said to be the last of Eight Vessells taken bound to Quebec with necessary Supplys for their Troops. However, while we are pleasing our selves with these Acquisitions, we should remember that the Want of these Supplys will be a Strong Stimulus to Charlton, to make a bold Push by the first opportunity over the Lake Champlain in hopes of furnishing himself at Albany; and increases the Necessity of the eastern States sending their troops to Tyonderoga immediately to supply the places of those who will return home when the Time of their Inlistments expires—the very next Week!

I have good Information from England that a certain Capt Furze who was in Boston the last year & gaind the Confidence & received the Civilities of the People, when he returned, gloried in the Deception and carried Intelligence to the British Ministry particularly of the Fortifications in and about Boston. Some of the people may remember him. How careful ought we to be lest while we mean only innocent Civilities to Strangers we expose our Councils & operations to Spies.   S. A.

RC (MB).
¹ Warren's October 24 and November 16, 1776, letters are in *Warren-Adams Letters*, 2:439–41.
² See John Hancock to Certain States, this date.
³ See New England Delegates to George Washington, December 12, 1776.
⁴ It cannot be determined precisely which letter Adams is alluding to, but see Secret Committee to the Massachusetts Assembly, December 4, 1776.
⁵ See Samuel Adams to James Warren, December 6, 1776.

⁶ This clothing was on the British transport *Mellish*, which was captured by John Paul Jones, commanding the Continental ship *Alfred*. See Morgan, *Naval Documents*, 7:110–11, 183–84; and Washington, *Writings* (Fitzpatrick), 6:356.

John Hancock to Certain States

Gentlemen,   Baltimore Decr. 25th. 1776.

Since I did myself the Honour of addressing you last on the Subject of the enclosed Resolve,[1] the Congress have received fresh Intelligence from Generals Schuyler & Gates, urging the Necessity of an immediate Compliance therewith. In Consequence of which they have ordered me to represent to you that without your immediate Aid and Assistance the important Fortress of Ticonderoga will unavoidably fall into the Hands of our Enemies, the Troops who at present garrison that and the adjacent Posts having determined not to continue there after the Term of their Inlistment expires.[2]

It is needless to use Arguments on the Occasion, or to point the dreadful Consequences, to Gentlemen already fully acquainted with them, of leaving the back Settlements of the New England States open to the Ravages of our merciless Foes. If any Thing can add to your Exertions at this Time, it must be the Reflection that your own most immediate Safety calls upon you to strain every Nerve. Should we heedlessly abandon the Post of Ticonderoga, we give up inconceiveable Advantages. Should we resolutely maintain it (and it is extremely capable of Defence) we may bid Defiance to Genl. Carlton and the Northern Army under his Command. But our Exertions for this Purpose must be immediate, or they will not avail any Thing. The thirty first of this Inst, the Time will expire for which the Troops in that important Garrison were enlisted, and Lake Champlain will, in all Probability be frozen over soon after. For the Sake therefore of all that is dear to Freemen, be entreated to pay immediate Attention to this Requisition of Congress, and let Nothing divert you from it. The Affairs of our Country are ·in a Situation to admit of no Delay. They may still be retrieved, but not without the greatest Expedition and Vigour.

If Nothing was at Stake but your *own* Peace and Security, I should not be so earnest on the Occasion. It is the Fate of Posterity (which depends on *our* Conduct) that stamps a Value on the present Cause. I beseech you therefore by all that is sacred—by that Love of Liberty and your Country, which you have always manifested—by those Ties of Honour which bind you to the Common Cause—by that Love of Virtue and Happiness which animates all good Men, and finally—by your Regard for succeeding Generations, that you will, without a Moment's Delay, exert yourselves to forward the Troops for Ticonderoga from your States agreeably to the enclosed Requisition of Congress.

I have the Honour to be, Gentlemen, your most obed. & very hble Servt.   J.H. Presid.

LB (DNA: PCC, item 12A). Addressed to the assemblies of New Hampshire, Massachusetts, and Connecticut.

[1] Apparently a reference to Hancock to Certain States, November 20, 1776.

[2] See JCC, 6:1038. Schuyler's December 10 letter to Hancock, dealing with the critical need for reinforcements at Ticonderoga, is in PCC, item 153, 509–12, and Am. Archives, 5th ser. 3:1160–61. Another letter on this subject from Gates to Hancock, written on November 27 and read in Congress on December 6, is in PCC, item 154, 1:121–24, and Am. Archives, 5th ser. 3:874–75.

Benjamin Harrison to the Maryland Council of Safety

Sir   Baltimore Decr. 25th. 1776
    Congress are in immediate Want of a fast sailing Vessell. Every Endeavor has been used to procure one without Success nor have they the least Chance left of getting one unless your honorable Board will spare Capt. Martin's Brig. I should by no Means ask the Favor, knowing how necessary this Vessel is to the State of Maryland, if the Occasion was not of the most pressing Nature. Should the Board be so obliging as to part with her, Congress expect to pay what the Vessel & Cargo cost with every Charge of Wages & Outfit. You'l please to lay this matter before the Board and favor me with their Answer by the Express.[1]
    I have the Honor to be, your obedt. Servant,
                                         Benja. Harrison

Tr (DNA: PCC, item 37).

[1] Harrison was probably writing on behalf of the Committee of Secret Correspondence. In their reply of the 26th the Maryland Council of Safety explained their reluctance to part with Martin's brig, the Friendship, and on the 30th they agreed to sell Congress the armed schooner Jenifer instead. Md. Archives, 12:553, 560–61. See also Committee of Secret Correspondence to the Maryland Council of Safety, December 29, 1776.

Benjamin Harrison to Robert Morris

Dear Sir,   Baltimore Decr 25. 1776
    Inclosed you have a Letter from the Committee of Secret Corres. to the Commissioners in France which youl please to Sign and send with the other Papers to those Gentn by the first opp[ortunit]y with proper orders for their being Destroyd rather than the Enemy should get them.[1] I need not suggest to you the Prejudice it would be to us if they should fall into their Hands.

Mr Deanes Letter is also enclosed that you may answer the mercantile parts of it. This would have been done sooner but you will see there were many Parts of it on which the advice of Congress was necessary, this occasiond the Delay. Binghams [letter] we have not had time to answer but hope to do it tomorrow. As soon as we do it shall be returnd.[2]

For Gods sake send us some News; we have none here but what a *Purviance* or a *Rush* Deal out to us. If you wish to please your Friends Come soon to us, but if you desire to keep out of the Damdest Hole in the World come not here. My Complimts. to my Friends. I wish you and them a Happy Xmass; a merry one you can not have Divided so far and on such on occasion from those you Love. I am, your affect. & Obedt Servt,

Benja Harrison

RC (MdBJ–G).

[1] See Committee of Secret Correspondence to the Commissioners at Paris, December 21, 1776. See also Morris to Harrison, December 29, 1776.

[2] These letters had been enclosed in Robert Morris to the Committee of Secret Correspondence, December 16, 1776.

Marine Committee to John Nicholson

Sir December 25th. 1776

As this severe weather is like to make ice, Captain Biddle will try to make a push with the Randolph and as it is of the utmost consequence that you should get to Carolina if possible I think it most for the public service that you should go down the Bay in company with him and I hope this will find you in readiness.[1] You will see the Ship as she comes down, and must join her as soon as you can, and you must concert with Captain Biddle the best plan you can think of for getting out. I am fearful an expedition is gone or will soon go against Charles Town, therefore you must proceed cautiously and get into the first safe harbour in that state that you can & give immediate notice to the president and the Continental Agents of your Arrival.

I am Sir by Order of the M. Committee, your hble servant,

Robert Morris V.P.

LB (DNA: PCC Miscellaneous Papers, Marine Committee Letter Book).

[1] Nicholson was captain of the Continental sloop *Hornet*.

Benjamin Rush to Richard Henry Lee

Dear Sir, Bristol Decemr 25. 1776

My letters I fear will prove troublesome to you but I cannot help it. Your industry as well as zeal in the Service of your country encourage me to convey every hint that occurs to me to your knowledge—being well convinced that if you think them of importance, you will *force* the congress to attend to them.

The Sufferings of our brave Continental troops from the want of cloaths exceed all description. I shall not give you or myself the pain of attempting to paint them. It becomes us to do every thing to remedy them as quick as possible, and guard against them for the future. For heaven's sake let it [be] a standing order of Congress that no subject should be broached there for three weeks to come but what relates to the cloathing and officering of the Army. I am in hopes we have got a sufficient stock of Woolens for the present year—But what shall we do for *linnens?* Every soldier in the British army is obliged to have *four* shirts, and to shift *twice* a week. Clean linnen is absolutely necessary to guard against lice and sickness. All the medicines in the world will not make an Army healthy without cleanliness. Suppose an Application is made to every man in America for one or two of his own shirts for the benefit of the Army? The application I am sure will be successful. Col: Griffin informed me that had our scheme for cloathing the Army with second hand cloaths proposed three months ago in Congress been adopted three fourths of the poor ragged fellows whose times are now expired would have reinlisted. Let nothing prevent the execution of this Scheme but a large supply of new linnen which I believe is not to be had. It would tend greatly to preserve the health of our Army if each soldier would have two flannen [*sic*] shirts instead of two linnen ones to wear in wet weather & in the fall of the year. But I fear we have not a sufficient stock of wool by us for that purpose.

Nothing new. Col: Griffin with only 800 men keeps How's whole army under constant alarms in New Jersey. He has had several successful skirmishes with them. Our militia who croud in daily call aloud for Action! Yours,   Benjn Rush

RC (ViU).

Matthew Thornton to Meshech Weare

Hond. Sir,   Baltimore, 25th Decr. 1776
The near Approach of the Enemy to Philadelphia, the Slowness of the Militia, & the advice of Friends, indus'd the Congress to adjourn to this Town, which is about 110 Miles Southwest from Philadelphia. By our last Advices the Militia are joining our army in great numbers, from which we have great hopes that Gl. How, & his army will Soon be in our power, or Return to New York. The Congress have encouragent of Assistance by the Spring. Nothing will be wanting on their part, to Support independence, Defeat the Enemy, & Render the united States, Great, Honorable, & Happy.

An inexcuseable Neglect in the Off[ice]rs, want of Fidelity, Honour, & Humanity, in the D[octo]rs, & Averice in the Suttlers, has Slain ten Soldiers to the Enemies one, & will Soon prevent everyman of Common Sense from puting his Life, & fortune in the Power of Such as Destroy both without pity, or mercy. I have propos'd to Congress, that every State, in future, Should Appoint one or more Suttlers, as they think proper for their own Men to be Supplied by a Committee Appointed by Said State, with everything Necessary for Sick, & well men, at a price Stipulated by said State, the Suttlers, & Committee to be paid by, & accountable to said States, & a Superintendent, who Shall have no Other Business but to See that every Soldier Belonging to the State, is properly Supplied, & Supported, agreeable to their Circumstances; & that proper Stopages be made for what they Receive when they are Receiving their wages.[1]

The Congress approve of the method, but Say it is the Business, & Duty of each State, to take Care of their own men, & they Expect they will. This may appear Expensive, but when it is Considered, that by this or Some better method that the Council, & Assembly think off we may Soon (when it is Published) have an army in the feild able to Defeat any Britain Can Send, & without it we Shall Soon have none But Officers, all which is Humbly Submited to the wisdom & prudence of the Honable Council, & Assembly, by him who has the Honour to be, Honble Gentn., Your Most Obedient Hble Sert.   Matthew Thornton

P.S. The Honble Col. Whipple is well. I have Received no Letter Since I left New-Hampshire. Please to take the trouble to present my Compliment to the Honble Council, & Assembly, & to Wm. Parker Esqr.

RC (NN).
[1] Congress had considered several proposals for regulating sutlers in the army on November 8 and 9, but it had deferred action. There is no further mention of this issue in the journals for 1776. *JCC*, 6:935, 937–38. See also Elbridge Gerry to John Wendell, November 11, 1776, note 3.

Oliver Wolcott to Laura Wolcott

My Dear   Baltimore Town 25t Decr. 1776
I Wrote to you the 13t from Philidelpa. by Tim. Dodd of Hartford wherein I informed you that the Congress had adjourned themselves hither. They Met on Business at this Place the 20t and will probably continue here a few Months. I Wrote to you Letters of the 11t and 5t Inst., also two others of the 24t and 16t last. By the Bearers of the Letters of the 5t and 11t I sent you some Books. I mention these Things a little particularly as some of my Letters may have miscarryed. I have recd. none from home but one from

Oliver Wolcott

Mr. Adams of the 15t Octo. which I have acknowledged and three from Mr. Lyman the last of the 23t Nov. He mentions his having sent one by Mr. Sherman which is not come to hand.[1]

You Excuse yourself from Writing to Me on Acco. of the Dificulty and uncertainty of Conveyance, but I should think if Letters were left with Mr. Stanton to forward them by Expresses which will probably pritty frequently pass thro Litchfield they might come safe, but you and my Freinds must consider the Delivery of Letters as a Matter of some Uncertainty but if Letters should fall into the Hands of the Foe, such as come from you and my Freinds I am sure I shall never be ashamed of, and as for mine they will find more trouble in Reading them, than Entertainment.

I am conveniently Situated in this Place and Lodge with a couple of Freinds, Dr. Hall formerly of Connecticut and Mr. Ellery of R. Island. By the Blessing of God I injoy Health except a slight cold which will soon go off. Nothing Material in respect of News since my last except the surprising and unexpected Capture of Genl. Lee which you have or will soon hear of.

I am still here alone from Connecticut which I do not Very Well know what else to attribute to except that affairs since last July Wear such a benign aspect as to render the Circumstance of a Deligation a Matter of a good deal of Indifferance.

My kindest Love to my Children and Freinds and May God grant you and them his chocist Favours. I am yours, with the tenderest Affection,   Oliver Wolcott

P.S. When I shall have the pleasure of Seeing You and my Family is Very uncertain, but it is not probable that it will be earlier than the next Spring. Take Care of your Health, and Suffer not yourself to be Anxious in Regard to any affairs of Life. The God who has hitherto taken Care of us will still I trust Grant his Protection to you and Me. I shall Write a Letter to Mr Lyman if I have time. Should I not I hope he will not take it Amiss, nor forbear to Write to me.

At present I have no other Objections against this Town of which in some future Letters I may give you a particular Acco. of, than that it is too Distant from my Freinds and is too dirty and too dear. You will I hope consider this Letter as Wrote in haste.

RC (CtHi).
[1] According to Robert Morris, Roger Sherman arrived in Philadelphia this day. Morris to John Hancock, December 26, 1776.

Samuel Adams to Elizabeth Adams

My dear Betsy   Baltimore in Maryland 26 Dec 1776
I have written to you once since I arrivd here, and am determind to omit no opportunity because I flatter myself you will at all times

be gratified in hearing from me. I am at present in good health and am exceedingly happy in an Acquaintance with Mr Samuel Purviance a Merchant of this Place, with whom I have indeed before corresponded, but I never saw him till I came here. He is a sensible, honest and friendly Man, warmly attachd to the American Cause, and has particularly endeard himself to me by his great Assiduity in procuring Relief in this part of the Continent for the Town of Boston at a Time when her Enemies would have starvd her by an oppressive Port bill.

Just now I receivd a Letter from my Son dated the 7th Instant, he tells me he had very lately heard from his Sister and that she and the rest of my Family were well. I pray God to continue your Health and protect you in these perilous times from every kind of Evil. The Name of the Lord, says the Scripture, is a strong Tower, thither the Righteous flee and are safe. Let us secure his Favor, and he will lead us through the Journey of this Life and at length receive us to a better.

We are now informd that the People of Jersey & Pennsylvania are in Possession of their Understanding and that they are turning out in great Numbers to the Assistance of General Washington. Had they done this early they would not have so deeply staind the Reputation of America. However I shall hardly think they will do their Duty at last if they suffer the Enemy to return without paying dearly for the barbarous Outrages they have committed in the Country, without Regard to Age or Sex.

Our Affairs in France & Spain wear a pleasing Aspect, but human Affairs are ever uncertain. I have strongly recommended to my Friends in New England to spare no Pains or Cost in preparing to meet the Enemy early in the Spring. We have a righteous Cause, and if we defend it as becomes us, we may expect the Blessing of Heaven.

Remember me to my Daughter, Sister Polly & the rest of my Family & Friends. Adieu, my dear,   S. Adams

RC (NN).

Elbridge Gerry to Joseph Trumbull

Dear Sir   Baltimore 26th Decr 1776

Your Favour of the 13th came to Hand Yesterday[1] & this Day Congress have ordered 400,000 Dollars to be sent You forthwith; the Residue can be better spared when this is expended, which You will give Notice of to Congress. You are also impowered to import Flower from Virginia or Maryland, & the Governor & Council of Virginia are desired to order 10,000 bb Flower to be provided on James, Rapahanock, York & Potomac Rivers & deliver to your

Order, with as much more as You shall direct. This is to be payed by your Order on the president of Congress for that purpose.[2]

I have wrote You several letters two of wch. were forwarded by General Mifflin & one by an Express wch. was sent to Congress by Governor Trumbull. Therein I desired a Bill of the Int[erest] & touched on other Matters wch. were mentioned in your Letter. General Lee's Captivity was very unexpected. I am glad We did not loose our Commissary. The King of Spain has opened his ports to our Commerce, privateers & prizes,[3] & I have no Doubt that France will engage in a War in the Spring; this then is the Time for America to exert herself, & to change the Aspect of Affairs in her Favour. I wish to See more of an interprizing Spirit in the civil as well as military Departments, & am with much Esteem your assured Friend & sert,   E Gerry

P.S. The Treasury have not yet been able to attend to your affair, but I believe will soon report upon it. Is there no possibility of obtaining full Supplies of Vegetables & Vinegar for the Army? The British Troops are preserved from Sickness by these Means only, & I fear We shall never have a Healthy & Vigerous Army without them.

RC (Ct).
[1] Trumbull's December 13 letter to John Hancock is in *Am. Archives*, 5th ser. 3:1202–3.
[2] For these December 26 resolves, see *JCC*, 6:1040–41. See also Gerry to Joseph Trumbull, December 7, and John Hancock to Joseph Trumbull, December 27, 1776.
[3] Although Spanish ports in Europe and the Americas were open to American merchantmen, privateers, and prize ships on equal footing with the British, only Portuguese prizes could be sold in Spanish ports. Commercial trading was virtually unlimited, and the Spanish government was secretly providing money and military supplies to the United States. Samuel F. Bemis, *The Diplomacy of the American Revolution* (New York: D. Appleton-Century Co., 1935), pp. 40, 54n.29; Buchanan P. Thompson, *Spain: Forgotten Ally of the American Revolution* (North Quincy, Mass.: Christopher Publishing House, 1976), pp. 23–47; and Morgan, *Naval Documents*, 6:607–8, 7:683, 785.

Francis Lewis to Robert Morris

Dear Sir   Baltimore 26 Decemr. 1776
The Congress think it absolutely necessary that a Number of Brass Field Pieces should be cast as soon as possible and have directed the Ordinance Board to request that you would direct an enquiry to be made for such persons as are capable of conducting that Branch.[1]

Mr Payne informed Congress that Mr Byers (who cast the Brass Cannon at New York) was then daily expected with his family at

Phila and where there is an Air Furnace at which he might be employed; Congress is therefore anxious to know if Byers is at Phila and can be there employed, or if any other person can be found capable of conducting that work.[2] It is necessary also to inform you that at Christeen I saw a quantity of Sea Coal, with some Copper, the latter said to be sent from New York: The Board of Ordinance imagine a work of this kind may be erected in the Vicinity of this place, it being more convenient, in getting supply, of Sea Coal from Virginia, provided the Mettle can be procured with a proper person to conduct the Work, the latter is not to be obtained here; And as Congress has this Affair much at hart, they intreat you to make the strictest inquiry you can & inform them.

Congress has this moment received letters from the General recommending in the most pressing terms the necessity of having a Number of Brass & Iron Cannon provided as early as possible for the next Campaigne on which he seems to say the fate of America in a great measure depends. He also strongly recommends an Augmentation of the Continental Battallions to 110—with five Battallions of Artillery—Thus far from the Ordinance Board.[3] *The following is a copy of a letter I this day received from Mr N. Shaw, junr of Nw London, dated 7th Inst. viz.:* [4]

"I wrote you 23d Ulto advising of the Ship Mary; being detained in this Port, since that I have not received any of yr favors. Have now to inform you that this day came an order from the Govr & Council of this state to have the Cargoe unladen and sent up to Norwich to the Mills with orders to have it ground & made into bread. I suppose the reason for this is that wheat is become a very scarce article this way, and the great probability of a move being made by the British Troops to Newport as they are undoubtedly gone to that place. I expect soon to have your directions relative to the ship, for I believe now she will not be able to get out of this Port, by reason of the Men of War which are cruzing up the harbour for these ten days past, if you approve of it I can get the Commissary Bills for the amount of the Cargoe pay in Phila."

As you have Mr Shaw's letter of the 23d Ulto in order to answer it I shall acquiesse in whatever directions you give him relative to the Ship, but should be glad of a possibility of sending her to the So. ward for Toba &c. . . .

Sir Yr very H. Servt.,   F. Lewis

P.S. I ordered some Effects to be shiped from St. Eustatia in the armed Vessell. Should she be returned with them beg you would dispose of them for me.

MS not found; text taken from *Stan V. Henkels Catalog,* no. 1183 (January 16, 1917), item 41, and Tr (DLC). The salutation, place-and-date line, complimentary close, and postscript all come from the DLC Tr, which Burnett made from the MS of Lewis' letter then in Henkels' possession.

[1] Lewis had just been made a member of the cannon committee on December 24. *JCC*, 6:1039. His references in this letter to the "Ordinance Board" and "Board of Ordinance" are probably to this committee since he was not a member of the Board of War and Ordnance.

[2] See also Robert Treat Paine to James Byers, November 3, 1776.

[3] Washington's December 20 letter to Hancock is in PCC, item 152, 3:69–79, and Washington, *Writings* (Fitzpatrick), 6:400–409. Enclosed in it was "A Plan for the establishment of a Continental Magazine" drawn up by Henry Knox, on which see *Am. Archives*, 5th ser. 3:1314. For the extensive grant of authority which Congress made to Washington on December 27, partly in response to this letter, see *JCC*, 6:1045–46.

[4] Shaw, the Continental prize agent in Connecticut, probably wrote this letter to Lewis in the latter's capacity as a member of the Marine Committee.

Robert Morris to John Hancock

Sir   Philada. Decemr. 26th. 1776

I have just received by the return of Pluckrose the Express your favour of the 23d and am very happy to find my Conduct meets the approbation of Congress. They may depend on my utmost exertions to promote the Publick good on every occasion that offers. And it is with singular pleasure I communicate any thing that will give you satisfaction as I know what follows must. Capt Charles Alexander whom I sent up to Colo Cadwallader for a few Tradesmen necessary to finish his Ship the Delaware, is just returned and says that whilst he was with the Colo. a Note came in from Trenton giving an Acct. that Genl. Washington is now Master of that place, that he had sent down to the Ferry 300 Prisoners, had taken all the Enemies baggage & Stores at that place, that the Action had been pretty hot for an hour or an hour & a half, that the British then run away towards Bordentown & our People after them. This Acct is just confirmed by a letter from Mr Barkly to Mr Mease who says Mr. Tilghman had come down to the Ferry & gave him the Acct. This Maneuvre of the Genl had been determined on some days ago but he kept it Secret as the nature of the Service would admit. Colo Cadwallader & Genl Ewing had orders to Cross the River from their respective Posts at the same time the Genl Crossed from his, but the Ice driving down from the Falls impeded & indeed prevented them from affecting their business. Colo Cadwallader got over 1000 men near Burlington but cou'd not land his artillery on Acct of the Ice & this day being such extream bad Weather, he was compelled to bring them back, but on receiving the advice from Trenton he determined to go again and as the weather is now clearing up, I am Confident he will be over this Night and I do suppose Genl Ewing will not remain on this side, so that if Genl Washington does but follow up the blow & pursue them downwards I think this will prove a Mortal Stroke to the Enemies intended expedition against this City. Colo Griffin is returned from his Expedition after a little Skirmishing as the Enemy brought too powerfull a body against him. However about 400 Jersey Militia remain at Mount Holly & I think Genl Putnam shoud reinforce them as here are lately come in a considerable number of Militia, indeed I believe he has sent over a reinforcement but tomorrow Morning I will speak to him on this subject. It is now too late at night. Mr Sherman arrived here yesterday. I have not seen him but am told he brings an Acct that Genl. Heath has Crossed the No River, retaken Fort Lee & Hackensack with all the baggage & Stores at those places & 130 Prisoners & that he was employing Waggons to remove the Stores into places of greater safety and from another quarter I am told Genl Washington previous to his Attack on Trentown had given Genl. Heath suitable orders.

You will observe I am not perfectly master of Genl. Washingtons plan but it appears to me, that if he has directed Genl. Heath to continue his March in the Enemies Rear, those that are between Hackensack & Trenton will be drawn off from Genl Washington and leave him to pursue the flying Hero's towards Burlington where I expect Colo Cadwallader will cut of[f] the Communication between them & about 200 Hessians & Highlanders that came to Moors Town against Griffin. If this is the plan, I think it well laid & if the General is properly supported in the Execution, why shall we not put a glorious end to the Campaigne of 1776. It must I had like to say it shall be so.

Capt Robison of the Andrew Doria tells me just now that he hears his Prize Sloop is got up to the Cheveaux de Frize. I hope it is true & as this is the first of King George's own Vessells that we have taken, I shou'd be glad the Congress wou'd Order her into their service and give the Command to Lieutt Dun of the Andw Doria who has been in the service from the first & is said to be an officer of Merit. Shou'd Genl Washington follow up his blow we may get time to fit out all these Vessells, but if Howe comes here we cannot do it for want of Tradesmen.

The letter for Genl Washington from Congress shall be sent to him in the Morning by Major Pierce and a Copy of the Resolves you enclosed.[1] I suppose there is a Copy in the letter to him but as you do not mention it I think it best to send them.

I am happy to find the attention Congress have paid to Genl Lee and flatter myself they will be well pleased to learn that I had wrote a letter to him enclosing a bill drawn by two Officers of the Royal Highland Emigrants on Major Small for £116 Sterlg that had been supplyed them by my Friends in Carolina where they are Prisoners. This letter [2] I sent open to Genl Washington who promised to send it in with a Flag & in that letter I told Genl Lee I hoped he wou'd be permitted to write me when he wanted more Money & he might depend on receiving it. Notwithstanding the supply sent in I shall desire Genl Washington to send a Flag to know if the Gold will be admitted and I will make a point to Collect it. Mr Walton is now here, we have sent for Mr Clymer & tomorrow we shall enter on business as Committee Men and if our best endeavours to serve the Publick can procure the approbation of Congress we shall have it. The enclosed letter from the Genl. to your Honor being directed to you *here* I judged it best to open it, supposing he meant it. The Contents of it I shall keep to myself, as indeed I shall of all other letters of that kind, but I mentioned to the General what I deemed good News from France & it had a good Effect. I am most truely Sir, Your obed Servt, Robt Morris

RC (DNA: PCC, item 137).
[1] See Hancock to Washington, December 23, 1776.
[2] Not found.

Robert Morris to George Washington

Dear Sir Philada. Decr. 26th. 1776
I have just received yours of yesterday and will duely attend to those things you recommend to my consideration.[1] At present I have to enclose you a letter from Congress which I suppose Contains their resolves of the 20th Inst. but as the President does not say in his letter to me that they are enclosed to you & as it is necessary you shou'd have them I take the liberty to send herewith a Copy of them.

I am well pleased to see the attention they pay Genl Lee and I shall make a point to Collect & send your Excellency soon as possible the one hundred half Johannes they order. Youl observe Mr. Clymer, Mr. Walton & myself are appointed a Committee to transact the Continental business here that may be necessary & proper, and I apprehend it will frequently be necessary that we shou'd know the substance of your Correspondence with Congress. Your letters to the President if sent open under our Cover shall always meet dispatch & their Contents kept secret, & when you think it improper we shou'd see them before the Congress Seal them & they shall go forward untouched & if you dont approve of submitting them to our inspection at all write us freely & your wishes in that respect shall be complyed with.[2]

We have just heard of your Success at Trenton. The acct is but imperfect but we learn you are master of that place & of all the baggage & Stores our Enemies had there & of 300 Prisoners and that your

Troops were still in pursuit of the flying Enemy. I have just wrote to Congress & told them thus much .as the substance of an Acct just come down & I told them further I had been informed that you had executed in this matter your part of a well Concerted plan, that Genl Heath at Hackensack had orders from you, & that Genl Ewing & Colo Cadwallader also had orders to Cross Delaware at the same time you did, but had been prevented by Driving Ice. Good News sets all the Animal Spirits to Work, the immagination is heated & I cou'd not help adding, that I expected Genl Heath was to Continue his march towards Brunswick which woud draw the attention of any Troops posted there & at Prince Town, while you wou'd pursue the flying Hero's to Bordenton & Burlington where Ewing & Cadwallader woud stop them & cut of their Communication with the 2000 Hessians & Highlanders that came after Griffin, nay I almost promised them that you shoud by following up this first blow, finish the Campaigne of 1776 with that eclat that your numerous Friends & admirers have long wished for. I Congratulate you most heartily on what is done & am with perfect esteem, Dr sir, Your Excellency's Most obedt servt,   Robt Morris

RC (DLC).
[1] Washington's December 25 letter to Morris is in Washington, *Writings* (Fitzpatrick), 6:436–38.
[2] For Washington's reply, see ibid., p. 441.

Executive Committee to Thomas Fleming

Sir   December 27th 1776.
     We have just received your letter of the 27th instant to the Secretary of the Board of war and are glad to find your Regiment on their March this way; but we cannot conceive it necessary to Send tents or Arms to the Head of Elk, as the Troops can quarter in Houses on their March or may come by Water from Christiana Bridge. Arms are not necessary as there is no Enemy in the way. Blankets, Shoes and Stockings we will provide if possible under our present circumstances.
     Genl. Washington has Struck an unexpected Stroke at Trentown where he now reigns master. We hope to drive the Enemy out of New Jersey and if you haste up you'l come in for a Share of the Glory. Mr Benjamin Hogeland at Christianna Bridge will supply you with Two thousand dollars which you'l please to Send a proper officer to receive and give a Receipt for it.[1] The amount will be charged to your Account therefore you must render an Accot. of the expenditure of it. On Behalf of the Committee of Congress left in this City to transact Continental business, I am Sir, Your very hble Sert.   Robt Morris

LB (DNA: PCC, item 133). Addressed: "To Colo. Flemming of the 9th Virginia Regt. or the Commanding Officer."
[1] Morris' letter to Hogeland of this date, ordering him to pay Fleming $2,000 at Head of Elk, is in PCC, item 133, fols. 12–13, and ,Am. Archives, 5th ser. 3:1439.

Executive Committee to Thomas Smith

Sir,[1]   Philada. Decemr. 27th 1776
The Congress have thought proper to appoint us a Committee to transact all Continental business in this City that may be necessary and proper, and they have empowered us to draw on the Loan Office for Such Sums of money as may be wanted, little Suspecting there was no such Office or Officer to be found in Philadelphia. For our parts we have been impatiently waiting your return, and are Sorry to say the public Service has Suffered by your absence. Had we been possessed of the Notes we could have borrowed considerable Sums which may probably be Otherways disposed of by this time. We expect your immediate attendance and are sir, Your hble Servts.

> Robert Morris
>
> Geo Clymer
>
> Geo Walton

LB (DNA: PCC, item 133).
[1] Thomas Smith (d. 1793) had been appointed Continental loan officer for Pennsylvania on December 5, 1776. *Journals and Proceedings of the General Assembly of the Common-Wealth of Pennsylvania* (Philadelphia: John Dunlap, 1777), p. 7.

John Hancock to Robert Morris

Sir,   Baltimore Decr. 27th. 1776.
The enclosed Resolves, which I do myself the Honour of forwarding, will inform you of the Steps taken by Congress in the present critical State of our Affairs.[1]
Your Favor of the 23d inst. came to Hand, and was immediately laid before Congress. The Uneasiness you mention therein, with Regard to your Want of proper Powers, is, no Doubt, by this Time removed, Congress having authorized the Committee in Philada. to adopt such Measures in the Business of the Continent as they shall judge proper.[2] You will therefore, in Conjunction with Mr. Clymer and Mr. Walton, act, not only in marine Matters, but in all others, as you shall think necessary and most conducive to the public Good.
I wrote you some Time ago per Express, informing you that Congress had appointed a Committee in Philada. to conduct all public

Business, and at the same Time enclosed you their Resolves. To them therefore, as well as to those herewith transmitted, I beg Leave to refer your Attention, and have only Time to assure you, that I am with great Esteem and Respect, Sir, your most obed. & very hble Servt.   John Hancock Presidt

[*P.S.*] The moment I can Steal a little time I will write you fully, till then you must Excuse me.

RC (DNA: PCC, item 58). In the hand of Jacob Rush, with signature and postscript by Hancock.
    [1] Presumably the resolves passed this day in response to the report of the "committee on the state of the army." *JCC*, 6:1043–46.
    [2] See *JCC*, 6:1032.

John Hancock to the
Pennsylvania Council of Safety

Gentlemen   Baltimore December 27th. 1776
    The great Importance to the Welfare of these United States of supporting the Credit of the Continental Currency, will suggest the Propriety of the above Resolve,[1] which I am commanded by Congress to transmit to you, and to request you will take Measures for an immediate Compliance therewith. I have wrote to the General to give you every necessary Assistance in carrying your Determinations on this Subject into effectual Execution. I have the Honour to be, Gentlemen, your most obedt. hble Sert.
                                           John Hancock Prest.

RC (PHC). In the hand of Jacob Rush and signed by Hancock.
    [1] This was a resolve of this date requesting the Pennsylvania Council of Safety to punish "all such as shall refuse continental currency." *JCC*, 1046. Its passage was prompted by intelligence contained in Robert Morris to Hancock, December 23, 1776.

John Hancock to the
Pennsylvania Council of Safety

Gentlemen   Baltimore December 27th. 1776
    Your favr. by Capt. Casdrop I duly Rec'd, and Communicated to Congress, in consequence of which they Directed Two hundred thousand Dollars to be Advanc'd you agreeable to your Request, you to be Accountable for the same, which Sum is committed to the Care of Capt Casdrop, I wish it safe to hand & that it may Answer

Valuable purposes.[1] Being much Engag'd can only Add that I am with much Esteem, Gentlemen, Your very huml Servt.

John Hancock Prest.

RC (PHi).

[1] Congress agreed to advance $200,000 to the council on December 24 in response to the council's December 20 request for a loan to meet the unexpected demands recently placed upon it. See *JCC,* 6:1037. The council's letter is in PCC, item 69, fol. 273; and *Am. Archives,* 5th ser. 3:1308–9.

John Hancock to Joseph Trumbull

Sir, Baltimore Decr. 27th. 1776.

After acknowledging the Receipt of your Favour of the 13th inst. I am to inform you, that some Time since I transmitted a Resolve, empowering you to import any Quantity of Rice from Carolina you should think proper. In Addition to that Resolve the Congress have come to the enclosed, authorizing you (agreeably to your own Plan) to import such Quantities of Flour and other Provisions from the Southern States, as you may judge necessary for the Support of the Army.[1]

The Delegates of Virginia will write immediately to the Governor and Council of that State, to contract for the Delivery of ten Thousand Barrels of Flour to your Order, for which Purpose you will please to send Vessels to take them in.[2] Your Draughts on me for Payment thereof, shall be duely honored.

I am, with Respect, Sir, your most obed., and very hble Sert.

John Hancock Presid

RC (Ct). In the hand of Jacob Rush and signed by Hancock.

[1] Congress passed the resolve authorizing the importation of rice on November 28 and the one concerning flour on December 26. *JCC,* 6:989, 1040. See also Elbridge Gerry to Joseph Trumbull, December 26, 1776.

[2] Congress had authorized the Virginia delegates to write such a letter on the previous day. *JCC,* 6:1041.

John Hancock to George Washington

Sir, Baltimore Decr 27th. 1776

The enclosed Resolves being of the utmost Importance, will naturally claim your Attention, without any particular Recommendation or Comment. They are ardently calculated to retrieve the Situation of our Affairs, and I trust will have the desired Effect.[1]

I have wrote to the Councils of Safety of Massachusetts Bay and Pennsylvania on the Subject of creating Magazines in their respective

States for both Arms and Ammunition.[2] The Commissions necessary
in Pursuance of the enclosed Resolves, shall be forwarded as soon
as possible. I have only Time to add, that I am with the most
perfect Esteem & Respect, Sir, your most obed. and very hble Sert.

John Hancock Prest.

RC (DLC). In the hand of Jacob Rush and signed by Hancock.

[1] For the resolutions of this date which significantly augmented Washington's
authority and were passed in response to the report of the "committee on the
state of the army," see JCC, 6:1043–46. Hancock explained the rationale behind
them more fully in his circular letter to the states, December 30, 1776, printed
below. See also Washington to Hancock, December 20, and Nathanael Greene to
Hancock, December 21, 1776, in Washington, Writings (Fitzpatrick), 6:400–409;
and Greene, Papers (Showman), 1:370–74.

[2] See Hancock to the Massachusetts Council, December 28, 1776.

Francis Lewis to the
New York Committee of Safety

Gentlemen,   Baltimore, 27th Decemr. 1776

Your favour of the 5th instant, per Lieut. Brit, I have received,
with your resolves relative to the frigate in Hudson's river, which
I this day laid before the marine committee, and meet their entire
approbation. They are of opinion that whatever vessels belonging
to the Continent, and are now in Hudson's river, should be also
secured in Esopus creek, or some other place of safety. The people
belonging to the brigantine and sloop may be disposed of at the
discretion of your Convention.[1]

Congress approves of your recommendation of Lieut. Victor Bicker,
Junr. for the marines, and as soon as the blank commisions are received from Philadelphia, one shall be filled up for him and forwarded to you.[2]

Your letter, directed to Captain Dennis, I thought it proper to
return you; his last place of residence was in Brunswick, which is
now in General Howe's possession. Perhaps you may hear of Captain
Dennis some where in your State. The rigging, &c. that belonged
to those vessels sunk into the North and East river, and now in
the possession of Captain Dennis, it is imagined may be of singular
service at Ticonderoga, of which General Schuyler should be informed. I am also directed to inform you that Congress much approves of the frigates being fitted out against the spring, and of your
directing a sufficient number of cannon to be cast at Salsbury, as
none for your purposes can be procured from these parts. I must
also beg that you would represent my present disagreeable situation
to the Honourable Convention, which is that of being the only

Delegate from the State of New-York attending Congress. My colleagues, Mr. Ph. Livingston and Colo. Floyd, departed for the northward upon the adjournment of Congress to this place, so that our State is now unrepresented in Congress, and of which the members highly complain; as there was never a more urgent necessity for its being full, than at this time, occasioned by several members being detached on committees, and as many as could be spared left Philadelphia to transact the necessary business there. I must beg leave to add, that from the late depreciation of Continental money, most necessaries of life are advanced here from three to five hundred per cent, to what they were at the commencement of our dispute. For instance, butter 4s. per lb.; loaf sugar 5s. and other necessaries in like proportion. I was asked at the rate of £300 per annum for a house, and now lodge in a paltry tavern with a bed scarcely fit to lie upon. At this rate I shall not be able long to subsist, and must soon think of removing to some cheaper part of the Continent, unless I am relieved by the Convention, for at present my expenses exceed my allowance.

I have the honour to be, Gentlemen, your very humble servant,
Fra. Lewis.

P.S. Congress has this day resolved to invest Genl. Washington with powers for six months to regulate the armies in such manner as he, with the advice of his general officers, shall think most conducive to promote the public good; of which I shall transmit to the Convention a copy in my next. The battalions are to be increased to 110. It is hoped you will raise one more, i.e. six.

I am to inform you, that when at Philadelphia there was, in the hands of Mr. Hayman Levy, purchased by him for the State of New-York, and packed up, sundry articles of clothing, to the amount of £11,000 and upwards, but at the time such was the hurry of the inhabitants to move their effects out of the city, that although I had obtained a press warrant from the Council of Safety for the purpose, the wagons were engaged by the citizens at the rates of 20s. per mile, and my warrant could not have the desired effect. I have since wrote from hence to both Mr. Robert Morris and Mr. Levy, to get them forwarded to Esopus,[3] but could wish your Commissary was sent to look after them, as I am convinced they must be wanted with you. In the then critical state of Philadelphia, Congress ordered them to be sent to General Washington, but I got that order rescinded.[4] The articles packed up in 32 casks, are as follows: White 4,061, check 1,939—6,000 shirts; 134 doz. milled hose; 1,109 pair leather breeches; 85 felt hats; 500 wooden canteens.

MS not found; reprinted from *Journals of N.Y. Prov. Cong.*, 1:763–64.

[1] The New York Convention's December 5 letter to Lewis and enclosed resolves are in *Am. Archives*, 5th ser. 3:355, 357. Both were in response to Lewis' letter to the convention of November 27, 1776.

[2] There is no mention in the journals of Lieutenant Bicker, who had been nominated for a lieutenancy in the marines by the committee of safety. *Am. Archives,* 5th ser. 3:355, 357.

[3] Lewis' letters to Hayman Levy and to Robert Morris have not been found.

[4] See *JCC,* 6:1001, 1012.

Robert Morris to John Hancock

Sir   Philada. Decr. 27th. 1776 11 oClock A.M.

Capt Peters informs me he has just seen a letter from Colo Cadwallader wrote late last night to the Council of Safety [1] wherein he says he has no acct from Genl Washington, but from private information that he can depend on, our Victory at Trenton has been compleat, the Killed, wounded & Prisoners are *very* considerable, that we have taken 16 pieces of their Cannon, a Wagon load of Hessian Arms with some Hessians were sent over the Ferry. Colo Cadwallader was to Cross over from Bristol this morning before day with his whole Force. Genl. Putnam is now sending him a reinforcement of 1500 men & the Gondolas under Command of Genl Mifflin who is returned from a Successfull excursion. We shall change the face of affairs & I hope soon to see you back here. I am respectfuly yours &c,   Robt Morris

P.S. Capt Peters will soon follow this but he must go via Lancaster.[2]

RC (DNA: PCC, item 137).

[1] Col. John Cadwalader's two December 26 letters, which the Pennsylvania Council of Safety enclosed in a letter of the 27th to President Hancock, are in PCC, item 69, fols. 303–8. Extracts are in *Pa. Archives,* 1st ser. 5:136–37.

[2] For the Board of War's order directing secretary Richard Peters "to repair to Baltimore as soon as possible," see Hancock to Robert Morris, December 23, 1776.

Robert Morris to Richard Henry Lee

Dear Sir   Philada. Decemr. 27th 1776

I am much obliged by the extract of a letter from London of the 21st Septr which you have been pleased to favour me with [1] and I fear there is but too much reason to suspect the generality of Scotchman as our most inveterate Enemies in the present Contest but I do not believe the misfortune of the two Ships at Hamburg to be oweing to any treachery.

The bills remitted to purchase the Goods at that place were many of them drawn by the Scotch Factors of Virginia & Maryland (for others coud not be got) drawn on their principals in London & Glasgow, and I suppose these principals have been at the pains to find out what channells the bills passed through & have thereby traced out the purposes for which they were remitted. I saw the

acct. of the Stoppage of these Vessells some time ago & was very uneasy at it knowing the Importance of the Cargoes they went for, but
still I have comforted myself with a firm dependence on the agent
I sent to manage the matter, who, tho a *Scotch Man* is a Man of
Strict honor, extreamly well versed in business & capable of extricat-
ing himself from difficulties so that I have at this moment a firm
reliance on receiving those Cargoes by some other Channell in the
Course of this Winter, and believe me if that Man deceives me I will
never trust another but I think it impossible. I am exerting myself
in your Service & will do every thing you wish in the business of
the Secret & Marine Committees. My Compts to your Brother & all
Friends as I am, Dr. sir, Your Obedt hble servt,

Robt Morris

P.S. Mr Jona Hudson writes me that he is desirous of serving the
Publick in such Capacity as he can be most useful. He is an active
dilligent Man in business and I believe a very honest one. I know
you like to employ such and if you serve him I believe you will
have satisfaction in doing it.

RC (ViU).
[1] For the "letter from London of the 21st Septr," see Richard Henry Lee to
Robert Morris, December 24, 1776.

Robert Morris to the Pennsylvania Council of Safety

Gentn   Philada. Decr. 27th 1776
Capt Cooke Commander of the Maryland Ship of War Defence
is the bearer of this Note. He came up with upwards 70 men to
assist in defence of this City. As the Gondolo's are going on Service
he offers to go in them as a reinforcement & if need be at the place
of Action he & his men will assist the artillery. I doubt not this
offer will be acceptable & if so the Council will give their officers
suitable directions. I have the honor to be Gentn, Your obed Sert.

Robt Morris

RC (DLC photostat).

Executive Committee to John Hancock

Sir   Philada. Decr. 28th. 1776
Your Committee at this place have opened their Office & given
publick Notice of their daily attendance to transact such Continental
business as may be proper & necessary in this place.[1] We wrote Genl
Washington of our appointment & proposed that he shoud forward

his dispatches to Congress through our hands unless when they might be of such a Nature as he wou'd not choose any persons shou'd see them before Congress. He approves this plan as it will ease his Correspondence with us & at the same time we shall receive information that will be necessary for our government in many affairs that will most probably come under our consideration.[2]

You have enclosed herewith the Generals Account of the Action at Trentown with a return of the Prisoners &c. Allow us to congratulate Congress on this Success, & to presage that if our good Fortune is well followed up our affairs will very speedily wear a pleasing Countenance. We take the liberty to enclose also an extract of a letter from Genl Cadwallader to Genl Putnam, by which it appears that our Enemies are Pannic-Struck. We hope our Troops will follow them up & not give them time to recover, & shall write in this Strain to Genl Washington with an assurance that every Man shall follow to his assistance that can be prevailed on to move from this State and we have not a doubt but their Spirits will now be up, and what they have before thought dangers will vanish before them like a Vision. You'l observe sir that Mr. Cadwallader is now a Brigadier General made so by our Council of Safety & you cannot conceive what general Satisfaction it gives. He is a Gentn of amiable private Character, fine Fortune, Numerous Connections, has a martial Spirit & has taken infinite pains to qualify himself for Command. He is beloved by his Troops & gains their confidence wherever he goes. Genl. Washington in a letter to Congress sometime past recommended their appointing this Gentn a Brigadier Genl. in the Continental service. His having recommended him for that purpose & our knowledge of his merits and a Conviction that it wou'd be vastly pleasing to all the associators of this State, prompts us to recommend to Congress to do it immediately. He now commands the Continental Colonels & they cannot complain that he is put over their heads. He is now leading on a valuable band of men in your service & the appointment will give Spirit & Vigour to their operations. The present Success will induce you to make other promotions & we hope this will not be neglected.

We are sorry to inform you that Capt Robisons information respecting his Prize was premature. She is not arrived nor have we heard further from below, altho the Fly has been sent down some days to reconnoitre. The Wasp is gone to Cruize outside the British Fleet, she retook a Schooner with Mollasses & Rum that had been taken by the Roebuck & has sent her into Egg Harbour.

We have the honor to remain, sir, Your obedt hble servts,

Robt Morris

Geo Walton

Geo Clymer

RC (DNA: PCC, item 137). Written by Morris and signed by Morris, Clymer, and Walton.

[1] The following notice, printed under the dateline "*Philadelphia*, Dec. 27, 1776," appeared in the *Pennsylvania Evening Post*, December 31, 1776. "The Honourable Congress having appointed a Committee of their body to transact such Continental business in this city as may be proper and necessary, the said Committee give this public notice, that they meet every day, and sit from ten to three o'clock, at their office in Front-street, where Messrs. Barclay and Mitchell lately dwelt, opposite to Messrs. Conyngham, Nesbit and Company. All persons charged with public letters for the Congress, Board of War, Marine, or other Committees, are desired to take notice hereof, as such letters will be opened or forwarded by the Committee as the case may require. ROBERT MORRIS, GEORGE CLYMER, GEORGE WALTON."

[2] Washington's December 27 letter endorsing Morris' suggestion that the general forward his letters to Congress through the Executive Committee unsealed is in Washington, *Writings* (Fitzpatrick), 6:441.

Executive Committee to George Washington

Dear Sir   Philada. Decemr. 28th. 1776

We have the pleasure to own receipt of your acceptable favour of yesterday by Colo. Bayler [1] & most sincerely do we rejoice in your Excellencys success at Trentown as we conceive it will have the most important publick consequences and because we think it will do justice in some degree to a Character we admire & which we have long wished to appear in the World with that Brilliancy that success always obtains & which the Members of Congress know you deserve. Permit us to Congratulate you on this success & to suppose it is only the beginning of more important advantages. You will excuse us for taking up so much of your time as will be necessary to read this letter which is not intended as an official letter of business but meerly to gratify our present feelings & to offer you such thoughts as occur on the present state of affairs without intending you the trouble of any reply as we know you have too much writing necessarily. It appears to us that your attack on Trentown was totally unexpected, the Surprize compleat, & the Success beyond expectation. Could Generals Ewing & Cadwallader have executed their parts no doubt but more good consequences must have followed instantly. However we apprehend it is not yet too late, as it appears by Genl Cadwalladers letter to Genl Putnam that the Enemy have abandoned all their Posts from Bordentown downward & fled with precipitation towards South Amboy. Its probable they are Seized with a panic whilst your Forces are flushed with success and such precious moments shou'd not be lost. We apprehend if your Victory is immediately pursued & no time allowed the Enemy to recover from their surprize you will have little difficulty in clearing the Jerseys of them. It is probable that those Troops whose times of enlistment are now expiring will follow their successfull General altho they wou'd have left him whilst acting a defensive part. Be that as it may, we have the pleasure to know that considerable bodies of associators are marching from every part of the State to your assistance. These have been put in Motion when our affairs were at the Worst but you have given a spring to the tardy Spirits & we think their Numbers will be greatly augmented. In short it is our opinion that you may from this time form a reasonable dependance on daily additions to your Force. Common Fame will double the Numbers of those that actually do turn out & if such reports reach our Enemies it will probably have great effect on their fears and assist wonderfully in causing them to evacuate their lately acquired territory in New Jersey. We have recd. a letter from Colo Fleming of the 9th Virginia Regiment which is on its march from the Eastern Shoar & we have ordered them a supply of money at the Head of Elk and the necessary Cloathing to be got in readiness against they come here.[2] We also expect the Pensylvania Regulars that have been lately raised in the back Counties of this State & we understand Militia & other reinforcements are coming from Maryland & Virginia. You may depend we will give every assistance in our power to forward these reinforcements to you & that we shall assist & advise far as we are able in every Publick department here. We have considered that part of your Excellencys letter of the 25th Inst.[3] to Mr Morris that relates to the Seamen in the two New England Battalions whose times expire with this Year, and shoud any of them obstinately persist in being discharged from your Service on New Years day We think it adviseable to prevail on them to come down here & assist in getting the Frigates out. When they come we will make the best bargain we can with them & if nothing else will do We will engage to send them home in one or two of those Ships. If they come on these terms we think Capt Read & his officers shou'd come with them that we may if possible get away the Washington as well as the Delaware. Congress are very anxious to have these ships out & will be pleased if this measure is pursued. We cannot avoid mentioning that we dont think it adviseable to exchange your Hessian Prisoners at this time. We think their Capture affords a favourable opportunity of making them acquainted with the Situation & Circumstances of many of their Country men who came here without a farthing of property & have by care & industry acquired plentifull Fortunes which they have enjoyed in perfect Peace & tranquility until these Invaders have thought proper to disturb & destroy those possessions. It will be proper to seperate the Officers from the Men & to Canton the latter in the back Counties which may be done by the Council of Safety untill the Congress are Consulted thereon. Your Excellency will excuse us for troubling you with our Sentiments on these matters & we think it necessary to appologize for doing so as its probable the whole has occurred to yourself. We remain with perfect regard & Esteem, Your Excellencys most Obedt. & most hble servants,   Robt Morris

Geo Clymer

Geo Walton

RC (DLC). Written by Morris and signed by Morris, Clymer, and Walton.
[1] See Washington, *Writings* (Fitzpatrick), 6:441.
[2] See Executive Committee to Thomas Fleming, December 27, 1776.
[3] See Washington, *Writings* (Fitzpatrick), 6:436–38.

John Hancock to the Massachusetts Council

Gentlemen,   Baltimore Decr. 28th. 1776. 5 O'Clock A.M.
    The Necessity of having proper Magazines established in Places of Security has induced the Congress to order three to be erected, one in Virginia, one in Pennsylvania, and one in Brookfield in Massachusetts Bay with an Elaboratory adjacent to each.[1] The foregoing Resolve respecting the Magazine & Elaboratory to be fixed at Brookfield, I am directed to transmit to you, and to request that you will be pleased to take such Measures as you judge necessary for the immediate Execution of it. I beg Leave to refer you to the Resolve, and am with every Sentiment of Esteem, Gentlemen, your most obed sert.[2]   J H Presid.

LB (DNA: PCC, item 12A). Hancock apparently also sent a similar letter to the Pennsylvania Council of Safety. See Hancock to Washington, December 27, 1776.
[1] See *JCC,* 6:1033, 1039, 1044.
[2] Hancock also wrote a letter this date to Thomas Cushing. This letter has not been found, but some indication of its content can be found in the statement in Cushing's January 16, 1777, reply "that I was oblidged to you for kindly offering to me the Care & management of Building the Two Ships, one for 74 Guns & the other for 36 Guns, which the Congress had determined to build in this State & that I chearfully Accepted the offer." Morgan, *Naval Documents,* 7:967. For Congress' November 20 resolve on the building of these two ships in Massachusetts, see *JCC,* 6:970.

William Hooper to Robert Morris

Baltimore December 28th 1776
    Mr Irwin this afternoon handed me your kind favour of the 23d [1] which was highly flattering to my feelings as it convinces me that I hold a place in your friendly remembrance, and gives me an opportunity to use my aid in behalf of the unfortunate. If my conduct in congress has, in your opinion, been featured with the lines of humanity, I hope it has never degenerated into unmanly milkiness and lost sight of a due respect to the safety of my Country. Under a proper restraint I never shall have occasion to regret it however

a contracted few may condemn me. Men see things thro different mediums, and to some of these to be unfortunate is to be criminal. It is enough for me my dear sir, that I have the approbation of yourself and a few others whom I sincerely love and esteem. It has very often given me an importance in my own eyes, that my feelings have been congenial with your's, and that we have together sympathized in the sufferings of the victims to this unnatural contest. Thank God, We can say and with truth too, that we have never sported with the Calamities of our fellow beings nor exercised power merely to shew that we possessed it.

I shall pay particular attention to the subject of Mr Irwins memorial and as I cannot perceive that there are grounds for a plausible pretext to refuse the prayer of it I confide that his application to congress will be attended with success. I have made known the purpose of his errand to Middleton, Harrison and Wilson and others "who can melt at human woe." The Delegates from Chas. town from whom opposition was to be expected if from any quarter, think him too undesigning, too well disposed, or too unfortunate to counteract his wishes—so at present it seems.[2]

I am well aware of the burden of publick business with which our removal hither has incumbered you. When in Philadelphia where we took a small share of it to ourselves I have been amazed how you waded thro' it, & found leisure for your own private concerns and the enjoyment of your friends. Congress seem unanimously sensible of the Obligations which they owe you, & you may boast of being the only man whom they all agree to *speak* & I really believe *think* well of.

I earnestly wish however that we could have you here for a little while. The transactions of this and a few preceeding days have in my opinion strongly proved the necessity of it. We have moved very rapidly in business and while some compliment themselves upon increasing Industry and application, I think I can find the cause else where & that the suddenness of decision may be truly attributed to ignorance of the Subject. We have been holding forth new lines to France, by offering what we have not to give & provided they will conquer the whole of Newfoundland & secure the fishing, that we will most bountifully & most graciously give them one half of it for their trouble. We have found out that the Duke of Tuscany is a potentate of much consequence, while some of us are such Ignoramuses as to think him very insignificant in the naval and military line and in this respect not worthy attention, & that in commercial matters his interest will attach him to us without much sollicitation. But I anticipate an amusement which you have to come, the Picture of our follies will be the more pleasing from being viewed at full length.[3]

We have given Genl Washington large and ample powers, fully

equal to the object if America means to contend and support him.[4] Thus the Business of War will for six months to come move in its proper channell & the Congress be no longer exercised about matters of which it is supremely ignorant.

A Plan is in agitation to appoint executive powers out of doors, and resolve the business of Treasury—Board of War—and of Commerce into the hands of persons not members of congress. A Committee is appointed for that purpose & you are a member of it.[5] You will be much wanted. I wish if your Attendance is impossible that you would reduce a few thoughts to paper upon the subject of a Chamber of Commerce which is the Hobby Horse & for which I fancy we are indebted to the Abilities of Mr P——e.[6]

I earnestly wish that the Congress could return to Philadelphia without hazarding the Ignominy of a second flight or the charge of Caprice. This dirty, boggy hole beggars all description. We are obliged except when the Weather paves the streets to go to Congress on Horseback, the way so miry that Carriages almost stall on the sides of them. When the Devil proffered our Saviour the Kingdoms of the World, he surely placed his thumb on this delectable spot & reserved it to himself for his own peculiar chosen seat and inheritance. As to the Inhabitants the congress can boast no acquaintance with them but what arises from their daily exorbitant claims upon our pockets.

Pray fall upon some expedient to give us true Intelligence, prevail upon some Friend that has leisure to write us what is authentick. What we pick up in this City comes thro' such mediums that it must be vitiated in its progress. One who believes everything he hears, & means to profit in his own importance by the recital of what is wonderful early alarmed us with an Account of Dickinsons Apostatization. I wish such would consider that when they thus brandish the fire brand of Censure it will scorch very deeply their *intimate connection*. Dont puzzle yourself for an explanation of this. I do not choose to commit names to paper, I will be explicit when I see you. I hope that the Report of A. Allen being with the Enemy will not prove true.[7] I have hitherto entertained such an exalted opinion of his virtues, that it will require almost more than human testimony to induce me to believe him an Apostate & a Villain.

The Congress meets tomorrow altho' it is Sunday. Why, Heaven knows, I cannot conceive unless it is to give us importance in the eyes of the very respectable Inhabitants of this place. But I have trespassed too long on your precious Moments. I meant a letter but have wrote a Book. Under every change of Circumstances, wherever my fortune may be cast & whatever that lot may be, my earnest wishes will ever be for the happiness of you and yours.

I am, with truth and sincerity, Dear Sir, Your most obedt humble ser't,   Will Hooper

[*P.S.*] Carter Braxton has lost his house & Furniture by fire.

RC (MdBJ-G).
¹ Not found.
² Thomas Irving, the royal receiver general of South Carolina who had been captured during Esek Hopkins' assault on New Providence in March 1776, received permission from Congress on January 2, 1777, to return to South Carolina "under his present parole" and place himself "under the direction of Governor Rutledge, or the executive power of that state." *JCC,* 7:9; and *Am. Archives,* 4th ser. 5:823, 867, 5th ser. 3:619, 791, 878, 899.
³ For Congress' continuing efforts to lay down the outlines of a foreign policy, see *JCC,* 6:1039, 1049–50, 1054–58.
⁴ See *JCC,* 6:1043–46.
⁵ For the appointment of this committee on December 26, see *JCC,* 6:1041–42. Support for the creation of executive boards consisting of persons not members of Congress had also been voiced a few days earlier by Samuel Chase—who had not yet returned to Congress since their departure from Philadelphia—writing to General Sullivan from Annapolis. See Samuel Chase to John Sullivan, December 18, 1776, note 2.
For further information on the results of the committee's deliberations, see Samuel Adams to John Adams, January 9, 1777, note 4.
⁶ Robert Treat Paine.
⁷ The report of John Dickinson's defection to the British was false, but the news of Andrew Allen's was true. *Am. Archives,* 5th ser. 3:1230, 1377, 1434. See also Benjamin Rush to Richard Henry Lee, December 20, 1776, note 3.

James Wilson to Robert Morris

Dear Sir   Baltimore 28th Decr. 1776
The Committee of Congress at Philadelphia are directed by a late Resolution of Congress to contract for erecting a Magazine at Carlisle.¹ I shall be at that Place in a short Time; and will give every Assistance in my Power to those whom you employ.
You are much wanted in Congress; tho' I know you are of essential Service at Philadelphia. I am, Dear Sir, Yours sincerely,
James Wilson

RC (DNA: PCC, item 78).
¹ For this resolution of December 27, see *JCC,* 6:1044.

Board of War to Robert Morris

Sir,   Board of War Decr. 29th. 1776
Be so kind as to order the muskets imported for the Continent in the Sloop   and the Andria Doria down to the Head of Elk to the Care of Mr Rudolph, this is directed by order of Congress, to arm three Virga Regiments that are order'd up without their arms.¹
You have Inclosed a List of Necessaries wanted to fit out the Virga. Horse, you'l please to order Towers to have them immediately pro-

vided all the other military Stores that came in the Vessels above, you'l plan to send to any place where you shall think they will be safe. We gave Mease orders to send Cloaths & Blankets to Elk for Colo Flemings Regt. I have wrote to him again on the subject [2] but for fear he should neglect it, wish you would Speak to him.

Congress have given up most of their Power to the General for the Term of six Months,[3] if this don't save your City nothing we can do will. They have also agreed to Establish Boards of War, Admiralty, Treasury & a Chamber of Commerce to be Composed of members out of Congress.[4] I had you Named to assist in forming the Plan & wish it was possible you could be here particularly to form the Latter. I can't indeed see the use of such a Chamber as it can have the Direction of nothing but the Congress Trade and that I think has been as well managed as it could be. Make my Compliments to my Friends. I wish most Heartily to be with them to Day at the Hill instead of attending Congress to hear what I am quite tired with. I forgot to tell you Poor Braxtons fine House is Burnt to the Ground with all his Liquors and a Quantity of Furniture. I am, your affect servt,   Benja Harrison

RC (MH-H).
  [1] See JCC, 6:1044.
  [2] Not found.
  [3] See JCC, 6:1045–46.
  [4] In reality Congress had done nothing more than appoint a committee to consider these innovations. JCC, 6:1041–42.

Charles Carroll, Barrister to the Maryland Council of Safety

Dear Sir   Mount Clare Decr 29t 1776
  By Direction of the Congress I Send you the Inclosed Resolves.[1] The Last Letters Bring us a Peice of Intelligence that it May be Material for you to Know.[2] One Mr Bevan a Person that May be Depended on Who was Taken by Capt Hammond Informed Mr Morriss that Hammond told him they were now Determin'd to Put a Total Stop to Our Trade and for that Purpose 6 frigates were to be stationed off Georgia & the Carolinas, 6 off the Capes of Virginia, and Six off Delaware. Their Signals and their Stations were fixed so as to form a Compleat Line along the Coast & that they were Determin'd to Keep their Stations During the Whole Winter. This I fancy it will be Difficult for them to do. However I thought it necessary yr. Board should Know their Plan. I am with Most Sincere Respects to you all, Dear Sir, Yr Obedt Hble Sert,
                                                            Chas Carroll

[*P.S.*] I have not as yet seen here any of our Delegates. Questions of the Greatest Magnitude every Day Agitated & Resolves Enter'd into & this State without a Representation or Voice.

RC (MdAA). Printed under the date December 21, 1776, in *Md. Archives*, 12:547.
   [1] Apparently the resolves of December 27 pertaining to the new levies and of December 28 requesting that blankets be supplied to the sick troops in Baltimore. See *JCC*, 6:1043, 1047.
   [2] See Robert Morris to John Hancock, December 23, 1776; and *JCC*, 6:1042.

Committee of Secret Correspondence to the Maryland Council of Safety

Sir,   Baltre. Decr. 29th 1776
   It is the Wish of the Committee of Secret Correspondence to avoid as much as possible doing Injury to the State of Maryland, for which Reason they return you many Thanks for your obliging Compliance with their Request as to the Brig but seing the great prejudice their taking of her would be to the State most willingly give her up, provided the Council will favor them with a small armed Schooner now in this port, which they hope will answer their purpose.[1] The price will be left to your honorable Board which it is expected will be what she cost the State. Your immediate Answer will much oblige your most humble Servant

FC (DNA: PCC, item 37).
   [1] For further information on efforts of the Committee of Secret Correspondence to secure a ship from the Maryland Council of Safety, see Benjamin Harrison to the Maryland Council of Safety, December 25, 1776.

Robert Morris to Benjamin Harrison

Dear Sir   Philada. Decr. 29th. 1776
   I recd yesterday yours of the 25th by Express with the Sundry enclosures with which I shall do the needfull, but I think you shou'd send Copies by some of the outward bound Vessells from Virginia & Maryland. There is a new Ship of Mr Archd. Buchanans near ready to Sail for France from Baltimore & I fancy your son must have either the Aurora, Gratz Brig or the Snow about Sailing, and I dont yet hear of any British Cruizers at the Capes of Virginia. If any do appear pray inform me of it. I must send you an order to receive from the Secret Committee abt. £2700 & send it down to Ben by the first opportunity. I have recd the Money here from Mr Hare & used it for the Secret Committee who must repay it and

Ben is to lay it out in Tobacco Concerning which I wrote him two posts ago.[1] I shall write additions to the letter to our Commissioners suited to our present Circumstances & send you Copies in due time. I detained this express untill this morning hoping to give you some news from Genl Cadwallader but no Accounts are yet come in. I wrote to Genl Washington & said every thing I cou'd say with decency to encourage a pursuit of our Enemies with his whole Force. Our Militia are daily coming in and I really hope to see him strong enough to drive these invaders out of New Jersey & then Congress may come back here. I believe it wou'd have an excellent effect were they to return immediately. Our Friends wou'd be inspirited & our external & internal Foes wou'd form favourable judgements of our supports & Strength from it. A few days more will determine whether it will be proper or not and soon as I can I will write a Publick letter on that Subject. Your Invitation to join you is very Civil, but you know I have always been satisfyed with Philadelphia & the Hills, and I have throughout this alarm been determined not to quit untill fairly drove off. At the same time I have been constantly prepared, my things Packed up, Horses & Carriage ready at any moment & constant means of intelligence had they approached.

I beg my Compts to all Friends & tell Ben Levy I expect he will be a very great Politician now the Great Council have removed to his quarters. We had a Merry Christmas at Smiths in spite of the times. The absence of my Family sits grievously hard on me as I never parted with them before, but my time is too much employed to dwell much upon any Subject and I am now pleasing myself with the thoughts of bringing them back. I dine at the Hills to day & have done so every Sunday. Thus you see I continue my old practice of mixing business & pleasure and ever found them usefull to each other. I am with great affection your Friend & Servant,

Robt Morris

RC (DNA: PCC, item 137).
[1] Morris' letter to Benjamin Harrison, Jr., has not been found.

Robert Morris to Richard Henry Lee

Dear Sir   Philada. Decr. 29. 1776

I have now to acknowledge the Rect. of your second letter of the 24th Inst. continuing the quotation from your London letter of the 21st Septr. for which I am much obliged.[1] The papers of the Secret Committee are sent away with my [own] & are now under care of one of my Clerks at Christiana Bridge but I very well remember that the propriety & necessity of sorting the Tobacco's

Shipped to Europe so as to suit the different Markets, struck me so forcibly that in one of the Committees letters to my Brother he was desired to employ proper persons to Inspect every Cargo that arrives & sort it in the manner I have mentioned. This you may [well?] remember if you think of it a little & [. . .] you'l see we have neither discovered ignorance nor inattention in this point. I shou'd have been glad you had mentioned the Gentns. Name that you wish to have joined with My Brother in this business. I shall readily Consent to every measure that tends to promote the Publick Good but it is necessary you will agree that I know who is to be joined to my Brother in a business of this kind, and if the Man meets my approbation there will be no difficulty in agreeing on the Measure. I wish the Secret Committee to buy the Ships you mention & hope they may be had reasonably. If the purchase is made there is Tobacco already bought to load them & I dont think you shou'd undertake any fresh purchases at this time because great Numbers of our People that had Continental Money on hand have gone down to buy Tobacco on the prospect of this City falling into the hands of the Enemy and I am fearfull they will raise prices. If we set up New purchases at this time it will assist in raising prices and if we remain quiet during the present alarm, we shall have an opportunity by & by of rebuying all the Tobacco now bought up on Speculation as none of the purchasers can export it & they will either grow tired or fearfull of keeping it long on hand.

I have borrowed a good deal of Money here for the Service of the Secret Committee & must draw some orders on them to repay it, therefore you'l please to be prepared for these drafts and I shall Account for the Amount.

You cannot conceive how I am vexed & mortifyed to find after the deal of pains & trouble I have taken that the Randolph Frigate is still at the Piers & Ice making in the River but the Officers of that Ship show great reluctance to go away without being compleatly manned & that is not possible. She might have been at Sea before now had they exerted themselves for that purpose but they have had constantly in view to wait for more Men. This has its foundation in a Noble principle which has hindered me from complaining to the Marine Committee, altho I have scolded the officers like a Gutter-Whore for their dilatoriness; they say they wish to Fight & not to run. I tell them they must run untill they can fight.

There are a Number of Soldiers in the two New England Regiments now with Genl Washington whose time expire with this year & will not reinlist. They are chiefly Fishermen or Seafaring Peoples and I have wrote the General to prevail on all that will not Continue with him to come down here to Man our Frigates & they shall carry them home. I think [this] a good plan as we shall by that me[ans get] some of the Frigates Manned for [Sea] & before they carry the others home they may pick up Seamen from Prizes &c. I have little time but remain, Dr sir, Your Obedt hble servt.

Robt Morris

P.S. I have just seen Mr. David Franks. He says Doctr Lee & Arthur Lee Esqr. had quitted London.[2]

RC (ViU).
[1] Not found.
[2] Morris apparently forgot which of Lee's brothers was the doctor; he should have written "Doctor Lee & William Lee."

Committee of Secret Correspondence to the Commissioners at Paris

Honble. Gentlemen   Baltimore 30 Decemr. 1776

You will be pleased to receive herewith copies of our letter of the 21st instant, and of it's inclosures, which we recommend to your attention. Since that letter was written, General Washington, having been reinforced by the Troops lately commanded by General Lee & by some Corps of Militia, crossed the Delaware with 2500 Men, and attacked a body of the enemy, posted at Trenton, with the success that you will see related in the inclosed hand bill.[1] We hope this blow will be followed by others that may leave the enemy not so much to boast of, as they some days ago expected, and we had reason to apprehend.

Upon mature deliberation of all circumstances, Congress deem the Speedy declaration of France and European Assistance so indispensibly necessary to secure the Independence of these States, that they have authorized you to make such tenders to France & Spain, as, they hope, will prevent any longer delay of an event that is judged so essential to the well being of North America.[2] Your Wisdom, we know, will direct you to make such use of these powers as will procure the thing desired on terms as much short of the concessions now offered as possible; but no advantages of this kind are proposed at the risk of a delay that may prove dangerous to the end in view. It must be very obvious to the Court of France that if Great Britain should succeed in her design of subjugating these States, their Inhabitants, now well trained to arms, might be compelled to become Instruments for making conquest of the French Possessions in the West Indies; which would be a sad contrast to that security & commercial benefit that would result to France from the Independence of North America.

By some accident, in removing the papers from Philadelphia to this place, the Secretary of Congress has mislaid the additional instructions formerly given you, by which you were impowered to negotiate with other Courts besides France. We think it necessary to mention this to you, lest the paper should have got into wrong hands, and because we wish to have a copy sent us by the first good opportunity.

We observe that Mr. Deane sent his dispatches for this Committee open to Mr. Bingham, but, though we have a good opinion of that Gentleman, yet we think him rather too young to be made acquainted with the business passing between you and us, and therefore wish this may not be done in cases of much importance.

The next opportunity will bring you the determination of Congress concerning the persons that are to be sent to the Courts of Vienna, Prussia, Spain, and the Grand Duke of Tuscany.[3] In the the meantime, it is hoped that, through the medium of the Ambassadors from those Courts to that of France, you may be so fortunate as to procure their friendly mediation for the purposes proposed by Congress. Our Andrew Doria of 14 Guns has taken a King's Sloop of War of 12 Guns after a smart engagement. In our last we say the Enemy made near 3000 Prisoners at Fort Washington but the number is fixed at 2634. The West Indiamen, taken by our Cruisers, amount to 250 Sail.

The Scarcity of Ships here is so great, that we shall find much difficulty in making the extensive remittances to France, that we ought, in due season, and therefore it will, in our opinion, be an object of great importance to obtain the consent of the Farmers General to send to Virginia & Maryland for any quantity of Tobacco they may chuse, or to the State of North Carolina for any quantity of Naval Stores, which may be wanted for publick use, or to supply the demands of private Merchants. The terms, both as to quantity & price, you will endeavour to learn and let it be made known to us with all possible expedition, that you may receive an answer thereon.

The Captain of the Armed Vessel that carries these dispatches has orders to deliver them himself, to you in Paris, and his vessel will expect his return in a different Port from the one he arrives at. He will take your directions about his return, and receive your letters, but the anxiety prevailing here to know your success renders it proper that he should return with all possible dispatch.[4]

Wishing you health, success, and many happy years we remain, Honble. Gentlemen, Your most obedt. & very huml Servts.

           Benja Harrison   Jno Witherspoon

           Richard Henry Lee   Will Hooper

P.S. The number of prisoners lately taken in the Jersies amounts to about 1100 and Gen. Washington is advancing upon the enemy who are retreating thro the Jersies towards New York.[5]

RC (PHC). In a clerical hand, signed by Harrison, Hooper, Lee, and Witherspoon, with postscript by Lee. Duplicate RCs are at PPAmP, PHi, and NjR. The letter at PHi was also signed by Robert Morris but does not contain the postscript.

[1] This reference is to a broadside on the battle at Trenton which is not listed in Evans, *Am. Bibliography,* and apparently does not survive. See, however, William Ellery to Nicholas Cooke, December 31, 1776, note 4.

[2] The commissioners' new instructions, which were adopted by Congress this day, are in *JCC,* 6:1054–58.

[3] These appointments were not completed until mid–1777.

[4] See Committee of Secret Correspondence to Larkin Hammond, January 2, 1777.

[5] This postscript was apparently added on the 31st, the day General Washington's December 27 letter containing this news was read in Congress. *JCC,* 6:1058.

Executive Committee to John Hancock

Sir   Philada. Decr. 30th. 1776

Mr. Thos. Smith the loan officer returned here this day. It seems he has Certificates for no more than Sixty thousand Dollars, and we have procured more than that Sum for him already wherefore we pray that an express may be immediately dispatched with Certificates for three or five hundred thousand Dollars as we shall use our utmost endeavours to get money into his office and doubt not but pretty good Success will attend our endeavours. We have given Mr Commissary Carpenter Wharton our order on Mr Mease for forty thousand dollars part of the Sum you sent him which arrived on Saturday night. Mr. Wharton produced the Generals orders for establishing Magazines of Provisions at Lancaster & York Town and we referred him to Congress for the Sums necessary for that purpose. We mean only to Supply him with what may be wanted to lay in stores between this & Lancaster, at this place & for what may be required in New Jersey, where we hope our Army will finally take up their Winter quarters. That State will suffer amazingly by both Armys. It is not what they Consume that does the mischief, but the destruction of Provisions first by one Side & then by the other will cause a Famine there. New Jersey has always supplyed very large quantities of Pork, but the Want of Salt, the Consumption & destruction of that article by both Armys will prevent it this year & we all know that very large supplys of it will be wanted next Summer for our Army. The lower Counties (say Delaware State) Maryland, Virginia & North Carolina have hitherto been exempt from the Ravages of War. Some of them have had tollerable good supplys of Salt and no doubt they will Cure as much Meat as they can. We think Congress shou'd immediately employ some prudent industrious person in each of these Governments to buy or Contract immediately for as much Salted provision as possible & Collect it into secure & proper places ready for use when wanted. Shoud this be neglected depend upon it you will repent next Summer and if it is not managed with Secrecy & prudence you will not only pay dear for what you get but poor individuals that cannot afford it will also suffer.

We think similar measures shou'd be taken in the Eastern states. The Commissary will buy all he can here & wish he possessed all the prudence and circumspection that we think requisite for executing that department as it ought to be.

We are told that the American Prisoners suffer amazingly in New York for want of some proper person to attend to them. Congress have allowed Mr. Franks to supply the British Prisoners here, and We think it wou'd be well done to send into New York an agent for our Prisoners whose business shou'd be to see them well supplyed with Cloathing and Provisions and to attend them constantly to prevent their enlisting in the Enemies service, but on the Contrary to engage all such whose times expire to reinlist with us. We are told General Howe wou'd admit such an agent (but he must hear nothing about inlistments we suppose) and if a Sensible Spirited American can be found whose mind will support him through accumulated insults to perform his duty with Fidelity We think a good Salary wou'd be well bestowed on him, but if the support of our Prisoners and proper regulations in the Medical departments are not attended to you cannot expect a permanent formidable Army & which above all things is now most wanted to save America.

The enclosed from the General came to hand this day but we keep it for the Post as the Contents do not require your immediate inspection by express. Since then Mr. Morris has received another letter from his Excellency requesting One hundred & fifty pounds in hard money for particular purposes in the publick service & it will be sent up this night. That letter is dated at Trentown this day. He then says "some of the Troops are yet on the other side of the River only waiting for Provisions." [1]

We have urged & will continue to press Mr. Commissary to push forward the supplys with all possible dilligence. Genl. Cadwallader had dispatched 100 Rifle Men, 100 Light Infantry & 100 Smart Active Lads to pursue our retreating Enemies in hopes of overtaking & keeping up their panic. Doctor Hodge says they were within 5 miles of the Enemies Rear when he passed them (not having seen the Doctr ourselves we do not know that time) & another person since come in reports that the general was within Eleven Miles with his main body, his Troops are fresh, full of spirit eager for an Action & march briskly. The Hessians are incumbered with a deal of Plunder & baggage which obliges them to move slow. We hope for another glorious Action & shall be happy to transmit you the account of it very soon. No doubt Sir Wm Howe Knight of the Bath & Genl. &c will be very angry at these doings in the Jerseys, and probably in his Wrath he will come over armed with vengeance & threaten destruc-

Robert Morris

tion, but we expect he must dance to a different Tune upon this March than he did on his late passage to Trenton for we have the pleasure to assure you with certainty, that the Face of things is totally changed, our People are full of Spirits & turn out freely so that Genl. Washington will find himself daily gathering fresh Strength and we shall not be surprized if New Jersey turns out in like manner.

We are now at the 31st Decr. 12 oClock & have just recd. your Honors letter of the 27th enclosing Sundry Important Resolves of Congress Copies whereof we shall dispatch to General Washington in half an hour. Every part that relates to this Committee shall be carefully attended to and no time shall be lost in carrying into execution such things as Congress have ordered.

We had yesterday the pleasure to see the Hessian Prisoners paraded in Front Street. They formed a line of two Deep up & down Front Street from Market to Walnut Street, and most people seemed very angry they shou'd ever think of running away from such a Set of Vagabonds. We have advised that both the officers & men shou'd be well treated & kept from Conversing with disafected People as much as possible. One of our Light Horse brought down ten prisoners this Morning that were taken near Prince Town & appear to have been a reconitering party, and a Captn Smith writes from Crosswix that nine Hessian officers were taken & one killed in that quarter, supposed to be part of those that fled from Trentown. No farther Acct yet from Genl. Cadwallader. Troops are Constantly coming in & marching for the Jerseys so that every thing may reasonably be expected in our favour. Six of the Enemies Ships are still in Delaware Bay so stationed that Capt Biddle cannot pass them, the Fly & Musquito employed in Watching them & the Wasp Cruizing outside of them. We intend to send a person to stay at Cape May to give us regular advice of their Motions which we are much in Want of. We are much hurried but ever remain sir, Your Obedt & devoted hble servts.

Robt Morris

Geo Clymer

Geo Walton

RC (DNA: PCC, item 137). Written by Morris and signed by Morris, Clymer, and Walton.

[1] For Washington's letters to Morris of December 29 and 30 mentioned here, see Washington, *Writings* (Fitzpatrick), 6:451, 457.

John Hancock to Philip Schuyler

Sir,   Baltimore Decr. 30th. 1776.

You will percieve, from the whole Tenor of the enclosed Resolves, which I have the Honour of transmitting, that Congress have paid every Attention to the Situation of the Northern Army, which the Circumstances of it required. On the 25th inst. they passed sundry Resolves urging the States of New Hampshire, Massachusetts Bay and Connecticut to send forward to Ticonderoga with the utmost Expedition a Body of four thousand five Hundred Troops. These Resolves I dispatched immediately accompanied with Letters wherein I informed them of the very critical Situation of that Fortress, as the Troops who at present garrison it, were resolved not to stay after the 31t of Decembr. the Day on which their Time expired.[1] Every Consideration that had a Tendency to induce them to comply immediately with the Requisition of Congress, I endeavoured to hold up to them in the most striking View. To the same Effect also I wrote them before Congress removed from Philada in Consequence of your representing that you wished Congress would stimulate them to a Compliance with your Letter on that Subject. These Measures, I trust will prove successful, and be attended with the Preservation of Ticonderoga during the Winter.

In Pursuance of the enclosed Resolve,[2] I have wrote to Govr. Trumbull desiring him to have twenty Eighteen Pounders cast with all possible Expedition and transported to Ticonderoga,[3] for which you will please to provide Carriages. I have likewise wrote to the Commissary General to procure Provisions for five thousand Men for eight Months to be sent to Fort Ann, and an equal Quantity to be lodged in Albany, and to be occasionally removed as Circumstances may make it necessary. He is also directed to send a sufficient Quantity of Salt to cure the Provisions, & by all Means to supply the Northern Army with Vegetables and Vinegar this Winter.[4]

The Congress have resolved that the present Mode of supplying that Army by the Commissary General under the Direction of the Commander in Chief, is more advantageous than that by a Contractor could possibly be.

As a General Hospital is to be erected on Mount Independence, the Congress are desirous that a Garden should be enclosed in the Neighbourhood of the same, that the Army may be the better supplied with Vegetables the ensuing Winter. You will therefore be pleased to appoint some suitable Person as an Overseer to see this Resolve carefully complied with.

The many Disorders that have crept into the Hospitals render it absolutely necessary that the strictest Enquiry should be made into the Conduct of the Directors, their officers, & Dependents, & that the offenders should be punished.

You will please to order the Commanding Officer of every Regiment to pay the greatest Attention to the Health of the Men under his Command, and to report any Misconduct or Neglect of the Surgeons to the General & likewise to the Congress.

I shall transmit to the State of Massachusetts Bay the enclosed

Resolve, by which they are requested to procure such a Quantity of Oakum and other Articles as you shall think proper to write for.

In Consequence of your Favour of the 10th inst which was laid before Congress, the Committee appointed to consider the same, are directed to send some Persons to Mr. Livingston, Govr. Trumbull, and to the State of Massachusetts Bay, to procure the Cannon & Ordnance Stores you mentioned in your Letter of that Date, as being immediately necessary for the Northern Department.[5]

The Congress have the firmest Reliance on your best Exertions to carry the enclosed Resolves into that Effect, and depend much on your Assistance in accomplishing their Views in that Quarter. Should we succeed in our Attempts to prevent the Incursions of the Enemy into the back Settlements of the New England & New York States, by a vigorous Defence of Ticonderoga and the adjacent Posts, the happiest Consequences to America must result from it—and the Glory of compleating this great Work, I trust will be reserved for you. As your Inclinations at all Times prompts you to undertake whatever has a Prospect of advancing the Good of your Country, so your Wisdom and Abilities will certainly enable you to execute the Task.

Genl. Gates arrived in this Town the Day before yesterday in a very poor State of Health, but is since much recovered.

The enclosed Copy of Resolves vesting Genl. Washington with very large and important Powers, the Congress were induced to pass in Hopes of retrieving thereby the present unfavourable Situation of our Affairs.[6] To them I beg Leave to refer you, and have the Honour to be with great Esteem and Respect, Sir, your most obed. hble. Sert.   J. H. Presid.

P.S. I most sincerely congratulate you on the Success of Genl. Washington. The enclosed printed Acct. will give you all the Particulars we are possessed of.[7] This may give a different Face to our Affairs and be productive of very happy Consequences. I have not Time to add, only to beg your Attention to the several Resolves enclosed. You will observe, Congress have laid an Embargo on the Exportation of Salted Provisions, and some other Necessaries.[8] Should any Thing material occur, you may depend, I will give you the earliest Notice of it. Wishing you the Compliments of the Season, I am your very hb Ser.   J.H. Presid.

[*P.S.*] I never have heard any thing of my Band of Musick, since I wrote you.

LB (DNA: PCC, item 12A).

[1] See Hancock to Certain States, December 25, 1776.

[2] All the resolves mentioned in the next six paragraphs were passed on November 28 and 29 and December 28 in response to the recommendations of the committee to which George Clymer's and Richard Stockton's report on the state of the northern army and accompanying documents had been referred. See *JCC*, 6:988–91, 1047–49; and Hancock to Schuyler, September 27, 1776, note 4.

[3] This letter has not been found.
[4] See Hancock to Joseph Trumbull, December 27, 1776.
[5] See *JCC*, 6:1050, 1052–53.
[6] See *JCC*, 6:1043–46.
[7] See Committee of Secret Correspondence to the Commissioners at Paris, this date, note 1.
[8] See *JCC*, 6:1054.

John Hancock to the States

Gentlemen,   (Circular)   Baltimore Decr. 30th. 1776.

Ever attentive to the Security of Civil Liberty, Congress would not have consented to the vesting such Powers in the Military Department as those which the enclosed Resolves convey to the Continental Commander in Chief, if the Situation of public Affairs did not require at this Crisis a Decision and Vigour which Distance and Numbers deny to Assemblies far removed from each other, and from the immediate Seat of War.[1]

The Strength and Progress of the Enemy joined to Prospects of considerable Reinforcement, have rendered it not only necessary that the American Force should be augmented beyond what Congress had heretofore designed, but that it should be brought into the Field with all possible Expedition. These Considerations induce Congress to request in the most earnest Manner, that the fullest Influence of your State may be exerted to aid such Levies as the General shall direct in Consequence of the Powers now given him, and that your Quota of Battalions formerly fixt may be completed with all the Dispatch that an ardent Desire to secure the public Happiness can Dictate. I have the Honour to be, with every Sentiment of Esteem, Gentlemen, your most obed. hble Servant,

                                                     J H Presidt.

[*P.S.*] The Resolve prohibiting the Exportation of sundry Articles, and the other Resolves enclosed, I beg Leave to refer to your particular Attention. I congratulate you on the Success of Genl. Washington in the Jerseys. The Particulars you will find in the Papers enclosed.[2]

LB (DNA: PCC, item 12A). Endorsed: "Note. The foregoing Letter I sent to all the States with the Resolves referred to, with this Variation—that the States of Virginia, Maryland, Delaware, Pennsylvania, New Jersey, and North Carolina are desired to order their New Levies to join Genl. Washington; the other States are addressed as in the foregoing Letter.

"To the Convention of New York the following was added—The enclosed Packett I beg the Favour you will please to order to be forwarded by a fresh Express to General Schuyler immediately. And I further request you will give my Express the best Route to Boston, and pray direct him to use all Dispatch on his Journey."

This letter undoubtedly was drafted by Richard Henry Lee, who with Samuel Adams and James Wilson had been appointed on December 28 "to prepare a circular letter to the several United States, explaining the reasons which induced Congress to enlarge the powers of General Washington, and requesting them to co-operate with him, and give him all the aid in their power." *JCC*, 6:1047. Lee's draft, dated December 29, is in the Lee Papers, PPAmP.

[1] Hancock sent the states the resolves passed by Congress on December 27 in response to the report of the "committee on the state of the army." *JCC*, 6:1043–46.

[2] This postscript was probably added on December 31. The resolve on exports was adopted on December 30 (*JCC*, 6:1054), but "the particulars . . . in the papers enclosed" is a reference to a broadside of the 31st. See William Ellery to Nicholas Cooke, December 31, 1776, note 4.

Robert Morris to the Continental Agents

Sir   Decemr. 30th 1776

The Bearer hereof Nicholas Eveleigh Esqr. is a Gentleman of fortune and established character in South Carolina and I beg leave to introduce him to your acquaintance, and to recommend him to your friendship. He has some commercial views in his journey to New England and this introduction may possibly be of mutual advantage which will please me exceedingly.

Our Loan office is just opened, and by way of setting a good example and ın order to make a beginning, I have given a considerable Sum of money and have persuaded Mr Eveleigh to carry with him continental Loan office notes to a large amount instead of the money because its lighter and safer carriage and because I think it will answer All his purposes equally if not better than the money. At any rate Eveleigh must not be disappointed. If he meets with any dificulty in getting money in Exchange for these Notes, when or where he wants it I must beg you will assist him and even if needfull that you will supply him out of the publick money you have in hand. This is but justice to the Credit of the Continent and it is essential to Mr Eveleigh, therefore I am sure you will not suffer any disapointment to take place. I am Sir your very hble Sert.

Robert Morris

LB (DNA: PCC, item 133). Addressed: "Copy of the foregoing letter to Danl. Tillinghast, Rhode Island, to Nath. Shaw, New London, to John Bradford, Boston, to John Langdon, Portsmouth—Continental Agents. Similar letters to this were given to Mr. Rose of So. Carolina."

Robert Morris to George Washington

Sir   Philada. Decr. 30th. 1776

I have just recd your favour of this day [1] & sent to Genl. Putnam to detain the Express untill I collect the hard Money You want which you may depend shall be sent in one specie or other with this letter & a list thereof shall be enclosed herein.[2]

I had long since parted with very Considerable Sums of hard money to Congress, therefore must Collect from others & as matters now stand it is no easy matter. I mean to borrow Silver & promise payment in Gold & will then Collect the Gold in the best manner I can. Whilst on this Subject let me inform you that there is upwards of 20,000 Dollars in Silver at Tyconderoga. They have no particular use for it & I think you might as well send a party to bring it away & lodge it in a safe place Convenient for any purposes for which it may hereafter be wanted.

I gave Mr Commissary Wharton an order for 40 thousand Dollars this morning & pressed him to attend most dilligently to your supplys. I will send for him again [to] know what is done & add Springs to his Movements if I can. I wish he was more silent, prudent &c but I fancy he is active. Whatever I can do shall be done for the good of the Service. I ever am, Dr sir, Your Excellencys Obedt hble servant,   Robt Morris

P.S. Hearing that you are in Want of a Q[uarte]r Cask of Wine, I have procured a good one which Mr Commissary Wharton will send up.[3]

RC (DLC).
   [1] See Washington, *Writings* (Fitzpatrick), 6:457.
   [2] At the foot of the LB of this letter the following note appears. "Accot. of hard Money sent: 410 Milled Dollars, 2 Eng. Crowns, ½ French Do., 10½ Eng. Shillgs." PCC, item 133, fol. 14. See also Morris to Washington, August 16, 1777.
   [3] Morris also wrote the following brief note to Washington this day. "I have recd your favour of Yesterday & will duely forward your dispatches to Congress & the other letters by Post. I am desired to put the enclosed letters in the way of being sent into New York and make no doubt Your Excellency will readily forward them by the first Flag after they reach Your hands. I am impatiently waiting for further News from Genl. Cadwallader & with constant wishes for Success remain sir Your Obedt Servt." Washington Papers, DLC.

Benjamin Rush to Richard Henry Lee

My dear sir,   Crossicks[1] Decem. 30. 1776
   There is no Soil so dear to a Soldier as that which is marked with the footsteps of a flying enemy. Every thing looks well. Our army increases daily, and our troops are impatient to avenge the injuries done to the state of New Jersey. The tories fly with the precipitation peculiar to guilty fear to Genl. Howe. A detachment from our body yesterday took four of them and kill'd one. Two of the former were officers in Howes new militia establishment.

We suffer much from the want of intelligence which can only procured by money that will pass in both camps. Howe owes the superiority & regularity of his intelligence above ours not so much to the voluntary information of the tories as to the influence of his gold. Pray send two or three thousand pounds in hard money im-

mediately to Gen Washington. It will do you more service than 20
new regiments. Let not this matter be debated, & posponed in the
usual way for two or three weeks. The salvation of America under
God depends upon its being done in an *instant*.

I beg leave for a moment to call off your Attention from the Affairs of the public to inform you that I have heard from good
Authority that my much hond father in law who is now a prisoner
with Gen Howe suffers many indignities & hardships from the enemy
from which not only his rank, but his being a man ought to exempt
him. I wish you would propose to Congress to pass a resolution
in his favor similar to that they have passed in favor of Gen. Lee.[2]
They owe it to their own honor as well as to a member of their
body. I did not want this intelligence to rouse my resentment against
the enemy. But it has encreased it. Every particle of my blood is
electrified with revenge—and if justice cannot be done to him in
any other way, I declare I will in defiance of the Authority of the
congress, & the power of the army drive the *first rascally tory I
meet with a hundred miles bare footed thro the first deep Snow
that falls in our country.*

Two small brigades of New England troops have consented to
serve a month after the time of their enlistment expires. There is
reason to believe all the New England troops in their predicament
will follow their example.

We have just heard that the enemy are preparing to retreat from
Princeton.

Advice. Gen Washington must be invested with dictatorial power
for a few months or we are undone. The vis inertia of the congress
has almost ruined this country. Yours,   B. Rush [3]

RC (PPAmP).
 [1] Crosswicks, N.J., a village southeast of Trenton where Gen. John Cadwalader's
troops were quartered from December 29 through January 1.
 [2] For Congress' response to this request, see the resolution of January 3, 1777,
concerning the treatment of Richard Stockton. *JCC*, 7:12–13. Stockton was the
first delegate to Congress to have the misfortune of falling into British hands,
and he suffered uncustomarily harsh treatment. Before obtaining his parole, he
was apparently forced to sign an oath of allegiance which later cast a shadow on
his reputation. For additional information on this subject, see John Witherspoon
to David Witherspoon, March 17, 1777, note 1.
 [3] The following day Rush also wrote a letter to his wife describing the recent
depredations of the Hessians. *Parke-Bernet Galleries Catalog*, no. 2661 (March 6,
1968), item 76.

George Walton to Richard Henry Lee

Dear Sir,   Philadelphia, Monday Evening, 30th Decr. 1776
I take it for granted that the Committee will write to Congress
in the morning, touching several matters of public concern. In the

mean time, as I am no. sleepy, permit me to obtrude two or three observations on your patience which I have made since I have had the pleasure of seeing you. Our soldiers, which have been taken prisoners by the enemy, are closely imprisoned in New-York; a miserable pittance to subsist upon; plundered of the better part of a most scanty apparel; and suffered to remain in that condition at this most inclement season. It is immaterial whether this treatment proceeds from an opinion that it is proper for rebels, or whether it is to starve the unfortunate into the humour of enlisting with the enemies of their country. Surely Congress is bound, indispensibly bound, to comfort and protect them as far as it is in its power. If we turn our eyes to those who have fallen into our hands, we shall find them free from almost the forms of restraint; fed on the fat of the land, in full possession of their all and quartered in our best barracks. This is lenity, gentleness, and humanity: but our enemies call it timidity. Congress threatens with the voice of thunder; but executes its purposes with the mildness of a Lamb. But could we once begin to act with spirit, and persevere with firmness, we should much sooner become more formidable to our enemies than by any other means. It is very far from my intention to insinuate that the unfortunate in our power should be made to suffer more than their situation necessarily creates; all I mean to suggest is, that Congress has taken no steps sufficient to remedy an inhuman pernicious evil. Suppose, for the present, a Commissary of prisoners was appointed and sent to New York, with power to purchase Cloathing & necessaries, & to give provisions in payment. To this Power Howe would not object. Besides the obligations of duty and humanity, and the frightful example to our new army, which prompt the necessity of something of this kind, it might be worked into an essential benefit. It is possible that such Commissary might prevail on these unfortunate people to re-enlist upon the prospect of being well cloathed. In this case the Continent would profit by their service as soon as an Exchange could take place. If we exchange them with out trying this expedient, we give an army [. . . .] [1] The enemy's force is now divided, and probably cannot be easily collected until the spring; but if you furnish them with two thousand effective men [it would?] at this time, be the ruin of our [. . .] [2] game is now in our hands; [. . .] [2] injured people obliges us to play it. If I am not mistaken in my conjectures, their conduct respecting General Lee will amount to a justification of any thing that it may be necessary to do on our part.

I am Dear Sir, you most Obedient Servant, Geo Walton

P.S. 31st Decr. The resolutions of Congress have just come to hand.[3] The Committee are pleased with them. Our great & good General will I have no doubt remedy these evils.

RC (ViU).
¹ Portions of seven lines missing.
² Approximately three words missing.
³ Undoubtedly the resolves of December 27, which among other things empowered Washington to appoint a commissary of prisoners. *JCC,* 6:1043–46.

James Wilson to Arthur St. Clair

My dear Sir   Baltimore Decr 30th 1776.
   With peculiar Pleasure I congratulate you on the Victory at Trenton.
   I hope the Tide is now turning, and will run high in our Favour.
   I have wrote to Genl Washington recommending Col. Irvine to a Regiment, and Mr. Robert Smith (a young Gentleman of great Merit, who studied law with me) to a Troop of Horse. You will oblige me much by adding your Influence to the Recommendation, and by letting me know the Result of it as soon as possible. I am, in Haste Dear Sir, yours sincerly,   James Wilson

Tr (DLC). Endorsed by Edmund C. Burnett: "Copied from original in the possession of Stan V. Henkels."

Committee of Congress to Walter Stewart

Sir,   Baltimore Decr 31 1776
   Congress having authorizd and directed us their Committee to appoint some suitable Person to apply to Mr Livingston Owner of a Furnace in the State of New York, and to Governor Trumbull who has the Direction of the Furnace in the State of Connecticut, also to the Council of the State of Massachusetts Bay, to procure such Cannon and Ordnance Stores as General Schuyler has represented to be immediately necessary for the Use of the Army in the Northern Department, we have thought of no One in whom we can more chearfully confide for the Performance of this important Business than yourself. And therefore we request you to undertake it, as Major General Gates has assurd us, that it is not inconsistent with the general Service or the Duty of that Station which you hold under his immediate Command.¹
   You have a List of the Ordnance and Stores that are wanted; and you will be pleasd to make your first Application to Mr Livingston for such of the Cannon and Stores as he can furnish.² You will then apply to Governor Trumbull to be furnishd by him with the Remainder; to be sent to General Schuyler as early as possible this

Winter. If you cannot be supplyd with the whole of the Stores in New York or Connecticutt, we desire you to apply to the Council of the Massachusetts Bay to make up the Compliment; to whom we have written as well as to Governor Trumbull requesting them to afford you all the Advice and Assistance you shall need in the Prosecution of this Business.

We doubt not but you will provide these Necessaries with all possible Dispatch and at reasonable Rates and see that they are in a Way of being forwarded to General Schuyler, to whom you will give Notice, and to us, of the Success you may meet with in your several Applications.[3]

We would mention for your Information, that Congress has contracted for Cannon to be cast in this State at the Rate of Thirty six Pounds ten Shillings per Ton. And the highest Price that has been given in Pennsylvania is Forty Pounds. We expect however that you will purchase them as the best Terms you can. The Proof of the Cannon must be according to the Practice in Woolwich.

We wish you a prosperous Journey and are very cordially, your Freinds & humble Servants,

Samuel Adams   Wm. Whipple

Richard Henry Lee   Benja Harrison

Ths. Heyward Junr.

RC (NHi). Written by Adams and signed by Adams, Harrison, Heyward, Lee, and Whipple.

[1] On December 29 Congress directed this committee to send a person to New York, Connecticut, and Massachusetts "to procure such cannon and ordnance stores" as were requested by Gen. Philip Schuyler in his December 10 letter to President Hancock. *JCC*, 6:1048–50; *Am. Archives*, 5th ser. 3:1160–61. Maj. Walter Stewart (ca. 1756–96), who was selected by the committee, was serving as aide-de-camp to Gen. Horatio Gates. In 1777 he was promoted to a regimental command, where he served until 1783. *Cyclopaedia of American Biography*.

[2] The committee wrote to Robert Livingston this day, soliciting his aid in procuring the supplies "on just and equitable terms, and timely enough to be transported to General Schuyler before the Winter." The RC of this letter is in the Livingston-Redmond Papers, NHpR; Adams' draft of it is in the Adams Papers, NN.

The committee also sent nearly identical letters this day to Gov. Jonathan Trumbull of Connecticut and to the Massachusetts Council. See *Am. Archives*, 5th ser. 3:1505–6; and the Adams Papers, NN.

[3] For some of Col. Stewart's subsequent difficulties in fulfilling this mission, see Committee of Congress to Jonathan Trumbull, Sr., February 12, 1777.

William Ellery to Nicholas Cooke

Sir,   Baltimore Decr. 31st. 1776.

I received your Letter of the 30th of November and laid it before

Congress; and took particular Notice of the very weak Condition
of our State.[1] Congress are sensible of its Situation, but as they have
by a late Resolve, which the President will by this Express transmit
to you, with a circular Letter in which the Reasons for their Doings are contained, delegated to and invested Genl. Washington
with the whole military Power for a limited Time, Applicaton will
properly be made to him in every Instance which respects the military Department. With Regard to the other Parts of your Letter,
which were ordered to be laid before Congress, as they required no
particular Observations none were made upon them either by Congress or Me.[2] I was extremely glad to receive so much particular
Information into the affairs of our State, and hope you will continue
to make Me acquainted with such Doings of the General Assembly,
from Time to Time, as may be thought proper to be communicated.
I should be glad to know whether We have any Powder Mills in
the State, whether they are going, and supplied with Salt Petre to
keep them in Motion. At present indeed, if any should have been
erected in the State of Rhode Island, they may be stopped by the
Enemy having entered our State; but I hope so large a Force will
soon be, if it should not be already collected as to give Security to
the Town of Providence and prevent them from making any Incursions into our State, confine them to Rhode Island, if not expell
them from thence, in which Cases all mechanical Business and
Manufactures may proceed. In my last of the 24th of this Instant,
notwithstanding the gloomy Appearance of our public Affairs, I
still expressed Hopes that Genl. Washington might be reinforced
by the Division under General Sullivan and the Militia from the
State of Pennsylvania, and thus reinforced be enabled to and drive
the Enemy from the Jersey. Genl. Sullivan with his Division and
some of the Troops from Ticonderoga, whose Time of Inlistment
had expired, under General Gates have joined Genl. Washington,
and also some of the Pennsylvania Militia. This and the glorious
Success of an Enterprize well planned by our General, and as well
executed on the Morning of the 26th have elevated my Hopes, and
give good Reason to expect that our cruel Foes may be drove from
Jersey. The President I suppose will send you an Account of that
Enterprize; but least he should omit it, and as We have been for
some Time unsuccessful, and this noble Exploit may exhilerate the
Spirits of my Countrymen under their present Situations, I can't
forbear inclosing you a Hand-Bill of the particulars, with some Additions on the Reverse made from Genl. Washingtons Letter of the
27th.[3] I heartily congratulate you on this noble, this unexpected
Event, an Event which although by no means decisive, yet by the
spirit it will give to the Troops in actual Service, to the Militia in
the neighbouring States to our Army, and to all the United States, is
of the greatest Importance. I hope and don't doubt but that it will

have a fine Effect upon the Troops which may be collected to support our State, and urge them on to some such Enterprize if they should have an Opportunity to execute it. Among other Things that fell into our Hands by the Victory at Trenton were four Standards, One of which is now in the Room where the Congress is held, and directly before Me. It is an Hessian Silken Standard. (The Battalions which were surprized and subdued were the Regiments of Landspatch, Kniphausen and Rohl). I would describe it if I were acquainted wtih Heraldry, and it were of Importance enough to engage your Attention. In the Center of a Green Field of about four by five Feet, is a decorated gilded Circle which incloses a Lion Rampant with a Dagger in his right Paw, and this Motto in the upper Part of it "Nescit Pericula." The Crest is a Crown with a Globe and Cross upon it. In the Corners are gilded decorated Circles with Crowns & Globes & Crosses on their Tops, and in their middle F L in Cyphers. A Broad Blaze extends from the Corners to the Peice in the Center, and three small Blazes are placed in the Field, One in the middle of the Side next the Staff, one in the opposite Side and One in the midst of the Lower Side or Bottom. How well the Motto suits the Conduct of the Troops where it was once waved I shall leave, and you Sir, with this sincere Wish that the Troops in our State may acquire like Trophies, and that this successful happy Enterprize may prove an Omen of future decisive Victory over our barbarous Foes. I continue to be with the greatest Esteem and Consideration, Your Honor's most obedient, humble Servant,

William Ellery

P.S. Inclosed you have a News-Paper which contains the first Number of Crisis, an animated useful Performance, and which ought in my Opinion to be reprinted every where in America.

The Express not going out so soon as was expected gives me an Opportunity to send you a printed Copy of Genl. Washingtons Letter and the Return of the Prisoners &c.[4] What I have called a Standard may be only One of the Colours mentioned in the Return. There is a Report that a Body of our Troops under Genl. Heath had taken Possession of Hakinsack and Fort Lee, and captured 130 Prisoners, a Number of Tories &c &c. I wish it may prove true. There indeed appears to be good Ground to credit it. I was just now told by a Gentleman who had convers'd with the Aid de Camp who bro't Genl. Washington's Letter, that his Excellency's Horse was wounded under him; and that We had taken more Prisoners than were mentioned in the Return and more Arms.[5]

W E

RC (R–Ar).

[1] This letter is in William R. Staples, *Rhode Island in the Continental Congress, 1765–1790* (Providence: Providence Press Co., 1870), pp. 101–4. There is no mention of this letter in the journals, but on December 26 Congress did read a

December 8 letter from Cooke announcing the British capture of Newport. See PCC, item 64, fol. 366; *Am. Archives*, 5th ser. 3:1131; and *JCC*, 6:1040.

[2] In his November 30 letter to Ellery, Governor Cooke revealed that the Rhode Island Assembly had "passed a resolve empowering me to grant commissions or letters of marque and reprisal to private vessels of war . . . until commissions be procured from Congress." Eventually this led to the passage of a resolve by Congress on April 5, 1777, validating the acts performed under the privateering commissions issued by Cooke up until that time but urging him in the future "not to grant any more commissions, to recal such as he may have issued, and to deliver out continental commissions in their stead." See Staples, *Rhode Island in the Continental Congress*, p. 104; and *JCC*, 7:226.

[3] See Committee of Secret Correspondence to the Commissioners at Paris, December 30, 1776, note 1.

[4] A broadside incorporating Washington's December 27 letter to Hancock about the American victory at Trenton as well as an enclosed "list of the prisoners, artillery, and other stores" was printed in Baltimore by Mary Katharine Goddard on December 31. Evans, *Am. Bibliography*, no. 15152. It is obviously to be distinguished from the "Hand-Bill" mentioned earlier in this letter with which note 3 above is concerned.

[5] This news was also transmitted this day by Richard Henry Lee to John Page. Lee noted that General Washington's letter contained a more exact account of the battle than had previously circulated and added, "Col. Baylor, who brought in this letter from the General says another party of Hessians was brought in just before he came away making the whole number of prisoners between 1000 & 1100." *Parke-Bernet Galleries Catalog*, no. 2569 (May 16, 1967), item 29.

Executive Committee to Thomas Nelson

Sir   December 31st 1776

You will find herein an account of Mr. Robert Jewell, keeper of the Continental State Prison in this City, ballance due him Two Hundred & Fifty two pounds 6s. 4 1/2d., also his account for the Salary of himself and Assistants £229.10. We thought it best these Accounts Should go through the Usual Forms, and you'l be good enough to lay them before the Treasury Board, who will either pass them as they Stand, or with Such alterations as they may judge proper. Mr. Jewell is an honest worthy man, indefatiguable in a dilligent execution of his duty. We also enclose you an Account of John Biddle for supporting Prisoners at Reading for Settlement whereof the Council of Safety referred him to us, and as we have no rule to go by, he agreed to wait your returns on this head. When these Accounts are passed if sent back to us we will pay the Parties agreeable to such directions as you may give. In the mean time we have advanced Mr. Jewell One thousand dollars in part of his demand & remain, Sir, Your Obedt. hble Servts.[1]

LB (DNA: PCC, item 133).

[1] The Board of Treasury reported accounts due Robert Jewell and John Biddle on January 8, 1777. See *JCC*, 7:22–23.

Executive Committee to George Washington

Sir   Philada. Decembr. 31st. 1776
We have the honor to enclose herein Sundry resolves of Congress just received from Baltimore by express.[1] We have barely taken time to read them over and finding them so important we wou'd not delay the express one moment. We find by these resolves your Excellencys hands will be Strengthened with very ample Powers & a new reformation of the army seems to have its origin therein. Happy it is for this Country that the General of their Forces can safely be entrusted with the most unlimited Power & neither personal security, liberty or Property be in the least degree endangered thereby. We shall loose no time in executing the matters assigned us by these resolves & are most truly Your Excellencys obt Servts,

> Robt Morris
>
> Geo Clymer
>
> Geo Walton.

RC (DLC). Written by Morris and signed by Morris, Clymer, and Walton.
[1] See Hancock to Washington, December 27, 1776, note 1.

William Hooper to Robert Morris

My dear Sir   Baltimore Decr. 31. 1776
This will be handed to you by Capt Allon from North Carolina. You will recollect the very favourable mention General Lee made of this Gentleman for an appointment in our Continental sea service. He has for sometime past been an officer in one of our North Carolina Reg'ts and from his spirited behaviour on Sullivants Island recommended himself to the notice of the General. I have been long acquainted with him & know him to be a Gentleman of strict honour & principle & as such beg leave to introduce him to your notice.

Hewes no doubt in his letter to you mentions a second piracy committed upon his property at Sea.[1] I shall remonstrate in the firmest tone to Congress against this procedure & if they will not bring the offender to Justice I have no business here. Pray write such a letter to me upon the Subject as I may make use of in Congress to assist our much injured friend. Your most Obedt Hb Svt,

> Wm Hooper

RC (PHi).
[1] In November the brigantine *Joseph*, jointly owned by North Carolina delegate Joseph Hewes and his business partner, Robert Smith, had been illegally taken by the Massachusetts privateer *Eagle*, making this the second such vessel in three

months to be thus captured by the *Eagle,* the first having been the *Fanny,* which was seized in September 1776 and subsequently released. For a fuller discussion of the first incident, see Hewes to William Tokeley, May 18, 1776, note; and for the second, Hooper to Morris, January 1, 1777, note 1. See also Secret Committee Minutes of Proceedings, October 27, 1776.

Thomas Nelson to Horatio Gates

Sir   Baltimore Decr 31st 1776

Being one of a committee appointed by Congress to prepare a plan for establishing a Board of War & Ordnance,[1] & not having a thorough knowledge of the Duties of these Boards, I have taken the Liberty to request the favor of you, when your health will permit, to furnish me with such a plan as you shall think best adapted to answer the designs of Congress. My not having the pleasure of a personal acquaintance with you, will, I hope, be a sufficient appology for my addressing you by Letter. I am Sir, Your Obedt hle Servt,

Thos Nelson jr.

RC (NHi).

[1] Undoubtedly the committee appointed December 26 "to prepare a plan for the better conducting the executive business of Congress, by boards composed of persons, not members of Congress." *JCC,* 6:1041–42.

Gates had arrived in Baltimore on December 28, "in a very poor State of Health." See John Hancock to Philip Schuyler, December 30, 1776. For an account of the general's activities during this period, which included renewing contacts with his political supporters in Congress who were sympathetic toward his aspirations for an independent command, see Paul D. Nelson, *General Horatio Gates* (Baton Rouge: Louisiana State University Press, 1976), pp. 75–80.

James Smith to Eleanor Smith

My dear Wife   Baltimore 31st Decembr. 1776.

On Christmas day I wrote you a few lines & also to Col. Hartley [1] & sent them by Young Martin Jehelberger, by the way of Hanover, & hope they came to hand safe. There is no Member of Congress here but Mr. Wilson & myself from Pensylva. I met with a kind Welcome from Congress, & every body here are extremely kind & obliging. Mr. Spear, Smith, Calhoon, Mrs. Ralf & Mrs. Neal & many others are like to worry me with kindness. This partly forced me out of my gloomy situation, & the agreable News from Genl Washington has given new life & Spirits to every body here. I have enclosed a hand Bill [2] with the Particulars of that affair which when you have Read, & Pegsy & Betsy & George & Jim have read it send it to Col. Hartly, or Donalson. I want Nothing but some more Cloaths & a private lodging, however my present lodging is tolerable, every body is Surprized I did not bring Mrs. Smith here. I have engaged Jas Graybill to go up & bring my Portmanteau down with what more Cloaths & linen you think proper, if you Cou'd send 2 Plain Shirts & a Night Shirt, & my Red Jacket & Uniform or blue Coat. Jas Grabill says he Can't go 'till to Morrow. I hear one of Genl. Washington's Aid de Camps is arrived here last night with a Hessian Standard. This place is much more Sociable than Philada. I have sent up the lock & key of the Portmanteau. I have no more time to write & remain, your loving & affectionate Husband,   Jas. Smith

[P.S.] My love & a buss to all the little folks.

RC (MeHi).
    ¹ Not found.
    ² See William Ellery to Nicholas Cooke, December 31, 1776, note 4.

William Whipple to Josiah Bartlett

My Dear Sir   Baltimore 31st Decr. 1776
    Your favor of the 25 Ultio came to hand Yesterday. I rejoice that you are recovering your health. The clouds have thicken'd exceedingly this way since you left Philada. but they now begin to disperse. The inclos'd will inform you of a successful Enterprise at Trenton & if our Troops follow their blow as is their intention I am in no doubt the Enemy will be obliged to leave Jersey, which will end the Campaign Gloriously on our part. A number of Light horse without their riders was taken at Trenton, not mention'd in the Genls. Letter & a considerable number of Prisoners Brot in since the inclos'd return.¹ There was about 2500 cross'd the River with Genl. Washington. One division was commanded by Sullivan, the other by Green. They were compos'd of those troops that came from the Northward, some with Lee & others with Gates. This event will have a very good effect. It puts new life into the Pensilvanians & will add greatly to our strength from Jersey. That People who have been treated with such Brutality by the British troops will be inspir'd with revenge so that the advantages the Enemy have gain'd in that Country will eventually operate against them. Thus the wise disposer of all things directs Human affairs.
    The Andw Doria is arriv'd at Philaa with a very valuable Cargo. On her passage from the West Indies she fell in with a British sloop of war which after an obstinate ingagement struck to the American Flagg, the Prize is not arriv'd.
    By a circular letter from the President You'll see that the Genl. is vested with almost Dictatorial Powers.² This measure was thot

absolutely necessary for the salvation of America. There is also measures taken (which I hope will be effectual) to prevent the abuses suffer'd by the Soldiers last campaign. I am in no doubt that the grevience so justly Complain'd off in every department will be redress'd so far as is possible, & the Causes of them remov'd.

Col. Poor is recommended by the Genl. for a Brigar. As there will soon be a considerable addition to the list of Genl. Officers, its probable that Gentn will be promoted.[3] I heartily wish some method could be adopted to bring Genl. Folsom into the Field, but how this can be effected I don't know. I hope proper measures are taken to compleat the new Levies. For Heavens sake & for the sake of everything thats valuable on Earth don't rest 'till this business is done. The Soldiers may be assur'd that the Causes of their Complaints will be remov'd. It is of the last importance that the Garrison at Ticonderoga shod immediately be reinforc'd. If the propos'd Army (which is to be increas'd to 110 Battalions) shod be compleated I am not in the least doubt that the Enemies of America will be completely vanquish'd next Campaign. The Tyrant will undoubtedly Summon Earth & Hell to his assistance to carry his Infernal plans into Execution. He has made another application to the Court of Russia but there is just reason to believe he has been unsuccessful. Every artifice has used to make the Court of France believe that an accomodation would take place, but Congress have Intructed their Commissioners to assure that and the other European Courts that they are determin'd to support the Independence of the American States. Affairs in France ware a very favorable aspect.[4]

Genl. Gates arriv'd here a few days ago very sick but is recovering. Business goes on briskly; more has been done in one week here then was done in two months in Philaa. Knowing Your discretion I write freely. Present my very Respectful Regards to Col. Weere, Dr Thompson, the Genl &c &c &c. A perfect restoration of Health, & that every Happiness may be Yours is the sincere wish of Your Affecte Friend & Hume St,   WW

Jany 2d. Missing the opportunity this was design'd by, I have the Pleasure to congratulate you on the arrival of the two Brigs Lexington & Friendship at this place. The former was taken as she was going into Delaware by the Peace Frigate of 32 Guns who took out all her officers & put on board 7 or 8 men but the weather being so bad they could not change the crews the Honest Tarrs took possession of her and Brot her safe to this place. These vessels have both very valuable Cargos on board.[5]

RC (NNPM).
[1] For this enclosure, see William Ellery to Nicholas Cooke, December 31, 1776, note 4.
[2] See John Hancock to the States, December 30, 1776.

[3] Enoch Poor was promoted to brigadier general on February 21, 1777. *JCC,* 7:141.

[4] See Committee of Secret Correspondence to the Commissioners at Paris, December 30, 1776.

[5] See John Hancock to Robert Morris, January 2, and Secret Committee to Robert Morris, January 4, 1777.

INDEX

In this index descriptive subentries are arranged chronologically and in ascending order of the initial page reference. They may be preceded, however, by the subentry "identified" and by document subentries arranged alphabetically—diary entries, letters, notes, resolutions, and speeches. An ornament (☆) separates the subentry "identified" and document subentries from descriptive subentries. Inclusive page references are supplied for descriptive subentries; for a document, only the page on which it begins is given. Eighteenth-century printed works are indexed both by author and by short title. Other printed works are indexed when they have been cited to document a substantive point discussed in the notes, but not when cited merely as the location of a document mentioned. Delegates who attended Congress during the period covered by this volume appear in **boldface type.**

Abbey, Kathryn, "Efforts of Spain," 367

Abely, Capt., 641, 642

Accommodation; *see* Reconciliation

Accounts: delegate, 188, 233, 345, 449, 465; state, 188–89, 285, 451, 521; secret committee, 206, 251-52, 413, 503–4, 528; treasury, 283; Georgia agent's, 387; prison, 712

Adams, Mr., 200

Adams, Abigail Smith (Mrs. John): letters to, 17, 29, 39, 58, 85, 86, 100, 107, 113, 158, 176, 211, 220, 237, 269, 302, 311, 318, 333; mentioned, 13, 41, 307

Adams, Andrew, 507, 508

Adams, Charles, 58, 85

Adams, Elizabeth Wells (Mrs. Samuel): letters to, 481, 509, 551, 590, 596, 616, 669; mentioned, 107

Adams, John: letters from, 3, 11, 12, 17, 18, 22, 27, 29, 39, 40, 42, 53, 54, 58, 60, 62, 69, 82, 85, 86, 90, 100, 101, 102, 107, 113, 121, 122, 158, 159, 176, 200, 211, 220, 237, 240, 260, 269, 270, 271, 286, 302, 306, 311, 318, 333; letters to, 51, 75; ☆ elected to Congress, xviii; attends Congress, xviii; proposes rotating Massachusetts delegates to Congress, 3; on unicameral legislatures, 3–4; requests military information, 4, 12–13, 19, 27–28, 62, 84; criticizes New Jersey elections, 11; opposes Negro militia battalion, 11; on New England's military service, 11, 240–41, 306; requests replacement as delegate, 12, 19, 211; requests horses, 13, 43, 85; on achieving popularity, 17; criticizes John Hancock and Robert Treat Paine, 18; favors military bounties, 23; on military duty, 23, 54–55, 61, 241–43; committee on spies, 26–27; on promoting Massachusetts officers, 28–29, 53, 60–61; praises Gen. Mifflin, 28–29; visits Charles Willson Peale, 39–40; describes Francis

584, 617, 620, 680–81, 692, 714; orders New York City kept undamaged, 97, 130, 279; medical committee, 103, 547; committee to meet with Lord Howe, 114–16, 119–29, 134–35, 137–44, 154–55, 157–63, 168, 171–75, 180–81, 183, 186–87, 292, 295–96, 302, 462–63, 633; sets state quotas for Continental Army, 128–29, 164, 173, 175, 181–82, 187–89, 191–92, 215, 228–31, 234, 250, 323, 681; settles northern department commissary dispute, 144–46, 155–56, 179; committee for Indian affairs, 170, 231; committee on schooner *Thistle*, 180–81; voting under articles of confederation described, 183; orders audit of southern department accounts, 188–89; establishes packet to North Carolina, 194; adopts articles of war, 221, 229–31, 237, 240, 256; committee on Gen. Schulyer, 227, 259–60, 314; committee on state of army, 231, 244–45, 253–54, 261, 294, 308, 319, 332–33, 678, 680; approves plan of treaties, 257–58, 302–3; appoints commissioners to France, 257–58, 264–65, 288–89, 302–3, 365, 368, 378–80; committee on establishing a military academy, 261; orders contractors paid, 283; urges full representation, 290, 295, 308, 347; recommends certification of army surgeons, 290, 307; delays consideration of articles of confederation, 295–96; refuses Gen. Schuyler's resignation, 303–4, 316; authorizes establishment of loan offices, 307–8, 325; recommends state committees on officers and troops, 332–33, 441–42; ranks navy captains, 336, 343, 406; unable to act on Jacob Sheafe petition, 343; reverses New Hampshire decision on *Elizabeth*, 343, 384; agrees to borrow money, 349; orders purchase of foreign vessels, 368; clears Gen. Wooster of misconduct, 391; appoints committee of intelligence, 394; adds to army bounty, 404; permits return of loyalist prisoners to North Carolina, 404, 426, 461; pays chaplain, 414; grants prize shares to American seamen, 425; intervention in Delaware criticized, 445; committee on hostilities, 449–50; appoints auditors to settle Virginia accounts, 451; establishes navy board, middle district, 453; pays Gen. Ward for remaining in command, 455, 463–64; rejects Maryland's proposed bounty, 458; opposes Massachusetts military pay increase, 458, 460, 478, 488, 513–14; grants Gen. Schuyler's request to visit Philadelphia, 459; reinstates officers' recruiting allowance, 459–60; paroles John Foxcroft, 460; orders army deserters punished, 460; urges economic measures, 462, 472–73; authorizes Washington to appoint officers, 466; regulates sutlers, 473, 513, 515; forbids communication between New York and New Jersey loyalists, 476; sets enlistment terms, 477–78, 504–5, 518–19, 526–27, 536–37, 544, 556; authority to form foreign alliances discussed, 530; committee to headquarters, 533–34, 544, 547, 549–50; pays committee account, 534; orders Gen. Mifflin to remain in Philadelphia, 546–47; visited by Indians, 556, 577–78; requests Maryland answer about Nanticoke Indians, 557; establishes lottery, 571–72; suspends William Franklin's exchange, 572; meets on Sunday, 581, 590, 689; selects Baltimore as seat, 590, 596, 603–4, 606, 615–16, 618; approves fast day, 596–97; deletes resolve from journals, 599; convenes at Baltimore, 622, 633, 640, 652, 654, 658–60, 666–67; accepts proposal for French loan, 633–34; authorizes purchase of French armed vessels, 634; appoints executive committee at Philadelphia, 642–44, 675, 677; sends money to Gen. Lee, 642–44, 675; approves Washington's conduct, 644; defers action on suttler regulations, 667; sends money to Joseph Trumbull, 670; authorizes purchase of military provisions, 679; creates arms magazines, 679–80; increases Washington's authority, 679–81, 688–89, 691, 710, 713, 715–16; offers share of Newfoundland fisheries to France, 688; committee on creating executive boards, 689–91, 714; prohibits export of salted provisions, 702–3; directs purchase of cannon, 709; validates Nicholas Cooke's letters of marque, 712; *see also* Accounts; Board of treasury; Board of war; Cannon committee; Committee of Congress; Committee of secret correspondence; Committee on clothing; Committee to Ticonderoga; Delegates; Executive committee at Philadelphia; Secret committee

Congress, president of; *see* Hancock, John

Congress (Continental frigate), 47, 359

Congress (Lakes galley), 394

Advisory Committee

☆ U.S. GOVERNMENT PRINTING OFFICE: 1979 O—252-741

767